World Philosophers
and
Their Works

World Philosophers and Their Works

Volume I

Abe, Masao — Freire, Paulo

EDITOR
John K. Roth
Claremont McKenna College

MANAGING EDITOR
Christina J. Moose

PROJECT EDITOR
Rowena Wildin

SALEM PRESS, INC.
Pasadena, California   Hackensack, New Jersey

Managing Editor: Christina J. Moose   *Project Editor:* Rowena Wildin
Research Supervisor: Jeffry Jensen   *Research Assistant:* Jun Ohnuki
Acquisitions Editor: Mark Rehn   *Production Editor:* Cynthia Beres
Photograph Editor: Karrie Hyatt

Some of the essays in this work, which have been updated, originally appeared in the following Salem Press sets: *World Philosophy: Essay-Reviews of 225 Major Works, Great Lives from History: Ancient and Medieval Series, Great Lives from History: Renaissance to 1900 Series, Great Lives from History: Twentieth Century Series, Great Lives from History: British and Commonwealth Series, Great Lives from History: American Women Series, Critical Survey of Literary Theory.*

Library of Congress Cataloging-in-Publication Data

World philosophers and their works / editor, John K. Roth.
    p. cm.
    Includes bibliographical references and indexes.
    ISBN 0-89356-878-3 (set) — ISBN 0-89356-879-1 (v. 1) — ISBN 0-89356-880-5 (v. 2) — ISBN 0-89356-881-3 (v. 3)
    1. Philosophers — Biography — Encyclopedias. I. Roth, John K.
B104.W67 2000
109—dc21   99-055143

First printing

Contents

Volume I

Contents

Publisher's Note

The three-volume *World Philosophers and Their Works* examines, in 231 alphabetically arranged chapters, 226 of the greatest world philosophers of all time, plus 5 of the most influential ancient works of indeterminable authorship—from ancient Greek and Chinese thinkers such as Pythagoras and Confucius to contemporary philosophers such as Holocaust survivor Elie Wiesel and feminist Alison M. Jaggar. Each chapter contains a 2,000-word biographical essay (or, in the case of the unattributable works, "Authorship and Context" overviews), followed by one or more 2,000-word overviews of representative works and ending in an annotated bibliography providing suggestions for Additional Reading. These philosophers and works are most frequently taught at the secondary and undergraduate levels, commonly referenced either directly or indirectly in our daily lives, and considered by both scholars and well-read laypersons to be among the most influential of all time.

Written with the needs of students and general readers in mind, the chapters present clear introductory discussions of the philosophers and 285 of their works. The entries in the encyclopedia are arranged in alphabetical order by the name of the philosopher or unattributable work: The chapter on the *I Ching*, for example, follows the chapter on Edmund Husserl and precedes the chapter on Luce Irigaray. Each chapter begins with a biographical overview: Birth and death dates and places, and major contributions are highlighted in ready-reference top matter, followed by approximately 2,000 to 2,500 words of text tracing the philosopher's life, the development of his or her thought, and the thinker's influence on the history of philosophy. For the five unattributable works, this first section instead traces the arguments and issues surrounding authorship and places the work in a larger historical context.

Following the biographical section of the chapter, one or more of the philosopher's works are examined in detail: These works have been selected as the ones most likely to be studied in the classroom or to be referred to in daily life. The top matter to this portion of each chapter details the work's provenance or publishing history, the category or categories of philosophical inquiry to which it belongs, and the principal ideas advanced. Bold-faced subheads faciliate the task of finding information within both the biographical essays and the essays that cover works. At the end of each chapter, the list of suggested Additional Reading provides sources that will aid in further investigation of the philosophers and their works; these have been carefully selected to include not only the "classic" secondary sources but also, where available, the best of recent, authoritative studies that are accessible to the student or general reader. Each bibliographical entry in Additional Reading is annotated to assist students and others in choosing sources to consult for more in-depth information.

World Philosophers and Their Works not only covers Western philosophers—from the Greeks, including Plato and Aristotle, through modern thinkers such as Paul M. Churchland, Martin Luther King, Jr., and Annette C. Baier—but also examines philosophical standouts from Asian and African cultures. Chapters in these volumes detail the lives and works of four African, eighteen Chinese and Japanese, and eight Asian Indian philosophers, as well as three Islamic and seven Jewish thinkers. The chronological range of coverage extends from ancient Chinese texts such as the *Dao De Jing* (transcribed sixth to third century B.C.E.) and the Greek Anaximander (c. 610 B.C.E.- c. 547 B.C.E.), through the Middle Ages (from Saint Augustine through thinkers such as Hildegard von Bingen, Averroës, Moses Maimonides, Jalāl al-Dīn Rūmī, Saint Thomas Aquinas), into the Renaissance (from Erasmus through René Descartes), the great seventeenth century and Enlightenment thinkers (John Locke, Baruch Spinoza, Gottfried Wilhelm Leibniz, his nemesis Voltaire, David Hume, Jean-Jacques Rousseau), to great modern influences on contemporary thought from Immanuel Kant and Georg Wilhelm Friedrich Hegel and Mary Wollstonecraft through Ludwig Wittgenstein and Karl Marx and Alison M. Jaggar.

The set contains a number of features designed to supplement the lengthy chapters, including more than 160 photographs and illustrations of the philosophers themselves. A list of the 285 works analyzed in these volumes organizes those works into one or more of twenty-seven subject categories and appears at the end of volume three as a Categorized List of Works for handy reference. For example, students wishing to learn more about the philosophy of mind or about feminist philosophy may consult the Categorized List of Works to identify classics of philosophy addressing those topics. The philosophers who wrote these works are listed in parentheses after the work's title, enabling readers to turn to the chapters (alphabetical by philosopher), in which the categorized work receives full treatment. Because most works of philosophy can be categorized in one or more of three large areas of inquiry—ethics, metaphysics, and epistemology—all works have received at least one of those designations.

The largest category is ethics, with 141 essays touching on this topic, closely followed by metaphysics (125), and epistemology (88). Other categories, more specific, are included as well: For example (and perhaps predictably), many of the works addressed in these chapters deal with religious issues: 32 are on philosophy of religion, 29 on philosophical theology, 7 on Jewish philosophy, 5 on Buddhism, and 3 on Islamic philosophy. Non-Western philosophy is the subject of 12 works on Chinese philosophy, 8 on Indian philosophy, 4 on Japanese philosophy, and 4 on African philosophy. Thirty-one works touch on political philosophy, 30 on social philosophy, 11 on philosophy of history, 3 on philosophy of law, and 2 on philosophy of education. The philosophy of science is the subject of 11 essays, and 3 deal specifically with the philosophy of mathematics. Other title overviews fall under the categories of aesthetics (17), philosophy of language (15), existentialism (14), logic (13), philosophy of

mind (8), philosophical psychology (8), pragmatism (8), feminist philosophy (4), and phenomenology (3).

At the end of the third volume, preceding the indexes, are three appendices that provide useful information in easily accessible formats. The Chronological List of Philosophers lists 572 philosophers (and a few unattributable ancient works) in chronological order, allowing students and general readers to gain a perspective on the development of philosophical thought from 900 B.C.E. to modern times. A list we have called More World Philosophers identifies 341 major philosophers worthy of additional study, along with their years of birth and death and brief descriptors indicating the ideas for which they are known or the schools of thought or movements with which they are identified. Finally, the Glossary provides simple, succinct definitions of more than 350 philosophical terms with which every student of philosophy should be familiar.

The third volume ends not only with a comprehensive and heavily cross-referenced subject Index but also with a Title Index. The former (which falls at the end of the volume) includes names of philosophers and historical figures, schools of philosophy, terms, titles of works, and other items discussed in the text. The latter includes the titles of the works surveyed in these volumes, in alphabetical order, with cross-references from foreign-language and other alternate titles.

Creating an encyclopedia of world philosophy requires the expertise of many people, primarily scholars of philosophy but also scholars of history and biography. Salem Press would like to thank the nearly 120 scholars who have contributed to this encyclopedia. Their names and affiliations follow the introduction. We would also like to thank the editor for the set, John K. Roth of Claremont McKenna College, who spent many hours at all levels to ensure that this reference work would cover an appropriate and broad range of philosophers whose continuing influence or innovative and significant new ideas have made their thought a solid part of the academic curriculum.

The Philosopher's Project

An Introduction

Since some philosophers lived in a different age—and perhaps in a culture completely different from ours—it is a good idea to try and see what each philosopher's *project* is. By this I mean that we must try to grasp precisely what it is that each particular philosopher is especially concerned with finding out.

—*Jostein Gaarder*, Sophie's World

A Novel About the History of Philosophy—that is how the Norwegian author Jostein Gaarder subtitled his best-selling *Sophie's World* (1991). It narrates the philosophical adventures of a teenager named Sophie Amundsen, who finds strange mail waiting for her when she comes home from school. Its messages ask questions. "Who are you?" and "Where did the world come from?" are the first two.

In more ways than one, those questions make Sophie wonder. Along with her, Gaarder's readers learn that the mysterious mail originates with the enigmatic Alberto Knox, who becomes Sophie's philosophy teacher. Before many pages are turned, the reader is drawn into Gaarder's project. One part of that project involves reflection about wonder. Pursuit of that theme, followed by consideration of several others, helps to explain the project tackled by these volumes of *World Philosophers and Their Works*.

Wondering About Wonder

Philosophy means "the love of wisdom," but that definition needs unpacking. Doing so requires reflection on wonder, which Plato regarded as philosophy's beginning. That reflection, in turn, invites inquiry about questions—their variety, power, and fundamental role in philosophy. Questions raised early in philosophy's history—their sources include Buddha and Confucius, Socrates and Plato, the Hindu sages who composed the ancient Upanishads, and African oral traditions, to mention just a few—provide much of the inspiration for *World Philosophers and Their*

Works, which discusses many of the most important thinkers and writings in the worldwide history of philosophy.

What do people wonder about? How does wondering feel? Where can wonder lead? Where should it go? What do such questions and responses to them reveal about philosophy? Ancient Greece produced some of the most influential approaches to such issues. There Aristotle's teacher was Plato (c. 427-347 B.C.E.), who had learned philosophy's way from Socrates (c. 470-399 B.C.E.). Little would be known of Socrates if we had to depend on his writings, for he apparently left none behind. Socrates preferred question-filled conversation, but Plato made sure that Socratic discussion was not lost when the talking stopped. Plato reconstructed versions of those Socratic inquiries in a series of classic dialogues. Although we cannot be sure where Plato blurred the line between historical fact and imaginative creation, he did preserve the memory and method of Socrates while developing ideas of his own.

Theaetetus (from Plato's middle period, 388-368 B.C.E.) is one of Plato's most important dialogues. Its name comes from a character in the narrative. A brilliant young man, Theaetetus knows mathematics. Plato has Socrates show, however, that even Theaetetus may not know as much as he thinks he does, because a clear account of what it means to know something is much harder to pin down than it seems. As Theaetetus and Socrates talk, experience becomes perplexing, and they find more questions than answers. Theaetetus says these puzzles amaze him. He wants to find out more about what the questions mean and what the answers to them are, but he confesses that thinking about the questions makes him dizzy.

Socrates understands how Theaetetus feels. Long ago one of Socrates' friends went to a sacred site at Delphi and asked the Oracle, a religious visionary, to indicate whether anybody was wiser than Socrates. "No one," the priestess replied. Socrates wondered about the Oracle's answer, for self-study made him feel that he lacked wisdom. His sense of wonder about the Oracle's meaning led Socrates to spend his life looking for people who were truly wise. This search was what made him ask so many questions. Socrates found that people often claimed to know more than they did. At least he was wiser than they in recognizing his own ignorance and working to move beyond it. Was that what the Oracle meant by suggesting that no one was wiser than Socrates?

Signs of a disposition similar to Socrates' exist in Theaetetus. They show the makings of a philosopher. In fact, their mutual friend, Theodorus, was right to call Theaetetus a philosopher, Socrates tells the young mathematician, because "wonder is the feeling of a philosopher, and philosophy begins in wonder." Plato's dialogue about Theaetetus and Socrates suggests several points that Aristotle (384-322 B.C.E.), who knew the account, summed up effectively later on. Aristotle agreed with Socrates that philosophy attempts to escape ignorance and that awareness of ignorance emerges from wonder. Wondering dwells in the human capacity to ask questions: who, what, where, when, and, above all, *why*?

Aristotle did not believe, however, that individuals plunge into philosophy originally or automatically at the level found in Theaetetus. Wondering develops. Driving deeper than it may at the beginning, wonder concentrates in time on things that are more rather than less important. Wondering what's for dinner, for example—important though that may be—is not on the same level as the questions about knowledge that concerned Socrates and Theaetetus.

We are likely to ask questions such as "What's for dinner?" before we wonder "What's knowledge?" Aristotle thought human beings naturally desire to know, so he believed that one kind of

wonder will probably lead to another. Although a kind of wonder may be aroused by questions such as "What's for dinner?," Aristotle argued that experience eventually provokes "wonder about less mundane matters such as the changes of the moon, sun, and stars, and the beginnings of the universe." At least initially, he added, the result of this wondering is "an awesome feeling of ignorance."

The feeling of wonder involves puzzlement, surprise, uncertainty, and unclarity. Such qualities link up with the dizziness of Theaetetus. Wonder also includes awareness, sensitivity, and amazement—features connected to the "awesome feeling" that Aristotle emphasized. In addition, it reflects wanting, yearning, and hope. Those elements relate to the desire and determination to know that Socrates embodied. Joy and gratitude can be aspects of wonder, too. They fit the idea that happiness involves philosophical pursuits. Socrates, Plato, and Aristotle shared the conviction that philosophy begins in wonder and reflects our need and capacity to ask insightful questions about fundamental matters. Failure to make our feelings of wonder the occasions for inquiry, they thought, dooms us to ignorance and folly. But if we discipline wonder to keep ourselves curious, it becomes a life-enhancing art. By encouraging us to think carefully, the art of wonder can lead from darkness into light. Of course, wondering that leads from darkness into light is a difficult path to take. The rewards can make the journey worthwhile, but that outcome is not simply assured. This we know because Socrates got into serious trouble for being a philosopher. Philosophy's sense of wonder invites reflection about that fact, too.

The word *philosophy* derives from two Greek words: *philein* ("to love") and *sophia* ("wisdom"). The practice of philosophy, if not the word itself, probably appeared in India even before its birth in the Greek world, but some traditions hold that the word *philosophy* was coined by Pythagoras, a Greek thinker who lived nearly two centuries before Socrates and called himself a lover of wisdom. Thus, philosophy is the love of wisdom, and, following that definition, a philosopher is or should be a lover of wisdom. Socrates fit that description. The love of wisdom, however, cost him his life.

Why did the love of wisdom get Socrates into such difficulty? If that is where philosophy leads, why should Sophie Amundsen or anyone else be introduced to it? Socrates' often-quoted reply to versions of the second question—"the unexamined life is not worth living"—also helps to provide an answer to the first. In a nutshell, Socrates challenged too many assumptions and beliefs that Athenian authorities preferred to leave uncriticized. In the *Apology* (from Plato's early period, 399-390 B.C.E.), which deals with Socrates' trial before an Athenian jury, Plato reports that Socrates made his famous claim about "the unexamined life" as he defended himself against charges of atheism and corrupting the city's youth.

Socrates posed too many hard questions about fundamental issues. He might wonder, for example, what is justice? What does justice mean? What, if anything, do all just acts have in common? Aristotle credited Socrates for being the first thinker to stress the importance of obtaining sound definitions for the most basic ideas. Indeed, getting truthful definitions for basic ideas such as justice was at the core of wisdom as far as Socrates was concerned. Such questioning, however, could make people intensely uncomfortable. If they could answer his questions at all, people were unlikely to withstand Socrates' further questioning as they tried to define key terms—good, true, right, wrong— that they used all the time. Unrelenting in his love of wisdom, Socrates questioned and questioned. He unmasked pretense, uncovered confusion, undermined dogmatism, undid false certitude, and, in general, left very little unexamined. This activity instructed and delighted the friends of Socrates—Plato among them—but it also put Athenian leaders on the defensive, which made them uneasy and angry.

Obtaining wisdom is a personal experience because wisdom is found, if it is obtained at all, only by the individual who seeks it. Socrates wanted people to discover truth for themselves. He believed they could do so if they tried; that is why he raised so many questions. But his questioning also suggested that the search for wisdom is a communal activity. The love of wisdom and the ways of thinking that encourage it require dialogue. If we are not to go astray, we need to be corrected by discussion with others. The journey and the destination are inseparable: Without the give and take of dialogue, we may settle too easily for an insufficiently examined "truth."

Among those who offered such "truth" were teachers known as Sophists. Typically, they taught that power, prestige, and property measure success. They also emphasized that the right techniques—for example, learning how to speak and argue cleverly—could produce those results. Like Socrates, the Sophists challenged traditional Athenian values. Unlike Socrates, they were more interested in getting ahead than in knowing the truth. Socrates contested their views. His dialogue with the Sophists showed their "wisdom" to be what we now call sophistry, for their "knowledge" was more apparent than real.

Dialogue requires what Socrates called dialectic, which is the core of what we still call the "Socratic method." Dialectic is the disciplined and sustained use of questioning, responding, and questioning some more. That rhythm is philosophy's heartbeat. Such inquiry weighs the strengths and weaknesses of different views. It aims at a more balanced and complete perspective than one's starting points provide.

Socrates was a master of dialectic, and Plato portrays him as the questioner par excellence. The context for Socrates' exercise of dialectic was typically a search for the wisdom he loved but felt he possessed inadequately. Publicly Socrates would engage people who presumed to be wise, and he would ask that they share their enlightenment. Unwittingly they would oblige and start to "tell" him about goodness, justice, truth, beauty, or whatever the fundamental topic might be. Then Socrates would probe away. His questions were revealing: "Knowledge" dissolved into opinion and usually into unsubstantiated opinion at that. "Wisdom" collapsed into ignorance, if not into sheer foolishness.

Socrates laced his dialectic with irony, a style that exposes incongruity between appearance and reality or between what might be expected and what actually occurs. Pretending to be more ignorant than he was and temporarily allowing others to seem wiser than they were, Socrates turned the tables with his questions. His thanks for revealing ignorance and foolishness? An indictment, a trial—and more. In court, Socrates argued brilliantly that he had done no wrong. On the contrary, he contended, his questioning benefited Athens and made it a better place than it could ever be if fundamental issues went unexamined. Because he was now an old man of seventy, Socrates suggested that Athens should show him respect and give him a pension instead of punishment by death. However, Socrates' ironic questioning upset Athens too much. He and his philosophy threatened the established order, and the jury's decision was unforgiving. The trial resulted in his conviction and execution. With the help of friends, Socrates could have fled prison and escaped the death sentence. By refusing the offer and drinking the poisonous hemlock instead, Socrates became an early martyr to philosophy and one of its patron saints.

What Wisdom Means

The wisdom Socrates loved was not a matter of collecting facts or obtaining information, though facts and information were very important to him. A person can have a lot of data and still be foolish—the opposite of wise. What Socrates wanted was understanding, insight, and ways of thinking that make sound judgments about truth and goodness. Socrates yearned for these but never claimed that he possessed them completely.

In his *Symposium* (from his middle period, 388-368 B.C.E.), a dialogue about love, Plato has Socrates explain further by noting that a philosopher, a lover of wisdom, "is in a mean between the wise and the ignorant." The philosopher does not possess wisdom lock, stock, and barrel. As the chapters in *World Philosophers and Their Works* help to show, no one does. However, the philosopher senses what is lacking and seeks what is not possessed or even completely obtainable. He or she does so because the lack of wisdom leads to folly and foolishness of the tragic kind that Athens produced when it took Socrates' life.

By making us aware of ignorance, wondering shows that we do not know as much as we may assume but also that we are not necessarily condemned to ignorance. The possibility of learning can create a yearning for the knowledge that goes beyond information to wisdom. That yearning can become passionate. When it does, love is the right word to use for the desire that keeps us asking and searching for wisdom.

Socrates' love of wisdom embodied at least four principles that define philosophy. Each of them has a place in a remarkable scene from the history of philosophy. Found in one of philosophy's most influential books, Plato's *Republic* (middle period, 388-368 B.C.E.), a classic dialogue on the nature of justice and the ideal state, that scene is his famous allegory of the cave.

An allegory is a story whose characters, circumstances, events, and the relations among them function symbolically to illustrate a basic idea. The idea illustrated by the allegory of the cave is that of philosophy itself—for the story that Plato has Socrates tell to Glaucon in book 7 of the *Republic* is about a crucial activity, the climb from the shadows and darkness of ignorance to the enlightenment of wisdom.

Socrates describes prisoners who spend their lives in a cave. Dwelling there since childhood, they are chained so that all they can do is watch the shadows cast on a wall by fire. They cannot even turn their heads to discover why the shadows exist. Behind the prisoners, there are objects moving before a fire that burns near the cave's entrance. Unaware, the prisoners mistake the shadows for reality. If "the unexamined life is not worth living," the prisoners' predicament is not a good one. Socrates suggests that those prisoners are like us—less than the fully human persons we might become. To move toward that full humanity, we need to be unchained from the bondage of taking experience for granted. This principle—our need to question and evaluate experience critically—is the first that defines philosophy Socratically.

In the allegory, at least one of the prisoners is set free, forced out of the cave, and even dragged into the sun's full light. This journey is anything but easy. The glare from the fire is blinding; the objects that made the shadows on the cave's wall cannot be clearly identified. Confused, the released prisoner may think that the previous circumstances were clearer, more comfortable, than the new ones. The disorientation may even get worse when the sun itself is glimpsed, for no one can look directly at the very source of light. Gradually, however, adjustment to the light can happen. Then confusion may give way to clarity. Disorientation can recede in favor of reorientation that reveals the difference between appearance and reality.

Here, then, is the second Socratic principle that defines philosophy: Appearance and reality are not the same any more than truth and falsity are identical or right and wrong are indistinguishable. Confusion reigns, disorientation rules, where those basic distinctions are blurred, forgotten, or left unexamined. It is hard work to distinguish appearance from reality. A philosopher-teacher such as Socrates or, in Sophie Amundsen's case, Alberto Knox, can lend a hand. Nevertheless, philosophy still requires inquiry for oneself. Socrates liked to call himself a gadfly who provoked others to think by prodding them, even against their will, into the light of the sun. A gentler image, although it too entails pain, was that of the midwife who helps a mother deliver the child within her. Both images, but especially the latter, suggest a third Socratic principle that defines philosophy: We can learn, and truth awaits discovery within our own experience if only we keep prodding one another and ourselves to give it birth.

As Socrates concludes the allegory, the former prisoner's enlightenment brings the true joy and happiness that only understanding can provide. If the former prisoner thinks about the cave, there is sympathy for those who remain within it, but the liberated one would endure almost anything rather than go back to living and thinking as before. Indeed, if the former prisoner had to return to the cave, he or she might appear ridiculous to those who had never left the cave. If the freed person tried to teach them, they might be so offended that they would try to put the teacher to death.

Plato alludes to Socrates' fate at the allegory's end, but he also has Socrates discuss the story with Glaucon. In that discussion, Socrates stresses that those who obtain philosophy's understanding have a responsibility: to reenter the cave and to try, even at the risk of life itself, to set the other prisoners free so that they will also see the light. To Socrates—and this is the fourth Socratic principle—philosophy meant freedom to inquire and responsibility to learn and teach. The questions of philosophy open the way to thinking that can free us to become the responsible men and women we ought to be.

The Questions of Philosophy

There are many kinds of questions, but not every one is a question of philosophy. What makes the difference? What are the questions of philosophy? To clarify those issues, consider some examples. "What time is it?" is a frequently asked question. The answer we seek is usually specific—for instance, "It is four o'clock." A different question might ask "What is time?" "Four o'clock" would not be very helpful in that case. It may be an instance of time, but it is not time itself. Philosophers need to know what time it is, but they are also likely to be concerned about the nature of time itself.

Another question might be: "Is it true that you are going out tonight?" This time, the answer could be a simple "yes" or "no." Such answers will not make sense if the question becomes "What is truth?" Few things are more important than being able to distinguish true judgments from false ones. Knowing how to do that well depends on having sound insight about the conditions that constitute truth. Philosophers need to know whether "yes" or "no" is the answer to a question with the form "Is it true that . . . ?" but they also want to know about the nature of truth itself.

"Is she a good doctor?" "Is this sculpture better than that one?" "Will the economy change soon?" "Was his decision fair?" Those are common questions, too. Sometimes they can be answered "yes" or "no," but often they require careful evaluation. That may be because we feel the need to wonder about some other questions along the way. These might include: "What does goodness mean?" "How can works of art be compared?" "What does change involve?" "What's the difference between fair and unfair treatment?" Questions of the latter kind, which defy quick and easy answers, guide the philosopher's search for wisdom.

Lines between philosophical and nonphilosophical questions are not hard and fast. They often blur into shades of gray. Asking "Is she a good doctor?" is a case in point. If that question wonders whether the doctor has mastered the latest surgical technique, it might not be very philosophical because its answer depends simply on easily obtained facts. However, that same question may wonder about a larger cluster of qualities evoked by the word "good." Among them, for example, might be signs of character, care, and conscientiousness that go beyond technique.

In any case, a question will be philosophical to the extent that it checks quick, easy, simple yes-or-no answers and invites instead inquiry that examines—critically and rationally—our most basic concepts and ideas, assumptions and beliefs. What is happiness? Are there some realities that never change? Does God exist? Why is there so much suffering? What purpose and meaning does life have? In what sense do human rights exist? To what extent can ignorance be overcome and enlightenment obtained? Those are just a few more examples of the questions of philosophy. One does not have to think about them very long to discover that they are not abstractions remote from our lives but rather expressions of concerns that are the closest to our hearts.

As *Sophie's World* suggests, every self-reflective person is likely to ask at least some of the questions of philosophy. Philosophers, however, sustain the inquiry that the questions provoke. Over time they have organized these investigations so that several major fields of inquiry—distinguishable but overlapping—characterize philosophy.

Traditionally, one major area of philosophy is *metaphysics*. That name appeared in the first century B.C.E. when a scholar named Andronicus edited Aristotle's writings. Not knowing how to classify some of those works, he grouped them after Aristotle's writings about topics then called physics. Hence, those writings got labeled *meta ta physica*—"after the physical works." The coincidence was a happy one because the Aristotelian writings now called *Metaphysics* did indeed deal with questions that come after physics in the sense that they go beyond that subject.

Metaphysics is by no means found only in the ancient Greek world. Focused on being and becoming, it pervades world philosophy. What is reality? What are its most general or ultimate qualities? What kinds of beings are there? Why do some things exist and not others? Why is there a world at all? Why do some things change while others remain the same? How are causes and effects related? Is there a human nature, and, if so, what is it? Are human beings free or determined? What are the connections, if any, between spirit and matter, mind and brain? Physics, or science in general, may have important things to say about these questions, but metaphysical questions, such as the ones just mentioned, go beyond those of science. The latter's perspectives and findings do not encompass everything that exists. Metaphysics tries to deal with nothing less than that.

Beliefs, judgments, theories, arguments—these, too, exist. So do truth and falsity, knowledge and error. Metaphysics involves these realities, but typically philosophy organizes inquiry about them under a category called epistemology. Taken from a Greek word for knowledge (*epistemē*), epistemology—or the theory of knowledge—is what philosophers often call the study of questions about knowledge and knowing.

What does knowing mean? Can I be certain of anything? What are the best ways to inquire? Does reason have limits, or is it possible, in principle, for us to know everything? To what extent is sense experience trustworthy? Does truth change or is it eternal? These are some of the questions that epistemology involves. When the questions ask "How do arguments work?" or "How do we know that reasoning is consistent or contradictory?," then issues about knowing lead to logic, another key area of philosophy. Like those that characterize metaphysics, the issues of epistemology and logic are as important as they are fundamental.

Good and evil, right and wrong, beauty and ugliness—these are also real. The ways in which they are and our knowing about them make these elements parts of metaphysics and epistemology. But philosophers also find that an emphasis on values deserves a focus of its own: What should we value? What should we care about and why? Most often this third major area of philosophy is identified as *ethics*. In that case the emphasis falls on questions such as: What makes one act wrong, another right? What is the difference between good and evil? How should we treat one another? How should we treat the environment in which we live? Are there eternal moral truths, or is moral judgment relative, simply a reflection of the time and place in which it occurs?

Closely related to ethics is social and political philosophy. Here the emphasis falls on inquiry about the communal and political nature of human life. For example, what are the best forms of government? What rights and responsibilities does political life entail? What authority should leaders possess, and what limits should be placed upon them? How does social organization affect individual existence? Can individuals exist apart from society? Closely related to both ethics and social and political philosophy is aesthetics, which concentrates on the values found in the arts and our experiences of beauty. What is art? Are there rational standards by which it can be judged, or is its evaluation a matter of taste and liking alone? Does art serve politics? Should it?

In addition to metaphysics, epistemology and logic, and value-oriented inquiries focusing on ethics, politics, society, and aesthetics, there are still other dimensions of world philosophy that intersect with those major fields while retaining an identity of their own. Typically these fields of inquiry are called "the philosophy of ____." The blank could be filled with religion, science, education, law, or some other discipline. In these cases, the philosopher's project will be to examine the methods, practices, findings, and implications of these particular areas of human experience.

The Adventures of Ideas

World Philosophers and Their Works contains biographies about some of the most important philosophers in world history and essays that are related to what the philosopher Alfred North Whitehead called "adventures of ideas." Describing major writings in philosophy's history, these essays aim to introduce philosophy to readers who are largely unacquainted with its key questions, major figures, and seminal texts, its delights and frustrations—even though these readers might already have puzzled over at least some of philosophy's issues without always realizing they were doing so. At it underscores the major contributions that these writers and texts have made, and why they have stood the test of time, *World Philosophers and Their Works* also shows four ways in which philosophy is *world* philosophy.

First, philosophy is world philosophy because *philosophy exists worldwide.* Here and there, philosophy appears everywhere. It does so because questioning is such a fundamental part of human

experience. The capacity to question takes individuals and communities on journeys that can scarcely be imagined in advance. Wherever questions are asked, philosophy is not far to find, for philosophy is defined by questions. The forms taken by philosophy's questioning are as diverse as the varied cultures in which they appear. Those forms include short essays and long discourses, but philosophy also finds expression in poetry, memoirs, and fiction. While writing is indispensable for philosophy's transmission, face-to-face discussion and community dialogue are essential, too. So is the thoughtful reflection that takes place in the silence of personal inquiry.

Second, philosophy is world philosophy because *philosophy has a history.* No one can date philosophy's birthday exactly. One reason is that philosophy's origins are not easy to separate from religion. Nevertheless, about 2500 years ago, distinctively philosophical ways of thought were quite independently under way in India, China, and the Greek world. Hinduism and Buddhism, two traditions whose spiritual emphases keep religion and philosophy closely intertwined, were emerging in India. They became most overtly philosophical when analytical questioning and argumentative commentary about the meaning of older traditions and texts asserted themselves. In ancient China, Confucius (551-479 B.C.E.) was planting the seeds of the ethical and political traditions that would bear his name and spawn diverse schools of interpretation, again characterized by analytical questioning and argumentative commentary. Only fragments of their writings remain, but in the Greek world even before Pythagoras introduced the word *philosophy*, thinkers such as Thales, Anaximander, Parmenides, and Heraclitus were discussing change, the world's origins, and the basic physical elements of the natural order through questioning and discussion that began to separate their inquiries from religion.

Third, philosophy is world philosophy because *philosophy's history, already pluralistic in its origins, has unfolded in diverse ways.* Their variety continues to increase as global communication permits greater contact between traditions that were previously much more isolated from each other. As the contents of these volumes show, wonder does not take place in a vacuum. The priorities of our questioning and inquiry depend on factors such as time, place, circumstance, and personal as well as communal experience. History shows that philosophy rarely deviates entirely from the basic priorities articulated by formative thinkers such as Buddha, Confucius, or Plato. Nevertheless, history also shows that philosophy takes turns and reaches destinations distant from its origins. It does so because one thinker may believe that another made a mistake or missed something important and took philosophy down the wrong path. Then criticisms and corrections are needed. The repetition of that pattern will be variously illustrated in the chapters in these volumes. But in contemporary philosophy, there is a particularly striking example.

To contextualize this example, note that it was the Delphic Oracle, a priestess, who sent Socrates on his philosophical quest. Socrates thought of himself as a midwife, and wisdom itself (*sophia*) is often portrayed as feminine, too. In Plato's dialogues, however, the characters invariably are men. Only occasionally do Plato's dialogues even speak about women. Although Plato's casting may have been unimaginative—even unenlightened—on that score, it did fit the social realities of Athens. There it was generally assumed that women would not have a part in such discussions, nor would they be occupied in other forms of public business. Plato's *Republic* had Socrates argue for a different position: In an ideal state, properly qualified women would have governing parts to play. Those views, however, tended to be exceptions to the rule. Aristotle, for example, believed that "nature's direction" best suited women to be subjects while men ruled. The assumption behind his conviction was that men's rational capacities were superior to those of women.

Human activity, which includes philosophy, owes much of its diversity to gender, sexuality, and the theory and practice those differences have produced in various cultures. Although shared and even common, the experiences of men and women can and do vary immensely. When Alexander Pope, the eighteenth century English poet, wrote that "the proper study of mankind is man," he invited inquiry about all of human experience. Several centuries later, there is well-founded suspicion—even considerable

agreement among men as well as women—that too much of the study has been improper. Such study has often neglected the particularities of women's experiences and construed humankind too specifically as if it really were *man*kind. Although men have no inherent right to dominate philosophy's way, historically they have done so all around the world. Therefore, what criticisms and corrections are needed? As women's voices become more influential, how will philosophy change? How should it? Such questions have become a priority in philosophy as never before.

By reconsidering what's most important, concerns about women and philosophy affect philosophy's self-understanding. Issues about truth and goodness still take center stage, but the dialogue's cast is different now. The approaches, methods, and findings in every area of philosophical inquiry are being altered. Diversity—including attention to ethnic differences, criticism of explicit or implicit racism in human thought, and concern about unprecedented ethical issues raised by modern science and environmental problems—marks its tone more than it did in ancient India, China, Africa, or Greece. Such changes indicate that what people wonder about, even how wonder feels and what gets done with wondering, depends significantly on adventures of ideas that will be increasingly global.

Over time, human beings have come to understand that they exist within a reality as varied as it is vast, complex, ordered, and mysterious. As creatures who think, inquire, and reason, we try to find out where in the world we are and not only where the world came from but what, in fact, it is. Fourth, then, philosophy is world philosophy because *philosophy seeks to interpret and understand the world.*

The word "*world*" can make us wonder. It invites questioning. Sometimes that word refers to Planet Earth. Such uses of *world* are complex enough, but even they are too simple, for the meanings of *world* are rightly more expansive than that. To speak of *the world* can be to speak about all that we can think and imagine—and maybe even more. It is even appropriate for us to observe that *the* world, whatever it may be, contains *worlds*, for one of the most amazing things about the world is not only the vast expanse of the heavens but also the realms of experience—art, for instance, politics, and commerce—that are part of our world. In addition, the natural order itself contains domains of animal, plant, and even so-called inorganic relationships so extensive and complex as to require ongoing revision of what we can rightly claim to comprehend. If philosophy did not try to understand the world—in all the rich and ambiguous senses of that term—it would not be itself. Philosophy was born to understand the world. It lives to pursue that aim.

A world with philosophy is very different from a world without it, for as philosophy tries to understand the world, it also changes the world and creates worlds of its own. Philosophy makes the world so different, in fact, that if the influence of the thinkers and texts discussed in these volumes of *World Philosophers and Their Works* were erased from history, the world would scarcely be recognizable. Think of it: No Buddha, no Socrates, no Confucius, no Aristotle—whatever the world might be without them, it would not be ours. With them and the influence of other major philosophical voices, world history contains not only individual philosophers and their works but also philosophical traditions that affect culture, politics, ethics, business, education, and a host of other factors.

Philosophy's Self-Defeat and Its Success

The world—or worlds—of philosophy make an impact on the world. As philosophy develops and changes, the world does, too. One way in which this happens involves our understanding of the results of inquiry. Human inquiry takes place in the world, not outside of it. Human inquiry also brings about changes in the world. As the world—or worlds—of philosophy interact with the world, our sense of the world's reality has to take account of the interaction. Doing so can result in even greater diversity within philosophy, for the meaning of that interaction can be interpreted in more than one way that makes sense.

In *Sophie's World*, Sophie Amundsen's world is not what it first seems to be. Not only is her world fictional, but also it is a world within other fictional worlds. Those worlds, in turn, are realms—important ones, because imagination is such a powerful dimension of experience—of our own

world. There are worlds within worlds, worlds within the world. These considerations point toward philosophy's variety, a theme that helps to focus further the historical development of philosophy displayed by *World Philosophers and Their Works*.

Philosophy's development is dialectical—that is, one thing leads to another but not always in expected ways. Philosophy's development is also paradoxical—that is, philosophy is self-defeating, but its self-defeat creates its most important contributions. To explain these points, note that every philosopher—at least those who have been most influential in world history—has a project. That project, moreover, involves elements that are in tension as much as they are related.

Notice first that the philosopher's project is shared with all philosophers. Wherever philosophy exists, it involves reflection on questions that are likely to interest every human being—no matter who they are, when they live, or where they are situated. True, these questions can be phrased in various ways, but they reflect common human interests in, and reasoned reflection on, topics such as the ones that the German philosopher Immanuel Kant (1724-1804) and the French thinker Henri Bergson (1859-1941) used to define philosophy.

For Kant, philosophy's defining issues were these: What can I know? What should I do? For what may I hope? The first question concentrates on what was previously identified as epistemology—inquiry about how we obtain knowledge, how we discern the differences between sound and erroneous judgments, appearance and reality, truth and falsity, and how we use and sometimes abuse language and argumentation that make claims about those matters. Kant understood the second question to deal with ethics, another major philosophical field that was previously mentioned. It involves inquiry about what is good, just, and right, and what is not. Its questions pertain not only to personal life but also to social policy and political power. Kant's third question, which is metaphysical in nature, focused on religion and indirectly—Kant doubted that philosophy could do more—on the fundamental nature of reality. It was prompted by the fact that all human beings die, which can make us wonder what, if anything, life means and what its ultimate destiny, if any, may be. Rare is the philosopher's project that does not attend in some way to questions universally raised by life's finite duration, the widespread impact of religion, and questions about what endures, perhaps eternally, beyond an individual's existence or even humanity's history.

Bergson would have been more comfortable than Kant in speaking of the category signaled by Kant's third question as metaphysics, that part of philosophy, we noted earlier, that considers what is fundamentally and ultimately real, including what our limited human points of view enable us—and prevent us—from saying about such matters. Metaphysics includes inquiry about the origins of the world and the human life that inhabits it. In addition, metaphysics involves questions about what we are doing here, an issue that not only is ethical but also can invite inquiry about the nature and structure of human action, freedom and determinism, even the relationship between causes and effects, mind and body, spirit and matter. To his first two defining philosophical questions—Where do we come from? What are we doing here?—Bergson added one more, a version of Kant's third theme: Where are we going? That question is about destination but also about direction. Where is history taking us? How should history be understood? To what extent can we govern it, and to what extent does it direct us?

Gaarder saw that, in one way or another, every philosopher's project deals with epistemology, ethics, and metaphysics. At the same time, he discerned something that brought to the fore philosophy's dialectical development and its paradoxical mixture of self-defeat and success. One of Gaarder's key insights was that philosophy's universality, its common ground, and the philosopher's specific interests are fundamentally linked. Buddha, for example, was profoundly disturbed by human suffering. His personal search for understanding launched a philosophical tradition of universal significance. Cause and effect relationships particularly puzzled the British philosopher David Hume (1711-1776). His specific efforts to understand them advanced a skeptical empiricism that continues to have global impact. Issues about women were of special importance to the French existentialist

Simone de Beauvoir (1908-1986). Her work changed philosophy's contemporary emphases and approaches. In addition, while the philosopher's particular concerns involve differentiation from and disagreement with other philosophical views, the individual philosopher's perspectives indicate that philosophy's diversity is inseparable from its unity. No one is likely to confuse Buddha, Hume, and Beauvoir, but the differences between them also reveal that their concerns are related, their interests overlapping. As each makes distinctive contributions, they all participate in philosophy's ongoing definition and help its singular identity to evolve.

As that evolution proceeds, philosophy's diversity—it results from the finding that no particular philosophical view deserves to have the last word—defeats philosophy insofar as philosophy's quest aims at what is taken to be the complete and final attainment of some single, unified, and knowable truth. Although philosophy defeats itself in this sense—indeed, because of its self-defeat—it achieves success of another kind. That success consists of awareness that, finite and limited though every philosopher's project surely is—no matter how grand or grandiose it may appear to be—philosophical inquiry can focus questions that humankind ignores at its peril. By doing so, philosophy dispels ignorance and creates insight by means of its questioning, which is often more persistent and penetrating than any other. These successes constitute philosophy's most important contributions to human life.

One philosopher's project, then, is both the same as and different from every other's. No philosopher is so different that the work he or she does cannot be properly placed in one or more of the three major philosophical fields: epistemology, ethics, or metaphysics. Within those fields, however, the opportunities for difference are considerable. Philosophers seize those opportunities.

Philosophers do so for at least two major reasons. First, one philosopher will honestly believe that previous thinkers missed something important. Correction seems needed. Self-proclaimed, modestly or immodestly, as more discerning, the successor conveniently steps up to provide it. For example, the Chinese philosopher Zhuangzi (c. 365-290 B.C.E.) introduced new interpretations into his Daoist tradition while also encouraging dissent against what he took to be the rigid formalism of Confucian ethics. Hume's skepticism was so challenging to Kant that the German philosopher spent much of his life trying to refute it and thus produced writings that rival Hume's in importance. Second, the history of philosophy suggests that philosophers want to be different. They may claim and sincerely believe that philosophical inquiry should ultimately produce universal and even eternal agreement among all who inquire rationally about a given issue. Nevertheless, the frequent implication is that such universal and eternal agreement entails accepting what a particular philosopher identifies as the direction to take, even if the philosopher adds the caveat that his or her views may need additional refinement, elaboration, or even further correction.

Philosophers are not copycats. Individually, their project is not primarily to say, "Oh, I just agree with Confucius" or "I think Aristotle is great—he got everything exactly right and there is nothing more to say." To the contrary, philosophers tend to think that no one—at least nobody before them—got much right (to say nothing of everything) and thus there is much that needs to be said that no one else can say as well. Philosophers may employ humility ironically (Socrates comes to mind), but humility is not usually the philosopher's most obvious virtue. It is no exaggeration to say that philosophers are stubborn, arrogant at times, even as they insist that philosophy's inquiry must be open-ended and self-corrective because, like every form of human inquiry, it is prone to error. In these ways, philosophers can be irritating. They may rub things the wrong way as far as conventional wisdom and received opinion are concerned. In addition, they may fall short of practicing the philosophical virtues that they preach.

Philosophy's virtues are persistent questioning, critical argumentation, boldly reasoned assertion and testing of hypotheses, and a deep commitment to discerning what is true, good, and right insofar as human minds are capable of doing so. At the end of the day, philosophy and philosophers are interesting, significant, and important because they hold that some fundamental views are true and others false, some key

ideas about reality are sound and others unsound, and they question, discuss, argue, and inquire about these matters. If hopes for complete acceptance of their particular views get dashed, they typically return to the fray expecting that greater clarity and insight will emerge. For instance, Buddha's search for enlightenment took years. Plato wrote many dialogues as he tried to clarify his views about virtue. If he had been satisfied too soon, we would not have the *Republic*, his masterpiece. Kant published *The Critique of Pure Reason* in 1781, but he was not content with the outcome and did extensive rewriting for the second edition, which appeared in 1787. By no means did Kant's second edition silence his critics, but philosophy is richer because Kant published the two versions of his famous *Critique*. If philosophy defeats itself by showing that the truth it seeks is harder to pin down than philosophy sometimes suggested it would be, philosophy still can claim important successes whenever the virtues of philosophical life are practiced well. That work produces corrected theories, new insights, criticism that provokes fresh inquiry, and persistent questioning that helps us to learn. No part of the philosopher's project, whether we think of the universality or the particularity of the project, is more valuable and important than that.

The richness of the philosopher's project resides not only in the fact that it involves complex relationships between universality and individuality, between philosophers' common concerns and their insistence on difference, but also in the fact that it depends on the ways in which particular groups of philosophers share enough specific interests and approaches that traditions or "schools" of philosophy begin to form. Often these traditions or schools originate with individual thinkers who exert such an important influence that a sustained following advances the founder's thought. Again, Buddha, Confucius, Plato, and Aristotle are four striking examples. Each of those formidable thinkers not only exerted far-reaching general influence on world philosophy and world history but also impressed later individuals so much that their particular ways of thinking—sometimes in style as well as substance—were consciously carried forward.

One tradition, moreover, usually leads to another. Buddha went beyond the Hinduism into which he was born. Aristotle's departures from Platonic thought developed a different philosophical approach in the Greek world. As both of these cases illustrate, the breaks between the earlier and the later movements were not absolute. To the contrary, the differentiation depended on reaction and response to what had gone before. Yet within the differentiation, new and often unexpected developments definitely do take place. The philosophical approaches of Zen Buddhism, which emerged in thirteenth and fourteenth century Japan, had clear connections to Buddha's original ways, but Buddha would not have been able to anticipate all that Zen philosophy contains. In the twentieth century West, influential philosophical outlooks such as Jean-Paul Sartre's existentialism, John Dewey's pragmatism, and Ludwig Wittgenstein's philosophy of language all had roots in an impatience with traditions—they often trace back to the German philosopher Georg Wilhelm Friedrich Hegel (1770-1831)—that made bold claims for the power of human reason to develop systematic metaphysical explanations. Sharing a more skeptical outlook, those three approaches emerged through rebellion against philosophy's past. Those rebellions took markedly different paths, and thus new traditions were formed.

Mavericks that they often tend to be, philosophers are not fond of being pigeonholed as members of a tradition or school, but the fact is that few, if any, philosophers are traditionless. There are philosophical "birds of a feather," and they do—more or less—flock together. The flocks, however, do not always mix and mingle easily. Disputes erupt. Rivalries form. These results are not only between philosophical traditions and schools but also within them. Such relationships keep philosophy on the move. One philosopher's project can be classified with those of others. Individual though they are, philosophers are social creatures, too. Certainly each one's work has distinctive approaches and themes. For example, just as people are unlikely to mistake Monet's painting for van Gogh's, it is not hard to see that Bertrand Russell's philosophizing is different from Martha Nussbaum's. Nevertheless, philosophers also belong to philosophical families whose members resemble one another. None of

these relationships stays absolutely fixed. Individually and sometimes together, philosophers break away from well-worn paths and blaze new trails. This process is ongoing and never-ending. It defeats the philosopher's project, because none of those projects proves to be entirely complete. In philosophy's self-defeat, however, wisdom is found. Even a project destined to be eclipsed can advance our knowledge and understanding. Perhaps especially a project bound to fail can help us to sift and sort what is most important and deserving of our loyalty.

Unintended Destinations
Alfred North Whitehead (1861-1947) came to the United States from England in 1924. Already he was famous for his work in mathematics and logic, but his prolific career continued during his years as a professor at Harvard University. There Whitehead developed what he called a "philosophy of organism." It understood reality to be an everlasting creative process in which becoming is ongoing and perishing is perpetual.

Among Whitehead's major achievements was his book *Process and Reality: An Essay in Cosmology* (1929). The constant change that characterized reality, noted Whitehead, also spilled over into philosophy. "In its turn," he wrote, "every philosophy will suffer a deposition." Elsewhere in *Process and Reality*, Whitehead made his frequently cited remark that the Western philosophical tradition could be regarded as "a series of footnotes to Plato." That point was not inconsistent with the first, although some have taken it to be so. For all his influence, Plato did not have the last word in philosophy. On the contrary, Plato's influence involved a "depositioning," a questioning of what he had to say that left even Plato's place unfixed.

The degree and timing vary, but all philosophies come and go. Some are virtually forgotten. Others, eclipsed for a time, return to enjoy a renaissance of interest. Still others, like Plato's, seem permanently to stand the test of time and exert lasting influence, but even among that select company none has the last word. Meanwhile the less influential philosophers and philosophies contribute to a conversation destined to continue as long as people ask questions that seek understanding and wisdom. Plato raised many of those questions; he also explored them in ways that bear remembering. However, Plato's most significant impact was that his thought launched countless philosophical journeys. Those journeys continue and begin anew to this day.

Whitehead's *Process and Reality* and Plato's *Republic* are examples of the philosophical masterpieces represented in *World Philosophers and Their Works*. Our world could conceivably be one in which only a single masterpiece of philosophy exists—the one that states everything that could be said and does so truthfully, once and for all, without any need for correction, revision, or elaboration. Nevertheless, the history of philosophy and human experience in general indicate that ours is not such a world. We neither possess nor are likely to obtain the truth once and for all, without any need for correction, revision, or elaboration. In our changing world, no philosophy can be *the* masterpiece, because no philosophical project can do everything.

Like the becoming and perishing about which Whitehead spoke, variety in philosophy is inescapable. In philosophy, variety's possibility inspires its actuality. The chance to see and say things differently encourages a thinker to take that chance. Philosophical diversity emerges mainly because one thinker disagrees with another and wants to "deposition" the philosophy found wanting. Yet the disagreement is not sheer disagreement any more than the intended depositioning requires total disappearance. Dissenting views take inspiration from outlooks that precede them. Aristotle differed with Plato, but Aristotle's inspiration and the philosophy it produced could scarcely have appeared without Plato's.

Wondering about the varieties of philosophy, the great American philosopher William James (1842-1910) once remarked that "the history of philosophy is to a great extent that of a certain clash of human temperaments." Philosophy, he thought, is intimately related to how we "see" the world. Much that people see is shared and apparently the same, and yet human seeing is not identical. Philosophers belong to human communities, and they depend on others. Yet, in the final analysis, they are not inclined to let anyone else do their seeing or thinking for them. They state

their own views, believing that what needs to be said is different in some significant way from anything else that has been said before.

No two philosophers—no two human persons—have ever agreed on everything. Nor are they likely to do so. They are different persons, who see differently, and therefore they want their thoughts to be different, too. Otherwise their writings would make far less sense than they do. As for those writings, important parts of their adventures live in the fact that words do not always express exactly what a philosopher thought he or she saw. Nor does a philosopher's theory always have the consequences that its author intended. Whitehead illustrated that point effectively. "Before Columbus set sail for America," Whitehead wrote, "he had dreamt of the Far East, and of the round world, and of the trackless ocean. Adventure rarely reaches its predetermined end. Columbus never reached China. But he discovered America."

The best philosophical writings often turn out to be voyages of discovery like that. So there is drama in philosophy. *World Philosophers and Their Works* contains a story that goes beyond the individual philosophers represented here. Taken together they establish a narrative in which anyone willing to read and think can take part.

Never Give Up

As Gaarder's story about Sophie Amundsen and Alberto Knox draws to its close, philosophy has taken them to many an unintended destination. Neither they nor Gaarder's readers are sure what will happen next, not least of all because the philosophical journey they have taken together makes the world different from what it was before. At the end of the book, Sophie is still facing in new ways the question "Who am I?," which started her encounters with Alberto and the world of philosophy. If the answer to that question, and to all the other questions of philosophy, is not crystal clear, Sophie has apparently taken to heart what may be the most important lesson: "A true philosopher," Gaarder writes, "never gives up." As well as any representative of world philosophy, the Spanish thinker José Ortega y Gasset (1883-1955) understood what that teaching means.

Born into an aristocratic family in Madrid,

Ortega studied philosophy at Spanish and German universities before receiving a teaching appointment at the University of Madrid in 1910. He taught there until the Spanish Civil War began in 1936, but meanwhile he was also active as a journalist and a politician. An opponent of monarchies and dictatorships, Ortega supported democracy in Spain. He served in the parliament of the Second Spanish Republic and for a time was Madrid's civil governor. When the political tide turned during the Civil War, he had to flee from his country. Not until 1948 was he able to return permanently to Madrid after years of exile in Argentina and several European states.

Much of Ortega's writing was first published in newspaper and magazine articles, and he often reworked this material for his numerous books. The best known of these is *La rebelión de las masas* (1929; *The Revolt of the Masses*, 1932), which sets forth Ortega's social philosophy. By the time of his death, Ortega was acknowledged to be among the outstanding thinkers in Spanish history and a major contributor to the existential tradition in philosophy. Sophie, Alberto, and virtually every thinker represented in *World Philosophers and Their Works*—almost any person, for that matter—could identify with key themes that were central to Ortega's philosophical project.

In *What Is Philosophy?*, a book published three years after his death, Ortega asserted, for example, that "life is a constant series of collisions with the future." What he called life's "unforeseen character" is present from the beginning and continues until the end. Ortega believed that every person's birth is something like a shipwreck that puts us, without previous consent, "in a world we neither built nor thought about." No one chooses to be born or to exist in the world we enter at birth. But soon enough, contended Ortega, living becomes "a constant process of deciding what we are going to do." That process makes human identity paradoxical, he thought, because one's life "consists not so much in what it is as in what it is going to be: therefore in what it has not yet become."

For Ortega, philosophy is rooted in our collisions with the future. Feeling, thinking, questioning as we do, the undecided, yet-to-be-determined, and therefore unknown elements of existence make philosophy "a thing which is inevitable."

Yet if philosophy is a form of life that arises naturally because we want to know what eludes us, what can philosophy accomplish? Ortega's response to that question produced an instructive adventure.

A first step, Ortega asserted, is to recall that philosophy comes into existence in response to the fact that life confronts us with what he called "dramatic questions" such as "Where does the world come from, whither is it going? What is the definitive power in the cosmos? What is the essential meaning of life?" To answer those questions completely, Ortega explained, requires nothing less than "knowledge of the Universe," and that is how Ortega defined philosophy. However, understanding what this definition involves also entails asking whether philosophy is really possible.

Part of Ortega's answer was, "I can't be sure that philosophy is possible." He had several reasons for saying this. No human being, for instance, knows what the Universe is as a whole. Even to speak about the "whole Universe" may hide as much as it explains, because *"Universe"* means "everything that is." Thus, said Ortega, the philosopher "sets sail for the unknown as such." The future of this voyage is profoundly uncertain; no one knows in advance how far it is possible to answer the questions of philosophy. The dilemma, moreover, is not simply that human intelligence may be too frail to know what is knowable. The origin of philosophy's difficulty lies deeper still. "There is also the chance," Ortega thought, "that the Universe may be unknowable for a reason which the familiar theories of knowledge ignore," namely, because "the world, the state of being, the Universe in itself, in its own texture, may be opaque to thought because in itself it may be irrational."

Recognizing that we may not be able to satisfy philosophy's hunger, Ortega nevertheless believed staunchly that we should make the attempt. We can know that we lack knowledge, Ortega thought, and thus we can at least try the philosophical quest. Philosophy is to that extent possible. As Sophie Amundsen came to understand, joining its adventures is one of the qualities that make us truly human.

Sophie's World: A Novel About the History of Philosophy begins with an epigraph from the German writer Johann Wolfgang von Goethe: "He who cannot draw on three thousand years" said Goethe, "is living from hand to mouth." *World Philosophers and Their Works* affirms that judgment. A record of the fact that true philosophers never give up, it extends an invitation to learn, to venture into the future, by joining their good company.

John K. Roth
Russell K. Pitzer Professor of Philosophy
Claremont McKenna College

List of Contributors

Christopher M. Aanstoos
State University of West Georgia

Patrick Adcock
Henderson State University

Bland Addison, Jr.
Worcester Polytechnic Institute

Emily Alward
Independent Scholar

Andrew J. Angyal
Elon College

Stanley Archer
Texas A&M University

Stephen M. Ashby
Bowling Green State University

Dorothy B. Aspinwall
University of Hawaii, Manoa

Bryan Aubrey
Independent Scholar

Richard Badessa
University of Louisville

Ann Marie B. Bahr
South Dakota State University

Robert Baker
Union College

Carl L. Bankston III
University of Southwestern Louisiana

Stephen F. Barker
The Johns Hopkins University

Dan Barnett
Butte College

David Barratt
Independent Scholar

Thomas F. Barry
University of Southern California

Jeffrey A. Bell
Southeastern Louisiana University

Raymond Angelo Belliotti
*State University of New York,
    Fredonia*

A. Cornelius Benjamin
University of Michigan

Richard P. Benton
Trinity College, Connecticut

Milton Berman
University of Rochester

Terry D. Bilhartz
Sam Houston State University

Wayne M. Bledsoe
University of Missouri, Rolla

David Boersema
Pacific University

Scott Bouvier
*California State University,
    Los Angeles*

David Warren Bowen
Livingston University

John Braeman
University of Nebraska-Lincoln

Wesley Britton
Harrisburg Area Community College

Kendall W. Brown
Hillsdale College

Fred Buchstein
John Carroll University

David D. Buck
Univeristy of Wisconsin, Milwaukee

Jeffrey L. Buller
Loras College

D. Burrill
*California State University,
    Los Angeles*

Michael Büsges
Rutgers University, New Brunswick

Edmund J. Campion
University of Tennessee

Sharon Carson
University of North Dakota

Thomas Cassidy
South Carolina State University

Christine R. Catron
St. Mary's University

John Y. Cha
Gustavus Adolphus College

Dipankar Chatterjee
University of Utah

Victor W. Chen
Chabor College

Pei-kai Cheng
Pace University

Drew Christie
University of New Hampshire

Thomas Clarkin
Independent Scholar

John Collinson
University of New Haven

Bernard A. Cook
Loyola University

Patricia Cook
Emory University

Robert C. Davis
Pikeville College

Frank Day
Clemson University

Whitaker T. Deininger
San Jose State University

David J. Depew
California State University, Fullerton

Willem A. deVries
University of New Hampshire

Thomas E. DeWolfe
Hampden-Sydney College

M. Casey Diana
University of Illinois

J. R. Donath
*California State University,
    Sacramento*

Joyce Duncan
East Tennessee State University

Val Dusek
University of New Hampshire

Marvin Easterling
University of Illinois

Robert P. Ellis
Worcester State College

Julia S. Falk
Michigan State University

Jean Faurot
California State University, Sacramento

Howard Z. Fitzgerald
Claremont Graduate University

Edwin D. Floyd
University of Pittsburgh

Karen Anding Fontenot
Southeastern Louisiana University

Robert J. Forman
Saint John's University

Douglas A. Foster
David Lipscomb College

Margot K. Frank
Randolph-Macon Woman's College

C. George Fry
Saint Francis College

Timothy Fuller
Colorado College

Jean C. Fulton
Humboldt State University

Keith Garebian
Independent Scholar

Jeffrey L. Geller
Pembroke State University

Albert J. Geritz
Fort Hays State University

John D. Glenn, Jr.
Tulane University

Irwin Goldstein
Loyola University of Chicago

Marc Goldstein
Independent Scholar

John T. Goldthwait
State University of New York, Plattsburgh

Nancy M. Gordon
Independent Scholar

James C. Griffith
Claremont Graduate University

Gil L. Gunderson
Monterey Institute of International Studies

Irwin Halfond
Mckendree College

Richard A. Spurgeon Hall
Methodist College

Gavin R. G. Hambly
University of Texas at Dallas

William S. Haney II
Maharishi International University

David Haugen
Western Illinois University

Robert M. Hawthorne, Jr.
Independent Scholar

Michael F. Hembree
Florida State University

Darryl L. Henry
Independent Scholar

Sally Hibbin
Independent Scholar

Stephen R. C. Hicks
Rockford College

Richard L. Hillard
University of Arkansas at Pine Bluff

Shawn Hirabayashi
Independent Scholar

John R. Holmes
Franciscan University of Steubenville

Pierre L. Horn
Wright State University

Ronald William Howard
Mississippi College

Kai-yu Hsu
Stanford University

Sue Hum
University of Akron

Dale Jacquette
Pennsylvania State University

Linda R. James
University of Wisconsin, Madison

Shakuntala Jayaswal
University of New Haven

Dwight Jensen
Marshall University

Randall M. Jensen
Claremont McKenna College

W. Paul Jones
Yale University

Cynthia Lee Katona
Ohlone College

Jacquelyn Kegley
California State College, Bakersfield

Amy Kind
Claremont McKenna College

Terry J. Knapp
University of Nevada, Las Vegas

Barbara Kramer
Santa Fe Community College

Robert B. Kruschwitz
Georgetown College

Gary Land
Andrews University

Robert E. Larsen
University of Minnesota

Richard M. Leeson
Independent Scholar

Leon Lewis
Appalachian State University

Terrance L. Lewis
Clarion University of Pennsylvannia

Thomas T. Lewis
Mount Senario College

John Linnell
University of Minnesota

Scott Lowe
University of North Dakota

Wei Luo
Independent Scholar

Reinhart Lutz
*University of California,
Santa Barbara*

Richard D. McGhee
Arkansas State University

Ian P. McGreal
*California State University,
Sacramento*

Kerrie L. MacPherson
University of Hong Kong

Paul Madden
Hardin-Simmons University

Grant A. Marler
Claremont Graduate University

Chogollah Maroufi
*California State University,
Los Angeles*

Eric L. Martin
Northeastern University

A. P. Martinich
University of Texas, Austin

Paul Marx
University of New Haven

Wallace I. Matson
University of California, Berkeley

Laurence W. Mazzeno
United States Naval Academy

Patrick Meanor
*State University of New York
College at Oneonta*

Michael W. Messmer
Virginia Commonwealth University

Diane P. Michelfelder
Utah State University

Leonard Miller
Cornell University

Mary-Emily Miller
Salem State College

Chris Moose
Independent Scholar

Robert A. Morace
Daemen College

Mario Morelli
Western Illinois University

Robert E. Morsberger
*California State Polytechnic
University*

Grosselin Nakeeb
Pace University

William Nelles
*University of Massachusetts,
Dartmouth*

Tammy Nyden-Bullock
Claremont Graduate University

Robert H. O'Connor
North Dakota State University

James H. O'Donnell III
Marietta College

Glenn W. Olsen
University of Utah

Joyce M. Parks
Independent Scholar

Bernard Peach
Duke University

Thomas R. Peake
King College

Mark Pestana
*City College of Chicago-
Richard J. Daley College*

R. Craig Philips
Michigan State University

Donald K. Pickens
North Texas State University

Arthur Pontynen
University of Wisconsin, Oshkosh

Richard H. Popkin
Washington University, St. Louis

Luke A. Powers
Tennessee State University

Lillian M. Range
University of Southern Mississippi

Thomas Rankin
Independent Scholar

Rosemary M. Canfield
Reisman
Charleston Southern University

Clark G. Reynolds
Independent Scholar

Patrick S. Roberts
Claremont Graduate University

Carl Rollyson
*Baruch College, City University of
New York*

Willem B. Roos
*Ingenieur-Akademie, Oldenburg,
Germany*

Joseph Rosenblum
*University of North Carolina at
Greensboro*

Andrew L. Roth
Independent Scholar

John K. Roth
Claremont McKenna College

Victor Anthony Rudowski
Clemson University

Nancy Ellen Rupprecht
Middle Tennessee State University

Priscilla K. Sakezles
University of Akron

Vicki A. Sanders
Paine College

Stephen Satris
Clemson University

Bernard Schlessinger
Texas Woman's University

June H. Schlessinger
University of North Texas

Calvin O. Schrag
Purdue University

Rose Secrest
Independent Scholar

Robert M. Seiler
University of Calgary

Roy Wood Sellars
University of Michigan

John C. Sherwood
University of Oregon

R. Baird Shuman
*University of Illinois,
Urbana-Champaign*

Anne W. Sienkewicz
Independent Scholar

Jack Simmons
Savannah State University

Julius J. Simon
University of Texas at El Paso

Erling Skorpen
University of Maine, Orono

Genevieve Slomski
Independent Scholar

Robert W. Small
Massasoit Community College

Roger Smith
Independent Scholar

Ira Smolensky
Monmouth College

Frederick Sontag
Pomona College

Bradley Starr
California State University, Fullerton

August W. Staub
University of Georgia

Leon Stein
Roosevelt University

Jean T. Strandness
North Dakota State University

Paul Stuewe
Independent Scholar

Susan A. Stussy
Independent Scholar

James Sullivan
California State University, Los Angeles

Roy Arthur Swanson
University of Wisconsin, Milwaukee

Glenn L. Swygart
Tennessee Temple University

Roy Talbert, Jr.
University of South Carolina- Coastal Carolina College

Paul C. L. Tang
California State University, Long Beach

Daniel Taylor
Bethel College

Terry Theodore
University of North Carolina, Wilmington

Nicholas C. Thomas
Auburn University at Montgomery

Evelyn Toft
Fort Hays State University

David Travis
Syracuse University

Paul B. Trescott
Southern Illinois University

Jack E. Trotter
Francis Marion University

George W. Van Devender
Hardin-Simmons University

Scott Vaszily
Northern Illinois University

Theodore Waldman
Claremont Graduate School

Marcia J. Weiss
Point Park College

Ron West
University of Nebraska at Omaha

Winifred Whelan
Saint Bonaventure University

John D. Wild
Independent Scholar

John F. Wilson
University of Hawaii, Manoa

John P. Windhausen
Saint Anselm College

Norman Wirzba
Georgetown College, Kentucky

Michael Witkoski
Independent Scholar

Shawn Woodyard
Independent Scholar

Lisa A. Wroble
Redford Township District Library

Keith E. Yandell
University of Wisconsin, Madison

Clifton K. Yearley
State University of New York, Buffalo

Kristen L. Zacharias
Albright College

Masao Abe

As the foremost exponent of Zen Buddhism for the West, Abe was instrumental in promoting and fostering interfaith dialogue between Western theology (both Jewish and Christian) and Buddhist philosophy.

Principal philosophical works: *Zen and Western Thought*, 1985; *The Emptying God: A Buddhist-Jewish-Christian Conversation*, 1990; *A Study of Dōgen: His Philosophy and Religion*, 1992; *Buddhism and Interfaith Dialogue: Part One of a Two-Volume Sequel to Zen and Western Thought*, 1995; *Zen and Comparative Studies: Part Two of a Two-Volume Sequel to Zen and Western Thought*, 1997.

Born: February 9, 1915; Osaka, Japan

Early Life

Masao Abe was the third of six children born to a doctor and his wife in Osaka, Japan. Abe wanted to study philosophy and religion at Kyoto University, but he was expected to pursue a career in the business world. He studied law and economics at Osaka Commercial University and worked for a company upon graduation. A few months before Japan attacked Pearl Harbor in December, 1941, Abe decided to end his career in business and study philosophy at Kyoto University. At the university, he worked with some of the major philosophers of the Kyoto School, including Hajime Tanabe, Keiji Nishitani, and most important for Abe, Shin'ichi Hisamatsu.

Abe taught at Kyoto Women's College and Ōtani University between 1946 and 1950. During the 1950's, he traveled to New York as a research fellow of the Rockefeller Foundation. He studied philosophy at Columbia University and worked closely with Zen Buddhist scholar D. T. Suzuki. He also met theologian Paul Tillich, with whom he would later have dialogues. Being in close proximity to Union Theological Seminary gave Abe the opportunity to study Christian theology with major figures such as Reinhold Niebuhr and John Knox. Abe's time at Columbia University and Union Theological Seminary laid the foundation for his work in interfaith dialogue.

Life's Work

For almost half a century, Abe acted as a teacher, scholar, mentor, philosopher, and interfaith dialogue partner for Christian theologians in major colleges and universities in the United States and Japan. His contributions were mainly in the areas of comparative philosophy, Asian studies, theology, and Buddhist studies. After Suzuki's death in 1966, Abe became the foremost interpreter and exponent of Zen Buddhism for the West.

The religion of Abe's family was Pure Land Shin Buddhism, although, according to Christopher Ives in his introduction to *The Emptying God*, Abe's mother was the only family member who could be considered religious. Ives states that during Abe's adolescent years, he became aware of what he felt was a negative effect he had on others and came to believe that he hurt others by the very living of his life. His struggles were partly resolved during his high school days when he read the *Tannishō* (c. 1290; *The Tannisho*, 1928), a compilation of talks by Shinran (1173-1262), the founder of the Pure Land sect to which Abe's family belonged.

According to the Pure Land school, people are living in *mappō*, the degenerate age of Buddhism, and therefore, because of their accumulated "sinfulness," people can no longer rely on their own efforts for salvation. The only means to salvation is faith in the bodhisattva Amida, who resides in the Pure Land. This doctrine of faith in Amida, called relying on "other-power," must have made a strong impression on Abe; years later, he was to have a powerful conversion experience of Amida's grace during his studies at Kyoto University.

Abe forsook everything he acquired through his business career when he entered Kyoto University in 1941 to study religion and philosophy. The motivating factor in Abe's decision to begin serious philosophical study was the struggle between his faith in Amida and his intellectual inquiries. The conflict between faith and intellect came to a head when Abe encountered the Kyoto philosopher and Zen teacher Shin'ichi Hisamatsu.

As recounted by Ives, Abe explains that the radical change from his faith in Amida to his awakening through Zen training and philosophy was a direct consequence of his studying under Hisamatsu. During his years in Kyoto, Abe felt as if he were doing battle with his teacher and mentor, who challenged his faith by asserting the illusory nature of human "sinfulness" and the "other-power" represented by Amida. Hisamatsu asserted that the key to Abe's struggle lay in realizing his "true self," his own Buddha-nature, not faith in Amida. Abe's struggle with the Zen of Hisamatsu and his subsequent acceptance of and awakening to the "Zen way" laid the foundations for the Zen standpoint underlying all of Abe's work.

Hisamatsu acted as a spiritual and religious mentor for Abe, and Keiji Nishitani helped cultivate the philosophical depth and subtlety apparent in Abe's work. Abe's use of philosophical discourse and his belief in the need to confront the issues of scientism, nihilism, and secularism facing modern humanity are directly inherited from Nishitani's stated philosophical mission.

The Western theologian who had the most influence on Abe was Tillich, whom Abe first met during his stay in New York as a research fellow of the Rockefeller Foundation. Abe originally went to New York to study with Tillich, but the theologian left to accept a position at Harvard. Abe did, however, attend the lectures and sermons that Tillich gave in New York, and after Abe returned to Japan, Tillich's visits to that country gave Abe more opportunities to dialogue with the Christian theologian. Abe stated that Tillich deepened his understanding and appreciation of Christianity and that he considered him one of the most

important dialogue partners for Buddhists. These encounters with Tillich no doubt strengthened Abe's belief in the need for interfaith dialogues.

After he began his academic career, Abe published hundreds of articles in English and Japanese in a variety of journals and magazines and circulated unpublished papers among colleagues and students on both sides of the Pacific Ocean. In 1985, a number of Abe's important essays on Zen and comparative philosophy were published as *Zen and Western Thought*. After the publication of this book, Abe continued to work on projects that included dialogues and critical exchanges with various Jewish and Christian theologians. Many of these exchanges were collected in *The Emptying God: A Buddhist-Jewish-Christian Conversation*. Topics included the notion of Buddhist emptiness and its relation to God, science and religion, the problem of evil, the Holocaust, and feminist theological responses to Buddhism.

Abe worked on special projects such as translations of the writings of Dōgen Zenji (1200-1253), the Zen monk who founded the Sōtō branch of Japanese Zen Buddhism and is considered one of Japan's foremost philosophical and literary figures. Many of these translations, done in collaboration with Norman Waddell, were published in the journal *The Eastern Buddhist*. Abe also wrote several interpretive articles on Dōgen's philosophical treatises, most of which appeared in the same journal. A number of these articles were collected and published as *A Study of Dōgen: His Philosophy and Religion*. These works display not only Abe's expertise in the philosophical discourse of the Kyoto School but also his mastery of textual scholarship.

One of the central concerns underlying Abe's activities and works on interfaith dialogue is the phenomenon of globalization, which increases the opportunities for people of different religions and cultures to interact. Abe perceived a need for constructive dialogue to bridge the gaps between people of different religious orientations. In Abe's view, it was imperative that representatives of the various religions of the world create a "space" within which meaningful dialogue can occur. He believed that the foundation for that dialogical space can be found in certain Buddhist concepts, particularly emptiness, which possesses the characteristics of nonsubstantiality, nonduality, and dynamic activity. He wanted to make clear, however, that he was not implying that Christians, for example, should become Buddhists. On the contrary, just as Buddhists must respond as Buddhists in creative and compassionate ways to the emerging phenomenon of globalization, so too must Christians respond as Christians. Indeed, in Abe's view, Jews, Christians, and Buddhists can learn from one another through interfaith dialogue while maintaining a commitment to their faiths.

Many of Abe's works on interfaith dialogue are collected in a multivolume sequel to *Zen and Western Thought*. The first volume, *Buddhism and Interfaith Dialogue*, directly addresses the issue of religious communication. In this volume, Abe engages in critical dialogue with a number of Jewish and Christian theologians representing a variety of positions. Abe, with his Buddhist stance, creatively and critically engages theologians with existential, feminist, mystical, and liberational orientations. The second volume, *Zen and Comparative Studies*, explores the main concepts of Zen Buddhism, its response to Western philosophy, its relation to Japanese culture, and Zen spirituality and practice. Its focal point and style mark a return to and expansion of the issues explicated in *Zen and Western Thought*. Abe also planned a third volume in this sequel, expected to be an explanation and interpretation of the leading figures of the Kyoto School, including Kitarō Nishida, Shin'ichi Hisamatsu, Keiji Nishitani, and Hajime Tanabe.

Much of Abe's work confronted the problem of nihilism/secularization that seems to accompany globalization. Like other philosophers of the Kyoto School, most notably Nishitani, Abe sought to disclose the foundations of the pervasive nihilism of the twentieth century. He believed that to overcome the profound sense of alienation that all people must eventually encounter, the Buddhist philosophy of emptiness must be incorporated in whatever worldview people hold. Abe brought these concerns to the notice of his colleagues and the students of many academic institutions, including Columbia University, the University of Chicago, the Claremont colleges and Claremont Graduate School, Carleton College, Princeton University, and the University of Hawaii.

Influence

As heir to Suzuki's role as the foremost exponent of Zen for the West, Abe has made significant contributions to a variety of intellectual fields, including translations and interpretive studies of traditional Zen treatises, comparative philosophy, and interfaith dialogue. He has continually explicated Zen philosophy within the context of the philosophical and theological currents in the West, thereby affording a bridge for those interested in pursuing comparative religious and philosophical study. Given his active role as Zen representative in interfaith dialogue during the last half of the twentieth century, Abe's work lays the foundation for critical discussion among representatives of the world's religions in the twenty-first century.

John Y. Cha

Zen and Western Thought

Type of philosophy: Buddhism, Japanese philosophy, metaphysics, philosophy of religion
First published: 1985
Principal ideas advanced:

◇ Although the Zen doctrine of absolute nothingness is sometimes misunderstood as merely a kind of nihilism, Zen goes beyond the duality of relative being and relative nonbeing.

◇ Buddha-nature, the positive term for absolute nothingness, paradoxically contains both being and nonbeing in an absolute manner; this paradox is termed the *logic of is/is not*.

◇ Using absolute nothingness as a standpoint, religion can confront and overcome the nihilism that results from modernity and globalization.

Masao Abe's work describes the main characteristics of the philosophy of the Kyoto School, explains the Zen Buddhist standpoint in the context of Western thought, analyzes Western philosophy and theology through dialogues, and confronts the problem of modernity. As the heir to D. T. Suzuki's role as the main exponent of Zen for the West, Abe explicated the fundamental standpoint of Zen philosophy in many contexts. He provided interpretive analyses of traditional Zen teachings and used the logic of is/is not to analyze Western thought. Like other philosophers of the Kyoto School, Abe was well acquainted with Western intellectual and religious traditions, but unlike his fellows, Abe addressed primarily a Western audience. Abe's work is constructive in that, through dialogues and critical exchanges, he attempts to articulate a standpoint that successfully confronts nihilism and revitalizes both Western and Eastern religion.

The Doctrine of Absolute Nothingness

In the opening pages of the work, Abe interprets a well-known Zen saying: Before one studies Zen, mountains are mountains and rivers are rivers; after one attains some insight, mountains are not mountains and rivers are not rivers; and when one becomes enlightened, mountains are really mountains and rivers are really rivers. For Abe, this short passage elucidates Mahayana Buddhism's central doctrine of absolute nothingness, or emptiness (*shunyata*). Abe's commentary on this passage explains the philosophical basis from which he compares Zen with Western thought and criticizes Western philosophy and theology.

Abe explains that before studying Zen, an individual affirms the existence of mountains and rivers, differentiates between them, and, most significantly, objectifies them—mountains are mountains and rivers are rivers. Objectification entails the positing of mountains and rivers as realities external to the internal subject, which Abe terms the *ego-self*. From the Zen standpoint, this duality between the subject (ego-self) and object (in this case, mountains and rivers) obstructs the realization of one's true self, or Buddha-nature. To inquire into the self in an objectified way throws the questioner into an infinite regression of subjects and objects. When one asks, "Who am I?" or "Who sees these mountains and rivers?" the very subject that perceives objects becomes an object. One can take this further by inquiring, "Who is asking these questions?" ad infinitum and never arrive at an awakening to the self, one's Buddha-nature.

Release from this infinite regression entails a full existential realization that Buddha-nature is

beyond the realm of objectifying thought, which frees one from the dichotomy of subject and object. From the Zen standpoint, this emptying of duality is the perception of nondifferentiation. The second phrase in the saying—mountains are not mountains and rivers are not rivers—refers to the realization that comes after the student of Zen gains some insight.

A subtle duality, however, still exists in this stage of nondifferentiation: a division between the state of differentiation and nondifferentiation. The realization of Buddha-nature requires a further negation, the negation of nondifferentiation. Abe calls this negation of negation *absolute negation* and contends that this absolute negation is, logically, an *absolute affirmation*. This paradox of the oneness of affirmation and negation, or what Abe calls the logic of is/is not, is the essence of Buddha-nature.

The Essence of Buddha-Nature

What is Buddha-nature? Abe answers this question by analyzing Dōgen Zenji's Buddha-nature theory. Dōgen's theory is based on his reinterpretation of the traditional Buddhist doctrine that all sentient beings *have* Buddha-nature. According to Dōgen, all beings, both sentient and nonsentient, *are* Buddha-nature. Part of Dōgen's project, according to Abe, is to undercut the tendency to objectify Buddha-nature as some sort of substantial existence. Abe identifies several aspects of Dōgen's view on Buddha-nature, including its *de-homocentric* nature, its nonsubstantiality, and its identity with worldly phenomena.

One of the central concerns in Buddhism is the problem of life and death in human existence and the emancipation from the suffering that entails this existence. Moreover, this emancipation is said to occur in human consciousness. Realizing one's Buddha-nature, therefore, has traditionally meant discovering that internal essence that transcends ordinary human existence. However, Dōgen sees this view as an objectification of Buddha-nature that will forever keep a person imprisoned in duality. For Dōgen, although the realization of Buddha-nature lies in human consciousness, the *reality* of Buddha-nature includes the entirety of worldly existence. This view is what Abe terms de-homocentric—the problem of life and death is located not in the human realm but in the appearance and disappearance of all worldly phenomena, both sentient and nonsentient. By emphasizing its de-homocentric nature, Buddha-nature is no longer objectified as a substance possessed by humans.

What is the relation between Buddha-nature and worldly existence? Dōgen asserts that all beings *are* Buddha-nature, thus signifying the *oneness* of Buddha-nature and worldly existence. According to traditional Buddhist doctrine, however, worldly existence is characterized by constant change, or impermanence, and is, therefore, not associated with the unconditioned, unchanging Buddha-nature. In contrast, Dōgen asserts that impermanence itself is Buddha-nature, thus continuing his efforts to undercut the tendency to objectify Buddha-nature. For Dōgen, Buddha-nature discloses itself as everyday phenomena such as grasses, trees, and stones. Furthermore, it is the moment-to-moment arising/disappearing of ordinary phenomena that marks the essence of Buddha-nature.

Practice and Enlightenment

Though the philosophical aspects of Zen are of great importance, Abe maintains that one must actualize philosophical insights in everyday life. The question then arises, if the moment-to-moment passing of phenomena constitutes Buddha-nature, how can one practice? If there is nothing beyond the here and now of everyday existence, then what purpose is there in meditation? Abe answers these questions with Dōgen's view on Zen practice, *shikantaza*, or "just sitting." Just as everyday life (all beings) and Buddha-nature are one for Dōgen, so too are practice and enlightenment. In other words, practice itself is enlightenment, and enlightenment is practice. For Abe, Dōgen's views on practice and enlightenment do not eliminate the reason for practicing Zen meditation but instead help the practitioner transcend self-centered human intention. According to Abe, therefore, shikantaza is the purest kind of practice.

Critical Analyses of Western Philosophy

Abe analyzes Western philosophy and theology based on the logic of is/is not. Eastern and Western thought differ significantly in their respective views on what Abe calls "negativity." Tradition-

ally, Western thought has favored the positive over the negative: being over nonbeing, life over death, permanence over impermanence. The positive principles of being, life, and permanence are considered primary, while nonbeing, death, and impermanence are viewed as secondary or derivative. In the East, however, the negative has always played a fundamental role in religions and philosophies. In fact, both being and nonbeing have equal force in many Eastern worldviews, particularly Buddhism.

Abe stresses that the Zen notion of nothingness is not the *relative nonbeing* that is the opposite of *relative being*. Rather, Zen nothingness is *absolute nonbeing*, which signifies a return to the original state of reality that existed before the division between positive and negative. This concept of reality is at odds with the traditional metaphysics of the West, including Platonism, which locates reality in the transcendent realm of ideal forms, and Christianity, which conceives of God as beyond this world. If Platonism and Christianity can be said to posit a *transcendent* reality, then Zen asserts, to use the philosopher Keiji Nishitani's term, a *trans-descendent* reality.

In his critical analyses based on the logic of is/is not, Abe examines modern philosophies that seem to advocate ideas similar to those of Zen Buddhism, including the philosophies set forth by Friedrich Nietzsche and Alfred North Whitehead. Nietzsche contends that in the face of the uncertainty and arbitrariness of the world, Western metaphysics and Christianity have hoisted false constructs (ideal forms, God) to avoid the nihility of existence. In so doing, they have imprisoned humanity in a false morality and cut it off from its natural birthright, spontaneity in life. Moreover, this avoidance entails the deception of positing a transcendent other, which offers comfort in the face of real existence but is in reality a lie.

Nietzsche claims that to truly live, one must face and endure nihility without recourse to any deception, including a higher reality or power. This facing up to the arbitrary uncertainty of existence is a return to life itself, which Nietzsche calls the innocence of becoming. This return to life is, furthermore, a commitment to live life with an awareness and abandonment of this deception of the transcendent.

While appreciating Nietzsche's challenge to transcendental constructs, Abe claims that Nietzsche still posits some kind of objective reality. Behind the false constructions of ideal forms or God lies a dynamic changing reality for the living subject. Therefore, even though the notions of unchanging substance and transcendent reality are relinquished, the innocence of becoming and natural life are still posited as a reality to be chosen by the human. Though Western metaphysics is radically changed in Nietzsche's philosophy, the subject/object duality still remains.

In Whitehead's philosophy of universal relativity, Abe finds much in common with the Buddhist notion of dependent arising. Both concepts assert that although individual entities are unique, they are also profoundly *interdependent*, so much so that each entity contains all other entities. Whitehead's philosophy of universal relativity and radical interdependence attempts to overcome the duality of separate substances (that each entity is a separate thing in itself).

Abe maintains that if Whitehead held that *all* entities fell under this radical interdependence, a true identity between the Buddhist doctrine of dependent arising and Whitehead's universal relativity would exist. However, Abe finds Whitehead's treatment of God a problem, specifically his notion of the nontemporal/nonspatial dimension of God. While at one level Whitehead contends that God and the world are both immanent in each other and also transcendent, God's primordial nature, being beyond space and time, is permanent. The primordial nature of the world, however, is a state of constant flux. According to Abe, Whitehead's view creates a subtle yet profound duality between God and the world, despite their overt interrelationship. Whitehead's formulation, therefore, does not transcend duality and is at odds with the Buddhist notion of interdependence.

Abe also engages Christian theology in critical dialogue, particularly the theology of Paul Tillich. While applauding Tillich's attempt at comparison, Abe discloses some misconceptions that Tillich has regarding Buddhism. For example, in his analysis of the Kingdom of God and Nirvana, Tillich explains that Christianity's aim is the unity of *everyone* and everything in the Kingdom of God, while in Buddhism, it is the unity of *everything* and everyone in Nirvana. The emphasis on *everyone* in Christianity signifies the superiority of humans over things in God's kingdom, while the emphasis on *everything* in Buddhism means that things are superior to humans in the realm of Nirvana. Abe takes issue with this formulation, explaining that although it is true that the immediate presence of all impermanent/empty things is Buddha-nature, the *realization* of this occurs only in human consciousness. In other words, while reality is identified with all things, both sentient and nonsentient, the awakening to this reality is actualized in the human realm, thus proffering humans a special, though not superior, status among things. In his analysis, Tillich violates the logic of is/is not by privileging things over humans and, therefore, has not understood the essence of Zen.

Another criticism of Tillich's work is the stand that the philosopher takes regarding religious encounters with the various secular movements of the twentieth century. These movements, including nationalism, scientism, Marxism, and liberal humanism, are analyzed by Tillich in the mode of an "observing participant," locating the discussion in the historic-cultural realm. Abe strongly maintains that one should confront these movements in the mode of a "self-staking participant," locating the encounter on the existential realm of personal faith and religious awareness. Abe contends that it is precisely a religious encounter with and an overcoming of nihilism that make religion a necessity in the modern world.

Zen and Western Thought was the first book-length study by the leading exponent of Zen for the West in the second half of the twentieth century. Its critique of Western philosophy and theology from the standpoint of Zen has provided a basis not only for a deeper understanding of Zen philosophy but also for interfaith dialogue.

John Y. Cha

Additional Reading

Cobb, John B., and Christopher Ives, eds. *The Emptying God: A Buddhist-Jewish-Christian Conversation.* Maryknoll, N.Y.: Orbis Books, 1991. This collection of nine articles—an initial essay by Masao Abe, responses by seven Western theologians, and a final rejoinder by Abe—

represents the extensive work taking place in the field of interfaith dialogue.

Heisig, James W., and John C. Maraldo, eds. *Rude Awakenings: Zen, the Kyoto School, and the Question of Nationalism.* Honolulu: University of Hawaii Press, 1994. This collection of articles addresses the relationship between the leading intellectuals of the Kyoto School and Japanese nationalism. Although previous works on the Kyoto School have dealt with theology and philosophy, this is the first book-length study in English on the school's political, social, and historical context.

King, Winston L. "The Existential Nature of Buddhist Ultimates." *Philosophy East and West* 33, no. 3 (July, 1983): 263-271. King analyzes the Buddhist concept of ultimate reality and its existential nature, from early to Mahayana Buddhism. He discusses the significance of Abe's interpretation of emptiness as a creative and active force.

Mitchell, Donald W., ed. *Masao Abe: A Zen Life of Dialogue.* Boston: Charles E. Tuttle, 1998. An assortment of essays honoring Abe's body of work.

John Y. Cha

Peter Abelard

Abelard developed the theory of conceptualism to reconcile Platonic idealism with nominalism. His use of the dialectic to explore Scripture helped shape Scholasticism, and many of his religious views, condemned as heretical in his own lifetime, subsequently influenced church doctrine.

Principal philosophical works: *Logica ingredientibus*, c. 1120; *Tractatus de unitate et trinitate divina*, c. 1120; *Dialectica*, c. 1120; *Theologia "summi boni,"* c. 1120; *Sic et Non*, c. 1123; *Logica "nostrorum petitioni sociorum,"* c. 1124; *Theologia Christiana*, c. 1125 (partial translation, *Christian Theology*, 1948); *Historia calamitatum*, c. 1132 (*The Story of My Misfortune*, 1922); *Theologia Scolarium*, c. 1135; *Ethica*, c. 1138 (*Abailard's Ethics*, 1935, also known as *Peter Abelard's Ethics*, 1971, and *Ethical Writings*, 1994); *Apologia*, c. 1141; *Dialogus inter philosophum, Judaeum et Christianum*, 1141-1142 (*Dialogue of a Philosopher with a Jew and a Christian*, 1979); *Letters of Abelard and Heloise*, 1713.

Born: 1079; Le Pallet, Brittany (now in France)
Died: April 21, 1142; the Priory of Saint-Marcel, near Chalon-sur-Saône, Burgundy (now in France)

Early Life

Peter Abelard was born in Le Pallet, Brittany, about 1079. His father, Berengar, was lord of the village and a knight in the service of the Count of Brittany. Because Abelard was the oldest son, his parents expected him to succeed to these titles. Nevertheless, they did not object when he showed more interest in intellectual than physical jousting. At age fifteen, Abelard left his parents, his three brothers—Raoul, Porcaire, and Dagobert—and his sister, Denise, to study under Roscelin of Compiègne. By 1100, he had moved on to Paris, where he attended the lectures of William of Champeaux, head of the cathedral school and archdeacon of Notre-Dame.

At the school, Abelard demonstrated the combination of brilliance and indiscretion that was to earn for him the title *Rhinoceros indomitus*, or the unconquerable rhinoceros. William, an extreme Platonist, maintained that universal concepts such as "tree" exist independent of any specific examples. Thus, there is no substantial difference between one maple tree and another, or between

an oak, a maple, or an elm. Moreover, the quality of "treeness" is independent of any individual example. In public debate, Abelard forced William, regarded as the leading dialectician of the age, to abandon this position and accept Abelard's own view of conceptualism. Without denying universal categories (which nominalists rejected), Abelard argued that one knows those universals only because of individual examples; if those specimens did not exist, neither would the universal.

Life's Work

Abelard's victory won for him the respect of his fellow students and the enmity of William; both factors prompted him to leave Notre-Dame and set up his own school, first at Melun (1102) and then at Corbeil, within five miles of the French capital. The rivalry with Abelard may have influenced William's decision to leave Paris as well; outside the city, he established a new monastery, dedicated to Saint Victor, where he continued teaching.

William's departure left a vacancy at the cathedral school, and after Abelard recovered from an illness that had caused him to return to Brittany, he was invited to assume the chair of his former master (c. 1108). As soon as William learned of the appointment, he hastened back to Notre-Dame and forced Abelard to leave. Retreating first to Melun, Abelard soon was teaching at Sainte-Geneviève, at the very gates of Paris, drawing all but a handful of the students from the cathedral.

His teaching was interrupted again in 1111 when his parents decided to take Holy Orders, a common practice among the elderly in the twelfth century. Abelard had to go to Brittany to settle the family estate; then, perhaps at the urging of his mother, Lucia, he went to study theology under Anselm of Laon.

Just as William had been the most noted logician, so Anselm was the most famous religious teacher of the period. Just as Abelard had shown himself a better logician than William, so he would prove himself a better teacher of theology than Anselm. Finding the lectures at Laon dull, Abelard absented himself frequently. Students loyal to the old master challenged this lack of respect, and Abelard retorted that he himself could teach more effectively. Considering the little time that he had devoted to the subject, such a boast seemed absurd; his fellow students challenged him to make good his claim.

Abelard readily agreed, promising to lecture the next day on Ezekiel, one of the most abstruse books in the Bible. Even his opponents thought that matters had now gone too far and urged him to take time to prepare. Abelard refused; thus, when he rose to speak, he saw only a few people in the audience, all eagerly waiting for the upstart to make a fool of himself. Instead, his exegesis was so brilliant that within two days, virtually all Anselm's students were attending Abelard's lectures and begging him to continue the series. Anselm thereupon forbade Abelard to teach anywhere in Laon.

By then, however, William's old post was vacant once more, and in 1112 or 1113 Abelard assumed it without opposition, inaugurating his ten-

ure by concluding his explication of Ezekiel. Handsome, of medium height, with piercing brown eyes, he was, as even his enemies conceded, "sublime in eloquence." As *magister scholarum* of the leading school in France, if not of northern Europe, he was immensely popular. In part, he owed this success to his unorthodox teaching methods. Rejecting the traditional *lectio*, in which the master read a text and then the commentaries on it, Abelard championed the *disputatio*, posing problems and resolving them through logic and careful textual analysis. Recalling those years, Héloïse wrote:

Peter Abelard holds the hand of his beloved Héloïse. This line drawing depicts their ill-fated love, which led to Abelard's castration. *(Library of Congress)*

Who among kings or philosophers could equal thee in fame? What kingdom or city or village did not burn to see thee? Who, I ask, did not hasten to gaze upon thee when thou appearedst in public, nor on thy departure with straining neck and fixed eye follow thee?

Among those impressed with Abelard's teaching was a canon of Notre-Dame named Fulbert, the uncle and guardian of Héloïse. She had been educated at the convent of Argenteuil, and, by the age of fourteen, she could read Latin, Greek, and Hebrew. "La très sage Héloïs," as French poet François Villon referred to her in 1461 in "Ballade des dames du temps jadis" ("Ballad of Dead Ladies"), may have already attended some of Abelard's lectures when in 1117 Fulbert invited Abelard to live with him on the Île de la Cité in the rue des Chantres. In return, the thirty-eight-year-old Abelard would tutor the seventeen-year-old Héloïse.

Tall, thin, with thick brown hair, gray eyes, fine features, a gracious manner, and intelligence, she might have tempted a saint left alone in her company: The sequel was not surprising. As Abelard recorded:

> More words of love than of our reading passed between us and more kissing than teaching. My hands strayed oftener to her bosom than to the pages; love drew our eyes to look on each other more than reading kept them on our texts.

Finally, even Fulbert realized his mistake and evicted Abelard, but Héloïse was already pregnant. To protect her from her uncle's anger, Abelard took her to Brittany, where their son, Astrolabe or Astrolabius, was born. To reconcile themselves to Fulbert, Abelard offered to marry Héloïse under the condition that the marriage remain secret, and Fulbert agreed.

Héloïse strongly opposed this step, recognizing it as the worst possible solution. If the purpose of the marriage was to lessen Fulbert's shame, secrecy would not satisfy him. Any marriage would also remove Abelard's prospects for advancement in the Church, and even his reputation as a philosopher would be diminished. She argued:

What harmony can there be between pupils and nursemaids, desks and cradles, books or tablets and distaffs, pen or stylus and spindles? Who can concentrate on thoughts of Scripture or philosophy and be able to endure babies crying, nurses soothing them with lullabies, and all the noisy coming and going of men and women about the house?

Moreover, she did not regard marriage as necessary to bind her to Abelard, to whom she was linked by a love stronger than any church vows.

Whether because of his desire to redeem Héloïse's honor, concern over Fulbert's possible vengeance, or fear that Héloïse might eventually marry another, Abelard rejected her sage advice, and they married, living apart to keep their union a secret. As Héloïse had predicted, Fulbert soon was boasting of his alliance with France's leading philosopher, and when Abelard and Héloïse denied having wed, Fulbert began to abuse his niece. Abelard thereupon removed her to the convent at Argenteuil, where she would be safe from Fulbert but close enough for him to visit.

Fulbert was now convinced that Abelard intended to force Héloïse to become a nun and thereby dissolve his marriage, leaving him free for ecclesiastical advancement. The enraged canon devised a revenge that would at once block such promotion and fittingly punish Abelard's lechery. Bribing Abelard's servant to leave the door unlocked, Fulbert, accompanied by some ruffians, burst into Abelard's bedroom one night and castrated him.

Paris rallied to Abelard's support. Fulbert was stripped of his canonry and expelled from the city. The two culprits who were apprehended—one of them Abelard's feckless servant—were blinded and castrated. Seeing his suffering as divine retribution, Abelard gave up his post at Notre-Dame and retired to the monastery of Saint-Denis, where he became a monk (c. 1119). He also ordered Héloïse to assume the veil, though she had no religious vocation; indeed, he insisted that she take her vows first. Was this another sign that he feared she might marry another? If so, he little understood her deep love for him.

At Saint-Denis, Abelard lost little time in making new enemies by pointing out that the monks were not adhering to the Benedictine rule. Therefore, when Abelard asked permission to resume teaching, the abbot gladly allowed him to establish a school at the priory, removed from the monastery. Students again surrounded him, and for them, he prepared *Tractatus de unitate et trinitate divina*, a work he would expand and revise several times over the next sixteen years.

Although the monks of Saint-Denis were delighted with Abelard's absence, others were not pleased with his teaching. Among the disciples of Anselm who still resented Abelard's behavior at Laon were Alberic of Reims and Lotulph of Novara. They maintained that a monk should not teach philosophy, that Abelard lacked the training to teach theology, and that his book, which sought to use logic to demonstrate the existence and nature of the Trinity, was heretical. They organized a council at Soissons in 1121 to try the book, and they secured Abelard's condemnation. Even the presiding papal legate regarded the decision as unjust and immediately allowed Abelard to return to Saint-Denis.

At the monastery, Abelard embroiled himself in further controversy by challenging the identity of the monks' supposed patron saint. So inflamed were passions against him that he fled to Provins. The friendly Count Theobald arranged for him to establish a hermitage near Troyes, and Abelard dedicated it to the Paraclete, or Holy Spirit. Again the orthodox objected; traditionally, hermitages were dedicated to the entire Trinity or to Christ, never to the Paraclete.

Students cared nothing about the name, though. Leaving the comforts of Paris, they came in the thousands to till the fields and build accommodations in order to listen again to the words of Abelard, who rewarded them with stimulating lectures and treatises. In *Sic et Non* (yes and no), Abelard responded to criticism that authority did not need the support of logic to establish faith. Abelard assembled some 160 seemingly contradictory statements by the church fathers and argued that only through reason could one reconcile these. *Ethical Writings* postulated that sin derives from intention, not action. Performing a good deed for evil purposes is not meritorious; committing wrong unknowingly is not sinful.

These heterodox views disturbed Bernard of Clairvaux and Norbert, archbishop of Magde-

burg. In his treatise on baptism (1125), Bernard rejected Abelard's view on sin, and Abelard was so uneasy about this opposition that around 1125 he accepted the post of abbot at the monastery of Saint-Gildas-de-Rhuys (in Brittany), a place so remote that even his devoted students did not follow him there.

The buildings at the Paraclete were abandoned but soon found another use. The abbot of Saint-Denis claimed the convent of Argenteuil and expelled the nuns. Around 1128, Abelard offered his former hermitage to a group under Héloïse, and they accepted. Soon the convent was so successful that other nunneries placed themselves under Héloïse's jurisdiction, and daughter institutions had to be established to house all the members.

Abelard did not fare as well in Brittany. As at Saint-Denis, his efforts to reform the dissolute monks met with hostility. Twice they tried to poison him; when he learned of a plot to cut his throat, he fled. Hiding and in despair, Abelard composed *The Story of My Misfortunes*. After a copy reached Héloïse, she promptly wrote to Abelard the first of a brief but poignant series of love letters that reveal how truly she meant her statement in 1118 that she would prefer to be Abelard's mistress than Caesar Augustus's wife.

Though her love had not abated, Abelard's had. "If . . . you have need of my instruction and writings in matters pertaining to God, write to me what you want, so that I may answer as God permits me," he replied to her impassioned lines, urging her to forget their former life together. Ever obedient, preferring Abelard's religious treatises to silence, she requested and received sermons, psalms, biblical exegeses, a rule more suitable for convents than that devised by Benedict for monasteries. As she had inspired Abelard to compose love poetry during their short time together, so now she served as a religious muse.

Abelard's movements in the early 1130's are unclear, but by 1136, he was again teaching in Paris. This return to prominence aroused his enemies, chief among them Bernard of Clairvaux, who saw in Abelard's reliance on reason a challenge to faith. Whether Bernard's extensive letter-writing campaign against Abelard would have succeeded is unclear, but in 1140, Abelard's students challenged Bernard to debate their master at an assembly at Sens. Bernard at first refused, knowing that he was no match for the *Rhinoceros indomitus*. Bernard's supporters insisted that he attend, however, and he finally agreed.

However, he had no intention of engaging Abelard in any intellectual combat. On the day before the scheduled encounter, Bernard persuaded the gathered religious leaders to condemn Abelard unheard; when Abelard entered the church of Saint-Étienne on June 3, 1140, Bernard began reading out a list of seventeen charges of heresy. Realizing that he was facing a trial, not a debate, Abelard immediately stopped the proceedings by appealing to Rome for judgment. He then left the church, intending to plead his case before the pope.

Bernard's letters moved faster than the aging Abelard, however, and Pope Innocent II owed his tiara to Bernard. At the abbey of Cluny, Abelard learned that Rome had confirmed Bernard's verdict, and the local abbot, Peter the Venerable, now urged Abelard to make peace with his old antagonist. Although Abelard consented, the rhinoceros remained unconquered. In *Dialogue of a Philosopher with a Jew and a Christian*, he still maintained that unless theologians could use reason, they could not defend their faith.

Abelard composed this treatise at the monastery of Saint-Marcel, near Chalon-sur-Sâone, in Burgundy, where he had gone for his health, and there he died on April 21, 1142. He had asked to be buried at the Paraclete, and so he was. Twenty-two years later, Héloïse was laid to rest beside him. According to a chronicler, as her body was lowered into the grave, Abelard reached up to embrace his wife. Over the centuries, their bodies were moved several times, and they lie in the famous Père-Lachaise cemetery in Paris beneath the inscription, "ABELARD: HELOISE—For Ever One."

Influence
In his epitaph for Abelard, Peter the Venerable called his friend "the Socrates of the Gauls, the great Plato of the West, *our* Aristotle." Yet Abelard was neither a secular philosopher nor a religious skeptic. As he wrote in his *Apologia*, "I do not wish to be a philosopher by dissociating myself from Paul; I do not wish to be an Aristotle by separating myself from Christ, since there is no

other name under heaven by which I can be saved."

Although Bernard was wrong to view Abelard as a heretic, he was right to see Abelard as a threat to the old order. Abelard's popularity as a teacher helped create the university system, which spelled the end of the power of monastic schools. His fusion of logic and theology fostered a new Scholasticism that was spread by his students, who included three future popes and the greatest classicist of the twelfth century, John of Salisbury. His manuscripts contributed to the era's intellectual renaissance.

Abelard is best remembered, however, for his association with Héloïse. Over the centuries, writers have found in their story an inspiration for poems, plays, and novels. A strange new twist to that famous story was introduced in the 1980's, when a computer-assisted stylistic analysis of the correspondence between Abelard and Héloïse suggested that all the letters, including those attributed to Héloïse, were in fact written by Abelard himself. Thus the possibility exists that Abelard was not only a philosopher but also, in a peculiar way, a gifted writer of fiction.

Joseph Rosenblum

Glosses on Porphyry

Type of philosophy: Epistemology, philosophical theology
First transcribed: Glossulae in Porphyrium, in *Logica ingredientibus*, c. 1120 (English translation, 1990; also as *Gloss on Porphyry*, 1994)
Principal ideas advanced:

◇ A universal is that which is formed to be predicated of many; because things cannot be predicated of many, only words are universals.

◇ A universal word is imposed on things because of a common likeness conceived by the person imposing the word.

◇ The common likeness of things is a function of the nature of things considered as causes of common conceptions.

◇ Universals signify existent things, namely, discrete individuals; but, in a sense, universals consist in the understanding alone.

⋄ Universal words are corporeal with respect to the nature of things, and they are incorporeal with respect to the manner in which they signify.

⋄ Universals signify sensible things, but because the intrinsic substance signified is naturally separated from the things signified, universals are, in that sense, insensible.

One of the most colorful and fascinating figures of the Middle Ages was Peter Abelard. Many who know little about the technicalities of medieval logic still know about his life and loves. Some mystery and much romance surround the events of his life, and beneath this fascination the fact that Abelard was undoubtedly one of the more skilled philosophers of the era is sometimes forgotten. For one thing, much less of his work has been translated than that of others from the same period who are, consequently, now better known. Furthermore, his particular doctrines have not gained the fame that came to others. No matter how important *Glosses on Porphyry* may be in a medieval setting, the idea of practicing philosophy through such commentary is not a currently accepted form. However, few were more responsible than Porphyry for the problems that dominated the Middle Ages, and Abelard's glosses concern crucial issues.

This work belongs to the branch of philosophy that Abelard, following the Roman philosopher Boethius, called "rational" (the other divisions being the "speculative" and the "moral"). It corresponds most nearly to what is called logic, although it comprehends a wider area of problems than formal logic does. Porphyry prepared an introduction for the *Categories* (in *Organon*, second Athenian period, 335-323 B.C.E.; English translation, 1812) of the Greek philosopher Aristotle, and it is this work upon which Abelard comments. Abelard's treatment of the problem of the status of universals really ended the argument in its all-absorbing attraction; from then on it was only one among a series of problems. Abelard, however, was condemned by his church because his doctrines seemed to lead to paganism.

Definition, division, and classification are the central logical problems to be considered first. Essential definition is the main issue, and consequently all these logical problems basically involve metaphysical issues. In Porphyry's mind, and Abelard's as well, logical division is division according to real structures actually present in nature. How are the creatures of the natural order divided? This question concerns the way of things as much as it does the ways of logical procedure, for in the medieval mind, the two are to be worked on until they become the same. The mind adjusts its classifications to the divisions it finds in nature. Logical investigation is ontological inquiry, and through it the structure of the world is grasped.

Universals

The prominent controversy regarding the status of universals is raised through logical inquiry, which has metaphysical overtones. Deciding whether universals are real is a necessary step before deciding about genus and species. People make divisions according to genus and species, but one cannot be content to do this as a logical convenience. The question is whether such division represents anything real, when it is obvious that every individual thing is singular and not universal, representative of the species but never the species itself. Abelard asks: Do universals apply to things or only to words, once one has been forced to study universals through the study of genus and species?

Abelard must first define a universal. Then, after quoting Aristotle and Porphyry, he refines his own definition: That is universal that is formed to be predicated of many. The question of the ontological status of universals has been raised by a logical question and formulated in logical terms. Abelard begins by supposing that things as well as words are included within this definition.

If things as well as words are called universal, how can the universal definition be applied to things also? Abelard begins to deal with this question by considering the views of those who have formulated this problem. Many, he says, solve this issue by asserting that in different things, there is present a substance that is essentially the same although the various things differ in form. Porphyry seems to assent to this solution in arguing that by participation in the species, many humans are one. Other philosophers are of different opinions, and Abelard begins to formulate his own solution by finding one opinion from among these that seems to him to be closest to the truth, namely, the suggestion that individual things are different from each other not only in their forms, but also in their essences. He concludes that things cannot be universals because they are not predicated of many.

In retrospect, there seems to be no question but that much early medieval interpretation of Aristotle was substantially influenced by Neoplatonic doctrines. Abelard, like many others, was working toward the empirical stress upon the unique individual, which came to be recognized as more accurate Aristotelian doctrine. In working on the problem of the status of universals, Abelard attempted to reconcile the Platonic suggestion that universals subsist independently of things with the Aristotelian view, which stressed the individual as primary and the universal as a function of the status of things, existing only in things.

Some philosophers maintain that the universal is merely a collection of many individual things, but this is too weak a status to assign to universals, in Abelard's view. He saw that, although a collection of humans is called a species, when the universal *human* is predicated of each individual, it is not the whole collection of humans that is predicated. A universal must be something other than a collection taken as a whole.

Abelard was trying to mediate between what he considered to be two extreme views, to work out a modified position that would give sufficient status to universals without making them in some sense more real than individuals. Being theologically oriented, he could not do away with universals or make them simply a product of language because they are present in God's understanding and important to God's way of knowing. On the other hand, like all those who became interested in Aristotle in the later Middle Ages, Abelard wanted to correct what he felt had been errors in previous ideas concerning universals and to stress the primacy of individuals and their status.

Words as Universals
Abelard, however, could not go along with those who called single individuals predicated of many things universals, on the ground that the many

things agreed with the individuals in certain respects. Neither a collection taken together, then, nor an individual thing could be called a universal; consequently, Abelard believed that universals belong to words alone. There are universal words and there are particular words. If this is so, what had to be done was to inquire carefully into the property of universal words. What is the common cause by which the universal word is imposed and what is the conception of the common likeness of things? More important, is the word called common because of a common cause (or respect) in which the things agree, because of a common conception, or because of both at once? These questions, Abelard found by his examination of other doctrines, form the heart of the issue concerning universals. Dealing with these questions is the only way to attempt to reach a solution.

In order to deal with the issues, Abelard argued, one must first be clear about the process of understanding itself. (This is typically Aristotelian.) When one understands the relation between the mind and the objects that it seeks to understand and how it comes to form that understanding, then one will learn the status of the universal. In other words, the universal is to be understood primarily as a part of the process of understanding itself. What Abelard found is that the understanding of universals differs and is to be distinguished from the understanding of particulars.

Abelard turned to theology and considered the question of universals as concerning the operation of God's mind. God must have universal conceptions in his mind as a necessary part of his creative function. Human beings, however, do not need such universal patterns. Universal conceptions exist in God's mind, but not in people's, and this is one measure of their difference. Humans have certain intrinsic forms that do not come to them through the senses, such as rationality and mortality. (Aristotle had also realized that not all knowledge could be formed from the senses and the apprehension of individuals.)

What, then, is responsible for the common reference of universal words? Is it caused by a common cause of imposition or a common conception? Abelard came to the conclusion that it is caused by both, but he regarded the common cause in accordance with the nature of things as having a greater force. There is, then, a source for universal conception in the things themselves from which the understanding forms its conceptions, although some universals result merely from the formation of common conceptions. The conception of universals is formed by abstraction.

Having come this far, Abelard believed that his analysis had provided the ground necessary to propose a solution to the question about universals and their status, the question Porphyry had originally raised. Universals signify things truly existent; they are not merely empty opinions. Nevertheless, in a certain sense, they exist in the understanding alone. Again, if one divides things into either corporeal or incorporeal and asks where in this division universals belong, the answer must be that they belong to both divisions. Universals in a sense signify corporeal things in that they are imposed according to the nature of things; yet in another sense, they signify incorporeal things, with respect to the manner in which they signify.

Universals are said to subsist in sensible things; that is, they signify an intrinsic substance existing in a thing that is sensible by its exterior form. However, although they signify this substance that subsists actually in the sensible thing, at the same time, they demonstrate the same substance as naturally separated from the sensible thing. Some universals are sensible with respect to the nature of things, and the same universal may be nonsensible with respect to the mode of signifying. Universals refer to sensible things, but they refer to them in an incorporeal manner. They signify both sensible things and at the same time that common conception that is ascribed primarily to the divine mind.

Singular words involve no such doubt as to their meaning. As things are discrete in themselves, so they are signified by singular words discretely, and the understanding of them refers to definite things. Universals do not have this easy reference, which is what makes them so difficult to understand. There is no definite thing, as is the case with singular words, with which they agree. Nevertheless, the multitude of things themselves is the cause of the universality of the nouns that are used to refer to them, because only

that which contains many is universal. Yet the thing itself does not have the universality that the thing confers upon the word.

In some sense such a solution as Abelard has proposed—a moderate realism—could be accused of not being definite. What he did was to reject extreme solutions and to set the limits of the question and the mode in which the question ought to be asked. Only an extreme position is likely to be clear; any solution that attempts to hold to a moderate view is always in danger of slipping over to one of the extremes and will suffer from appearing to hold both extreme positions at once.

Yet the value in Abelard's analysis is the raising of the problems, the cast given to the question, and the elucidation of the difficulties involved in any solution. The subtle analysis is illuminating in its own right, and understanding it gives us an appreciation both of Abelard and of the tradition that set his problems for him.

Frederick Sontag, updated by John K. Roth

Additional Reading

Abelard, Peter. *Abelard and Heloise: The Story of His Misfortunes and the Personal Letters*. Translated by Betty Radice. London: Folio Society, 1977. Peter Abelard's account of his life and his and Héloïse's letters are available in many translations. This work provides primary information about Abelard's life from his birth until about 1132.

Bowden, John. *Who's Who in Theology: From the First Century to the Present*. New York: Crossroad, 1992. Provides helpful information on Abelard and his thought and discusses other thinkers who helped form the context for Abelard's reflections.

Clanchy, M. T. *Abelard: A Medieval Life*. Malden, Mass.: Blackwell, 1997. This historical work interprets Abelard's life, thought, and historical circumstances in accessible ways.

Copleston, Frederick. *A History of Philosophy: Medieval Philosophy*. Garden City, N.Y.: Doubleday, 1962. A leading historian of Western philosophy emphasizes Abelard's contribution to controversies about metaphysics and the theory of knowledge.

Grane, Leif. *Peter Abelard: Philosophy and Christianity in the Middle Ages*. Translated by Frederick

Crowley and Christine Crowley. New York: Harcourt, Brace and World, 1970. An excellent survey of Abelard's life set against the history, religion, and philosophy of the twelfth century. The work contains a good summary of Abelard's views on metaphysics and religion.

Luscombe, David Edward. *The School of Abelard: The Influence of Abelard's Thought in the Early Scholastic Period*. Cambridge, London: Cambridge University Press, 1969. This study shows how Abelard influenced Western philosophy. Includes an extensive bibliography of works by and about Abelard.

Marenbon, John. *The Philosophy of Peter Abelard*. New York: Cambridge University Press, 1997. A good account of Abelard's thought and his contributions to the history of philosophy.

Rinser, Luise. *Abelard's Love*. Translated by Jean M. Snook. Lincoln: University of Nebraska Press, 1998. Focuses on Abelard's relation to Héloïse.

Sikes, Jeffrey Garrett. *Peter Abelard*. Cambridge, London: Cambridge University Press, 1932. An older but still useful biography that pays special attention to Abelard's views on religious and philosophical matters.

Starnes, Kathleen M. *Peter Abelard, His Place in History*. Washington, D.C.: University Press of America, 1981. A helpful study that offers important insights about the development of Abelard's thought and its significance in Western philosophy.

Worthington, Marjorie. *The Immortal Lovers: Heloise and Abelard*. Garden City, N.Y.: Doubleday and Co., 1960. A popular, well-written biography of the two lovers. Good on twelfth century background.

Joseph Rosenblum, updated by John K. Roth

Theodor Adorno

Adorno, one of the major figures in the Frankfurt School of Marxist social philosophy, attempted to fuse philosophy and sociology in his writings. He developed a negative dialectic designed to advance philosophical materialism.

Principal philosophical works: *Kierkegaard, Konstruktion des Ästhetischen*, 1933 (*Kierkegaard: Construction of the Aesthetic*, 1989); *Dialektik der Aufklärung*, 1947 (with Max Horkheimer; *Dialectic of Enlightenment*, 1972); *Philosophie der neuen Musik*, 1949 (*Philosophy of Modern Music*, 1973); *Minima Moralia: Reflexion aus dem Beschädigten Leben*, 1951 (*Minima Moralia: Reflections from Damaged Life*, 1974); *Prismen: Kulturkritik und Gesellschaft*, 1955 (*Prisms*, 1967); *Zur Metakritik de Erkenntnistheorie: Studien über Husserl und die phänomenologischen Antinomien*, 1956 (*Against Epistemology: A Metacritique, Studies in Husserl and the Phenomenological Antinomies*, 1982); "Soziologie und empirische Forschung," 1957 ("Sociology and Empirical Research," 1970); *Drei Studien zu Hegel*, 1963 (*Hegel: Three Studies*, 1993); *Jargon der Eigentlichkeit: Zur Deutschen Ideologie*, 1964 (*Jargon of Authenticity*, 1973); *Negative Dialektik*, 1966 (*Negative Dialectics*, 1973); *Ästhetische Theorie*, 1970 (*Aesthetic Theory*, 1984); "Commitment,"1974.

Born: September 11, 1903; Frankfurt am Main, Germany
Died: August 6, 1969; Visp, Switzerland

Early Life

Theodor Adorno was born Theodor Wiesengrund in 1903 in Frankfurt am Main, Germany. His mother, the daughter of a German singer and a French army officer (whose Corsican and originally Genoese ancestry accounts for the name Adorno, the name by which Theodor was known after his emigration from Germany), was a talented singer from whom he inherited a love of music; his father was a successful wine merchant of Jewish extraction. While attending secondary school, Adorno studied privately with Siegfried Kracauer, the German historian and social critic. From 1925 to 1928, he studied music with Alban Berg and Eduard Steuermann in Vienna. Returning to the University of Frankfurt in 1928, Adorno wrote his qualifying paper on the aesthetics of philosopher Søren Kierkegaard.

In 1931, he became a lecturer at the university, where he became involved with the Institut für Sozialforschung (Institute for Social Research) and published numerous articles in its journal, *Zeitschrift für Sozialforschung*. The institute was established by a group of radical Marxist scholars whose goal was to assess modern society through an interdisciplinary study of its cultural and philosophical phenomena. Soon after Adolf Hitler's rise to power in Germany, the institute moved to the United States; Adorno officially joined in 1938, when he moved to New York City. In 1941, Adorno moved to Los Angeles and continued to write prolifically, although most of his manuscripts remained unpublished until after his return to Germany in 1949. While in Los Angeles, he renewed his acquaintance with composer Arnold Schoenberg and assisted Thomas Mann with the musical sections of his novel *Doktor Faustus* (1947; *Doctor Faustus*, 1948). He became assistant director of the Institute for Social Research in 1950 and codirector, with Max Horkheimer, in 1955. He continued to teach and publish numerous essays and books until his death in Visp, Switzerland, in 1969.

Life's Work

Adorno's work is difficult to codify or systematize, as *Negative Dialectics*, one of his major philosophical works, reveals. The self-contradictory

Theodor Adorno. *(Archive Photos)*

term "negative dialectics" is meant to affirm the idea and value of an ultimate synthesis, while negating its existence in individual instances. Adorno argues that every theory about the world, as it is formed, tends to become reified by the mind and to be invested with the prestige and permanency of an object, thus effacing the very dialectical process from which it emerged. It is this optical illusion of the substantiality of thought that negative dialectics attempts to dispel.

Adorno's negative dialectics is not Marxist dialectical materialism in the conventional sense of the term. Reviving Karl Marx's "materialist" critique of Georg Wilhelm Friedrich Hegel, Adorno, as well as his colleagues at the Institute for Social Research, believed that there was no ontological primacy of spirit over matter and no logical priority of the thinking subject over the

material object. Consequently, they sought a principle that would legitimize both the intellectual comprehension of the world and its radical critique; they also relentlessly attacked the opposition between culture as a superior sphere of human endeavor and material existence as a lesser aspect of the human condition.

The goals and methods of the institute (later known as the Frankfurt School), as well as the historical situation out of which it arose, are important factors to consider in any discussion of Adorno's work. Under the directorship of Max Horkheimer, Adorno's longtime colleague and collaborator, the institute's theorists focused on the interdisciplinary nature of "social research." This social research, however, is not to be confused with sociology or *Geisteswissenschaft* (cultural sciences) as practiced in German universities, which fostered a tradition of treating intellectual history in a social vacuum. Rather, Adorno and fellow members of the Frankfurt School devoted themselves to what became known as *kritische Theorie*, or critical theory.

Using the dialectical method, critical theory's practitioners engaged in a dialogue with both other schools of Marxist thought and with a changing historical situation (the success of the Russian revolution and socialism's advance eastward). The two poles of critical theory's dialectic (as opposed to Hegel's dialectic between subject and object, or mind and matter, based on the primacy of the absolute subject) were praxis (more specifically, the relation of theory to praxis) and reason (*Vernunft*, or an appreciation of the dialectical relations beneath surface appearances). Praxis, in the sense in which it is used here, has been defined as "a kind of self-creating action, which differed from the externally motivated behavior produced by forces outside man's control. . . . One of the earmarks of *praxis*, as opposed to mere action, was its being informed by theoretical considerations." One of the institute's major tasks was to explore how the social and cultural order could be transformed through praxis.

Adorno, who shared the interdisciplinary goals and methods of the Institute for Social Research, investigated literature and many other cultural forms in his role as a critic of modern culture:

The task of criticism must not be so much to search for the particular interest-groups to which cultural phenomena are to be assigned, but rather to decipher the general social tendencies which are expressed in these phenomena and through which the most powerful interests realize themselves. Cultural criticism must become social physiognomy.

What distinguishes Adorno's sociology of art from its more orthodox Marxist counterparts (the theory of Georg Lukács, for example) is its refusal to reduce cultural phenomena to an ideological vehicle of class interests. In Adorno's view, art not only expresses and reflects social tendencies but also serves as the last preserve of individual subjectivity in the face of historical forms that threaten to crush it. A dialectical critique of art, Adorno argues, "takes seriously the principle that it is not ideology in itself which is untrue but rather its pretention to correspond to reality."

In a widely read essay entitled "On Commitment," Adorno argued that Bertolt Brecht's plays are fundamentally flawed, both aesthetically and politically, by the author's heavy-handed political didacticism and oversimplified presentation of such realities of the contemporary world as capitalism, fascism, or communism. Even more destructive are Brecht's tendencies to "preach to the converted" and to distort "the real social problems discussed in his epic drama in order to prove a thesis." Echoing Friedrich Engel's injunction (in a letter to Ferdinand LaSalle, May 8, 1859) that "the more the author's views are concealed the better for the work of art," Adorno goes on to say that "the gravest charge against commitment is that even right intentions go wrong when they are noticed, and still more so, when they then try to conceal themselves." Critics of Adorno have pointed out that his treatment of "committed" writing is often narrow and one-sided; in attacking polemics, Adorno himself turns polemicist.

In this same essay attacking the theory and practice of "committed" literature in the works of Brecht and Jean-Paul Sartre, Adorno praises Franz Kafka and Samuel Beckett as true models of a critical, revolutionary art. Instead of the artificially reconciled and positive outlook of the directly "political," Beckett's "dissonant" (exhibit-ing a state of unresolved tension) and "negative" art refuses to pacify and console.

> Kafka's prose and Beckett's plays . . . have an effect by comparison with which the officially committed works look like pantomimes. . . . By dismantling appearance, they explode from within the art which committed proclamation subjugates from without, and hence only in appearance. The inescapability of their work compels the change of attitude which committed works merely demand.

Adorno believed that Beckett was the one truly outstanding literary figure to emerge after World War II, and he even intended to dedicate *Aesthetic Theory*—published posthumously—to the author.

In a 1959 essay on Beckett's *Fin de partie* (1957; *Endgame*, 1958), Adorno describes the play as a continuation of Kafka's relentless reminder of the death of personality in the contemporary world; still, this abandonment of selfhood had now advanced further. In Adorno's view, Beckett's work is not ahistorically "existential" but powerfully suggestive of the absence of the self.

> Instead of excluding the temporal from existence, . . . [Beckett] subtracts that which time—the historical trend—is in reality preparing to annul. He extends the trajectory of the subject's liquidation to the point where it shrinks to the here-and-now. . . . History is excluded because it has dried up the power of consciousness to conceive history: the power of memory . . . All that appears of history is its result, its decline.

Adorno writes that in Beckett's art "all that remains of freedom is the impotent and ridiculous reflex of empty decisions."

Equally pessimistic is Adorno's famous statement on the place of art in the modern world: "To write poetry after Auschwitz is barbaric." He meant that even art that is "dissonant" is inadequate, because it contains hopeful language and imagery that have the power to elicit aesthetic enjoyment. The horror vanishes; the sound of despair becomes a "hideous affirmation." Yet the work of Beckett (and Arnold Schoenberg) provides a glimpse of hope by its capacity to express even the slightest of contemporary society's horrors. In Adorno's view, as long as their discordant sounds are heard and appreciated, their artistic power will enable them to keep alive the possibility of a "consonant" utopia in their honest acknowledgment of its absence.

In his discussion of the modern novel, Adorno argues that traditional bourgeois realism is no longer a historically viable option. Only the type of fragmentation of personality and narrative "standpoint" that appears, for example, in the works of such writers as Marcel Proust, James Joyce, or Robert Musil could adequately represent the extent of individual alienation, torment, and impotence in contemporary life. Telling a traditional realistic story from a single narrative perspective would nullify collective guilt and suggest that the individual still has independent meaning and power in society. On the other hand, modern novelists who disjointedly interrupt narration present it from multiple perspectives, reveal the power of objects in the unconscious of thoughts of powerless "characters," and construct the whole through associational logic of the parts are more "truthful" in their representation of contemporary life, according to Adorno. Yet these novelists' techniques must serve to demonstrate, in a potentially critical way, the disintegration of individual subjectivity.

One legacy of Adorno's (and the Frankfurt School's) critique of modern culture is that it enriched and challenged traditional Marxist criticism and better equipped it to assess both the modernist revolt and the crisis of liberal bourgeois society in the postwar era. In contemporary Western culture, in which traditional art is reduced to what Adorno and Horkheimer in *Dialectic of Enlightenment* call "the culture industry," that is, to a form of mere entertainment, Adorno points out that artists are obliged to create works that demand intellectual activity of themselves and of the audience.

In stressing the need for formal preoccupations and self-reflectiveness in both art and criticism, in rejecting the classical notion of organic unity, romantic subjectivity, or realist "reflection," and in emphasizing the fragmentary, ephemeral, and relativist nature of "truth" (although remaining primarily rooted in the Austro-German cultural tradition), Adorno eventually came to accept much of what the modernist revolt had attempted to achieve.

Influence

Adorno was among the first philosophers and critics to propose a consistent theory of popular culture and to analyze the various aspects and functions of the modern cultural market, mass cultural consumption, and what he and Horkheimer called the "culture industry" (the task of which is to supply the cultural market with products specifically designed to induce a state of relaxation or escape). In essays written as early as 1941, Adorno describes the need of the masses for distraction as both a product and a result of the existing capitalist economy.

Genevieve Slomski

Negative Dialectics

Type of philosophy: Epistemology, metaphysics
First published: Negative Dialektik, 1966 (English translation, 1973)
Principal ideas advanced:
◇ Negative dialectics, the pursuit of nonidentity, aims to dispel the illusion of the substantiality of thought.
◇ Negative dialectics rejects all transcendental elements and critiques the German tradition of idealism, with its concept of the world as constituted by thought.
◇ Martin Heidegger's dogmas about Being are metaphysical sleight-of-hand.
◇ Immanuel Kant's pronouncements on free will are subjectively repressive; spontaneity allows reason to escape from the subject's passivity.

Theodor Adorno was one of the principal figures in the Frankfurt School of Marxist social philosophy that flourished between 1923 and 1970. Dismayed by the sudden rise of capitalism in Germany after World War I, the Frankfurt thinkers rejected both metaphysics and scientific rationalism in focusing on understanding how capitalism worked in modern society. The school's founders included Max Horkheimer, director for a while of the movement's Institute for Social Research and collaborator with Adorno on the important book *Dialektik der Aufklärung* (1947; *Dialectic of Enlightenment*, 1972).

The school soon abandoned class analysis in favor of the study of culture and authority, and although its members deplored the fragmentation of learning in the universities and attempted to fuse sociology and philosophy, they usually specialized themselves. Adorno, for example, was a brilliant musicologist and student of culture. Adorno's Marxism was cooled by the events in Russia during the 1930's and tempered by such non-Marxist influences as philosophers Friedrich Nietzsche, Arthur Schopenhauer, and Georg Wilhelm Friedrich Hegel. The institute relocated in the 1930's to New York, where Horkheimer and Adorno continued writing despite Adorno's deep antipathy to the United States. In 1950, Herbert Marcuse stayed on in the United States, but Horkheimer and Adorno returned to Frankfurt, Horkheimer as the university rector and Adorno as a chaired professor. They continued their own Western Marxist polemics and criticized the "culture industry," but they also attacked the communist regimes to the east. Indeed, E. B. Ashton, translator of *Negative Dialectics*, describes the book as "an apologia for deviationism, a Marxist thinker's explication of his inability to toe the lines laid down today for proper Marxist thinking." The movement produced one substantial later thinker, Jürgen Habermas, but by 1969, Adorno was dead and the movement spent.

Negative Dialectics is an extraordinarily difficult work unless the reader is well versed in philosophy, especially German idealism of the last two centuries and the writings of Karl Marx. The usual problems of translating German metaphysics are greatly compounded by Adorno's expecting from his readers a deep familiarity not only with Immanuel Kant, Hegel, and Nietzsche but also with the later thinkers Martin Heidegger, Walter Benjamin, and Georg Lukács. Finally, Adorno's often paratactic style (his translator confesses that he at first judged *Negative Dialektik* "untranslatable") concedes nothing to any reader and adds a layer of obliquity to an already dark text.

Adorno divides his four-hundred-page tome into a long introduction that he says "expounds the concept of philosophical experience." This is followed by "Part 1: Relation to Ontology," which is divided into "The Ontological Need"

and "Being and Existence." Part 2 consists of "Negative Dialectics: Concept and Categories," and part 3, "Models," has sections on "Freedom," "World Spirit and Natural History," and "Meditations on Metaphysics." Adorno breaks down each of these sections into brief essays averaging a couple pages each, but the frequent difficulty in following the thread of his arguments from essay to essay appears in his translator's admission that he found himself "translating entire pages without seeing how they led from the start of an argument to the conclusion."

Negative Dialectics

Informing *Negative Dialectics* throughout is the linking of the subject-object dichotomy in Hegel's idealism with the Enlightenment's subjection of nature through reason, the theme of Adorno and Horkheimer's early work *Dialectic of Enlightenment*. The contemptuous epithet "bourgeois idealism" suggests the complicity of society with science: The mind (subject) shapes nature (object) to produce what Adorno perceives as a monstrous technocracy that refutes Marx's hope for a beneficent evolution in the "relations of productivity."

Philosophy lives on, Adorno says in the introduction to his work, because it failed to achieve the mission Marx assigned it of changing the world. The old systems, or "conceptual shells," linger like "relics," and Hegel's dialectic is due for an overhaul. Hegel's idealism envisioned the objective world as somehow identical to, or constituted by, thought; but Adorno avers that "dialectics says no more . . . than that objects do not go into their concepts without leaving a remainder," and it is this remainder, the "untruth of identity," that enables dialectics: "[Negative] [d]ialectics is the consistent sense of nonidentity." Negative dialectics reveals its affinity with Jacques Derrida's celebrated notion of différance when Adorno asserts: "What we differentiate will appear divergent, dissonant, negative for just as long as the structure of our consciousness obliges it to strive for unity." The philosophical materialism that Adorno strives to formulate through negative dialectics would destroy the subject's stranglehold and free nature from the grip of reason.

Adorno concludes his introductory remarks by stating that he "is prepared for the attacks to which *Negative Dialectics* will expose him. He feels no rancor and does not begrudge the joy of those in either camp who will proclaim that they knew it all the time and now he was confessing." Adorno anticipated these attacks resulting from remarks such as this:

> In the East, the theoretical short circuit in the views of individuality has served as a pretext for collective oppression. The party, even if deluded or terrorized, is deemed a priori superior in judgment to each individual because of the number of its members. Yet the isolated individual unhampered by any ukase may at times perceive objectivities more clearly than the collective, which is no more than the ideology of its functionaries, anyway.

Existentialism and relativism get disposed of as summarily as Stalinism. Relativism is the "doctrinal embodiment" of bourgeois skepticism, which is "obtuse." As for existentialism, the dogma of freedom of choice is "illusionary."

Criticisms

In the chapters on "The Ontological Need" and "Being and Existence," Adorno critiques philosophers Heidegger and Jean-Paul Sartre, jabbing at Being and existentialism with caustic wit. The "need" he identifies is for a materialism that is not "shrouded in vapors." Hegel's idealism, embodied in the mind's increasing control of nature, threatens the world with "the very calamity [technology] is supposed to protect us from." Adorno's contempt for Heidegger appears in references to "the corny tremolo of the phrase 'obliviousness of Being'" and to the existentialists' "posturing as metaphysically homeless and nothingness-bound" as "ideology, an attempt to justify the very order that drives men to despair and threatens them with physical extinction." Heidegger's Being is an "aura without a light-giving star." Heidegger's account of the word "Being" implies transcendence, not "entwinement," the appropriate understanding; and it abandons dialectics to achieve an immediacy beyond subject and object. Heidegger's assertion of a Being without entity is hocus-pocus, and in ontologizing the ontic, he made something out of nothing. Adorno's final verdict is brutal. Characterizing existentialism as a "Platonic prejudice"

for power without Gorgias's saving devotion to the ideal of justice, he says, "Of the eternal idea in which entity was to share . . . nothing remains but the naked affirmation of what is anyway—the affirmation of power."

Only some idea can be given of the tortuous arguments in "Negative Dialectics: Concept and Categories," which often have a theological cast to them, their burden being a scrutiny of Kant's and Hegel's views on the subject-object relationship. Kant represents Western "peephole metaphysics," in which the pure "in-itself" peeps out. However, there is "no peeping out" from the object, says Adorno. In Hegel's idealism, thought (the subject) somehow creates, or is identical to, matter (the object), and the perceived domination of matter by mind becomes in Adorno analogous to the dominance of individuals by an exploitative economic system:

> When we criticize the barter principle as the identifying principle of thought, we want to realize the ideal of free and just barter. To date, this ideal is only a pretext.

To seek totality, or identity, is a false goal, for it is out of nonidentity that ideas can be "salvaged." Dialectical thought—the negative dialectic—is the pursuit of nonidentity.

Responding to Lukács's *Geschichte und Klassenbewusstsein* (1923; *History and Class Consciousness*, 1971), Adorno asserts in his brief note on "Objectivity and Reification" that dialectics cannot be reduced to reification and that the true cause of human suffering will be lost in the "lament over reification." Reification is a secondary worry, for people's woes issue from their social conditions, not from their perceptions of reality:

> The meaningful times for whose return the early Lukács yearned were as much due to reification, to inhuman institutions, as he would later attest it only to the bourgeois age. Contemporary representations of medieval towns usually look as if an execution were just taking place to cheer the populace.

Models of Negative Dialectical Thought

Part 2 offers models of negative dialectical thinking. The essay "Freedom" becomes a dialogue with Kant on free will, a "metacritique" of Kant's

Kritik der praktischen Vernunft (1788; *The Critique of Practical Reason*, 1873). Kant taught that reason, working through its servant will, created reality, "untrammeled by the material," in Adorno's words. Adorno admits that freedom demands "full theoretical consciousness," but, always attentive to the role of the object, insists that something more is needed, "something physical which consciousness does not exhaust," and he finds this in the spontaneity that he identifies as the "part of action that differs from the pure consciousness." In this spontaneity lies the arbitrariness that enables reason's escape from the subject's passivity. Adorno refers twice to the fact that in Kant's ethics, "the dogmatic doctrine of free will is coupled with the urge to punish harshly, irrespective of empirical conditions," a result that to Adorno reveals the repressiveness of Kant's understanding of freedom as obedience. These reflections lead Adorno to what is always murkiest in his thinking: a sudden transition from metaphysics to ideology. Statements such as "In their inmost core, the theses of determinism and freedom coincide" and "surely it is only in a free society that the individuals would be [metaphysically] free" offer all the intuitive certainty of declarations about the mystery of the Holy Trinity.

Adorno's Influence

The impact of *Negative Dialectics* cannot be assessed apart from a general consideration of Adorno's influence. Many of his left-wing critics in the 1960's judged that Adorno's negative dialectics had fragmented the Frankfurt School's original effort to construct a critical theory. One of his most sympathetic students, Martin Jay, admits that "a lengthy journey through the thicket of Adorno's prose does give the impression of passing the same landmarks with uncomfortable frequency." Even though Jay concedes that Adorno may have been an "ambitious failure," he urges that he be given the benefit of the doubt.

In 1998, however, two substantial, largely favorable, and well-written studies of Adorno appeared: Simon Jarvis's *Adorno: A Critical Introduction* and Eric L. Krakauer's *The Disposition of the Subject: Reading Adorno's Dialectic of Technology*. These penetrating commentaries reveal the power of Adorno's works to stimulate minds decades

after his death. Krakauer's explication of the dialectic of technology draws heavily on Adorno and Horkheimer's *Dialectic of Enlightenment*, which contains ideas that were widely disseminated and could be sensed frequently in the polemics of the 1980's and 1990's. Among Adorno's successors, Jürgen Habermas is a significant figure whose work was touched by Adorno.

Frank Day

Additional Reading

Buck-Morss, Susan. *The Origin of Negative Dialectics: Theodor W. Adorno, Walter Benjamin, and the Frankfurt Institute*. New York: Free Press, 1977. Traces Theodor Adorno's intellectual development and outlines his major theories. Emphasizes the influence of Walter Benjamin on his thought.

Hohendahl, Peter Uwe. *Prismatic Thought: Theodor W. Adorno*. Lincoln: University of Nebraska Press, 1995. A wide-ranging introduction to Adorno and his work, with emphasis on his aesthetic writings. Includes chapters providing biographical context on Adorno's exile to the United States during World War II and his return to West Germany in the 1950's, as well as on his writings on literature, mass culture, sociology and philosophy of art, and language. An epilogue summarizes Adorno's place in contemporary criticism.

Huhn, Tom, and Lambert Zuidervaart, eds. *The Semblance of Subjectivity: Essays in Adorno's Aesthetic Theory*. Cambridge, Mass.: MIT Press, 1997. Twelve essays exemplify a broad range of approaches to Adorno's writings on aesthetics. Includes selective bibliographies of English translations of Adorno's work and of articles and books in English on Adorno and his relation to critical theory.

Jameson, Fredric. *Late Marxism: Adorno, or, The Persistence of the Dialectic*. New York: Verso, 1990. Detailed readings of three major works by Adorno, *Dialectic of Enlightenment*, *Negative Dialectic*, and *Aesthetic Theory*, documenting their contributions to contemporary Marxism and exploring Adorno's emphasis on late capitalism as a total system within the forms of culture.

_____, ed. *Marxism and Form: Twentieth-Century Dialectical Theories of Literature*. Princeton, N.J.:

Princeton University Press, 1971. Jameson's first chapter, "T. W. Adorno, or, Historical Tropes," analyzes Adorno's dialectical method and pessimistic critique of modern culture, chiefly with reference to his *Philosophy of Modern Music*.

Jarvis, Simon. *Adorno: A Critical Introduction.* New York: Routledge, 1998. Surveys the development of Adorno's thought and sketches the intellectual and institutional contexts from which it emerged. Offers explications of Adorno's work as a critic of society and culture, of his aesthetic theory, and of his work on epistemology and metaphysics.

Jay, Martin. *Adorno.* Cambridge, Mass.: Harvard University Press, 1984. A lucid introduction to Adorno's work, beginning with his key images of the force field and his extension of Benjamin's concept of constellation. These metaphors are then used to map five major areas of Adorno's intellectual concerns: Marxism, aesthetic modernism, cultural conservatism, Judaism, and deconstructionism.

Krakauer, Eric L. *The Disposition of the Subject: Reading Adorno's Dialectic of Technology.* Evan-ston, Ill.: Northwestern University Press, 1998. This work draws on Adorno and Max Horkheimer's *Dialectic of Enlightenment* to explain the dialectic of technology.

Lichtheim, George. *From Marx to Hegel.* New York: Herder and Herder, 1971. Analyzes the German intellectual tradition and historical status of Marxism. His chapter on Adorno provides biographical and historical context and briefly surveys his major writings.

Lunn, Eugene. *Marxism and Modernism: An Historical Study of Lukács, Brecht, Benjamin, and Adorno.* Berkeley: University of California Press, 1982. A comparative study of the treatment of Marxism and modernism in the writings of four important theoreticians of Marxist aesthetics, focusing on the period from 1920 to 1950. Contains six useful bibliographies on Marxism; on modernism; on the Brecht-Lucács and Benjamin-Adorno debates; on works by or about each of the four authors; and a general listing of key works on German and European social, political, and cultural history.

Genevieve Slomski, updated by William Nelles

Louis Althusser

Combining linguistic structuralism and concepts from Freudian psychoanalysis, Althusser formulated a modern version of scientific and antihumanist Marxism in which structures and process take precedence over individual subjects in accounting for history.

Principal philosophical works: *Montesquieu: La Politique et l'histoire*, 1959 (in *Politics and History*, 1972, later published as *Montesquieu, Rousseau, Marx*, 1982); *Pour Marx*, 1965 (*For Marx*, 1969); *Lire le Capital*, 1965 (with E. Balibar, R. Establet, P. Macherey, and J. Ranciere; *Reading Capital*, partial translation, 1970); *Lénine et la Philosophie*, 1969 (*Lenin and Philosophy and Other Essays*, 1972); *Réponse à John Lewis*, 1973 (in *Essays in Self-Criticism*, 1976); *Éléments d'autocritique*, 1974 (in *Essays in Self-Criticism*, 1976); *Philosophie et philosophie spontanée des savants*, 1974 (in *Philosophy and the Spontaneous Philosophy of the Scientists and Other Essays*, 1990); *L'Avenir dure longtemps*, 1992 (*The Future Lasts a Long Time*, 1993, also published as *The Future Lasts Forever*, 1993); *Écrits sur la psychanalyse: Freud et Lacan*, 1993 (*Writings on Psychoanalysis: Freud and Lacan*, 1996); *Sur la philosophie*, 1994; *Écrits philosophiques et politiques*, 1994-1995 (2 volumes).

Born: October 16, 1918; Birmendrëis, Algeria
Died: October 22, 1990; near Paris, France

Early Life

Louis Althusser was born in Algeria to a banker and his wife. Althusser's mother married his father after the death of her true love, his father's brother, in World War I. Althusser attended French secondary schools whose faculty and students for the most part embraced monarchistic and religious views, and he also held conservative opinions. In 1937, he became involved with the youth movement of the Catholic Church. During World War II, he was captured by the Germans and spent the duration of the conflict in a prisoner-of-war camp. After the war, Althusser became associated with the left-wing worker-priest movement. In 1946, he became involved with Hélène Rytman, a longtime anti-Nazi communist activist who was eight years older than he. He lost his Catholic faith, and in 1948, at the beginning of the Cold War, he joined the French Communist Party (PCF) but continued his connection with the worker-priest movement until it was dissolved by the pope. His relation with Rytman, who was his companion for thirty-five years, was difficult because she had been ex-

pelled from the PCF for alleged treason and Althusser was ordered by the party not to have contact with her, an order he disobeyed.

Althusser attended the École Normale Supérieure in Paris. He was particularly influenced by the philosophers of science Gaston Bachelard, Jean Cavailles, and Jules Canguileme. He wrote a thesis on Georg Wilhelm Friedrich Hegel under Bachelard and received a second place in the *agrégation de philosophie*, a difficult postgraduate examination for teaching positions at *lycées* and universities in France, in 1948. He became a tutor and spent the rest of his academic career at the university where he had studied.

Life's Work

Althusser published relatively little during the 1950's. At the end of the decade, he published *Politics and History*, a work on the eighteenth century social philosopher Montesquieu. In this work, Althusser formulated his notion of historical process without either a goal or a subject. In the early 1960's, he wrote a series of articles concerning the early works of Karl Marx, which appeared in 1965 as *For Marx*. He also collaborated with several others to write a much longer book, *Reading Capital*. These works had immense influence, but he fell into a severe depression and was hospitalized soon after they appeared.

In *For Marx*, Althusser argues that Marx's early, humanist works are not truly Marxist and that Marx did not develop the concepts specific to Marxism until the publication of *Die deutsche Ideologie* (1845-1846; *The German Ideology*, 1938). Althusser considers Marx's works between 1845 and 1857 to be transitional, and the works thereafter to be mature. His opinion is much like the orthodox view of the Socialist and Soviet Communist Parties. However, Marxist humanists, including Jean-Paul Sartre, Erich Fromm, and Herbert Marcuse, claim that Marx is part of the humanist tradition, given the existentialist and Hegelian language of Marx's *Jungendschriften* (1844; *Early Manuscripts*, 1959). Althusser argues that Marx's method rejected the humanism of German philosopher Ludwig Feuerbach and the idealism of Hegel for a new analysis of history. At one point, Althusser claims that Marx did not fully free himself from humanism until the publi-

cation of *Randglossen zu Adolph Wagner* (1879; *Notes on Wagner*, 1974).

Althusser claims that the individual is not the center of Marx's philosophy and that history is a process without a subject. Using Bachelard's concept of an epistemological break (similar to American philosopher Thomas S. Kuhn's notion of paradigm shift and scientific revolution that appeared decades later), Althusser claims that Marx created a new science and approach to history. He follows German socialist Friedrich Engels in comparing the shift from the concept of profit in the classic economics of English economist David Ricardo to the concept of surplus value in Marx to the shift from chemistry of the imaginary substance phlogiston to the chemistry of oxygen as an element.

In *Reading Capital*, Althusser "symptomatically" reads Marx's *Das Kapital* (1867, 1885, 1894; *Capital: A Critique of Political Economy*, 1886, 1907, 1909), noting significant lapses and absences in much the same way that a psychoanalyst would

Louis Althusser. *(Jacques Pavlovsky/Sygma)*

interpret a patient's words. He argues that Marx's philosophy has to be extracted from his economic writings and is not revealed in his explicit philosophical remarks. According to Althusser, Marx's conception of history was not purposive in that it was not structured by a goal. He denies that Marx was an historicist—an individual who claims all concepts and structures are in process and that history is goal-oriented or teleological. Marx's *Das Kapital* is not a historical narrative but rather an analysis of the structures of capitalist society. These structures are not themselves in process but account for process. Borrowing the notion of overdetermination from psychoanalyst Sigmund Freud, Althusser claims that historical events are overdetermined, that they are intersections of causes working at a number of different levels. Societies—slave, feudalistic, capitalist, and socialist—are organized according to the modes of production, which can appear in various social formations. Although various structures can appear in a given society, there is a dominant structure, the primary determining structure of that type of society. Although the political, legal, and ideological superstructures have relative autonomy from the economic base, they are eventually determined by it.

In the title essay of *Lenin and Philosophy and Other Essays*, Althusser shifts his position on the role of philosophy. To Althusser, philosophy had previously been a "theory of theoretical practice" (he considered theory to be a kind of practice) and a guarantor of the objectivity of science, but because philosophy is unable to give absolute justifications, he came to regard it as a locus of the struggle between classes. The extreme rationalism of his earlier works gives way to a limited role for philosophy in persuasion and in giving plausible accounts, not ultimate justifications. Althusser criticizes his earlier works as guilty of "theoreticism," a term that his critics applied to all of his work.

In "Idéologie et appareils idéologiques d'état" (1970; "Ideology and Ideological State Apparatuses" in *Lenin and Philosophy*), Althusser moves away from Marx's view of ideology as false, inverted ideas and toward a notion of ideology as the medium through which people find meaning in everyday life. Althusser delineates the institutions (such as school, church, and state)

that maintain and propagate ideology for the self-reproduction of society. In his "Philosophy and the Spontaneous Philosophy of the Scientists," Althusser takes the sharply dichotomized relation between science and ideology set forth in *Reading Capital* and renders it subtler. He recognizes that science is awash in ideology and that it is influenced by ideological conceptions such as religion, politics, and philosophy. Althusser attempts to reconcile the objectivity of science with a historical and contingent account of the way in which scientific theory is generated, a problem not only for Marxists but also for science studies in general in the late twentieth century.

Althusser's own theory of knowledge somewhat resembles that of German philosopher Immanuel Kant. For Althusser, knowledge is not extracted from given facts or sense experiences. Experience itself is already structured by ideology and theories. Theoretical work involves the processing of the deliverances of experience (Knowledge I) by the methods and techniques of theorizing (Knowledge II) to produce genuine theoretical concepts (Knowledge III). Although Althusser believes in the objectivity of knowledge, he does not believe that people have direct access to reality; people experience reality only as something mediated through concepts.

One of the traditional philosophers whose views greatly influenced Althusser was the seventeenth century rationalist Baruch Spinoza. Spinoza, like the early Althusser, identifies logical consequence with causality and holds that the universe is completely deterministic. Althusser likens Spinoza's pantheist God (who is an immanent cause of the universe, not a separate creator) to Althusser's own notion of structures as immanent causes of society. Althusser rejects empiricism and claims that the correct theory corresponds to real structures. Spinoza's notion that all knowledge is true to some extent (insofar as it represents, even if confusedly, some reality) is used by Althusser to account for his claim that knowledge is objective but is not a direct revelation of reality.

In addition to structuralist linguistics and the French philosophers of scientific change, one of the major influences on Althusser was psychoanalyst Jacques Lacan. Althusser claimed that he set out to read Marx the way that Lacan had read the works of Sigmund Freud. Lacan and Althusser rejected Freud's hydraulic and energy flow imagery from nineteenth century physics in favor of a linguistic model. Lacan claimed that the unconscious is timeless and is structured like language. Althusser similarly claimed that social structures are timeless and that implicitly they are structured like language. Althusser wrote several essays comparing Marx and Freud as well as Marx and Lacan. He also corresponded with Lacan. These writings are collected in *Writings on Psychoanalysis: Freud and Lacan.* Althusser's lifelong series of bipolar swings from manic to depressive states, mental breakdowns, and experience with various kinds of psychiatry were not described by him until his posthumously published autobiographical work, but these collected writings show that his involvement with the concepts of psychoanalysis was not merely theoretical.

Althusser's academic career abruptly ended in 1980 when he reported to police that he had strangled Hélène Rytman, his wife of four years and companion of thirty-five years. He was placed in a mental institution and released some eighteen months later. He lived in retirement for eight years and continued to write on the Italian Renaissance political theorist Niccolò Machiavelli and on ancient Greek atomists such as Democritus and Epicurus. He would occasionally surprise Paris passersby by loudly proclaiming that he was indeed the great Althusser. He wrote *The Future Lasts Forever* to explain his crime and mental illness. It was published after his death in 1990. Many of the unpublished writings from the last decade of his life later were collected and published.

Influence

Althusser's influence is wide, varied, and often unacknowledged. His intransigent Marxism-Leninism (he claimed that Soviet political leader Joseph Stalin was too humanistic) offended many people of other political persuasions. After he strangled his wife, his name was anathema to many feminists who had earlier used his ideas. During the 1960's, he influenced a number of leftist sociologists, economists, and political theorists in France, including anthropologist Em-

manuel Terray and political sociologist Nikos Poulantzas. Though Poulantzas committed suicide and many others renounced Marxism to become "new philosophers," Althusser's influence lingered. Pierre Bourdieux, though critical of Althusser, imported his methods into the study of sociology. Swedish scholar Gören Therborn developed an Althusserian analysis of politics. By the 1970's, his influence on British leftist social science and philosophy was considerable. In the United States, the concept of the reproduction of society through education has had a great impact on the sociology of education, though the concept is generally used without reference to Althusser. In literary studies, Althusser's view of writing as a kind of production permeated the work of Pierre Macherey and the journal *Tel Quel* in France as well as the Birmingham Center for Contemporary Cultural Studies and the journal *Screen* in Britain.

After Althusser's incarceration and the decline of communist and socialist movements during the 1980's, explicit Althusserianism all but disappeared, and many ex-Althusserians became postmodernists. Postmodernists (who, unlike Althusser, reject scientific objectivity and rationality) often use Althusserian formulations of decentered totality and process without a subject but attribute the notions to philosophers Michel Foucault, Jacques Derrida, or Jacques Lacan. Althusser once taught Foucault, who before 1970 was quite structuralist. American Foucaultians emphasize the roots of Foucault's views in Friedrich Nietzsche's philosophy but suppress the Althusserian aspect. Postmodernists sometimes denounced Althusser in the classroom and at conferences but mined his texts for ideas useful in their own research.

Val Dusek

The Future Lasts Forever

Type of philosophy: Philosophy of history, ethics, political philosophy
First published: L'Avenir dure longtemps, 1992 (English translation, 1993; also published as *The Future Lasts a Long Time,* 1993)

Principal ideas advanced:
◇ Philosophy is "perennial" in that it again and again plays out the same struggle between oppressors and the oppressed.
◇ Science, rather than the delusions and distortions of everyday beliefs and experiences, should serve as a foundation for philosophy.
◇ Baruch Spinoza's rationalist monism (doctrine of the universe as a single substance) was made idealistic by George Wilhelm Friedrich Hegel but was again made material by Karl Marx.

Although most of Louis Althusser's works are impersonal and academic, this work is personal and autobiographical. Althusser describes how he strangled his wife and his life before the murder. To avoid his being tried as a murderer, his friends and doctor prevented Althusser from testifying at his trial. Althusser wrote the main part of this work to give his own account of what happened and to counter the various theories that were presented in the press and in philosophical literature, linking his Marxism, his structuralism, and even his philosophy as a whole with the killing of his spouse.

Althusser notes that the work of Jean-Jacques Rousseau is a model for this type of self-examination and mentions the diary of a parent-murderer edited by Michel Foucault. Althusser mixes autobiographical reminiscences with psychoanalytical reflections and accounts of his own intellectual development and works. Structuralism is often claimed to be totally nonexperiential and abstract, lacking reference to concrete human experience. This work mixes poignant stories of various human experiences with accounts of intellectual work. Althusser was intellectually involved with Lacanian psychoanalysis in addition to being a psychiatric patient undergoing a variety of treatments from psychoanalysis to electric shock therapy. He used concepts from psychoanalysis in his account of social theory. In this work, he uses psychoanalytic theory to examine his own life and reflects on his relationship with the psychoanalytic theorist Jacques Lacan.

Althusser's memoir opens powerfully with his sudden realization that while giving his spouse a neck massage, he had unwittingly or unconsciously strangled her to death. He rushes out of his university apartment to get a nearby psychiatrist and other colleagues. Before the police arrive, he is spirited away to a mental institution.

The Formative Years

Althusser describes his earliest childhood. His mother's true love was killed in World War I, and she married his brother, who became Althusser's father. She named her son Louis after her dead lover, and Althusser feels that his mother maintained a relationship with the original Louis through her son. His father was highly intelligent and knowledgeable about world politics and economics, but he was a cold person and played no role in raising the children. When challenged, he would leave the house in a rage. Althusser's mother was highly neurotic and considered herself a martyr. Althusser loved his grandfather, a forester who spoke with him as an equal and taught him botany. Althusser was born at his grandfather's Algerian forestry house and felt more loved by his grandfather than by his parents.

Althusser attended secondary school in Marseilles and Lyons in France. The atmosphere of the schools was highly conservative. Although Althusser was not unhappy at school and had friends, he was slow to establish relations with women. Althusser claims to have been a virgin until his late twenties.

Althusser joined the French army at the beginning of World War II and was soon captured by the Germans. He spent the entire war in a prisoner-of-war camp where he actually felt secure and met several men who became models for him. These men, natural leaders, organized the prisoners and deceived or manipulated the Nazi guards in various ways. One camp incident seemed particularly symbolic to Althusser. He knew that escapees were quickly captured as warnings were sent to neighboring regions. He and some friends attempted to deceive the Nazis into thinking that they had escaped by hiding within the camp. When the Nazis thought they were long gone, they planned to run away. To Althusser, this unsuccessful ruse came to symbolize his later relations with social organizations.

Althusser and Rytman

After the war, released from the camp, Althusser was disoriented and at a loss. During this period, he met and fell in love with Hélène Rytman, who had been involved in the anti-Nazi resistance. Their relationship was extremely difficult because both were neurotic and had had very bad relationships with their parents. Althusser experienced his first severe depression after making love to her. Through Rytman, a member of the French Communist Party (PCF), Althusser learned of the struggles of the workers and of political activism and organizing. Althusser lost his Roman Catholic faith and soon joined the PCF. Rytman had kept a Nazi prisoner alive in order to extract information from him but was accused of having betrayed the party and was expelled. Althusser was ordered not to associate with her but disobeyed, leading to many difficulties.

Marxism vs. Althusserianism

Althusser believed that the point of philosophy was to aid in the struggle of workers against the state and the capitalists. Marx had said that philosophers had tried only to understand the world rather than to change it. Althusser agreed that the point was to change the world for the better, but he felt that Marx was wrong about philosophers. Philosophers of the past—including Plato, Niccolò Machiavelli, Thomas Hobbes, Baruch Spinoza, and Immanuel Kant—had developed their theories with an eye to either changing or preserving the social order in which they lived.

Althusser originally defined philosophy as the "theory of theoretical practice" (considering theory itself to be a kind of practice), but he later claimed that philosophy was a class struggle in the realm of theory. Althusser states that philosophy sets forth viewpoints and theses that cannot be decisively proved. It supplies the outlook and framework for political action and scientific theories that can be evaluated by their consequences. According to Althusser, philosophy has no history because it replays the same oppositions, such as the one and the many, over the centuries. Thus, it can be termed "perennial philosophy," which does not mean it expresses eternal truths but rather that it plays out the struggle between the oppressors and oppressed. Philosophy has no history, just as ideology has no history for Marx because it simply reflects the real social and economic developments of history. For Althusser, the

struggle between idealism and materialism in philosophy expresses in theory the struggle between rulers and the ruled in social life.

Althusser believes that science, unlike philosophy, does not express the struggle between the ruling class and the oppressed. Science, he believes, can achieve genuine representation of reality, even if always only approximate and partial. Although the problematic aspects of science are influenced by religion and politics, the activity of science transforms the raw material of observations and facts into genuine theoretical knowledge. For this reason, Althusser always rejected the theory of the "two sciences" that was held by the Communists under Joseph Stalin. Under this theory, science is divided into bourgeois (capitalist) science and socialist science. Althusser recalls with disgust how one party official berated a leading biologist and party member, claiming that even "two plus two equals four" was true only from a bourgeois standpoint. This sort of view led to Soviet support for agriculturally harmful biology.

Althusser rejects the attempt by Jean-Paul Sartre and Maurice Merleau-Ponty (whom he considers the better philosopher) to ground Marxism on a phenomenological intuition or description of direct experience. He criticizes the phenomenological philosophy for taking for granted as intuitively self-evident certain experiences of everyday life. For Althusser, these experiences are distorted by unconscious repression of individual psychology and social oppression of structures of force and authority. These distorted experiences cannot serve as a foundation for philosophy. One must use science to pass from appearance to an essence that is different from appearance (Marx) or to structures (Althusser). Marxist social analysis is necessary to break through the delusions and distortions of everyday beliefs and everyday experiences.

Machiavelli and Spinoza

Two philosophers whom Althusser discusses favorably in this work are Niccolò Machiavelli and Baruch Spinoza. Machiavelli, according to Althusser, developed a theory of political activity rather than a justification for political rule. Machiavelli's theory of actual political strategy has not developed since his time. Marx had only fragments of such a theory, and, consequently, though he had a detailed economic theory of social development, he really lacked a theory of political strategy apart from rules of thumb. Machiavelli wrote before the parliamentary state and did not develop a theory of the social contract. Unlike the later social contract theorists, such as John Locke, Machiavelli did not justify the legitimacy of the state in terms of an imaginary citizens' agreement but described the actual strategies by which the ruler imposes his will as force and deceit. For this reason, he is far more realistic than the social contract theorists.

Of all the traditional philosophers, Spinoza garners the most praise from Althusser. Althusser sees Spinoza as developing a brilliant analysis of how ideologies are generated in his discussion of the Hebrew prophets. Althusser also foresees much of Sigmund Freud's theory of personality and drives in Spinoza's theory of *conatus* and theory of emotions. Furthermore, Spinoza rightly treats thought as a bodily process, not a separate activity of a spiritual nature. Spinoza's third kind of knowledge, which grasps a singular case that is also universal rather than a general law of correlated qualities or events, is for Althusser the sort of knowledge one finds in Machiavelli and Marx. According to Althusser, Spinoza's rationalist monism (doctrine of the universe as a single substance) was made idealistic or spiritual by Georg Wilhelm Friedrich Hegel but was then again made material by Marx, who was perhaps Spinoza's only true follower in his economic theory if not in his explicit philosophy.

Conflict, Isolation, and Death

Although Althusser disagreed with the PCF's earlier Stalinist doctrine of the two sciences, the party's later support of Marxist humanism, its bureaucratic manipulation of the workers' movement, and its refusal to give support to the students' and workers' uprisings of 1968, he remained a member of the party. He justifies this by arguing that if an individual is committed to the workers' movement and to social change in France, that person has to be part of the PCF in order to have any effect. He claimed that a Communist is never alone, but that those leftist intellectuals who broke with or stayed outside the party were isolated and had no real influence on

the workers and mass movements. Althusser openly criticized the PCF and hoped to influence it to change.

By the late 1970's, communist and socialist movements were on the retreat in most parts of the world. Althusser finally openly rejected the PCF in several speeches and articles. This was an extremely difficult time for him and his longtime companion, Hélène Rytman, whom he married in the late 1970's. She threatened suicide, and he fell into depression. They isolated themselves from their friends and colleagues, and not long after, Althusser inadvertently or unconsciously strangled Rytman.

By the time *The Future Lasts Forever* appeared, Althusser's theories seemed dated to many because they had been associated with the revolts of 1968 and Marxism, Maoism, and other movements that had declined during the privatization of the capitalist countries during the 1980's and the collapse of the Eastern Bloc communist governments in the early 1990's. His strangling of his spouse and subsequent incarceration in a mental institution discredited him in the eyes of many followers and gave further ammunition to those who already opposed his Marxism and structuralism. However, this work made many readers more sympathetic with Althusser the man and revived interest in his theories. Despite the horror of his crime, Althusser's narration put a human face on a man whose "theoreticism" and abstraction had been notorious. His decades-long struggles with depression and mental illness were unknown to most readers. French reviewers seemed more upset with him for his continued allegiance to materialism and his rejection of relativism than they were with his murdering his companion. American reviewers for the most part used the book to reiterate already held opinions concerning the evils of French theory, Marxism, and even philosophy. Nevertheless, the work led readers to return to Althusser's theoretical treatises and to see his work not just as a product of political struggles within the PCF and French intellectual fads but in relation to philosophers of the past.

Val Dusek

Additional Reading
Callari, Antonio, and David F. Ruccio. *Postmodern Materialism and the Future of Marxist Theory:*

Essays in the Althusserian Tradition. Hanover, N.H.: University Press of New England, 1996. Contains several insightful essays, some by European students and contemporaries of Louis Althusser such as Étienne Balibar, Emmanuel Terray, and Antonio Negri, and some by American economists.

Callinicos, Alex. *Althusser's Marxism.* London: Pluto Press, 1976. A helpful, brief, sympathetic introductory overview of Althusser's earlier work by a philosopher.

Elliot, Gregory, ed. *Althusser: A Critical Reader.* Cambridge, Mass.: Blackwell, 1994. The best selection of articles on Althusser, including several by eminent European philosophers Paul Ricoeur and Axel Honneth and historians Eric Hobsbawm and Pierre Vilar.

_____. *Althusser: The Detour of Theory.* New York: Verso, 1987. Excellent coverage of the relation of French leftist politics to Althusser's theoretical positions by the author of the best available biographical essay on Althusser, which appears in both the Callari and Ruccio and the Elliott anthologies cited in this bibliography.

Ferry, Luc, and Alain Renaut. *French Philosophy of the Sixties: An Essay on Antihumanism.* Amherst: University of Massachusetts Press, 1990. This attack on postmodernism by two French neoliberals partly attributes the course of French philosophy and sociology after May, 1968, to the baneful, indirect influence of Althusser.

Payne, Michael. *Reading Knowledge: An Introduction to Barthes, Foucault, and Althusser.* Malden, Mass.: Blackwell, 1997. This work contains two brief but lucid chapters on Althusser as well as a section on his discussion of art.

Resch, Robert Paul. *Althusser and the Renewal of Marxist Social Theory.* Berkeley: University of California Press, 1992. An excellent and extensive wholly sympathetic treatment of Althusser's philosophy and theory of history and politics as well as treatments of a number of other structuralist Marxists and students of Althusser. Contains much information on Althusser's philosophy of science and his philosophical predecessors.

Schaff, Adam. *Structuralism and Marxism.* New York: Pergamon, 1978. A readable criticism of Althusser and structuralism by a Polish Marxist who moved from orthodoxy to humanism.

Schmidt, Alfred. *History and Structure: An Essay on the Hegelian Marxist and Structuralist Theories of History.* Cambridge, Mass.: MIT Press, 1981. A member of the Frankfurt School of critical theory compares Althusser's structuralism with "historicist" and humanist approaches to history and attempts a rapprochement between the two, although he is much more sympathetic to the historicist-humanist approach.

Smith, Stephen. *Reading Althusser.* Ithaca, N.Y.: Cornell University Press, 1985. A clear exposition and criticism focusing on the earlier Althusser. Smith claims Althusser is led into relativism and nihilism in a reading influenced by the conservative political theorist Leo Strauss.

Spinker, M., ed. *The Althusserian Legacy.* London: Verso, 1993. This collection of essays features an interview with Jacques Derrida on Marxism and Althusser and also contains the speech Derrida gave at Althusser's grave.

Thompson, Edward P. *The Poverty of Theory and Other Essays.* New York: Monthly Review Press, 1978. The title essay is an attack against Althusser's abstraction and "theoreticism" by a leading British social historian.

Val Dusek

Anaxagoras

By devising a philosophical system to explain the origins and nature of the physical universe that overcame the paradoxes and inconsistencies of earlier systems, Anaxagoras provided an indispensable bridge between the pre-Socratic philosophers of the archaic period of Greek history and the full flowering of philosophy during the Golden Age of Greece.

Principal philosophical works: Only fragments exist, fifth century B.C.E. (*The Fragments of Anaxagoras*, 1981)

Born: c. 500 B.C.E.; Clazomenae, Anatolia (now in Turkey)
Died: c. 428 B.C.E.; Lampsacus, on the Hellespont (now the Dardanelles, Turkey)

Early Life

Virtually nothing is known of Anaxagoras's parents, his childhood, his adolescence, or his education. Born into a wealthy family in an Ionian Greek city around 500 B.C.E., he almost certainly was exposed to the attempts by Ionian philosophers, especially Parmenides, to explain the physical universe by postulating that everything is made from a single primordial substance. Anaxagoras apparently realized even before he was twenty years old that such an assumption could not explain the phenomena of movement and change, and he began to devise a more satisfactory system.

He grew to adulthood during the turbulent years of the wars of the Greek city-states against the Persian Empire. His own city, Clazomenae, forced to acknowledge the suzerainty of Darius the Great in 514 B.C.E., joined the Athenian-aided Ionian revolt against Persia in 498. That revolt was ultimately suppressed in 493. Anaxagoras's childhood was spent during a time when the echoes of the great victory of Athens over Darius at Marathon in 490 were reverberating throughout the Hellenic world.

According to tradition, Anaxagoras became a resident of Athens in 480 B.C.E. That a young scholar should be attracted to the intellectual and artistic center of Greek civilization is not surprising, but it is doubtful that this change of residence took place in 480. Xerxes I chose that year

Anaxagoras of Clazomenae. *(Giraudon/Art Resource)*

33

to attempt to realize Darius's dream of conquering the Greek polis, but his plans were frustrated and his great host scattered at the battles of Salamis and Plataea. The next year, the Ionian cities of Asia Minor again rose in rebellion against Persia and in 477 joined with Athens in the Delian League. The League succeeded in expelling the Persians from the Greek states of Asia Minor. It seems more likely that the young Anaxagoras came to Athens after the alliance between the Ionian cities and the Athenians.

While in Athens, Anaxagoras became friends with the young Pericles and apparently influenced him considerably. Several classical scholars have concluded that Anaxagoras's later trial was engineered by Pericles' political rivals in order to deprive Pericles of a trusted friend. Convicted of impiety after admitting that he thought the Sun was a huge mass of "hot rock," Anaxagoras went into exile at Lampsacus, where many young Greeks came to study with him before his death, probably in 428 B.C.E..

Life's Work

Sometime in or shortly after 467 B.C.E., Anaxagoras published his only written work, apparently entitled "On Nature." Of this work, only seventeen fragments totaling around twelve hundred words have survived, all recorded as quotations in the works of later generations of philosophers. That so few words could have inspired so much study is ample testimony to Anaxagoras's importance in the evolution of Greek philosophy and natural science.

Anaxagoras's book was an ambitious attempt to explain the origins and nature of the universe without recourse (or so it seemed to many of his contemporaries) to any supernatural agents. Other Ionian philosophers, notably Parmenides, had preceded Anaxagoras in this endeavor, but their systems were logically unable to explain the multiplicity of "things" in the universe or to explain physical and biological change in those things because they had postulated that all things are made from the same basic "stuff." Anaxagoras overcame the logical inconsistencies of this argument by postulating an infinite variety of substances that make up the whole of the universe. Anaxagoras argued that there is something of everything in everything. By this he

meant that, for example, water contains a part of every other thing in the universe, from blood to rock to air. The reason that it is perceived to be water is that most of its parts are water. A hair also contains parts of every other thing, but most of its parts are hair.

In the beginning, according to the first fragment of Anaxagoras's book, infinitely small parts of everything in equal proportion were together in a sort of primal soup. In fragment 3, he proposes a primitive version of the law of the conservation of energy, saying that anything, no matter how small, can be divided infinitely, because it is not possible for something to become nonexistent through dividing. This idea of infinite divisibility is unique to the Anaxagorean system; no philosopher before or since has proposed it.

This universal mixture of all things acquired form and substance, according to fragment 12, through the actions of *nous*, or "mind." Mind is not of everything (though it is a part of some things), nor is a part of everything found in mind (though parts of some things are found in mind). Mind set the primal soup into rotation and the different things began to "separate off," thus forming the universe. The rotation of the primal mixture not only separated everything according to its kind (but not perfectly because everything still contains parts of every other thing) but also supplied heat through friction. Among other things, friction ignited the Sun and the stars. Considerable disagreement over the exact meaning that Anaxagoras was trying to convey with the term "mind" has colored scholarly works on his work since Aristotle and continues to be a controversial issue.

Anaxagoras's system not only enabled him and his students to describe all existing objects, but it also permitted the explanation of physical and biological change. It was the introduction of the idea of mind and its action as a formative agent in the creation of the universe for which Anaxagoras became famous and which rejuvenated Socrates' interest and faith in philosophy.

Sometime after 467 B.C.E., Anaxagoras was accused of and tried for impiety (denying the gods) and "medism" (sympathizing with the Persians). The actual date of his trial and subsequent banishment from Athens is still hotly debated among classical scholars. A traditional date accepted by many historians was once 450 B.C.E., but this seems unlikely for several reasons. By 450, the charge of medism could hardly have been a serious one, because the Persian wars were long since over. Also, had he been in Athens in 450, the young Socrates would almost certainly have met Anaxagoras personally, but Socrates' own words indicate that he knew Anaxagoras only through his book. Finally, Anaxagoras's friend Pericles would have been fully able to protect his mentor from political opponents in 450. An earlier date for his exile from Athens seems likely. Some scholars have attempted to solve this problem by postulating that Anaxagoras visited Athens one or more times after being exiled shortly after the publication of his book. This seems the most reasonable explanation to reconcile the dispute, especially since several ancient sources place him in Athens as late as 437.

One of Anaxagoras's most notable achievements during his stay in Athens was to postulate the correct explanation for a solar eclipse. Anaxagoras was apparently the first to argue that an eclipse occurs when the Moon (which he said was a large mass of cold rocks) passes between Earth and the Sun (which he said was a larger mass of hot rocks). He may have reached this conclusion after the fall of a large meteorite near Aegypotomi in 467, which excited wide discussion throughout the Hellenic world.

After leaving Athens, Anaxagoras spent his remaining years as the head of a flourishing school at Lampsacus. How his philosophical system may have changed over the years between the publication of his book and the end of his life is unknown. He died at Lampsacus, probably in 428 B.C.E..

Influence

The thesis that Anaxagoras greatly influenced Socrates and Aristotle is easily proved by their elaborate discussions of his system in their own words. Through those two most influential of all Greek thinkers, Anaxagoras had a profound impact on all subsequent generations of philosophers and natural scientists in the Western world. Some of Anaxagoras's critics, both ancient and modern, accuse him of merely substituting the word "mind" for "God" or "the gods." Thus in

their estimation, his philosophy becomes merely a humanistic religion. Other critics have dismissed Anaxagoras's teachings as simplistic and unworthy of serious consideration. His supporters, from Aristotle to the present, have defended him as a pioneering thinker who provided much of the inspiration for the flowering of post-Socratic philosophy during the Golden Age of Greece and the Hellenistic world.

Early critics and supporters alike may have missed an important point in the Anaxagoras fragments. Late twentieth century work on Anaxagoras points out that his concept of mind giving form to the universe is not far removed from the position of some modern physicists who argue that our perception of the universe is determined by our own senses, which provide an imperfect understanding at best. Anaxagoras may well have been trying to express this same concept (that without cognitive perception there is no form or substance to the universe) without possessing the technical language to do so.

Paul Madden

Anaxagoras: Fragments

Type of philosophy: Metaphysics
First transcribed: fifth century B.C.E. (*The Fragments of Anaxagoras*, 1981)
Principal ideas advanced:

◇ The universe is infinite and is composed of infinitely divisible matter.
◇ Everything that exists contains portions of every other kind of thing, but particular things are recognized by their most obvious characteristics.
◇ Mind is matter considered as conscious and knowing.
◇ Originally the universe was homogeneous and motionless, but as a result of the whirling influence of mind, the universe became differentiated and ordered.

Anaxagoras held that the universe is infinite in extent and composed of mind and matter, but mind is a special kind of matter. There is no empty space.

Matter

Matter is not composed of primary units; it is infinitely divisible. "Nor is there a least of what is small, but there is always a smaller; for it cannot be that what exists should cease to be by being cut." If you take a piece of a certain kind of matter—a hair, say, or a steak—and begin cutting, no matter how finely you cut it the pieces will still have the characteristics of hair or flesh. "How can hair come from what is not hair, or flesh from what is not flesh?"

Nevertheless, we eat bread, and the bread (we say) becomes hair and flesh. This is not accurate, Anaxagoras says: "The Greeks follow a wrong usage in speaking of coming into existence and passing away; for nothing comes into existence or passes away, but there is mingling and separation of things that exist. Therefore, they would be right to call coming into existence mixture, and passing away separation." The "coming into existence" of the hair is really mixture, then, and the "passing away" of the bread is separation. However, this prompts one to ask: Mixture and separation of what? Any crumb of bread, however tiny, has all the properties of the whole loaf. Bread is not *made of* bits of hair and flesh. Likewise a hair is not separable into microscopic breadcrumbs. How then can hair be a "mixture" into which bread enters, while at the same time it cannot "come from what is not hair"?

The answer is that "The things that are in one world are not divided nor cut off from one another with a hatchet." Although bread contains no particles of hair, it nevertheless contains hair fused or dissolved in it. In general, "all things will be in everything; nor is it possible for them to be apart, but all things have a portion of everything. . . . And in all things many things are contained, and an equal number both in the greater and in the smaller of the things that are separated."

A loaf of bread contains "portions of everything"; that is, it contains or rather *is* a complex of *all* the sensible qualities. The same is true of every crumb of the loaf. (Anaxagoras was notorious for asserting that snow is black—in the sense that even the purest white stuff yet contains a portion of every "thing," including blackness.) Yet the loaf does not appear to our senses as a primordial chaos. "Each single thing is most mani-

festly those things of which it has most in it." It presents us with a definite, restricted set of qualities, such as brownness, moisture, bread-smell, and bread-taste. Hair as we know it is black, shiny, oily. Hair is in bread in the sense that blackness, shininess, and oiliness are all there, but relatively in such small quantities that "the weakness of our senses prevents our discerning the truth." If we were presented (*per impossibile*) with a loaf of "pure" bread, we could not distinguish it from an ordinary loaf by looking at it, smelling it, or tasting it; but it would not nourish us. Our insides, however, are able (in an unexplained manner) to separate out the traces of hair and flesh.

Anaxagoras used the word "seeds"—"seeds of all things, having all sorts of characteristics both of color and of savor," "a multitude of innumerable seeds in no way like each other"—to indicate the diversity of quality-things to be found in even the smallest bit of matter. However, the word has no atomistic implications; anything, however large or small, that has a trace of hair in it is a hair "seed." The word occurs only twice in the extant fragments, both times in a description of world formation, and all that is signified is that the original mixture of all things has the potentialities in it for eventual separation into the most diverse kinds of objects.

Mind

Mind, like blackness or the smell of bread, is a real stuff; consequently, it has location ("it is certainly there, where everything else is") and occupies space ("it is the thinnest of all things and the purest"). Although this seems sufficient evidence to make it a kind of matter, it must be remembered that Anaxagoras does not make a distinction between stuff and the qualities of stuff; indeed, refusal to make this distinction is the key to his philosophy. Mind has or *is* the properties that in our experience we find it to have: It is conscious and cognitive ("it has all knowledge about everything") and powerful, manifesting itself as will power or *élan vital* in living things ("mind has the greatest strength; and it has power over all things, both greater and smaller, that have life"). It is unique in not entering into mixtures: "All other things partake in a portion of everything, while Mind is infinite and self-ruled, and is mixed with nothing but is alone, itself by itself."

Anaxagoras argued that "if it were not by itself, but were mixed with anything else, it would partake in all things if it were mixed with any; for in everything there is a portion of everything, and the things mixed with it would hinder it, so that it would have power over nothing in the same way that it has now being alone by itself." The thought seems to be that if mind mixed, it would lose its peculiar power just as the blackness in snow or the breadness in hair does; but this is impossible, both because what is essentially active cannot become passive and because our minds are experienced as unities. Also "it would partake in all things if it were mixed with any"; rocks and clods would be alive—an absurdity.

However, although mind is not mixed with anything, it is *present* in some living things: "In everything there is a portion of everything except Mind, and there are some things in which there is Mind also." The power of mind is to initiate activity (motion) in these things and to move and "set in order all things" from outside. Anaxagoras also says "All Mind is alike, both the greater and the smaller." It is the same mind stuff that is present in people as in other animals and vegetables. Humans' greater intelligence is due not to possession of a superior grade of mind but to our having hands.

World Creation

Like every other Greek philosopher, Anaxagoras held that nothing can come from nothing, nor can anything utterly vanish. The totality of world stuff is fixed: It is "all," and "we must know that all of them are neither more nor less; for it is not possible for them to be more than all, and all are always equal." However, the world of moving, changing, differentiated things that we know is not eternal. Anaxagoras postulated a primeval condition of homogeneity and motionlessness:

All things were together, infinite both in number and in smallness; for the small too was infinite. And, when all things were together, none of them were plain, because of their smallness. . . . But before they were separated off, when all things were together, not even was any color plain; for the mixture of all things prevented it—of the moist and the dry, and the warm and the cold, and the

light and the dark, and of much earth that was in it, and of a multitude of innumerable seeds in no way like each other.

It is perhaps permissible to think of this initial condition as a gray, dim, damp, tepid, dirty vastness, or if you prefer, a luminosity: "Air and fire prevailed over all things, being both of them infinite; for amongst all things these are the greatest both in quantity and size." That is, a homogeneous mixture of all things would look like air and fire, because those are what are most plentiful.

At some point in this mass, mind started a whirl: "And Mind had power over the whole revolution, so that it began to revolve in the beginning. And it began to revolve first from a small beginning; but the revolution now extends over a larger space, and will extend over a larger still." We *see* the whirl of the heavenly bodies still going on overhead.

The centrifugal force of the whirl caused separation out of the homogeneous mass, "as these things revolve and are separated off by the force and speed. And the speed makes the force. Their speed is not like the speed of any of the things that are now among men, but in every way many times as fast." He continues, "And when Mind began to move things, separating off took place from all that was moved, and so much as Mind set in motion was all separated. And as things were set in motion and separated, the revolution caused them to be separated much more."

The separation resulted not just in differentiation but in a natural *order*: "And all the things that are mingled together and separated off and distinguished are all known by Mind. And Mind set in order all things that were to be . . . and that now exist, and this revolution caused the separating off, and the thin is separated from the thick, the warm from the cold, the light from the dark, and the dry from the moist. . . . The thick and the moist and the cold and the dark came together where the earth is now, while the thin and the warm and the dry and the bright went out towards the further part of the sky." However (it is not clear how), "from the earth stones are solidified by the cold, and these rush outwards more than water." They are the Sun, Moon, and stars, the Sun and stars being heated to incandescence by their motion, while the Moon, lower down and not moving so fast, shines by the reflected light of the Sun. The process described is only a local one. Anaxagoras reasoned that mind must "set things in order" in other parts of the boundless universe, producing other worlds.

> We must suppose . . . that men have been formed in them, and the other animals that have life, and that these men have inhabited cities and cultivated fields as with us; and that they have a sun and a moon and the rest as with us; and that their earth brings forth for them many things of all kinds of which they gather the best together into their dwellings, and use them. Thus much have I said with regard to separating off, to show that it will not be only with us that things are separated off, but elsewhere too.

Anaxagoras followed Anaximenes in holding that the earth is a flat disc held up by the air. The Sun, he said, "is bigger than the Peloponnese." He correctly explained winds as spawned by the thinning of the air by the sun. He theorized that earthquakes are caused by the air above striking on the air under the earth; the movement of the latter causes the earth, floating on it, to rock. He understood the causes of eclipses, but thought that some lunar eclipses are caused by the interposition of invisible bodies between the Sun and Moon. This theory was evidently intended to explain the eclipses that occur when the sun is still above the horizon.

Contrary to the theory of Empedocles, according to which perception is a process of uniting constituents of the sense organs with like things outside them, Anaxagoras held that perception is essentially an irritation by substances unlike those that compose the organs. He worked this theory out with considerable subtlety. We see light because the pupils of our eyes are dark; this explains also why we cannot see at night. We perceive warmth and cold only when in contrast our skin is colder or warmer than the object felt; when they are at the same temperature, there is no sensation. Salt, sweet, and sour tastes are known because though these qualities are in us, there is a deficiency that makes possible a contrast. It follows that all perception is subliminal pain, as is proved by the fact that any prolonged or violent sensation is felt as painful.

A Thorough Rationalist

Anaxagoras was aware of the Italian philosophers—the Pythagoreans, Parmenides, Empedocles, and Zeno—and in some respects adopted their views (concerning eclipses), in others made concessions to their arguments (in rejecting a vacuum), and sometimes argued against them (his doctrine of infinite divisibility seems to stem from an attempt to refute Zeno). Primarily, however, Anaxagoras was the continuator of the Milesian school. His conception of the "beginning" and of the process of world formation, for instance, was an elaboration of Anaximander's. Like the Milesians, he was a thorough rationalist: There is no trace of mysticism in his work, and if he had any emotional reaction to his vision of the nature of things, no report of it has come down to us. The Milesians still talked of "god" and "the divine" in connection with the cosmic process, although these terms had become mere abstract labels for stuffs and mechanisms. In Anaxagoras, on the other hand, even the words have disappeared. Nor was his mind an object of worship; it was not a personality, and (as Socrates complained) it was not even a cosmic designer. It was just the projection of human cognition and will ("known" in experience as initiator of motion) without any moral or religious attributes.

In one respect, Anaxagoras's explanation of things was more consistent than that of any of his predecessors: Having postulated that nothing can come from nothing, and that "things are what they seem to be" (that is, the sensible qualities *are* literally the constituents of the things), he had no difficulty (as Empedocles did) in accounting for the diversity of objects of experience. However, at the same time this success was a great failure, for if there are as many principles of explanation as there are things to be explained, how can one be said to "explain" anything? Everything comes from *just* what it is. However, to say that visible, concentrated hair comes from obscured, diluted hair is not to satisfy the demand that impels us to ask for explanations. Granted that we do not want to be told that hair comes from nothing, we still look for *some* sense in which "hair comes from what is not hair."

Thus the philosophy of Anaxagoras, in being the logical conclusion of the assumption that "things are what they seem to be," was—like many logical conclusions—also a cul-de-sac. Like Parmenides' similar working out of the implications of monism, it closed off one way of investigation and in doing so assured that the next advance in Greek thought (made by the atomists) would consist in denying the premise on which it rested.

Anaxagoras was the first to bring philosophy to Athens. He was also the first philosopher to suffer from Athenian religious and political bigotry. Tried and convicted of "impiety" (for his statements about the Sun and Moon) and allegiance to a foreign power (Persia), he was, it seems, condemned to death but escaped to Lampsacus in Ionia, where he spent the rest of his days as an honored schoolteacher.

Wallace I. Matson

Additional Reading

Barnes, Jonathan. *The Presocratic Philosophers*. London: Routledge, 1993. Includes a chapter on Anaxagoras, reconstructing his philosophy from a careful examination of the fragments.

Davison, J. A. "Protagoras, Democritus, and Anaxagoras." *Classical Quarterly* 3 (1953): 33-45. Establishes Anaxagoras's position vis-à-vis other Greek philosophers and shows his influence on the "atomist" school that succeeded him. Also contains some information on his early life not available elsewhere in English and argues for an early date for his exile from Athens.

Gershenson, Daniel E., and Daniel A. Greenberg. *Anaxagoras and the Birth of Physics*. New York: Blaisdell, 1964. This controversial work suggests that the Anaxagoras fragments are not really the words of Anaxagoras, but rather his words as interpreted by later philosophers, notably Simplicius, who succeeded him. Contains a good, if somewhat theoretical, explanation of Anaxagoras's system.

Guthrie, W. K. C. *A History of Greek Philosophy*. Vol. 2 Cambridge, England: Cambridge University Press, 1965. Contains the most complete account available of Anaxagoras's life. Puts his life and teachings in the context of his times.

Kirk, Geoffrey S., John E. Raven, and M. Schofield. *The Presocratic Philosophers*. 2d ed. Cambridge: Cambridge University Press, 1983. One chapter contains a scholarly account of Anaxagoras's philosophy; includes Greek text of fragments.

Mansfield, J. "The Chronology of Anaxagoras's Athenian Period and the Date of His Trial." *Mnemosyne* 33 (1980): 17-95. Offers the most convincing arguments concerning Anaxagoras's arrival in Athens, his trial, and his banishment. Also contains references to Anaxagoras's relationship with Pericles and the political motives behind the former's exile.

Mourelatos, Alexander P. D. *The Pre-Socratics: A Collection of Critical Essays*. Princeton: Princeton University Press, 1993. Includes two essays by eminent scholars, Gregory Vlastos and G. B. Kerford, which attempt to reconstruct Anaxagoras's philosophy in a way that makes it logically consistent. Both focus on his materialism.

Schofield, Malcolm. *An Essay on Anaxagoras*. Cambridge, England: Cambridge University Press, 1980. A clear, witty exposition of the philosophy of Anaxagoras and his importance in the history of philosophy. Perhaps the best work on Anaxagoras's system and its meaning available in English.

Taylor, A. E. "On the Date of the Trial of Anaxagoras." *Classical Quarterly* 11 (1917): 81-87. A good discussion of the backdrop against which Anaxagoras's sojourn in Athens was played and the political and intellectual milieu during which his book was written.

Paul Madden, updated by Priscilla K. Sakezles

Anaximander

Anaximander realized that no ordinary physical element could be the source of the world's diversity; instead, he saw that the fundamental stuff must be an eternal, unlimited reservoir of qualities and change.

Principal philosophical works: Only a fragment exists, sixth century B.C.E. (*The Anaximander Fragment*, 1982; commonly known as *On Nature*)

Born: c. 610 B.C.E.; Miletus, Greek Asia Minor
    (now in Italy)
Died: c. 547 B.C.E.; probably Miletus

Early Life

Anaximander was a fellow citizen and student of Thales, the Milesian usually credited with having inaugurated Western philosophy. Thales, some forty years older than his protégé, put none of his philosophical thought in writing and maintained no formal pedagogical associations with pupils. Yet Thales' cosmological views (as reconstructed by historians) doubtless inspired Anaximander, and Anaximander finally expanded on Thales' ideas with innovative leaps in conceptual abstraction.

Life's Work

Anaximander was known in his day for his practical achievements and his astronomical discoveries. Anaximander is said to have been chosen by the Milesians as the leader for a new colony in Apollonia on the Black Sea. He traveled widely and was the first Greek to publish a "geographical tablet," or a map of the world. The map was circular and was centered on the city of Delphi, because Delphi was the location of the *omphalos*, or "navel" stone, that was thought to be the center of Earth. Anaximander is also said to have designed a celestial map and to have specified the proportions of stellar orbits. In addition to the celestial map, he built a spherical model of the stars and planets, with Earth located at the center and represented as a disk or cylinder whose height was one-third its diameter. The heavenly bodies were rings of hollow pipe of different sizes that were placed on circling wheels in ratios of three to six to nine, in proportion to the magnitude of Earth. This model was dynamic; the wheels could be moved at different speeds, making it possible to visualize patterns of planetary motion. Anaximander is also credited with inventing the sundial, or gnomon, and with having discovered the zodiac.

All these eclectic interests and discoveries illustrate, with elegance, Anaximander's particular genius, namely, his rational view of the world. This way of thinking was quite an innovation at a time when both scientific and protophilosophical thought took their content from the mythical and literary traditions and thus were marked by vagueness and mystery. Anaximander viewed the world as steadily legible; he had the expectation of its rational intelligibility. His map of the world and his model of the heavens show his anticipation of symmetry and order. Earth, he argued, remained at rest in the center of the cosmos by reason of its equidistance at all points to the celestial circumference; it had no reason to be pulled in one direction in preference to any other. He projected the celestial orbits in perfect and pleasing proportions, and he anticipated regular motions.

Anaximander's mapping and modeling techniques themselves were products of his rationalistic thinking. Models and maps relocate some set of unified phenomena into a new level of abstraction. Implicit in map and model design is the assumption that the abstractions will preserve the intelligible relationships present in the world that they reproduce. Thus Anaximander's introduction of models and maps represents a tremendous and utterly original conceptual leap from the world "seen" to the world's operations understood and faithfully reproduced by the abstracting human mind.

Anaximander's rational view of the world received its fullest and most innovative expression in his philosophy of nature. Here one finds the first unified and all-encompassing picture of the world of human experience in history that is based on rational deduction and explanation of all phenomena.

In order to understand Anaximander properly, his terminology must be put into its historical context. What Anaximander (and Thales as well) understood by "nature" is not quite the same as its modern sense. In Ionian Greece, *physis* denoted the process of growth and emergence. It also denoted something's origin, or source, that from which the thing is constantly renewed. Nature, in the Ionian sense of *physis*, had nothing to do with matter; even Aristotle was mistaken in thinking that it did. In fact, no word for matter even existed in Anaximander's day. It is also important to note that Anaximander's thought is reconstructed entirely from ancient secondary sources. The one extant fragment of Anaximander's own words is the quotation of an ancient historian. Thus, any explication of Anaximander's thought is to some extent conjectural and interpretive.

Anaximander's philosophy of nature arose in part as a response to Thales' ideas on nature. Thales held that water was the nature of everything. This meant, in the light of the ancient idea of *physis*, that water was the origin of everything, that everything was sustained by, and constantly renewed from, water. This notion does not have any allegorical or mythical connotations in Thales' formulation. Water is the ordinary physical stuff in the world, not some engendering god such as the Oceanus of

Thales' predecessors. That is why Thales is the first philosopher: He had a theory about the origin of things that competed with ancient creation myths.

Anaximander agreed with Thales that the origin of the things of the world was some common stuff, but he thought that the stuff could not be some ordinary element. He rejected Thales' conception on purely logical grounds, and his reasoning was quite interesting. How could any manifestly singular stuff ever give rise to qualities that pertained to things differently constituted, such as earth and fire? What is more, if water were the source of things, would not drying destroy them? Thus, reasoned Anaximander, the thing with which the world begins cannot be identical with any of the ordinary stuff with which humans are acquainted, but it must be capable of giving rise to the wide multiplicity of things and their pairs of contrary qualities. What therefore distinguishes the source from the world is that the source itself is "unbounded": It can have no definite shape or quality of its own but must be a reservoir from which every sort or characteristic in the world may be spawned. Therefore, Anaximander called the source of

Anaximander of Miletus. *(Hulton Getty/Liaison Agency)*

things this very name: *apeiron*, Boundlessness, or the Boundless. Anaximander designated the Boundless an *arche*, a beginning, but he did not mean a temporal beginning. The Boundless can have no beginning, nor can it pass away, for it can have no bounds, including temporal ones.

Thus the eternal source, the Boundless, functions as a storehouse of the world's qualities, such that the qualities that constitute some present state of the world have been separated out of the stock, and when their contrary qualities become manifest, they will, in turn, be reabsorbed into the reservoir. When Earth is hot, heat will come forth from the Boundless; when Earth cools, cold will come forth and heat will go back. For Anaximander, this process continued in never-ending cycles.

The cause of the alternating manifestations of contrary qualities is the subject of the single existing fragment of Anaximander's own words, the remains of the first philosophy ever written. Out of the Boundless, Anaximander explains, the worlds arise, but

> from whatever things is the genesis of the things that are, into these they must pass away according to necessity; for they must pay the penalty and make atonement to one another for their injustice according to the ordering of Time.

History has produced no consensus of interpretation for this passage and its picturesque philosophical metaphor for the rationale of the world. Anaximander was probably thinking of a courtroom image. Each existing thing is in a state of "having-too-much," so that during the time it exists it "commits injustice" against its opposite by preventing it from existing. In retribution, the existing thing must cede its overt existence for its opposite to enjoy and pay the penalty of returning to the submerged place in the great Boundless reservoir. This cycling, he added, is how time is ordered or measured. Time is the change, the alternating manifestation of opposites.

Here is the apotheosis of Anaximander's rational worldview. The world's workings are not simply visible and perspicuous, but neither are they whimsical and mysterious. The hidden workings of things may be revealed in the abstractions of the human mind. The world works, and is the way that it is, according to an eternal and intelligible principle. What is more, this world and its workings are unified, indeed form a cosmos. The cosmos, in turn, can be understood and explained by analogy with the human world; the justice sought in the city's courts is the same justice that sustains everything that human perception finds in the universe.

Influence

Classical antiquity credited Thales with having pioneered philosophy. Anaximander, with his scientific curiosity and his genius for abstract insight, poised philosophical inquiry for new vistas of exploration; his new philosophical approach inaugurated penetrating, objective analysis. His principle of the eternal Boundless as the source of the world's multifarious qualities and change forms the conceptual backdrop against which twenty-five centuries of science and natural philosophy have developed.

Two particular innovations of Anaximander have never been abandoned. First, his extension of the concept of law from human society to the physical world continues to dictate the scientific worldview. The received view in Anaximander's time—that nature was capricious and anarchic—has never again taken hold. Second, Anaximander's invention of the use of models and maps revolutionized science and navigation and continues to be indispensable, even in people's daily lives. All scientific experiments are models of a sort: They are laboratory-scale contrivances of events or circumstances in the world at large. Purely visual three-dimensional models continue to be crucial in scientific discoveries: The so-called Bohr model of the atom played a crucial role in physics; the double-helical model was important to the discovery of the structure and function of DNA. Maps are taken for granted now, but if human beings had relied on verbal descriptions of spatial localities, civilization would not have proceeded very far.

Thus, Anaximander's innovations and influence persist. Indeed, it is difficult to imagine a world without his contributions. Anaximander himself could hardly have seen all the implications of his discoveries, for even now one can only guess at the future direction of abstract thought.

Patricia Cook

On Nature

Type of philosophy: Metaphysics

First transcribed: sixth century B.C.E. (*The Anaximander Fragment*, 1982; commonly known as *On Nature*)

Principal ideas advanced:

◇ The universe arose out of an infinite Boundless—a mass of undifferentiated material.

◇ The basic material of the universe was none of the elements (earth, air, fire, water), but something intermediate.

◇ The world was generated when the hot and the cold were separated from the Boundless by its eternal motion.

◇ The earth is shaped like a drum and is surrounded by fire-filled hoops of mist with holes on their inner sides (the Sun, Moon, stars).

◇ Justice is achieved in nature by a process of a return of all things to their origins.

Thales of Miletus is traditionally credited with having been the first philosopher because he was the first to put forward a nonmythological account of the origin and nature of things. However, we know no more of his views than that he claimed that all things originated from water, and it is unlikely that he worked out this thesis in detail. It remained for his "pupil and successor" Anaximander to produce the first comprehensive natural philosophy, a system of astonishing acumen and sophistication.

Anaximander conceived his problem to be that of explaining how the present constitution of the universe developed out of a primordial condition of simplicity. Apparently he did not consider the possibility that things had always been much the same. To this extent, he inherited the notion of evolution from Near Eastern mythologies, which all told of how the world had been fashioned out of a preexisting "chaos" or homogeneous matter, usually water. However, in rejecting divine personal agency and in substituting a (more or less) continuous process for separate acts of creation, Anaximander radically transformed the idea.

The Boundless

Anaximander postulated an undifferentiated stuff out of which the world arose, which he called the Boundless, or *apeiron*. This stuff was not any of the traditional elements, earth, air (mist), fire, and water, but "something intermediate." Because it was no more wet than dry and no more hot than cold, it was presumably damp and tepid. In opposition to Thales, who had held the basic stuff to be water, Anaximander conceived it as neutral, on the ground that the elements "are in opposition to one another—air is cold, water moist, fire hot—and therefore, if any one of them were infinite, the rest would have ceased to be by this time." This is the first recorded philosophical *argument*, a criticism of a predecessor's view supported by an appeal to reason rather than to revelation or to a special mode of insight.

The Boundless was supposed to be infinite in extent and "ageless and deathless," that is, infinite in time. Anaximander called it "divine" but only because of its agelessness and deathlessness; he did not attribute to it any characteristics of personality or (as far as we know) intelligent consciousness.

The Boundless was also said to "encompass all the worlds," implying an infinite or at least indefinitely large number of individual worlds like the one we inhabit. The initial step in the generation of a world occurs when as a result of its eternal motion (we are not told how) "something capable of begetting hot and cold out of the eternal is separated off." The hot and the cold (conceived as *things*, not as qualities of a substance) separate, and at the same time, a motion in rotation is imparted to them. The hot, which is fire, encircles—"like the bark around a tree"—the cold, which contains earth, mist, and water. In due course, earth, mist, and water separate, the earth remaining at the center of the whirl, the water collecting in a ring around the earth, which is in turn enclosed in a circle of mist. The fire around the mist and water heats them until pressure builds up and, combined with the centrifugal force of the whirl, results in a cosmic explosion. The mist causes the fire to be contained in gigantic hoops, resembling inner tubes, that circle around the earth.

Anaximander's Cosmology

The earth in Anaximander's cosmology is shaped like a drum, the diameter being three times as great as the depth. Human beings live on one of the flat surfaces. Though supported by nothing, the earth remains at the center "because of its equal distance from everything." The surface of the earth, which was at first entirely submerged, is now partly dry, and it keeps getting drier through continued evaporation. "The sea is what is left of the original moisture. The fire has dried up most of it and turned the rest salt by scorching it."

Fire-filled hoops of mist, at distances of eighteen and twenty-seven earth-radii, surround the earth and revolve around it. Each of these hoops has on its inner side one hole ("like the nozzle of a bellows," or like the valve-hole of an inner tube) through which the fire shines. The hoop eighteen earth-radii out is the Moon; the outermost is the Sun. The diameter of the Sun—that is, of the opening in the sun-hoop—is as great as that of Earth. Eclipses and the Moon's phases are explained as obstructions over the holes. (We are not told what blocks them.) The stars are the innermost hoops, presumably at a distance of nine earth-radii from the earth. Anaximander would understandably infer that they were the hoops nearest us, for otherwise the hoops of Sun and Moon ought to appear as black bands in the night sky; but these thin, faint star-hoops would not interfere with the greater lights of the Sun and Moon.

Even if Anaximander did not affirm the rotation of the earth, his model of the world contains two very important new ideas. One is that of *an earth without material support*. All earlier, and indeed many later, cosmologists thought themselves obliged to explain the earth's fixity by providing supports. Anaximander, seeing that such shifts only moved the problem back a step or two without solving it, declared boldly that the earth stays at the center "because of its equal distance from everything."

The other new idea is that of *explanation in terms of a theory involving postulated entities*. Anaximander certainly could not *see* the hoops; only the "breathing-holes" were visible. Why did Anaximander postulate the hoops, instead of the simpler and more commonsense conception of fiery spheres or discs? Ancient sources give no hint; however, Anaximander may have reasoned that heavy bodies near the earth tend to move toward the center of concentration of mass, that

is, toward the center of the earth. The earth, being a very heavy body, should likewise move toward the greatest concentration of mass, if there is one. There *appear* to be at least two of these concentrations: the Sun and the Moon. Therefore, if the Sun and Moon are what they appear to be, Earth ought to move toward them (or they toward us). Because this does not happen, the earth must really be equidistant from these bodies, despite appearances. This condition could hold only if the bodies surround the earth symmetrically, that is, are hoops, of which only the "breathing-holes" are visible. The idea of mist wrapping up fire, which seems strange to us, was natural enough to Anaximander; lightning emerging from clouds easily suggests such a notion. We know that Anaximander explained lightning in some such way: "When the wind is shut up in a cloud and bursts forth violently, the tearing of the cloud makes the noise of thunder, and the rift gives the appearance of a flash."

A Scientific Thinker

If this conjectural restoration of Anaximander's reasoning is correct, then Anaximander grasped the essential nature of theoretical explanation: of a law or natural regularity holding universally (in this instance, gravitation) and accounting for or generalized from observation (falling bodies on the earth's surface), leading to the hypothesis of unobserved entities (the hoops) in order to render other observed phenomena (the Sun and Moon *not* falling) consistent with the law. This is nine-tenths of "scientific method" as now understood. Had he devised (or admitted the necessity of) some test of the hoop hypothesis, he would have had the other tenth. Even if he did not reason in this way, it seems that the hoops must have played this role of hypothetical entities in respect to some general theory, for there was no traditional or mythological incentive for supposing them. In consequence, the scientific nature of Anaximander's thought is established.

An Evolutionary Theory

The power and originality of Anaximander's thought are displayed preeminently in his biology. Mythmaking, even when it assumed a development of the cosmos as a whole, always conceived of animals, including humans, as having appeared on the scene from nowhere, in their latter-day forms, either as special creations of the gods or in some unexplained manner. In sharp contrast to this sort of facile storytelling, Anaximander worked out a theory of animal evolution based on the ideas of adaptation to environment and survival of the fittest.

His starting point was the observation that "while other animals quickly find food by themselves, man alone requires a lengthy period of suckling. Hence, had he been originally as he is now, he would never have survived." That is to say, a theory of the world that in general is evolutionary is incompatible with the human species having appeared all at once (possibly as babies), for if it had, the species could never have survived in the "state of nature." It follows that animals whose young are long immature must be the products of gradual development (presumably including socialization) from some other kind of life not so ill-fitted for the world.

Furthermore, the theory that in the beginning there had been no dry land suggested, if it did not require, that all life originated in the sea. Hence "living creatures arose from the moist element as it was evaporated by the sun." The transition from marine to terrestrial life occurred thus: "The first animals were produced in the moisture, each enclosed in a prickly bark. As they advanced in age, they came out upon the drier part. When the bark broke off, they survived for a short time." As for human beings, they too were "like other animals, namely fish, in the beginning. . . . At first human beings arose in the inside of fishes, and after having been reared like sharks, and become capable of protecting themselves, they were finally cast ashore and took to land." The mention of sharks was not fanciful but based on the observation that certain sharks of the eastern Mediterranean hatch their eggs inside their bodies, which makes them seem akin to mammals.

The Father of Scientific Rationalism

Anaximander wrote a book, the Western world's first scientific treatise, of which one sentence, or part of a sentence, has been preserved: Things return to their origins "as is ordained; for they give satisfaction and reparation to one another for their injustice according to the ordering of time." It is clear from this that Anaximander's philosophy made use of the concept of justice, pervasive in Greek thought, according to which there is an impersonal and inexorable force in nature charged with keeping things balanced. In society and in the world at large, every person, state, and element has its allotted portion, and "injustice," the encroachment of anything beyond its bounds, is followed automatically and surely by restorative retribution. The notion lies at the root both of Greek moral ideas and the conception of "laws of nature"; in the fragment of Anaximander it is evidently being developed in the direction of the latter. It would be risky to infer anything more as to Anaximander's worldview from this half sentence. In particular, it by no means shows that Anaximander viewed the universe as "inherently moral" in any sense that we would naturally give to that expression.

Even allowing for the fact that in Greek and other Near Eastern thought before the sixth century B.C.E. there existed a discernible tendency toward "rationalization" of traditional myths, and that the myths themselves contained the kernels of evolutionary and natural-law concepts, it is hardly an exaggeration to say that Anaximander single-handedly invented science and philosophy as we know them. Above all, he put rationalism on such a firm foundation that, among the educated, it took mythology a thousand years to overthrow it; and even then it did not perish utterly.

Any naturalistic worldview at the beginning of the sixth century B.C.E. would be remarkable; it is staggering to find that the very first philosophy contained such transcendently important ideas as an unsupported earth, theoretical explanation involving inferred entities, and animal evolution from marine organisms to humans in accordance with a principle of adaptation—and, quite possibly, the earth's rotation and "gravitation" in addition.

It is not surprising that Anaximander's immediate successor, Anaximenes, was incapable of such daring speculation. He accordingly taught a more "commonsense" philosophy in which the earth was held up by "mist," the unobservable hoops were abolished, and the Sun, Moon, and stars were "like fiery leaves," floating in the air. He was, so to speak, the first positivist. The belief that the earth needed a support continued to be held in Anaximander's homeland for a century, down to and including Anaxagoras. However, at first, the Pythagoreans adopted Anaximander's astronomy, hoops and all. Later, scientists Nicolaus Copernicus and Johannes Kepler were strongly influenced by Pythagorean theories. Unfortunately Anaximander's equally promising beginnings in biology bore no fruit. Though Empedocles also recognized the principle of adaptation, the details of his evolutionary theory were fantastic; and after his time, the authority of Aristotle in favor of fixity of species put an end to evolutionary speculation in the ancient world; its revival two thousand years later owed nothing to Anaximander.

Wallace I. Matson

Additional Reading

Barnes, Jonathan. *The Presocratic Philosophers*. London: Routledge, 1993. This book includes a chapter on Anaximander, focusing on his evolutionary theory, his account of the stability of the earth, and his view of the *apeiron*, or the Boundless.

Brumbaugh, Robert S. *The Philosophers of Greece*. New York: Thomas Y. Crowell, 1964. This volume contains a short chapter on Anaximander's life and accomplishments. Emphasizes cartography and engineering. Includes a reproduction of the first map designed by Anaximander.

Burnet, John. *Early Greek Philosophy*. 4th ed. New York: Barnes & Noble Books, 1945. A detailed scholarly analysis of Anaximander's thought in the context of comparisons with, and influences on, other pre-Socratic philosophers.

Guthrie, W. K. C. *The Earlier Presocratics and the Pythagoreans*. Vol. 1 in *A History of Greek Philosophy*. Cambridge, England: Cambridge University Press, 1962. This is the best work to consult for a thorough, dependable, and readable overview of Anaximander's philosophy. It focuses on Anaximander's cosmology and his view of the *apeiron*.

Kahn, Charles H. *Anaximander and the Origins of Greek Cosmology*. New York: Columbia University Press, 1960. Indianapolis, Ind.: Hackett, 1994. Surveys the documentary evidence for Anaximander's views, reconstructs a detailed cosmology from documentary texts, and devotes an entire chapter to analysis and interpretation of Anaximander's fragment.

Kirk, Geoffrey S., John E. Raven, and M. Schofield. *The Presocratic Philosophers*. 2d ed. Cambridge, England: Cambridge University Press, 1983. One chapter contains a scholarly account of Anaximander's philosophy; includes Greek text of his fragment and testimony.

Seligman, Paul. *The Apeiron of Anaximander: A Study in the Origin and Function of Metaphysical Ideas*. Westport, Conn.: Greenwood Press, 1975. Originally the author's University of London dissertation, this book includes numerous chapters focusing specifically on Anaximander's view of the *apeiron* and the meaning and role of *adikia* (injustice). It presupposes no prior knowledge on reader's part but is very scholarly and detailed in its examination of the texts.

Taylor, C. C. W., ed. *From the Beginning to Plato*. Vol. 1 in Routledge History of Philosophy. London: Routledge, 1997. Contains a chapter on the Ionian philosophers, in which Anaximander's cosmology is examined. This section on Anaximander is brief, readable, and very accessible to the nonspecialist.

West, M. L. *Early Greek Philosophy and the Orient*. Oxford: Clarendon Press, 1971. Contains a substantial chapter examining Asian elements in the philosophy of both Anaximander and Anaximenes.

Wheelwright, Philip, ed. *The Presocratics*. New York: Macmillan, 1966. A primary source. Contains the Anaximander fragment in translation. Also contains testimonies from Aristotle and other Greek and Latin sources who read and commented on Anaximander's treatise.

Patricia Cook, updated by Priscilla K. Sakezles

Saint Anselm

Combining a tenacious attachment to principle with a penetrating mind, Anselm maintained the independence of the English church while making major contributions to the inductive argument for the existence of God.

Principal philosophical works: *Monologion*, 1076 (*Monologium*, 1903; better known as *Monologion*); *Proslogion*, 1077-1078 (*Proslogium*, 1851; better known as *Proslogion*); *Cur deus homo*, 1098 (*Cur Deus Homo: Or, Why God Was Made Man*, 1854-1855); *De humani generis redemptione*, 1099 (*Meditations Concerning the Redemption of Mankind*, 1701); *De conceptu virginali et de originali peccato*, 1099-1100 (*Concerning Virginal Conception and Original Sin*, 1954); *De processione Spiritus Sancti*, 1102 (*The Theology of Saint Anselm Concerning the Procession of the Holy Spirit to Confute the Opposition of the Greeks*, 1953); *De concordia praescientiae et praedestinationis et gratiae dei cum libero arbitrio*, 1107-1108 (*The Harmony of the Foreknowledge, the Predestination, and the Grace of God with Free Choice*, 1976); *Theological Treatises*, 1965-1967 (3 volumes); *Anselm of Canterbury*, 1975-1976 (4 volumes); *The Letters of Saint Anselm of Canterbury*, 1990-1994 (3 volumes).

Born: c. 1033; Aosta, Lombardy (now in Italy)
Died: April 21, 1109; Canterbury?, Kent, England

Early Life

Saint Anselm was born about 1033 in Aosta, an Alpine town now in Italy, near the St. Bernard Pass. His parents were wealthy; Gundulf, his father, was a Lombard who assumed the extensive property of his wife, Ermenberger of Aosta, who may have been related to German royalty. They had one other child, a daughter, Richera, younger than Anselm. Ermenberger's piety was the most important influence on the young Anselm. Placed under the tutelage of a strict disciplinarian, the young boy nearly lost his mind until his mother restored him to normality with kindness.

At age fifteen, Anselm decided to become a Benedictine monk, but the abbot of Aosta refused to accept the underage boy for fear of offending Gundulf. Anselm responded by pursuing worldly amusements, only to be recovered again by his pious mother. When Ermenberger died, Anselm resumed worldly pursuits and had repeated conflicts with the censorious Gundulf. At the age of twenty-three, around the year 1056, he left home with a clerical companion. Anselm made his way to the monastery at Becin Normandy, taking up studies with the celebrated teacher, Prior Lanfranc. Anselm was determined now to become a scholar and a monk and avidly pursued literary studies. When his father died, he briefly considered returning to Burgundy to administer the family estates but instead chose the religious life in 1060. Hence, at age twenty-seven, he was accepted into the monastery at Bec by Abbot Herlwin. Three years later, as a result of his scholarship and exemplary commitment to monastic duties, Anselm succeeded Lanfranc as prior when the teacher left to become abbot of St. Stephen's Monastery in Caen.

Life's Work

As prior, Anselm set aside time each day to render advice in person and in writing to others, even those of high position, and to his nephew, also named Anselm. At night, he corrected the books of the monastic library or wrote devotional literature. Rejecting the prevailing instructional methods for the education of young boys, which included severe constraints and physical beatings, Anselm, recalling his own unhappy experience at the hands of the tutor in Aosta, stressed a blend of kindness and punishment, freedom and discipline. While still at Bec, he wrote *Monologion*, followed a year later by *Proslogion*.

Fifteen years after becoming prior, Herlwin died. Anselm was elected abbot in 1078, and in the following year, he was consecrated. That year, he journeyed to England to examine the English properties of the monastery but also to visit with his old teacher, Lanfranc, now the Archbishop of Canterbury. At Lanfranc's request, Anselm addressed the religious at Canterbury on sundry theological and monastic topics. It was there that Anselm met his future biographer and lifelong friend, Eadmer.

When William the Conqueror lay dying from a wound at Rouen, he sent for Abbot Anselm to hear his confession. Anselm's own illness prevented his arrival, and the king died in 1087.

Saint Anselm. *(Library of Congress)*

After Lanfranc died in May, 1089, King William Rufus (William II) seized the opportunity to tax the clergy and acquire the revenues of the English churches and monasteries. No new archbishop was allowed to be appointed; the king sought to use his added revenues for a military campaign in Normandy. English nobles invited Anselm to come and intercede with the king on behalf of the oppressed churchpeople. His visit with the king in September, 1092, was, however, unsuccessful. When King William became seriously ill the following year, he was frightened into naming Anselm as the new Archbishop of Canterbury. Anselm demanded that all the former lands of the see be restored to church control, that additional properties long claimed by the see be recognized, and that the king take him as his personal counselor. William accepted the first demand but not the other two. With considerable reluctance, Anselm consented and was consecrated archbishop on December 4, 1093, by Thomas of Bayeux, Archbishop of York. Anselm was sixty years of age. Although there may have been the customary election of the archbishop, the records do not reveal one.

As an administrator of church affairs, Anselm is best remembered for his protection of ecclesiastical independence and properties from the depredations of English royalty. Shortly after his consecration as archbishop, King William Rufus demanded a gift of one thousand pounds. Anselm refused for fear that the public would perceive such a large gift as simony. When the king refused his offer of five hundred pounds, Anselm ordered the sum given to the poor. King and primate also quarreled over the former's insistence on possessing the revenues of the abbeys.

Anselm wished to go to Rome in 1095 to receive the symbol of papal approval, the archiepiscopal pallium (a woolen shoulder vestment that was a sign of investiture) from Pope Urban II. King William refused to recognize Urban as pope and so denied Anselm's request for a safe-conduct document.

The papal election was disputed between Urban and Clement III, and England had not yet decided which individual to recognize. Anselm did not deny the king's right to withhold support for a pope whose election was disputed; rather, he held that his support for Urban was announced before his own acceptance of the see. Normandy had accepted Urban, but a convocation of English bishops and nobles in 1095 resulted in the craven submission of the bishops to King William. The nobles, however, supported Anselm and negotiated a truce. Anselm agreed not to go to Rome. William sought to deal with the pope; determining that Urban was, indeed, the rightful pontiff, he asked that the pallium be delivered to himself for bestowal on someone other than Anselm. The Roman agents refused to accept his scheme, and the pallium arrived in Canterbury for Anselm only on June 10, 1095.

During the next two years, 1095-1097, church-state disputes ceased, and Anselm was able to administer routine affairs of the Church, such as consecration of new bishops and erection of buildings. During these years he also began work on his famous book, *Cur Deus Homo*. He even raised two hundred pounds to aid the king's temporary acquisition of Normandy when Robert, his brother, accepted Urban's appeal to go on the First Crusade. Still, William angered Anselm by refusing to consider other church reforms.

Hence, in 1097, Anselm again wished to travel to Rome; as before, William refused. The king feared papal interference with his own prerogatives and, this time armed with the support of both bishops and nobles, informed Anselm that if he left for Rome, he could not return. After personally blessing the king, Anselm left for Italy in November, 1097, whereupon the king confiscated all of his properties. Anselm's reception in Rome was unusually warm. While resting in Apulia, he finished *Cur Deus Homo*. The pope did not accept his request to be relieved of his see. Anselm attended the Council of Bari in 1098, which concerned the filioque doctrine that caused such division with the Church in the East. The address that Anselm delivered at the council later formed the basis of his book *The Theology of Saint Anselm Concerning the Procession of the Holy Spirit, to Confute the Opposition of the Greeks*. This gathering specifically denounced King William

of England for simony and would have excommunicated the king had it not been for Anselm's intercession. In Rome the next year, Anselm attended the Vatican Council of 1099, which declared for excommunication of laypersons who invested church offices. Stopping in Lyons on his way home, Anselm wrote *Concerning Virginal Conception and Original Sin* and *Meditations Concerning the Redemption of Mankind*. A number of miracles were attributed to him during these months. Before he reached England, both Pope Urban II and King William II died, the latter by an assassin's arrow.

The new English king, Henry I, William's brother, quarreled with Anselm on the very same issues and demanded that the archbishop be reinvested and render homage for his see. Henry secured a truce in order to send agents to Rome to beg the pope to relax the recent decrees. During this respite in the quarrel, Anselm pleased the king by allowing him to marry Mathilde of Scotland, who was charged with having entered a convent as a nun. The archbishop's council decided otherwise, and Anselm blessed the royal marriage on November 11, 1100. Once again, he served the king's interest by supporting his claim to Normandy vis-à-vis that of his brother, Robert, and so helped to avert a war. When Pope Paschal's letter arrived and maintained the former decrees, however, Anselm concluded that he must obey Rome. In 1103, Anselm began his second exile, traveling to Rome to see Pope Paschal II. The king and pope were deadlocked over who held the right of investiture. The archbishop had agreed to go to Rome to clarify the situation, but the pope reiterated his positions, doing so in a manner designed to soothe and compliment the English king. Anselm went to Lyons again, to study with his friend, Archbishop Hugh. After written negotiations between Anselm and Henry proved fruitless, the two parties agreed to meet in Normandy in July, 1105. There they were reconciled, and Anselm returned to Canterbury in September, 1106. The English bishops were chafing now under royal taxes and finally came to Anselm's support. Hence, at the conference at Westminster, the king promised never again to invest bishops and abbots with the ring and crosier, and Anselm agreed to render homage to the king for the temporal possessions of the archbishopric, a formula that was approved by Pope Paschal II. This agreement was the model for the Concordat of Worms in 1122, which resolved a similar dispute within the Holy Roman Empire.

Anselm wrote a work called *The Harmony of the Foreknowledge, the Predestination, and the Grace of God with Free Choice* between 1107 and 1108. The next year, he became seriously ill; he died on April 21, 1109. He was called Beatus by the new archbishop, Theobald; Saint Thomas Becket requested his canonization in 1163. Sometime before Becket's martyrdom on December 29, 1170, Anselm may have been formally canonized, but no explicit record has been discovered. Others contend that his canonization was only executed by the notorious Borgia pope, Alexander VI, in 1494. Pope Clement XI declared him a doctor of the Church in 1720.

Influence

Intellectually, Anselm's contributions to philosophy and theology were pivotal in the transition from early medieval thought to the Scholasticism of the later era. Anselm always regarded belief in God as something in accordance with unaided reason, yet his approach was still Platonic rather than Aristotelian. In *Monologion*, he sought not only to demonstrate the reasonableness of belief in God but also to explicate his attributes. In his most remembered work, *Proslogion*, Anselm argued that the very idea of perfection implied its existence. Although Saint Thomas Aquinas later rejected Anselm's ontological argument, it was defended by French philosopher René Descartes in the seventeenth century, and it has continued to interest philosophers of religion.

Anselm's successful defense of church prerogatives in the face of royal demands was crucial to the maintenance of limited authority that marked late feudal England and that was a lasting political legacy of English history for the modern era. Indeed, the triumph of limited government in Western history can in part be attributed to the fact that the contests between church and state in the Middle Ages were between equal forces, neither of which was able to dominate the other. The compromise of Westminster between Anselm and King Henry was just such a case.

John D. Windhausen

Monologion *and* Proslogion

Type of philosophy: Epistemology, metaphysics, philosophical theology
First transcribed: Monologion, 1076 (*Monologium*, 1903; better known as *Monologion*); *Proslogion*, 1077-1078 (*Proslogium*, 1851; better known as *Proslogion*)
Principal ideas advanced:
◇ Because everything good must have a cause, because the cause is goodness, and because God is goodness, God exists.
◇ Because whatever exists must have a cause, because a cause depends upon the power to cause, and because God is that power, God exists.
◇ Because degrees of value or reality depend upon reference to absolute excellence and reality and because God is absolute excellence and reality, God exists.
◇ Because God is the being than whom no greater can be conceived and because it is better to exist in fact than to exist merely in the imagination, God must exist in fact.
◇ God is not substance but essence (the Father) and a set of essences (the Son); as Father, he is the efficient cause (the creator) of all that exists; as Son, he is the formal cause (the idea).

Saint Anselm was an Augustinian Christian whose fame rests to a great extent on his belief that faith is prior to reason, a belief he expresses in the well-known words of the *Proslogion*: "For I do not seek to understand that I may believe, but I believe in order to understand. For this I also believe—that unless I believed, I should not understand." After one has accepted on faith the revelations given through Scripture and through the church fathers, reason is able to fulfill its secondary role of clarifying meanings and providing proofs. Yet Anselm was an ambivalent figure, for despite his emphasis on the priority of faith, he felt a very strong need to support it with proofs. Indeed, he extended the scope of reason considerably further than did the Scholastics who followed him, for they would not have thought of trying to prove doctrines such as those of the Trinity and the Incarnation. His rationalism led others to characterize him as the first of the Scholastics.

The Three Proofs

Anselm delivered three proofs of the existence of God in his earlier work, *Monologion*. According to the first argument, the goodness of things in this world must be caused and must therefore stem from one thing that is good or from many. However, if many causes have their goodness in common, it is by virtue of this goodness that they cause good things; therefore, there must be a common source. In either case, whether the cause be one or many, a single, unitary source of goodness is indicated. Because it is the source of all goodness, this source is not good because of something else but is itself goodness. (Notice that this argument depends on a realistic doctrine of essences that will allow an essence such as *goodness* to function not only as a form but also as an active First Cause.) God is Goodness itself, not merely something that possesses goodness.

The second argument follows a similar course with respect to existence. Because whatever exists must have a cause and because an infinite regress of causes is impossible, there must be either one ultimate, nonfinite cause or several causes. If there is but one cause, one has encountered God. If there are several, then either they support one another mutually or they exist independently. The former is impossible, for that which is supported cannot be the cause of that which supports it. However, if there are several independent ultimate causes, each must exist through itself, and therefore they must share this common power. Now, because it is this common power that is the source of all else, there cannot be several causes but only one. (This proof also depends on the doctrine of essences.) God is not something that has this supreme power; he *is* this power.

The third proof depends on the fact that things in the world can be ranked according to their degrees of "dignity," goodness, or reality. For instance, Anselm says, everyone will admit that a horse represents a higher degree of reality than a piece of wood, for the horse is animate; similarly, a person outranks a horse, for he or she is rational. However, the sequence of degrees of reality cannot be an infinite one, for there must be some boundary, some limiting value by which all the rest are measured, a value that is real absolutely. If there should be several things that share

this degree of reality, it is nevertheless the case that they are equal because of the common excellence they share. This excellence is the absolute reality that is the source of all relative degrees of reality.

The Ontological Argument

Apparently Anselm thought these proofs too complex, for in *Proslogion*, he says that he searched a long time for a simpler proof. The result is the well-known ontological argument. When people think of something, Anselm says, and people are really thinking of it and not just uttering the associated verbal symbol, that thing is in their understanding. Of course, people need not understand that it exists, for they may be thinking of something that they believe does not exist, as in the case of those "fools" who say in their heart that God does not exist, or people may be thinking of something about whose existence they are uncertain. However, in any of these cases, if people are thinking of something, if they understand *it*, then *it*, and not something else, is in the understanding. This point applies to people's thought of anything, including God. However, in the case of God, people are thinking about a unique thing, for they are thinking about the greatest thing conceivable, the being "than which nothing greater can be conceived." Now if a being exists in the understanding alone, it cannot be the greatest conceivable thing, for a being that exists in reality as well as in the understanding would be greater. Consequently, because God is the greatest being conceivable, he must exist in reality as well as in the understanding. Or, to put it another way, if the greatest conceivable being exists in the understanding alone, then it is not the greatest conceivable being—a conclusion that is absurd.

This argument met opposition from the monk Gaunilo, who criticized Anselm in his *Liber pro insipiente* (eleventh century; *In Behalf of the Fool*, 1903). First, Gaunilo says that because God's nature is essentially mysterious, people do not have an idea of him. People may think they do, but they have only the verbal symbol, for when they hear the word "God," what are they to think or imagine? The proof fails, then, for the term "God" does not denote any *conceivable* thing. Second, Gaunilo says that if the argument were sound, people could prove the existence of other things. By way of example, he invites his readers to think of an island that is blessed with more good features and is therefore better than any actual land with which they are acquainted; then he suggests that people must admit its existence, because if it exists in the mind alone, it would not be as good as lands that are known to exist. Third, he says that an idea or concept is only a part of the understanding and that the existing object, if there is one, is something else. It does not follow from the fact that an idea occurs that something quite different in status also occurs. The fact that I am thinking of a being, thinking of it as the greatest conceivable being and therefore thinking of it as existing necessarily, does not provide the slightest evidence that there actually is such a being, for the thought of a necessarily existing being is one thing and a necessarily existing being is another.

Anselm replies to the first objection by saying that the proof does not require a complete understanding of God, but only that one understands this much: that whatever else he may be, God is such that no greater being than he can be conceived. Even the "fool" must admit this much before he or she can refuse to believe. In reply to the second objection, he says that God, unlike the blessed isle, is not thought of simply as the greatest thing of a certain type, or even as the greatest thing of all, but as the being than which nothing greater can be conceived. This latter concept can refer to only one thing, and that thing quite obviously is not the blessed isle. Later proponents of the argument, such as French philosopher René Descartes, make the same point by asserting that existence is contained in the essence of only one thing—namely, the greatest conceivable being.

The third objection is more difficult to handle. It seems to pinpoint an obvious defect, yet Anselm and many others were not daunted by it. In his reply to Gaunilo, Anselm hardly seems aware of it, for he simply repeats again, as if the objection had not been raised, that if people understand a thing, then it exists in the understanding. Most people are likely to feel more at home with Gaunilo's theory of ideas than with Anselm's, so Anselm's doctrine must be reconstructed so that people can see why the objection seemed so un-

important to Anselm. To do so, the nature of the divine being whose existence is supposed to be proved by the argument must be explored a little further.

The Essence of God

Anselm regarded God as self-caused, but the nature of this causation is quite mysterious. God could not have functioned as his own efficient, material, or instrumental cause, for all these causes must be prior to their effect, and not even God could exist prior to himself. For a similar reason, God did not create himself. Yet he does exist through himself and from himself. By way of explication, Anselm presents us with a model, that of light. Light illuminates another thing by falling on it, but it also lights itself, for it is lucent. Its lucidity must come from itself, though, of course, it does not fall upon itself. Now, he says, in God, the relation between *essence, to be,* and *being (existing)* is like the relation between *the light, to light,* and *lucent.* The implication is that the essence of God, the being he enjoys, and the generating of this being are one and the same thing. Like his master Saint Augustine, Anselm conceived of God as an active essence, an activity that necessarily exists, not simply because it is active, but because its activity is the activity of existing.

In other places, too, Anselm indicates quite clearly that God is not a substance having matter and form. First, he points out that if God were such a substance, he would be composite, a state impossible in a being that is the unitary source of all and in a being that has no prior cause. Furthermore, God cannot be a substance possessing such qualities as justness, wisdom, truth, and goodness; for if he were, he would be just, wise, true, and good through another and not through himself. God does not *possess* justness and wisdom; he *is* justice and wisdom. That is, as was indicated in the earlier proofs, God is identical with these essences, and because in him they are one and the same essence, God is an essence.

Creation

This same conclusion is reached by another route, that of creation. As pure spirit, God creates the matter of the world *ex nihilo,* but he creates it according to a model he had in mind prior to the creation. That is, as Augustine had said earlier, all the essences that are manifested in the world existed in God's thought prior to the creation. Insofar as this network of essences is the model according to which the world is created, it is the formal first cause of the world (Augustine had called the divine ideas "the reasons"), and as first cause, it is identical with God. Following Augustine, Anselm says that insofar as God *is* this expression of the world, he has an intelligence; he is wisdom, the word, the Son. However, the important point as far as the ontological argument is concerned is that God is not thought of as a substance in the ordinary sense, but as an essence (the Father) and also as a set of essences (the Son) that function respectively as efficient and formal cause of the world. Again, as in the proofs of *Monologion*, God the Creator is thought of as an acting essence. In God the Father exists the highest degree of reality an essence can enjoy—that of an eternally acting essence that exists in and through itself.

Anselm's doctrine of creation throws still further light on the ontological argument. It is to be noted that the essences that exist prior to creation are not created, for they are the eternal exemplars. As the Son, they are sustained by God insofar as he is the ground of all, but because they *are* the intellect of God, they are not the products of a mind and they do not depend for their existence on being in a mind. Thus, there are essences that do not enjoy the highest degree of reality but that do enjoy a degree higher than that which they would if they were mind dependent. As Anselm says, prior to their manifestation in matter, they were not nothing. Because they are consubstantial with God, they are beings in their own right. Anselm leans as far in the direction of a Platonic realism as his theology will allow him.

Anselm was not clear about the manner in which general ideas are apprehended, but he insists that these ideas are the essences just discussed. This follows not only from his realistic doctrine of ideas but also from his theory of truth. When a thing is apprehended truly, its nature is apprehended, but if it exists truly, then it manifests truly the essence God intended it to manifest. Hence, when people think truly, they are apprehending one or more of the essences that constitute the intellect of God. (Thus, God is

Truth.) This is not to say that people apprehend essences as they exist in God, for in God these essences are exemplars, but what people apprehend does come directly or indirectly, clearly or obscurely, from God. Because the ideas in people's understanding *come* into their understanding, their existence does not depend on people's understanding and is not restricted to their occurrence there. This is what Anselm means when he says that the things people understand are in their understanding.

Essences and Reality
In speaking as if people already knew that these essences constitute the mind of God, it might seem that people beg the question that is to be settled by the ontological argument, but an account of Anselm's doctrine of creation serves to illuminate the way in which he thought of God and of essences. In both *Proslogion* and *Monologion*, Anselm emphasizes the proposition that essences are characters that may be shared in common by many things and that they are ontologically prior to these things. One can assume that he would agree with Augustine, whom he follows in so many respects, that the eternity and immutability of self-evident truths and of the essences involved in them, and the fact that many minds can share the same ideas, are sufficient evidence that general ideas are not created by mutable and independent minds. At any rate, the argument presupposes that because they are not mind dependent, essences can occur elsewhere than in minds. Thus, one can conceive of an essence enjoying a higher degree of reality, such as existing in the physical world or, perhaps, existing in such a way that it is self-sustaining. That some of the essences one apprehends also enjoy a higher degree of reality cannot be denied, for they are manifested as material objects. The only question, and the interesting one, is whether any essence one can apprehend also enjoys the supreme degree of reality. It would be worth examining the various essences one apprehends to see if there is any case where this is so. Anselm says we are led to a positive answer in the case of one and only one essence, that of the "being than which none greater can be conceived," for in this case alone, the essence is such that it necessarily exists.

To do justice to Anselm and understand the strong appeal this argument had for him and many others, one must be clear about the fact that throughout the argument he is talking about an essence. The premises are premises about an essence and the conclusion is a statement about this very same essence. It is not, as Gaunilo insisted, a conclusion about something else. Gaunilo's objection would be valid, as it is in the example of the blessed isle, if Anselm had concluded that an essence has been manifested in matter. However, because manifestation in matter is always an accident, this is not something that could be discovered by examining an essence alone. It is crucial to the argument that existence in matter should not be thought of as the highest level of existence and that the being concerned should not be thought of as a composite of form and substance. The argument can move only from essence to Pure Essence, or *essentia*. That is, it can reveal to one only something more about essence, and this is just what it does when it shows that one of the essences one apprehends is an active self-sustaining essence.

This discussion does not show that Anselm's argument is sound, but perhaps it does show that the whole question centers on two radically different theories about ideas, essences, and objects. Historically, philosophers who have found Anselm's argument acceptable have leaned toward a Platonic or Neoplatonic realism in which the role of essences is emphasized and that of matter minimized. The proof was not accepted by the Aristotelians who dominated the philosophic world for four or five centuries after Anselm, nor by the nominalists and empiricists who have dominated so much of philosophic thought in the last three hundred years; but it is adopted in one form or another by Descartes, Gottfried Wilhelm Leibniz, Baruch Spinoza, and Georg Wilhelm Friedrich Hegel, who, despite the fact that they diverge radically from one another, are each influenced, directly or indirectly, by Plato, Plotinus, or Augustine.

Leonard Miller, updated by John K. Roth

Additional Reading

Barth, Karl. *Fides Quaerens Intellectum*. Translated by I. W. Robertson. London: SCM, 1960. One of the twentieth century's greatest Protestant theologians explores Saint Anselm's understanding of religious faith.

Bencivenga, Ermanno. *Logic and Other Nonsense: The Case of Anselm and His God*. Princeton, N.J.: Princeton University Press, 1993. Explores the logic of Anselm's arguments for the existence of God, especially the ontological argument.

Copleston, Frederick. *A History of Philosophy: Medieval Philosophy*. Garden City, N.Y.: Doubleday, 1962. An excellent historian of Western philosophy provides a readable account of Anselm's thought and its significance in the medieval period.

Davis, Stephen T. *God, Reason, and Theistic Proofs*. Edinburgh: Edinburgh University Press, 1997. A thoughtful discussion of traditional attempts to prove the existence of God, including Anselm's ontological proof.

Eadmer. *The Life of Saint Anselm, Archbishop of Canterbury*. Translated and edited with an introduction and notes by R. W. Southern. Oxford: Clarendon Press, 1979. The principle source for biographical information on Anselm, this work is important not only for what it reveals about Anselm but also for what it tells about the community of monks that shaped him and his thought.

Evans, G. R. *Anselm and Talking About God*. Oxford: Clarendon Press, 1978. Explores Anselm's view about what can—and cannot be said—about God. Analyzes, in particular, Anselm's understanding of language and logic.

Hartshorne, Charles. *Anselm's Discovery: A Reexamination of the Ontological Proof for God's Existence*. La Salle, Ill.: Open Court, 1965. A sympathetic interpretation of Anselm's ontological argument for God's existence by one of the twentieth century's eminent philosophers and theologians.

Hopkins, Jasper. *A Companion to the Study of St. Anselm*. Minneapolis: University of Minnesota Press, 1972. A helpful guide to a full range of Anselm's thought. This work systematically analyzes Anselm's philosophical themes (truth, freedom, and evil) as well as his theological concerns (Trinity, Incarnation, and Redemption).

Morris, Thomas V. *Anselmian Explorations: Essays in Philosophical Theology*. Notre Dame, Ind.: University of Notre Dame Press, 1987. Morris shows how Anselm's philosophy and theology contain approaches and insights that can inform contemporary reflection.

Rogers, Katharine A. *The Neoplatonic Metaphysics and Epistemology and Anselm of Canterbury.* Lewiston, N.Y.: Edwin Mellen Press, 1997. This study focuses on the Platonic influences on Anselm's understanding of reality and knowledge.

Southern, R. W. *Saint Anselm: A Portrait in a Landscape.* New York: Cambridge University Press, 1990. This work analyzes Anselm's thought and situates his life in its historical context. The work considers not only the theological and devotional aspects of Anselm's life and its monastic context but also matters involving history, politics, and economics.

John D. Windhausen, updated by John K. Roth

Kwame Anthony Appiah

Combining intimate knowledge of life in Africa with a philosopher's care for ideas and a reader's appreciation of culture, Appiah critically analyzed the racial myths by which European culture views Africa, and those that inform the pan-African movement.

Principal philosophical works: *Assertion and Conditionals*, 1985; *For Truth in Semantics*, 1986; *Necessary Questions: An Introduction to Philosophy*, 1989; *In My Father's House: Africa in the Philosophy of Culture*, 1992; *Identity Against Culture: Understandings of Multiculturalism*, 1994; *Color Conscious: The Political Morality of Race*, 1996 (with Amy Gutmann).

Born: May 8, 1954; London England

Early Life

Kwame Anthony Appiah (also known as Anthony Appiah and K. Anthony Appiah) was born in London, England, to Enid Margaret Appiah, an art historian and writer, and Joe Emmanuel Appiah, a lawyer, diplomat, and politician from the Asante region, once part of the British Gold Coast Colony but now part of Ghana. He grew up principally in Kumasi, the capital of Asante. In his preface to *In My Father's House: Africa in the Philosophy of Culture*, he describes growing up in his father's world—filled with barrister wigs and dark suits—and in that of the Asante palace royalty (to which he was closely related on his father's side) without experiencing any sense that they were separate worlds or that they were radically different from the world of his mother's family in England. When Appiah was eight years old and hospitalized for an illness, he was visited by both Queen Elizabeth and President Kwame Nkrumah of Ghana on the same day. This acceptance of differences without the identification of contradictions would inform his adult writing, which is often animated by the recognition of the diversity of cultural inheritances.

As a writer, Appiah followed in the footsteps of his mother, a writer of children's books under the name Enid Elizabeth "Peggy" Cripps;

Kwame Anthony Appiah. *(Jane Reed/Harvard University)*

however, there can be no mistaking the early and crucial influence of Anthony's father. A dedicated pan-Africanist and nobleman, the senior Appiah distinguished himself first during World War II in West Africa and then after the war in London as a leader of the West African Students Union. He attended the 1945 pan-Africanist conference along with W. E. B. Du Bois and Kwame Nkrumah and twenty-seven years later was one of the few surviving members of that conference to attend a 1972 pan-Africanist conference. An early supporter of President Nkrumah as well as an early challenger who led an opposition party, Appiah was jailed by Nkrumah for his political activity but, according to his son Anthony, left as an enduring legacy to his children the lesson to be completely untempted by racism.

Life's Work

Kwame Anthony Appiah was educated at Clare College in Cambridge, England, where he received his B.A. in 1975, his M.A. in 1980, and his Ph.D. in 1982. Throughout the 1980's, he taught at Yale University, Cornell University, Duke University, and Harvard University, where he continued to teach in the 1990's along with his friend and frequent collaborator, Henry Louis Gates, Jr. Appiah's earliest publications as an adult were poems published privately in the 1970's; this interest in literature would remain a part of his professional career. Though his first three books, *Assertion and Conditionals*, *For Truth in Semantics*, and *Necessary Questions: An Introduction to Philosophy*, show an ability to write about complex philosophical issues in language that is clear and accessible to general audiences, they did not find wide audiences. These works, written before he focused his attention on the philosophical issues related to race and culture, were not widely reviewed, made no discernible impact on the study of philosophy, and quickly went out of print. Similarly, while the 1991 publication of a mystery novel, *Avenging Angel*, firmly established his professional interest in literature, its Anglophilic tone and setting do not give any sign of the complex questioning of nationality that would emerge in his philosophical writing.

The appearance of *In My Father's House* in 1992 was a watershed for Appiah's career. By reevaluating concepts of race, nationality, and culture,

Appiah brought a fresh perspective to the ongoing debate about the importance of race at a time when Afrocentrism, of which Appiah is highly critical, was beginning to be nationally and internationally articulated, especially, though not only, on college campuses. Afrocentrism, as opposed to Eurocentrism, looks at the world from a black African perspective. Appiah's goal in writing *In My Father's House* was to expose the bad biology that underlies the pan-Africanism that extends from Alexander Crummell and W. E. B. Du Bois to the late President Nkrumah of Ghana. Though he is sympathetic to the goal of African unity, he points out that most people who have sought such unity have had to assume the existence of some stable African essence, an assumption that paves over the multicultural mixture of local and regional and ever-changing cultures that is modern Africa. Though he stops far short of articulating a vision, Appiah's goal is to posit a nonracially biased alternative for grounding pan-Africanism based loosely on the notion of a fraternity of nations. A mixture of philosophy, literary criticism, history, and autobiography, *In My Father's House* received the Annisfield-Wolf Award and the Heskovitz Award of the African Studies Association for the best work published in English on Africa and established the ideas Appiah would spend the bulk of the decade exploring.

In My Father's House was widely and usually favorably reviewed, and its publication vaulted the author onto the stage of public intellectual debate, giving him a role he clearly relished. Though Afrocentrism is not a specific target of *In My Father's House*, in 1993, shortly after the book's publication, Appiah wrote an essay and book review of Clinton M. Jean's *Behind the Eurocentric Veils: The Search for African Realities* (1991) entitled "Europe Upside Down: Fallacies of the New Afrocentrism," in which he targeted the works of Molefi K. Asante and Cheik Anta Diop, the founders of Afrocentrism in the United States and in Africa respectively. Picking up on his central point in *In My Father's House*, that the concept of race corresponds to no biologically or socially unifying principle in human beings, Appiah skewers the biologism that is often associated with Afrocentricity and questions the reliability of Asante's knowledge of Africa and Diop's defense of the

African origins of Greek culture. Essentially, he sees Afrocentrism as an extension of the race solidarity concepts proposed by Crummell and Du Bois, a discourse he faults for being more concerned with self-esteem and sociopolitical aims than with truth, an argument that brought him the wrath of Asante and his followers.

His association with Henry Louis Gates, Jr., a man who has been his colleague throughout his professional career, has proved productive for both men. They have jointly edited several volumes in a series of collections of critical perspectives on black writers (including Zora Neale Hurston, Langston Hughes, Richard Wright, Toni Morrison, and Gloria Naylor), a collection of essays on the nature and defining characteristics of social identity, a book called *Identities* (1995), a reference work entitled *The Dictionary of Global Culture* (1997), and the journal *Transitions*, which is devoted to issues of concern to black life and culture and is written for a general college-educated audience. Of these enterprises, *The Dictionary of Global Culture* has proven to be the most popular and the most controversial. Written as a standard multicultural reference work, it was widely reviewed after its publication. The reviews often revealed the reviewers' biases regarding multicultural education. Those who supported the trend toward multicultural education praised the volume's wealth of hard-to-find information on non-Western cultures and figures. Those who opposed the trend noted that the work lacked or contained inadequate entries on key figures in Western culture.

Color Conscious, Appiah's collaboration with Amy Gutmann, dean of the faculty at Princeton University, marks an attempt to return to the considerations raised in *In My Father's House* but with a greater emphasis on their Anglo-American context. Appiah returns to the biological theory of race he attacked in *In My Father's House*, criticizing it from more a historical perspective. He traces its growth from the racism of U.S. president Thomas Jefferson to the reorientation of race theories in the nineteenth century to accommodate Social Darwinism, to the further reorientation of these theories in the period after poet and critic Matthew Arnold, when biology was replaced by culture in the discourse on racial definition. Appiah arrives at what he calls an "ana-

lytical notion" of racial identity, which encourages the reader to acknowledge the reality of the idea of race as formative but not determinative in the development of identity. Belonging to a specified group still expresses something meaningful about a person but not everything about the individual. In her essay, Gutmann explores how such a notion of race might function in matters of social policy, particularly in preserving affirmative action. Though it is not as groundbreaking as *In My Father's House*, Appiah's contribution to *Color Conscious* is a fruitful development of ideas initiated in that earlier work, one that displays the same articulate and knowledgeable persona and has been widely praised.

Influence
Appiah has established himself as a thinker of considerable significance on the concept of race and African identity. His genealogy of the biological underpinnings of Du Bois's theory of race has become a necessary reference point for further discussions of Du Bois's thought. Similarly, in drawing distinctions between postmodernism and postcolonialism, two movements with much in common that have too often been conflated as a single movement, he has made a significant contribution to clarifying the biases regarding the reception of non-Western art and the assumptions that are sometimes shared by the creators of such art. Not least of all, *In My Father's House* constitutes a worthy, analytic contribution to the growing body of postcolonial African philosophy.

However, Appiah's most important contribution might be less a result of what he has written than of how he has written it. Appiah's professional career began at a time when the humanities were highly specialized and growing increasingly separate: Criticism was written by critics, philosophy by philosophers, and fiction by creative writers. In addition, the philosophy of identity was growing increasingly informed by a politics of resentment and anger. His greatest contribution might be his example in showing how gracefully the boundaries between supposedly separate disciplines can be crossed, how fruitful it is to do so, and how unnecessary anger is to inform a philosophical search for concepts to advance the common good.

Thomas Cassidy

In My Father's House

Africa in the Philosophy of Culture

Type of philosophy: African philosophy, aesthetics, ethics

First published: 1992

Principal ideas advanced:

◊ The concept of race advanced by Alexander Crummell and W. E. B. Du Bois in the late nineteenth and early twentieth centuries was based on incorrect biological concepts.

◊ The pan-African movement and the artists who embraced the idea of an African essentialism have frequently been informed by this obsolete idea.

◊ Though postmodernism and postcolonialism have often been conflated as different expressions of the same artistic idea, they are in fact quite distinct, as a glance at postcolonial art reveals.

◊ To reject the concept of an African essence does not mean to reject African identity; however, it does mean to focus on the important differences between African cultures.

In My Father's House is a collection of essays written over a period of about six years. When Kwame Anthony Appiah was writing these essays, there was much debate among African and African American writers about the status of race as a concept. The argument that racial differences are real and significant, which had long been used in the United States to justify segregation and unequal treatment, was being used by African American leaders and artists to defend affirmative action against those who saw no need for the continued existence of such programs in the face of the civil rights gains of the 1960's. These leaders argued for the existence of distinctive African and African American forms of expression. At the same time, there was a growing body of what has been termed black public-sphere intellectual writing. Black writers with academic backgrounds, including Cornel West, Charles Johnson, bell hooks, Houston Baker, Jr., and Henry Louis Gates, Jr., increasingly directed their debates on issues of race and identity toward a general, nonacademic audience. Though

In My Father's House, unlike the works of West and the other black intellectuals, makes little attempt to focus on the most controversial issues of black life in the United States, it does touch on the same ideas, and its cross-disciplinary approach makes it significant to a large, general audience interested in the importance of the idea of Africa in culture.

A Father's Influence

In My Father's House opens with a brief autobiographical sketch in which Appiah presents his current work in terms not only of his own life but also that of his father, Joe Appiah. His father was a dedicated pan-Africanist and lawyer in Ghana who befriended Kwame Nkrumah, the first president of independent Ghana, when he was a young man and who broke with Nkrumah to form an opposition party. Appiah's father never stopped working for African unity and cooperation but was completely untempted by racism. The title of Appiah's work, *In My Father's House*, part of a passage from the Bible (John 14:2) that concludes "In my father's house are many mansions," refers to the beliefs that Appiah's father inculcated in him—that it is possible to believe in African unity without resorting to notions of race founded on anger or hatred and that there is no such thing as a monolithic African essence—core ideas that Appiah explores throughout the book.

The Concept of Race

Appiah begins with an examination of the racial beliefs of Alexander Crummell and W. E. B. Du Bois, two black Americans born in the nineteenth century (the former a role model for the latter) who worked for diasporic unity among people of African ancestry and who each eventually migrated to Africa. Appiah finds in Crummell's thought an intrinsic racism, which assumes that race determines identity and which also saw Africa as a negative space, one in need of the enlightenment and culture that Americans of African ancestry could bring to the continent. By contrast, he finds in the writings of Du Bois an extrinsic theory of race, one that replaces the intrinsically determinative feature of biology with the extrinsically determinative feature of socio-history. Taking his cue from Georg Wilhelm Friedrich Hegel, who saw the history of the world as the history of great peoples, Du Bois asserts that each race has a message for humanity and that the message of blacks was only beginning to be heard. Du Bois wants to move beyond the basic features of color and hair in his definition of African identity but ends up defining race only in terms of the suffering and insult those of African ancestry have endured at the hands of Europeans and Euro-Americans. Du Bois employs the negative terms of the Euro-American tradition to define being black first and foremost as not being white. Appiah argues that only under these terms could anyone see unity among the diverse populations of sub-Saharan Africa. Although Du Bois's theorizing is more complex than Crummell's, Appiah asserts that it is ultimately as unproductive in that it rests upon an identification of a black "race" that was actually invented to justify racism and that has no basis in human biology, sociology, or anthropology.

The "Essence" of Africa

After attacking the notion of race, Appiah investigates the uses to which the concept has been put in the construction of national literatures. The very notion of studying "English" or "American" literature is based, he points out, less on the raw merit of the literature to be studied than on a belief that in studying the poetry of a people, one is in fact studying the "essence" of a people. At every stage of development, race partisanship has been a crucial, determining factor in deciding what gets studied, and only in the last few decades of the twentieth century was this type of partisanship cast in the role of something that had to be overcome by the inclusion of works of African or African American literature on a reading list for students. Appiah would like to see an end to chauvinistic claims of autonomy that are fostered by the assertion of a self-contained body of literature. Although cultural differences are indeed real, virtually all of the cultural background that an audience needs can usually be found through a sensitive reading of individual texts.

Appiah generally supports Nigerian novelist Chinua Achebe's position that African assimilation of Western art forms is a historical fact that African art will inevitably express, but he speaks against—though not directly opposes—writer

Wole Soyinka's essentialist notion of an African essence expressed in art. Appiah's most in-depth example of the dangers of asserting an autonomous "we" in a body of literature comes in the form of his exploration of the works of Soyinka, especially his commentaries on literature in *Myth, Literature, and the African World* (1976). Appiah finds Soyinka guilty of making the same mistake as Du Bois does in that Soyinka extrapolates an assumed racial essence from the content of his cultural background. African literature draws upon a belief in African religious beliefs and a belief in the power of the community. Using Soyinka's own writing, Appiah points out that it draws most heavily on Yoruba beliefs from a region in what is now Nigeria and that it is impossible to extrapolate from that any African "essence." Although Appiah insists that "African literature" is a meaningful concept and that African cultures do share significant aspects, to generalize too broadly is to repeat the mistake of Du Bois in defining Africa in terms of its history of suffering at the hands of Europe. African identities—but not an African essence—can be expressed in literature.

Postcolonialism vs. Postmodernism

One of the most useful essays in the book sets forth a careful distinction between the varieties of postcolonialism and postmodernism. Because postmodernism (which rebelled against the high seriousness and secular certainties of the modernist period) appeared in the Western world about the same time that postcolonialism (which rebelled against the dictates of colonialism) appeared in the non-Western world, these concurrent movements have often been conflated as different expressions of the same spirit. Taking as his starting point a postcolonial Yoruba sculpture entitled *Man with a Bicycle* (a photograph of which adorns the cover of the 1992 Oxford edition of *In My Father's House*), Appiah traces the work's postcolonial aesthetics not to the culture of postmodernism but to the culture of modernism, the culture that informs much postcolonial African art and literature. The situation is by no means simple, however. If postmodernism is the term used to denote the period after the end of overarching metanarratives, as philosopher Jean-François Lyotard asserts, then postcolonialism, which by its nature must resist the metanarratives of the European empire, would seem to be the natural home for postmodernity. In fact, though, much postcolonial art seeks to posit not an end to all narratives but instead a counternarrative to the European narrative of empire. Postcolonialism seeks a universal ground of truth that can establish at least that the wrongs suffered by African peoples are in fact wrong. The Western narrative of modernity is incorporated into African forms and turned against the Western narrative of colonialism, which is rejected. Returning to the Yoruba statue, this reasoning allows a bicycle to become an African machine not because of who made it, but because it is a machine that will get the rider to town faster than his feet.

African Unity and Identity

Though the last essay, an epilogue titled "In My Father's House," adds little to the philosophical content of the entire book, it adds much to the book's overall value. The author's father, Joe Appiah, died while the book was being written, and this epilogue traces the power struggle that erupted in his family over how and when the funeral should be held. Partly this chapter is important in that it brings the reader deeper into Appiah's world, filling in the picture suggested by his autobiographical comments throughout the book, and partly because it gives the reader the fullest glimpse into how the traditional ways of the Asante people coexist with and adapt to the flux that was Ghana in the late twentieth century. In Ghana, Joe Appiah had been a lawyer, a diplomat, and an important politician, who often found himself in opposition to the father of Ghana's independence, President Kwame Nkrumah. In the kingdom of Asante, part of modern Ghana, Appiah had been a nobleman and nephew to the king. Accordingly, the struggle over the details of his funeral turned into a struggle over lineage and, implicitly, rank in the royal family. Although this story does not add to concepts already listed, it does serve as a vivid representation of what Appiah means when he calls for a recognition of the variety of local African identities that are themselves always in flux.

What if anything, then, do Africans have in common that makes them African, and what can serve as the basis of any future pan-Africanism?

What little Appiah has to offer about the first question sounds remarkably like Du Bois. African cultures do share a history of forced incorporation of Western languages, literatures, and culture. The difference between his view and Du Bois's is that Appiah cautions against trying to make this the basis for a mystical essence. About the second question, pan-Africanism, Appiah is almost as vague, but he makes it clear that he would like to see the emergence of a sense of fraternity between African nations, one that would be quick to recognize common interests without wallpapering over the very real differences that exist between Africans.

Appiah's work is still emerging, but the most significant consequence of his work in *In My Father's House* is likely to be his deconstruction of any identity formation based on an us-against-them ideology. Though he acknowledges that Europe and Africa have often defined themselves against one another, such a definition is ultimately too paltry to do justice to the rich variety of African and European identities. Further, to define oneself antagonistically against the other is to continue the game of domination and resistance. It would be a mistake to say that his arguments have convinced those committed to an Afrocentric or black nationalist perspective, but even the negative responses he has received indicate that he has certainly hit a nerve.

Effect on Literature and Scholarship

Although *In My Father's House* is a philosophically informed, cross-disciplinary work, it probably has had the greatest impact in the study of literature, particularly in African and African American literary criticism, and in that field, the chapter on Du Bois has had the greatest impact. Though *In My Father's House* is critical of Du Bois's race theory, it is also respectful of the man, his aims, and his accomplishments. Furthermore, there can be no denying that the recurring use of autobiography as a unifying motif in *In My Father's House* has had a great deal to do with the book's impact on a general audience, or that Du Bois's landmark work, *The Souls of Black Folk* (1903), serves as the model that makes possible this mixture of philosophy, literary criticism, sociology, history, and autobiography. Whatever criticisms Appiah has of Du Bois, the book itself honors a debt to the man by keeping alive a personal but scholarly form of the essay collection that Du Bois raised to an art form.

Most important, *In My Father's House* established Appiah as a spokesperson for African scholarship in North America, and his seeming ease with the intellectual background of Africa, Europe, and North America has made him an articulate spokesperson. The widespread attention *In My Father's House* received has helped call attention to the true diversity of philosophical and cultural traditions associated with Africa.

Thomas Cassidy

Additional Reading

Appiah, K. Anthony. "Reconstructing Racial Identities." *Research in African Literatures* 27, no. 3 (Fall, 1996): 68-72. This article is Kwame Anthony Appiah's reply to an earlier edition of the journal that featured four essays on his work. In his reply, Appiah cites his lack of a clearly articulated alternative to a racially conceived notion of African ancestry as the major shortcoming of *In My Father's House*.

Bell, Bernard W., Emily Gosholz, and James B. Stewart, eds. *W. E. B. Du Bois: On Race and Culture*. New York: Routledge, 1995. This collection of essays on the importance of W. E. B. Du Bois as a cultural figure begins with a spirited exchange of views by authors Lucius Outlaw and Robert Gooding-Williams on the validity of Appiah's attack on Du Bois's theory of race. Outlaw disagrees with Appiah's criticisms, while Gooding-Williams tries to show that Du Bois himself was already anticipating and replying to the concerns Appiah raises.

Gates, Henry Louis, Jr., ed. *"Race" Writing and Difference*. Chicago: University of Chicago Press, 1986. This compilation of articles that originally appeared in the journal *Critical Inquiry* in 1985 and 1986 deals with issues related to the definition of race and the difference it makes in arts and culture. Besides printing the original version of an essay on Du Bois, "The Uncompleted Argument: Du Bois and the Illusion of Race," that served as the basis for Appiah's essay on Du Bois in *In My Father's House*, this collection is notable for the

reply by Houston A. Baker Jr., "Caliban's Triple Play," in which he notes the shortcomings of Appiah's biological dismissal of the category of race, comments that, though short, have proven to be the core of most objections to Appiah's work.

Houessou-Adin, Thomas. "The Big Con: Europe Upside Down." *Journal of Black Studies* 26, no. 2 (November, 1995): 185-200. Houessou-Adin, a student of Molefi K. Asante, one of the founders of Afrocentrism, replies to Appiah's attack on the movement. Though the reply is needlessly personal, a failing that considerably lessens its overall merit, it does point out some Appiah's mistakes in his account of Afrocentrism and is of note as an example of an Afrocentrist reply to Appiah's criticism of the philosophical underpinnings of that movement.

Imbo, Samuel Oluoch. *An Introduction to African Philosophy*. Totowa, N.J.: Rowman & Littlefield, 1998. This well organized book concentrates on the ethnophilosophy question of the nature and function of African philosophy. Imbo also pits Leopold Senghor's negritude philosophy against Appiah's universalism.

Nicol, Davidson. "Race Ethnohistory and Other Matters: A Discussion of Kwame Anthony Appiah, *In My Father's House: Africa in the Philosophy of Culture*." *African Studies Review* 36, no. 3 (December, 1993): 109-116. An excellent and mostly approving review of the importance of Appiah's work by a scholar familiar with much of the same material and who therefore brings an informed perspective to his discussion.

Research in African Literatures 27, no. 1 (Spring, 1996). The entire issue is devoted to an investigation of *In My Father's House*. These essays are mostly by four scholars of African philosophy and culture. Though the scholars find much to correct and question in Appiah's work, they find more to laud, and much of their work is in applying the philosophical concerns Appiah develops to other works and to considering further ramifications of his work for Africans and African Americans.

Thomas Cassidy

Hannah Arendt

One of the most challenging political philosophers of the twentieth century, Arendt adopted an Aristotelian approach to explore the origins of totalitarianism, the structure of human consciousness, and the nature of violence and evil.

Principal philosophical works: *Der Liebesbegriff bei Augustin*, 1929 (*Love and Saint Augustine*, 1996); *The Origins of Totalitarianism*, 1951; *The Human Condition*, 1958; *Between Past and Future*, 1961; *Eichmann in Jerusalem: A Report on the Banality of Evil*, 1963, rev. 1964; *On Revolution*, 1963; *Men in Dark Times*, 1968; *On Violence*, 1970; *Crises of the Republic*, 1972; *The Jew as Pariah: Jewish Identity and Politics in the Modern Age*, 1978; *The Life of the Mind*, 1978; *Essays in Understanding, 1930-1954*, 1994; *Between Friends: The Correspondence of Hannah Arendt and Mary McCarthy*, 1995.

Born: October 14, 1906; Hannover, Germany
Died: December 4, 1975; New York, New York

Early Life

Hannah Arendt was the only child of Paul Arendt and Martha (Cohn) Arendt, a German-Jewish couple who lived in Hannover. Arendt's father was an engineer, and the family moved to the town of Königsberg, the former capital of East Prussia, where the young Hannah grew up. She attended the University of Königsberg shortly after World War I, receiving a bachelor's degree from that institution in 1924. Later that same year, she began postgraduate study with the existentialist philosopher Martin Heidegger at the University of Marburg. Arendt met Hans Jonas (her future colleague at the New School for Social Research) when she and Jonas were the only two Jewish students to enroll in a New Testament seminar offered at Marburg by the biblical scholar Rudolf Bultmann.

Arendt's education continued at the University of Heidelberg, where she studied philosophy under Karl Jaspers. During her years at Heidelberg, Arendt began to be influenced by Jaspers's Christian existential philosophy and his view that each individual is ultimately responsible for his or her own actions. In 1928, when Arendt was only twenty-two years old,

the University of Heidelberg granted Arendt a doctorate. The following year, her dissertation, *Love and Saint Augustine*, was published. In September of 1929, Arendt married the young Jewish

Hannah Arendt. *(Library of Congress)*

philosopher Günther Stern, whom she had met in 1925 during her postgraduate training in Marburg.

As the National Socialist movement (the Nazis) began to gain power in Germany, Arendt felt that her Jewish heritage was placing her in increasing danger. She fled to Paris in 1933 and began to work for Youth Aliyah, a relief organization that attempted to find homes in Palestine for Jewish orphans. Her relationship with Stern began to deteriorate during the 1930's, and the couple obtained a divorce in France in 1937. Arendt's activity in relief work continued, however, until 1940, when she married Heinrich Blücher, a professor of philosophy. Blücher was to remain one of Arendt's most important mentors during the course of their thirty-year marriage.

In 1941, France was invaded by the Nazis, forcing Arendt and Blücher to move to the United States. From 1944 until 1946, Arendt performed humanitarian work for the Conference on Jewish Relations in New York City. At the same time, she worked to preserve the writings of several Jewish authors, many of whose works had been suppressed by the Nazis during World War II. In 1946, Arendt assumed the position of chief editor for Schocken Books, remaining at that post until 1948. She applied for American citizenship in 1950 and was granted full citizenship during the following year.

Life's Work
Arendt began to draw the attention of international scholars in 1951 with the publication of her first major book, *The Origins of Totalitarianism*. In this work, Arendt suggested that the roots of both communism and Nazism could be traced not only to the imperialism of the nineteenth century but also to the anti-Semitism rampant throughout Europe at that time. Arendt's thesis initially met with mixed reviews. Many scholars praised the extensive research that was reflected in *The Origins of Totalitarianism* and concurred with its view that the rise of modern dictatorships resulted from the collapse of the nation-state. Nevertheless, many critics also rejected Arendt's view that anti-Semitism had been a decisive factor in shaping all forms of totalitarianism in the twentieth century. Arendt was criticized for taking too personal a view of modern

history and for failing to be objective in her interpretation of events. Since the original publication of *The Origins of Totalitarianism*, however, Arendt's central thesis has gained considerable academic support.

In 1958, Arendt's Walgreen lectures delivered at the University of Chicago were published as *The Human Condition*. With its groundbreaking distinction between work, labor, and activity, and its optimistic view that political activity can enhance civilization, this book improved Arendt's reputation as a scholar. One of Arendt's most influential works, *The Human Condition* uses an Aristotelian approach to address issues of concern in modern society. Nevertheless, several critics found the book's prose style to be extremely dense, even awkward. Arendt's literary style continued to be criticized following the publication of several of her later works.

Arendt became the first woman to hold the rank of full professor at Princeton University when she accepted the position of visiting professor of politics in 1959. Soon after, her major study of modern society and its values, *Between Past and Future*, was published. In this work, Arendt argued that by rejecting both tradition and authority, modern society had deprived itself of the basis for establishing generally approved standards of behavior. Her view that moral relativism had left the twentieth century without a shared system of values was to be echoed repeatedly in the decades that followed.

In 1963, Arendt completed the work that was to reach her largest general audience. *Eichmann in Jerusalem: A Report on the Banality of Evil* began as a series of articles for *The New Yorker* magazine. Adolf Eichmann, a leading official of the Nazis, had been captured in Argentina by agents of the Israeli intelligence service in May of 1960. His war-crimes trial in Israel attracted international attention and inspired *The New Yorker* to send Arendt to Jerusalem for her perspective on the trial.

Coining the phrase "the banality of evil," Arendt characterized Eichmann not as a Nazi fanatic but merely as an officious bureaucrat whose personal ambition had caused him to be responsible for horrific actions. Unlike the prison guards and the executioners who took an active role in exterminating the Jews, Eichmann was (in

Arendt's view) little more than a "paper shuffler" whose duties had resulted in unimaginable suffering. The Nazi regime, Arendt continued, did not arise because of the fanaticism of a few of its leaders but because of a collapse of conscience throughout Europe. Jewish leaders themselves, Arendt contended, were not wholly guiltless in permitting the Holocaust to occur. To imply that one person was single-handedly responsible for the murder of millions was to attribute more power to him than any individual can possibly have. Finally, Arendt's book criticized the Israeli government for its conduct of the trial.

With the publication of *Eichmann in Jerusalem*, Arendt found herself once again on the defensive for her views. Although many scholars had regarded her interpretation of history as excessively Zionist in *The Origins of Totalitarianism*, there were some critics who now accused her of being anti-Semitic for criticizing the Israeli court in *Eichmann in Jerusalem*. Despite years of service to Jewish relief organizations, Arendt found her book condemned by the Jewish humanitarian league B'nai B'rith ("Sons of the Covenant") as a "distortion" of history.

Despite this criticism, Arendt's academic career continued to prosper. In the same year that *Eichmann in Jerusalem* was published, Arendt accepted a professorship from the highly prestigious Committee on Social Thought at the University of Chicago. Her book *On Revolution*, a philosophical and political comparison of the French and American revolutions, was also released at this time. In 1967, Arendt left Chicago to begin teaching at the New School for Social Research in New York City. During that same year, Arendt was the only nonspecialist invited to speak at Harvard University at a conference commemorating the fiftieth anniversary of the Russian Revolution.

Arendt's collection of intellectual profiles, *Men in Dark Times*, appeared in 1968. Despite the title of that work, its most influential essays were those that dealt with women, including the German socialist leader Rosa Luxemburg and the Danish author Isak Dinesen. *On Violence*, Arendt's philosophical essay dealing with the use of force in society, was published in 1970.

That same year, Arendt's second husband, Heinrich Blücher, died. Although Arendt men-

tioned to friends at the time that she would not be able to continue her work without Blücher, she soon occupied herself with several major projects. *The Jew as Pariah: Jewish Identity and Politics in the Modern Age* helped to restore Arendt's tarnished reputation in the Jewish community. *The Life of the Mind* was envisioned as a three-volume work, only about half of which was ever completed. In this massive study, Arendt attempted to explore what she regarded as the three major activities of human consciousness: thought, will, and judgment. Both *The Jew as Pariah* and the completed portions of *The Life of the Mind* were published posthumously.

Arendt died suddenly in New York on December 4, 1975, the victim of an apparent heart attack. Four days later she was eulogized at Riverside Memorial Chapel in New York City by Jonas, her longtime friend and colleague at the New School for Social Research, and the novelist and essayist Mary McCarthy, who served as Arendt's literary executor.

Influence
Arendt's political philosophy resulted from the union of three independent strands in her intellectual training: Arendt's Jewish heritage led her to seek philosophical explanations for human suffering and exposed her to the threat of anti-Semitic totalitarianism; her familiarity with the existential philosophy of Heidegger, Jaspers, and Bultmann encouraged her to develop an emphasis on individual responsibility; and her study of the Greek and Roman classics led her to adopt the methods of classical philosophy in her study of the problems afflicting modern society.

Criticized both for excessive Zionism and anti-Semitism in her writing, Arendt was, in the end, an original thinker who resisted all categorization. Her rigorous philosophical analysis of political issues and, in the last decade of her life, of human consciousness made her works among the most influential texts in political philosophy to be written since World War II. Running counter to the pessimistic tone found in a great deal of modern scholarship, Arendt viewed political life as a potentially heroic activity that is fully in keeping with the highest values of Western culture.

Jeffrey L. Buller

The Origins of Totalitarianism

Type of philosophy: Ethics, political philosophy
First published: 1951
Principal ideas advanced:

◇ Anti-Semitism developed in response to the Jews who were perceived as a threat to international domination in Germany, Austria, and France; the slogan of "death to the Jews" crystalized European domestic policy.

◇ Nineteenth century European imperialism led directly to the two world wars in the twentieth century because it employed international expansionist policies, used "race" as grounds for anti-Semitic movements, played a role in the decline of the nation-state and dissolution of multiparty systems, and caused the emergence of masses of stateless peoples without rights under national law.

◇ Through social atomization, the masses are forced into structures of homelessness and uprootedness precipitated by the terror that is the essence of totalitarianism.

◇ The goal of totalitarian domination, in its modern forms of racism and communism, is the total control of humans through organized domination in every sphere of life, thus not only isolating humans from each other but also ultimately making them superfluous.

Although Hannah Arendt never tired of disassociating herself from the class of "paid professional thinkers," *The Origins of Totalitarianism* is nonetheless a tour de force of political philosophy. It combines her unique talent for attention to historical detail, rigorous philosophical analysis resulting from her training in Germany between the two world wars, and her predilection for the disciplines of historical research and political science. The direct occasion for this particular text was Arendt's successful flight from the oppression that she, a German Jew, was bound to endure under the Nazis and her conclusions about what she considered to be the crisis of the twentieth century: the emergence of totalitarianism as a new form of government and with it mass destruction of humans. Although the bulk of this text is taken up by her presentation of an analysis of the social and phenomenological origins of to-

talitarianism as a movement and its remarkable successes, her conclusions also provide some suggestions on how such social phenomena might be avoided.

Arendt divides this text into three major parts: "Anti-Semitism," "Imperialism," and "Totalitarianism." The emergence of anti-Semitism as a sociohistorical phenomenon paves the way for the political policies of imperialism, not only Europe's race-based policies but also the Soviet Union's classless-society policies. The imperialists saw Jewish claims to chosenness and a national-tribal entity as a threat to their own policies of global domination. Arendt presents both anti-Semitism and imperialism as forerunners of totalitarian structures, total and ruthlessly consistent social organizations.

Anti-Semitism

In part 1, Arendt explores the origin and formation of anti-Semitism, which she identifies as a secular, nineteenth century ideology, distinct from the centuries-old Christian and Islamic religious traditions of Jew hatred. She locates its origin in the equally long history of Jewish-Gentile relations and the late-nineteenth century reaction of Gentiles to emancipated and assimilated Jews.

She limits the scope of her analysis to Jewish history in central and western Europe, ranging from the roles of the Court Jews in early modernity to the Dreyfus affair in France at the end of the nineteenth century. The official emergence of anti-Semitic political parties in the 1870's and 1880's began the process that inevitably ended in what has come to be known as the "final solution," that is, the response of the Nazis in Germany to the presence of the Jews as a distinctive subgroup within European nation-states. For Arendt, the historical roots of anti-Semitism demonstrate how it served as the catalyst for the expansionist imperialist policies that ultimately resulted in Nazi totalitarianism. She points out that, ironically, Jewish and anti-Jewish affairs became used for events that, while having little to do with actual Jews, nonetheless targeted Jews as their chief victims.

Arendt at first considers how the Jewish community transcended established national boundaries and what effects that had. Although Jews were instrumental in the nineteenth century development of the European entity of the nation-state because of their supranational status (their "homelessness"), economic resources, and perceived international contacts, precisely because of their status as transnational entities, they were perceived as threats to the aspirations of newly emergent overarching movements such as pan-Germanism and pan-Slavism. As an inter-European element, the Jews served as the primary competition for supranational groups, such as the All-German Union in Germany, the anti-Semitic pan-Germanists led by Georg von Schönerer in Austria, and the anti-Semitic, antirepublic, antidemocratic, anti-Dreyfusards in France.

Arendt successfully provides a fabric for understanding how the extermination of the Jews, or any ethnic group, en masse and individually, is not possible without broad social support. Anti-Semitism as a political movement needed the passionate fanaticism of social forces to create the attitudes or moods of extermination. With such a mood, it then becomes easier to argue that vices must be exterminated, or, as she puts it, that one gets rid of unwanted bedbugs by poison gas.

Imperialism
In part 2, Arendt analyzes imperialism as a preparatory stage to the coming catastrophe of totalitarianism. Imperialism was born when ruling classes came up against national limitations to their economic expansion and thus devised the new tenet that the inherent law of the capitalist system is constant economic growth and that expansion should be the political goal of economic policy. From 1884 to 1914, the slogan of "expansion for expansion's sake" was used to justify conquering foreign peoples for the sake of the nation and also as a business guideline as companies brutally exploited foreign peoples. Significantly, many of the pioneers of this expansion were adventurous Jewish financiers. However, the export of money had to be followed by the export of power in order to protect the tremendous capital risks, thus eliminating the Jews from the power struggle to follow.

It was only through the national instruments of violence that foreign investments could be rationalized and integrated into the national economy. The police and army were exported and

thus separated from the national body (setting a precedent for the police state), and they also became representatives of the state. Without the ethical structures of the national body to constrain it, police-led capitalism created its own realities. Quickly, it became obvious that only unlimited power could beget unlimited money. Hence, because expansion was a permanent policy, violence and power became the conscious aims of a body politic, and violence administered for violence's sake was allowed to continue until there was nothing left to violate. What is new in imperialist expansion is precisely the model that is set up of unlimited expansion aimed at unlimited accumulation of capital that brings about aimless accumulation and violent use of power.

At the heart of Arendt's analysis is an application of Hobbesian political philosophy. English philosopher Thomas Hobbes's social theory entails that individuals accumulate control in a kind of absolute isolation and to their own advantage and are thus driven to realize that they can pursue and achieve their goals only with the help of the majority. Individuals, driven solely by personal interests, conclude that the pursuit of power is the fundamental drive of all humans because each person is equally capable of killing the other. For Arendt, Hobbes is a philosophical scoundrel in promoting a philosophy of the war of "all against all" that became the theoretical basis for the identification of nations as tribes with no interconnections or human solidarity. Such a philosophy legitimizes the foundation of a naturalistic ideology that reduces humans and their instinct of self-preservation to a least common denominator shared with the lower forms of the animal world. This leads to Arendt's insight that racism was the main ideological weapon of imperialistic politics, which helps explain the transition of imperialist ideas in Germany to totalitarian ones.

The other major element characteristic of imperialism is its bureaucratic rule. The creation of nation-states through the Versailles peace treaty at the end of World War I spawned millions of minorities with no place to call home. The bureaucratic response was to assimilate or eliminate them, which then led to the problem of statelessness and the coordinated institution of internment camps for undesirables or "displaced persons." According to Arendt, to deal with the influx of millions of undesirable refugees, the police assumed political control in all countries throughout Europe and thus were able to erect concentration camps and coordinate internment efforts. The first loss suffered by the stateless and rightless refugees was the loss of their homes, which "meant the loss of the entire social context into which they were born and in which they established for themselves a distinct place in the world." Loss of government protection followed, but what was unprecedented in this loss was the impossibility of finding a new home—there was no place where these unwanteds were welcome.

Totalitarianism

The final part of Arendt's text focuses on totalitarian movements and governments, in particular, how various movements became established and retained power and control. The most central ideas are that the success of a totalitarian movement depends on the selflessness of its adherents; its aim in and skill at organizing the masses; its elimination of all anomalies, even those in its own ethnic base; and the presence of the masses for support and continuation. The masses are those who by sheer numbers, neutrality, or indifference cannot be organized into groups of common interest and hardly ever vote. To establish totalitarian rule, the mob-inspired bourgeoisie must be able to organize themselves politically (which they started to do in the imperialist period) in order to influence the politically indifferent masses and gain their support.

In Europe, there arose the phenomenon of the mass human, who possessed a kind of selflessness that diluted the forces of self-preservation and engendered a pervasive mood that the individual, being expendable or superfluous, does not matter. After the leaders of totalitarian movements attracted the masses and gained their obedience, they conducted repeated purges that lead to mass atomization of the populace and blind loyalty from individuals who, because of total isolation from family, friends, comrades, and even acquaintances, could find their place in the world only via membership in the movement and the political party to which it gave birth. Total domination followed, exercised not only externally but also from within such that, according to Hitler, even "thinking . . . [exists] only by virtue of giving and executing orders." No one is allowed to even pause to stop and think, let alone resist. Total loyalty to the leader and his new version of history extended even to elite intellectuals, who began to distrust traditional views of world history and adopted cynical views that the old views were only a facade used to fool people.

For the Nazis, anti-Semitic propaganda was a way to coalesce an atomized society. However, the true goal of totalitarian propaganda is not persuasion but organization; the masses have to become a living organization, a *Volksgemeinschft*, or "community of the people." Such an organization can only be achieved by creating an entire people of sympathizers in a hierarchy of onion-like, fluctuating front organizations meant on the one hand to deceive and protect the members from outside contamination and on the other to provide a bridge with the "normal" nontotalitarian world. Hence, the Nazi and Bolshevik totalitarian movements developed a form of government Arendt calls permanent revolution, practiced in the constant liquidation of party members in the Soviet Union and in the ever-changing radicalization of the standards of race selection in Nazi Germany. In the totalitarian movement's "struggle for total domination of the total population of the earth," the final use of state power is to establish secret police to help constantly transform its fiction into reality, finally erecting "concentration camps as special laboratories to carry through its experiment in total domination."

As the totalitarian movement subsumes all other goals to its goal of total global conquest, which can be achieved only through total organization and domination in every sphere of life, it becomes a short step from the doctrine of "everything is possible" to "everything is permitted." Thus, concentration and extermination camps were created to destroy the juridical, moral, and spontaneous aspects of humans. There is no justice in the internment process—who gets chosen is totally arbitrary and lawless—and survivors were not allowed to remember or grieve for those were killed, destroying even the meaning of death. The disallowing of spontaneity and freedom is the most horrible act because it robs humans of their uniqueness, packing them so closely together in the death machine that all distance and difference is lost. The cold, ruthless, systematic killing of individuality that occurred in the late stages of extermination, when the Schutzstaffel (SS) took over the camps, exemplifies the final and most horrible triumph of the totalitarian system.

Arendt's Conclusion

Arendt provides a thorough and compelling argument that the causes of the two world wars in the twentieth century have identifiable roots that are tied up in two major movements, anti-Semitism and imperialism, which together provided the grounds for totalitarianism. Avoiding and condemning sweeping generalities, she examines in consuming detail the perplexities of how such events have driven humans to become more attentive to the task of comprehending reality in the forms of the power that we have come to exercise on ourselves both for good and for evil. Her conclusion is that our traditional heritage has produced dehumanizing sociopolitical forces of anti-Semitism, imperialism, and totalitarianism, demonstrating the ongoing need to guarantee human dignity with a "new political principle, in a new law on earth, whose validity this time must comprehend the whole of humanity while its power must remain strictly limited, rooted in and controlled by newly defined territorial entities." Only in such a comity, she argues, where humans receive equality by rights only and not by race, class, or party membership, will we be able to carry on the traditions of liberal individualism with its ideals of humankind, the dignity of each human and common responsibility of each for all.

Julius J. Simon

Additional Reading

Benhabib, Seyla. *The Reluctant Modernism of Hannah Arendt*. Thousand Oaks, Calif.: Sage Publications, 1996. Drawing on Arendt's cultural background, life experiences, and philosophical influences, Benhabib has provided a critical account of Arendt's thought.

Bernstein, Richard J. *Hannah Arendt and the Jewish Question*. Cambridge, Mass.: MIT Press, 1996. Bernstein argues how certain events in Arendt's life and how she responded to these events directed her thinking and greatly influenced her body of work.

Bradshaw, Leah. *Acting and Thinking: The Political Thought of Hannah Arendt*. Toronto: University of Toronto Press, 1989. Deals with the problem of evil and Hannah Arendt's major texts on totalitarianism, revolution, democracy, the life of the mind, and political responsibility. Contains notes, bibliography, and index.

Carnovan, Margaret. *Hannah Arendt: A Reinterpretation of Her Political Thought*. Cambridge, London: Cambridge University Press, 1992. Contains chapters on *The Origins of Totalitarianism*, *The Human Condition*, and on Arendt's view of morality and politics, philosophy and politics, and republicanism. Carnovan believes that Arendt is "widely misunderstood" because her views are original and disturbingly unorthodox.

Figal, Günter. *For a Philosophy of Freedom and Strife: Politics, Aesthetics, Metaphysics*. Translated by Wayne Klein. Albany: State University of New York Press, 1998. This book consists of essays ranging in subject matter from aesthetics to political philosophy. Contains studies on Hannah Arendt and others.

Isaac, Jeffrey C. *Arendt, Camus, and Modern Rebellion*. New Haven, Conn.: Yale University Press, 1992. Covers totalitarianism, power, humanism, rebellion, and democratic politics. Isaac argues that Albert Camus and Arendt were distinctive in arguing for a common human condition that makes a politics of human rights imperative.

Tlaba, Gabriel Masooane. *Politics and Freedom, Human Will and Action in the Thought of Hannah Arendt*. Lanham, Md.: University Press of America, 1987. Examines freedom and action, freedom and politics, nonpolitical issues (labor, socioeconomic factors, violence), totalitarianism, and the continuity of Arendt's thought.

Carl Rollyson

Aristotle

Building on Plato's dialogical approach, Aristotle developed what is known as the scientific method. In addition, he founded the Lyceum, a higher institute of learning (similar to Plato's Academy), which, with its vast collections of biological specimens and manuscripts of verse and prose, housed the first research library.

Principal philosophical works: Second Athenian period (335-323 B.C.E.): *Analytica priora* (*Prior Analytics*, 1812); *De poetica*, c. 334-323 B.C.E. (*Poetics*, 1705); *Analytica posterioria* (*Posterior Analytics*, 1812); *Aporemata Homerika* (*Homeric Problems*, 1812); *Aristotelous peri geneseōs kai phthoras* (*Meteoroligica*, 1812); *Athenaiōn politeia* (*The Athenian Constitution*, 1812); *De anima* (*On the Soul*, 1812); *Ethica Nicomachea* (*Nicomachean Ethics*, 1797); *Metaphysica* (*Metaphysics*, 1801); *Organon* (English translation, 1812); *Physica* (*Physics*, 1812); *Politica* (*Politics*, 1598); *Technē rhetorikēs* (*Rhetoric*, 1686); *Topica* (*Topics*, 1812); middle period (348-336 B.C.E.): *Tōn peri ta zōia historiōn* (*Zoology*, 1812).

Born: 384 B.C.E.; Stagirus, Chalcidice, Greece
Died: 322 B.C.E.; Chalcis, Euboea, Greece

Early Life

Aristotle was born in the town of Stagirus, located on the northeast coast of the Chalcidice Peninsula in Greece, most likely in 384 B.C.E. His father, Nicomachus, was a physician and a member of the clan, or guild, of the Asclepiadae, as had been his ancestors; the family probably migrated from Messenia in the eighth or seventh century B.C.E. Aristotle's mother was from Chalcis, the place where he sought refuge during the last year of his life. Both parents died while Aristotle was very young.

Aristotle was adopted and reared by Proxenus, court physician to Amyntas II of Macedonia (an occasional source suggests that Nicomachus also held this position, but others disagree); it is likely, therefore, that young Aristotle lived part of his youth at Pella, the royal seat. He may even have learned and practiced surgery during this time.

Aristotle's early environmental influences helped determine his outlook: his detached, objective way of looking at a subject, his interest in biological science, and his universality. In his early life, Aristotle was surrounded by physicians and princes, not philosophers. When he

was eighteen, he was sent to Athens for training in the best school available, Plato's Academy, where he would spend the next twenty years. Thus ended the first of the four phases of Aristotle's life.

Life's Work

Aristotle's career divides itself naturally into three periods: the twenty (some say nineteen) years at Plato's Academy, from 368 to 348; the thirteen years of travel, from 348 to 335; and the return to Athens, or the years in the Lyceum, from 335 to 323.

When young Aristotle arrived at the Academy, Plato was away on a second journey to Syracuse. When the master returned the following year, however, Aristotle became his prize student and ardent friend. Although most of Aristotle's earlier works have been preserved only in fragments, usually in quotations within works by later scholars of the Peripatetic school, several are attributed to this period and the one that followed.

As Plato's method was dialogue, Aristotle, like other students at the Academy, began writing in dialogue. Aristotle was influenced by Plato about the time the master altered his own form, moving toward dialogues other than those with Socrates as questioner and main speaker. Aristotle, in turn, made himself the main speaker in his own dialogues. Some scholars consider *On the Soul* the best of Aristotle's works from this period. This work treats the soul and immortality and is imitative of Plato's *Phaedros* (middle period dialogue, 388-368 B.C.E.; *Phaedo*, 1675). Critic Werner Jaeger believes that each of Aristotle's early dialogues was influenced by a particular Platonic dialogue, that the student was still dependent on the master as far as metaphysics was concerned but independent in the areas of methodology and logic.

About 347 B.C.E., the death of Plato (and possibly the choice of a new leader of the Academy) caused Aristotle to leave Athens, and Philip II's destruction of Stagirus caused the philosopher to look elsewhere for a new home. With a fellow Academic Xenocrates, Aristotle left Athens for Mysia (modern Turkey), accepting the invitation of Hermeias, a former fellow student at the Academy who had risen from slavery to become ruler of Atarneus and Assos.

Aristotle presided over his host's small Platonic circle, making of it a school modeled after the Academy. He married Pythias, niece and adopted daughter of Hermeias, after the ruler's death; they had a daughter, also named Pythias. His wife lived until late in Aristotle's so-called second Athenian period. After three years came another move, this time to Mytilene on the nearby island of Lesbos; it is possible that Theophrastus found him a suitable place of residence there. Having begun research in marine biology at Assos, Aristotle continued this work at Mytilene. During these years (c. 347-343 B.C.E.), he probably wrote *Peri philosophias* (on philosophy; lost manuscript known only through others' mention of the work), *Ethika eudēmeia* (*Eudemian Ethics*, 1811), and early portions of *Physics*, *Metaphysics*, and *Politics*.

In 343, Aristotle accepted Philip's invitation to move to Pella and become tutor to his thirteen-year-old son, Alexander (the Great). The tutoring lasted until Alexander became regent in 340. It is uncertain whether Aristotle remained in Pella or moved to Stagira, which had been rebuilt by Philip in honor of Aristotle. With the assassination of Philip in 335 and the resultant accession of Alexander, Aristotle returned to Athens.

This time Aristotle's purpose was not to attend the Academy but to found its greatest competitor. The Lyceum was situated on rented property just outside the city, since an outsider could not own Athenian land. The school housed many biological specimens, including the marine specimens Aristotle himself had collected. It is said that Alexander became his old teacher's benefactor, donating eight hundred talents and instructing all under his command throughout the world to preserve for Aristotle any unusual biological specimens. The site was probably to the northeast of the city, where lay a grave sacred to Apollo Lyceius and the Muses, a place where Socrates had enjoyed walking.

Aristotle. *(Library of Congress)*

In addition to specimens, the Lyceum housed hundreds of manuscripts and numerous maps. The objects in the museum were used to illustrate Aristotle's lectures and discussions. In the mornings, he used the peripatetic (walking) method by strolling through the trees, discussing with more advanced students difficult (esoteric) subjects; in the evenings, he would lecture to larger groups on popular (exoteric) subjects. Logic, physics, and metaphysics were discussed; lectures included rhetoric, sophistic, and politics. In turn, Aristotle seems to have prepared and made available two types of notes: preliminary ones, from which he lectured, and more polished treatises, based on the discussions. Many of these have survived as his later, published works. They are in the form of treatises rather than dialogues.

With the death of Alexander and the rise of feelings in Athens against Macedonians, especially those who had been close to Alexander, Aristotle left Athens for his mother's birthplace of Chalcis, where he died a year later of a disease that had afflicted him for some time.

In his later years at Athens, Aristotle was described as well dressed, enjoying the easy life of self-indulgence. He was bald and thin-legged with small eyes, spoke with a lisp, and had a mocking disposition and a ready wit. After the death of his wife, he lived with a mistress, Herpyllis, in a permanent but nonlegal relationship. Together, they had a son, whom Aristotle named Nicomachus, after his father.

Influence

Aristotle's influence—not only on medieval and Renaissance thought but also on modern science—cannot be understated. When Aristotle returned to Athens to found and preside over the Lyceum, he perfected his scientific method, whereby he established logical systems of substantiation before arriving at tentative conclusions—a method that has continued to modern times. Through his teaching, he influenced a few advanced students and the large public groups who heard his lectures. Through the Peripatetic school, his work continued for centuries and many of his writings were preserved to influence those who lived in even later ages. He learned from and utilized the thought of Greek philosophers from Thales to Plato, extending their ideas

and synthesizing them. He perfected the method of Socrates (who had intended such an extension himself) by reaching conclusions rather than probing endlessly. Along with Plato, Aristotle became the most influential of Western philosophers, advancing Greek philosophy to its greatest height.

George W. Van Devender

Metaphysics

Type of philosophy: Metaphysics
First transcribed: Metaphysica, second Athenian period, 335-323 B.C.E. (English translation, 1801)
Principal ideas advanced:

◇ True knowledge is the knowledge of ultimate causes.
◇ There are four types of causes: the formal cause (a plan or type); the final cause (a purpose); the material cause (matter, that which is used); and the efficient cause (that which initiates change).
◇ The study of being as being involves the attempt to discover first principles of explanation.
◇ The individual thing to which properties belong is the only true substance; substances are subjects but never predicates.
◇ Because properties attach themselves to individuals of a certain kind, the kind may also be called "substance"; thus, the essence of a thing is, in this sense, its substance.
◇ Matter is potentiality, the capacity to be something; matter is unlimited that is able to be limited by form; when matter is limited by form, there is actuality.
◇ Forms, or universals, exist only in things.
◇ The process of change cannot go on to infinity; there must be an unmoved First Mover that is eternal substance and actuality; such a First Mover is good; it is divine thought thinking only of thought.

The Islamic philosopher Avicenna reported that he had read Aristotle's *Metaphysics* forty times and still had not understood it. Such a comment is illuminating both for metaphysics as a subject matter and for Aristotle's treatise. Both are difficult to understand, but Aristotle's work, baffling as it is, remains one of the best sources on metaphysics. Its structure is somewhat puzzling, probably because Artistotle's students, not the philosopher himself, assembled the work from their notes. Therefore, Aristotle did not name the treatise. It was placed in the collection of his writings *after* the treatise *Physica* (second Athenian period, 335-323 B.C.E.; *Physics*, 1812) and so earned the name of *meta-*(after the) *physics*.

Accidental as this title seems, it still describes the content of the treatise fairly accurately. In modern times, much of the *Physics* (the discussion of the infinite) might be classed as metaphysics, and some of the topics of the *Physics* (change and movement) are repeated in the *Metaphysics*; however, the *Metaphysics* does go beyond the *Physics*. First principles, not the principles of natural movement alone, are the subject. The *Metaphysics* takes up questions beyond those of physical nature as such and moves on not only to first principles but also to an Unmoved Mover. It is true that *Metaphysics* stands somewhat alone in Aristotle's writings. Much of the general interpretation of Aristotle's other works will vary according to the way in which the *Metaphysics* is either bypassed or interpreted. That is, this treatise rightly occupies a metaphysical (basic) position within Aristotle's vast writings.

Causes and Substance

Book *Alpha,* which begins with the famous sentence, "All men by nature desire to know," is sometimes called the first history of philosophy. In it, Aristotle reviews the theories of the pre-Socratics and of Plato, and much of the information available about the pre-Socratics comes from Aristotle's accounts. Aristotle works out his own theories through a critical appraisal of other doctrines, indicating the strong and the weak points of each theory and incorporating the strong points in his own view.

Aristotle first gives a brief epistemology, describing the modes for gaining knowledge and, finally, for the achievement of wisdom. Such true knowledge can only be a knowledge of causes, particularly of ultimate causes. It is this that leads Aristotle to consider previous theories and types of cause, ending in the famous doctrine of the four kinds of cause: the *formal* cause (the plan); the *final* cause (the purpose); the *material* cause (that which is used); and the *efficient* cause (that which initiates change).

Such a theory of causation is crucial to metaphysics, because what one wants is knowledge of truth, and one cannot know truth without its cause. In order to demonstrate that this can be done, Aristotle must affirm the existence of a first principle and the impossibility of either an infinite series or infinitely various kinds of causes. If it were otherwise, knowledge could not be obtained. Thus, a great deal of the treatise is devoted to proving that the kinds of causes are definite in number and that the existence of a first principle is certain. Knowledge comes through a grasp of causes; but if the kinds of causes were infinite in number, knowledge would be impossible (the mind can handle only finite entities). The disproof of an actual infinite, the limitation of causes to four, and the establishment of the existence of a first cause of motion—all are central if metaphysics is to achieve wisdom.

Book *Beta* turns to the problem of substance. How many basic kinds of entities are there and what is it that is most stable and underlies change? Are the principles that govern both perishable and imperishable things one and the same? "Being" and "unity" are two difficult concepts, and Aristotle considers whether they are themselves substances or merely properties of things. Inevitably he becomes involved in the Platonic theory of forms. Although rejecting forms as substances, Aristotle still agrees with Plato that individuals as such are never knowable and that the knowledge of any individual thing is of its universal properties.

Definition of Metaphysics

In book *Gamma*, Aristotle begins with the definition of metaphysics as the science that investigates "being as being." Other branches of philosophy treat various particular kinds of things, but metaphysics considers the one starting point of all things, the first principles and highest causes. Because being falls immediately into genera, the various sciences correspond to these genera. Yet certain properties are peculiar to being as such, and the philosopher seeks to discover the truth about these.

To complete such basic inquiry, the philosopher must first find principles that are certain, and Aristotle provides a statement of the principle of noncontradiction as an example. Few principles can have the certainty that such a principle has, and one cannot demand demonstration of all things. Basic axioms cannot be proved, although they can be established indirectly by intuition or by the impossibility of their opposite being true. The starting point of demonstration cannot be demonstration but something accepted as true in itself. What metaphysicians must develop is a grasp of the basic principles that lie behind all demonstration, and then they ought to demand demonstration only of matters in which such proof is possible. They must grasp the principles of being itself.

Philosopher's Lexicon

At first glance, book *Delta* seems puzzling. Sometimes called the philosopher's lexicon, it appears to be (and is) simply an extended series of definitions of crucial terms. On closer inspection, these terms prove to be the basic metaphysical vocabulary (made up of such terms as "beginning" and "cause"). Metaphysics has always proceeded by spending time on the definition of a few key words. However, instead of attempting to give a single definition for each of these thirty or so terms, what Aristotle does is to list several common or possible meanings that may be given to each term. He does point up the more important meanings and focuses on any of metaphysical significance, but on the whole, the book is a straightforward analysis of various common meanings given to these philosophically important terms.

The four causes are listed again in this book (they are not always defined in the same terms). The term "necessity" is of some special interest, since Aristotle uses it in the positive sense ("cannot be otherwise"), very much as Plato uses "eternal," whereas "necessity" for Plato in the *Timaeos* (last period dialogue, 360-347 B.C.E.; *Timaeus*, 1793) is a symbol of nonrationality and chaos. Aristotle denies unity as an overreaching concept and makes it merely an attribute of things. The philosopher also defines "substance" as the individual thing that is the bearer of properties and is not itself a property.

Aristotle's other doctrines can be seen through these definitions, that priority means complete actuality and absence of potency, that what is complete and excellent is what has attained its end or purpose. In defining "accident," Aristotle is far from being a rigid determinist. Some aspects of the world are necessary, but events without a definite cause (except that of chance) are equally present; they are accidental. Through definitions of crucial terms, Aristotle built an outline of his view of the world's basic structure.

Scholars argue that the *Metaphysics* was not composed as a continuous work; rather, it represents a collection of pieces on similar topics. This becomes evident when, after the lexicon, the next section begins again on the concept of knowledge through comprehending the principles and causes of things. However, this time the discussion leads into the definition of physics, mathematics, and metaphysics. Physics theorizes about such beings as admit of being moved by but are not separable from matter. Mathematics deals with things that are immovable but presumably do not exist separately, only as embodied in matter. Metaphysics (first science) deals with things that both exist separately and are immovable and eternal. Of the accidental, there can be no scientific treatment whatsoever, in these branches of science or elsewhere.

Substance

Next Aristotle returns to the crucial question of substance, which he calls "first in every sense." The essence or the universal, the genus, and the substratum (that which underlies a thing) are all called substance. In deciding which of these meanings of substance is primary, Aristotle is never completely clear. As far as knowledge is concerned, essence is prior. However, Aristotle does not consider Plato's forms to be self-subsistent substances; forms, or universals, exist only in things. At the other extreme, matter as pure potentiality is unknowable in itself, and there is no definition for the individual as such.

The causes of substances are the objects of Aristotle's search, but sensible substances all have matter and are thus subject to potentiality. Essence certainly attaches to the form and to actuality, and in that sense, the form of the thing has a prior claim to be called substance. Substance is the primary category, and all other categories depend on it. In virtue of the concept of substance, all other beings also are said to be. It is clear that actuality is prior to potency. "Potency" is every principle of movement or rest, whereas substance or form is actuality.

Prime Mover

Arguing that eternal things are prior in substance to perishable things, Aristotle begins his argument for the existence of an eternal Prime Mover. No eternal things exist potentially (and on these grounds, he excludes the existence of an actual infinite). Nothing that is necessary can exist potentially. Yet such eternal and necessary substances must exist, for if these did not exist, nothing would exist. In things that are from the beginning, in eternal things, there is nothing bad, nothing defective, nothing perverted. How is there to be order unless there is something eternal and independent and permanent? In pursuing the truth, one must start from the things that are always in the same state and permit no change.

The process of change cannot go on to infinity. It is necessary that there should be an eternal unmovable substance. It is impossible that movement should either have come into being or cease to be. Movement also is continuous in the sense that time is. There must, then, be a principle whose very essence is actuality. There is something that moves without being moved, being eternal substance and actuality. The object of a desire moves in this way; it moves without being moved. The final cause, then, produces motion as being loved or desired, but all other things move by being moved.

Such a First Mover exists of necessity, and its mode of being is good. The heavens and the world of nature depend on such a principle. This substance cannot have any magnitude, being without parts and indivisible. The nature of divine thought is that it thinks of that which is most divine and precious, and it does not change. Change would be for the worse (involving potentiality, as it must). Because it must be of its own nature that divine thought thinks, its thinking is a thinking on thinking. The divine thought and its object of thought are one.

The *Metaphysics* contains at this point Aristotle's consideration of the Platonic forms and his rejection of their separate and eternal existence. Aristotle does not deny that there are universal forms; knowledge requires them. What Aristotle refuses to do is to give them an independent and prior existence outside particulars. Aristotle then closes the *Metaphysics* with a consideration of the status of mathematical objects. This section has often been a puzzle to scholars, for Aristotle seems to attribute certain views to Plato that are not to be found within the extant Platonic dialogues. Aristotle treats Platonic forms as if they were all thought by Plato to be numbers. These and other unexpected references to unknown Platonic theories have led scholars to guess that Aristotle knew (as Plato's pupil) of later theories developed by Plato in the Academy but not reflected in the written dialogues. Such a puzzle is only one among many generated by the *Metaphysics*. The book is both repetitious and vague in some of its theories and unsystematic in its structure. The parts do not all fit together, and yet it has never failed to attract students to its study. It remains a classical source of metaphysics, and its problems and theories continue to be debated. It is impossible to understand the book in its entirety, and it is equally impossible to dismiss it. It remains a classical training ground for learning abstract theorizing on fundamental problems.

Frederick Sontag, updated by John K. Roth

Nicomachean Ethics

Type of philosophy: Ethics
First transcribed: Ethica Nicomachea, second Athenian period, 335-323 B.C.E. (English translation, 1797)
Principal ideas advanced:
◇ The good is that at which all things aim; the good for humanity is happiness, and happiness is the realization of humanity's essential nature.
◇ The virtue, or excellence, of a thing is the full development of the potentialities of its essential nature; because a human being is essentially a rational animal, the good for humanity is activity of the soul in accordance with reason.

- ◇ To act in accordance with reason, to be virtuous, usually involves choosing the mean between extremes of conduct; for example, the virtue *courage* is the mean between rashness and cowardice.
- ◇ Some kinds of acts are inherently bad, and no temperate action is possible in such cases: for example, adultery and murder.
- ◇ The good life involves friendship with virtuous people and development of the intellectual virtues.
- ◇ The highest good for humanity is the contemplative life.

Italian poet Dante Alighieri's description of Aristotle as "the master of those who know" has an appropriate ambiguity: It suggests Aristotle's mastery of his predecessors' knowledge and also his influence, paralleled only by Plato's, on his philosophical descendants. Both aspects of this mastery are prominent in *Nicomachean Ethics*. It is to Aristotle's credit that he gives full recognition to the contributions of other philosophers, and it is to his glory that so many basic ethical ideas of later philosophers are found in this great seminal work. Although scholarly explanations of the work differ, it is generally agreed that the work was not intended for publication in its present form; it is a version of Aristotle's ethics as stated by his son, Nicomachus. The *Eudemian Ethics,* a record composed by one of Aristotle's pupils, Eudemus, supplements this work.

Nicomachean Ethics is part of a vast scientific and philosophical system to which a teleological view of the universe is basic: All things are to be understood in terms of their purposes, the ends toward which they tend and which are inherent in their forms and integral to their natures. Defining the end or good of humanity by reference to its nature, Aristotle's ethics is a kind of naturalism, but not a reductionism failing to distinguish a higher sense of "nature" from one meaning simply "whatever is or occurs." It thus suggests (though it does not fully develop) the crucial difference between the factual and the ideal. The normative element, the "oughtness," of virtue is determined by the end or good by which virtue is understood. There is thus no non-natural, self-subsistent, or supernatural source of obligation, but this is no loss to an ethics grounded firmly in the Aristotelian psychology and metaphysics.

The Good

Aristotle's psychological approach appears when he begins his investigation of the final good by reference to what he regards as a general fact of human and animal behavior. He cites the dictum of a predecessor that the good is "that at which all things aim." However, there are many aims; some goods are desired for themselves, some for the sake of others. To avoid an infinite regression of goods merely instrumental to others, intrinsic goods must be presupposed; if one good appears to be more ultimate than any other, this will be the chief good. Its criteria will be finality and self-sufficiency—it will be valued for its own sake and its achievement will leave nothing to be desired. Everyone agrees, Aristotle notes, that happiness is thus final and self-sufficient; one desires other goods for the sake of this happiness but never this for the sake of others. However, this general agreement is merely verbal; specific descriptions of happiness are so varied that a detailed inquiry is obviously needed.

Among previous theories of the good is that of Aristotle's teacher, Plato, who held that good is a self-subsistent essence, a universal form, or idea, in which all particular good things participate, and by which alone they are good. Aristotle objects, however, that if nothing but this form is good intrinsically, the good would be both empty of content and unattainable. In the practice of arts and sciences aiming at their own particular ends, it does not seem that a knowledge of this universal good is prerequisite. Hence Aristotle turns to a search for the specifically human good.

This must be found in humanity's own form and function *qua* human. To understand the latter, consider briefly the Aristotelian concept of matter and form, derived but considerably altered from that of Plato. Except for pure matter and pure form, terminal limits posited by the system rather than experienced differences in reality, the matter and form of any given thing are its two aspects of potentiality and actuality, separable only in analysis. Matter is the stuff, form the structure; matter is the *thatness*, form the *whatness*, of things. Matter without form is hardly conceivable, and form without matter is empty abstraction. Form is not mere structure, however, for what a thing is or becomes when its potentialities are actualized depends not only on shape or organization but also on function. The traditional illustration here is that of the acorn, which is a potential oak tree. Relative to the tree, the acorn is matter—an unrealized possibility that will eventuate in the actuality or form, oak tree. However, the tree in turn may be matter for a higher form in case, say, it is made into a piece of furniture, and obviously the acorn itself must mature into the form, "oak tree seed," before it can function as material for the future tree. Thus the end or *telos* of the acorn is integral to its nature, and its "good" is to fulfill its formal function well—to become a strong, well-shaped tree.

Virtues

Humanity's end must likewise be found in form, which is soul. "Soul" here does not have the connotations given it in Christian tradition; it is not an entity but rather a level of function of living bodies. Even plants have the nutritive function or vegetative "soul"; lower animals have this plus a sensory and appetitive or desiderative soul; the human soul has a higher level, the rational. Now the *excellence* or *virtue* of each thing, according to the meaning of the Greek *aretē*, lies in the efficiency of its peculiar function; therefore "human good turns out to be activity of soul in accordance with virtue, and if there are more than one virtue, in accordance with the best and most complete."

Two broad divisions in the human soul are the irrational and the rational; the former includes the vegetative, over which reason has no direct control, and the appetitive, partially amenable to rational guidance. The rational part includes the calculative and scientific functions. Corresponding to each of these are various kinds of excellence ranged under the two main types, moral and intellectual virtues.

To reach a definition of the first type, Aristotle observes that well-being is achieved through a mean between two extremes, either of which destroys it, as the athlete's fitness is maintained by the proper amount of food, neither too much nor too little. However, this is not an arithmetical mean; the proper amount of food for a wrestler would be too much for a businessperson. Applying this concept to attitudes, emotions, and conduct, Aristotle develops a relational ethics that is not relativistic in the pejorative sense: "Virtue . . . is a state of character concerned with choice, lying in a mean, i.e., the mean relative to us, this being determined by a rational principle . . . by which the man of practical wisdom would determine it. Now it is a mean between two vices, that which depends on excess and that which depends on defect." (Examples of virtues appropriate to certain activities and attitudes are shown in the accompanying table.)

Virtue lies in feeling or acting rightly in relation to time, objects, people, motives, and manner. Though the mean is variable because some means lie nearer one or the other extreme, there *is* a mean for most situations—that middle course recognized by the practically wise or good person. Aristotle himself notes, however, that this account of virtue and vice is not exhaustive; there are some acts and passions inherently bad, such as spite or envy, adultery or murder—there are no mean (right) ways of feeling or doing these.

Neither does the theory apply in the same way to a major virtue, justice. As a particular virtue (rather than as the Platonic justice comprehending all other virtues), justice involves the sharing of external goods such as honor or money; and the mean is an intermediate amount, while both

Activity or Attitude
1. Facing death
2. Experiencing pleasure/pain
3. Giving and taking money
4. Attitude toward honor/dishonor
5. Assertion
6. Giving amusement

Vice of Excess	Virtue (Mean)	Vice of Defect
1. Rashness	Courage	Cowardice
2. Self-indulgence	Temperance	Insensibility
3. Prodigality	Liberality	Meanness
4. Empty vanity	Proper pride	Undue humility
5. Boastfulness	Truth telling	Mock modesty
6. Buffoonery	Ready wit	Boorishness

extremes are injustice. Distributive justice is a geometrical proportion between persons judged by merit and goods awarded. If *A* and *B* are persons and *C* and *D* are things, this justice can be formulated thus: *A:B :C:D*. Equality is thus not between persons or quantities; it lies in proportional relation. Rectificatory justice involves only the righting of wrongs in which the gain of one party equals the loss of the other, and the persons themselves are treated as equals. Because Aristotle disclaims universality for the concept of virtue as a mean, the objection of some critics to the inconsistency of his account or justice seems pointless.

The virtues and vices tend to be self-perpetuating; states of character are both causes and effects of corresponding actions. However, although both acts and character are voluntary, specific choices precede acts, and development of character is gradual and not so obvious. Nevertheless, people are responsible for both; even ignorance of the right is inexcusable if caused by carelessness. The very attractiveness of false goods is due to one's character, just as that which is not really wholesome may appear so to a diseased person. Herein lies the distinguishing feature of the good person: Although each character has its own concept of the noble and pleasant, the good person sees "the truth in each class of things, being as it were the norm and measure of them."

Though Aristotle's ethics is not a deontological system, it clearly was intended to develop "the sort of person that the right rule prescribes." The temperate person, for example, "craves for the things he ought, as he ought, and when he ought; and this is what rational principle directs." However, virtuous people are not burdened with a restrictive, puritanical sense of obligation; instead, they enjoy the best life by realizing their highest potentialities as human beings. This is illustrated by Aristotle's description of properly proud people: Pride, a mean between vanity and humility, "seems to be a sort of crown of the virtues; for it makes them greater, and it is not found without them." Proud people think themselves to be *and are* worthy of great things. They are courageous, honorable and honored, noble, disdainful of the petty, liberal, dignified yet unassuming, frank in expressing their loves and hatreds, people of few but great deeds. They are

independent and incapable of centering their life in another, except for friends.

Friendship
Aristotle writes at length of friendship's necessity to the good life. There are three types: friendships based on utility, those maintained for pleasure alone, and those between similarly virtuous people loved because of their goodness. The last kind is highest, rarest, and most durable.

The topic of friendship raises questions of the relations between benevolence and self-love, and Aristotle anticipates such later writers as Scottish philosopher David Hume and Bishop Joseph Butler. Our estimate of "self-love," he points out, requires distinction between higher and lower senses of the term. Selfish concern for wealth or physical pleasure is of course blameworthy, but the true lover of self is one who seeks that most fitting to one's highest nature—the just, temperate, and noble. If all sought for themselves the highest good, self-love would make for the greatest common welfare. True self-love thus involves beneficence and occasionally sacrifice of wealth or even life itself for the sake of friends and country. Thus the good person needs friends in order to exercise virtue fully.

The Intellectual
The good person also needs the second major type of virtue, the intellectual, for the moral involves choice, and choice is defined as "either desiderative reason or ratiocinative desire." Good choice, then, presupposes right desire and true reasoning. The rightness and truth are measured against the right rule by which Aristotle avoids subjectivism: "There is a mark to which the man who has the rule looks . . . there is a standard which determines the mean states which we say are intermediate between excess and defect." However, pure, contemplative intellect does not directly motivate, its end being truth *per se;* therefore it is the practical or productive intellect that aims at the truth in harmony with right desire.

Practical wisdom is the intellectual virtue most intimately connected with moral virtue: "It is a true and reasoned state of capacity to act with regard to the things that are good or bad for man." It is deliberation about the contingent, not the eternal, for its concern is with selecting the best means to the good life; therefore, it is a function of the productive intellect that can command and sometimes control the irrational soul, the feelings and desires. Practical wisdom is thus a virtue of the calculative level, the lower of the two rational parts of the soul. Because it must not only calculate the means but also recognize the ends, "it is not possible to be good in the strict sense without practical wisdom, nor practically wise without moral virtue." Thus, intellectual virtue is not mere cleverness.

Practical wisdom presupposes *intuitive reason*, which grasps first principles, universals, and ultimate particulars or specific facts, the raw materials with which practical wisdom does its work. Intuitive reason also furnishes the first principles with which another intellectual virtue, *scientific knowledge* (logical or mathematical demonstration) operates. This virtue concerns only the eternal, the logically necessary. However, the highest form of wisdom involves not only knowledge of the logical implications of first principles but also comprehension of the principles themselves.

Hence Aristotle, calling *philosophic wisdom* the combination of scientific knowledge and intuitive reason, specifies that it must be directed to the highest objects and be properly completed. From this it follows that it is not directed toward the highest human good, because "man is not the best thing in the world," not as divine, for example, as the heavenly bodies. However, though not directed toward the highest human good, it *is* that good. Should a critic object that philosophic wisdom, being merely contemplative, is thus useless, Aristotle reminds us that it makes humanity happy not as an instrument but as the actualized end, the highest human activity. Practical wisdom's command of the body is not a mark of superiority to contemplation but rather prepares the way for its coming, as medicine is instrumental to health.

Happiness

Before one can fully appreciate Aristotle's concept of happiness, it is necessary to review his treatment of pleasure, regarded by many philosophers as the *summum bonum*. As usual, Aristotle considers arguments on both sides in some detail. He concludes not only that pleasure is a

good but also that there are cogent reasons for thinking it the chief good: Everyone agrees that its opposite, pain, is bad. Both beasts and humans aim at pleasure (and at the start Aristotle had accepted the view that "the good is that at which all things aim"), and because pleasure is a necessary accompaniment of each activity carried to its unimpeded fulfillment, happiness would seem to be the fruition in pleasure of at least some or perhaps all activities.

This latter consideration enters into Aristotle's final formulation of happiness, but there are compelling reasons for denying that pleasure per se and without qualifications is the chief good. Pleasures differ in kind, just as do activities, and because there is a pleasure proper to each activity, their values are concomitant. Some pleasures complete acts that are vicious, and some hinder the fulfillment of more worthwhile activities. As Plato argued, it appears that the desirability of pleasure can be augmented by addition of other goods, such as that of wisdom, but one criterion of the final good is self-sufficiency. Pleasure, then, is but an ingredient of that good, happiness.

The modern reader must be careful not to identify this happiness with euphoria. Aristotle's happiness is a state of being, not just one of feeling. It is an activity, and since virtuous activity is also desirable for its own sake, happiness is virtuous activity. As the chief good, it involves the highest virtue, which is contemplative. Contemplation is capable of more continuity than other actions; it requires fewer material necessities, and its pleasures are pure and lasting. No immediately practical results follow from it, so again it appears to be loved for itself alone. As the highest human activity, it seems most like that of the gods, and indeed it belongs to the most authoritative element in people:

> that which is proper to each thing is by nature best and most pleasant for each thing; for man, therefore, the life according to reason is best and pleasantest, since reason more than anything else *is* man. This life therefore is also the happiest.

Although this may strike the modern reader as an overly rationalistic or perhaps academic conclusion, Aristotle tempers it by adding that such happiness requires a complete life, including the satisfaction of bodily needs. He recognizes that few people have the ability or the opportunity to lead the life of contemplation. He claims that happiness on a secondary level is the morally virtuous life, for the moral virtues, after all, directly concern human nature in its "all too human" aspects because it is a mixture of reason and the irrational appetites. Indeed, most people are incapable of being good through reason and self-discipline alone; they need the aid of legislation. This idea provides the subject of Aristotle's next work, the *Politica* (second Athenian period, 335-323 B.C.E.; *Politics*, 1598).

If Aristotle's method should appear too speculative for the leading scientists of his day, he reminds his readers that what he has said must be reviewed and tested by reference to the facts, and should it clash with them, it must be considered mere theory. However, should the reader adopt this alternative, it must be with reluctance when the theory is seen as an integral part of Aristotle's whole system. To find the most distinctive human excellence in reason and yet to allow for the most tonic exercise of the senses and appetites by conceiving both as the full fruition of humanity's natural potentialities and to see this actualization as part of a universally purposeful process, is to share one of philosophy's most stirring ethical convictions.

Marvin Easterling, updated by John K. Roth

On the Soul

Type of philosophy: Metaphysics, philosophical psychology
First transcribed: De anima, second Athenian period, 335-323 B.C.E. (English translation, 1812)
Principal ideas advanced:
◇ The soul is the actual development of the potentialities of life; it is the body's source of movement, the essence of the living body, and the purpose for which the body exists.
◇ Sensation is the process of receiving into oneself, by means of the sense organs, the forms of things.
◇ The mind is that part of the soul by which the soul knows and thinks.

On the Soul is divided into three books. The first consists mainly of a review of the opinions of Aristotle's predecessors about the soul, and refutation of their errors. The second book and the first part of the third define the soul and describe and explain the nutritive and sensitive faculties. The rest of the third book treats the intellect.

The original meaning of the word *psychē* was "breath," and in the earliest Greek literature it had come to stand for "breath-soul," being identified with vital functions in general, while a separate blood-soul was held to be the seat of consciousness. Aristotle seems to have been unaware of this view. By his time, *psychē* meant "life-principle," whether simple or complex, the inner cause of vital movements of all kinds.

Theories of the Soul

Aristotle begins by describing in detail the views about the soul held by his predecessors, finding them to fall into two groups: first, those according to which the soul is one of the elements (earth, air, fire, water) or some combination of them, or a special (material) soul-substance, and second, the doctrine that the soul is the harmony of the body. Theories of the first kind have in common the characteristic of trying to account for bodily movements by postulating a power of self-movement in the soul. Aristotle says they are mistaken, for the soul cannot have any motion at all. The theories require it to have a natural motion, and if it had, it would (by Aristotle's doctrine of motion) have a natural place toward which it moved, a condition manifestly impossible. Aristotle treats the harmony theory very literally and unsympathetically. He interprets it as meaning that the soul is the ratio of the elements that go to make up the body, and he points out that because, for example, the ratio of elements in bone is different from that in flesh, there would have to be as many souls in one body as there are different kinds of tissues.

It is curious that Aristotle does not discuss the immortality of the soul. As is well known, belief in personal immortality was not widely held in Greece; however, Plato and some of his Pythagorean predecessors had taught transmigration. Aristotle declares almost at the outset that he is not inclined to think that the soul can exist separate from its bodily substratum—though he makes an exception for the intellect, which he says "seems to be an independent substance implanted within the soul and to be incapable of being destroyed." To the familiar argument that mental powers are observed to decline along with bodily ones, he replies that senility is not a defect of the mind as such, but a progressive incapability of the body to use the mind aright. This exception does not constitute an endorsement of belief in *personal* immortality, for thinking is impersonal. The arguments of Plato are not even mentioned.

Actuality and Potentiality

In book 2, Aristotle defines the soul as the "first grade of actuality of a natural body having life potentially in it." It is "'the essential whatness' of a body." It is not really possible to understand these definitions without prior acquaintance with the whole of Aristotle's physics and metaphysics; but it is hoped that the following explanation suggested by Aristotle's discussion of causes will be of some help.

There are four questions that can be raised about a couch. (1) What is it made of (what is its *material cause*)? (2) What sort of thing is it (what is its *formal cause*)? (3) How was it made (what was its *efficient cause*)? (4) What is its purpose (what is its end or *final cause*)? When all these questions are satisfactorily answered, then (and only then) is it possible to understand the couch. So, in general, artificial objects are produced when someone takes raw materials and by moving them imposes a form on them for a certain purpose. The process of making a couch is to be looked upon as a movement from the potential to the actual. A heap of cloth, springs, and wood is potentially a couch; the maker's activity moves these ingredients from the state of potentiality to that of being actually a couch. These terms, however, are only relative; what is potentially a couch (the matter of a couch) is at the same time actually cloth, springs, and wood.

The world consists of particular things. Those that are not artificial are natural, and the significant difference between natural and artificial things is that while the latter have their form imposed on them from outside, the former have their own internal principles of motion (in the broadest sense, including growth). Hence everything is to be understood in the way a couch is understood: as a particular thing, a *this*, consisting of a certain matter that takes on a certain form or whatness—that is, it undergoes a process of development from a condition of potentiality to a state of actuality. It is possible to understand an acorn when one knows that it is a potential oak tree, that it is the sort of thing that has the internal power of developing (organizing itself and other matter) into (not just anything but specifically) an oak tree.

Articles of furniture are classified according to their shapes. The whatness of a table is distinguished from the whatness of a chair by mere outline. However, even in this instance, the difference in form amounts to a difference in *function*. What makes a thing a knife is not its shape but its ability to cut: The form of whatness of a knife is cutting. It is in an analogous sense that Aristotle declares the soul to be the essential whatness of a living body.

A bar of unsharpened steel is potentially a knife. When it is shaped and sharpened, it is actually a knife. However, the word "actually" is ambiguous. The object is actually a knife both when it is actually cutting something and also when it is resting in a scabbard, in a condition to cut. The actuality of the knife in the scabbard Aristotle calls the "first grade of actuality" to distinguish it from the second grade, manifested only when the knife is cutting. Therefore, for the first definition of soul, the soul is not an ingredient of a body or an extra organ; it *is* the organization and functioning of the body. If a body has life potentially in it, the soul is the actuality (developed potentiality) of life. It is the "first grade" of actuality because not all the vital functions are in exercise at every moment. Hence, the immortality of the soul is out of the question. Further, it is as meaningless to ask whether soul and body are one as to wonder whether a piece of wax and its shape are one or two. It is not wrong to say that the animal is its body *plus* its soul, if care is taken to realize that this is to be interpreted in the same sense as the statement that the pupil *plus* the power of sight constitute the eye. (It appears that Aristotle's own doctrine was not so far as he thought from the harmony-of-the-body theory.)

The Soul and Life

The soul is the life-principle. However, what is it to live? It may mean "thinking or perception or local movement and rest, or movement in the sense of nutrition, decay and growth." Plants have the power of nourishing and reproducing themselves, as do all living things, "in order that, as far as their nature allows, they may partake in the eternal and divine. That is the goal toward which all things strive, that for the sake of which they do whatsoever their nature renders possible." Animals have in addition the faculty of moving from place to place, and sensation that makes movement feasible; all animals have at least the primary sense of touch and taste, which is a kind of touch. Only humans are endowed with the power of thought, which "is capable of existence in isolation from all other psychic powers." However, although Aristotle distinguishes thus radically between thinking and the other psychic powers of reproduction, nourishment, and sensation, it is probably a mistake to attribute to him the doctrine that humanity has three (separate or separable) souls.

In all senses of cause except material cause, the soul is the cause of the body. It is the body's source or origin of movement (efficient cause), the essence of the whole living body (formal cause), and the purpose for which the body exists (final cause).

The Senses

The remainder of book 2 treats of the faculty of sensation and of the five senses. "By a 'sense' is meant what has the power of receiving into itself the sensible forms of things without the matter," as the wax receives the imprint of the seal. ("Sensible form" seems to mean any form that can be perceived. Thus, shapes are sensible forms, souls are not.) The process of sensing is this: The sense organ consists of two or more of the four elements in a certain ratio, the combination being such as to be suitable matter for receiving a certain range of sensible forms. When I see a hippopotamus, there is no hippopotamus (natural body, matter and form) *in* my eye. What is there is the matter of the eye, which has now taken on the sensible form of the hippopotamus and is in consequence *qualitatively* identical with the hippopotamus. I cannot see sounds or hear colors

because the matter of the eye is such as to be the potentiality only of colors, the ear only of sounds. The power of the sense organ to perceive, then, is the ratio of the elements in its composition.

On sight, Aristotle says, "What is visible is color and color is what lies upon what is in its own nature visible." In order that something may be seen, there must exist a colored object, a transparent medium, and light. They are related as follows: All transparent things—air, water, and the "uppermost shell of the physical Cosmos"— contain a certain substance that has the power of becoming transparent. It is *actually* transparent, however, only when excited to actuality by fire, or something resembling fire (such as the phosphorescence of certain fungi and decaying flesh). Light is not a body; it is the activity of the transparent medium. When the medium is actually transparent, color is able to set it in motion, thus to communicate the sensible form to the eye.

Aristotle's discussion of sound and hearing is very accurate. He knows that sound is transmitted by vibration of the air, and he knows something of the anatomy of the ear. He remarks that voice, being "sound with a meaning," indicates the presence of soul. Voice is not just air knocking against the windpipe: one must hold one's breath to speak, using the confined air as an instrument.

Aristotle observes acutely that a study of touch raises the problem whether touch is or is not a single sense. For several pairs of opposites, not just one, are perceived by touch: hot and cold, dry and moist, hard and soft. People are inferior to other animals in some of the senses, notably smell, but exceed them all in touch and in its subsense, taste. This, Aristotle says, is the explanation of humanity's superior intelligence and of the superiority of one person to another: "It is to differences in the organ of touch and to nothing else that the differences between man and man in respect of natural endowment are due; men whose flesh is hard are ill-endowed by nature, men whose flesh is soft, well-endowed." Only solutions can be tasted, Aristotle argues. The organ of taste must be something dry that can be liquefied.

All sensation is *via* a medium. The Greek atomist Democritus erred in supposing that one can see through a vacuum. One cannot see something placed directly on the eye or hear something on the eardrum. Neither can one smell something in the nostril, unless one is breathing in. (Aristotle was puzzled, however, to find that some bloodless animals, which do not breathe, nonetheless can smell. He suggests that over the intranasal organ of smell people have some sort of curtain, analogous to the eyelid, which is raised only when people inhale. This the bloodless animals presumably lack.) Even the sense of touch has its medium, to wit, the flesh, which is not itself the sense organ.

Book 3 begins with a complicated proof that there could not be a sixth sense, nor a need for one. Aristotle continues with a discussion of the relation of the sensible object to the percipient sense. They are distinct, though their activity is one and the same: For example, the hearing and the soul are "merged in one." Both must be "found in that which has the faculty of hearing; . . . actual hearing and actual sounding appear and disappear from existence at one and the same moment." However, Aristotle is no Berkeleian: as *potentialities,* one of them may exist without the other. It is wrong to say that without sight there is no white or black; this description applies only to the actualities, not to the potentialities.

There follows an obscure passage in which Aristotle seems to say that after all one does need—and indeed, has—a sixth sense, a "common sense" that discriminates between sensations in different modalities: How else could one tell that sweet is different from white? This passage serves as a transition to the consideration of thinking and imagining that occupies most of the rest of the book.

Thought and Imagination

Thinking is different from perceiving (a doctrine denied by some ancient philosophers), for perception does not admit of error, while thinking does, and all animals perceive, but very few think. Imagining is different from both, as being in the province of the will and not productive of emotion.

Thinking is part imagination, part judgment. Imagination is "that in virtue of which an image arises for us." It is not sensing, for it takes place in dreams; it is not always present, as sense is; imaginations are mostly false, while sensations are always true; when one (in fact) sees a person, one does not say that one imagines it to be a

person; and visions appear to one even when one's eyes are shut. Nor is imagination knowledge or intelligence or opinion, for brutes imagine but do not believe. Nevertheless, imagination is impossible without sensation: one does not imagine what one has never sensed. Imagination is "a movement resulting from an actual exercise or a power of sense."

Mind is "the part of the soul with which the soul knows and thinks." Thinking, though it is not perceiving, is sufficiently *like* perceiving to enable one to conclude that mind is capable of being affected by forms: "Mind must be related to what is thinkable, as sense is to what is sensible." It follows that mind can have no nature (no combination of *matter* and form) of its own; for unlike the senses, the matter of which restricts their potentialities each to a certain range of possible sensations, mind is not limited in its objects. Hence, mind "before it thinks is not actually any real thing. For this reason, it cannot reasonably be regarded as blended with the body." It is (potentially, not actually) "the place of forms."

The mind so far described, however, is only "passive mind." In the extremely short, obscure, and important fifth chapter, Aristotle says that though passive mind "is what it is by virtue of becoming all things," there is "another which is what it is by virtue of making all things: this is a sort of positive state like light, for in a sense light makes potential colors into actual colors." This kind of mind "is not at one time knowing and at another not. When mind is set free from its present conditions it appears as just what it is and nothing more: this alone is immortal and eternal (we do not, however, remember its former activity because, while mind in this sense is impassible, mind as passive is destructible), and without it nothing thinks."

The remainder of the book is in the main a sort of appendix in which topics previously treated are considered further.

The great conception of *On the Soul* is that of soul as the *function* of the body. On this account, it is the only ancient treatise that is akin in its viewpoint to modern psychology and philosophy of mind. It is tragic that Aristotle's great authority, which sufficed to canonize so many errors for so long in other departments of science and philosophy, did not prevail in psychology.

Aristotle, like the tragic heroes he describes in *De poetica* (c. 334-323 B.C.E.; *Poetics*, 1705), was not blameless in the matter: His flaw was his abandonment of his own doctrine in order to sing the ode to "active mind." Although the progress of many a science has consisted in throwing off Aristotelian shackles, the reverse is true in psychology, in which Aristotle's insight had to wait almost until the twentieth century to be rediscovered.

Wallace I. Matson

Organon

Type of philosophy: Logic, metaphysics

First transcribed: Organon, second Athenian period, 335-323 B.C.E. (English translation, 1812)

Principal ideas advanced:

◇ Of the categories—substance, quality, quantity, relation, action, affection, place, time, position, and state—substance is the most important, for the other categories are properties of substance.

◇ Primary substances are the subjects of properties; they are not themselves properties: for example, individual people are primary substances.

◇ Secondary substances are the classes of which primary substances are members: for example, the class "human" is a secondary substance.

◇ The propositional form "If all *B* is *A*, and all *C* is *B*, then all *C* is *A*" is an axiom of logic by reference to which arguments of syllogistic form can be reduced and criticized.

◇ Scientific arguments depend upon ultimate premises established either by induction or by intuition.

The six treatises that make up Aristotle's *Organon* are the first writings on logic as an independent discipline to appear in Western civilization. The title has been used to refer to the collection since at least the sixth century, but there is no evidence that Aristotle himself referred to the treatises by this name. Aristotle's word for what today is called formal logic was "analytics." Traditionally, the treatises have been ordered as follows: *Cate-*

gories, On Interpretation, Prior Analytics, Posterior Analytics, Topics, and *On Sophistical Refutations.* This order is based on the contents: *Categories* treats of terms, *On Interpretation* treats of propositions, *Prior Analytics* treats of syllogisms. The remaining three treat of kinds of argument; *Posterior Analytics* of apodictic (necessary) syllogisms, *Topics* of dialectical (debatable) syllogisms, and *On Sophistical Refutations* of unsound arguments (informal fallacies). However, Aristotle did not write the treatises in this order, and there is no evidence to support the rather common misconception that Aristotle regarded them (except for the *Prior* and *Posterior Analytics*) as successive chapters in a systematic treatise on logic. The *Categories, Topics,* and *On Sophistical Refutations* are early works, *On Interpretation* was probably written some time later, and the two *Analytics* were written last. The *Categories* is perhaps as much a work on metaphysics as it is on logic; it has considerable historical significance, but its logical content is rather meager.

There is a wealth of material discussed in the six works, but it is of very uneven importance. Large portions are tedious and out of date, while other sections are first-rate philosophy and surprisingly modern. What follows is a very brief summary of the contents of each treatise, with a somewhat more detailed account of the *Categories* and the two *Analytics*.

The Six Treatises

The Greek word *kategoria*, from which the word "category" is derived, ordinarily is used simply to mean "predicate." *Categories* is concerned with the ten ultimate kinds of predicates people can use in communicating with one another. There are references to the categories throughout the Aristotelian corpus, but at various places in his writings, Aristotle departs from the list given in *Categories.* Those listed in *Categories* are substance, quality, quantity, relation, action, affection, place, time, position, and state. Aristotle specifies what he means by each category and points out its peculiar characteristics. This work has had considerable historical importance.

On Interpretation opens with some grammatical distinctions. Nouns, verbs, sentences, and various kinds of propositions are characterized, and the relations between various propositional forms are traced. The traditional square of opposition has its roots in *On Interpretation*. The four traditional *A, E, I,* and *O* forms of propositions are discussed, although the matter of the distribution of predicate terms is not raised. (*A*: All *S* is *P*; *E*: No *S* is *P*; *I*: Some *S* is *P*; *O*: Some *S* is not *P*.) It is one of the more controversial treatises because it is the source of the view (which has plagued philosophers as gifted as Gottfried Wilhelm Leibniz) that all propositions must finally be resolved into subject-predicate propositions, a view that modern logicians reject.

Prior Analytics and *Posterior Analytics* are Aristotle's mature account of the formal theory of the syllogism and of what is today called "scientific method."

Topics concerns itself with the dialectical syllogism; that is, with questions that are matters of "opinion" (in the Platonic sense). The work is an early one, and probably its contents are largely commonplaces from the Academy regarding questions that can profitably be debated. Aristotle offers commonsense advice about how to attack or defend the various views an educated Greek of fourth century Athens might expect to encounter. The work is rather tedious for the modern reader. Its significance lies in the seriousness with which Aristotle treats the problems the Sophists offered to settle cheaply. It is also a reminder of the often forgotten fact that philosophy, for the Greek, was a conversational business. To philosophize, for the Greek, was to *talk*, not to reflect in private. Such a conception of philosophy as this undoubtedly led Aristotle to focus attention on the syllogism as the instrument of logical argument, since the syllogism is most effective and convincing in debate.

On Sophistical Refutations, although an early work, has been held in high regard by philosophers in all periods. It is concerned with what are today called "material fallacies." The fundamental distinction Aristotle draws between fallacies resulting from language and fallacies of relevance is still a common approach to the discussion of fallacies. Many of the fallacies he identified are still included in logic books and called by the names he gave them; for example, amphiboly and accent.

Scholarship has shown that so-called traditional logic, although attributed to Aristotle, is actually a synthesis made in late antiquity of some Aristotelian doctrine together with elements from an independent Stoic logic. Stoic logic is now largely lost, but it did play into the rather crude misunderstanding of Aristotle that came to be known as traditional logic. Aristotle is the discoverer of the logic of propositional functions, the branch of logic in which the range of values for the variables is terms. The Stoics discovered the logic of truth functions, or the propositional calculus, the branch of logic in which the range of values for the variables is propositions. The categorical syllogism is Aristotle's discovery; hypothetical syllogism is a discovery made by the Stoics. The extent of Aristotle's influence, however, is indicated by the name "hypothetical syllogism," which has been given to a Stoic inference form that is not syllogistic at all. The barrier traditional logic raises often prevents both a proper recognition of the Stoic achievement and a sound historical approach to and appreciation of Aristotle's syllogistic.

Categories

The ten ultimate predicates Aristotle lists in *Categories* may be separated into two divisions, substance and the remaining nine. Substance is by far the most important; it is presupposed by all the others—they are really all characteristics or properties of substances. Within the broad category of substance, Aristotle distinguishes primary and secondary substance. Philosophers have often held that Aristotle's primary substance was the substratum of later metaphysics. Aristotle says that it is neither "predicable of" nor "present in" a subject, and he lists as examples the individual person or the individual horse. Secondary substances are the species of which primary substances are members; "person" and "horse," for example, are illustrations of secondary substances. One might get closer to Aristotle's doctrine if one recognizes that practically everything he meant by substances could be included if one talked merely about that which is symbolized by whatever word may stand as the subject of a proposition.

However, it would be going beyond the doctrine of *Categories* to charge Aristotle with a substratum view of primary substance. Actually, Aristotle seems to mean by primary substance merely the commonsense notion of a living individual thing. After all, the term "thing" is metaphysically vague and its mere occurrence in a passage is not sufficient ground for inferring that Aristotle held a substratum doctrine. Examination of the words "predicable of" and "present in" (a subject) reveals insufficient support for a substratum view. The remarks Aristotle makes immediately following the distinction between primary and secondary substance show that by "predicable of," he means the relation between a genus or species and one of its members (for example, the species *man* is "predicable of" the *substance* Socrates), while "present in" refers to the relation between a substance and one of its attributes (for example, the *attribute* rational is "present in" the *substance* Socrates).

Before dispensing with this question, however, it is important to note a remark that Aristotle makes shortly following the section discussed above. He states that primary substances are most properly called substances as a result of the fact that they are the "entities which underlie everything else," and that everything else is predicated of or present in them. In another place, he states that primary substances are called primary because they "underlie and are the subjects of" everything else. Now although "underlies" immediately suggests "substratum," it is important to bear in mind that the substratum doctrine was not fully developed until the medieval period, long after Aristotle's death. One should beware of anachronism and avoid attributing to Aristotle a view that was not current until after his time. If nothing is attributed to him that cannot be supported by the statements he makes in *Categories*, it is clear that he does not there hold such a view. For the words "present in" and "predicable of" do not by themselves entail a substratum view, and "underlie and are the subjects of" are words that show that Aristotle treats "underlie" as equivalent in meaning to "are subjects." It would therefore seem wiser to recognize that there is not sufficient evidence to support the view that *Categories* sets forth a substratum view. What Aristotle had in mind when he spoke about primary substances was simply individual living things without the metaphysical and epistemological frills that decorate the substratum doctrine.

Analytics

Considerable interest has developed in Aristotle's syllogistic as it is presented in *Prior Analytics*. Viewed on its own merits, apart from the additions and revisions of "traditional logic," the doctrine of *Prior Analytics* is seen to be surprisingly modern and innocent of many of the charges often made against it. It lacks the refinement of contemporary functional calculi, but it nevertheless is a surprisingly sophisticated formal, axiomatic system, needing but little to make it a completely acceptable logical calculus.

A modern logical calculus includes four elements:

1. A set of terms that are undefined (within the calculus) or "primitive" and that serve as a basis for defining all other terms in the system. Examples of such primitive terms in a logical calculus are "not" and "if . . . then . . . " and the notion of a variable.

2. Formation rules that specify which expressions are to be included as well-formed and which expressions are inappropriate or not well-formed. For example, everyone recognizes implicitly that "The instructor is tardy" is a sensible English sentence and that "The stone sang a solo" is inappropriate or not well-formed. The formation rules explicitly state the conditions well-formed expressions must meet.

3. Certain axioms or postulates from which the theorems of the system are derived. Euclid's axiom that the shortest distance between two points is a straight line is an example—taken from geometry rather than logic, of course— of an unproved axiom.

4. A set of rules specifying how the theorems are to be derived from the axioms.

Aristotle does not call his primitive terms by that name, but he uses "not" and "and" and "if . . . then . . ." as primitives, taking it for granted that the reader can also use them, and offering no definitions for them. In the case of variables, however, he has clearly and self-consciously arrived at the modern point of view. Throughout *Prior Analytics*, he uses letters of the alphabet in stating his syllogistic forms, and only after stating them formally does he give examples of terms that can be substituted for the variables. For example, he discusses syllogistic forms of the first figure using the letters *A*, *B*, and *C*, and then often lists terms that can be taken as values for these variables, terms such as "horse," "man," and "animal."

Prior Analytics does not include any specific formation rules because Aristotle presupposed that he and his readers were able to recognize well-formed expressions and to rule out inappropriate expressions. He did not recognize the theoretical importance of such rules. Nor did he include explicitly stated inference rules for passing from axioms to theorems. However, a great number of proofs appear in the course of the treatise, and the proof techniques that are appropriate for deriving the theorems from the axioms are given names. Thus Aristotle illustrated the rules of proof, even though he did not lay them down as a modern logician would. The axioms are the valid moods of figure one, and the theorems are the valid moods of the other figures. The proof techniques are the techniques of "reduction," and Aristotle makes it clear that all valid moods in the second and third figures can be derived from figure one either by "conversion" (later called "direct reduction" by logicians) or by *reductio per impossible* (later called "indirect reduction" by logicians).

The axiomatic character of *Prior Analytics* is what is most often overlooked by contemporary logicians and scholars. Aristotle is usually credited with the well-known syllogism:

> All men are mortal
> Socrates is a man
> ∴ Socrates is mortal

The form known as *Barbara*—figure one, mood *AAA*—is also usually attributed to Aristotle. However, neither of these is to be found in Aristotle. He did write about something that resembles these traditional forms, but it was quite different theoretically. Compare the traditional form *Barbara* with Aristotle's form:

Barbara	Aristotle's form
All *M* is *P*	If all *B* is *A*, and all *C*
All *S* is *M*	is *B* then all *C* is *A*
∴ All *S* is *P*	

Barbara is an inference rule. It justifies asserting the conclusion on the basis of the two premises.

There are three propositional forms in *Barbara*, together with the special word or symbol "therefore," the sign or mark of an inference. Aristotle's form, however, has only one proposition, and no word "therefore." It is a propositional form, not a rule of inference. Aristotle's form is really an axiom, one of four that correspond to the four valid moods of the first figure in the same way that the two forms above correspond. As axioms, then, in Aristotle's axiomatic syllogistic, there are propositions corresponding to the four valid moods of figure one. As theorems, derived by reduction, there are the valid moods of figures two and three.

There is one additional point that should be made about Aristotle's axioms, however. Contemporary logicians do not try to establish the truth of their axioms; they merely assume them and deduce their consequences. Aristotle tried to justify his axioms by appealing to the *dictum de omni et nullo*; this was his definition of the first figure. Aristotle regarded the *dictum* as self-evidently true, and he said that the first figure, which it defined, was the "perfect" figure.

The *dictum* as the definition of the first figure leads to the last point about the doctrine of *Prior Analytics*. Aristotle, as is commonly known, recognized only the first three figures. He has sometimes been charged with error here, but, as he defined the figures, there are only three. The basis for his division is the width of the middle term. If the middle term is predicated of both the major and the minor, the syllogism is second figure. If the major and the minor are both predicated of the middle, the syllogism is third figure. If the middle is predicated of one extreme, while the other extreme is predicated of the middle term, the syllogism is first figure. These exhaust the possibilities, of course, and the last definition includes both the traditional first and fourth figures. In fact, Aristotle did recognize and list the valid moods of the fourth figure, even though he (somewhat uncomfortably) treated them as strange first figure moods.

In *Posterior Analytics*, Aristotle's account of scientific method, the philosopher stresses two features of scientific knowledge: its factual character and its necessary character. To know something, for Aristotle, meant knowing that an event occurred, and it meant knowing the cause of the event; this is the factual character. In addition, scientific propositions "cannot" be false; they are not merely contingently true; this is the necessary character of such knowledge. For Aristotle, then, science consists of a series of propositions that are logically systematic, have factual reference, and are necessarily true.

What gives the collection of propositions logical order is, of course, the syllogism. Scientific propositions are syllogistically demonstrated conclusions from true premises. However, the premises must also have been demonstrated; otherwise the conclusion is merely consistent, not necessarily true. However, it is obvious that not all premises can be syllogistically demonstrated. Ultimately the regress of demonstrations must come to an end. At this point, one has reached premises that must be justified in another manner. Aristotle offers a justification for such first premises, and this justification is the most fascinating part of *Posterior Analytics*.

Aristotle lists six characteristics of ultimate premises. Ultimate premises

1. must be *true* propositions about things that exist (matters of fact)
2. they must be *primary*, by which Aristotle means logically indemonstrable
3. they must be *immediate;* that is, they must be self-evident
4. they must be *better known* than the conclusions that follow from them
5. they must be *prior* to the conclusions in a logical sense
6. they must state the *causes* of the events referred to by the conclusions

Aristotle mentions two methods of establishing such ultimate premises, induction and intuition. The induction he is speaking about in *Posterior Analytics*, however, is perfect induction, and so the question ultimately turns on the account of intuition.

At the very end of *Posterior Analytics*, Aristotle describes intuition as a process involving the following steps:

1. sense perception
2. retention of the sense percept in the soul following the removal of the external stimulus
3. memory
4. experience as the product of repeated memories

5. abstraction of the universal—"the one in the many"—from experience

Here it is revealed, however, that the justification of first premises has led to the problem of the role played by the active intellect, a matter that is more fully—though not completely satisfactorily—dealt with in Aristotle's psychology, his treatise *De anima* (second Athenian period, 335-323 B.C.E.; *On the Soul*, 1812).

This brief survey should make it clear that Aristotle's claim to the title Father of Logic is a just one. He marked out many of the problems of logic and offered solutions that in many cases retain their fascination and pertinence. Of course, he made mistakes and his system of logic is incomplete by modern standards. However, he closes *Organon* with the comment that there was nothing written on the subject before him. He then asks to be excused for his mistakes but thanked for the light he has shed on the matter. Surely Western civilization is deeply in debt to Aristotle for his contributions to logic.

Robert E. Larsen

Physics

Type of philosophy: Metaphysics, philosophy of science

First transcribed: Physica, second Athenian period, 335-323 B.C.E. (English translation, 1812)

Principal ideas advanced:

◇ To know a thing involves understanding first principles.

◇ Matter is potentiality, form is actuality; to each form there corresponds a special matter.

◇ There are four types of causes: the material cause (matter); the formal cause (the kind); the final cause (the purpose); and the efficient cause (that which initiates change); in addition, change and spontaneity are kinds of causes.

◇ Nature, defined as a principle of motion and change, is a cause that operates for a purpose.

◇ The infinite is potential, never actual.

◇ Place is the innermost motionless boundary of that which contains; time is the number of motion in respect to before and after.

◇ There are three kinds of change: qualitative, quantitative, and local.
◇ There must be an Unmoved Mover that by eternal rotary motion imparts motion to all things.

In modern times, with the growth of natural science, most of the topics treated by Aristotle in *Physics* would be classified as metaphysics. The collection of treatises bearing that name has come to stand for any speculative question concerning first principles, and in that light the topics of the *Physics* are closer to metaphysics than to modern questions of physics. Aristotle begins by considering the number and character of the first principles of nature, and he goes on to argue against Parmenides' speculative theories. Nevertheless, the topics here considered do concern first principles of the physical world, and the work is still a classic in its grasp of issues fundamental to all physical inquiry.

Book 1 opens by stating that it is first principles that one must come to know. To know a thing means to grasp its first principles and to have carried the analysis out to the simplest elements. One proceeds from things more obvious and knowable to one to those principles more clear and knowable by nature. The first question is whether the first principles involved are one or more than one. As a physicist, Aristotle takes it for granted that the things that exist by nature are, either all or some of them, in motion. Speculative theories to the contrary (the idea of "Being as one and motionless"), he dismisses.

One of the famous questions of the *Physics* now begins to develop: whether there is an actual infinite in the category of quantity. The infinite *qua* infinite, Aristotle firmly believed, is unknowable; it is primarily this epistemological difficulty that plagues Aristotle about the infinite. The principles of physical nature cannot be either one or innumerable. A finite number is sufficient, and an infinite number would be unknowable.

In dealing with coming into being and change, Aristotle uses potentiality and actuality as explanatory concepts. What desires form is matter, and matter is the origin of potentiality and form the symbol of actuality. "Matter" Aristotle defines as the primary substratum of each thing, from which it comes to be without qualification and which persists in the result. "Nature" Aristotle defines as a source or cause of being moved and of being at rest in that to which it belongs primarily. However, no thing has in itself the source of its own production.

In book 2, Aristotle returns to the basic problems of physics. Form is more nearly nature than matter, for a thing is more properly said to be when it has attained fulfillment (fully formed) than when it exists potentially. However, one also speaks of a thing's nature as being manifest in the process of growth by which its nature is attained. Aristotle makes a distinction between physics and mathematics. Physical objects contain surfaces, volumes, lines, and points (the subject matter of mathematics), but the mathematician does not treat them as the limits of a physical body. He separates them, for in thought they are separable from motion. The objects of physics are less separable than those of mathematics. Such things are neither independent of matter nor definable in terms of matter only. Of course, matter is a relative term; to each form there corresponds a special matter.

Causes
Aristotle changes topics again, this time to define the four types of causes:

1. that out of which a thing comes to be, the matter, or *material cause*
2. the form or the archetype, the *formal cause*
3. the end, or purpose, the *final cause*
4. the primary source of change or coming to rest, the *efficient cause*

Aristotle adds chance and spontaneity to these four causes, an addition that is often overlooked because these latter two causes are not amenable to knowledge, and yet any complete account must include them. Chance is unstable and is thus inscrutable.

Nature belongs to the class of causes that act for the sake of something, and therefore it is amenable to intelligence. Those things are natural that, by a continuous movement originated by an internal principle, arrive at some completion. Nature is a cause, a cause that operates for a purpose. Nature is to be defined as a "principle of motion and change." The fulfillment of what exists potentially, insofar as it exists potentially, is motion. It is not absurd that the actualization of one thing should be in another.

Place and Time

In book 3, Aristotle turns to the problem of the existence of an infinite, and he readily admits that many contradictions result whether or not one supposes an infinite to exist. Is there a sensible magnitude that is infinite? This is the physicist's problem. Aristotle begins by assuming that number is a numberable quantity. Having concluded that the sensible infinite cannot exist actually, Aristotle goes on to discuss whether it might have potential existence. The infinite has turned out to be the contrary of what is said to be. The infinite is potential, never actual. Its infinity is not a permanent actuality but consists in a process of coming to be, like time and the number of time.

Place is the concept under consideration in book 4. Now if place is what primarily contains each body, it would be a limit. The place of a thing would be its form. However, the place of a thing is neither a part nor a state of it but is separable from it. Place would not have been thought of if there had not been a special kind of motion; namely, that with respect to place. Aristotle concludes that the innermost motionless boundary of what contains is place. Furthermore, places are coincident with things, for boundaries are coincident with things and also with places.

After place, Aristotle begins his famous consideration of time. Aristotle considers it evident that time is not movement nor is it independent of movement. People perceive movement and time together. Time, he concludes, is just this— the number of motion in respect to before and after. Time, then, is a kind of number. Just as motion is a perpetual succession, so also is time. Time and movement define each other.

It is obvious, then, that things that always are cannot be in time; time by its nature is the cause of decay because change removes what now is. Yet because time is the measure of motion, it is also indirectly the measure of rest. In conclusion one asks: Will time fail? Surely not, if motion always exists. Time has being in the same way that motion does. Every change and everything that moves is in time.

Motion

In book 5, Aristotle begins to move the argument from motion toward the motionless. The goal of motion, he insists, is really immovability. Only change from subject to subject is motion, and there are three kinds of change: qualitative, quantitative, and local. In respect to substance, there is no motion, because substance has no contrary among things that are. Change is not a subject. There must be a substratum underlying all processes of becoming and changing.

Book 7 begins by asserting that everything that exists is in motion and must be moved by something. However, this series cannot go on to infinity. Therefore, the series must come to an end, and there must be a first movement and a first moved. This is Aristotle's argument for the existence of an Unmoved, Prime, or First Mover from the very nature of motion itself. A great deal of the force of the argument derives from the requirements of Aristotelian knowledge. Knowing and understanding imply that the intellect has reached a state of rest and has come to a standstill, and this can be so only if the mind can find a satisfactory explanation for the origin of motion. Nevertheless, time is uncreated and motion is eternal. There must always be time.

It is clear that there never was a time when motion did not exist and that the time will never come when motion will not be present. There must be three things: the moved, the movement, and the instrument of motion. However, the series must stop somewhere. Because the kinds of motion are limited, there will be an end to the series. Consequently, the first thing that is in motion will derive its motion either from something that is at rest or is from itself. However, that which is itself independently a cause is always prior as a cause, and this argues for the source of motion in something itself at rest. That which primarily imparts motion is itself unmoved.

There must necessarily be some such thing, which, while it has the capacity of moving something else, is itself unmoved and exempt from all change—this is the crux of Aristotle's argument. Because motion is eternal, that which first causes movement will also be eternal. It is sufficient, he feels, to assume only one movement, the first of unmoved things; and this will be eternal and the principle of motion to everything else. The first movement must be something that is one and eternal. If the first principle is permanent, the universe must also be permanent because it is continuous with the first principle. However, motion is of two kinds. Some things are moved by an eternal unmoved movement and are therefore always in motion. Other things are moved by an agent itself in motion and changing, and so they, too, change their motion.

Locomotion, Aristotle feels, is the primary motion. Yet it is possible that there should be an infinite motion that is single and continuous. This motion is rotary motion, since rectilinear motion cannot be continuous. There cannot be a continuous rectilinear motion that is eternal. On the other hand, in motion on a circular line are found singleness and continuity. Rotation is the primary locomotion. Every locomotion is either rotary or rectilinear or a compound of the two. Rotary motion can be eternal, and therefore, it is prior as motion.

Aristotle concludes that there always was and always will be motion throughout all time. The first movement of this eternal motion is unmoved, and rotary motion alone can be eternal and is primary. If the series comes to an end, a point is reached at which motion is imparted by something that is unmoved. The only continuous motion, then, is that which is caused by the Unmoved Mover, and such a First or Unmoved Mover cannot have any magnitude, is indivisible, and is without parts.

Aristotle's conclusion to *Physics* is really only an introduction to the repetition and extension of some of the arguments later to appear in the book of edited writings entitled *Metaphysica* (second Athenian period, 335-323 B.C.E.; *Metaphysics*, 1801). Yet in this preliminary book most of the crucial concepts concerning physical nature are given a basic definition. The first principles of physics have been enumerated and defined. All that lies beyond physics is metaphysics.

Frederick Sontag

Poetics

Type of philosophy: Aesthetics, ethics
First transcribed: De poetica, c. 334-323 B.C.E. (English translation, 1705)

Principal ideas advanced:

◇ Poetry is imitation of human life in its universal aspects.
◇ The arts differ according to the medium, manner, and objects of imitation.
◇ Tragedy is the imitation of serious action, achieving through pity and fear a catharsis of those emotions.
◇ The tragic hero is a person better than most who brings about his or her own downfall because of a character flaw.
◇ The three most important moments in a tragedy are the reversal of fortune, the discovery of the critical fact that hastens the denouement, and the suffering—the final submission of the hero.

Poetics was one of Aristotle's briefest works, and only half of it has been preserved. Nevertheless, it contains so many fruitful insights and canons of literary art that it has been turned to constantly by literati and philosophers since Aristotle's time. It has a history of varying interpretations, as well as variant manuscripts. The present review makes use chiefly of the translation and commentary of S. H. Butcher.

Unlike most of Aristotle's work, *Poetics* contains little argument. Rather, it simply analyzes poetic art as it existed in Aristotle's time and as he understood it. The lasting influence of the work attests to the worth of his observations. Modern readers must make adjustments for the narrower scope and achievement of literature of that day and for the specific nature, particularly in metrics, of the Greek language.

Poetics treats tragedy and (very briefly) epic poetry. A second portion on comedy has been lost. All the kinds of poetry, Aristotle finds, are modes of imitation of character, emotion, and action, but they differ in respect to the medium of imitation (which includes rhythm, meter or language, and harmony or tune); the manner of imitation (that is, whether staged as a play, or sung, or narrated); and the objects of imitation. The objects of all artistic imitations are actions, and these always have some degree of moral quality. Hence people must be portrayed as either better than in real life, worse, or the same. The difference between tragedy and comedy, Aristotle affirms, is that tragedy aims at representing people as better than they actually are and comedy as worse.

Tragedy

Aristotle defines tragedy as "an imitation of an action that is serious, complete, and of a certain magnitude; in language embellished with each kind of artistic ornament, the several kinds being found in separate parts of the play; in the form of action, not of narrative; through pity and fear effecting the proper purgation of these emotions." The terms of this definition have undergone much interpretation. Butcher states that action (*praxis*) for Aristotle included the whole life of the mind, as well as mere motion of the body—an inner energy working outward. This is the object imitated by drama and other arts; and under this interpretation, dramatic action is much more than physical action alone. Imitation (*mimesis*) was a term used disparagingly by Plato, and perhaps popularly, to which Aristotle gave a new meaning. Because the object of poetic imitation was human life and human nature, imitation meant an expression of the universal element in human life. Aesthetically, the real and the ideal come together in this way; the ideal is the real freed from limitations of alien influences and chance and enabled to work out its own development from beginning to end. Thus imitation became a creative process that could improve on nature.

Purgation (*katharsis*) is applied, in the definition, to pity and fear, by which the spectator is moved. Reference to *Politica* (second Athenian period, 335-323 B.C.E.; *Politics*, 1598) to *Technē rhetorikēs* (second Athenian period, 335-323 B.C.E.; *Rhetoric*, 1686), and to contemporary medical writings shed more light on this purgation than *Poetics* alone does. Aristotle considered pity and fear to be painful emotions. Pity is what one feels upon observing another in a situation in which he would fear for himself. Just as the playing of frenzied music has the effect of calming those possessed (an actual practice in Aristotle's times), the presentation of events arousing pity and fear would allay these emotions latent in the spectator, and thus bring pleasure. These are the universal elements of human nature that it is proper for tragedy in particular to imitate.

Tragedy requires six parts: rhythm, song, metrical wording—these three are the kinds of orna-

ment that embellish the language—spectacle (the staging of the play), character of those portrayed, and their thought. What the completeness of tragedy requires, however, is that the piece have a beginning, a middle, and an end. A beginning is that which does not necessarily follow anything but is naturally followed by something else. An end is what must follow another thing but need not be followed by anything. A middle both follows and must be followed by something else. As to magnitude, the imitation should not be so long as to give difficulty in remembering or comprehending the action; but within this limitation, the longer it may be, the finer a creative production. Further, it must be long enough to allow naturally a change from good to bad fortune, or bad to good. The action must be both single and complete, such that to add or subtract an element of plot would disorganize or disrupt, rather than enhance, the action. In these descriptions, Aristotle recognized the dramatic principle of unity of action, which, along with the unities of time and place that he suggested, were zealously observed in neoclassical times.

Plot, Aristotle says, is the very soul of tragedy. Being the arrangement of the incidents, it is what portrays the action. "For Tragedy is an imitation, not of men, but of an action and of life, and life consists in action, and its end is a mode of action, not a quality." Character determines people's qualities, and these together with their thought determine their actions. Dramatic action, therefore, does not aim at the representation of character; character is subsidiary to the action.

Aristotle approves the origin of the plots of most Greek tragedies in Greek myth. In telling the nature of tragedy, he states that a poet is unlike a historian, not writing about what has happened but rather about what may happen. Thus he acknowledges the transformation of events by the poetic imagination. Plato had barred poets, whom he considered immoral falsifiers, from the ideal republic until they could write poetry convincingly arguing for their own reinstatement. In other words, poetry should be didactic or argumentative and have a moral purpose. Aristotle in *Poetics* attempts to rehabilitate poetry from this low estimate. He shows here a function of poetry that Plato had entirely overlooked, for if poetry imitates what ought to happen rather than what has happened, it imitates the universal rather than the particular. Hence poetry, Aristotle concludes, is a more philosophical and a higher thing than history.

Aristotle recognizes three parts of the plot of tragedy, calling plots complex when so divided and simple if there were no divisions. One part is reversal of the situation, or *peripeteia*, such as when an act of the hero produces the opposite from the intended effect. Another is recognition or discovery, *anagnorisis*, in which a character acquires knowledge of a fact, producing love or hate toward another character. These two, when simultaneous, are most effective in arousing pity or fear. The third part of the complex plot is the final suffering. It does not turn upon a surprise as do the others, but like them will be most effective as a probable or natural outcome of other events.

What of the person chiefly concerned in these actions? The tragedy must not bring a perfectly virtuous person from prosperity to adversity, nor raise a bad person from adversity to prosperity, nor yet depict a villain receiving his or her deserts, for none of these would both satisfy the moral sense and inspire pity and fear. The remaining possibility is of a person not eminently good and just but unmarked by vice or depravity, who is brought to adversity by some error or fault (*hamartia*). Here Aristotle seems perhaps to contradict the earlier statement that tragedy shows people better than in real life, for such would seem to be "eminently good" people. Part of the difficulty lies in the translation of *hamartia*, which has variously been rendered "tragic flaw," conveying the idea of a radical character trait such as excessive pride, or "error in judgment," conveying simply a mistaken interpretation of some event. At any rate, Aristotle seems to intend a hero who falls short of perfection yet is better than people usually are, and whose virtue and shortcomings both are related to the events of the drama in which the character is set.

Therefore, the best tragedy will have a complex rather than simple plot, and because it concerns the sort of character described above, it will show a change from prosperity to adversity. The fear and pity that come from the structure of the tragedy, such as when a hero intends or performs harm to a person without knowing him to be his father or his son, is superior to the fear and pity

arising from the spectacle alone, as when one sees the violent act performed.

Four requirements are laid upon character. First, it must be good. Any speech or action that shows moral purpose will express character, and if the purpose is good, will express good character. Second is propriety; any trait must be appropriate to the person in whom depicted. Third, the character must be true to life. Last, it must be consistent; or if inconsistent, at least consistently inconsistent. The construction of both plot and character should aim at the necessary, the probable, and the rational. If deviations occur, they must be outside the scope of the tragedy. Both the complication and the unraveling of the plot must arise out of causes within the plot itself, and a *deus ex machina* should be used only for events antecedent or subsequent to those of the plot. Although the depiction of character should be true to life, it should be yet more beautiful, like a portrait.

The two stages of the plot are the complication and the unraveling or denouement. The complication contains everything up to the turning point to good or bad fortune. The unraveling extends from the beginning point of the change to the end of the play. The dramatist should master both. With respect to existing tragedies, there are four types:

1. the complex, depending entirely on reversal of the situation and recognition
2. the pathetic, in which the motive is passion
3. the ethical, where the motives are moral
4. the simple

If possible, poets should attempt to combine all elements, to produce the best type, the complex. They should not attempt to take an epic structure, which has a multiplicity of plots, and make it into a tragedy. Even the chorus should be regarded as one of the actors, and the choral songs should share in the action rather than serve as mere interludes.

As to thought, little needs to be added to what has been said in *Rhetoric*. Thought makes up every effect produced by speech and has as subdivisions (1) proof and refutation; (2) the excitation of the feelings such as pity, anger, fear; and (3) the suggestion of degree of importance (amplification). Just as incidents should speak for themselves without verbal exposition, the speeches should effectively produce the speaker's desired effect on their own strength.

Poetic Diction

Turning to the diction of poetry, Aristotle classifies words as either current, strange, metaphorical, ornamental, newly coined, lengthened, contracted, or altered. The latter five are used by poets for their immediate purposes of expression or meter. A word is strange if used in another country, current if in general use in one's own. Metaphor is the transference of a name from one thing to another by certain relationships that Aristotle carefully describes. It may transfer a name from a genus to a species, from species to genus, from species to species, or by analogy or proportion. In metaphor by analogy or proportion, the second term is to the first as the fourth term is to the third; for example, old age is to life as evening is to day, so one may speak of "the evening of life." Sometimes one of the terms is lacking, with no word existing to fill its place, but such a metaphor may still provide expression. A poet says "sowing the god-created light" where some unnamed process is to light as sowing is to seed. A command of metaphor is the greatest mark of a good writer, yet it cannot be taught by another and is a mark of genius. Other embellishments may be employed to secure good effect by causing style to depart from the normal idiom—only, of course, in due proportion and with propriety. The use of these devices of language can achieve greater clarity of style. The perfection of style is to be clear without being mean.

The Epic

The epic, Aristotle declares, in many ways is like tragedy. It should be constructed on dramatic principles. It too should resemble a living organism in its unity, having as its object a single action with a beginning, a middle, and an end. Epics, like tragedies, can be divided into four kinds: the simple, complex, ethical, and pathetic. Epics have the same parts excepting song and spectacle—that is, rhythm, poetic language, character, and thought.

The epic differs from tragedy in scale and meter. It has a special capacity for enlarging the dimensions of tragedy, for narrators can transcend the limits of the stage. Epics can achieve greater diversity of materials and can narrate simultaneous events, thus adding mass and dignity. As to meter, nature has revealed the proper one, the heroic or iambic hexameter that is the gravest and weightiest; for experience has shown others more suitable to other compositions and leaves only this still in use.

Poets should obtrude into the narrative as little as possible; many have failed, not realizing that it is not in this respect that they imitate. Homer excels in this, as he does also with respect to magnitude and unity. Again, Homer has shown the way in telling false things skillfully. He recounts one event such as would be caused by another, the earlier actually being false or impossible; and thus makes the reader fallaciously infer that the impossible event did occur. The diction should be elaborated in the pauses of incident, not in the action, so as not to obscure character and thought.

In a chapter near the end of *Poetics*, Aristotle lists certain criticisms such as might be applied to a poet's work and offers replies that the poet might make. Some dozen criticisms are gathered around five general objections: that the works are either impossible, irrational, morally harmful, contradictory, or contrary to artistic correctness. To provide a basis to combat such charges, Aristotle draws attention ti the following statements.

The poet, as an imitator, can imitate one of only three objects—things as they were or are, things as they are said or thought to be, or things as they ought to be. The vehicle of expression is language. The standard of correctness must be acknowledged to be not the same in poetry and politics, just as it is not the same with poetry and any other art. The faults of poetry may be either essential or accidental. If a poet poorly imitates, through want of capacity, the error is essential. However, if the error is of imputing a wrong gait to a horse or a wrong treatment to a physician, this error is not essential to the poetry but accidental.

When something is challenged as impossible, it must be justified by reference to artistic requirements (a probably rendered impossibility being preferred to an improbable possibility), or to a higher reality (the ideal sometimes serving the artist better than the actual), or to received opinion (popular report sometimes receiving greater acceptance than the actuality). The irrational and the depraved are justly censured when introduced with no artistic necessity. Seeming contradictions should be examined, as in dialectic, by asking whether the same thing is meant in both cases, in the same relation, and in the same sense. Again, if a description is called factually untrue, poets may reply that they have described things not as they are but as they ought to be; or as people say them to be, such as the tales about the gods.

Further, if the morality of a particular act or saying is challenged, one must point out that one cannot look to that alone but must consider by whom it is done or said, and to whom, when, how, and why. Aristotle here hints, but fails to say directly, that the aesthetic question of whether an immoral act should be depicted is different from the "political" question of whether that act is moral.

Various objections are met by a due regard for language, as when the critic has missed metaphorical intent, an ambiguity, or some legitimate sense of the word used, such as its usage among a foreign people.

In his last chapter, Aristotle attacks the existing opinion that the epic is a higher form of art than the tragic. His opponents have said that the more refined is the higher, and that whatever is received as best by the better sort of audience is the most refined. The art that imitates anything and everything is most unrefined, since boorish audiences are pleased only when something of their own is thrown in, and tragedy provides gesture and spectacle to appease such an audience. The epic, not needing these, must be the higher of the two.

Aristotle meets this argument first by diverting its force. The censure attaches not to the poetic but to the histrionic art—and the deliverer of an epic may be just as guilty of excessive gesture as an actor. Further, not all gesture and spectacle, but only bad acting, should be condemned. Again, tragedy can secure its effect without being staged, by the mere reading, so that if this fault were present, it would not be an inherent but an accidental one. Furthermore, tragedy is superior, having not only all the elements of epic but also the accessories of song and spectacle, which produce the most vivid of pleasures; and it attains its end within narrower limits than does epic, a concentrated effect being more pleasurable than one more diluted. Finally, the tragedy is superior in unity, any epic being capable of providing the material for several tragedies. Tragedy, then, fulfills its proper function better and is a higher art than epic poetry.

John T. Goldthwait

Politics

Type of philosophy: Ethics, political philosophy
First transcribed: Politica, second Athenian period, 335-323 B.C.E. (English translation, 1598)
Principal ideas advanced:

◇ The morally virtuous person performs acts according to a rational mean between extremes of excess and deficiency; so also does the state.

◇ The good states are monarchies, aristocracies, and polities (constitutional governments); the corresponding bad states are tyrannies, oligarchies, and radical democracies.

◇ Polities that lean toward the democratic form of government possess the greatest political stability and are least liable to revolutions.

◇ The art of government involves the use of practical wisdom.

◇ Because the best life is one that combines action with contemplation, the ideal state aims at providing sufficient external goods to permit the pursuit of virtue and happiness.

Aristotle's *Politics* combines description with judgments about the ideal political community. Its eight separate books make up a work that, most scholars insist, was never intended to be one finished product. There is debate about the ordering of the existing books. However, in spite of the work's variety, several dominant themes and interests prevail throughout. One theme is the characteristic Aristotelian stress on the purposive quality of political life—the view that a state, like any other entity in nature, has a nature understandable in terms of a purpose. Consequently, one cannot properly determine the nature of citizenship unless one first knows what, in general and particular, the state is established to accomplish. Another, yet related, theme concerns the way in which political life is viewed as an important, organized means to the ethical development of its members. Though the state is logically prior to the individual, according to Aristotle, its purpose centers in the production of the maximum human good. The *Politics* presupposes the ethical teachings found in Aristotle's famous work on ethical life. The primary question for Aristotle is not whether people will act politically—because it is their natures so to act—but rather whether they will act well.

Aristotle's insistence on the natural basis of human political activity accounts for his central concern with the proper education of the state's citizens. Learning is induced by nature, habit, and reason. Education can influence habit and reason by modifying natural capacities, directing them to selected ends or kinds of action. Aristotle's conception of the way in which human ethical capacities develop affects what he says about human political roles. Two broad classes of ethical facts exist—one of them moral, the other intellectual. These classes are interdependent. The moral virtues are learned. They result from habitual kinds of conduct. The morally virtuous person performs acts according to a rational mean between extremes of excess and deficiency that require prudential judgments in specific contexts demanding action. The chief aim of the moral virtues is action rather than contemplation, doing rather than theorizing. Political activity expresses the range of virtuous actions insofar as human beings must live in associations and devote attention to the family and to the public affairs of a commonwealth.

Citizenship and the State

The matter of what makes good citizenship possible is a complicated one. Good citizenship must occur in relation to some actually existing state, of which there may be different kinds. Thus, there can be "good" citizens of "bad" states. Good citizenship need not coincide with human goodness. A good citizen of a bad state will acquire a character that produces acts foreign to the character of the morally good person. Although Aristotle preferred a state that encouraged moral activity on the part of its members, he showed sufficient realism to recognize the possibility of a

wide range of states and to admit that citizenship exists as a function of the end sought after by any actually existing state. Aware of the conditions needed to produce an ideal state, Aristotle nevertheless wanted also to describe and to classify existing and possible types of political units.

Aristotle's sense of the variety of political possibilities becomes clear in his criticisms of Plato's utopian scheme sketched so brilliantly in the latter's *Politeia* (middle period dialogue, 388-368 B.C.E.; *Republic*, 1701). Aristotle disagrees with Plato's abolition of private property and his advocacy of social communism of wives and children. Aristotle insists that Plato's recommendations are wrong in terms of both their end and their means. There can be too great a unity in any existing state. Plato's political thought wrongfully sought after an impossible kind of unity in suggesting abolition of property and the private family. Such recommendations could never lead, as means, to the minimal unity any state requires. They would increase the chances of dissension in the state. Aristotle argues that differentiation of functions is a law of nature—that things actually differ. Political philosophers must accept this fact and not seek to alter the unalterable.

In *Nomoi* (last period dialogue, 360-347 B.C.E.; *Laws*, 1804), written later than the *Republic*, Plato softened some earlier political suggestions by abandoning his theory of social communism. Aristotle also criticizes the *Laws* on several grounds: It fails to discuss foreign relations; it makes new states too large in territory; and it fails to limit property, population, or the respective roles of ruler and subject. Just as Aristotle insists that philosophers must never seek greater certainty in ethics than the subject-matter permits, so he argues that the political philosopher must recognize that judgments must conform to an inevitable relativity in types of political systems. "Since there are many forms of government," Aristotle asserts in book 3 of *Politics*, "there must be many varieties of citizens, and especially of citizens who are subjects." Nevertheless, he agrees with Plato that the best states—however specialized the functions of their citizens—seek the common interests of all.

When Aristotle describes existing states of his own day and age, he mentions the three that he considers best: Sparta, Crete, and Carthage. During his lifetime, Aristotle also directed a study of the various constitutions, showing his interest in the empirical details of political life. Yet his empirically minded studies never paralyzed his independent judgments about the values of what he studied. Thus, Aristotle pointed out that Sparta was fit only for conducting war; the Cretan state was too narrowly a rule of the rich (oligarchy) whose cities remained safe only because of their accidental geographical inaccessibility; and the Carthaginian state relied on a policy of emigration to keep down domestic insurrection. The best existing states fail to measure up to what is possible. Aristotle realized that a description of what exists politically need not suffice either as a basis for classifying possible type of states or as a means of making clear the nature of an ideal state. In various portions of his *Politics*, he devotes attention to such matters.

The Types of States

Like Plato, Aristotle claims that there are three broad types of states, each possessing a corresponding possible perversion. The so-called "good" types are monarchy, aristocracy, and polity. The corresponding perversions (or so-called "bad" types) of these are tyranny, oligarchy, and radical democracy. By "radical democracy," Aristotle means a state that permits an absolutely unrestricted suffrage and the right of all, without qualification, to hold office.

This classificatory scheme hides a great complexity, especially of degree, because Aristotle thinks both monarchy and aristocracy allow for at least five possible forms. The classification also contains puzzles. One is that though oligarchy is listed as a possible perversion of aristocracy, Aristotle indicates that the best state (practically, though not ideally) is a polity. A polity is defined as a state that mixes rule by the rich with rule by the poor. Ideally, then, a polity requires existence of a significantly entrenched middle class, whose interests moderate the extremes and receive furtherance through the state's machinery. A polity therefore requires a constitution that expresses elements of oligarchical interests.

To achieve a balance between oligarchy and democracy is difficult because each type of state emphasizes a different end. Oligarchy rests on the assumption that people's political rights ought not to be equal but rather based proportionately on their possession of wealth. Democracy stresses human equality—that each shall count as one in political affairs. Neither is absolutely correct. Virtue stands as the sole general aim of statecraft, meaning that any form of political organization that produces virtuous conduct is politically justifiable. Aristotle understood that polity results from a compromise. It involves a mixed constitution. Polities may come into being in several different ways, but their constitutions must find a mean that mingles some property qualifications with offices open to lot or election. Aristotle's comments about the value of a polity result, in part, from his unwillingness to consider absolute kingship the best political unit. Admitting that an absolute king who rules according to the spirit of law produces an excellent model for governing, Aristotle suggests that the rule of law receives less abuse if reserved for many citizens. He objects to monarchy because, in his estimation, it evolved as a response to the problems of a primitive social order. Monarchy often becomes simply hereditary. Its additional weaknesses are that it is subject to the passions of a single man and that no king can adequately handle all the affairs of ruling.

Revolution

The need of continuity and stability in a state receives ample recognition in Aristotle's *Politics*. Yet all political systems are subject to revolutions. Existing forms of government share two general aims, "an acknowledgment of justice and proportionate equality." People fail to translate these aims of government into adequate practice, producing conditions from which revolutions spring. In one example, Aristotle shows how the democrats' emphasis on equality leads them to think that people are equal in all things, while the oligarches' insistence on human inequality spurs them to claim too much for themselves. In any state in which both equalities and inequalities fail to receive proper balancing, hardened parties tend to arise that encourage revolution on behalf of a more thorough realization of their own partial interests. The citizens possessing the highest right to rebel—people who stand out for their virtuous conduct—are those who, by their nature, seem least willing to take part in rebellions.

A student of revolutions needs to understand, first, the general feeling or attitude of those who rebel; second, the specific motivation of any rebellion (its objects); and third, the immediate factors that cause the rebellion. In all revolutions, a general cause exists in the desire for equality. This leads inferiors to revolt in hopes of attaining equality. It also causes people who are genuinely capable to rebel to achieve superiority over those who are in fact not their equals. The motivation for rebellion centers around "the desire of gain and honour, or the fear of dishonour and loss; the authors of them want to divert punishment or dishonour from themselves or their friends." Other causes play important roles. These causes of revolution include contempt, fear, insolence, a disproportionate increase in some aspect of the state, and excessive superiority. Other kinds of causes of rebellion include intrigues at elections, unjust differences in the elements in the state, lack of care, and neglect of trivial issues over a period of time.

What causes an actual revolution depends often on the type of constitution involved. For example, Aristotle claims that democracies usually enter revolutionary times because of the demagogic intemperance of the leaders. Oligarchic states must guard against revolution-producing causes of two kinds—severe oppression of the people and personal political rivalries between important oligarches in the state. Revolutions occur in aristocratic states when too few qualify for honors and in constitutional states when the constitution itself permits lack of justice. Aristotle insists that mixed constitutions that lean toward the democratic possess, in general, the greatest stability.

Public Officers

The analysis of the causes of revolutions leads Aristotle to consider how constitutions may be preserved. Obedience to the spirit of existing law requires planned defense in any moderately stable state. Such obedience extends even to small matters. Like Plato, Aristotle shows suspicion of alteration when he writes that "men should guard against the beginning of change." This remark shows that despite his awareness of variety, Aristotle adopted a conservative political stance. In democracies, offices should rotate frequently; and a number of institutions are required in cases

where the governing class is numerous. Aristotle advocates a fairly wide personal participation in government. He wrote for a small Greek city-state, limited in territory and numbers. For this reason, many of his observations about participation in governing seem irrelevant or foreign to modern states whose extensive territories require an underpinning of bureaucratic machinery. Aristotle makes clear, however, that magistrates and others who perform public offices should never make money. Public service should exist as a self-justifying activity of the virtuous citizen.

The moral tone of much of Aristotle's treatment of politics is apparent in his recommendations about the qualifications of those who wish to hold office in the state. In each existing state, office holders must show loyalty to the contents of the constitution. They must also possess administrative abilities of a high order and express the kind of virtue that their particular state requires. In the case of democratic governments, Aristotle never makes clear how office holding by lot or election can guarantee that able administrators will rule. He does insist that only those who are citizens can qualify for office, and he excludes from the citizen body slaves and mechanics. Aristotle shares the cultural prejudices of his own age when he confines the virtues of the governing class (the citizen body) to the well-born and the aristocratic.

A reliance on common sense runs throughout the *Politics*. Aristotle realizes that, once the purposes of governing are understood in principle, any state requires the practical wisdom of sound leadership. Individuals must apply their knowledge of principles to specific situations. At this point, the art of governing passes beyond the sphere of scientific prediction and control. Indeed, Aristotle makes clear that each and every form of state is subject to change and possible revolution, including the most tyrannically controlled states. He also indicates an unusual sensitivity to the ways in which any political form—say, democracy—must adapt itself to the special geographical and cultural circumstances with which it must in practice operate.

Forming an Ideal State

In the final portion of the *Politics* (books 7 and 8), Aristotle discusses the way in which to form an ideal state as well as the educational practices necessary for its maintenance, once established. The treatment of these issues depends upon Aristotle's conception of human nature. The human soul contains an element that is subservient to a rational principle of control. This is the desiring aspect of human nature that is amenable to command and persuasion. Each person also possesses a unique capacity for rational comprehension. The best life, in Aristotle's view, is that which combines action with contemplation. Happy people will enjoy external goods, goods of the body, and spiritual (intellectual) goods in some appropriate proportion. Goods of the soul exist as that to which the other goods are a necessary and enjoyable means. Individuals and states need sufficient external goods to permit the pursuit of virtue and happiness. Aristotle treats such a view as axiomatic, beyond argument.

To the question of which is the more preferable, the life of a philosopher or that of a statesman, Aristotle's answer is that political activity is not degrading, though political power can never stand as the highest good. Aristotle claims that natural capacities, developed in a proper order, can lead to the realization of the philosopher's ideal of wisdom. An important aspect of Aristotle's attitude toward the functions of political philosophizing is the manner in which he relates its aims to common sense. The political philosopher acts not so much like the scientific theorist, discovering new theories, as like the practical person who rediscovers the applicability of rules evolved in the history of political communities.

When he discusses the formation of an ideal state, Aristotle considers a small state. Its population and territory must be controlled. There must be a sufficient economic base to make the state self-sufficient. Agricultural workers, mechanics (artisans), and men of commerce are excluded from the body of the citizens. Slaves possess no rights at all. Only soldiers, priests, and rulers qualify for the rights of citizenship. These groups alone own land. Each citizen, in addition, should perform the functions of soldiering, act as priest, and rule at different periods in life. A hard distinction should hold between rulers (citizens) and subjects (noncitizens). In addition, in any ideally formed state, attention is given to the city's planning from the standpoints of utility and beauty.

Education functions to perpetuate the state. Potential citizens learn to obey in order later to know how to rule. The legislative body of the state holds responsibility for the education of the citizens. The aim again is the production of the good person. The humanistic aim of well-rounded human development is emphasized. Physical fitness is encouraged to stimulate practical and contemplative efforts. The legislative body exercises a moral watchfulness over the content of the music and tales heard by the potential citizens. Legislators control the age of marriage, determine the physical requirements of parentage, decide when exposure takes place (the Greek practice of putting infants out to die), and oversee the duration of existing marriages. These educational arrangements serve, for Aristotle, as necessary ingredients in the political perpetuation of the state.

The lasting features of Aristotle's *Politics* are its emphasis on the moral justification of a state and the way in which the philosopher accepts the inevitability of a wide range of existing states. Through the work also runs a firm defense of common sense as the touchstone of all political philosophizing. Aristotle attempted to make sense out of politics rather than to impress individuals by proffering complicated theories. There can be no blueprint guiding the statesman's prudential judgments. Aristotle's classical work has inspired people in different times and places when political events have forced them to seek sanity rather than drama in their political thought.

Whitaker T. Deininger, updated by John K. Roth

Additional Reading

Ackrill, J. L. *Essays on Plato and Aristotle*. New York: Oxford University Press, 1997. This work contains important and insightful reflections on two of the most influential thinkers in Western philosophy.

Adler, Mortimer J. *Aristotle for Everybody: Difficult Thought Made Easy*. New York: Scribner's 1997. A reliable interpreter provides an account that introduces Aristotle's thought in accessible fashion.

Bar On, Bat-Ami, ed. *Engendering Origins: Critical Feminist Readings in Plato and Aristotle*. Albany: State University of New York Press, 1994.

Feminist perspectives are brought to bear on Aristotle's philosophy in significant ways.

Barnes, Jonathan. *Aristotle.* New York: Oxford University Press, 1982. A reliable study designed for readers who want an introduction to Aristotle's thought.

_____, ed. *The Cambridge Companion to Aristotle.* New York: Cambridge University Press, 1995. An excellent guide to Aristotle's thought, which features significant essays on major aspects of his work.

Broadie, Sarah. *Ethics with Aristotle.* New York: Oxford University Press, 1991. This carefully done book concentrates on Aristotle's ethical theory and its implications.

Brumbaugh, Robert S. *The Philosophers of Greece.* Albany: State University of New York Press, 1981. An introductory study that discusses Aristotle's philosophy within the larger context of the Greek world.

Cooper, John M. *Reason and Human Good in Aristotle.* Cambridge, Mass.: Harvard University Press, 1975. Cooper's book is a study of the "theoretical backbone" of Aristotle's moral philosophy—his theories of practical reasoning and of human happiness.

Copleston, Frederick. *A History of Philosophy: Greece and Rome.* Garden City, N.Y.: Doubleday, 1962. A leading scholar of Western philosophy discusses Aristotle's life as well as his logic, metaphysics, ethics, politics, and aesthetics.

Edel, Abraham. *Aristotle and His Philosophy.* New Brunswick, N.J.: Transaction Books, 1996. A careful and helpful study by a veteran interpreter of Western thought.

Ferguson, John. *Aristotle.* Boston: Twayne, 1972. Assisting the general reader in the study of Aristotle's works, this book discusses Aristotle's life and his views about nature and psychology and also offers perspectives on Aristotle's lasting influence.

Jones, W. T. *A History of Western Philosophy: The Classical Mind.* New York: Harcourt, Brace & World, 1969. Combines historical interpretation of Aristotle's far-reaching thought with relevant readings from Aristotle's writings.

Kenny, Anthony. *Aristotle on the Perfect Life.* New York: Cambridge University Press, 1980. This work focuses on Aristotle's views about human nature, ethics, and politics.

Lear, Jonathan. *Aristotle and Logical Theory.* New York: Cambridge University Press, 1980. A detailed study of Aristotle's views on logic and their continuing significance for understanding human reasoning.

McLeisch, Kenneth. *Aristotle.* New York: Routledge, 1999. An excellent biographical introduction to the thoughts of the philosopher, clearly presented and requiring no special background. Bibliography.

Mulgan, R. G. *Aristotle's Political Theory: An Introduction for Students of Political Theory.* Oxford: Clarendon Press, 1977. Seeks to bring the major themes and arguments in Aristotle's political theory into sharper focus than they appear in the *Politics* itself.

Randall, John Herman, Jr. *Aristotle.* New York: Columbia University Press, 1960. An older but reliable survey of Aristotle's philosophy.

Robinson, Timothy A. *Aristotle in Outline.* Indianapolis, Ind.: Hackett, 1995. Accessible to beginning students, this clearly written survey covers Aristotle's full range of thought.

Rorty, Amélie Oksenberg, ed. *Essays on Aristotle's 'Ethics.'* Berkeley: University of California Press, 1981. An important collection of essays that concentrates on various facets of Aristotle's influential moral philosophy.

Strathern, Paul. *Aristotle in Ninety Minutes.* Chicago: Ivan Dee, 1996. A brief, easily accessible, introductory overview of Aristotle's philosophy.

George W. Van Devender,
updated by John K. Roth

Saint Augustine

Renowned for his original interpretations of Scripture and extensive writings—in particular, his *Confessions*—Augustine was the greatest Christian theologian of the ancient world.

Principal philosophical works: *Contra academicos*, 386 (*Against the Academics*, 1943); *De beata vita*, 386 (*The Happy Life*, 1937); *De ordine*, 386 (*On Order*, 1942); *Soliloquia*, 386 (*Soliloquies*, 1888); *De immortalitate animae*, 387 (*On the Immortality of the Soul*, 1937); *De musica*, 389 (*On Music*, 1947); *De magistro*, 389 (*On the Teacher*, 1924); *De vera religione*, 391 (*Of True Religion*, 1959); *De sermone Domini in monte*, 394 (*Commentary on the Lord's Sermon on the Mount*, 1875); *De doctrina Christiana*, books 1-3, 396-397, book 4, 426 (*On Christian Doctrine*, 1875); *Confessiones*, 397-400 (*Confessions*, 1620); *Annotationes in Job*, 400; *De Genesi ad litteram*, 401-415; *De civitate Dei*, 413-427 (*The City of God*, 1610); *De Trinitate*, c. 419 (*On the Trinity*, 1873).

Born: November 13, 354; Tagaste, Numidia
Died: August 28, 430; Hippo Regius, Numidia

Early Life

Aurelius Augustinus was born of middle-class parents, Patricius and Monica, in the Roman province of Numidia (now Algeria). His pious mother imbued him with a reverence for Christ, but as he excelled in school, he found the Catholic Church's teachings and practices unsatisfactory. As he studied at nearby Madauros and then Carthage, he was swayed by various philosophies. From 370 to 383, with the exception of one year in Tagaste, he taught rhetoric in Carthage. Part of these early years were wasted (he later regretted) on womanizing, but this experience created in him a lifelong sensitivity to overcoming the desires of the flesh. Upon the birth of an illegitimate son, Adeodatus, in 373, Augustine identified himself with the prophet Mani, who had preached a belief in the spiritual forces of light and darkness that also included Christ as the Redeemer. Hoping to explore the tension in this dualism, Augustine was disappointed by the shallow intellect of the Manichaean bishop Faustus and became disillusioned with that faith.

Desirous of a fresh outlook and a better teaching position, Augustine sailed to Rome in 383 and the next year began teaching rhetoric in Milan. There he was awakened to the potential of Christian theology by the sermons of Saint Ambrose and, in particular, the Neoplatonism of Plotinus. In this philosophy—the beliefs of Plato adapted to Christianity by Plotinus—the individual can know true existence and the one God only by searching within to attain unity with God's love. Only spiritual faith, and not reason or physical appearances, can provide the ultimate answers. At first a skeptic, Augustine began his inner search and in 386 had a mystical experience in which he believed he had discovered God. Resigning his teaching position, Augustine converted completely to Christianity and was baptized by Ambrose at Milan in the spring of 387.

Life's Work

Augustine plunged into the cause of discovering and articulating God's will as a Christian philosopher. He did so with such zeal that a steady stream of treatises flowed from his pen. He returned to Numidia in 389 and established a monastery at Hippo, intending to live there quietly and write. He was ordained as a priest in 391, and he became bishop of Hippo in 396. Therefore, instead of developing his theological ideas systematically, Augustine revealed them in sermons, letters in reply to queries for guidance, tracts against separatists, and books. In addition, he wrote a lengthy autobiography of his early life, *Confessions*.

God, in Augustine's view, is at the center of all events and explanations. Such a theocentric philosophy depends on Holy Scripture; for Augustine, the Psalms, Genesis, and the First Letter of John were especially important. His commentaries on the Psalms and Genesis are famous treatises, along with *On the Trinity* and *The City of God*.

God, as "the author of all existences" and "the illuminator of all truth," is wisdom itself and therefore the highest level of reality. The second level is the human soul, which includes memory,

understanding, and will. By looking to God, one discovers the true knowledge that God has already bestowed upon oneself. All things emanate from that ultimate authority. Through faith, one gains truth; the use of reason is only secondary. The third and lowest level of reality is the human body.

A human's greatest ethical happiness can be realized only by aspiring to God's love. Human beings are endowed with the free choice to do good or evil, but God by divine grace may bestow the greater freedom of enabling a person to escape an attraction to evil. Similarly, revelation frees the mind from skepticism. By grappling with the elusive problem of evil, Augustine managed to bring better focus to an issue of universal concern to all religions.

Also a practical thinker, Augustine was an acute observer of the natural universe. By focusing on God in nature, however, and believing that true knowledge came only through spiritual introspection, he came to regard physical things as least important and science as having little utility. Faith rather than reason provides the ultimate truth. By the same token, Augustine viewed history optimistically; humankind was saved by Christ's sacrifice on the cross, the premier event of the past.

The collapse of Roman hegemony to barbarian invasions, even as Augustine preached his sermons on faith, caused many doubters to blame Christianity for Rome's decline. Augustine refuted this accusation in *The City of God*. He envisioned two cities: the heavenly City of God patterned after the biblical city of Jerusalem, which means "vision of peace," and an earthly city similar to the biblical Babylon and permeated with evil. Whereas perfection is the hallmark of the City of God, Augustine offered important guidelines for the conduct of human cities. Earthly

Saint Augustine, far right, is depicted with Saints Ambrose, Gregory, and Jerome in this line drawing. *(Library of Congress)*

"peace" he defined as harmonious order, a condition whereby a person, a community, or a state operates by the ideals of felicity (good intentions) and virtue (good acts) without suffering under or imposing dominion. No pacifist, Augustine believed that a nation might go to war but only on the authority of God and then to achieve a "peace of the just." "Good men undertake wars," he wrote to Faustus the Manichaean in 398, to oppose evil enemies. "The real evils in war are love of violence, revengeful cruelty, fierce and implacable enmity, wild resistance, and the lust of power."

The greatest challenge to Augustine's teachings centered on the issue of how an individual might escape the evils of the flesh—whether by one's own choice or by the initiative of God through divine grace. Augustine insisted on the latter and regarded the Pelagians as heretics for arguing the former view. As Saint Paul taught, each person is guilty of Original Sin, must admit it, and can accept salvation only from God's grace through the Holy Spirit. Indeed, Augustine concluded early in his episcopate that God decides which elected souls will receive divine grace—a clear belief in the predestination of each individual. The barbarian army of the Vandals was at the gates of Hippo when Augustine died.

Influence

Augustine was a genius of Christian philosophy and has been venerated since his death. That all subsequent Christian thinkers owe him an immense debt is evident from the continuous outpouring of reprints of his vast works and discussions concerning his ideas. He brought focus to the major issues that continue to challenge the Church to the present day, and he motivated key figures to adopt aspects of his thinking outright. In the early Middle Ages, Charlemagne founded the Holy Roman Empire in the mistaken belief that Augustine's *The City of God* had been written as a blueprint for a divine kingdom on earth. Saint Thomas Aquinas accepted Augustine's notions of predestination for the later Middle Ages, as did theologian John Calvin during the Protestant Reformation. The power of Augustine's theology has remained undiminished through the ages.

Clark G. Reynolds

Confessions

Type of philosophy: Metaphysics, philosophical theology
First transcribed: Confessiones, 397-400 (English translation, 1620)
Principal ideas advanced:

◇ How can an eternal God be the cause of anything evil?
◇ God is not the cause of evil, for evil has no genuine existence; evil is the absence of good, the corruption of possibilities, as in the human will.
◇ Only the parts of creation, not the whole, can partake of evil, which is the privation of good.
◇ By faith, the corruption of the human will is cured.
◇ The question as to what God was doing before he created the world is a senseless question, since "before" the Creation would make sense only if God had not created time; God's creative acts are not in time.

Saint Augustine, the greatest theologian of the disintegrating ancient Roman world, came to Christian faith partly "from the outside" after a trying spiritual and intellectual pilgrimage. His *Confessions* recounts episodes from a restless life finally blessed by religious peace and certainty. The work opens and closes with ardent praise for God's goodness and mercy. The details of Augustine's autobiographical passages achieve significance only in the focus of a deeply experienced conversion. After the conversion, Augustine sees everything from a new perspective.

The book is the first and perhaps most universally read of its genre. Examples of this type of literature in the modern world can be found in aspects of the novel and in straightforward autobiographies. Perhaps no other Christian writing of its kind has so influenced despairing persons or suggested so wide a range of psychological insights into the human quest after religious meaning in existence. Augustine writes of guilt and forgiveness from the vantage point of one who, threatened by the apparent worthlessness of life and haunted by a terrifying realization of the nature of human egoism, overcomes anxiety through a self-authenticating faith in Christ. In a world of chaos and impending destruction this faith speaks out joyously and compellingly in the *Confessions*.

Reinterpreting the Past

The psychology of human belief is such that, given any series of experiences, people can reinterpret the significance of earlier items in the light of later ones. Likewise, people can judge the significance of any later experience in terms of an earlier one. People's judgments about what is important in their experiences need not follow a simple chronological ordering. Augustine writes like a man who obviously judges that an item in his experience is not only centrally but also, in some sense, finally crucial. He reports this conversion experience in book 7 of his *Confessions*. The significance of all his experiences is to be decided in relation to his achievement of God's "grace"; however, *that* experience is final, self-authenticating, and in principle beyond any possibility of doubt or reinterpretation. It is also the standard measure of value. Consequently, Augustine's conversion to the Christian faith leads him to reconsider even selected aspects of his earlier life in its light. Among these are his childhood sins, including a youthful theft of some pears; his strong sexual appetites, which drew him to concubines and produced an illegitimate son; his philosophical "errors" prior to the discovery of his Christian "truth"; and his relations with a beloved Christian mother and half-pagan father.

The *Confessions* includes confidential admissions of a man who seems preoccupied with the problem of human guilt, even inordinately so. Augustine's association of Christian faith with sexual abstinence explains the extent of his guilt feelings—though, of course, it does not explain the Christian emphasis on asceticism. So difficult and austere a standard of human conduct, once applied in human practice, may well cause even earlier slight transgressions to appear momentous. Such reasoning may well enable an unsympathetic reader to understand Augustine's otherwise puzzling concern about a childish theft of pears. Given a Christian belief in the basic sinfulness of human acts, even seemingly trivial actions may take on great personal significance—since formerly trivial items making up a great

part of an individual's personal life will be those very ones over which convinced Christians will think they should have control. It is as if, following his conversion, Augustine wants to say that how sinful humankind really is may be learned from an examination of seemingly unimportant acts of his, including those of his childhood.

An Intellectual and Spiritual Quest

Two major currents dominate the predominately autobiographical books of *Confessions* (books 1 through 9). One current is an apologetic account of Augustine's intellectual search after comprehension or wisdom among some of the important "schools" popular in fourth century Roman civilization. The other is a current of continuous intellectual rootlessness—a sense of "being taken in" by a philosophical position that proves only temporarily satisfying. He describes the reasoned effort to understand the meaning of human existence in philosophical terms, which goes side by side with the experienced failure of each tentatively grasped solution. The certainty for which Augustine thirsts is not to be found in philosophy alone. Faith, and only Christian faith, is able to bring certainty, but his intellectual restlessness continues even after conversion. This restlessness receives serious attention in the contents of books 10 through 13. Nonetheless, even the philosophical quest has altered. Where previously faith was to be judged by reason, now reason is to be employed in a context involving faith.

Augustine's intellectual and spiritual quest lasted from his nineteenth until his thirty-third year. At that age, he experienced total conversion to Christianity. He tells how, reading from Cicero, he earlier became interested in religious issues and even turned to the Scriptures without understanding; he "was not such as could enter into it, or stoop my neck to follow its steps." He turned next to the astrologers, hoping in some material mode to discover deity. In the process, he became obsessed by the problem of evil.

He came to Carthage as a teacher of rhetoric and, while "for this space of nine years . . . we lived seduced and seducing, deceived and deceiving in divers lusts," sought intellectual clarification among the Manichees, a group of people who thought a kind of divine knowledge was possible. He became disillusioned by a Manichee spokesperson, who proved unable to put some of Augustine's doubts to rest. From Carthage, Augustine traveled to Rome. He did this against his mother's entreaties. In Rome, he was temporarily attracted to the philosophical Academics, whose chief ability was criticism and whose philosophical tenets tended toward skepticism. Still concerned about evil—which he thought of as a kind of substance—Augustine became a catechumen in the Catholic Church. Moving to Milan, where he was at last joined by his mother, and continuing to live with the concubine who bore him a son, Augustine worried about evil, became attracted to the Platonic philosophers who sensed the ultimate unity of Being, heard Saint Ambrose preach, and after a trying emotional episode was converted to Christianity.

Evil, Time, and Memory

The remainder of the *Confessions* is devoted to discussions of specific religious and philosophical topics. Three problems dominate the later books. One is the problem of evil, which had proved such a stumbling block to Augustine's acceptance of the Christian faith. Two others are time and memory, discussed in books 10 and 11, respectively. Divorced from the autobiographical nature of the earlier books, books 10 through 13 contain some of the most significant of Augustine's intellectual reflections. These books indicate the extensiveness of Augustine's intellectual questioning following his emotional conversion. These books also discuss the biblical notion of the creation of the world as well as the ways in which Scripture may be interpreted.

Because the Christian faith requires beliefs that do not always seem to meet the demands of reason, Augustine's anguished effort to understand the origin and nature of evil proved a persistent one. His first step involved denying the Manichean dualism that made God finite and evil an objective reality. If evil were real, then God as the cause of all created things would have to contain positive evil. Intellectually, a part of Augustine's development here resulted from his reading of Platonist writers. God is to be viewed as eternal rather than as infinite. Therefore, no spatial or temporal being could be God. Yet the problem of evil remained. How can an eternal God as creator of a temporal-spatial order pro-

duce anything evil? The demands of the Christian faith permitted only one solution—the denial that evil is a substance, a genuinely objective existent.

Augustine later confesses: "And I sought 'whence is evil,' and sought in an evil way; and saw not the evil in my very search." There can be no positive evil in the world, according to Augustine's final position on the matter. There is corruption, of course. This includes the corruption of people's will. However, the perversion of the human will is a human responsibility; God cannot be seen as the cause of such perversion. Corruption is rather the absence of good, a privation and a lack rather than a positively existing thing. It is the failure of parts of the system of Creation to harmonize for which God is not causally responsible. It is doubtful that Augustine's "solution" of the problem of evil is a clearly rational one. Rather it seems to follow from the need of faith to discover a satisfactory position that will not involve denial of God's immutability. Whatever has been caused by God to exist must be good. Evil cannot therefore possess a positive existence. It must be treated as an absence of positive goodness. Because God is a creator—though not of a universe *in* time since there could have been no time before the world's existence—his immutability and absolute goodness exclude the possibility that anything could be evil from God's perspective. The parts alone and not the whole of Creation can include evil even as privation. If one's faith demands the denial of genuinely existing evil, clearly, then, whatever corruption may exist results from humankind's will. This corruption is to be cured, for Augustine, by faith in "my inmost Physician." In other writings, he defends his argument that God's foreknowledge of events is not incompatible with human freedom; God's foreknowledge of how people will act is not the cause of such action.

Yet Augustine's mental inquiry continued long after his conversion. The philosopher in him would not completely give way to faith. One example is his discussion of the human memory. Although inconclusive, this discussion raises a number of fascinating questions about the phenomenon of human mental activity. The fact of faith is that Augustine loves his God. However, *what* is it that he loves? He knows this is a unique kind of love, but he desires some clear notion of the nature of its object. He does not love bodily beauty, light, melodies, harmony of time, or the earth when he loves God. What then can he love? The earth answers when asked: "I am not he"; and heaven, moon, sun, and other created bodies reply only: "He made us." Yet Augustine is certain he loves something when he loves God—"a kind of light, melody, fragrance, meat, embracement of my inner man." Eventually, he seeks the answer within his own consciousness. "And behold, in me there present themselves to me soul, and body, one without, the other within." God made his body, which is the corporeal aspect of his manhood. However, his body cannot tell him what he loves when he loves God. It must then be the soul ("mind") by which Augustine can love his God. Mental activity must be the means by which one can know the object of one's love in loving God; yet God must exist "beyond" one's own mind. This concern with mental activity ("soul") leads Augustine into his puzzlement over memory.

The memory enables Augustine to recall images rather at will, including images of the different separate senses such as touch and hearing. He can also recall items from his past personal life. He can combine these images freshly as well as consider future contingent possibilities. "Great is the force of this memory, excessive great, O my God"; so great, Augustine concludes, that it appears bottomless. Though it is by memory that Augustine knows whatever he does, he cannot comprehend the full extent of his self. "Therefore is the mind too strait to contain itself." However, how can one get into one's own mind? Whatever is known mentally as an image came originally through the senses, as Augustine knows well. Yet he now remembers images even in the dark that are not the objects originally sensed. The memory is also an active capacity that knows reasons, laws, and numbers. It is capable of cognition. His memory recalls notions of truth and falsity. It also contains emotions such as desire, joy, fear, and sorrow—which are the four great perturbations of the mind. He knows what he recognizes in naming memory but only by virtue of that which he names. Puzzlingly, Augustine even remembers forgetfulness. Augustine argues that remem-

bering God is much like rummaging in the memory for something temporarily seeming to be lacking and finally saying, "This is it." However, one, remembering, can never say, "This is it," unless it is somehow a remembered thing that has been temporarily forgotten. "What then we have utterly forgotten, though lost, we cannot even seek after."

Seeking God in the memory is, for Augustine, something like seeking happiness, if indeed they are not the same. However, in seeking, people are "looking" for *something*. If the mind is essential to this search, then *what* is sought after must be like something once known but now forgotten. To say that God resides in memory is to assert that God can be known through the agency of mental activity. Yet God cannot reside in a specific part of memory. It is ultimately a mystery. Loving God is like seeking happiness. The soul ("mind") is nonetheless often tempted to seek knowledge of the object of its love through the senses. However, it is obvious that what the eye, ear, nose, tongue, and fingers sense are specific things—bodily things—greatly unlike God. A mind-body dualism is characteristic of Augustine's thought. Though bodily things may be aspects of God's creation, they are not God. Mental phenomena must be the means by which people can know God. Strangely, however, people do not always love God, at least not consciously. God must somehow reside in memory even when people's mental activities are not searching for him. Coming to know God suggests a discovery. Augustine's moving words express this: "Too late loved I Thee, O Thou beauty of ancient days, yet ever new! too late I loved thee!"

The nature of time also puzzles Augustine. This puzzlement arises partly from Augustine's belief that in some sense God created the world from nothing. Yet on the view that time may be infinite, having no beginning or end, a skeptic may ask what God was doing before he created the world. Augustine refuses to commit himself to the notion of a finitely created spatial-temporal world. If time is infinite, then the world is equally so; and both time and the world exist as created by God. God's creative act stands "outside" time. God is therefore eternal rather than infinite. This view probably stems from Plato's influence. As eternal, God contains neither spatial nor temporal parts. God exists in an eternal "present," possessing neither pastness nor futurity.

Augustine attempts to show how this view can prove meaningful through an analysis of the psychology of human time. People speak of things as past, present, and future. Clearly, the past and future are in some sense nonexistent. They do not exist except in relation to some present. The past is finished and done with; the future is not yet here. Time moves only relative to some present measuring unit. What and where is this present for humankind? The present as a unit of measurement can in itself have no parts. Yet no unit of time is in principle removed from the possibility of further subdivision. This suggests that one spatializes time, but even the person who is aware of the movement of time can measure such movement only in the present. This present cannot itself be measured while operating as the necessary norm of measurement. Analogous to this human present, though absolutely unique, is God's eternity, God's present. Augustine "sees" an eternal God as involving a timeless present containing no temporal subdivisions whatever. God contains all possible reality and yet has neither past nor future. This view is related to Augustine's belief that God has complete knowledge of events, including historical ones—as if all events are somehow immediately, nontemporally available to God.

Whitaker T. Deininger

The City of God

Type of philosophy: Metaphysics, philosophical theology, philosophy of history
First transcribed: De civitate Dei, 413-427 (English translation, 1610)
Principal ideas advanced:
◇ The essential nature of humankind is will, and no one wills the true God to be God unless the person is touched by divine grace.
◇ Theology is faith seeking understanding; humankind has faith in order to understand.
◇ History has at its beginning the Creation, at its center, Christ, and, as its consummation, the judgment and transformation.

◇ Because God had foreknowledge, he knew that humankind's will would be misdirected and that evil would thereby come into the world; but he also knew that through his grace, good could be brought from evil.
◇ History is divided by two cities formed by alternative loves: the earthly city by the love of self and the heavenly city by the love of God.

The whole of Christian thought may be seen as variations on the essential positions of two men—Saint Augustine and Saint Thomas Aquinas. This contention is closely related to another—that the history of philosophy is wisely seen as variations on the work of Plato and Aristotle. It is inevitable that when religious thinkers express the content of their faith, they will use the most appropriate words, concepts, and even systems available in their culture. Consequently, Augustine was a Platonist, Thomas was an Aristotelian. Any attempt to gloss over this fundamental difference between these two leading theologians of Christendom is to pervert both.

In the thirteenth century, Thomas was very influential in establishing Aristotelian empiricism, thereby creating a momentous division between philosophy and theology. Thomas held that there were certain areas unique to each discipline, while other matters could be properly understood from either perspective. The Trinity and Incarnation, for example, could be known only through revelation; the nature of the empirical world was properly the jurisdiction of philosophy and was almost perfectly understood by Aristotle. However, God's existence, and to a certain extent his nature, could be known either through revelation or by the processes of natural reason, operating on sense perception. Thus, natural theology was strongly defended as a legitimate discipline and a fitting handmaiden of the Catholic Church.

Plato as Inspiration
Augustine, however, writing eight centuries before, drew his inspiration from Plato, strongly tempered by the theology of Saint Paul. For Plato, "knowledge" through the senses was inferior to intuitive knowledge, which he defined as knowledge of the essential nature of all things without which people perceive only dim shadows in a

darkened cave. Augustine coupled this Platonic distrust of the senses with his preoccupation with the problem of evil and his own personal problems of morality. At first, this concern had driven him to the position of Manicheanism, a philosophy that holds to a metaphysical dualism of good and evil and to the inherent evil of matter. Disillusioned by the naïveté of this philosophy's spokesperson, Augustine turned to Neoplatonism, finding there a suitable explanation of evil in terms of a theistic universe, intuitively understood. "I found there," he said, "all things but one—the Logos made flesh."

The significance of this omission rested in Augustine's common confession with Paul: "I can will what is right, but I cannot do it. For I do not do the good I want, but the evil I do not want is what I do. . . . Wretched man that I am! Who will deliver me from this body of death?" Truth is not a matter simply of knowledge but of action; the problem is not knowing the truth but living the truth. With this awareness came Augustine's baptism of Neoplatonism into the Christian worldview—the result has been called a complete break with all previous understandings of humankind.

"Faith Seeking Understanding"

In opposition to the Greek philosophers, Augustine insisted that to know the truth is not necessarily to do the truth, for the essential nature of humankind is not reason but will. Human beings are so created that they have no option but to love, to orient their being to some object, principle, or person with an ultimate devotion. The supreme object willed by people characterizes their total being and endows them with presuppositions, motivations, rationale, vitality, and goal. There is no person without such a faith, "religion," or "god." One does not reason *to* such an object, but reasons *from* it. No one believes in the true God, the God of moral demand, unless the individual wills it; but no amount of persuasion can change an unwilling will. Since human beings are essentially self-centered, they will always will something other than the true God to be god—human beings will create god in their own image. Only when human beings are touched by divine grace can they will God alone as true center.

Consequently, there must be no severance of theology and philosophy: There can be no reasoning *to* faith, to truth; there can only be reasoning *from* faith. Only from the rightly oriented will, the mind already turned toward the redeeming God, can human beings discover truth. The keystone of Augustinianism is this—"I believe in order to understand," or even better, theology is "faith seeking understanding." The same applies to morality, for every "virtue" that makes no reference to God is a vice. This insistence, essentially discounted by Thomas Aquinas and the philosophers of much of the medieval period, was revived as an essential proclamation of the Protestant Reformation. Through Danish philosopher Søren Kierkegaard, it has become an adapted tenet of existentialism.

From Apology to Theology

This understanding is the foundation for Augustine's magnum opus, *The City of God*. Augustine's writing career was largely consumed in apologetics, in defending orthodox (Nicene) Christianity against its antagonists both within and without the Church. Occasioned by the sack of Rome in 410, *The City of God* arose as an answer to pagan critics who insisted that Christianity was the principal cause of the weakening of the Roman Empire. The reasons documenting this charge ranged from the religious position that avowal of the Christian God had elicited the vengeance of the true pagan gods, to the secular charge that Christian otherworldliness had undermined the internal solidarity of the empire. With a brilliant display of concerned patience, Augustine produced one of the most detailed, comprehensive, and definitive apologies ever written. Augustine not only answered major charges but also dealt with every conceivable attack. He answered the critics in terms of the Christian position and defended his answers in detail from the writings of the honored spokespeople of the empire throughout its history. Augustine's second purpose with this work was to help Christians who had been weakened or perplexed by persecution and by the disastrous events of history.

Yet from this apology emerged what has made this not only a work of historic interest but also a classic. *The City of God* is one of the first attempts at a theology or philosophy of history. Although Greek concepts of history differed somewhat, they were essentially in agreement that history was cyclic, characterized by an endless round of recurring events. In effect, there was no *telos*, no final goal, toward which history moved. Augustine's apology developed the cosmic implications of Christian revelation, defending history as a linear pattern. The Christian God is Triune; that is, God operates in the three eternal modes of creator-sustainer, redeemer, and inspirer. History as the plane of divine activity has as its beginning Creation, as its center point God's redemptive act in Jesus Christ, and continues in the Spirit toward the consummation, the judgment, and transformation of all into a new heaven and a new earth. From the perspective of faith, the pattern of history is visible and the meaning of life perceivable. Augustine's work set the basic view of much of the Middle Ages and of Western culture, and he, perhaps more than any other person, provided the fundamental theology of Christendom.

The situation confronting Augustine was fraught with theological difficulties. He could easily counter petty charges, pointing to the Church as a refuge during the sacking, to Christian teachings as having tempered pagan bloodthirstiness, and to pagan respect for possessions of the Christian God. Equally easy was Augustine's proof of the moral decadence of Rome, a condition with disastrous consequences that had long been warned against by the Roman orators. Although Augustine may have had an apology of this scope in mind at first, the work, once begun, held vast implications. Involved here were the problems of Divine Providence, the justification of evil in a theistic world, the reconciliation of unmerited suffering, and the meaning of a history interrupted by disasters. Nothing short of a cosmology, a total worldview, could do justice to the questions forcing such an apology.

God, Evil, and Free Will

The overarching problem was Providence. If God does not know what evils will occur, is he God? If he does know, is God not then either impotent or evil? Augustine answers the first question in the negative—God must have foreknowledge to be God. The problem exists only if one holds that

infallible foreknowledge implies necessity. For Augustine, God can know all things without undermining free will, for the free wills themselves are included in the order of causes that God foreknows. It is God's knowledge of a thing that gives it not only being but also its specific nature; therefore, it is the very fact of God's knowledge of humankind's free will that makes it free—it is known as free and not as determined. Freedom does not mean uncaused but self-caused, and it is the very self that God knows even more intimately than the self does. Consequently, God's knowledge of a person is that the individual will sin, not that the person will be forced to sin.

In this manner, God's immediate responsibility for evil is met. Yet there is a larger problem, for God still permits people in their freedom to do evil. The Roman Empire provided the framework for Augustine's answer. The empire, at its beginning, was dedicated to truth, justice, and the good of humankind—it was blessed by God. However, love of liberty became love of domination, desire for virtue became intoxication for pleasure, and glory in well-doing became vaunted pride. Herein is portrayed the dilemma of humankind from the beginning. In the beginning, God created all things and continues to create, for all would relapse into nothingness if he were to withdraw his creative power. All that God created is good, yet mutable; having been created from nothing, it is absolutely dependent on God. Everything was graduated according to being, and the opposition of contraries serves to heighten the beauty of the universe. It was with the act of creation that time began, for time means movement and change—none of these applies to God. As a result, God's foreknowledge applies to *all* time, for his eternal envisagement is unchangeable; although God knows what people in their freedom will do, he also knows what he will do to bring from every evil a greater eventual good. It is in knowing all time as present that the evil in each human is redeemed. For Augustine, everything adds to God's cosmic whole; even sinners beautify the world.

Nothing, however, is evil by nature, for all natures are created by God. Evil can be nothing but privation, lack of good. Only the will, not one's nature, is the source of evil. Both the highest of the angels and Adam became inflated by pride in their God-given capacities, craving to become ends in themselves—"ye shall be as gods." Thus evil entered the world, for humankind made what was good into an evil by elevating it as the *supreme* good. Sex, for example, is a good but is made evil when claimed as the center and meaning of life. It is not the thing turned to, but the turning itself, that is evil. Since people are sustained in being by their relation to the supreme good, any substitution of a lesser good brings with it a disruption in which their nature is injured. Although by such action people come to approximate a nonentity, God does not revoke his nature totally, but sustains people enough for them to be aware of their self-inflicted loss.

The result is a creature frustrated in the conflict between nature and will: "O Lord. Thou hast made us for Thyself, and we are restless until we find our rest in Thee." People, in first not wanting to will what they could, will to do what they cannot. This is evil as privation—the impotence of an essentially good nature. Because God alone truly exists, that which is opposed to God is nonbeing; in willing less than fullness of being, people do not create evil but give to nonbeing the existential status of being. Expressed in another way, sin is living the lie of believing oneself to be self-created, self-sustained, and self-dependent. Such confusion establishes the duality, the fall, of creation—death is the most obvious consequence. Evil then has no efficient cause but a deficient one—the will. As humankind is insubordinate to God, the "flesh" becomes insubordinate to the will.

The Two Cities
According to Augustine, evil is misdirected love. Adam's sin so altered the nature of humankind that the human will is incapable of redirecting itself and no longer regarding itself as center. Therefore, for most of humankind, history is simply cyclic. However, God's foreknowledge includes not simply the fall of humankind, but God's election of some people through grace to a redirected love. For these people, history is linear, marked at its center by Jesus Christ, moving toward consummation in eternal life. Therefore, in God's cosmic plan, there are two histories, indicated by two cities. The existence of these cities was permitted by God to show the consequences

of pride and to reveal what good can be brought from evil by Grace.

Augustine states, "A people is an assemblage of reasonable beings bound together by a common agreement as to the objects of their love." History, from beginning to end, is divided by the two "cities" formed by these alternative loves—"the earthly by the love of self, even to the contempt of God; the heavenly by the love of God, even to the contempt of self." Of the first parents, Cain belonged to the city of people and Abel to the city of God. However, since all are condemned by God, those in the latter are there only because of God's undeserved election.

Augustine's descriptions of these cities is all the more interesting because he refuses to overstate his case. In the first place, he refuses, for the most part, to equate the human city with historic Rome or the divine city with the visible Church—the churches are "full of those who shall be separated by the winnowing as in the threshing-floor." These are invisible cities, and their members are interspersed in these institutions, to be separated only at the end of history. In the second place, he refrains from painting the human city with totally black strokes—"the things which this city desires cannot justly be said to be evil, for it is itself, in its own kind, better than all other human good. For it desires earthly peace for the sake of enjoying earthly goods, and it makes war in order to attain to this peace." This city is characterized not by its goods but by its supreme love of them.

With meticulous care, Augustine traces the history of both cities, carefully explaining scriptural history as both literal and allegorical of the abiding presence of the city of God. Augustine sees Christ's coming prophesied and prepared for throughout history, in event, figure, and word. Because not even the Jews held that they alone belonged to God, Augustine maintains that it cannot be denied that other people and nations prophesied concerning Christ, and therefore, many of these may belong to the heavenly city.

After his resurrection, Christ opened the Scriptures to the disciples so that they could understand the eternal foundation of history and God's dual plan. However, the instruments of God's grace to the elect were Christ's death, resurrection, ascension, and the sending of the Holy

Spirit. Through his Incarnation, God became mediator, partaking of humanity so that in its purification by atonement on the cross, humanity could be resurrected with him in glory and so that through faith humankind could participate in his divinity. Faith begins purification not only of the will and thus of one's nature but also of the mind. As Augustine says, impregnated with faith, reason may advance toward the truth. Theology and philosophy belong together because will and reason are inseparable, both in impotence and in restoration.

Throughout history, those of the divine city will know suffering at the hands of the human city, yet, being of the elect, they will not fall again. No evil will be permitted although ultimately evil results; through suffering, God bears witness to himself, and through suffering, the believer is tempered and corrected. Members of the divine city (striving for the ideal balance of contemplation and action) obey the laws of the earthly city and are concerned with the necessities that do not undermine faith. To the end, the true Church goes forward "on pilgrimage amid the persecutions of the world and the consolations of God." Its life is aimed at universal love, and its endurance based on the hope of future happiness. The peace of the city of God is "the perfectly ordered and harmonious enjoyment of God and of one another in God." However, in this life such peace is more the "solace of misery," and righteousness consists more in forgiveness than in the perfecting of virtues. The peace of the unbeliever is earthly pleasure, but in the life to come it will be an eternal misery of the will and passions in conflict. Expressed in terms of sin, history began with humankind's ability to sin or not to sin; it will end for the elect with humankind's higher freedom, the ability not to be able to sin, for in true freedom, sin no longer has delight.

With meticulous detail, often disturbing in its literalness, Augustine outlines the epochs of future history, climaxing with the "new heaven and the new earth." Such an attempt escapes the charge of speculation, Augustine believes, because it has as its point of departure scriptural revelation, interpreted from the perspective of the Christ event. Throughout these reflections, there is a tension that has its roots in Augustine's

own life. On one hand is the rejection of this world in otherworldliness, holding alone to God's unfailing omnipotence and justice, and the eternal duality of heaven and hell. On the other hand, Augustine is world-affirming, straining for a transformational vision of which God's love gives foretaste. Both have their basis expressed in one of Augustine's concluding statements, emerging not only as a statement of faith but also as a yearning hope issuing from his own tempestuous life. Speaking of that which is to be, he says that "then there shall be no more of this world, no more of the surgings and restlessness of human life."

W. Paul Jones

Additional Reading

Ancient Christian Writers: The Works of the Fathers in Translation. Westminster, Md.: Newman Press, 1946. Out of fifty-seven volumes in this collection of early Christian theologians, eight volumes (9, 12, 15, 22, 29, 30, 41, and 42) are devoted to Saint Augustine. Includes background and biographical material. Helps in understanding Augustine's doctrinal views.

Augustine, Saint. *The Essentials of Augustine.* Selected with commentary by Vernon J. Bourke. New York: New American Library, 1964. A topical collection of excerpts from Augustine's major writings.

Brown, Peter. *Augustine of Hippo.* Berkeley: University of California Press, 1967. One of the best biographical accounts of Augustine, this book uses a chronological approach to reveal how Augustine's writings evolved during his lifetime. Heavily annotated.

_____. *Religion and Society in the Age of Augustine.* New York: Harper & Row, 1972. This volume places Saint Augustine in his historical context.

Clark, Mary T. *Augustine.* Washington, D.C.: Georgetown University Press, 1994. A good biographical sketch of the life of Augustine, including his long search for truth that led to his conversion to Christianity. Evaluates many of Augustine's ideas. Gives an excellent summary of the nature and impact of *The City of God.*

Deane, Henry. *The Political and Social Philosophy of Saint Augustine.* New York: Columbia University Press, 1963. A treatment of the theological basis of Augustine's belief about the "fallen man" or the idea of Original Sin and the resulting sinful nature of man. Also covers morality and justice, the state and order, the church, heresy, and Augustine's philosophy of history.

Elshtain, Jean Bethke. *Augustine and the Limits of Political Power*. Notre Dame, Ind.: University of Notre Dame Press, 1995. Written to show the relevancy of Augustine's political theories to modern politics. Author tries to adapt *The City of God* to twentieth century conditions. Although some of the arguments are good, Elshtain's conclusions are not entirely realistic.

Evans, G. R. *Augustine on Evil*. Cambridge, England: Cambridge University Press, 1982. Begins with Augustine's thoughts on the nature of humankind as a young pagan philosopher, then shows the changes in his thinking after his conversion to Christianity. Epilogue covers later philosophers and their interpretations of Augustine's ideas.

Scott, T. Kermit. *Augustine: His Thought in Context*. New York: Paulist Press, 1995. Discusses the philosophies and the ideologies that influenced Augustine's early life, then traces his spiritual search and the results of that search. Interprets Augustine in light of his own time. Good discussion of Augustine's doctrine of predestination.

Smith, Warren Thomas. *Augustine: His Life and Thought*. Atlanta, Ga.: John Knox Press, 1980. A very well-written and readable biographical account of Augustine's early life, home and parents, years of searching, conversion to Christianity, and life as a Christian leader. Puts Augustine's writings in the context of defending the doctrines of the Christian church.

Clark G. Reynolds, updated by Glenn L. Swygart

Sri Aurobindo Ghose

Aurobindo was a political leader who worked for the independence of India from British rule before he devoted himself to spirituality. His writings in praise of traditional Indian culture helped revitalize the culture and protect it form the onslaughts of British culture.

Principal philosophical works: *The Life Divine*, 1914-1919 (serial), 1939-1940 (revised and enlarged book); *Ideas and Progress*, 1915-1916 (serial), 1920 (book); *The Ideal of Human Unity*, 1915-1918 (serial), 1919 (book); *Heraclitus*, 1916-1917 (serial), 1941 (book); *The Human Cycle*, 1916-1918 (serial, as "The Psychology of Social Development"), 1949 (book); *Essays on the Gita*, 1922; *Essays on the Gita: Second Series*, 1928; *The Riddle of This World*, 1933; *The Synthesis of Yoga*, 1948; *The Foundations of Indian Culture*, 1918-1921 (serial), 1953 (book); *The Hour of God*, 1959; *The Essential Writings of Sri Aurobindo*, 1998.

Born: August 15, 1872; Calcutta, India
Died: December 5, 1950; Pondicherry, India

Early Life

Sri Aurobindo Ghose was born in Calcutta, India, on August 15, 1872. His father, Krishna Dhan Ghose, was a respected physician who, after receiving his preliminary degree, went to England for further study. His father returned the year before Aurobindo was born with not only a secondary degree but also a love of England and an atheistic bent. In 1879, Aurobindo was taken with his two elder brothers to be educated in England. Ghose arranged for them to board with the Drewetts, cousins of an English friend. He asked that the boys be given an English education without any contact with Indian or Eastern culture. Mrs. Drewett, a devout Christian, went a step further and did her best to convert them. Aurobindo remained in England for fourteen years, supported at first by his father, then through scholarships.

Aurobindo was first taught by the Drewetts. In 1884, he enrolled in St. Paul's School in London. A prize student, Aurobindo in 1890 went to King's College at the University of Cambridge with a senior classical scholarship. In the same year, he passed the

Sri Aurobindo Ghose. *(Library of Congress)*

open competition for preparation for the Indian Civil Service. He scored record marks in Greek and Latin. Aurobindo was also fluent in French and taught himself enough German and Italian that he could read Johann Wolfgang von Goethe and Dante Alighieri in their native tongues. He also wrote poetry, an avocation that would lead to some published work. Other than poetry, Aurobindo's only extracurricular activities were general reading and membership in the Indian Majlis, an association of Indian students at Cambridge. It was in this association that Aurobindo first expressed his desire for Indian independence.

In 1892, Aurobindo passed the classical tripos examination in the first division. He did not, though, apply for his B.A. degree. He also completed the required studies for the Indian Civil Service but failed to pass the riding exam. It was suggested that his failure was the result of his inability to stay on the horse, but Aurobindo claimed to have failed expressly by not presenting himself at the test. His reason for doing so was his distaste for an administrative career. It happened that a representative of the Maharaja of Baroda was visiting London. He was petitioned by friends of Aurobindo, and Aurobindo was offered an appointment in the Baroda service. He left for India in 1893.

Aurobindo began with secretariat work for the maharaja, moved on to a professorship in English, and culminated his career in the service as vice principal of Baroda College. By the time he had left Baroda, Aurobindo had learned Sanskrit and several modern Indian languages, and he had begun to practice yoga.

Life's Work

At the time of Aurobindo's return to India, the Indian Congress, presided over by moderates, was satisfied with the current state of affairs. At best they would petition the colonial government with suggestions. Dissatisfied with the effect they were having on conditions in India, Aurobindo began political activities in 1902. Prevented from public activity while in the Baroda service, he established contacts during his leaves. His original intent was to establish an armed revolutionary movement that would, if necessary, oust the English. Toward this end, he helped organize

groups of young men who would acquire military training.

In 1905, with the unrest caused by the Bengal Partition, Aurobindo participated openly in the political scene. He took a year's leave without pay and then, at the end of the year, resigned from the Baroda service. In his political work, he met other Indians desiring Indian independence. Most notable among these was Bal Gangadhar Tilak. Eventually, with Tilak and others, Aurobindo formed the Nationalist Party. With Tilak as their leader, they overtook the congress with their demand for *swadeshi*, or India's liberty. Content to remain behind the scenes, Aurobindo concentrated on propaganda. He helped edit the revolutionary paper *Bande Mataram*, which called for a general boycott of English products, an educational system by and for Indians, noncooperation with the English government, and establishment of a parallel Indian government.

Aurobindo eventually moved into the limelight, which resulted in several arrests. Finally, in 1908, he was imprisoned for a year while on trial for sedition. Though acquitted, his and the other leaders' arrests effectively disrupted their movement. Upon his release, Aurobindo found the party organization in disarray. He tried to reorganize but had limited success. In 1910, responding to a spiritual call, Aurobindo retired from political life and went to the French Indian enclave, Pondicherry.

Aurobindo's spiritual life had a gradual growth that was marked by a few specific events. Contrary to the usual method of following a guru, Aurobindo practiced by himself, calling on masters only when he believed that he needed help. He began his practice in 1904. In 1908, feeling stifled, he consulted the guru Vishnu Lele. Following Lele's instructions, after three days of meditation, Aurobindo achieved complete silence of the mind, or Nirvana.

The next event that marked Aurobindo's development occurred when he was incarcerated. He spent most of his time meditating and reading the Bhagavad Gita and the Upanishads. The realization came to him of spiritual planes above the conscious mind and of the divinity in all levels of existence. It was at this time that the seed for the work that would consume the rest of his life took root. It was not until 1910 that Aurobindo was told by an inner voice that he was to go to Pondicherry. In Pondicherry, Aurobindo began his work in earnest. His purpose was to cause the manifestation of the divine, via the supermind, into the lower levels of existence, and thus move humankind toward its ultimate evolutionary goal. Aurobindo did not, though, remove himself from the world. He received visitors, continued his reading, and corresponded with disciples and friends.

In 1914, Aurobindo met Paul and Mira Richard. Paul persuaded Aurobindo to write a monthly periodical to put forth his thinking. This became the *Arya*, which was published until 1921. Some of Aurobindo's major works, including *The Life Divine*, *The Synthesis of Yoga*, and *The Human Cycle*, appeared as serials in this publication and were later published in book form. Mira Richard came to be Aurobindo's main disciple, then his spiritual partner. She left Pondicherry with Paul in 1915 but returned to stay in 1920. When Aurobindo and Mira met, Mira found the spiritual leader to whom she had been introduced psychically as a youth. She came to be known as the "Mother" and eventually took over the management of Aurobindo's household.

With more time to concentrate on his spiritual task, Aurobindo succeeded in penetrating the veil between the upper and lower planes of consciousness. On November 24, 1926, he accomplished the descent of what he termed the "Overmind." All that remained was for him to bring the final plane via the "Supermind" into the physical, and thus divinize, or transform, life on this plane. That India's independence came on his birthday was significant to Aurobindo: He saw it as an affirmation of his efforts.

Aurobindo, with his task not yet complete, died on December 5, 1950, in Pondicherry. His passing, though, was not like that of the average man; witnessed by outside observers, among whom were doctors, his body did not decompose for five days. The Mother announced that Aurobindo had come to her and explained his *mahasamadhi*, or the leaving of his body. Humanity was not ready for the descent of the Supermind because Aurobindo had found too much resistance on this plane. He explained that he would return by manifesting himself in the first person who achieved the Supermind in the physical.

Influence

Aurobindo was a spiritual man driven to serve others. His success in education was largely for the satisfaction of his father. Involvement in politics was his attempt to serve his fellow Indian. He saw that for India to thrive spiritually and physically, Indians would have to throw off the yoke of the English. Aurobindo's retirement was in part the effect of a shift of focus. He saw life in universal rather than national terms. The development of what he saw was needed by India for true change was needed by all humankind.

Aurobindo helped organize a movement that ignited a fire in Indians and that led eventually to their independence. His spiritualism has been the subject of many religious and philosophical writings and a few international symposiums. His ashram, or commune, continued to grow after his death, and in 1968, Auroville was founded.

Shawn Hirabayashi

The Foundations of Indian Culture

Type of philosophy: Epistemology, Indian philosophy, metaphysics
First published: 1918-1921 (serial), 1953 (book)
Principal ideas advanced:

◇ The idea of Indian culture accepted by many in the West is a caricature of what India really represents.

◇ The core of Indian spirituality is the quest to realize the absolute divine consciousness, which is also the essence of the human self, in individual human consciousness.

◇ The final stage of Indian spirituality is still evolving and when realized will transform human life into a "divine superlife."

The essays that comprise *The Foundations of Indian Culture* were first published in Sri Aurobindo Ghose's philosophical journal *Arya*, from December, 1918, to January, 1921. They were later revised before publication in book form.

The immediate stimulus for these essays was a book entitled *India and the Future* (1917) by William Archer, an English writer. Written from the standpoint of Western rationalism, this work was an extremely negative account of Indian life and culture. Archer concluded that the entirety of Indian philosophy, religion, art, and literature was a mass of barbarism. Aurobindo believed that Archer had been deliberately unfair and that he was profoundly ignorant of the beliefs about which he wrote. At a time when India was still under British rule and heavily dominated by Western ideas and values, Archer's denigration of Indian culture expressed an attitude that was all too common, prompting Aurobindo to embark on a wide-ranging defense of his native land and traditions.

The Foundations of Indian Culture is a collection of essays falling into three main parts. The first contains three essays under the title, "The Issue: Is India Civilized?," and the second holds a series of essays entitled, "A Rationalistic Critic on Indian Culture." The third part consists of "A Defence of Indian Culture," which is divided into four sections, "Religion and Spirituality," "Indian Art," "Indian Literature," and "Indian Polity."

Cultural Values
In his first essays, Aurobindo argues that a culture is to be valued to the extent that it encourages a natural harmony of spirit, mind, and body, and a civilization must be judged by how it expresses that harmony in its fundamental ideas and ways of living. A culture may be material, as in Western society, or predominantly spiritual, as in India. This poses the question of whether the future hope of humanity depends on a mechanized, utilitarian society based on reason and science or on a spiritual, intuitive, and religious civilization, in which every aspect of the culture works together to advance the progress of the soul toward a higher spiritual consciousness.

For Aurobindo, the answer is clear. Although he does not dismiss the contributions the West has made to human progress, he argues that it is the spiritual traditions of India that can inspire the rest of the world to grasp the unity of all humankind, based on the knowledge of a universal divine consciousness. This will be a unity in which diversity will flourish, rather than a spurious unity in which one culture simply obliterates all others. To this end, India must live up to the highest ideals of its tradition and defend itself against the infiltration of alien ideas.

A Defense of India
"A Rationalistic Critic on Indian Culture" contains Aurobindo's refutation of many of the claims made by Archer, whom Aurobindo sees as representative of a whole school of Western authors who had denigrated India. Archer's main charges were that Indian culture was riddled with superstitions, irrationality, and immorality; it did not encourage individual responsibility; and it was defeatist in its ability to keep pace with the modern world. Moreover, the prominence given to the theory of karma and reincarnation encouraged a passive otherworldliness, the effect of which was enervating and inimical to the exercise of the individual will.

Against this barrage of criticism, Aurobindo denies at length that India embodies a pessimistic, world-negating philosophy. He points out that India's ancient civilization was founded on the four pillars of human life: the fulfillment of desire and enjoyment of the world (*kama*); material, economic goals and the needs of mind and body (*artha*); ethical conduct (*dharma*); and finally spiritual liberation (*moksha*). The fourth pillar was attainable only after the first three had been reached. At its best, Indian spirituality has a profundity that secular Western culture, which recognizes only what is tangible and can be grasped by the rational mind, cannot match. It represents a "high effort of the human spirit to rise beyond the life of desire and vital satisfaction and arrive at an acme of spiritual calm, greatness, strength, illumination, divine realization, settled peace and bliss."

From this basis, Aurobindo proceeds to his detailed defense of Indian culture. First, he tackles the spirit of Indian religion, which differs profoundly from what he regards as the Western concern with dogma and creed. Indeed, many Westerners have difficulty in accepting that Hinduism is in fact a religion because it has neither a single leader nor a governing ecclesiastical body and seems to be able to admit the validity of all beliefs and spiritual experiences. Aurobindo points out that in India, dogma, or fixed intellectual belief, is the least important aspect of religion; what matters is the religious spirit.

The fundamental idea in Indian religion is the belief in a transcendent, infinite, eternal, or absolute dimension to existence, from which all finite manifestations of life are derived. This absolute eternal consciousness manifests in a multitude of apparently different forms merely for the purpose of its own play. Thus the absolute is the ultimate essence of the human self, and the goal of human life is the realization of this supreme truth, which could also be termed a state of god realization. Although in India, there are many different sects and conflicting philosophies, all accept these truths as the essential basis of religion.

Aurobindo stresses at length the generally tolerant spirit of Indian religion. Although he concedes that there have been outbreaks of fanaticism and persecution, they have not been on the scale of what took place in the West. India recognized the need for variety in spiritual experience and was ready to acknowledge the validity of new spiritual teachers who have enlarged the religious tradition. At its best, Hinduism has found a correct balance between spiritual order and spiritual freedom. Order and stability were supplied by family and communal traditions, the Brahmans (priests and scholars), and the succession of gurus (spiritual teachers) who not only preserved the tradition from generation to generation but also made innovations in it. The Hindu willingness to develop and grow, to build freely on the foundations of tradition, is also apparent in the way its authorized scriptures kept growing in number and in the fact that it allowed wide differences in interpretation of its central texts, such as the Bhagavad Gita and the Vedas, which has prevented their being used as instruments of tyranny rather than enlightenment.

Continuing his contrast of India with the West, Aurobindo argues that Western religions mistakenly believe that a true spirituality can be experienced by the intellect or emotions, or through building systems of ethics or cultivating aesthetic beauty. However, for Indians, genuine spiritual life is a deeper, more inward experience, because the inmost self is beyond the intellect or the emotions, however discriminating or subtle those may be. Anything less than this, in Indian tradition, is considered to be ignorance or at best a merely superficial form of knowledge.

Given this perspective, the ultimate goal of Indian spiritual culture is to uplift all aspects of life, to "divinize human nature." Aurobindo identifies this as the third stage in the evolution of Indian spirituality, and it is not yet complete. The first stage occurred at the dawn of the Vedic era. The Vedas, the most ancient of Indian scriptures, recorded humanity's first intimation of the divine as mediated through the forms of external nature. The Vedas also spoke of a deeper spiritual truth, knowledge of which was reserved for initiates, who understood the function and essence of the gods in their inner as well as their outer meanings. The second, post-Vedic, stage is characterized by the rise of epic literature and of philosophy. The Vedic gods lost their original significance and a new pantheon appeared, centering on the trinity of Brahma, Vishnu, and Shiva. The third stage will fully arrive at some point in the future, when all people, rather than only a few, will "found their whole life on some fully revealed power and grand uplifting truth of the Spirit." Only then will India be able to say that it has fulfilled its spiritual mission to the world.

Art and Literature
In his chapters on Indian art, by which Aurobindo means architecture, sculpture, painting, music, dance, and drama, he answers the charge often made by Westerners that Indian art is not "realistic." Aurobindo points out that much of the inspiration behind Western art is outward life and external nature, whereas the purpose of Indian art is to disclose through symbols some aspect of the infinite divine self.

Of the five chapters that survey three thousand years of Indian literature, Aurobindo devotes the first three chapters to the Vedas, the Upanishads, and the two heroic epic poems, the Mahabharata and the Ramayana. Vedic poetry is distinguished by the constant awareness of the infinity and the ability to translate that into diverse imagery. The Upanishads add an intellectual, philosophical dimension that is not present in the Vedas. Aurobindo points out that the philosophy of the Upanishads can also be found in much of the most influential philosophy of the West, including that of Pythagoras, Plato, the Neoplatonists, the Gnostics, and later German metaphysicists. Indeed, according to Aurobindo, there is hardly a philosophical idea of any substance that does not have its seed or authority in the varied Upanishads.

In his final essays, Aurobindo disputes the common perception that Indian culture, despite the greatness of the spiritual life it provides, has been a failure at the social, economic, and political levels. He argues that ancient India was governed wisely and well; the old system endured for a long time until invasion and conquest by foreigners combined with the decadence of the ancient culture caused it to crumble.

Aurobindo's Impact
In 1914, when Aurobindo first began publishing *Arya*, where the essays that make up *The Foundations of Indian Culture* first appeared, his ambitions were high. He intended the journal to reach a global audience and set out a new paradigm of human knowledge that would incorporate the heights of yogic experience. He also wished the journal to communicate his vision of the future development of humanity.

Aurobindo's initial achievements may have been more modest. The *Arya* had only a limited circulation, mostly confined to India. However, although readership was small, many readers responded to Aurobindo's words. In the aftermath of the destruction caused by World War I and the apparent soullessness of a rapidly growing industrial civilization, thoughtful young Indians saw in Aurobindo's essays a revival of the true spirit of Indian thought, as well as deep insights into the contribution Indian spirituality could make to the modern world. Many journeyed to Aurobindo's ashram in Pondicherry to learn more from him.

When the essays were published in book form in 1953, they reached a much wider audience. India had recently gained its political independence from Britain and no longer had to endure the belittling of its traditions by a foreign culture.

The Foundations of Indian Culture, like the works of Swami Vivekananda and Sarvepalli Radhakrishnan, is an outstanding exposition of the Vedantic tradition to a West that was becoming increasingly aware of the limitations of its own secular culture and was ready, at least in some quarters, to learn from the wisdom of the East.

Bryan Aubrey

Additional Reading
Bolle, Kees W. *The Persistence of Religion*. Leiden, the Netherlands: E. J. Brill, 1965. A study of Tantrism as a vehicle to examine India's religious history, with a chapter on its manifestation in Aurobindo's philosophy. It offers a different perspective of Aurobindo's work.
Bruteau, Beatrice. *Worthy Is the World: The Hindu Philosophy of Sri Aurobindo*. Rutherford, N.J.: Fairleigh Dickinson University Press, 1971. A good introduction to Aurobindo's philosophy. It contains an interesting biography of Aurobindo's spiritual life and a good bibliography.
Cenkner, William. *The Hindu Personality in Education: Tagore, Gandhi, Aurobindo*. Columbia, Mo.: South Asia Books, 1976. Surveys Aurobindo's life and thought, with a focus on his writings on the problem of national education. Includes a glossary, bibliography, and index.
Heehs, Peter. *Sri Aurobindo: A Brief Biography*. New York: Oxford University Press, 1989. A concise account that attempts to give equal attention to all aspects of Aurobindo's life: domestic, scholastic, literary, political, revolutionary, philosophical, and spiritual.
Iyengar, K. R. Srinivasa. *Sri Aurobindo: A Biography and a History*. 4th rev. ed. Pondicherry, India: Sri Aurobindo International Centre of Education, 1985. A voluminous and influential—and frankly reverential—account of Aurobindo's life and writings.
Mathur, O. P., ed. *Sri Aurobindo Critical Considerations*. Bareilly: Prakash Book Depot, 1997. This book provides criticism and interpretation of Aurobindo's work. Includes examination of Aurobindo's poetry.
Mukherjee, Jugal Kishore. *Sri Aurobindo Ashram: Its Role, Responsibility, and Future Destiny, an Insider's Personal View*. Pondicherry: Sri Aurobindo International Centre of Education, 1997.
Pandit, Madhav P. *Sri Aurobindo*. New Delhi: Munshiram Manoharlal Publishers, 1998. A readable account of Aurobindo's life. Includes a bibliography and an index.
Purani, A. B. *The Life of Sri Aurobindo*. 3d ed. Pondicherry, India: Sri Aurobindo Ashram, 1964. Despite its complicated organization and a devoted view, this work is perhaps the most authoritative biography of Aurobindo. It has

excellent documentation of Aurobindo's early life and is filled with quotations from Aurobindo.

Sethna, K. D. *The Vision and Work of Sri Aurobindo*. Pondicherry, India: Sri Aurobindo Ashram, 1968. The first three chapters, in which Sethna debates with a Western philosopher via correspondence, offer a good, clear explication of Aurobindo's philosophy. In later chapters, there is a tendency toward proselytism.

Van Vrekhem, Georges. *Beyond the Human Species: The Life and Work Sri Aurobindo and the Mother*. St. Paul, Minn.: Paragon House, 1998. An informative and interesting biography of Sri Aurobindo.

Shawn Hirabayashi, updated by William Nelles.

J. L. Austin

Austin was a leading spirit of the post-World War II philosophical trend variously called "Oxford philosophy," "ordinary language philosophy," or "analytic philosophy" and the teacher of many leading philosophers and linguists.

Principal philosophical works: "Other Minds," 1946; "Ifs and Cans," 1956; "A Plea for Excuses," 1956; *Philosophical Papers*, 1961; *Sense and Sensibilia*, 1962; *How to Do Things with Words*, 1962.

Born: March 26, 1911; Lancaster, England
Died: February 8, 1960; Oxford, England

Early Life

John Langshaw Austin was the second of five children born to Geofrey Langshaw Austin and his wife, Mary Bowes-Wilson. Austin's father was an architect who after World War I became an administrator at St. Leonard's School in St. Andrews, Scotland. Austin, an intellectual prodigy, excelled in Greek studies while a student at Shrewsbury School and later attended Balliol College of the University of Oxford. In 1931, he won the Gaisford Prize for Greek Prose.

Life's Work

Austin approached philosophy from a background in classical studies and linguistics. In 1933 he won a fellowship to study at All Souls College, and in 1935 he became a fellow and tutor in philosophy at Magdalen College. Austin believed philosophy taught students how to think clearly. Thinking clearly required truthful prose, which could be obtained only by making sure that each word, clause, sentence, and sequence of thought was accurate; prose that was accurate in each of its parts would be accurate as a whole. Austin believed that the process of making prose truthful would immunize students and philosophers against the confusion, myth mongering, and intellectual trickery that arose from shoddy thinking in philosophy.

Austin believed the best way of doing philosophy was in a group. During 1936 and 1937,

Austin became the leading spirit of a small group of young philosophy dons at Oxford University who began meeting weekly to discuss issues of mutual concern and importance. He suggested to group members, who included such notable thinkers as A. J. Ayer, Isaiah Berlin, and Stuart Hampshire, that the discussions be informal. These discussions were the origin of the philosophical trend known as Oxford philosophy.

Before World War II, Austin concentrated on problems in the history of philosophy, especially the work of Aristotle. When war broke out in 1939, Austin had been teaching philosophy for four years and had published only one article. In 1940, he joined the British Intelligence Corps. His first assignment was to analyze the German Order of Battle. The next year, Austin married Jean Coutts. The couple eventually had four children, two boys and two girls.

In 1942, Austin directed a newly formed small section to provide the intelligence needed for an invasion of Europe. In 1943, Austin's section was enlarged, renamed the Theatre Intelligence Section, and transferred to the Twenty-First Army Group. Before the D day invasion, Austin was busy collecting and analyzing military information on the coastal defenses of northern France and on the German military command and control in the area. Austin and his colleagues prepared a guidebook, *Invade Mecum*, for the invading Allied armed forces. Historians credit Austin more than any other single person with being responsible for the life-saving accuracy of the D day intelligence. During this period, Austin helped the Allies solve the problems of identifying the launching sites of the German V-weapons and solve the problem of their intended use. He also helped collect and analyze intelligence for future military operations. Later, Austin interrogated prominent enemy prisoners to gather military intelligence. In September, 1945, Austin left the army as a much-decorated lieutenant colonel. For his work in the planning of the D day invasion, Austin was awarded the Office of the Order of the British Empire, the French Croix de Guerre, and the American Officer of the Legion of Merit. After the war, Austin returned to practicing philosophy at Oxford University and resumed his fellowship at Magdalen.

From the beginning, Austin was determined to reduce whatever he could to plain prose—the language used by ordinary people in ordinary situations, not the language of philosophers. He thought philosophers had overlooked important distinctions embedded in everyday speech and therefore were using ordinary language improperly. This misuse of language made them stagnate and rendered them unable to solve important problems. Austin's method of attack was to seize on a topic and carve it into smaller and smaller pieces. He approached problems by taking a real or imagined situation and asking what should be said about it. He minutely examined which words are and may be used in a situation as well as when certain words are not and cannot be used in order to determine the distinctions among the words. He determined what should be said when and in what situations in order to understand the realities people use the words to represent. For example, Austin described a situation in which each of two people has a donkey in a field. One person wants to shoot his donkey. Instead, he shoots the other person's donkey. Austin explores whether the shooting is a mistake or an accident and why the incident is described that way.

During the influential Saturday morning sessions of the late 1940's and 1950's at Oxford, Austin wrestled with his often-cantankerous colleagues to get them to accept an argument that was right, pertinent, and generally true. Austin's goal was to explode logjams in discussions over the central questions of philosophy. He believed philosophers should work in collaboration, not in competition and alone. He wanted the sessions to be occasions on which philosophy was done, not studied. These informal but intense sessions greatly influenced the participants, and through them, the course of philosophy and linguistics at Oxford and elsewhere in the English-speaking world, including the United States. Participants in the Saturday morning sessions learned to examine the features of ordinary language and its usage carefully before they developed a foundation for their philosophical thinking. Austin wanted philosophers to think of philosophy more as a science than as an art and to regard it as a tool for investigating and settling matters.

Austin believed that the investigation of ordinary language was key to resolving philosophical problems and that words are tools. The stock of words embodies all the distinctions people over the centuries have found worth drawing and the connections they have found worth making. When philosophers examine what people should say when and what words they use in which situations, they are looking at the realities people use words to talk about or represent. In sharpening the use of words, the philosopher is sharpening people's understanding of the real world. Ordinary language, according to Austin, is not the last word on reality. It is only the first word. Specialized language should supersede ordinary language only if the new vocabulary is necessary and useful. Austin started with ordinary language and proceeded from it. He wanted philosophers and others to understand the ambiguity, context, and purpose of words and then proceed to the world the words represent.

Austin's method featured three steps. First, Austin collected all the linguistic idioms and expressions relevant to a particular topic such as excuses, often using a dictionary to aid his research. In one of his essays, "A Plea for Excuses," he discussed the distinctions between the words "mistake," "accident," and "inadvertent." Second, the philosopher imagined, as precisely and in as much detail as possible, different situations in which the expressions could be said to be appropriately used. The philosopher gave an account of the meanings of the expressions or terms and determined their interrelationships. He attempted to discover what is present in those cases where people use one term and not another. Third, he investigated how people can "say" something by doing something or performing certain acts. He distinguished between two kinds of speech: making certain noises and uttering words according to grammatical rules. Austin also identified actions that indicate how an utterance is to be interpreted when, for example, a person is asking or answering a question, as well as actions that convince, persuade, or cause an effect.

In 1952, Austin was appointed to the White's Chair in Moral Philosophy. He taught at Oxford until his death from cancer in 1960. During his tenure, he held a number of important administrative faculty posts. He became a delegate of the prestigious Oxford University Press in 1952 and served as chair of the publisher's finance committee until his death. In 1955, he delivered the William James Lectures at Harvard University and in 1958 was a visiting professor at the University of California, Berkeley.

In his philosophical activities, Austin focused on whether the discussion advanced the solution of the problem at hand. He believed that one of the principal tasks of the philosopher is to make distinctions. Austin described his way of doing philosophy as "linguistic phenomenology," a term he admitted was a mouthful. He argued that one good way to begin in philosophy is to make distinctions using ordinary speech. Where ordinary speech makes a verbal distinction, it is highly probable that there is a distinction to be made. Austin contended that one's native language offers a ready-made and enormous stock of discriminations and that using this stock of discriminations merely makes good sense. If one wants to know whether to distinguish between two cases, one should consider whether one speaks about the two cases in the same way. If one does not speak of them in the same way, they probably can be distinguished and the distinction is an important one. Austin believed that philosophers should look to language to find pointers that indicate important distinctions and that they often need to examine language itself. He examined language through his focus on "speech acts": what kinds of actions are performed while speaking, how they are done, and how they might be right or wrong.

Austin held no views about the proper objective of philosophy; however, he was distressed, even scandalized, by the lack of agreement and progress in philosophy. He believed that the best way to reach agreement was through cooperative discussion of well-defined questions among collaborators. He thought that the team approach to resolving philosophical questions was superior to the solitary composition of lectures, articles, and books. He regarded cooperative philosophy not only as the best method of practice but also as the only instrument to ensure progress in philosophy. A cooperative discussion conducted with sufficient care for detail could lead to the resolution of some long-standing philosophical problems. He also thought that philosophers had altogether underestimated the subtlety and complexity of ordinary language and the distinctions found within it. He believed that philosophers must drop their theoretical preconceptions in order to study ordinary language.

Influence

Austin taught people how to philosophize usefully. He was above all a teacher—a tough teacher who offered explicit directions for profitable study and provided lists of required assignments. He was a stickler for sound preparation and disapproved of sloppy work and lazy effort.

When Austin died at age forty-eight, he was a leader among philosophers not only at Oxford University but also in Britain and the rest of the English-speaking world. His major contribution was to clear the minds of philosophers and to help them pursue the truth. Friends and enemies, students, and later commentators generally agree that Austin exercised a powerful intellectual authority. Austin's influence is remarkable because he published only seven papers during his lifetime. The most influential of these papers were "Other Minds" (1946), "Ifs and Cans" (1956), and "A Plea for Excuses" (1956). His three books, *Philosophical Papers*, *Sense and Sensibilia*, and *How to Do Things with Words*, were published posthumously from lecture notes. Austin's work reoriented the research of many philosophers and laid the groundwork for the standard theory of speech acts, later developed by his student John Searle and others. Austin influenced the course of the philosophy of language. He championed the idea that philosophers must speak and think clearly if they are to be useful.

Fred Buchstein

How to Do Things with Words

Type of philosophy: Epistemology, philosophy of language
First published: 1962
Principal ideas advanced:

◇ There appears to be a contrast between merely saying something and doing something; this is the contrast between "constative utterances," such as stating, and "performative utterances," such as promising.

◇ Detailed examination of this contrast shows that it is not fruitful: To say something is to do something; in fact it is to do many things.

◇ Locutionary acts consist, among other things, of uttering words with a sense and reference.

◇ Illocutionary acts are governed by conventions and include such things as promising, swearing, and stating.

◇ Perlocutionary acts are natural acts, such as persuading or angering, consequent upon illocutionary acts.

How to Do Things with Words is a collection of J. L. Austin's William James Lectures at Harvard in 1955; it was first published posthumously in 1962. Austin's views on the matters discussed in the lectures were first formed in 1939, and he made some use of them in his address, "Other Minds," to the Aristotelian Society in 1946. Between 1952 and 1959, he lectured on the same topic, sometimes under the title "Words and Deeds." Much of Austin's philosophical reputation rests upon his incisive and acerbic criticism of the views of other philosophers—for example, his withering attacks on the views of A. J. Ayer and G. J. Warnock in *Sense and Sensibilia* (1962). The lectures in *How to Do Things with Words*, however, are constructive philosophy. Austin invented speech act theory, and his theory has been used, revised, and extended not only by philosophers but also by linguists, linguistic anthropolo-

gists and sociologists, cognitive psychologists, and speech communication theorists.

Austin begins his lectures in a remarkably modest way: "What I shall have to say here is neither difficult nor contentious; the only merit I should like to claim for it is that of being true, at least in parts." He then recounts, with approval, attempts to recognize that some so-called statements are strictly nonsense and to determine why they are nonsense. He also lauds the discovery that some statements do not purport to state facts but aim to evince emotion or to prescribe or otherwise influence conduct. These efforts and discoveries have developed piecemeal, he thinks, but also amount to a revolution in philosophy, about which he says, "If anyone wishes to call it the greatest and most salutary in its history, this is not, if you come to think of it, a large claim." What he proposes is a theory that describes the utterances that masquerade as statements. He calls such utterances "performatives."

Performatives

Performatives have two characteristics: First, they do not describe or "constate" anything at all and are not true or false; second, to utter the performative sentence is not merely to say something. Austin's first examples of performatives are "I do," uttered by a bride or groom; "I name this ship the *Queen Elizabeth*," uttered by someone smashing a bottle of champagne against the bow of a vessel; "I give and bequeath my watch to my brother," as occurring in a will; and "I bet you sixpence it will rain tomorrow." Based upon these examples, it might be tempting to think that to say the right words is the same as to do the action at issue. However, that is not correct. In general, the words have the proper effect only if uttered in appropriate circumstances, and only if the participants are doing certain other physical or mental things—for example, breaking the bottle of champagne. Further, for some acts, words are not necessary at all. Marrying might be accomplished by cohabiting and betting accomplished by inserting a coin into a slot machine.

Austin's examples of performatives are sufficient to prove that there is some distinction to be drawn between them and constatives: "But now how, as philosophers, are we to proceed? One thing we might go on to do, of course, is to take it all back: Another would be to bog, by logical stages, down. But all this must take time."

Constatives are true or false; however, performatives are not—instead, because they are types of actions, they can be done well or badly. Austin, in his doctrine of infelicities, concentrates on how they can be performed badly; for one way to learn how a machine works is to see in what ways it can break. As a kind of action, performatives are subject to all the defects that any action is; as linguistic acts, they have some special problems. Without pretending that the list is exhaustive or that its items are mutually exclusive, Austin mentions three conditions for performatives, conditions which, if contravened, give rise to infelicities:

First, a conventional procedure having a conventional effect must exist, and it must require that certain words be uttered by certain persons in certain circumstances; and the persons and circumstances must be the right ones for invoking the conventional procedure.

Second, the procedure must be performed correctly and completely.

Third, when the procedure requires certain thoughts, feelings, or intentions to act subsequently in a certain way, the participant must have them and in fact perform the intended action.

If an action is infelicitous for contravening either the first or second condition, the action is a misfire; the attempted performative is a failed attempt and the act is null and void. If an action is infelicitous for contravening the third condition, the performative is successful but defective because it "abuses" the procedure. This classification is helpful and instructive even though the borders between the three conditions are not always clear, and it is not always possible to decide whether an infelicity belongs to one kind or another. Austin believed that philosophers should attend to these deficiencies in the classification. "We must at all cost avoid over-simplification, which one might be tempted to call the occupational disease of philosophers if it were not their occupation."

Although performative utterances are not true or false if they are felicitously, that is, nondefectively, performed, they are related to statements that are true. For example, if a person felicitously utters, "I apologize," it is true that the individual apologizes, true that the person had offended or otherwise injured the addressee, true that the person commits himself to not repeating the injury, and so on. The way in which a performative is related to some true statements is analogous to the way in which constatives are related to some true statements. The sentence "All men blush" *entails* "Some men blush." Saying "The cat is on the mat" *implies* that the speaker believes that the cat is on the mat. The sentence "All Jack's children are bald" presupposes that Jack has children. So constatives are more like performatives than first appeared to be the case; they are being assimilated.

There are other reasons for assimilating constatives. The truth of "I am stating that John is running" depends upon the felicity of the speaker's saying or having said, "John is running." So at least some constative utterances have felicity conditions. On the other side of the distinction, some performatives are false: The warning "I warn you that the bull is about to charge" is a false warning if the bull is not about to charge.

Explicit Performatives

These matters raise doubts about the performative/constative distinction. Is there a way to make the distinction in grammatical terms, by grammatical criteria? Many, but not all, performatives have their main verb in the first-person-singular, present tense, active, indicative mood, but "You are hereby authorized . . . ," "Passengers are warned . . . ," "Notice is hereby given . . . ," and "Turn right" are exceptions. Thus, neither person, number, tense, voice, nor mood can be used as a simple criterion. The first-person, active, present tense remains, however, an attractive base upon which to build a criterion. An asymmetry exists between a performative verb in this form and the same verb in other persons, tenses, and moods. If one utters "I had bet," "He bets," or "They (might) have bet," one describes a certain action; but no action is described if one utters the words "I bet." Rather, to say "I bet" (in the right circumstances, frame of mind, and so on) is, roughly, to bet. Austin's strategy for devising a criterion is, then, to make a list of verbs having this asymmetry and to "reduce" other performative utterances to this form, which Austin calls "explicit performative" form.

Explicit performatives should be considered a development of language that evolves out of "primary performatives," which are vague and less explicit because they serve more than one purpose. "I will," in contrast with "I promise that I will," can be used for a prediction, expression of intention, or promise. Explicit performatives do the work that mood, tone of voice, cadence, adjectives, adverbs, particles, and sundry other things do in primary performatives. The imperative mood is indeterminate between giving an order, advice, permission, or consent, where the corresponding performative verb is determinate. Depending on how the sentence "It's going to charge" is uttered (depending upon its phonological contour), the act is a warning, a question, a charge, or a statement. The particles "therefore," "although," and "moreover" become, respectively, "I conclude that," "I concede that," and "I add that" in explicit performative form.

Although all this is instructive, it fails to serve the purpose of yielding a criterion of explicit performatives, for it is not always easy to determine whether an utterance is performative. "I assume that . . . " can be performative but may not be, and one can assume things without saying anything at all; and "I agree that . . . " may be performative or merely descriptive of the speaker's attitude. Another problem is that "I state that . . . " seems to be performative and yet is paradigmatically constative. The performative/constative distinction, then, cannot be sustained as a fruitful one, and it has, as promised, bogged down.

The Locutionary Act
Up to this point Austin has been contrasting saying and doing. A new approach is required, one that focuses on the senses in which saying can be doing. Austin notices that every case of saying something, in the full sense, what he calls the "locutionary act," is a case of doing something. Every locutionary act consists of a *phonetic* act, a *phatic* act, and a *rhetic* act. The phonetic act is the

act of merely uttering noises; a parrot is capable of performing a phonetic act. The phatic act is the act of uttering certain words in a grammatical sequence, that is, noises that belong to a language, and of uttering those words *as* belonging to a language. The *as* requirement is important; a parrot utters words but because it is not aware of them *as* words or *as* having a meaning, it does not perform a phatic act. The rhetic act is the act of uttering the words with a more or less definite sense and a reference. The terms "sense" and "reference" are those of German philosopher Gottlob Frege, but the doctrine is Austin's. For Frege, all meaningful words have both a sense and reference; for Austin, reference belongs to words that are correlated to objects by "demonstrative conventions"; sense belongs to those words that are correlated to general things by "descriptive conventions."

The difference between the phatic act and the rhetic act is brought out by the different ways of reporting them. A phatic act is reported by direct quotation: He said, "The cat is on the mat." A rhetic act is reported by indirect quotation: He said that the cat is on the mat. The difference is critical. One who reports a phatic act is claiming, in effect, to be offering a verbatim report of the speaker's words and is not committed to the proposition that its speaker had achieved any reference; there might have been no cat to which to refer. A person who reports a rhetic act is not claiming that its speaker used the very words in which the report is cast; the speaker might have said, "The feline pet is lying upon the fabric used for protecting the floor." The person is committed to the proposition that the speaker's words had a definite sense and reference.

Illocutionary and Perlocutionary Acts
To report a rhetic act is not to report a speech act fully, for such a report leaves out the force of the utterance. Was his saying that I was to go to the store an order or merely advice or a suggestion? The force of a speech act is its "illocutionary force"; the act is an *illocutionary* act. The illocutionary act is governed by and conforms to conventions, and it should not be confused with something else that is done in a speech act, a *perlocutionary* act. A perlocutionary act is an act that produces certain effects on the feelings,

thoughts, or actions of the audience, or even the speaker, as a consequence of the illocutionary act. These effects are natural consequences and not conventional ones, such as follow illocutionary acts. Although it is only a rough linguistic guide, people commonly report illocutionary acts as things done *in* saying something and perlocutionary acts as things done *by* saying something. In saying it, one *warns* another person (illocutionary act); by saying it, one *persuades* another person (perlocutionary act). These linguistic formulas do not, however, yield a criterion. *By* saying something, a person might have been joking or insinuating, but joking and insinuating are not perlocutionary acts. And *in* saying something, a person might have made a mistake, but making a mistake is not an illocutionary act.

Statements

The original contrast between performatives and constatives was a false dichotomy. Illocutionary acts are performative, in Austin's original sense of that term, and some of them have truth values. "I state that . . ." is on a par with "I argue that . . ." and "I promise that . . ." Like performatives, statements have felicity conditions. A statement often presupposes the existence of a referent, so if no referent exists, the attempted statement fails. Also, like performatives, statements require that the speaker be in a certain position; without evidence, the speaker cannot state when the world will end, although he or she may guess or prophesy it. Stating, it appears, is not unique; it is just one of many kinds of evaluation, and statements are not simply to be evaluated in terms of truth and falsity. Statements can be correct or incorrect, fair or unfair, exaggerated, precise, apt, misleading, or rough.

Statements belong to one category of illocutionary acts. Austin tentatively distinguishes five such categories: *verdictives, exercitives, commissives, behabitives,* and *expositives*. Verdictives, as the name implies, are typified by the kind of judgment issued by a jury, judge, umpire, or arbiter; they include estimates and appraisals. Exercitives are exercises of power; they include appointing, voting, ordering, and warning. Commissives commit the speaker to a course of action; they include promising, swearing, and declaring. Behabitives concern attitudes and social

behavior; they include apologizing, congratulating, and condoling. Expositives indicate how an utterance fits into a conversation; they include arguing, replying, objecting, and stating.

Austin ends his lectures by commenting on his failure to relate his theory to traditional philosophical problems. The failure was deliberate; "I have purposely not embroiled the general theory with philosophical problems . . . ; this should not be taken to mean that I am unaware of them. . . . I leave to my readers the real fun of applying it in philosophy."

A. P. Martinich

Additional Reading

Berlin, Isaiah, L. W. Forguson, D. F. Pears, G. Pitcher, J. R. Searle, P. F. Strawson, and G. W. Warnock. *Essays on J. L. Austin.* Oxford: Clarendon Press, 1973. This book of memoirs of J. L. Austin written by former students offers criticism and commentary on his work. These essays show what Austin tried to do as a philosopher and why.

Burr, John R., ed. *Handbook of World Philosophy: Contemporary Developments Since 1945.* Westport, Conn.: Greenwood Press, 1980. This survey of world philosophy covers Austin among many other philosophers. The book reveals that no agreed-upon doctrines, method of analysis, or terminology exist in the study of philosophy, a viewpoint that Austin would appreciate. The work shows how philosophy spread internationally after World War II.

Cavell, Stanley. *Philosophical Passages: Wittgenstein, Emerson, Austin, Derrida.* Cambridge, Mass.: Blackwell, 1995. Cavell, a noted American philosopher, demonstrates the subtle power of Austin's thought. He also notes the importance of Austin as a teacher and an early influence on his own work.

Dummett, Michael. *Truth and Other Enigmas.* Cambridge, Mass.: Harvard University Press, 1978. The author is critical of Austin's work and influence on other philosophers.

Fann, K. T. *Symposium on J. L. Austin.* London: Routledge & Kegan Paul, 1969. This collection contains commentaries on Austin's philosophy by well-known philosophers, many of whom knew Austin personally.

Gill, Jerry, ed. *Philosophy Today No. 1.* New York:

Macmillan, 1968. The author provides selected writings on analytic philosophy from Austin and Ludwig Wittgenstein as well as many of their contemporaries.

Graham, Keith. *J. L. Austin: A Critique of Ordinary Philosophy*. Sussex, England: Harvester Press, 1977. This work provides a review of Austin's philosophy and explores why Austin was influential, especially in the realm of language analysis.

Hacker, P. M. S. *Wittgenstein's Place in Twentieth-Century Analytic Philosophy*. Oxford: Blackwell, 1996. This benchmark survey provides a history of philosophy in England before, during, and after World War II. The author comments on Austin's place in the history of philosophy.

Lepore, Ernest, and Robert Van Gulick, eds. *John Searle and His Critics*. Cambridge, Mass.: Blackwell, 1991. Searle developed ideas that originated with Austin and other philosophers associated with Oxford University.

Passmore, John. *A Hundred Years of Philosophy*. New York: Basic Books, 1966. Passmore concentrates his historical survey on philosophical activity in England. He contends that Austin exercised an intellectual authority that was nothing short of remarkable from the end of World War II until his death in 1960.

Warnock, J. L. *J. L. Austin*. New York: Routledge, 1989. This book reviews Austin's seven philosophical papers and his major ideas.

Williams, Bernard, and Alan Montefiore, eds. *British Analytical Philosophy*. New York: Humanities Press, 1966. This survey provides examples of philosophers' thinking about linguistic and philosophical problems that were of concern to Austin and Wittgenstein.

Fred Buchstein

Averroës

Jurist, physician, and philosopher, Averroës was one of the last of a line of medieval Muslim scholars who sought to reconcile the truths of revealed religion and dialectical reasoning. He exercised an overwhelming influence upon Latin thought through his commentaries on Aristotle.

Principal philosophical works: *Talkhis kitab al-maqulat*, 1174 (*Averroës' Middle Commentaries on Aristotle's "Categories" and "De interpretatione,"* 1983); *Averroës' Three Short Commentaries on Aristotle's "Topics," "Rhetoric," and "Poetics,"* wr. before 1175, pb. 1977); *Kitab fasl al-maqāl*, 1179-1180 (*On the Harmony of Religion and Philosophy*, 1961); *Tahāfut al-tahāfut*, 1180 (*The Incoherence of the Incoherence*, 1954); *Tafsir Ma ba'da al-tabi'ah*, 1190 (*Ibn Rushd's Metaphysics: A Translation with Introduction of Ibn Rushd's Commentary on Aristotle's Metaphysics, Book Lambda*, 1984); *Be'ur le-sefer hanhagat ha-medinah le-Aplaton*, 1194 (*Commentary on Plato's "Republic,"* 1956).

Born: 1126; Córdoba (now in Spain)
Died: 1198; Marrakech, Morocco

Early Life

Abu al-Walid Muhammad ibn Ahmad ibn Muhammad ibn Rushd, generally known as Ibn Rushd and to the medieval Christian West as Averroës, was born in 1126 into a distinguished Spanish-Arab family of jurists in Córdoba, the former capital of the Umayyad Caliphate in Spain. His grandfather, who died in the year of his birth, had been a distinguished Malikite jurisconsult, who had held the office of chief *qadi* (Muslim judge) of the city, as well as *imam* (prayer leader) of its great mosque, still one of the most celebrated monuments of early Islamic architecture. Averroës's father was also a *qadi*, and in the course of time, Averroës too would follow the family calling. His biographers state that he was given an excellent education in all the branches of traditional Islamic learning, including medicine, in which he was the pupil of a celebrated teacher, Abu Jafar Harun al-Tajali (of Trujillo), who may also have initiated him into a lifelong passion for philosophy. The young scholar was also influenced by the writings of one of the most famous thinkers of the previous generation, Ibn Bajja of Saragossa, known to the Latin Scholastics as Avempace.

By 1157, Averroës, now thirty years old, had made his way to Marrakech in Morocco, at that time the capital of the North African and Spanish empire of the Almohads, where he was perhaps employed as a teacher. Averroës lived during a very distinctive period in the history of Islam in Spain and the Maghrib. A century before his birth, the disintegration of the caliphate of Córdoba had led to the fragmentation of Muslim Spain among the so-called Party Kings (*muluk al-tawaif*), who in turn had been overthrown by the Berber tribal confederacy of the Almoravids (*al-murabitun*, "those dwelling in frontier fortresses"). These fanatical warriors from the western Sahara had quickly succumbed to the hedonistic environment of Spanish Islam, only to be replaced by another wave of Berber fundamentalists, the Almohads (*al-muwahhidun*, "those who affirm God's unity"). Under 'Abd al-Mu'min (reigned 1130-1163), who assumed the title of caliph, the Almohads conquered all southern and central Spain as well as the North African littoral as far east as modern Libya.

Within the context of the cultural and intellectual history of the Muslim West, the Almohads played a highly ambiguous role. The spearhead of a puritanical movement sworn to the cleansing of Islam of latter-day accretions and to a return to the pristine mores of the days of the Prophet and the "rightly guided caliphs" (*al-Khulafa al-Rashidun*), they were also the heirs, through their conquests, to the intellectually precocious and culturally sophisticated traditions of Muslim Spain. The ruling elite seems to have dealt with this paradox by developing a deliberate "double standard": Within the walls of the caliph's palace and of the mansions of the great, the brilliant civilization of an earlier age continued to flourish, while outside, in street and marketplace, obedience to the Shari'a, the law of Islam, was strictly enforced at the behest of the clerical classes, the *ulama* (persons learned in the Islamic "sciences") and the *fuqaha* (those learned in jurisprudence). The life of Averroës himself points to a similar dichotomy. Outwardly, he was a *qadi* and a *faqih*, a judge and a jurisprudent; inwardly, he was a *faylasuf*, a philosopher with an insatiable urge to pursue speculative inquiry by rational argument and to delve deep into the infidel wisdom of the ancients.

In 1163, 'Abd al-Mu'min was succeeded by his son, Abu Ya'qub Yusuf, who throughout his reign (1163-1184) was to be a generous patron and friend to Averroës. Apparently, it was a contemporary scholar, Ibn Tufayl (c. 1105-1184), known to the Latins as Abubacer, who first presented Averroës to Abu Ya'qub Yusuf, probably around 1169. Tradition relates that, at their first meeting, the caliph began by asking Averroës about the origin and nature of the sky. While the latter hesitated, uncertain as to how to reply to questions that raised dangerous issues of orthodoxy, the caliph turned to converse with Ibn Tufayl, and in so doing revealed his own extensive learning. Reassured, Averroës embarked upon a discourse that so displayed the depth and range of his scholarship that the delighted caliph thereafter became his ardent disciple. It was on this occasion, too, that Abu Ya'qub Yusuf complained that the existing translations of the works of Aristotle were too obscure for comprehension and that there was need for further commentaries and exegeses. Ibn Tufayl

remarked that he himself was too old to assume such an undertaking, at which Averroës agreed to assume the task that was to become his life's work.

Life's Work

Averroës is inextricably linked with Aristotle because he became famous in the Christian West for his commentaries on the works of Aristotle. Since the end of antiquity, no one had studied the writings of Aristotle, or what passed for his writings, so carefully as Averroës, and in his numerous commentaries, many of which are now lost or are known only through Hebrew or Latin translations, he set out to remove the exegetical accretions of earlier ages. The Great Commentator, as the Latin Scholastics liked to call him, did not perhaps have a very original mind, but he did have a highly analytical one, capable of great critical penetration.

Averroës. (*Library of Congress*)

129

Averroës understood Aristotle better than his predecessors had because his powers of analysis enabled him, almost alone in the Arabo-Aristotelian philosophical tradition, to circumvent the glosses superimposed upon Aristotle by a spurious tradition that had for so long concealed the real Aristotle, consisting of such works as the *Theologia Aristotelis* derived from Plotinus, the *Liber de causis* of Proclus, and the commentary on Aristotle of Alexander of Aphrodisias. This "contamination of Aristotle," as one scholar has described it, laid upon medieval Arab and Jewish scholars alike the temptation to undertake "a synthesis in the systems of Plato and Aristotle," but this was a false trail that, for the most part, Averroës avoided following, largely on account of his intellectual acuity. On the other hand, he was a man of his times. Preoccupied as he was with political thought and its relationship to personal conduct, he nevertheless did not have access to Aristotle's *Politica* (second Athenian period, 335-323 B.C.E.; *Politics*, 1598). He was therefore forced to rely upon Plato's *Politeia* (middle period work, 388-368 B.C.E.; *Republic*, 1701) and *Nomoi* (later period work, 365-361 B.C.E.; *Laws*, 1804) and Aristotle's *Ethica Nicomachea* (second Athenian period, 335-323 B.C.E.; *Nichomachean Ethics*, 1797) and was heavily dependent upon his predecessor al-Farabi. Averroës had no knowledge of Greek. Therefore, he was compelled to study both Aristotle and Aristotle's Greek commentators in Arabic translations made from Syriac or, more rarely, from the original Greek. This fact alone makes his achievement the more remarkable. It helped him that, from the outset of his career as a scholar, his unabashed admiration for Aristotle as a thinker drove him to try to uncover the authentic mind beneath the palimpsests of later generations, the mind of the man who, in his words, "was created and given to us by divine providence that we might know all there is to be known. Let us praise God, who set this man apart from all others in perfection, and made him approach very near to the highest dignity humanity can attain."

Although Averroës has come to be known first and foremost as a philosopher, to his contemporaries he was probably regarded primarily as a jurist and a physician. In 1169, the year that saw the beginning of his long and fruitful intellectual

friendship with Abu Ya'qub Yusuf, he was appointed *qadi* of Seville, where, always preoccupied with his writing, he complained of being cut off from access to his library in Córdoba. He returned to the latter city as *qadi* in 1171, but it seems that throughout the 1170's he traveled extensively within the caliph's dominions, perhaps undertaking roving judicial commissions for the government. In 1182, he was summoned to Marrakech to succeed Ibn Tufayl as the caliph's physician. He had already written extensively on medical subjects, for in addition to the celebrated *Kitab al-kulliyat* (c. 1162-1169; a seven-part encyclopedia of medical knowledge, later translated into Latin as *Colliget*), he had written several commentaries on Galen. It is not certain how long he served as Abu Ya'qub Yusuf's physician, for not long afterward he was appointed chief *qadi* of Córdoba, the post that his grandfather had formerly held. Since Abu Ya'qub Yusuf was killed in battle at Santarém (Portugal) in 1184, it is possible that the prestigious appointment was made by Abu Ya'qub Yusuf's son and successor, Abu Yusuf Ya'qub (reigned 1184-1199), nicknamed al-Mansur, "the Victorious." For most of his reign, Abu Yusuf Ya'qub showed himself as well disposed toward Averroës as his father had been, but during 1195, the philosopher experienced a brief period of disgrace and danger.

The Christian powers of the north were mustering their forces, and Abu Yusuf Ya'qub needed to rally his subjects for the approaching struggle. For that, he needed the unqualified support of the *ulama* and *fuqaha*, which in turn involved his unequivocal commitment to orthodoxy. The *fuqaha* insisted that Averroës be silenced for spreading doctrines that were subversive of faith, such as the Aristotelian theory of the eternity of the world, which denied God's act of creation, and for his rejection of the divine knowledge of particulars, which called into question God's omniscience. Averroës was compelled to appear before some kind of hostile gathering in Córdoba, his books were publicly burned, and his enemies bombarded him with false accusations and scurrilous libels. His actual punishment, however, was quite mild—temporary exile to the town of Lucena, south of Córdoba—and it cannot have done much to assuage the wrath of his foes. Shortly afterward, the caliph won a great victory over the Christians at Allarcos, midway between Córdoba and Toledo (July 19, 1195), the last triumph of Muslim arms in the peninsula. In consequence, he apparently felt less dependent upon the goodwill of the *fuqaha*, and upon returning to his capital of Marrakech he summoned Averroës to join him. The old man (for he was now in his seventies) did not have long to enjoy his restoration to favor. He died in 1198 in Marrakech, where his tomb still stands, although he was subsequently reinterred in Córdoba. Abu Yusuf Ya'qub died within months of the passing of his most celebrated subject.

As a thinker, Averroës was in the mainstream of Muslim Scholasticism, as well as being one of its last significant practitioners. Like his great predecessors in the Muslim East, he sought to establish an honored place for philosophy within the broader context of Islamic thought and learning. Contrary to the later and quite erroneous Christian notion of him as a champion of rationalism who denied the truths of revealed religion, Averroës was a devout Muslim who never set philosophy on a pedestal in order to challenge religious belief. Throughout his life, he stoutly denied that there was any inherent contradiction between philosophical truth, as established by the speculative thinker, and the certainties of faith embodied in the Qur'an and the Shari'a, the religious law that provided the social bounds within which the Muslim community and individual Muslims lived their lives—and that, as a *qadi*, it was his duty to uphold. In his celebrated *The Incoherence of the Incoherence*—a defense of philosophy against the attacks made upon it by the eleventh century theologian and mystic al-Ghazzali in his *Tahafut al-falasifa* (1095; *The Incoherence of the Philosophers*, 1958)—he takes it as axiomatic that the philosopher will subscribe to the teachings of the highest form of revealed religion of the age in which he lives (by which he meant Islam). In *On the Harmony of Religion and Philosophy*, he assumes the compatibility of philosophical truth and revelation: Where there appears to be a conflict, that is the result of human misunderstanding, as in the case of diverse interpretations of Scripture. The Muslims, he writes, "are unanimous in holding that it is not obligatory either to take all the expressions of Scripture in their apparent meaning or to extend them all

from their apparent meaning to allegorical interpretation. . . . The reason why we have received a Scripture with both an apparent and an inner meaning lies in the diversity of people's natural capacities and the difference of their innate dispositions with regard to assent." In other words, people can believe only what their natural abilities allow them to comprehend, and this affects, among much else, the relationship between religion and philosophy as well as the philosopher's place in society.

Influence

Averroës was one of the most formidable thinkers in the entire intellectual history of Islam, but he was also, in a very real sense, the end of a line. In the Muslim East, of which he lacked direct experience, the heritage of speculative philosophy had long since withered away in the face of Ash'arite orthodoxy and a growing preoccupation with transcendent mysticism. In the Muslim West, which was his home, the end came more rapidly and more completely. Fourteen years after Averroës's death, the Almohads went down in defeat in one of history's truly decisive battles, Las Navas de Tolosa (1212), which heralded the end of Muslim rule in Spain and, with it, Arabo-Hispanic civilization. Thereafter, the intellectual life of the Muslim West, to which Averroës had contributed so much, slowly drew to its close.

Yet Averroës, whom the Muslim world soon forgot, enjoyed a posthumous and enduring fame in lands that he had never visited and in a civilization that, had he known it, he would probably have despised. A principal component of the twelfth century European Renaissance was the work of the translators of Toledo (reconquered by Alfonso VI of Castile from the Muslims in 1085), who made available in Latin the riches of Arabic, Hebrew, and Greek thought. When the pace of translation intensified during the thirteenth century, attention centered on the works of Aristotle and on the Aristotelian commentaries of Averroës. Among Christian translators were Michael Scott, Hermann the German, and the Italian, William of Lunis. No less prominent were the Jewish translators: Jacob Anatoli, Solomon ben Joseph ibn Ayyub, Shem-Tob ben Isaac ibn Shaprut, and Moses ben Samuel ibn Tibbon. As a result of this activity, Averroës became, along with Aristotle, one of the most explosive elements in the development of medieval Christian thought.

Misread and misunderstood, Averroës became the personification of human reason, unaided by divine illumination, arrogantly pitting itself against Providence. In 1277, the Bishop of Paris censured 219 errors held by Aristotle or Averroës, by which time his alleged disciples, the Latin Averroists, headed by Siger of Brabant, were drawing upon themselves the magisterial denunciations of Saint Thomas Aquinas, whose schematic endeavor to reconcile faith and reason nevertheless derived from the labors of Averroës a century earlier. Dante Alighieri, encountering him in Limbo, was correct in his emphasis when he wrote, *Averroès, che'l gran comento feo* ("Averroës, who made the Great Commentary"), but even he could not have imagined the extent of Averroës's influence on the intellectual history of late medieval Europe.

Gavin R. G. Hambly

The Incoherence of the Incoherence

Type of philosophy: Islamic philosophy, metaphysics, philosophical theology

First transcribed: Tahāfut al-tahāfut, 1180 (English translation, 1954)

Principal ideas advanced:

◇ Because any series of causes necessary through another cause must ultimately depend upon a cause necessary in itself (a first cause), God, as the First Cause, exists.

◇ God did not create the world in time, either by willing it at the moment of creation or by willing it eternally, for to act in time is to change, and God is changeless because he is perfect.

◇ God, as First Cause and Unmoved Mover, does not act in time but produces immaterial intelligences that, because of their imperfection, can change in time.

◇ The being of existent things is inseparable from their essence.

Averroës, the last of the great Islamic philosophers, lived roughly one hundred fifty years after Avicenna, his philosophic rival, and about three generations after al-Ghazzali, the greatest of Muslim theologians. In his controversy with these two men, he concerned himself primarily with the defense and purification of Aristotle, whom he followed as closely as he could. Because he, too, accepted such spurious works as *Theologia Aristotelis* (derived from Plotinus), his interpretation is still permeated by Neoplatonic elements, but to a lesser extent than that of Avicenna. The success of his endeavor is indicated by the fact that he was known to Scholastic writers as *the* Commentator and that no less a person than Saint Thomas Aquinas had him constantly at hand as he wrote his *Summa contra gentiles* (c. 1258-1260; English translation, 1923) and his various commentaries on Aristotle.

The Incoherence of the Incoherence was written in reply to mystic al-Ghazzali's book, *Tahā-fut al-falāsifa* (1095; *Incoherence of the Philosophers*, 1958), in which al-Ghazzali attacked the philosophers, and in particular Avicenna, for advocating doctrines that were incompatible with their faith. As the title of his own book suggests, Averroës came to the defense of the philosophers. Adopting a position similar to that of the later medieval thinkers who distinguished between revealed and natural theology, Averroës scrupulously avoided denying any tenet of his faith; nevertheless, he sided firmly with the philosophers. His interpretations of religious doctrines were so far removed from those of the theologians that even though he was studied carefully by Hebrew and Christian philosophers, he was not recognized to any great extent by his Islamic contemporaries. Averroës's book plays a very important role in the long controversy between the philosophers and the theologians because it is concerned chiefly with the nature and existence of God and with the relationship between God and the cosmos. Averroës does not spell out his position in detail, for he agrees on the whole with the earlier commentators on Aristotle and with the version of Aristotle he receives from them. In particular, he agrees largely with Avicenna, disagreeing on those points, and they are important points, where he thinks Avicenna departs from Aristotle.

A First Cause and Time

Averroës agrees with Aristotle that there is a First Cause, and he accepts a modified version of

Avicenna's proof from contingency. Objects whose existence is contingent rather than necessary must have a cause. If the cause is itself contingent, and if its cause is contingent, and so on, there would be an infinite regress and therefore no cause at all, a conclusion that, it can readily be seen, denies the assumption that contingent objects must have a cause. Hence, any series of contingent objects must be preceded in existence by a necessary cause that is either necessary through another or necessary without a cause—necessary in itself. However, if we have a series of causes each of which is necessary through another, once more we have an infinite regress and thus no cause. Hence, any series of causes necessary through another must depend on a cause necessary in itself—a First Cause.

The nature of this First Cause and of the way in which it causes is illuminated by Averroës's discussion of creation. Averroës agrees with the philosophers against al-Ghazzali that the world was not created in time. The philosophers had argued that if the world was created in time, it was created directly or indirectly by God, because an infinite regress of causes is impossible. If God created it in time, then he acted at a time and therefore underwent a change in time; but unquestionably, this is an impossible state of affairs because God is perfect and changeless. To al-Ghazzali's objection that God did not act in time but decreed from all eternity that the world should come into being at a certain time, Averroës replies that even if God had so willed from all eternity, he must also have acted at the time of creation in order to implement his decision, for every effect must have a contemporaneous cause. Consequently, the philosopher's objection cannot be avoided. It can be shown similarly that the cosmos is incorruptible; that is, that there is no time at which it will come to an end, for this too would require a change in God. Change occurs only within the world and then only when one thing is changed into another. The world itself is eternal and everlasting.

Al-Ghazzali had already attacked Avicenna on this point, asserting that the followers of Aristotle now have a problem on their hands, for they must give some account of how an eternal First Cause produces things that have a beginning in time. The problem is complicated by the fact that

Averroës and Avicenna agreed with Aristotle that because the world is eternal, infinite temporal sequences do occur. For instance, there was no time when the celestial sphere began to move and no time when the first person appeared. Why not, chides al-Ghazzali, agree with the materialists that because there is an infinite sequence of causes, a First Cause is not only superfluous but impossible?

In reply, Averroës asks us to consider the case of the infinite sequence of past positions of a celestial sphere. Like Avicenna, he says that so far as the sphere is concerned this sequence is an accidental infinite, for the motion of the sphere at any given moment does not cause the motion it has at any other moment. First, if motion did cause motion there would be an infinite regress of causes and therefore no cause at all. Second, because motion is continuous, there are in it no discrete units that have a beginning and an end and therefore no units that could stand in a causal relationship to one another. Finally, because the cause must be contemporaneous with the effect, the causal relation cannot span an interval of time, and past motion cannot influence present motion. In the case of the celestial sphere, the motion it has at any given moment follows, not from the motion it had at some previous moment, but from its desire at that moment to emulate the perfection of the associated Intelligence. Through all eternity, this Intelligence has sustained it in motion from moment to moment by continuously acting as its final cause. Because this Intelligence is itself a being whose existence is necessary through another, one is led back to the First Cause, the Unmoved Mover who stands behind the world. The Mover itself does not operate in time nor does it cause time directly, but it does produce an Intelligence that, because it is immaterial, is changeless, but that, because it is imperfect, is able to produce change of position in the sphere and thus to produce change in time.

Averroës's treatment of the infinite sequence of humanity begetting humanity is somewhat different from the preceding argument, for in this case there are discrete objects that do seem to cause one another successively. However, here, too, Averroës says the sequence is, in itself, an accidental infinite. To be sure, the sequence does depend upon humans, but only in several secondary senses. First, as he puts it, the third person can come from the second only if the first person has perished. That is, because the amount of matter in the universe is limited, human bodies can continue to come into existence only if others perish. Second, through the phenomena of conception and growth, people are the instrument by which God produces other people. However, having functioned in both cases as a material cause by providing suitable matter, the human role is complete, for no body can produce a form in another. Directly or indirectly, the First Mover is the source of the eternal form that, when individuated by matter, animates that matter. Here again Averroës describes the Mover or one of the Intelligences as operating eternally as a final cause, again and again drawing forth from complexes of matter the form that is contained in them potentially.

Plurality

Averroës then considers the question raised by al-Ghazzali as to how it is possible for the plurality in the world to arise from the Mover, who is simple. Avicenna had argued that only one thing can emanate from God, but that this thing, the First Intelligence, is able to generate more than one thing by contemplating both itself and the Mover. Averroës replies, first, that because thought and its object are identical, the Intelligence is really identical with its thought of God and with its thought of itself and, therefore, that these thoughts are identical with each other. Hence, there is no plurality of thought and no plurality of creation.

Second, he says that when Avicenna insists that only one thing can come from God, he is thinking of the Supreme Intellect as if it were a finite empirical one, but this concept is a mistake. Because our intellect is limited by matter, any particular mental act can have only one object, but because God is not so limited he can think all things even though his simplicity and changelessness preclude a plurality of acts. If it is argued that to think of all things is to have many thoughts and that because thinker and thought are identical, God must be plural, Averroës replies that when God thinks all things, he does not think them discursively as people do. People

either entertain images, a process that unquestionably involves spatial apprehension and thus spatial plurality, or they understand concepts by genus and species, a process that again introduces plurality. In either case, because people apprehend the object of thought by abstracting it from its material context, they apprehend it imperfectly. God, who is perfect, does not apprehend the nature of things in these ways and therefore does not apprehend them as either individual or universal. In some manner that people do not understand, he comprehends that which is plural to people but does not comprehend it as numerically plural. (This is a particular application of the general principle that any property or capacity attributed to God must be attributed only by analogy.) God, then, is the source of all plurality even though he is simple and changeless.

The Avicennian Cosmology

Averroës accepts the Avicennian cosmology in its general outlines. The First Mover produces a number of pure intelligences that may produce others and that cause the motions of their respective spheres or, in the case of the Agent Intellect, preside over generation and corruption in the sublunar world. The Mover is the efficient cause of these intelligences, producing them by means of a power that it emanates, and the final and formal cause insofar as it is the thing they seek to emulate. They in turn are the efficient, final, and formal causes of the motion of the spheres. Averroës agrees with Avicenna that though prime matter is not created, the existence of material things depends upon the Mover who is the source of the forms and also the agent, final, and formal cause of the manifestation of any form in matter.

However, despite this agreement Averroës disagrees with Avicenna on a number of points. Some, such as the number of intelligences (more than forty), and the nonlinear order of the intelligences (the Mover may have produced all of the intelligences of the principle spheres directly) are unimportant, but others are crucial. Averroës insists that the intelligences really are simple in that they do not contemplate themselves in several essentially different ways. The spheres are not composites of soul and body even though they are animate, and God is the source of plurality. Consequently, God does not function as Avicenna says he does. Whether by intention or not, Avicenna left the impression that God's role in the creative process was completed when he produced the First Intelligence and that the further creative acts were contributed piecemeal by the various intelligences acting from their own natures. In locating the source of plurality in God, Averroës is insisting that direct responsibility for the whole creative process rests with God. It is true, he says, that the intelligences are creative agents, but they are the Mover's subordinates who, out of respect for him, implement his commands throughout the cosmos. Setting aside the theological analogy, a theory such as this means that God's essence functions as the efficient, formal, and final cause of the First Intelligence, that this intelligence is an imperfect manifestation of the essence of God, that God as thus reflected functions once more as the efficient, formal, and final cause of an Intelligence or soul inferior to the first one, and so on down through the hierarchy.

Averroës also differs from Avicenna in that he loosens the Avicenna bonds of necessity. To be sure, in some sense God acts necessarily, but this is not logical necessity, for the world God contemplates and thus produces is the best of all possible worlds. Similarly, the various intelligences respond to God, not because it would be contradictory not to, but because they respect him. There is a definite normative element permeating the system. On the general issue of the relation between God and the world, Averroës does not differ from Avicenna as greatly as he frequently says he does; nevertheless, his modifications are important and they do result in a weakening of the Neoplatonic elements, a fact that was appreciated by later Aristotelians.

Existence and Essence

Another historically important feature of Averroës's philosophy is his rejection of Avicenna's sharp distinction between essence and existence. Avicenna had insisted that except in the case of God, existence is an accident that happens to an essence. For Avicenna, existence is a condition that must be satisfied by an essence before it can occur outside a mind, a property that must be added to it. Therefore, the existence of a material

object does not stem from its essence, but from what happened to its essence. However, Averroës insists that the very being of an existent thing is its essence, that its being depends upon the essence and not upon what happens to the essence. For him, the terms "being" and "existence" are not verb terms, but substantives applied primarily to the object itself and secondarily to the essence that makes it the sort of thing it is. Because the object is a being or existent in virtue of its essence, it is impossible to separate essence and existence save in thought. The essence itself may be regarded as an existent in a secondary sense of that term, but in this case it is impossible to separate essence and existence even in thought.

This difference between the two men is reflected in their views, inasmuch as Avicenna is very much concerned with how things come into existence and Averroës shows himself to be more concerned with the manner in which things change. Thus, in their proofs of the existence of God, Avicenna moves from the contingent existence of things to a necessarily existing ground, whereas Averroës proceeds from the occurrence of motion to an unmoved mover. Again, whereas Avicenna's Giver of Forms is bringing essences into existence by impressing them on suitably prepared matter, Averroës's Agent Intellect is coaxing out forms nascent in complexes of matter. Averroës insists correctly that Avicenna is moving away from Aristotle and that he himself is truer to their common master. Later, Saint Thomas Aquinas and his followers follow Avicenna in making a sharp distinction between essence and existence, but they acknowledge Averroës's objection by transforming existence from a property into an act of being that is prior in principle to essence. On the other hand, William of Ockham and the Averroists of the fourteenth, fifteenth, sixteenth, and seventeenth centuries insist that Averroës is right and that Avicenna and Thomas are wrong.

Leonard Miller, updated by John K. Roth

Additional Reading

Copleston, Frederick. *A History of Philosophy: Medieval Philosophy*. Garden City, N.Y.: Doubleday, 1962. Provides a good overview of medieval Islamic philosophy, and the contributions made by Averroës in particular.

Davidson, Herbert A. *Alfarabi, Avicenna, and Averroes on Intellect: Their Cosmologies, Theories of Active Intellect, and Theories of Human Intellect.* New York: Oxford University Press, 1992. A significant study of the most important Arabic philosophers from the medieval period.

Hitti, Philip K. *Makers of Arab History.* New York: St. Martin's Press, 1968. This collection of popular biographies includes a lively introductory account of Averroës and his thought.

Kogan, Barry S. *Averroes and the Metaphysics of Causation.* Albany: State University of New York Press, 1985. A detailed analysis of Averroës's theory of causation and his understanding of the nature of reality.

Leaman, Oliver. *Averroes and His Philosophy.* New York: Oxford University Press, 1988. A helpful overview of the philosophy of this leading Arabic thinker.

Wahbah, Murad, et al., eds. *Averroes and the Enlightenment.* New York: Prometheus Books, 1996. Significant essays concentrate on Averroës's influence on the Western philosophical tradition.

Watt, W. Montgomery. *Islamic Philosophy and Theology.* Edinburgh: Edinburgh University Press, 1962. A compact and still useful general account of Islamic philosophy that helpfully interprets Averroës's place in that tradition.

Gavin R. G. Hambly, updated by John K. Roth

Avicenna

Avicenna was the first Islamic thinker to synthesize the philosophy of Aristotle and Plato with Islamic traditions. His writings on medicine were studied in Europe as late as the seventeenth century.

Principal philosophical works: *Kitab al-Qanun fi al-tibb*, early eleventh century (*A Treatise on the Canon of Medicine of Avicenna*, 1930); *Kitab al-Najat*, early eleventh century (commonly known as *The Book of Deliverance*; partial translation, *Avicenna's Psychology*, 1952); *Kitab al-Shifa'*, early eleventh century; *Danish Nama'i 'Ala'i*, early eleventh century (partial translation, *Avicenna's Treatise on Logic*, 1971).

Born: August or September, 980; Afshena, Transoxiana Province of Bukhara, Persian Empire (now Uzbekistan)
Died: 1037; Hamadhan, Persia (now Iran)

Early Life

Abu 'Ali al-Husain ibn 'Abdallah ibn Sina was born in 980 to Abd-Allah of Balkh (now in Afghanistan), the well-to-do governor of an outlying province under Samanid ruler Nuh II ibn Mansur. Avicenna may have descended from a Turkish family on his father's side, but his mother, Sitara, was clearly Iranian.

After his brother Mahmud was born, the family moved to Bukhara, one of the principal cities of Transoxiana and capital of the Samanid emirs from 819 to 1005. Exhibiting an early interest in learning, young Avicenna had read the entire Qur'an by age ten. His father was attracted to Isma'ili Shi'ite doctrines, preached locally by Egyptian missionaries, but Avicenna resisted his father's influence. There was much discussion in his home regarding geometry, philosophy, theology, and even accounting methods. Avicenna was sent to study with an Indian vegetable seller who was also a surveyor. Through this man, Avicenna became acquainted with the Indian system of calculation, which made use of the zero in computations.

Avicenna. *(Library of Congress)*

A well-known philosopher came to live with the family for a few years and had an extraordinary influence on the young scholar. Abu 'Abd Allah al-Natili stimulated Avicenna's love of theoretical disputation, and the youth's earlier readings in jurisprudence enabled him to tax al-Natili's powers of logic daily. The tutor convinced Abd-Allah that Avicenna's career should be only in learning. Avicenna was studying Aristotelian logic and Euclidean geometry when the teacher decided to move to a different home. Soon Avicenna had mastered texts in natural sciences and metaphysics, then medicine, which he did not consider very difficult. He taught physicians and even practiced medicine for a short time. At the age of sixteen, he engaged in disputations on Muslim law.

For the next year and a half, Avicenna returned to the study of logic and all aspects of philosophy, keeping files of syllogisms and praying daily at the mosque for guidance in his work. He became so obsessed with philosophical problems and so anxious to know all that he hardly took time to sleep. Aristotle's *Metaphysica* (second Athenian period, 335-323 B.C.E.; *Metaphysics*, 1801) became an intellectual stumbling block until his reading of a work by Abu Nasr al-Farabi clarified many ideas for him. Soon all of Aristotle became understandable, and Avicenna gave alms to the poor in gratitude.

When Sultan Nuh ibn Mansur of Bukhara became ill, he sent for Avicenna on the advice of his team of physicians. Because of his help in curing the ruler, Avicenna gained access to the palace library, thus acquainting himself with many new books. When not studying, Avicenna was given to drinking wine and satisfying a large sexual appetite that he retained to the end of his life. Avicenna claimed that after the age of eighteen, he learned nothing new, only gained greater wisdom. When the palace library was destroyed in a fire, critics blamed Avicenna, who, they said, wished to remove the sources of his ideas. There is no proof of that charge.

Life's Work

Avicenna's writing career began in earnest at the age of twenty-one with *al-Majmu* (1001; compilation), a comprehensive book on learning for Abu al-Hasan, a prosodist. Then he wrote *al-Hasil wa*

al-mahsul (c. 1002; the sun and substance), a twenty-volume commentary on jurisprudence, the Qur'an, and asceticism. There soon followed a work on ethics called *al-Birr wa al-ithm* (c. 1002; good works and evil). The sponsors made no copies of them, a matter of some concern to the author.

His father died in 1002, and Avicenna was forced to take government service. He reluctantly left Bukhara for Gurganj, the capital of Khwarazm, where he met Emir Ali ibn Ma'mun. From Gurganj, he moved to Fasa, Baward, Tus, Samanqan, and thence to Jajarm on the extreme end of Khurasan. He served Emir Qabus ibn Wushmagir until a military coup forced Avicenna to leave for Dihistan, where he became ill. After recovering, he moved to Jurjan.

In Jurjan, Avicenna met his pupil and biographer, Abu 'Ubaid al-Juzjani, who stayed with him throughout much of the remainder of his life. Juzjani thought him exceptionally handsome and wrote that when Avicenna went to the mosque on Friday to pray, people would gather to observe at first hand "his perfection and beauty." While in Jurjan, Avicenna wrote *al-Mukhtasar al-awsat* (the middle summary on logic), *al-Mabda' wa al-ma'ad* (the origin and the return), and *al-Arsad al-kulliya* (comprehensive observations). He also wrote the first part of *A Treatise on the Canon of Medicine of Avicenna*, *Mukhtasar al-Majisti* (summary of the Almagest) and numerous other treatises. One modern scholar lists one hundred books attributed to Avicenna; another says that Avicenna's works include several hundred books in Arabic and twenty-three in Persian.

From Jurjan, Avicenna next moved to al-Rayy, joining the service of al-Saiyyida and her son, Majd al-Dawlah. Civil strife forced him to flee to Qazwin; from there he moved to Hamadhan, where he managed the affairs of Kadhabanuyah. He was called to the court of Emir Shams al-Dawlah to treat the ruler for colic, after which Avicenna was made the vizier of his emirate. Because of a mutiny in the army, however, the emir was forced to discharge him. After matters calmed down, Avicenna was called back and reinstated as vizier. During this period, public affairs occupied his daytime hours, and he spent evenings teaching and writing. When the emir died, Avicenna went into hiding, finishing work on his *Kitab al-Shifa'* (book of healing). He was arrested for corresponding with a rival ruler, but when Emir 'Ala' al-Dawlah attacked Hamadhan four months later, Avicenna was set free.

Avicenna left Hamadhan for Isfahan with his brother, two slaves, and al-Juzjani to serve Emir 'Ala' al-Dawlah. The emir designated every Friday evening for learned discussions with many other masters. Not present was a famous scholar and rival of Avicenna, Abu al-Rayhan al-Biruni, with whom he carried on a rather bitter correspondence. They had been clients at many of the same courts but never at the same time. At Isfahan, Avicenna completed many of his writings on arithmetic and music. He was made an official member of the court and accompanied the emir on a military expedition to Hamadhan.

When he was rebuked by the emir's cousin, Abu Mansur, for feigning expertise in philology, Avicenna was so stung by the criticism that he studied this subject frantically, compiling his discoveries in a book entitled *Lisan al-'Arab* (the Arabic language). During these years, he conducted experiments in medicine and astronomy. He introduced the use of medicinal herbs and devised an instrument to repair injured vertebrae. He understood that some illnesses arose from psychosomatic causes, and he wrote extensively on the pulse, preventive medicine, and the effects of climate on health. On May 24, 1032, he observed the rare phenomenon of Venus passing through the solar disk.

When he became ill in Isfahan, one of his slaves filled his meal with opium, hoping for his death and an opportunity to steal his money. Avicenna managed to recover under self-treatment but soon had a relapse, dying in 1037. Most authorities say that he died and was buried in Hamadhan.

Influence

A Treatise on the Canon of Medicine of Avicenna remained a principal source for medical research for six centuries. Between 1470 and 1500, it went through thirty editions in Latin and one in Hebrew; a celebrated edition was published on a Gutenberg press in Rome in 1593. Avicenna's principal literary contribution was the invention of the Rubaiyat form, quatrains in iambic pentameter, later made famous by Omar Khayyám.

Most important of all, Avicenna's philosophical system helped stimulate a genuine intellectual renaissance in Islam that had enormous influence not only in his own culture but also in Western Europe. European scholars Saint Thomas Aquinas, Averroës, John Duns Scotus, Albertus Magnus, and Roger Bacon learned much from Avicenna, even though they disagreed on some particulars.

Most intriguing to the medieval Scholastics was Avicenna's insistence upon essences in everything, the distinction between essence and existence (a notion derived from al-Farabi), the absence of essence in God (whose existence is unique), and the immortality of the soul (which animates the body but is independent of it).

According to some scholars, Avicenna's insistence upon observation and experimentation helped turn Western thought in the direction of the modern scientific revolution. His theories on the sources of infectious diseases, his explanation of sight, his invention of longitude, and his other scientific conclusions have a truly remarkable congruence with modern explanations. The application of geometrical forms in Islamic art, his use of the astrolabe in astronomical experiments, and his disputations on the immortality of the soul demonstrate Avicenna's universal genius.

John D. Windhausen

The Book of Deliverance

Type of philosophy: Islamic philosophy, epistemology, metaphysics

First transcribed: Kitab al-Najat, early eleventh century; commonly known as *The Book of Deliverance* (partial translation, *Avicenna's Psychology*, 1952)

Principal ideas advanced:

◇ God is the eternal, unmoved First Mover, who exists necessarily by his own nature and who eternally generates the first created being, a pure intelligence, by a creative act of thought.

◇ The First Intelligence creates the Second Intelligence and also the first celestial sphere and its soul; the Second Intelligence produces the Third Intelligence and the second celestial sphere; the process continues to the Tenth Intelligence, the Giver of Forms.

◇ Souls are vegetable, animal, and human; the human soul is characterized by the faculties of growth, reproduction, nutrition, motion, perception, and reason.

◇ There are five external senses and five internal senses; the internal senses are common sense, representation, imagination, estimation, and recollection.

◇ Reason has two faculties: the practical and the theoretic; faculty may develop to the stage of Actual Intellect, as activated by the Tenth Intelligence; knowledge then consists of discovering the necessary relations between universals.

In the year 529, Justinian closed the Schools of Athens, but fortunately for the West, Greek learning had been transmitted to the Near East, principally through the institutions of Alexandria and the Christian communities of Syria and Persia. Later, after the advent of Islam, this learning was fostered and developed by various Islamic philosophers and eventually carried across North Africa into Spain, where it flourished in such places as Toledo and Cordova. From the eleventh to the thirteenth centuries, it trickled and then flooded into Western Europe to augment the Christians' meager and unbalanced knowledge of Greek philosophy.

Avicenna was, perhaps, the most important Islamic philosopher. Besides being a prolific writer on philosophy and religion, he was a court scholar and physician, an active politician, a civil administrator, and the writer of medical texts that were standard works in Europe through the seventeenth century. Of his approximately one hundred works, the two most important are the philosophic encyclopedia, *Kitab al-Shifa'* (early eleventh century; book of healing), the bulk of which was known to late medieval thinkers, and an abridgment of it, *Kitab al-Najat*, commonly known as *The Book of Deliverance*. This essay is based primarily on the section of the work dealing with Avicenna's philosophy of mind, which was translated by F. Rahman and published under the title *Avicenna's Psychology*.

In order to discuss Avicenna's philosophy of mind and his epistemology, it is necessary to outline the system within which it is elaborated. Avicenna regarded himself as an Aristotelian, but his Aristotelianism, like that of both his predecessors and successors, was influenced by the pressure of religious considerations and by the fact that the Aristotle transmitted to him had become colored by Stoic and Neoplatonic elements.

The modifications in Aristotle's philosophy are evident in Avicenna's notion of God, his doctrine of creation, and his cosmology. He describes God not only as an eternal, unchanging, immaterial unmoved mover but also as a being whose existence is necessary because his essence is identical with his being, as the one who is indivisible, as true perfection, as pure benevolence, and as a continuously active Agent Intellect who, by emanation, creates the cosmos and all that is in it. Because intellect and will are identical in a pure intelligence, God can create simply by thinking. When he contemplates himself, he automatically generates the first created being, which is, because it stems from him, a pure intelligence.

God and the Intelligences

The First Intelligence can also create by contemplation, but because it is a finite intelligence, it can contemplate and create in different ways. In contemplating God, it creates the Second Intelligence. In contemplating its own essence and in knowing that it is a contingent being characterized by potentiality, it creates the body of the first celestial sphere. In contemplating itself and in knowing its existence as necessary in that it flows necessarily from God, it generates the soul of the first celestial sphere.

Because the celestial sphere is attached to a body, its soul is not a pure intelligence and therefore does not create, but it does seek to emulate the perfection of its creator, the First Intelligence. It does so by contemplating the intelligence and by perfecting its own body. Because the only change simple celestial matter can undergo is a change of position, the soul perfects celestial matter by circular motion. Hence, the First Intelligence is the final cause of both the existence and motion of the first sphere. The Second Intelligence, by contemplating the First Intelligence and by contemplating itself in the twofold manner, produces the Third Intelligence and the body and soul of the second celestial sphere, that containing the stars. In a similar manner, further intelligences and spheres are produced as the creative process works down through the spheres of Saturn, Jupiter, Mars, the Sun, Venus, Mercury, and the Moon. The Tenth Intelligence does not produce a sphere, but it does produce sublunar things by providing souls and forms and by uniting them with suitably disposed complexes of sublunar matter. These complexes of matter come about as the four Aristotelian elements combine and recombine under the influence of the celestial spheres. The Tenth Intelligence is the Agent Intellect, or Giver of Forms, which looms large in Avicenna's psychology and which provides a linkage between Aristotle's Active Intellect and the Active Intellect of the Scholastics.

Avicenna agrees with Aristotle and disagrees with the theologians in claiming that this creative process is not a temporal process and that it is not creation out of nothing. Creation is not a temporal event, since time is the measure of change and thus presupposes the existence of matter, and it is not a temporal process because a cause must be contemporaneous with its effect. Furthermore, creation is not *ex nihilo* because form can only be imprinted on matter that is already available. Consequently, God, matter, the cosmos, and creation itself are eternal. Things exist because God exists, because he contemplates himself necessarily, and because their existence flows directly or indirectly from this contemplation. Insofar as it explains why things exist, the theory of emanation suggests a nontemporal sequence of active, efficient causes grounded in the supreme efficient cause, but it also suggests a hierarchy of essences following from one another in sequence. When God contemplates his own essence, he sees the network of implications that flow from it and thus, unlike Aristotle's God, knows the cosmos in detail.

Avicenna's views influenced much subsequent philosophy. Many, if not all, of the later Christian philosophers appreciated the proof of God's existence from the existence of contingent things, the notion of God as an agent, the step in the direction of a suitable creation theory, the doctrine of intelligences as a foundation for a study of angels, God's knowledge of the world, and the identity of essence and existence in God but their

sharp separation in other things. They objected to the eternity of the world, the denial of creation *ex nihilo*, the piecemeal emanation of the created world, the determinism, and the doctrine of the Agent Intellect.

The External and Internal Senses

Avicenna's reliance on Aristotle, and in particular on Aristotle's *De anima* (second Athenian period, 335-323 B.C.E.; *On the Soul*, 1812) is evidenced from the beginning of his psychology when he classifies souls as vegetable, animal, and human. The vegetable soul is characterized by the faculties of growth, reproduction, and nutrition; the animal has, in addition, those of motion and perception; and the human being is completed by the faculty of reason. There are really two faculties of motion in the animal soul: a psychic one characterized by desire and anger, which incite motion toward objects or away from them, and a physical one that actually moves the body by contracting and relaxing the muscles. There are five external senses, each operative when the form of the sensed object is impressed on the physical sense organ. For instance, when light falls on an object, it transmits an image through the transparent medium, and this image is impressed on the vitreous humor of the eye where it is apprehended by the psychic faculty of sight.

Avicenna's analysis of the internal sense goes considerably beyond that of Aristotle, who did not distinguish explicitly between internal and external senses, and it anticipates in considerable detail that of the Scholastics. There are five internal senses: fantasy or common sense, representation, imagination, the estimative sense, and the recollective or retentive sense. These are unique faculties, each being associated with a different part of the brain. The common sense receives images transmitted to it by the five external senses, enabling people both to know that they differ from one another and to collate the data received from them. The function of representation or sense memory is to preserve the data received by the common sense. An external sense, such as vision, abstracts the form of a particular object from its matter, but it can do so only in the presence of the object, seeing the form with all the determinations imposed upon it by that matter and seeing it as being present in matter.

The form in the representative faculty is still particular, but it is not seen as being present in or presented by matter. This further abstraction makes memory possible. Imagination is the faculty that enables people to separate and combine the images preserved by representation.

The estimative faculty detects the intentions of animate things and the effects of inanimate ones, thus enabling people to discover their significance for their welfare. On the first occurrence of such an insight, such as the sheep's recognition that the skulking wolf means it no good, the response is an instinctive one in which the estimative sense operates on the images of common sense or representation to abstract the intention. Later it also seems to work by association, for after sense memory has stored up past correlations of a certain sort of visual data, say, with subsequent pain, the occurrence of such a visual datum will trigger the associated image of pain in the imagination and the estimative sense will then note the evil of that object.

Avicenna and the Scholastics note that intentions are not the objects of any of the five external senses, yet they insist, without explaining how it is possible, that intentions can be grasped only by attending to the images of common sense or representation. These intentions are particulars, but because they are nonsensible, apprehending them marks a yet higher degree of abstraction—an immaterial thing is abstracted from a material thing in which it exists only accidentally. Avicenna also points out that noncognitive judgment is involved in this process and that this is the supreme judging faculty in the animal. Furthermore, it is the function of this faculty to guide the two motive faculties. The function of the recollective or retentive faculty is to retain the judgments or insights of the estimative faculty, just as the representative retains the images of sensible things.

The apprehension of particulars occurs only through bodily organs, for a spatial thing can be present only to another spatial thing. This is so even in the case of the faculties of imagination, representation, and estimation, despite the fact that they operate in the physical absence of the object. To demonstrate this point, imagine two squares of exactly the same size that are separated from each other, then ask yourself how

it is possible for there to be two separate squares. Because the difference cannot be accounted for as a difference of form, it must be the consequence of the same form being manifested in two different places. That is, there must be two images impressed on different areas of the middle ventricle of the brain, which is the physical seat of the psychic faculty of imagination. The point is a general one: The determinate features of imagery can be accounted for only if the form perceived by the faculty is at the same time a form manifested in matter. This line of reasoning, which does not appear in Aristotle, influenced the Scholastics and reappears quite explicitly in the works of the French philosopher René Descartes.

Reason

Reason is divided into practical and theoretic faculties. With the help of the theoretic faculty, the practical faculty elaborates basic moral principles such as "Tyranny is wrong," "Lying is wrong"; it considers purposes, deliberates, initiates behavior, and produces in the faculty of appetite such responses as shame and laughter.

The theoretic faculty can occur in various degrees. It may be dormant; it may develop to the point where it possesses the primary principles of thought, such as "The whole is greater than its part" and "Things equal to a third are equal to one another"; or it may perfect its potentiality by grasping the secondary principles as well and thus be in a position to think without the further acquisition of any other principles. These are the various degrees of the Potential Intellect. Finally, the intellect may actually think, exercising the capacities it has perfected at the prior stage. It is then called the Actual or Acquired Intellect. This last stage is not attained unless the Potential Intellect is activated by the Agent Intellect, the Tenth Intelligence.

In order to achieve its end of contemplating pure forms, theoretic reason must complete the process of abstracting forms from matter, a process already initiated by the external and internal senses. That is, it must turn to the imagination, to the images of particular objects, and, through the agency of the Agent Intellect, grasp the forms appearing there free of all the materially imposed determinations they still exhibit. This process of abstraction can be bypassed only by highly gifted individuals, such as the prophets, whose intellects are illuminated directly by the Agent Intellect, or the Giver of Forms. Reason recognizes that these pure forms could be manifested in many particular cases, so it regards them as universals; however, it also sees that these forms need not have been manifested at all, and therefore that they are, in themselves, neither particular nor universal.

Though he departs from Aristotle in holding that a form is not restricted to its occurrence in matter, Avicenna is not quite a Platonic realist, for he does not admit that a form can exist or subsist by itself. He introduces the famous doctrine of *ante rem*, *in rebus*, and *post rem*, a doctrine accepted later by Saint Thomas Aquinas and other philosophers as the solution to the problem of universals. The essences are *ante rem* insofar as they are the exemplars in the Giver of Forms, *in rebus* insofar as they are manifested in sensible objects, and *post rem* insofar as they are grasped free of material considerations by the human intellect.

Immateriality and the Soul

Knowledge involves the discovery of necessary relations between universals, relations noted directly by intuition, which is a kind of illumination, or established indirectly by syllogistic reasoning. Although his model seems to be that of a body of knowledge derived by reason alone from universals and self-evident truths, Avicenna does point out that much knowledge about the world, though certain, is based partly on experience. Having noted the constant conjunction between things such as humankind and rationality and day and being light, and constant disjunction such as its not being both day and night, one must conclude that the noted constancy reveals a necessary conjunction or disjunction. Thus one must acknowledge necessary truths about the world, truths such as "Humankind is rational," "If it is day, then it is light," and "Either it is day or it is night." However, apart from this sort of assistance and the assistance of the internal senses as providers of data, the intellect does not need the assistance of the body. It does not operate through a physical organ, for it can know itself and is not disrupted by strong stimuli, as

the physical organ of sight is disrupted by a dazzling light. Furthermore, as is required by a faculty that apprehends pure forms, it is an immaterial faculty.

In defending his view that the soul is an immaterial substance, Avicenna invokes his famous "man in the void" argument. Suppose, he says, that a man is created in a void and suppose that his feet, hands, and other physical parts are separated from him in such a way that he has no sensation of them. Under these circumstances, he would have no experience of an external world and no experience of his body; nevertheless, he would still be conscious of himself. Consequently, the self he is conscious of must be an immaterial thing. Furthermore, since he can think of himself without thinking that he has a body, having a body is not essential to being a self and therefore is excluded from the nature of the self. That is to say, the immaterial self exists in its own right independently of other things and is therefore a substance. If it is associated with a body, the association is accidental. The soul is an entelechy because it governs and guides the body, but it is no more the form of the body than the pilot is the form of the ship.

This soul did not exist before the existence of its body, for if there were a number of preexisting souls, they would have to differ from one another; to do so is impossible because they would not differ in form nor would they be individuated by matter. If there were one preexisting soul, it would have to be shared by all men—an absurd idea. Therefore, the individual soul is created when there is a body suitable for it. By binding itself closely to its body, the soul is influenced permanently by the peculiar nature of the body and the particular events that befall it. Because the soul is a simple substance, it survives the death of the body, carrying over into the hereafter the individuality it has acquired.

In these various respects, Avicenna departed from the Aristotelian view of the soul in order to satisfy the requirements of theology. Therefore, the later Jewish and Christian philosophers welcomed his guidance when they encountered Aristotle. Avicenna's position and arguments and those of Descartes are similar; the influence of the "man in the void" argument is particularly evident in Descartes's work.

The Active Intellect and the Human Intellect

To complete the survey of Avicenna's psychology, one must consider the relationship between the human intellect and the Active Intellect. The human intellect does not achieve its highest status, that of apprehending universals and the relations between them, unless it is activated by the Tenth Intelligence, which is the Active Intellect, or Giver of Forms. Avicenna describes the Active Intellect as radiating a power that illuminates the potentially intelligible but actually sensible forms of imagination, thereby making them intelligible and present to a suitably prepared mind. In this way, Potential Intellect becomes an Actual or Acquired Intellect. In this process, images are important for two reasons: first, one must abstract the form from an image of the object if one is to grasp the form as the form of an object, and second, one must compare and contrast images in order to raise one's intellect to a level where the divine illumination is able to enlighten it. It is to be noted that the Active Intellect, not the human intellect, abstracts the intelligible form from the image in the imagination. One's dependence on the Giver of Forms is evinced further by the fact that because one has no intellectual memory, one must reestablish contact with it every time one thinks. Later, Saint Thomas Aquinas and others objected to Avicenna's Active Intellect and insisted on fragmenting it into individual Active Intellects occurring as faculties of individual human souls, thus making each person responsible for the activating of Potential Intellect. They also feared, though Avicenna himself did not, that as long as people all shared the same Active Intellect, personal immortality was jeopardized. Also, they introduced intellectual memory and insisted that when intellection occurs, the knower and the known become one.

Because the human intellect is able to contact the Giver of Forms more easily on subsequent occasions, it is able to perfect itself, approaching the ideal of constant contemplation of the forms. By emulating the Giver of Forms, which contains all intelligible forms, the soul prepares itself to enjoy a higher and worthier status when it leaves the body. Insofar as it is the emulated intelligence, the Giver of Forms is a final and formal cause as well as an agent, and insofar as it functions in these ways, it brings the human soul into the sequence of efficient, formal, and final causes that stems from and culminates in God.

Besides influencing later Jewish and Christian philosophers in the various ways already indicated, Avicenna had a great influence on the work of Averroës, another great Islamic philosopher. Averroës presents a critical but sympathetic evaluation of Avicenna.

Leonard Miller

Additional Reading

Afnan, Soheil M. *Avicenna: His Life and Works*. London: George Allen & Unwin, 1958. The author stresses the impact of Avicenna's philosophy upon the thinkers of the Arabic-speaking world.

Arberry, Arthur J. *Avicenna on Theology*. London: John Murray, 1951. This important brief work contains Avicenna's own autobiography and its continuation by his disciple and companion, Abu 'Ubaid al-Juzjani, as well as Arberry's discussion of Avicenna's defense of monotheism and the immortality of the soul.

Avicenna. *The Life of Ibn Sina: A Critical Edition*. Translated by William E. Gohlman. Albany: State University of New York Press, 1974. Contains an annotated edition of Avicenna's autobiography, the contemporary account of his life by al-Juzjani, and a critical examination of the bibliography about Avicenna.

Brown, H. V. B. "Avicenna and the Christian Philosophers in Baghdad." In *Islamic Philosophy and the Classical Tradition: Essays to Richard Walzer*, edited by S. M. Stern, Albert Hourani, and Vivian Brown. Columbia: University of South Carolina Press, 1973. A clear presentation of Avicenna's philosophical differences with both Aristotle and the Peripatetic thinkers of the Baghdad school, despite his fundamental adherence to the rationalism of Aristotelian traditions.

Copleston, Frederick. *A History of Philosophy*. Vol. 2. Westminster, Md.: Newman Press, 1955. Copleston clarifies not only the contributions of Arab philosophy to European medieval thought but also the diversity within this Islamic renaissance. Particular attention is focused upon Avicenna and Averroës.

Corbin, Henry. *History of Islamic Philosophy*. Translated by Liadain Sherrard. London:

Kegan Paul, 1993. A detailed discussion of Islamic philosophy with a section on Avicenna.

Davidson, Herbert A. *Proofs for Eternity and the Existence of God in Medieval Islamic and Jewish Philosophy*. Oxford: Oxford University Press, 1987. Davidson provides discussions of proofs of the existence of God in the philosophical writings of these two faiths, including Avicenna's views.

Fakhry, Majid. *A History of Islamic Philosophy*. 1970. 2d ed. New York: Columbia University Press, 1983. Excellent presentation of Islamic philosophy with a long chapter on Avicenna.

Goodman, L. E. *Avicenna*. London: Routledge, 1992. A thorough account of Avicenna's philosophy, sensitive to both his historical context and his contemporary relevance.

Leaman, Oliver. *An Introduction to Medieval Islamic Philosophy*. Cambridge, London: Cambridge University Press, 1985. Discussion, for beginners, of the issues in Islamic philosophy, including Avicenna.

Maurer, Armand A. *Medieval Philosophy*. New York: Random House, 1962. Reprint. Toronto: Pontifical Institute of Mediaeval Studies, 1982. Maurer presents a summary of Avicenna's arguments on being, necessity, and essence; on proofs for the existence of God; on the doctrine of creation; and on humankind's intuitive knowledge of the soul. Although an Aristotelian, Avicenna, according to Maurer, also had links with the Neoplatonists and the later followers of Saint Augustine.

Nasr, S. H., and Oliver Leaman. *History of Islamic Philosophy*. Parts 1, 2. London: Routledge, 1996. Thorough treatment of Islamic philosophy with a chapter on Avicenna.

Ormsby, Eric L., *Theodicy in Islamic Thought*. Princeton, N.J.: Princeton University Press, 1984. Discussion of Al-Ghazzali's *Best of All Possible Worlds* with multiple references to Avicenna.

Sharif, M. M., ed. *A History of Muslim Philosophy*. Vols. 1, 2. Wiesbaden, West Germany: Otto Harrassowitz, 1966. Multiauthored discussion of Islamic philosophy in connection with other disciplines.

John D. Windhausen, updated by Keith E. Yandell

A. J. Ayer

Ayer introduced the Austrian philosophy of logical positivism to the English-speaking world and continued the British empiricist and skeptical tradition of John Locke, George Berkeley, and David Hume. His contributions were primarily to the field of epistemology.

Principal philosophical works: *Language, Truth, and Logic*, 1936, 2d ed. 1946; "Verification and Experience," 1937; *The Foundations of Empirical Knowledge*, 1940; *Philosophical Essays*, 1954; *The Problem of Knowledge*, 1956; *The Concept of a Person and Other Essays*, 1963; *The Origins of Pragmatism*, 1968; *Metaphysics and Common-Sense*, 1969; *Russell and Moore: The Analytical Heritage*, 1971; *Possibility and Evidence*, 1972; *Bertrand Russell*, 1972; *The Central Questions of Philosophy*, 1973; *Part of My Life*, 1977; *Hume*, 1980; *Philosophy in the Twentieth Century*, 1982; *More of My Life*, 1984.

Born: October 29, 1910; London, England
Died: June 27, 1989; London, England

Early Life

Alfred Jules Ayer's father came from the French area of Switzerland and his mother from Belgium, although she was raised in England. The couple was residing in London when their only child was born in 1910. Ayer spent much of his early life in solitude, enjoying stamp collecting and reading. By age seven, he was in a boarding school, and when he was almost thirteen, he received a scholarship to Eton. There he first read philosophy, including works by contemporary thinkers Bertrand Russell and G. E. Moore, and though confirmed in the Church of England, he became a lifelong "militant" atheist. At the suggestion of his maternal grandfather, whom Ayer identified as the greatest influence on his life, in 1929 he entered Oxford University with the intention of becoming a barrister.

In Christ Church College at Oxford, he studied ancient history and philosophy. His principal tutor was Gilbert Ryle, who would later gain recognition and wide influence as the author of *The Concept of Mind* (1949). Isaiah Berlin, philosopher of political theory and intellectual history, became a lasting friend of Ayer when the two met through the Jowett Society, the undergraduate philosophical group of which Ayer was secretary.

After completing three years of study, Ayer, at Ryle's recommendation and despite a desire to work with Ludwig Wittgenstein at Cambridge, spent an academic year (1932-1933) in Vienna, where he participated in the weekly meetings of a group of Austrian philosophers, physicists, and mathematicians who developed the perspective of logical positivism and called themselves the Vienna Circle. They sought to rid philosophy of its metaphysical speculation and to unite the natural sciences. Their leader was Moritz Schlick, professor of philosophy at the University of Vienna, whose lectures Ayer attended. The observations made in the circle provided the basis for Ayer's *Language, Truth, and Logic*, which would introduce Ayer to the world of professional philosophy.

Life's Work

Language, Truth, and Logic was the first systematic introduction of logical positivism for the English reader and became Ayer's best-known and most widely read work. Ayer held that logical positivism was a natural extension of the British empirical tradition of John Locke, George Berkeley, and David Hume and logically followed from the work of Bertrand Russell and Ludwig Wittgenstein, particularly the latter's "Logisch-philosophische Abhandlung" (1921; best known by the bilingual German and English edition title of

Tractatus Logico-Philosophicus, 1922, 1961).

Logical positivism rested on the premise that all propositions could be sorted into two classes: The first contained propositions that were either true by form (tautologies from mathematics and logic or definitional claims such as "All unmarried men are bachelors") or verifiable (testable) by some empirical means. The second category contained all remaining propositions. These were deemed to be neither true nor false but rather nonsensical. That is, the latter class of propositions were not merely untrue claims about the world—they really were not claims at all, for they could not meet the most fundamental test of any proposition, which is that a proposition must make a meaningful claim. The meaningfulness of a claim was to be assessed by the principle of verification. It was this principle that allowed for the sorting of propositions into their appropriate and respective category or class.

The principle of verification asserted that a claim was "factually significant" if one knew what observation or evidence could lead to demonstrating its truth or falsity. One was not required to be able to actually carry out the observations (for example, at the time of Ayer's writing, a statement such as "The surface of Mars is made of volcanic rock" could not be directly verified); however, one needed to be able "in principle" to specify that the observations could be made. No observations even in principle, however, could be given for or against metaphysical claims such as "God is good" and "The beautiful is sublime." Hence, they were dismissed as nonsensical.

Logical positivism promised to move philosophy beyond the realm of endless distinctions and arguments by assigning it the task of analyzing whether a proposition was meaningful. Thus, the proper method of philosophy was logical analysis; clarification and critical analysis was its goal. The task of determining whether the propositions were true or false could be left to science. Philosophy would be rid of the endless speculative metaphysical discussions that formed and defined much of its history. Moreover, philosophy could serve to unify the sciences and become their foundation. Philosophy would become the logic of science.

One set of propositions remained problematic, however. These were moral or ethical claims. Some logical positivists had addressed them with the doctrine of utilitarianism, but Ayer's solution was an emotive theory of value. He regarded ethical claims not as propositions (assertions of fact) but rather as expressions of emotion. They reflected the feelings or attitude of the speaker. Ayer applied similar reasoning to aesthetic values, as well as claims about the existence of God. Theological propositions contained no factual content; they were not false, merely nonsensical. They failed the principle of verification, which Ayer once described as an "axe."

A. J. Ayer. *(AP/Wide World Photos)*

Other traditional problems in philosophy were resolved or disappeared. Logical positivism showed the way to resolution of the problem of induction, the grounds of rationality, the proper form of reductionism, the nature of truth and necessary truths, the relation of mind to matter, and the nature of self and sense-experience. Logical positivism appeared to overthrow and discard much of what had passed as the great philosophy of Western civilization (though much of it, Ayer said, dealt with analysis rather than substantive claims). It was a doctrine especially suited to an age of scientific aspiration and advancement.

In 1946, Ayer modified some aspects of his original claims. He tried to give a more precise meaning to "empirically verifiable," the notion that was at the heart of the principle of verification. He also tried to address the criticism that the principle was neither a tautology nor a proposition testable by observation, and therefore, the dichotomous classification of propositions by logical positivism failed. Though Ayer would move beyond the specific claims made in *Language, Truth, and Logic*, the commitment to empiricism and logical analysis found in this work would permeate all his subsequent philosophical views.

Ayer held a research lectureship (1932-1935) at Oxford when he wrote *Language, Truth, and Logic* and later a research studentship (1935-1940). The approach of World War II led to a commission as a military intelligence officer in the Welsh Guard. He served for a while in New York City, where in his spare time, writing under a pseudonym, he was the film critic of *The Nation*, reflecting a passion for the cinema he had developed at Oxford. He later served in West Africa and France. After the war, Ayer returned briefly to Oxford as Dean of Wadham College before being appointed Grote Professor of Philosophy and Logic at London University (1946-1959). He returned to Oxford as Wykeham Professor of Logic (1959-1978) and was knighted in 1970.

Ayer's subsequent work spans more than a dozen volumes, and though it includes some works in the history of psychology, the bulk of his interests concentrate on epistemology and skepticism, that is, what is the basis for what people claim to know. No easy summary can be

offered except to say that he developed the line of analysis from the British empiricists (Locke, Berkeley, and Hume) and strongly followed in the tradition of Russell. Within this general framework, he continued to modify his views and explore their implications.

The 1940's marked the publication of Ayer's phenomenalistic views (contrasted with his later constructivistic position) in which he introduced the concept of a sense-data language to deal with the problem of the relationship between physical objects and people's perception of them. It was this work that J. L. Austin of the ordinary language approach to philosophy criticized in his posthumous lecture notes published as *Sense and Sensibilia* (1962).

Ayer regarded *The Problem of Knowledge* as his best work. He addressed the foundation of inductive leaps from sense-data to physical objects, from another's behavior to their mind, and from the present to the past. He sided with the view of skepticism and concluded that induction is "primitive" and no rational basis can be given for it, though he rejected the idea that this undermined the very possibility of knowledge. In this regard, Ayer's position may be viewed as a creative extension of Humean empiricist and skeptical ideas into mid-twentieth century philosophy.

The last period in Ayer's philosophical development was his constructionism, which also may be traced to Hume and which contrasts with his early phenomenalism. Through constructionism, Ayer sought to explain how people's perception of the physical world may be built up from the coherence of neutral sense-qualities, or quale, such as greenness and loudness.

In the latter decades of his life, Ayer held the leading position among British philosophers. His frequent contributions to British Broadcasting Corporation (BBC) broadcasts made him a public figure, and he was invited to lecture widely in the United States, Europe, and the Far East. He gave the William James Lectures at Harvard in 1970 and later in the same year the John Dewey Lectures at Columbia. Though the policy at Oxford required him to retire upon reaching age sixty-seven, Ayer remained active until the very end of his life. Shortly before his death, he offered for general readership a small volume on the meaning of life. It reflected his long-standing atheism, which was not modified by a near-death experience. When death did overtake him, Ayer had nearly completed his responses to a set of papers prepared for a volume on his work in the Library of Living Philosophers series and was scheduled to return to the United States for a visiting term at Bard College.

Influence

Ayer is best remembered as leaving a fine exposition of other's ideas, though he did introduce his own qualifications. His book, *Language, Truth, and Logic* remains the most accessible source for the ideas advanced by logical positivism, which had an enormous influence in philosophy until the late 1940's and a continuing influence in the social sciences until the 1960's. Beyond its historical significance, the work is recognized as an excellent model of philosophical writing. It displayed a simple elegance in composition and clarity.

The ultimate value of Ayer's contributions are easily overshadowed by his those of his contemporaries Ludwig Wittgenstein and Sir Karl Popper, whose work receives continued attention beyond the limits of academic philosophy. Ayer's influence was greater in Britain; his ideas never became the reason for Americans or others to venture to England as had the ideas of Wittgenstein and other members of the ordinary language movement. The later work of Ayer remains largely the province of professional philosophers and did not reach as large an audience as did *Language, Truth, and Logic*. Late in life, when asked to reflect on twentieth century philosophy, Ayer placed Russell and Wittgenstein in the "premier" division of influence, and himself, Ryle, and W. V. O. Quine in the "first division," categories he borrowed from Scottish football.

Terry J. Knapp

Language, Truth, and Logic

Type of philosophy: Epistemology, philosophy of language
First published: 1936
Principal ideas advanced:

◇ Metaphysics is impossible because metaphysical statements are meaningless.
◇ A sentence is factually significant if and only if there is a method of verification that an observer can adopt to determine the truth or falsity of the sentence; when experience cannot settle an issue, the issue has no factual meaning.
◇ The propositions of philosophy are not factual but linguistic; they are not factual reports, but either definitions of words in use or expressions of the logical implications of such definitions.
◇ Value statements and statements declaring duties are neither true nor false; they express the feelings of the speaker.

In *Language, Truth, and Logic*, Sir A. J. Ayer presents a modified version of logical positivism that he prefers to call "logical empiricism." However, the doctrines, particularly their implications for philosophy, are largely those of logical positivism, and the work serves to bring these together succinctly and vigorously. Therefore, the book has had great importance as a positivistic document and as a center of controversy about positivistic tenets. In it, Ayer offers to solve the problems of reality, perception, induction, knowledge, meaning, truth, value, and other minds. He presents no great new idea; rather, he has modified and brought into logical consistency solutions proposed by others. In the introduction to the 1946 second edition, Ayer provided further explication and modified a few beliefs, but essentially his position remained unchanged.

The Verification Principle

Ayer attacks metaphysics, saying that he will deduce the fruitlessness of attempting knowledge that transcends the limits of experience from the "rule which determines the literal significance of language." The sentences of metaphysics, failing to meet this rule, are meaningless.

Ayer finds the criterion of meaning in the verification principle. "We say that a sentence is factually significant to any given person, if, and only if, he knows how to verify the proposition which it purports to express—that is, if he knows what observations would lead him, under certain conditions, to accept the proposition as being true, or reject it as being false." Another possible kind of meaningful sentence is the tautology. However, any sentence that is neither a tautology nor a verifiable proposition (by this criterion) is a mere pseudoproposition, a meaningless sentence.

Certain provisions qualify this tenet. Ayer distinguished practical verifiability and verifiability in principle. Some sentences are not practically verifiable because of inconvenience or the present state of science and culture. If one knows what observations would decide such a matter if one were in a position to make them, the proposition is verifiable in principle. A further distinction is that between "strong" verifiability and "weak" verifiability. According to the "strong" theory, advanced by the Vienna Circle of logical positivists, a sentence is meaningful only if it is conclusively verifiable empirically; according to the "weak" theory, it is meaningful if experience may render it probable. Ayer chooses the "weak" theory on the basis that because no empirical demonstration is ever 100 percent conclusive, the "strong" theory leaves no empirical statement meaningful. By using the "weak" theory, Ayer believes he allows general propositions of science and propositions about the past, which previous positivistic writers found problematic, to have meaning. The proposed principle rules out such assertions as the statement that the world of sense is unreal and such questions as whether reality is one substance or many. No experience could decide these issues, so they have no literal significance. Metaphysicians have usually been misled by the grammar of language so that they posit an entity ("substance," "Being") where grammar requires a noun as the subject of a sentence, even though thought may exert no such requirement.

By the abandonment of metaphysics, the philosopher is freed from the function of constructing a deductive system of the universe from first principles, for first principles cannot come from experience, whose propositions are only hypotheses and never certain. However, if they are taken a priori, they are only tautologies, which cannot apply to the universe as factual knowledge.

The problem of induction can be set aside as unreal. It is the attempt to prove that certain em-

pirical generalizations derived from past experience will hold good also in the future. It must have either an a priori or an empirical solution. However, in the first case, it is improper to apply tautologies to experience, for they cannot apply to matters of fact; and in the second, one simply assumes what one set out to prove. Because Ayer can conceive no test that would solve the "problem" through experience, he concludes that it is not a genuine problem. In actuality, people place their faith in such scientific generalizations as enable them to predict future experience and thus control the environment; there is no general logical problem about this practice.

Definitions

A common mistake is to assert that without a satisfactory analysis of perception, one is not entitled to believe in the existence of material things. Rather, the right to believe in their existence comes simply from the fact that one has certain sensations, for to say the thing exists is equivalent to saying the sensations are obtainable. The business of philosophers is to give a correct definition of material things in terms of sensations. They are not concerned with the properties of things in the world but only with how people speak of them. The propositions of philosophy are not factual, but linguistic in character: "They do not describe the behavior of physical, or even mental, objects; they express definitions, or the formal consequences of definitions." Philosophy is a department of logic. It is independent of any empirical, not to say metaphysical, assumptions. Often propositions that are really linguistic are so expressed as to appear to be factual. "A material thing cannot be in two places at once" is actually linguistic, recording "the fact that, as the result of certain verbal conventions, the proposition that two sense-contents occur in the same visual or tactual sense-field is incompatible with the proposition that they belong to the same material thing." The question "What is the nature of X?" asks for a definition, which is always a linguistic statement.

Philosophical analysis essentially provides definitions. However, such definitions are not the most frequently occurring kind, that is, *explicit*, or synonymous, definitions giving an alternative symbol or symbolic expression for the term to be defined. Rather, they are *definitions in use*, which are made by showing how a sentence in which the definiendum (expression that is being defined) occurs can be translated into equivalent sentences that do not contain the definiendum or any of its synonyms. An example taken from English philosopher Bertrand Russell defines "author" in the sentence, "The author of *Waverley* was [Sir Walter] Scott," by providing the equivalent, "One person, and one person only, wrote *Waverley*, and that person was [Sir Walter] Scott." Such definitions clarify sentences where no synonym for the definiendum exists and where available synonyms are unclear in the same fashion as the symbol needing clarification. A complete philosophical clarification of a language would first enumerate the types of sentences significant in that language, then display the relations of equivalence that hold between sentences of various types. Such a set of definitions would reveal the structure of the language examined, and any truly philosophical theory would hence apply to a given language.

Some symbols denote simple sense-contents and others logical constructions, the latter making it possible to state complicated propositions about the elements of the logical constructions in a relatively simple form. However, logical constructions are not inherently fictions. Rather, material things are among such logical constructions. The definition in use will restate the definiendum, naming a material thing by translating it into symbols that refer to sense-contents that are elements of the material thing. In other words, roughly, to say something about a table is always to say something about sense-contents. The problem of the "reduction" of material things into sense-contents, long a chief part of the problem of perception, is a linguistic problem readily solved by providing definitions in use. To accomplish this reduction, Ayer stipulates that two sense-contents *resemble* each other *directly* when there is either no difference, or only an infinitesimal difference, between them and *indirectly* when they are linked by a series of direct resemblances amounting to an appreciable difference. He stipulates further that two sense-contents are *directly continuous* when within successive sense-fields there is no difference, or only an infinitesimal difference, between them, with respect to the

position of each in its own sense-field and *indirectly continuous* when related by an actual, or possible, series of direct continuities. Any two of one's sense-contents, then, are elements of the same material thing when they are related to each other by direct or indirect resemblance and by direct or indirect continuity.

Ayer assumes that the object of a theory of truth is to show how propositions are validated. Like all questions of similar pattern, the question "What is truth?" calls for a definition. Consequently, no factual theory is needed to answer it. The real question discussed most of the time in "theories of truth" is "What makes a proposition true or false?"

Analytic and Synthetic Propositions

Ayer adopts the distinction between analytic and synthetic propositions. Each has its own validation. "A proposition is analytic when its validity depends solely on the definitions of the symbols it contains, and synthetic when its validity is determined by the facts of experience." While "Either some ants are parasitic or none are," an analytic proposition, is undubitably and necessarily true, it provides no actual information about ants. As a tautology, it has no factual content and serves only to help us understand matters of language. The valid propositions of logic are true by tautology and are useful and surprising in revealing hidden implications in our sentences. They can help us gain empirical knowledge, but it is not the tautologies that render empirical knowledge valid. Whether a geometry actually can be applied to physical space is an empirical question that falls outside the scope of the geometry itself. There is therefore no paradox about the applicability of the analytic propositions of logic and mathematics to the world.

Synthetic propositions, Ayer affirms, are validated by experience. Experience is given in the form of sensations. Sensations are neither true nor false; they simply occur. Propositions about them are not logically determined by them in one way or another; hence, while these are perhaps largely dependable, they may be doubted. Similarly, they may be confirmed by additional experience. In other words, "Empirical propositions are one and all hypotheses." In fact, whenever a verification is carried out, it is applied to an entire system of hypotheses—a principal one, together with supplementary hypotheses that often are adjusted by the verification rather than by the principal hypothesis. Therefore, the "facts of experience" can never *per se* oblige one to abandon a particular hypothesis because one may ever continue without contradiction to explain invalidating instances in various ways while retaining the principal hypothesis. One must, of course, retain a willingness to abandon it under certain circumstances because of experience, or else one makes of it not a hypothesis but a definition. It must be granted that one is not always rational in arriving at belief—that is, one does not always employ a self-consistent accredited procedure in the formation of one's beliefs. That a hypothesis increases in probability is equivalent to saying that observation increases the degree of confidence with which it is rational to entertain the hypothesis.

The exposition of synthetic propositions, every one of which is a rule for the anticipation of future experience, constitutes Ayer's validation of the verification principle, for it comes to just what the verification principle states, that the literal significance of an empirical proposition is the anticipated sense-contents entailed in it.

Statements of Value and Religion

To account consistently for statements of value with empirical principles, Ayer holds that descriptive ethical sentences are empirical statements and that normative ethical sentences are "absolute" or "intrinsic," not empirically calculable, and indefinable in factual terms. The normative symbols in a sentence name no concepts, add nothing to the factual content. Thus, normative sentences are not capable of being true or false. They simply express certain feelings of the speaker. They are not even *assertions* that the speaker has a certain feeling, for such assertions would be empirical and subject to doubt. Thus the question of their having any validity at all is removed.

How, then, can one dispute about value? Ayer maintains that actually one never disputes about questions of value but only about questions of fact. The pattern usual in such a dispute is to exhibit to one's opponent what one believes to be the facts, assuming a common framework of value statements, and attempting to bring the opponent to one's way of seeing the facts.

As to religious knowledge, one cannot appeal to tautologies for factual truth about God, for these are mere stipulations of one's own. Nor can one have empirical propositions about God, for one can conceive of no experience that would bring one different sense-contents if God exists than if he does not. Hence, the notion is metaphysical and meaningless.

The Self and Knowledge of the World

Ayer applies a complete phenomenalism to the traditional problems of the self and knowledge of the world. He denies that the given needs a logical rather than sensory justification. Further, he rejects the pattern of subject-act-object as an account of perception. He defines a sense-content not as the object but as a part of sense-experience, so that the existence of a sense-content always entails the existence of a sense-experience. Hence, the question of whether sense-contents are mental or physical is inapplicable. Such a distinction can apply only to the logical constructions that are derived from them. The difference between mental and physical objects lies in differences between the sense-contents, or in the different relations of sense-contents that constitute objects.

The self may be explained in similar terms. "It is, in fact, a logical construction out of the sense-experiences which constitute the actual and possible sense-history of a self." To ask its nature is to ask what relationship obtains between sense-experiences for them to belong to the sense-history of the same self. Rather than retain the metaphysical notion of a substantive ego, one can identify personal identity simply in terms of bodily identity, and that in turn is to be defined in terms of the resemblance and continuity of sense-contents. To say anything about the self is always to say something about sense-contents. One knows other selves empirically, just as one knows physical things and one's own self empirically.

Ayer urges the unity of philosophy with the sciences. Rather than actually validating scientific theory, the philosopher's function is to elucidate the symbols occurring in it. It is essential to the task that the philosopher understand science. Philosophy must develop into the logic of science.

Observation-Statements

As well as providing further exposition, Ayer's introduction to the second edition contains some modifications of doctrine that deserve notice. In the interim between editions, he came to accept a belief of the logical positivists that he opposed in the first edition, that some empirical statements may be considered conclusively verified. These are "basic statements," referring to the sense-content of a single experience, and their conclusive verification is the immediate occurrence of the experience to which they refer. As long as these merely record what is experienced and say nothing else, they cannot be factually mistaken, for they make no claim that any further fact could confute. However, this change makes little difference to the chief doctrine, Ayer maintains, for the vast majority of propositions are not of this sort.

Ayer introduces the term "observation-statement," to designate any statement "which records an actual or possible observation." To remove the objection that, as originally stated, the principle allows any indicative statement whatever to have significance, Ayer amends its expression to say that the principle of verification requires of a literally meaningful, nonanalytic statement that it should be either directly or indirectly verifiable. For it to be directly verifiable, it must be an observation-statement, or it must entail at least one other observation-statement not entailed by the other observation statements alone. To be indirectly verifiable, first, in conjunction with certain other premises, a statement must entail one or more directly verifiable statements not deducible from the other premises alone and, second, the other premises must include no statement that is not either analytic, or directly verifiable, or indirectly verifiable independently.

Ayer gives up the position that a priori propositions are linguistic rules, for they can properly be said to be both true and necessary, while linguistic rules cannot be called true and are arbitrary. Descriptive linguistic statements of contingent empirical fact of language usage are, however, the basis for statements of logical relationships—which are necessary truths. Ayer admits doubts as to whether his account of the experiences of others is correct, yet says, "I am not convinced that it is not." He confesses error in

assuming that philosophical analysis consists mainly in providing "definitions in use." Such a result is the exception rather than the rule; and in fact, for statements about material things, such definition becomes impossible because "no finite set of observation-statements is ever equivalent to a statement about a material thing."

Finally, rather than classify philosophical statements alongside scientific statements, Ayer states that "it is incorrect to say that there are no philosophical propositions. For, whether they are true or false, the propositions that are expressed in such a book as this do fall into a special category . . . asserted or denied by philosophers." Lexicographers are concerned with the use of particular expressions; however philosophers are concerned with classes of expressions; and their statements, if true, are usually analytic.

John T. Goldthwait

Additional Reading

Austin, J. L. *Sense and Sensibilia*. New York: Oxford University Press, 1962. A widely read response from an ordinary language perspective to A. J. Ayer's early epistemological formulations. Austin dismissed Ayer's views as "weak" and "full of jokes."

Foster, John. *The Philosophical Arguments of Philosophers: Ayer*. London: Routledge & Kegan Paul, 1985. A systematic and detailed presentation of Ayer's philosophical views as contained in his major works. A high-level work, but probably the most authoritative secondary source on Ayer's views.

Griffiths, A. Phillips. *A. J. Ayer Memorial Essays*. Cambridge, England: Cambridge University, 1991. An excellent collection of commentaries on Ayer's contributions to philosophy by those who knew him personally. Includes a British Broadcasting Corporation interview with Ayer conducted during the last year of his life.

Hahan, Lewis, E., ed. *The Philosophy of A. J. Ayer*. Library of Living Philosophers series. La Salle, Ill.: Open Court, 1992. Ayer responds to twenty-one of the twenty-four papers addressing his work. Also contains Ayer's essay "My Mental Development" and a bibliography of his publications. The best survey of his life's work.

Hanfling, Oswald. *A. J. Ayer*. New York: Routledge, 1999. An excellent biographical introduction to the thoughts of the philosopher, clearly presented and requiring no special background. Bibliography.

_____. *A. J. Ayer: Analysing What We Mean.* London: Phoenix, 1997. An examination of Ayer's work and his contribution to philosophy.

MacDonald, G. F., ed. *Perception and Identity: Essays Presented to A. J. Ayer with His Replies to Them.* London: Macmillan, 1979. A set of essays honoring Ayer upon his retirement from Oxford, made more useful by the inclusion of his responses to each paper.

Magee, Bryan. *Modern British Philosophy.* New York: St. Martin's Press, 1971. Interviews with leading British philosophers including A. J. Ayer and his early mentor Gilbert Ryle. A sound and easily understood presentation of Ayer's views.

Priest, Stephen. *The British Empiricists: Hobbes to Ayer.* New York: Penguin Books, 1990. An excellent source for placing Ayer's work in the tradition from which it emerged.

Terry J. Knapp

Gaston Bachelard

Bachelard was a major figure in the "criticism of science" school, which argues that scientific activity involves merely observing and analyzing reality. Bachelard pointed out that reality, or the "real world," is constantly changing, and therefore attempts to approximate reality do not involve concrete knowledge of things.

Principal philosophical works: *Essai sur la connaissance approchée*, 1927; *Étude sur l'évolution d'un problème de physique: La Propagation thermique dans les solides*, 1927; *La Valeur inductive de la relativité*, 1929; *Le Pluralisme cohérent de la chimie moderne*, 1932; *L'Intuition de l'instant: Étude sur la "Siloë" de Gaston Roupnel*, 1932; *Les Intuitions atomistiques: Essai de classification*, 1932; *Le Nouvel esprit scientifique*, 1934 (*The New Scientific Spirit*, 1984); *La Dialectique de la durée*, 1936; *L'Expérience de l'espace dans la physique contemporaine*, 1937; *La Psychanalyse du feu*, 1938 (*The Psychoanalysis of Fire*, 1964); *La Formation de l'esprit scientifique: Contribution à une psychanalyse de la connaissance objective*, 1938; *Lautréamont*, 1939 (English translation, 1986); *La Philosophie du non: Essai d'une philosophie du nouvel esprit scientifique*, 1940 (*The Philosophy of No: A Philosophy of the New Scientific Mind*, 1968); *L'Eau et les rêves: Essai sur l'imagination de la matière*, 1942 (*Water and Dreams: An Essay on the Imagination of Matter*, 1983); *L'Air et les songes: Essai sur l'imagination du mouvement*, 1943 (*Air and Dreams: An Essay on the Imagination of Movement*, 1988); *La Terre et les rêveries de la volonté: Essai sur l'imagination des forces*, 1947; *La Terre et les rêveries du repos: Essai sur les images de l'intimité*, 1948; *Le Rationalisme appliqué*, 1949; *L'Activité rationaliste de la physique contemporaine*, 1951; *Le Matérialisme rationnel*, 1953; *La Poétique de l'espace*, 1957 (*The Poetics of Space*, 1964); *La Poétique de la rêverie*, 1960 (*The Poetics of Reverie*, 1969); *La Flamme d'une chandelle*, 1961 (*The Flame of a Candle*, 1988); *Le Droit de rêver*, 1970 (*The Right to Dream*, 1971); *Études*, 1970; *L'Engagement rationaliste*, 1972.

Born: June 27, 1884; Bar-sur-Aube, France
Died: October 16, 1962; Paris, France

Early Life

Gaston Bachelard was born in a small town about two hundred kilometers south of Paris. His father and his grandfather were shoemakers, and he grew up in modest circumstances. He finished secondary school in his hometown of Bar-sur-Aube, served briefly as a teaching assistant, and then became a clerk in the telegraph and post office in the town of Remiremont in 1903. Bachelard served in the military as a telegraphist and then returned to the postal service in 1907. He was assigned to the Gare de l'Est post office in Paris, where he began to pursue further education.

Intending to become an engineer, Bachelard took up the study of mathematics at Lycée Saint-Louis in Paris in 1909. He received his first di-

ploma, a *licence* in mathematics, at the age of twenty-one. In the summer of 1914, Bachelard married a schoolteacher from his region. One month later, World War I broke out. He again entered the military and fought in the trenches for more than three years, receiving the Croix de Guerre medal.

At the end of the war, Bachelard returned to Bar-sur-Aube. In his mid-thirties, married, and with a daughter, Bachelard gave up his ambition to become an engineer and took a job teaching physics and chemistry in his old secondary school. He also began to study philosophy. In 1920, Bachelard's wife died and he obtained his *licence* in philosophy. Two years later, he earned another degree, the *agrégation*. In 1927, after completing two dissertations, he received his doctorate from the Sorbonne. He continued to teach at the secondary school in Bar-sur-Aube for three more years, but he also taught classes at the University of Dijon. At the age of forty-four, Bachelard published his first book aside from his dissertations, *La Valeur inductive de la relativité* (the indicative value of relativity). The following year, he was appointed to the chair of philosophy at the University of Dijon.

Life's Work

Bachelard is an unusual figure in intellectual history because he was both a philosopher of science and a literary analyst. In his early work on the philosophy of science, Bachelard maintained that all scientific knowledge is approximation. When we know things, we attempt to approximate them by measuring them. He distinguished between the first approximation of our everyday senses and the second approximation of modern scientific knowledge. The second approximation does not involve seeing things but calculating them. The modern scientist has access only to the mathematical measurements of relations among things. Therefore, the objects of the scientist's knowledge are mathematical relations, rational constructions of the human mind. These constructions do involve something that is measured, though, so the philosopher of science must see knowledge in the connection between empirical experimentation and the systems of rational interpretation that thinkers impose on the results of experiments.

In *The New Scientific Spirit*, Bachelard looked closely at scientific epistemology, at how scientists know things, and at how thinking, particularly in images, influences scientific thought. This concern with images marked an important turn in Bachelard's thought because it would lead to his later interest in literature. He maintained that the post-Einstein era was the time of "the new scientific mind." The old scientific mind of the Newtonian era saw reality as something to be discovered through experiments. From the new scientific perspective, experimental investigations are directed by the questions that we ask, and experimental results make sense only because human reason imposes an order on them. One consequence of this back-and-forth movement between rationality and empiricism is that scientists must attempt to look critically at the human tendency to think in images and to inter-

pret information in terms of the experiences of the senses. A second consequence is that scientific knowledge is dialectical; it moves back and forth between thought and empirical results and moves forward by the opposition between the two.

The dialectical nature of science led it forward. Bachelard saw science progressing through breaks with older ways of thinking. The three major periods of scientific thought were the prescientific period, which included classical antiquity and the sixteenth through part of the eighteenth century; the scientific period, which extended from the late eighteenth to the beginning of the twentieth century; and the era of the new scientific mind, which began with Einstein's theory of relativity in 1905.

Because science progresses through breaks with older ways of thinking, Bachelard believed that the philosopher of science must be continually analyzing the commonly accepted images of the world that shape the thinking of scientists. The philosophy of science should, in other words, be a form of psychoanalysis. In *La Dialectique de la durée* (the dialectic of duration) and *L'Expérience de l'espace dans la physique contemporaine* (the experience of space in contemporary physics), Bachelard turned his attention to two of the fundamental frameworks for images of the world: time and space.

Toward the end of the 1930's, Bachelard reached his fullest development as a philosopher of science and gradually began to turn his attention to literature. In 1937, he was named a *chevalier* of France's Legion of Honor for his work. The following year, he published *La Formation de l'esprit scientifique: Contribution à une psychanalyse de la connaissance objective* (the formation of the scientific spirit: contribution to a psychoanalysis of objective knowledge) which drew loosely from the concepts and terminology of Freudian psychoanalysis. This work argued that scientific thinking and the teaching of science required an analytic examination of patterns of thought from the past that could block the quest for knowledge. In *The Philosophy of No: A Philosophy of the New Scientific Mind*, Bachelard argued that the scientific mind of the post-Einstein era required a new logic that would go beyond traditional Aristotelian logic. The dialectical logic that Bachelard suggested required con- tinually breaking down received notions in science in order to go beyond those notions.

Bachelard's movement toward literature first became evident in 1938 with the publication of *The Psychoanalysis of Fire*. The author's scientific interests provided the starting point for this book. He wanted to analyze the subconscious processes leading scientists to form images of fire that would affect scientific thought. Over the course of the book, though, he began to concern himself with literary images of fire. He identified "complexes," clusters of emotions and ideas that were expressed in fire images.

With *Lautréamont*, Bachelard produced his first book explicitly and exclusively concerned with literature. The subject of the book was the nineteenth century French poet Isidore Ducasse, better known by the pen name Le comte de Lautréamont. Lautréamont was an author much admired by the Surrealists for the violent, irrational, dreamlike images that ran through his principal work, *Le Chants de Maldoror* (1874; *The Lay of Maldoror*, 1922). Bachelard saw Lautréamont's writing as an example of a new literary mind, analogous to the new scientific mind in the effort to go beyond naïve realism in exploring ways of looking at the world.

Bachelard left the University of Dijon in 1940 when he was named to the chair of history and philosophy of science at the Sorbonne. He also became director of the Institute of the History of Science. Although he had achieved recognition for his work on science, he began to concentrate on the analysis of literary images. Over the next decade, he followed a path he had begun with *The Psychoanalysis of Fire*, examining the literary and psychological significance of water, air, and earth, the rest of the classic four elements of the prescientific worldview.

In 1942, he published *Water and Dreams: An Essay on the Imagination of Matter*, in which he looked at images of water. By the time he had written this book, his interest had definitively moved from how the imagination affects knowl-

Gaston Bachelard. *(Archive Photos)*

edge of the external world to the role of the external world in the reality of the human imagination. He followed his study of water images with a study of images of air in *L'Air et les songes: Essai sur l'imagination du mouvement* (*Air and Dreams: An Essay on the Imagination of Movement*). The French words *songes* and *rêves* can both be translated in English as "dreams," but *rêves* carries a sense of drifting as in "daydreaming" and *songes* implies intent and will in the act of dreaming. This is an important distinction because Bachelard saw the aerial imagination as having a dynamic, upward-moving quality. He treated the fourth element, earth, in his books *La Terre et les rêveries de la volonté: Essai sur l'imagination des forces* (earth and reveries of will: an essay on the imagination of forces) and *La Terre et les rêveries du repos: Essai sur les images de l'intimité* (earth and reveries of repose: an essay on images of intimacy). The dynamic and material images that Bachelard discussed in his books on the elements were clusters of ideas shared among humans, similar to psychoanalyst Carl Gustav Jung's archetypes, which were expressed in works of literature.

Bachelard returned to epistemology, the study of the nature and process of knowledge, with *La Rationalisme appliqué* (applied rationalism), *L'Activité rationaliste de la physique contemporaine* (the rationalist activity of contemporary physics), and *Le Matérialisme rationnel* (rational materialism). In these books, Bachelard looked once again at the issue that had concerned him before his turn to literature, the dialectic of rationalism and empiricism. After his retirement from the Sorbonne in 1954, though, he went back to literary phenomenology.

The Poetics of Space considered space as a psychological and literary phenomenon. For Bachelard, lived-in space differs from the objective space of geometry. The importance of the former lies in its qualities for the imagination. *The Poetics of Reverie* looked at how reverie, or daydreaming, takes shape through poetry. In this book, Bachelard drew once again on the work of Jung. The Swiss psychoanalyst's distinction between *animus* and *anima*, the masculine and feminine principles in the psychology of each individual, was particularly important for Bachelard's analysis of reverie. Poetry is produced from a human tendency to organize and form projects (the *animus*, or "masculine" tendency) and the simultaneous tendency to dream (the *anima*, or "feminine" tendency).

The last book published in Bachelard's lifetime was *The Flame of a Candle*, a meditation on the psychological nature of flame and light. In 1961, he was awarded the Grand Prix National des Lettres. The following year, Bachelard died. His death did not end publication of his works, however. Three books, *The Right to Dream*, *Études* (studies), and *L'Engagement rationaliste* (the rationalist engagement), were published posthumously. *The Right to Dream* was particularly notable because it expressed Bachelard's view that daydreaming is one of the highest functions of human life.

Influence

Bachelard's reputation has been limited chiefly to his native France, where he exercised a great influence on a number of key French thinkers. As one of the founders of the "criticism of science" school, he helped to develop the idea of science as a human activity, dependent on human perspectives, rather than as knowledge of a nonhuman world. This aspect of his work showed up in the late twentieth century in the writings of thinkers such as Michel Foucault.

Bachelard's psychological insights have sometimes been compared to those of Jung and Sigmund Freud. His claim that daydreaming is not a private matter but part of a collective experience was especially intriguing to many interested in human psychology. Bachelard's suggestion that the imagination in its free state reverts to images of the four traditional elements of earth, air, water, and fire was a stimulating contribution to psychoanalysis.

The defense of the free imagination in his works after the 1930's contributed to the appreciation for nonrational functions of the human mind. Dreaming and imagining, in his writing, were portrayed as essential activities with as much value as scientific enterprise.

Carl L. Bankston III

The Psychoanalysis of Fire

Type of philosophy: Aesthetics, epistemology, philosophical psychology
First published: La Psychanalyse du feu, 1938 (English translation, 1964)
Principal ideas advanced:

◇ Thinking in the modern scientific era continues to be influenced by images from older ways of thinking about the world.

◇ Scientific progress requires that the philosopher of science psychoanalyze the objects of knowledge in order to make conscious the unconscious imagery attached to them.

◇ Fire, as one of the four elements of the prescientific view of the world, is a major subject of prescientific, poetic imagery.

◇ The images that cluster around the idea of fire may be identified in psychoanalytic terms as complexes.

◇ By identifying the various complexes associated with fire, the psychoanalysis of fire not only removes obstacles to scientific thinking, but it also provides insight into poetic thinking.

Gaston Bachelard began his career as a philosopher with writings about the philosophy of science. In these early writings, he maintained that scientific thinking had entered a new phase following Albert Einstein's work on relativity. The scientific understanding of things had moved beyond seeing the world as composed of concrete objects or as things perceived by the senses. Instead, the new scientific mind had become a matter of comprehending the world as mathematical measurements. Knowledge was no longer knowledge of things or of the perception of things by the senses. Knowledge was a relationship between the empirical results of experimentation and the rational formulation of experiments and interpretation of results.

Because the world is known by the way the mind formulates and tests questions, Bachelard maintained, understanding processes of thought is critical to engaging in scientific activity. Even though science had entered a new era in the early twentieth century, older ways of thinking still influenced people and shaped the types of questions that people asked. In order to move beyond these older ways of thinking, the philosopher of science must be continually analyzing the commonly accepted images of the world that shape the thinking of scientists. This meant that philosophy of science should be a form of psychoanalysis.

Psychoanalysis

Psychoanalysis emerged in the late nineteenth and early twentieth centuries in the theories of Sigmund Freud. Freud maintained that neuroses, or emotional problems, were the result of psychological conflicts, especially conflicts of a sexual nature, that people had pushed out of their conscious minds into their subconscious minds. Dealing with these neuroses involved analyzing the thoughts of patients in order to bring the conflicts to consciousness. One of Freud's closest followers, Carl Gustav Jung, broke with Freud over the sexual nature of psychological conflicts. Jung maintained that the unconscious was more than the personal experiences of individuals. In

Jung's view, each individual's unconscious mind contains clusters of ideas in the form of images, known as archetypes, that are common to all people. Resolving unconscious conflicts was, then, a matter of analyzing an individual's particular arrangement of shared archetypes.

Bachelard shared with Jung the view that understanding thought meant analyzing the unconscious patterns of thinking that people held in common. Bachelard's initial intention in writing *The Psychoanalysis of Fire* was to analyze the unconscious prescientific patterns of thought about fire in order to free scientific thought from these prescientific patterns. This was important because fire was one of the four basic elements of the prescientific worldview, along with earth, air, and water, which became subjects of later books by Bachelard. In the process of writing the book, though, Bachelard became interested in the psychological and literary importance of the image of fire. In this turn toward the "irrational," Bachelard was influenced by the surrealists, artists and philosophers who believed that the mind had a reality of its own that should be explored. He was also affected by literary and anthropological writings on mythology, particularly by the works of Sir James G. Frazer.

Fire Images and Ideas

In the introduction to *The Psychoanalysis of Fire*, Bachelard asserts that fire, which had seemed for centuries to be one of the basic elements of nature, is no longer a reality for science. He points out that many chemistry books no longer mention fire or flame. Science sees fire only as an appearance produced by molecular events. Despite the scientific unreality of fire, though, it remains a basic experience of all people, including scientists. Therefore, the way that we perceive fire continues to be part of our unconscious experience, and images or metaphors based on this unconscious experience can influence the ways that we think about the world.

Bachelard refers to the ideas that cluster around the image of fire as "complexes," a term taken from Freudian and Jungian psychoanalysis. In the first chapter, he examines what he terms the "Prometheus complex." Prometheus was the character in Greek mythology who stole the secret of fire from the gods and brought it to humanity. Fire, in this myth, was a source of great and godlike power. It is also a forbidden source of power. As children, we experience the forbidden and awesome character of fire when our parents order us not to play with it. Thus, fire is an image of the will to intellectuality, of the will to know, and we achieve knowledge by seizing that which is forbidden to us and by trying to know more than our parents and more than our teachers. For these reasons, Bachelard claims that the Prometheus complex of fire is the intellectual equivalent of Freud's Oedipus complex, the set of psychological drives that impel youngsters to take the positions of their parents.

Another cluster of ideas about fire is the "Empedocles complex," the subject of Bachelard's second chapter. Fire is a source of reverie, of daydreaming. people who sit before a fireside identify with flames, the flickering inspires thoughts that have no practical aim, and through these thoughts, people lose themselves in the blaze. Fire, then, is an image of the blended instincts for self-assertion and living and for self-abandonment and dying. Bachelard refers to fire as an image of self-loss through reverie as the Empedocles complex because the Greek mythological figure Empedocles threw himself into a volcano, fusing himself with the power of fire.

The "Novalis complex" is a third fire complex. Bachelard argues that from prehistoric times, fire has had a connotation of sexuality and intimacy. Fire, before the time of matches, was made by rubbing until the rubbing produces warmth, sparks, and flame. Citing eighteenth century authors and mythological lore collected by Bachelard's English contemporary, James Frazer, Bachelard points out that fire has continued to carry an implication of sexual pleasure. Applying this insight to the interpretation of literature, Bachelard suggests that the poetry of the German Romantic Novalis (pen name of Friedrich Leopold, Freiherr von Hardenberg) makes extensive use of erotic fire and that the poetry of Novalis could be seen as a return to the primitive inner heat.

The sexual nature of fire is one of its most important psychological characteristics, and Bachelard devotes his fourth chapter to sexualized fire. In the imagination, fire propagates and generates itself. In prescientific thinking, men dif-

fer from women because the former have a greater bodily heat that enables them to inseminate and propagate. Bachelard reminds his readers that fire had a sexual characteristic in alchemy.

Throughout his book, Bachelard shifts between using fire images for literary interpretation, as in his Novalis complex, and explaining away fire imagery as a primitive barrier to true scientific knowledge. In the fifth chapter, he seems to remind himself that his original purpose was to analyze old unconscious views that interfere with the progress of abstract and mathematical knowledge. He examines intuitions about fire as epistemological obstacles. Fire provides examples of two such obstacles. One of these he calls the "substantialistic obstacle." The other he terms the "animistic obstacle." People have a tendency to think about fire as a substance and a tendency to think about fire as a living thing. Both of these ways of thinking about fire and other phenomena impede scientific progress. He cites older scientific writings that portrayed fire as a substantial reality rather than as a process. He gives examples of writings and myths that presented fire as something that feeds itself. Bachelard maintains that in these examples, fire is personalized, and he asserts that the scientist must avoid personalizing knowledge.

After returning to his goal of purging scientific knowledge of the unconscious influence of prescientific imagery, Bachelard once again shifts back to a more appreciative approach to that imagery. In the sixth chapter, Bachelard stops attempting to psychoanalyze objective knowledge. In discussing what he terms the "Hoffman complex," Bachelard suggests that alcohol is the creator of language. Alcohol is a rich subject for the imagination of the elements because it is "fire water." It combines both of these primary images. The Hoffman complex is a reference to the works of the German Romantic writer Ernst Theodor Amadeus Hoffman, who wrote dreamlike fantasies inspired by alcohol. Bachelard suggests that dreaming, like the fire-water of alcohol, is not to be avoided but used carefully.

Finally, Bachelard considers idealized fire. Fire is seen as something that purifies everything. He once again cites the poet Novalis, who spoke of love being transformed into a flame and of the transformed flame burning up everything earthly and impure. Fire consumes matter, and by consuming matter, it transforms it into light.

Bachelard concludes by suggesting that his book can serve as a basis for a chemistry or physics of reverie, or daydreaming. He no longer tries to explain away prescientific imagery and takes the position that analyzing this imagery can provide understanding of poetic activity and of thinking. He insists that fire is an intense and painful human experience and that the complexes attached to fire are painful. These complexes, such as the firelike sublimation of sexuality, can give rise to neurosis, but they can also lead to the writing of poetry.

A Turning Point

The Psychoanalysis of Fire is an important book in Bachelard's own philosophical development because it marks his turn from the rationalistic philosophy of science to the analysis of literature. In this work, he begins to argue that poetic images and daydreaming have their own value and are to be appreciated and understood in their own terms. It is also the first of his books on the four elements, in which he works out his view that the ways in which people see the physical world are representations of their psychological world. At the same time, the book demonstrates how scientific thinking and poetic thinking are related to one another because the two are ways in which the mind engages in a continual dialogue with the objects of the world.

As an extension of Jungian psychology, *The Psychoanalysis of Fire* demonstrates one of the ways in which human beings may project their own psyches on the world around them. Bachelard's insights in this book have often been compared to those of Freud and Jung. His view that the primitive mind, the mind uninhibited by the rationalism of science, reverts to the traditional elements of fire, earth, air, and water has been seen as an intriguing argument by many practitioners of psychoanalysis. Bachelard's complexes, or constellations of ideas and emotions associated with the element of fire, provided new ways of thinking about both psychology and mythology.

Although Bachelard began writing this book with the intention of making a contribution to the philosophy of science, it became best known to literary critics and achieved its greatest influence in literary criticism. The approach he began to develop in this, his first work on the psychoanalytic significance of the four elements, has been applied by literary analysts to the writings of such diverse authors as Albert Camus and Ray Bradbury.

Carl L. Bankston III

Additional Reading

Caws, Mary Ann. *Surrealism and the Literary Imagination: A Study of Breton and Bachelard.* The Hague, the Netherlands: Mouton, 1966. This book compares Gaston Bachelard's theories with those of the founder of the Surrealist movement, André Breton. It is useful for those interested in Bachelard's later work and for those attempting to understand Bachelard in the context of twentieth century French intellectual history.

Champigny, Robert. "Gaston Bachelard." In *Modern French Criticism: From Proust and Valéry to Structuralism*, edited by John K. Simon. Chicago: University of Chicago Press, 1972. A discussion of Bachelard's contribution to modern literary criticism.

Kushner, Eva M. "The Critical Method of Gaston Bachelard." In *Myth and Symbol: Critical Approaches and Applications*, edited by Bernice Slote. Lincoln: University of Nebraska Press, 1963. Kushner looks at the role of images in Bachelard's method of literary criticism.

Lecourt, Dominique. *Marxism and Epistemology: Bachelard, Canguilhem, and Foucault.* London: NLB, 1975. A Marxist treatment of Bachelard's scientific theories. This book is primarily helpful for the view it gives of Bachelard's connections with the celebrated French philosopher Michel Foucault. Lecourt argues that Bachelard and other philosophers rejected positivism and accepted an evolutionary view of the history of science.

McAllester, Mary, editor. *The Philosophy and Poetics of Gaston Bachelard.* Washington, D.C.: University Press of America, 1989. A collection of writings on Bachelard's literary and philosophical work.

Privitera, Walter. *Problems of Style: Michel Foucault's Epistemology.* Albany, N.Y.: State University of New York Press, 1995. An examination of the philosophy of Michel Foucault that deals with Foucault's intellectual connections with Bachelard.

Smith, Roch C. *Gaston Bachelard*. Boston: Twayne, 1982. This is the best overall view of Bachelard's life and work available in English. It is intended as an introduction, but it may be difficult for general readers to follow at some points. To some extent, this difficulty may be a matter of Bachelard's philosophy rather than of Smith's exposition of that philosophy. Because much of the work published on Bachelard in English deals with Bachelard the literary analyst rather than Bachelard the philosopher of science, Smith's work is a valuable contribution to the English-speaking reader's

understanding of Bachelard's early scientific work.

Tiles, Mary. *Bachelard: Science and Objectivity*. Cambridge, England: Cambridge University Press, 1985. Tiles looks at Bachelard's critique of scientific knowledge. She maintains that his emphasis on breaks in the continuity of scientific thinking is in agreement with contemporary philosophy of science.

Toupance, William F. *Ray Bradbury and the Poetics of Reverie: Gaston Bachelard, Wolfgang Iser, and the Reader's Response to Fantastic Literature*. San Bernardino, Calif.: Borgo Press, 1997. An imaginative application of the ideas of Bachelard and others to the work of science fiction writer Ray Bradbury.

Carl L. Bankston III

Francis Bacon

The first to use English instead of Latin for a philosophical treatise with his *Advancement of Learning*, Bacon is credited with the formulation of modern scientific thought. His *Essayes* is widely admired for its worldly witticisms and has become a classic of the form.

Principal philosophical works: *Essayes*, 1597, 1612, 1625; *The Twoo Bookes of Francis Bacon of the Proficience and Advancement of Learning, Divine and Humane*, 1605 (enlarged as *De Augmentis Scientiarum*, 1623; best known as *Advancement of Learning*); *De Sapientia Veterum*, 1609 (*The Wisdom of the Ancients*, 1619); *Instauratio Magna*, 1620 (*The Great Instauration*, 1653); *Novum Organum*, 1620 (English translation, 1802); *Historia Ventorum*, 1622 (*History of Winds*, 1653); *Historia Vitae et Mortis*, 1623 (*History of Life and Death*, 1638); *New Atlantis*, 1627.

Born: January 22, 1561; London, England
Died: April 9, 1626; London, England

Early Life

Francis Bacon was born January 22, 1561, at York House in London, to Sir Nicholas Bacon, Lord Keeper of the Seal of England, and his second wife, née Ann Cooke, who was related to nobility through her sister, the wife of Sir William Cecil, the later Lord Treasurer Burghley. In 1573, at the age of twelve, Bacon entered Trinity College, Cambridge, which he left in 1576 for Gray's Inn, thus following in his father's steps and beginning a legal career.

After a brief visit to the French court in the entourage of Sir Amias Paulet from 1576 until his father's death in 1579, Bacon stayed with the Inn and was called to the bar in 1582, two years before he began to complement his legal work with an ambitiously undertaken political career that commenced with his membership in Parliament.

After advancement to the position of Queen's Counsel in 1589, Bacon's career stalled under Elizabeth I, whom he seemed to have offended in a parliamentary debate regarding the implementation of regal subsidiaries in 1593; his enemies at court used the opportunity to bar his way to promotion, seeing in Bacon (not wholly unjustly) not only an ambitious, prolific writer of political ad-

vice but also an unscrupulous seeker of preferment. Again, on the personal level, his friendship with the young earl of Essex did not bring him hoped-for political gain; in 1601, after Essex's ill-

Francis Bacon. *(Library of Congress)*

163

considered rebellion against the queen, Bacon's position required him to partake in the prosecution of his former friend.

Although the publication of *An Advertisement Touching the Controversies of the Church of England* (1589) had brought Bacon political advancement, his later work of political advice did not professionally benefit him. During a long period of arrested political development until Elizabeth I's death, Bacon showed himself stubborn and inclined to use the common practice of patronage and favoritism to lobby for a higher position. In his own office, he became a rather successful mediator of conflicts and tried hard but finally ineffectively to smooth the waves after Essex's insubordination preceding his open revolt against the queen.

A later painting shows Bacon as a tall, bearded officer wearing his regalia and insignia proudly; the picture suggests the reserved, somewhat unemotional yet nevertheless personally sensitive character that his later biographers have asserted on the basis of accounts from Bacon's chaplain and secretary William Rawley. At forty-five, he married Alice Barnham, daughter of a London alderman, who survived him; they had no children.

Life's Work

His long period of relative political inactivity under Elizabeth I gave Bacon time to write the first ten of his *Essayes*, which saw publication in 1597, and again, because of their popularity, in 1612 and in 1625, both times with significant enlargements that brought the total number to fifty-eight. A master of the essay form, which he helped to forge, Bacon looked at people and their government realistically, free of passionate idealism and zeal for the betterment of humankind. What his critics have called his Machiavellian and emotionless coldness nevertheless facilitated a witty discourse on the world as it really is and not as it should be in the eyes of reformers. With this was coupled political advice, as in his essays "On Dissimulation" or "On Plantations," which portrayed the shortsightedness, greed, and abuses of his time.

The *Advancement of Learning* represents his first step toward the formulation of a new method of looking at the natural world—through the eyes of the experimenting and hypothesizing scientist who has purged all visions of religious allegory, Platonic metaphysics, or Aristotelian dialectics.

Bacon's political fortunes changed in the reign of James I; he ascended from his knighthood in 1603 through the office of attorney general (1613) to the high position of Lord Keeper in 1617 before he was made Lord Chancellor and Baron Verulam and ultimately created Viscount Saint Albans in 1621, at the age of sixty.

During these years of success, Bacon wrote *The Great Instauration*, the planned preface for six different works, never completed, intended to describe a restoration of human knowledge. The work is a powerful model for radical change in the pattern of Western scientific thought, characterized by Bacon's clear sense of ordering and classification. *Novum Organum*, also published in 1620, contains Bacon's argument for a "new logic," the discovery of a finite number of "natures" or "forms" lying at the base of the natural world, and an exhaustive description of natural history.

After he had reached the zenith of his power, Bacon's fall came when old enemies charged him with bribery; he admitted to the charges because he not only had indeed taken gifts from suitors, which was more generally acceptable, but also had accepted donations from individuals whose cases were pending with him as their judge (and in which he often decided against them despite the offerings given). Bacon resigned from his office, was fined forty thousand pounds, was briefly imprisoned in the Tower of London, and was banished from the court. He made slow progress at rehabilitation, but at the time of his death in the house of Sir Arundel in 1626, he had not yet received full royal pardon from the new king Charles II.

Influence

Although his public fall from grace as a result of misconduct in office linked Bacon to his literary model Seneca, who showed similar excellence in thought and corruption in public life, the British naturalist and statesperson must be remembered for his new, practical approach toward the natural environment; his proposed outlook at science contains the seeds of modern scientific thought.

In his last, unfinished work, *New Atlantis,*

posthumously published in 1627, Bacon argues that there is no conflict between the free pursuit of scientific exploration and the dogmas of the Christian religion. He sums up the ancient Hebrew view of the natural world as there to use and explore rather than as the manifestation of sundry natural deities, and he connects this thought to the idea that scientific research is ultimately undertaken so that God (the final spiritual authority) "might have the more glory" in the "workmanship" of the scientists and people "the more fruit" in the "use" of their discoveries.

On a final note, Bacon's idea, expressed in the utopian *New Atlantis*, for an organization dedicated to the free pursuit of all natural sciences that would collect and display its findings in central "houses," has been realized in the British Royal Society and the British Museum.

Reinhart Lutz

Novum Organum

Type of philosophy: Epistemology, philosophy of science

First published: Novum Organum, 1620 (English translation, 1802)

Principal ideas advanced:

◇ To acquire knowledge about the world, one must interpret the particulars given in sense experience.

◇ Various false ideas and methods have handicapped people in their attempt to study nature impartially; they are the Idols of the Tribe (conventional beliefs that satisfy the emotions), the Idols of the Cave (erroneous conceptions resulting from individual predilections), the Idols of the Market Place (confused ideas resulting from the nonsensical or loose use of language), and the Idols of the Theater (various systems of philosophy or other dogmatic, improperly founded assertions).

◇ The discovery, investigation, and explanation of Forms (the properties of substances) by controlled observation and experimentation, using tables of instances by reference to which inductive generalizations can be made, is the philosophical foundation of all knowledge.

This important work in scientific methodology was part of a larger work, *Instauratio Magna* (1620; *The Great Instauration*, 1653), which was to consist of a preface and six parts (the *Novum Organum* was to be the second) but was never completed. Even this work itself is partial, as is indicated by the fact that the author listed in aphorism 21 of book 2 a number of topics that he proposed to discuss but never did. The content of the book clearly indicates that he considered it to be a correction of, or a supplement to, Greek philosopher Aristotle's logical writings, the *Organon* (Second Athenian Period, 335-323 B.C.E.; English translation, 1812). A large portion of Bacon's text is devoted to a demonstration of the futility, if not the error, of trying to understand nature by the deductive method. People cannot learn about the world, he insists, by arguing, however skillfully, about abstract principles. On the contrary, people must *interpret* nature by deriving "axioms from the senses and particulars, rising by a gradual and unbroken ascent, so that the method arrives at the most general axioms last of all. This is the true way, but as yet untried." In this work, Bacon disclosed the rules of a new "inductive logic."

The work is divided into two books, the first concerned mainly with setting down the principles of the inductive method and the second with the method for collecting facts. Book 1 is further divided into two parts, the first of which is designed to purge the mind of the wrong methods (aphorisms 1-115), while the second is planned to correct false conceptions of the method that Bacon is proposing (aphorisms 116-120).

Humankind and Nature

Bacon begins by showing that the relation of humankind to nature is such that humankind can know the world only by being its servant and its interpreter. In humankind, knowledge and power meet, for people can control nature only if they understand it: "Nature to be commanded must be obeyed." Humankind can modify nature only by putting natural bodies together or by separating them. Moreover, people's control over nature has been very much limited because people have chosen to spend their time in "specious meditations, speculations, and glosses," which are well designed to systematize the knowledge

165

that they already have but poorly designed for the discovery of new ideas. The syllogism, for example, serves only to give stability to the errors of tradition; it deals with such unsound notions as substance, quality, action, passion, and essence rather than with those that have been abstracted from things by the proper inductive methods.

Bacon writes that there are three methods commonly employed for understanding nature. He describes these metaphorically in aphorism 95 as those of the ant, the spider, and the bee. The ant is an experimenter, but it only collects and uses. The spider is not an experimenter, but it makes cobwebs out of its own inner substance. The bee takes the middle course; it gathers material from the flowers but transforms and digests this by powers of its own. Natural philosophy is exemplified neither by the ant nor by the spider; it does not gather material from natural history and from mechanical experiments and store it away in memory, nor does it rely solely on the powers of the mind. Like the bee, it alters and digests the particulars that are given in experience and then deposits them in memory.

In further clarification of his method, Bacon suggests that there is an important distinction between the Anticipation of Nature and the Interpretation of Nature. Anticipations are collected from very few instances; they are sweeping generalizations that appeal to the imagination and thus produce immediate assent. Indeed, if all people went mad in the same manner, they might very well agree on all Anticipations. However, Interpretations are obtained from widely dispersed data; they cannot produce consent because they usually disagree with accepted ideas. Anticipations are designed to be easily believed, and Interpretations are designed to master things.

The Doctrine of the Idols

One of the contributions to scientific methodology for which Bacon has become famous is his doctrine of the Idols. These are false notions and false methods that have taken possession of people's minds, have become deeply rooted in them, and strongly resist people's efforts to study nature impartially. Bacon believes that people can guard against these only if they are aware of what these notions and methods are and how

they mislead thinking. He calls them the Idols of the Tribe, the Idols of the Cave, the Idols of the Market Place, and the Idols of the Theater. The first Idols have their foundation in human nature itself, the second in the individual human being, the third in the vagueness and ambiguity of language, and the fourth in the dogmas of philosophy and the wrong rules of demonstration.

The Idols of the Tribe are found in the belief that all celestial bodies move in perfect circles, which arises because people are predisposed to find more order and regularity in the world than actually exists; superstitions, which are accepted because people are reluctant to abandon agreeable opinions even when negative instances arise; unwillingness to conceive of limits to the world, or of uncaused causes, and the resulting eternal search for principles that are ever more and more general; the swaying of people's beliefs by emotions rather than by reason; the deceptions that arise because of the dullness and incompetency of the sense organs; and people's proneness to prefer abstractions to the concrete realities of experience.

The Idols of the Cave are caused by the mental and bodily peculiarities of the individual. People become attached to certain beliefs of which they are the authors and on which they have spent much effort. For example, some people see resemblances and overlook differences; others reverse these; both err by excess. Some people worship the past and abhor novelty; others reverse these; truth, however, is to be found in the mean between these extremes. Similar examples are to be found in the respective overemphasis on particles rather than structure, both of which distort reality.

The Idols of the Market Place are the most troublesome of all. They are words that are names of things that do not exist (Fortune, Prime Mover, Element of Fire) and words that are names of things that exist but are vague and confused in their meanings. One example of these vague names is the word "humid," which may apply in its many meanings to flame, air, dust, and glass.

The Idols of the Theater are subdivided into those of Systems of Philosophy and those of False Arguments. Among the former are the Sophistical (exemplified by the Greek philosopher Aristotle, who corrupted philosophy by his logic and his theory of the categories), the Empirical (exemplified by the alchemists and all those who leap to generalizations on the basis of a few, "dark" experiments), and the Superstitious (exemplified by those who employ their philosophies to prove their theologies). The False Argument idols are found when people improperly extract the forms of objects from the objects themselves, and when, in a spirit of caution, they withhold judgment even though a truth has been well demonstrated or dogmatically assert a conclusion without sufficient grounds. The only true demonstration is experience, not by means of careless experiments, experiments in play, or experiments performed repeatedly with only slight variations until one wearies in the process, but by planned and controlled experiments whose motive is true understanding rather than an "overhasty and unreasonable eagerness to practice."

The Progress of Science
Bacon shows that if traditional natural philosophy is examined, it is easy to see why it has not met with success. In the first place, it was largely disputational—a feature that is most adverse to the acquisition of truth—and primarily dialectical. Much of it was argued by itinerant scholars, who put their wisdom up for sale and were primarily concerned with defending their own schools of thought. In addition, these people had the disadvantage of there being no historical knowledge other than myths on which they could base their conclusions, and they had very limited geographical knowledge. Furthermore, such experimental knowledge as existed was largely a kind of "natural magic" that had almost no utility, philosophy not having realized, apparently, that it, like religion, must show itself in works. Indeed, it proved sterile, not only of mechanical progress but also of theoretical development; it thrived under its founders, remained stagnant for a few years, then declined and disappeared. As a result, many of its advocates not only apologized for the limited character of their knowledge by complaining of the subtlety and obscurity of nature and of the weakness of the human intellect but also argued defensively that nature was completely beyond the reach of humankind and essentially unknowable. To claim

that the soundness of Aristotle's philosophy has been demonstrated by its long survival is fallacious, Bacon argues; it has survived not because of the consensus of the judgments of free minds (the only real test of truth) but because of the blind worship of authority. "If the multitude assent and applaud, men ought immediately to examine themselves as to what blunder or thought they have committed."

According to Bacon, science has progressed slowly over the history of humankind for several reasons. In terms of the total history of humankind, the few centuries that had elapsed since the Greeks was not a long period; people should therefore not be too hasty in disparaging the meager results of humanity's attempt to understand the world. The poverty of results in natural philosophy can be explained by the great concentration of effort on study in the other areas of thought: religion, morals, and public affairs. Furthermore, the sciences have failed to progress because the natural philosophy on which they must be based for sound support has not been forthcoming: Astronomy, optics, music, and the mechanical arts lack profundity and merely glide over the surface of things. In addition, the sciences have remained stagnant because their goal has not been clearly formulated and the method for attaining this goal has not been stressed; people have tended to rely mainly on their wits, on an inadequate logic, and on simple experiment. "The true method of experience first lights the candle, and then by means of the candle shows the way; commencing as it does with experience duly ordered and digested, not bungling or erratic, and from it educing axioms, and from established axioms again new experiments; even as it was not without order and method that the divine word operated on the created mass."

Any tendency to praise the accomplishments of the mechanical arts, the liberal arts, and alchemy should be tempered by the recognition of how ignorant people still are in these areas; much is known, but much remains to be known. Much of which poses as knowledge, Bacon insists, has been set forth with such ambition and parade that one easily comes to feel that it is more nearly complete and perfect than it really is. Its subdivisions seem to embrace all fields, but many of these fields prove to be empty and devoid of content. Even worse, much of what is practiced in the arts is pure charlatanism, claiming without grounds to prolong life, alleviate pain, bring down celestial influences, divine the future, improve intellectual qualities, transmute substances, and much more. The main defects of such arts are to be found in their combination of littleness of spirit with arrogance and superiority. They aspire to very little but claim to accomplish very much; they engage in trifling and puerile tasks but claim to solve all problems.

On the positive side, Bacon believes that there are strong grounds for hope. Knowledge is so obviously good that it bears the marks of Divine Providence on its surface. All that is required is that people should realize that they need a new science, a new structure built on a new approach to experience. The old science is inadequate. "Nothing duly investigated, nothing verified, nothing counted, weighed, or measured, is to be found in natural history: and what in observation is loose and vague, is in information deceptive and treacherous." Accidental experiments must be replaced by controlled experiments—"of light" rather than "of fruit," which are designed simply for the discovery of causes and axioms. Data should be arranged in Tables of Discovery (which Bacon discusses in book 2), and from these people should ascend to axioms educed from these particulars by a certain rule, and then descend again to new particulars. In this activity, understanding, which is prone to fly off into speculation, should be hung with weights rather than provided with wings. The induction that is based on simple enumeration of accidentally gathered data is a childish thing; it should be replaced by one that examines the axioms derived in this way to see whether they are applicable to new particulars not included in the original enumeration and whether they should be extended to wider areas or modified and restricted to what the new experience discloses.

Corrections of Misconceptions

The second section of book 1 is devoted to a correction of the misconceptions of the Baconian method. Bacon assures the reader that he is not trying to set up a new sect in philosophy and not trying to propose a new theory of the universe.

He is not even willing to promise any new specific scientific discoveries that may occur as a result of the introduction of the new method. He grants that his method probably contains errors of detail, though he believes these to be minor in character. Among the results that he is able to show, some will be claimed by others to be trivial, some to be even mean and filthy, and some to be too subtle to be readily comprehended. In reply to these charges, Bacon repeats the statement of the poor woman who, having asked for a grant from a haughty prince and been rejected on the grounds that such an act would be beneath his dignity, replied, "Then leave off being king." If Bacon is criticized on the grounds that his method is presumptive, since he claims with one blow to have set aside all previous sciences and all earlier authors, his reply will be that with better tools one can do better things. Thus, he is not comparing his capacities with those of his predecessors but rather his skill at drawing a perfect circle by means of a compass with that of his predecessors who would draw a less perfect one without this instrument. To the charge that in urging caution and suspension of judgment, he is really denying the capacity of the mind to comprehend truth, he can answer that he is not *slighting* the understanding but *providing for* true understanding, not taking away authority from the senses but supplying them with aids.

Fact-Collecting Methods

Book 2 is concerned with the method for collecting facts. To explain this method, Bacon first shows what he means by "Forms." Every body may be regarded as a collection of "simple natures." Gold, for example, is yellow, malleable, heavy, nonvolatile, noncombustible. These constitute the Form of gold, for in gold these properties meet. Anyone who knows what these properties are and is capable of transforming a body that does not possess these properties into one that does can create gold. The Form of gold can therefore also be called the "law" of gold, for it is a description of the nature of this substance and of the various ways in which it may be created or generated. Although in the world itself there exist only bodies, not empty Forms, the discovery, investigation, and explanation of Forms is the philosophical foundation of all knowledge and all operations on objects. A limited number of "simple natures," or Forms, exist, and every body can be understood as a compound of such natures.

"The Form of a thing is the thing itself, and the thing differs from the Form no other wise than as the apparent differs from the real, or the external, or the thing in reference to humankind from the thing in reference to the universe." Therefore, people must set up procedures that will enable them to distinguish the true Form from the apparent Form. These procedures are employed in the setting up of Tables and Arrangements of Instances. These are obtained by the collection of particulars discovered in nature. "We are not to imagine or suppose, but to discover, what nature does or may be made to do." However, since nature is so various and diffuse, it tends to distract and confuse people as it presents itself. Consequently, the particulars must be arranged and organized so that understanding may be able to deal with them. These tables and arrangements enable people to use induction and to educe axioms from experience.

The three kinds of such tables are Tables of Essence and Presence, a Table of Deviation, and Tables of Degrees or Comparisons. Tables of Essence and Presence consist of collections of all known instances of a given nature, exhibiting themselves in unlike substances. As an example, Bacon gives a long list of instances of heat—in the sun, in meteors, in flame, in boiling liquids. A second kind of collection is a Table of Deviation, or of Absence in Proximity. These instances are cases where heat is absent—for example, in moonlight, light from the stars, and air on mountaintops. Finally, there are Tables of Degrees or Tables of Comparisons. These involve noting the increase or decrease of heat in the same substance or its varying amount in different subjects. For example, different substances produce different intensities of heat when burned; substances once hot, such as lime, ashes, and soot, retain their former heat for some time; dead flesh, in contrast to living flesh, becomes cold. These three tables are devices by which people assure themselves that where the nature is present, the Form will be present; where the nature is absent, the Form will be absent; and where the nature varies quantitatively, the Form will vary quantitatively.

Applying the Inductive Process
The next step is to apply the inductive process to data arranged in tables. If people follow their natural inclination and proceed simply on the basis of affirmative cases, the results will be fancies, guesses, and ill-defined notions, and the axioms must be corrected every day. God and the angels may have the capacity to extract Forms solely from affirmative cases; but humankind must proceed by affirmation, negation, and variation. What is obtained by this process, however, is only the Commencement of Interpretation, or the first vintage. Bacon presumably means by this what present-day scientists would call a *hypothesis*, that is, a tentative interpretation that is employed as a guide to the selection of further instances (such as Prerogative Instances, which he discusses in great detail). On the basis of the hypothesis we then proceed either to collect the instances by controlled observation or to produce them by experimentation.

A. Cornelius Benjamin

Additional Reading

Anderson, Fulton H. *Francis Bacon: His Career and His Thought*. Los Angeles: University of Southern California Press, 1962. Discusses the public life of Francis Bacon. Based on a series of lectures, the book links Bacon's philosophy to his politics. Attempts to relate Bacon's philosophy to twentieth century problems are not entirely successful.

Bowen, Catherine Drinker. *Francis Bacon: The Temper of a Man*. Boston: Little, Brown, 1963. A very readable and interesting biography that brings Bacon to life but is still historically accurate. The author's favorable treatment forgives Bacon for all of his faults except his coldness toward women.

Church, R. W. *Bacon*. London, 1881. A nineteenth century biography that has stayed amazingly fresh over the years. The author's readable, precise style provides an enjoyable encounter with Bacon. Emphasizes Bacon's personality.

Farrington, Benjamin. *The Philosophy of Francis Bacon*. Liverpool, England: Liverpool University Press, 1964. A valuable discussion of Bacon's philosophical concepts. The author includes good translations of Bacon's minor

Latin writings; making them available to a broader audience.

Jardine, Lisa. _Francis Bacon: Discovery and the Art of Discourse_. Cambridge, England: Cambridge University Press, 1974. Begins with a discussion of the dialectical methods of sixteenth century Europe. Discusses Bacon's theory of knowledge, which Bacon referred to as logic. Analyzes Bacon's major writings and gives clear evaluations of them. Author includes a good bibliography; divided into time periods.

Sessions, William A. _Francis Bacon Revisited_. New York: Twayne, 1996. This book by a leading Bacon scholar begins with an excellent biographical sketch and a chronology of Bacon's life, including the rise and fall of his political career. Integrates his major writings with the events of his life. Last chapter emphasizes Bacon's utopian work, _New Atlantis_. Bibliography of primary and secondary sources.

Stephens, James. _Francis Bacon and the Style of Science_. Chicago: University of Chicago Press, 1975. Emphasizes Bacon's concern about the communication of knowledge, specifically the need for a philosophy of communication. Includes Bacon's attempt to use science in this philosophy. Discusses Bacon's psychology of discovery, his plan to exploit human passions and imagination, and his doctrine of literate experience (uniting philosophy and rhetoric). Examines Bacon's approval of fable-making as a way to pass knowledge on to future generations.

Wallace, Anthony F. C. _The Social Context of Innovation: Bureaucrats, Families, and Heroes in the Early Industrial Revolution, as Foreseen in Bacon's New Atlantis_. Princeton, N.J.: Princeton University Press, 1982. An interesting discussion of how Bacon's ideas in _New Atlantis_ paved the way for many of the inventions of the Industrial Revolution. Includes twenty-five illustrations of those inventions and how Bacon's political positions helped promote them.

White, Howard B. _Peace Among the Willows: The Political Philosophy of Francis Bacon_. The Hague, Netherlands: Martinus Nijhoff, 1968. Title based on an actual event when Bacon prayed among a grove of willow trees for peace in the world. Author discusses how others have shared that dream, with the same disappointments. Includes Bacon's hope that science would be used to improve conditions in the world.

Reinhart Lutz, updated by Glenn L. Swygart

Annette C. Baier

Baier's work in traditional philosophical fields demonstrated the worth of women philosophers, and her theory of "appropriate trust" created a middle ground between male and female values.

Principal philosophical works: *Postures of the Mind: Essays on Mind and Morals*, 1985; "The Need for More than Justice," 1987; *A Progress of Sentiments: Reflections on Hume's Treatise*, 1991; *Moral Prejudices: Essays on Ethics*, 1994; *The Commons of the Mind*, 1997.

Born: October 11, 1929; Queenstown, New Zealand

Early Life

In her preface to *Moral Prejudices*, Annette C. Baier commented on how fortunate she was to be born to parents who urged their daughters to pursue their interests, whatever they might be. She also expressed gratitude toward the high school English teacher who introduced her class to the Socratic method of inquiry, motivating her to become a philosopher. Although there were very few women in that field, Annette's family encouraged her as did her philosophy professors at the University of Otago, where she enrolled in 1947.

After earning her bachelor's and master's degrees in philosophy from the University of Otago, in 1952, Baier left her native country for Oxford University and began graduate work at Somerville, a prestigious college for women. There she came into contact with prominent philosophers Philippa Foot and Elizabeth Anscombe, who were quietly but firmly pressing for a greater presence of women's voices in philosophical discourse. Foot was a leading opponent of the philosophy of Immanuel Kant and of the Kantian tradition, which feminists saw as bolstering the male-dominated power structure. Baier, too, came to reject Kantian ideas and to embrace those of Kant's contemporary, the Scottish philosopher, David Hume, who seemed to be more supportive of feminism.

At Oxford, Baier's faith in the possibility of a universal moral system based on reason, of which she had become convinced after reading the classical philosophers, was gradually replaced by a profound skepticism. In 1953, when she read the *Philosophische Untersuchungen/ Philosophical Investigations* (1953, bilingual German and English edition) of the Austrian/British philosopher Ludwig Wittgenstein, Baier began to wonder whether she had chosen the right discipline, for she saw that if philosophical analysis was impossible, as Wittgenstein suggested, there could hardly be any future for a philosopher.

It would be years before Baier found the answers she sought, and then, as she explains in the preface to *Postures of the Mind: Essays on Mind and Morals*, they came through interaction with students and through careful rereading of Wittgenstein and Hume. After receiving a B.Phil. from Oxford in 1954, Baier returned to New Zealand, became a teacher, and began to rethink everything she had been taught. From 1956 to 1958, she held a position as lecturer at the University of Auckland in New Zealand; the following year, she taught at the University of Sydney.

Baier married another philosopher who would also attain prominence, Kurt Erich Maria Baier. Kurt Baier was an Austrian-born Australian, who, after studying law in Vienna, had received a B.A. and an M. A. from the University of Melbourne and a D.Phil. from Oxford. When he left Australia to join the philosophy faculty at the University of Pittsburgh, Annette Baier followed him. As a result, her own academic career suffered, for as a married woman academic who had taken her husband's name and accompanied him to the United States, she was perceived as being, if not indifferent to advancement in her profession, at least readily available for exploitation.

From 1963 to 1969, Baier taught at Carnegie Mellon University, first as a part-time lecturer, then as a senior lecturer, and finally as associate professor. In 1973, she joined the faculty of the University of Pittsburgh. She was to remain there throughout the rest of her academic career, first as associate professor, then as professor, and finally as Distinguished Service Professor.

Life's Work

In dedicating *Postures of the Mind* to her parents, Baier recognized how important their encouragement had been to her. She frequently comments on the support received from her husband and her colleagues, who are often credited in her notes with helping her to refine her ideas. However, Baier merits high praise for her own determination. It took a long time for her to attain the recognition she deserved. By the time *Postures of the Mind* appeared, the author was in her fifties, and even though almost all of the essays in her book had been published previously, none of them had appeared in print before 1976.

During the years after her arrival in the United States, Baier had not only been seeking an academic home but had also been working on Wittgenstein, Hume, and her own approach to ethics. Meanwhile, she had become increasingly active in her profession, not only teaching but also reading papers at conferences and submitting essays for publication in scholarly journals. To cite some examples, her article "Act and Intent" appeared in a 1970 issue of *Journal of Philosophy*, "The Search for Basic Actions," in a 1971 issue of *American Philosophical Quarterly*, and "Ways and Means," in 1972 in *Canadian Journal of Philosophy*. However, these early essays were not included in *Postures of the Mind*, partly because of space limitations but, more important, according to the author, because when she looked back at these early efforts, she realized that although her conclusions were still the same, there were some

radical changes in the way she arrived at them.

By 1976, however, Baier felt comfortable about what she thought and why she thought it. The title of a paper published that year in the *Philosophical Quarterly* and reprinted in *Postures of the Mind* exudes a new assurance: It is called simply "Realizing What's What." In 1976, one of her essays was selected to appear in an edited work; "Intention, Practical Knowledge, and Representation," which Baier had read in 1975 at the Winnipeg Conference on Action Theory, was included in *From Action Theory*, edited by M. Brand and D. Walton. This essay constitutes the third chapter of *Postures of the Mind*.

In the preface to that volume, Baier admits that her choice of discipline was doubtless influenced by her habit of challenging anything that someone else says is incontrovertibly true. The essays in *Postures of the Mind*, she explains, were written over a period of some ten years, during which she was "liberating" herself from the ideas she had acquired during her years of study. More specifically, *Postures of the Mind* was inspired by a discussion of "particles" in the *Essay Concerning Human Understanding*, by the English philosopher John Locke, in which it was suggested that one should not view particles, or atoms, separately, but as they are connected to others. In her essays, Baier rejects not only the belief that atoms can be examined individually, as the British empiricists held, but also the Kantian notion that there are universal laws governing the behavior of atoms.

Postures of the Mind is divided into two sections. In the first, "Varieties of Mental Postures," Baier considers Wittgenstein's ideas as to cultural influences on thought and behavior and explores at length such matters as emotion and memory. In the second section, the author points out what she sees as the weaknesses in Kant's philosophy and the strengths in that of Hume. Baier parts from Wittgenstein when she rejects religion, advocating instead a purely secular faith, based on trust in human beings and in the development of the human community.

It is evident from the many responses to Baier in scholarly journals that she was now considered a Hume scholar who should not be ignored. However, one reason she was so interested in Hume was that she saw in him support for feminism. After pondering the psychologist Carol Gilligan's book *In a Different Voice* (1982), Baier had become convinced that any ethical system must take into account essential differences in gender. In her own essay, "Hume, the Women's Moral Theorist?," published in *Women and Moral Theory* (1987), edited by Eva Kittay and Diana T. Meyers and later reprinted as a chapter in *Moral Prejudices*, Baier stated some of the ideas that she would amplify in her next book, *A Progress of Sentiments: Reflections on Hume's Treatise.* As an analytic feminist, Baier refuses to reject either the traditional analytic method as rational and therefore male and to discard all the male philosophers of the past as being hopelessly sexist. Instead, she believes that if a woman looks carefully and analytically at the works of some of these male philosophers, she may discover in them perceptions in accordance with feminine wisdom that have hitherto gone unremarked. Thus when Hume insists that morality must be derived from such human emotions as sympathy and compassion rather than from cold reason, Baier sees him as supporting the validity of a feminist approach to ethics.

A Progress of Sentiments aroused considerable controversy in the academic world. Baier's new and highly original interpretation of Hume was acknowledged as a real contribution to Hume scholarship, and some scholars agreed with many of the ideas she advanced, for example, that Hume sees the human reason as gradually developing from preoccupation with abstract theory to a more useful interest in morality. However, many expressed reservations about her conclusions, for instance, her insistence that Hume effectively discarded reason in favor of passion as a basis for ethics. Others rejected her analysis, sometimes rather cavalierly dismissing it as a feminist reading.

In her third major work, *Moral Prejudices: Essays on Ethics*, Baier brought together a number of her lectures and some previously published essays. Although Hume is the subject of two of them, the fact that in the titles of these chapters he is referred to as a candidate for "the Women's Moral Theorist" and "the Reflective Women's Epistemologist" indicate that the primary emphasis in this volume was not on the interpretation of Hume but on feminist ethical theory.

In 1998, the American Academy of Arts and Sciences chose Baier as one of four in the philosophy and theology category to be elected a fellow of the academy. Forty-four years had passed since she left Oxford and began to reevaluate all that she had been taught. Finally, however, she had been recognized for her achievements not only as a Hume scholar but also as one of the major women philosophers of the late twentieth century.

Influence
When Baier's mentors at Somerville College called for women's voices to be heard in philosophy, they could not have had any idea that their student would some day be considered so important. Instead of taking the easier route to fame by discarding tradition and approaching philosophy from a strictly feminine point of view, she mastered the analytical techniques that men had long considered their own property. Baier's study of Hume, then, not only demonstrated her own scholarly skills but also proved that women were as capable of analysis as men. Along with other analytical feminists, Baier refused to reject the entire philosophical tradition as too sexist to be worth considering and instead worked to redeem it by rereading important works and, where it seemed useful, by reinterpreting them.

Baier's theory of "appropriate trust" has also influenced the course of ethical thought by seeking a middle ground between the male emphasis on justice, order, and obligation and such feminine values as love, caring, and nurturing. Thus, unlike more radical feminists, Baier sees no point in confrontation between the genders but hopes to find a basis for compromise.

Finally, it will probably never be known how much Baier has influenced her students, her readers, and the young women who may follow in her footsteps. By daring to enter a male-dominated discipline, by courageously working through the difficulties inherent in the role of an academic wife, and by rising to all the intellectual challenges with which she was presented, she has proven herself to be the kind of woman whom everyone can respect and in whom women can take great pride.

Rosemary M. Canfield Reisman

Moral Prejudices

Essays on Ethics

Type of philosophy: Ethics
First published: 1994
Principal ideas advanced:

◇ Men and women see the world differently and therefore advance different values; however, some male philosophers, notably David Hume, are closer to the feminine perspective.

◇ Men see justice as the highest virtue and consider obligation the proper basis of morality; women see caring as the primary virtue and believe ethics should be founded on love.

◇ Though love is risky, it can be made less so if the traditional theological and patriarchal assumptions are rejected.

◇ Trust, too, is risky, but it is the only possible basis for a system of morality to which both men and women can subscribe.

◇ A system of morality for both men and women must balance rights and responsibilities and must make sure that responsibilities are shared.

◇ Although it is likely that women philosophers will have an important role in shaping new ethical systems, they will not speak with a single voice any more than men philosophers do.

◇ Men and women alike must seek common ground on ethical matters, but they should also be able to appreciate diversity.

As Annette Baier explains in the preface to *Moral Prejudices: Essays on Ethics,* she borrowed the title for her collection from an essay by David Hume called "Of Moral Prejudices," in which he questions the traditional assumption that men are meant to be independent and women dependent on men. The title seemed appropriate, she continues, because she appreciates Hume's willingness to attack stereotypes and because she not only studies moral prejudices but also recognizes them in herself, for example, her very real anger about the way women have been treated over the centuries. However, Baier knows that no society can be based on rage and confrontation. Philosophical inquiry, she believes, should look for ways to reconcile the genders, without making

either of them subservient to the other. In the preface, Baier explains that because the fourteen essays in this volume were written for various audiences and on several different topics, which in some cases were assigned, the book should not be read as if it were a single entity, advancing a coherent philosophical system, even though there are stylistic similarities in the essays as well as thematic links.

Male and Female Perspectives

Baier begins her collection by asking, "What Do Women Want in a Moral Theory?" Although she admits that as yet there are too few women philosophers for anyone to answer the question by perusing their works, she does agree with psychologist Carol Gilligan that there is a basic difference between the way men look at the world and the way women see it. Men emphasize obligation, while women emphasize relationships, caring, nurturing, and love. The author then advances the idea for which she is best known, that a moral theory whose central concept is trust could bring together men and women in a way that the prevailing men's theories have never done.

In her second essay, Baier considers "The Need for More than Justice." She begins by pointing out that it is African Americans and women who have most challenged the prevailing male assumption that justice is the most important of the virtues. Having learned to distrust "justice" as too often a justification for oppression, those who have been oppressed and those who can empathize with them stress humanitarianism, or what Gilligan calls "care," as the principle on which ethics should be based.

The epigraph to "Unsafe Loves" quotes Hume on the two ultimate values in this world, love and friendship. The questions Baier considers in this essay are, first, how to define love, and, second, whether it is a good idea to love someone. After summarizing the ideas of several philosophers, including those who believed the only safe love was that of a human being for God, Baier settles down with Hume, whose biological approach seems to her both realistic and sensible. Although the love of one human being for another is always risky, in part because it involves power games, one can at least reduce the level of danger by eliminating theological and patriarchal notions from one's idea of what love should be.

In her fourth essay, "Hume, the Women's Moral Theorist?," Baier argues that Hume often saw the world as a woman would see it, rather than from the viewpoint of a man. She then proceeds to compare German philosopher Immanuel Kant and Hume on five different issues, pointing out that in every instance, Kant adhered to what Gilligan identified as the male perspective, while Hume did just the opposite. Baier's "Hume, the Reflective Women's Epistemologist?" also deals with Hume, but most of the essay is devoted to an analysis of Hume's ideas on epistemology, or the theory of knowledge, rather than to comparisons of his views with those of other philosophers. Although Baier admits that Hume shares some of the prejudices of his age, such as the idea that women restrain and refine the more energetic gender, she offers evidence to show that he opposed all tyranny, including that inherent in a patriarchal society.

Trust, Violence, and Rights
The next four essays all explore the issue of trust. "Trust and Antitrust" presents various examples in order to develop an adequate definition. Trust, Baier concludes, means making another the custodian of something one cares about. She discusses trust as it operates between adults and as it applies in child rearing. She also deplores the male obsession with contracts, which she thinks are both unreliable and essentially immoral. It is preferable, she argues, to depend on one's own judgment.

In "Trust and Its Vulnerabilities," Baier presents some specific examples of situations in which trust was betrayed, either by another individual or by an institution. She concludes that it is almost impossible to make a set of rules that guide one in determining whom to trust and whom to distrust, whom to offer another chance, even how to react after a breach of trust becomes evident. "Sustaining Trust" begins by pointing out the degree to which all people are vulnerable and goes on to suggest how to differentiate between trust that has no real basis and trust that is based on good judgment. Finally, in "Trusting People," Baier offers support for her belief that

trust should be considered the primary virtue and that therefore every effort should be made to bolster the trustworthiness of individuals and of institutions.

The tenth essay in *Moral Prejudices* concerns a very different issue, violence, and specifically terrorism. After pointing out that what are called in the title "Violent Demonstrations" will not themselves bring about the changes the demonstrator desires but will merely publicize the cause, Baier proceeds to consider the motivations of terrorists and to suggest moral responses to what are evidently immoral, if often understandable, actions. She concludes by urging the study not only of what makes individuals violent but also of how they can be reared to be gentle.

"Claims, Rights, Responsibilities" and "How Can Individuals Share Responsibility?" are both incisive discussions of important philosophical concepts. In the first of these essays, Baier illustrates how human beings claim rights but also compromise concerning their claims, often trading one right for another. She also explains the relationships among the concept of rights, the development of language skills, and the increasing awareness of oneself as an individual. However, she also points out that without a sense of responsibility, the assertion of rights will never produce a civilized society. Baier begins the second essay by tracing the conflict between individualism, or libertarianism, and communitarianism, a conflict linked inevitably with the matter of responsibility and with the question of the status of women. As long as women were considered the responsibility of men, for example, they could never make their own decisions, and as long as women's responsibilities within the home and within society were assigned by the patriarchs who ruled both, women were little more than servants. Nothing changed until women finally claimed their rights and took the responsibility for revising the male and female roles in the family and in society. Asserting that many of our ideas are derived from Kant's form of individualism, which is actually elitist, sexist, and patriarchal, the author ends her essay with a call to Americans to reject Kant and become true philosophical revolutionaries. In "Moralism and Cruelty: Reflections on Hume and Kant," Baier compares the statements of the two philosophers on such matters as crime and punishment, guilt, and shame. Rather than espousing the rigid moralism of Kant, she encourages her readers to become Humeans, holding that the worst vice is cruelty and that gentle mockery is often the best way to remedy wrongs.

Women Philosophers

In the final essay in *Moral Prejudices*, entitled "Ethics in Many Different Voices," Baier returns to the subject her Oxford mentors had emphasized so many years before. Now, she reports, there are many more women's voices in philosophy. The plural is important, for, as she points out, women philosophers do not speak with a single voice. Indeed, they differ as markedly, both in manner and in matter, as men do. One issue that concerns the author is the professional risk women encounter when they specialize in feminist philosophy or even are candid about their feminist interests; another is that of timing, because the very years when young academicians need to concentrate all their energy on obtaining tenure are those when women are most likely to be bearing and rearing children. If the academic world altered its invidious practice of measuring a scholar's worth by the quantity of published works rather than on their quality, this problem could be solved.

From these practical matters, Baier moves to a personal testimony on the impact one woman philosopher had on her own thought. If anyone knew about evil and forgiveness, Baier comments, it was the German-born Jewish writer and activist Hannah Arendt. The author admires Arendt not only for her accomplishments but also for the breadth of her vision. The book concludes by urging contemporary women ethicists not to limit themselves but to listen to all the voices, old and new, male and female; perhaps even to become a bit androgynous; and certainly to appreciate the beauty of diversity.

Criticism and Impact

Moral Prejudices became a subject of discussion and even of controversy as soon as it appeared. It was argued, for example, that Baier had done herself a disservice by basing her analyses on the theory of gender differences. However, one reason for the book's importance was that it does

explore the differences in perspective between men and women and, even more significant, the dissimilarities between men philosophers and women philosophers, particularly as to ethical issues.

The theory of "appropriate trust" proposed by Baier in earlier works and discussed at length in this volume has also provoked criticism. It is argued, for example, that trust alone cannot solve the social problems Baier mentions in *Moral Prejudices* (terrorism and genocide, for instance), not to mention disagreements about responsibilities in the home and gender-related problems in the workplace. However, because the author made it clear that this volume of essays was never intended as an outline of a new ethical system, it is likely that subsequent books will deal with such objections.

Perhaps the greatest impact of *Moral Prejudices* will be in its influence upon women readers and philosophers. Although it does not contain a blueprint for social harmony, at least it contains some interesting suggestions as to how women could influence society. If feminine values prevailed, and if everyone insisted on gentleness as the aim of child rearing and on mutual respect rather than competition as a guideline for adults, including husbands and wives and academics, the result could well be a much more satisfactory world.

Rosemary M. Canfield Reisman

Additional Reading

Code, Lorraine. *What Can She Know?: Feminist Theory and the Construction of Knowledge*. Ithaca, N.Y.: Cornell University Press, 1991. Much of the third chapter of this volume is devoted to an interpretation of Baier's concept of "second personhood" and to a comparison of her view to the ideas advanced by philosophers Caroline Whitbeck and Sara Ruddick. A good summary of Baier's position on this important issue.

Gilligan, Carol. *In a Different Voice*. Cambridge, Mass.: Harvard University Press, 1982. A landmark study of gender differences from a psychologist's point of view, suggesting that while men see justice as the foundation of morality, women base their ethical judgments on sympathy, or caring. One of the major influences on Baier and other feminist philosophers.

Gowans, Christopher W. "After Kant: Ventures in Morality Without Respect for Persons." *Social Theory and Practice* 22 (Spring, 1996): 105-129. In this critical discussion of works by Baier and Michael Philips, the author defends Immanuel Kant and argues for the concept of autonomy, which Baier rejected. According to the author, in *Moral Prejudices*, Baier not only fails to do justice to Kant, but her feminist reading of Hume also is open to question. This thoughtful essay is a useful summary of the main points raised by Baier's critics.

Held, Virginia, ed. *Justice and Care: Essential Readings in Feminist Ethics*. New York: Westview Press, 1995. Eleven essays on feminist issues fill this volume. Baier's "The Need for More than Justice" gains a new significance when read along with related works, some of which disagree sharply with her point of view. A helpful index directs readers to specific references to Baier in essays by other writers. The editor's brief but pithy introduction is a good starting point for the study of the ethical theory controversy among women philosophers.

Tong, Rosemarie. *Feminine and Feminist Ethics*. Belmont, Calif.: Wadsworth, 1993. A lucid, well-organized volume. After four chapters on the historical and theoretical background to feminist ethics, the author discusses the major writers in the field, explaining each writer's theories and outlining their opponents' arguments. In the chapter "Feminist Approaches to Ethics," the author presents the ideas of Alison Jaggar, Sheila Mullett, and Susan Sherwin before turning to Baier and her concept of appropriate trust. Objections to the theories advanced by these writers are then summarized. Includes index.

Walker, Margaret Urban. *Moral Understandings: A Feminist Study in Ethics*. New York: Routledge, 1998. Finds traditional, maternal approaches to ethics very different from those of feminists or lesbians. There are many references to Baier, and a passage from *Moral Prejudices* is used as the epigraph to one chapter. Five of Baier's books are listed in the bibliography. Perceptive and readable. Has a full index.

Rosemary M. Canfield Reisman

Mikhail Bakhtin

Bakhtin had a profound impact on the philosophy and interrelatedness of language and society, on the extension of linguistics and literary theory, and on modern philosophical systems.

Principal philosophical works: *Freidizm: Kriticheskii ocherk*, 1927 (probable author, as V. N. Voloshinov; *Freudianism: A Marxist Critique*, 1973); *Formal'nyi metod v literaturovedenii: Kriticheskoe vvedenie v sotsiologicheskuyu poetiku*, 1928 (probable author, as P. N. Medvedev; *The Formal Method in Literary Scholarship*, 1978); *Marksizm i filisofiya yazyka*, 1929 (probable author, as Voloshinov; *Marxism and the Philosophy of Language*, 1973); *Problemy tvorchestva Dostoevskogo*, 1929; *Problemy poetiki Dostoevskogo*, 1963 (*Problems of Dostoevsky's Poetics*, 1973, 1984); *Tvorchestvo Fransua Rable i narodnaya kul'tura srednevekov'ya i Renessansa*, 1965 (*Rabelais and His World*, 1968); *Voprosy literatury i estetiki*, 1975 (*The Dialogic Imagination*, 1981); *Estetika slovesnogo tvorchestva*, 1979; *Speech Genres and Other Late Essays*, 1986; *The Architectonics of Answerability*, 1988.

Born: November 16, 1895; Orel, Russia
Died: March 7, 1975; Moscow, Soviet Union

Early Life

Mikhail Mikhailovich Bakhtin was born November 16, 1895, in the provincial capital of Orel, Russia. Untitled and unpropertied, he came from a noble family who, like their city, dated back to the late Middle Ages. His father and grandfather were owner and manager, respectively, of state banks. The third of five children, Mikhail was closer to his elder brother Nikolai than to his three sisters or his parents. A German governess taught the boys Greek poetry in German translation.

When Bakhtin was nine years old, the family moved to Vilnius, the Russian-ruled capital of Lithuania. In this multiethnic center, his outlook was broadened even though the schools and church that he attended were Russian. He was influenced by new cultural and literary movements such as Symbolism and by the spirit of revolutionary change. A lifelong process of debate and dialogue was begun between Bakhtin and his brother and others. Bakhtin's extensive reading included the works of philosophers Friedrich Nietzsche and Georg Wilhelm Friedrich

Hegel. Six years later, Bakhtin's family moved to Odessa, a major city of the Ukraine. Bakhtin attended and finished the school known as the First Gymnasium; he then attended the University of Odessa for one year, studying with the philological faculty. At sixteen, he contracted osteomyelitis.

From 1914 to 1918, Bakhtin attended the University of St. Petersburg, rooming with his brother Nikolai. Of several professors, the most influential was Faddei F. Zelinsky, credited with laying the foundation for Bakhtin's knowledge of philosophy and literature. Bakhtin's graduation in 1918, following Nikolai's departure for the White Army in 1917 and eventual self-exile to England, marked the end of the preparatory stage of his life.

Life's Work

From 1918 through 1929, Bakhtin established lifelong friendships with artistic and intellectual people, developed and expressed his own ideas, did extensive work on his own writings, married, and saw his first works published. He became the center of a series of informal groups of people from a wide variety of backgrounds, areas of achievement, and political and ideological persuasions. At Nevel, to which he and his family moved in 1918, members of the Bakhtin circle included Lev Vasilyevich Pumpiansky, Valentin Nikolayevich Voloshinov, and the musician Maria Veniaminova Yudina. Bakhtin maintained his personal and philosophical commitment to Christianity at a time when all religions were suppressed in the Soviet Union. His first known publication was a two-page article in a local periodical in 1919 entitled "Iskusstvo i otvetstvennost" (art and responsibility). The ideas he expressed in this article were later developed into those of his mature works.

In 1920, Bakhtin moved to nearby Vitebsk, where his circle expanded to include new members such as Ivan Ivanovich Sollertinsky and Pavel Nikolayevich Medvedev. In addition to writing and keeping notebooks, Bakhtin taught at Vitebsk Higher Institute of Education and held several other positions. The worsening of his osteomyelitis was complicated by typhoid in 1921, and he was nursed by Elena Aleksandrovna Okolovich; their fifty-year marriage began later that year and ended with her death in 1971.

Bakhtin spent 1924 through 1929 in Leningrad, where he lived on a progressively reduced medical pension. His health prohibited public activity, but he was able to meet with members of his circle and to lecture in private apartments. Works published by his friends contained his ideas but also his friends' Marxist ideology, thus making them politically acceptable for publication. Opinion varies as to authorship of these collaborative works. Some scholars believe that Bakhtin wrote them in their entirety; some believe that he composed the bulk of these texts, with his friends adding the requisite ideology; others are convinced that the works were actually written by those under whose names they were published and merely reflect the influence of Bakhtin. One work signed by the scientist Ivan Ivanovich Kanaev questions the claims of vitalism. Of the four works attributed to Medvedev, the best known is *The Formal Method in Literary Scholarship*. One of Voloshinov's seven titles is *Marxism and the Philosophy of Language*. Only these twelve works are questioned; other books signed by these men are accepted as theirs, thus providing scholars with a basis for comparison.

The year 1929 was a turning point in Bakhtin's life. He was arrested and sentenced to exile in Siberia for ten years for political and religious reasons (he was never tried). He also published his first major work under his own name (and the first since 1919): *Problemy tvorchestva Dostoevskogo* (expanded as *Problemy poetiki Dostoevskogo*, 1963; *Problems of Dostoevsky's Poetics*, 1973, 1984). Bakhtin's sentence in Siberia was reduced for reasons of health; a good review of his book by the minister of education and the fact that the questioners believed him to be the author of the disputed texts probably also helped his case.

He was allowed to go to Kustanai from 1930 to 1934, traveling without guard and choosing his own work. After a year of unemployment, he found work as an accountant for the local government and later taught local workers his clerical skills. Here as elsewhere, he was well liked. In 1934, he chose to remain for two more years; that same year, he published an article based on his observations there.

In 1936, Bakhtin ended his self-exile by moving to Saransk and teaching in the Mordovian Pedagogical Institute. The next year, for political reasons, he moved to Savelovo, about one hundred kilometers from Moscow. In 1938, the first of a series of misfortunes overtook him: His right leg was amputated. An article on satire he was asked to contribute to a literary encyclopedia never appeared because the volume was canceled. As a result of the vicissitudes of wartime, several works by Bakhtin that had been accepted and were awaiting publication did not appear. In 1940, he lectured on the novel at the Gorky Institute in Moscow, writing a dissertation for that institution on François Rabelais, which was published in an expanded version as *Rabelais and His World*, a work rivaling *Problems of Dostoevsky's Poetics* in importance. In 1941, he began teaching German in the Savelovo schools while working on yet another important endeavor: articles about the novel, collected as *The Dialogic Imagination*, in which he expanded his ideas on polyphonic communication to dialogic communication, which included the self and others or the author, characters, and reader. From 1942 to 1945, he taught Russian in Savelovo.

In 1945, Bakhtin returned to Saransk, where he was promoted to the rank of docent and made department chairman. In 1946, he submitted his dissertation, defending it the following year. The committee compromised and granted him the lesser degree of candidate in 1951, precluding publication at that time. In 1957, he saw his institute become a university. The next year, he was promoted to chairman of the department of Russian and foreign literature at this newly formed institution.

Recognition came slowly. With few publications in his own name, Bakhtin was little known beyond his own circle of friends. Attention to the book on Fyodor Dostoevski marked a change: Vladimir Seduro, an American, mentioned the book in a published work in 1955; the next year, his old antagonist, the Formalist critic Viktor Shklovsky, treated the Dostoevski book in a Soviet work; in 1958, the influential Slavicist Roman Jakobson, a pioneering figure in the application of linguistics to literary study, having mentioned Bakhtin to members of the International Conference of Slavists in 1956, shared preview copies of his review of Shklovsky's book, publishing his review in 1959. Young intellectuals led by Vadim Valerianovich paid Bakhtin homage and pressed for publication of his works. The revised Dostoevski book and the revised dissertation, 1963 and 1965, established his reputation. Other works followed, some posthumously.

Poor health forced both of the Bakhtins to move to Moscow in 1969 and to nearby Grivno in 1970. Bakhtin's wife died of a heart condition in 1971. Bakhtin then moved first to a hotel for writers and in 1972 to his own apartment at 21 Krasnoarmeyskaya Street in Moscow, where he lived and, in spite of osteomyelitis and emphysema, wrote until his death on March 7, 1975. His funeral ceremonies were both civil and religious.

Influence

For much of his life, Bakhtin was a relatively obscure figure, though in his last years he attained a measure of fame among literary specialists in the Soviet Union and saw his work begin to appear in the West. In the decade following his death, as previously unpublished works became available and early works were reissued, there was an explosion of interest in Bakhtin, to the extent that he has become one of the most influential literary theorists of the twentieth century.

In part Bakhtin's influence can be attributed to his appeal to critics and readers who value plu-

ralism and cultural diversity. Most of the now widely used terms and concepts that Bakhtin introduced to critical discourse directly reflect his sense of literature as an interplay of voices, of meanings, of languages. "Dialogic" thinking recognizes this multiplicity (or "heteroglossia," as Bakhtin termed it); "monologic" thinking attempts to suppress it. Bakhtin's pluralism and his emphasis on the social context of meaning have made an impact not only on literary studies but also on linguistics, philosophy, theology, and the social sciences.

George W. Van Devender

The Dialogic Imagination

Type of philosophy: Aesthetics, ethics, social philosophy
First published: Voprosy literatury i estetiki, 1975 (English translation, 1981)
Principal ideas advanced:
◇ The novel is the most liberated and liberating of the genres and as a genre may be distinguished from epic and poetry in terms of its openness both to the living present and to language in all its variety.
◇ The novel has its own distinctive prehistory and chronotopes (that is, ways of organizing time and space).
◇ The novel must be studied in terms of the ways it incorporates diverse, intersecting voices and speech types rather than on the basis of abstract formal properties.

The Dialogic Imagination consists of translations of four of the six essays published in 1975, the year of Mikhail Bakhtin's death. The publication of *The Dialogic Imagination* was the result of interest in Bakhtin on the part of a new generation of Russian literary scholars who sought to rescue Bakhtin from the obscurity forced on him during the Stalinist era.

To gain a proper appreciation of the essays, it is important to understand not only how they finally came to be published and what Bakhtin espoused but also what he rejected and wrote against. Chief among the ideas he rejected was monologism (of which Stalinism was the most obvious example); it was also the topic about which Bakhtin was least able to write openly. Bakhtin's rejection of monologism extends to his rejection of any system that claimed to offer a complete, scientific explanation of language in general and literature in particular. At a time when formalism and structuralism were in favor throughout Europe and especially in the Soviet Union, Bakhtin developed a very different, deeply historical approach, one that saw language not as abstract and scientifically classifiable but as intensely social, indeed as a ceaseless struggle of opposing, intersecting forces. For Bakhtin, then, the multiple meanings of a living utterance exceed any system's capacity for fixing, explaining, and containing them. Thus, rather than seeking unity in diversity, Bakhtin explored the diversity within language's apparent unity by attending closely and sensitively to the "the social atmosphere of the word" and "the dialogic orientation of a word among other words."

The Epic and the Novel

The first of *The Dialogic Imagination*'s four essays, "Epic and Novel," was written in 1941 and first published in 1970 (and in expanded form in the 1975 collection). It offers a succinct and relatively straightforward introduction to one of Bakhtin's most important ideas, in effect defining one genre, the novel, by contrasting it with another, the epic. According to Bakhtin, what distinguishes the epic is the complete separation of its world from contemporary reality (the time of its narration) and by means of this separation, the creation of a valorized past: absolute, closed, complete, uncontaminated by the present, above all unchanging, and therefore both inhuman and ahistorical.

The novel is everything the epic is not. It is alive, liberated, and liberating; this is its aesthetic and its ethic. Anticanonical, unfinalized and unfinalizable, the novel is less a carefully defined genre than an antigenre, whose plasticity and formlessness define or constitute its form. The novel intersects with other genres, which it critically examines, using parody and other means to expose their limitations and conventionality. Freely absorbing other literary as well as subliterary and extraliterary forms, the novel proves itself the most omnivorous, fluid, and organic of the genres and therefore the most resistant to theoretical explanation. Written one year earlier (1940), and first published three years earlier (1967), the collection's second essay, "From the Prehistory of Novelistic Discourse," follows much the same line of thought. It traces the novel back to its roots in those forms (Socratic dialogue, Menippean satire, folklore, carnival, popular laughter) which, unlike the epic, emphasize what is low, present, contingent, and parodic. These are the forms that prepare the way for the novel as "the genre of becoming."

Chronotopes

The collection's remaining essays are much longer and more complex. Written in 1937-1938 and revised in 1973, "Forms of Time and Chronotope in the Novel" concerns "the intrinsic connectedness of temporal and spatial relationships that are artistically expressed in literature." ("Chronotope" literally means "time-place.") Bakhtin's interest is not in the way literature reflects the world (he rejected naïve realism); instead it is with the ways in which literature organizes the world spatially and temporally, as he demonstrates by analyzing a number of representative chronotopes.

Not surprisingly, the earliest chronotope, that in a Greek romance, is also the most abstract and static. Its settings are vaguely exotic but otherwise indefinite; the adventures themselves are interchangeable and both causality and development entirely lacking. The world of the Greek romance is one in which much happens but nothing actually changes, least of all the hero, who emerges from his many adventures exactly as he began and always will be. Bakhtin then considers genres that begin to include all that the Greek romance excludes: first, the adventure novel of everyday life, with its striking mix of adventures and quotidian existence, its use of wandering as an organizing structure, and emphasis on change, albeit of a spasmodic kind such as metamorphosis, and second, ancient biography and autobiography, with their emphasis on the "exteriority of the individual," an individual who exists either as an already existing potential or as "an organic human collective."

Bakhtin takes notice of the realism in folklore

and of the way the world of chivalric romance is subject to chance (miraculous) occurrences and the way the heroes of these romances are at once individualized and symbolic. In the encyclopedic dream visions of the late Middle Ages (Dante Alighieri's in particular), Bakhtin emphasizes the "struggle between living historical time and the extratemporal other worldly ideal," which is to say "the struggle between two epochs and world-views." Especially important to Bakhtin's theory of the novel's development are those works in which rogues, clowns, and fools figure prominently because of the ways in which they expose conventionality (the rogue's flouting of all that is socially acceptable, the clown's play, and the fool's incomprehension).

The lengthy discussion of the Rabelaisian chronotope contains the main points that Bakhtin explores more fully in his *Tvorchestvo Fransua Rable i narodnaya kul'tura srednevekov'ya i Renessansa* (1965; *Rabelais and His World*, 1968), an expanded and revised version of his 1940 doctoral dissertation. The most obvious feature of the Rabelaisian chronotope is expansiveness, but Bakhtin is more interested in its basis in folklore, its emphasis on feasts and deaths, its rhythm of destruction and construction, and the demise of the medieval metaphysic and the rise (or birth) of a less transcendent, more authentic worldview in which the individual, instead of being sealed off from the natural world, is open to it and made an integral part of it. The Rabelaisian chronotope contrasts sharply with that of the idyll, which, even though it develops a special relationship to place, is nonetheless "severely limited to only a few of life's basic realities." The severely circumscribed spaces that figure so prominently in the nineteenth century novels of Honoré de Balzac, Stendhal, and others, on the other hand—the parlors and salons, for example—open up new possibilities. They serve as crisis points and thresholds—points of intersection for characters and speech types alike.

Dialogism and the Novel

The last essay in *The Dialogic Imagination* is also the earliest of the four to be written (1934-1935) and arguably the most interesting if at times the most confusing. As Bakhtin points out at the beginning of "Discourse and the Novel," "The prin-

cipal idea of this essay is that the study of verbal art must overcome the divorce between an abstract 'formal' approach and an equally abstract 'ideological' approach." Defining the novel as a diversity of voices and speech types, Bakhtin here contrasts it not with the epic (as in *The Dialogic Imagination*'s opening essay) but with poetry. Unlike poetry, which Bakhtin faults for giving rise to the idea of "a purely poetic, extrahistorical language," novelistic discourse "cannot forget or ignore." Against the monologism of poetry (and the epic) and its "Ptolomaic" conception of language, he posits the novel's essential dialogism, its Galilean "decentering" of meaning and liberating sense of "linguistic homelessness." This liberation gives rise both to the centripetal forces that seek to limit meaning and to a speaker's yearning not just to speak but to be heard and responded to—important ideas that Bakhtin discusses elsewhere. Rather than excluding or limiting heteroglossia ("another's speech in another's language," serving two speakers, each with his or her own intentions), the novel intensifies it. Indeed, Bakhtin explains the development of the novel as "a function of the deepening of its dialogic essence," which leaves "fewer and fewer neutral, hard elements" outside its relativizing gaze.

Bakhtin turns his attention to the stages in the novel's development. One of his most interesting observations concerns the difference he finds in the way the Baroque novelists of the eighteenth century approached heteroglossia and incorporated it in their work, whether condescendingly from above or more enthusiastically from below. Another is the part played in the novel's development by the English comic novel with its parodic recycling and stylization of literary language. Unfortunately, not all of this important essay is quite so clear or provocative, least of all the perhaps overly fine distinctions he makes between different kinds of hybrid constructions.

A Novel Theorist

The first book by Bakhtin to appear in English translation was *Rabelais and His World*, a work well suited to the interests of the iconoclastic late 1960's. The second, *The Dialogic Imagination*, appeared thirteen years later. Drawing on the rediscovery of Bakhtin in the Soviet Union, it heralded the emergence of Bakhtin in the West as a major literary theorist. Although there are important differences between the two books (ones that a number of Bakhtin scholars have subsequently tried to minimize in an effort to reshape Bakhtin as an essentially conservative thinker), the most significant difference has to do with the circumstances surrounding their reception, specifically, the way *The Dialogic Imagination* was hailed as an important contribution to the growing field of narratology and as a viable but by no means reactionary alternative to other poststructuralist theories, deconstruction in particular.

In 1984, Michael Holquist and Katerina Clark published a biography of Bakhtin and his *Problemy poetiki Dostoevskogo* (1963; *Problems of Dostoevsky's Poetics*, 1973, 1984), an expanded version of a 1929 publication, was translated into English. The work contains Bakhtin's fullest treatment of the overall argument of *The Dialogic Imagination* and many of its main points as well. From these two works, the Bakhtin who was once known for his work on carnival (in the Rabelais book) has emerged as the novel's most important and influential theorist, both because of the stimulating albeit idiosyncratic way he has traced the novel's history and because he has examined so scrupulously the question of "who speaks" in the novel and "under what conditions." As Bakhtin points out in "Discourse in the Novel," "this is what determines the word's actual meaning. All direct meanings and direct expressions are false."

Robert A. Morace

Additional Reading

Danow, David K. *The Thought of Mikhail Bakhtin: From Word to Culture*. New York: St. Martin's Press, 1991. This gracefully written introduction is a clear and accessible presentation of Mikhail Bakhtin's thought for readers encountering the philosopher for the first time.

Dentith, Simon. *Bakhtinian Thought: An Introductory Reader*. New York: Routledge, 1995. This anthology reprints excerpts from Bakhtin's key works and presents well-researched critical guides to the concepts in those works.

Emerson, Caryl. *The First Hundred Years of Mikhail Bakhtin*. Princeton, N.J.: Princeton University Press, 1997. An indispensible book for those who wish to explore the ongoing world of Bakhtin scholarship. It provides an in-depth overview of the issues debated by Russian Bakhtinians as well as those debated by Bakhtin scholars of the English-speaking world.

Emerson, Caryl, and Gary Saul Morson. *Mikhail Bakhtin: Creation of a Poetics*. Stanford, Calif.: Stanford University Press, 1990. Though it is a little too detailed to be an accessible introduction to Bakhtin's philosophy, this is an invaluable companion to anyone trying to read his entire body of work.

Holquist, Michael, and Katerina Clark. *Mikhail Bakhtin*. Cambridge, Mass.: Harvard University Press, 1984. This critical biography of Mikhail Bakhtin is notable in part for its assertion that selected works of Bakhtin's associates, Pavel Medvedev and Valentin Voloshinov, were in fact the work of Mikhail Bakhtin, dictated to his friends and published under their names when he was out of favor with the Stalinist government. No definitive resolution of this issue has ever appeared.

Vice, Sue. *Introducing Bakhtin*. New York: Manchester University Press, 1997. Though this may not be the most definitive guide to Bakhtin's thought available, its use of contemporary references in long discussions of Bakhtin's concepts of heteroglossia, polyphony, dialogism, and the carnival make it helpful for those coming to his work with only a basic knowledge.

George W. Van Devender,
updated by Thomas Cassidy

Roland Barthes

Barthes made significant contributions to semiology and structuralism and was one of the most important literary critics and aestheticians of the twentieth century.

Principal philosophical works: *Le Degré zéro de l'écriture*, 1953 (*Writing Degree Zero*, 1967); *Michelet par lui-même*, 1954 (*Michelet*, 1986); *Mythologies*, 1957 (English translation, 1972); *Sur Racine*, 1963 (*On Racine*, 1964); *Essais critiques*, 1964 (*Critical Essays*, 1972); *La Tour Eiffel*, 1964 (*The Eiffel Tower and Other Mythologies*, 1979); *Éléments de sémiologie*, 1964 (*Elements of Semiology*, 1967); *Critique et vérité*, 1966 (*Criticism and Truth*, 1987); *Système de la mode*, 1967 (*The Fashion System*, 1983); *S/Z*, 1970 (English translation, 1974); *L'Empire des signes*, 1970 (*Empire of Signs*, 1982); *Sade, Fourier, Loyola*, 1971 (English translation, 1976); *Nouveaux essais critiques*, 1972 (*New Critical Essays*, 1980); *Le Plaisir du texte*, 1973 (*The Pleasure of the Text*, 1975); *Roland Barthes par Roland Barthes*, 1975 (*Roland Barthes by Roland Barthes*, 1977); *Fragments d'un discours amoureux*, 1977 (*A Lover's Discourse: Fragments*, 1978); *Image-Music-Text*, 1977; *Sollers écrivain*, 1979; *La Chambre claire: Note sur la photographie*, 1980 (*Camera Lucida: Reflections on Photography*, 1981); *Le Grain de la voix: Entretiens, 1962-1980*, 1981 (*The Grain of the Voice: Interviews, 1962-1980*, 1985); *A Roland Barthes Reader*, 1982; *L'Obvie et l'obtus*, 1982 (*The Responsibility of Forms*, 1985); *Le Bruissement de la langue*, 1984 (*The Rustle of Language*, 1986); *The Semiotic Challenge*, 1988.

Born: November 12, 1915; Cherbourg, France
Died: March 26, 1980; Paris, France

Early Life

Roland Gérard Barthes was born into the heart of the French bourgeoisie of Cherbourg on November 12, 1915. His father died in a World War I battle in 1916, leaving the family in reduced circumstances, although his mother learned the trade of bookbinding and kept the household together. Roland's early brilliance at the *lycée* pointed to a career in the high academic circles reserved for graduates of the École Normale Supérieure; however, he contracted tuberculosis in 1931 and was forced to attend a lesser institution, the Sorbonne. In 1937, he was declared unfit for military service because of his illness, and he taught from 1939 to 1941 in *lycées* in Biarritz and Paris. He was, however, forced to abandon teaching when the tuberculosis flared up again, and he spent the war years in a Swiss sanatorium. After the war, he taught in Romania and Egypt before returning to France. During this period, he became further acquainted with literary criticism

and linguistics and produced his first important book, *Writing Degree Zero*.

Life's Work

The distinguishing mark of Barthes's career was his refusal to be confined to one field of study, one critical position, or one group. He continually sought new areas to investigate after having made significant contributions to areas such as linguistics or semiology. Some have accused him of not developing or testing insights or breakthroughs he made; he has left it to others to complete systems in which he made seminal contributions. This refusal to be restricted to one position in a period of ideological rigidity is very attractive. A new work from Roland Barthes was always a new starting point for fresh investigations and never a mere recovering of old ground.

Through the 1940's and 1950's, Barthes worked in a branch of the French cultural service dealing with teaching abroad, and he was given a scholarship to study lexicology in 1950; however, he used that time to write his first books in the field of literary criticism. *Writing Degree Zero* is a

Marxist rewriting of French literary history that was influenced by Jean-Paul Sartre and is, in part, an answer to Sartre's *Qu'est-ce que la littérature?* (1947; *What Is Literature?*, 1949). Barthes was associated until the late 1970's with the journal *Tel Quel*, which stood for a more formal approach to literary works. In his first book, Barthes identifies two distinct periods of French literature. The first, or classical, runs from 1650, when the writers of that time began to see the "literariness" of language, to 1848, the year of revolution in all of Europe. The second period (or modern) began in the revolution and continues to the present; it is marked not by the representational mode of the early period but by a questioning and experimental type of literature. Later, in *S/Z*, Barthes defined two types of literary writing: the readerly (or the representational) and the writerly (the experimental). In this respect, he was the champion of the new, avant-garde literature. He was a supporter of the experiments of Alain Robbe-Grillet in the novel and defended him against received critical opinion. In *S/Z*, Barthes created a critical context in which these new writers could be discussed and understood.

Michelet and *On Racine* show Barthes moving away from the Marxism of Sartre to seeing a literary work as a system with codes or rules for functioning. In the book on Michelet, Barthes used many of the concepts of phenomenology in which the writer's ideology is ignored. Barthes discovered in Michelet the use of opposing substances, such as warm and dry. These substances show the "existential thematics" of Michelet; Michelet's thought is dismissed as of no interest. *On Racine* is more consciously structuralist and psychoanalytic, as Barthes examines the conflict between authority and the "primal horde." Barthes ignored the usual academic and historical view of the work in order to reveal its structure as composed of interior and exterior "spaces." His irreverent treatment of the most sacred of French classics engendered a challenge from the academic world. Raymond Picard accused Barthes and his criticism of being a

fraud, and Barthes replied with a defense of the new criticism that won the day. Barthes has consistently opposed a merely academic view of literature. Ironically, as a result of the notoriety of the Racine book and his innovative work, Barthes was appointed to teach at an academic institution, although it was not one of the first rank. He became a full-time teacher at the École Pratique des Hautes Études in 1962.

In *Mythologies*, Barthes is a semiologist examining the signs and signifiers found in popular culture as well as in literature. For example, Barthes examines wrestling as a system in which spectacle outweighs sport. In a similar fashion,

Roland Barthes. *(Holtz/Sygma)*

185

striptease is seen as a sport that is "nationalized" and expresses the essence of the French. The aim of the book is demystification, to show that assumptions about a practice or institution as being natural are false; they are instead strictly structured codes of culture. The book also tends to treat serious subjects in a playful way and trivial ones with great seriousness in an amusing and enlightening manner.

Mythologies was very popular, but once more Barthes refused to repeat or develop a successful mode. Next Barthes became a structuralist, and it is in this capacity that his greatest works were written. In *Critical Essays*, he defined structuralism as an "activity," not as a system. Structuralism's primary tools were the binary oppositions of Ferdinand de Saussure's linguistics, especially the opposition of the diachronic and synchronic and of *langue* (the language as a whole) and *parole* (the individual utterance). Perhaps the most thoroughgoing structuralist work Barthes produced is *S/Z*, in which he analyzed a story by Honoré de Balzac, "Sarrasine," in exhaustive detail. Barthes divides the analysis into codes: There is the proairetic code, which deals with plot; the hermeneutic code, which deals with suspense and enigmas; the semic code, which deals with character and other stereotypes; the symbolic code, which takes the reader from literal details to the level of symbolism; and the referential code, which deals with social and cultural aspects of the work. It is a monumental dissection of one short story, and the commentary tends to swamp the text. It does show how various types of critical apparatus can be applied to a specific literary work, but they remain fragments, as Barthes refused to combine the codes into a unified system. Some critics have seen in this refusal the seeds of poststructuralism or deconstruction. The book takes structuralism as far as it can go in revealing the "system" of a work, but it remains tantalizingly incomplete.

Barthes turned from structuralism to what is the key element of his later work, feeling. *The Pleasure of the Text* is a discussion and description of the many ways in which the reader derives pleasure from a literary work. One of the most important ways that the reader gains pleasure is not, for Barthes, from aesthetic contemplation of the whole but by ignoring the "whole" and "drifting" to passages that catch the interest and

attention of the reader. For Barthes, the pleasure of the text is equated with the body, and the pleasure derived from the text is compared to sexual bliss. It is a more personal way of looking at literature than the systems Barthes discovered earlier using linguistics as a tool.

Barthes had become an eminent figure in French intellectual life by this time, and he was appointed to a chair at the prestigious Collège de France in 1976. Barthes refused to be a traditional academic as he continued to emphasize pleasure and feeling in his critical work. In *A Lover's Discourse: Fragments*, he attempts to codify the language of love by using such texts as Johann Wolfgang von Goethe's *Die Leiden des jungen Werthers* (1774; *The Sorrows of Young Werther*, 1779), and he traces the typical gestures and maneuvers of love. Each aspect of the language of love is illustrated and discussed. In "Making Scenes," for example, Barthes traces the etymology of words used in such scenes and finds that they take the rhetorical form of stichomythia. Love may have had a very defined code for Barthes, but his analysis was not merely intellectual, and it did not become more important than the object it described. *A Lover's Discourse* became Barthes's most popular book, testifying to the accuracy of his analysis and observations.

One of the last works by Barthes was *Roland Barthes by Roland Barthes*, an autobiography done in fragments and memories. It contains lists of such things as "I Like" and "I Don't Like." There are a few revealing sections in the book; Barthes includes a fragment on the "Goddess H" that speaks of the pleasures of homosexuality and hashish. There are also photographs of the young Barthes and his bourgeois environment at the beginning, but the rest of the book is arranged in alphabetical order for each topic he discusses. There is no narrative in this "autobiography," but a picture of the essential Barthes does emerge. One aspect of Barthes that is revealed in the book is his opposition to *doxa*, or received opinion. He was always opposed to the rigidity of received authority.

Barthes's fertile mind continued to produce new and challenging works, such as his study of Japan, *Empire of Signs*, and a book on photography, *Camera Lucida: Reflections on Photography*, 1981). His reputation as an intellectual was international. In early 1980, Barthes was tragically killed after a laundry truck struck him as he attempted to cross a Paris street near the Collège de France.

Influence

Barthes is one of those rare individuals who made significant contributions to many fields. He was one of the first to see the applicability of semiology to a wide range of topics. He was not the first to discover how the structures of linguistics could be applied to all of the human sciences, but he was one of its most elegant practitioners. *S/Z* is one of the finest and fullest structuralist analyses extant. Furthermore, Barthes pointed the way for poststructuralism and showed how literary criticism could reveal not unity but fragmentation. He also never lost sight of the importance of emotion in literature and life and of the dangers of completing and fixing any system of thought. He freed criticism from a narrow academic view and led it to the multiplicity of voices it currently enjoys.

James Sullivan

Mythologies

Type of philosophy: Aesthetics, epistemology
First published: 1957 (English translation, 1972)
Principal ideas advanced:

◇ Myth is a type of speech, a message, a mode of signification, a form.
◇ Everything can be a myth, including objects if they mean something.
◇ Mythology is part of semiology and of ideology.
◇ There is a tridimensional pattern in myth: signifier, signified, and sign.
◇ In myth, there are two semiological systems: a linguistic system (language-object) and myth itself (metalanguage).
◇ Myths can be deciphered only through naming concepts, but there is no fixity in mythical concepts because these are condensations of certain sets of knowledge.
◇ Myth plays on this analogy between meaning and form.

◇ There are three ways of reading and deciphering myth, based on focusing on meaning or form or both at the same time.

This classic of semiotics is composed of discrete essays written one a month for about two years (from 1954 to 1956) on diverse topics suggested by French daily life. It shows how heterogeneous phenomena can be interpreted as myth or metalanguage because they are cultural moments and constitute their own language. Philosopher Ferdinand de Saussure's distinction between language and discourse generated Roland Barthes's investigation of mundane mythologies as active language. Barthes did not consider semiology a grid but an imaginative play with signs, very much like Gaston Bachelard's phenomenology. Barthes's tactic of codifying or classifying phenomena flies in the face of philosophers who consider systems to be absurd, including Søren Kierkegaard, Friedrich Nietzsche, and Ludwig Wittgenstein. It makes for antilinear discourse, and the style permits philosophy to become a performance with multiple meanings.

Mythologies is divided into two sections. The first is a series of short essays on diverse subjects of French bourgeois life; the second is a philosophical essay on myth. The book is a set of commentaries in the form of short semiological investigations of the operations of myth on the daily sensibilities of social human beings and of the bourgeoisie (the class that assigns value to things).

Signs

Every phenomenon is a set of signs. For example, professional wrestling, the subject of Barthes's first essay in the book, is not a sport but a "spectacle of excess" where everything (the wrestler's physique or temperament or technique or an individual moment of competition) is a sign of something else. The wrestler's body expresses through gesture a temperament—ignobility, suffering, defeat, or justice—that is the signified message.

In this way, even wrestling becomes a language, a "diacritic writing" that can be read by means of "gestures, attitudes, and mimicry which make the intention utterly obvious." Indeed, wrestling is a theatrical spectacle, where the wrestler's mask (of suffering, arrogance, ridiculousness, and so on) provides "the image of passion, not passion itself." Therefore, wrestling conforms to images of the great themes of its own mythology, and it accomplishes what its public expects.

The fundamental question is what really lies beneath a gesture or sign. Barthes asserts that a seemingly straightforward signifier transmits a code or set of codes that triggers a message (the signified), converting it into a new mythology. To this end, he focuses on so-called mass culture in order to expose the bourgeoisie as the enemy of myth because this class appropriates phenomena to nationalize them and treat them as social property. Food, drink, cookery, and toys become signs of national character, just as automobiles, the Domenici trial, detergents, striptease, and certain pastimes constitute a new metalanguage of the French bourgeoisie.

In showing how even food and drink can be seen as nationalized basic elements that follow the index of patriotic values, Barthes fans out his semiology into sociopolitical criticism. The essay on wine shows how this drink is considered a French possession and shares a sanguine mythology with steak, except that the mythology of wine bears contradictions, for the drinking of it is both a pleasure as well as a gesture of decoration. Yet, because the production of wine is deeply involved in French capitalism—whether that of "the private distillers or that of the big settlers in Algeria who impose on the Muslims, on the very land of which they have been dispossessed, a crop of which they have no need, while they lack even bread"—the mythology of wine is not innocent.

Barthes can take something as apparently innocuous as toys and turn them into an intriguing system of signs: "French toys *always mean something*, and this something is always entirely socialized, constituted by the myths or the techniques of modern adult life." He can look at the sleek new Citroen and see in its bodywork, upholstery, and accessories the actualization of petit-bourgeois advancement. The colorful rich glazes of ornamental cookery become for him a clever appeal to the working-class' need for gentility.

The Bourgeois Myth
Barthes criticizes the bourgeoisie because of its effects on art and mythology. He condemns bour-

geois art for "naturalizing" phenomena and for giving rise to an essentialist mythology that costs people dearly in language and reality. Barthes cites the case of the Gaston Dominici murder trial of 1952, in which an eighty-year-old Provencal landowner was convicted of murdering three persons found camping near his land. Barthes shows how the judiciary used unreal clichés and epithets from Latin translations and French essays to decorate a psychology posited on categories of action and soul-states straight out of traditional literature. Such a case demonstrates how people can be deprived of language when two conflicting languages, that of official law and that of the uneducated goatherd, grope blindly without ever touching each other or understanding their own psychology.

What Barthes means by the essentialist nature of bourgeois myth can be seen in his essay "Blue Guide," in which he discusses the Spanish typology that masks reality by codes that reduce a land and its people to picturesque essences: "In Spain, for instance, the Basque is an adventurous sailor, the Levantine a light-hearted gardener, the Catalan a clever tradesman and the Cantabrian a sentimental highlander." Ironically, "Blue Guide" expresses a mythology that is obsolete for part of the bourgeoisie itself, because in reducing geography to a description of a world of monuments, "Blue Guide" fails to account for the present and renders the monuments themselves undecipherable or senseless.

New Mythologies
The second part of the book is a substantial essay called "Myth Today," which outlines Barthes's theory of new mythologies. It postulates myth as a type of speech, not just of any type but as communication or message. Speech is not restricted to an oral form; it can consist of modes of writing or of representations, such as photography, cinema, reporting, sport, shows, and publicity, all of which are discourses that support mythical speech. In fact, we are dealing with particular images for particular significations, so even objects become speech if they mean something.

There is a tridimensional pattern in myth because we are dealing with three different terms: signifier, signified, and sign. For example, roses can be a signifier of passion (the signified). The third term, which is the unification of the first two, is roses weighted with passion (the sign or meaning).

Myth has two semiologial systems: a linguistic system, which is the language with which myth builds itself (Barthes calls this "language-object"); and metalanguage (myth itself) which speaks about the first. Barthes provides two distinct examples of mythical speech. In the first, the Latin phrase *quia ego nominor leo* ("because my name is lion") is clearly an example of the grammatical rule about predicate agreement. It really tells us little about the lion. Therefore, there is a signified (*I am a grammatical example*) and a signification in the form of a correlation between signifier and signified, for neither the naming of the lion nor the grammatical example is a separate entity. Barthes's second example is the cover of *Paris-Match* magazine in which a young black man in French uniform is saluting something. Barthes presumes that the man is probably saluting the French tricolor. There is a signifier (a black soldier giving the French salute); there is a signified (a mixture of Frenchness and militariness); and finally, there is "a presence of the signified through the signifier."

The meaning of each myth belongs to a history, that of the lion or that of the black man, and so the meaning is *already* complete because it is based on a past, a memory, a comparative order of facts and ideas. The Latin example calls up a certain period when Latin grammar was taught by example to some children whose linguistic habits trained them to see the illustrated grammatical rules as something worthy of note. In the saluting black soldier example, the concept of French imperiality is tied to the general history of France, its colonial adventures, and its present difficulties. However, when both these examples become form, they void themselves of their contingencies; in other words, they empty themselves until only images or gestures remain.

Meaning presents form, and form always outlasts meaning. The paradox is a signal one for there is never any contradiction or split between meaning and form. Indeed, myth can have no meaning without motivated form. For French imperiality to successfully deploy the image of a saluting black man, there must be an indentification between the black man's salute and that of the French soldier. French imperiality can be given many other signifiers beside a black man's salute—a French general pinning a decoration on a one-armed Senegalese, a nun handing tea to a bed-ridden Arab, a white schoolmaster teaching black children—so this leads to the idea that there is no fixity in mythical concepts because, being based on a condensation of certain sets of knowledge, they can alter, disintegrate, or disappear.

Barthes produces three different readings of myth by focusing on meaning (a full signifier) or form (an empty signifier) or both at the same time. The first two types are static and analytical: The focus on form fills the myth literally (the saluting black man is a symbol or example of French imperiality); a focus on meaning, which distinguishes meaning from form, yields a distortion (the saluting black soldier becomes the alibi of French imperiality). The third type of focus is dynamic and yields an ambiguous signifier: The saluting black man is no longer a symbol or alibi; he is "the very *presence* of French imperiality."

Bourgeois Ideology
There are two languages that resist myth: One is mathematical (this is a finished language that admits no parasitism); the other is poetic (this is essentialist, seeking to be an antilanguage because it believes there are no ideas but in things themselves). The essentialist attitude is what also informs bourgeois ideology, which continuously seeks to transform the products of history into essential types, as in the Basque identity's being expressed ethnically by a Basque chalet. This attitude also reveals language's ability to *signify* rather than represent reality.

Bourgeois ideology transforms the reality of the world into an image of the world; in other words, the world supplies myth with a historical reality, and myth gives back a natural image of this reality. Although the status of the bourgeois is contingent on historical factors, humanity is represented as something universal and unchanging. Bourgeois ideology expresses myth's capacity to provide a natural justification for historical intention. Therefore, the semiological definition of myth in a bourgeois society is *depoliticized speech*. When the image of the black soldier states French imperiality without explaining it, the myth abolishes the complexity of French colonialism and accepts it as something *natural*, thereby depoliticizing reality and its language.

The book concludes with seven rhetorical forms of bourgeois myth. Barthes contends that the bourgeoisie, while admitting some of its small evils, conceals its large ones. History becomes the servant of the bourgeois, and the petit bourgeois is unable to imagine the Other because that threatens his or her secure existence. Bourgeois mythology is a tautology that assumes its own causality and explains itself by killing rationality. It does not accommodate choice; instead, it seeks merely to endorse itself by a quantification of quality and by an appeal to universalism. Bourgeois aphorisms belong to metalanguage because they are an overlayer for a world already made, established on common sense (that is, something arbitrarily assumed to be its own truth), and held to be unchanging.

A System of Cultural Criticism

Mythologies is widely known in the West as a seminal work by a French critic who popularized cultural criticism. The book is an example of structural method and semiological analysis, for it considers phenomena as systems. This concept of system is justified on a methodological level beyond the result of any particular configuration.

Mythologies demonstrates a short, summative, expository style that is, as Susan Sontag claims, recognizably French, for it stems from "the idiosyncratic essays published between the two world wars in the *Nouvelle Revue Française*." Barthes's theory has influenced every philosopher-critic (from Claude Lévi-Strauss to Susan Sontag) who seeks an eccentric discourse on form, for the essays reconstitute the structure of phenomena while formulating their meaning. The disposition to codify or classify phenomena is exercised by semiology's famous triad of signified, signifier, and sign without appearing to be a static taxonomy. *Mythologies* helped Barthes and his successors explore the language-systems of many other phenomena, such as photography, Japanese culture, Nazi ideology, and eroticism, before Barthes went on to his great project of the reading of the self.

Keith Garebian

Additional Reading

Calvet, Louis Jean. *Roland Barthes: A Biography*. Bloomington: Indiana University Press, 1995. This comprehensive account of Barthes's life frequently provides connections between Barthes's biography and his literary production. Includes numerous photographs, a bibliography, and an index.

Culler, Jonathan. *Roland Barthes*. New York: Oxford University Press, 1983. The best short study of Barthes's works. Culler divides the protean Barthes into such areas as "Mythologist" and "Hedonist," which enables the reader to see the range of Barthes's mind. Contains clear, direct, and insightful discussions.

Knight, Diana. *Barthes and Utopia: Space, Travel, Writing*. Oxford, England: Clarendon Press, 1997. Knight thoroughly examines Barthes's work, thereby placing his work into larger political and theoretical contexts.

Lavers, Annette. *Roland Barthes: Structuralism and After*. Cambridge, Mass.: Harvard University Press, 1982. The most detailed study of Barthes's literary criticism. Lavers discusses not only Barthes's thought but also critics who influenced and were influenced by him. Scholarly.

Moriarty, Michael. *Roland Barthes*. Stanford, Calif.: Stanford University Press, 1991. A lucid introduction to Barthes's writings, usefully equipped with definitions, illustrations, and relevant contextual background for the benefit of new readers of his work. Includes primary and secondary bibliographies and a brief "Biographical Appendix."

Payne, Michael. *Reading Knowledge: An Introduction to Barthes, Foucault, and Althusser*. Malden, Mass.: Blackwell, 1997. Barthes's principal works are introduced and carefully examined. Payne also devotes a section to the study of Barthes's important work, *S/Z* .

Sontag, Susan. "Writing Itself: On Roland Barthes." In *A Barthes Reader*. New York: Hill & Wang, 1982. Sontag provides a sympathetic and revealing introduction to Barthes's thought and an excellent selection of Barthes's writing. Students who wish to read Barthes might begin here.

Stafford, Andy. *Roland Barthes, Phenomenon and Myth: An Intellectual Biography*. Edinburgh: Edinburgh University Press, 1998. Stafford examines the influences on Barthes's work and how that work was received.

Wasserman, George. *Roland Barthes*. World Authors series. Boston: Twayne, 1981. A brief biographical section is followed by a critical overview of Barthes's works. Includes a bibliography, a chronology, and an index.

James Sullivan, updated by William Nelles

Georges Bataille

Bataille developed a philosophy of excess and exuberance. His claim that human beings need to break rules and pass boundaries in order to realize a sense of the sacred influenced many later thinkers generally identified with postmodern trends in philosophy.

Principal philosophical works: *L'Expérience intérieure*, 1943, rev. ed. 1954 (*Inner Experience*, 1988); *Le Coupable*, 1944 (*Guilty*, 1989); *Sur Nietzsche*, 1945 (*On Nietzsche*, 1992); *La Part maudite*, 1949 (3 volumes; *The Accursed Share*, volume 1, 1988, volumes 2-3, 1991); *L'Érotisme*, 1957 (*Eroticism, Death, and Sensuality*, 1986); *Les Larmes d'Éros*, 1962 (*The Tears of Eros*, 1989); *Œuvres complètes*, 1970-1988; *Théorie de religion*, 1974 (*Theory of Religion*, 1989); *Visions of Excess: Selected Writings, 1927-1939*, 1985.

Born: September 10, 1897; Billom, Puy-de-Dôme, France
Died: July 8, 1962; Paris, France

Early Life

Many of the details of Georges Bataille's early life come from his own writings. It is difficult to know, then, to what extent a painful childhood produced his fascination with the bizarre and to what extent his fevered imagination shaped his presentation of his own background. According to Bataille, his father suffered from blindness and general paralysis brought on by syphilis. The disease gradually drove his father insane, and madness apparently intensified the older Bataille's dislike of the Catholic religion, because he refused to have a priest present when he died and expired ranting against the Roman Catholic Church. Georges Bataille's youthful Catholic piety and lifelong attraction to religious feeling may have stemmed from rebellion against this anticlerical father.

In 1900, the family moved from Bataille's birthplace to the nearby city of Reims. Bataille dropped out of school temporarily in 1913 and became a devout Catholic in 1914, just before the outbreak of World War I. The Germans advanced on the city, and Bataille and his mother evacuated, abandoning his father, who could not be moved because his syphilis was in an advanced state.

Young Bataille entered the seminary of Saint-Fleur in 1917, intending to become a monk. The following year, he produced his first-known published work, a six-page pamphlet on Notre Dame de Reims, a cathedral that had been nearly destroyed by German shelling. Bataille foretold the restoration of the cathedral and the restoration of the medieval Catholic spirit of its original builders. However, Bataille lost his faith in 1920, apparently as a result of a romantic involvement with a woman.

Bataille did not lose his interest in things medieval along with his faith. At the famous École de Chartres, he trained to be a librarian specializing in medieval texts. He also obtained a fellowship to study at the School of Advanced Hispanic Studies in Madrid. While traveling in Spain, he witnessed the gory death of a bullfighter, a scene that left a deep impression on him. In 1922, he submitted his thesis on a medieval romance to the École de Chartres, then obtained a position as a librarian at the Bibliothèque Nationale, where he would remain until poor health forced him to resign in 1942.

Life's Work

During the 1920's, Bataille published a number of scholarly articles on numismatics, the study of old coins. He also began to lead a second life, one that moved him into the French intellectual and artistic avant-garde. During World War I, disillusionment with the values of European society had led a number of young intellectuals to take up the movement known as Dada, a rebellion against all artistic and social standards. Under the leadership of poet and theorist André Breton, some of the Dadaists formed the Surrealist movement. While Dada was largely dedicated to pure revolt and ridicule, the adherents of Surrealism proposed to create new values out of the unconscious and the irrational.

In 1924, Bataille became friends with Michel Leiris, who was to become involved with Surrealism. Although Bataille had difficult relations with the Surrealists and was often regarded as an enemy by Breton, Bataille and the Surrealists became part of the same Parisian intellectual milieu. Bataille's fictions and philosophical writings display the hallucinatory, dreamlike quality and exotic, incongruous images associated with Surrealism.

Leiris was one of the few readers of Bataille's first book, *W. C.*, written in 1926 and later burned unpublished by the author. According to Leiris, *W. C.* displayed Bataille's characteristic obsessions with sexuality, excrement, violence, and death. The following year, 1927, Bataille wrote the essay "L'Anus solaire" (published 1931; "The Solar Anus," 1985), in which he proclaims the sacred connection of all things through parody and sex. Although the essay does not take the form of an argument, it essentially maintains that the verb "to be" (the copula) unifying objects is the same as copulation unifying bodies. With the death of God, there is nothing to maintain the stability of this unification; therefore, all things can become parodies of all other things, and unstable copulation becomes the melting of bodies into bodies in perverse sexuality.

One doctor, a Dr. Dausse, who read *W. C.* and "The Solar Anus" was so shocked by the obsessive character of the writing that he arranged for Bataille to begin treatment with the psychotherapist Adrien Borel. Familiarity with psychotherapy intensified Bataille's interest in the role of unconscious drives in human experience. The therapy also helped him to continue to write by clarifying his own emotional complexities. While in therapy, he entered into a brief marriage with the actress Sylvia Makles, later the wife of psychoanalytic theorist Jacques Lacan, and had a child.

Bataille's first published book was the novel *L'Histoire de l'oeil* (1928; *The Story of the Eye*, 1977), which appeared under the pseudonym Lord Auch. The novel is an erotic fantasy, influenced by the Marquis de Sade, marked by bizarre, perverse imagery. In 1929, Bataille and a group of associates from the Surrealist movement founded the journal *Documents*, in which Bataille published a series of essays. These essays, based on things such as photographs of toes and the genitals of plants, dealt with the constantly shifting boundaries of ideas and objects in a godless world.

While editing *Documents*, Bataille began to read Marxist literature and started to expand his previously self-absorbed speculations into social philosophy. He made contact with the anti-Stalinist Democratic Communist circle and contributed articles in which he developed his ideas about expenditure as the basis of economic activity to the Democratic Communist journal *La Critique Sociale*. He moved further in the direction of political and social philosophy when he attended the lectures of the celebrated philosopher Alexandre Kojève on Georg Wilhelm Friedrich Hegel and Karl Marx from 1934 to 1939.

As a consequence of this growing concern with social philosophy, Bataille, Leiris, and former Surrealist Roger Caillois founded a group known as the College of Sociology in 1937. The College of Sociology sponsored lectures by some of continental Europe's best-known intellectuals, including Jean-Paul Sartre, Claude Lévi-Strauss, and Walter Benjamin. Bataille also established a secret society known as Acéphale that published a review of the same name and held mysterious rituals in order to create an atheistic, ecstatic religion. In a more public fashion, the College of Sociology dedicated itself to developing a "sacred sociology," which explored the role of the sacred in creating human society.

The College of Sociology and Acéphale broke up with the onset of World War II. During the war years, Bataille appeared to move away from his social concerns. His most important productions at this time were the three books that he later named the *La Somme athéologique* (summa atheologica). These were *Inner Experience, Guilty*, and *On Nietzsche*. Intended to recall the *Summa theologiaea* (c. 1265-1273; *Summa Theologica*, 1911-

1921) of Saint Thomas Aquinas, these writings explore the contradictions, paradoxes, and absence of ultimate definitions in establishing standards and bounds in a universe without a god. *Inner Experience*, the most widely read book of *La Somme athéologique*, attempts to create an atheistic version of religious mysticism from the self-contradictory human urges to be separate from the surrounding universe and to achieve union with it.

Following the war, Bataille returned to social and political philosophy with his three-volume *The Accursed Share*, based on an article on the notion of expenditure that he had written during the College of Sociology period. The concepts of surplus and waste were at the core of Bataille's thinking on economic and social relationships. Bataille maintained that living organisms receive more energy than they need for survival. If the excess energy cannot be spent in growth, it must be expended as waste. The basic problem of humanity and, indeed, the basic problem of living matter in general is the expenditure of excess energy or useless consumption.

Bataille referred to consumption as a luxury. He identified three luxuries in nature: eating, death, and sexual reproduction. Each luxury is an establishment of relations between self and not-self. Eating wastes energy because through being eaten, more efficient systems such as simple plants and animals lower on the food chain are lost to less efficient systems. These eaters and predators impose heavier burdens on the environment, are further from self-sufficiency, and squander more life in each moment of existence.

In death, a system squanders all its energy, yielding it all to the surrounding environment. Destruction creates an absolute unity between self and not-self. The paradoxical nature of squandering becomes clearest in sexuality. Through sexuality, individuals give up their own energies and their own possibilities for growth for the species. According to Bataille, all economic transactions and all social relationships are products of the need to give up excess.

The works Bataille composed after World War II offer the most coherent statements of excess and expenditure as the foundations of human society. In 1946, Bataille founded the journal *Critique*. In this journal, he published early works by philosophers who would come to dominate the French intellectual scene, including Roland Barthes, Jacques Derrida, and Michel Foucault. As Bataille's reputation grew, some of the works that he had written earlier were made more widely available or were published for the first time. His novel *Le Bleu du ciel* (1957; *Blue of Noon*, 1978), for example, was written in 1935 but first published in 1957.

Throughout the last two decades of his life, Bataille suffered from recurrent tuberculosis and from continual financial difficulties. Remarrying after the war, he supported himself by returning to work as a librarian, first in Charpentras and later in Orleans. In 1961, Pablo Picasso, Max Ernst, Joan Miró, and other artist friends of Bataille held an art auction to raise money for the ailing Bataille. With the proceeds of this auction, he was able to purchase an apartment in Paris and live comfortably for a short time as something of a cult figure, admired by many of the leading intellectuals in France. Until shortly before his end in 1962, Bataille worked steadily on a last book of meditations on sexuality and death.

Influence

Despite the disturbing quality of his writing, Bataille was an influential figure both because of his role in intellectual networks during his lifetime and because of the continuing impact of his ideas after his death. Bataille took part in many of the central movements of the French avant-garde. He participated in Surrealism and was, at the same time, a major critic of Breton's Surrealist movement. As a founder of the College of Sociology, Bataille helped provide a forum for some of France's most brilliant philosophers and social thinkers. His journal *Critique* introduced many of the philosophers, such as Derrida and Foucault, who would later become known as poststructuralists.

Bataille's greatest impact on Western philosophy was probably his concept of transgression, the continual breaking of boundaries, as an act that disintegrates the traditional philosophical distinction between subject and object and between self and not-self. In an article entitled "Homage to Bataille," published in *Critique* in 1963, Foucault acknowledged Bataille as basic to the formation of his own philosophy. Foucault and others known as poststructuralists tended to see acts of transgression as acts of liberation from social and intellectual limits. Because sexuality is a fundamental human impulse, Foucault and other poststructuralists have also followed Bataille in seeing sexual transgression as a particularly important means of liberation.

Bataille's critics often object to the violence and nihilism, or rejection of all values, in his work. Nevertheless, Bataille offered intriguing insights into the role of the irrational in human thoughts, actions, and social relations.

Carl L. Bankston III

Inner Experience

Type of philosophy: Aesthetics, ethics, philosophy of religion

First published: L'Expérience intérieure, 1943, rev. ed. 1954 (English translation, 1988)

Principal ideas advanced:

◇ Without God, there is no ultimate transcendent reality outside the individual human to be approached through mysticism.

◇ The impulse toward mystical experience is a result of the human desire to surpass the limited, individual existence and to achieve union with all that exists outside the self.

◇ The desire to surpass a limited individual experience is, taken to the extreme, a desire to become everything; however, since there is no God, in the form of a being with distinct objective existence, there is also no ultimate state of union.

◇ At the same time that humans have the desire to become everything, they also have the contradictory urge to establish personal autonomy, a separate existence.

◇ Mystical experience is a matter of breaking down the boundaries between the individual and everything outside the individual; this breaking of boundaries is termed transgression.

◇ Sexual transgression is a particularly important way of breaking down boundaries because sex involves unions between individuals and persons or objects outside individuals.

◇ The urge to establish autonomy means that individuals are constantly creating new boundaries as they break down existing boundaries.

◇ Therefore, mystical experience is a continual process of creation and transgression, of continually establishing and surpassing limits.

Inner Experience was one of three books written by Georges Bataille during World War II in an attempt to express his philosophy of the sacred in human life. The other two volumes were *Le Coupable* (1944; *Guilty,* 1988) and *Sur Nietzsche* (1945; *On Nietzsche,* 1992). After the war, Bataille reworked these books somewhat and named them *La Somme athéologique* (summa atheologica). This general title was intended to recall the *Summa theologiaea* (c. 1265-1273; *Summa Theologica,* 1911-1921) of Saint Thomas Aquinas, the principal statement of Catholic religious philosophy during the Middle Ages. Bataille envisioned his work, in contrast to that of Aquinas, as an atheistic religious philosophy.

In style, *Inner Experience* and the other two books have little in common with the systematic, logical exposition of Aquinas. Instead, they are chiefly aphoristic, consisting of fragmented exclamations and images. This is consistent with Bataille's intent in offering an alternative to the thinking represented by Aquinas. Although traditional philosophy is held together by a supreme being from whom all reason is derived and toward whom all reason proceeds, Bataille's philosophy has no supreme being or center to maintain a systematic logic.

Although Bataille was an original thinker, *Inner Experience* shows the influence of a number of currents of thought. These include religious mysticism, Dada and Surrealism, and the vitalist tradition that gave rise to modern existentialism. Although the general title *La Somme athéologique* echoes Saint Thomas Aquinas, the rapturous tone of *Inner Experience* recalls the writings of Christian mystics such as Saint Theresa of Avila and Saint John of the Cross. In his youth, Bataille was a devout Catholic and briefly planned to become a monk. Even after losing his faith, the premodern Christian religious heritage remained a part of Bataille's background because he was educated as a medieval librarian.

Surrealist and Vitalist Influences

Religious mysticism was a premodern influence on Bataille, and other influences were distinctly antimodern. The scientific, rational, and progressive attitudes characteristic of the modern perspective emerged with the development of industrial civilization. During World War I, many Europeans began to feel disillusioned with modern society. Among intellectuals, the disillusionment gave rise to the Dada movement, an artistic and philosophical rebellion against progress and rationality. Surrealism followed Dada, replacing Dada's pure rebellion with an exaltation of the irrational, the unconscious, and the life of dreams. Bataille had close personal connections with many members of the French Surrealist movement and his writing often shows the spontaneity and startling, hallucinatory imagery associated with Surrealism.

The vitalist reaction against modernism opposed the logic and science of the modern worldview with intuition, instinct, and personal experience. In the nineteenth century, thinkers such as Søren Kierkegaard and Friedrich Nietzsche asserted the primacy of flowing existence over abstract logic. The early twentieth century philosopher Henri Bergson, whose teachings inspired the existentialist Jean-Paul Sartre, helped to make the vitalist approach a central part of French intellectual life by presenting a vital impulse, approachable only by intuition, as the fundamental reality. Bataille's own views of inner experience as intuitive and irrational in character owe a great deal to this vitalist trend in French thinking.

A Commentary on the Mystical Experience

Inner Experience is an unusual philosophical work. Both the style of the book and the ideas in it are difficult for most readers. It does not present a systematic argument or relate a narrative. Instead, it consists of loosely organized fragments. Its style often seems to have more in common with poetry than with traditional philosophical prose, and the author's intent in writing is as much to induce a rapturous, hypnotic state of mind in himself and in the reader as it is to give voice to ideas. In part, the book consists of a commentary on the mystical experience that unfolds as the author tries to evoke such an experience through his writing. In part, it consists of autobiographical pieces that describe Bataille's own mystical experiences.

The 1954 edition, which is the edition that was translated into English, consists of five parts. The first part, entitled "Sketch of an Introduction to *Inner Experience*," comes closest to traditional philosophical exposition. In this section, Bataille defines his concept of inner experience and describes his method for achieving this state. Inner experience is similar to religious mysticism insofar as both involve rapture and ecstasy, or the surpassing of the limitations of the usual self. Loss of self in Bataille's state, though, does not lead to any ultimate union with God. Rapture, or the surpassing of the self, has no goal beyond itself.

According to Bataille, one reaches rapture through "dramatization." Although his use of this term is obscure, dramatization apparently involves breaking the boundary between oneself and the supposedly external world by investing the world with emotional intensity and then allowing the words or images used to achieve that intensity to dissolve into nothingness. From this perspective, religious rituals would be a means of dramatizing existence, of bestowing a special intensity on objects and actions. This type of intensity is, according to Bataille, experience at the extreme limit of the possible. At the end of the first part of this work, Bataille slips into a series of observations on how Hindus, Christian mystics, and the philosopher Nietzsche have attempted to surpass the limits of ordinary existence.

The second part, entitled "The Torment," resembles the inspired writings of the Christian mystics. It is a poetic evocation of the anguish entailed in the urge to ecstasy and of the release from anguish when one reaches the ecstatic state. Giving his own ecstasy at a French monastery on the Isle of Wight as an example, Bataille proclaims that ecstasy is not achieved by knowledge but by the realization of "non-knowledge." Knowledge is a relationship between a subject and an object. Ecstasy is a matter of erasing the distinction between the subject and the object.

The first two parts, then, basically involve setting up something like a reasoned argument for the necessity of going beyond reason and then plunging into a state beyond reason. The third part, "Antecedents to the Torment (or the Comedy)," is a collection of Bataille's writings from the 1930's. These are chiefly aphorisms on the flow of life and on gaining access to the universal.

The fourth part, "Post Scriptum to the Torment (Or the New Mystical Theology)," returns to something like a philosophical argument. It is a series of meditations on God, René Descartes, Georg Wilhelm Friedrich Hegel, Friedrich Nietzsche, ecstasy, and fortune. Despite the references to the philosophers, these are not logical analyses or refutations, but reflections on the nature of knowledge and activity. Bataille refers to both knowledge and activity as "projects," or the pursuit of goals. Bataille rejects "projects," or goal-oriented activities, because these involve postponing existence while pursuing a goal outside present existence. Following Nietzsche's proclamation of the death of God, Bataille announces that there are no ultimate standards and no goals to be achieved. The only projects that are acceptable are those projects, like this book, whose ultimate purpose is to lead beyond themselves and then destroy themselves, to become purposeless.

God, Bataille indicates in his meditation on the supreme being, is beyond all things and therefore is nothingness and has knowledge of his own nothingness. God is thus an atheist. Observations such as these make it clear that Bataille's "atheism" differs radically from that of the scientific materialist. In fact, Bataille points out in his meditation on the sixteenth century philosopher Descartes, modern science is based on rational discourse, which is founded on an intuition of an ultimate reality. If the ultimate reality is groundless, though, rational discourse becomes an illusion.

The dialectical reasoning of nineteenth century philosopher Hegel, Bataille maintains, is also ultimately illusory and unsatisfying. Hegel argued that consciousness creates reality when the known confronts the unknown and the confrontation results in a new and higher form of the known. However, for Bataille, non-knowledge is the source of all knowledge, and the movement of knowledge is toward its own empty, illusory character.

Having established his "new theology" as an antitheology, an argument for the nonexistence of God and for mysticism as movement toward emptiness, Bataille finally moves beyond even fragmentary prose. In the fifth part, "Manibus Date Lilia Plenis" ("Give Lilies by the Handful"), he breaks into rapturous poetry on the glories of union with the ultimate, which is the final mystical self-annihilation.

Inner Experience was controversial from the time it was first published. The celebrated philosopher Jean-Paul Sartre published an article entitled "Un Noveau Mystique" ("A New Mysticism") in 1947, objecting to the book's obscure language, its emotionalism, and its mystical elitism. While claiming to destroy the sovereign self, Sartre maintained, Bataille was actually creating a myth of a higher, mystical self, a false and antidemocratic ideal. Further, Sartre felt that the book reached no conclusions, led nowhere, and was therefore ultimately pointless.

A Theory of Political Economy

The ideas on the sacred that Bataille developed in *Inner Experience* and the other books of the war years did, however, lead to a further progression in Bataille's own thinking. Bataille contrasted "projects," work and other goal-oriented activities, with the sacred; he maintained that projects were illusory and the emptiness of the sacred was the true origin of action. These views led Bataille, in the three-volume *La Part maudite* (1949; *The Accursed Share*, 1988, volume 1; 1991, volumes 2-3), to develop a theory of political economy. Bataille maintained that economic systems, like organisms, grow because they accumulate energy as they seek to surpass their own limitations and to become what they are not. When they reach the limits of growth, they can only become what they are not by squandering their energy and by self-destruction. Thus, whether one agrees with Bataille's political economy or not, one may see his mystical views as premises for some intriguing and original conclusions about the irrational basis of human social and economic relations.

Bataille's Admirers

Although the obscurity and apparent nihilism of works such as *Inner Experience* have repelled some readers, others have been drawn to Bataille by precisely those qualities. The philosopher Michel Foucault praised Bataille for his violation of boundaries and for his destruction of the philosophical subject. Other philosophers of the French poststructuralist trend, such as Jacques Derrida, have admired Bataille for his playful self-contradictions and self-refutations, which they see as the refusal to accept an ultimate truth.

Bataille began to attract a following (or a cult, some critics might say) among American academics during the 1980's and 1990's. The English translation of *Inner Experience* appeared at approximately the same time that translations of many other works of this author became available, and it was widely discussed in academic circles concerned with modern European thinking.

Carl L. Bankston III

Additional Reading

Bataille, Georges. *Visions of Excess: Selected Writings, 1927-1939*, edited by Allan Stoekl. Minneapolis: University of Minnesota Press, 1985. A collection of Bataille's early writings, with a helpful introduction by the editor that can provide general readers with some insight into the development of Bataille's thinking.

Drury, Shadia B. *Alexandre Kojève: The Roots of Postmodern Politics*. New York: St. Martin's Press, 1994. Examines the influence of the ideas of Alexandre Kojève, a Russian thinker who introduced the philosophy of Georg Wilhelm Friedrich Hegel to many French thinkers, including Georges Bataille. Chapter 8 looks specifically at how Kojève's Hegelian teachings affected Bataille's philosophical views.

Hollier, Denis, ed. *The College of Sociology, 1937-1939*. Translated by Betsy Wing. Minneapolis: University of Minnesota Press, 1988. A collection of writings by Bataille and his colleagues, during the period of the College of Sociology, on their attempts to develop a sacred sociology. In addition to writings by Bataille, it includes lectures by other participants such as Michel Leiris and Roger Caillois. The editor is one of the foremost French authorities on Bataille and his circle. Hollier's discussion of the College of Sociology in the foreword will provide useful background for readers seeking to learn about Bataille and French intellectual circles on the eve of World War II.

Land, Nick. *The Taste for Annihilation: Georges Bataille and Virulent Nihilism (An Essay in Atheistic Religion)*. New York: Routledge, 1992. A philosophical essay on Bataille's ideas on the sacred. The writing is difficult and the book is probably best suited for readers who already have some familiarity with Bataille's work.

Nadeau, Maurice. *The History of Surrealism*. Translated by Richard Howard. New York: Macmillan, 1965. The authoritative history of the Surrealist movement, written by one who participated in it. This work explains the intellectual climate that shaped Bataille's thoughts and writing.

Polizzotti, Mark. *Revolution of the Mind: The Life of André Breton*. London: Bloomsbury, 1995. This biography of the leader of the Surrealist movement offers readers a view of the radical intellectual and artistic circles that surrounded Bataille in Paris. It also gives a history of the difficult relations between Breton and Bataille and discusses Bataille's criticisms of the Surrealists.

Richardson, Michael. *Georges Bataille*. New York: Routledge, 1994. The most thoroughly researched and dependable biography of Bataille available in English. It also offers a readable introduction to Bataille's thinking.

Stoekl, Allan. *Politics, Writing, Mutilation: The Cases of Bataille, Blanchot, Roussel, Leiris, and Ponge*. Minneapolis: University of Minnesota Press, 1985. An examination of the use of language in the writings of Bataille and his colleagues. Stoekl sees Bataille and the others as precursors of deconstructionist philosophers and literary critiques, such as Jacques Derrida and Michel Foucault, who look at writing and other forms of expression as reflections of political and social relations.

Carl L. Bankston III

Pierre Bayle

Bayle was a great skeptical arguer, criticizing philosophical theories both old and new and exposing the weaknesses of Catholic and Protestant theologies. His criticisms helped pave the way for modern toleration and provided the principal arguments for the Enlightenment.

Principal philosophical works: *Lettre sur la comète*, 1682 (*Miscellaneous Reflections Occasion'd by the Comet Which Appear'd in December, 1680*, 1708); *Critique générale de l'histoire du calvinisme de M. Maimbourg*, 1682; *Commentaire philosophique sur ces paroles de Jésus-Christ "Contrain-les d'entrer,"* 1686 (*A Philosophical Commentary on These Words in the Gospel, Luke XIV, 23: "Compel Them to Come In, That My House May Be Full,"* 1708); *Dictionnaire historique et critique*, 1697, 1702 (*An Historical and Critical Dictionary*, 1710).

Born: November 18, 1647; Carla-le-Comte, France
Died: December 28, 1706; Rotterdam, the Netherlands

Early Life

Pierre Bayle was born in the small town of Carla-le-Comte, near the Spanish border south of Toulouse, where his father was a Calvinist minister. He grew up during the increasing persecution of Protestants in France. He was first sent to a Calvinist academy at Puylaurens. Next, he attended the Jesuit college in Toulouse because there was no advanced Protestant school left in his area. His studies with the Jesuits led him to consider the controversial arguments used by Catholics to convert the Protestants. On the basis of intellectual considerations, he soon became a Catholic, the worst thing a son of an embattled Calvinist minister could do. He soon redeemed himself by converting from Catholicism back to Protestantism, again on the basis of intellectual arguments. This second conversion made Bayle a *relaps*, someone who has returned to heresy after having abjured it. As such, he was subject to banishment or imprisonment. For his protection, he was sent to the University of Geneva to complete his studies in philosophy and theology.

To earn his living, Bayle returned to France in disguise and was a tutor in Paris and Rouen. In 1675, he became professor of philosophy at the Calvinist academy at Sedan, where he was the

Pierre Bayle. *(Library of Congress)*

protégé of the fanatically orthodox Protestant theologian Pierre Jurieu, who was to become his bitterest enemy. Bayle and Jurieu taught at Sedan until it was closed by the French government in 1681. They then went to the Netherlands as refugees and were reunited as faculty members of the new academy in Rotterdam, the École Illustre, and as leading figures in the French Reformed Church in that city.

Life's Work

Bayle's career as an author began shortly after his arrival in Rotterdam. He published a work he had drafted in France, *Miscellaneous Reflections Occasion'd by the Comet Which Appear'd in December, 1680*, in which he began his critique of supersition, intolerance, bad philosophy, and bad history. This was followed by *Critique générale de l'histoire du calvinisme de M. Maimbourg* (general criticism of Father Maimbourg's history of Calvinism), an examination of a very polemical history of Calvinism by a leading Jesuit. In 1684, Bayle edited *Recueil de quelques pièces curieuses concernant la philosophie de M. Descartes*, a collection of articles about Cartesianism, which was then under attack by the Jesuits. The collection contained articles by Nicolas de Malebranche, Bayle, and others. From 1684 to 1687, Bayle published a learned journal, *Nouvelles de la République des Lettres*, in which he commented on the theories then appearing of Gottfried Wilhelm Leibniz, Malebranche, Antoine Arnauld, Robert Boyle, and John Locke, among others.

Because of his acute judgment, which appeared in his early writings, Bayle became one of the central figures in the Republic of Letters and was in direct contact with many of its leading personalities. From 1684 to 1685, Bayle devoted himself exclusively to scholarly writing. His brothers and his father died in France as a result of the religious persecution against Protestants. He declined the opportunity of an advantageous marriage offered by the Jurieu family. He rejected a position as professor at the University of Franeker, preferring to remain in Rotterdam, contending against various kinds of opponents.

In 1686, Bayle published *A Philosophical Commentary on These Words in the Gospel, Luke XIV, 23: "Compel Them to Come In, That My House May Be Full."* This essay was directed against the Catholic persecution of the Protestants in France. In it, Bayle developed the most extensive argument of the time for complete toleration, going further than Locke did in *A Third Letter for Toleration* (1692). Bayle advocated tolerating Muslims, Jews, Unitarians, and atheists as well as Catholics (who were then persecuted in the Netherlands). Bayle's views used skeptical arguments as a basis for complete toleration of all views, claiming that an "erring conscience" had as many rights as a nonerring one because it was impossible to tell who was right or wrong.

Bayle's tolerance brought him into conflict with his erstwhile mentor, Jurieu, who became the theorist of intolerance and a dominant figure in the French Reformed Church while in exile. Their differences became so great that Jurieu denounced his colleague as a menace to true religion and a secret atheist. During the late 1680's, Bayle began a furious pamphlet war against Jurieu and criticized the liberals who sought to develop a rational, scientifically acceptable version of Christianity. Bayle's many controversies led to his dismissal from the Rotterdam professorship in 1693. The rest of his life was devoted to skeptical, polemical scholarship.

Bayle's greatest work, *An Historical and Critical Dictionary*, began as an effort to correct all the errors he had found in previous dictionaries and encyclopedias and was a way of skeptically criticizing philosophical, scientific, and theological theories. The dictionary consists almost exclusively of articles about deceased people and defunct movements, with a few articles about places. Bayle decided to omit persons who had been adequately dealt with in the previous biographical dictionary of Louis Moreri from 1674. Thus, many famous people, such as Plato and William Shakespeare and René Descartes, are missing, while many obscure people are given articles of substantial length. The format of Bayle's dictionary, in folio volumes, was to set forth a biography of a personage on the top of the page, with long footnotes below, and with notes to the notes on the side. This gives the book a look somewhat like that of an edition of the Talmud.

The core of the dictionary is in the notes and the notes to the notes, in which Bayle digressed to discuss and dissect old and new theories on a variety of subjects. He skeptically challenged

Scholastic philosophy, Cartesianism, and the new philosophies of Leibniz, Malebranche, Ralph Cudworth, Baruch Spinoza, Locke, and Isaac Newton. He challenged Catholic and Protestant theologies and sought to show that they were unable to give a consistent or credible explanation of the problem of evil. Throughout *An Historical and Critical Dictionary*, Bayle claimed that his skepticism was a means of undermining or destroying reason in order to make room for faith. He cited Blaise Pascal to show this. Throughout the work, however, Bayle questioned the moral or religious sincerity of the leading figures of the Old Testament, the church fathers, and the religious leaders of the Reformation. He reported all varieties of immoral sexual conduct, unethical practices, and hypocritical behavior of everyone from Noah and his children, to the heroes of Greek mythology, to kings and queens, to saints and church leaders.

An Historical and Critical Dictionary shocked the learned and religious worlds. The French Reformed Church tried to ban it; it was attacked by many, with the result that it quickly became a best-seller. In the second edition (1702), Bayle promised his church that he would explain what they found most outrageous: his article on King David, his defense of atheists, his Pyrrhonian skepticism, and his inclusion of so much obscene material. He wrote four lengthy clarifications of these matters, which only infuriated his opponents more. The clarification on skepticism became one of his most important statements on the relationship of skepticism and religion. The material in the second edition became basic to discussions of philosophy and theology in the eighteenth century. It was used extensively by George Berkeley, David Hume, Voltaire, and many others.

In the four years after the appearance of the second edition of the dictionary, Bayle wrote several works continuing his attacks on his many opponents, particularly his orthodox, liberal, and rational opponents. Critics insisted that he was trying to undermine all philosophy, science, and religion. He insisted that he was a true believer, trying to destroy reason to buttress faith.

Influence

Bayle was one of the most important skeptical arguers of the seventeenth century, who pro-

vided what was called "the arsenal of the Enlightenment." His many critical works, especially *An Historical and Critical Dictionary*, raised the central problems and questions of the time, challenging all the philosophical and theological solutions that had been offered previously. From the time that Bayle was alive and continuing after his death, there has been debate about his real intentions. Some see him as a chronic outsider, criticizing all views while apparently maintaining just a modicum of religious faith.

Regardless of his intent, Bayle influenced thinkers for the next hundred years. Leibniz wrote *Essais de théodicée sur la bonté de Dieu, la liberté de l'homme, et l'origine du mal* (1710; *Theodicy: Essays on the Goodness of God, the Freedom of Man, and the Origin of Evil*, 1952) in an attempt to answer Bayle's skeptical attacks on religious solutions to the problem of evil. Berkeley and Hume took some of their basic argumentation from Bayle, and French Enlightenment figures from Voltaire onward built on his criticisms. German philosopher Immanuel Kant used him as a source for the antinomies of pure reason. American politician Thomas Jefferson recommended Bayle's works as one of the initial purchases for the Library of Congress. Bayle continued to be influential until *An Historical and Critical Dictionary* was replaced by modern encyclopedias, and his skepticism was replaced by modern scientific positivistic views. In the late twentieth century, a strong revival of interest in his writing and impact occurred among scholars. He has since been recognized as one of the seminal figures in eighteenth century thought.

Richard H. Popkin

An Historical and Critical Dictionary

Type of philosophy: Epistemology, philosophy of religion
First published: Dictionnaire historique et critique, 1697, 1702 (English translation, 1710)
Principal ideas advanced:
◇ Because reason is useless, humanity should turn to faith.
◇ The traditional philosophical and theological

arguments prove nothing; skeptical criticism can demolish any theory.

◊ By consistently employing the arguments of philosophers, one can no longer be certain even of the existence of external objects, to say nothing of their qualities.

◊ Such Christian doctrines as those concerning the Trinity, the Fall, Transubstantiation, and Original Sin, if self-evidently true, contradict other propositions that are also self-evidently true.

◊ There is no faith better established on reason than that which is built on the ruins of reason; true people of faith accept beliefs for which they can give no rational justification.

Pierre Bayle's *An Historical and Critical Dictionary* is a compendium of arguments, tending toward a skeptical view, for and against almost every theory in philosophy and theology. In the eighteenth century, it was called the "Arsenal of the Enlightenment," and it played a very important role in intellectual discussions throughout the first half of that century. Significant criticisms of the major and minor philosophers and theologians of the time appear throughout *An Historical and Critical Dictionary*. Thinkers such as George Berkeley, David Hume, and Voltaire used the work as a source of arguments and inspiration. Remaining in vogue until it was no longer useful as a reference work, the last edition appeared in 1820.

The Dictionary

Bayle's *An Historical and Critical Dictionary* was begun as a series of corrections to a previous biographical dictionary, but it grew until it became an enormous work in its own right. It consists, formally, of a series of articles in alphabetical order, giving biographical information and historical data about all sorts of people, places, and things, some historical, some mythological. Many of the people discussed are obscure theologians or philosophers with strange theories. The meat of *An Historical and Critical Dictionary* appears primarily in the footnotes, which occupy most of the space, appearing below the text on the huge folio pages in double columns of small print. Many of the footnotes contain digressions that allow Bayle to bring up all of his favorite

disputes. An important, interesting, or exciting digression can appear almost anywhere. In the article on "Rorarius," for example, Bayle launches into one of the first and most significant criticisms of Gottfried Wilhelm Leibniz. The footnotes are also interspersed with spicy tales about the love lives and sexual practices of various famous people, and with profane versions of Bible stories. In the course of the thousands of footnotes, virtually every theory ever propounded is attacked, and a recurring theme appears—humanity, realizing the uselessness of rational endeavors, should turn to faith.

When the work first appeared, it was immediately attacked and banned in France for its anti-Catholic, antireligious, skeptical views, as well as for its obscene content. It was similarly criticized in Holland by Bayle's own church, the French Reformed Church of Rotterdam, which demanded an explanation for the material contained in *An Historical and Critical Dictionary*. The author insisted that he had been misunderstood. The obscenities, he said, represented reports of actual historical facts, and he could not be held responsible for the actions of historical personages, many of them long dead. As to the other charges, he insisted that they were entirely without foundation. His intention was to support the faith of his church by exposing the weaknesses of all rational theories, so that people, seeing this, would turn away from philosophy and science, to faith. His opponents contended that Bayle had made such a mockery of the faith that he could not possibly be seriously advocating it.

To answer the charges, Bayle wrote some appendices to the dictionary, plus additional footnotes, and incorporated them into the next edition, that of 1702. These additions were considered so much more dangerous and heretical than his original work that they produced another storm of attacks, as well as a series of answers on Bayle's part. For the rest of his life, Bayle fought to vindicate his contention that his general, overall view was the same as that of John Calvin and of all of the most orthodox theologians. The liberal and the orthodox Calvinists fought against this claim and tried to unmask their opponent as a true heretic. Bayle kept pointing out that his most extreme orthodox opponents really said the same things as he did. However, as one of them observed, "When I say it, it is serious. When he [Bayle] says it, it turns out comical."

Controversy and Debate

Bayle has been interpreted, by most critics, as being the earliest figure in the Enlightenment to use his scholarship and his critical abilities for the purpose of destroying all confidence in religion, both through undermining the reasons given by theologians for the faith and through making the faith appear ridiculous. On the other hand, some scholars have argued that Bayle was sincere, that he was actually defending religion rather than opposing it, using the same sort of irrational "defense" later employed by philosopher Søren Kierkegaard. Neither the information about Bayle's life nor an analysis of his writings results in a definitive solution of the mystery of his *real* intentions. However, regardless of what he may have thought he was trying to accomplish, the impact of Bayle's thought in the eighteenth century caused many thinkers to doubt traditional philosophical and theological arguments and to doubt the philosophies and religions as well. Bayle also supplied much of the ammunition used by the skeptical philosophers of the Age of Reason.

In the wide range of articles and issues dealt with in *An Historical and Critical Dictionary*, some deserve special notice because of either their influence or their content. The longest article, on Spinoza, was notorious in its day because it presented the first defense of Spinoza's character as a saintly human being, in contrast to the grim rumors of the time that Spinoza must have been a villainous person to have advocated the philosophy that he did. However, while defending Spinoza's character, Bayle also engaged in his favorite sport, that of decimating other people's theories. The article on "Rorarius" presents the first serious discussion that had appeared in print of Leibniz's novel metaphysical theory. (When Leibniz wrote a lengthy response, Bayle enlarged the footnotes in "Rorarius," in the second edition, to discuss Leibniz's defense as well as some new criticisms of his own.) The philosophies of Malebranche, John Locke, and Sir Isaac Newton are all subjected to devastating criticisms in the article on Zeno of Elea.

Two of the articles on early religious groups, one on the Manichaeans and the other on the Paulicians, deal with the problem of evil, arguing that it is not possible to disprove the Manichaean theory that there is an evil as well as a good God or the theory that God is author of evil. These two articles unleashed a storm of controversy and led to the writing of two famous answers, that of Leibniz, in his *Essais de théodicée sur la bonté de Dieu, la liberté de l'homme, et l'origine du mal* (1710; *Theodicy: Essays on the Goodness of God, the Freedom of Man, and the Origin of Evil*, 1952) and that of William King, Archbishop of Dublin, in his *Origins of Evil* (1739). Both Hume and Voltaire used Bayle's arguments on the subject of evil in their attacks on traditional theology.

Questioning Reality

In the article on Zeno of Elea, especially in the footnotes G and H, Bayle levels his attacks on modern metaphysical systems. He tries to show that, on the basis of the premises of a philosopher such as René Descartes, no satisfactory evidence can be offered to show that an external world exists or that it can be consistently described in mathematical terms. First, Bayle argues that the same sort of skeptical evidence that led modern philosophers to doubt that real objects possess the secondary qualities that we perceive, such as color, smell, and heat, should also lead these philosophers to doubt whether real objects possess the primary, mathematical qualities, such as extension. The reality of secondary qualities is denied by almost all seventeenth century philosophers. They all point out that because these qualities are perceived differently at different times, under different conditions, and by different people, the real object cannot possess these variable properties. Bayle then contends that if this argument is considered adequate, it should also be applied to a quality such as extension. The same object appears big to an individual at one time, small at another. One's perception of its size differs from that of other persons. Hence, extension, like color, is no more than an idea in one's own mind and is not a characteristic of real objects.

Further, Bayle gathers together all the arguments from philosophers such as Malebranche to show that there is no genuine evidence that real objects even exist. It cannot be demonstrated that they do. All of the information that is offered as evidence could be due to the actions of God on us, without requiring the actual existence of objects corresponding to our ideas and feelings or causing them. If it is answered that God would be deceiving us if he made us believe in the existence of real objects when there really were none, Bayle answers, in the article on Pyrrho of Elis, that God makes peasants think that snow is white, and the philosophers claim this is a delusion, so why cannot God also delude the philosophers into thinking objects exist? To conclude this subject, Bayle endorses Malebranche's view that it is faith only, and not reason, that can justify our beliefs about the real existence of things. Hence, we ought to be content with the light of faith and give up the hopeless pursuit of truth by means of reason.

The Skeptic's Argument

The longest and most explicit statement of this theme (and the one that was most often debated in the eighteenth century) occurs in footnotes B and C of the article on Pyrrho. The discussion begins as a comment on the observation in the text that it is fitting that Pyrrhonian skepticism is detested in the schools of theology. Bayle points out that Pyrrhonism, complete skepticism, is a danger only to theology, not to science or politics. Practically every scientist *is* a skeptic because scientists doubt that it is possible to discover the secret causes and springs of nature. Instead, the scientists look only for descriptive information and probable hypotheses about nature. Regarding politics, the skeptics are not dangerous because they are always willing to follow the laws and customs of society as they have no dogmatic moral or legal principles. However, skepticism can be a great danger to religion, because religious doctrines should be completely certain. If not, there will be no firm conviction. Fortunately, however, Bayle points out, skepticism has little effect on people, either because of the grace of God, their education, their stupidity, or their natural inclinations.

To show the merits or the dangers of skepticism, Bayle tells a story about a discussion between two abbots. One asserts that it is incomprehensible to him that there are still any skeptics

around because God has given us the Revelation. The other replies that both the "new philosophy" and Christian theology provide excellent ammunition for any skeptic. The philosophy of thinkers such as Descartes leads, as the article on Zeno shows, to a complete skepticism about the nature and existence of the real world. By consistently employing the arguments of seventeenth century philosophers, we can no longer be sure whether objects possess *any* qualities, including those of extension and motion, and we cannot even be sure that there are any objects.

Further, Bayle insists, we cannot even be sure of the dogmatic philosophers' contention that something is true, because we cannot be certain of the criterion of truth. Philosophers have said that self-evidence is the sure mark of truth. However, the skeptical abbot declares, if Christianity is true, then there are self-evident propositions that must be false, and so, self-evidence cannot be taken as the standard for measuring what is true. Bayle then argues that the Christian doctrines of the Trinity, Transubstantiation, the Fall, and Original Sin contradict various self-evident propositions of philosophy such as that two things not different from a third are not different from each other, that a body cannot be in several places at the same time, that one ought to prevent evil if one can, and so on. In passing from the shadows of paganism to the light of Scripture, the abbot points out, we have learned the falsity of a great many self-evident notions.

Then the skeptical abbot answers the possible objection that all of the evidence against the criterion of truth depends on evaluating God and his actions by human standards, and these may not be the correct criteria for some judgments. If this objection is taken seriously, then we are again led to complete skepticism because we are then unable to know what is true in God's world if we cannot employ our own judgmental standards.

The arguments of the skeptics, Bayle contends, cannot be answered by human reason, and they expose the weakness of our rational faculties. Thus we are made to feel the need for a guide different from reason—namely, faith. In footnote C, this point is explored further, first by pointing out that complete skepticism is the greatest achievement of human rationality, but that even so, it is completely self-defeating. One cannot even believe that skepticism is true without ceasing to be a skeptic. The attempt to become completely dubious about everything by means of reason finally leads one to give up reasoning entirely and to turn to a more secure guide, faith. Skepticism is portrayed as the best preparation for religion because it reveals the total and hopeless inadequacy of reason as a means for finding truth. One is then ready to accept Revelation without question. In a later defense of this theory, Bayle asserts that there is no faith better established on reason than that which is built on the ruins of reason.

Faith and Reason

This total irrationalism and acceptance of religion on blind faith was bitterly attacked by theologians everywhere. In the second edition of *An Historical and Critical Dictionary*, Bayle added a more detailed (and more antirational) exposition of his views in the appendix explaining the article on Pyrrho. There he argued that the world of reason and the world of faith are two totally different and opposing realms. If one looks for evidence, one cannot have faith, and the search for evidence will end only in complete skepticism. If one completely abandons the quest for evidence, then faith is possible. In fact, the more irrational one's beliefs are, the more this means that such beliefs cannot be based on any evidence whatsoever (otherwise, there might be some reason for them). The true and complete person of faith, then, according to Bayle's rendition of the case, is the person who accepts a belief for which he or she can give no justification and no reason of any kind. Bayle, in keeping with the other French skeptics from Michel Eyquem de Montaigne onward, cites as his Scriptural authority for this interpretation of religion Saint Paul's antirational pronouncements in the first chapter of his first letter to the Corinthians.

Opponents immediately pointed out that this irrationalism would destroy religion rather than defend it. There would be no reason left for accepting a religion, no standards by which to tell what is true or false, and no way of distinguishing the true religion from all the others. In fact, the critics claimed, Bayle's religion without reason would actually be a form of madness, or superstition, which neither Bayle nor any other

"reasonable" man could possibly accept. Bayle fought back during the last years of his life, attacking the reasons his opponents offered for their religious views and for their criticisms and insisting that all of the most orthodox theologians had said exactly the same thing as he was saying.

Whether Bayle was sincere or not, the arguments he presented to show that religion could not be based on reason became basic ingredients in the deistic, agnostic, and atheistic views developed in the course of the Enlightenment. His arguments against modern philosophy became crucial themes in the theories of Berkeley, Hume, and Voltaire. *An Historical and Critical Dictionary* was all important in transforming the intellectual world from its metaphysical and theological phase to the skeptical and empirical phase of the Age of Reason.

Richard H. Popkin

Additional Reading

Bayle, Pierre. *Historical and Critical Dictionary, Selections*. Translated by Richard H. Popkin and Craig Brush. Indianapolis: Bobbs-Merrill, 1965. This work includes forty of Pierre Bayle's articles on important intellectual and moral figures throughout history. It provides a glimpse into the seventeenth century mind in general and Bayle's philosophical views in particular. In addition to these translations, an introduction to Bayle's life and an annotated bibliography are included.

Chappell, Vere, ed. *Port-Royal to Bayle*. Vol. 4 in *Essays on Early Modern Philosophers*. New York: Garland, 1992. Contains a wealth of articles from the past thirty years on early modern philosophy. There are four articles on Bayle. Each article is accompanied by a helpful introduction, biography, and introduction. Other philosophers covered in this volume are Antoine Arnauld, Blaise Pascal, and Samuel Pufendorf.

Critical Spirit, Wisdom and Erudition on the Eve of the Enlightenment. Amsterdam: APA-Holland University Press, 1998. A look at Bayle's philosophy.

Kearns, Edward John. *Ideas in Seventeenth-Century France*. New York: St. Martin's Press, 1979. This book considers the political and religious climate in which the scientific revolution took place in France. Kearns takes a detailed look at Bayle, René Descartes, Pascal, Bernard le Bovier de Fontenelle, and others.

Kilcullen, John. _Sincerity and Truth: Essays on Arnauld, Bayle, and Toleration_. New York: Oxford University Press, 1988. The author discusses issues of morality, toleration, and conscious in Bayle's philosophy and considers it in relation to Arnauld's views on philosophic sin. Includes an introduction, bibliography, and index.

Labrousse, Elisabeth. _Bayle_. Translated by Deny Potts. New York: Oxford University Press, 1983. Discusses Bayle's place in intellectual history and offers an important interpretation of his philosophy.

Mason, H. T. _Pierre Bayle and Voltaire_. London: Oxford University Press, 1963. An investigation into the relationship between the philosophies of Bayle and Voltaire. Mason particularly examines the extent to which Voltaire borrowed from Bayle.

Nadler, Steven. _Causation in Early Modern Philosophy_. University Park: Pennsylvania State University Press, 1993. This work consists of essays examining seventeenth century philosophers and their approaches to the problem of causation. Philosophers covered include Bayle, Descartes, Gottfried Wilhelm Leibniz, Nicolas Malebranche, and Anne Conway.

Popkin, Richard H. _The High Road to Pyrrhonism_. San Diego, Calif.: Austin Hill Press, 1980. Several of the articles in this work concern Bayle's influence and skepticism.

Robinson, Howard. _Bayle the Skeptic_. New York: Columbia University Press, 1931. This work portrays Bayle as a precursor of Enlightenment atheism.

Sandberg, Karl C. _At the Crossroads of Faith and Reason: An Essay on Pierre Bayle_. Tucson: University of Arizona Press, 1966. This work looks at Bayle in the context of Protestant theology. Sandberg portrays Bayle as a sincere Calvinist.

Richard H. Popkin,
updated by Tammy Nyden-Bullock

Simone de Beauvoir

De Beauvoir cut across traditional academic fields to produce important works of literature, criticism, and philosophy. Her political activism made her a pioneer of the late twentieth century women's movement as well as a leading figure in human rights, peace, and social reform efforts.

Principal philosophical works: *Pour une morale de l'ambiguïté*, 1947 (*The Ethics of Ambiguity*, 1948); *Le Deuxième Sexe*, 1949 (*The Second Sex*, 1953); *Privilèges*, 1955 (partial translation, "Must We Burn Sade?," 1953).

Born: January 9, 1908; Paris, France
Died: April 14, 1986; Paris, France

Early Life

Simone de Beauvoir was born in Paris on January 9, 1908, the eldest of two daughters of Georges Bertrand and Françoise Brasseur de Beauvoir. Although her family was descended from the aristocracy, it teetered precariously on the brink of financial solvency, maintaining the status of upper-middle-class gentility with difficulty. De Beauvoir had a relatively happy childhood, which she described graphically in the first volume of her autobiography, *Mémoires d'une jeune fille rangée* (1958; *Memoirs of a Dutiful Daughter*, 1959). She especially treasured the summers that she spent at her grandfather's rambling estate at Meyrignac in Limousin, where she developed what would become lifelong passions for reading and hiking. In 1913, de Beauvoir was enrolled at the private school Cours Désir.

In her autobiography, de Beauvoir depicted herself as a precocious young girl chafing at the restraints placed upon her both by society and by other persons' wills. The personal and ideological problems in her parents' marriage, created primarily by tension between her mother's religious piety and her father's cynical agnosticism, led de Beauvoir to conclude that intellectual and spiritual life were mutually exclusive. This enabled her to reject both the Catholic religion and the social role of "dutiful daughter" imposed upon her by her parents. As de Beauvoir entered her second decade, she developed an attraction for her cousin Jacques Laiguillon. Although she had strong feelings for him, she was afraid that their love would trap her into becoming a bourgeois wife, a role that she rejected as completely as she had the life of a "dutiful daughter."

In 1928, after completing her undergraduate education, she began working at the École Normale Supérieure on her *agrégation de philosophie*, a difficult postgraduate examination for teaching positions at *lycées* and universities in France. The next year, she met Jean-Paul Sartre, a fellow philosophy student. For the first time in her life, de Beauvoir found a soul mate who was her intellectual equal, a man with whom she knew she always would be compatible. In 1929, they passed the *agrégation* and began a liaison that would last a lifetime. During the same year, however, her happiness was marred by the death of her closest childhood friend, Elizabeth "Zaza" Mabille; this event marked both the end of the first volume of de Beauvoir's memoirs and her childhood.

Life's Work

Next to her work, the most important thing in de Beauvoir's life was her relationship with Sartre. Because neither of them wanted children, they rejected the notion of traditional marriage in favor of a bond that they called an "essential" love, which was to be permanent but which would not exclude what they deemed "contingent" love af-

207

Simone de Beauvoir. *(Archive Photos)*

Despite ominous clouds on the French political scene, in the prewar era de Beauvoir and Sartre remained oblivious to the world around them, burying themselves in their work, their friends, and each other. The outbreak of World War II in 1939, however, marks an important watershed in de Beauvoir's life. Sartre's induction into the army brought de Beauvoir face to face with social and political reality. They jointly adopted the philosophy of personal commitment, realizing that they had a responsibility to humanity as well as to themselves. During the German invasion of France in June, 1940, Sartre was taken prisoner, and de Beauvoir, like many other Parisians, fled the capital only to return when the reality of defeat and German occupation became obvious. On April 1, 1941, Sartre was released and returned to Paris. Although de Beauvoir and Sartre worked on the fringes of the French Resistance, they were not active participants in it.

During the war, both de Beauvoir and Sartre abandoned their teaching careers to concentrate on writing. De Beauvoir's first novel, *She Came to Stay*, was an immediate success, and from 1943 on, both she and Sartre were established as major new talents on the French intellectual horizon. In 1945, de Beauvoir, Sartre, and others founded the journal *Les Temps modernes* as a vehicle for independent left-wing intellectual viewpoints. The same year, the novel that she had written during the war, *Le Sang des autres* (1945; *The Blood of Others*, 1948), was published to almost universal critical acclaim as the quintessential existentialist novel of the Resistance.

Her philosophical treatise *The Ethics of Ambiguity*, a secular breviary of existentialist ethics, was published in 1947, the year de Beauvoir first journeyed to the United States. There she met novelist Nelson Algren and began her first serious "contingent" love affair. Her four-year relationship with Algren resulted in a proposal of marriage, which she rejected both because of her commitment to Sartre and because of her disinclination to leave France. After several transatlantic visits, the affair ended in bitterness when de

fairs. In 1931, Sartre did suggest that they marry, but de Beauvoir refused his proposal, arguing that they were not being true to their own principles.

In 1931, de Beauvoir was appointed to teach in a *lycée* in Marseilles. The next year, she transferred to Rouen, where she was reprimanded by *lycée* authorities for questioning women's traditional role in society. Sartre, also in Rouen, met Olga Kosakievicz, a former pupil of de Beauvoir, with whom he fell in love. They experimented with a trio, which failed primarily because of de Beauvoir's jealousy; the incident furnished her with the plot for her first novel, *L'Invitée* (1943; *She Came to Stay*, 1949). In 1936, she was transferred to Paris, where Sartre was able to join her the following year.

Beauvoir used their relationship as a basis for her novel *Les Mandarins* (1954; *The Mandarins*, 1956), which won the prestigious Prix de Goncourt for literature in 1954.

Throughout her life, de Beauvoir, an avid traveler, visited most of the world's exciting venues, recording her thoughts and storing her memories for use in her writing. In the fall of 1949, her most famous book, *The Second Sex,* was published. This massive work discusses the role and condition of women throughout history from biological, psychological, historical, sociological, and philosophical perspectives. Two of its most important tenets—the concept that man has defined himself as the essential being, the subject, who has consigned woman to the subordinate position of object or "Other," and the idea that there is no such thing as "feminine nature," that one is not born a woman but becomes one through social conditioning—served as an important basis for the resurrection of the women's liberation movement in the mid-twentieth century.

In 1952, de Beavoir began her second "contingent" liaison, this time with Claude Lanzmann, a filmmaker and journalist seventeen years her junior. This affair, which ended in 1958, was to be the last important romantic interlude in her "essential" love relationship with Sartre.

Two important changes occurred in de Beauvoir's life during the last half of the 1950's. First, her political views hardened and grew more bitter as the culpability of the French army in the torture of Algerians became increasingly obvious and the world moved closer to the brink of nuclear war. De Beauvoir's commitment to political activism intensified at this time, and she embarked on a series of public demonstrations against Charles de Gaulle, French torture in Algeria, nuclear war, and social injustice. The second major change was in de Beauvoir's writing. She all but abandoned fiction for several years in order to begin the first of what would become a four-volume autobiography and a variety of other nonfiction works. She would not return to the novel form until the publication of *Les Belles Images* (1966; English translation, 1969), which was followed in 1968 by her last major work of fiction, *La Femme rompue* (1967; *The Woman Destroyed*, 1968). These two volumes are shorter than her four earlier novels but, like them, follow in a long tradition established by French women writers who have focused their work on women's lives and ambitions.

In 1967, de Beauvoir increased her commitment to political activism, raising the issue of women's rights in Israel and taking part in Bertrand Russell's Tribunal of War Crimes, which met in Copenhagen to investigate U.S. involvement in the Vietnam War. The following May, she and Sartre became active supporters of the revolutionary students at the Sorbonne. During this phase of her politically active life, de Beauvoir was preparing *La Vieillese* (1970; *The Coming of Age*, 1972), a lengthy but critically acclaimed study of aging that attacked modern society's indifference to the problems of the elderly.

In 1969, de Beauvoir was elected to the consultative committee of the Bibliothèque Nationale (national library) as a "man of letters." Soon thereafter, she became actively involved in the women's movement, joining a series of demonstrations led by the Mouvement de la Libération des Femmes in 1970. The next year, she signed the "Manifesto of 343," a document bearing the signatures of French women who publicly admitted to having had illegal abortions. Soon after the publication of the manifesto, de Beauvoir publicly declared herself to be a militant feminist, explaining that she had eschewed the reformist, legalistic feminism of the past but eagerly embraced the radical movement of the 1970's. In 1972, she joined street demonstrations protesting "crimes against women" and the next year began a feminist column in *Les Temps modernes*. She renewed this feminist commitment by becoming president of the Ligue des Droits des Femmes (French league of the rights of women) in 1974, the same year in which she was selected to receive the Jerusalem Prize for writers who have promoted the freedom of the individual.

On April 15, 1980, the lifelong "essential" love of de Beauvoir and Jean-Paul Sartre ended with the latter's death. The following year, de Beauvoir published *La Cérémonie des adieux* (1981; *Adieux: A Farewell to Sartre*, 1984), a sober narrative that recorded Sartre's mental and physical decline with a brutal honesty that seemed to her to be the final tribute she could pay to him. Although de Beauvoir wrote no major literary works after Sartre's death, she remained politically active. She died of pneumonia in a Paris hospital on April 14, 1986, and was entombed with Sartre's ashes in the Montparnasse Cemetery. More than five thousand people attended the funeral to which women's organizations throughout the world sent floral tributes.

Influence

De Beauvoir lived her adult life in a way that illustrated the most important tenets of existentialist ethics, especially the concepts of social responsibility and commitment. Her development from a politically indifferent young woman to a socially committed adult and, finally, to a mature woman militant in the causes of women's liberation and human rights is chronicled in the four volumes of her autobiography. Although de Beauvoir's existentialist views are presented somewhat didactically in her nonfiction and philosophical essays, in her novels they are infused with nuances of ambiguity and expressed in less strident prose. She used literature to present the real world to her readers by stripping away the insulating layers of hypocrisy that she believed bourgeois society installs to obscure truth. In this way, she believed, words could be enlisted as a weapon to help obliterate selfishness and indifference in the modern world.

In the post-World War II era, de Beauvoir became one of the most visible and influential left-wing advocates of social justice, peaceful coexistence, and women's liberation. Because her life and work supported her belief in sexual and social equality, de Beauvoir contributed immeasurably by word and by example to elevating the consciousness of men and women as well as improving the quality of their lives. She is one of the most important writers of the twentieth century because of both the literature that she created and the legacy of social and political commitment that she provided.

Nancy Ellen Rupprecht

The Second Sex

Type of philosophy: Ethics, existentialism, feminist philosophy

First published: Le Deuxième Sexe, 1949 (English translation, 1952)
Principal ideas advanced:

◇ The human female has unnecessarily acceded to second-place social and sexual status.
◇ Sexual differentiation is not prerequisite to the perpetuation of the species.
◇ The human being is his or her body, but the body is something other than the self.
◇ Immanence, or physicality, is the limitation of the self to the body; transcendence, or the exceeding of physical limitations, is the projection of the self toward extraphysical satisfactions by which one justifies one's existence.
◇ Women have been held to the stagnation of immanence; men have consistently enjoyed the elevation of transcendence.
◇ The subordination of women to men can end when women refuse to be reduced to immanence and, as a matter of habit, nurture the self in projects that are predispositional to transcendence.

Although *The Second Sex* is similar to the tradition of profeminism manifest in Mary Wollstonecraft's *A Vindication of the Rights of Woman* (1792), Florence Nightingale's *Cassandra* (1860), and John Stuart Mill's *The Subjection of Women* (1869), it is unlike these works in subjectively describing rather than objectively deploring the inferior status of women. Simone de Beauvoir's lyricism never congeals into a manifesto. *The Second Sex* is less a dissertation than a huge collection of philosophical essays variously oriented from biology, mythology, history, and literary criticism in book 1 ("Facts and Myths") and sociology and psychology in book 2 ("The Life Experience"). Her lifelong erotic and collegial companionship with philosopher Jean-Paul Sartre, along with her brief love affair with American writer Nelson Algren, were evidence of the integrity of her views on the veritable equality of the sexes: In both relationships, her choices were on her own terms.

Her commitment to existentialism informs much of her analytical writing and scholarly observation in *The Second Sex*. According to de Beauvoir, existentialism—inherent in Edmund Husserl's phenomenology and Martin Heidegger's ontologicalism (as distinct from ontology) and broadcast in Sartre's theory of man as freedom—is, as Beauvoir explains in "Existentialisme et la sagesse des nations" (1963, existentialism and conventional wisdom), an optimistic, not a pessimistic, philosophy. De Beauvoir writes as a free woman who is convinced that transcendent freedom, although traditionally skewed to men, is biologically and psychologically also a property of women. The other major mode of thought in *The Second Sex* is Marxist socialism, which, in its ostensible egalitarianism, is accepted by de Beauvoir as more conducive to women's freedom than Western capitalism.

Woman as the Other

De Beauvoir's biological data disclose a characteristic but not an inevitable or necessary dependence of procreation upon sexual differentiation; the human female is seen sexually to renounce her individuality and therewith her potential for transcendence, while the male human's sexuality, benefiting from this renunciation, remains consistent with his individuality. De Beauvoir denies not the physiological but the psychological necessity of sexual differentiation at the human level: In renouncing her capacity for transcendence, woman brings her sexuality into a state of incompatibility with her individuality. Moving from biology to Freudian psychiatry, de Beauvoir notes psychoanalysis's inability, in its assumption of the male libido as axiomatically primary, to explain why women constitute the Other.

The second part of book 1 is a historical survey of the hierarchy of the sexes from the earliest nomads and workers of the soil through classical antiquity, the European middle ages, and the French Revolution to modern times. The summary begins with the observation that the world has always been man's and concludes with the assertion that while the modern woman is in a position to free herself from domestication, her choices continue to be made, not naturally, but on the basis of man's definition of her and his dreams about her.

The third part is subtitled "Dreams, Fears, Idols" and elaborates upon the alterity of woman through myths. Alterity is a justification, by means of nonvalid exaltation of the Other, of demeaning the Other. One can positively affirm woman's subordinate status in human society and compensate for doing so by attributing ideal qualities to her. Placing woman on an imaginary pedestal thereby entitles man to keep her in a veritable pit. De Beauvoir illustrates alterity by proceeding from "every creation myth" through the mythic presentations of woman as both idol and slave and as the source of life and the agent of death to the Oedipus myth, reflecting man's denial of a mother's carnality while sublimating his erotic desire for her.

The Myth of Woman

The examination of the myth of woman in the works of five male authors—Henri de Montherlant, D. H. Lawrence, Paul Claudel, André Breton, and Stendhal—is perhaps the real heart of the text. De Beauvoir's passage from mythology to literary criticism establishes the mythic, or contrived, conviction of man that woman is by nature a creature of immanence. The attitudes of the writers chosen by de Beauvoir move from the lowest to the highest regard for woman; however, even the highest is a manifestation of alterity.

Montherlant is uncompromisingly negative: Woman is an incomplete being (the female athlete being his only, and grudging, exception); her influence upon man is always perverse and destructive. The Greek warrior Achilles, for example, was vulnerable only on that part of his body touched by his mother. Montherlant's ideal woman, according to de Beauvoir, is benignly stupid and submissive, ever ready to yield to man without demanding anything from him.

The only non-French examplar in de Beauvoir's gallery of authors is the British Lawrence, who, she says, sees man and woman as two antithetical streams, convergent but never confluent. This failure of unity is due to the impossibility of mutual renunciation. For Lawrence, man and woman must, but in fact cannot, lose their differential identities and obliterate any sense of give and take as they engage in the sexual act. However, even if the ideal were realizable in this, the male stream must surge in superiority as it enriches the vacuous and passive female flow. Lawrence, in de Beauvoir's reading, vigorously applauds the superiority of man; and his "true" woman unreservedly accepts her status as the Other.

De Beauvoir then denounces Claudel's Catholicism and its consignment of the origin of sin to woman. Claude's divine ordination is that woman ensures her salvation only by serving as auxiliary to man's salvation. Woman is the perennial servant, whose grandest virtues are loyalty and fidelity. She is made for renunciation. De Beauvoir allows that Claudel's sublimest characters are women, but she complains that, in his work, existence is transcended for men and is merely continued for women. In this context, Claudel's woman fulfills herself by choosing to accomplish her God-given duty as the Other.

Breton is shown by de Beauvoir to resemble Claudel in positing woman's existence as an instrument of man's salvation, but as a celestially inspired guide more than as a handmaid of the Lord. She is Beauty and Poetry and, through her vocation of love, leads man to his perfection. De Beauvoir credits Breton with saying that all existence derives its meaning from woman. She also quotes his conclusion that the fusion of existence and essence is realized in the highest degree precisely and exclusively through love; it is, however, a love by which woman gives and man receives.

Alterity's nonvalid exaltation of woman and its propagation of her romantic mystery are disdained by de Beauvoir's relatively good example of myth in an author, Stendhal (Marie-Henri Beyle). A sensual love of women dating from his childhood predisposed Stendhal to see women as they really are, human beings of flesh and blood without any spiritually ingrained mystery. He believed that women, freed from the seriousness of romantic aspiration, could equal men in all areas of achievement. For all his admiration of woman on her own terms, however, Stendhal, according to de Beauvoir, nonetheless limits the terrestrial destiny of woman to her relation to man.

Love and a Woman's Life

Book 2 is one and a half times as long as book 1 but noticeably less trenchant. It ruminately investigates woman's passage in life from the experiences of childhood through those of maturity and old age. The book's thesis is that a person is not born a woman but becomes one. Woman is shown by de Beauvoir to adapt herself, at every stage of her life, to the place in a male world that man has laid out for her. She shows the young girl to be conditioned to femininity and to feel

shame in the alterity and inferiority incumbent upon it. In sexual initiation, the woman serves as object while the man retains his subjective independence. As she ages, woman loses her servitude in proportion to her loss of effectiveness. Taught only to devote herself to someone, she finds in old age that her devotion is no longer wanted by anyone.

Recourse to lesbianism, love, marriage, narcissism, or religion can be integral with independence, but all of these options lack the transcendence that freedom must engender in an individual. To love authentically, according to de Beauvoir, a woman must assume the contingence of her mate—his failings and limitations—and she should never idolize him; love in this sense is not a type of salvation but a human relationship. To be free authentically, a woman must project her freedom through practical action within human society. De Beauvoir claims that the free woman is just being born. Once woman abandons a quest for transcendence within her immanence and pursues transcendence in authentic action, and once man learns to react to woman as a human equal, there can arise a true human confraternity (*fraternité*), one that is not confounded by female otherness.

Feminism and Existentialism

The Second Sex was received initially more as a suffragist tract than as an existentialist approach to woman's situation. In the 1980's and after de Beauvoir's death, the reverse came to be true. De Beauvoir came to be read as one dispassionately celebrating existentalist authenticity and focusing on woman, who as an individual, has the human capacity for economic and erotic independence in the context of transcendence.

The waves and currents in the women's liberation movement after the 1960's and 1970's tended to wash away the importance of *The Second Sex* to the movement; people started to take issue with de Beauvoir's favor of personal commitment over collective revolt. Writers such as Elaine Marks and Renée Weingarten, in the late 1980's, berated de Beauvoir for her naïveté and general compliance with the world of men. In the same decade and in the next, however, a new estimate of de Beauvoir's influence and importance appeared in the writings of Lisa Appignanesi, Mary

Evans, Margaret Crosland, Deirdre Bair, and many others. A new attention to de Beauvoir's lucidity and common sense checked the hostility of militant feminists.

Roy Arthur Swanson

Additional Reading

Appignansei, Lisa. *Simone de Beauvoir*. London: Penguin, 1988. This is a significant appraisal of Simone de Beauvoir's concept of the independent woman. Appignanesi aptly explicates de Beauvoir's existentialist ethics and her suppositions of woman's subjectivity.

Bair, Deirdre. *Simone de Beauvoir: A Biography*. New York, Summit Books, 1990. This very reliable biography covers the philosophical life of de Beauvoir as Beauvoir's inquiry into the nature of woman. Chapter 28 is an entertaining and edifying précis of *The Second Sex*.

Berghoffen, Debra B. *The Philosophy of Simone de Beauvoir: Gendered Phenomenologies, Erotic Generosities*. Albany: State University of New York Press, 1997. Berghoffen takes note of de Beauvoir's differences from Jean-Paul Sartre and details the philosophical eroticism in *The Second Sex* and other books as well as de Beauvoir's ethics of the erotic.

Brown, Catherine Savage. *Simone de Beauvoir Revisited*. Boston: G. K. Hall, 1991. Contains chapters on de Beauvoir's life, on her role as a woman writer, her early fiction and drama, later fiction, philosophical and political studies, and her memoirs. Brown aims at a focused study, criticizing the emphasis on anecdotal reports and biography.

Fallage, Elizabeth. *The Novels of Simone de Beauvoir*. London: Routledge, 1988. Contains chapters on de Beauvoir's radicalism and on individual novels, including *She Came to Stay* and *The Blood of Others*, and on her short-story cycles. Biographical notes and bibliography are included.

Francis, Claude, and Fernande Gontier. *Simone de Beauvoir: A Life a Love Story*. New York: St. Martin's Press, 1979. A lively, well-documented biography for general readers, less comprehensive than Bair's.

Fulbrook, Kate, and Edward Fulbrook. *Simone de Beauvoir and Jean-Paul Sartre: The Remaking of a Twentieth-Century Legend*. New York: Basic Books, 1994. This work revises previous interpretations of the relationship, relying on new documents (letters and memoirs) that show how the two fashioned their legend.

Moi, Toril. *Simone de Beauvoir: The Making of an Intellectual Woman*. Cambridge, Mass.: Blackwell, 1997. Two chapters in the study are particularly important. Chapter 3 recounts the hostile reception of de Beauvoir's work by those in France and elsewhere who did not accord de Beauvoir, as a woman, the intellectual strength and integrity of male philosophers. Chapter 6 juxtaposes de Beauvoir's ethics of ambiguity and "alienation and the body" in *The Second Sex*.

Simon, Margaret A., ed. *Feminist Interpretations of Simone de Beauvoir*. University Park: Pennsylvania University Press, 1995. This work features several essays on *The Second Sex*, de Beauvoir's relationship with Sartre, *The Mandarins*, and her views on the Algerian war. Bibliography and index.

Carl Rollyson and Roy Arthur Swanson

Jeremy Bentham

Bentham's lifelong philosophical analysis of English law laid the foundations for early nineteenth century political reforms that saved England from violent social revolution.

Principal philosophical works: *A Fragment on Government*, 1776; *An Introduction to the Principles of Morals and Legislation*, 1789; *"Panopticon": Or, The Inspection-House*, 1791; *Panopticon: Postscript; Part I*, 1791; *Panopticon: Postscript; Part II*, 1791; *A Protest Against Law Taxes*, 1793; *Management of the Poor*, 1796; *Traités de legislation civile et pénale*, 1802 (3 volumes; *Theory of Legislation*, 1840, 2 volumes); *Théorie des peines et des récompenses*, 1811 (2 volumes; *The Rationale of Reward*, 1825; also known as *The Rationale of Punishment*, 1830); *A Table of the Springs of Action, Shewing the Several Species of Pleasures and Pains, of Which Man's Nature Is Susceptible*, 1815; *"Swear Not at All": Containing an Exposure of the Needlessness and Mischievousness, as well as Anti-Christianity, of the Ceremony of an Oath*, 1817; *Church of Englandism and Its Catechism Examined*, 1818; *An Analysis of the Influence of Natural Religion on the Temporal Happiness of Mankind*, 1822 (as Philip Beauchamp).

Born: February 15, 1748; London, England
Died: June 6, 1832; London, England

Early Life

Jeremy Bentham was born in London on February 15, 1748, the son of a prosperous English lawyer named Jeremiah Bentham. The elder Bentham wanted his son to have advantages that he had missed, so the father was delighted at his precocious son's ability to read at the age of three. Young Bentham accordingly was sent to the Westminster School and then on to Oxford University by the time he was twelve. Because of his youth and small stature, this "dwarfish phenomenon," as Bentham called himself, never engaged in the normal activities of the boys his age. While his peers played cricket, he contented himself with badminton. His world was contained within the boundaries of books and ideas.

At Westminster School, Bentham encountered his first acknowledged intellectual battle with the English law. All the students at the school were required to sign an oath supporting the Thirty-nine Articles of Religion of the Church of England. Already an advocate of logical thinking, the young prodigy privately believed that the articles were so irrational and contrary to the Scrip-

tures that the Church was forcing perjury on those required to sign them. In this instance, and throughout his entire life, however, Bentham obeyed the law and did the expected but privately agonized over what he had done, vowing silently to battle for the reform of the English legal system, not to mention the Church of England.

Perhaps no other scholar in English history spent so much time studying and writing about the law and the legal system but practically no time practicing it. Once the brilliant youngster finished his course of study at Westminster, he entered Oxford University. Toward the middle of his third year at Oxford, he attended a lecture by the most famous English legal scholar of his day, William Blackstone, the first of whose *Commentaries on the Laws of England* would be published beginning in 1765. The fifteen-year-old student eagerly attended the presentation given by the forty-year-old jurist, the first professor of English law at Oxford. Diligently, Bentham attempted to follow the lecture by recording its essentials in notes, but he could not. There were so many internal fallacies and illogical premises in what Blackstone pronounced that Bentham gave up his attempts at note taking.

In this incident may be seen the beginnings of

Bentham's lifelong battle against English law and the legal system that supported it. Although Blackstone might marvel at the "glorious inconsistency" of the English law, Bentham denounced it as an abhorrent mass of confusion, designed to be manipulated by those with the money and patience sufficient to retain the proper attorneys.

Most repugnant to Bentham throughout his lifetime of intellectual jousting was falsehood. At Westminster School, he had despised being forced to sign the Thirty-nine Articles of Religion; he believed not only that the statements were lies but also that his signature compounded the prevarication. Subsequently, in his attendance at Blackstone's lecture, he encountered English law as an even greater fabric of falsification. Especially frustrating to him was the notion of fiction in law, a method by which legal entities might be created or destroyed at the whim of the court and its attorneys. Appalled at this practice, Bentham declared that "in English law, fiction is a syphilis, which runs in every vein, and carries into every part of the system the principle of rottenness."

Life's Work

Although Bentham read law at Lincoln's Inn after he took his master's degree from Oxford in 1766 and was called to the bar in the following year, he was never a successful practicing lawyer. Instead, he spent each day in his rooms reading and writing about the law or conversing with the other law students who came to call. He set himself the daily task of writing more than fifteen folio practice pages of commentary on English law or society. These trial pages, or drafts, dealt with numerous subjects of interest to him. The dedication and intensity with which Bentham labored were so consuming that he suffered bouts of psychosomatic blindness. Only the loving attendance of his friends brought him through these extremely depressing periods.

In the course of his long life, many thousands of pages were written, many on subjects he never fully developed and many of which were never published. His first publication was a critique of Black-

stone, printed anonymously in 1776 under the title *A Fragment on Government.* So brilliant and masterful was this work that it was attributed to many great minds of the time. Ironically, when his proud father accidentally revealed the true authorship of the essay, the headline-hungry public no longer was interested.

Bentham's accomplishment did, however, bring him to the attention of William Petty, Lord Shelburne, who introduced him to the world of the nobility by extending his patronage to the young intellectual. Perhaps most important, Shelburne helped broaden Bentham's criticisms of English law to include constitutional law along with his ongoing considerations of civil and penal law. Although Shelburne could never provide Bentham an office of political power, he did afford him an insight into the functions of the enlightened minority within the English political establishment.

Jeremy Bentham. *(Library of Congress)*

In what Bentham thought, said, and wrote for the next seventy years, he did what few Englishmen had ever dared and did so successfully. As his intellectual godson John Stuart Mill explained: "Bentham broke the spell. . . . Who, before Bentham, dared to speak disrespectfully in express terms, of the British Constitution, or the English Law?" He was not, however, merely a "negative philosopher," wrote Mill, but a person of questioning spirit who demanded the "why" of everything and then applied his "essentially practical mind" toward a system of solutions for the problems that he saw.

Fourteen years after his first published work, Bentham introduced his proposition commonly known as the principle of utility, or the utilitarian idea. In *An Introduction to the Principles of Morals and Legislation*, Bentham proclaimed that through legislation the government could achieve the greatest good for the greatest number. Whether Bentham realized it or not, he had in effect launched a major reform crusade in English politics, the ultimate results of which would not be realized until the various social changes undertaken by English reformers had passed through Parliament after the Reform Bill of 1832.

Despite the implicit radicalism of his ideas, Bentham continued to live his rather ordinary existence as legal scholar and budding political philosopher. Two events that influenced his thinking in major ways were his trip to Russia for a visit with his brother Sam in the 1780's and his correspondence with the political leaders of the French Revolution in the 1790's.

From his travels abroad and his lengthy correspondence in response to the queries from his friends in France about reorganizing government and society there, Bentham drew new inspiration for his critiques of his own society. He became convinced that the very framework of English society needed a thoroughgoing revision based on his utilitarian principles. Made independently wealthy by his father's death in 1792, Bentham could thereafter use the family home at Queen Square Place and the income from the estate to support himself, his ideas, and any social experiments he might choose to undertake.

Bentham and his brother Sam did attempt to implement one philanthropic scheme, a model prison which was grandly named the Panopticon.

From Sam's architectural knowledge was drawn the plan for the building laid out in the shape of a wheel. In the model prison, the keeper resided in the center of the wheel where he could see all the prisoners. By a clever structural arrangement of floors and walls, the inmates could not see one another or the keeper but were imprisoned in isolation, away from the corrupting influences of one another. Although many applauded the Benthams' theories, lack of government support forced them to abandon their plans. Not until 1813 did the British government attempt to repay them for the money they had spent trying to persuade Parliament to adopt their plan.

However intellectually and emotionally democratized Bentham may have become, he did not take up his role as inspiration for a political movement until after 1808, when he met James Mill. Mill's writing and activism helped turn Bentham's political teachings into practice. Out of this background developed politicians known as the Benthamites, who sometimes were called the Philosophical Radicals, or the utilitarians. Within a little more than a decade, the publications of James Mill, coupled with the activities of his son, John Stuart Mill, brought the utilitarians into public prominence. Convinced that nothing positive would be written about them either by the Whig *Edinburgh Review* or the *Tory Quarterly Review*, the utilitarians used their mentor's financial backing to launch the *Westminster Review*.

In the twilight years between 1820 and Bentham's death in 1832, the elderly sage still drew a circle of admirers, disciples, and curiosity seekers to his home in London. By this time, Bentham's hearing had failed so badly that within an hour, visitors often found themselves exhausted from raising their voices to be heard. His voice continued to be heard, however, even after his death. To further the goal of spreading Bentham's ideas, his followers established University College, London. There his bones rest, dressed in his usual clothing, a wax model of his head atop the auto-icon, and his skull at his feet.

Influence

The emergence of the Benthamites into political activism was by no means the first occasion on which Bentham's ideas aroused controversy and criticism. No one could engage in a lifelong critique of English law and society without awakening the wrath of powerful individuals determined to protect the establishment. Bentham's responses to criticism were sometimes regarded as petty and perhaps uninformed. As John Stuart Mill explained, however, Bentham's reactions were peculiar because the great philosopher was "essentially a boy. He had the freshness, the simplicity, the confidingness, the liveliness and activity, all the delightful qualities of boyhood, and the weaknesses which are the reverse side of those qualities—the undue importance attached to trifles, the habitual mismeasurement of the practical bearing and the value of things, the readiness to be either delighted or offended on inadequate cause."

Despite this criticism, which some scholars regard as unfounded, Mill praised Bentham as one of the two men (Samuel Taylor Coleridge was the other) to whom England was "indebted not only for the greater part of the important ideas which have been thrown into circulation among its thinking men in their time, but for a revolution in its general modes of thought and investigation." For more than fifty years, Bentham had labored to bring order out of chaos of the English legal system by providing a logical basis for codification that would render the law at once comprehensible and just.

Bentham's investigation into the legal system, moreover, was so fundamental that his conclusions reached far beyond simple matters of law. The critical scholar saw how the entire fabric of society was interwoven with the law. Hence, he attacked not only laws, courts, and attorneys, but also prisons, poor relief, municipal organizations, rotten boroughs, Parliament, the established clergy, the titled nobility, and the idle landed gentry. Some of his followers would even go so far as advocating the abolition of the monarch; others fought for the principle of a vote for every adult Englishman.

Even as age overtook Bentham physically, the ideas that he had so long espoused were finally becoming accepted by new English political leaders. Reform did not mean revolution, as the emerging politicians understood, so Great Britain in the next decades could carry out change without the turbulence of the French Revolution of 1789. Thanks for this accomplishment, in large

measure, should go to a mild little man whose life testified to the notion that the pen and the written word, indeed, were mightier than the sword and its conquests.

James H. O'Donnell III

An Introduction to the Principles of Morals and Legislation

Type of philosophy: Ethics
First published: 1789
Principal ideas advanced:

◇ The first principle of moral philosophy is the principle of utility, which states that every person is morally obligated to promote the greatest happiness of the greatest number of persons.

◇ The principle of utility takes account of the fact that all people are governed by an interest in securing pleasure and in avoiding pain.

◇ Only the consequences of acts are good or bad; intentions are good or evil only insofar as they lead to pleasure or pain.

◇ Because suffering is always bad, all punishment is bad; but punishment must sometimes be administered in order to avoid the greater suffering that an offender against society might bring to others.

Jeremy Bentham's aim in writing *An Introduction to the Principles of Morals and Legislation* was to discover the foundations for a scientific approach to penal legislation. Because he found these in human nature, rather than in statutes and precedents, his work is also a book on morals.

Two distinct elements appear in Bentham's theory. The first is a psychology of motivation according to which all the actions of people are directed toward pleasures or away from pains. The second is a principle of social ethics according to which each person's actions ought to promote the greatest happiness of the greatest number of persons. That the two principles are independent in their origin and application is not altered by the fact that happiness, according to Bentham, consists in nothing other than pleasure and the avoidance of pain.

Utility

The obligation to promote the happiness of the greatest number Bentham called *the principle of utility*. In the manner of the eighteenth century, he frankly admitted that this first principle of his philosophy cannot be proved, because a chain of proof must begin somewhere, and there can be no principle higher than a first principle. The principle, he said, is part of "the natural constitution of the human frame," and people embrace it spontaneously in judging others if not in directing their own actions. Bentham believed that, in addition to this principle, there are in humans social motives, including "goodwill" or "benevolence," which work in harmony with the principle of utility; but the inclination to kindness is one thing and the principle of utility something else. The latter is an intelligible rule that lies at the foundation of all morals; hence, also of legislation.

What chiefly distinguished Bentham from other eighteenth century moral philosophers was, first, that he recognized only one ultimate principle of morals and, second, that the principle that he maintained was one that admitted of empirical application. The Age of Reason commonly appealed to a whole array of self-evident principles, intuitive convictions, and laws of nature. However, Bentham complained that none of them provided an external standard on which people could agree. In many instances, the alleged truths of nature were an expression of the principle of utility, but at other times they were nothing but expressions of private feelings, prejudices, and interests. The principle of utility, on the other hand, made it possible to define good and evil, right and wrong, in terms that everyone understood and accepted.

> Nature has placed mankind under the governance of two sovereign masters, *pain* and *pleasure*. . . . The *principle of utility* recognizes this subjection, and assumes it for the foundation of that system, the object of which is to rear the fabric of felicity by the hands of reason and of law.

These fundamentals having been laid down, Bentham devoted the remainder of his work to detailed analyses of the psychology of human behavior, chiefly as it bears on problems of social control. His aim was to find the natural divisions of his subject and to arrange the matter in tables that would be of help in drawing inductions.

Pleasures and Pains

First, Bentham treated of pleasures and pains. Legislators, he said, have a twofold interest in these. Inasmuch as the general happiness consists in pleasure and the avoidance of pain, legislators must consider these as ends or final causes; however, because, as legislators, they have to employ motives, they must also consider them as instruments or efficient causes. It is the latter consideration especially that makes it necessary to consider the *sources* of pain and pleasure. Legislators are advised that, in addition to such internal motives as people have toward benevolence, there are several external forces or "sanctions" that reinforce virtue and right. The physical sanction is the pain and loss that nature attaches to certain imprudent acts; the religious sanction is fear of divine displeasure or hope of divine favor; the popular sanction is the favor or disfavor of other people. Political sanction is a fourth source of pain and pleasure, being the rewards and punishments that the ruling power of the state dispenses in cases where the other sanctions are not effective.

The *value* of particular pains and pleasures is obviously relevant in connection with the ends of legislation, but not less so in connection with the means, because the deterrent must be made to outweigh the temptation to crime if it is to serve its purpose. Bentham believed that it is possible to estimate the amount of a pain or pleasure, and he suggested seven calculable factors: intensity, duration, certainty, propinquity, fecundity, purity, and extent. Besides the quantitative side of pain and pleasure, Bentham recognized that there are different kinds of pains and pleasures, and he devoted a chapter to tabulating them. Perceptions, he held, are usually composite, made up of more than one pain or pleasure or both. He undertook to analyze them into their simple parts and to enumerate these. Besides pleasures of the senses he noted pleasures of acquisition and possession, of skill, of friendship, of a good name, of power, and even of malevolence. Besides pains of the senses, he recognized the pains of privation (desire, disappointment, regret) and the kinds of pains that are opposite to the pleasures listed above. Lawmakers, according to Bentham, must have all these in view. When they consider an offense, they must ask what pleasures it tends to destroy and what pains to produce in order, on one hand, to estimate its mischief to the public and, on the other, its temptation to the wrongdoer. Furthermore, when they consider the punishment, they must take into account the several pains that the state has the power to inflict.

Besides these accounts of the general value of pains and pleasures, a special chapter is devoted to individual differences. Bentham listed thirty-two factors that influence people's sensibilities to pain and pleasure, reminding lawmakers that there is no direct proportion between the cause of pain or pleasure and its effect because differences of health, sex, education, religion, and many other conditions must be taken into account.

Actions and Motives

Bentham then considered human *action*. Legislators are interested in acts in proportion to their tendency to disturb the general happiness; hence, their judgment has regard only to consequences, not to motives. Bentham distinguished carefully between the intention of an act and its motive. The intention of an act, he maintained, may have two things in view, the act and its consequences, but not equally: One must intend at least the beginning of the act, as, for example, when one begins to run; but one may have none of the consequences in view and rarely does one have more than a few. To make his point, Bentham took the story of the death of William II of a wound received from Sir Walter Tyrrel when they were stag hunting, diversifying it with different suppositions. Had Tyrrel any thought of the king's death? If not, the killing was altogether unintentional. Did he think, when he shot the stag, that there was some danger of the king's riding in the way? If so, the act was intentional but obliquely so. Did he kill him on account of hatred and for the pleasure of destroying him? If such was true, the deed was ultimately intentional. Such examples show that intention involves, besides the motive or will to act, an understanding of the circumstances in which the action takes place. It is the latter that, according

to Bentham, must chiefly be taken into account when an intention is praised or blamed, for it is the consequences that are properly good or evil; the intention is good or evil only in so far as the consequences were in view from the start.

Bentham maintained that the will or motive of an intentional act is neither good nor evil. One desire is as legitimate as another, and the pleasure that a person receives from injuring an enemy is, considered by itself, a good, however we may judge the act in terms of its consequences. Bentham was alert to the role that fictitious entities play in human discourse and noted the difficulties that they place in the way of exact analysis. For example, "avarice" and "indolence" are supposed to act as motives, although they correspond to nothing in the human heart. Similarly, real motives, such as the pleasure of eating or of sexual satisfaction or of possession, are obscured by calling them "gluttony," "lust," and "covetousness." To help clear up the confusion, Bentham goes over the whole catalog of kinds of pleasures and pains and notes how many of them have several names. Thus, pleasures of wealth are called "pecuniary interest" (a neutral term); "avarice," "covetousness," "rapacity," and "lucre" (terms of reproach); and "economy," "thrift," "frugality," and "industry" (terms of approval), according to the circumstances and one's estimate of their consequences. However, the motive, in each case, is the same, and may neither be praised nor blamed.

Nevertheless, some motives are more harmonious with the principle of utility than others. Bentham classified the motives as *social* (goodwill, love of reputation, desire for friendship, and religion), *dissocial* (displeasure), and *self-regarding* (physical desire, pecuniary interest, love of power, and self-preservation). However, not even the purest social motive, goodwill, always coincides with the principle of utility, particularly when it confines itself to the interests of a limited set of persons.

Bentham recognized that when one is contemplating an act, one is frequently acted on by many motives which draw one in different directions. Some of them are more likely to prompt mischievous acts, others to oppose them. The sum of the motives by which one is likely to be influenced make up one's disposition. "Disposition" was, in Bentham's view, another fictitious notion that represents no more than one person's estimation of how another person is likely to behave. Nevertheless, so far as it can be estimated, the disposition of an offender is important to know. Also Bentham admitted that judgments of good and bad do apply to dispositions, as they do not to single motives. He suggested that the degree of depravity of a criminal's disposition is inversely proportional to the strength of the temptation needed to prompt the person to a mischievous act.

Consequences and Punishment

True to the principle of utility, however, Bentham maintained that, strictly speaking, only the *consequences* of an act are good or bad. Pleasures and pains are real, as dispositions are not. Also acts and intentions, which are internal to the doer, are good or evil only as they attach to consequences. Bentham devoted approximately the last half of his book to distinguishing and classifying mischievous acts. The main division is between primary mischief, which is suffered by one or more individuals whose happiness is directly affected by the offense, and secondary mischief, which is the alarm or danger apprehended by the citizenry from the presence of the offender at large in their midst. Penal legislation must take account of both because the latter diminishes the general happiness (by disturbing people's sense of security) no less than the former.

Bentham's principles for penal legislation are frankly calculative. The lawmaker must estimate the strength of temptation to do mischief and make the punishment sufficiently severe to act as a deterrent. Bentham argues that there is no kindness in making the punishment light because if it is strong enough, persons disposed to crime will not have to endure it, whereas if it is too light, they will. Severity, of course, is not the only thing to be considered. Applying his method of calculating the amount of pleasure and pain, Bentham argued that the certainty and proximity of the punishment must also be taken into account, as well as its appropriateness.

There is no detailed account in *An Introduction to the Principles of Morals and Legislation* of the purposes of punishment. However, in a footnote, referring to a separate work called *Théorie des*

peines et des récompenses (1811, 2 volumes; *The Rationale of Reward*, 1825; also known as *The Rationale of Punishment*, 1830), the author explains that the principal end of punishment is to control action, whether that of the offender or of others who might be tempted to similar misdeeds. It may work through reformation of the person's disposition, through prohibiting action, or through making the individual an example. Bentham recognized that vindictive pleasure is also a good, but he could not tolerate making it a basis for punishment.

Like his liberal disciple John Stuart Mill (as in *On Liberty*, 1859), Bentham held that all punishment is mischief and to be admitted only for the exclusion of greater evil. In many cases, to use his words, "punishment is not worth while." This is the case when the act was freely entered into by the party injured, when the penalty cannot be efficacious (for example, when it comes too late), or when the evils of detecting and prosecuting the crime are more costly than the evils they are intended to prevent. In some cases, the mischief is better countered in other ways—for example, the disseminating of pernicious principles should be overcome by educating people in wholesome ones.

The limitations of effective penal legislation were a matter of primary concern to Bentham. He emphasized private ethics and education as more important than legislation. His view of ethics is usually designated "enlightened self-interest" because he maintained that in most instances people's motives for consulting the happiness of others are dictated by their own interest. However, he conceded that there are occasions when social motives act independently of self-regarding motives. Private ethics he called the art of self-government; education, the art of governing the young. Admittedly these do not always achieve their full intention, but it is dangerous and unprofitable to try to make up for their defects by criminal procedures.

Bentham was especially critical of the jurisprudence that existed at the time, and he distinguished his approach to the subject by coining a new name. A book of jurisprudence, he said, could have one of two objects: to ascertain what the law is, or to ascertain what it ought to be. Most books are devoted to the former—he called them "expository"; his was devoted to the latter—he called it "censorial" jurisprudence, or the *art of legislation*.

Jean Faurot

Additional Reading

Davidson, William Leslie. *Political Thought in England: The Utilitarians from Bentham to J. S. Mill*. Ralph Curtis, 1979. Outlines the development of utilitarianism, clearly differentiating Jeremy Bentham and John Stuart Mill. Offers insights into Bentham's moral, social, and political philosophy and his theories of education and prison reform.

Halévy, Elie. *The Growth of Philosophic Radicalism*. 1901. New York: A. M. Kelley, 1949. London: Faber, 1952. The classic analysis of the emergence of the Benthamites. Halévy writes with great clarity for the general reader. Exceptional bibliography.

Himmelfarb, Gertrude. *Victorian Minds*. New York: Alfred A. Knopf, 1968. The second of these essays uncovers Bentham's obsession with the Panopticon, his rejected plan for a model prison. Examining the actual plans, Himmelfarb reveals a darker side of Bentham's intended prison reforms and questions whether Bentham shared the democratic ideals of his later adherents.

Long, Douglas G. *Bentham on Liberty: Jeremy Bentham's Idea of Liberty in Relation to His Utilitarianism*. Toronto: University of Toronto Press, 1977. Long has concluded that Bentham, in searching for a science of humanity and society, believed that liberty was secondary to security in establishing a plan for social action.

Lyons, David. *In the Interest of the Governed: A Study in Bentham's Philosophy of Utility and Law*. Oxford: Clarendon Press, 1991. An interpretation, suitable for advanced undergraduates, of *An Introduction to the Principles of Morals and Legislation*. Argues that Bentham has a dual standard of interests: community interest is the criterion of right and wrong in public or political affairs, whereas personal interest is the proper standard for "private ethics." Comprehensive bibliography.

Mack, Mary Peter. *Jeremy Bentham: An Odyssey of Ideas*. New York: Columbia University Press, 1963. This magisterial biography of Bentham's first forty-four years draws from unpublished as well as published sources. The standard modern study of Bentham, scholarly yet written for the general reader.

Mill, John Stuart. *On Bentham and Coleridge*. Edited by F. R. Leavis. New York: G. W. Stewart, 1951. The classic and essential account of Bentham by his intellectual godson and heir, who was himself a leader of the utilitarians.

Rosen, F. *Bentham, Byron, and Greece: Constitutionalism, Nationalism, and Early Liberal Political Thought*. New York: Oxford University Press, 1992. This book offers insights into Bentham's political philosophy.

Rosenblum, Nancy L. *Bentham's Theory of the Modern State*. Cambridge, Mass. Harvard University Press, 1978. Highlights in readable fashion Bentham's anticlassical views of the state and particularly of legislation. For Bentham, laws are neither the foundation of an ideal, unchanging order nor the instrument of character formation but an expression of utility.

Semple, Janet. *Bentham's Prison: A Study of the Panopticon Penitentiary*. New York: Oxford University Press, 1993. This interesting story of Bentham's attempt to build a prison offers insights to his difficult character.

Steintrager, James. *Bentham*. Ithaca, N.Y.: Cornell University Press, 1977. An interpretation of Bentham's political thought, somewhat opposed to Mill and Halévy. Takes pains to dissociate Bentham from some aspects of what later became known as utilitarianism. For advanced undergraduates.

James H. O'Donnell III, updated by Grant A. Marler

Henri Bergson

By rejecting the mechanistic view of life held by the noted positivists of his day, Bergson focused renewed attention on the importance of the human spirit, its creative potential, and its inherent freedom, thereby opening new intellectual vistas to many creative artists.

Principal philosophical works: *Extraits de Lucrèce*, 1884 (*The Philosophy of Poetry: The Genius of Lucretius*, 1959); *Quid Aristoteles de loco senserit*, 1889; *Essai sur les données immédiates de la conscience*, 1889 (*Time and Free Will: An Essay on the Immediate Data of Consciousness*, 1910); *Matière et mémoire: Essai sur la relation du corps à l'esprit*, 1896 (*Matter and Memory*, 1911); *Le Rire: Essai sur la signification du comique*, 1900 (*Laughter: An Essay on the Meaning of the Comic*, 1911); *Introduction à la métaphysique*, 1903 (*An Introduction to Metaphysics*, 1912); *L'Évolution créatrice*, 1907 (*Creative Evolution*, 1911); *L'Énergie spirituelle*, 1919 (*Mind-Energy: Lectures and Essays*, 1920); *Durée et simultanéité*, 1922, 1923, 1926 (*Duration and Simultaneity with Reference to Einstein's Theory*, 1965); *Les Deux Sources de la morale et de la religion*, 1932 (*The Two Sources of Morality and Religion*, 1935); *La Pensée et le mouvant*, 1934 (*The Creative Mind*, 1946); *Écrits et paroles*, 1957-1959; *Œuvres: Édition du centenaire*, 1959.

Born: October 18, 1859; Paris, France
Died: January 4, 1941; Paris, France

Early Life

Henri Louis Bergson was born into a sophisticated, multinational family in the year that Charles Darwin published *On the Origin of Species* (1859), a book that profoundly affected Bergson's thinking and against whose dispassionate view of human existence he reacted significantly. Bergson's father, Michel, studied piano under Frédéric Chopin before leaving his native Warsaw to pursue a career in music elsewhere in Europe and in Great Britain. There he met Katherine Levinson, a beauty of Irish-Jewish lineage. He soon married her and took British citizenship.

Henri, although born in Paris, was taken to London as an infant and remained there until he was eight, whereupon the family resettled in Paris. There Bergson spent most of his remaining years, taking French citizenship as soon as he turned twenty-one. He attended the Lycée Fontane, later renamed the Lycée Condorcet, from the time he was nine until he was nineteen, the year in which he published his first article, a prizewinning solution to a problem in mathematics, in the *Annales de mathématiques* (annals of mathematics).

Equally gifted in the sciences and the humanities, Bergson decided upon entering the École Normale Supérieure to concentrate on philosophy. Earning his degree and license to teach in 1881, he taught first at the Lycée d'Angers, then at the Lycée Blaise Pascal in Auvergne. His *Time and Free Will: An Essay on the Immediate Data of Consciousness* was published when he was thirty, at which time he also completed his doctoral dissertation, in Latin, on Aristotle, which won for him a Ph.D. from the University of Paris.

Returning to Paris in 1891, he married Louise Neuberger, a cousin of Marcel Proust. Bergson taught at the Lycée Henri IV until 1900, when he was appointed to the chair in Greek philosophy at the prestigious Collège de France. Before assuming this position, he had published *Matter and Memory*, which was concerned with how the brain's physiology is related to consciousness. He found neurophysiological explanations of consciousness frustratingly limited because they failed to explain satisfactorily the roots of recollection.

Life's Work

Bergson gained considerable attention and some celebrity through his early publications, but his *Laughter: An Essay on the Meaning of the Comic*, a short study of the essence of the comic, placed him in the company of the more significant thinkers of his day. Bergson's theory is that people laugh as a result of a mechanistic impediment, physical or mental, to the usual progression of any activity in life. Using such classic writers as Jonathan Swift, Charles Dickens, and Molière to support and illustrate his contentions, Bergson considered laughter a release of tensions caused by a situation in which the flow of life is impeded by the mechanical.

Following this book was *An Introduction to Metaphysics*, in which Bergson defends intuition against the analytical approach of science, which had been adopted by many humanistic disciplines in an attempt to make them seem more scientific and therefore more credible. Bergson considers analysis, dependent on abstract symbols for its expression, to reside outside humans and outside knowledge, whereas intuition resides within them. It is through intuition, Bergson contends, that humans approach reality in the Platonic sense.

The study for which Bergson is best known is *Creative Evolution*, a work that changed the thinking of a whole generation of creative people. Bergson accepts Darwin's evolutionary theory but interjects into it the notion of the *élan vital*, the life energy that Darwin in his mechanistic, analytical approach denies. Perhaps the most influential concept in Bergson's thought at this time was that humans do not exist in time, but rather that time exists in humans, a notion with which William Faulkner experimented in his writing.

This distinction is at the heart of Bergson's departure from that considerable legion of intellectuals who, in his day, were trying to apply scientific method to all intellectual concerns. Although never antiscientific, Bergson nevertheless insisted that science must be kept in a proper relation to human intuition and that humans must revere it less than intuition, the quintessential humanizing element in all intellectual processes.

Creative Evolution, widely read by intellectuals, also had considerable appeal to a more general reading public, largely because of Bergson's clarity of expression and overall persuasiveness. Bergson departed from Darwin in postulating that human evolution was not simply a routine, mechanistic alteration of the species but that inherent in it was a creative process that had purpose. Obviously, Bergson was moving away from science toward religion, and he was embraced happily by Roman Catholic and other Christian thinkers of his time.

Immediately before World War I, Bergson was at the peak of his influence, lecturing in Europe, Great Britain, and the United States. As war encroached upon Europe in 1914, he was inducted into the French Academy. In that year, he was the Gifford Lecturer at Scotland's University of Edinburgh. He gave his first series of lectures, "The Problem of Personality," in the spring, but he

Henri Bergson. *(The Nobel Foundation)*

could not return to give his final lectures in the fall because war had erupted.

He wrote two thoughtful essays, "The Meaning of War" and "The Evolution of German Imperialism," in both of which he tried to analyze according to his own philosophy the reasons for the conflict. He cast the French as those who represented individual freedom and their opponents as those who venerated the masses rather than the individual. During the war, Bergson served as a French diplomat to Spain and the United States, and at the war's end, he embraced Woodrow Wilson's League of Nations, becoming president of its Commission on Intellectual Cooperation.

Shortly after the end of the war, Bergson's health began to fail. Badly crippled with arthritis that occasionally caused paralysis of his limbs, he was unable to go to Stockholm in 1928 to receive the 1927 Nobel Prize in Literature that had been reserved and that he was awarded the following year. The award speech in Stockholm stressed Bergson's role in freeing the creative imagination and indicated his profound influence on artists of his day. He was praised for breaking out of the stultifying mold in which he was educated, for forging beyond it to celebrate the greatness of the human spirit and its creative potential.

Bergson's last book, *The Two Sources of Morality and Religion*, completed at a time when he was extremely ill and suffered from blinding migraine headaches, has to do with his conception of God. This conception was largely Christian, although Bergson remained a Jew. In a will that he executed in 1937, Bergson indicated that he would have become a Roman Catholic at that time had he not felt compelled to support his fellow Jews at a time when their futures and their very lives were being seriously threatened by the Nazi incursions.

Because of Bergson's international celebrity, his age, and his membership in the French Academy, which he once served as president, France's Vichy government excused him from resigning his official offices and registering with the government as Jews were required to do. To show his support for his Jewish compatriots, however, Bergson, then eighty-one years old, resigned his honorary chair in philosophy at the Collège de France. He registered with the government as a Jew, having to stand in line on a bitterly cold,

damp day, when he was already ill, until he was served. In consequence, he developed a lung inflammation that resulted in his death on January 4, 1941.

Influence

Bergson sought to free his fellow intellectuals from the constricted scientific approach to learning that dominated much of the philosophical thinking of his day and that has since continued to dominate intellectual circles. Frequently accused of being antiscientific, Bergson, who understood the sciences well, wanted merely to control the extent to which scientific method was used in pursuits that were essentially nonscientific.

Bergson's most appreciative audience was found among graphic artists, composers, and writers, many of whom felt constrained by the scientific bias of contemporary society. Thinkers such as Bertrand Russell complained that much of Bergson's work was based on opinion rather than on hard research data; it is hard to deny that such was the case. One cannot ignore, however, the incredible promise that Bergson's writings and his idea of the creative force, the *élan vital*, stirred in a broad range of writers who derived from his writing precisely the kind of justification they required to validate their activities.

Writing about consciousness, Bergson outlined a methodology for many modern writers who were grappling with the stream-of-consciousness technique in writing and other arts. Writers such as Thomas Mann, Marcel Proust, Virginia Woolf, and Paul Valéry, as well as painters such as Claude Monet and Pablo Picasso, imbibed the spirit that emanated from Bergson's writing and translated it into their own media, thereby creating challenging art forms. It is for this kind of contribution that Bergson will be remembered.

R. Baird Shuman

An Introduction to Metaphysics

Type of philosophy: Epistemology, metaphysics
First published: Introduction à la métaphysique, 1903 (English translation, 1912)

Principal ideas advanced:

◇ Metaphysics is the science that uses intuition.

◇ Intuition is a kind of intellectual sympathy by which one understands an object by placing oneself within it.

◇ Intuitive knowledge is superior to analytic knowledge because intuitive knowledge is both absolute and perfect, while analytic knowledge is relative and imperfect.

◇ Science depends on symbols and employs the analytic method; consequently, science deals with classes rather than with individual objects; it can grasp time, motion, change, and the self only by reducing the fluid to the static.

◇ Intuition, on the other hand, reveals reality as a changing, restless flux—a kind of creative mobility that can never be understood by the use of static concepts.

This famous essay first appeared in the *Revue de Metaphysique et de Morale* in January, 1903. Published in book form in 1912, it has been translated into many languages and constitutes what many philosophers consider to be the best introduction to Bergson's philosophy. Strictly speaking, the title is misleading. The book is not an introduction to metaphysics but rather an introduction to the *method* of metaphysics, or *intuition*. Although there is a close relation between Bergson's view of the world and his conception of the intuitive method, the emphasis in this book is predominantly on the latter. Metaphysics, in fact, is defined by Bergson as the science that uses intuition.

Intuition and Analysis

Neither the term "intuition" nor the concept of a direct and immediate way of knowing objects was original with Bergson. A number of rationalists had used the word to describe the awareness of certain basic notions that exhibit a kind of transparency as to their truth and are commonly spoken of as self-evident. Mystics have often described the culmination of their mystic experiences, in which they see God face to face, as an intuitive experience. Many philosophers have recognized, as Bergson did, the need for a direct, as well as an indirect, way of knowing and have variously characterized intuition as "acquaintance," "sensation," "introspection," "instinct,"

and "feeling." To Bergson goes the credit for extracting what is common to all of these conceptions of immediacy and for portraying the intuitive method in a clear and forceful manner by means of a wide range of vivid examples.

Intuition is defined by Bergson as "the kind of intellectual sympathy by which one places oneself within an object in order to coincide with what is unique in it and consequently inexpressible." In contrast, the method of analysis attempts to grasp the object by portraying the features that it possesses in common with other things. Analysis, therefore, always sees an object partially—from a certain perspective—rather than in its individuality and in terms of its peculiar properties. Intuition gives us what the object is in itself; analysis provides only the shell or the husk.

Of all the metaphors that Bergson uses to contrast the method of intuition with that of analysis, the spatial one is perhaps the most frequent. Consider the contrast between entering into an object and moving around it. Because of spatial perspective, an object appears different from various points of observation—larger or smaller, of different shapes, sometimes of varying colors. To identify the object with any one of these appearances would be a mistake. All such knowledge is relative and partial. However, the object has a true character of its own; otherwise it would not be capable of exhibiting itself in these many ways. We could not determine this character merely from the many appearances, for there would be an infinity of such manifestations, and we could not create the object by merely adding them together. However, if we can intuitively grasp the object by "entering into it," we can see its essential nature and we can predict what the various perspectives will be. This knowledge does not depend on a point of view nor does it use any symbols. Hence it is *absolute* rather than *relative*.

Bergson illustrated the difference between intuition and analysis by examining the two methods by which we come to know a character whose adventures are portrayed in a novel. After the author has portrayed the hero through his speech and behavior, we feel that we understand him. However, this knowledge is superficial and unreliable unless we can succeed at some time in identifying ourselves with him, unless we *become* the hero and experience his feelings and drives. Once we have done this, we can see that his speech and behavior flow naturally from his personality; we are able, having seen him from the inside or absolutely, to account for his actions relative to varying situations. Having grasped his unique nature, we are able to recognize what he has in common with other people—what may be known of him through descriptions, symbols, and analysis.

Intuitive knowledge, according to Bergson, is not only absolute but perfect, whereas analytic knowledge is imperfect. Try to ascertain what the inner meaning of a poem would be by examining its translations into all possible languages, each with its own shade of meaning, and each correcting the other. The individual translations would be only symbolic representations and could never add up to the true meaning of the poem; they would all be imperfect because they were partial, and even their sum could not give the intended meaning.

Analysis and intuition are the respective methods of positive science and metaphysics. Science works with symbols: words, numbers, diagrams, graphs. It makes comparisons between forms and reduces complex forms to simple ones; it deals with *classes of things*, not with the *individual objects*. Metaphysics, on the other hand, attempts to grasp the world without any expression, translation, picture, model, or symbolic device. It is the study that claims to dispense with symbols.

Self, Duration, and Motion

From the many illustrations that Bergson gives of the contrast between the intuitive and the analytic methods, three may be selected for special emphasis. These are to be found in our knowledge of the *self*, *duration*, and *motion*.

According to Bergson, as I first look at myself, I see three things: a series of perceptions of the external world, a group of memories that adhere to the perceptions, and a crowd of motor habits or urges. However, as I examine these elements more carefully, they seem to recede from my true self, which begins to take on the character of the center of a sphere with the perceptions, memories, and tendencies radiating outward toward the surface. The self that I discover here is not like any flux that I know because the successive

stages merge into one another, each retaining something of what has just passed and each giving a hint of what is still to come. It is not like a series of discrete elements but more like the unrolling of a coil or the rolling up of a thread on a ball. Or it can be compared to a spectrum of colors, with insensible gradations from one hue to the next. However, none of these metaphors is quite adequate. The spectrum, for example, is something that is ready-made, while the self is a living, growing, developing being, with retentions of what has taken place in its past existence and expectations of what is to come. The inner life of the self has variety, continuity, and unity—yet it is not merely the synthesis of these, for they are themselves abstract and static concepts, while the self is characterized by mobility.

Both empiricists and rationalists miss the real self, for they try to find it in its *manifestations*, which they mistake for its *parts*, not realizing that these are really *partial expressions* of a *total impression* obtained through intuition. Empiricists can find in the personality nothing but a series of psychical events, which they call "states of the ego." However, the ego eludes them because they have only a very confused notion of what it is that they seek; they are looking for an intuition but are using in this search the method of analysis, which is the very negation of intuition. No matter how closely the states are joined or how thoroughly the intervals are explored, the ego escapes. We might as well conclude that Homer's *Iliad* (c. 800 B.C.E.; English translation, 1616) has no meaning because we fail to find it between the letters of which it is composed.

Rationalism is no more successful. It, too, begins with the psychical states. However, it realizes that the unity of the personality cannot lie merely in the series of percepts, images, and feelings. Hence, it concludes that the self must be something purely negative—the absence of all determination, form without content, a void in which shadows move. Small wonder that the rationalist finds it hard to distinguish Peter from Paul; if the ego itself is devoid of determination, the individual self must be also. Thus the empiricist tries to construct the unity of the self by filling in the gaps between the states by still other states, and the rationalist tries to find the unity in an empty form. The empiricist reduces the string of beads to the unstrung beads; the rationalist to the unbeaded string; *both* lose the reality with which they began. What is needed is a new empiricism that will define the self through an intuitive examination of the self. This definition can hardly produce a concept at all because it will apply to only one object. However, certainly no concept of the self can be reached by taking sides with empiricism or with rationalism. Only from an intuition of the self in its uniqueness can we descend with equal ease to both philosophical schools.

Bergson offers the idea of duration as another illustration of what happens when we try to understand the world through analysis. From one point of view, duration is *multiplicity*; it consists of elements that, unlike other elements, encroach on one another and fuse. If we try to "solidify" duration by adding together all of its parts, we fail; we find that we get not the mobility of the duration but the "frozen memory of the duration." From another point of view, duration is *unity*. However, it is a moving, changing, and living unity, not at all like the abstract and empty form that pure unity demands. Shall we then try to get duration by combining multiplicity and unity? No sort of mental chemistry will permit this; we cannot get from either of them or from their synthesis the simple intuition of duration. If, however, we start with intuition, then we can easily see how it is unity and multiplicity, and many other things besides. Unity and multiplicity are only standpoints from which we may consider duration, not parts that constitute it.

Bergson shows the error in trying to understand the world through analysis. Movement can be considered as a series of potential stopping points; these are points through which the moving object passes, its positions at various times during its motion. Now suppose there were an infinite number of such potential stoppages. Would there be motion? Obviously not. If the object were judged to be *at rest* at each of these positions, no sum of them—finite or infinite—would constitute motion. If the object were judged to be *in motion* at each of these positions, then we should not really have analyzed motion; we should only have broken up a long motion into a series of shorter ones. Passage is movement, and stoppage is immobility, and the two

have nothing in common. We try to get mobility from stoppages to infinity, and then, when this fails to give us what we want, we add a mysterious "passage from one stoppage to another." The trouble is, of course, that we have supposed rest to be clearer than motion, and the latter to be definable from the former by way of addition. What we should recognize is that mobility is simple and clear, and that rest is merely the limit of the process of slackening movement. Given an intuition of motion, rest becomes easily understood; without this intuition the motion can never be grasped, whether approached from rest or from any of the other points of view that constitute notes of the total impression.

Through the intuition of movement, we can know it *absolutely* rather than *relatively*. Bergson uses the spatial "inside" and "outside" distinction to sharpen the contrast between the two methods of knowing. When we know motion absolutely, we insert ourselves into the object by an act of imagination. When we know it relatively, we see it only as a function of coordinate systems or points of reference, or as dependent on our own motion or rest with reference to it. The only way really to understand motion is to move. Motion has an interior (something like states of mind), and when we intuit motion, we sympathize with this inner nature. We no longer view the motion from outside, remaining where we are, but from within, where the movement really is.

Two Problems

Bergson admits that there are certain difficulties in accepting the intuitive method. One difficulty is that the adoption of the intuitive method requires a change in our ordinary habits of thinking. When we try to understand an object, we customarily pass from the concept to the thing rather than the reverse. Concepts are abstractions and generalizations; they portray only what is common to objects, not what is peculiar to them. If we try to capture an object by putting concepts together, we are doomed to failure, for a concept can only circumscribe an object, creating a circle that is too large and does not fit exactly. Realizing this in the case of any one concept, we add another concept, which is also too large but which partially overlaps the previous circle and thus cuts down the area within which the object is to be found. We continue the process to infinity, confidently believing that we will finally reach an area so small that it will contain *only* the object, will characterize it uniquely, and thus will coincide with it. However, although the area does coincide with the *properties*, it does not coincide with the *object*; the identity of the properties and the object can be grasped only if we start with the object, not if we start with its properties. If we know the thing, we can understand its properties, for from a unity we can proceed to the various ways of viewing that unity; but once the unity has been divided into many symbolic expressions, it can never be restored. There will ever remain a gap between the object, which is a unique member of a class, and the class of which the object is the only member. To avoid this predicament, we have only to reverse the usual methods of thinking. Instead of starting with concepts and trying to get objects, we should start with intuitively grasped objects and then proceed to symbolize their aspects and properties. Only in this way can inconsistent concepts be harmonized, and only in this way can concepts be molded to fit their objects.

A second difficulty in accepting the intuitive method is that it seems to displace science and render all of its conclusions worthless. However, Bergson cautions against this inference on the grounds that both science and the analytic method have an important practical role to play. To illustrate, let us return to the concept of *motion*. We saw that motion cannot be grasped in its essence by thinking of it as an infinite series of positions occupied by the moving object. Suppose we wish to stop a moving object—as we might well wish to do for certain practical reasons. It will then be very important for us to know where the object is at a precise moment. Science, by the analytic method, can provide us with this information. Indeed, the need for this kind of information accounts for the exactness and precision of science, for its well-defined concepts, and for the method of inductive generalization that it so effectively employs. Through the centuries, increased emphasis on the techniques of logic has brought about great improvement in the scientific method. This, in turn, has increased our control over the world. However, we do not thereby penetrate deeper into the heart of nature.

We can use nature better; we can see better how it will behave toward us and how we should behave toward it, but we do not have the intellectual sympathy that is identical with true understanding. Every concept is a *practical question* that we put to reality. Reality replies in the affirmative or in the negative. In doing so, however, it hides its true identity.

What sort of a world is it that is revealed by intuition? For an answer to this question, we must turn to Bergson's other works. In *An Introduction to Metaphysics*, he states only a few conclusions. Reality is external, but it can be directly experienced by mind. It is characterized primarily by such words as *tendency, mobility, change,* and *flux.* It is a world *being made* rather than a world *ready-made.* It is better understood as a "longing after the restlessness of life" than as a "settling down into an easy intelligibility," as a world of soul than as a world of idea.

In this way, Bergson tells us about intuition. His success in this attempt, however, leads us to wonder if, in the achievement of his goal, he has destroyed the very thesis of his book, that the true nature of intuition cannot be communicated by means of abstract, general, or simple ideas. Perhaps his reply would be that he has not really analyzed intuition. What he has done is to select illustrations of intuition so skillfully that we have been able in each case to identify ourselves with intuition and thus to receive an intuition of intuition.

A. Cornelius Benjamin

The Two Sources of Morality and Religion

Type of philosophy: Ethics, philosophy of religion
First published: Les Deux Sources de la morale et de la religion, 1932 (English translation, 1935)
Principal ideas advanced:
◇ There are two kinds of morality: compulsive and ideal.
◇ There are two kinds of religion: popular and dynamic.
◇ Corresponding to the two kinds of morality and the two kinds of religion are two kinds of

societies, the closed and the open, and two kinds of souls, the enslaved and the free.

◇ The two sources of morality and religion are the practical needs of humans and societies and the idealistic impulse.

◇ Humans rise above the static patterns of compulsive moralities and popular religions, achieving freedom in open societies, when they recapture, through mystical intuition, their original vital impetus.

In no sense was Henri Bergson's philosophy a mere compilation of the scientific findings of his time. Nevertheless, his kind of empiricism required him to investigate on his own principles the subject matter of various sciences. His early works may be viewed as studies in psychology. In *L'Évolution créatrice* (1907; *Creative Evolution,* 1911), he turned to biology. His last great work, *The Two Sources of Morality and Religion,* took him into the fields of sociology and cultural anthropology. Here he made the *élan vital* (vital impulse) the key to understanding morality, religion, and history. The work is admittedly more speculative than its predecessors. Whereas in *Creative Evolution,* he had tried to "keep as close as possible to facts," in this later work, he permitted himself to argue from "probabilities" on the grounds that "philosophical certainty admits of degrees." Whenever possible, philosophic intuition should be "backed up by science"; however, where science falls short, Bergson maintained, it is legitimate to appeal to the testimony of great prophetic and mystical teachers. The author regarded this work as a valuable confirmation of the thesis presented in *Creative Evolution.* Others have found it rewarding for the fresh perspectives it has brought to social studies.

As the title indicates, the author's approach was a genetic one. Understanding of the phenomena under investigation meant seeing how they were necessitated by the evolutionary impulse. Bergson's contribution was to suggest that morality and religion cannot be understood in terms of one kind of explanation only. Followers of Auguste Comte, Herbert Spencer, and Karl Marx had tried to explain all morality and religion as arising out of the needs of society. Bergson went a long way with them; but he insisted that because some morality and religion

are, in the usual sense, antisocial, they must be traced to another source; namely, the spiritual vision of exceptional people. In fact, according to Bergson, all historical systems of morality and religion are blends, combining idealistic with pragmatic elements. This amalgamation takes place because people's lives are so largely dominated by intelligence, which moderates the seemingly extravagant claims of mystical insight even as it relaxes the hold of tradition and habit. Bergson denied that it is possible to explain either moral obligation or religious belief on intellectual grounds: Reason is emphatically not one of the two sources from which morality and religion arise. Nonetheless, its presence is felt.

To make his thesis plain, Bergson discussed morality and religion under separate chapters. His argument is that there are two kinds of morality and two kinds of religion. Corresponding to these, there are two kinds of souls and two kinds of societies.

Morality

The first kind of morality is a *common, compulsive morality* demanded by society for its protection. Bergson regarded social life as a device of the life impulse for increasing its mastery over matter and enhancing its freedom. Social life is an evolutionary advance because the true individual is found only in society. However, there are grades of social life. Insects have purchased their efficient organization only at the expense of adaptability. It was the gift of intelligence that enabled humans to break out of the hard and fast regulations imposed by instinct. The problem for humans is that of preserving the social organism. Bergson imagines, as an example, that an ant momentarily endowed with sufficient intelligence asks itself whether it is in its interests to perform the onerous tasks imposed upon it by the group. He concludes that were it to consider long enough, it might at last arrive at the conclusion reached in the history of human thought by John Stuart Mill and resume its labors, happy in the belief that its interests are identical with those of the group. Meanwhile, however, it will perish unless instinct draws it back with the imperative, "You must because you must." Such, according to Bergson, is the sense of obligation that lies at the basis of common morality. Closely connected with habit, it is a weakened form of instinct. Intellect, far from providing a basis for moral obligation, is what obligation was designed to overcome. Moral obligation operates impersonally in a compulsive manner and has its analogies in somnambulistic behavior. However, moral compulsion is not natural in the sense that animal instincts are. Bergson denied that acquired characteristics—such as moral compulsions—are inherited. Moral patterns must be learned by each generation from its predecessor and may be modified in the process. Therefore, the moralities of civilized nations differ radically from those of primitive peoples. However, obligation as such is the same in all societies and everywhere exercises identical control.

Contrasted with morality of this compulsive kind is that which works under the attraction of an *ideal*. For example, ordinary people feel obliged to render what they think of as justice to their friends (such as returning a favor) and to their enemies (such as exacting vengeance). However, rare individuals have caught a glimpse of a higher kind of justice, what we call "social justice," that makes no distinction between friends and enemies and treats all people as equals. It is impossible, according to Bergson, to explain the origins of the latter as a development or modification of the former. Customary morality speaks for an existing order that demands to be perpetuated; the higher morality speaks for a vision that inspires in sensitive people a demand that the existing order be changed. It does not ordinarily require great effort either to learn or to practice common morality; but an ideal morality requires constant propaganda even to keep it alive and is practiced only at the expense of personal discipline and self-denial. Accordingly, we have to look not to the masses for its origins but to exceptional persons who have had a vision of reality in its unity and striving. Prophets through their preaching and mystics through their example call on humankind to enter a truer way. Their teaching, not subject to the vicissitudes of history and tradition, is a perennial source of insight and motivation to lesser people.

Religion
Analogous to the first kind of morality is *popular religion*, which Bergson calls *static*. Like con-

science, by which nature secures the individual's submission to the welfare of the group, religious belief is a protective device, invented by vital impulse to overcome the hazards that attend the use of intelligence in the "human experiment." Instinctive acts are performed without thinking and without any doubt as to whether they will be effective, but intelligent acts are complex; and deliberations concerning means and ends would paralyze human activity altogether if nature did not come to the rescue and teach humans to invent necessities where none exist. This is what lies at the bottom of myth. A myth is a kindly hallucination that fills up the gaps left by our understanding, permitting humans to act with assurance and ease.

The hunter, facing a beast at bay, needs to believe that his arrow is directed after it leaves his hand; and the farmer is comforted by the belief that there are powers that preside over the seed that he has planted in the earth. Somewhat in the same way, humans need assurance in the face of death, which has never threatened the nonreflective animal as it does humans. The belief in an afterlife neutralizes doubt and fear and provides humans with the sense of self-mastery. In these ways, provident nature preserves its favorite, humans, making it possible for them to benefit by intelligence without being destroyed by it.

In Bergson's view, myth and magic pass over into religion in the same proportion that humans accustom themselves to think of environing powers in personal terms. The *mana*, which anthropologists claim is the basis of the religious response, Bergson took to be an expression of purposive activity. In magical practices, humans suppose that they employ this mysterious power themselves; in religious acts, they seek the cooperation of unseen beings who, they believe, have even greater *mana* at their disposal. For Bergson, religion is not primarily a matter of knowledge, nor is it based on poetic imagination. It has its origins in practical needs, and it provides a scaffolding for human activity.

Opposed to this static religion, which has no cognitive worth, is the *dynamic* religion that has its source in mysticism. Bergson was sparing in his use of the ambiguous term "mysticism"; like American philosopher William James, he regarded mystical insight as a definite kind of experience that most of us never directly share. The visions of mystics bypass the constructions of myth and imagination as well as those of rational argument and yield immediate experience of reality in its character as a whole. Bergson held that the Greeks, because of their intellectualism, never attained a full-blown mysticism. In India, it developed further but frequently was blighted by a speculative tendency or perverted into hypnotic trance. The prophets of ancient Israel contributed the vision of a God as just as he was powerful: However, his transcendence above the world and the particularism of his purpose were residues of static belief. Only the Christ of the Gospels—to whom we owe the truth that God is love—was completely open to divine reality. The great mystics of the Church are "the imitators, and original but incomplete continuators, of what the Christ of the Gospels was completely." Christ's influence is also seen, according to Bergson, in the mystics of Islam and such modern Hindus as Ramakrishna and Vivekananda. (Bergson, as was noted, was a Jew, although in his latter years he showed sympathy for Roman Catholicism.)

According to Bergson, genuine mysticism is not pessimistic or antisocial or quietistic. The vision of God as love generates in its beholders charity toward all God's creatures, stirring in them the desire to lead all people into the higher form of life that has been disclosed to them. Furthermore, it releases energies in them and opens their eyes to possibilities that are sealed off from ordinary people. God works through these beholders. They become the agent of the evolutionary impulse in its purpose to transcend the present stage of human life. However, as always, divine freedom must adjust its steps to material conditions. In order to draw people upward to higher freedom, mystics accommodate their teaching to the capacity of their hearers. To get a portion of the truth accepted, mystics have to compromise, for humanity understands the new only as it is incorporated into the old.

Dynamic religion is the result of this compromise. It does not come into being through a natural development of the static, but by the deliberate adaptation of old forms to new ends. Like the higher ethics, dynamic religion requires a constant effort to keep it from lapsing completely into familiar static forms. Indeed, a constant ten-

sion exists between the "civic" and "universal" functions that all of the higher religions seek to perform.

Societies and Souls

The whole problem is illuminated by Bergson's distinction between "closed" and "open" societies and the types of souls that correspond to them. Natural societies are *closed societies*: examples are families, clans, city-states, and sovereign nations. They exist to serve the interests of their own members and take no responsibility for the rest of humanity. "Self-centeredness, cohesion, hierarchy, absolute authority of the chief"—such are the features of the closed society. The *open society*, by contrast, is largely an ideal existing in the minds of chosen souls. In principle, it embraces all humanity, but in practice, the most that ever is achieved is an enlarging here and there of closed societies. Such enlargement, according to Bergson, never takes place of itself but only as a result of propaganda carried on by dedicated people, who may effect more or less far-reaching transformations of the existing order. "But after each occasion the circle that has momentarily opened closes again. Part of the new has flowed into the mould of the old; individual aspiration has become social pressure; and obligation covers the whole." Bergson regarded modern democracy as in principle an "open society," founded as it is on the ideals of liberty, equality, and brotherhood of all people. Thus, it rests on foundations quite different from those of Athenian democracy. Nevertheless, the tensions between the demands of nation-states and the service of humankind remain; in fact, our Western democracies, too, are "closed societies."

Cultural Evolution

In a final chapter entitled "Mechanism and Mysticism," Bergson explains the bearing of these investigations on the thesis set forth in *Creative Evolution*: that in humans the divine impulse toward freedom is destined to realize itself. Does the history of the human race support this thesis? Bergson's answer was affirmative. However, he had to depart from the simplicities that characterize most theories of cultural evolution. They assume that through intelligence, humans have progressed thus far toward liberty and justice.

Bergson maintained that intelligence was not a sufficient explanation and that had it not been supplemented by a halo of "intuition," it would have proved fatal to humans. What enables humans to rise above the static, ingrown patterns of natural societies is the capacity, never entirely lost to him, of recapturing in his own self, through the mystic vision, the original vital impetus, and moving forward with it toward higher unity and greater freedom.

Viewing the situation in modern times, Bergson lamented the fact that humans seem to have fallen slave to the machine. He was unwilling, however, to subscribe to any kind of economic determinism. Industry, which came into existence to satisfy real needs, has taken a different direction and fostered artificial ones. This can be corrected, and by simplifying his way of life, humans can make machines a benefit. "The initiative can come from humanity alone, for it is humanity and not the alleged force of circumstances, still less a fatality inherent to the machine, which has started the spirit of invention along a certain track." Bergson thought that a new mysticism, with an attendant ascetic discipline, might well be in the offing, which would renew in humans a sense of their high calling. In view of the breakdown of popular religion, psychical research seemed to him also to bear some promise, by restoring to the masses belief that life is more than meat and the body more than raiment. He concludes:

> Mankind lies groaning, half crushed beneath the weight of its own progress. Men do not sufficiently realize that their future is in their own hands. Theirs is the task of determining first of all whether they want to go on living or not. Theirs the responsibility, then, for deciding if they want merely to live, or intend to make just the extra effort required for fulfilling, even on their refractory planet, the essential function of the universe, which is a machine for the making of gods.

Jean Faurot

Additional Reading

Alexander, Ian W. *Bergson: Philosopher of Reflection*. New York: Hillary House, 1957. This book provides an introspective look into Henri Bergson's theories of knowledge and consciousness. It is lucid and direct in presenting the salient parts of Bergson's philosophy and theology, noting the effects of his thinking on creative artists.

Gunter, Pete A. Y., ed. *Bergson and the Evolution of Physics*. Knoxville: University of Tennessee Press, 1969. Gunter and his contributors try to show that Bergson was not antiscientific and that his emphasis on the *élan vital* and on intuition is positive for science rather than negative as it has often been portrayed.

Hanna, Thomas, ed. *The Bergsonian Heritage*. New York: Columbia University Press, 1962. The eleven essays in this collection, drawn from a convention held at Hollins College to commemorate the centennial of Bergson's birth, present assessments of Bergson's impact on theological thought and on literature. The book also contains reminiscences by people who knew him at the Sorbonne and the Collège de France.

Kolakowski, Leszek. *Bergson*. New York: Oxford University Press, 1985. A concise overview of Bergson's major ideas, written as an elementary introduction to his work for the general student.

Lacey, Alan R. *Bergson*. New York: Routledge, 1989. Surveys most of Bergson's major writings with a focus on Bergson as a philosopher of process and change. Bibliography, index.

Moore, Francis C. T. *Bergson: Thinking Backwards*. New York: Cambridge University Press, 1996. Brief and accessible exposition of the content and significance of Bergson's most influential ideas.

Mullen, Mary D. *Essence and Operation in the Teaching of St. Thomas in Some Modern Philosophies*. Washington, D.C.: Catholic University Press, 1941. Mullen shows the effect that Bergson had on the developing Thomism of Jacques Maritain, a debt that Maritain acknowledged. The portions of this book that deal with Bergson are chronicles of a spiritual journey that caused Bergson to see the Church as a creative force.

Pilkington, Anthony Edward. *Bergson and His Influence: A Reassessment*. Cambridge, England: Cambridge University Press, 1976. This five-chapter book presents an initial overview of

Bergsonism, then devotes one chapter each to Bergson's influence on Charles Péguy, Valéry, Proust, and Julien Benda. The chapter on Benda contains interesting insights into Bergson's theory of mobility.

Russell, Bertrand. *The Philosophy of Bergson*. Cambridge, England: Cambridge University Press, 1914. Russell, more devoted to an undeviating scientific method than Bergson, looks with considerable skepticism on Bergson's theories of knowledge and dependence on intuition in shaping arguments. He particularly questions Bergson's *Creative Evolution*, in which the theory of the *élan vital* is fully expounded.

R. Baird Shuman, updated by William Nelles

George Berkeley

Berkeley put forth a novel theory of sense perception that led to the denial of the existence of physical objects. Serving as the link between John Locke's commonsense materialism and David Hume's skepticism, Berkeley's ideas spanned the philosophical gap between classical traditionalism and the emergence of modern science.

Principal philosophical works: *An Essay Towards a New Theory of Vision*, 1709; *A Treatise Concerning the Principles of Human Knowledge*, 1710; *Three Dialogues Between Hylas and Philonous*, 1713; *De motu*, 1721; *Alciphron: Or, The Minute Philosopher*, 1732; *The Theory of Vision: Or, Visual Language, Showing the Immediate Presence and Providence of a Deity, Vindicated and Explained*, 1733; *The Analyst: Or, A Discourse Addressed to an Infidel Mathematician*, 1734; *A Defense of Free-Thinking in Mathematics*, 1735; *The Querist*, 1735-1737; *Siris: A Chain of Philosphical Reflexions and Inquiries Concerning the Virtues of Tar Water and Divers Other Subjects*, 1744.

Born: March 12, 1685; in or near Kilkenny, County Kilkenny, Ireland
Died: January 14, 1753; Oxford, England

Early Life

George Berkeley was born on March 12, 1685, in or near Kilkenny, in County Kilkenny, Ireland, the eldest son of William Berkeley. Little is known of his boyhood, but there is evidence that he was a precocious child. In 1696, he attended the Kilkenny School, and in 1700, Trinity College, Dublin, where he studied mathematics, logic, languages, and philosophy. He was graduated in 1704 and received his M.A. in 1707, becoming a Fellow of Trinity College. During this period, the principal influences upon his thought were the ideas of English philosopher John Locke and the continental thinkers Nicolas Malebranche and Pierre Bayle. Berkeley had begun the line of thought that he was to pursue in his later major works, that is, his argument for the immateriality of objects, based on the subjectivity of sense perceptions. Before the age of thirty, he had published three of the most important philosophical works in eighteenth century England, books that have become classics in English philosophy. All three were published within a four-year period, from 1709 to 1713, *An Essay Towards a New Theory*

of Vision, *A Treatise Concerning the Principles of Human Knowledge*, and *Three Dialogues Between Hylas and Philonous*.

Life's Work

In *An Essay Towards a New Theory of Vision*, Berkeley's design was to show how human sight conceptualizes distance, magnitude, and the location of objects and whether ideas of sight and touch are similar or different. His goal in *A Treatise Concerning the Principles of Human Knowledge* was to demonstrate that an uncritical acceptance of materialism inevitably leads to skepticism and atheism. In *Three Dialogues Between Hylas and Philonous*, Berkeley refines and extends these ideas, arguing in dialogue form that the notion of a "material substratum" is a meaningless verbal abstraction.

Even though these books, as an example of English prose, are superb in style and clarity, they were, when they appeared, either dismissed, ridiculed, or ignored. Common sense convinced most people that "matter" was real enough, and Dr. Samuel Johnson's declaration, "I refute him thus," upon kicking a large stone, was refutation enough.

In 1709, Berkeley was made a deacon in the Church of England and was ordained a priest in

1710. That same year, Berkeley traveled to London, where he met writers Joseph Addison, Sir Richard Steele, Alexander Pope, and Jonathan Swift. Berkeley was present at the first night of Addison's play *Cato* (1713) and wrote a lively description of the evening. He wrote essays for Steele's *The Guardian* (1713) against the ideas of the freethinkers. Pope praised Berkeley, and Swift presented him at court.

In 1713-1714, Berkeley traveled on the Continent, where he probably met and conversed with Malebranche. He returned there in 1716-1720, serving as tutor to George Ashe, son of the Bishop of Clogher. On his return, he published *De motu* (of motion), in which he argued against Sir Isaac Newton's notion of absolute space, time, and motion and made reference to his ideas on immaterialism. This work also earned for Berkeley the title as "precursor of Mach and Einstein." He retained his fellowship at Trinity College until 1724, when he became dean of Derry.

Disappointed at having failed to attract the interest of educated English society in his philosophical theories, Berkeley turned his attention toward propagating Christianity and educating American Indians, even settling on a scheme to

George Berkeley. *(Library of Congress)*

build a college in Bermuda for that purpose. He was granted a charter, with the Archbishop of Canterbury acting as trustee and Parliament allotting a grant of twenty thousand pounds for the project. There was, however, some opposition to the plan, and the project was eventually abandoned.

In 1728, Berkeley married Anne Forster, an intelligent and well-educated woman, and they moved to Newport, Rhode Island. The marriage was a happy one and six children—four sons and two daughters—would be born to the couple. Returning to Ireland in 1731, Berkeley was appointed Bishop of Cloyne. There he administered

his diocese with skill and grace for eighteen years. At the time of his leaving America, he had donated generously of his books and money to Yale University, and it is interesting to note that the United States honored his largess 150 years later when the university town of Berkeley, California, was given his name.

In Ireland, Berkeley's writing continued. He produced works on religious apologetics, optics, and mathematics. In his later work, he attacked Deism, analyzed geometrical optics, and raised questions concerning the theory of physical fluxions. (On this latter issue, throughout his lifetime, he was a constant opponent of Newton.)

These topics appear in many of his later writings.

Alciphron, *The Theory of Vision*, *The Analyst*, and *A Defense of Free-Thinking in Mathematics* all reflect the same general objective: to mount a critical attack against materialism, religious free-thinking, and atheism. Berkeley's position, although not an idiosyncratic view of matter, perception, and mathematics, is essentially negative. It is an attempt to destroy what had become the generally accepted eighteenth century viewpoint on these issues. His opponents, he argued, find the entities of religious belief mysterious and difficult to understand, but they are no more mysterious or difficult to believe, he concluded, than the scientific picture of the world offered by Galileo and Newton. He who can digest, he writes, the notions of force, gravity, fluxions, and infinitesimals should not be squeamish about accepting the hidden points of divinity.

The Querist, in contrast, is a treatise on economics and an analysis of the relations among work, production, and wealth. *Siris* is a curious piece written toward the end of Berkeley's life, in which he maintains that tar water (resinous residue of pine and fir trees) is an efficacious medical treatment against famine and dysentery. *Siris* is a pious book pervaded with mysticism, yet, at the same time, it contains Berkeley's most systematic and penetrating account of the philosophical assumptions of science. In *Siris*, Berkeley achieved what he had sought in all of his other books—a large, sympathetic readership. The book was an instant success, going through six editions in the first year.

After 1745, Berkeley continued to be active in public affairs, speaking out often on political events. In 1752, the Berkeleys moved to Oxford, where Berkeley entered Christ Church College. Berkeley died suddenly on January 14, 1753, and was buried in Christ Church Chapel.

Influence

As a man whose life was ideas, Berkeley's life must be evaluated in terms of the contribution he made to empiricist philosophy. His works serve as the philosophical bridge between John Locke's notions of common sense and the skepticism of David Hume. Yet in a fundamental way, Berkeley stands alone. He was a more tenacious empiricist than Locke, for he insisted that the senses are the avenue of knowledge. Moreover, while Berkeley rejected every noetic intuitive device as an access to knowledge, as did Hume, his conclusions do not end in skepticism. Berkeley's method of direct sensory experience leads neither to Locke's contradictions nor Hume's doubt and agnosticism but to an irresistible vision of God. Berkeley argued that the source of intellectual confusion can be traced to Galileo's, Newton's, and Locke's hypothesis that something called "matter" exists independent of the mind and sensory experience. It is, Berkeley declares, quite the other way around. Sensory experiences do not lead to doubt and an abstracted notion of "substratum" called matter, but rather to a direct manifestation of the reality of mind or spirit. As a human entity, mind or spirit is finite and temporal; as a divine entity it is infinite and eternal. It is, on the one hand, "inner," the private sensation that induces thought, memory, dreams, imagination; on the other hand, it is "outer," the public sensory entities that reveal the nature of the external world of objects. In Berkeley's view, experience never provides an account of materiality standing apart from the reality of mind.

Berkeley further argued that the empirical method offers no sensory distinction between objective and subjective qualities; in fact, primary qualities are as subjective as the senses of color, taste, and sound. Berkeley's point is that experience is a complex of visual, factual, and locomotor sensations, a product of the mind. All that is known is comprehended as immediacy, in Berkeley's well-known phrase, *esse es percipi* (to be—that is, reality—is that, and only that, which is perceived).

Berkeley started with the lofty goal of solving the philosophical problems of his time and ended with a book for curing bodily ills. Sadly, no clear assessment of his great philosophical contribution was available during his lifetime. It took the next great British empiricist, David Hume, to demonstrate the significance of Berkeley's philosophical skepticism and its systematic doctrine of immaterialism.

Berkeley's influence on contemporary philosophy is significant. He taught the Anglo-American philosophers who followed him that there is a conceptual difference between the subjective, inchoate impressions spun within imagination and memory, and objective reality that requires cognitive order, vividness, and repetition. Berkeley insisted unequivocally that claims about the external world, if they are to have meaning, must be verbal declarations about undiluted sensory experience. For this reason, contemporary philosophical phenomenalism owes him much. "The table I write on," he wrote, "I say, exists, that is, I see and feel it, and were I out of my study I should say it existed, meaning thereby that if I was in my study I might perceive it, or that some other spirit does perceive." In the language of contemporary phenomenology—meaningful utterances about sense-data require sensate experience, and the meaningfulness of unsensed assertions requires, at least conditionally, an accounting of what sensory experience must occur if the utterance is going to be more than empty nonsense. Contemporary theories of knowledge learned this lesson well from Berkeley's unrelenting view of empiricism.

D. Burrill

A Treatise Concerning the Principles of Human Knowledge

Type of philosophy: Epistemology, metaphysics
First published: 1710
Principal ideas advanced:

◇ The belief in abstract ideas had led to the supposition that material objects are quite different from sensations; the fact is that material objects are nothing but collections of sensations given a common name.
◇ *Esse es percipi*; to be is to be perceived—this is a truth concerning all material objects.
◇ If it be argued that ideas are copies of material objects, consider whether anything could be like an idea but an idea.
◇ The distinction between primary and secondary qualities (between such structural properties as figure, motion, and shape, on the one hand, and color, odor, and sound, on the other) on the ground that the former are objective, the latter subjective, cannot be maintained: The primary qualities depend on the secondary; they are equally subjective.

◇ There is no independently existing material substratum; a distinction between the world of illusion and the world of reality can be maintained by realizing the greater vividness and coherency to be found in veridical sensations.
◇ The order in nature is created and maintained by God, who secures the reality of all things by his perception.

The idea that "all those bodies which compose the mighty frame of the world, have not any subsistence without a mind—that their *being* is to be perceived or known" will hardly seem obvious to anyone unfamiliar with George Berkeley or with idealism. This startling statement has considerable shock value, but it is true to Berkeley's bold metaphysical thesis that reality is mental or spiritual in nature.

The statement's emphasis on perception reveals its author's epistemological and methodological approach: empiricism. Although not all empiricists would accept Berkeley's conclusions and not all metaphysical idealists would accept his method, none would deny his importance in the traditions of both empiricism and idealism. That his method and even his immaterialism have influenced some modern physicists and that his analytical technique is valued even by such antimetaphysicians as the logical positivists are proofs of the classical status Berkeley's work has enjoyed.

His aims, however, were primarily those of a metaphysician and theologian; he wished to undermine skepticism and atheism by refuting materialism, to demonstrate God's existence and immateriality, to show the immortality of the soul, and to clarify current scientific and philosophical confusions. The latter are due, he claimed, not to inherent defects in people's mental faculties but to their use: "We have first raised a dust and then complain we cannot see." Berkeley intended to settle this dust and to destroy materialism.

Abstraction
A chief cause of obscurity, Berkeley states, is the doctrine of abstract ideas, the theory that the mind can abstract from particular qualities a clearly conceived notion of what is common to them, but which itself is otherwise like none of

them, or that the mind can separate in thought what cannot be separated in reality. An example of the first abstraction would be a notion of color that is neither red, blue, green, and so forth, or of extension that has neither size, shape, line, plane, nor surface; an illustration of the second would be an abstract idea of color or motion without extension.

Berkeley finds such abstraction psychologically impossible and challenges the reader to conceive such an idea as that of a triangle with all of the general and yet none of the specific characteristics of triangles. However, must Berkeley then deny the universality of ideas essential to rational demonstration such as geometrical proofs relevant to all triangles? No—ideas may be general without being abstract; one generalizes particular ideas by temporarily disregarding their unique features, while one's demonstrations concern only features shared. However, this universality in *function* must not be mistaken for abstract *conception*; the latter is actually without content and unintelligible.

Berkeley claims that the confused belief in abstract ideas arises from language: The assumption is that general names signify precise abstract ideas indispensable to thinking and communication, but this is false. Attention should be paid not to words but to ideas themselves. Because ideas are perfectly transparent, being known directly, the verbal controversies and errors springing from abstraction can be avoided. Thus, Berkeley sets the stage for a far-reaching application of the foregoing conclusions to an analysis of the nature and existence of the objects of knowledge.

Objects of Knowledge
The objects of knowledge, Berkeley writes, are ideas of three kinds: sensations, ideas originating in the mind's own passions and activities, and those of memory and imagination. He first deals with "sensible" objects. Through sight, one knows color; through sight and touch, one knows size and shape; through touch, hardness; and through smelling, odors. Certain constant collections of such ideas are considered one object or thing and accordingly named, such as "apple" or "tree." However, obviously perceived ideas require a perceiver, and this is spirit or mind, not

itself an idea. Careful examination shows that thoughts and ideas have no existence external to minds; hence "sensible" things or physical objects do not exist apart from their perception in minds—*esse es percipi*: For them to *be* is to be perceived.

The typical reaction to this conclusion is to accuse Berkeley of denying the reality of the physical world and even the evidence of his senses. However, Berkeley explains that when one says that a table *exists*, this means that someone sees and feels it or will do so on occasion. The very meaning of "existence" or "being" applied to perceptible objects is exhaustively described in terms drawn from perception—nothing else can meaningfully be said about them. To think that sensible objects or their alleged metaphysical substratum, matter, exist "without" (external to) the mind is to entertain an unintelligible abstraction and a clear contradiction. People commonly think that houses or mountains exist unperceived. However, what are these but objects of the senses? Is it not self-contradictory to think that sensations or ideas exist unperceived? When one imagines that one can think of unperceived objects, one is merely thinking of objects while forgetting the perceiver, but meanwhile one *is* perceiving or thinking of them. One cannot conceive the inconceivable.

However, the common belief that matter exists even when it is unperceived will not die easily, so Berkeley tries to anticipate every possible objection. One of the first arises from the "representative" theory of perception, which grants that ideas occur only in minds but holds that they represent or copy things outside minds. Berkeley's most direct answer is that ideas can resemble nothing but other ideas. How could a color represent something uncolored, or a sound something inaudible?

Both rationalists and empiricists such as René Descartes and John Locke held that in describing one's knowledge of the physical world, one must distinguish sensed qualities, which are mostly subjective, from others that are wholly objective. These philosophers argue that "primary" qualities such as figure, motion, spatial location, and shape are inherent in objects themselves and are perceived without distortion or addition by the observer. However, "secondary" qualities such as color, sound, and taste are so obviously variable that they must be contributed by the subject's mind, though of course originally caused by action upon him of the primary qualities. Thus color qualities are subjective but caused by motion of light—color is "in the mind" but motion is "out there." Because qualities must qualify something (it was assumed), the primary qualities subsist in matter, the reality of which they are the appearances. Thus primary qualities really do represent or copy the external world.

However, this theory is fallacious, Berkeley holds; if it admits that secondary qualities are in the mind, it must concede that primary qualities are also, because both types are inseparable actually and conceptually. Can one conceive of an extended, moving body that has no color or temperature? Also, the arguments that secondary qualities are subjective apply equally to the primary. Consider size; one's estimate of size depends on the nature and position of one's sense organs. Berkeley's *Three Dialogues Between Hylas and Philonous* (1713) makes this point by noting that what will seem minute to a person may appear mountainous to a mite. Even number varies with point of view, as when a given length is considered as one, three, or thirty-six (yard, feet, or inches). However, finally, the copy theory leads to utter skepticism by insisting that ideas represent something wholly unlike ideas and by distinguishing between "mere appearance" and "reality," for it thus posits an external world forever unknowable.

Still, belief in a material substratum or support of sensed qualities will persist. Yet matter cannot literally "support" qualities, since "support" is itself a spatial term and space is perceptual. Even if there were such a substance, the problem of knowledge would remain. Knowledge stems from either sense or reason; the former yields only immediate objects of perception, or ideas, as even the materialists hold. However, reason cannot bridge the gap between ideas and matter because it would then have to argue from what one knows—ideas—to something quite alien; and materialists themselves admit no logically necessary relationship between ideas and matter. Furthermore, it sometimes happens, and conceivably always could happen, that one entertains ideas when no external bodies are supposed present, as

in the case of dreams. Finally—and here Berkeley broaches a problem Descartes could not solve—how could matter possibly act on spirit to produce ideas? The more one insists on their substantial differences, the less conceivable is causal interaction.

However, if one denies the reality of external bodies, will it not sound very odd to say that one eats and drinks ideas? Of course, agrees Berkeley; but his argument is about truth, not terminology. People may use common speech, even the term "matter" itself, as long as they refer only to the sensible world. If an opponent boasts his senses' superiority to any argument whatever, Berkeley is only too glad to join him, for he denies nothing actually perceived. "It were a mistake to think that what is here said derogates in the least from the reality of things." Berkeley intended to refute skepticism and atheism not by denying reality but by showing the impossibility of the materialistic account of it.

Existence and Reality

Yet if his theory is true, can it distinguish reality from illusion—for example, real from merely imaginary fire—since everything perceived consists only of ideas? If there is any doubt, Berkeley answers, put your hand in the real fire, and you will sense a pain lacking in the imaginary one—but can you suppose pain existing externally to a mind? Fantasy and illusion are differentiated from the real world by obvious differences in their ideas; those of the latter are more vivid, constant, and coherent; their regular, predictable order constitutes the laws of nature, and they are independent of people's wills as imagination is not. In fact, this independence marks the one legitimate sense in which one speaks of "external objects"; sensed qualities are external to finite spirits' wills but not to that of the eternal Spirit, God, of whose will they are a perceptible expression.

Critics point out that if the existence of things depends on perception, they will exist and cease to exist with the occurrence and cessation of perception, and therefore, this theory is absurd. Berkeley counters by asking whether the statement that a table continues to exist when everyone leaves the room means anything more than that *if* one were still there one would perceive it, or if one were to return, one would once again see it. From the reliability of nature's order, one can both reconstruct the past and predict the future, in neither of which are there *present* finite minds as perceivers, but this is wholly consistent with saying that objects and events are only what they are perceived to be (in past, present, or future). If no finite minds existed at all, whatever remained would nevertheless be perceived by the omniscient, eternal Spirit. Clearly, the strength of Berkeley's arguments here lies in the difficulty of *describing* an existent known to no mind whatever.

However, is this really a plausible account of nature? Must not any scientific explanation of natural events presuppose causal efficacy resident either in matter itself or in primary qualities such as extension and motion? Berkeley answers in the negative; he has already shown that the notion of matter explains nothing at all because it is incomprehensible and the primary qualities are ideas. Ideas are inert or inactive, having no causal power; there is no *idea* of causation in addition to those of successive events. Yet one gains a *notion* of causality from one's own volition; one finds that one can produce and manipulate some ideas at will. However, if action is the prerogative of spirit, and if finite minds could not possibly produce the vast and intricate system of ideas called nature, it follows that nature is the work of the infinite Spirit.

The Infinite Spirit

Suppose, however, that one grants both the existence of this Spirit and the extremely complicated mechanism of nature. To what purpose did God create such a powerless machine if he wished merely to communicate with finite minds? Why not do it directly? Berkeley meets this objection by observing that if anything were superfluous, it would be an unknowable, ineffectual corporeal substance; it is possible, on the other hand, to give a rationale for nature.

Its orderly mechanism, while not indispensable to God, is still instrumental to human learning and profit. Observing the conjunction of fire and heat, people learn not that the idea of fire *causes* the idea of heat, but that the former *signifies* that the latter will follow. Single ideas are like words, and the laws of nature like the grammar

of a language; however, just as it is unwise to study only grammar and neglect meaning, so it is folly for science to concentrate only on mechanical laws and neglect the final causes (purposes) they express, those determined by God's wisdom and goodness. This does not derogate from science, but redirects it to explication of phenomena as signs rather than as effects of physical causes. Thus the hypothesis of matter is unnecessary even to physics.

Why, then, is belief in matter so pervasive? Partly because people found that objects of sensation seemed to be independent of themselves and thus supposed that such ideas exist externally. Philosophers saw the error of this supposition, but in trying to correct it by positing the external existence of matter, they substituted another mistake, unaware of the internal contradictions involved. Furthermore, the operations of the eternal Spirit are so lawful that it was not imagined they were those of a *free* spirit rather than those of rigidly mechanical causes; and although they clearly point to his being, still there is no collection of sensed qualities making God visible or tangible as people are.

In the foregoing considerations, the existence of spirit has been assumed on the basis of only one argument—that because ideas are not self-subsistent and matter is a nonentity, ideas can exist only in a different substance, spirit. However, if they are inactive and one can thus have no ideas of spirit, how does one *know* that spirit exists? Berkeley says that people have a *notion* of spirit because they understand the terms describing it and its activities, a notion people get "by inward feeling or reflection." Other spirits are known by reasoning from analogy with one's own; one perceives their effects and infers other minds as causes. A spirit's existence consists not in being perceived but in perceiving; it is "one simple, undivided, active being—as it perceives ideas it is called the *understanding*, and as it produces or otherwise operates about them it is called the *will*." No more than a notion of matter can be abstracted from sensed qualities can the existence of spirit be abstracted from its cogitation.

An interesting consequence follows from this in conjunction with Berkeley's analysis of time; time cannot be abstracted from the succession of ideas one experiences, and so the duration of a spirit depends on the ideas and activities occurring within it. Therefore, Berkeley concludes, the spirit always thinks, the notion of a literally thoughtless mind being unintelligible. He asserts, "*Spirits* and *ideas* are things so wholly different. . . . There is nothing alike or common in them." Because spirits are indivisible, incorporeal, and unextended, it follows that they are not subject to the laws of nature and hence enjoy immortality.

Berkeley's arguments for God's existence have been given in part; the eternal Spirit must exist as the only sufficient cause of nature. When one considers the lawfulness, perfection, beauty, and design of the whole system, it is obvious that the characteristics of nature suggest the character of God. God's existence is in a sense known more certainly than that of any other spirit because one can constantly perceive God's effects, even in those ideas by which one communicates with other people. If one does not realize this fact fully, it is because one is "blinded with excess of light."

However, granted the existence of God, Berkeley is still faced with the problem of evil. Why does God's universe contain pain, monstrosities, sorrow, death? Is the cumbersome machinery of nature very obviously turned directly by the hand of God? Berkeley answers that natural events occur according to rules of the greatest simplicity and generality; without such regularity, there could be no human foresight. What seems like waste from the human viewpoint—countless blighted plants, little fish devoured by parents, and so forth—can be understood as necessary to the riches of God. The apparent defects of nature really augment its beauty, and seeming evil contributes to the good of the whole. Even the mixture of pain with pleasure is necessary for humanity's guidance. Clear understanding of these truths instills that holy fear that is the chief motive to virtue, and indeed "consideration of God and our duty," was Berkeley's chief aim in writing the book.

Merits and Criticisms
To what extent did Berkeley achieve his announced aims? The complete answer cannot be given in brief, just as Berkeley himself could not make all the grounds and implications of his phi-

losophy clear at once. Many readers find themselves unable to refute Berkeley's arguments, yet they remain unconvinced by them; and many professional philosophers have given long and profound attention to the problems he raises. A great merit of this book and of the *Three Dialogues Between Hylas and Philonous* is that Berkeley was thorough and clever in foreseeing and forestalling possible objections. Yet criticisms exist that, while insufficient to prove a diametrically opposite position such as materialism or even a more moderate realism, nevertheless show that Berkeley's conclusions do not necessarily follow from his premises.

He was probably correct in his insistence on the dangers of abstraction, although he sometimes seems to have confused conception with visualization. Many thinkers today would agree also with his demand that terms and statements describing the physical world be defined and verified by reference to sensory experience. However, can one infer from this experience that the world is ultimately mental or immaterial in nature? Berkeley's argument seems either to beg the question or to depend on ambiguous terms. A fair but condensed statement of it seems to be this:

1. Physical objects are objects of knowledge
2. Objects of knowledge are ideas or sets of ideas
3. Ideas and sets of ideas are in the mind, or mental
4. Therefore, physical objects are in the mind, or mental

However, "objects of knowledge" is ambiguous, unless one already grants that the world is mental; in the first sentence, it means "nonmental things," but in the second, it means "constituents of knowledge." Of course, the constituents of knowledge are ideas by definition, but this fact does not bestow upon knowledge the power to *constitute* the real nature of what would not otherwise have been considered ideal or immaterial. Whether or not one perceives or conceives a "physical" object is actually irrelevant to the object itself.

Still, this criticism does not prove that physical objects are independently real or that the term "matter" has a meaning describable in terms not ultimately derived from perception. Berkeley has a strategic advantage in the fact that all people are caught in what American philosopher Ralph Barton Perry called "the egocentric predicament": In a sense people are forever imprisoned within their own consciousness because they must always use thought as a bridge to the "outside." However, this advantage can also be a liability, for Berkeley's skepticism about external reality can be turned against people's knowledge of other minds, the eternal Spirit, and even their own minds considered as substantial entities. Scottish philosopher David Hume and subsequent philosophers, for example, have not agreed that an indivisible, incorporeal self can be discovered by inward reflection. Many of Berkeley's conclusions, such as his account of the self's continuity by saying that the spirit always thinks, have the appearance of absurdities demanded by his premises rather than of facts verifiable by experience. Hence, "spirit" itself may turn out to be an abstraction to be relegated to the company of "matter."

In Berkeley's later writings, the purity of his empiricism is diluted by noticeable amounts of rationalism, and even in *A Treatise Concerning the Principles of Human Knowledge*, there are assumptions hardly empirical in origin or confirmation, such as his facile acceptance of the traditional attributes of God—eternal, infinite, omniscient— as obviously pertaining to that Spirit. Berkeley's arguments for God's existence, which are the traditional cosmological and teleological "proofs," would have to meet the devastating criticisms produced by such philosophers as Hume and Immanuel Kant before they could be acceptable to a modern reader. However, even were the being of an infinite, omnipotent, omniscient Spirit granted, the traditional problem of evil posed by comparison of such a Creator with the created universe is one to which Berkeley offers only the usual but ineffective answers. Hume showed in *Dialogues Concerning Natural Religion* (1779) how ill such answers suit even an empirical theism.

Although it is doubtful that Berkeley accomplished some of his chief aims, it is certain that he achieved much by the method of his efforts. If he unintentionally undercut his own metaphysics by settling the dust of materialism, philosophy since has been able to learn from his experience.

Marvin Easterling, updated by John K. Roth

Three Dialogues Between Hylas and Philonous

Type of philosophy: Epistemology, metaphysics
First published: 1713
Principal ideas advanced:

◇ The universe is composed not of matter but of minds and spirits; material objects, conceived of as nonmental substances existing outside consciousness, do not exist.

◇ The universe of sensible objects is a projection of the mind; the existence of sensible objects is comparable to that of objects in dreams or hallucinations.

◇ The view that tables, chairs, and other sensible objects exist independently of being perceived leads to skepticism about the existence and nature of such a realm.

◇ Perceptions are not caused by material substances.

◇ An infinite being causes and coordinates all perceptual experiences.

In *Three Dialogues Between Hylas and Philonous*, George Berkeley defends the view that matter does not exist, that the universe contains minds or spirits but no realm of atoms and molecules. Berkeley argues that things that are normally considered material objects—stones, trees, shoes, apples—have no existence outside the minds and experiences of conscious beings. Like an object in a dream, a stone has no existence outside consciousness. If all conscious beings were to stop perceiving some sensible object—the moon, for example—that object would cease to exist. Although Berkeley's book owes its philosophical greatness to the many important arguments that are presented in support of the main thesis, the work is also notable for the simplicity and clarity with which the ideas are conveyed. The ideas are presented in the form of a dialogue between Hylas, a materialist, and Philonous, the representative of Berkeley's idealism.

Perception as the Basis of Reality
The main argument in the work centers on an examination of the set of properties of which sensible objects are composed. Berkeley first examines the properties that philosophers have called

"secondary qualities" (heat, taste, sound, smell, color) and argues that these properties have no existence outside sensations and perceptions in the minds of perceivers. He then argues that the same sorts of considerations will show that what have been called the "primary qualities" of sensible objects—extension (length and width), shape, hardness, weight, motion and other characteristics—also have no existence outside the perceptions of conscious beings. In arguing that *every* property that a sensible object has exists only as a sensation or a property of a sensation within a mind, Berkeley is showing that the entire sensible object has no existence outside the mind. For Berkeley, a cherry is nothing over and above the sensations experienced in connection with it. "Take away the sensations of softness, redness, tartness, and you take away the cherry," he writes.

Secondary Qualities Exist Only in the Mind

Berkeley begins his argument by reference to heat. Intense heat, like intense cold, is pain; it is intrinsically unpleasant. Pain, like pleasure, is a kind of experience; it is something that cannot exist outside someone's consciousness. Therefore, when someone feels intense heat or intense cold, Berkeley reasons, what he feels is in his own mind, not in some inert, unfeeling object existing outside his consciousness. To be aware of intense heat is simply to be aware of a particular kind of pain sensation.

To the objection that intense heat is a *cause* of pain and not itself literally "pain," Berkeley replies that when one is perceiving intense heat, the heat of which one is aware is not distinguishable from the pain sensation of which one is aware. In perceiving the heat, the person is not aware of *two* things, heat *and* a pain sensation, but of only one thing, a painful sensation.

The temperature that an object appears to have differs under different circumstances, Berkeley proceeds. If one's left hand is hot and one's right hand cold and both hands are immersed in a bowl of water, the water seems cool to the left hand and warm to the right hand. From this fact, Berkeley concludes that the heat that one feels cannot be a feature of some object existing outside one's mind. No single object could have the incompatible properties of

warmth and coolness at once. Berkeley concludes that the warmth and coolness that one perceives are sensations within one's own experience. What one thinks of as *the* "temperature" of the water is simply the sensation experienced in connection with the water. The sensation is in the consciousness of the person perceiving the temperature, not in an unfeeling object outside one's consciousness.

These arguments concerning heat can be paralleled for the other secondary qualities of sensible objects. A sweet taste is a form of pleasure; a bitter taste is intrinsically unpleasant or painful. Because pleasure and pain are necessarily mental phenomena, a sweet or bitter taste, because it is a pleasure or pain, must itself be a mental phenomenon, Berkeley reasons. Furthermore, the taste that people perceive in an object varies under different conditions. A food that one finds sweet at one time may seem bitter or tasteless another time. The taste a food has when one is sick differs from its taste when one is well, Berkeley writes. What differs in the two cases, he reasons, is not the alleged external object but the experience had when tasting the food. In each case, one has different taste sensations, and these taste sensations, which *are* the taste of the food, exist in the mind of the person doing the tasting. Berkeley considers the fact that some people delight in the very food that others find repulsive to be further proof that the taste of a food is not a property inherent in the object that allegedly exists outside people's minds but a sensation undergone by the people who taste the food. Similar arguments support the claim that odor or smell is a sensation within someone's mind.

As happens with other secondary qualities, the *color* that an object appears to have varies under different conditions. A cloud that appears to be some shade of white under most conditions may appear red or purple when perceived at sunset, Berkeley writes. Someone who holds that color is an inherent property of the clouds will need to say that not all the colors that may be perceived in an object are the true color of the object and that some of these colors are only apparent.

How then is the true color to be distinguished from the colors that are said to be merely *apparent*? It might be suggested that the true color is the one the object presents when it is viewed under white light. However, this suggestion raises problems. An object presents a somewhat different color under candlelight from that which it presents under daylight, Berkeley notes. Indeed, there are many different intensities and shades of what we call "white light," and each of these intensities and shades is as normal and common as the others. Yet each shade and intensity leads to a somewhat different color being perceived in an object.

One might reply that the true color of an object is the color that is perceived when the object is given the most close and careful inspection possible. However, this suggestion also runs into serious problems. To examine an object in the closest and most careful manner possible is to examine the object under a microscope, Berkeley writes. However, when an object is examined under a microscope, the microscope does not simply present *one* color to the eye, a color which one could label the true color; rather, the microscope (like the naked eye) presents numerous colors to the eye, and the particular color one sees in an object depends on the magnification one gives to the microscope. To pick out one color from the various colors which are perceived and call it the true color of the object would require a choice which has no justification.

A further problem for someone who maintains that color is a property inherent in objects exterior to minds is the fact that objects under the same conditions present different colors to different perceivers. Objects that appear yellow to people with jaundice appear other colors to people without jaundice, Berkeley writes. Furthermore, given the structural differences between the eyes of animals and those of people, it is probable that some animals perceive colors in objects that are different from those that people perceive, Berkeley reasons. To pick out any of these perceived colors and call it the true color would involve an arbitrary, unjustifiable decision. The view that an object has a true color Berkeley considers untenable in face of the above facts. From these considerations, Berkeley concludes that *all* colors perceived in sensible objects are simply visual sensations in the minds of those perceiving the color.

The accounts that scientists give of perception are often consistent with Berkeley's account of secondary qualities and may even be interpreted as supporting it, Berkeley writes. Although scientists do, of course, believe in a material world existing external to consciousness that causes people to hear sounds and see colors, they often think of hearing or seeing as a matter of having certain auditory or visual sensations. Scientists say, for example, that when an object causes air to move in a certain manner and this air strikes the eardrum, a certain neurological activity is produced, and the neurological activity causes one to experience the sensation of sound. Color is seen, they say, when light rays, after being reflected off some object, enter the eye and stir the optic nerve such that a message is communicated to the brain, upon which the person experiences the sensation of color. To say, as these scientists do, that sound and color are sensations is to say that they are mental phenomena. The view that "secondary qualities" are nothing but sensations in the minds of conscious beings, although strange in relation to common sense, did not originate with Berkeley. The view had been previously defended by John Locke. Berkeley's most radical departure from previous philosophical opinion was in his claim that all properties of sensible objects, including the primary qualities, could be shown to have no existence outside the minds of perceivers.

Primary Qualities Exist Only in the Mind

If the existence of perceptual variation is reason to conclude that the secondary qualities do not exist outside minds, Berkeley reasoned, then philosophers have the same reason to conclude that the primary qualities also lack existence outside minds. Like the secondary qualities, the primary qualities give rise to radical perceptual variations. The extension that an object appears to have varies as the object is perceived from different positions, Berkeley explains. The visible extension that a tree has, the extension that it has in relation to the expanse of a perceiver's field of vision, grows larger as the perceiver approaches the tree and shrinks as the perceiver moves away from the tree. When a perceiver is near, a tree may appear to be a hundred times larger than it does from a great distance. (Imagine how much larger the moon would look if one could see it from a distance of only ten miles.) It does not help to reply that the tree has the same size in feet and inches whatever one's distance from it, for the visible extension of a foot or an inch itself is not a constant, and it too goes through the same variations as one approaches or recedes from it. A twelve-inch ruler looks large from very close but tiny when perceived from a distance. Furthermore, Berkeley argues, a sensible object may present differing visible extensions at one and the same time. The foot of a mouse, which seems tiny to a person, would seem to be of considerable extension to the mouse. An object that extends over a large portion of the field of vision of a mouse would extend over a small portion of the visual field of a person. Berkeley concludes that the extension of a sensible object is not a property of an object that exists outside consciousness but a property of a sensation in the mind of a perceiver.

The types of considerations which show that the extension of a sensible object has no existence outside a mind also show that shape, hardness, and the other primary qualities are only properties of sensations within the minds of perceivers. The shape, hardness, and motion which an object appears to have also vary from one perceiver to another and vary for a single perceiver when the object is viewed under different conditions.

One might think that the fact that objects are perceived as being at a distance from the person perceiving them proves that the objects cannot be inside the perceiver's mind. Berkeley responds to this objection with the observation that even in dreams and hallucinations objects are experienced as being at a distance and outside the mind, yet in spite of these appearances these imagined objects do not exist outside the mind of the person imagining them. Thus it clearly is possible for an object to be experienced as being at a distance from oneself even when the object is really not outside one's own mind.

Another reason the primary qualities must be in the mind with the secondary qualities, Berkeley writes, is that all sensible qualities coexist. When one perceives a table, the extension and shape that one perceives are joined to the color. The shape outlines the color. If the color that is perceived is in one's mind, then so are the extension, shape, and motion that are experienced as being together with the color.

It might be supposed that when one perceives an object one has an image in one's mind that copies or mirrors a material world existing outside one's mind—a world that is the cause of the image. Although it is the mental image and not the material world of which a perceiver is directly aware, the image provides accurate information about the external, material world, it may be said. Berkeley finds serious problems in this view. First, if it is admitted that all the primary and secondary qualities of objects exist only within minds, then there are no properties remaining for this so-called "material substance" outside the mind to have. Talk of material substance in this context becomes meaningless. Furthermore, it is not possible, Berkeley argues, for an image that is continually undergoing radical changes (which one's perception of sensible objects is doing) to be a copy of some set of objects that remains unchanged throughout this period (as the alleged material substance is assumed to do).

A further problem with this view, Berkeley argues, is that the model of perception that it presents leads to a severe skepticism about the alleged material world. According to this view, one who perceives a sensible object is not directly aware of the material world but only of the image in one's mind. That this image, which is said to be a copy of a material world outside the mind, does indeed copy or resemble the object alleged to be the original could not be known. If one's knowledge of the alleged original is derived entirely from one's familiarity with the image that is said to be the copy, there is no independent means of checking that the "copy" is actually like the original. Indeed, because in this view people are never directly aware of the alleged material world, it follows that it is not possible even to know whether this outside, unexperienced world exists. The existence of a mental image does not itself guarantee that there is an external object causing the image, for it is logically possible for someone to have exactly the same perceptions or mental images even if no world of material objects exists.

Reality as Spirit

If what one considers *real* objects are like objects in dreams and hallucinations in having no existence outside the mind, how then does Berkeley distinguish the former from the latter? Berkeley explains that the perceptions one considers real are vivid and consistent in a way that those that one does not consider real are not.

What then is the cause of people's perceptions of sensible objects if not a world of material substance corresponding to those perceptions? Berkeley reasons that because one does not cause or coordinate one's own sensations, one's sensations must have a cause outside oneself, and this cause, Berkeley concludes, is an omnipresent infinite Spirit. From the order, beauty, and design with which one's sensations appear Berkeley concludes that the designer is wise, powerful, and good "beyond comprehension."

Irwin Goldstein

Additional Reading

Berman, David. *Berkeley*. New York: Routledge, 1999. An excellent biographical introduction to the thoughts of the philosopher, clearly presented and requiring no special background. Bibliography.

_____. *George Berkeley: Idealism and the Man*. New York: Oxford University Press, 1994. This worthwhile analysis of George Berkeley's distinctive philosophical positions focuses on his religious thought. Contains considerable information about Berkeley's life and his considerable influence.

Bonk, Sigmund. *"We See God": George Berkeley's Philosophical Theology*. New York: Peter Lang, 1997. A good analysis focusing on Berkeley's spiritual thoughts.

Dancy, Jonathan. *Berkeley: An Introduction*. New York: Basil Blackwell, 1987. Dancy provides a helpful introduction that is useful for beginning students.

Foster, John, and Howard Robinson, eds. *Essays on Berkeley: A Tercentennial Celebration*. New York: Oxford University Press, 1985. This collection contains important interpretations of Berkeley's philosophy by leading scholars in the field.

Jones, W. T. *A History of Western Philosophy: Hobbes to Hume*. New York: Harcourt, Brace & World, 1969. Offers a clear and accessible introduction to the key theories in Berkeley's philosophy.

Muehlman, R. G., ed. *Berkeley's Metaphysics: Structural, Interpretive, and Critical Essays*. University Park: Pennsylvania University Press, 1995. A good collection of essays that analyze and criticize Berkeley's metaphysical idealism.

Richie, A. D. *George Berkeley: A Reappraisal*. Manchester, England: Manchester University Press, 1967. Richie argues that the key to understanding Berkeley is found in his theory of vision.

Turbayne, Colin M. *Critical and Interpretive Essays*. Minneapolis: University of Minnesota Press, 1982. Turbayne's essays explore key aspects of Berkeley's theory of knowledge and metaphysics.

Urmson, J. O. *Berkeley*. Oxford: Oxford University Press, 1982. A reliable commentary on Berkeley's thought by an influential twentieth century philosopher.

Warnock, G. J. *Berkeley*. London: Penguin Books, 1953. This introduction is particularly useful in its account of Berkeley's views of science, mathematics, and language.

D. Burrill, updated by John K. Roth

Isaiah Berlin

Drawing upon the liberal heritage of Western civilization, Berlin advocated viewing history and ideas from a plurality of viewpoints, the better to provide realistic and reasonable answers to the conditions and problems of human existence and society.

Principal philosophical works: *Karl Marx: His Life and Environment*, 1939; 1959, 1963; *The Hedgehog and the Fox: An Essay on Tolstoy's View of History*, 1953; *Historical Inevitability*, 1955; *The Age of Enlightenment*, 1956; *Four Essays on Liberty*, 1969; *Vico and Herder*, 1976; *Concepts and Categories*, 1978; *Russian Thinkers*, 1978; *Against the Current*, 1979; *Personal Impressions*, 1980; *The Crooked Timber of Humanity: Chapters in the History of Ideas*, 1990; *The Magus of the North: J. G. Hamann and the Origins of Modern Irrationalism*, 1993; *The Sense of Reality: Studies in Ideas and Their History*, 1996; *The Proper Study of Mankind*, 1997.

Born: June 6, 1909; Riga, Latvia, Russian Empire (now Latvia)

Died: November 5, 1997; Oxford, England

Early Life

Isaiah Mendelevich Berlin, the son of Jewish parents, was born in 1909 in Riga, a major city in the Baltic nation of Latvia, which had been part of the Russian Empire since the eighteenth century. Both Berlin's father, Mendel Berlin, and his mother, Marie Berlin, spoke Russian. They were very interested in the arts, especially writing and music; throughout his life, Isaiah Berlin displayed a keen appreciation for and enjoyment of literature and opera.

World War I began in 1914, and by 1915, German armies were pressing close to Riga. The Berlins moved into Russia for greater safety, first to Adreapol and then, in 1917, to the capital, Petrograd (modern-day St. Petersburg). In Petrograd, the young Berlin witnessed first the moderate February Revolution, which brought Prince Aleksandr F. Kerensky to power, and then the more violent Bolshevik Revolution in November, led by Vladimir Lenin and Leon Trotsky. It was during this time that Berlin saw a former czarist police officer dragged away, pale and struggling, to his almost certain death by a mob, an action that, as he remembered years later, "gave me a lifelong horror of physical violence."

When Latvia achieved its independence in 1919, the Berlins returned to Riga, where they endured the extreme hardships of the postwar years. Berlin later recalled standing in line for up to five hours to buy bread or other food. Berlin's father, a committed Anglophile, had friends and business acquaintances in Britain, and in 1921, the family moved to England, living in London before settling in Hampstead. While in Britain, the young Berlin grew fluent in English but retained his knowledge of Russian by reading the great classics of Russian literature.

After establishing himself as an outstanding student in preparatory school, Berlin received a scholarship to attend Corpus Christi College of Oxford University in 1928. While there, he edited an intellectual periodical, *The Oxford Outlook*, and made a lifelong friend of the poet Stephen Spender. His time at Oxford confirmed his choice of career: an intellectual, whose service to the public in both government and the academy would be appreciated primarily because of his own independence of thought and interests.

Life's Work

After graduation, Berlin became a lecturer in philosophy at New College, Oxford. Soon after, he was elected to a fellowship at All Souls College. He was commissioned to write a biographical and critical study of German political philoso-

Isaiah Berlin. *(Library of Congress)*

pher Karl Marx for the Home University Library; ironically, he was not the first choice of the editors. With perhaps equal irony, *Karl Marx: His Life and Environment* was Berlin's only full-length book; although a prolific writer, he would confine himself to essays and collections throughout his lengthy and productive career.

Berlin's *Karl Marx* was, in many ways, the first serious consideration of Marx as a philosopher and political thinker in the noncommunist world. It gave Marx the respect he deserved for having acutely isolated and analyzed the failures and inequities of unrestrained capitalism and honored him for his criticisms of the often hypocritical stances of bourgeoisie democracy but did not shrink from noting that Marx, in his view of the inevitable trend of human history, had failed to foresee either fascism or the welfare state. In

short, in this relatively brief work, Berlin described Marx the man, Marxism the philosophy, and Marxism's fatal contradictions.

Chosen in 1938 as a fellow of New College, Berlin spent the first years of World War II teaching. In 1941, he was sent by the British Foreign Office to the United States, first to New York and then to Washington, D.C. He was responsible for drafting reports on the political mood in the United States. Later Winston Churchill would state that Berlin's dispatches were the ones he most prized and enjoyed during the war years. They were published as *Washington Despatches, 1941-1945* (1981).

Berlin was transferred to Moscow in 1945 and remained there until the following year. While in the Soviet capital, he met a number of writers and intellectuals, among them the novelist and poet Boris Pasternak and the poet Anna Akhmatova. He was especially impressed with Akhmatova and later wrote movingly of their meeting and her influence on him in his work *Personal Impressions*. His regard for Akhmatova was not one-sided, for the Russian poet was impressed enough by Berlin to write a poem about the visit, and she felt that the Soviet dictator Joseph Stalin was so suspicious of the meeting that it was a small, but real, cause of the Cold War.

During the war, Berlin had decided that his interests were less in pure philosophy than in the history of ideas, especially those of political science. In 1950, he returned to All Souls College and began his examination of how, and perhaps why, people believe what they do and how they act upon those beliefs. One of his central concepts was that there was no single, universal answer to the perpetual questions of human existence; each culture and age, even each individual, approached life from a unique perspective. It is the task of the historian of ideas to understand and articulate these perspectives rather than to force them into one falsely coherent whole.

The Hedgehog and the Fox, published in 1953, was one of the first fruits of this new direction. In this work, which has won classic status, Berlin examines the two contrasting visions of history and human life that writers and historians have created. His title comes from a fragment by the Greek poet Archilochus that reads, "The fox knows many things, but the hedgehog knows one great thing." Hedgehogs see everything as related; they possess a unitary inner vision. Foxes see many different phenomena but may not perceive essential connections; they have a vision of variety. According to Berlin, the writers and philosophers Dante Alighieri, Plato, Georg Wilhelm Friedrich Hegel, Fyodor Dostoevski, and Marcel Proust are hedgehogs. The writers and philosophers William Shakespeare, Herodotus, Aristotle, Michel Eyquem de Montaigne, Johann Wolfgang von Goethe, Alexander Pushkin, and James Joyce are foxes. Tolstoy, the focus of Berlin's perceptive study, was the saddest of all creatures, the born fox who agonized all his life because of his desire to be a hedgehog.

In 1956, already in his late forties and apparently a confirmed bachelor, he married Aline Halban, daughter of a noted European banker; she was a widow with three sons. The following year, he was knighted by Queen Elizabeth II. The knighthood was only one of the many honors and awards bestowed upon Berlin during his lifetime. He was also awarded the British Order of Merit, made a Commander of the British Empire, and named as a fellow of the British Academy, where he served as vice president from 1959 through 1961 and as president from 1974 to 1978. His distinguished body of work also earned him the Erasmus, Lippincott, and Agnelli Prizes, along with the Jerusalem Prize for his lifelong defense of civil liberties.

In 1957, now Sir Isaiah, he was elected to the Chichele Chair of Social and Political Theory at Oxford. His inaugural lecture, "Two Concepts of Liberty," contrasted "negative liberty" (freedom from others—who can command me?) and "positive liberty" (freedom of action—what can I make happen in the world?). This lecture made a significant contribution to political thought in the twentieth century and became the centerpiece of Berlin's best-known work, *Four Essays on Liberty*.

The new Oxford graduate college Wolfson chose Berlin as its first president in 1966, in large part because of his intense personal involvement in raising funds and support for the institution. While president, Berlin was also on the faculty of City University of New York, where, from 1966 to 1971, he was professor of humanities. He retired from the Wolfson presidency in 1975.

After Berlin's retirement, he published numerous works, including *Vico and Herder*, which examined two of the most influential thinkers of European history, and four volumes of collected essays, which displayed his wide-ranging and perceptive appreciation of thinkers from Niccolò Machiavelli to Karl Marx and of their influence on contemporary philosophical and political thought and action. He was especially interested in Russian thinkers. The writer and theorist Alexander Herzen was a particular favorite of his; both Herzen and Berlin wrote of an intense, innate rejection of absolutist philosophies such as communism or fascism, which demanded sacrifice and suffering, even death, from people in the present for the sake of some future utopia.

Although Berlin profoundly distrusted the hyperrationalism of the eighteenth century European Enlightenment, which sought to smooth all human knowledge into a single orderly and untroubled synthesis, he also rejected the Romantic irrationalism that followed in the nineteenth century. Two of his most important works examine the premises and results of such philosophies: "Joseph de Maistre and the Origins of Fascism," collected in *The Crooked Timber of Humanity*, and *The Magus of the North: J. G. Hamann and the Origins of Modern Irrationalism*.

As he grew older, Berlin remained intellectually active, continuing to write his graceful and perceptive essays on a variety of subjects ranging from philosophical history to opera, one of his lifelong loves. A culminating anthology, *The Proper Study of Mankind*, was published in 1997. On November 5 of that year, Sir Isaiah Berlin died.

Influence

Berlin's enduring legacy to philosophy and the history of ideas was his stress on the importance of a pluralistic point of view, the belief that there is no single, ultimately objective way of viewing the world, human existence, or the goals of individuals or societies. Throughout his long and productive career as a teacher, lecturer, and writer, he forcefully presented the view that human life cannot be viewed as a unified whole and that goals—though equally valuable, valid, and desirable—may be incompatible.

"Life can be seen through many windows, none of them necessarily clear or opaque, less or more distorting than the others," Berlin wrote, explaining one aspect of his fundamental approach to the study of ideas. It was one that he developed and articulated throughout his career.

A second key element for Berlin was his passionate insistence on locating his theoretical and philosophical discussions in specific individuals and their activities and writings. Thus, Berlin's examination of Marxism is directly related to Karl Marx himself; his discussions of the origins of modern totalitarianism are rooted in the life and writings of Joseph-Marie de Maistre. Berlin consistently moves from the specific to the general, always keeping his perceptions and observations fixed on the tangible and particular.

One contribution that probably can be attributed solely to Berlin is the concept of negative and positive liberty that he first articulated in his inaugural lecture as Chichele Chair of Social and Political Theory at Oxford. Negative liberty is the degree to which people are left alone—by others, the law, the state—to do as they please. Positive liberty is the ability people have to control life around them—to command others to do as they please. The subtle yet crucial distinction between these two forms of liberty and how they can exist in a free society steeped in the liberal tradition of Western civilization is one of Berlin's most profound and lasting teachings.

Michael Witkoski

Four Essays on Liberty

Type of philosophy: Ethics, political philosophy
First published: 1969
Principal ideas advanced:

◇ Historical determinism—the belief that events happen according to large historical patterns that individuals are incapable of changing or even influencing to any great degree—cannot be proven, and human beings intuitively ignore the concept in their actions.

◇ Historians use words full of value judgments (especially moral ones), and complete objectivity is not possible.
◇ "Positive" liberty allows one to influence the actions of others; by contrast, "negative" liberty reduces the influence of others over one.
◇ "Monism," or the unity or harmony of human goals, is an illusion; there is no single, universal truth for all humanity; each individual, nation, and culture is different.

Over a period of almost a decade, from 1949 through 1959, Isaiah Berlin turned his attention to the issue of individual liberty in an essay and three lectures that were later collected and published as *Four Essays on Liberty*. Each essay addressed a specific aspect or problem associated with liberty, such as whether history followed a predetermined course or how much power the state could or should have in a democracy. Collectively, the pieces form a coherent presentation of Berlin's thoughts and observations on this topic.

Four Essays on Liberty is especially concerned with how the twentieth century treats the concept and practice of individual liberty. The opening essay, "Political Ideas in the Twentieth Century," was published in the journal *Foreign Affairs* in 1949. World War II had recently ended, and the Cold War had just begun. The horrors of the totalitarian regimes of Nazi Germany, fascist Italy, and militaristic Japan were still vivid, and the brutal repression of Stalinist Russia was becoming better known. In such a setting, the civil and political rights of individuals were seen to be extremely fragile and the concept of liberty in need of review and reinforcement.

The First Essay

In the opening essay, Berlin notes that how people look at history and what they regard as the facts change over time and reflect specific periods. During the nineteenth century, there was a belief in progress and in rational solutions to the problems affecting human beings and society. That belief disintegrated in the twentieth century, giving rise to what Berlin calls an intellectual barrier between the two centuries and their view of the world and history.

In the twentieth century, people came to understand and stress the importance of the unconscious and irrational forces in human beings, and many came to believe that the answer to most problems is to remove the problem rather than solve it through rational thought and argument. For example, the problems associated with human liberty (such as dissidents, extremist political groups, or demonstrations) can be removed by eliminating the desire for liberty among the people. This was a solution shared equally by Nazi Germany and the Soviet Union when these governments denounced "bourgeois liberty" as hollow and useless.

Such an approach would create a perversely "ideal society" in which disturbing questions simply would not be raised because they could not even be conceived. This is the vision of George Orwell in *Nineteen Eighty-Four* (1949) and, slightly altered, that of Aldous Huxley in *Brave New World* (1932). Such a world can be achieved, Berlin argues, when there is a growing desire among people to accept security at the price of personal liberty. To avoid this fate, it is necessary to have less faith in systems and more trust in human intelligence operating in a condition of maximum freedom.

The Second Essay

Human freedom in a different context is the theme of the second essay, "Historical Inevitability." Berlin, the biographer of Karl Marx and his ideas, knew very well that certain philosophers and historians believed that they had discerned large patterns in the procession of historical events, and from these patterns, they had deduced the laws that history was obliged to obey. The result was historical inevitability. For the Marxist, it was historically inevitable that once capitalism had reached the point where its internal contradictions were intolerable, the proletariat would spontaneously sweep away the old system, the state would wither away, and the socialist utopia would arrive. Other scholars and other factions had different versions of what was historically inevitable but shared the same underlying belief that they had discovered the laws of history.

This, Berlin writes, is not part of an empirical theory but a metaphysical attitude. Historical inevitability is much better at explaining the facts after they happen than in predicting them before

they occur. Moreover, a belief in historical inevitability is not shared by most human beings, who normally act as if they retained the freedom to make choices and decisions unconstrained by abstract historical laws. Berlin is thankful for this because he believes that determinism "is one of the great alibis, pleaded by those who cannot or do not wish to face the fact of human responsibility."

The Third Essay

Human responsibility is at the heart of the book's third and most important essay, "Two Concepts of Liberty." Human beings can be responsible if and only if they have a certain amount of freedom to determine how they will think and act. Berlin posits that such liberty can be of two sorts. There can be "negative" liberty, which essentially asks the question, "How much can a person be left alone?" Contrasted to this is "positive" liberty, which asks "To what degree can a person influence his surroundings, especially the actions of others?"

Negative liberty is important because all people give up some personal liberty for social order but people must retain a minimum amount of liberty to preserve their humanity. The more a person is uncommanded by the state, organizations, or others, the more negative liberty he or she retains—in other words, the more the individual is left alone. The concept and practice of negative reality are most important in dealing with the modern state, which has increasingly sought to control the behavior of its citizens. Negative liberty can be a danger when individuals, businesses, or other groups are left free to do actual harm to others, as when industry unregulated by government pollutes rivers or when employers exploit their employees. As Berlin notes, "Freedom for the wolves means death for the sheep."

Positive liberty comes from the wish of individuals to be their own masters, but it also can lead to a desire to be the master of others. Without a system that provides for checks and balances, this can lead to excessive control, even tyranny. As Berlin notes, positive liberty has more often been perverted than negative liberty, which is why he urges caution.

Both forms of liberty are good and desirable,

but both can lead to situations where people desire equally valuable but irreconcilable goals. For Berlin, there is no absolute standard for setting the limits of negative or positive liberty; each society and ultimately each human being must decide where to draw that line.

The Fourth Essay

The book's final essay, "John Stuart Mill and the Ends of Life," looks at an individual who has drawn such lines. Mill, whose father's teaching enabled him to read Greek at age five and to know algebra and Latin by the age of nine, established modern liberalism with the publication of *On Liberty* in 1859. Berlin's study of Mill reveals the extent and expanse of the British philosopher's contributions to the theory of liberty.

As a thinker, writer, and political leader, Mill was concerned above all with the extension of individual freedom, especially freedom of belief and speech. Time after time, he argued for the right of unpopular, even dangerous, groups and individuals to express their views freely and openly. Mill passionately believed that human society needed variety and that tolerance of the ideas of others was necessary for this variety.

Mill believed that human beings wish to curtail the liberties of others for one of three reasons: the desire for power, a wish for conformity, and the belief that there is a single, universal answer to each important question or issue. The first two reasons are irrational, Mill argues, and the third has been proven wrong by history. History has repeatedly demonstrated that human knowledge is never complete and that different individuals, nations, or civilizations can have different goals, equally valid but not necessarily in harmony with one another.

Mill's most important and enduring contribution, Berlin believed, was his constant, untiring insistence that it is the freedom to choose and to experiment that distinguishes human beings from the rest of nature. This, above all else, is what liberty is expected to preserve.

Berlin's Impact on Philosophy

Four Essays on Liberty is perhaps the quintessential Berlin work: not a sustained, full-length book, but a collection of essays focused on a few specific topics and approaching them from divergent directions that in the end find coherence and unity. As individual works, the parts of *Four Essays on Liberty* had caused considerable discussion, even controversy, among serious writers and thinkers. Berlin prepared a long and carefully written introduction for *Four Essays on Liberty* that addressed the points that had been raised. This was only one more stage of a philosophical dialogue that ran throughout Berlin's life and career.

Two major ideas emerged from *Four Essays on Liberty* that have had profound and lasting impact on political philosophy. The first idea was the concept of "negative" and "positive" liberty—briefly, how much one can escape control contrasted with how much one can control others. Although this distinction has become commonplace since the publication of Berlin's essay, he was the first major political thinker systematically and eloquently to articulate the distinction and its importance, and his discussion of this topic has been hailed as one of the major contributions of his career.

The second major idea, which was even more central to Berlin's entire philosophy, was the view that human beings, whether as individuals or as members of a society, pursue goals that cannot be viewed as forming a unified whole. Goals equally valid for their particular groups often contradict one another. There is no single, universal truth that is valid for every society, in all places, and at any time (the concept of monism). Berlin demonstrated in terms of classical empiricism that monism is not a valid theory to explain human behavior and human history.

Four Essays on Liberty placed these two ideas on the philosophical record, where they have remained essential elements in the continuing development of political science. Their enduring impact has been to underscore the need for tolerance and generosity in debates on political goals and activities and to inject a healthy dose of skepticism about the reality of ultimate, universal truths for which individual human beings and their liberties must be sacrificed. After these two points were clearly stated by Berlin, they have come to form a part of any serious discussion of political philosophy or the rights and liberties of the individual in society.

Michael Witkoski

Additional Reading

Berlin, Isaiah, and Ramin Jahanbegloo. *Conversations with Isaiah Berlin*. New York: Charles Scribner's Sons, 1992. In a question-and-answer format, Isaiah Berlin discusses a wide range of topics, including his personal history, intellectual development, and opinions on philosophy and philosophers. Berlin's responses to questions on such topics as "two kinds of liberty" are direct and lucid, and the biographical sections, especially those dealing with Berlin's life as a young boy in Russia during the Bolshevik Revolution of 1917, are fascinating.

Galipeau, Claude. *Isaiah Berlin's Liberalism*. New York: Oxford University Press, 1994. A thoughtful consideration of Berlin's version of liberalism and how it differs from and yet is linked to the traditions of classical liberalism. Galipeau is especially good at placing Berlin's thought in relationship to modern world politics, the excesses of which were often in direct, if not brutal, conflict with his more humane and humanitarian stance.

Gray, John. *Isaiah Berlin*. Princeton, N.J.: Princeton University Press, 1996. A thoughtful examination of Berlin's belief in the existence of values that while different are equally important. The central thesis of the book is that Berlin's work is based on a principle that might be called "value-pluralism," meaning that ultimate human values are objective but diverse and may often conflict.

Margalit, Edna, and Avishai Margalit, eds. *Isaiah Berlin: A Celebration*. Chicago: Chicago University Press, 1991. This collection draws together essays that touch on the wide range of Berlin's interests, from opera to political science to philosophy. Although a number of the pieces included here are valuable, the essay by celebrated legal scholar Ronald Dworkin on "Two Concepts of Liberty" is especially illuminating for those wishing to understand the full impact of *Four Essays on Liberty*.

Ryan, Alan, ed. *The Idea of Freedom: Essays in Honor of Isaiah Berlin*. Oxford: Oxford University Press, 1979. A useful collection of essays that shed light on Berlin's philosophy of history and his views on the history of philosophy.

Michael Witkoski

Bhagavad Gita

Written sometime between 200 B.C.E.-200 C.E., the Bhagavad Gita is one of the most revered and celebrated texts in Hinduism. It is a primarily a practical religious text—one concerned with moving its readers toward salvation—and only secondarily concerned with doctrine.

Authorship and Context

Although the authorship of the Bhagavad Gita cannot be traced to an individual, someone inserted the Bhagavad Gita, composed c. 200 B.C.E.-200 C.E., into the Mahabharata, an ancient and highly popular Indian Hindu epic. The Mahabharata, which consists of some 180,000 lines, is the product of a process of oral transmission and was probably written down by 400 B.C.E. The title means "the great story of the Bharatas," and it recounts the tale of the Kauravas (depicted as demons incarnate) and the Pandavas (depicted as sons of gods or as gods incarnate). The Kauravas and the Pandavas are cousins fighting one another for the Bharata kingdom with the latter enjoying the advice and support of Krishna (who is depicted as the god Vishnu incarnate). The Mahabharata describes itself as the fifth Veda, the Vedas being viewed as eternal, unauthored *schruti* (spoken revelation) or authoritative scripture. Unlike the four other Vedas, the Mahabharata was available to the poor, the low caste, and the uneducated as well as to the affluent, the high caste, and the learned; it was also available to women as well as to men. Its focus—at least on one very plausible reading, is *bhakti* (devotion) to Vishnu or Krishna.

The Bhagavad Gita ("the song of the blessed lord") became part of the great Indian epic and shared in its popularity. Strictly, it is not officially *schruti* or scripture according to the Hindu Vedantic tradition, but *smriti*—a remembered, traditional text. Not only is its author unknown; some scholars believe that the work had multiple authors. Nonetheless, its practical status is that it is a fully authoritative Hindu text. It is highly popular among ordinary believers, and it is nearly mandatory that the leading Vedantic scholars comment on it. Thus Samkara, Ramanuja, and Mahdva—leading scholars in different Hindu schools of thought—all wrote commentaries on the Bhagavad Gita. Its relative brevity—some seven hundred verses—makes it easy to separate from the Mahabharata as a devotional text with its own powerful influence.

The Bhagavad Gita is a mainstream text in the Hindu religious tradition in which reincarnation and karma are basic assumptions. This tradition is based on two basic assumptions: that every person is subject to the law of karma and that every person is subject to a beginningless and potentially endless cycle of reincarnation. The law of karma guarantees that each person will reap the benefits and suffer the costs of his or her actions; good actions yield benefits and bad actions yield costs. The benefits and costs do not all come in any one lifetime, and whenever one dies with benefits or costs due to one, one must be born into a new life with a new body and receive the benefits and costs still due from past lives. It is difficult but possible in a given lifetime to have suffered all the costs due to one, to avoid wrong actions, to have received all the benefits, and to perform good actions without concern for their effects (and thereby avoiding generating benefits). Thus it is possible to die without benefits or costs remaining due to one, in which case one escapes the cycle of reincarnation, which is the goal of religious belief and practice.

Salvation is conceived in terms of escape from the cycle of reincarnations and freedom from all karmic benefits and costs. In monotheistic Indian religions, the supreme being can release one from the cycle of rebirths given one's repentance of wrong actions and trust in the supreme being's grace. One's body, in this view, is merely the vehicle that one takes through the course of a given life, to be left behind at death and replaced by another body that is one's vehicle in the next life. One way in which one's karmic benefits and costs can bear fruit is in the quality of the vehicle in which one takes the next ride, specifically in features such as the health, strength, and beauty of one's body and more significantly, the caste into which one is born.

The Bhagavad Gita examines some of the tenets of Hinduism through the characters of Arjuna and Krishna. Arjuna is a member of the warrior class; it is his caste duty to participate in a war that his community is waging. However, Arjuna—dressed for battle and observing his army and the enemy forces gather for conflict—is himself unwilling to fight because he has relatives on both sides. He may well be called upon to kill some family member that he loves. Krishna, Arjuna's charioteer, argues that Arjuna's duty is to fight. Even if he kills a relative, he merely destroys that person's body. The real person will not die. Each person must do his duty as defined by his caste; only this will further his progress to liberation from the cycle of birth and death. Not inactivity, but disinterested activity done as sacrifice to God and in accord with the duties that are consequent on one's status in society, lead to escape from the cycle of reincarnation. This doctrine involves the idea that it is desire for consequences that keeps one attached to this world and the notion that detachment is essential to escape. This is also occurs in the Buddhist tradition.

Disinterested right action is one among several suggested ways to liberate the self from reincarnation. Another suggested path is asceticism, which, in one of its more extreme forms, might require wandering through India clad only in a loin cloth with a beggar's bowl as one's only other possession, eating only what one is given. Less austere versions involved abstinence from all sexual activity, no use of alcoholic beverages, and dedication to meditation. Still another path is that of esoteric knowledge gained from learning

the language in which the sacred texts are written and studying those texts under the guidance of recognized pundits. Neither of these paths, of course, are likely to be attractive or available to most people. The path that Krishna recommends does not require a change of caste, a forsaking of family or society, a lifetime of scholarship, an embracing of impoverished asceticism, or membership in a separate sacred society.

Another path is that of devotion—trust in the supreme being's gracious willingness to forgive the repentant sinner. This path is not difficult to combine with the path of disinterested good action, particularly insofar as one's failures are at least in principle forgivable. This path is, of course, monotheistic—it requires that a god exists and can be prayed to, is willing to forgive a repentant sinner, and to release the devotee from karmic consequences and the cycle of reincarnations—to provide enlightenment in the form of salvation from karma and rebirth.

Given its popularity, it is not surprising that the various religious and philosophical traditions provide interpretations of the Bhagavad Gita that accord with their own fundamental tenets. Two major readings of the Bhagavad Gita's content derive from the Advaita Vedanta, which sees the work as a monistic text, and the Vsistadvaita and Dvaita Vedanta, which see it as a theistic text.

Advaita ("nondual") Vedanta offers a monistic reading of the Vedas and Upanishads, which serve as the central doctrinal scriptures of Hinduism. A monistic view of the world holds that there is one kind of thing and only one thing of that kind. All that exists is *nirguna* ("not quality," or "qualityless") Brahman. While admittedly there seems to be a plurality of things, all of them possessing qualities, how things seem is held to be illusion, and the reality is that there is only qualityless Brahman. There are passages in the Bhagavad Gita that seem to teach this.

Vsistadvaita (qualifiedly nondual) Vedanta holds that Brahman has qualities and is distinct from all else in the sense that Brahman with qualities could exist in the absence of all else. It also regards the world (the things that exist and are not Brahman) as Brahman's body. Dvaita (dualistic) Vedanta also holds that Brahman possesses qualities, but it denies that the world is properly said to be Brahman's body. It is not clear that in the end the doctrinal differences between Vsistadvaita Vedanta and Dvaita Vedanta are as deep as they may seem, but it is quite clear that they are much closer to one another than either is to Advaita Vedanta. For example, each is theistic rather than monistic. For both, Brahman has qualities, is an appropriate object of worship, and can and does answer prayer, forgive sins, and provide release from the reincarnation cycle. Brahman is not viewed as qualityless. There are Bhagavad Gita passages that seem to teach that the theistic view of Brahman is correct.

The Bhagavad Gita is often interpreted as a text intended to bring about a synthesis of competing religious positions and to make religious enlightenment available to everyone rather than simply to monks or Brahmans. If so, this puts certain features of the work into a different perspective. For example, the work contains both monistic and theistic passages, so it appears that the Bhagavad Gita teaches contradictory doctrines. However, if the text aims at synthesis and making enlightenment widely available, then another interpretation of this apparent contradiction may be correct. Although the assertion of these two logically incompatible doctrines cannot be termed synthesis, a doctrine that says that monism is true but those who embrace theism come as close to the truth as they are able and they too will receive enlightenment (or the reverse case), would provide a synthesis of means of salvation without proposing that contradictions are true. Of course, monists will interpret the Bhagavad Gita as stating that monists receive enlightenment by seeing the truth and theists receive enlightenment in spite of not doing so, and theists will interpret the work as stating that theists receive enlightenment by seeing the truth and monists receive enlightenment in spite of not doing so, but through these ideas, the presence of contradictory passages is explained. The theistic version of this sort of reading has at least one advantage: It can explain how false belief can still lead to enlightenment (God's grace is deep) whereas it is hard to see what sort of explanation monism could give of false belief leading to enlightenment. This suggests that perhaps, in the end, the Bhagavad Gita is a fundamentally theistic text.

Keith E. Yandell

Overview

Type of philosophy: Ethics, metaphysics, philosophy of religion
First transcribed: Bhagavadgita, c. 200 B.C.E.-200 C.E. (*The Bhagavad Gita*, 1785)
Principal ideas advanced:

◇ One's true self is one's undying soul that is divine in nature.
◇ Even though one's phenomenal nature is a projection of the ever-active matter (*prakrti*), one can avoid the inherent bondage of a material mode of existence by cultivating even-mindedness and detachment.
◇ Practice of detachment is possible through self-knowledge and devotion to God and is to be initiated in the performance of righteous acts that uphold social order.
◇ Such practice leads to freedom from the fetters of action through the conquest of passion and ego-consciousness and contributes to an awakening of one's latent divinity by taking one closer to God.
◇ Whenever righteousness declines and lawlessness abounds, God descends into this world in human form to restore order; he is the Supreme Person, the personified Absolute Being, who is the abode of all beings; yet he remains distinct from his creation in power and personality.

The Bhagavad Gita, the most revered text in Hinduism, literally means "the song of the blessed lord." The spiritual poem consists of the God-incarnate Krishna's discourse with a despondent warrior, Arjuna. Throughout the discourse, the Bhagavad Gita attempts to synthesize the various ideas in the Hindu philosophy of its time into its own brand of theism. Yet, in spite of its philosophical profundity, it remains a delightfully easy-to-read poem with an almost lyrical beauty. This is one important reason for its appeal to people of all levels of understanding.

Composed of eighteen chapters, the Bhagavad Gita is a small part of the popular Hindu epic, the Mahabharata, which is believed to have been an orally transmitted text written down about 400 B.C.E. The epic, one of the Vedas (authoritative scripture), was available to the poor and members of the lower caste. A tale of cousins fighting for the Bharata kingdom, it emphasizes *bhakti* (devotion) to Vishnu or Krishna.

The Hindu Tradition

To understand the Bhagavad Gita's importance in the Hindu tradition requires some familiarity with dominant trends and ideas in Hinduism. Broadly speaking, the Hindu tradition makes a distinction between the pursuit of God as the personified supreme being, to be reached primarily through devotion, and the mystical quest for the undifferentiated One. In the latter, monistic, tradition, it is believed that any characterization of the supreme reality, including identifying it as God with his various attributes in their perfection, is an attempt to impose limitations on the absolute, which is beyond name and form. The supremely real is to be known through an exalted type of direct intuitive awareness that transcends all relativity and conceptual limitations. In ancient India, this view was taught in the Upanishads, which asserted an identity between a person's true self (*atman*) and the absolute (*Brahman*). According to this philosophy, a mystical, nondiscursive knowledge of such an identity is the ultimate experience of one's life. Such a realization liberates one from material bondage.

A seeker of God in theistic Hinduism, on the other hand, strives for God-realization through self-surrender, devoted service, and rituals. This seeker sees God as the supreme person with many-splendored attributes who never lets a devotee down. This view finds its most definitive expression in the philosophy of the Bhagavad Gita, composed at a time when the Hindu religion was trying to make a comeback with its own answer to the Buddha's practical philosophy. The Buddha's emergence had been made possible mainly because of the post-Upanishadic slump in the Hindu tradition. At that time, the common people were bewildered by the excesses of the Vedic sacrificial ritualism and by the all-too-nebulous metaphysical teachings of self-realization (*atma-jnana*) as found in the Upanishads. What they needed and were looking for was a practical guide to everyday living and a philosophy of salvation understandable in human terms, which they found in the Buddha and, a few centuries later, in a resurgence of Hinduism, made possible through the popular appeal of the Bhagavad Gita and through the emergence of the *dharma* texts, which contained systematic explanations of household and social duties.

The Bhagavad Gita emphasized the element of loving devotion (*bhakti*) to a personal God. As opposed to the Vedic hierarchy, the promise of salvation was offered to all people who would put their faith in Krishna. The importance of self-knowledge was deemphasized but not denied; rather, such knowledge was to be blended with selfless action and devotion. The Bhagavad Gita found meaning in diverse spiritual orientations and put them together into its own broad conception of religious quest, thereby making its philosophy appeal to a wide range of people.

Krishna and Arjuna

The Bhagavad Gita's story is set in the dramatic context of a war in which the good and the evil sides are clearly marked. Krishna, the human-incarnate of the Hindu god Vishnu, is the charioteer of Arjuna, who is the most gifted warrior on the good side that is destined to overcome the evil forces. When the two sides are about to engage in the war, Arjuna, realizing that the war means killing some of his own relatives and benefactors who are members of the other side, becomes dejected and refuses to fight. In order to advise Arjuna that he should do what must be done, Krishna gives a sermon that constitutes the body of the Bhagavad Gita. The dramatic setting of the story in the battlefield is highly symbolic, suggestive of the spiritual struggle of a human soul in which Arjuna, the confused self, looks for an excuse to withdraw from the battle, but Krishna, the divine in humanity, charioteers the soul.

To get Arjuna back to his task, Krishna starts his teaching with the Sāmkhya idea that a person's true self, which is the soul, is eternal and indestructible. The initial thrust of his message is to persuade Arjuna to get out of his despondency; hence, some of Krishna's points, at this stage, are meant more as persuasive appeals than as spiritual insights. Accordingly, the idea that a person's true self is eternal is used, to start with, to convince Arjuna that he should not be perturbed by the prospect of the mere physical death he might cause people to undergo; after all, their souls are indestructible. Although this ploy seems to be a rationalization for killing, it should be understood in its proper perspective. Arjuna is faced with a crisis of resolve: He is rightfully assigned to do something that he now finds unnerving, improper, and distasteful. To show him the importance of doing his duty (*svadharma*) and of not being swayed by external considerations in the face of what must be done, Krishna teaches him how to accept the inevitable in the right spirit.

The rightness of Arjuna's fighting the battle, because he is a warrior by caste, is not really in question. It was already decided that to fight was the only right and honorable option available to Arjuna and his clan. Arjuna's last-minute self-doubt and his consequent decision not to fight are, then, indications of failure of nerve and weakness of resolve on his part. As a result, it is Krishna's task to see that Arjuna comes out of his confusion and secures the necessary strength to do what must be done. Being Arjuna's guru and a shrewd judge of human character, Krishna knows that a confused person like Arjuna who is in need of help will not be impressed by a reasoned discourse on the rightness of a proposed course of actions or by a gospel of spiritual wisdom. Rather, what he needs is some reassurance and practical persuasions. Accordingly, Krishna tries to provide them both by using, almost to the point of sophistry, the deeply cherished Hindu ideas of the imperishability of soul and the inevitability of death and reincarnation. He also tries to appeal to Arjuna's honor by reminding him of his caste duty to fight a just war and by citing the possible consequence of his being branded as a coward if he backs out of the battle at the last moment.

Gradually, however, Krishna takes Arjuna to progressively higher planes of awakening by leaving out sophistry and the appeal to his base emotions and by providing more substantive discourses on human nature, life's goal, and God. This practical teaching procedure, in which the teacher comes down to the disciple's level and then gradually takes him to a deeper understanding of the issues commensurate with his ability, is a standard feature in a guru-disciple relationship in Hinduism. In such teaching, many of the earlier points of persuasion, meant to take one out of one's spiritual lethargy, are to be ignored or grown out of in a later phase of realization. Krishna's initial effort to make Ar-

juna come back to his senses, together with his later offering of more profound discourses, serves as an excellent demonstration of this progressive teaching technique.

It is seemingly ironic that the Bhagavad Gita, which is one of the most definitive texts on love and nonviolence, starts with an apparent rationalization for killing. However, the irony disappears when it is understood that Arjuna is not really given a lesson on killing but is told to differentiate between real love and false compassion, to understand death and not be afraid of it, and to realize that there is much more to a person than his fleeting nature and perishable body—namely, his undying soul that is divine in nature. Because these points are presented in the context of a battle and in the initial guise of the advice to kill, they illustrate the real-life import of the teachings and dramatize the importance of spiritual serenity in the midst of unnerving situations. Like the progressive teaching method, the advocacy of spirituality in juxtaposition to material concerns is another technique in the Hindu tradition.

Detachment

In order to emphasize the need for even-mindedness as a prelude to having control over oneself in the midst of action and hence to being able to better perform action, Krishna moves on to a discourse of detachment in action. In the course of his teaching, it becomes clear that such detachment is not only necessary if one is to be unperturbed by extraneous considerations while performing action, but also if one is to attain purity of soul and conquest of passion and ego-consciousness. These in turn are said to be conducive to spiritual liberation (*moksha*), humanity's ultimate salvation.

Krishna initially develops the idea of detachment by elaborating on the nature of work and its "fruit" (*phala*). He advocates right attitude toward work to avoid its inherent bondage and illustrates the fundamental difference between eternal, nonactive human souls and transient, ever-active matter, which is the real locus of action. Perhaps the most celebrated account of detachment in any Hindu scripture is contained in the second chapter of the Bhagavad Gita, where Krishna asks Arjuna to set his heart only on his work and never on its fruit or result. A person who is moved by success or failure, Arjuna is told, is not an even-minded person settled in wisdom. To be mentally detached from one's work one need not renounce work or be indifferent to what must be done; rather, one is asked to be indifferent to the *fruits* of one's action. That is, after taking utmost care to do what is right, one must not worry or be apprehensive about the results, for, according to Krishna, one has access only to one's work, not to its results.

In the later chapters, Krishna points out that the results of work must be surrendered to God as sacrifice; any outcome must be acceptable as God's gift. The emergence of the totality of God in the Bhagavad Gita is a gradual but sure one: It starts in chapter 4 and goes on until chapter 15, climaxing in the eleventh chapter where Krishna reveals his divine form to Arjuna in all its terrifying majesty. These chapters contain discourses on God's nature, the nature of soul and matter and their relation to God, and, above all, the importance of loving self-devotion to God. They also dwell on the idea of work in the spirit of sacrifice as a means to detachment.

The Vedas prescribed undertaking sacrificial rituals to obtain the desirables from the gods. The Upanishads deemphasized the rituals, substituting inward subjective quest in their place. The Bhagavad Gita reintroduced the notion of sacrifice, but not in the Vedic sense. If work cannot be avoided because the world is sustained by work, and yet if attachment to its fruit creates fetters (*karma*), then the way out, according to the Bhagavad Gita, is through a detached performance of one's work where God is the object to whom the result is offered as sacrifice. The cardinal teaching in the Bhagavad Gita seems to be that doing one's work in the right spirit, as sacrifice, involves an integrated discipline (*yoga*) of action, knowledge, and, above all, devotion, and that such a *yoga* not only enables one to undertake activities without anxiety for gain and safety but also is a spiritual exercise that takes one closer to God.

Divine Incarnation

Accompanying the idea of personal devotion in the Bhagavad Gita is the notion of divine incarnation (*avataravada*). In chapter 4, Krishna declares that whenever righteousness declines and lawlessness arises, he appears in this world in human form to set things right. This idea is especially important to a devotee because it provides a personal touch to one of the persistent themes of the Bhagavad Gita, which is that God's laws are moral laws and whoever strives to establish righteousness (*dharma*) is actually doing God's service and is dear to him. It reveals that God is concerned about what goes on in his creation, and, therefore, it conveys hope to the faithful. In the context of this declaration, it makes all the more sense why Arjuna is asked to engage in action to uphold righteousness, and why, in the Bhagavad Gita, so much emphasis is placed on the importance of devoted performance of righteous work, in the spirit of sacrifice, as the preferred means to God-realization.

The idea of divine incarnation, popular among the Hindus, has helped them view all prophets of all religions as fulfilling the divine promise, and thus it has made them generally tolerant toward other religions. In fact, the Bhagavad Gita itself champions this attitude: Throughout the gradual unfolding of the supremacy and priority of God, Krishna repeatedly mentions that whenever one shows devotion to God in whatever form, God responds to one in the same manner. Although the Bhagavad Gita favors an integrated *yoga* of devotion that is to be carried through wisdom and proper action, it leaves room for other forms of devotion; and, what is more, it also acknowledges paths to spiritual freedom even without devotion. In chapter 12, Krishna admits that the seekers of wisdom who strive after the Upanishadic "Unmanifest" also reach God; but he thinks that the path of devotion to a personal God is an easier one. However, he declares that if the Bhagavad Gita's preferred path is not suitable for someone, then that person should resort to another method.

The Bhagavad Gita repeatedly asserts the fundamental difference between one's true self, which is one's soul and which is nonactive by nature, and the ever-active material nature (*prakrti*) that forms one's body and mind (the subtle body). However, the Bhagavad Gita avoids a Sāmkhya-type dualism, which is the basis of the later philosophy of the *yoga*, by postulating a personified absolute being, God, who manifests himself both in selves and matter (which are parts of him) and yet remains distinct from them in power and personality. Isvara, the personal god who is symbolized as Lord Vishnu and whose incarnate is Krishna, is the creative aspect of this supreme being; it is through Isvara that God creates and sustains the world and dwells in everything. Brahman, the Upanishadic absolute, is said to be the unmanifest form of the Bhagavad Gita's God, the supreme person (*purusottama*), yet the Bhagavad Gita insists that God is more than all his forms.

Consistent with this position that asserts the supremacy of God over everything else, the Bhagavad Gita makes God the abode of Brahman. Philosophical difficulties aside, what is clearly evident in these characterizations is an attempt to meet the Upanishadic challenge by making a personified absolute being the foundation of all possible beings, including the one immutable Brahman, and by making devotion not only a viable but also the most important path to the realization of this highest reality. The Bhagavad Gita's whole idea is to demonstrate that love of God, so far from being just a convenient device disposable at the dawn of knowledge, is also the very anchor of such knowledge, which, without it, is inadequate.

Dipankar Chatterjee

Additional Reading

Carr, Brian, and Indira Mahalingham, eds. *Companion Encyclopedia of Asian Philosophy*. London: Routledge, 1997. First-rate presentation of Indian philosophy, and Asian philosophy generally, including the context of the Bhagavad Gita.

Deutsch, Elliot. *The Bhagavad Gita*. New York: Holt, Rinehart & Winston, 1968. Translation, with introduction, of the Bhagavad Gita.

Lipner, Joseph. *The Face of Truth*. Albany: State University of New York Press, 1986. Excellent account of Ramanuja's Vsistadvaita theology and philosophy.

Mahadevan, T. P. *The Philosophy of Advaita*. Wiltshire: Compton Russell, 1997. Highly recommended study of Samkara's Advaita Vedanta perspective.

Sharma, B. N. K. *Philosophy of Sri Madhvacarya*. Delhi: Motilal Barnasidas, 1986. Excellent study of Madhva's Dvaita Vedanta philosophy and theology.

Yandell, Keith E. "On Interpreting the Bhagavad Gita." *Philosophy East and West* 32, no. 1 (January, 1982): 37-46.

Keith E. Yandell

Maurice Blanchot

One of the leading novelists and literary critics of the post-World War II generation in France, Blanchot decisively influenced the work of philosophers such as Jacques Derrida and is widely recognized as a forerunner of the school of literary theory known as deconstruction.

Principal philosophical works: *Faux pas*, 1943; *Le Très-Haut*, 1948 (*The Most High*, 1996); *La Part du feu*, 1949 (*The Work of Fire*, 1995); *L'Éspace littéraire*, 1955 (*The Space of Literature*, 1982); *L'Entretien infini*, 1969 (*The Infinite Conversation*, 1993); *La Folie du jour*, 1973 (*The Madness of the Day*, 1981); *L'Éscriture du désastre*, 1980 (*The Writing of the Disaster*, 1986); *Après coup*, 1983 (*Vicious Circles: Two Fictions and "After the Fact,"* 1985); *La Communauté inavouable*, 1983 (*The Unavowable Community*, 1988).

Born: September 22, 1907; Quain, Saone-et-Loire, France

Early Life

Of Maurice Blanchot's personal life, very little is known. Born of a wealthy family, he received a B.S. degree from the University of Strasbourg and a graduate degree from the University of Paris, Sorbonne. At Strasbourg in 1925, Blanchot met philosopher Emmanuel Lévinas, a fellow undergraduate. Their friendship, which would endure, arose from shared literary and philosophical interests. Otherwise, the two young men were poles apart. Lévinas, a Jew, was a Lithuanian immigrant and politically a liberal; Blanchot was, in these early years, a monarchist. Through Lévinas, however, Blanchot was introduced to two philosophers whose work proved to be central to his intellectual development: Edmund Husserl and Martin Heidegger.

During the 1930's, Blanchot was visibly active as a right-wing political journalist, and the extent of his involvement with the fascist movement in France has been a matter of some controversy. Like many young men of the period, Blanchot was deeply disturbed by the failure of parliamentary democracy to provide effective leadership for a France still debilitated by the economic and social chaos produced by World War I and threatened by the rising power of the Nazis in Germany. His first journalistic efforts were for the

traditionalist *Journal des débats*, a prestigious mouthpiece for the French oligarchy, and within a short period, he had risen to become its editor in chief, a position he maintained until 1940, when France fell to the German invasion.

Although as leading editorialist for the *Journal des débats*, Blanchot was often highly critical of the centrist government of Leon Blum, his most vitriolic attacks upon the political establishment were published in the fascist journals *Combat* and *L'Insurge*. Appalled particularly by the government's capitulation to the League of Nations in Geneva in 1936, which allowed the German reoccupation of the Rhineland, and by the government's policy of neutrality toward Spain, which was then involved in a civil war, Blanchot adopted an increasingly violent rhetorical stance that culminated in the late 1930's in a number of articles that attempted to justify acts of revolutionary terrorism against the democratic regime. Most controversial, however, has been the suggestion that Blanchot's involvement with *Combat* and *L'Insurge* somehow amounted to an endorsement of the distinctly anti-Semitic content of the two journals. If this were the case, then Blanchot's post-World War II writings, deeply sympathetic to the plight of the Jews during the Holocaust, might be considered tainted or intended somehow to suppress his own complicity with the persecutions carried out under the German occupation. However, Blanchot's own writings from the 1930's present little evidence of anti-Semitic leanings.

Life's Work

World War II seems to have marked a turning point in Blanchot's career. During the war years, he began to move toward a more moderate French nationalism, as evidenced by his participation in the Resistance. In addition, the primacy of political involvement gave way to his literary interests. Before the end of the war, he published two novels, *Thomas l'Obscur* (1941; *Thomas the Obscure*, 1973) and *Aminadab* (1942), and two critical works, one of which, *Faux Pas* (1943), brought together a number of essays from the prewar period. In *Faux Pas*, Blanchot's theoretical antecedents become apparent; the influence of the French poet Stéphane Mallarmé and that of the novelist/poet Le Comte de Lautréamont are also evident. Most important, though, is the philosophical influence of Martin Heidegger, whose radical phenomenology is evident in Blanchot's claims for the quasi-mystical character of language as that which lies at the foundations of human existence. With Heidegger, Blanchot seeks to overturn the traditional view that ordinary, instrumental language precedes poetic language. Poetic discourse, rather, is the originary language out of which historical communities emerge.

The seminal theoretical statement from this period in Blanchot's career appeared in a work entitled *The Work of Fire*. In this work, several other important influences are in evidence in addition to that of Heidegger. The first of these is Georg Wilhelm Friedrich Hegel, the great German philosopher, by way of Alexander Kojève, whose lectures on Hegel—first published in 1947—shaped the philosophical reception of Hegel in France for the entire post-World War II generation in France. At the core of Kojève's interpretation of Hegel's phenomenology is the claim that Hegel's philosophy is one of death. Death is understood in this context as the power of negation—a central aspect of the Hegelian dialectic—or the possibility of nonbeing that dwells within being itself. According to Kojève, the pressure of nonbeing, or negation, in the midst of being (time) gives rise to creative activity—a philosophy of action understood as existential struggle. Such are the terms of authentic existence for

the common lot of men and women; but for the literary artist or intellectual, work in the everyday sense of the term must fall short of authenticity. The intellectual or literary artist, Kojève argues, sets up an ideal universe, a fiction in opposition to the "real" world. The artist's creativity is thus a deception, a fraud.

Blanchot, while accepting Kojève's claim that literary production is not an authentic "work" in the Hegelian sense of the term, insists that literature nevertheless possesses its own proper negativity, a creative principle whose warrant lies not in producing meaning in and for the world but in abolishing the world, in substituting for the "real" an absolute imaginary world. In "Literature and the Right to Death," the most important theoretical essay in *The Work of Fire*, Blanchot develops a philosophy of literature that is very close to that of Georges Bataille, with whom he had been closely associated since 1940. For both Blanchot and Bataille, the power of negation is not merely a moment in the movement of the spirit toward synthesis, as in the Hegelian dialectic; rather, negation becomes for these thinkers a sufficient end unto itself. It follows that literary creation cannot be a matter of moral action or engagement with the world but must instead be a struggle against its own structures or conventions. Literature, in this quasi-gnostic sense, must take the form of the fragmentary rather than the whole; it must seek not a false synthesis but a creative disintegration.

To carry out this new conception of literary creation, Blanchot developed a fictive vehicle called the *récit*, essentially a highly fragmentary form of the novel. Among his first efforts in this direction was the 1950 revision of his earlier *Thomas the Obscure*. What had been in 1941 a conventional novel, albeit inspired by the subversive tradition of Lautréamont and Mallarmé, was transformed through a process of rigorous negation into something radically new on the literary horizon. What this process of negation entailed was a massive paring down of sentences, anticipating in certain respects the "minimalist" style of more recent fiction, followed by a wholesale elimination of characters, leaving only the anti-hero, Thomas, who is a writer, and a few others whose personae are so unstable, so evanescent that it is hard to call them characters. Lastly, related to this instability of character, Blanchot completely eliminated all psychological depth, abetted by an artfully contrived slippage of conventional pronouns, so that an "I" is confused with or replaced by, almost at random, a "he," a "they," or a "she." In short, Blanchot continues the attempt already evident in James Joyce's novels, to dissolve the very concept of identity.

Blanchot continued to produce a number of *récits* and collections of short fiction through 1973, pursuing relentlessly the literary program he had begun in the 1940's. Perhaps most notable among these fictional experiments is *The Madness of the Day*, for it is here that Blanchot carries the dissolution of identity to the most extreme lengths. In *The Madness of the Day*, the "hero" is in fact nameless. His identity, such as it is, consists in an unfinished series of fragmented replies to a group of institutional authorities who have, by all appearances, imprisoned him and have insisted upon interrogating him in a manner that suggests their desire to transform him into a more conventional identity like themselves—a character with a history, a story with a beginning, middle, and end. In its inconclusiveness, its stubborn refusal of closure, *The Madness of the Day* invites its readers to complete or, rather, continue the process of creative negation which it has begun.

Alongside his experimental fiction, Blanchot produced a steady stream of critical essays. Until 1968, when editor Jean Paulhan died, most of these essays appeared in the prestigious French literary journal *Nouvelle Revue française*. They were subsequently collected into a series of volumes, several of which have been translated into English. Blanchot was given almost complete freedom by Paulhan to choose his subject matter, and his monthly contributions to the journal were diverse, ranging from occasional essays on specific authors such as Franz Kafka, Stéphane Mallarmé, Johann Christian Friedrich Hölderlin, Samuel Beckett, Herman Melville, Marguerite Duras, Rainer Maria Rilke, Thomas Mann, and Marcel Proust—just to name a few of the most prominent—to more explicitly theoretical essays in dialog with philosophers whose work, like that of Martin Heidegger, Emmanuel Lévinas, and Ludwig Wittgenstein, explores the problematics of writing and interpretation. One of the most important of these collections is *The Space of Literature*. In this work, Blanchot's foremost concern is the self-reflexive or self-questioning mode that the act of writing in a posthumanist age must assume. Here again the influence of Heidegger is important, but primarily through the continuing reinterpretation of Heidegger provided by Lévinas. Whereas for Heidegger the originary "gift of Being" is represented as an act of generosity, for Lévinas the emergence of the existential subject into Being is associated with horror and anonymity. This condition of anonymity may even be said to be prior to all foundations: That is, it precedes the foundations of any world at all, real or imagined, fictional or nonfictional.

For both Lévinas and Blanchot, this anonymity at the very heart of Being negates the possibility of any traditional notion of self-presence or representation, for anonymity signifies a perpetual absence. In one of the most often cited essays in *The Space of Literature*, "The Gaze of Orpheus," Blanchot reads the well-known myth of the origins of poetry in a manner that reflects his perception of the paradoxical *impossibility* that haunts the possibility of representation. Here Orpheus's failure to heed the command of the god of the underworld, to refrain from gazing into the face of his beloved Eurydice, suggests the necessity for indirection and dissimulation in the creation of a work of art. If a work of art is to escape the darkness of original anonymity and obscurity and emerge into the light of creation, it must do so by way of a detour, through partial blindness.

Other important critical works from the latter half of Blanchot's career include *The Infinite Conversation* and *The Writing of the Disaster*. In the latter work, which is now regarded as the summation of his career-long preoccupations as a critic and theorist of writing, Blanchot abandons any attempt to present his thought in the traditional essay form. Indeed, it might be said that here his fictional techniques fuse with his theoretical presentation, resulting in a highly fragmentary meditation, not only on writing but also on the very conditions of Being. In *The Writing of the Disaster*, Blanchot returns to his engagement with Hegelian dialectic; however, as his title indicates, this engagement is informed by an acute sense of historical disaster, or of the place of disaster in history. Here, more than in his earlier works, he attempts to locate the act of writing within an ethical dimension.

Influence

In seeking to recuperate the late Romantic preoccupation with self-consciousness in literature, or with literature understood as a vehicle for an escape from self-consciousness, Blanchot's work—both fictive and critical—served as a powerful influence, first, in French literary and philosophical circles, and second, by way of his effect on Jacques Derrida, on Anglo-American criticism. The foremost school of poststructuralist literary theory in the Anglo-American sphere, decontruction, is largely the creation of the Yale critics Paul de Man and Geoffrey Hartman, who were in turn deeply influenced by the work of both Derrida and Blanchot. Derrida has frequently voiced his debt to Blanchot, and Hartman has written at length of Blanchot's relation to Mallarmé and Heidegger. In deconstruction, one can detect the clear presence of a number of ideas that were either pioneered by Blanchot or given impetus by his writings. Among these ideas are the post-Hegelian claims for the importance of negation as a feature of authentic writing: the noninstrumentality of literature, which places it at odds with production of meaning; the self-referentiality of language, which follows from its freedom from instrumentality; and the essential anonymity of language and writing, the notion that the author is but the vehicle for an autonomous writing that speaks through the individual.

Jack E. Trotter

The Writing of the Disaster

Type of philosophy: Aesthetics, ethics
First transcribed: L'Écriture du désastre, 1980 (English translation, 1986)
Principal ideas advanced:
◇ The language of authentic writing belongs to the realm of the "neutral," that is, the realm of nonmeaning, separated from both being and nonbeing.

◇ To write *of* "the disaster" is to write from *within* the disaster, which lies outside history and thus outside all production of meaning and all systems of thought, including the dialectic.
◇ Writing situated within the neutral is *passive* writing, whose vehicle is the *fragment*.
◇ Passivity is that movement of thought (and writing) that seeks to undermine dialectical recuperation; passivity is resolutely antithetical, resisting any final synthesis.

The Writing of the Disaster may best be understood within the context of Maurice Blanchot's ongoing concern to create a fragmentary writing that explores the extremes of human experience. Such a mode of writing, or thinking (and for Blanchot these amount to much the same thing), seeks not to provide answers but to provoke questions about the fundamental problems of life and death, memory and forgetfulness, and culture and anarchy. Whereas earlier in his career as writer and critic, Blanchot had sought, in dialogue with French philosophers Emmanuel Lévinas and Georges Bataille, to explore the Hegelian mode of negation—the moment of antithesis in the dialectic—in *The Writing of the Disaster*, he seeks to go beyond negation, to explore the realm of the *neutre*, or the neutral. The concept of the neutral, as developed by Lévinas, denotes a passive position between being and nonbeing, a space that cannot be identified with the activity of the production of meaning or with productivity of any kind. Rather than the finished work or thought, Blanchot promotes the fragment, which is not to be mistaken for the aphorism—the latter being in some sense "finished," or closed. Fragmentary writing, by its nature, seeks its own erasure; it is self-consuming and eludes the possibility of unity, totality, or continuity.

The Writing of the Disaster is not simply a meditation upon fragmentary writing but is itself composed in a highly fragmentary, elliptical style. Lacking chapter headings, subdivisions, or any of the usual markers of linear development, *The Writing of the Disaster* defies conventional summary in the most flagrant terms. However, it is possible to isolate the central thread of the argument while keeping in mind that any such attempt must betray the essence of the work.

For Blanchot, writing is not so much the concrete expression of ideas, of words on a page expressed in a particular style, as it is a mental process, a thinking that is already writing as well as a thinking that is pure anticipation. Authentic writing is writing that is forever seeking its own origins and questioning its own possibility. Following in the steps of German philosopher Martin Heidegger, Blanchot conceives of poetic language as something extremely rare and elusive and yet omnipresent; it is everywhere and nowhere at once and is essentially authorless. People are not the speakers of language; they are the vessels through which language speaks to the world. However, the possibility of affirmation that Heidegger found in a language of negation is no longer a possibility in the modern world. Language has depleted or exhausted its powers of negation. All attempts at unitary meaning are now meaningless or absurd. This is one way of thinking about Blanchot's use of the term "disaster," though again it must be noted that the disaster is not, finally, situated within the historical process.

Fragmentary Writing

Fragmentary writing is neither negation nor affirmation but is situated between the two, within the neutral. Fragmentary writing is *outside* conventionally understood language. It is writing at the margins or rather writing that has abdicated the quest for a center and is thus marginal only with respect to conventional notions of expression. Because fragmentary writing neither affirms nor denies, it is unnecessary and inherently implausible. It is not something that could be said to "occur,' insofar as occurrence implies an end, a purpose. It is purposeless writing and seeks with infinite patience to dissolve the purposes of the instrumental world. A writing of the fragment must have some affinity with German philosopher Friedrich Nietzsche's "eternal return," for such a writing must "occur" always as if for the first time, without a past, without reference to any future that might be conceived as part of some progress toward an end, or *telos*, of history.

In fragmentary writing, no authorial "I" exists that might assume responsibility for the writing. Any such "I" is a mere fiction, for that which one

calls the "I" is merely a vessel for the eruption of language into the world. Thus to write *of* the disaster is to speak the disaster, to abdicate the "I" that would impose its illusion of purpose upon the world. Having been deprived of its relation to an author, fragmentary writing confronts the world as the perfectly arbitrary, thus erasing any possibility of presence. Rather, writing of the disaster is the writing of absence, of death.

Fragmentary writing employs words to invoke silence, the silence that is the death of meaning. Through paradox, through dissimulation, through the suppression of all pretension to represent reality (as in a mirror), it seeks to evoke a certain undertone—the cry of the heart that is embedded in the silence that surrounds and underlies all language. To write in this manner, Blanchot asserts, is to write without desire, to cultivate an almost mystical renunciation of the desiring self. This condition of renunciation Blanchot frequently refers to as belonging to passivity, to *patience*.

Related to this act of self-erasure is the issue of *seriousness*. Fragmentary writing is writing that refuses the serious, refuses to take itself seriously. A model of such a posture, frequently mentioned by Blanchot, is the Marquis de Sade, whose apparent seriousness is, properly understood, a subtle mockery of seriousness. Rather, de Sade is a master of detachment, of neutrality.

An important aspect of the neutrality of fragmentary writing is that it does not pretend to change anything, least of all the world. The fragment comes into play where progress, or the faith in progress, has collapsed, where all systems of thought and action cease to compel allegiance. The fragment makes no effort to modify systems of thought; it cannot be taught. Its passivity functions as a corrosive element, revealing the futility of all dominant disciplines and ideas. The fragment can belong to no theoretical structure and exists only in the in-between realm, in the space of nonrelation between our ideals and our practice. The fragment conceptualizes nothing. Faced with an event such as the Holocaust, which defies all efforts at conceptualization, the fragment can function ethically to heighten our awareness of the horror that cannot be expressed and that must not be reduced to the level of the merely conceptual lest the actuality of the horror be forgotten. For Blanchot, the Holocaust represents that point in history at which meaning is swallowed up, consumed in an apocalyptic fire that makes nonsense of historical progress. What remains in the wake of the Holocaust is silence.

Writing, Death, and the Child

Central also to Blanchot's concerns in *The Writing of the Disaster* is the relation between writing and death, or dying. To write the disaster is to think endlessly, just as to become aware of one's mortality is to know that one is endlessly dying. The disaster is thus always, like death, at the threshold of consciousness, of thought. To write of the disaster is to write (or to think) in the manner of one's dying. Just as death is the eclipse of purpose, of living to secure some purchase in the world for the self, so writing-as-dying is to abandon both purpose and power—the power to effect an alteration in the reality that impinges upon the self or ego. To write, Blanchot argues, is no longer to think of death as something awaiting us in the future but to think of it as that which has always already happened. This, too, is another way to understand the disaster, as the knowledge that death has already taken place, that it exists within people as a past—a past that people may recognize by the traces that it deposits, moments of forgetfulness. This awareness of death as *prior* to all experience is the realization that death is not personal—for individuality requires the projection of a future death, a unique lifeline. However, death is that which has always already happened; thus, death is profoundly impersonal and anonymous and so must the act of writing-as-dying be an anonymous writing.

Closely related to the theme of death is the figure of the *infans*, or child. One may begin to write or to speak authentically only when one has put to death the *infans* within oneself. The *infans* stands for that in each person which has not yet begun to speak; it is the child that each individual has been in the eyes and expectations of others—parents and society. That child is, in psychoanalytic terms, the narcissistic image or representation of the self that each person harbors. To remain a prisoner of this representation is to exist in a kind of limbo, from which the effort to escape can lead to madness. Yet to attempt to kill the *infans* is a glorious risk, even if in fact the *infans* cannot be killed.

Blanchot's Impact on Literature, Philosophy

In France, Blanchot's reputation as both a novelist and a literary theorist was established as early as the 1940's and has continued to grow over subsequent decades. Within a small but prestigious circle of literary artists and philosophers, Blanchot's influence in France has been direct and substantial. In the English-speaking world, his influence has been for the most part more indirect (and somewhat belated) but no less substantial.

As a forerunner of the *nouveau roman*, or New Novel, of the 1950's and 1960's, Blanchot's impact has been decisive. At least a decade before the appearance of the controversial novels of such practitioners and theorists of the New Novel as Alain Robbe-Grillet and Michel Butor, Blanchot's *récits* pioneered many of the techniques they employed. Among the techniques that the New Novel inherited by way of Blanchot (and, to some degree, Bataille) were the use of the fragment to undercut linear closure; the cultivation of an anonymous or impersonal narrative voice; the de-emphasizing of metaphor and figurative language generally; the radical questioning of identity and reduction of character; and the abandonment of any attempt at social relevance. In the English-speaking world, these techniques became widely dispersed but are especially evident in the works of such experimental novelists as Donald Barthleme and, more recently, Paul Auster (who translated some of Blanchot's writings).

In addition, Blanchot's influence as a literary theorist and philosopher can be discerned in the poststructuralist language theory of deconstruction, especially as practiced by Jacques Derrida and his disciples. Blanchot was among the first group of theorists to assimilate Alexandre Kojève's critique of the Hegelian dialectic and was also steeped in the works of late Romanticism, Nietzsche, Heidegger, and the European avant-garde, so he was in a unique position to draw together the various strands of what is now termed the poststructuralist critique of reason, or logocentrism, a critique shared by most poststructuralists. For Derrida and his many Anglo-

American deconstructionist followers, logocentrism is evident everywhere in the great tradition of Western philosophical discourse but especially in the traditional view of language, which presumes a real rather than a merely conventional relation between a signifier and that which it signifies. In opposition to this view, the deconstructionists establish a claim, already implicit in much of Blanchot's view of language, that any relation between language and the reality it describes is purely conventional and thus arbitrary. If this is true, then it follows that all interpretation of a signifying chain (a text) is equally arbitrary, itself a fiction. More radically, every sign is always already an interpretation of other signs, and there can be no escape from this play of signifiers. The result will be a criticism, much like Blanchot's, that regards any attempt to impose a unitary meaning upon a text as misguided and will celebrate those works of literary art that, like Blanchot's *récits*, seek to implode and dissolve the traditional conventions of representation.

Jack E. Trotter

Additional Reading

Bruns, Gerald L. *Maurice Blanchot: The Refusal of Philosophy*. Baltimore, Md.: The Johns Hopkins University Press, 1997. Bruns attempts to show that Maurice Blanchot's literary theory and practice may be understood as a type of philosophical anarchism. This is most apparent in Blanchot's fictive techniques, particularly his use of the fragmentary style. Bruns examines a number of important works, including *The Writing of the Disaster*, in some detail, and attempts to draw parallels between the literary and political concerns of the writer. Blanchot's influence on poststructuralist theorists such as Jacques Derrida and Jean-Luc Nancy is also discussed.

Hartman, Geoffrey H. *Beyond Formalism: Literary Essays, 1958-1970*. New Haven, Conn.: Yale University Press, 1970. In an essay entitled "Maurice Blanchot: Philosopher-Novelist," first published in 1960, Hartman introduces Blanchot's work to an English-speaking readership. Hartman has since become associated with the Yale school of deconstruction, and

readers of a literary-critical bent will find this essay an interesting example of the manner in which Blanchot's criticism was received by an American academic at a time when the New Criticism, or formalism, was still dominant.

Hill, Leslie. *Blanchot: Extreme Contemporary*. New York: Routledge, 1997. Hill's study seeks to provide a comprehensive view of both the life and works of Blanchot and is especially strong in demonstrating his philosophical debt to Georges Bataille and Emmanuel Lévinas. While much of this study will be accessible only to those readers already well-versed in literary theory and philosophy, the first chapter, entitled "An Intellectual Itinerary," will be of use to anyone seeking a detailed account of Blanchot's political activities in the 1930's, including his connections with the French fascists.

Mehlman, Jeffrey. *Legacies of Anti-Semitism in France*. Minneapolis: University of Minnesota Press, 1983. This highly controversial work includes a chapter entitled "Blanchot at *Combat*: Of Literature and Terror," in which Mehlman attempts to establish ideological connections between Blanchot's early political writings with rightist journals such as *Combat* in 1930's France and his later fictional and especially theoretical works. Mehlman's essential argument is that Blanchot's early advocacy of terrorism against the prewar French regime is later transmuted into a kind of philosophical terrorism.

Murray, Kevin D. S., ed. *The Judgment of Paris: Recent French Theory in a Local Context*. North Sydney, Australia: Allen & Unwin, 1992. This collection includes a highly accessible essay by David Odell entitled "An Introduction to Maurice Blanchot," which provides a brief but insightful overview of Blanchot's career as writer and theorist, focusing particularly upon the influences of Hegel and Bataille. His most interesting claim is that Blanchot's work is best understood as a gnostic revision of Hegelian dialectic, especially the late theoretical meditation, *The Writing of the Disaster*.

Jack E. Trotter

Boethius

Combining Greek philosophy and his Christian Roman heritage, Boethius articulated a solution to the contradiction between divine omniscience and the freedom of human will that laid the foundation for medieval thought.

Principal philosophical works: *De consolatione philosophiae*, 523 (*The Consolation of Philosophy*, late ninth century).

Born: c. 480; Rome, Italy
Died: 524; Pavia, Italy

Early Life

Anicius Manlius Severinus Boethius was born into the patrician Roman family of the Anicii, whose members figure prominently in Roman history as far back as the Third Macedonian War in the second century B.C.E. The Manlius and Severinus families also could boast of eminent forebears. Boethius's own father held several important offices under Odovacar, the first Germanic ruler of the Italian peninsula. In 480, the supposed year of Boethius's birth, the old Roman families were adjusting and contributing to the reign of a "barbarian" king. When Boethius's father died, perhaps in the early 490's, another distinguished Roman, Quintus Aurelius Memmius Symmachus, became the boy's guardian.

An old tradition that Boethius was sent to Athens to study Greek has no basis in fact; he might as well have been sent to Alexandria, which by the late fifth century had replaced Athens as a center of Greek studies. Wherever he studied, it is clear that Boethius mastered Greek at a time when it was becoming a lost skill in Rome, and in the process, he developed a strong interest in the great Greek philosophers on whom Roman thinkers had depended heavily for centuries. It is likely that Plato's *Politeia* (c. 388-366 B.C.E.; *Republic*, 1701) convinced him of the advisability of philosophers entering public life, and he combined an ambitious program of study and writing with public service. As a young man, he married Rusticiana, his guardian's daughter, with whom he had two sons. Boethius may have met the Ostrogothic king Theodoric, who had displaced Odovacar, in 500 when the ruler, who maintained his headquarters at Ravenna, visited Rome. In any event, many of the traditional Roman offices persisted, and Boethius rose to the consulship in 510, when he was about thirty.

Life's Work

Boethius's earlier writings cannot be dated with any confidence. Of his five theological tractates, *De Trinitate* (*On the Trinity*), dedicated to his father-in-law, Symmachus, shows his determination to use reason in support of a doctrine he recognized as standing firmly on a foundation of Christian faith. His interest in harmonizing revealed religion with the discoveries of pre-Christians thinkers foreshadows the work of the medieval Scholastic philosophers many centuries later. *On the Trinity* represents his attempt to reconcile for intellectual Christians the seemingly contradictory doctrines that God was one but consisted of three persons.

In addition to the tractates, Boethius wrote on all four subjects of the ancient quadrivium—arithmetic, music, geometry, and astronomy—although his works on the last two subjects have not survived. His most voluminous extant works, however, deal with one of the subjects of the trivium: logic. He translated treatises by Aristotle and Porphyry, wrote commentaries on these works as well as on Cicero's *Topica* (c. 45-44 B.C.E.; *Topics*, 1848) and produced original monographs on such subjects as categorical syllogisms and systems of logical classification. His overriding ambition, to harmonize the philosophies of Plato and Aristotle, probably bogged down amid the pressures of his public career.

After serving as consul, he became a Roman senator according to ancient tradition, and in 520 or 522, he obtained an important post with authority over most other government positions, the *magister officiorum*, or master of offices. This appointment would have involved moving to Theodoric's court at Ravenna and leaving behind the library at Rome that had sustained his scholarly endeavors. Also in 522, his sons were both appointed as consuls, although Boethius himself at this time could not have been much more than forty years of age.

With family prestige at this high point, Boethius was drawn into the struggle between Italy's Ostrogothic king and the Roman senate. Theodoric, who had been educated in Constantinople and who owed his kingship to the eastern Roman emperor Zeno, brought with him a substantial retinue of his Germanic brethren, many of them subscribers to the Arian heresy, which held—contrary to the Catholic position established at the Council of Nicea in 325 C.E.—that Jesus was not coeternal with God. Theodoric's Roman subjects, as well as the emperor of the eastern Roman Empire (technically his ruler), were Catholic. Despite the potential for ethnic and religious conflict, Theodoric established a reputation for tolerance, impartiality, and devotion to the goals of peace and prosperity. Yet he also imprisoned, tortured, and eventually executed the renowned scholar and previously trusted official, Boethius.

Like philosophically minded civil servants before and after his time, Boethius found much to distress him in government, including rampant corruption. "Private pillage and public tributes," as he put it, depleted the treasury, and when he interceded to protect principled officials from the clutches of greedy courtiers, he made influential enemies. His troubles mounted when he rose to the defense of a fellow former consul and senator named Albinus, who was suspected of treason. It appears that Boethius was motivated primarily by a desire to defend the reputation of the senate as a whole from suspicions of complicity in the alleged treachery. Boethius apparently admitted to the suppression of evidence that he considered damaging to the integrity of the senate, a course of action inevitably leading to charges against him. Accused of plotting against Theodoric in favor of Justin I, the reigning eastern emperor, Boethius was conveyed to Pavia in 522 and imprisoned there. Under the strain of a conviction he considered entirely unjustified, he produced his masterpiece, *The Consolation of Philosophy*. If his previous writings and his government service had made him a notable man, this work commanded the attention of the West for more than a thousand years thereafter.

Although conceived as a tribute to philosophy and exhibiting features of his plan to synthesize the best in Greek philosophy, *The Consolation of*

Boethius. *(Library of Congress)*

Philosophy endures as a human record of doubt, discouragement, and suffering transformed by a rethinking of basic philosophical tenets into a triumph of the spirit. Even more than his Christian faith, philosophy sustained Boethius in his two years of confinement. To dramatize the conflicts within him, Boethius resolves his mental and emotional state into two components represented by the discouraged prisoner and an awesome visitor to his cell, Lady Philosophy. She listens to his complaints and gradually brings him around to the reaffirmation and fuller understanding of conviction, which his ordeal has undermined. At length she convinces Boethius that no human or divine necessity stands in the way of the most valid exercise of the will: the pursuit of virtue.

Though presumably reconciled to his unjust sentence, Boethius reached no reconciliation with his accusers, and he died in prison in 524, either from the effects of torture or by explicit order. Almost immediately, his friends and admirers began to regard him as a martyr for his faith; his local followers in Pavia acclaimed him as a saint. The existing evidence suggests that he suffered and died not for specifically religious convictions but for moral and political ones. Even after his other works ceased to be generally read, *The Consolation of Philosophy* continued to attract readers and translators. Two of England's greatest monarchs, Alfred the Great in the ninth century and Queen Elizabeth I seven centuries later, became philosopher-kings enough to make their own translations. Like his beloved Plato, Boethius had found a form for his philosophy that earned for it the status of a literary classic.

Influence

Although Boethius possessed both literary ability and the discipline of a professional writer, it took imprisonment to make him a philosophical poet. His earliest admirers valued not only his thought but also the integrity and courage that shine through both metrical and prose sections of *The Consolation of Philosophy*. These readers, members of an increasingly Latinate culture, could hardly have appreciated fully his efforts to keep the West in touch with Greek antiquity. At the same time, the rise of vernacular tongues and the Catholic Church's adaptation of Latin to its own purposes

meant that the classical Latin verse forms that Boethius could still practice proficiently became a lost art. In this sense, he can be considered the last of the classical Latin poets as well as one of the last representatives of Greco-Roman culture.

Boethius became that quintessentially medieval scholar, the Catholic theologian, and although little of the theologian shows through in his last work, there is not the slightest reason to believe that he ever abjured Christianity. On the contrary, he was believed to have been put to death for trying to protect the Church from persecution by heretics. None of his medieval enthusiasts saw anything remarkable in his exclusion of specifically Christian doctrine from *The Consolation of Philosophy*. He was simply operating as a philosopher and thus keeping theology and philosophy distinct.

In time, Boethius's versatility was bound to recommend him to scholars, among them the recoverers of the Greek heritage that had slipped almost completely from sight in the centuries between the breakup of the Roman Empire and its comeback through Arabic sources beginning in the eleventh century. Successive waves of intellectuals, from the Scholastics of the twelfth and thirteenth centuries to the scientists of the sixteenth and seventeenth centuries, were in a better position than were early medieval people to understand the import of Boethius's pursuit of Greek learning. By modern times, Boethius could be seen as a pivot between the ancient and medieval worlds generally, between classical and Christian Latinity, and between pre-Christian Hellenism and Renaissance Humanism.

Robert P. Ellis

The Consolation of Philosophy

Type of philosophy: Ethics, philosophy of religion
First transcribed: De consolatione philosophiae, 523 (English translation, late ninth century)
Principal ideas advanced:
◇ Boethius, a political prisoner, complains to Philosophy, personified as a fair lady, that virtue is not rewarded; he questions God's justice.

◇ Philosophy answers that God is the source of all things and that, through study of God's nature, Boethius can rediscover his own true nature.

◇ Human possessions come through good fortune; anyone who realizes this and who does not become attached to material possessions can lose them with equanimity.

◇ Because nature is always inconstant, people should seek to be masters of themselves and to bear changes of fortune with a calm mind.

◇ Truth, happiness, and even divinity may be found within a person; one should exercise one's God-given freedom to raise oneself in accordance with the vision of the divine nature.

This classic of prison literature bears all the marks of great Roman philosophical writing. Formulated as a dialogue between the prisoner Boethius and Lady Philosophy, it exhibits the unique Roman quality of combining literary appeal with technical philosophy. Philosophy in Greece was for the most part academic and theoretical, but when transplanted to Rome, it became the basis for a way of life, as did Stoicism. It is often said that philosophy in Rome was eclectic and unoriginal; it is more accurate to say that the original Roman element was to mold philosophy into forms that could deal effectively with serious and perennial human problems. Like other philosophical writers of the era, Boethius took full advantage of his knowledge of Plato, Aristotle, the Stoics, and Neoplatonism, blending classical sources as the means to develop his own views. His attempt was not to construct a novel metaphysics but to apply philosophical views to the solution of pressing problems—particularly his own need to reconcile his fall from prominence into political imprisonment that would eventually result in his death.

Boethius opens with a lament about the sudden reversal of his circumstances, a lot that has reduced him from the role of a consul to that of a prisoner in a dungeon near Milan. As he accuses Fortune of being fickle, Philosophy, in the form of a fair lady, appears to him in his cell and attempts to answer his doubts about the justice of the world. She joins him in lamenting his present plight but tells him it is time to search for healing rather than to complain. She chides him for his lack of courage in his present state, reminding him of Plato's struggle and of Socrates' valiant death. Philosophers, she tells him, have always been at variance with the ways of humankind and therefore have always been subject to attack. To oppose evil people is the chief aim of all philosophers, a course that cannot help leading them into trouble repeatedly. Therefore, philosophers must learn to reconcile their lives to fate, to conquer the fear of death, and to show themselves unyielding to good and bad alike.

The Question of Justice

Ever since human beings have been able to speak, they have complained that their just lives have not been properly rewarded, either by God or by their fellow humans. Boethius continues this complaint, that his prison sufferings prove the injustice of the world when they are considered as the reward for the just life he has lived. Wicked people make attacks on his virtue, and all because he is too honest ever to have engaged in deceit. Why does God allow a wicked person to prevail against innocence? Echoing the biblical Job and a chorus of others, Boethius questions God, whose ways are unnatural to him. "If God is, whence come evil things? If he is not, whence came good?" Thus Boethius phrases the age-old question of why evil exists. Why should he be exiled, condemned to death without an opportunity to defend himself, because of his too great zeal for the Roman senate?

Furthermore, Boethius argues, Philosophy has also been dishonored in this process, for Boethius has never sought perishable riches but has instead "followed after God." Thus, in his misfortune, Philosophy's wisdom is also brought under question. In return for kindness he has received persecutions. Even his reputation has been stained. Honest people are crushed with fear; wicked people oppress good people and prosper by doing so. At this point, Philosophy scolds Boethius mildly: She tells him that his mind is so beset by passions that nothing can come close enough to him to bring any healing. Philosophy then asks the basic question on which the argument will rest: Is the universe guided by a rule of reason, or are its events random and guided by chance? If it is the latter, then no explanations for misfortune can be given. If it is the former, however, then one can question the reason and hope for a reasonable reply.

First, one must ask if all things have an aim and end. Is there a goal to which all nature tends? Boethius and his questioner agree that all things have their source in God. Then, if the beginning can be known, why not also the end of all things? Even more important than such cosmic questions, which establish the framework for a person's life, is the fact that Boethius seems to have forgotten who he is and what his role as a human being can be. He can rediscover his true nature, fortunately, through one spark within him: his knowledge of the hand that guides the universe. Through his knowledge of God and God's purpose within the world, Boethius can perhaps recover a true knowledge of his own nature.

Fortune, Change, and Death

What needs to be considered first, Philosophy urges, is the way of Fortune. Life cannot stand still; change must be understood. Anyone who complains over lost possessions has mistakenly assumed them to be his private property rather than the gift of Fortune. To rise to the top is not a guarantee that the next phase may not be to sink to the bottom. Fortune, not one's own just deserts, may bring one alternately high and low. These are the rules of the game, and understanding them prevents unnecessary misery. If one is violently attached to one's position and possessions, they do not really bring satisfaction but cause one to desire more. If one is not so attached, then one will not be so disturbed by the loss of position and possessions.

Nature constantly changes. Why, then, should humans alone wish to be exempt from cyclical flow? One thing alone is certain: Nothing that is brought to birth is fixed or constant. Because these are nature's ways, nothing is wretched unless one thinks it so. On the other hand, if one bears everything that comes with a calm mind, then one will find one's lot blessed. Why seek happiness without, when it really lies within? If one is the master of oneself, then one possesses all that it is important not to lose, and even fickle Fortune cannot take that from one. Fear alone prevents a person from being happy. Self-mastery excludes fear, and only a life based on inner calm-

ness can ignore the raging passions that always threaten to destroy. In the light of this knowledge, why would anyone embrace as his good anything outside the self?

No fame or power appears lasting when compared with eternity. Death has no regard for high position, however great, but claims high and low alike. Even ill fortune has its blessings: It distinguishes true friends from doubtful acquaintances. The loss of riches is a gain because it reveals one's true friends, a possession greater than riches. Love rules the universe, and people can be happy if their hearts are ruled by love. Happiness is, after all, a person's highest good. Friends, who are one chief source of happiness, depend upon virtue more than upon Fortune's uncontrollable ways. They may argue over means, but they agree in their highest good and happiness.

The person who would gain true power must subdue his own wild thoughts—so Philosophy consoles Boethius. Because God is humanity's author, no one is degenerate or base except the person who leaves the Creator. Because God and the highest good form a union, every happy person is, in happiness, divine. If it is truth for which one searches, one should turn the light of an inward gaze upon oneself. It is of no use to search elsewhere: Truth, happiness, and even divinity may be found within human beings themselves. God governs the universe for the highest good. Anyone who turns thought away from the light above is in danger of losing whatever he or she has won below, having lost a sense of direction.

The Reason for Evil

Next comes the age-old question: If there exists a good ruler of the world, why do evils exist and, what is worse, seem to go unpunished? Philosophy answers: Power is never lacking to the good, while the wicked are weak. Yet all people, good and bad alike, seek to arrive at the good, although by different means. Bad people seek the same ends that good ones do, but they do it through cupidity. Such is the weakness of wicked people that it is hard to allow that they are human beings at all. The power of evil is no power at all, especially because nothing evil ever reaches happiness. The wicked person is oppressed by passions; all good people become happy by virtue of the very fact that they are good. Therefore, as honesty is itself the reward of the honest, so wickedness is itself the punishment of the wicked. The person who loses this inner goodness ceases to be a human being and turns into a beast.

One should love good people, for it is their due, and show pity for the evil, because to be oppressed by the disease of feeble wickedness is much more worthy of pity than of persecution. Providence is a guide for all, and there is no such thing as chance. Yet all who have reason also have the freedom of desiring and of refusing, although the working of human reason cannot approach the directness of divine foreknowledge. Such foreknowledge does not bring necessity to bear upon things as they come to pass. A person may sometimes rise to see all things as God might see them and sometimes sinks down and fails to grasp such connections at all. That person's freedom is preserved by a lack of vision.

A Difference in Perspective
Near the end, having raised the question of a divine vision of all things, Boethius turns to the question of whether there are universals, and it is here that much of the famous medieval controversy takes its start. What is comprehensible to the senses and to the imagination cannot be universal, yet reason holds to be universal what is really an individual matter comprehensible to the senses. It sees from a general point of view what is comprehensible to the senses and to the imagination, yet this is not a knowledge of real universals but only a way reason has of comprehending. Nothing set in time, for instance, can at one moment grasp the whole space of its lifetime. God, of course, sees all things in his eternal present, but human beings do not. Seen from God's perspective, an event may seem necessary: When examined in its own nature, it seems free and unrestrained.

In this dialogue, Philosophy has the last word, and that refers to the theological problem of the difference in perspective between God and humankind. Consolation comes in trying to raise oneself to see the events of the world as God views them. Dejection, then, is caused by a too limited, a too human perspective; Philosophy's

job is to raise human sights, to give people divine vision. Since Philosophy can accomplish this, she is humanity's hope of consolation. Any individual's turn of fortune is not understandable in isolation; it must be placed in the total scheme of things, and to do this is to philosophize. Philosophy does not change events or reverse Fortune, but it does provide the understanding with which the events of life may be not only accepted but also enjoyed. When Fortune reverses itself, the first cry is for restoration. Philosophy teaches that humanity's chief need is not for change but for understanding.

Impact in the Middle Ages
The Consolation of Philosophy was widely known in the Middle Ages, and Boethius, in fact, was the source of several of the prominent philosophical questions of that later period. It is still debated, however, whether Boethius was himself a Christian. It seems likely that he was, although his writings contain no specific Christian doctrine. Perhaps, like the early writings of Saint Augustine, his intellectual discussions were intended to be strictly philosophical, even though his formal religion was Christianity. As Richard Green put it in his introduction to his translation of *The Consolation of Philosophy*, "As a Christian, Boethius had to arrive at Augustine's affirmation of divine omniscience and human freedom; as a logician and speculative philosopher, he formulated a solution, based on the difference between human and divine knowledge, which was to be authoritative for centuries to come."

Although Boethius's work has indeed exerted enormous influence for centuries, it is largely neglected today—more often read in the contexts of historical or literary studies rather than within professional philosophical circles. According to the usual standards of philosophical argument, no real argument or analysis supports the points introduced. In some sense, there is not a novel doctrine here; all parts may be traced to preceding classical sources. Nevertheless, *The Consolation of Philosophy* remains a classic, both because of its historical situation, in that it came to be a source for philosophical argument, and because it raises an interconnected series of important philosophical and theological problems. Its answers are not original, but they are classical and the problems themselves perennial. It is perhaps for this reason that the work's influence has extended so broadly and has lasted so long; to this day, readers of Boethius's work extract from it insights that they can associate with their own lives.

Frederick Sontag

Additional Reading

Barrett, Helen M. *Boethius: Some Aspects of His Times and Work*. 1940. Reprint. New York: Russell and Russell, 1965. This book, one of the older works on Boethius, provides a solid historical survey, sets Boethius firmly in this context, and interprets the scanty details of his life in a balanced and sensible way.

Chadwick, Henry. *Boethius: The Consolations of Music, Logic, Theology, and Philosophy*. Oxford: Clarendon Press, 1981. Unlike other writers, who have tended to concentrate on the Christian, the poet, the philosopher, or the educational theorist, Chadwick aims to show Boethius's career as a unified whole. He has succeeded in writing the most comprehensive book about Boethius's life and work.

Gibson, Margaret, ed. *Boethius: His Life, Thought, and Influence*. Oxford: Basil Blackwell, 1981. This book contains a variety of Boethian material, including two valuable biographical essays. John Matthews studies Boethius as a thoroughgoing Roman affirming ancient traditions and offices against the Ostrogothic king. Helen Kirkby stresses Boethius's determination to continue the Roman habit of enriching Latin culture with Greek philosophical and educational thought.

Hoenen, Maarten J., and Lodi Nauta, eds. *Boethius in the Middle Ages: Latin and Vernacular Traditions of the Consolatio Philosophiae*. New York: Brill, 1997. A collection of essays that focus on how views of the *Consolatio* have changed. The first part of the book explores the Latin tradition, while other sections are devoted to the vernacular traditions.

McInery, Ralph. *Boethius and Aquinas*. Washington, D.C.: Catholic University of America Press, 1990. Boethius, the last Roman and first Scholastic philosopher, came down to modern thought through his primary medieval commentator, Saint Thomas Aquinas. McInery refutes claims of modern scholars that Aquinas's understanding of Boethius is faulty, concluding that Aquinas correctly understood Boethius. For advanced undergraduates.

Pieper, Josef. *Scholasticism: Personalities and Problems of Medieval Philosophy*. New York: McGraw-Hill, 1964. The author argues that Boethius, a century after Saint Augustine, still lived intellectually within classical philosophy and politically within the Roman Empire, although his listeners and readers did not. Boethius, Pieper notes, was the first thinker to turn to those who had come from the north into the ancient world.

Procopius. *Procopius, with an English Translation by H. B. Dewing*. London: W. Heinemann, 1914-1940. Volumes 3 and 4 of this set include Procopius's *The Gothic War* and incorporate for the first time details of Boethius's life in the record of political struggle in the Italian peninsula. Procopius was a Byzantine historian whose life overlapped that of Boethius.

Reiss, Edmund. *Boethius*. Boston: Twayne, 1982. Reiss argues the case against accepting too literally the autobiographical details in what he regards as a highly polished work of fictional art. He tends to reject the assumption that the quotations and other specific knowledge demonstrated in *The Consolation of Philosophy* constitute a feat of memory by a prisoner without access to a library.

Scott, Jamie S. *Christians and Tyrants: The Prison Testimonies of Boethius, Thomas More, and Dietrich Bonhoeffer*. New York: P. Lang, 1995. A collection of material from three philosophical giants that was produced while they were imprisoned.

Robert P. Ellis, updated by Chris Moose

Saint Bonaventure

Bonaventure combined an early commitment to the ideals of Saint Francis of Assisi with great preaching and teaching abilities; he wrote several works on spiritual life and recodified the constitution of the Franciscans. Bonaventure proved himself a defender of both human and divine truth and an outstanding witness for mystic and Christian wisdom.

Principal philosophical works: *Breviloquium*, 1257 (English translation, 1946); *Itinerarium mentis in Deum*, 1259 (*The Journey of the Soul to God*, 1937; also known as *The Wind's Road to God*, 1953; better known as *The Journey of the Mind to God*, 1993); *De triplici via*, 1260 (*The Enkindling of Love, Also Called the Triple Way*, 1956); *De perfectione vita ad sorores*, 1260 (*Holiness of Life*, 1923); *Legenda maior*, 1263 (*Here Begynneth the Life of the Gloryous Confessoure of Oure Lorde Ihesu Criste Seynt Francis*, 1515; also known as *The Life of the Most Holy Father Saint Francis*, 1635; better known as *The Life of Saint Francis of Assisi*, 1868); *De sex alis seraphim*, 1263 (*The Virtues of a Religious Superior: Instructions by the Seraphic Doctor*, 1920); *Collationes de Decem Praeceptis*, 1267 (*St. Bonaventure's Collations on the Ten Commandments*, 1995); *Collationes de septem donis Spiritus Sanctis*, 1268 (English translation, 1950); *Collationes in Hexaemeron*, 1273 (*Collations on the Six Days*, 1970); *De reductione artium ad theologiam*, before 1274 (*On the Recution of the Arts to Theology*, 1938); *The Works of Bonaventure: Cardinal, Seraphic Doctor, and Saint*, 1960-1970 (5 volumes).

Born: 1217 or 1221; Bagnoregio, Papal States (now Italy)
Died: July 15, 1274; Lyons

Early Life

Bonaventure was born either in 1217 or 1221 in Bagnoregio—in the Viterbo Province, Papal States. Not much is known of his family. His father was a medical doctor, Giovanni di Fidanza. (Fidanza was not a family name, but the name of a grandfather.) His mother was called Maria di Ritello, or simply Ritella. He was very ill as a boy and was said to have been saved from death by the intercession of Saint Francis of Assisi. Bonaventure recorded his cure in his life of Saint Francis. It is recorded that the young Bonaventure received his early schooling at the Franciscan friary in Bagnoregio. He showed scholastic ability and was sent to study at the University of Paris in 1235 or 1236.

It was in Paris that Bonaventure met many of the Franciscan friars and entered the Franciscan order (in either 1238 or 1243). Called Giovanni since birth, he received the name Bonaventure soon after entering the order. In accordance with the Franciscan regulations of the time, he was considered a member of the Roman province of his birth. After receiving a master of arts degree from the University of Paris in 1243, he studied theology at the Franciscan school in Paris for the next five years, under Alexander of Hales and John of La Rochelle until their deaths in 1245. He probably continued with the masters Eudes Rigauld and William of Meliton; later, he was influenced by the Dominican Guerric of Saint-Quentin and the secular master Guiard of León.

During these years, Bonaventure began teaching the brothers in the local Franciscan friary. In 1248, he became a teacher of Scripture, lecturing on the Gospel of Luke and other portions of the Bible. From 1250 or 1251 to 1253, he lectured on the *Sententiarum libri IV* (1148-1151; *The Books of Opinions of Peter Lombard*, 1970, 4 volumes; commonly known as *Sentences*) at the University of Paris. This work was a medieval theology textbook written by Peter Lombard, a twelfth cen-

Saint Bonaventure. *(Library of Congress)*

Yet the secular masters opposed the Mendicants, and although Bonaventure presented at least three series of disputed questions in Paris between 1253 and 1257, some authors claim that he was not accepted into the guild, or corporation, of the masters of the university until October 23, 1257.

Life's Work

The years between 1248 and 1257 proved to be a productive time for Bonaventure. He produced many works, not only commentaries on the Bible (not all of which have survived) and the *Sentences* but also the *Breviloquium*, which provided a summary of his theology, showing his deep understanding of Scripture, early church fathers (especially Saint Augustine), and philosophers (particularly Aristotle). He adapted the older Scholastic traditions, perfecting and organizing a fresh synthesis. Bonaventure urged that the theologian be allowed to draw on logic and all the profane sciences. He thought of truth as the way to the love of God. In 1256, he and the Dominican Thomas Aquinas defended the Mendicants (Franciscans and Dominicans) from an attack by William of Saint-Amour, a university teacher who accused the Mendicants of defaming the Gospel by their practice of poverty and wished to prevent them from attaining any teaching position.

The Franciscan order itself was experiencing an internal struggle, between those who wanted a more rigorous poverty and those who wanted to relax the strict views of poverty established by Saint Francis. Pope Alexander IV commanded the minister general of the Franciscans, John of Parma, to resign his office. A chapter gathering was called at Rome late in January, 1257. Because of his defense of the Franciscans and the fact that he was an exemplary person patterning himself after Saint Francis, Bonaventure was elected minister general on February 2, 1257. He was to hold that post for seventeen years.

By placating the Spirituals (who opted for a more rigorous poverty) and reproving the Relaxati, Bonaventure reformed the order in the spirit of Saint Francis. The restoration of peace and reconciliation of opponents, a special talent of Bonaventure, was accomplished through extensive visits to all the provinces of the order and through his own practice of the Franciscan way

tury Italian theologian. Bonaventure's commentaries on Scripture and the *Sentences* enabled him to receive the licentiate and doctorate from the chancellor of the University of Paris. The chancellor acted in the name of the Church; therefore, this licentiate allowed Bonaventure to teach anywhere in the Christian world at the end of the 1252-1253 academic year. He was placed in charge of the Franciscan school in Paris, where he taught until 1257.

Paris at that time was a hotbed for theological study. Thomas Aquinas had arrived to study in 1252; he and Bonaventure became good friends.

of life. It was during these travels, despite health problems, that his reputation as a preacher was earned. His election to office had ended his teaching career, but it created preaching opportunities. Throughout Europe, his eloquence, knowledge, and simplicity caught the attention of high dignitaries and the laity. He also administered the order, presiding over the general chapters and guiding the continued growth of the Franciscans.

Bonaventure's new tasks did not prevent him from continuing his writing. In his visits to the provinces in October, 1259, he stopped at La Verna. There he wrote *The Journey of the Mind to God*. At this time, without ceasing to be a Scholastic, Bonaventure became a mystic, aligning himself more clearly with the inner life of Saint Francis. He merged Augustine's intellectual contemplation of truth with the Dionysian notion of truth as the ecstatic knowledge of God. He used as his model Saint Francis, whose vision of the seraphim at La Verna had shown how the heights of contemplation could be reached. Bonaventure also had the example of Brother Giles of Assisi, although to a lesser degree than Saint Francis. He wrote other works in this period, including *The Enkindling of Love, Also Called the Triple Way* and *Holiness of Life*.

In 1260, Bonaventure was in France preparing for the Pentecost Chapter at Narbonne, which was to codify the Franciscan ordinances into a new set of constitutions. It was this chapter that charged him with writing a new biography of Saint Francis. To gather material, Bonaventure visited all the places that had been significant to Francis and interviewed those of the early friars who were still alive. While working on this project, he presented himself to the new pope, Urban IV, elected in August, 1261. Late in that year or in the following year, Bonaventure was forced to submit the previous minister general, John of Parma, to a trial because of John's continued adherence to Joachism. On April 8, 1263, Bonaventure was in Padua for the transferral of the relics of Saint Anthony, and on May 20, he was in Pisa for a general chapter where some forty liturgical statutes and rubrics were introduced, ending about fifty years of work in the Franciscan order. Bonaventure gave each of the thirty-four provincials present a copy of his new *The Life of Saint Francis of Assisi*. That year, he also wrote *The Virtues of a Religious Superior: Instructions by the Seraphic Doctor*.

In 1264, he spent some time at the papal court, and in the spring, he gave a sermon on the Body of Christ at a consistory of Urban IV. In March, 1265, he was at Perugia to present himself to the new pope, Clement IV. In November, the new pope nominated Bonaventure to be Archbishop of York, but he refused the post. At the general chapter at Paris, May 16, 1266, Bonaventure continued to correct abuses in the order, especially those regarding matters of poverty. The chapter also ordered that all other biographies of Francis be destroyed because Bonaventure had provided a new one.

Until as late as mid-1268, Bonaventure lived at a small friary in Mantessur-Seine, France, where he continued his ascetical writings and preached at the university. His Lenten conferences of 1267 (on the Ten Commandments) and 1268 (on the gifts of the Holy Spirit) attacked current trends. On July 8, 1268, he was in Rome receiving the Archconfraternity of the Gonfalonieri into spiritual communion with the Franciscans, staying in Italy through the chapter of Assisi in May. When he returned to Paris, he found that Gerard of Abbeville, a teacher of theology, had renewed the charge of William of Saint-Amour against the Mendicants. Bonaventure responded by upholding the Christian faith while denouncing unorthodox views in a work that was not only a refutation of heretical opinions but also the presentation of a positive theology of religious life in imitation of Christ. It showed that Bonaventure was less interested in external regulations than building up an inner spirit of prayer and devotion and creating right attitudes using the examples of Christ and Francis. Here one can see Bonaventure's doctrine of illumination, discussed in *The Journey of the Mind to God*, in operation: the cooperation given the soul when it acts as the image of God.

In June, 1272, Bonaventure was in Lyons for the Pentecostal General Chapter. The following spring, 1273, he was in Paris for the last time; there, he began work on *Collations on the Six Days*, his theological testament to refute those who exaggerated the rationalism of Aristotle in opposition to the inspiration of the Scriptures. In this same year, Pope Gregory X named him the Cardinal Bishop of Albano, Italy. He proceeded with the pope to Lyons for the Second Council of Lyons and was consecrated as bishop November 11 or 12, 1273. In the capacity of legate, Bonaventure helped the pope prepare for the Council of Lyons, which opened on May 7, 1274. To continue his work at the council, he resigned as minister general of the Franciscans. Bonaventure continued to lead in the reform of the church, reconciling the secular (parish) clergy with the Mendicants. He preached at least twice at the council and effected a brief reunion of the Greek church with Rome.

Bonaventure died unexpectedly on July 15, 1274, leaving his last work unfinished. He was buried on July 15 in the Franciscan church in Lyons, with the pope attending. At the fifth session of the council, July 16, all priests of the world were ordered to celebrate a mass for his soul.

The impression Bonaventure made on contemporaries is summarized in the notes of the Council of Lyons, which indicate sorrow at his death. He was canonized on April 14, 1482, by Pope Sixtus IV, who also enrolled him with the mass and office of a confessor bishop. On March 14, 1588, another Franciscan pope, Sixtus V, gave Bonaventure the designation Doctor of the Church. In 1434, his body was transferred to the church dedicated to Saint Francis in Lyons, with an arm taken to his native Bagnoregio. During the Huguenot uprising in France, his body, except the head, was destroyed by fire. His head was destroyed by fire during the French Revolution.

Influence

Bonaventure is properly considered the second father of the Franciscans and a prince of mystics. He personified the ideals of Saint Francis of Assisi in teaching, in preaching, in writing, and in living his life. He had an immediate and a lasting influence on the Scholastics of the thirteenth century. He was an influential guide and teacher of spiritual life, particularly in Germany and the Netherlands. His influence has been maintained through the Roman College of Saint Bonaventure, founded by Pope Sixtus V in 1587. He was depicted in medieval art, and modern scholars consider him one of the foremost men of his age, a true contemporary of Saint Thomas Aquinas.

Mary-Emily Miller

The Journey of the Mind to God

Type of philosophy: Epistemology, metaphysics, philosphical psychology
First transcribed: Itinerarium mentis in Deum, 1259 (*The Journey of the Soul to God*, 1937; also known as *The Wind's Road to God*, 1953; better known as *The Journey of the Mind to God*, 1993)
Principal ideas advanced:

◇ The six stages of the soul's powers correspond to the six stages of the ascension unto God.
◇ God is reflected in the traces in the sensible world.
◇ In considering the powers of the self, through self-love, self-knowledge, and memory, the mind comes closer to God.
◇ Memory, intelligence, and will are recognized as reflecting God's trinitarian nature.
◇ By disciplined contemplation, we are led even closer to the divine.
◇ In recognizing the necessity of God's being for our understanding, the mind's work is done.
◇ The final stage is the mind's abandonment of intellectual powers in the mystical knowledge of God.

Both the size and the title of Saint Bonaventure's most famous little work belie its contents. From its diminutive size, one might take it to be a meditation on some single point; from its title, one might easily come to think of it as vague and mystical. Actually the opposite of both of these common impressions is the case. *The Journey of the Mind to God* belongs in the company of the *Summa Theologiae* (c. 1265-1273; *Summa Theologica*, 1911-1921) of Saint Thomas Aquinas, although its brevity indicates the quite different temper of its author. Bonaventure, the "Seraphic Doctor," does not use the elaborate compendium method. Yet in brief compass, he presents a view of nature, humanity, and God no less comprehensive than that contained in a many-volumed work.

As to its "mystical" qualities, this work does reflect classical mysticism but Bonaventure's presentation of this viewpoint is both detailed and highly technical. To sketch completely the structure that Bonaventure outlines would require a quite detailed study. It is rational in every detail—right up to the point at which reason finds its own end and realizes its own boundaries. Reason will be left behind, and ecstatic vision will become the goal, but this does not transpire until the very peak of possible human understanding has been reached. Only when reason has done its utmost at description and explanation can a way be seen to transcend reason. In this brief work, what we find is an elaborate, intricate, and technical view, rational to its core, but aimed from the beginning at finding reason's limiting point in order thereby to leave it behind.

What is perhaps hardest for the modern mind to grasp is that Bonaventure both begins and ends with God. The modern prejudice that must be overcome here is the same one that plagues Saint Anselm's famous "ontological argument." The contemporary philosopher is addicted to the primacy of a theory of knowledge. Before any question is asked, the modern reader must inquire whether, methodologically considered, the quest is justifiable and the object knowable. Bonaventure and a host of others, on the other hand, pose the ultimate question of God at the outset just as if it were answerable. Only through the technical process of attempting to construct the answer can the success or the failure of the endeavor be discovered. The process of the attempt itself is the source of our correction. The limits of the question are recognizable, not at the beginning, but only at the end of the argument.

Not unlike the Greek invocation of the muses in the face of a difficult task, Bonaventure in the prologue calls upon God to enlighten him in his quest. His use of the term "Father of Light" for God and his stress upon illumination place Bonaventure well within the Augustinian and Neoplatonic tradition. God is to be immediately addressed at the outset of all serious consideration because he is cast in the role of a first principle and as such is central to any knowing process.

The work has a devotional element. Francis of Assisi, the founder of Bonaventure's order, is mentioned reverentially, and Bonaventure himself claims to have undergone a vision like that experienced by Francis. However, coupled with this theme must be the awareness that Bonaventure served as a highly successful administrator, in fact as minister general of his order. This obvious organizational skill, which daily must have

called for the solution of dozens of practical problems, is balanced against the visionary quality of his writing.

Stages of Ascension
Bonaventure describes six stages of ascension to God. Their delineation is purely technical and rational, but Bonaventure, at the same time, considers prayer one means of becoming enlightened about them. To minds so used to splitting spirituality and rationality completely, such duality in Bonaventure's thought is hard to grasp. To do so, however, is also to come close to understanding the special feature of *The Journey of the Mind to God*. For all natural objects have a double side: They at once are parts of a structured natural order discoverable by reason and at the same time, when properly viewed, may come to be seen as traces of God. Such divine traces are uncoverable in many places; he begins with those that are corporeal and outside people (as contrasted to those spiritual and interior).

The mind has three principal aspects, one of which is animal or sensual, another of which makes it capable of introspection, and a third in virtue of which it is able to look above itself and to grasp levels of existence higher than its own natural order. Because all natural objects have a divine side, the six stages of the soul's powers correspond to the six stages of the ascension unto God. To describe the levels of ascent to God is to delineate the soul's powers; to set forth the soul's capacities is to outline the levels through which God is to be approached.

Theology itself has three modes: symbolic, literal, and mystical. The symbolic gives proper interpretation to sensible things; the literal corresponds to an intelligible level, and the mystic transcends the level of rationality. All three are properly theology. However, none of these is to be undertaken without preparation because rectitude of the will and the clarity of unimpeded vision are necessary. Then the sensible world may be taken up for consideration, and it will be transformed upon reflection into a veritable Jacob's ladder, the sense world being as it is so full of the traces of God.

We proceed by transposing natural qualities into a divine setting. Weight, number, and measure provide a basis for grasping the power, wisdom, and immense goodness of the Creator. One inquires after the origin, course, and terminus of the natural order, then a grasp of the various levels of natural organisms can be acquired. From this one moves to consider God as a counterpart of these levels and of this order, as spiritual, incorruptible, and immutable. The natural order is a plenitude, full of every level and variety of kind. Such munificence is a source of natural illumination for the mind in its search for the proper road to God.

God is reflected in his traces in the sensible world and is known not only through but also in them. Bonaventure sees the natural world as being both good and beautiful, so that to an eye sensitive to such structure, God can actually be seen without taking our eyes away from the world of the senses even for a moment. The five senses are like doors. Through apprehending motion, we are led to the cognition of spiritual movers, as a progress from effect to cause.

Our senses lead us to apprehension, then to delight in the natural order, and finally to judgment, which operates by abstraction and renders the sensible objects intelligible. Then, following Saint Augustine's *De musica* (389; *On Music*, 1947), Bonaventure regards number as the outstanding exemplar of God to be found in the physical world. All Platonists have been fascinated with the intelligible and yet nonsensible properties of number, especially its relation to the qualities of rhythm and proportion. The invisible things of God come to be seen, being grasped in and through the changing, sensible world. Like a sign, the sensible order leads the discerning mind to the intelligible; seeing this, we are led to turn from an outward vision and to consider the mind itself.

Grasping how divine things may be seen as reflected in the order of nature leads us to turn inward to consider ourselves, and here divine images appear most clearly. For the natural psychical phenomena are self-love, self-knowledge, and memory. Here Bonaventure follows Augustine's classical model and finds in these a representation of the divine Trinity. Particularly in memory the soul is most like an image of God, for God lives with all objects eternally present, and the soul imitates this power in the grasp of its own power of memory. We cannot understand

the being of any particular object until we come to understand Being-in-itself. Memory, intelligence, and will form in us a second reflection of God's trinitarian nature, so that when the mind considers itself, it rises through itself as through a mirror to the contemplation of the divine Trinity.

Having brought the mind so close to God, Bonaventure turns to inquire why not all people see God clearly in themselves. His answer is that most people lie so buried in the world of the senses that they are unable to regard themselves as in God's image. Here, for the first time, specifically Christian doctrine enters because Bonaventure sees in Christ a mediator who accomplishes this needed purification and illumination. Spiritual hearing and vision must be recovered.

After the conversion of the mind to a new direction comes the disciplining of the self. Bonaventure outlines the "steps" of Bernard of Clairvaux to bring the soul to vision through humility and the inculcation of strict habits of thought. We must learn contemplation, and this requires a strict order in the soul. The acquired habits of the rationally ordered soul yield powers capable of leading us to the divine.

We have learned to contemplate God *outside* us in his traces in the natural and sensible order, *inside* the self through the trinitarian structure of the soul's powers, and finally *above* the mind as the contemplative powers are strengthened by discipline. We may fix on Being-itself, rejecting, as all Neoplatonism does, any positive status for nonbeing. Here a little dialectical exercise on Being and nonbeing convinces us that Being is actually what first enters the intellect and that this is the Being of pure actuality. Thus, analysis indicates the immediate orientation of all intellection toward Being-itself and therefore toward God. Because this orientation is at the foundation of every intellective act, it only remains for the mind to become aware of just how necessary its orientation toward God is for our understanding in every instance. For intellect to operate, the Being of the divine being must be ever present as a referent and standard.

Only because we are accustomed to the lesser beings of the sensible world do we fail to recognize the mind's natural orientation and nearness to God. As the eye seems to see nothing when it sees pure light, so we seem to see sensible images and lesser beings and do not recognize the highest Being. The darkness that seems to surround Being-itself, in comparison with the ease of grasping lower objects, can be disclosed as the fullest illumination of the mind. The purest being, necessary for every grasp of impure beings, appears only by contrast to be empty of content.

At the height we reach the traditional Platonic and Neoplatonic name for God, the Good. The fecundity of the Good is given as a rational necessity for the multiplicity of a Trinity within God, as more adequately expressing the fullness of the Good than could any less multiple first principle. Yet Bonaventure is quick to add that such rational arguments do not make the Trinity comprehensible. Because it is incomprehensible, it is not fully understandable.

The Goal and Beyond

Having arrived at the end of the sixth step, our mind's work is done, and it rests. The mind, having traversed the whole of the sensible order, then the intelligible realm, has finally understood itself and disciplined itself to raise itself to consider God. However, the end of this gigantic and rigorous activity is rest. The mind has reached the place at which it has done all it can do; nothing more is within its power and so it must rest. Rationally it has exhausted itself and has reached its limit. Reason, illumination, devotion, and discipline have brought the mind to the pinnacle of its powers and transformed it in the process of the journey, although at the end it sees that the final vision was never far away. At the outset the goal was near but not seen. It was present from the beginning (Being-itself), but our powers were not then sufficient to grasp it directly.

What remains? By looking at sensible things, the mind passed beyond them and then turned to consider itself. Now it passes not only beyond sensible things, by way of a rational dialectic, but beyond even itself. In this final passage, if the rational discipline has been perfected, all intellectual operation should at this point be abandoned. All our affection should be transferred from ourselves to God. The final step is most certainly mystical, but mysticism enters only at this final point and not before. No one can know this final phase who has not experienced it, and even to the mind undergoing the experience, it seems like moving into death and darkness to leave rational structure behind. However, the soul, having set out to find God, is now at the terminus of its itinerary and willingly surrenders what it could not have surrendered before (the guidance of its rational powers) and passes over into what appears to be (as contrasted with structured reason) darkness.

How shall a modern mind appraise such a scheme and its importance to philosophy? The immediate concentration on God, the mixture of philosophy with religious discipline, and the view of all mundane things as immediately reflecting God—all of these are nearly the opposite of the modern approach. In some basic sense, modern philosophers as well as most Protestant theologians are fundamentally rationalists, and to them Bonaventure's ultimate mysticism seems strange. Consequently, *The Journey of the Mind to God* has an important function to fulfill as an example of a possible and different approach.

Historically its significance cannot be overestimated. In any form of the religious life, Neoplatonism has always been extremely influential, and Bonaventure represents a philosophical and a theological view that has for centuries been closely associated with devout practice. Since philosophy's divorce from theology in the modern period, philosophy has become largely academic. *The Journey of the Mind to God* is an example of how a philosophical view can be intimately associated with, and even be determinative for, a way of life.

Out of a religious desire to see God, this philosophical view arises as a disciplined guide. Such desire actually causes us to seek for and to see aspects of the natural order that might otherwise have remained unnoticed. A more abstract intellect may derive its philosophical problems internally simply from philosophical discussion. Bonaventure finds his questions through the attempt to guide the soul toward God. Neither approach to philosophy or theology excludes the other, but a secular and a rationalistic age has trouble recognizing the legitimacy of a philosophy generated from such a practical (and in this case religious) goal.

Perhaps the most interesting comparison is to remember that Bonaventure was a contemporary of Thomas Aquinas. The two considered together offer a fascinating contrast. Both represent the use that was made of philosophy in the Middle Ages. Thomas has had wide circulation in non-Catholic and even in nonreligious circles. Bonaventure is still widely read within religious orders and in theological circles that do not receive as much public notice.

Bonaventure's work could be considered purely as a devotional classic if it were not for its elaborate technical structure and his use of "Being" as God's primary name. Nothing indicates the presence of an abstract metaphysician more than his preference for the traditional name "Being" as opposed to more personal names for God. God is discussed in his role as a metaphysical first principle and not as an object of worship. In fact, except for the trinitarian reference, little specifically Christian or biblical doctrine is discussed. It is only by contrast to modern anti-metaphysical interests that this work seems "religious." Actually by comparison, it is both technical and abstract.

In considering Being and nonbeing, Bonaventure adopts the traditional Neoplatonic role of giving nonbeing status only as a privation of Being, not as anything independent of or opposed to it. In fact, upon analysis, it appears that nothing within the natural order can be known unless Being itself has first entered the intellect. In this way, God is involved in even the simplest act of cognition, as a prerequisite for any apprehension. For a particular being to be known, Being itself must be present to the intellect, a fact that may not be recognized until after the analysis of Being and nonbeing has been carried out.

Bonaventure stresses unity, the traditional Neoplatonic attribute of God. He possesses no diversity, and it is primarily this central characteristic of unity that places God above intellection and forces reason ultimately to transcend itself. Although God is close to and visible through the natural order, his nature is quite different, reflecting none of the multiplicity of nature's variety. Because of such a basic dissimilarity, any persons who would have the vision of God must finally leave themselves behind, insofar as they are rational creatures dealing with multiple objects.

Being, which is absolutely one, is seen also to be the Good, but the different ontological level involved here forces the apprehending mind to pass beyond the multiple sensible world and also beyond itself as a discursive mind. It is not so much Bonaventure's view of the order of nature that dictates this as it is his view of the divine nature. Just as Bonaventure begins with God, so any criticism of his whole scheme must start by attempting to set forth and to defend a different view of the divine nature.

In order to see the point of Bonaventure's theory of knowledge and his theory of the orders of nature, each must be seen in its relation to his view of the divine nature, coupled with his ethical and religious goal of seeing God. In order to criticize the Seraphic Doctor's theories, we also must begin with a theory of the divine nature. As that is altered, so also are the theory of knowledge, and the view of nature and of human psychology.

Frederick Sontag, updated by John K. Roth

Additional Reading

Bettoni, Efrem. *Saint Bonaventure.* Translated by Angelus Gambatese. Notre Dame, Ind.: University of Notre Dame Press, 1964. A reliable and accessible introduction to Saint Bonaventure's life and thought.

Carpenter, David A. *Revelation, History, and the Dialogue of Religion: A Study of Bhartari and Bonaventure.* Maryknoll, N.Y.: Orbis, 1995. Carpenter's comparative study of the Indian philosopher Bhartari and Bonaventure sheds important light on the relations between diverse religious and philosophical traditions.

Copleston, Frederick. *A History of Philosophy: Medieval Philosophy.* Garden City, N.Y.: Doubleday, 1962. An eminent historian of Western philosophy provides a good overview of Bonaventure's contributions to medieval philosophy.

Cousins, Ewert. *Bonaventure and the Coincidence of Opposites: The Theology of Bonaventure.* Chicago: Franciscan Herald Press, 1978. This work explores the philosophical theology of Bonaventure with clarity and insight.

Gilson, Étienne. *The Philosophy of St. Bonaventure.* Translated by Illtyd Trethhowan and Frank J. Sheed. Patterson, N.J.: St. Anthony Guild Press, 1965. A great interpreter of Roman Catholic thought provides an interpretation of Bonaventure that is of lasting significance.

Malloy, Michael P. *Civil Authority in Medieval Philosophy: Lombard, Aquinas, and Bonvaventure.* Lanham, Md.: University Press of America, 1985. The work explores medieval political philosophy and situates Bonaventure in that tradition.

Prentice, Robert P. *The Psychology of Love According to St. Bonaventure.* St. Bonaventure, N.Y.: Franciscan Institute, 1957. Explores how the experience and concept of love affects Bonaventure's understanding of the nature of God and humankind.

Quinn, Mary Bennett. *To God Alone the Glory: A Life of St. Bonaventure.* Westminster, Md.: Newman Press, 1962. A worthwhile biographical treatment of Bonaventure.

Ratzinger, Joseph. *The Theology of History in St. Bonaventure.* Chicago: Franciscan Herald Press, 1971. An important Catholic thinker explores Bonaventure's views about history and providence.

Rout, Paul. *Francis & Bonaventure.* Liguori, Mo.: Triumph Books, 1997. A useful study of Saint Bonaventure's life and thought.

Shahan, Robert W., and Francis J. Kovach, eds. *Bonaventure and Aquinas: Enduring Philosophers.* Norman: University of Oklahoma Press, 1976. Draws together reflections that compare two of the most influential and different thinkers in the Western medieval tradition.

Tracy, David, ed. *Celebrating the Medieval Heritage: A Colloquy on the Thought of Aquinas and Bonaventure.* Chicago: University of Chicago Press, 1978. Tracy compiles significant interpretations of Bonaventure's thought by important late twentieth century interpreters.

Mary-Emily Miller, updated by John K. Roth

Dietrich Bonhoeffer

Bonhoeffer defined the concept of Christian discipleship, especially as it related to the Lutheran Church in Germany during the 1930's. He provided a unique combination of theology and political ethics that made him a leader in German resistance to Adolf Hitler and also led to his untimely death in 1945.

Principal philosophical works: *Sanctorum Communio*, 1930 (*The Communion of Saints*, 1963); *Akt und Sein*, 1931 (*Act and Being*, 1962); *Nachfolge*, 1937 (*The Cost of Discipleship*, 1948); *Gemeinsames Leben*, 1939 (*Life Together*, 1954); *Ethik*, 1949 (*Ethics*, 1955); *Widerstand und Ergebung: Aufzeichnungen aus der Haft*, 1951, rev. eds. 1964, 1970 (*Letters and Papers from Prison*, 1953, rev. eds. 1967, 1971).

Born: February 4, 1906; Breslau, Germany (now Wrocław, Poland)
Died: April 9, 1945; Flossenbürg, Germany

Early Life

Dietrich Bonhoeffer was born in Breslau, Germany (now Wrocław, Poland), on February 4, 1906. His father was Karl Bonhoeffer, a well-known physician and psychiatrist. There were eight children in the family, of whom Dietrich and his twin sister, Sabine, were the sixth and seventh, respectively. The family soon moved to Berlin, where Karl Bonhoeffer became professor of psychiatry at the University of Berlin. It was there that Dietrich spent his childhood.

The realism that later characterized the philosophy and theology of Bonhoeffer was imparted to him by his father and through the influence of his mother, who was from one of the leading intellectual families in Germany. The family home became a meeting place for friends and neighbors representing some of the most brilliant minds of the day. Among the visitors were Adolf von Harnack, an eminent historian of Christian doctrine, and Ernst Troeltsch, a philosopher and theologian. The influence of these men helped place Bonhoeffer in the liberal spectrum of Christian theology as well as at the forefront of the ecumenical movement.

At the age of sixteen, Bonhoeffer dedicated his life to the study of theology and to service in the Lutheran Church. He entered the University of

Tübingen in 1923 and was matriculated at the University of Berlin the following year. He remained in Berlin for the completion of his formal education. During his years at the university, Bonhoeffer became a follower of the post-World War I theology of Karl Barth, soon to become known as Neoorthodoxy. These ideas enhanced Bonhoeffer's realism and helped him to accept the tremendous suffering and destruction of the recent conflagration, as well as Germany's lowered status in the community of nations.

When Bonhoeffer was twenty-one, he presented his doctoral dissertation to the faculty at Berlin. The dissertation, *The Communion of Saints*, published in 1930, was praised by many, including Barth.

Bonhoeffer left Berlin in 1927 to serve two years as an assistant minister to a German-speaking congregation in Barcelona, Spain. He proved to be a tremendous help and encouragement to the church and its elderly pastor. Back in Berlin in 1929, Bonhoeffer soon became a lecturer in systematic theology at the university. Before settling into the routine, however, he went to the United States for a year of additional study at Union Theological Seminary in New York City. Somewhat surprised by the lack of interest in serious theology on the part of American students at the seminary, Bonhoeffer was impressed by their social concern for the poor and needy. Bonhoeffer was well prepared for his life's work when he returned to Berlin in 1931. He was ready to face the challenges to Germany and the world in the person of Nazi leader Adolf Hitler.

Life's Work

By the time Bonhoeffer began lecturing full-time, he was identified with the ecumenical movement, which sought to unite Christians around the world, and also with the ideas of Barth, whom Bonhoeffer soon met at a seminar in Bonn. The students at the university were at first skeptical about the youthful professor but were soon drawn to him by the depth and relevance of his views.

Bonhoeffer's rising popularity in Berlin coincided with the rising popularity of the National Socialist German Workers' (Nazi) Party throughout the country. The Bonhoeffer family had been deeply affected by the defeat of Germany in 1918 and by the humiliation of the nation in the Treaty of Versailles, but they strongly opposed the ultranationalistic philosophy and the superior race ideology of the Nazi Party. Even while outside the country, Dietrich was kept informed about the growing Nazi influence, particularly as it related to the Jews. His twin sister, Sabine, was married to Gerhard Leibholz, whose father was a Jew, although Gerhard had been baptized as a Lutheran.

Bonhoeffer was soon dismayed by the paralysis of the German Christians regarding Nazi ideology. His realism, as well as his theology, compelled him to speak out against that ideology. On February 1, 1933, two days after Hitler had become chancellor of Germany, Bonhoeffer addressed the German public on radio and urged them not to adopt an ultranationalistic leader who could easily become a national idol. The broadcast was cut off the air before the speech was completed. In the minds of Nazi leaders, Bonhoeffer was already a marked man.

Most Lutheran leaders succumbed to Nazi pressure and formed the German Christian Movement, a vital part of German nationalism. Bonhoeffer and a minority formed what became

Dietrich Bonhoeffer. (*Deutche Presse Agentur/Archive Photos*)

known as the Confessing Church, seeking to purify the church through discipline. These leaders were shocked by parallels being drawn between Jesus and Hitler. Unable to accept such ideas, Bonhoeffer went to Great Britain in the fall of 1933, answering the call to pastor two German-speaking congregations in South London. During his eighteen months there, he studied the Sermon on the Mount and the idea of Christian discipleship. The result was his best-known book, *The Cost of Discipleship*. In this absorbing volume, Bonhoeffer criticized what he called the "cheap grace" being preached in many churches. He defined cheap grace as "the preaching of forgiveness without requiring repentance." Bonhoeffer then advocated costly grace, which "is costly because it costs a man his life, and it is grace because it gives a man the only true life. . . . Above all it is costly because it cost God the life of his Son."

In 1935, Bonhoeffer was called back to Germany by the Confessing Church to lead a clandestine seminary, eventually located in Finkenwalde, Pomerania. This seems to have been a profitable and pleasant time for Bonhoeffer and the small group of students; in 1937, however, the seminary was closed by the Gestapo. Following the closing, Bonhoeffer became active in the Resistance movement dedicated to the overthrow of Hitler. From 1937 to his arrest in 1943, Bonhoeffer lived in temporary places of refuge, such as the Benedictine Abbey at Ettal. His spare time during these years was used to write *Ethics*, a work he regarded as his greatest contribution as a theologian.

As the clouds of war began gathering over Europe, Bonhoeffer's friends urged him to leave Germany and continue his work abroad. He did return briefly to London and in June, 1939, visited the United States; however, he soon felt constrained to return to his homeland. Before leaving, Bonhoeffer wrote to Reinhold Niebuhr, an American Neoorthodox leader, and declared, "I shall have no right to participate in the reconstruction of Christian life in Germany after the war if I do not share the trials of this time with my people." Taking advantage of one of the last opportunities to do so, Bonhoeffer returned to Berlin on July 27, 1939.

In the spring of 1941, a major conspiracy was organized to assassinate Hitler and overthrow the Nazi government. Bonhoeffer's role in this plot was to use his ecumenical contacts in Great Britain and the United States to convince the Allies to stop fighting while the overthrow was in progress. The unsuccessful attempt was made in July, 1944, but by then, Bonhoeffer had been in prison for more than a year. He was arrested on April 5, 1943, at his parents' home in Berlin, along with his sister Christel and her husband, for helping smuggle fourteen Jews into Switzerland.

For the next two years, Bonhoeffer wrote and ministered from various German prisons. The writings were later edited and published by his close friend, Eberhard Bethge, under the title *Letters and Papers from Prison*.

Bonhoeffer's final days were spent in the concentration camp at Flossenbürg. On April 9, 1945, by a special order from Nazi Schutzstaffel leader Heinrich Himmler, Bonhoeffer was hanged. About the same time, his brother Klaus and two brothers-in-law were executed elsewhere for Resistance activities.

Influence

Bonhoeffer had a clear understanding of the relationship between church and state. He first clarified the difference between state and govern-

ment. By state, Bonhoeffer meant an ordered community; by government, he meant the power that creates and maintains order. The Nazi system, therefore, was government representing only the rulers and not the full German state. Bonhoeffer believed that the New Testament teaches that the basis of government is Jesus Christ and that only from Christ does government have authority on earth. By this simple concept, Bonhoeffer destroyed the foundation of Nazi ideology, including the exaltation for the German state and the attempt to use the church as an instrument of governmental power.

This Christocentric view of government was also used by Bonhoeffer to justify the involvement of the Confessing Church in the Resistance. He declared this involvement to be the responsibility of the church because of "the persecution of lawfulness, truth, humanity and freedom" that permeated the Nazi system. Although he was basically a pacifist, this combination of theology and ethics made Bonhoeffer a leading spokesperson for the Resistance. Behind all that Bonhoeffer preached and practiced was his emphasis on discipline, which he urged all Christians and all Germans to follow.

Glenn L. Swygart

Letters and Papers from Prison

Type of philosophy: Ethics, philosophical theology
First published: Widerstand und Ergebung: Aufzeichnungen aus der Haft, 1951, rev. eds. 1964, 1970 (English translation, 1953, rev. eds. 1967, 1971)
Principal ideas advanced:

◇ The world has "come of age" and is freed from ecclesiastical and religious guardianship.

◇ A "religionless Christianity" can serve this world.

◇ The church is not some abstract Bride of Christ and needs to justify its space in the modern world.

◇ God's apparent removal from the world is a positive.

◇ Humankind and the church must share in the sufferings of God by adopting a "secret discipline."

◇ Christian faith unites Christology, transcendence, and discipleship, thereby freeing the Christian for life in a secular world.

In this book, published posthumously after being smuggled out of prison, Dietrich Bonhoeffer tries to reconcile sociological ideas concerning the church as a human organization with the theological idea of the church as a divine society on earth. In so doing, he follows both his doctoral dissertation, *Sanctorum Communio* (1930; *The Communion of Saints*, 1963), which first introduced the theme, and *Akt und Sein* (1931; *Act and Being*, 1962), which was chiefly concerned with philosophical postulates of theology. Bonhoeffer, who in 1933 helped found the Confessing Church, which battled against National Socialism (Nazism) in Germany, focused on the earthly dimension of the church and its political responsibility. Influenced by philosophers such as Immanuel Kant, Martin Heidegger, Karl Barth, and Søren Kierkegaard, Bonhoeffer, who was one of the leading Lutheran theologians during the Nazi period, urged Christians to imitate Christ with respect to obedience, penance, and discipline so that the church might save the world, which was becoming increasingly secularized.

After his arrest and during incarceration, Bonhoeffer completed *Ethik* (1949; *Ethics*, 1955), which acknowledged the world's disunion with God. Bonhoeffer believed that one knows oneself as an individual apart from God and therefore knows only oneself, outside God. One's shame is a recognition of estrangement from the source of knowledge of good and evil. This book complements the *Letters and Papers from Prison* (written during the last two years of his life), a work that also shows a growing feeling of abandonment in a world without God. Both books reveal Bonhoeffer as a sociologist of religion who portrays Christ not as an isolated historical figure who founded Christianity, but as a collective person who is the foundation of the church.

Letters and Papers from Prison consists of letters to Bonhoeffer's parents and an unnamed friend (probably his editor, Eberhard Bethge), miscellaneous papers (including an outline for a book), five poems, and reflections on prison life. This work, which made him internationally famous because of its deep inspirational and controversial nature, enables the reader to reconstruct the last days of an extraordinarily sensitive man. Intimate details of his life fuse with disastrous events occurring outside his prison cell, but Bonhoeffer's real legacy is not simply the model of spiritual courage he provided before his hanging but also the key he provided for unlocking a revolutionary theology and ecclesiology.

The letters and papers express an acute awareness of the world in its manifold glories and deprivations. Despite the repressive nature of his imprisonment, Bonhoeffer is able to turn his solitude into a way of taking himself out of himself. He turns his thoughts to life and its meaning. Acting on the belief that prison life is not so different from life anywhere else, he uses his reading, meditating, and writing to allay anxieties about the future. The Bible and Christian hymns serve as "vehicles of spiritual realities" (June 14, 1943), just as simple gifts or parcels from family and friends reassure him of spiritual bonds among people. The early letters evoke a palpable sense of worldliness despite his transcendental thought. For one thing, Bonhoeffer confesses to weakness when he feels his peace and placidity wavering and his heart becoming defiant or despondent. Yet, the counterpoint is a better understanding of life.

Worldliness and Christians

Bonhoeffer's appreciation of the worldliness of life in the Old Testament leads him to rethink concepts of the "ultimate" and "penultimate." He claims that one must first turn to this world if one is to understand the meaning of the Christian life of faith. "This-worldliness" (the "penultimate") of Christian life is a means of witnessing the "ultimate" (the one and only interest of theology). However, the goodness of life and the love of the world cannot resolve the tension between this world and "the transcendent." Transcendence is necessary, but it has a proper time and place. Genuine transcendence means accepting the life God gives one with all its blessings, loving it and drinking it in full, grieving over what one has wasted or neglected. Bonhoeffer brings together in one letter the false and proper views of transcendence, advocating a "religionless Christianity" that directs one to this world and to

God simultaneously. By living in this world, the Christian bears witness to God.

History and contemporary events teach Bonhoeffer that "it is the unexpected that happens, and that the inevitable must be accepted." Life in wartime is grim, but he eagerly anticipates a reconstruction of international society, both materially and spiritually, based on Christian principles. Convinced that human life extends far beyond physicality, he is able to perceive how a pattern is created for the whole of existence and what materials are or should be used for this purpose (February 20, 1944).

Bonhoeffer integrates theology and ecclesiology in the process of arguing that though the church occupies space in the world, the nature and justification of that space needs to be rethought. This space is still related to divine revelation, but it is not the only area where revelation can be discussed. Bonhoeffer attempts to provide a different perspective or picture of Christ's form in the modern world and of humanity's conformation with Christ. He is willing to explore "a time of no religion at all," an age that the church must redeem and serve (June 8, 1944). He interprets contemporary history as a liberating force and sees the "god of explanation," of a priori religious postulates, disappearing from Western history, and therefore, he considers the world to have "come of age." Humanity has decided to be emancipated from God, church, and pastor. As a consequence, God is no answer to humanity's problems, or so it seems at first. His letter of July 16, 1944, claims that this historical trend must be acknowledged if Christianity is to be honest and true to its message. Bonhoeffer takes issue with Karl Barth, his great teacher, for his "positivist doctrine of revelation," which urges people to swallow doctrine whole or not at all (April 30, 1944). He also argues against Rudolf Bultmann's famous essay on mythology and the New Testament, claiming that although you cannot, as Bultmann imagines, separate God from miracles, you do have to be able to interpret both in a nonreligious way. Religious mythology is true, but the concepts must be reinterpreted so as not to make religion a "precondition of faith" (May 5 and June 8, 1944).

Bonhoeffer's "nonreligious interpretation" recognizes the contribution of Barth and Bultmann, but it refuses to claim that eternal and universal Christian truth may be discovered independently of the secular historical setting of the New Testament. Consequently, it raises a paradox: On the one hand, his Christ is a worldly man who claims for himself and the Kingdom of God the whole of human life in all its manifestations. On the other, his triumphant Lord in a salvation myth suffers and is humiliated in this world before being crucified.

Active Participation in Life

Bonhoeffer's Christological vision leads to his exhortation to share "in the sufferings of God at the hands of a godless world" by adopting a "secret discipline." This latter phrase is mentioned twice in the prison letters, the first reference occurring in the middle of his initial thoughts about religionless Christianity and the second during a discussion of a nonreligious interpretation of biblical concepts (April 30 and May 5, 1944). Bonhoeffer seeks to protect the "secrets" of Christian faith (such as preaching and the Sacraments) against profanation. He appears to be arguing that the church must not cast away its great terms such as "Creation," "Fall," "Atonement," "regeneration," and "Holy Ghost." However, if the church cannot relate them to the secular world, showing their essence in worldly life, then the church must keep silent. Christians derive strength from living a worldly life and sharing in Christ's Lordship over it, through the discipline and humility of holding their peace during the union with God's suffering.

The problem of theology is language, and Bonhoeffer differentiates between "qualified speech" and "qualified silence." There is a proper time and place for silence as regards the ultimate, and that time has come in this secularized age. Dogmatic theology and apologetics must remain silent and secret, and nonreligious Christians must grope and stammer to find words free of pious jargon yet consistent with the life of the modern world. Christians derive strength from living a worldly life and sharing in Christ's Lordship over it, through the discipline and humility of holding their peace while sharing in the suffering of God.

Christ's life among people and his suffering and death merge into a single vision (July 18 and

July 21, 1944). This concept becomes the climax of Bonhoeffer's theology: "Man is challenged to participate in the sufferings of God at the hands of a godless world. He must therefore really live in the godless world, without attempting to gloss over or explain its ungodliness in some religious way or other" (July 18, 1944). To be a Christian, claims Bonhoeffer, is not to be religious "in a particular way" on the basis of some method or other, but "to be a man—not a type of man but the man Christ creates in us." Therefore, it is not the "religious act" that makes a Christian, but "participation in the sufferings of God in worldly life." The religious act is "always something partial," but "faith is something whole, an act of one's life." Jesus does not invite people to a new religion but to life itself in which "the knowledge of death and resurrection is ever present" (July 18, 1944). By living as a human, Christ gave meaning to people's lives.

Finding Christ through this identification with the world means that people accept full responsibility for the world's history, structures, laws, and influences. This is not an escape into the transcendent but an active Christian participation in secular, political, social, and economic life. It is a style of life that leads people to God through the world.

Letters and Papers from Prison had a vital impact on Christian philosophy. Despite the fragmentary nature of the writing and its palpable spiritual unrest, Bonhoeffer was, in an important sense, a forerunner of the "Honest to God" controversy. As a Lutheran, he obviously went far beyond his church's typical concern with doctrines of the two kingdoms and of salvation by faith. His concept of the modern church breached the idea of a doctrinaire institution with dogmatic truth; instead, it sought to reveal a human organization that could restructure the world in Christ despite events that challenged faith. As such, Bonhoeffer became a forerunner of such theologians as Gregory Baum and Daniel Berrigan, who played active roles as sociopolitical dissenters. Bonhoeffer's theology allowed for a confrontation between the secret discipline, which makes possible a mundane existence, and the godless world come of age. Although this confrontation or dialectical tension, which gives Christian life a distinctiveness, left itself open to various interpretations, it helped change the shape of Christianity and its role in the secular world.

Keith Garebian

Additional Reading

Bethge, Eberhard. *Dietrich Bonhoeffer: Man of Vision, Man of Courage.* New York: Harper & Row, 1970. Written by a friend, relative, and associate of Bonhoeffer, this volume and others by Bethge are the basic authority for any study of Bonhoeffer.

Bonhoeffer, Dietrich. *Dietrich Bonhoeffer: Witness to Jesus Christ.* Edited by John W. De Gruchy. Minneapolis, Minn.: Fortress Press, 1991. A compilation of Bonhoeffer's most important writings in chronological order with a valuable introduction to the development of Bonhoeffer's thought written by De Gruchy.

Bosanquet, Mary. *The Life and Death of Dietrich Bonhoeffer.* New York: Harper & Row, 1968. Perhaps the clearest and most objective biography. Much information is from Bonhoeffer's twin sister and from Bethge.

Marsh, Charles. *Reclaiming Dietrich Bonhoeffer: The Promise of His Theology.* Oxford: Oxford University Press, 1994. An evaluation of Bonhoeffer's writings in the context of modern German philosophy, especially post-Kantian notions of self. A useful examination of the theological interchange between Bonhoeffer and Karl Barth.

Morris, Kenneth Earl. *Bonhoeffer's Ethic of Discipleship: A Study in Social Psychology, Political Thought, and Religion.* University Park: Pennsylvania State University Press, 1986. A study of faith and politics in the modern world. Morris examines the influence that family played in the determination of Bonhoeffer's psychological makeup relative to the influence of religion and politics.

Ott, Heinrich. *Reality and Faith: The Theological Legacy of Dietrich Bonhoeffer.* Translated by Alex A. Morrison. Philadelphia: Fortress Press, 1972. This is an exhaustive study of Bonhoeffer's theology and its impact.

Rasmussen, Larry. *Dietrich Bonhoeffer: Reality and Resistance.* Nashville, Tenn.: Abingdon Press, 1972. A good summary of how Bonhoeffer's theology shaped his political ethics and led him into the resistance.

Robertson, Edwin. *The Shame and the Sacrifice: The Life and Martyrdom of Dietrich Bonhoeffer*. New York: Macmillan, 1988. An excellent and later evaluation of Bonhoeffer's influence. It includes some interesting insights into the resistance and those who survived.

Weikart, Richard. *The Myth of Dietrich Bonhoeffer: Is His Theology Evangelical?* San Francisco: International Scholars Publications, 1997. This books tries to debunk the questions surrounding Bonhoeffer's theology.

Young, Josiah U. *No Difference in the Fare: Dietrich Bonhoeffer and the Problem of Racism*. Grand Rapids, Mich.: Eerdmans, 1998. An examination of Bonhoeffer's contribution to the theology of race relations. Contains a bibliography and index.

Glenn L. Swygart, updated by Darryl L. Henry

Pierre Bourdieu

Using methods and theories from sociology and anthropology, Bourdieu developed a theory of human action as practice based and argued that this perspective transcends a false distinction between subjectivism and objectivism.

Principal philosophical works: *Les Héritiers*, 1964 (with Jean-Claude Passeron; *The Inheritors*, 1979); *Esquisse d'une théorie de la pratique*, 1972 (*Outline of a Theory of Practice*, 1977); *La Distinction: Critique social du jugement*, 1979 (*Distinction: A Social Critique of the Judgement of Taste*, 1984); *Le Sens pratique*, 1980 (*The Logic of Practice*, 1990); *Ce que parler veut dire: L'Économie des échanges linguistiques*, 1982 (*Language and Symbolic Power*, 1991); *An Invitation to Reflexive Sociology*, 1992 (with Loic Wacquant).

Born: August 1, 1930; Denguin, France

Early Life

The son of a civil servant, Pierre Bourdieu was born on August 1, 1930, into a lower-middle-class family in the Béarn, a rural region of southeastern France. In the early 1950's, Bourdieu attended the prestigious École Normale Supérieure, an elite teacher-training school in Paris. During these formative years, Bourdieu's thinking was particularly influenced by Jean-Paul Sartre's existentialism and Claude Lévi-Strauss's structuralism, as well as by the classical sociological writings of Émile Durkheim, Max Weber, and Karl Marx. Bourdieu graduated with a degree in philosophy, although he did not write a thesis. He refused to comply with this standard requirement in protest against what he described as the authoritarian nature of the education available at the École Normale Supérieure.

After a year of teaching, Bourdieu was conscripted into the French army and, in 1956, was sent to Algeria. Bourdieu's experience in Algeria was pivotal in his development as an intellectual. His stay in Algeria, then a French colony, exposed him to the clash between indigenous and European civilizations. There he observed at first hand the breakdown of traditional social structures caused by the colonial situation and the impact of European civilization.

Life's Work

When Bourdieu returned to France in 1960, he retained his original interest in seeking answers to philosophical questions—about the nature of mind, agency, and personhood—but he sought to address those questions in terms of concepts, methods, and perspectives adapted from the social sciences, including the disciplines of anthropology and sociology.

In the 1960's, Bourdieu held a series of important positions within French academic culture, including director of the École Pratique des Hautes Études (1964) and the founder and director of the Centre de Sociologie Européene (1968). These positions furthered the development of Bourdieu's scholarly career. He began to publish profusely on a diverse array of topics and became internationally prominent and influential as a social theorist. In 1981, Bourdieu was named the senior chair in sociology at the most elite and prestigious French academic institution, the Collège de France, a far remove from his origins as the son of a civil servant from a rural community.

Bourdieu characterized himself as an "oblate," a term that conventionally refers to a child from a poor family entrusted to a religious foundation to be trained for the priesthood. In using this term to describe himself, Bourdieu acknowledges the importance of France's educational system in the development of his thinking, career, and social position. Bourdieu's self-characterization simultaneously conveys his understanding of professional academics as a sort of secular "priesthood" and acknowledges the extent to which his rise to a position of prominence in that social order cannot be explained exclusively in terms of his own individual effort.

In his research and through his studies, Bourdieu repeatedly sought to show that what seems "natural" in society is, in fact, socially constructed. That is, the "natural" or typically taken-for-granted order of any social system is actually the product of specific social actions, relationships, and institutions. Whether addressing marriage among the Kabyle of Algeria, the structure of France's educational system, or the role of social science in politics, Bourdieu was concerned with exposing—and analyzing—what might be called the covert functions of social institutions. The institutions of marriage, education, and social science (to name only a few) function to produce and reproduce relationships of power and influence among different classes of people.

According to Bourdieu, social life consists of a struggle for predominance among the members of different classes. The struggle, however, is not the war of "all against all" envisioned by philosopher Thomas Hobbes, in which physical strength is the crucial determinant of privilege. For Bourdieu, social life is akin to a well-regulated game, but one in which the rules of the game are understood and used correctly only by a privileged few, those who established these rules. The crucial determinant of superior social standing is "a feel for the game."

This game is complicated because the players, privileged or otherwise, are not necessarily aware of how the organization of the game systematically produces unequal results. Bourdieu argued that neither the privileged classes nor those without special privileges are wholly conscious of the ways in which the established rules work to the benefit of the game's privileged players. Consequently, those who succeed in the game understand their successes as the confirmation of natural, personal gifts; those who participate in the game without success interpret their failures as the result of their personal lack of skill, talent, or determination. Thus, the organization of the game not only serves to accrue further

privileges to those players who already possess them but also provides a justification or legitimation of this (unequal) outcome.

Bourdieu first systematically presented this account of social order in *The Inheritors*, which he coauthored in 1964 with Jean-Claude Passeron. *The Inheritors* investigated the relationship between French students' social origins and their academic success. Education, Bourdieu and Passeron concluded, operates to reproduce and legitimize divisions among different social classes. Members of privileged classes are more likely to be able to afford advanced education for their children. In addition, as students, children from privileged backgrounds are better prepared to succeed in school because their upbringing has made them familiar with the unspoken and undeclared rules of the game in that environment. Officially, such students succeed because they are "gifted," but in reality, Bourdieu argued, these gifts are only a reflection of their privileged social backgrounds.

What exactly have the privileged students in Bourdieu's study inherited? Bourdieu argued that the skills and sensibilities necessary for social success are forms of cultural and symbolic capital. Bourdieu used the term "capital" to link this pair of concepts to Karl Marx's analysis of economic capital. However, whereas Marx and other social theorists focused on the distribution of material wealth (in the form of money, property, and stocks, for example) as the basis for divisions among classes, Bourdieu emphasized how the transmission of other valuable, but not strictly economic, resources contributes to class division.

Thus, Bourdieu argued that knowledge, skills, taste, and sensibility constitute forms of "cultural capital," while prestige, honor, and fame constitute forms of "symbolic capital." Like economic capital, cultural and symbolic capital can be transmitted. Parents may pass on to their children not only their household and savings but also their knowledge, social skills, and status. Moreover, in some cases, the different forms of capital may be exchanged or used as equivalents. For example, the cultural capital of an elite education—made official in the form of the academic diploma—may contribute to an individual's chances of securing a job that pays a high wage, and in turn, the accumulation of economic capital may also be a source of prestige. Bourdieu concluded that the transmission of cultural and symbolic capital is no less crucial to the production and reproduction of social classes than the transmission of material capital.

In *Outline of a Theory of Practice*, Bourdieu developed the theoretical concepts of "habitus" and "field" in an effort to analyze the relationship between individuals' knowledge, skills, and sensibilities and the situations in which those individuals act. Bourdieu used the term "habitus" to designate individuals' socially and culturally acquired capacities. These capacities allow individuals to respond "naturally," in any given social situation, in a way that is immediate and appropriate. In developing the concept of habitus, Bourdieu emphasized that individuals are not necessarily aware of all of the choices that they make, or of the strategic benefits that result from those choices. "Field" in turn refers to the situations in which individuals live and act. Bourdieu contended that any field has its own balance of power that defines and regulates it.

Dissatisfied with prior accounts of human agency that emphasized either individuals' subjective orientations to the world or the objective constraints of the world on individual agency, Bourdieu argued that habitus and field stand in interdependent relationship to each other. Thus, in any given situation, when acting, individuals adapt their habitus to the specifics of the field; and, in doing so, they produce and reproduce the balance of power that defines and regulates that situation. In this way, *Outline of a Theory of Practice* develops a recurrent theme in Bourdieu's work, the notion that all action is strategically oriented, even when individuals are not necessarily aware—or wholly aware—of the ways in which their actions serve their own interests, individually and as members of a class.

Throughout his work, Bourdieu drew attention to the ways that language, as a social institution, functions as a form of symbolic capital and must therefore be understood as a source of symbolic power. He addressed this theme explicitly in the collection of essays published as *Language and Symbolic Power*.

Bourdieu criticized the structuralist accounts of language and language use developed by Ferdinand de Saussure and Noam Chomsky. According to Bourdieu, both Saussure and Chomsky employed theoretical distinctions that hid language's function as a form of symbolic power. Saussure distinguished between *langue*, or language as a system of signs, and *parole*, or speech as the realization of the system by particular speakers; and Chomsky distinguished between "competence," the capacity of an ideal individual to produce an infinite number of utterances, and "performance," the actual use of language in specific, concrete situations. Bourdieu objected to these approaches on the grounds that their theoretical distinctions—between *langue* and *parole*, competence and performance—assume a preestablished set of linguistic practices as dominant and legitimate.

By contrast, Bourdieu argued that language use in any given situation is the product of a complex set of social, historical, and political conditions that the theories of Saussure and Chomsky ignore. Bourdieu demonstrated that an understanding of language must take into account the part played by language use in the construction of social reality and the contribution that it makes to the constitution of classes. Through language use, Bourdieu contended, humans create more or less authorized ways of seeing and interpreting the social world, and any adequate philosophical or scientific analysis of language must, therefore, take account of how individuals and classes use language in struggle against one another for the symbolic authority to impose a certain vision of the social world as legitimate and, indeed, natural.

Influence

A philosopher by training, Bourdieu's most immediate contributions were to the social scientific disciplines of anthropology and sociology. His theoretical and empirical studies of education, especially the links between social background and academic success, became the foundations of the sociology of education. Likewise, his conception of cultural and symbolic capital and his explanation of their transmission attained the status of orthodoxy in social scientific accounts of class and social stratification. Although there may have been disagreement about specifics, the fundamental aspects of the perspective that

Bourdieu developed became widely accepted in the social sciences.

Almost certainly, one basis for the general acceptance and even popularity of Bourdieu's work is its promise as a set of tools for critical reflection on the relationship between self and society—a central theme in philosophy, even if Bourdieu's approach is largely sociological. By Bourdieu's own account, his work was intended to encourage readers to recognize their own social status and their personal identities not as individual achievements but instead as the product of social structures and classification systems that shape individuals' tastes, attitudes, and conduct. Such recognition, Bourdieu contended, may lead individuals to rethink how their own conduct contributes to—and might potentially transform—the social world in which they act and live.

From this perspective, the diverse scope of Bourdieu's work is unified by its recurring inquiry into the conditions for the realization of individuals' authentic selves—as practical, social agents. This emphasis should contribute to his work's enduring significance in the field of philosophy.

Andrew L. Roth

Outline of a Theory of Practice

Type of philosophy: Epistemology, social philosophy

First published: Esquisse d'une théorie de la pratique, 1972 (English translation, 1977)

Principal ideas advanced:

◇ Contrary to objectivist accounts of human action as rule governed and subjectivist accounts of it as ideally oriented, human action is practical and strategic.

◇ Previous accounts of human action that have emphasized either objectivist or subjectivist perspectives fail to recognize the difference between theories about practice and practice itself.

◇ By advancing the theoretical concept of the habitus and empirically investigating its operation in actual instances of practice, the false dilemma between objectivism and subjectivism can be overcome.

◇ The habitus refers to individuals' socially organized capacities for acting appropriately in any given situation.

◇ These capacities are strategic in character, advancing individuals' interests, yet not completely available to individuals for self-conscious reflection.

When Pierre Bourdieu wrote *Outline of a Theory of Practice,* structuralism and structural Marxism were the dominant modes of thought in his native France. Fearful that advances in the understanding of actual human conduct would falter because of the developing orthodoxy of these perspectives, Bourdieu wrote *Outline of a Theory of Practice* to offer an alternative to the accounts of human action provided by structuralism and by abstract sociological theory. As the book's title suggests, the argument that Bourdieu advanced as an alternative was not yet complete; as an "outline" of a theory of practice, this book stands as a point of departure for an approach that Bourdieu continued to develop and refine in numerous other publications after the appearance of *Outline of a Theory of Practice.*

Bourdieu's *Outline of a Theory of Practice* is an unusually complex book, and the author's stated intention is to challenge his readers. As a reflection on scientific practice, *Outline of a Theory of Practice* promises to "disconcert both those who reflect on the social sciences without practicing them and those who practice them without reflecting on them." Neither the presentation of Bourdieu's argument nor the construction of his sentences is straightforward.

The book's argument does not follow an obvious, linear progression. Concepts introduced and employed in one section may be reintroduced under different definitions and with altered emphases, giving the reader the impression that the development of Bourdieu's argument is more like a rocky, twisting path—which sometimes doubles back on itself and other times disappears altogether—than a unobstructed, straight sidewalk. Bourdieu requires that his reader actively work, sentence by sentence, to understand his argument. Nevertheless, *Outline of a Theory of Practice* is a rewarding text to those willing to take the time to understand Bourdieu's challenging argument.

Action and Practice

The book has two aims: first, to evaluate why previous accounts of human action, in philosophy and especially social science, have failed to adequately explain human action, and second, on the basis of this critique, to develop an original account of how human action should be understood. For Bourdieu, the key to an adequate understanding of human action is "practice."

As Bourdieu employs the term, "practice" can refer both to conventional or routinized ways of doing something (such as marriage customs or ways of speaking) and to disciplined training (such as an athlete practicing a particular skill). Human action is "practical" in at least two senses of the term. First, action is composed of and conducted through practices; and, second, action is never abstract, it is always oriented to some actual outcome. Bourdieu quotes approvingly from Karl Marx's "Theses on Feuerbach" (1888): "All social life is essentially *practical*. All mysteries which lead theory towards mysticism find their rational solution in human practice and in the comprehension of this practice."

Bourdieu argues that previous theories of human action fail because they do not come to terms with human action as a practical matter. Moreover, Bourdieu proposes that the failure of these theories is partly the consequence of theorists' inability or unwillingness to acknowledge that theorizing about human action is, itself, a form of practical human action. These two themes recur throughout the four sections of *Outline of a Theory of Practice*.

Rules and Social Action

The book's first section is titled "The Objective Limits of Objectivism." Bourdieu uses the term "objectivism" to refer to analyses of the social world in terms of the object relations that structure human conduct. His treatment of objectivism focuses on accounts of human action that explain action as rule-governed.

It is frequent and even conventional in a great deal of social philosophy, anthropology, and sociology to argue that social action is orderly insofar as it is governed by socially shared rules. From this perspective, in any given situation individuals know how to act because they apprehend the situation and recognize the rule, or rules, that direct action in that situation.

Bourdieu rejects this perspective as too simple. According to him, rules could not possibly determine social action because those rules and the situations in which they apply (or do not apply) always require active interpretation. Far from having their actions determined by rules, practical actors engage in what Bourdieu describes as the "'art' of necessary improvisation." Thus, Bourdieu contends, norms and rules should be understood as providing interpretive resources for strategic action.

Bourdieu presents an example from his ethnographic fieldwork among the Kabyle of Algeria to illustrate his point. Bourdieu studied the social organization of kinship and marriage among the Kabyle. According to Kabyle custom, the most appropriate and desirable form of marriage involved the union of "patrilateral parallel cousins" (that is, marriage to a specific member of one's kin). However, only 3 percent or 4 percent of Kabyle marriages involved parallel cousins. Analyzing this discrepancy, Bourdieu concluded that the official rules of marriage among the Kabyle did not determine who would marry whom. In actual practice, the Kabyle invoked the rule of marriage between parallel cousins selectively, only as specific circumstances required. What mattered in practice, Bourdieu contended, was not the official rule, but the strategies that different parties involved in a potential marriage employed in order to advance their own interests.

The Habitus

If an objectivist explanation of human action as rule-governed fails, then what is the alternative? Bourdieu addresses this question in the book's second, and perhaps most important section, "Structures and the Habitus." "Habitus" is originally a Latin word associated with Aristotelian philosophy, referring to a habitual or regular condition, state or appearance, especially of the body.

Bourdieu uses the term "habitus" to refer to the organized production of practices (the organized ways of doing things) that are both regulated and regular, even though they are not the product of obedience to rules. The habitus is, Bourdieu elaborates, a system of "dispositions," "tendencies," "propensities," or "inclinations."

In using this cluster of terms to describe the habitus, Bourdieu alerts the reader to the tacit, typically taken-for-granted character of the organization of practice. Dispositions constitute "practical sense," the basis on which humans act in any given situation. Individuals need not be conscious of how their actions are organized—nor need they be wholly aware of how their actions are strategically organized—in order to advance their own interests as individuals and as members of a class. Therefore, the habitus contributes to the production, and reproduction, of the existing social order "invisibly," without individuals' conscious awareness, even though the habitus exists only through those individuals' own actions. The habitus comes to have a structuring function even though it is not in itself a structure, although individuals may (mistakenly) apprehend the habitus as such. In this way, the reproductive function of the habitus is hidden, resulting in the production of a commonsense world endowed with the appearance of objectivity.

The habitus is the key to Bourdieu's conception of humans as active agents, although they cannot be wholly conscious of their own agency. Bourdieu writes, "Each agent, wittingly or unwittingly, willy nilly, is a producer and reproducer of objective meaning." Bourdieu emphasizes that this point is especially true for humans who attempt to construct systematic theories of human action.

A Critique of Theories of Practice

The book's third section, "Generative Schemes and Practical Logic: Invention Within Limits," focuses specifically on Bourdieu's critique of the methods and perspectives of social science. Bourdieu introduces the section by remarking that the idea of a "point of view" on practice is possible only if one "stands back so as to observe." That is, to have a "point of view" on practice—to be an *observer* of practice—is to detach oneself from practice itself. Having a "point of view" on practice is, Bourdieu asserts, the privilege of those who hold high positions in the social structure.

Bourdieu includes in this privileged group both social scientists and philosophers who have attempted to produce systematic theories of prac-

tice. These theories fail for two reasons. Some theories of practice fail to recognize that the objects of knowledge are socially constructed; these theories slip into a form of positivist materialism, in which individuals' capacities as sense-making agents are ignored. Alternatively, other theories of practice fail to recognize that insofar as the objects of knowledge are socially constructed, they are constructed in and through practical activity; in this case, the objective character of social structures is ignored, and these theories become a sort of idealist intellectualism.

This critique is summarized in the handful of densely written, challenging paragraphs that introduce this section of the book. Bourdieu proceeds to devote the bulk of the section to detailed ethnographic analysis of the rituals, myths, and practices that constitute the yearly calendar of the Kabyle of Algeria. The purpose of these extensive descriptive passages is to demonstrate Bourdieu's critique that theories of practice that attempt to portray practice in systematic terms can never wholly account for actual instances of practice.

The ideal version of the Kabyle calendar that an anthropologist might construct is not, and cannot be, the same as the calendar as it is experienced and used by the Kabyle themselves. The more that the scholar attempts to exert a firm grasp on the phenomenon by creating a systematic description or analysis of it, the more the phenomenon slips away, like sand through the fingers of a tightly clinched fist. Bourdieu writes: "The problem is that the calendar cannot be understood unless it is set down on paper, and that it is impossible to understand how it works unless one fully realizes that it exists only on paper." The scholar is thus left holding not the thing itself but a model of it. The Kabyle calendar, as rendered by a scholarly observer, is, Bourdieu contends, a "synoptic illusion," bearing little resemblance to the Kabyle experience of social time.

With regard to theories of practice, Bourdieu argues that any scheme of perception is necessarily developed in and acquired through actual practice and that through this process of formation, these schemes of perception come to function as if they have an objective status. This is the case, according to Bourdieu, whether or not the schemes of perception belong to and are employed by either laypersons or scholarly analysts. Because social scientists (and, to some extent, philosophers) have failed to recognize the practical origins of their own schemes of perception (that is, the practical origins of their own theories), they have correspondingly failed to provide adequate accounts of practice itself.

Bourdieu concludes the section by claiming that the Greek philosopher Plato's remark, "The philosopher is a mythologist," must be taken "literally." Bourdieu identifies theorists' unacknowledged preoccupation with the logic or systematics of their own theories as, itself, a form of mythmaking: "Logical criticism inevitably misses its mark: Because it can only challenge the relationships consciously established between words, it cannot bring out the incoherent coherence of a discourse that, springing from underlying mythic or ideological schemes, has the capacity to survive every *reductio ad absurdum*." For Bourdieu, the actual organization of practice exists independently of scholarly attempts to provide systematic, logical accounts of it.

In the final section of *Outline of a Theory of Practice*, Bourdieu introduces a theory of "symbolic power," based on his critique of previous social theory and his development of the concept of the habitus. This sketch of "symbolic capital" and its relation to the habitus serves as the basis for the continuation of Bourdieu's theory in his subsequent books, including *La Distinction: Critique social du jugement* (1979; *Distinction: A Social Critique of the Judgement of Taste*, 1984) and *Le Sens pratique* (1980; *The Logic of Practice*, 1990).

Outline of a Theory of Practice contributed significantly to Bourdieu's stature as one of the most important social theorists in the second half of the twentieth century. Bourdieu's work undertakes the general project of understanding society and social relations as well as the more specific task of understanding the relationship between the historical pattern of social relations (in the form of "structures") and the actual actions and interactions of real people (as evidence of their "agency"). For scholars and other individuals who treat the constitution of society, the organization of social relationships, and the ex-

planation of human agency as issues of enduring significance for philosophy and the social sciences, Bourdieu's work continues to be influential.

Andrew L. Roth

Additional Reading

Brubaker, Roger. "Rethinking Classical Social Theory: The Sociological Vision of Pierre Bourdieu." *Theory and Society* 14 (1985): 745-775. A somewhat specialized (though still accessible) account of Pierre Bourdieu's writing, Brubaker's article critically evaluates Bourdieu's position relative to the founding figures of sociological theory, including Karl Marx, Max Weber, and Émile Durkheim.

Calhoun, Craig, Edward LiPuma, and Moishe Postone, eds. *The Social Theory of Pierre Bourdieu*. Chicago: University of Chicago Press, 1993. A dozen essays by Anglo-American commentators, addressing the work of Bourdieu from interdisciplinary perspectives. In the final essay, Bourdieu responds to the issues and themes raised by the other contributors.

Fowler, Bridget. *Pierre Bourdieu and Cultural Theory: Critical Investigations*. Thousand Oaks, Calif: Sage, 1997. Sets Bourdieu's theory and methods in their intellectual context and offers a critical survey of his thinking on capitalism, modernity, and contemporary culture. Fowler includes a substantial discussion of the relationship between Bourdieu's work and that of philosopher Jürgen Habermas.

Jenkins, Richard. *Pierre Bourdieu*. London: Routledge, 1992. One of the best, most accessible introductions to Bourdieu's work. In concise, readable prose, Jenkins reviews the full range of Bourdieu's scholarly output and offers an even-handed critique of it.

Robbins, Derek. *The Work of Pierre Bourdieu: Recognizing Society*. Boulder, Colo.: Westview Press, 1991. Provides a chronological account of the development of Bourdieu's work. Instead of comparing Bourdieu's work with that of other social theorists, Robbins examines how Bourdieu has developed and reconfigured his own methods and concepts over time.

Andrew L. Roth

F. H. Bradley

In the history of British philosophy, Bradley represents a point of view that is fundamentally idealist. He was a vigorous, gifted, brooding critic of England's empirical philosophers.

Principal philosophical works: *Ethical Studies*, 1876; *The Principles of Logic*, 1883; *Appearance and Reality*, 1893; *Essays on Truth and Reality*, 1914; *Aphorisms*, 1930; *Collected Essays*, 1935.

Born: January 30, 1846; Clapham, Surrey, England
Died: September 18, 1924; Oxford, England

Early Life

Francis Herbert Bradley was the fourth child of the Reverend Charles Bradley, an Evangelical minister, and Emma Linton Bradley. Little is known about his early life. He was educated at Cheltenham (1856-1861) and Marlborough (1861-1863), and in 1865 he attended University College, Oxford. In 1870, at the age of twenty-four, he became a fellow at Merton College, Oxford, where he remained until his death in 1924. A year after arriving at Oxford, he contracted a kidney disease that disabled him and left him sick and suffering, sardonic, and sometimes bitter. Fortunately, his fellowship allowed him to pursue scholarship without the added burden of teaching or lecturing, tasks that his disability would never permit. His illness made him something of a recluse, which, in some measure, accounts for his biting, often cruel prose.

Bradley's frail constitution frequently forced him to take shelter from Oxford's severe winters on the southern coast of England or on the French Riviera. On one sojourn to Saint-Raphael in the winter of 1911, he became friends with Elinor Glyn, who was later to depict him as "the sage of Cheiron," in her book *Halcyone* (1912). In appearance, Bradley had a thin face, fine eyes, and a long nose. Fastidious in his habits, he was affable, courteous, and a good conversationalist, although it was said that he did not suffer fools gladly. He is said to have had a small shooting gallery constructed above his living quarters where he practiced routinely. He claimed to be a good marksman and was known to employ his skill on cats.

Life's Work

Bradley had strong political opinions. He was a conservative, perhaps even reactionary, with a lifelong dislike for the English Liberal Party and a specific disgust for its famous leader Prime Minister William Ewart Gladstone. In particular, he was angry at Gladstone for, as he said, betraying General Charles Gordon at Khartoum in the Egyptian Sudan in 1885. For Bradley, Gladstone represented what Bradley characterized as a degrading social sentimentality, an inviolate pacifism, and a false humanitarian notion of the natural equality of persons.

Almost nothing is known about Bradley's private life, except that he dedicated all of his books to "E. R.," an American woman named Mrs. Radcliffe who lived in France. Bradley met her while on holiday in Egypt, and although she had absolutely no literary or philosophical interests, he laid out for her, voluminously, his complete metaphysical system in a series of letters, which she later destroyed. Although his philosophical system had its roots in German soil (specifically in the ideas of Georg Wilhelm Friedrich Hegel, Johann Friedrich Herbart, and Arthur Schopenhauer), he had little time or sympathy for German philosopher Immanuel Kant.

Bradley died of blood poisoning on September 18, 1924, the same year that he was recipient of England's highest literary award, the Order of Merit. The external events in Bradley's life made little mark on him—primarily because as a philosopher, the events of moment were internal and mental—and there can be no understanding of Bradley the man apart from Bradley the philosopher.

Bradley has been described as a man of caustic epigrams and poetic metaphors. He was probably Great Britain's finest philosopher of metaphysics in the nineteenth century. He wrote numerous articles and reviews but only four book-length pieces of major importance: *Ethical Studies, Principles of Logic, Appearance and Reality*, and *Essays on Truth and Reality*. His *Aphorisims* appeared posthumously in 1930, and his *Collected Essays* was published in 1935. Throughout Bradley's works, there is an obsessive criticism of empiricism, or what he refers to as that branch of philosophy's devotion to "sense experience." Empiricism is, Bradley argues, a shallow, surface view of the world with two rather "contemptible" qualities: first, a naïve devotion to the idea that raw sense-data are philosophically significant, and second, a pedestrian attachment to the doctrine of utilitarianism. Utilitarianism, he insists, is the inevitable philosophical result of the ill-conceived dogmas of empiricism. When Bradley was at the height of his powers, his two most illustrious adversaries were the Englishman Bertrand Russell and the American William James. Both men were empiricists and utilitarians.

An analysis of Bradley's thought is difficult because so much of what he wrote is enigmatic and obscure. A primary question for Bradley was that of how one obtains knowledge. Bradley rejected as contradictory the notion that knowledge can be obtained from the senses, as was claimed by the empiricist philosophers John Locke and David Hume. For Bradley, knowledge should begin and end with an analysis of meaning. The proper role of philosophical investigation is understanding the use and meaning of language. This powerful redirection of philosophy from an analysis of sensate ideas in the mind to an analysis of the structure and meaning of language would become a dominant theme in Anglo-American philosophy, owing much to Bradley's initial critical assessment of empiricism.

For Bradley, proper philosophical study is the examination of rationality; that is, it is understanding the "internal connection" that mental ideas have to one another, the internal relations of species, kind, and class (in more contemporary terminology, the investigation into conceptual elements of signs, symbols, and semantics). In other words, the primary interest of philosophy should be in the laws of intelligibility, rather than in particular physical facts or specific sensations as the empiricists had believed. Universal understanding transcends empirical sensations; it requires absolute knowledge. Such knowledge should embrace the logical possibilities of past, present, and future, the real and the imagined. Furthermore, all conceptual worlds are internal and theoretically complete.

Thus, rather than identifying information about an object, such as a lemon, by collecting sense-data, Bradley would begin with the proposition that the lemon exists—in particular, that it possesses qualities. More important, the object, for Bradley, is more than the sum of these qualities. Empiricist Locke had recognized that there is more to things than the sum of their parts, and he called this not-sensed element underlying the sensory ideas "substance." Yet for Locke, substance is unknowable precisely because it is not sensed, a conclusion that leaves those who sense in a state of skepticism about the reality of substance—a position that was acceptable to almost no one except Locke's philosophical heir, Hume.

Bradley argues that the confusion fostered by this notion of substance ends in a rational contradiction. Ostensibly, when one says that a lemon is yellow, one never means that "lemon" and "yellow" mean the same thing, that they are equivalent terms, as two plus three and four plus one are equivalent sets. Yellow, rather, is a quality of lemon; lemon is more than the color yellow. The empiricists would add that the lemon is also ellipsoid in shape. Yet this, for Bradley, leads to confusion, for to say that being an ellipsoid is identical with being a lemon is contradictory, because it means that a lemon is identical with that which is yellow, which it is not, and with that which is ellipsoid, which it is not; finally, it means that that which is yellow is identical with that which is ellipsoid, which it is not. Thus, the empiricist must argue that a lemon is the sum of all its sensed qualities, not merely one of them in contradiction to some others. Hence, the "substance" of a lemon, for the empiricist, must be the collection of all of these discrete qualities taken together: yellow, elliptical, sour, and so forth. A collective relationship of these qualities constitutes the lemon's substance.

It is at this point that Bradley declares empiricism worthless. Suppose, for example, that a lemon is defined as a yellow object that is elliptical and sour. Then yellow is the subject of the proposition declaring it so, and elliptical and sour are predicates of this proposition. Yet it is as possible to define a lemon with sour as the subject and yellow and elliptical as its predicates. These combinations are, in other words, interchangeable. What this demonstrates, Bradley argues, is that these qualities are interchangeable as subjects and predicates, and hence, it is the relationship in which people think and talk about these qualities that properly establishes the meaning of "lemon." Thus, a lemon is something more than the sum of its sensed qualities; it is a cognitive entity. Yet one should not assume that there is a kind of Lockean substance underlying the sensed qualities because this only sustains the contradictions that the limits of sense perceptions produce.

For Bradley, there is an Archimedean point on which any definition of reality is to be balanced: That point is freedom from contradiction. In order to escape contradiction, all qualities must be internally related to all other elements of experience in a single conceptual system. This "transcendent" view of reality, however, requires Bradley to employ the language of the European Idealists, most particularly the discourse of the post-Hegelians. Therefore, reality, the "substance behind" appearances, is not material, it is mental. In Bradley's words, it is a conceptual "unity of all multiplicity." Human knowledge is filled with contradictions; nevertheless, it is also a part of a wider and higher relation: It is part of "absolute experience." Thus, appearances (sense-data) are manifestations in lesser degree of something conceptually truer, morally higher, and aesthetically more beautiful. Collectively for society, idealized experience is nearer to the heart of things. Higher idealized experience draws society closer to ideals of perfection, closer to its historical myths about God. Reality, thus, is idealized experience, not sensible experience. Bradley thus changed the focus in philosophy from observation of phenomena to an examination of pure reality, which is mental.

Influence

Oxford philosopher Gilbert Ryle observed that when Bradley began his career, the burning issues in philosophy were between theologians and antitheologians. They were issues of faith and doubt. When he died in 1924, philosophical energies had turned to ratiocinative technique and rigor. Transcendental dicta had lost their influence, and the technicalities of logical theory, linguistic meaning, and the investigation of scientific methodology had changed the tone and temperament of philosophers. Theologians had withdrawn from the battle with scientists, claiming that their endeavors were conducted in different domains: Religion spoke to the needs, aspirations, and hopes of supplicants, while science was searching for explanations of the world's operations. Theology thus maintained a certain immunity from the restrictive, austere propositions of science, enabling theological language to become more subjective and introspective. It became the language of feeling and aspirations, a verbal instrument of communal persuasion and solidarity. Within these limits, only the most literal believers would fear the quantitative onslaught of science.

Bradley, however, had no sympathy with this verbal compromise. He believed it to be a futile, crippling solution. Scientific knowledge is not in another domain; it is, rather, an attempt to understand reality. Theology and metaphysics should do no less, according to Bradley. Transcendental philosophy had been abandoned because it was unable to withstand the inexorable successes of science.

For more than two centuries, English philosophy had attempted to imitate the method of science with a philosophy of "mental science," a science of sense experience. This method failed. In fact, it produced only circumlocutions and contradictions. Bradley led philosophy into the realm of logical and semantical discourse, where its primary task was a search for meaning and understanding. Thought and judgment became the primary function of conceptual inquiry. Bradley's philosophical method begins and ends with the premise that truth is the systematic application of self-consistent coherent propositions that are derivatively appropriate, in a rationally unifying fashion, to all aspects of human experience. He envisioned a rationally coherent metaphysics that would replace an antiquated theology and supplant the spiritually bereft notions of science.

D. Burrill

Appearance and Reality

Type of philosophy: Metaphysics
First published: 1893
Principal ideas advanced:

◇ The distinction between primary (sensed) qualities of physical objects and secondary (structural) qualities is based on appearance; in reality, there is no such distinction.

◇ Upon analysis, it turns out that space, time, objects, and selves are appearances, not realities; the concepts do not stand up because alleged differences vanish when it is discovered that definitions are circular, empty, or inconsistent.

◇ The logical character of reality is that it does not contradict itself; the metaphysical character of reality is that it is one; and the epistemological character of reality is that it is experience.

◇ Reality, or the Absolute, must be because appearances are the appearances of reality.

◇ In judgment, an idea is predicated on a real subject; a judgment is true insofar as it predicates harmonious content, removing inconsistency—but because predicates are ideal, every truth is but a partial truth, every error but a partial error.

F. H. Bradley wrote with the confidence of a leader in the mainstream of British philosophy between the 1870's and the 1920's. His speculation, strongly influenced by Georg Wilhelm Friedrich Hegel, was highly metaphysical; and his intention was to arrive at ultimate truths about the universe as a whole. His general method was to show that the world regarded as made up of discrete objects is self-contradictory and, therefore, a world of appearances. The real is one, a world in which there are no separate objects and in which all differences disappear. Curiously

enough, Bradley's conclusions about reality have not been of primary interest to philosophers in the latter half of the twentieth century. It is, rather, his critical method that they have found important, his destruction of the world of appearance.

In the preface to *Appearance and Reality*, Bradley describes metaphysics as "the finding of bad reasons for what we believe on instinct, but to find these reasons is no less an instinct." He warns the reader that many of the ideas he presents must certainly be wrong, but because he is unable to discover how they are wrong, others will have to be critical of his conclusions.

If metaphysics is so liable to error, why should Bradley bother to study it, much less write more than six hundred pages about it? He reminds readers that they have all had experiences of something beyond the material world and that they need metaphysics to understand these experiences, at least insofar as they admit of being understood. Metaphysical speculation on its constructive and critical side protects people from the extremes of cross materialism and dogmatic orthodoxy. The study of metaphysics teaches that either of these solutions is too simple, that both are peremptory. "There is no sin, however prone to it the philosopher may be," Bradley says, "which philosophy can justify so little as spiritual pride."

Appearance

Appearance and Reality is divided into two parts. In the first part, "Appearance," Bradley deals with some of the recurring problems of philosophy, such as quality, relation, space, time, causation, and self. His general intention was to show that these problems have been formulated in such a way that no determinate solution can be found for them, that the world viewed from their perspective is contradictory and, therefore, appearance.

The first problem with which Bradley deals is the division of the properties of objects into primary and secondary qualities. According to this theory, primary qualities are those spatial aspects of things that are perceived or felt, and all other qualities are secondary. Primary qualities are constant, permanent, self-dependent, and real. Secondary qualities—such as color, heat, cold, taste, and odor—are relative to the perceiver.

In one of his arguments against this view, Bradley grants that secondary qualities are mere appearances because he wishes to show that the same thing is true of primary qualities. If an object has secondary qualities, even though they are relative to the perceiver, they must have some ground in the object. A thing can be relative only if the terms of the relation are real. For example, in the sentence, "The table is to the left of the chair," the relation, "to the left of" can hold only if there are a table and a chair. Consequently, to show that a quality is relative is to show that it is grounded in an object. The ground or terms of the relation must be real for the relation to hold. Consequently, secondary cannot mean unreal, as some proponents of the theory seem to argue that it does. Again, primary qualities must also be perceived and would be relative for the same reason given for secondary qualities. The division of the properties of objects into primary or secondary qualities turns out on close examination to be mistaken. This division, which has seemed real to many philosophers, is merely an appearance.

The structure of Bradley's argument, which often recurs in this section of the book, can be stated as follows: Some opponent maintains that x is different in kind from y, but both x and y are seen to depend on a. The opponent takes a as the defining property of x; therefore it is inconsistent not to take it as the defining property of y. Thus x and y are not different in kind. The opponent defined them from different points of view and concluded that they were different in kind from the difference in definition. The alleged difference is merely one of appearance.

Bradley's argument that space is unreal or an appearance involves the question of whether space has an end. If one thinks of a small portion of space, one thinks of it as bounded. The space between the table and the chair is bounded by the table and the chair. However, space itself cannot be bounded. What would be outside it? However, precise boundaries determine space. This difficulty arises from regarding space first of all as a relation with the table and chair as its terms and then regarding it as a quality that is unlimited. Space cannot be a relation because any space can be divided into smaller spaces. However, to divide space is to have a relation with

another relation as its terms. "Space," says Bradley, "is essentially a relation of what vanishes into relations, which seek in vain for their terms. It is lengths of lengths of—nothing that we can find."

However, if space is a quality, it must have limits because it is a quality in contrast to some other quality. However, this other quality does not exist. If it did, space would be a relation. According to Bradley, the philosophers who have thought of space as real have wanted to think of it both as infinite and ideal and as limited and experienced. Neither of these views by itself is enough, but one can be maintained only at the expense of the other.

A similar argument applies to time. If time is composed of units, it has no duration. If it has duration, it has no units and no before or after. As he had said of space, Bradley avers, "Time . . . must be made and yet cannot be made of pieces."

The world seems to be made up of things or objects. However, what is a thing? A minimum qualification for being a thing is to be located somewhere and probably at some time. However, one cannot make clear the notions of spatial or temporal location. Not only must a thing be located but also it must have qualities; yet here again is a notion to which one cannot give any determinate meaning. In Bradley's analysis, the world of this and that has disappeared.

If the external world is appearance, what of the self? Surely here is a constant point of reference. However, the world "self" has many meanings. If the self is defined in terms of what is not self, that is, the external world, then this external world must have some meaning. If the self is understood by self-examination, then it is at once subject and object—an impossibility.

Now that objects and selves have become appearances, Bradley has only the world of things-in-themselves to deal with. However, if things-in-themselves are absolutely unknown, then their existence itself is unknown; and to the extent that things-in-themselves are known, they are not things-in-themselves.

In the section on appearance, whatever Bradley examined turned out to be appearance, to be inconsistent with itself. However, it was not proved that these inconsistent entities have no connection with the real. Reality completely divorced from appearance would have no meaning. One must look for some way in which appearance and reality can be joined, and it is to this problem that the second part of the book, "Reality," is devoted.

Reality

Bradley maintains that there are three fundamental properties of reality: logical, epistemological, and metaphysical. The logical character of reality is that it does not contradict itself. This immediately differentiates reality from appearance. The metaphysical property is that reality is one, another characteristic to be contrasted with appearance. The epistemological property is that reality is experience. This is Bradley's way of putting the central doctrine of German idealism that the real is the rational. For him, to be rational is to be in some mind. A rational, nonmental world could at best be merely potentially rational. However, to be in some mind is to be experience. These three principles, as Bradley develops them, are seen to be constitutive of all reality and, as such, are metaphysical principles.

Reality, taken as the totality of all that exists, Bradley calls the Absolute. There must be such a reality because something can be an appearance only if it is the appearance of something. The problem now is to show how such things as appearance, evil, finite objects, error, time, and space are related to and are compatible with this Absolute.

Before the question of the Absolute can be settled, truth must be defined. What is a real object? Bradley says that every real thing has at least two properties, existence and characteristics. One has to be able to say that the entity *is* and *what* it is. However, to be able to say something is, one must have ideas, and through judgment, an idea is predicated of a real subject. Existence, then, is contained in the subject, and the predicate contains an ideal character that it relates to the real subject. According to Bradley, "Truth is the object of thinking, and the aim of truth is to qualify existence ideally." Furthermore, "Truth is the predication of such content as, when predicated, is harmonious, and removes inconsistency and with it unrest." However, a truth is never wholly adequate. The predicate is only ideal, not real. Therefore, every truth is a partial truth and is

capable of being expanded and extended indefinitely toward more truth.

If one can account for truth, one must also account for error. The Absolute exists and what is not a part of the Absolute does not exist. Error seems to be an exception. It cannot exist as part of the Absolute because it is in contradiction with it and is hence, error. It cannot be nonexistent because people really do make errors. It is as naïve to think that there is no error as it is to think that there is no evil in the world. On the other hand, there is a sense in which error is a partial truth. The subject and predicate refer to real things and the relation asserted between them does exist. However, this partiality is also the source of error. It is a partiality that must be supplemented to become truth. Its error is in its one-sidedness; but in spite of that, it expresses one side or aspect of the Absolute.

If solipsism were true, it would be a forceful argument against the Absolute. The argument in favor of solipsism may be stated as follows: Whatever I am conscious of is an experience. However, every experience is my private experience. Therefore, all I can know are various states of my own mind. Bradley's answer to this view is through definitions of the term "experience." There are two meanings that the term may have. One is that experience is a succession of bare mental states, unrelated to one another. This meaning of experience is not enough for solipsists because they must be able to talk about a self or mind that is the agent or subject of the experiences. Thus the experiences on which solipsism is based must be more than bare mental states. They are experiences that go beyond the moment of feeling. However, solipsists may say that experience in going beyond the present moment stops short at the self. Even for them, this self must have a past and a future, which are constructed by inference from the present self. However, in the same way that solipsists infer the existence of other states of their own selves, they could infer other selves. The truth in solipsism is that one can know the universe only through one's own experiences and sensations. Its falsity is that it wishes to stop the expansion of experience at an arbitrary point. For Bradley, the expansion of experience, once begun, cannot stop short of the Absolute.

Are things more or less real and statements more or less true? Bradley says, "The Absolute considered as such, has of course no degrees; for it is perfect, and there can be no more or less in perfection." However, if the Absolute is perfectly real and statements of it perfectly true, then true statements of anything other than the Absolute must be less true and refer to something less real. It seems odd to say that one thing is less real than another. One would be inclined to think that a thing is either real or not: This chair is real; ghosts never are. However, it is easy to see Bradley's difficulty. Either every statement must be of the Absolute, or some must be less true than others. The same consideration must be applied to existence. Properly speaking, only the Absolute exists, and you, I, and the gatepost exist only partially.

No propositions are adequate to the Absolute; and Bradley says, "There will be no truth which is entirely true, just as there will be no error which is totally false. With all alike, if taken strictly, it will be a question of amount, and will be a matter of more or less." However, even this doctrine must have a proviso: "Our thoughts certainly, for some purposes, may be taken as wholly false, or again as quite accurate; but truth and error, measured by the Absolute, must each be subject always to degree."

Bradley discussed morality in *Ethical Studies* (1876). In *Appearance and Reality*, he treats goodness as a metaphysical category. One might ask the question, "Is the Absolute good?" The answer is that good is an incomplete category, simply one aspect of perfection. Beauty, truth, and so on are good, but they are something else besides. Good is limited in its scope; but, limited, it cannot be a property of the Absolute. "Goodness, as such, is but appearance which is transcended in the Absolute."

Surely, then, the Absolute must be God. However, the God of religion must be an object to humanity. The God of religion must be available. However, if God has these properties, then he is appearance. The logic of development in Bradley's metaphysics cannot be suspended even for God. If God is another name for the Absolute, then he is unavailable to humanity. However, if he is not the Absolute, then he is subordinate to it. The God of religion must remain in the

world of appearances. Thus religion would have little to recommend it if it were knowledge. The essential factor in religion is not knowledge. It is, Bradley says, "the attempt to express the complete reality of goodness through every aspect of our being."

Most of the doctrines attributed to Bradley have been negative. Many of the things in which people most firmly believe are revealed as appearances, half-truths at best. However, only the Absolute is true. What can one say about it? One can only approach a description of the Absolute because no statements are infinite as statements of this sort would have to be. The Absolute is perfection. Insofar as a statement approaches perfection, insofar as the system approaches completeness, one's statements become more nearly true. A statement will be more nearly complete to the extent that its opposite is inconceivable. A statement is inconceivable when its truth would falsify a system of truths. Thus a true statement is one related to other truths within a system, and the more comprehensive the system, the more nearly true the statement.

Truth about the Absolute is only one part of the Absolute itself. Truth refers to statements that are abstract, but the Absolute itself is reality and concrete. Philosophy, the concern of which is truth, can only hope to be partial at best. Bradley says, "Truth, when made adequate to Reality, would be so supplemented as to have become something else—something other than truth, and something for us unattainable." However, there are degrees of truth; and insofar as their limits are determined, truths are genuine.

In an early chapter of *Appearance and Reality*, Bradley states that "what is *possible*, and what a general principle compels us to say *must be*, that certainly *is*." There is some sense in which this statement is the key to what Bradley does in *Appearance and Reality*. His sharp, critical mind led him to reject much of what common sense would admit. The few principles that remain, he accepted reluctantly because they seemed to him impervious to attack. What could he construct with the material that he had left? Logical necessity led him into a world in which no one could feel at home, a world that transcends the scope of philosophy and even of language.

John Collinson

Additional Reading

Bradley, James, ed. *Philosophy After F. H. Bradley: A Collection of Essays*. Bristol, England: Thoemmes Press, 1996. These essays deal with both historical and present-day issues. Representing some of the most acute analysis and assessment available, they presuppose some philosophical sophistication and, in a few essays, some understanding of the rudiments of symbolic logic.

Eliot, T. S. *Knowledge and Experience in the Philosophy of F. H. Bradley*. New York: Columbia University Press, 1989. Originally submitted in 1916 as Eliot's Harvard doctoral dissertation, this is a beautifully argued and independent exposition of F. H. Bradley's epistemology as conveyed in *Appearance and Reality*. Defends Bradley against the views and criticisms of Alexius Meinong and Bertrand Russell.

Ingardia, Richard. *Bradley: A Research Bibliography*. Bowling Green, Ohio: Bowling Green State University Press, 1991. A selective, research-oriented bibliography, which lists more than a thousand secondary sources published through June, 1990. It opens with a charming memoir of Bradley by Brand Blanshard.

Mander, W. J. *An Introduction to Bradley's Metaphysics*. Oxford: Clarendon Press, 1994. Centers on the relation between thought and reality and uncovers Bradley's core beliefs about the logical structure of reality, space, and time. Difficult in places but still the best single introduction to Bradley's metaphysics and some opposing viewpoints. Excellent bibliography.

_____, ed. *Perspectives on the Logic and Metaphysics of F. H. Bradley*. Idealism Series. Bristol, England: Thoemmes Press, 1997. This collection of papers spans a wide range of philosophical concerns regarding Bradley and his influence. Useful for advanced undergraduates.

Manser, Anthony R., and Guy Stock, ed. *The Philosophy of F. H. Bradley*. Oxford: Clarendon Press, 1984. This superb collection of papers relates Bradley's thought to contemporary philosophy. It covers the philosophy of history, ethics, the nature of punishment, political philosophy, the theory of judgment, epistemology (somewhat technical), truth, and skepticism.

Muirhead, John. *The Platonic Tradition in Anglo-Saxon Philosophy*. London: Allen & Unwin, 1931. Reprint. New York: Humanities, 1967. This is a good, though brief, account of Bradley's philosophical development, particularly his reaction to Immanuel Kant and Georg Wilhelm Friedrich Hegel. Muirhead's work is somewhat informal but still accurate and worthwhile.

Saxena, Sushil Kumar. *Studies in the Metaphysics of Bradley*. London: George Allen & Unwin; New York: Humanities Press, 1967. Charges that Bradley has been the victim of unfair criticism, and clarifies and defends Bradley in his debate with Bertrand Russell on relational forms. Suitable for undergraduates.

Sprigge, T. L. S. *James and Bradley: American Truth and British Reality*. William James and Bradley dominated the philosophy of the United States and Britain, respectively, in their time. This study demystifies Bradley's metaphysics, theories of judgment and truth, and concept of the self. Comprehensive bibliography.

Stock, Guy, ed. *Appearance Versus Reality: New Essays on Bradley's Metaphysics*. Oxford: Clarendon Press, 1998. Though challenging to read, this is the best source for those who wish to understand Bradley's place in relation to the twentieth century analytic tradition.

Wollheim, Richard. *F. H. Bradley*. London: Penguin Books, 1960. Reprint. Chicago: Open Court, 1993. Explains Bradley's hierarchy of knowledge or experience, his esoteric ethical thought, and his condemnation of British empiricism. Recommends *The Principles of Logic* as an introduction to Bradley's thought. This lucid book is an excellent starting point for undergraduates and the general reader.

D. Burrill, updated by Grant A. Marler

Giordano Bruno

With his daring and speculative theories in astronomy and philosophy, Bruno anticipated many of the achievements of modern science, but his stubborn personality and arcane interests brought him into inevitable conflict with the authorities of his time.

Principal philosophical works: *Cantus Ciraeus*, 1582; *De umbris idearum*, 1582; *De la causa, principio e uno*, 1584 (*Concerning the Cause, Principle, and One*, 1950); *De l'infinitio universo e modi*, 1584 (*On the Infinite Universe and Worlds*, 1950); *La Cena de le Ceneri*, 1584 (*The Ash Wednesday Supper*, 1975); *Spaccio de la bestia trionfante*, 1584 (*The Expulsion of the Triumphant Beast*, 1713); *Cabala del cavallo Pegaseo*, 1585; *De gli eroici furori*, 1585 (*The Heroic Frenzies*, 1959).

Born: 1548; Nola, near Naples (now in Italy)
Died: February 17, 1600; Rome

Early Life

Giordano Bruno was born in 1548 in Nola, in what is now Italy. He was the son of Juano Bruno, a professional soldier, and his wife, Fraulissa Savolino. As a child, Bruno was named Filippo; he took the name Giordano when he entered the Dominican Order. He was sometimes known as "the Nolan," after the town of his birth, and he often referred to himself in this fashion in his works.

From contemporary records and his own writings, Bruno seems to have been a particularly intelligent and impressionable child. He left several accounts of odd, almost visionary experiences in his youth, including an extended, quasi-mystical dialogue with the mountain Vesuvius that first revealed to him the deceptiveness of appearances and the relativity of all material things. These were to become two dominant themes in his philosophy.

As a youth, Bruno was sent to Naples, where he attended the Studium Generale, concentrating in the humanities, logic, and dialectic. It is clear that Bruno had a thorough grounding in Aristotle and his philosophy and also was well acquainted with the works of Plato and the writings of the Neoplatonists, who were then creating considerable intellectual activity and controversy, especially in Italy.

In 1565, when Bruno was seventeen, he entered the Dominican Order, moving within the walls of the monastery of San Domenico in Naples. There he took the name Giordano. Bruno's decision to enter the Dominican Order is puzzling, for in retrospect, it clearly stands as the major mistake in his often-turbulent life. Although he was well suited for the intellectual studies of the Dominicans, he was quite unfit for the accompanying intellectual discipline and submission required for the monastic and clerical life. His thoughts were too wide-ranging and innovative to be restrained within traditional confines, a situation that eventually placed him in mortal conflict with the Church.

Bruno spent eleven years in the monastery of San Domenico. He studied Saint Thomas Aquinas, Aristotle, and other traditional figures but at the same time was reading in the mystical doctrines of the Neoplatonists, the new works of Desiderius Erasmus, and the works of other reformers and seems to have become suspiciously well acquainted with the works of heretics such as Arius. These unorthodox diversions brought him into conflict with the Dominican authorities, and reports were made that Bruno was defending the Arian heresy. Arius had taught that God the Father and God the Son were not the same in essence. When the Dominicans learned that Bruno was suspected of defending Arianism, charges were prepared against him. Learning of this, he fled the monastery in 1576. He was age twenty-eight, and he would spend the rest of his life in exile or in prison.

Life's Work

When Bruno fled the monastery, he embarked on twenty-one years of wandering throughout Europe. Many of his stops lasted merely a matter of months, and the most productive, for only three years. Controversy and conflict dogged him on his travels—much of it a result of not only his daring and speculative thought but also his unrestrained attacks on those who opposed him in any degree and his innate lack of common sense or practical judgment. Employment was difficult, and income was insufficient and insecure. Yet, during this period, Bruno wrote and published an enormous body of work whose content far outpaced even the most advanced thinkers of his time.

Bruno's first extended sojourn was in Geneva. There, safe from the power of the Church, he soon plunged into local intellectual conflicts. In 1579, he published a scathing attack on Antoine de la Faye, a noted professor of philosophy at the University of Geneva. Bruno's assault was more than an academic exercise, for he seemed to undermine de la Faye's theories, which were the basis for the quasi-theological government of Geneva. Bruno, the renegade Dominican on the run, had put himself in disfavor with the Calvinists of Switzerland. He was arrested, then released; he soon left Geneva, moving first to Lyons, then to Toulouse, France. In 1581, Bruno went to Paris, where he found his first real success. He lectured on his own techniques of memory, and the results were so impressive that King Henry III summoned Bruno to court to explain his methods. As a result, the king appointed Bruno to the Collège de France. Bruno held the post for two years, lecturing on philosophy and natural science and publishing a number of books, many of them on his art of memory.

Still, he managed to alienate many fellow professors and intellectuals in Paris. Some were outraged by his arrogant and self-proclaimed superiority, while the more conventional were troubled by his unorthodox views and desertion of his monastic vows. In 1583, Bruno left for London, with a letter of recommendation to the French ambassador Michel de Castelnau.

The London period, from 1583 through 1585, was the most productive of Bruno's career. Perhaps he was stimulated by the intellectual climate of England, for not only did he deliver a series of lectures at Oxford, explaining the Copernican theory, but also he had among his acquaintances noted figures of the English Renaissance such as Sir Philip Sidney, Sir Walter Raleigh, and Sir Fulke Greville. In 1584, Bruno produced a series of six dialogues expounding his philosophy; three of these dealt with cosmological issues and three with moral topics.

In *The Ash Wednesday Supper*, Bruno laid the foundation for his scientific theories. He began with the view of Nicolaus Copernicus that the sun, rather than the earth, was the center of the

Giordano Bruno. (*Library of Congress*)

307

solar system. Bruno recognized that the sun was itself a star, and he concluded that other stars must have their attendant planets circling them. He came to the conclusion that the universe was infinite, and that it therefore contained an infinite number of worlds, each world capable of having intelligent life on it. Such a theory ran counter to the traditions of both the Catholic Church and the newer Protestant faiths.

Bruno continued the development of his theories in *On the Infinite Universe and Worlds*. He systematically criticized the prevailing Aristotelian cosmology and, in its place, put forth a precursor of the modern theory of relativity later developed by Albert Einstein. Bruno maintained that sensory knowledge could never be absolute, only relative, and it is this relativity that misleads humans in their attempts to understand the universe. Human perceptions are incapable of truly and completely comprehending the universe, and that universe itself can be accurately comprehended only as a total unity, rather than in isolated parts. Therefore, neither senses nor imagination can be fully trusted, but only reason, which allows humans to penetrate to the divine essence of creation.

Bruno also developed a theory that the universe was composed of "minima," extremely small particles much like the atoms proposed by the ancient Roman philosopher Lucretius. Like Lucretius, Bruno thought that certain motions and events were inevitable and that the universe develops inexorably out of inherent necessity. In order to resolve the conflict between this deterministic view and free will, Bruno postulated that the universe itself was divine; he projected a universal pantheism in which the Creator manifests himself through and within creation.

Finally, Bruno resolved the difficulty of the relationship of human beings to God, of the finite to the infinite, or ignorance to knowledge. These were long-standing puzzles to theologians and philosophers, for it seemed impossible that humans' limited minds could comprehend or understand the perfect and infinite attributes of divinity. Bruno believed that there was an identity of opposites at work in which the essential elements of creation and divinity are found in all parts of the universe. Opposition is only relative and illusory; on the most fundamental level,

everything is the same, and everything is therefore divine.

In 1585, Castelnau was recalled to Paris, and Bruno, left without a patron, was forced to leave England. For the next six years, he wandered through Europe, accepting and losing posts at a number of universities in Germany and the Holy Roman Empire. He continued to write and publish prolifically, including his special area of study, memory, and, in the fall of 1591, he received an invitation from a Venetian nobleman, Zuane Mocenigo, to come to Venice and teach him the art of memory.

Bruno accepted, believing that he would be safe in Venice, which was at that time a fairly liberal and independent state that carefully guarded its freedom from the papacy. There was a dispute between Bruno and his patron, however—apparently the nobleman believed that he was being cheated and that Bruno planned to flee to Germany—and on May 23, 1592, Bruno was arrested by the Venetian Inquisition. He was questioned through September, but no decision was made.

On February 27, 1593, Bruno was delivered into the hands of the Roman Inquisition, and for the next seven years, he was held in prison, repeatedly questioned and examined and urged to recant his heresies and confess his sins. Bruno tried to play a crafty game, willing to admit minor infractions but pretending not to comprehend how his cosmological and philosophical writings could run counter to the teachings of the Church. Finally, in February, 1600, the Inquisition found him guilty and delivered him to the secular authorities for punishment. When Bruno heard the decision, he replied, "Perhaps you who pronounce my sentence are in greater fear than I who receive it." On Saturday, February 17, 1600, Bruno was burned in the Square of Flowers in Rome.

Influence

Bruno was a philosopher of great insight and imagination, yet a thinker who could link science to magic and yoke philosophical understanding to mnemonic tricks. He was poised amid the thought and traditions of the Church, the mystical teachings of the Neoplatonists, and the rapid advances of the sciences, especially astronomy.

From the combination of these three traditions, he forged a new and highly individual vision of the cosmos and humankind's place in it.

Bruno's influence was recognized by both scientists and humanists in the years following his death. Scientists, even to modern times, admire the startling insights that he drew concerning the infinite number of worlds in an infinite universe. Bruno's early recognition of the concept of relativity and the place that it must play in humanity's conception and understanding of the universe is also a prime legacy that Bruno left to science. Humanists of the period were profoundly influenced by his insistence on the need for tolerance in matters of religion and belief. Perhaps because Bruno himself was so often a victim of the intolerance of the age, he was especially eloquent in his plea for patience and understanding.

Finally, Bruno combined the sense of infinite expansion and relativity of all things with a new approach to human knowledge and culture. He refused to divide the world into the sacred and the profane, the Christian and the heathen, the orthodox and the heretic. Instead, he saw human life and culture as a single strand and the universe as a divine manifestation that carried with it all knowledge and truth. To Bruno, the cosmos was God's creation and therefore all good, and humanity's role was not to judge but to understand.

Michael Witkoski

Concerning the Cause, Principle, and One

Type of philosophy: Metaphysics, philosophical theology

First published: De la causa, principio e uno, 1584 (English translation, 1950)

Principal ideas advanced:

◇ Knowledge of the first cause and principle of the universe can be acquired only with difficulty through the study of remote effects.

◇ God is the first principle of all things in that, as the world soul pervading all nature, his nature is the nature of all things.

◇ God is the first cause of all things because all things have being as the result of the informing action of the world soul.

◇ There is but one substance; but one may distinguish *form*, the power to make, from *matter*, the power to be made.

◇ Matter is passive potency in that it can be more than it is; but it is also act in that it contains the forms that, given the efficient cause, it unfolds.

◇ The universe is one, infinite, immobile; all multiplicity is in appearance only.

Giordano Bruno's *Concerning the Cause, Principle, and One* is the work of one of the most brilliant and courageous philosophers of the Italian Renaissance. He was a man of faith with an independent and creative mind. His views did not win favor with the Dominicans with whom he had allied himself, and he was forced to leave the Order. He moved from place to place, provoking criticism wherever he settled. In France and England, he produced some of his most famous works, but he finally had to move on. He spent some time in Germany and Switzerland. When he went to Venice in 1591, he became a victim of the Inquisition. He was tried, imprisoned in Rome, and finally burned at the stake because of his refusal to recant.

His philosophy of the universe is in the grand tradition of metaphysics and theology in that it describes an infinite universe that is God, and it attempts to explain how a world that presents a bewildering number of aspects to those viewing it from various perspectives can nevertheless be regarded as a unity. Perpetuating Neoplatonic ideas and showing the influence of Plotinus, Bruno used his philosophic and poetic resources to build an image of a universe made perfect by the light of God that affects the existence and nature of everything. God is the principle, the cause, and the unity of the infinite universe.

Bruno, like seventeenth century philosopher Gottfried Wilhelm Leibniz, used the idea of the unity of body and soul, or *monad*, and a manifestation of divine energy. *Concerning the Cause, Principle, and One* prepares the way for the idea of the monad by describing God as the world soul pervading all being.

The first dialogue of the work introduces

Filoteo, a philosopher who serves as the figure of Bruno. It presents a good-humored defense of philosophy, but not without suggesting the difficulties that come to one who has the courage of his convictions. The conversation is with two friends, Heliotropio and Armesso. Bruno, in the "Introductory Epistle," describes the first dialogue as "an apology, or something else I know not what, concerning the five dialogues of 'Le cena de le ceneri,'" *The Ash Wednesday Supper*, one of his satirical dialogues.

Cause

With the second dialogue, the proper body of the work begins. The interlocutors are Alexander Dixon, described as having proposed the subject matter to Theophilus, who is Filoteo (or Teofilo), or Bruno; Gervasius, not a philosopher, a person who "neither stinks nor smells" and who "makes jokes of the things that Polyhymnius says"; and Polyhymnius, a "sacrilegious pedant . . . one of the most rigid censors of philosophers."

Theophilus, the lover of God (whose name means literally that), explains to the others that it is only with the greatest difficulty that the first cause and principle is known; the divine substance, because of its infinitude and distance from its effects, can be known only through traces, the remote effects of its action. To call God first principle and first cause is to say the same thing from different points of view; God is first principle "inasmuch as all things are after him . . . either according to their nature, or according to their duration, or according to their worthiness." God is first cause "inasmuch as all things are distinct from him as the effect from the efficient." Theophilus explains that the term "principle" is more general than the term "cause": a point is the principle of a line but not its cause. Principle has to do with the nature of a thing, cause with its production.

God is then described as "universal physical efficient cause" and as "universal intellect." In response to a question from Dixon, Theophilus explains what he means by "universal intellect." The intellect is the most real and proper faculty of the world soul; it illumines the universe and is the mover of all things; it is the "world architect"; it is what the Magi regarded as the seed sower, what Orpheus called the eye of the world, what

Empedocles regarded as the distinguisher, what Plotinus called the father and progenitor, the "proximate dispenser of forms," and what Theophilus himself calls "the inner artificer."

Dixon wonders what the formal cause (the idea, the plan) of the universe is, if God, or the universal intellect, is the efficient cause (what brings things to existence); he ventures the answer that the formal cause is the "ideal concept" in the divine intellect. Theophilus agrees, and he supplements Dixon's remark that the final cause (the purpose) of the universe is the perfection of it by saying that the final cause, as well as the efficient cause, is universal in the universe. A problem disturbs Dixon: He wonders how the same subject can be both the principle and the cause of natural things. Theophilus answers that although the soul informs the entire universe and is an intrinsic and formal part of it—the principle of the universe—nevertheless, considered as governor and efficient cause, it is not a part.

Theophilus then comes forth with an idea that startles Dixon, the claim that the forms of natural objects are souls and that all things are animated. Although Dixon is willing to concede that the universe is animated, he has not considered that Theophilus would regard every part as animated, and he protests, "It is common sense that not all things are alive." Theophilus is insistent; everything has a vital principle. This claim is too much for Polyhymnius: "Then my shoes, my slippers, my boots, my spurs, my ring and my gloves will be animate?" Gervasius assures him that they are because they have within them "an animal such as you." Theophilus finally reassures them by saying that tables as tables, glass as glass, and so forth, are not animate, but as composites of matter and form, they are all affected by spiritual substance and in that sense are animated by spirit. However, not everything having soul is called animate. There is an intrinsic, formal, eternal principle in all things; it is the One in all things, the world soul in every part, the soul of all parts. Although distinctions can be made between forms, all forms are finally unified in one substantial ground. However, the world soul is not present corporeally; it does not stretch out to cover the universe; rather, it is present in its entirety in every part as the formal principle of every part.

Form and Matter

When the discussion is resumed (in the third dialogue), Theophilus mentions philosophers who have taken matter as primary and as the only reality. Confessing that he himself once held this view, he adds that he has come to the opinion that there are two forms of substance in the world: form and matter, active potency and passive potency, the power to make and the power to be made. Neither matter nor form can be dissolved or annihilated, although changes of form are common. There is, then, the one soul and formal principle that is the cause and principle of all things; there are the forms supplied by that principle; and there is one matter, the "receptacle of forms."

Matter is regarded as a potency and as a substratum. Potency is either active or passive. Passive potency is common to all matter; it is the capacity to be other than in actuality it is. Only the One is all that it can be, for it contains all being; consequently it contains all that which is passively potent as well as all other being. However, death, corruption, vices, and defects, according to Theophilus, are neither act (actively potent) nor passively potent. God is both absolute act and absolute potency, and he cannot be apprehended by the intellect except in a negative way.

After some jesting between Polyhymnius and Gervasius—the theme being that matter is like woman, stubborn, inconstant, never satisfied with its present form, and so forth—Theophilus resumes (in the fourth dialogue) his discussion of matter, arguing that matter is the substratum of all beings, both corporeal and intelligible. He quotes Plotinus's remark that "if this sensible world is the imitation of the intelligible world, the composition of this is the imitation of the composition of that." Other reasons are offered in support of the thesis that there is only one matter. Matter in itself has no determinate dimensions and is indivisible; it is only in virtue of form that what is capable of receiving dimension actually acquires it. However, matter, even when deprived of form, is not pure potency; matter as deprived of form is not like darkness deprived of light, but like "the pregnant . . . without its progeny, which she sends forth and obtains from herself." Matter is that which unfolds "out of its own bosom" that which it has enfolded; it contains within itself all the forms that it is capable of taking on; it is not a pure nothing, but a subject. Form could not arise to inform the matter that enfolds it were matter pure potency.

The fifth dialogue begins with the words of Theophilus: "The universe is, then, one, infinite, immobile." The multiplicity in the universe, the change, the diversity—all this is in appearance and relative to the senses; properly considered, every part of the universe is, in its mode of being, the One. Despite the existence of particular things, everything is one in substance, being, form, and matter; and there is but one cause and principle of all things. Properly speaking, there are no distinctions if one considers the substance of things; for there is but one substance, the infinite, the world soul, the divine intellect. To Polyhymnius, who hears but does not understand and begs for an example, Theophilus explains how a unity can account for apparent multiplicity; he uses an example from arithmetic: A decade is a unity, but is embracing; a hundred is more embracing, although still a unity; a thousand is even more embracing. However, the one is the highest good, the highest beatitude, perfection; it is "the unity which embraces all."

Theophilus, having faithfully served as the apologist of the philosophy of the Nolan (Bruno of Nola), closes with words of praise: "Praised be the Gods, and extolled by all the living be the infinite, the simplest, the most unified, the highest, and the most absolute cause, principle, and the one."

Ian P. McGreal

Additional Reading

Boulting, William. *Giordano Bruno, His Life, Thought, and Martyrdom.* New York: E. P. Dutton, 1916. A classic biography that gives a favorable account of Giordano Bruno's life. Contains an index.

De León-Jones, Karen Silvia. *Giordano Bruno and the Kabbalah: Prophets, Magicians, and Rabbis.* New Haven, Conn.: Yale University Press, 1997. A study of Bruno's Kabbalistic system. Includes useful appendices, a bibliography, and index.

De Santillana, Giorgia. *The Age of Adventure: The Renaissance Philosophers.* Boston: Houghton

Mifflin, 1957. An introduction to Bruno and his philosophy. Discusses Bruno's influence on later thinkers.

Gatti, Hilary. *Giordano Bruno and Renaissance Science*. Ithaca, N.Y.: Cornell University Press, 1999. Gatti reevaluates Bruno's contribution to the new science and argues against some current views that hermetic and occult traditions shaped the new science. Gatti portrays Bruno as a significant scientific thinker.

Greenberg, Sidney. *The Infinite in Giordano Bruno: With a Translation of His Dialogue; 'Concerning the Cause, Principle, and One.'* New York: King's Crown Press, 1950. The first part of this work traces the history of the problem of infinity up to the time of Bruno. Then special attention is given to Bruno's own theory of infinity.

Horowitz, Irving Louis. *The Renaissance Philosophy of Giordano Bruno*. New York: Coleman-Ross, 1952. A general introduction to Bruno's ontology and a detailed analysis of the interaction of his system and method.

Kristeller, Paul Oskar. *Eight Philosophers of the Italian Renaissance*. Stanford, Calif.: Stanford University Press, 1964. The book consists of lectures on the philosophy of the Italian Renaissance. Gives special attention to Bruno, Pico, Petrarch, and others.

Michel, Paul Henri. *The Cosmology of Giordano Bruno*. Translated by R. E. W. Maddison. Ithaca, N.Y.: Cornell University Press, 1973. This work examines Bruno's cosmology and argues that such an examination is justified by its historical context. Includes a biographical section that attempts to separate Bruno's history from his legend.

Ordin, Nuccio. *Giordano Bruno and the Philosophy of the Ass*. New Haven, Conn.: Yale University Press, 1996. This work explores Bruno's use of the image of the donkey in a literary and philosophic sense. Includes an iconographical collection and an index.

Paterson, Antoinette Mann. *The Infinite Worlds of Giordano Bruno*. Springfield, Ill.: Charles C Thomas, 1970. Includes chapters on Bruno's cosmology, theory of knowledge, and theory of virtue. Also contains a bibliography and appendices on Bruno's execution and Gottfried Wilhelm Leibniz's letters about Bruno's philosophy.

Singer, Dorothea. *Giordano Bruno: His Life and Thought*. New York: Henry Schuman, 1950. This biography includes illustrations and very useful appendices on the history of Bruno's writings and their publication. In addition, there is an annotated translation of Bruno's work, *On the Infinite Universe and Worlds*.

Yates, Frances. *Giordano Bruno and the Hermetic Tradition*. Chicago: University of Chicago Press, 1964. The preeminent Bruno scholar claims that Bruno's work is best understood as an expression of Neoplatonism, magic, and Egyptian religion.

_____. *Lull and Bruno*. Boston: Routledge & Kegan Paul, 1982. The section "Essays on Giordano Bruno in England" examines Bruno's lectures on Copernicus at Oxford and his views of religion and the established church.

Michael Witkoski, updated by Tammy Nyden-Bullock

Martin Buber

One of the greatest Jewish philosophers of the twentieth century, Buber postulated an interpersonal relationship between God and humans. This theoretical relationship, which he called "I-Thou," profoundly affected diverse thinkers of all faiths.

Principal philosophical works: *Die Geschichten des Rabbi Nachman*, 1906 (*The Tales of Rabbi Nachman*, 1956); *Die Legende des Baalschem*, 1908 (*The Legend of the Baal-Shem*, 1955); *Daniel: Gespräche von der Verwirklichung*, 1913 (*Daniel: Dialogues on Realization*, 1964); *Ich und Du*, 1923 (*I and Thou*, 1937); *Die Chassidischen Bücher*, 1928 (*Tales of the Hasidim: The Early Masters*, 1947, and *Tales of the Hasidim: The Later Masters*, 1948); *Königtum Gottes*, 1932 (*The Kingship of God*, 1967); "Die Frage an den Einzelnen," 1936 ("The Question to the Single One," 1947); *Gog u-Magog*, 1941 (*For the Sake of Heaven*, 1945); *Torat ha-Neri'im*, 1942 (*The Prophetic Faith*, 1949); *Moshe*, 1945 (*Moses*, 1945); *Be-pardes ha-Hasidut*, 1945; *Or haganuz*, 1946 (partial translation, *From the Treasure House of Hassidism: A Selection from "Or haganuz,"* 1969); *Netivot be-Utopyah*, 1947 (*Paths in Utopia*, 1949); *Zwei Glaubensweisen*, 1950 (*Two Types of Faith*, 1951); *Bilder von Gut und Böse*, 1952 (*Good and Evil*, 1953); *An Der Wende*, 1952 (*On Judaism*, 1967); *Tsedek veha-'avel 'al-pi tseror mizmore Tehilim*, 1950 (*Good and Evil: Two Interpretations*, 1953); *Gottesfinsternis: Betrachtungen zur Beziehung Zwischen Religion and Philosophie*, 1953 (*Eclipse of God: Studies in the Relation Between Religion and Philosophy*, 1953); "Elemente des Zwischenmenschlichen," 1954 ("Elements of the Interhuman," 1965); *Der Mensch und sein Gebild*, 1955 (*Man and His Image-Work*, 1965); "Dem Gemeinschaftlichen folgen," 1956 ("What Is Common to All," 1965); "Das Wort, das gesprochen wird," 1960 ("The Word That Is Spoken in Word and Reality," 1965); *The Knowledge of Man*, 1965; *Between Man and Man*, 1965; *The Philosophy of Martin Buber*, 1967.

Born: February 8, 1878; Vienna, Austro-Hungarian Empire
Died: June 13, 1965; Jerusalem, Israel

Early Life

Mordecai Martin Buber was born in Vienna on February 8, 1878, the son of Carl and Elise (née Wurgast) Buber. When Martin was only four years old, his mother mysteriously disappeared. (It was discovered later that she had eloped with another man.) The motherless boy was sent to Lemberg (now Lvov, Ukrainian Soviet Socialist Republic) to live with his paternal grandparents. His grandfather, Salomon Buber, was a landowner, grain merchant, mine operator, and philologist. He was also one of the last great scholars of the Jewish Enlightenment, responsible for authoritative critical editions of the Midrash, a special class of Talmudic literature comprising interpretations of the Bible, wise sayings, and stories.

Buber's grandmother, Adele, was also a lover of words. A rebel who taught herself to read and write in an era when such things were proscribed for the women of her class, she arranged for young Martin to be tutored at home until he was ten years old. Because the household of Salomon and Adele Buber was one in which many languages were spoken, Martin learned the integrity of the "authentic word," the word that cannot be paraphrased. The boy, not having many playmates, made a game of creating conversations between people of different languages, imagining what a German would think when talking with a Frenchman, or a Hebrew with an ancient Roman.

When Buber was nine, his father remarried, and the boy began spending summers on his fa-

Martin Buber. *(Library of Congress)*

ther's estate. There he developed a love of horses. More important however, he learned to relate to the world in a way that became the basis for his most famous work, *I and Thou*. He later credited his father, a farmer who knew how to relate directly, one-on-one, both to animals and to his fellows, with teaching him to practice "immediacy."

At the age of ten, Buber was enrolled in the local *Gymnasium*, where he studied until he was eighteen. The school was primarily Polish; Jews were the minority. At the school, Christians and Jews alike were obliged to participate in daily devotional exercises. Buber would later recall that he and the other Jewish children would stand through these prayers, head bent, feeling only that the services meant nothing to them. The experience left the man with a lifelong antipathy toward missionary work.

Buber moved from his grandparents' home into his father's townhouse at the age of fourteen. At eighteen he finished his studies at the *Gymnasium* and entered the university.

Life's Work

Buber spent his first year of university study in Vienna, a city of mixed German, Jewish, and Slavic influences. In Vienna, Buber discovered the living theater and became acquainted with many contemporary writers. At the University of Vienna, he studied literature, art history, and philosophy and wanted to become a poet.

In the winter of 1897-1898, the young man studied at the University of Leipzig and in the summer of 1899 at the University of Zurich. His subjects included philosophy, history of art, literary history, psychiatry, Germanics, classical philosophy, and national economy. Buber soon discovered a preference for seminars over lectures. He worked in a psychological seminar and was the only nonmedical student in the physiological institute. He belonged to a number of intellectual and social clubs, including the literary society.

Buber met two people in 1899 who would change his life forever. One of these was Gustav Landauer, a socialist who led and taught a group known as the Neue Gemeinschaft, or New Community. Founded by Heinrich and Julius Hart, the New Community believed in divine, boundless moving upward, as opposed to comfortably settling down. It saw in the ideal future a communal settlement in a new age of beauty, art, and religious dedication. Buber's relationship with Landauer prompted him to change his major course of study from literature and the history of art to German mysticism.

Even more important than his friendship with Landauer, though, was Buber's marriage to Paula Winkler, a fellow student in Zurich. One year his senior, Paula was probably his superior intellectually when the two met. That meeting was to have inestimable meaning for Buber, compensating as it did for the "mismeeting," a word coined by Buber, between his unforgotten mother and himself. Reared as a Roman Catholic, Paula converted to Buber's faith before the two were wed, giving up her earlier life and family for him. It has been said that the existential trust that underlies *I and Thou* would not have been possible without Buber's relationship with Paula.

It was Paula's strength that enabled Buber to be decisive about the direction of his life. With her help and encouragement, he found his path through Hasidism, a form of Jewish mysticism. Paula also increased his self-confidence. Buber believed marriage to be the lifestyle most suitable for people. He dedicated his books to his wife, as in this poem from *Tales of the Hasidim*:

> Do you still know, how we in our young years
> Traveled together on this sea?
> Visions came, great and wonderful,
> We beheld them together, you and I.
> How image joined itself with images in our
>   hearts!

Paula and Martin had two children, Rafael and Eva. Paula was a writer of fiction who published under the pseudonym of George Munk.

Buber joined the Zionist movement in 1898, and was a delegate to the Third Zionist Congress in 1899. Although he addressed the congress on behalf of the propaganda committee, he stressed the importance of education over propaganda. He became editor of the Zionist movement's *Die Welt*. He wrote his doctoral dissertation on German mysticism and received his Ph.D. from the University of Vienna in 1904, then withdrew for five years to concentrate on the study of Hasidism, long regarded as occult and disreputable by most modern thinkers. Hasidism had flourished in the isolated villages of Poland during the mid-eighteenth century. While the movement stressed inward renewal, it was also characterized by exuberant manifestations of spiritual experience. Buber's study ultimately resulted in three books on Hasidism, *For the Sake of Heaven*, *From the Treasure House of Hassidism: A Selection from "Or haganuz,"* and *Be-pardes ha-Hasidut* (the origin and meaning of Hasidism).

At the start of World War I, Buber founded the Jewish National Committee, which was devoted to wartime work on behalf of Eastern European Jewry. In 1916, he started a monthly magazine called *Der Jude*, for eight years the most impor-

tant organ of the Jewish renaissance movement in Central Europe. Buber believed strongly in Utopian socialism and envisioned a world in which people would live communally and in direct personal relationship with one another. From 1926 to 1930, he coedited another journal, *Die Kreatur*.

In 1923, Buber published *I and Thou*, a basic formulation of his philosophy of dialogue. He published in 1925, in collaboration with Franz Rosenzweig, a German translation of the Bible, in which the translators attempted to preserve the original literary character of the Hebrew Bible as a work meant to be spoken rather than simply read silently. Buber held the only chair of Jewish philosophy at a German university when he became professor of comparative religion at the University of Frankfurt (1925-1933). In 1933, he became director of the Central Office for Jewish Adult Education in Germany after Jews were barred from all German educational institutions. In 1935, he was finally forbidden to speak at Jewish gatherings in Germany.

Buber moved his family to Palestine in 1938 and became professor of philosophy at the Hebrew University. Not surprisingly, he was very active in public affairs in Israel. He pressed for a peaceful settlement of the Arab-Hebrew disputes and was a strong advocate for rapprochement and a joint Arab-Israeli state. He was the first president of the Israel Academy of Sciences and Humanities (1960-1962). In his later years, Buber lectured outside Israel, widely influencing Jewish and Christian thinkers alike. He served at the end of his life as a counselor for kibbutz members. Buber died in Jerusalem on June 13, 1965.

Influence

Buber's beliefs often ran contrary to contemporary thought. His interpretation of Hasidism, for example, came under fire again and again, and his interpretation of the revelations in the Bible remains controversial. His study of Hasidism changed scholarly opinion about the subject; it is now considered one of the great mystical movements of the world. As a member of the Zionist movement, he favored a renewal of Jewish culture over the creation of a Jewish state, an unpopular stand among his peers. In Israel, he argued for the peaceful coexistence of Hebrews and Arabs.

Buber believed that the only real evil is refusing direction because the only possible direction is toward God, the theme of *Good and Evil*. He believed strongly in a "living God," one with whom it is possible to have a direct personal relationship. He wrote of the inseparability of people's relationship to God and to others. The old theory of the duality of existence was reinterpreted. Rather than two worlds, the sacred and the profane, there are, according to Buber, two ways to respond to the mundane world. The world may be perceived as a thing to be experienced, a distant thing, or the individual may enter into direct relation with the world and experience the immediacy of God. In this immediacy is the key to eternity, because time becomes meaningless and the relation is all. For Buber, faith becomes an entrance into the whole of reality, because when one stands in direct relation to the world, one speaks the words "I-Thou." Buber believed that dialogue with God, not monologue about God, is the root of the Hebrew faith.

Joyce M. Parks

I and Thou

Type of philosophy: Ethics, Jewish philosophy, philosophical theology
First published: Ich und Du, 1923 (English translation, 1937)
Principal ideas advanced:
◇ There is no independent "I" but only the "I" existing and known in objective relation to something other than itself, an "It," or as encountered by and encompassed by the other, the "Thou."
◇ Just as music can be studied analytically by reference to its notes, verses, and bars, or encountered and experienced in such a manner that it is known not by its parts but as a unity, so the "I" can relate itself analytically to something other, "It," or it can encounter the other, "Thou," so as to form a living unity.
◇ The "Thou" stands as judge over the "It," but as a judge with the form and creative power for the transformation of "It."

◇ Each encountered "Thou" reveals the nature of all reality, but finally the living center of every "Thou" is seen to be the eternal "Thou."
◇ The eternal "Thou" is never known objectively, but certitude comes through the domain of action.

Since its publication in 1923, *I and Thou* has become an epoch-making work. This slender volume, perhaps more than any other single work, has helped to mold contemporary theology. For example, the Neoorthodox tradition in recent Protestantism has appropriated in a rather wholesale manner Martin Buber's "I-Thou encounter," the "Eternal Subject," and other features. Although Neoorthodox Protestants reinterpret these concepts from a radical Protestant context, other Christians, such as philosopher Paul Tillich, have developed systems that are in fundamental agreement with Buber's fuller understanding of these ideas. Perhaps at no other point do liberal and orthodox Christian thinkers find so rich a place of meeting.

For Judaism, on the other hand, Buber's writings have been a new leaven. It is not true, as some have maintained, that Buber was a rebel from basic Judaism, that he was simply a Jew by birth and an existentialist by conviction. Rather, Buber combined the rich heritage of Judaism, some of it long neglected, with certain insights of contemporary thinking. No other writer has so shaken Judaism from its parochialism and applied it so relevantly to the problems and concerns of contemporary people.

Buber's writing is often rhapsodic in quality, frustrating the searcher for clear and distinct ideas; his key work has been aptly called a "philosophical-religious poem." Yet this is as it should be, for Buber is no system builder, but the imparter of a way of life. At its center is a unique type of relation, one universally available and yet almost universally neglected. His task is not so much one of detailed and logical exposition, but one of evoking, eliciting, educing this relation, which is its own proof.

Hasidism
Quite early, Buber's youthful mastery of Jewish thought, life, and devotion came into tension with European intellectualism, especially the

thought of Germans Immanuel Kant and Friedrich Nietzsche. Buber's tentative resolution was that of mysticism, particularly as developed by the postmedieval Christian mystics. However, a sense of rootlessness drew him back toward Judaism, first in the form of emerging Zionism, not so much as a political movement as a cultural renaissance. Here, in the venerable roots of Jewish religioculture, Buber found an alternative to humanity's modern plight of overcommercialism and superintellectualism. However, it was in Hasidism that his answer became crystalized. This pietist conservative Jewish movement, emerging in eighteenth century Poland, moved him to withdraw from active life for five years of intensive study. The teachings stressed not monastic withdrawal, but joyous life in communities of this world, worshiping in every practical activity.

Around the same time, Buber encountered translations of Søren Kierkegaard's work. Kierkegaard's insistence on total involvement and absolute commitment, on the priority of subjective thinking, on truth as existential or lived truth, and his stress on the centrality of the individual—all of these elements made immediate contact with Buber's newfound religious devotion. The resulting tension of existentialism and Hasidism was creative for Buber. The emphasis of Hasidism on the warmth of community tempered the cold stress of Kierkegaard on the lonely and anxious individual; the latter's pessimism concerning humanity was largely dissolved by the general Jewish confidence in God-given human potential. On the other hand, the existentialist stress on authentic existence grounded in the totally free and responsible decision of the self transformed Buber's earlier concern with mystic absorption and the illusory nature of the commonplace world. In personal experiences resulting from people seeking him out for help, Buber learned the utter necessity of religion as a this-worldly faith, as a total devotion transforming every aspect of common life together. The unique "I-Thou" was no longer understood as a state of the absorbed individual in unity with an Absolute, but as a permeating relationship with all life—a lived experience, not of loss, but of transformation and fulfillment in reciprocity. With this key awareness, Buber's religious philosophy was fully formed, and it emerged in his *I and Thou*.

I, It, and Thou

Quite clearly, this work is an essay in epistemology; it is epistemology, however, not simply in the traditional sense of understanding the nature and ascertainable truth of commonsense perception, but in the sense of exploring in sweeping fashion the possible "modes" or types of "knowing." It is Buber's thesis that strict empiricism is only one of several kinds of relations with reality and that a life founded on this mode alone is anemic to the core. Although he refuses to argue the point, Buber assumes that the plurality of modes corresponds with dimensions within reality itself. Such a contention stands within a time-honored tradition, whether it be Greek philosopher Plato's distinction between sense impression and *noesis* or philosopher Teilhard de Chardin's distinction between the "inner" and "outer" aspects of all things. Such a distinction, Buber holds, cannot be logically argued, for logic is simply the instrument of one of these modes and does not apply to others. Verification is thus intrinsic to the mode itself; it is self-verifying and requires no further "proof."

Buber's key affirmation is this: "To man the world is twofold, in accordance with his twofold attitude." This overarching attitude is expressed in every language by the words indicating "I," "It," and "Thou." "It" and "Thou" do not signify different things, Buber insists, but two different relations possible between the same self and the same "object." This is an interesting contention, first developed in detail by Kierkegaard, for in general parlance the ground for such distinction is usually held to be within the object itself. Underlying Buber's position is a radical rejection of French philosopher René Descartes's famed *Cogito, ergo sum* ("I think, therefore I am"). There is no such thing as an independent "I" that, internally certain of its own existence, moves externally to God and the world. Rather, there is no "I" in itself but only the "I" existing and known in these two basic ways.

The "I-It" relation is the realm of objectivity, the realm of "experience," which is generally understood as perceiving, imagining, willing, feeling, and thinking. It includes all activities of the "I" in which there is an object, a "thing," whose existence depends on being bounded by other "things." Here one experiences and extracts knowledge concerning the "surface of things." Above all, the "I-It" experience is unilateral; in it the "I" alone is active, and the object perceived has no concern in the matter nor is it affected by the experience.

This experience, as well as the "I-Thou," occurs in regard to three spheres—our life with nature, with people, and with intelligible forms. For example, to use Buber's most difficult illustration, in an "I-It" experience with a tree, I may look at it, examine its structure and functions, classify it, formalize the laws of its operation, see it in terms of its numerical components or control, and shape it by activity. However, not only may I experience the tree, but I may enter into relationship with it—this is the mode of "I-Thou." Here I am "encountered" by the tree; I become bound to it, for it seizes me with "the power of exclusiveness." Although this relation is totally different in kind from the "I-It" experience, it is not strictly different in "content." In it, one does not have to reject or forget the content of objective knowledge; rather, all of the above enumerated components become indivisibly united in the event which is this relation—"Everything belonging to the tree is in this: its form and structure, its colours and chemical composition, its intercourse with the elements and with the stars, are all present in a single whole."

Although objective knowledge is always of the past, the relation of the "I-Thou" is always present, a "filled present." Above all, characteristic of this relation is its mutuality. Yet we cannot say that in this relation the tree exhibits a soul, or a consciousness, for of this we can have no experience. The relation is undifferentiated, and to inquire of its constitutive parts is to disintegrate what is known only as an indivisible whole. Such a wholeness is all-consuming and absolute—a "He" encountered as a "Thou" is a "whole in himself" and "fills the heavens." What Buber means is not that the "He" alone is existent but rather that this relation is such that "all else lives in *his* light."

To one not naturally inclined to Buber's way of thinking, the best available illustrations, as Buber's own examples clearly indicate, are from the arts. In fact, Buber maintains that the "I-Thou" relation is the true source of art. Music can be analyzed in terms of notes, verses, and bars;

this is the realm of the "I-It." This same music, however, may be encountered in a living relation in which each component is included, yet experienced not as parts but as an inseparable unity. In artistic creativity, a form that is not an offspring of the artist encounters him or her and demands effective power. This calls for sacrifice and risk—risk, for endless possibility must be ended by form; sacrifice, because the work consumes the artist with a claim that permits no rest. Buber's interpretation of this artistic form is helpful in understanding the "content" of the "I-Thou" encounter. Says Buber, "I can neither experience nor describe the form which meets me, but only body it forth."

Buber begins a transition from the exclusive relation of the "I-Thou" to the inclusive, concerned life that he espouses, in contrast to the mystic. The "I-Thou" is consummated in activity, activity that inevitably partakes of the "I-It" experience, but activity that is redeemed, for in being the creative and transforming ground of activity, the "I-Thou" relation is exhibited in its fullness. This creative tension of "It" and "Thou" in the practical life is exemplified in such contrasts as those between organization and community, control and mutuality, and individuals and persons. The "Thou" stands as judge over the "It," but a judge with the form and creative power for its transformation. In existential living, the fathomless dimension of the "Thou" is creatively incarnated, as it were, into the commonplace world of the "It." As an "It," the created object will be scrutinized with all the instruments of "objectivity," but as a living embodiment of a "Thou," it has the capacity to lift its perceiver from the commonplace to the all-pervasive dimension of the Thou in which all things fundamentally participate. As Buber continually insists, such relation is not simply subjective, for then it could have no mutuality: "To produce is to draw forth, to invent is to find, to shape is to discover." This relation of "I-Thou" is subjectivity and objectivity in a totality that transcends the "I-It" quality of either in isolation.

"Thou" and "Thou"

Buber inevitably passes from the field of epistemology to that of metaphysics. If it be true that the relationship of "I-Thou" is a valid mode of apprehending reality, a relationship grounded in the very nature of reality, a further question is unavoidable—what is the relation of "Thou" to "Thou," each of which is apprehended as *the* totality and as *the* illuminator of the whole? It is Buber's answer to this question that distinguishes him from aesthetic philosophers such as George Santayana and Bernard Bosanquet and marks him as a religious philosopher. He begins by perceiving love as the unique quality of the "I-Thou" relation, love as a "metaphysical and metapsychical fact." This is the nature of the relationship between "Thou" and "Thou," and the "I" as it participates in that which is the constituting relation of all. At this central point, Buber comes intriguingly close to Christianity:

> Love is responsibility of an I for a *Thou*. In this lies the likeness . . . of all who love, from the smallest to the greatest and from the blessedly protected man . . . to him who is all his life nailed to the cross of the world, and who ventures to bring himself to the dreadful point—to love *all* men.

Or again, the "I-Thou" relation is one in which a person "calls his *Thou Father* in such a way that he himself is simply Son." There can never be hatred of a "Thou"; hatred can be only against a part of a being. The "Thou," the whole, can only be loved, for this is the very nature of the mutual relation.

Because each encountered "Thou" reveals the inmost nature of all reality, we see that everything can appear as a "Thou." This is so because in the "I" is an "inborn Thou," an a priori of relation. We see this, Buber affirms, as the child's fundamental guide to action from the instinct to make contact by touch and name, to its blossoming in tenderness and love, and its perfection in creativity. All of these emerge from the inherent longing of an "I" for the "Thou." Throughout life "I-Thou" encounters continue, but they are not ordered, for they are only "a sign of the world-order." Increasingly one sees this to be so, for every "Thou" inevitably becomes an "It"; but humans cannot rest content with only a momentary "I-Thou" relation. The inborn "Thou" can be consummated only in a direct relation with the "Thou" that cannot become "It." All lesser "Thou's" whet the soul for the relation that is

abiding, for which all others are mere foreshadows. Through them the "I" sees that the "Thou's" are such only because they possess a "living Centre," that "the extended lines of relations meet in the eternal "Thou."

Witness to this is exhibited for Buber even in the practical realm. People can live in mutual relation only when they first take their stand in mutual relation with a living center. A great culture rests on an original, relational event from which a special conception of the cosmos emerges. Loss of this center reduces a culture to the impotence of a mere "It." Likewise, marriage is consummated by a couple's mutual revealing of the "Thou" to each other; only thereby do they participate in the "Thou" that is the unifying ground in which mutual relations in all realms are possible. Whatever name one gives to this "Thou," if one really has "Thou" in mind, despite one's illusions, one addresses the true "Thou" that cannot be limited by another. Even though one regards oneself as an atheist, one stands in a relation that gathers up and includes all others.

This meeting of the "Thou" is a matter both of choosing and being chosen. One can prepare, yet because all preparations remain in the realm of "It," the step from that realm is not humanity's doing. Therefore, the word "encounter" is the only one appropriate. Epistemologically, the particular encounters are prior; metaphysically, the central Thou is eternally prior. Through the former, we are addressed by the latter; ours is the response. It is here that we reach the apex of Buber's position: "In the relation with God unconditional exclusiveness and unconditional inclusiveness are one." This relation means neither the loss of world nor the loss of the "I," but a giving up of self-asserting instinct by regarding all in the love relation of the "Thou." The world of "It" cannot be dispensed with, nor is it evil; it becomes demonic only when the motivating drive is not the will to be related but, for example, in economics is the will to profit or, in politics, the will to power. Buber's ethic can be clearly stated—a person participating in awareness of the Thou

> serves the truth which, though higher than reason, yet does not repudiate it. . . . He does in communal life precisely what is done in

personal life by the man who knows himself incapable of realising the *Thou* in its purity, yet daily confirms its truth in the *It*, in accordance with what is right and filling for the day, drawing—disclosing—the boundary line anew each day.

Such a life is characterized by action filled with meaning and joy, and possessions radiating with "awe and sacrificial power." These are the truths of primitive humanity, encountering with wonder the immediacy of life, but now purified of superstition and fitted for civilized community. To hallow life is to encounter the living God; to encounter this "Thou" is to hallow life—this is the paradox that best summarizes Buber's thought.

It is in this relation that Buber sees true theology resting. Its basis is not dogma, a content once and for all delivered. It is a compulsion received as something to be done; its confirmation is its product in the world and the singleness of life lived in obedience to it. This is the meaning of revelation, revelation that is eternal and ever available. It must be completed in theology, in objectification, but the abiding sin of religion is to substitute the objectification for the relation, to make the Church of God into a god of the church, to make the Scripture of God into a god of the scripture. The mystery at the foundation of theology cannot be dispelled, yet language can point in the right direction. For Buber the affirmations "God *and* the world" or "God *in* the world" are still in the "I-It" realm; but the declaration "the world in the Thou" points to the true relation. With hesitation, Buber attempts to say more, drawing heavily upon the artistic analogy. The God-human relation is characterized by the polarity of creatureliness and creativity, of being totally dependent on God and yet totally free. For Buber this tension can only mean that while we need God in order to exist, God needs us for the very meaning of life. That is, "there is a becoming of the God that is"—herein is the eternal purpose of our existence. Mutual fulfillment, which is the "I-Thou" relation, must mean, in the final account, that we are cocreators with God in cosmic fulfillment.

Such declarations will raise immediate questions for the logical philosopher. Is this absolute idealism, pantheism, panpsychism, or process philosophy? In what sense is this the theistic worldview of traditional Judaism, centered in the God of providence and history? Buber's refusal to be of any help here shows the degree to which he is not a philosophic system builder but an existentialist and, above all, a religious thinker. The problem for him is not so much to know as it is to act in lived awareness of the omnipresent "Thou."

However, at least this much can be said. In Buber, we have the general Kantian position taken to a religious conclusion. The realm of the "Thou" is the realm of the noumenon; here is to be found no causality but the assurance of freedom. The realm of "It" is the phenomenal realm, the realm of necessity, causality, and the objectification of all according to finite categories. However, for Buber the noumenal is more than a postulate or an inference. Similar to Kant's impact of the moral imperative and the encounter of beauty and sublimity in *Kritik der Urteilskraft* (1790; *The Critique of Judgment*, 1892), the noumenon is encountered through the total self. Finally, as in Kant, the eternal "Thou" is never known objectively, but certitude of it comes centrally through the domain of action.

W. Paul Jones

Additional Reading

Bach, H. I. *The German Jew: A Synthesis of Judaism and Western Civilization, 1730-1930.* Littman Library of Jewish Civilization. New York: Oxford University Press, 1984. This volume discusses Martin Buber's work in the context of a history of German Jewry. An excellent survey, providing valuable background for the understanding of Buber's thought and philosophy.

Breslauer, Daniel S. *Martin Buber on Myth: An Introduction.* New York: Garland, 1990. A thorough introduction to Buber's thought on myth dealing with such subjects as "the Bible," "Eden," "Language," and "Hasidism." Includes a bibliography and index.

Diamond, Malcolm L. *Martin Buber: Jewish Existentialist.* New York: Oxford University Press, 1960. A reading of Buber's works in the context of modern existential philosophy. Includes a selected bibliography and index.

Friedman, Maurice S. *Martin Buber and the Eternal.* New York: Human Sciences Press, 1986. A solid introduction to Buber's thought in terms of Western and Asian religion, existentialism, and religious education. Includes an index.

_____. *Martin Buber's Life and Work*. Detroit, Mich.: Wayne State University Press, 1988. A full, authoritative biography on Buber including extensive chapter notes and an index.

Kepnes, Steven. *The Text as Thou: Martin Buber's Dialogical Hermeneutics and Narrative Theology*. Bloomington: Indiana University Press, 1992. Discusses how Buber's hermeneutics were influenced by the ideas of Romanticism. Includes a major section on "narrative theology."

Kohanski, Alexander S. *An Analytical Interpretation of Martin Buber's "I and Thou."* Woodbury, New York: Barron's, 1975. A complete introduction to *I and Thou*. Includes an introduction and glossary.

Moore, Donald J. *Martin Buber: Prophet of Religious Secularism*. 2d ed. New York: Fordham University Press, 1996. Includes a biographical portrait of Buber and discussions of his "critique of religion." Contains a bibliography and index.

Silberstein, Laurence J. *Martin Buber's Social and Religious Thought: Alienation and the Quest for Meaning*. New York: New York University Press, 1989. Discussions of Buber's religious thought as it relates to social imperatives. Includes notes, bibliography, and index.

Streiker, Lowell. *The Promise of Buber*. Philadelphia: Lippincott, 1969. Discusses Buber's philosophy of dialogue. Contains a suggested reading list of Buber's works and an index.

Vermes, Pamela. *Buber*. Jewish Thinkers series/ New York: Grove Press, 1988. This volume provides a concise and well-informed introduction to Buber's thought and works.

Joyce M. Parks, updated by Richard M. Leeson

Joseph Butler

Besides having provided the classical theory of the ethics of conscience and the standard critique of psychological egoism, Butler presented a very influential version of the argument from design as to the existence of God and a powerful theory of personal identity.

Principal philosophical works: *Fifteen Sermons Preached at the Rolls Chapel*, 1726 (revised and enlarged as *Fifteen Sermons to Which Are Added Six Sermons Preached on Public[k] Occasions*, 1765); *The Analogy of Religion Natural and Revealed, to the Constitution and Course of Nature*, 1736; *A Charge Deliver'd to the Clergy of the Diocese of Durham*, 1751.

Born: May 18, 1692; Wantage, Berkshire, England
Died: June 16, 1752; Bath, Somerset, England

Early Life

Born into a Presbyterian family, Joseph Butler was the youngest of eight children. He switched from Presbyterian to Anglican sympathies and entered Oriel College, Oxford, in 1714. He was ordained deacon, then priest, in 1718, and from 1718 to 1776 he was a preacher at Rolls Chapel, where he delivered the sermons that were published in 1726 as *Fifteen Sermons Preached at the Rolls Chapel*. In 1722, he added the rectory at Haughton-le-Skerne, and in 1726, he left this for Stanhope, County Durham. Here he wrote *The Analogy of Religion Natural and Revealed, to the Constitution and Course of Nature*, which, assuming Deism to be right in its positive claims, argues for a continued journey to full Christian belief. The Deists accept belief in an all-powerful, all-knowing, all-good God and in life after death. To this, Butler adds the claims of orthodox Christian belief. Appointed Clerk of Closet in 1736, he was in constant attendance to Queen Caroline until her death in late 1737. In 1738, he was given the see of Bristol, added the deanery of Saint Paul's in 1740, and became Bishop of Durham in 1750. He died in 1752.

Life's Work

Joseph Butler's thought is systematically complex because he continually balances two themes—an *enough* theme and a *not too much* theme. People have, he contends, enough evidence to determine that there is a God whose existence explains the order and intelligibility of nature and the obligations of conscience and who has given them the Bible as his Revelation. However, there is not so much evidence that people are coerced by it to believe in God or to live in accord with God's revealed will. Butler insists on both the reliability of people's rational capacities to provide them with the knowledge they need in order to do their duty and save their souls and the limits of those capacities and the data available to them to leave people free to wander if they choose. More formally put, there are elements of both constrained rationalism and subdued skepticism in Butler's thought. The key to understanding him is coming to see exactly what is balanced and how that balance is created.

Butler's self-appointed philosophical task is to answer Deistic criticisms of orthodox Christianity. Deism is the view that there exists an omnipotent, omniscient, morally good God who created the world and placed in human nature the capacities necessary for proving that God exists and determining God's will, along with the capacity to live in accord with that will. It rejects any notion of historical revelation, partly because historical claims are inherently logically contingent and partly because historical revelation is inherently given to some particular people at some particular time and thus is not equally available to all people at all times. Claims of religious importance, Deists hold, are always universal. Such claims make no reference to particular persons, groups, events, or times. Butler sees no reason to accept this assumption.

One important theme in Butler's works is that probability is the guide of life. By the word "probability," Butler has in mind something much simpler than the full doctrine of probability later held by John Maynard Keynes and Rudolf Carnap. For Keynes and Carnap, for any two logically contingent propositions *A* and *B*, each has some objective probability given the other, even if their meanings indicate no mutual relevance. Thus "Sheep grow wool, not silk" and "Some ice cream is peppermint flavored" each has some specific probability given the other. Further, each has an intrinsic probability—a probability given necessary truths and nothing else. Even necessary truths and self-contradictions receive probabilities, 1 and 0, respectively, according to this scheme. Butler's account has no such complexity. When Butler speaks of probability, he has in mind that we can possess evidence in favor of some proposition being true without that evidence being sufficient for us to be sure that it is true. Although Mary can see the dirt on the newly mopped floor, she cannot be sure that it was Tim who tracked it in, though she may rightly take the presence of the dirt as evidence that he did.

Butler's theory of knowledge is implicit; he produced no systematic work in epistemology. He was strongly influenced by John Locke's *An Essay Concerning Human Understanding* (1690), which says that probability "is likeness to be true, the very notation of the word signifying such a proposition, for which there be arguments or proofs to make it pass, or be received as true." We can see that the statement "Nothing can have incompatible properties" is necessarily true; we need nothing more. However, for the statement, "The chair has one leg shorter than the others," we need evidence. Some evidence is better than other evidence; sitting in the chair and finding that it is unstable confirms our visual sense that one is leg is short. A close examination of the chair provides better evidence than a quick look at the chair from a distance. Different degrees of evidence yield different "likenesses to be true." Relative to at least the simpler among necessary truths, we can have certainty—justified complete confidence that what we believe is true. Relative to most of the logically contingent propositions that we believe, we lack certainty. This is not an escapable feature of things; it is an inherent part of our condition.

Butler is correct; any time you believe any logically contingent proposition whose truth, unlike your belief that you exist, is not entailed by your believing it, you could be wrong. Strength of belief makes no difference here. No matter how strong your belief, you may be wrong; you lack certainty, and this lack is inescapable. However, it might have been the case that every time you came to believe that a logically contingent proposition was true, you were right. You might also have superb evidence for everything you

Joseph Butler. *(Library of Congress)*

believe, evidence that yielded a very high degree of likeness to be true. This is not our typical condition. We usually deal with evidence that yields a much lower degree of likeness of truth. Butler claims that probability is our guide regarding religious beliefs as it is regarding other beliefs whose denial is not self-contradictory.

Butler holds that among our religious beliefs, we may properly include belief in our survival of the death of the body. One element in Butler's argument for this is what is naturally called a principle of continuance. He writes, "There is in every case a probability, that all things will continue as we experience they are, in all respects, except those in which we have some reason to think that they are."

This passage can be interpreted as referring to the existence of what philosophers call substances—things that have qualities, are not themselves qualities, and typically endure over time. It amounts to the claim that "If a substance X exists at time T then, without any reason to think otherwise, it is reasonable to suppose that it will exist at time T-plus-one." It is a claim about things such as cats and mountains rather than about lights and noises. It is also an epistemological claim—a claim about what is reasonably believed. Behind this epistemological claim is some such thesis such that "If X exists at time T, then if X is not fatally interfered with, X will exist at T-plus-one." This is a metaphysical claim—a claim about how things universally and necessarily are, independent of thought. Butler is, of course, a monotheist and thus believes that whatever exists other than God is created and sustained in existence by God. Therefore, he also holds the metaphysical and theological claim that "If God sustains X in existence at time T, then unless God has some reason not to do so, God will sustain X in existence at T-plus-one."

Butler, however, wants to argue for people's survival after death without appealing to T. The most obvious objection to the idea that humans survive death is the fate of the body. Because upon its death, the body makes none of the motions previously characteristic of it, it gives every appearance of having lost all of those powers whose exercise one associates with personhood. How, then, can Butler speak of survival?

There are several relevant considerations. First, he holds that what is essential to being a person is being a self-conscious substance—a mind. Second, he holds that there is no necessity that a mind be embodied. Third, he contends that a human person is a mind that is embodied in a human body; once that body dies, the mind is no longer able to use that body as a means of acting in the physical world. It is not the mind's power to act but its power to act through (what was) its body that ends with death. Fourth, what one observes when someone dies is a body no longer capable of movement. One *infers* that the mind that acted through the body no longer exists. That inference requires some such claim as "A person is identical to his or her body or else his or her body, being a living organism, is a logically necessary condition of her existence." However, this claim—a summary of several varieties of materialism—is not something confirmable by observation. The observed data relative to death no more require a materialist than a nonmaterialist metaphysic, and their significance sharply differs as one switches from on metaphysical view to the other.

Butler is also famous for holding a conscience view of ethics and for his denial of psychological egoism. His view of conscience is that this is the standard name for our rational capacity for understanding and judging the motives we have, enabling us to act in what we consider the proper way even if our strongest motives would lead us to act otherwise. He denies that a person is to be thought of as a prisoner of psychological forces with the prize of one's actions going to the strongest forces. Instead we are able to judge our motives and act against them if they would lead us to act wrongly.

Psychological egoism is the view that we can act only from motives that target our own perceived self-interest—only in ways that we at least believe will benefit us. Acting for anyone else's interest is not in our makeup. Butler distinguishes between selfishness—concern merely for our own interests—and self-interest. The latter term refers to our concern for our well-being as self-conscious beings, a condition of respect for the self as a self-conscious agent. We cannot hold this high view of ourselves consistently without granting an equal worth to other self-conscious agents; therefore, rational self-interest is inconsistent unless altruism—recognition of the worth of any self-conscious agents—is added.

Butler's view relates to a contemporary criticism of the sort of moral philosophy that he espouses—more precisely, to the combination of ethics and metaphysics that he embraces. This criticism arises from a view that holds that a person is not an enduring self-conscious being but is rather composed of momentary states—of what might be called person bites (analogous to sound bites). The objection goes as follows. Suppose Joe, at time *T*, is composed of person bites *A* and *B*. Consider Joe at time *T*-plus-one-thousand and his contemporary Jill. Joe at this later time, let us suppose, is composed of person bites *X* and *Y*, and Jill is composed of person bites *Q* and *R*. The claim is that person bites *A* and *B* (Joe at *T*) is no more identical with persons bites *X* and *Y* (Joe at T-plus-one-thousand) than they are with person bites Q and R (Jill at T-plus-one-thousand). Therefore, this theory concludes, selfishness is irrational. However, in fact, selfishness is irrational in Butler's view because it assumes the necessary falsehood that one's own status as a self-conscious being is more worthy of respect than the same status as found in every other person. Further, Butler's claim is that moral worth resides in enduring self-conscious persons, not in person bites. Although it seems clear that Butler's persons can be responsible, have consciences, and operate as rational agents, it is not clear that this is true of a person bite or a series of person bites. Indeed, the very lack of identity on which the objection rests calls into question whether these things can be true of person bites, singly or in a series.

Influence

Butler made important contributions to moral philosophy and ethics through his analytical methods and influential arguments. His *Fifteen Sermons Preached at the Rolls Chapel* and *The Analogy of Religion Natural and Revealed, to the Constitution and Course of Nature* continue to be read as presentations of the argument from design and of conscience theory in ethics. His methods of argument influenced such diverse later thinkers as David Hume and John Henry Newman.

Keith E. Yandell

Fifteen Sermons Preached at the Rolls Chapel

Type of philosophy: Ethics, metaphysics
First published: 1726 (revised and enlarged as *Fifteen Sermons to Which Are Added Six Sermons Preached on Public[k] Occasions*, 1765)
Principal ideas advanced:
◇ An examination of human nature reveals not only how humans behave but also how they ought to behave.
◇ Human nature, according to God's plan, is expressed properly when the passions are controlled by self-love and benevolence, and when the latter are controlled by conscience.
◇ Desires have external objects—such as building a house; the theory that all people act to secure their own happiness is mistaken, for people often desire particular external objects without considering the satisfaction to come from securing such objects.
◇ The fact that pleasure is often the consequence of achieving what we desire does not imply that pleasure is the object of desire.
◇ The claim that people are all basically selfish even though they desire objects other than pleasure is in error; it depends on linking compassion to fear, but experience shows no necessary correlation.
◇ If self-love is enlightened, the course of action it prescribes will coincide with that of benevolence.

Joseph Butler was the most influential Anglican theologian of the eighteenth century. During his own time and for some time thereafter, his fame as a religious philosopher rested primarily on his very influential book *The Analogy of Religion Natural and Revealed, to the Constitution and Course of Nature* (1736), in which he argued for an enlightened theology designed to woo the Deists back into the fold of the church. However, his enduring philosophical reputation rests on his *Fifteen Sermons Preached at the Rolls Chapel* and *A Dissertation Upon the Nature of Virtue* (appended to his 1736 work), in which he expounds his views about human nature and morality. Indeed, his refutation of psychological egoism, the doctrine that people are always motivated by their own self-interest, is a classic. Butler's refutation and the analysis of human nature on which it is based are also dealt with in the preface to the *Fifteen Sermons Preached at the Rolls Chapel*, in Sermons 1, 2, 3, 11, and 12, and in the dissertation.

Human Nature

Butler's analysis rests on the thesis that an examination of human nature will reveal not only how people behave but also how they ought to behave. This thesis, in turn, rests on the assumptions that God wants people to act in certain ways, that he has given humans such a nature that they will naturally act in these ways if that nature is not corrupted, and therefore, that these ways can be discovered by examining God's handiwork. Human nature has a hierarchical structure, with people's many impulses, passions, and desires providing the base, the more general and reflective concerns for oneself and others providing the intermediate level, and the supreme faculty of conscience providing the apex. Consequently, human nature is expressed fully and properly not in a life dominated by impulse but in one in which these are exercised under the guidance of self-love and benevolence and in which the latter are controlled in turn by conscience.

Prior to the exercise of rational control, people are creatures of impulse, appetite, passion, and desire, acting in a multitude of ways. Without direction, they seem to be impelled by a host of specific desires to a host of specific and unrelated ends. These desires, or affections, seem to have several important characteristics that distinguish them from the higher principles. On their first appearance, and usually thereafter, they occur spontaneously, without premeditation or deliberation. These affections exist before they become subject to any control or regulation that the mature personality exercises over them, and they tend to move spontaneously toward particular goals. Although the goal is sometimes sought deliberately, it is not chosen deliberately. Finally, Butler says, affections have external objects such as eating food, kicking someone, or building a house—objects external in the sense that they are not states of the agent. That is, for instance, the object of hunger is the consumption of food, not the relief of a feeling of discomfort or the produc-

tion of a pleasant sensation. Note that when Butler speaks of hunger he is not speaking of a state of metabolism or of a feeling in the stomach but of a desire for something, the desire for food.

Butler's point is that the crudest form of psychological egoism is false, for in many, if not most, cases, when people desire something, they do not have in mind their own welfare. If an angry person springs up and attacks a persecutor, the attacker would not ordinarily be thinking that this is the appropriate action to maximize happiness. If asked what he or she wanted, the angry person might speak of a wish to get even, to save face, or to kick the other person; these are the things the individual intends to accomplish.

Of course, Butler agrees, many of our impulsive or passionate acts do bring pleasure to ourselves or to others, whether we had this result in mind or not. Indeed, affections can be classified according to whether they promote the private or the public good. Thus, the desire for food does tend to keep one alive, even though this is not usually what one has in mind; and the desire for esteem does lead one to treat others considerately, even though the object of one's desire is not their welfare. According to Butler, intelligent agents will recognize these tendencies of the affections to augment either their own or others' general welfare, come to value these two wider possibilities as ends in themselves (if they do not already), and hence be led to satisfy their affections as a means to the achievement of these ends. Emerging from this heterogeneous group of affections are two more general and comprehensive desires: the desire to maximize our own happiness and the desire to maximize that of others. These two desires are present in every normal person.

Self-Love

We do desire our own welfare, but this desire is not to be classified with the affections because it is not a passion or an appetite that arises spontaneously and drives impulsively toward a specific goal only to die away when it has been satisfied. Rather, it is a deliberately cultivated, long-enduring desire whose object is such that it cannot be satisfied once and for all at any given time or through the occurrence of any particular event. Furthermore, it functions not merely as a psychological drive but as a principle according to which we deliberately plan what ends to pursue to enhance our overall welfare. Finally, as experience shows, it is a very powerful motive that exerts a natural authority over the affections; the affections ought to be subordinated to it.

Nevertheless, while it is superior to affections, self-love cannot achieve its object unless they achieve theirs, for pleasures occur only as a by-product of the pursuit and satisfaction of affections. Although Butler is not specific, he has in mind such things as the pleasure we experience in pursuing our objective, the satisfaction we experience because we have attained it, and any other pleasures that may follow upon its attainment. For example, although one goes to the fields because of a desire to obtain food, one may enjoy the walk, enjoy digging in the earth, enjoy the satisfaction of gathering the number of potatoes intended for the meal, and enjoy the physical satisfaction that follows the meal. Though an affection and self-love may seek the same thing, the one seeks it for itself, whereas the other seeks it insofar as its pursuit and attainment bring pleasure to the pursuer. Self-love can attain its own end only by letting selected affections pass into action.

Butler suggests that the intimate relationship between self-love and the satisfaction of affections has led some noted egoists, such as Thomas Hobbes, into the error of identifying the particular affections with the principle of self-love or of regarding them as just so many expressions of it. However, the fact that our actions do lead to enjoyment, which is exploited by self-love, does not indicate that the only thing we seek is such enjoyment or that because such enjoyments occur we must have been seeking them. Indeed, if we did not seek something other than pleasure, we would experience no pleasure. The conclusion that we must be egoists does not follow from the fact that all affections belong to the self, from the fact that we never act unless we have such affections, or from the fact that all satisfied affections bring pleasure to the self.

However, there is still room for a subtler egoism, for the egoist might admit that the object of an affection is not the welfare of the agent but insist that insofar as the affections are under the direction of self-love, the overriding considera-

tion is always one's own welfare. Insofar as one acts reasonably, one acts prudently. This type of egoism can be refuted only if there are actions that are not subsumed under the principle of self-love or subsumed under it alone.

Benevolence

There are such actions, Butler says, for most people do act part of the time in a genuinely benevolent fashion. He realized that he would have to defend this position against the most sophisticated egoist. Hobbes argued that what appears to be benevolence is really subtly disguised selfishness. Thus Hobbes claimed that when one feels pity for another person, one is really feeling thankful that one has escaped the calamity and fearful lest such a thing should happen to oneself in the future. One feels more "sympathetic" toward one's unfortunate friend than one does toward strangers because one's friend's life is much more like one's own, and therefore the probability of a similar calamity befalling one is higher.

Butler admits that such selfish reflections might occur, but he insists that they must be distinguished from genuine compassion. Hobbes's view requires equating compassion with fear. If this view was correct, the more compassionate one is, the more fearful one would be, but this is simply not the case. In addition, the more compassionate a person is, the more people admire that individual; but the more fearful a person is, the less people admire him or her. Also, although it is true that the sight of friends in distress evokes greater compassion than the sight of others in distress, it is quite questionable whether the sight of friends in distress raises in us greater fear for ourselves than does the sight of others in distress. This is the classic refutation of Hobbes's doctrine, a refutation that was accepted and polished by philosophers David Hume and Adam Smith.

Butler supports his position, not simply by criticizing his opponents but by drawing our attention to the way people behave. Human behavior will show, he says, that we do have a propensity to help each other, a propensity that cannot be confused with self-love. He offers examples to support this view. In some cases, an apparently benevolent action may be performed solely for the satisfaction it gives the agent or for the sense of power experienced. Yet, what of the person who was not in a position to help another but who nevertheless rejoiced when a third party assisted the second? Also, what of the person who assist one individual rather than another where the choice between the two could not be accounted for in terms of the sense of power? Are there not cases where the choice is made in terms of need? If you examine your own behavior, will you not find it ridiculous to try to explain your benevolent behavior entirely in terms of your love of power, of being dominant, or of hoped-for reciprocation? Nor will it do to reply that acting benevolently gives you pleasure. First, this does not mean you sought that pleasure, and second, the action would not have given you pleasure unless you had a concern for the other person. In this way, Butler answers the more sophisticated egoist.

Although Butler clearly maintains that there is genuinely benevolent action that cannot be explained away, he is not as clear as he might be about the status of benevolence. There are some passages in which benevolence is spoken of as an affection, but there are many others in which it is spoken of as a rational principle. It is true that benevolence is not as strong a motive as self-love, and it is also true that the scope of its application is more restricted, for whereas every affection has consequences that affect the agent, not every affection has consequences that affect others. Most of the passages in which Butler speaks of benevolence as an affection occur when he is making these contrasts, and consequently they seem designed to emphasize the contrasts rather than to express his full view about benevolence. In view of the numerous passages in which benevolence is spoken of as a principle, it seems reasonable to conclude that Butler was not being inconsistent, that he meant that insofar as benevolence transcends spontaneous compassion, it becomes a principle functioning as a guide and having a relationship, like that of self-love, to a multitude of affections. Because it is psychologically weaker, it needs to be fostered and cultivated in a manner in which self-love does not, but it has a similar function and enjoys the same sort of authority over the affections.

Because these principles are coequal in authority, one might expect conflicts in interest between them, but Butler believes that if self-love is really enlightened, the course of action it prescribes will coincide with that of benevolence. No one who is callous to one's fellows will be really happy, not only because this involves thwarting natural affections of sympathy and the like but also because such behavior invites a similar reaction on the part of those so treated. Furthermore, even though it should appear that the selfish will prosper more on this earth than the benevolent, one should not overlook the fact that there is an afterlife in which God will at least compensate for the earthly imbalance. Once again, because two different motives suggest the same actions, we must be wary of falling into the error of identifying them or repudiating one of them. Butler sometimes leaves himself open to misunderstanding on this point when he writes that we are never required to act against our own self-interest. However, when he said this he was pointing out to his worldly and sophisticated congregation that benevolent action does not have consequences that are incompatible with those pursued by self-love. He was not suggesting that benevolence should be placed under the dominance of self-love but rather that if there is a conflict, we had better check to see if we really have discovered what is to our self-interest, for the conflict provides *prima facie* evidence that we have not.

Conscience

These two principles, self-love and benevolence, do not involve duty, but in humans there is a faculty whose function it is to point out what is right and wrong, the faculty of conscience. It should be noted that we must distinguish between action motivated by compassion or benevolence on the one hand and that motivated by a sense of duty on the other. Of course, benevolence and conscience may, and frequently do, suggest the same course of action, but the motivation is different. As the supreme faculty, conscience should stand above and coordinate the activities of the other principles. Its supremacy does not rest on its power, for impulse and self-love often override it, but it carries the mark of authority, as is evidenced by the feeling of wrongdoing or guilt we experience when we do not heed it. "Had it strength as it has right, had it power as it has manifest authority, it would absolutely govern the world." The existence of conscience indicates in yet another way the inadequacy of the egoist's position.

Conscience is not a criterion used in reaching decisions or planning courses of action, as are the rational principles of benevolence and self-love, but a faculty that makes pronouncements about what is right or wrong. It tells us *what* to do and *what* to approve of, but not *why*. Butler suggests that God might be a utilitarian, but he insists that we cannot be, for certain things are simply seen to be praiseworthy or unpraiseworthy quite apart from any tendency they might have to further or hinder the public welfare. Thus, for instance, conscience reveals the baseness of treachery and the meanness of a small mind as well as the praiseworthiness of fidelity, honor, and justice. Conscience does not proceed by reasoning, nor does it seek to justify its deliverances in terms of some underlying principle; it simply pronounces on specific matters and does so with authority. It functions in all "plain honest men" as the vice-regent of God, cutting in a direct and simple manner through the moral perplexities of their daily lives.

Butler believed not only that there is no conflict between conscience and benevolence but also that there is none between conscience and self-love. There cannot be if we are clear about what is to our self-interest. After all, God intends that we should be happy, and conscience is the faculty he has given us to ensure that we do as he intends. Consequently, as Butler saw it, human nature exhibits a complexly structured system of motives, resting on the affections that are controlled by the principles of self-love and benevolence and capped by the faculty of conscience that has authority over all. When developed as God intended it should be, it is a nature in which these various factors supplement and complement one another to produce an integrated and harmoniously organized life.

Butler did not develop his views fully, but he traced out in bold outline a view that embodies the classic refutation of psychological egoism, ancient or modern. Butler is one of the most important moral philosophers of the eighteenth century.

Leonard Miller, updated by John K. Roth

Additional Reading

Cunliffe, Christopher, ed. *Joseph Butler's Moral and Religious Thought*. Oxford: Clarendon Press, 1992. An excellent collection of essays on Joseph Butler's philosophy; the central topics are illuminatingly treated.

Duncan-Jones, Austin. *Butler's Moral Philosophy*. Hammondsworth, England: Penguin, 1952. This book-length discussion of Butler's moral philosophy also contains the best short biographical sketch on the bishop.

Jeffner, Anders. *Butler and Hume on Religion*. Stockholm: Diakonistyrelsens Bokforlag, 1966. Excellent discussion of Butler's philosophy of religion.

Mossner, E.C. *Bishop Butler in the Age of Reason*. New York: B. Blom, 1971. Places Butler's view in the intellectual controversies of his time.

Penelhum, Terence. *Butler*. Routledge & Kegan Paul, 1985. A clear, careful, judicious discussion of Butler's philosophy.

Waring, E. Graham, ed. *Deism and Natural Religion*. New York: Frederick Ungar, 1967. A generous selection from the English deists, whose beliefs Butler addressed in his works.

Keith E. Yandell

Albert Camus

Camus's philosophical and literary writings established his reputation as the moral conscience of France during the 1940's and 1950's. With understated eloquence, he reaffirmed the intrinsic values of individual freedom and dignity in the face of such evils as Nazism, Stalinism, and colonial exploitation.

Principal philosophical works: *L'Envers et l'endroit*, 1937 ("The Wrong Side and the Right Side," 1968); *Noces*, 1938 ("Nuptials," 1908); *L'Étranger*, 1942 (*The Stranger*, 1946); *Le Mythe de Sisyphe*, 1942 (*The Myth of Sisyphus*, 1955); *La Peste*, 1947 (*The Plague*, 1948); *L'Homme révolté*, 1951 (*The Rebel*, 1953); *L'Été*, 1954 ("Summer"); *La Chute*, 1956 (*The Fall*, 1957); *Carnets: Mai 1935-février 1942*, 1962 (*Notebooks*, 1963); *Carnets: Janvier 1942-mars 1951*, 1964 (*Notebooks*, 1963); *Lyrical and Critical Essays*, 1968 (includes "The Wrong Side and the Right Side," "Nuptials," and "Summer"); *La Mort heureuse*, 1971 (wr. 1936-1938; *A Happy Death*, 1972); *Le Premier homme*, 1994 (*The First Man*, 1995).

Born: November 7, 1913; Mondovi, Algeria
Died: January 4, 1960; near Villeblevin, France

Early Life

Albert Camus had a very difficult childhood. When he was born on November 7, 1913, his parents Lucien and Catherine were living in the small Algerian city of Mondovi, where his father worked for a vineyard. His parents were very poor. The very next year, Lucien was drafted, and he died in October, 1914, as a result of wounds received during the Battle of the Marne. His widow, Catherine, already partially deaf, suffered a stroke soon after Lucien's death, and this stroke permanently affected her speech. She moved to Algiers with her two sons, Albert and Lucien. They lived with her domineering mother, Catherine Sintes, in the working-class neighborhood of Belcourt. The harsh conditions of Camus's youth taught him to value independence, personal responsibility, and human dignity.

Camus did very well in grammar school and earned a scholarship to the prestigious Grand Lycée of Algiers, where he developed a profound interest in philosophy and literature under the guidance of his teacher, Jean Grenier, to whom he would later dedicate two philosophical works,

"The Wrong Side and the Right Side" and *The Rebel*. At the age of seventeen, however, he became gravely ill with tuberculosis, from which his lungs never fully recovered. Camus did, however, resume his studies, and in 1936, he defended his master's thesis on the problem of evil in the writings of Plotinus and Saint Augustine. Although his mother was Catholic, Camus was an agnostic. His medical problems prevented him from being offered a teaching position in Algeria.

Between 1935 and his move to France in 1942, he worked as a journalist in Algiers. He also became involved with a theatrical troupe in Algiers, first as an actor and then as a playwright and director. He wrote his first play, *Caligula* (pb. 1944; English translation, 1948), in 1938-1939. He temporarily joined the Algerian Communist Party, but he soon became disillusioned with communism. His distrust of communism greatly influenced his political opinions. In 1940, he married Francine Faure. Two years later, he moved permanently to France in order to join the French Resistance. Francine stayed in Algeria from 1942 until 1944. She rejoined Camus in 1944 after the liberation of Paris. Camus and Francine had two children—twins, Catherine and Jean, born in 1945.

Life's Work

Although Camus published two well-crafted volumes of short stories in the 1930's, his work was then appreciated only in Algeria. His international reputation as a writer and philosopher dates from the publication in occupied Paris of *The Stranger* and *The Myth of Sisyphus*.

The Stranger is a first-person narrative whose principal character, Meursault, does not even have a first name. Meursault, an Algerian office worker, is alienated from society. He is incapable of expressing strong emotions, even at his mother's wake and burial. He has no real ambition or sensitivity to the feelings of his lover Marie. Meursault does not truly respect the dignity of other people. Raymond, a close friend, is a pimp, and Meursault sees nothing wrong with this amoral profession. Meursault kills an Arab who has been following Raymond. Although Meursault is clearly guilty, he should still receive a fair trial. Impartial justice, of course, no longer existed in occupied France. The presiding judge overtly favors the prosecutor, who is allowed to introduce numerous irrelevant and damaging remarks about Meursault, whose incompetent or corrupt lawyer never protests effectively. Nazi collaborators in France denounced *The Stranger* as a dangerous novel because it held the French judicial system up to ridicule. In an early essay on *The Stranger*, philosopher Jean-Paul Sartre noted perceptively that these collaborators had not fully understood *The Stranger*. This novel clearly condemns the legal injustices committed by the Nazis and their collaborators, but it also reaffirms the French republican ideals of liberty, equality, and fraternity. The Nazis wanted nothing to do with the moral values of the French Third Republic, which they had destroyed in 1940.

Camus's next major work was his 1942 philosophical treatise *The Myth of Sisyphus*. According to Greek mythology, Sisyphus was condemned for eternity to push a large rock to the top of a mountain. Every time he reached the summit, his rock rolled back into the valley. Despite the apparently absurd nature of his task, Sisyphus never gave in to the forces that were trying to destroy his spirit. Camus imagines that Sisyphus was being punished because he had rebelled against the arbitrary power of the gods. Camus transforms Sisyphus into a moral hero who resists evil. Many readers have interpreted *The Myth of Sisyphus* as an ethical defense of the French Resistance. In the last paragraph of this work, Camus describes Sisyphus at the bottom of his mountain. Sisyphus must decide whether it is worth the effort to continue his fight for human dignity. Sisyphus will not give in to evil. Camus ends *The Myth of Sisyphus* with the thought-provoking remark, "We must imagine Sisyphus to be happy." Sisyphus realizes that he is mor-

Albert Camus. *(The Nobel Foundation)*

331

ally superior to the evil forces that seek to destroy him.

Three years after the liberation of France, Camus published his most extended reflection on the evil of Nazism. His powerful 1947 novel *The Plague* takes place in the walled Algerian city of Oran. *The Plague* is technically a series of diary entries, but readers do not discover until the very last chapter that Dr. Bernard Rieux kept this diary. Camus describes Oran as a typical modern city with which any reader can identify. The plague suddenly breaks out, and the walls of Oran are closed in order to prevent this epidemic from spreading to other cities. For the inhabitants of Oran, this plague symbolizes the absolute evil against which they must fight. The political and moral implications of *The Plague* were clear to Camus's contemporaries. The closed walls of Oran may represent the closed frontiers of those countries occupied by the Nazis, or they may refer more directly to the walls around the Nazi death camps. In plague-ridden Oran, crematoriums are used to dispose of the numerous corpses. This clearly reminds Camus's readers of the crematoriums used by the Nazis in their concentration camps.

For highly diverse reasons, characters such as the agnostic Dr. Rieux, the journalist Rambert, and the modest civil servant Joseph Grand all decide to fight the plague. The incredibly destructive power of evil is illustrated when Camus describes the painful death of Judge Othon's young son. The screams from this dying child cause Father Paneloux to question his belief in a just God, and they almost destroy Judge Othon's will to live. The gruesome death of his young child is reminiscent of the suffering of millions of equally innocent children and adults whom the Nazis murdered. At the end of this novel, the plague itself is over, but its effects will last for years and generations to come. Camus ended this powerful novel by reminding his readers that evil can never be permanently eradicated, because a plague may break out at any time in another "happy city." *The Plague* was such an extraordinarily effective novel that the members of the Swedish Academy seriously considered giving Camus the Nobel Prize in 1947. Camus was then only thirty-four years old, and the youngest previous Nobel laureate had been Rudyard Kipling, who was forty-three years old when he received his Nobel Prize in Literature in 1907. In 1957, the Swedish Academy would honor Camus with the Nobel Prize in Literature.

During the last twelve years of his relatively short life, Camus became very involved in the theatrical life of France. His plays stressed both the absolute need to respect human life and the danger of political theories that try to justify the use of violence as a means of changing society. Among his most important contributions to the theater were *L'État de siège* (pr., pb. 1948; *The State of Siege*, 1958), *Les Justes* (pr. 1949; *The Just Assassins*, 1958), and *Requiem pour une nonne: Pièce en deux parties et sept tableaux/d'apres William Faulkner*, his 1956 adaptation of William Faulkner's *Requiem for a Nun* (1951). His major philosophical work from this period was his 1951 book *The Rebel*, in which he argued against all uses of violence as a technique for social change. *The Rebel* provoked an extremely negative reaction from Sartre, who believed that violence was sometimes justifiable. Camus considered Sartre's arguments to be both specious and dangerous. The rupture between Camus and Sartre would be permanent. In 1956, Camus published *The Fall*, a marvelously ironic novel about an amoral lawyer named Jean-Baptiste Clamence. During the last year of his life, Camus worked on *The First Man*, a novel about his own youth. When he died in an automobile accident on January 4, 1960, the unfinished manuscript of *The First Man* was found in Camus's attaché case. Although he died at the relatively young age of forty-six, Camus was a very prolific writer with extremely varied interests.

Influence
Camus's refusal to propose simplistic answers to complex moral and social problems alienated him from many French intellectuals on both the political left and right. He refused, however, to compromise his ethical beliefs in order to placate even influential critics such as Jean-Paul Sartre and François Mauriac. Personal integrity was indispensable for Camus. He courageously resisted all attempts to limit basic freedoms. He fought in the French Resistance; he was once expelled from his native Algeria because he had written newspaper articles denouncing the mistreatment of

Arabs by the French colonial authorities; and he frequently criticized political abuses in countries such as Francisco Franco's Spain and communist Hungary and East Germany. When he received the Nobel Prize in Literature in December, 1957, his acceptance speech stressed that a conscientious writer should convey to others the interrelated values of truth and liberty. His profound insights into the human condition have enriched the lives of readers from many different cultures.

Edmund J. Campion

The Rebel

Type of philosophy: Ethics, existentialism, political philosophy
First published: L'Homme révolté, 1951 (English translation, 1953)
Principal ideas advanced:

◇ When a person who is slave to the absurd conditions in the environment declares that there is a limit to what can be endured or approved, that person becomes a human and exists.

◇ In creating value through rebellion, the rebel creates values for all people and becomes part of the human community.

◇ Those who attempt to rebel by becoming nihilists or utopians fail to achieve authentic rebellion.

◇ The genuine rebel combines the negative attitude of one who recognizes the relativity of values with the positive attitude of one who makes an absolute commitment that gives rise to spiritual values.

From French revolutionist Maximilien Robespierre to Soviet political leader Joseph Stalin, lovers of justice and equality have fallen time and again into contradiction and ended by outraging the humanity they were committed to save. *The Rebel* seeks to understand the failure of a century and a half of revolution and, by returning to its source in the spirit of revolt, to recover the ideal that has eluded the ideologues.

Albert Camus's book is, in one respect, a history of the whole anti-God, antiauthoritarian movement in literature, philosophy, and government. The historical study is divided into three parts. The first, entitled "Metaphysical Rebellion," examines a gallery of "immoralist" authors beginning with the Marquis de Sade and ending with André Breton. A longer section, called "Historical Rebellion," traces the fortunes of political nihilism both in its individualist and collectivist forms. A third part, "Rebellion and Art," briefly indicates the manner in which the same analysis may be carried over into the fine arts, particularly the history of the novel. Thus, the body of this considerable work is a series of essays in literary and historical criticism.

However, the introductory and concluding essays are of a different sort. In them, Camus conducts a phenomenological investigation into the data of revolt, analogous to German philosopher Max Scheler's study of resentment and Camus's own earlier analysis of the absurd. These essays, which are the most original part of the book, provide the norm by which the failures of nihilism are judged and point the direction of a more humane and creative endeavor.

Nihilism

The essay *Le Mythe de Sisyphe* (1942; *The Myth of Sisyphus*, 1955) was addressed to the problem of nihilism that engrossed the minds of intellectuals at the close of World War I. In it, Camus presents his variant of existentialism, according to which one who has been confronted with the meaninglessness of existence gives one's own life a modicum of dignity and significance by holding the posture of revolt. Honest people, says Camus, act according to their beliefs. If one affirms that the world is meaningless, one is bound to commit suicide, for to go on living is to cheat. According to Camus in this youthful work, the only honest reason for one's putting up with the irrationality of things is to be able to feel superior to the forces that crush one. To the person of the absurd, the world becomes as indifferent as one is to the world. One bears one's burden without joy and without hope, like Sisyphus, who was condemned to roll his rock up the hill anew each day; but one preserves a titanic fury, refusing any of the palliatives offered by religion or philosophy or by the distractions of pleasure or ambition.

When *The Rebel* was written, ten years later,

the fashionable nihilism of the period between the wars was no longer relevant. The fall of France led to the taking of sides by many intellectuals, including Camus. The problem of suicide gave way to that of collaboration. People who had cultivated indifference suddenly found that they could not overlook the difference between Nazi collaborator Pierre Laval and Charles de Gaulle, leader of anti-Nazi forces outside France.

The new concern is plainly evident in Camus's novel *La Peste* (1947; *The Plague*, 1948), where it is abundantly clear that those who are strong ought to bear the burdens of the weak. In this pest-hole of a world, no individual can stir without the risk of bringing death to someone. However, although all people are contaminated, they have the choice of joining forces with the plague or of putting up a fight against it. The immediate objective is to save as many as possible from death. However, beyond this, and, in Camus's eyes even more important, is the task of saving people from loneliness. It is better to be in the plague with others than to be isolated on the outside.

Rebellion

In *The Rebel*, Camus tries to show that solidarity is logically implied even in the absurdist position; for to perceive that life is absurd, there must be consciousness, and for there to be consciousness, there must be life. However, the moment human life becomes a value, it becomes a value for all people. In this way, absurdism may be extended to prohibit murder as well as suicide. However, it offers no creative solution to an age of wholesale exportation, enslavement, and execution. People must turn, instead, to a different kind of revolt—that which on occasion is born in the heart of a slave who suddenly says, "No; there is a limit. So much will I consent to, but no more." At this moment, a line is drawn between what it is to be a thing and what it is to be a person. Human nature is delineated, and a new value comes into being. To be sure, the universe ignores it, and the forces of history deny it. However, it rises, nonetheless, to challenge these; and in so doing creates a new force, brotherhood. Out of rebellion, Camus wrenches a positive principle of politics as French philosopher René Descartes had found certitude in the midst of doubt. "I rebel," says Camus, "therefore *we* exist."

Although the first stirrings of rebellion are full of promise, the path they create is straight and narrow, and few follow it to the end. Like the moral virtues in Aristotle's *Ethica Nicomachea* (second Athenian period, 335-323 B.C.E.; *Nicomachean Ethics*, 1797), it is a mean between two extremes. If rebels think out the implications of the impulse that moves within them, they know that they must never kill or oppress or deceive other people. However, in the actual world, such a policy makes them accessory to the crimes of others. Therefore, they must on occasion perform acts of violence in the interest of suffering humanity. The difficulties of taking arms against oppression without becoming an oppressor are so great that it is small wonder most would-be rebels slip into one false position or another.

In *The Myth of Sisyphus*, Camus went to great lengths to show the inauthentic responses to the absurd made by the existentialists Søren Kierkegaard, Franz Kafka, and Jean-Paul Sartre, who, according to Camus, rejected literal suicide, but substituted a kind of "philosophical suicide" by making believe that it is possible to escape absurdity. In *The Rebel*, Camus's chief line of argument is to show that the great heroes in the literature of revolt and in the history of revolution, almost without exception, fall away from authentic rebellion. For some, the dominant impulse is to negate the forces that frustrate humanity's development: With them rebellion passes into hatred, and they can think of nothing but destruction. For others, the impulse is to enforce order and realize a standard good: Love of their fellow man gives place to an abstract goal that they must achieve at any cost. The former are nihilists, the latter utopians.

World Deniers and Affirmers

Camus's discussion in "Rebellion in Art" provides a clear instance of the two kinds of false rebellion. All art, in his opinion, is essentially a revolt against reality. Art both needs the world and denies it. However, contemporary art has allowed itself to be sidetracked. Formalism gravitates too exclusively toward negation, banishing reality and ending in delirium. Realism, however (he specifies the "tough" American variety), by reducing humans to elemental and external reactions, is too eager to impose its own order on the world. Both arise, in a sense, out of the spirit of revolt, protesting the hypocrisy of bourgeois conventionality; both fail as art, inasmuch as they lose touch with the springs of revolt. Marcel Proust is Camus's example of a genuine artist: Rejecting those aspects of reality that are of no interest to people while lovingly affirming the happier parts, he re-creates the universe by redistributing its elements after the heart's desire. This suggests that the creative way is not that of "all or nothing" but that of moderation and limit. The order and unity that make for genuine art do minimal violence to the matter they undertake to re-form. The artist remains, above all, a friend of humanity.

Camus's classification of rebels into world deniers and world affirmers provides only a rough basis for division when he comes to consider the great figures in the history of revolt. The difficulty is that the contradictions into which their extremism leads renders them at last almost indistinguishable. Nevertheless there is merit in retaining the groupings. Under "Metaphysical Rebellion," the Marquis de Sade's advocacy of universal crime and Alfred de Vigny's Satanism exemplify rebellion that took the way of negation. With them can be placed Arthur Rimbaud, who made a virtue of renouncing his genius, and the Surrealist André Breton, who talked of the beauty of shooting at random into a street crowd. On the other side are the partisans of affirmation: Max Stirner with his absolute egotism and Friedrich Nietzsche with his deification of fate. In "Historical Rebellion," Camus looks at anarchists and nihilists such as Mikhail Bakunin and Dmitry Pisarev, for whom destruction was an end in itself. However, they are more than balanced by the revolutionaries, whose ambition in overthrowing the present order was but a means toward fulfilling the destiny of a race or of humankind—Italian dictator Benito Mussolini and German Nazi Adolf Hitler, German philosopher Karl Marx and Russian Communist leader Vladimir Ilich Lenin.

The Problems of Rebellion

The section "Metaphysical Rebellion" deals with those whose revolts were centered in the realm of imagination. Camus finds their archetype not in Prometheus, the figure from Greek mythology who stole fire from Zeus and gave it to humankind, but in the biblical figure Cain, who killed his brother Abel, because rebellion presupposes a doctrine of creation and a personal deity who is held to be responsible for the human condition. Their temper is that of blasphemy rather than of nonbelief; and when these rebels go so far as to deny that there is a God, their protest, lacking an object, turns into madness. The fictional Ivan Karamazov, from Fyodor Dostoevski's *Bratya Karamazovy* (1879-1880; *The Brothers Karamazov*, 1912), is more instructive than real-life rebels. Indignation causes him to reject God on the grounds that a world that entails suffering ought never to have been permitted. However, he discovers that, having rejected God, there is no longer any limit; "everything is permitted." Ivan acquiesces in the murder of his father—before going mad. Ivan rejects grace and has nothing to put in its place. This is the tragedy of nihilism.

"Historical Revolt" was directed less immediately against God than against the absolutism of divine right kings and the prerogatives of feudal lords and bishops. However, it has its metaphysical dimension. In rejecting the old order, the revolutionaries were also rejecting grace, without, however, falling into nihilism; for instead of concluding that all things are permitted, they immediately divinized justice. They repudiated Christ, but retained the apparatus of an infallible institution within which alone salvation is possible. In place of the madness of Ivan Karamazov, they find themselves swallowed up in despair. Their conclusion is a direct contradiction of their original premises: Starting from unlimited freedom they arrive at unlimited despotism.

In Camus's opinion, just as the nineteenth century revolted against grace, the twentieth must revolt against justice. The kingdom of humanity that the revolutionaries sought to substitute for the kingdom of God has retreated into the distance, and the goal has been brought not a step nearer. The fault is in the nature of revolution itself, which, as the word indicates, describes a full cycle. In rebellion, the slaves rise up against their master; in revolution, they aspire to take their masters' place. Thus, the champions of justice have merely substituted a new domination for the old. In many ways, the new is less tolerable than that which it replaced. For the rule of

God at least allowed humanity to preserve the human image; but when the sacred disappeared, humanity's dignity disappeared with it. It is a principle of all revolutions, says Camus, that human nature is infinitely malleable; in other words, there is no special human nature. Under the kingdom of grace there was; and rebels insist that there still is. Rebellion rediscovers humanity, affirms that people are not mere things, insists that a distinctive nature sets people apart from all other beings and, at the same time, unites each person with every other human. From this point of view, the only alternative to grace is rebellion.

The Values of the Spirit of Rebellion

No doubt enough has been said about the defections into which rebels are prone to fall. Like many a preacher, Camus finds it easier to criticize the failures of others than to present a clear-cut statement of what authentic rebellion entails. We have, of course, his stories and dramas to fill out the picture. However, so far as the present essay is concerned, the only vivid illustration of genuine revolt is found in his account of a group of Russian terrorists (the most exemplary were brought to trial in 1905) who combined nihilism with definite religious principles. Camus calls them "fastidious nihilists." "In the universe of total negation, these young disciples try with bombs and revolvers and also with the courage with which they walk to the gallows, to escape from contradiction and to create the values they lack." They did not hesitate to destroy; but by their death they believed they were re-creating a community founded on love and justice, thus resuming the mission the church had betrayed. They combined respect for human life in general with the resolution to sacrifice their own lives. Death was sought as payment for the crimes that the nihilists knew they must commit.

Transposed into a more moderate key, what Camus seems to be advocating is a life of tension in which contradictions may live and thrive. There must be a way between that of the Yogi and that of the Commissar, between absolute freedom and absolute justice. In this world, people have to be content with relative goods; but they do not have to give them anything less than their absolute commitment. This is humanism, though hardly of the Anglo-Saxon utilitarian variety. The values born of the spirit of rebellion are essentially spiritual. The rebel wills to serve justice without committing injustice in the process, to use plain language and avoid falsehood, to advance toward unity without denying the origins of community in the free spirit.

Politically, Albert Camus takes his stand with syndicalist and libertarian thought: Opposed to the revolutionists who would order society from the top down, he favors a society built out of local autonomous cells. Far from being romantic, he holds that a communal system is more realistic than the totalitarian, based as it is on concrete relations such as occupation and the village. His stand is not new: From the time of the Greeks, the struggle has been going on (especially around the Mediterranean) between city and empire, deliberate freedom and rational tyranny, and altruistic individualism and the manipulation of the masses. It is the endless opposition of moderation to excess in people's attempt to know and apply the measure of their stature, their refusal to be either beast or god.

Jean Faurot

Additional Reading

Brée, Germaine. *Camus and Sartre: Crisis and Commitment*. New York: Delacorte, 1972. This book accurately describes similarities and differences between Albert Camus and French philosopher Jean-Paul Sartre. Brée disagrees with other Camus biographers who contend Camus was insensitive to the situation of Arabs in Algeria.

Bronner, Stephen Eric. *Albert Camus: The Thinker, the Artist, the Man*. Impact series. New York: Franklin Watts, 1996. This title provides a thorough, detailed account of the life and work of Camus. Bronner assumes, however, that the reader is familiar with key places and figures in Camus's life. Black-and-white photos and chronology put events and Camus's influence on history and literature into perspective.

Fitch, Brian T. *The Narcissistic Text: A Reading of Camus' Fiction*. Toronto: University of Toronto Press, 1982. This creative book examines Camus's major works of fiction from the perspective of reader-response criticism. Fitch stresses the numerous ambiguities in *The Stranger*, *The Plague*, and *The Fall*.

Lazere, Donald. *The Unique Creation of Albert Camus*. New Haven, Conn.: Yale University Press, 1973. This fascinating psychoanalytic reading of Camus's works enriches appreciation of Camus's style. Lazere's final chapter summarizes American critical reactions to Camus's works.

Lottman, Herbert R. *Albert Camus*. Garden City, N.Y.: Doubleday, 1979. This is an extremely well-documented biography of Camus. Lottman based this book on extensive interviews with people who knew Camus well.

Merton, Thomas. *Albert Camus' 'The Plague': Introduction and Commentary*. New York: Seabury Press, 1968. This book proposes a profound theological interpretation of *The Plague*. Thomas Merton, a Trappist monk and a famous writer, shows that the two sermons delivered by Friar Paneloux in this novel distort the traditional Christian concept of grace.

Rhein, Phillip H. *Albert Camus*. New York: Twayne, 1969. This excellent general study of Camus's works defines well the originality of his contributions to French literature and philosophy.

Todd, Olivier. *Albert Camus: A Life*. Translated by Benjamin Ivry. New York: Knopf, 1997. A captivating account of the philosopher's life. The book includes a great many details and anecdotes of Camus's life in Algeria before moving to France. Fewer details are given for the subject's later life, however. Todd uses interviews with those who knew Camus, drawing on details, memories, and anecdotes to portray the depth and character of this existentialist philosopher.

Edmund J. Campion, updated by Lisa A. Wroble

Rudolf Carnap

Carnap became leader of the logical positivists. They regarded logic, mathematics, and physics as genuine knowledge, but metaphysics and ethics as cognitively meaningless. Carnap's main strategy was to construct artificial languages in formal symbolism.

Principal philosophical works: *Der Raum: Ein Beitrag zur Wissenschaftslehre*, 1922; *Physikalische Begriffsbildung*, 1926; *Der logische Aufbau der Welt*, 1928 (*The Logical Structure of the World: Pseudoproblems in Philosophy*, 1967); *Abriß der Logistik*, 1929; *Wissenschaftliche Weltauffassung*, 1929 (with H. Hahn and O. Neurath); *Logische Syntax der Sprache*, 1934 (*The Logical Syntax of Language*, 1937); *Philosophy and Logical Syntax*, 1935; *Foundations of Logic and Mathematics*, 1939; *Introduction to Semantics*, 1942; *Formalization of Logic*, 1943; *Meaning and Necessity*, 1947; *Logical Foundation of Probability*, 1950; *The Continuum of Inductive Methods*, 1952; *Dear Carnap, Dear Van: The Quine-Carnap Correspondence and Related Work*, 1990 (with W. V. O. Quine).

Born: May 18, 1891; Ronsdorf, Germany
Died: September 14, 1970; Santa Monica, California

Early Life

Rudolf Carnap was born in northwest Germany to parents who were earnestly religious but tolerant of the beliefs of others. During adolescence, his studies of science led him to drop his religious beliefs in favor of secular humanism. He attended the Universities of Jena and of Freiburg im Breisgau, studying mathematics, physics, and philosophy.

At Jena, between 1910 and 1914, Carnap attended the classes of Gottlob Frege, a philosophical mathematician little known at that time. Frege had anticipated Alfred North Whitehead and Bertrand Russell by originating quantificational symbolism in logic and using it in the attempt to demonstrate rigorously that all mathematics of number is strictly reducible to logic. Under Frege's influence, Carnap came to distinguish sharply between symbols and what the symbols stand for, thereby avoiding much confusion in the philosophy of mathematics, and also to distinguish sharply between analytic truths (knowable on the basis of principles of pure logic together with explicit definitions) and synthetic truths (knowable only on the basis of some kind of immediate experience). However, Carnap rejected Frege's metaphysical views about the reality of abstract entities.

Carnap's studies were interrupted by military service in World War I. On his return, he committed himself to graduate work in philosophy. His doctoral dissertation, published in 1922, dealt with the philosophy of space. It was influenced by the neo-Kantianism he had absorbed from his professors, but it also showed his keen interest in new developments in physics. Soon his philosophical work began to show the influence of Russell, who in 1914 had called for a new breed of thinkers who would resolve philosophical problems by using the techniques of mathematical logic to construct formalized systems.

Life's Work

Carnap's philosophical career began to blossom in 1925 when he was invited to lecture at the University of Vienna, where Moritz Schlick had assembled a group of philosophers, mathematicians, and scientists actively concerned with the philosophy of science. This group held regular meetings and came to be known as the Vienna Circle. They were impressed by Carnap, and Schlick obtained a teaching position, starting in

1926, in philosophy at Vienna for Carnap. Carnap later looked back on this period as a time of especially fruitful discussion and cooperative research among this lively group of largely like-minded thinkers. Carnap began to play a leading role in the drafting of manifestoes and the editing of publications aimed at spreading the philosophically radical doctrines of this new movement, and his writings soon became more extensive and influential than those of any other member. The movement came to be called logical positivism, though Carnap preferred to call it logical empiricism.

The members of the Vienna Circle had been impressed by Ludwig Wittgenstein's "Logisch-philosophische Abhandlung" (1921; best known by the bilingual German and English edition title of *Tractatus Logico-Philosophicus*, 1922, 1961) and drew some of their doctrines from it. However, Wittgenstein did not find Carnap congenial; Carnap's conception of philosophy could hardly have pleased him. Carnap's view was that the goal of philosophy should be to work out rational reconstructions of scientific language that needed clarifying. In each case, his strategy was to construct a formalized artificial language containing precisely defined symbols that could serve as improved replacements for the terms occurring in ordinary scientific discourse. For him, these were just technical problems requiring technical solutions. Carnap had no interest in the mystical or in other philosophical perplexities with which Wittgenstein became obsessively concerned.

Carnap's most important work from his Vienna period was *The Logical Structure of the World*. In this book, he attempted to sketch a rational reconstruction of all talk about physical objects in the world. He tried to show how, in a formalized language, sentences using physical-object terminology could in principle be completely translated into sentences that merely report immediate sense experience. This was Carnap's reformulation of the view that earlier philosophers had termed phenomenalism. It became part of the program for what Carnap called the

"unity of science," his goal being a single, logically unified language system in which all science could be expressed.

Russell had already worked on this project, but Carnap's treatment was fuller. Even Carnap, however, left the project very incomplete, with many logical gaps unbridged. Notably, rather than starting with sentences about small bits of sensory content as Russell had, Carnap, under the influence of Gestalt psychology, began with sentences about momentary total experiences. Also, unlike Russell, Carnap did not think it imperative to treat immediate experience as the starting point. He mentioned that sentences about publicly observable physical objects could also serve as an acceptable starting point. Thus, he showed his cavalier attitude toward the traditional idea that empirical knowledge of objects

Rudolf Carnap. *(AP/Wide World Photos)*

must be based on private sensory experience. He held that choice of a starting point is merely a matter of convenience.

After five years in Vienna, Carnap moved to the German University of Prague, where he remained through 1935, continuing to maintain contact with his colleagues in Vienna. During his Prague period, he published a very readable short book, *Philosophy and Logical Syntax*, in which he provides a forceful statement of the overall outlook of logical positivism. In it, he makes a sharp distinction between empirical (synthetic) sentences, which he says have factual content only if they are verifiable through observation, and a priori (analytic) sentences, which lack content and merely reflect linguistic conventions. All other sentences have no cognitive meaning and are incapable of truth or falsity, he maintains.

Carnap dismisses the statements of metaphysicians. For example, Carnap states that the disagreement between realists and idealists about whether physical objects really exist is nonsense, for there is no verifiable difference between the opposing answers. He also dismisses as nonsensical all ethical and value judgments (except perhaps those that are tautologies). To say that a state of affairs is right or good is merely to vent one's subjective emotional response, he holds; it is never to make an observationally verifiable claim, and therefore such remarks are incapable of truth or falsity. At a later time, Carnap explained that his advocacy of this noncognitivist view of ethics never affected his own strong ethical and political views. He advocated socialism, pacifism, world federalism, and kindly treatment of everyone. Critics might complain that it is incoherent for Carnap to advance views about how society ought to operate when he regards these very views as wholly subjective and incapable of being true. However, Carnap was unfazed by such criticism.

The major work of Carnap's Prague period was *The Logical Syntax of Language*. In this technical book, Carnap undertakes an overarching construction of languages suitable for expressing mathematics and science, attending only to their syntax (the formation rules and transformation rules governing combinations of symbols). He distinguishes sharply between an object-language and a metalanguage; the former speaks about objects of some type, such as numbers or physical things, while the latter speaks about the former. It is not safe to speak about the syntax of a language within that language itself, as this readily leads to contradictions; however, Carnap holds, in opposition to Wittgenstein, that every language can be spoken about in some suitable metalanguage.

Of special philosophical interest is the "principle of tolerance" that Carnap puts forward in this book. This is the principle that anyone may choose to use any language whatever, so long as it is made clear exactly what the syntactical rules of that language are. Some languages may prove to be more useful than others, but none is more correct than any other. In the light of this principle, Carnap proposes to dissolve the controversy in philosophy of mathematics between those who say that numbers are real, independently existing entities (part of "the furniture of the universe") and others who say that there are no such things as numbers, only numerals. Carnap's response is that both sides are mistaken to think they are in opposition. Speaking in either of these two ways is fine as long as everyone realizes that there is no fact of the matter and that the seeming problem is no problem at all.

The rise of Nazism in Germany affected the turbulent German minority in Czechoslovakia, making life increasingly difficult there for Carnap. In 1936, he moved to the United States, becoming a professor at the University of Chicago. He became a U.S. citizen in 1941. At Chicago, he was pleased with his students but did not find his philosophical colleagues as stimulating as he would have wished, for most of them were committed to doing philosophy in ways he regarded as metaphysical. Carnap left Chicago in 1952, spent two years at the Institute for Advanced Study in Princeton, New Jersey, and in 1954 moved to the University of California, Los Angeles, where he continued teaching until his retirement.

Carnap's early view was that only a limited range of sentences is empirically meaningful, but in "Testability and Meaning" (1936-1937), he greatly broadened this, conceding empirical meaningfulness to far more sentences. Also Carnap abandoned his former view that the logic of language can be treated solely in terms of syntax. He decided that semantics (which takes account of relations between symbols and what they refer to) is also needed. His *Meaning and Necessity* is a technical work proposing semantical rules for concepts such as necessity and possibility.

Much of Carnap's effort during his later years was devoted to the topic of probability, which he saw as vital to science. In *Logical Foundations of Probability*, he construed probability as a logical relation between a sentence expressing data and another sentence expressing a hypothesis. His goal was to construct a language for science providing rules for evaluating the probability of any hypothesis sentence relative to any set of data sentences. The book is long and elaborate, yet makes only limited headway toward a plausible general account of probability. His construction leaves him with some implausible results: that universal hypotheses always have zero probability and that the probability of all particular hypotheses will decline whenever a new predicate is introduced into the language. In subsequent years, Carnap continually modified his theory, never achieving complete success but never giving up the hope of constructing a formal theory that would fully serve as a rational reconstruction of scientific talk about probability.

Influence

Carnap became a major figure in philosophy because his intellectual energy and extensive publications marked him as the leader of logical positivism. Throughout his career, he remained generally faithful to its central iconoclastic outlook, though he frequently modified its details. Carnap's influence has continued to be felt strongly in the philosophy of science. His favored method in philosophy, that of creating formalized languages in order to provide rational reconstructions of key notions in science, was admired by many in its time and still has followers. A danger with this method is that its practitioners may lose themselves in the intricacies of their formal constructions and may not succeed in shedding much light on the philosophical problems with which they started.

Beginning in the 1930's, W. V. O. Quine was both an admirer and a major critic of Carnap. Especially noteworthy is Quine's attack on the distinction between analytic and synthetic sentences, an attack aimed especially against Carnap. Quine takes for granted that a scientific study of language must be behavioristic and insists that if one limits oneself to behavioristic observations of the language use of others, one cannot establish any legitimate distinction between sentences that are analytic and sentences that are synthetic for these people. Carnap was unconvinced by this criticism.

Stephen F. Barker

Philosophy and Logical Syntax

Type of philosophy: Epistemology, logic, philosophy of language
First published: 1935
Principal ideas advanced:
◇ Philosophy is the logical analysis of meaningful language.
◇ Meaningful language is either the language of logic and mathematics (involving analytic sentences) or the language of science (involving empirically verifiable synthetic sentences).
◇ Metaphysics and ethics are not legitimate parts of philosophy, for their language is meaningless.
◇ Logical analysis is logical syntax, and logical syntax is the study of the manipulation of signs in accordance with the rules of a language.

Rudolf Carnap's *Philosophy and Logical Syntax* is the substance of three lectures that he gave at the University of London in 1934. As a result, the book is short, outlining the essentials of the logical positivism of the Vienna Circle from the viewpoint of probably the best known and perhaps the most influential member of the group.

Logical positivism had its origin in a seminar conducted in the 1920's by Moritz Schlick at the University of Vienna. A number of the members of this group, the original Vienna Circle, were scientists reacting against those idealist philosophers who pontificated, sometimes in almost complete ignorance, about the aim and function of science. Part of positivism's program was the explicit rejection of this kind of irresponsible philosophizing. Another characteristic concern of the group was a strong interest in logic, an interest that grew out of its members' admiration for the work that had been done on the foundations of mathematics toward the close of the nineteenth century and in the early twentieth century, particularly the work of Alfred North Whitehead and Bertrand Russell in their *Principia Mathematica* (1910-1913). These interests quite naturally led the Vienna group to deliberate regarding philosophy's proper business. They decided that philosophy is properly the analysis and clarification of meaningful language. By meaningful language, they meant the language of empirical science together with the language of mathematics; all other language, they held, lacked cognitive meaning. The Vienna Circle philosophers gave expression to this conviction in their criterion of empirical meaning, a widely known and vigorously debated tenet of logical positivism.

Verifiability Criterion

Carnap spends the first chapter of *Philosophy and Logical Syntax* discussing the implications of the verifiability criterion. At one point he states that only the propositions of mathematics and empirical science "have sense" and that all other propositions are without theoretical sense. However, he does not do much with mathematical propositions—with "analytic" propositions, as positivists sometimes labeled the propositions of logic and mathematics. He spends most of his time with "synthetic" propositions; that is, with propositions whose truth value cannot be determined simply by referring to their logical form. As examples of this analytic-synthetic distinction, consider the two propositions: "The ball is red," and "Either the ball is red or the ball is not red." One cannot know whether the first one is true or false without in fact examining the ball, but one can know that the second proposition is true without looking at the ball. It is true by virtue of its logical form. A sentence that is true or false by virtue of its form alone is analytic; a sentence whose truth value is determined by the (nonlinguistic) facts is synthetic.

Carnap holds the view that the only synthetic propositions that make sense are those propositions whose truth value can be determined by consulting the evidence of sense. These propositions, he further believes, are all to be found within the domain of empirical science. He uses the word "verification" in the usual logical positivist sense; that is to say, a proposition is verifiable if its truth value can be determined by reference to sense experience. The only synthetic propositions that make sense, then, are verifiable propositions, and these are all scientific propositions. This is the verifiability criterion of empirical meaning.

A Definition of Philosophy

It is Carnap's view, then, that philosophy is the logical analysis of meaningful language, and meaningful language is restricted either to analytic propositions (logic and mathematics) or to empirically verifiable propositions (natural science). This theory implies that certain traditional areas of philosophy are no longer to be regarded as legitimate. Carnap rejects what he calls traditional metaphysics because it is made up of propositions that he feels are neither analytic nor empirically verifiable. As examples of metaphysical sentences, he mentions sentences about "the real essence of things," "things in themselves," and "the absolute." In addition, Carnap rejects traditional philosophical ethics. He believes the usual utterances of ethical philosophers—such as "Killing is wrong"—mislead people by virtue of their grammatical form. They look like propositions, and so philosophers have given arguments to show that they are either true or false. Carnap, however, believes that what is grammatically an assertion, "Killing is wrong," is logically not an assertion at all, but rather a disguised command, "Do not kill." However, commands are neither true nor false and hence cannot be propositions. Ethics, then, is necessarily ruled out of the domain of philosophy.

Ethics and metaphysics are thus ruled out of philosophy proper. However, there must be something to them; otherwise why have people been so concerned about them? Here Carnap also has a simple answer. Metaphysical and ethical utterances express deep feelings and emotions, and that is why people are so concerned about them. However, Carnap points out, although these utterances resemble those of the lyric poet in that they express emotion and evoke a profound response in the reader, they nevertheless do not make theoretical or cognitive sense—they are meaningless from a philosophical and scientific point of view.

However, not only metaphysics and ethics suffer from Carnap's determination to rid philosophy of the burden it has borne. Epistemology and psychology also suffer as a result of his reforming zeal. Psychology's legitimacy lies in its being an empirical science, and, as such, it is not the philosopher's concern. Epistemology is, Carnap suspects, a hybrid of psychology and logic. Philosophers must continue to do the logic, but they should give over the psychology to the behaviorists. The proper domain of the philosopher, after rejecting metaphysics, ethics, psychology, and epistemology, is to perform logical analysis on the language of the scientist. There can be no misunderstanding of Carnap's intention here, for he writes, "The only proper task of *Philosophy* is *Logical Analysis*."

Pragmatics, Semantics, and Syntax

In other writings, Carnap has taken some pains to identify what he means by logical syntax. In the *Foundations of Logic and Mathematics* (1939), he has perhaps made the distinctions most clearly. In this work, he distinguishes pragmatics, semantics, and syntax as parts of the general philosophical concern with language that he calls "semiotic." The first distinction that needs to be made here is between language that is about language and language that is not about language. One might, for example, assert the proposition: "The ball is red." In this case, one would be using language to talk about the nonlinguistic world, to talk about a ball. However, one might then go on to talk about the proposition that refers to the red ball; one might say: "The proposition 'The ball is red' has four words in it." In this case, the proposition is not about objects (such as red balls) but about language itself. Such language about language is called "metalanguage"; language about objects is called "object language." The general theory of an object language, stated in a metalanguage, is what Carnap means by "semiotic." However, semiotics has three branches: pragmatics, semantics, and syntax. Pragmatics is an empirical study of three elements that can be distinguished in the use of a language—linguistic

signs, the meanings (Carnap calls them "designata") of the signs, and the users of the signs. Pragmatics studies all three elements. Oversimplifying, pragmatics may be likened to the activity of an anthropologist constructing a dictionary for a tribe he or she is studying. The anthropologist studies and records how the tribespeople use words, how the words are spelled and combined, and what the words indicate.

Semantics is an abstraction from pragmatics. The semanticist (in the Carnapian sense) restricts his concern to the words or signs and their designata or meanings. He abstracts from users to focus solely on the signs and their designata. There are two kinds of semantics: descriptive and pure. Descriptive semantics is an empirical study of signs and their matter-of-fact meanings in popular usage; pure semantics, on the other hand, is not an empirical study but a normative one that lays down rules regarding the signs and what their proper designata are. A pure semantical system is an artificial language consisting of rules specifying designata for a collection of linguistic signs. An example of a pure semantical sentence might be: "The predicate word 'large' designates the property of being large in a physical sense." This specifies how the word "large" is to be used in a given artificial language, and it implies that such common language expressions as "That's a large order" are incorrect in the semantical system in which the rule occurs.

Syntax represents yet another level of abstraction. Pragmatics includes signs, designata, and users. Semantics ignores the users and focuses its attention solely on signs and their designata. Syntax ignores the designata of the signs as well as ignoring the users. It is concerned only with the signs and the rules in accordance with which they can be combined and manipulated. Again, one may oversimplify and say that the subject matter of syntax is the traditional rules of logical deduction, provided one adds that the rules are formulated in a more abstract and formal way than is customary. Very roughly speaking, then, pragmatics may be likened to making a dictionary of usage; semantics may be likened to specifying the exact and unambiguous definitions of words in, say, a technical treatise; and syntax may be likened to constructing a formal set of rules of logic.

Formation and Transformation Rules

In his second chapter, Carnap attempts to characterize and illustrate logical syntax somewhat more fully. He says syntax is a "formal" theory, meaning that syntax abstracts from all concerned with the sense or meaning of the signs and confines itself strictly to the forms of the signs or words. It consists entirely of rules specifying how signs—regarded simply as shapes or designs or sounds—may be combined and manipulated. Within this formal theory, there are formation and transformation rules. The formation rules, in effect, define what is to be regarded as a proper sentence. The ordinary person's rejection of Russell's well-known example of an ill-formed sentence—"Quadruplicity drinks procrastination"—is made by virtue of an appeal to the implicit formation rules of the English language. Ordinarily, of course, people abide by the implicit formation rules of English. Carnap's formation rules are intended to make explicit these implicit rules that people follow. The other group of rules, the transformation rules, specify what manipulations can be performed on the well-formed sentences identified by the formation rules. The transformation rules are the rules of logical deduction expressed in syntactical terms. Carnap states that the two primitive terms in a logical syntax are "sentence" and "direct consequence." That is to say, syntax attempts to identify what are proper sentences and also to specify how people are to draw their logical consequences.

There are other important syntactical terms in addition to "sentence" and "direct consequence," however. Carnap spends a fair amount of time in the second chapter defining and illustrating these additional syntactical terms. He defines "valid" as the property a sentence has if it is a direct consequence of the null class of premises. Putting this into a different logical terminology, one could say that a proposition that is validly inferred from tautologies is itself a tautology; Carnap means by "valid" what is often called "tautologous." Carnap then defines "contravalid" so that it corresponds to the usual notion of self-contradiction. These two classes of sentences, the valid and the contravalid, make up the class of "determinate" sentences; all other sentences (sometimes called "contingent sentences" by other logicians) are called "indeterminate."

The syntactical transformation rules serve to isolate the valid and contravalid sentences. These rules are called "L-rules" by Carnap. However, one may make other inferences that depend not on these logical rules but on certain laws of natural science; for example, Newton's laws or the laws of thermodynamics. Scientific laws such as these, which also serve to justify drawing the consequences of sentences, Carnap calls "P-rules" to distinguish them from the L-rules. Carnap is then able to distinguish additional kinds of sentences; namely, P-valid and P-contravalid sentences.

Additional terms are defined in this second chapter. Enough have been mentioned here, however, to enable us to see what it is that Carnap is trying to do. He is making many of the usual distinctions and defining many of the usual terms of traditional logic. However, he is doing it in a slightly different way from that characteristic of traditional logic. He has avoided the usual basic logical terms "true" and "false," since they depend on the question of the meaning of the propositions that are said to be either true or false. He has also avoided the usual logical term "implication," and has replaced it with "direct consequence." All of this is intentional and novel. Carnap sees it as being implied by his definition of syntax as a *formal* theory. He can describe a language and lay down rules for manipulating it without ever dealing with the question of the meaning of the words and sentences, and, consequently, without ever worrying about the subject matter with which the language deals. He is not doing physics or chemistry or biology; rather, he is manipulating symbols, symbols that might be assigned meanings later on so that they become words and sentences in a theory of chemistry, physics, or biology. However, as Carnap sees it, he has sharply separated the work of the philosopher-logician from the work of the scientist. Furthermore, abstracting from the meanings of the words and sentences enables the philosopher-logician to concentrate on the properly logical matters and avoid the tangles that often impede progress in the sciences. Best of all, the philosopher-logician has a legitimate activity in which to engage, one that benefits the scientist and that also circumvents the morasses of much traditional philosophy.

Pseudo-object Sentences

Just how Carnap feels he has avoided the morasses of traditional philosophy is best seen by looking at his discussion of what he calls "pseudo-object sentences." Carnap feels that many times philosophers have combined syntactical predicates with nonsyntactical subjects. The result is neither one thing nor another; they are not statements in the object language nor are they statements in the metalanguage. They are, however, responsible for many of the disputes of traditional metaphysics about the reality or nonreality of entities such as universals. One example will perhaps illustrate Carnap's distinction fairly clearly. He distinguishes three sentences:

The rose is red.

The rose is a thing.

The word "rose" is a thing-word.

No disputes arise over the first sentence, which Carnap defines as a real object-sentence in the material mode of speech. It is a sensible sentence that everyone understands and knows how to handle. Nor do disputes arise over the third sentence, which Carnap describes as a syntactical sentence in the formal mode of speech. Most people do not speak this way, but when they do (that is, when they are philosophical syntacticians), they make sense and avoid confusion. Unfortunately, philosophers have too often spoken in the manner of the second sentence, which Carnap calls a pseudo-object sentence. They then believe they are speaking about roses, and they begin debating and defining, getting further and further mired in the morass of bogus entities. One should speak either with the vulgar about red roses or with the sophisticated about thing-words. However, one should beware of speaking with the metaphysicians about rose-things.

Pseudo-object sentences are likely to give rise to pseudo-questions. This is the burden of the final chapter of Carnap's book. Logical positivism offers hope, he feels, for genuine progress in philosophy because it identifies the errors of earlier philosophies, and it provides a technique for avoiding them. The problem of universals, for example, is not a real problem; it is a pseudo-problem that results from confusing the "formal mode" of speech and the "material mode" of speech, from being deceived by pseudo-object sentences such as "The rose is a thing." People should speak in the formal mode about "predicate words" and not in the material mode about universals as things.

The position Carnap states in *Philosophy and Logical Syntax* has been stated much more fully in other of his works, especially in his earlier *Logische Syntax der Sprache* (1934; *The Logical Syntax of Language*, 1937). In some of his later works, he modified some of his earlier views—most notably, perhaps, by admitting semantics to philosophical legitimacy along with syntax. However, in its essentials, his position remained as stated in *Philosophy and Logical Syntax*. It is a view that has influenced contemporary philosophy greatly, and it is genuinely novel—a notable achievement in as ancient a discipline as philosophy. It probably has not had the influence outside philosophy that the intrinsic merit of the position deserves. This lack of widespread influence is quite probably the result of Carnap's tendency, in his more extended writing, to use a formidable and forbidding battery of technical apparatus including strange terms and Gothic script. He unfortunately did not completely rid himself of a Germanic fascination with architectonics and a tendency to identify the profound with the unfamiliar. He also suffered from a tendency to oversimplify and trivialize the views he opposed. His rejection of the excesses of some idealist philosophers is understandable, but less acceptable is his simple "resolution" of the problems with which the idealists wrestled by defining them out of existence as "pseudo-problems." However, despite Carnap's lack of understanding and sympathy for philosophical problems other than his own, he brought great skill to bear on the problems that did interest him. Carnap was a great innovator and an original thinker of enormous stature who strove to develop a logic that does not rest on any prior theory of meaning.

Robert E. Larsen

Additional Reading

Ayer, A. J., ed. *Logical Positivism*. Glencoe, Ill.: Free Press, 1959. This anthology of writings by logical positivists contains three papers by Rudolf Carnap, others by his associates, and a useful introduction by the editor, who favored the movement.

Cirera, Ramon. _Carnap and the Vienna Circle_. Amsterdam: Rodopi, 1994. A vigorous survey and interpretation of the philosophical views of Carnap and his colleagues in the Vienna Circle.

Coffa, J. Alberto. _The Semantic Tradition from Kant to Carnap_. Cambridge, England: Cambridge University Press, 1991. This study traces connections between the views of Carnap and those of his predecessors regarding language and a priori knowledge.

Friedman, Michael. "Logical Truth and Analyticity in Carnap's _Logical Syntax of Language_." In _History and Philosophy of Modern Mathematics_, edited by William Asprey and Philip Kitcher. Volume 11 in _Minnesota Studies in the Philosophy of Science_. Minneapolis: University of Minnesota Press, 1988. In this article, Friedman, a leading philosopher of science, provides an incisive description and criticism of this central work of Carnap's.

Goodman, Nelson. _Ways of Worldmaking_. Indianapolis, Ind.: Hackett, 1978. A discussion of the method of logical construction in philosophy by one of its practitioners.

Hintikka, Jaacko. _Rudolf Carnap_. Dordrecht: Reidel, 1975. A large collection of personal reminiscences of Carnap and discussions of his thought by colleagues and students who remember him with admiration.

Katz, Jerrold J. _Cogitations_. New York: Oxford University Press, 1986. Chapters 4, 5, and 6 present a view of analytic truth differing from Carnap's yet not accepting Quine's criticisms of Carnap.

Quine, Willard V. _From a Logical Point of View_. Cambridge, Mass.: Harvard University Press, 1953. The papers "On What There Is" and "Two Dogmas of Empiricism" contain explicit and implied criticisms of Carnap's position.

_____. "Truth by Convention." In _Readings in Philosophical Analysis_, edited by Herbert Feigl and Wilfred Sellars. New York: Appleton-Century-Crofts, 1949. An important early criticism of Carnap's notion of analytic truth.

Richardson, Alan W. _Carnap's Construction of the World_. Cambridge, England: Cambridge University Press, 1998. Richardson studies Carnap's first major book and rejects the widespread interpretation that Carnap, in this book, aims to carry out Bertrand Russell's epistemological program.

Schilpp, Paul, ed. _The Philosophy of Rudolf Carnap_. Volume 11 in _The Library of Living Philosophers_. La Salle, Ill.: Open Court, 1963. Contains Carnap's autobiography, twenty-six substantial descriptive and critical essays by others, Carnap's lengthy replies to these commentators, and a bibliography of Carnap's writings.

Urmson, J. O. _Philosophical Analysis: Its Development Between the Two World Wars_. Oxford: Clarendon Press, 1956. Part 2 of this short, readable book describes logical positivism and criticizes its philosophical approach.

Weinberg, J. R. _An Examination of Logical Positivism_. London: Routledge, 1936. Weinberg's survey of the then-very-new doctrines of logical positivism is for the most part breathlessly admiring although he has a few reservations.

Wittgenstein, Ludwig. _Tractatus Logico-Philosophicus_. London: Routledge & Kegan Paul, 1922. The logical positivists borrowed several important doctrines from this dark but seminal work while rejecting its metaphysical aspect.

Stephen F. Barker

Stanley Cavell

Cavell's unusual areas of interest and interdisciplinary treatments of traditional and nontraditional topics expanded the boundaries of modern American philosophical discourse, provided a bridge to European philosophical thinking, and tied the concerns of philosophy to everyday life.

Principal philosophical works: *Must We Mean What We Say? A Book of Essays*, 1969; *The World Viewed: Reflections on the Ontology of Film*, 1971; *The Senses of Walden*, 1972; *The Claim of Reason: Wittgenstein, Skepticism, Morality, and Tragedy*, 1979; *Pursuits of Happiness: The Hollywood Comedy of Remarriage*, 1981; *Themes Out of School: Effects and Causes*, 1984; *Disowning Knowledge: In Six Plays of Shakespeare*, 1987; *In Quest of the Ordinary: Lines of Skepticism and Romanticism*, 1988; *This New Yet Unapproachable America: Lectures After Emerson After Wittgenstein*, 1989; *Conditions Handsome and Unhandsome: The Constitution of Emersonian Perfectionism*, 1990; *A Pitch of Philosophy: Autobiographical Exercises*, 1994; *Philosophical Passages: Wittgenstein, Emerson, Austin, Derrida*, 1995; *Contesting Tears: The Hollywood Melodrama of the Unknown Woman*, 1996.

Born: September 1, 1926; Atlanta, Georgia

Early Life

Stanley Louis Cavell was born in 1926 in Atlanta, Georgia, to Irving and Fannie Goldstein, central European Jewish immigrants. His mother was a professional pianist who provided musical interludes during film screenings. He attended the University of California, Berkeley, where he was a student of Ernest Bloch and earned his A.B. in music in 1947. He did graduate work at the University of California, Los Angeles, from 1948 through 1951 and attended the Juilliard School of Music. While in New York, rather than focusing on music, he spent his time reading the works of Sigmund Freud and writing, and he finally decided to study philosophy. He received a Ph.D. from Harvard University in 1961. He held a number of appointments, including election as a junior member to the Harvard Society of Fellows (1953-1956), an assistant professorship in philosophy at the University of California, Berkeley (1956-1962), and a year at the Institute for Advanced Studies in Princeton, New Jersey. In 1963, he became the Walter M. Cabot Professor of Aesthetics and General Theory of Values at Harvard University.

Life's Work

Cavell's early philosophical interests and his professional direction were profoundly affected by his reading of Ludwig Wittgenstein's *Philosophical Investigations* (1953, bilingual German and English edition) and by British philosopher J. L. Austin's arrival at Harvard in 1955. Both of these philosophers were interested in language and linguistics and the ways in which philosophical problems and linguistic issues and concerns are connected. Their influence on Cavell is emblematic of his interest in reconciling continental and analytic philosophical perspectives, drawing on the best of both, and following his own personal interests in the philosophical arena.

Although language had been a significant concern of philosophers since Blaise Pascal in the seventeenth century, Wittgenstein was a central figure in the development of linguistic philosophy. The central principle of linguistic philosophy is that traditional philosophical problems are not truly problems but misunderstandings or confusions based on imprecise or misused language. Wittgenstein was fundamentally concerned with language as a component of philosophical activity and preoccupied with the significance of meaning in the context of actual use and real life.

In Austin's hands, interest in meaning and its nuances evolved into concern with the application or use of language as an act. The result was the development of "speech act" theory, which was based on the premise that speech is a form of action, and "ordinary language" philosophy, which focuses on the ways in which different contexts influence and illuminate meanings. In postwar European and English-speaking nations, philosophers and cultural critics began to be interested in analyzing how philosophically central terms such as "knowledge" and "truth" were used in common, everyday speech. They also created and investigated artificially logical languages, which were not burdened by the messiness and spontaneity of ordinary language.

Austin came to Harvard from Oxford to give the 1955 William James Lectures, eventually published as *How to Do Things with Words*, the seminal monograph on the theory of speech acts and ordinary language published in book form in 1962 after his death. Cavell attended one of the seminars given by Austin, and there he began to feel he had at last found the direction he wanted to take. He had been reading and writing and doing what he thought might be understood as "philosophy" but had not really identified with the discipline as it was taught at universities. Austin's emphasis on the ordinary and natural was the key that allowed Cavell to focus on the philosophical threads of his myriad interests. He was hired as an assistant professor at the University of California, Berkeley, in 1956, and completed his dissertation, "The Claim to Rationality: Knowledge and the Basis of Morality," in 1961. In 1962, he returned to Harvard after accepting a tenured Harvard junior fellowship and in 1963 accepted the Walter M. Cabot professorship.

Under the dual influences of Wittgenstein and Austin, Cavell began to focus his energy and intellect on finding his own voice as a philosopher. He had understood himself as a somewhat bifurcated intellect, studying toward a professional degree, on one hand, while reading and writing outside the bounds of his nominally chosen profession, on the other. Cavell discovered that he, Wittgenstein, and Austin shared an interest in the ordinary and everyday that was not part of the mainstream of professional philosophy of their times. In addition, he was drawn to Austin's radical vision of the philosopher's relationship to language, which, for Cavell, had a literary flavor that he found most congenial. He began to think of the tasks of professional philosophy as a series of texts to be read and understood rather than as a series of problems to be solved.

This view no doubt influenced both the form and the content of his first book, *Must We Mean What We Say?*, a series of philosophical essays published in 1969. It is an eclectic collection, demonstrating Cavell's wide-ranging interests and education. There are prototypical philosophical treatments of Wittgenstein, Austin, and Søren Kierkegaard. Several other essays consider fundamental philosophical questions of knowledge, meaning, and aesthetics. Many of the essays introduced concerns and themes and areas of interest, such as music and literature, to which Cavell would return again and again in later works. For example, in the essay, "The Avoidance of Love: A Reading of *King Lear*," Cavell linked his interest in philosophical skepticism to an exploration of literary tragedies, a use of playwright William Shakespeare's works that resurfaced a number of times in his writing over the next thirty years.

Cavell focused a great deal of his energy on skepticism and the ways in which this perspective affects both people's views of the world around them and the traditions that shape the meanings of skepticism. For example, the first half of *The Claim of Reason* included a reinterpretation of Wittgenstein's *Philosophical Investigations* and focused on what Cavell saw as the work's two main ideas—the notions of criteria and grammar—and how these two concepts underpin Wittgenstein's response to both philosophical skepticism and his definition of the relationship of philosophical thinking and everyday experiences. This does not express a concern with a philosophical "problem" in the historical sense of the term but rather is an effort to discover and understand fundamental ways of thinking and being. For Cavell, skepticism is the expression of what philosophers René Descartes and David Hume described as a radical doubt about people's ability to know, with any certainty, that the world and their experience of it actually exist.

Cavell's version of skepticism is not a modern position of existential indifference but a position of constant reevaluation and frailty. It is another way of describing people's sense of distance from the world in which they live and those who live there with them.

Skepticism has been a central theme of Cavell's treatments of various works of literature, including Shakespeare's plays and American Ralph Waldo Emerson's essays. Influenced by the work of French poststructuralists such as Jacques Derrida and Paul de Man, Cavell's "critical" readings of these authors are informed by a reconceptualization of philosophy as a kind of literary act. In this context, Emerson holds a special place of importance in Cavell's pantheon of philosophical heroes; he is the fountain of the best and most important concepts in American thinking. In Cavell's readings of the Transcendentalists, especially Emerson and Henry David Thoreau, published as *The Senses of Walden*, the philosopher unearths the kind of active skepticism that was a major component of his arguments in *The Claim of Reason*. For Cavell, Emerson's call for self-reliance on the part of American "scholars" is a call to think, write, and act in ways that are centered in individual perceptions and ways of self-expression. Cavell's perspective on Emerson supports his understanding of the role of the philosopher as something of a rebel against society's rules and customs—one who takes "endless responsibility for one's own discourse, for not resting with words you do not happily mean."

Underpinning all of Cavell's thinking and writing, from the very start of his career, was an interest in expanding the boundaries of the philosopher's sphere of activity and influence. As a result, he turned his attention to nontraditional areas of investigation, especially in the field of aesthetics. In his studies of popular film, Cavell found rich resources and rewards for his philosophical imagination. For instance, in *The World Viewed*, Cavell considers the significance of the reality portrayed in films and the audience's response to that world. For Cavell, film is an art form worthy of a discussion informed by readings of philosophers such as Martin Heidegger and Thomas S. Kuhn. In *Pursuits of Happiness*, Cavell's viewing of Hollywood comedies of the 1930's and 1940's leads him to meditate on the fundamental philosophical questions of "knowing" and "unknowingness" and how this genre of film reveals the workings of modern skeptical consciousness and gender awareness. Cavell even turns his philosophical eye to television, and in "The Fact of Television," one of the essays in *Themes out of School*, reworks these themes as they play out on the small screen.

What is perhaps most striking about Cavell's work is the consistency of his interest in the ways in which philosophy can contribute to people's understanding of the world around them, on both rarefied occasions and as they lead their everyday lives. Cavell returns again and again, refining and redefining, to questions of experience and meaning in a variety of settings and under a variety of conditions. His interest in experiences and ideas that are unequivocally American and his sympathetic understanding of English and continental philosophical traditions and trends allow him to play a unique role in contemporary philosophy. He tests the boundaries of the philosophical enterprise and expands them by opening dialogues between philosophy and other disciplines such as psychoanalysis. Cavell's work is simultaneously traditional philosophy, art review, literary scholarship, and cultural criticism.

Influence

Cavell's work is best known for its grounding in and elevation of Wittgenstein, its exploration of the centrality of skepticism, and its central preoccupation with issues that arise from everyday experience. Cavell is one of the most socially engaged contemporary American postanalytic philosophers; he contextualizes and reevaluates philosophical skepticism as a modern attempt at self-definition, self-examination, and self-awareness.

He is also one of the most consistently "American" of philosophers, retrieving and recasting the Romantic philosophical heritage of American philosophy articulated by Emerson and Thoreau. His long-term interest in Wittgenstein and his belief in the centrality of Wittgenstein's work to any understanding of the world of everyday-experience led Cavell to question the professionalization and narrowing of philosophy as a discipline, course of study, and a way of understanding the world.

Arguably, however, Cavell's most significant contributions to the discipline have come in the ways in which he placed philosophical inquiry at the center of cultural and artistic criticism. He has written widely on diverse subjects such as ethics, epistemology, and aesthetics. He has demonstrated that philosophy belongs at the center of all the humanities as an intersection that reveals the relationships among these disciplines and the questions they ask about experience and as a lens through which important thinking and significant writing is shaped.

J. R. Donath

Must We Mean What We Say?

A Book of Essays

Type of philosophy: Epistemology, philosophy of language
First published: 1969
Principal ideas advanced:

◇ The legitimate areas of interest in contemporary philosophy must be extended and broadened.

◇ Questions about language are really questions about the world around one and one's place in it.

◇ Philosophy is more a study of texts than it is an examination of problems.

◇ There is no distinction between philosophy and metaphilosophy.

The title piece in *Must We Mean What We Say?*, which consists of a series of chronologically arranged essays, was written as a symposium paper in 1957. The essays in the book range from relatively short reviews to more developed meditations and fall into one of three categories: examinations of topics in epistemology, aesthetics, and the philosophy of language; focused, critical studies of individual philosophers such as J. L. Austin, Søren Kierkegaard, and Ludwig Wittgenstein; and interpretations of specific literary texts such as William Shakespeare's *King Lear* (produced c. 1605-1606) and Samuel Beckett's *Endgame* (1958). One of Stanley Cavell's areas of

special interest is the philosophy of aesthetics, and five of the ten essays in this volume are directly concerned with aesthetic matters.

In his preface to *Must We Mean What We Say?*, Cavell warns his readers not to try to categorize his essays as either literary criticism or what he calls "straight philosophy," in part because he feels these two approaches are so intertwined in his work that they would be difficult to separate. He engages in a kind of criticism that allows him to treat a number of issues and concerns from a consistent, fundamentally philosophical perspective. Although one of the themes that runs through many of the volume's essays is an exploration of the relationships between philosophy and literature and the philosopher and the author, Cavell is also very interested in the concept of the "modern" as it is understood in both philosophical circles and in larger arenas of experience. A third overarching concern that surfaces in several of the essays is an attempt to replace philosophy's emphasis on knowledge as an ideal with a primary goal of something more like sensitivity or sensibility. *Must We Mean What We Say?* is not simply a collection of essays, it is a book that integrates several themes by presenting them in a number of different contexts.

Ordinary Language Philosophy

The title essay, "Must We Mean What We Say?," is a defense of "ordinary language philosophy" as it was practiced at Oxford in the 1950's by philosophers such as Cavell's teacher, J. L. Austin. Austin, an instructor and working philosopher, is the subject of the fourth essay in the collection, "Austin at Criticism." Cavell called Austin's work and his classes and lectures at Harvard the most important influences in his philosophical life. Austin was very interested in the nuances of linguistic meaning and stressed that "ordinary language," the language people actually use, is a result of evolutionary changes in meanings and use. For Austin, philosophers tend to make fundamental missteps when they oversimplify and mix words that, while similar, have real differences in meaning.

By the late 1950's, when Cavell's essay on Austin first appeared, ordinary language philosophy was a force on American university campuses, and Cavell's goal was to defend not only the procedures of this approach but also Austin's conclusions against critics such as Benson Mates. In this essay, Cavell concentrates on what people commonly say and mean in an attempt to address issues of philosophical obscurity and confusion. In particular, he is interested in highlighting the necessity of understanding not only the empirical and scientific meaning of speech but also the intentions of the speaker and the rules of language being used. This matter of the rules of discourse was especially important because although these rules are often informal and therefore cannot be systemized, they nonetheless underpin both usage and meaning. For Cavell, people must mean what their words mean, since the ways they live and use language in everyday life will not allow them to say one thing but mean another. Therefore, argues Cavell, people must be very careful about what they say. Austin's (and by implication, Cavell's) interest in the everyday and the ordinary as a sphere of philosophical inquiry is in part a call to philosophers to return to their natural habitats, to back away from a reliance on theories, and to embrace truths and logical ideas that people recognize and acknowledge for themselves, as individuals and members of specific communities of meaning.

Wittgenstein and Modernity

Cavell expands and redirects the arguments of "Must We Mean What We Say?" in the second essay in the book, "The Availability of Wittgenstein's Later Philosophy," a scathing attack on David Poole's *The Later Philosophy of Wittgenstein* (1958). In this review, interest in "meaning what we say" leads Cavell to consideration of the differences between the modern and the traditional in philosophical practice. Perhaps because he finds Poole's oversimplification of Wittgenstein's writings offensive, he spends several pages discussing Wittgenstein's style as a self-conscious philosophical strategy parallel to the therapeutic approach of Sigmund Freud, father of psychoanalysis. Cavell also focuses on what he views as the inadequacies of Poole's traditional approach to Wittgenstein's radically original—and by extension—modern ideas. Cavell's interest in, and treatment of, Wittgenstein's literary style and the issue of modernity are both themes that resurface in other essays in the collection.

For example, in his third essay, "Aesthetic Problems of Modern Philosophy," Cavell demonstrates that changes in philosophical practice and focus are characteristic of shifts wrought by the advent of the modern era and that these changes are also reflected in endeavors such as literature. At the heart of these changes is a movement away from an overriding concentration on knowledge and its origin, nature, and limits. Instead, Cavell argues, a modern philosopher will be more comfortable with a model that includes concern for matters of sensibility. In this essay, Cavell applies Wittgenstein's methods to issues in aesthetics. His goal is to point out the similarities in beliefs among aesthetic and ordinary language philosophers and Wittgenstein. Philosophy, like art criticism and aesthetics, often centers on questions of whether or not a person sees or experiences an artifact or an event in a certain way. He suggests then, that, given those similarities, it is not surprising that modern philosophers are becoming interested in questions of philosophical style and the application of aesthetic judgments to philosophical writing. As a result, Cavell suggests, a "new literary-philosophical criticism" is developing. It is a distinctly modern vision of philosophy and well suited to discussions of modern expressions in such arts as film, music, and literature.

Art and the Modernist Sensibility

If the critical thinking of disciplines such as literary study can illuminate philosophy, philosophy can be fruitfully brought to bear as a critical tool in examining various works of art. Therefore, *Must We Mean What We Say?* includes studies of several artistic subjects, such as music (Cavell's bachelor's degree from the University of California, Berkeley, was in music, where he studied with the composer Ernest Bloch) and plays by Samuel Beckett and William Shakespeare. In "Music Discomposed" and its companion essay, "A Matter of Meaning It," Cavell describes a number of modern threads in musical composition and criticism since Ludwig van Beethoven that he believes are rooted in a clear break with traditional values. This break with the past did not merely result in new musical forms but also led to a breakdown in the very structures that are used to judge artistic products and people's responses to them. These essays develop the argument that contemporary composers such as Igor Stravinsky, Béla Bartók, and Arnold Schoenberg found themselves in a modernist predicament. New systems of rhythm, duration, dynamics, and other musical elements appeared, and the ways in which composers understood themselves and their enterprise underwent fundamental changes. For Cavell, the loss of tradition as a measure of beauty and appropriateness left a vacuum of authority and led to what might best be described as the "modern" artistic vision of the world—one filled with ambiguities, unresolvable problems, and significant difficulties.

This sort of examination of the modernist sensibility is an important theme in Cavell's reading of Samuel Beckett's *Endgame*, described in the chapter entitled "Ending the Waiting Game." Underpinning Cavell's interpretation of Beckett's play is his sense that when most literary interpreters review Beckett's work, they neglect to consider the central problem of modern artists—that they must create in the absence of any of the recognized, traditional conventions that had previously shaped and ordered their enterprise—and therefore misunderstand his vision. Cavell's treatment of the play emphasizes the ways in which *Endgame*'s effectiveness depends on a contrast between the seeming ordinariness of its action and the extraordinary ways in which Beckett infuses the language of the play with meaning. Cavell pays special attention to the play's grammar and the ways in which conceptual issues are reinforced or undercut by the words Beckett chooses to put into the mouths of his characters. What he admires in Beckett is the skill with which the playwright delivers his message. Cavell's meditation on the meaning of the play leads him to consider such diverse sources as the film *Dr. Strangelove: Or, How I Learned to Stop Worrying and Love the Bomb* (1964) and the poetry of Rainer Maria Rilke in a discussion of ideas about the end of the world revealed in works of modern art.

Shakespeare and Skepticism
Cavell's long reading of Shakespeare's *King Lear*, "The Avoidance of Love," which takes up a quarter of the book, is the final, most ambitious essay in *Must We Mean What We Say?* and brings together a number of Cavell's themes. The essay, a

major contribution to Shakespeare criticism, is divided into two major parts: a critical reading and an examination of dramatic criticism using the play as a case study. Cavell's interpretation of this difficult play suggests that its major theme is how people avoid love and what results from such avoidances. Running through this analysis is an interest in the philosophical concept of skepticism, which is also the focus of the essay on "Knowing and Acknowledging," in this volume, and which continues to periodically draw his attention.

These essays not only are concerned with interpreting the play in terms of avoidance of love and skeptical consciousness but also are infused with the philosophical preoccupations of the whole book, such as the perils of saying more (or less) than one means and the self-deception that can result from not acknowledging the meaning of what one says. For example, Cavell interprets *King Lear* from the perspective of the modern predicament, which leads him to discuss the possibility of writing tragedies in the modern world. Cavell uses the play to consider how disagreements in dramatic criticism are in many ways parallel to those in philosophy, particularly in terms of the difficulties critics have in seeing the obvious (perhaps because they, too, are caught up in avoidance behaviors). This essay on *King Lear* draws together a careful reading of the text, an interest in performance and the audience's responses, and analytical approaches in the sort of literary philosophy for which Cavell has become known.

An Interdisciplinary Influence
Must We Mean What We Say? is a personal, individual work that is embedded in the singular sensibility of its author. Cavell's earliest work, *Must We Mean What We Say?*, is best known for its sympathetic treatment of ordinary language philosophy and the later works of Wittgenstein. First published in 1969, it received very little notice at first but gradually aroused enough interest to be reprinted in 1976. Its chronological organization allows the reader to follow Cavell's intellectual development and to appreciate his ability to expand the world of philosophical discourse beyond its traditional boundaries. Throughout his career, Cavell continued to write about both

traditional and nontraditional philosophical topics in a highly literate style.

The nature of Cavell's future contributions to the discipline of philosophy were also first demonstrated in the essays collected in *Must We Mean What We Say?* His interdisciplinary interests and his innovative combinations of art and cultural criticism are always supported by his fundamental belief that philosophy and other sorts of knowledge, such as literature, can be mutually illuminating and should be explored in relationship to one another.

J. R. Donath

Additional Reading

Bates, Stanley. "Self and the World in *Walden*." *The Thoreau Quarterly* 14 (Summer/Fall, 1982). This entire issue is devoted to Stanley Cavell's *The Senses of Walden*.

Borradori, Giovanna. *The American Philosopher: Conversations with Quine, Davidson, Putnam, Nozick, Danto, Rorty, Cavell, MacIntyre, and Kuhn*. Translated by Rosanna Crocitto. Chicago: University of Chicago Press, 1994. This work contains a nineteen-page interview with Cavell that focuses on his interests in Ludwig Wittgenstein, Ralph Waldo Emerson, and J. L. Austin and his work on skepticism. The introduction provides a good contextualization of Cavell within trends and issues of modern American philosophy.

Fischer, Michael. *Stanley Cavell and Literary Skepticism*. Chicago: University of Chicago Press, 1989. An evaluation of Cavell's often difficult to understand but significant contributions to literary criticism and theory. Focuses on Cavell's investigations of tragedy, Romanticism, skepticism, and Wittgenstein. Contextualizes Cavell in current critical literary theory.

Fleming, Richard, and Michael Payne, eds. *The Senses of Stanley Cavell*. Lewisburg, Pa.: Bucknell University Press, 1989. A collection of essays "inspired by" various aspects of Cavell's work in literary, film, and philosophical studies. A very dense interview with Cavell begins the volume, and a short conversation acts as a coda. Excellent bibliography.

Gould, Timothy. *Hearing Things: Voice and Method in the Writing of Stanley Cavell*. Chicago: University of Chicago Press, 1998. A significant analysis of Cavell's work that highlights his evolution as a philosopher and makes the connection between his various interests.

Meyerowitz, Rael. *Transferring to America: Jewish Interpretations of American Dreams*. Albany: State University of New York Press, 1995. This book provides an analysis of the work of Stanley Cavell and others from a psychoanalytic point of view.

Smith, Joseph H., and William Kerrigan, eds. *Images in Our Souls: Cavell, Psychoanalysis, and Cinema*. Baltimore, Md.: The Johns Hopkins University Press, 1987. In addition to an essay by Cavell on the "unknown woman" melodrama, the volume includes essays that draw on Cavell's writings about film in their discussion of a number of psychological themes in films.

Wheeler, Richard P. "Acknowledging Shakespeare: Cavell and the Claim of the Human." *Bucknell Review* 32, no. 1 (1989): 132-160. A readable treatment of Cavell's uses of William Shakespeare's plays to illuminate important philosophical issues, especially the relationship between philosophical skepticism and literary tragedy.

J. R. Donath

Aimé Césaire

Césaire wrote poems, plays, and essays describing the struggles he faced as a black Martinican educated in a Western, French colonial system. He called colonialism morally and spiritually indefensible and blamed it for what he saw as the decline of civilization in the West.

Principal philosophical works: *Cahier d'un retour au pays natal*, 1939, 1947, 1956 (*Memorandum on My Martinique*, 1947; better known as *Return to My Native Land*, 1968); *Les Armes miraculeuses*, 1946 (*Miraculous Weapons*, 1983); *Soleil cou coupé*, 1948 (*Beheaded Sun*, 1983); *Discours sur le colonialisme*, 1950 (*Discourse on Colonialism*, 1972); *Corps perdu*, 1950 (*Disembodied*, 1983); *Et les chiens se taisaient*, 1956; *Toussaint Louverture*, 1960; *Ferrements*, 1960 (*Shackles*, 1983); *Cadastre*, 1961 (revised editions of *Soleil cou coupé* and *Corps perdu*; *Cadastre: Poems*, 1973); *La Tragédie du Roi Christophe*, 1963 (*The Tragedy of King Christopher*, 1969); *Une Saison au Congo*, 1966 (*A Season in the Congo*, 1968); *State of the Union*, 1966 (includes abridged translation of *Miraculous Weapons* and *Shackles*); *Une Tempête, d'après "La Tempête" de Shakespeare: Adaptation pour un théâtre nègre*, 1969 (*The Tempest*, 1974); *Œuvres complètes*, 1976; *Moi, Laminaire*, 1982; *Aimé Césaire: The Collected Poetry*, 1983; *Lyric and Dramatic Poetry, 1946-82*, 1990; *La Poésie*, 1994.

Born: June 25, 1913; Basse-Pointe, Martinique

Early Life

Aimé Fernand Césaire was born in 1913 in Basse-Pointe, a town on the northeast coast of the West Indian island of Martinique. Although his family was poor, they were not from the impoverished class of illiterate farmworkers that made up the majority of the black population of Martinique. Aimé's father was a local tax inspector, while his mother contributed to the welfare of the six children by making dresses. Aimé was the second eldest of the children. It was his grandmother, Eugénie, who taught him to read and write French by the time he was four. The family made a concerted effort to imbue their children with French culture and literature; his father read stories to his children, not in Creole, the primary language of black Martinicans, but in French. He particularly favored the prose and poetry of Victor Hugo.

When Aimé was eleven, the family moved to the capital of Martinique, Fort-de-France, where he attended the Lycée Schoelcher. It was during his years at this school that the young Césaire came under the influence of Eugène Revert, a teacher of geography, who introduced his students to the specific richness of the Martinican botanical and geological landscape. Revert also encouraged Césaire to further his education by recommending him for acceptance at a well-known preparatory school in Paris, the Lycée Louis-le-Grand, where he readied himself for entrance to the distinguished École Normale Supérieure, also in Paris.

During his time at the Lycée Louis-le-Grand, he met and developed a deep friendship with a fellow classmate, Léopold Senghor of Senegal, who later became both the president of that African republic and a highly respected poet. Senghor then collaborated with a friend and fellow poet of Césaire, the French Guianan Léon-Gontran Damas, in forming a newspaper called *L'Étudiant noir* (the black student), a publication that brought together young blacks from Africa and the West Indies and created the opportunity for an intercultural mix that eventually gave birth to the concept of negritude. In the group that formed around *L'Étudiant noir*, Aimé Césaire met a Martinican woman, Suzanne Roussy, whom he married in 1937 and who later helped him create and edit the well-known journal *Tropiques*.

During his time at the École Normale Supérieure, Césaire was introduced to the literary and anthropological works that would determine the direction of his artistic and political vision: the writing of James Joyce, Virginia Woolf, Marcel Proust, Arthur Rimbaud, Stéphane Mallarmé, the black poets of the Harlem Renaissance, and the anthropologists Maurice Delafosse and Leo Frobenius. The last two scholars revealed to Césaire that Africa possessed its own highly articulated history, art, and civilization, while one of his professors introduced him to the idea of a black cultural archetype that went beyond geographical borders.

With all these influences brewing within the imagination of the young Césaire, he began in 1936 the poem that was to make him famous throughout the world and upon which his literary reputation was permanently based. The long poem *Return to My Native Land* documented his spiritual journey from adolescence to adulthood through the various cultural, linguistic, and moral conflicts that he was forced to confront as a black Martinican educated in a Western, French colonial intellectual system. By the time he returned to Martinique after seven years of European schooling, he was already beginning both a literary and a political career that would establish him as one of the greatest black writers of the twentieth century.

Life's Work

Césaire combines a number of seemingly contradictory roles within a single career. All of them, however, stem from his overwhelming conviction that the political is always the personal and that a person's work, whether it be writing poems or running a city government, embodies his or her belief system. After earning his degree at the prestigious École Normale Supérieure in Paris, he returned in 1940 to teach languages and literature at his former school, the Lycée Schoelcher. He and his wife founded and edited their own West Indian version of *L'Étudiant noir*, calling it *Tropiques*, which helped promulgate the concept of negritude to the politically naïve natives

of the West Indies. Following World War II, Césaire decided that the only way to help his country improve its economic and political situation was to become an active member of the government. After retiring from teaching, he was sent to Paris as a deputy to the French Assembly. In 1946, he returned to become the mayor of Fort-de-France, and finally founded and became president of his own political party, the Progressive Party of Martinique. He held a deputy's seat in the French Assembly until 1993, when he retired from the political arena. Concurrent with his exceptionally active political activities, he published five major volumes of poetry, four full-length plays, and three major political and historical prose works.

Aimé Césaire. *(AP/Wide World Photos)*

The key to understanding all of his multifaceted scholar's activities and production is the concept of negritude, a word that Césaire first used in his revolutionary long poem *Return to My Native Land*. The word has come to represent the affirmation that one is black and proud of it, an idea that became in the 1960's "Black Is Beautiful." This neologism was created by Césaire, Senghor, and Damas and referred to blacks who had been dominated and oppressed politically, culturally, and spiritually by Western values. The word expressed a total rejection of assimilation with white culture and urged an exploration and a celebration of their unique racial roots. The Western values most antithetical to the values embodied in the idea of negritude were rationalism, Christianity, individualism, and technology. Césaire, particularly in his poetry, celebrates the ability of the black soul to participate in the energies of nature and not to control them by technology; he rejects the zeal of the Christian missionaries in their attempt to destroy ancient, pagan rituals. Most important, however, is his dismissal of the Western concept of individualism symbolized by its apotheosis of the hero to a semidivine status. He celebrates, rather, the loss of the individual ego in the collective effort toward a communal idea in which all may participate. In all of his poetry, plays, and prose works, Césaire expresses in varying degrees his loyalty to the tenets of negritude in one form or another.

The first and most influential work written by Césaire is his long poem *Return to My Native Land*. It is a classic example of a writer who writes himself into political action by rejecting all the values that he has just spent seven years assimilating in France. He had recently received his degree from France's most distinguished university, the École Normale Supérieure, had mastered the French language and its literature, yet had also assimilated the techniques and visions of the prevailing European aesthetic movement, Surrealism. Indeed, André Breton, the founder of the Surrealist literary movement, declared that Césaire handled the French language "as no white man can handle it today." Jean-Paul Sartre theorized that Césaire used the techniques of Surrealism to liberate himself from the stuffy conventions of French literature, while other critics recognize Césaire's difficult, exuberant wordplay and unorthodox metaphors, mixed with African and Caribbean imagery and history, as attempts to forge a new language that can express the violently chaotic nature of the black collective unconscious from which his imagination proceeds.

Three major themes dominate *Return to My Native Land* and chart the poem's spiritual journey while simultaneously embodying the principal tenets of negritude. Césaire identifies "suffering" as the primary mode through which blacks experience the world. From the recognition of this suffering, which becomes the agent of his awakening to consciousness, the fictive voice in the poem learns to hate and reject the white world of racism, colonialism, and slavery. The poem concludes with hope not only for black redemption and unity but also for worldwide celebration of the common values of all races. By celebrating his specifically black Martinican heritage, he celebrates the world in all its diversity.

Césaire's attempt to reject the values of a white, colonial European society led him to a lengthy flirtation with Communism. He and a number of his fellow poet-politicians found that Marxism gave them a revolutionary stance in the same way that Surrealism had given them a modernist perspective and, therefore, an individual voice in expressing the yearnings of their people. Césaire's famous *Lettre à Maurice Thorez* (1956; *Letter to Maurice Thorez*, 1957) announced his break with Communism, finding its goals as incompatible as French colonialism or any other foreign influence in relieving the poverty of his fellow Martinicans. He had returned, in effect, to the same conclusions of his earlier rejection of colonialism as a civilizing force that had been the major theme of his *Discourse on Colonialism*. His next important prose work was a biographical and historical study of Toussaint-Louverture, the revolutionary liberator of Haiti, called *Toussaint Louverture*. From this documentary treatment of Haiti's earliest hero, Césaire's attention focused on specific black heroes rather than on theoretical treatises that only the well educated could comprehend, and he began a series of plays that had historical figures as their main characters, who would be recognized by the people of the West Indies.

By the early 1960's, Césaire, whose poetry had become virtually inaccessible to the common person, made a conscious effort to reach a larger audience by choosing topics that would be recognizable and, more important, comprehensible both to the people of his own area and to the rest of the world. His choice of famous black figures and his treatment of them in rather straightforward dramatic structures demonstrated his dedication to propounding black causes. His first highly successful play was *The Tragedy of King Christopher*, the story of the rise of a young slave to the status of self-declared King of Haiti and his subsequent fall. Henri Christophe's tragic flaw is that once he attains his position of power, he loses sight of his primary reason for driving out the tyrannical French colonials and becomes obsessed with expanding his power base, thus becoming as cruel and greedy as the departed French.

Césaire's next play, *A Season in the Congo*, treats the tragic career of the revolutionary leader Patrice Lumumba, the first president of the Republic of the Congo. His earlier ambitious dreams for his people collapsed into power struggles among competing black leaders and led to his assassination in 1961 in spite of heroic efforts by the United Nations. By the late 1960's, a number of literary critics declared Césaire the leading black dramatist writing in French. Both these plays are highly crafted, impeccably executed literary works that entertain audiences while at the same time registering their political points with subtlety, wit, and exquisite poetic language. His last play of this period, *The Tempest*, is an adaptation of William Shakespeare's play. In this play, Césaire uses Prospero as the white, colonial conqueror, or the "man of reason." Caliban becomes a metaphor for the black man, the instinctual, nature-loving slave, or victim of Prospero. Ariel becomes in this political allegory the mulatto, or man of science, a combination of the European and black sensibilities but equally repressed by the rationalistic Prospero.

After the writing and production of these three highly acclaimed plays of the 1960's, Césaire devoted himself to his political duties and responsibilities as the mayor of Fort-de-France and, more important, his role as deputy in the French National Assembly for Martinique. As a result, he spent much of his time in Paris, attending to his civic responsibilities as a participant in the governance of France and its international interests. He was also reelected many times to head his own political party, the Progressive Party of Martinique.

Influence

Césaire made a major contribution to the worldwide black rights movement in that he is recognized as one of its most honored spiritual leaders. He began to assume that spiritual leadership role with the publication of *Return to My Native Land*. In this poem, certainly one of the major long poems of the twentieth century, he charts the spiritual journey of a colonial black man through the abstractions of Western civilization to his return to the spiritual and instinctual sustenance of his native Martinique. Because of his concern for the welfare of his suffering people, he turned to a more accessible literary format and wrote three plays that eschew the former Surreal intellectuality and instead realistically document the tragic destinies of two actual black historical figures: Christophe and Lumumba. Concurrent with both his poetic and dramatic productions is a consistent barrage of brilliantly scathing prose works condemning the pernicious effects of slavery, racism, and, most important, colonialism.

Some scholars of the African American movement view Césaire's career as not within the mainstream of either American or African social transformation. Although they include him as a major literary and spiritual leader, he is viewed by some as torn between the claims of his black identity and those of his French heritage. He is, obviously, committed to the French parliamentary system, having served as its Martinican deputy from 1946 to 1993, and has never advocated any kind of revolutionary overthrow of any government in the West Indies or Africa. His writings demonstrate that he sees himself as heir to the great French intellectual poets, philosophers, and statesmen. To the dismay of more radical black leaders, he appears to believe in the humanistic principles inherent in the French political and social heritage. Though these ideas may appear paradoxical, they are not mutually exclusive, although they do seem to preclude him from ever being viewed as a serious revolutionary, activist leader. More than any of his literary or political achievements, Césaire will be most remembered and honored for his invention of the term negritude and his first use of it in one of the country's most compelling poems.

Patrick Meanor

Discourse on Colonialism

Type of philosophy: Ethics, political philosophy
First published: Discours sur le colonialisme, 1950 (English translation, 1972)
Principal ideas advanced:
◇ Colonialism as practiced by the European powers does not have a single human value, is morally and spiritually indefensible, and is ultimately responsible for European civilization's decline into decadence.
◇ Colonialism is neither a philanthropic nor an evangelical operation but is based entirely on economic exploitation and racist assumptions.
◇ The historical effect of colonial operations has been the destruction of great civilizations in Africa, Asia, and the Caribbean.
◇ Ethnographic studies by unbiased scientific explorers have repudiated the lies and distortions of propagandists and apologists defending the colonial powers.
◇ Contact between differing cultural communities can be beneficial when there is a mutual recognition of alternative patterns of development.
◇ The rule of force of traditional colonial oppressors may be ending but the influence of modern technology and the lure of industrialization may result in another kind of enslavement as pernicious as the conquests of the past.

In what has been described as a "shocking upset," Aimé Césaire, a Communist Party member, was elected to the municipal council of Fort-de-France shortly after the close of World War II and was chosen by the members of the council to be the mayor of the city. This made him a member of the French Prèmiere Assemblée National Constitutante, the body responsible for the formation of the Fourth Republic. As a deputy in the assembly,

he was able to combine his solid educational background in literature and history with the immediate experience of parliamentary debate and deliberation and to hear all of the arguments that were made by French politicians for the continuation of the foreign empire that France had maintained for several centuries.

Although he was never a dogmatic Communist and broke with the party after the suppression of the Hungarian revolution in 1956, Césaire was interested in Marxist thought and felt that the tide of history was running against all of the old colonial arrangements. The revolutionary activities of the Viet Minh in Indo-China had already made it clear that armed resistance to a colonial government would not be easy to suppress, and French colonies along the Mediterranean coast, particularly Algeria, had begun to demand changes in their governmental arrangements. Césaire's visit to Haiti in 1944 also contributed to his conviction that political independence and cultural autonomy for a colonial state was a real possibility. On the other hand, when the government of the United States, at the insistence of Secretary of State John Foster Dulles, backed away from a promise made at the Geneva Conference of 1954 to support free elections in French Indo-China, Césaire felt that the United States might be moving into a position of control just as the old colonial powers were beginning to loosen the grip they had on territories in the Third World. Césaire knew and admired the work of the writers of the Harlem Renaissance and recognized aspects of the same racist attitudes he had heard in the French Assembly in the bigotry that American writers such as Langston Hughes, Jean Toomer, and Claude McKay described in their works.

Civilization Destroyed
Césaire begins his indictment of colonialism with a series of defining statements pointing to a serious flaw in Western civilization. Asserting that a civilization unwilling to recognize its problems, incapable of solving them when they are impossible to avoid, and then duplicitous in attempting to camouflage them is "decadent" and "dying," Césaire declares that "two centuries of bourgeois rule" have led to a situation that is "morally, spiritually indefensible." To support this judg-

ment, he refutes the claim commonly made by representatives of colonial powers that their regimes are intended to be philanthropic enterprises or evangelical missions and shows that these regimes are mercantile endeavors designed to extend the economic structure of their own societies. Contact between civilizations that have followed different paths of development are crucial in sustaining healthy growth through a juxtaposition of varying perspectives because "a civilization that withdraws into itself atrophies," but throughout history, Césaire claims, not "a single human value" has been the result of colonial expeditions.

At the crux of his critique of colonialism is the effect the process has on the colonizing country. Césaire interlaces his commentary with examples of atrocities committed by colonial regimes, assuming that the evidence he cites is irrefutable, but in enumerating the ways in which these atrocities *decivilize* the colonizer," brutalizing and degrading the humane traditions of Western thought, he is advancing a position that was previously hardly mentioned. By gradual degrees, the colonizing process leads back to the inhabitants of European powers, resulting eventually in an acquiescence in barbarism, culminating in the rise of the Nazis. Césaire connects colonizing efforts in lands far from Europe, their consequences ignored by European citizens, to the emergence of Adolf Hitler, who attempted to colonize all of Europe itself. He supports this by quoting extensively from spokespersons for official government positions who explained their country's foreign policies in racist language that Césaire labels "howling savagery," likening these people to the Nazi propagandists whose genocidal programs were defended on supposedly scientific grounds. Césaire's strongest criticism here is for the so-called humanists who did not speak out and resist the hatemongers. His conclusion is that "a civilization that justifies colonization—and therefore force—is already a sick civilization."

Although Césaire is utilizing a mode of reasoned discourse to advance his thesis, he is better known as a Surrealist poet, and he uses poetic language to dramatize his argument. The directly personal voice of a witness emerges as he decries the brutalization he has observed. "I see force,

brutality, cruelty, sadism," he declares, "I am talking about societies drained of their essence, cultures trampled underfoot, institutions undermined, lands confiscated, religions smashed, magnificent artistic creations destroyed, extraordinary *possibilities* wiped out." The righteousness of his anger is evident in this mode as he attempts to undercut the quasi-scientific pseudo-objectivity of the apologists.

A student of African civilizations at a time when most Europeans were taught that the term was an oxymoron, Césaire introduces the idea that such significant advances in human thought as the invention of arithmetical calculation and astronomical systems by people living in North Africa, and such sophisticated examples of artistic expression as the bronzes of Benin and the sculpture of the Shango (in what is now known as Nigeria) are endeavors comparable to or beyond what was accomplished in Europe to that point in time. Summarizing, he concludes the first half of his discourse by exclaiming, "The idea of the barbaric Negro is a European invention."

A Call to Action
The second part of the discourse is a call to action. Césaire, basing his economic analysis on a Marxist construct common to the French intellectuals (including Jean-Paul Sartre) who were his contemporaries, sees colonialism as a part of a capitalist social order that by its nature excludes most people from the rewards of their labor. Assuming that his audience shares his basic assumptions, he directs his words to the attentive "comrade" who is ready to challenge the "enemies" of a genuinely civilized society.

Continuing in the poetic mode he finds comfortable, Césaire identifies these "enemies" in a colorful catalogue of invectives, excoriating "venomous journalists, goitrous academician . . . the hoodwinkers, the hoaxers, the hot-air artists, the humbugs" among others, supporters of "plundering capitalism" who he insists are "answerable for the violence of revolutionary action." Balancing solid scholarship with exhilarating bursts of vivid language, Césaire continues his citation of prominent sociologists and academicians whose theories about the Bantu need for dependence, or the Madagascan rejection of personal responsibility are justification for the "Occidental obligation" to these people. Lacing his remarks with a withering sarcasm, Césaire applauds the efforts of these men to keep under control the more vicious methods of colonialist administrators who are "less subtle and more brutal," but ruefully observes that those who resort to force to compel obedience have become less interested in appeals to world opinion and that Hitler is the culmination of the colonialist program. This leads him back to his initial position that modern European civilization has been seriously compromised and corrupted by two centuries of colonialism.

Descent into Darkness

Recapitulating, Césaire restates his fundamental position that colonialism *"cannot but bring about the ruin of Europe,"* and then moves toward an affirmative conclusion by counterposing the work of ethnographers (who respect the cultures they examine) with theoreticians of imperialism (whose preconceptions about the cultures they describe results in racist dismissal). Deftly selecting passages that effectively illustrate the biases of the defenders of colonialism, Césaire sees them as proof of his contention that "the West has never been further from being able to live a true humanism," and warns that the United States may pose the greatest threat to a restoration of humane values as "American high finance" replaces European soldiers to "raid every colony in the world."

In a sense, Césaire is using the United States as a symbol of the mechanization of the modern world in accordance with its ascendance as a superpower after World War II. His hope is that Europe (by which he means the West) will become what he calls "the awakener of countries" in the spirit of the great achievements of the Enlightenment that formed the basis for his own classical education. If not, he foresees a descent into "the pall of mortal darkness" for European civilization and maintains that the only way that Europe can redeem itself is through revolution—an idea that he does not discuss in detail but which was a part of his continuing commitment to a Marxist view of history that persisted even after he rejected the dogma of the Communist Party.

The Legacy of a Pioneer

Césaire's *Discourse on Colonialism* was a groundbreaking venture into previously unmentionable territory, introducing an issue that was not regarded as appropriate for consideration by the Western powers before World War II. It was a sensitive subject immediately following the war because of fears of Soviet expansion into a power vacuum, the unease felt by countries such as France and Great Britain, which had been devastated by the war, and by countries such as Germany and Japan, which had temporarily lost any influence they might have had in global politics. The principles of democracy that had theoretically guaranteed the autonomy of all people were not always actually applied in terms of international politics as the Cold War made the West cautious about radical changes in governmental arrangement. Nonetheless, it was becoming increasingly difficult for Great Britain and France to justify a continuataion of their colonial empires, and the end of British rule in India set a precedent for change.

Colonialism had been under attack prior to Césaire's essay, but many of the more persuasive critics were dismissed as Communist sympathizers, a charge made easier by what was often a Marxist foundation (or parallel) to their critique. Césaire's essay was so singular in its style that it attracted immediate attention, although some who agreed with the thrust of his attack were unsettled by the vituperative nature of his language and imagery, and there are sections in which discourse verges on diatribe. While his accusations are far less controversial decades later, it is the vivid and gripping nature of his mode of expression that still compels attention, indicating that a philosophical inquiry may be written in a form not usually associated with the tradition.

Césaire was particularly a pioneer in his emphasis on the value of ancient African civilizations, an expression of the Afrocentric position that became both popular and controversial in the late twentieth century, and his accusation that "bourgeois Europe . . . extirpated 'the root of diversity'" anticipates the multicultural concerns that have become a major component of sociopolitical thinking. While his warning about U.S. domination is somewhat alarmist, his comment about factories in the former colonial countries making products for foreign corporations is an accurate forecast of the practice of many Western manufacturers, and his ruminations about the effect of colonialism on the colonizers have been borne out by the intermixing of people from the colonies into European countries, especially France and Great Britain where the contributions made by citizens born elsewhere but now integrated into society have given the European nations a new strength and vitality, as Césaire hoped they would.

Leon Lewis

Additional Reading

Arnold, A. James. Introduction to *Césaire's Lyric and Dramatic Poetry 1946-82*, by Aimé Césaire. Translated by Clayton Eshleman and Annette Smith. Charlottesville: University Press of Virginia, 1990. Provides a succinct introduction to Aimé Césaire's life and work. Offers critical observations that supplement and extend many of the readings in Arnold's important *Modernism and Negritude*.

_____. *Modernism and Negritude: The Poetry and Poetics of Aimé Césaire*. Cambridge, Mass.: Harvard University Press, 1981. This work is certainly the definitive study of Césaire's poetry and its relationship to both negritude and modernism. Highly readable and elegantly written.

Davies, Gregson. *Aimé Césaire*. New York: Cambridge University Press, 1997. A generally chronological examination of the evolution of Césaire's poetic and intellectual development and its connection to his aesthetics and politics.

Frutkin, Susan. *Aimé Césaire: Black Between Worlds*. Coral Gables, Fla.: Center for Advanced International Studies, University of Miami, 1973. A short but clearly written document on Césaire's career. Frutkin covers the biographical details, both actual and intellectual, in a thoroughly convincing manner. While pointing out Césaire's undeniable contribution to various African American movements, she places him accurately between the two worlds of his French heritage and his black identity.

Kennedy, Ellen Conroy, ed. *The Negritude Poets*. New York: Viking Press, 1975. An excellent collection of translations of French poetry written by black writers from the Caribbean, Africa, and the Indian Ocean area. Kennedy's preface to Césaire's work serves as an informative introduction to his work, his career, and his literary significance. Although purists may wince, her abridgment and summary of *Return to My Native Land* might make Césaire's difficult work more accessible to the beginner.

Patrick Meanor, updated by William Nelles

Patricia Smith Churchland

By building a bridge between philosophy and neuroscience, Churchland demonstrated that empirical study of the brain is crucial to the philosophy of mind.

Principal philosophical works: *Neurophilosophy: Toward a Unified Science of the Mind-Brain*, 1986; *The Computational Brain*, 1992 (with Terrence J. Sejnowski); *On the Contrary: Critical Essays, 1987-1997*, 1998 (with Paul Churchland).

Born: July 16, 1943; Oliver, British Columbia, Canada

Early Life

From a very young age, Patricia Smith Churchland was interested in how things work. As she speculated in an interview published in *Speaking Minds: Interviews with Twenty Eminent Cognitive Scientists* (1995):

> Maybe it's because I grew up on a farm, and as a kid I had to solve, as a matter of daily life, a lot of practical problems. If an irrigation pump did not work or a cow was having trouble calving, we had to figure out how the thing worked and do what we could to fix it.

In this way, Churchland's childhood provided her with a mechanistic understanding of the world that has significantly influenced her approach to philosophy, particularly to the philosophy of mind. Much in the way that she once attempted to understand the workings of irrigation pumps, she has throughout her philosophical career attempted to understand the workings of the human brain or, as she usually puts it, the "mind-brain."

Churchland received a bachelor's degree from the University of British Columbia in 1965 and then entered graduate school in philosophy at the University of Pittsburgh. Her time at Pittsburgh was important to her philosophical development for several reasons, not the least of which was that her schooling there planted the seeds of skepticism about what is often called "ordinary language philosophy." Owing primarily to the works of the Austrian philosopher Ludwig Wittgenstein and the British philosopher J. L. Austin, ordinary language philosophy was the dominant school of Anglo-American philosophical thought in the 1950's and 1960's. Reacting against early twentieth century philosophers such as Gottlob Frege and Bertrand Russell, who claimed that philosophy required a technical language of its own, ordinary language philosophers argued that philosophical problems could best be solved by attending to the ordinary meanings of words, that is, by doing conceptual analysis. While working toward her M.A. degree at Pittsburgh, Churchland developed a growing uneasiness about the tenability of conceptual analysis as a philosophical method. In particular, she became frustrated with philosophers' attempts to develop a theory of the mind by way of a priori reflection on ordinary mental concepts. Even within the strongly Wittgensteinian climate of Oxford University, where she studied from 1966 to 1969, Churchland's disdain for a priori philosophy, and what she saw as its antiscientific narrowness, grew.

This disdain was shared by her husband, Paul M. Churchland; together, they began to explore the view that the way to make progress in philosophy of mind was to look to science, and in particular, to the neurosciences. Though many philosophers at that time were arguing that empirical science had little to offer a philosophical study of the mind, the Churchlands began to steer a different course, becoming more and more convinced that the key to understanding cognition lay in understanding the processes of the brain. This conviction would remain at the center of Patricia Churchland's work throughout her philosophical career.

Life's Work

Churchland began her academic career as an assistant professor of philosophy at the University of Manitoba, Canada, in 1969. During her early years at Manitoba, she and her husband had two children, Mark in 1972 and Anne in 1974. She also published her first article, "Logical Form and Ontological Decision," which appeared in *Journal of Philosophy* in 1974. It was soon followed by several other well-received articles in professional journals, and her substantial publication record no doubt paved the way to her promotion to the rank of associate professor in 1977.

Throughout this time, however, Churchland's frustration with a priori philosophy continued to grow, and by the mid-1970's she was seriously disenchanted with the current state of the discipline. One of the sources of her frustration was functionalism, a theory that was then beginning to dominate philosophy of mind. Functionalism views the mind as an information-processing system based on a computational analogy. Roughly, functionalists compare the relationship between mind and brain to the relationship between program and computer. In keeping with this comparison, functionalists believe that understanding the brain, seen simply as a piece of "hardware," is largely irrelevant to understanding the program, human cognition, that it runs. This assumption, though widely shared, struck Churchland as misguided. She firmly suspected that there was much to be learned about human cognitive processes by understanding the brain, the center of such processes. Deciding to explore this suspicion for herself, she turned to science and began a systematic, empirical study of the brain.

Given her childhood on the farm, once Churchland decided that she wanted to learn neuroscience, it is not surprising that she would choose a hands-on approach

rather than simply immerse herself in books. She began a course of study at the University of Manitoba Medical Center, conducting experiments and dissections and observing patients with brain damage in neurology wards at the Health Sciences Centre in Winnipeg. After achieving the level of mastery of neuroscience expected of the medical students, she began to take graduate-level courses in neurophysiology, and ultimately she did considerable work in a neurophysiology laboratory, headed by Larry Jordan, that was doing research on how the spinal cord controls locomotion.

Her laboratory work was important not only because it gave her a basic grounding in neuroscientific techniques but also because it helped reorient her thinking about what empirical re-

Patricia Smith Churchland. *(Courtesy of Patricia Churchland)*

search is important to philosophy. Churchland had immersed herself in neuroscience in an attempt to shed some light on cognition. As a result, her neuroscientific interests primarily concerned topics such as perception and memory. Although Jordan's work on locomotion initially seemed to her to be tangential to her main focus, she gradually became convinced that animal movement is closely tied to cognition. How an animal moves, she learned, is at a very fundamental level connected to how it represents the world.

Churchland spent the academic year 1992-1993 at the Institute for Advanced Study in Princeton, New Jersey, at which time she wrote much of *Neurophilosophy: Toward a Unified Science of the Mind-Brain*. Upon returning to the University of Manitoba, she was promoted to the rank of full professor in 1983. However, the following year, both she and her husband Paul departed Manitoba to assume professorships in the department of philosophy at the University of California, San Diego (UCSD). When the Churchlands arrived in San Diego, they joined a vibrant, interdisciplinary community studying cognition, including such cognitive science luminaries as Francis Crick, James McClelland, and David Rumelhart. UCSD is regarded as the West Coast birthplace of cognitive science (the Massachusetts Institute of Technology is generally recognized as the East Coast birthplace) and was the site of the first research institute for cognitive science, the Center for Human Information Processing.

While at UCSD, Churchland began to work closely with Terrence Sejnowski, a professor of biology and the director of the Institute for Neural Computation. The two also worked together at the Salk Institute, where Churchland became an adjunct in 1989. Both were associated with the Salk Institute's Computational Neurobiology Lab (CNL), a laboratory devoted to investigation into the computational aspects of the brain. The research at CNL led to numerous collaborations between Churchland and Sejnowski, the most notable of which is *The Computational Brain*. In this book, Churchland and Sejnowski advance a heterodox theory of neural representation commonly known as "connectionism" or "parallel distributed processing." According to the con-

ventional wisdom among artificial intelligence (AI) researchers, the brain can be understood on the model of digital computers. This analogy involves two basic assumptions: first, that cognitive processes consist of symbol manipulation; second, that these processes run sequentially. The connectionist rejects both of these assumptions. In particular, connectionism views the brain's representations not in terms of symbols but in terms of a pattern of activity that is distributed across a network of neurons. In the years following the publication of *The Computational Brain*, connectionism gathered steam and became more than a minority view.

Churchland's frequent collaborations with Sejnowski as well as with numerous other cognitive scientists underscore the interdisciplinary nature of her work. Viewing cognitive science as in need of contribution from a multitude of disciplines—not only the neurosciences, such as neuropsychology, neuroanatomy, and neurophysiology, but also experimental psychology, linguistics, and molecular biology—Churchland reserved a key role for philosophy. According to Churchland, it is the philosopher's job "to synthesize and theorize and ask the questions everyone else is either too embarrassed or too focused or too busy to ask."

In 1992-1993, Churchland served as the president of the Pacific Division of the American Philosophical Association (APA). Her presidential address, "Can Neuroscience Teach Us Anything About Consciousness?," stands as an excellent précis of her distinctive take on the interconnections between philosophy and neuroscience. Originally published in 1993 proceedings of the American Philosophical Association, this paper was later reprinted in *The Nature of Consciousness* (1997), a widely used anthology of articles on consciousness. Other pieces of Churchland's work were also reprinted in influential anthologies, such as *Mind and Cognition* (1990), and in the *Encyclopedia of Neuroscience* (1988).

Influence

Churchland became the recipient of many awards and grants, but one award deserves special mention. In 1991, Churchland was one of thirty-one individuals awarded a MacArthur

Foundation fellowship. Every year since 1983, the MacArthur Foundation has awarded between twenty and forty such fellowships, often referred to as the "genius" awards (although that is not a label the MacArthur Foundation itself uses). Through these substantial monetary awards, the MacArthur Foundation aims to recognize and reward individuals who have exhibited special creativity, whether by making or finding something new or by drawing together things that have previously seemed unconnected.

It is in this latter respect that Churchland's work is most influential. Her unique synthesis of philosophy and neuroscience broke down the walls between these two disciplines, opening bidirectional lines of communication. She became arguably the philosopher best informed about the state of neuroscience in the 1980's and 1990's and, as such, almost singlehandedly introduced philosophers to a wealth of information about the brain and the nervous system, conveying technical neuroscientific results in a fashion accessible to the nonscientist. Most important, however, she not only conveyed the details of the scientific research but also extracted the philosophical implications of such research. Insofar as such implications have threatened the traditional philosophical conception of the mind, Churchland may have encountered resistance from fellow philosophers, but at the same time she undoubtedly commands their respect.

Amy Kind

Neurophilosophy

Toward a Unified Science of the Mind-Brain

Type of philosophy: Metaphysics, philosophy of mind, philosophy of science
First published: 1986
Principal ideas advanced:
◇ Because philosophers cannot develop an adequate theory of the mind without understanding the brain, neuroscience has utmost importance for philosophy.
◇ Because scientific researchers need an overarching framework, a "synoptic vision," to make sense of the results of their empirical research, philosophy has utmost importance for neuroscience.
◇ The isolationist methodology commonly adopted by researchers in cognitive psychology and artificial intelligence is a mistake. Instead, there should be an interanimation between "top-down" and "bottom-up" strategies for studying the workings of the brain.
◇ Folk psychology, our commonsense theory of the mind, is inadequate. What should ultimately revise or perhaps even replace it is a mature neuroscience.

Broadly speaking, theories in the philosophy of mind are of two sorts: dualist and materialist. Dualist theories, such as the one associated with French philospher René Descartes, claim that there are two fundamentally different kinds of substances in the world: physical substances such as the body and mental substances such as the mind. In contrast, materialist theories claim that there are only physical substances; hence, on a materialist view, mental states are standardly understood to be physical states of the brain.

Patricia Smith Churchland falls squarely in the materialist camp, believing that the mind should be identified with the brain. In fact, she approaches her study in terms of neither the "mind" nor the "brain" but rather in terms of the "mind-brain." As its subtitle suggests, *Neurophilosophy* lays the groundwork for a theory of the mind-brain and, according to Churchland, this theory must be informed not only by philosophical work but also by neuroscientific research. Toward this end, Churchland's primary aim in the book is to bridge the gap between neuroscience and philosophy, acquainting researchers in these fields with one another.

History of Neuroscience
Part 1 of *Neurophilosophy* aims to introduce philosophers to some elementary neuroscience. The book opens with a historical sketch of the science of nervous systems, beginning with Galen, the third century B.C.E. Greek anatomist and physician, and ending with the invention of the electron microscope in the 1950's. Although this overview is organized chronologically, the historical details nonetheless suggest a unifying

theme: the progress of science away from vitalism and toward a mechanistic materialism.

As Churchland explains, the vitalists viewed the motion of muscles in terms of a psychic breath of air, or *pneuma*. Although through the centuries there were occasional refinements to the theory, such as Descartes's introduction of a mechanistic connection between the vital spirit and the body, vitalism remained scientific orthodoxy through the first half of the seventeenth century. At that time, the theory suffered its first real threat, stemming from the work of Dutch biologist Jan Swammerdam. In experiments on the leg muscles of frogs, Swammerdam was able to produce muscle contractions purely mechanically, thereby suggesting the superfluousness of vital spirits. Such experiments themselves were not enough to loosen the grip that vitalism held on the scientific imagination, but they did lead to further research, such as the nineteenth century work of Hermann von Helmholtz. A student of the father of modern physiology Johannes Müller, Helmholtz applied the law of conservation of energy to biology. As Churchland describes in some detail, this application produced experimental results showing that the chemical reactions ordinarily occurring in a human body were sufficient to generate all of the organism's physical activity. There was no need, in other words, for a psychic spirit or breath of air. In this way, Helmholtz was profoundly influential in overturning the vitalistic conception and was responsible for ushering in the modern-day, mechanistic understanding of the nervous system.

In the hundred years between Helmholtz's experiments and the invention of the electron microscope, what Churchland calls the "neuron paradigm" was established. Scientists developed a basic framework for neuroscientific research, and the science of nervous systems thereby began to blossom. After guiding her philosophical audience on a tour of early research into the neuron, Churchland abandons her historical approach. The remainder of part 1 involves a thematic discussion of theories concerning the functioning and anatomy of neurons. After summarizing scientific findings about neurons themselves, she provides a description of how these basic elements of nervous systems are configured

into networks. Her discussion of the structure of nervous systems aims to refute the "bramblescape" theory, according to which such systems are fundamentally a hodgepodge of neurons. Someone who labors under the misconception that nervous systems are merely a hopeless tangle will quite naturally be skeptical about the promise of neuroscience. Thus, to defend the neuroscientific enterprise against such skepticism, Churchland carefully describes five different dimensions of neuronal organization: pathways, laminae, topographical maps, columns, and nervous-system development.

Churchland's discussion of functional neuroanatomy also sets the stage for her discussion of the importance that philosophy has for neuroscience in part 2 of *Neurophilosophy*. As she writes,

> With so much known about the neuroanatomy and neurophysiology of nervous systems, what is now needed are theories of brain function that will begin to pull the data together, to pose new questions, and to compete for epistemological space.

Philosophy must play an essential role, Churchland thinks, with respect to the development of overarching theories that can guide neuroscientific research.

Rejection of Folk Psychology

In this way, Churchland assigns to philosophers an important role in the development of a theory of the mind-brain, but it is important to note that she does not think that the needed philosophical work can be done from the armchair, so to speak. Churchland argues persuasively that an adequate theory of the mind must be informed by empirical research. She thus calls for the rejection of what is usually referred to as "folk psychology," our commonsense understanding of mental states and processes.

Folk psychology consists of a vast network of rough generalizations, usually invoking propositional attitudes such as beliefs and desires, that explain behavior. For example, two such generalizations are as follows: (1) When a person desires to bring about some state of affairs *S* and believes that her doing action *A* is the best way to bring about *S*, then (other things being equal) she will do *A*; (2) When a person desires to prevent some state of affairs *S* and believes that *S* will result from her doing action *A*, then (other things being equal) she will refrain from doing *A*. Philosophers of mind have generally assumed that any adequate theory of the mind must, to at least a significant extent, respect the generalizations of folk psychology and account for the propositional attitudes it posits. Churchland thinks that this assumption is deeply mistaken. Advances in physics came only when physicists were willing to reject many of the commonsense presuppositions of folk physics, and advances in medical science came only at the expense of many of the commonsense presuppositions of folk medicine. Likewise, Churchland argues that we must be willing to reject common sense when it comes to psychology, the science of the mind.

This negative assessment of folk psychology is often referred to as "eliminative materialism." It was first put forward by Paul Feyerabend in the early 1960's, but its leading proponents throughout the 1980's and the 1990's were Churchland and her husband, Paul. Throughout the second part of *Neurophilosophy*, Patricia Churchland calls upon much of her husband's published work on eliminative materialism in an attempt to make her case against folk psychology.

First, Churchland claims that folk psychology should be viewed as a theory. She believes that it then becomes apparent how unsatisfactory it is. Advancing considerations from both neuroscience and philosophy, she argues that the inadequacies of folk psychology require that it must eventually be significantly revised or simply replaced with an alternative theory. The replacement theory she envisions, and for which she attempts to lay the groundwork throughout *Neurophilosophy*, should ultimately come from a matured neuroscience.

Along these lines, she argues that neuroscience and psychology need to develop in conjunction with each other and, moreover, that they must rely on some philosophical theory to guide this development. Philosophy offers folk psychology as a start, but as the sciences continue their joint endeavor, a new philosophical theory needs to emerge to replace the outmoded folk theory. Painting an apt picture of the codevelopment she envisions, she likens the two sciences to two rock climbers ascending a wide chimney by bracing their feet to the walls and their backs to one another.

Search for a Theory of Neuroscience

Having surveyed the neuroscientific and the philosophic terrain in parts 1 and 2, respectively, in the final part of *Neurophilosophy* Churchland attempts to survey the theoretical terrain. As she notes, though neuroscientists know a significant amount about the structure of nervous systems, they lack a theoretical framework in which to make sense of their experimental results. Against the claims of many neuroscientific researchers that it is still too early for theorizing, or that theorizing is too abstract, Churchland argues that the organizational and motivational value of theories should not be underestimated. Though much of her book seems to be directed toward philosophers, attempting to convince them of the importance of neuroscience, the opening section of part 3 seems clearly aimed at neuroscientists, attempting to convince them of the importance of philosophy.

According to Churchland, the search for a theory should be guided by the following question: What sort of organization in neuronlike structures could produce the output in question (motor control, visual perception, memory, and so on), given the specified input? An ideal theory, or proto-theory, will have what she calls a "Galilean combination" of simplification, unification, and mathematization. Churchland does not herself offer such a theory, but rather, in the remainder of the book, surveys three theoretical ventures in an attempt to show what shape a unified theory of the mind-brain might take.

The tensor network theory, the first theory that Churchland presents and the one to which she devotes the most attention, targets the problem of sensorimotor control by providing a general framework for understanding the computational architecture of nervous systems. In an attempt to make this very complicated theory accessible, Churchland relies on a cartoon story whose main character is the crablike critter Roger. When Roger spots an object, its position is represented in terms of his visual space. However, to reach the object, he has to represent it in terms of his motor space. The tensor network theory aims to explain how visual space representations can be converted into motor space representations. One important contribution of the theory is its postulation of a nonsentential model of representations, thereby counting directly against the folk psychological presumption in favor of sentencelike symbols in the head. Insofar as philosophers and other cognitive scientists who are proponents of a sentential theory of representation argue that their theory is the only game in town, the tensor network theory shows them wrong and offers what Churchland thinks is a promising alternative.

The second theory that Churchland discusses, stemming primarily from the work of Geoffrey Hinton and Terrence Sejnowski, is a connectionist one. This is the theory she later explores in considerable depth in collaboration with Sejnowski in *The Computational Brain* (1992). Her brief discussion of this theory aims to show that neuroscientific research counts against a sequential model of cognition; the connectionists offer an alternative model according to which cognition proceeds by parallel processing. Finally, the third theory presented, owing to the work of Francis Crick, addresses the neurobiological mechanisms that underlie visual attention. One reason Churchland highlights this theory in particular is that it serves as an example of the co-evolution of neurobiology and psychology.

In the end, however, the details of each of these theories are less important than the picture they present of what a neuroscientific theory could look like, that is, how it would be possible to explain the emergence of macro-level phenomena such as visual attention, learning, and movement from the micro (neuronal) level. Churchland thus concludes on a note of optimism: The end of the twentieth century, in her opinion, is a "monumentally exciting" time. As she notes, "we appear to have embarked on a period when an encompassing scientific understanding of the mind-brain will, in some nontrivial measure, be ours." The arguments that such a scientific understanding must come from both neuroscience and philosophy are her unique contributions to the endeavor.

The highly technical nature of published neuroscientific research once presented philosophers with an excuse for ignorance. One of the important contributions of *Neurophilosophy* was to deprive philosophers of this excuse, presenting a sketch of neuroscience that started from scratch but did much more than merely scratch the surface. In a similar vein, the book has served to remind philosophers of the vast wealth of empirical data with which their theories of the mind must be consistent. Part of the impact of *Neurophilosophy* has been to ease the philosopher out of the armchair and into the empirical world.

Amy Kind

Additional Reading

Bechtel, William. "Connectionism and the Philosophy of Mind: An Overview." In *Mind and Cognition*, edited by William Lycan. Oxford, England: Blackwell, 1990. Bechtel provides a useful, general survey of some of the philosophical issues surrounding connectionism, the theory of the mind that Churchland puts forward in both *Neurophilosophy* and *The Computational Brain*.

Campbell, Keith, et al. "Commentaries on *Neurophilosophy*." *Inquiry* 29 (1986). In a special issue devoted to a symposium on Churchland's book *Neurophilosophy*, six commentaries are followed by replies from Churchland.

Churchland, Patricia Smith. "Take It Apart and See How It Runs." In *Speaking Minds: Interviews with Twenty Eminent Cognitive Scientists*, edited by Peter Baumgartner and Sabine Payr. Princeton, N.J.: Princeton University Press, 1995. This interview finds Churchland discussing her approach to philosophy, how she initially became interested in neuroscience, and her views on the discipline of cognitive science. The volume also contains an interview with Churchland's husband, Paul, entitled "Neural Networks and Commonsense."

McCauley, Robert N., ed. *The Churchlands and Their Critics*. Oxford, England: Blackwell, 1996. The first half of this anthology contains nine essays on the works of both Patricia and Paul Churchland. The contributors come from a wide variety of fields, such as philosophy, neurology, neuroanatomy, and psychology. In the second half of the anthology, the Churchlands jointly respond to their critics. Their responses proceed thematically, covering five major topics: the future of psychology (both folk and scientific), the impact of neural network models on the philosophy of science, semantics in a new vein, consciousness and methodology, and moral psychology and the rebirth of moral theory. Suitable for advanced students.

Stich, Stephen. *From Folk Psychology to Cognitive Science: The Case Against Belief*. Cambridge, Mass.: MIT Press, 1983. The argument that Stich launches against folk psychology makes many points of contact with Churchland's work. Especially relevant is chapter 10.

Amy Kind

Paul M. Churchland

An analytic philosopher and proponent of eliminative materialism, Churchland maintained that advances in the neurosciences and artificial intelligence are the key to understanding cognition. A leading defender of scientific realism, he held that scientific theories present a literally true account of the world, especially of the unobservable world.

Principal philosophical works: *Scientific Realism and the Plasticity of Mind*, 1979; *Matter and Consciousness: A Contemporary Introduction to the Philosophy of the Mind*, 1984, rev. ed. 1988; *Images of Science: Essays on Realism and Empiricism, with a Reply from Bas C. Van Fraassen*, 1985 (edited with C. A. Hooker); *A Neurocomputational Perspective: The Nature of Mind and the Structure of Science*, 1989; *The Computer That Could: A Neurophilosophical Portrait*, 1994; *The Engine of Reason, the Seat of the Soul: A Philosophical Journey into the Brain*, 1995; *On the Contrary: Critical Essays, 1987-1997*, 1998 (with Patricia Smith Churchland).

Born: 1942; Vancouver, British Columbia, Canada

Early Life

Paul Montgomery Churchland, a dual American/Canadian citizen, was born in Vancouver, Canada, in 1942. He studied at the University of British Columbia, Vancouver, from 1960 to 1964, and graduated with a B.A. (honors) in philosophy, physics, and mathematics. From 1964 to 1967, he studied at the University of Pittsburgh, one of the world's leading centers for studies in the philosophy of science. He received his Ph.D. from this institution in the fields of philosophy of science and philosophy of mind. In 1966, Churchland served as an instructor in philosophy at the University of Pittsburgh at Greensburgh and then moved to the University of Toronto, where he served as a lecturer in philosophy from 1967 to 1969, moving in 1969 to the University of Manitoba, where he rose from assistant professor to full professor.

Life's Work

In 1982-1983, Churchland was a member of the Institute for Advanced Study in Princeton, New Jersey. In 1984, Churchland became a professor of philosophy at the University of California, San Diego. At that university, he served as department chair from 1986 to 1990 and was a member

of the Cognitive Science Faculty, a member of the Institute for Neural Computation, and a member of the Science Studies faculty.

An important component of Churchland's philosophy deals with the metaphysical mind-body problem, posed in its sharpest form by the French philosopher René Descartes, called the father of modern philosophy. Descartes asked: What do human beings have that material objects do not have that allows human beings to cognize, to learn languages, and to learn mathematics? He argues that human beings must have an immaterial, nonspatial mind over and above a material, spatially located brain that inanimate objects and lower life forms do not have. Descartes called this mind "mental substance," the essence of which is thinking. This substance is to be contrasted with material substance, the essence of which is extension, the occupying of space. These two substances are the basis of Descartes's metaphysical dualism. (For Descartes, there was also a third substance, divine substance, or God.) These substances have necessary existence and need nothing else for their existence. For Descartes, the separation of material substance from mental substance meant that science (which deals with material substance) would never have to come into conflict with religion (which deals with mental substance, or spirit, or soul). Nevertheless, a problem immediately arose as to the nature of the causal interaction between an immaterial, non-spatial mind and a material, spatial body. Descartes held that the interaction occurred in the pineal gland, but this answer simply postpones the problem rather than solving it. To this day, no generally received answer to this mind-body problem has been provided by philosophers, psychologists, or neuroscientists.

Although few modern scholars hold Descartes's theory of *substance dualism*, there are, nevertheless, many varieties of contemporary dualism. *Popular dualism*, for example, holds that the mind is a spiritual substance yet fully possessed of spatial properties in intimate contact with the brain. Other dualistic theories claim that the mind is a *property* of the material brain. For example, *epiphenomenalism* holds that the mind is an emergent property of the brain that is not causal to other events, whereas *interactionist property dualism* holds that mental states emerge from the brain but can causally interact with the brain and other parts of the material body. A sophisticated form of dualism centers on the notion of *supervenience*. Things of kind *A* supervene on things of kind *B* when the presence or absence of things of kind *A* is completely determined by the presence or absence of things of kind *B*. It is sometimes argued that the mental supervenes on the physical but that mental categories are not identical with nor reducible to any physical categories.

In contrast to these dualistic theories, *reductive materialism*, more often called "the identity theory," holds that mental states *are* physical states of the brain. An even more popular materialist theory is *functionalism*, which holds that the defining feature of any type of mental state is the set of causal relations it bears to environmental effects on the body, other types of mental states, and bodily behavior. So pain, for example, typically results from bodily injury, causes annoyance and distress, and causes wincing, blanching, and the nursing of the injured area. Any state that plays exactly the same functional role is pain, according to functionalism. A third type of material-

ism is *eliminative materialism*, which holds that the theory of mental states is impoverished, not simply incorrect. There are *no* mental states, only brain states.

Eliminative materialism is the philosophical theory held by Churchland. He argues that the position is supported by advances in the neurosciences. Neuroscientists routinely produce color-coded images of the actual patterns of activity in the brain when people read, attend to different features of visual stimuli, encode and retrieve memories, and perform other cognitive tasks. Other neuroscientists produce very detailed maps of the primate cortex that distinguish dozens of specialized processing areas. Much support for eliminative materialism is also found in studies of cases of brain damage, degeneration,

Paul M. Churchland. *(Courtesy of Paul Churchland)*

and disequilibrium. For example, lesions to the connections between the secondary visual cortex and the secondary auditory cortex of the left hemisphere may result in the inability to identify perceived colors, while lesions to the secondary auditory cortex of the left hemisphere results in the more drastic effect of total and permanent loss of speech comprehension, while bilateral damage to the hippocampus results in the inability to retain new memories.

Nevertheless, eliminative materialists such as Churchland must still account for the phenomenon of introspection and the "qualitative feel" of people's alleged mental states. The eliminative materialist must account for the differences people claim to perceive, for example, in pain, their understanding of a mathematical problem, and their believing or knowing a fact. A strong case can be made that these latter phenomena are best explained under some dualist theory of mind-brain.

The argument from introspection in favor of a dualism of mind-brain is a serious problem for Churchland. He responds to it by invoking a robust scientific realism, which is, basically, the position that scientific theories provide a literally true account of the world. Moreover, Churchland claims that, if scientific theories are successful at explaining and predicting phenomena, then there is good reason to believe that the entities that the theories postulate really exist, even if they are not directly perceivable through the senses. For example, the standard model theory of matter claims that electrons, protons, quarks, and other subatomic entities exist even if people do not directly perceive them with their senses. As Churchland argues, when one experiences a warm summer day as 70 degrees Fahrenheit, what one is experiencing is the mean kinetic energy of the air molecules, which is about 6.2×10^{-21} joules, whether one realizes it or not, for heat is the mean kinetic energy of molecules. If one does not perceive it that way, one can learn to do so.

This realism is important for Churchland, for it allows him to formulate a response to the argument from introspection, the strongest argument against the eliminative materialism that Churchland embraces. Churchland argues that, with suitable training and knowledge, one can eventually introspect one's brain states directly. This claim undercuts the dualist position that one introspects one's mental states that exist over and above the brain. However, this leads to one of the most controversial of Churchland's theses, for he claims that eventually one can directly introspect such brain states as spiking frequencies in specific neural pathways and dopamine levels in the limbic system, based on a realist account of current and successful neurophysiological theories.

To support this controversial claim, Churchland presents the case of the musical prodigy who, at a very early age, can distinguish between sound pitches. Very soon, with more training and study, the young person can distinguish between different instruments of the orchestra. As the prodigy matures and becomes a talented young conductor, he or she can distinguish when instruments in an orchestra are playing in tune and when they are not. Churchland then draws an analogy with the introspection of brain states. He claims that people will have to learn the conceptual framework of a matured neuroscience if they are to introspect brain states directly and that they will have to practice its noninferential application. Eventually they will reach the stage analogous to that of the mature conductor who can now experience phenomena that were impossible to experience at an earlier stage of development. Churchland thinks that the amount of self-apprehension gained by direct introspection of brain states is more than worth the effort of training and study. Several problems arise with regard to Churchland's argument. The most obvious problem concerns the precision of his argument by analogy.

As an eliminative materialist, Churchland is quick to use parallel distributive processing (PDP) from artificial intelligence research as a model of cognitive processes. Such digital computers function solely as symbol manipulators, and it is unclear whether any symbol manipulator—whether a computer or a human being—can ever possess intentionality, the state of having meanings that point to, or are about, features of the world. Typically, intentionality is said to be "the mark of the mental." The philosopher John Searle argues that mere symbol manipulators cannot have semantics or meanings and thus cannot have intentionality. Thus, according to the computational model of conscious intelligence held by Churchland, a brain that simply manipulates symbols cannot account for people having meanings that are about the world. However, as many philosophers hold, a dualist theory of mind-brain can. Meanings (or propositions) are just the objects of mental states.

Searle uses his famous Chinese room argument (of which there are several versions) to argue his case. Suppose Searle himself is a central processing unit (CPU) of a digital computer and understands no Chinese at all. If Searle is given rules of syntax, he can string together Chinese characters and output them in such a way that a person fluent in Chinese could read the resulting string of symbols, understand them, and respond. However, he, Searle, cannot respond even though as a CPU he gives the *appearance* of knowing what the symbols mean. Searle argues that the meaning of the symbols has intentionality, and hence the Chinese speaker can understand and respond appropriately to the output sentence in a way that Searle as a mere symbol manipulator cannot. Therefore, brains or computers that can only manipulate symbols according to a program cannot have intentionality. Intentionality can be had only by objects that have a conscious mind, such as the Chinese speaker. Searle claims that his argument holds independently of technological advances in computer design. This argument presented a serious challenge to Churchland's eliminative materialism and the associated view that the material brain is merely a neurocomputer.

Churchland countered Searle's argument with his own "luminous room" argument. Churchland asked the reader to imagine a small, closed-off room that is completely dark. The occupant of this room is the scientist James Clerk Maxwell, who claims that light is nothing other than electromagnetic waves. Maxwell shakes a bar magnet that produces such waves. An outside critic points out that the room is completely dark, so light cannot possibly be electromagnetic waves. Churchland says that all Maxwell needs to do is claim that the room is indeed lit, albeit at a grade too poor to be detected. All that is needed for visible light is that the electromagnetic waves be speeded up in order to produce visible light. The same is true for Searle's argument, claims

Churchland. All that is needed is that the syntax of a language be sufficiently complex in order for people to detect the meaning and thus the intentionality of symbol manipulation. Churchland's argument, however, again suffers from problems arising from analogy. Scientists, for example, do not say there is light unless it is visible, even if moving electromagnetic waves are present. More important, it is not clear that speeded-up electromagnetic waves giving rise to visible light is analogous to increased syntactical complexity of language giving rise to meaning.

Paul C. L. Tang

The Engine of Reason, the Seat of the Soul

A Philosophical Journey into the Brain

Type of philosophy: Metaphysics, philosophy of mind, philosophy of science
First published: 1995
Principal ideas advanced:

◇ The neural sciences (neuroanatomy, neurophysiology, neurochemistry) and artificial intelligence research have recently contributed, and will continue to contribute, to a greater understanding of the brain and of cognitive processes.

◇ There is no mind or spirit or soul over and above the brain as has been traditionally claimed by many philosophers and theologians.

◇ All cognitive processes can be explained entirely in terms of the brain.

◇ The brain *is* the self.

◇ This revolutionary treatment of cognition and the self will also result in reconceptions of consciousness, philosophy, science, society, language, politics, and art.

◇ The technology that will arise from this neural net approach to brain function could have important medical and legal consequences.

In the seventeenth century, French philosopher René Descartes argued that humans have an immaterial mind (also called "soul" or "self" or "spirit") over and above the material brain. This position is known as mind-body dualism. The mind is the origin of thought ("the engine of reason") as well as "the seat of the soul." For Descartes, the mind causally interacts with the brain, although this interaction is difficult to explain. Modern dualists have not been successful either, and this problem has led many philosophers, psychologists, and cognitive scientists in general (such as neuroanatomists, neurochemists, artificial intelligence researchers, scientifically trained philosophers) to argue for *materialism*, the view that denies there is such an entity as "the mind" and claims that there is only one entity, the material brain. In *The Engine of Reason, the Seat of the Soul*, Paul M. Churchland holds this position, a position supported by studies on brain-damaged and brain-lesioned patients. For example, postmortem examinations of the brains of people who had Alzheimer's disease reveal material plaques and tangles throughout the fine web of synaptic connections of the neurons of the brain that embodies all of one's cognitive skills and capacities for recognition.

Moreover, Churchland is impressed with the tremendous advances in the neurosciences and in AI research that allows modeling of brain processes. Modeling enables cognitive scientists to represent brain function as massively parallel distributive processing (PDP) of recurrent neural nets that carry out vector-to-vector transformations or vector completions. This model (perhaps theory) of human cognitive brain processes will effect, Churchland claims, a revolution in understanding of the self, consciousness, all cognitive processes, science, art, and much else besides. His book is intended to convey the possibilities and excitement of this revolution.

Churchland's book is divided into two parts. Part 1 describes the enormous anatomical complexity of the brain and links this complexity to artificial neural networks in computer modeling that imitate parts of the brain. Part 2 explores the consequences of this neuroscientific approach to cognition and soul and, in the process, delves into the nature of consciousness and shows how the new neuroscientific approach can be applied in many other domains besides the study of consciousness, such as science, philosophy, ethics, law, and medicine.

The Brain

Churchland begins by describing the enormous structural capacity of the human brain to represent the world. For example, a standard television screen contains about 200,000 pixels, the tiny dotlike elements that are easily seen if one peers very closely at the screen. However, the human brain has approximately 100 billion nerve cells, or neurons, each of which can also take on a full range of activation levels (or "brightness values" when compared to pixels). Counting each neuron as a pixel, one can calculate that the brain's representational capacity is about 500,000 times greater than a television screen's representational capacity.

Churchland then asks the reader to consider one of the twin towers of the World Trade Center in New York City. Imagine the entire outside surface—all 500,000 square feet of the skyscraper—to be tiled with 500,000 television screens so that each seventeen-inch screen is glued next to each other and facing outward. Assuming there are about 200,000 pixels per square foot, one can calculate that there are 100 billion pixels in this setup that correspond to the 100 billion neurons in the human brain. This is the *minimum visual representational power* of the human brain, for the brain can also represent reality in many other dimensions, including, for example, social, moral, and emotional.

Churchland then asks the reader to picture that the skyscraper's pixels are embedded in a thin sheet of aluminum foil that covers the entire building. He then imagines someone scrunching this great expanse of foil into a ball about the size of a large grapefruit, which is approximately the volume of the human brain. These 100 billion pixels (analogous to neurons) can still represent the world even if they are folded out of sight.

Furthermore, Churchland considers the *manner* in which the brain represents the world. He argues that AI research gives the best answer in terms of artificial neural nets that involve parallel distributive processing. The brain is treated as an advanced neurocomputer. Neural nets represent the world by means of *vectors*, which are simply lists of numbers or sets of magnitudes. (Note that this use of the word "vector" is different from its use in physics, where "vector" refers to a magnitude, such as velocity, that also has a direction.)

For example, on the tongue, there are four distinct kinds of receptor cells. The vector coding scheme for taste, such as the taste of a peach, might have a substantial effect on one of the four types of cells, a minimal effect on a second type, and an intermediate effect on the third and fourth types. Taken together, this precise pattern of relative stimulations constitutes a type of neural "fingerprint" that uniquely characterizes the taste of peaches. Or more exactly, a specific taste is a pattern of spiking frequencies across the four neural channels that convey information of these activity levels away from the mouth and to the rest of the brain. Basically, the same system, *mutatis mutandis*, can be used to represent sensory coding for color, smell, and the more complex actions of facial recognition and use of the human motor system.

Cognition

Churchland turns to a discussion of cognition, which involves learning or "training up a network." One famous example concerns a submarine's sonar system detecting the difference between a mine echo or a rock echo. The sonar system network contains thirteen sonar input cells, and each cell codes the total energy contained in the sonar echo at exactly one of the thirteen sampled frequencies. Each echo is thus characterized by a distinct activation vector across the input population of cells. The cells of the sonar machine at the input layer all project to a second layer and then on to a third layer that consists of only two cells, whose job it is to signal mine or rock, as the case may be. This is also called "vector-to-vector transformation." If the output vector relaxes into a final configuration of (1,0), or close to this, then the sonar has detected a potentially dangerous, explosive mine; when the final configuration is (0,1), or close to this, the sonar has detected a harmless rock.

As the network is trained up, scientists initially have no idea how to configure its connection weights. Hoping to get lucky, they set the weights at small random values and prepare to teach the network on a substantial training set of recorded sonar echoes, half of them returned from real mines placed by the scientists on the ocean floor and half of them returned from visually identified rocks. Using a well-known method of back propa-

gation of synaptic weight adjustments, the scientists cycle the information repeatedly through the training set until the network has assumed an overall synaptic weight adjustment that minimizes the mean squared error at the output layer. That is to say, the scientists continue to instruct the network until it has learned to make the mine-rock distinction as reliably as it can.

This network described is quite real. Churchland cites the work of Paul Gorman and Terry Sejnowski, who have created such a network that topped out at a performance level of 100 percent on the training set. When tested on echoes from outside the training set, the network generalized to these new samples very well, identifying better than 90 percent of them correctly. The training up of a network regularly produces a partitioning of its higher level activation spaces into a hierarchial structure of categories and subcategories producing a framework of concepts that subserve the skill acquired. For example, the sonar network displays two categories with prototypical cores. The sonar example is a model of how the human brain learns, and the research program is extended to neuroscience as to which parts of the brain have sufficient neuroanatomical and neurophysiological complexity to allow for such vector-to-vector transformations.

Churchland extends the discussion from simple forms of sensory coding, to vector coding at the scale of many thousands or even millions of neurons, to the emergence of categories and their central prototypes as carefully crafted areas of activation space, and to recurrent neural processing at the level of animal locomotion and visual interpretation in humans. The central phenomenon at the level of recurrent networks is the phenomenon of *vector completion* of partial inputs often aided by the brain's recurrent manipulation of the relevant population of representing neurons. That is, vector completion can represent the phenomenon of someone's recognizing—perhaps slowly at first, but then suddenly—some unfamiliar, puzzling, problematic situation as being an instance of something (a prototype) well known to that person. Churchland traces out this idea in terms of many salient discoveries in science, such as Descartes's "whirlpool" interpretation of the various planetary motions; Isaac Newton's "deflecting force" interpretation of the Moon's elliptical orbit around Earth; and Albert Einstein's "straight-line in non-Euclidean space-time" interpretation of the Moon's elliptical orbit around Earth. Thus, Churchland claims, some of the most sophisticated intellectual achievements involve the same activities as vector processing, recurrent manipulation, prototype activation, and prototype evaluation, which can be found in some of the simplest of cognitive activities, such as recognizing a dog in a low-grade photograph.

Consciousness

In part 2, Churchland deals with the fascinating but difficult puzzle of consciousness. This phenomenon appears unique to human beings and beyond scientific and purely *physical* explanation. Traditionally, philosophers have argued that the phenomenon is basically a *subjective* occurrence, accessible only to the creature that has it. Churchland argues against this classical view.

Churchland begins by reviewing a number of similar arguments for the classical view advanced by philosophers such as Gottfried Wilhelm Leibniz, Thomas Nagel, John Searle, and Frank Jackson. Nagel's argument was advanced in his seminal 1974 paper, "What Is It Like to Be a Bat?" Nagel argues that no matter how much one might know about the neuroanatomy of a bat's brain and the neurophysiology of a bat's sensory apparatus, one will never know "what it would be like" to have the bat's sensory experience. Even if scientists could track the neuroactivation patterns, one would never know what they are like from the unique perspective of the creature that possesses them; their intrinsic character as felt experiences would still be unknown to us. A purely physical science of the brain, Nagel and others argue, does have a limit on the capacity of understanding as it reaches the subjective character of the contents of one's consciousness.

Churchland responds by arguing that Nagel fails to make a distinction between *how one knows something* and *the thing known*. Churchland argues that the existence of a unique first-person epistemological access to a conscious phenomenon does not entail that the phenomenon is nonphysical in character. For example, the difference between *X*'s knowledge of her facial blush and *Y*'s knowledge of *X*'s facial bluish lies not in the thing known but rather in the manner of knowing it. The blush itself is a physical entity.

Churchland then proposes seven provisional criteria of adequacy that a neuroscientific theory of consciousness must try to reconstruct. Consciousness involves short-term memory, is independent of sensory inputs, displays steerable attention, has the capacity for alternative interpretations of complex or ambiguous facts, disappears in deep sleep, reappears in dreaming, and holds the contents of several basic sensory modalities within a single, unified experience. Churchland takes up each of these criteria of consciousness and shows how they can be explained by treating the brain as a recurrent neural network. Churchland cites some areas where such neuroprocessing could occur, such as Roldofo Llinas's view that the contents of consciousness lie within the layers of the interactively connected primary sensory cortex rather than, as Churchland himself holds, the sparser pathways of the grand recurrent loop that connects all the pathways from cortex to intralaminar nucleus.

Churchland's position that all cognitive processes and the phenomenon of consciousness can be reduced to brain processes representable as a testable theory of recurrent neural nets is a powerful and carefully argued position. He is at pains to warn the reader several times that he may be wrong. Arguments have been raised against his position, but no definitive answer has been reached.

Paul C. L. Tang

Additional Reading

Bechtel, William. "What Should a Connectionist Philosophy of Science Look Like?" In *The Churchlands and Their Critics*, edited by Robert N. McCauley. Oxford, England: Blackwell Scientific Publications, 1996. The author is also a major figure in the field of philosophy and cognitive science. He holds that traditional philosophy of science has been little concerned with the psychology of science, and that the general sentential approach of traditional philosophy of science is ineffective. Bechtel nevertheless questions Paul M. Churchland's claim that theories and explanations are best understood in terms of representations in the heads of scientists.

Clark, Andy. "Dealing in Futures: Folk Psychology and the Role of Representations in Cognitive Science." In *The Churchlands and Their Critics*, edited by Robert N. McCauley. Oxford, England: Blackwell Scientific Publications, 1996. This article is written by another major leader in the field of philosophy and cognitive science. Clark agrees with the Churchlands that connectionist models can contribute very valuable, new resources for understanding human cognition. However, he forcefully rejects Churchland's claim that this outcome impugns folk psychology.

Flanagan, Owen. "The Moral Network." In *The Churchlands and Their Critics*, edited by Robert N. McCauley. Oxford, England: Blackwell Scientific Publications, 1996. Flanagan defends Churchland's moral network theory. He examines the potential of this theory for making sense of moral learning, knowledge, practices, and standards. He applauds the way the theory illuminates the biological, psychological, and social forces shaping the moral lives of human beings, while the normative component of the theory can assess right and wrong, good and bad.

Fodor, Jerry, and Ernie Lepore. "Paul Churchland and Stated Space Semantics" and "Reply to Churchland." In *The Churchlands and Their Critics*, edited by Robert N. McCauley. Oxford, England: Blackwell Scientific Publications, 1996. In both of these articles, the authors argue that Churchland's state space version of a network account of semantics is wanting. They argue that Churchland has remained committed to two positions that are incompatible.

Lycan, William G. "Paul Churchland's PDP Approach to Explanation." In *The Churchlands and Their Critics*, edited by Robert N. McCauley. Oxford, England: Blackwell Scientific Publications, 1996. Lycan discusses Paul Churchland's prototype activation account of explanatory understanding. Lycan argues that if explanation concerns either quasi-logical relations between sentences or the natural relations between the affairs those sentences represent, then Churchland's objections to the traditional deductive-nomological model of scientific explanation are ineffective.

McCauley, Robert N. "Explanatory Pluralism and the Co-evolution of Theories in Science." In *The Churchlands and Their Critics*, edited by Robert N. McCauley. Oxford, England: Blackwell Scientific Publications, 1996. The author is a leader in the field of the philosophy of cognitive science. He discusses Churchland's account of intertheoretic relations in science and the implications for a scientific psychology as opposed to folk psychology. He argues that the earlier continuum model advanced by Churchland and his wife, Patricia Churchland, is vastly oversimplified, leading to unwarranted expectations about the elimination of psychology in favor of advanced neuroscience.

Paul C. L. Tang

R. G. Collingwood

Collingwood stimulated international interest with his efforts to harmonize philosophy and history. His effort to explain what was meant by the term "philosophy of history" resulted in its becoming a respected discipline in Great Britain and the United States.

Principal philosophical works: *Religion and Philosophy*, 1916; *Speculum Mentis*, 1924; *Outlines of a Philosophy of Art*, 1925; *An Essay on Philosophical Method*, 1933; *The Principles of Art*, 1938; *An Autobiography*, 1939; *An Essay on Metaphysics*, 1940; *The New Leviathan*, 1942; *The Idea of Nature*, 1945; *The Idea of History*, 1946; *Essays in Political Philosophy*, 1989.

Born: February 22, 1889; Cartmel Fell, Lancashire, England

Died: January 9, 1943; Coniston, Lancashire, England

Early Life

Robin George Collingwood, the only son of William Gershom Collingwood, a professional painter, archaeologist, and secretary and biographer of English art critic John Ruskin, inherited a great appreciation of the arts and archaeology from his parents. He was home-schooled until the age of thirteen; his early education included formal lessons, provided by his father, in Greek, Latin, and history, along with readings in geology, astronomy, and physics. His mother, an accomplished pianist, instilled in her son a lifelong love for classical music. As a youth, Collingwood learned to play the piano and violin and demonstrated a commendable talent for painting. He continued to paint and compose music throughout his adult life, and his paintings merited exhibits at Oxford University.

Collingwood's formal education included five years at Rugby, followed by four years of study at Oxford, where he graduated with honors and was elected tutor in philosophy in 1912. Although he died at the age of forty-three after developing pneumonia, Collingwood had a very distinguished career at Oxford. He simultaneously held positions as lecturer in philosophy and Roman history and later held the post of professor of metaphysical philosophy until declining health forced him to resign in 1941. In 1915, he received an M.A. degree from St. Andrews University and was awarded an honorary LL.D. from the same institution in 1938.

World War I interrupted Collingwood's academic career from 1915 to 1918, when he served in the admiralty intelligence in London. Upon returning to Oxford in 1918, he married Ethel Winifred Graham; their marriage produced a son and a daughter. A second marriage, to Kathleen Frances Edwardes in 1942, resulted in the birth of another daughter.

Life's Work

From 1911 to 1934, Collingwood's interest in archaeology resulted in his becoming the most highly regarded authority in his day on Roman Britain. His research and publication of *The Archaeology of Roman Britain* (1930) and *Roman Britain and the English Settlements* in the *Oxford History of England* (1936) helped to shape his philosophical thought. Other formative works include *Religion and Philosophy* and *Speculum Mentis*, in which he attempted to demonstrate the mental unity between five forms of human experience: art, religion, science, history, and philosophy. In two of his works, *An Essay on Philosophical Method*, which critics hailed as his best work, and *An Essay on Metaphysics*, he increasingly proposed a notion of philosophical inquiry that depended on the study of history.

Collingwood wrote other distinguished works on important topics in philosophy, but they defy any systematic classification. *Outlines of a Philosophy of Art* was one of his early works; two other works, *The Idea of Nature*, which he began in 1934, and *The Idea of History*, started in 1936, were published posthumously. In *The Principles of Art*, published in 1938, Collingwood dealt with various examples of historiography that he described as pseudohistory, a theme that would reoccur in his work on the philosophy of history. (This theme was taken up in Collingwood's *Principles of History*, an unpublished manuscript presumed lost and discovered in 1995.) Also in this work, he articulated a "theory on the mind," a concept that was the basis of his fascination with the "history of thought," a topic that holds a major place in *The Idea of History*. During the late 1930's, Collingwood's failing health caused him to abandon several works in progress to write *An Autobiography*. His last major work, *The New Leviathan*, was a description of the modern European mind. In this work, he sought to convince his contemporaries that history was the only hope civilization had to realize the Socratic dictum, "Know thyself." History for Collingwood was an adventure in self-discovery through the use of philosophy.

In *An Autobiography*, Collingwood wrote that "the chief business of twentieth century philosophy is to reckon with twentieth century history." He predicated this statement on his conviction that for history to be meaningful, historians must make it so. Instead of concentrating on documenting a sequence of events or debating the credibility of sources, Collingwood maintained that history should concentrate on three objectives: looking for a deeper and clearer insight into the conditions that render historical knowledge possible, elucidating the presuppositions upon which historical inquires are founded, and clarifying the principles according to which these inquiries proceed. Failure to formalize a philosophical framework reduced history to chaos, which, to Collingwood, was unacceptable. Inspired by such notable philosophers as Wilhelm Dilthey and Benedetto Croce, Collingwood abandoned the prevailing desire of some scholars to provide an all-embracing synoptic vision of the entire historical process and concerned himself, instead, with an understanding and justification of historical procedures.

The best single source on Collingwood's philosophy of history is his posthumously published treatise *The Idea of History*, which contains seven essays written between 1935 and 1939. In this seminal work, Collingwood maintained that true history exists only when the historian is able to relive the past in his own mind. He formulated his idea of history in reaction to what he termed "scissors-and-paste" history or the "commonsense" approach, which defined history as knowledge of the past based on the report of someone who actually observed the occurrence. The observer was deemed the "authority" and the believer was the historian. Although Collingwood recognized the importance of credible sources, he argued that historical events are understandable only when historians penetrated the mind of past actors. It is only when historians immerse themselves in the thought patterns of the past and rethink the past in terms of their own experiences that the significance and patterns of past civilizations can be discovered. Contrary to the commonsense view of history, Collingwood's scheme made historians their own "authorities" in that they are the interpreters of the evidence.

History is far more than the stringing together of names, dates, places, and events from carefully studied primary sources. Obviously historical evidence must be credible, but as Collingwood argued, it is not enough for historians to know "exact chronology" because each event in history is an action and historians must think their way into the action. Historians must discern the thought of their agent. In *The Idea of History*, Collingwood states, "Man is regarded as the only animal that thinks, or thinks enough, and clearly enough, to render his actions the expression of his thoughts." When historians note that a fortress has been built, the fortress becomes a document to be read. Actions, like written documents, express reflective thought that must be interpreted. When historians try to determine the purpose of the fortress, they are seeking to enter the mind of the person who built it. Historians must look "through" events in history to ascertain the thoughts within them, just as historians must look "through" a document to deduce the thoughts of the writer. Stated in its briefest form, history to Collingwood was the study of *res gestae*, or things done by human beings in the past. The subject matter of history is reflective thought—acts done on purpose. Thus, Collingwood saw history as a set of human actions that were expressive of rational thought or as a science of thought that dealt with the rational aspects of human activity.

Collingwood's ideas on the "inside-outside" theory of historical action shed light on his perceptions regarding the reconstruction of the past. Historians investigating any historical event need to distinguish between what may be called the "outside" and the "inside" of the event. For Collingwood, the "outside" of an event includes that which can be described in terms of bodies and their movement: For example, Julius Caesar and his army crossed the Rubicon on a specific day, or Caesar was slain on the floor of the Roman senate. The "inside" of these events can be explained only in terms of "thought," such as Caesar's willful defiance of Roman law and the clashing of constitutional viewpoints between Caesar and his assassins. Historians are never to limit themselves to one of these concerns to the exclusion of the other. Those historians whose task begins and ends with the discovering of the "outside" of an event produce an incomplete history. Every event is an action, and historians must think their way into the action to become part of the thought process of the actors. Human actions are the grist of history, and these actions are both discernable and understandable when they are perceived to be rational efforts enacted by the agents of history to solve problems of significance to them. Historians must use their own powers of rational action to reconstruct a spatiotemporal picture of the past in which they are able to reenact the thought that went into the events being described. In other words, to understand the drafting of the U.S. Constitution, it is necessary to reenact the thoughts of the framers of the Constitution. For Collingwood, this is an achievable exercise because each person has the capacity to think within any given culture.

Influence

Collingwood's labors to establish a philosophy of history bore fruit. His philosophy of history sparked a major controversy among his successors regarding the role of historians. Two of the major criticisms of Collingwood's philosophy of history involve the degree of autonomy he assigned to historians in their reconstruction of the past and the process whereby the past is reconstructed. As stated in *The Idea of History*, historians have no other authority than themselves. The "thoughts" and "ideas" of the historian are "autonomous, self-authorizing, and possessed of criterion to which his so-called authorities [primary sources] must conform and by reference to which they are criticized." The historian alone decides what criteria and sources will be used to explain the events of the past. Also, where gaps exist because of the absence of source material, it is the historian who fills the gaps based on the individual's own methodological principles.

With regard to reconstructing the past, Collingwood states that historians infer what happened in the past by means of their "a priori imagination." Stated another way, historians' reconstruction of the past is the work of their imagination, and it is a priori, or necessary. His use of "a priori" has a double meaning. First, when historians use their imagination to fill gaps, the interpolations must be logically deduced from the sources, whether written documents or the actions of the agents. Second, the act of interpolation is essential for any historical knowledge to be discovered. Using their a priori imagination, historians create a mental picture of the past and then evaluate sources based on how they conform to their imagined picture.

When Collingwood refers to the reconstruction of the past as "imagination," he does not mean that it is fictitious. If historians know from their sources that an army was in one location on a given date and in another location at a later date, they must "imagine" that a journey has occurred. The use of the imagination must be limited, however, to what the evidence allows as a possibility. For Collingwood, the imagination was an ontological condition for understanding and without it, historical knowledge would be impossible. This does not mean, as some critics have suggested, that Collingwood's philosophy of history is based in radical subjectivity, as he qualifies the autonomy of the historian and the use of the imagination.

Although Collingwood's philosophy of history appears to be individualistic, making each person his own historian, this must be qualified. Human action, he maintained, is predicated on human experience, but each society accepts certain absolutes (worldviews) that serve as a framework for human experience. People rarely question their own worldviews, but use these absolute presuppositions to address specific problems. Tribespeople perceived the natural world to be controlled by the actions of gods, and modern societies entertain a mechanistic view of the world, whereby everything has a natural explanation. For historians to be able to reenact the past, they must learn to think within the framework of the past, adopting their absolutes for the purpose of reenacting the thoughts that led the agent to provide certain solutions to existing problems.

Collingwood's efforts to explain "what is history" and describe the role of the historian in the reconstruction of history were crucial to the establishment of the philosophy of history as a discipline in the twentieth century.

Wayne M. Bledsoe

An Essay on Metaphysics

Type of philosophy: Epistemology, philosophy of history
First published: 1940
Principal ideas advanced:

◇ Any intelligible statement finally rests upon certain absolute presuppositions.
◇ Ordinary presuppositions are either true or false, but absolute presuppositions are neither true nor false, for they are not factual.
◇ Although it is a mistake to treat absolute presuppositions (such as the belief in the uniformity of nature) as if they were factual propositions to be confirmed by sense experience, it is also a mistake to suppose metaphysics impossible and to narrow rational investigation to empirical inquiry.
◇ The metaphysician is a kind of historian whose task it is to discover absolute presuppositions in the thought of others.

In designating his philosophical books "essays," R. G. Collingwood, who preserved a keen sense for etymologies, meant to imply that they were not general "treatises," and he made no claim either to comprehensiveness or to system. On the contrary, each essay was written to make a special point.

These remarks apply to the work at hand, both to its outline and to its texture. It is far from being a "metaphysical" book, in the usual sense of that word. Instead of propounding the author's metaphysics, it is a lively statement of the importance of metaphysics, sharpened by a polemic against certain antimetaphysical tendencies, and it is enforced by three extended illustrations (which make up half of the volume).

Absolute Presuppositions

Collingwood argued that any intelligible statement, if fully fathomed, rests upon a series of presuppositions that terminate in one or more absolute presuppositions. This is not a mere matter of fact but a consequence of the nature of the understanding itself. Not merely philosophy, but everything that is included under science (taken in the sense of systematic thought about a determinate subject matter) involves logical or a priori elements.

Writing on board a freighter, Collingwood took as an example a cord that the crew had stretched above the deck. He recognized it as being a clothesline. However, this supposition presupposes another thought, namely, that the line was put there on purpose. Had this assumption not been made, the thought that identified it as a clothesline would never have occurred. In other words, every thought that can be put into words is the answer to some question and can be understood only if the question is sensible. However, a sensible question rests upon other thoughts that, if put into words, are likewise answers to questions—and so on, until one finally comes to a thought that is not the answer to any question. It is an absolute presupposition.

Inquiries and Metaphysics

Collingwood is almost as well known as a historian (of Roman Britain) as he is as a philosopher, a circumstance that shaped his views on metaphysics. As an excavator, he formulated and was instrumental in giving currency to the methodological principle: Never dig except to find the answer to a question. As a historian, he brought new clarity to the concept that the only subject matter of history is the thoughts of people who lived in the past. "Why did Caesar invade Britain? Did he achieve his purpose? If not, what determined him to conclude the campaign?" Armed with questions of this sort, the archaeologist becomes something more than an antiquarian and the historian something more than an editor of texts: They become scientists. They increase the store of relevant knowledge by following philosopher Francis Bacon's advice about interrogating nature.

Collingwood relates that it was this kind of intellectual discipline that overthrew in his mind the claims of the Oxford realists under whom he had studied philosophy. He abandoned their claim that knowledge is made up of simple truths that are independent of each other and immediately knowable; he maintained, to the contrary, that a fact is meaningful only as it fits into an inquiry. Moreover, he argued, a particular inquiry is always part of a more comprehensive undertaking—civilization itself—that gives it backing and direction, for at any given moment, people of a living culture are engaged in solving the problems of human existence, starting from certain beliefs and commitments. These considerations are commonly called metaphysics, after the treatise by Greek philosopher Aristotle in which they were first systematically considered.

In Aristotle's thinking, according to Collingwood, two quite different inquiries are confused. Aristotle perfected the logic of classification by genus and species. He saw that at the bottom of the table there must be *infimae species* that are fully differentiated and that, by the same logic, at the top there must be a *summum genus*, which, because it is completely undifferentiated, may be designated by the term Pure Being. In a different context, Aristotle dealt with the structure of the sciences. Aristotle understood—much better than the philosopher Plato—the necessity of delimiting a particular subject matter and defining the presuppositions that it involves. He saw that this task was a distinct one that required a new science to deal with it, which he called first philoso-

phy, wisdom, or theology. At this point, according to Collingwood, Aristotle made a mistake. Influenced excessively by the ontological tradition from Parmenides to Plato, Aristotle supposed that the first principles of the sciences could be identified with the Pure Being of his logic of classification. In Collingwood's view, in the history of Western philosophy, metaphysics has had great difficulty extricating itself from this confusion, and philosopher Immanuel Kant's *Kritik der reinen Vernunft* (1781; *The Critique of Pure Reason*, 1838) is a notable attempt to set it free. Kant's transcendental aesthetic and the analytic pursue the proper task of metaphysics, which is seeking for absolute presuppositions; and the transcendental dialectic exposes the fallacies of pseudometaphysics, which seeks to fit these absolute matters into a conditional scheme of things.

Antimetaphysics

There is a significant agreement, at this point, between Collingwood and various present-day antimetaphysical groups. He insists that much of what is traditionally called metaphysics is bad science because it seeks to treat transcendental issues as matters of fact. Ordinary presuppositions are factual: They can be stated as propositions and are either true or false. However, absolute presuppositions are not factual: They do not answer any question and are neither true nor false. Properly speaking, they are not propositions at all.

However, if Collingwood agrees with the realists and positivists in assailing the claims of ordinary metaphysics, his emphasis on the importance of absolute presuppositions represents a significant protest against this group. In his opinion, their radical empiricism is a species of antiintellectualism. Such empiricism accounts for truths such as: "This is the back of my hand," but it breaks down when called upon to account for complex truths that make up natural science, not to speak of ethics and politics. He sees it as part of a dangerous tendency in the contemporary world that he broadly designates as irrationalism and, in its philosophical expression, as antimetaphysics.

The second part of *An Essay on Metaphysics* is given over to the discussion of two characteristic expressions of this antimetaphysical tendency. The first is pseudopsychology. Collingwood has no quarrel with psychology as long as it sticks to its subject. It began as a distinct science when sixteenth century thought began to insist on a sharp distinction between mental (logical) and physiological (mechanical) explanations of human conduct. Emotion or feeling did not seem to fit in either of these realms; therefore, psychology arose to deal with this third realm. Properly, psychology deals with problems of motivation that cannot be accounted for by either mechanical or rational means; however, according to Collingwood, these problems do not include those of ethics, aesthetics, and religion. These are rational pursuits, each with its own logic and presuppositions. They are mental sciences that fall outside the province of psychology. Collingwood states that these pursuits have been included under psychology partly because of what Collingwood terms the irrational tendency of the nineteenth century, describing it as "a kind of epidemic withering of belief in the importance of truth." He cites Sigmund Freud's *Totem und Tabu* (1913; *Totem and Taboo*, 1919) as an example of the errors and confusions that arise when a great psychoanalyst tries to apply psychological techniques to a rational pursuit. If the presumptions of psychology are not turned back, science itself is doomed. Citing at length three instances of careless thinking to be found in standard psychology books, Collingwood calls psychology a deliberate conspiracy to undermine scientific habits.

The other characteristic expression of antimetaphysics is positivism. Collingwood admits that it has greater respect than does psychology for the autonomy of humanity's rational activity; but in maintaining that science is made up entirely of empirical truths, it is a victim of the same irrationalist infection. Philosopher John Stuart Mill set the pattern when he maintained that the principle of uniformity in nature is an inductive inference, whereas it is the absolute presupposition on which induction depends. Philosopher Francis Herbert Bradley, according to Collingwood, disclosed his own positivist affinities when he defined metaphysics as "the finding of bad reasons for what we believe on instinct." Mill saw rightly enough that the science of his day presupposed belief in the uniformity of nature;

however, he introduced radical incoherence when he treated it as a proposition that must be verified by experience.

The irrationalist propensities of positivism become most clear, however, in the dictum of the logical positivists that any proposition that cannot be verified by appeal to observed facts is nonsensical. That is to say, because they cannot be treated as factual statements, the absolute presuppositions of science, ethics, and politics are subrational. Collingwood agrees with A. J. Ayer's strictures on pseudometaphysics (a science that would treat absolute presuppositions as if they were facts), but he blames Ayer for what seems to him to be merely a petulant attack arising from the lunatic fear that in some way metaphysics is a threat to science. The threat that Collingwood sees is the habit of mind that narrows rational investigation to the limits of sense verification.

Theology and Science

The remainder of the book is given to three examples that illustrate the thesis that metaphysics is the science of absolute presuppositions. The first is an illuminating account of the role theology has played in Western intellectual history. One of the names that Aristotle gave to the science of first principles was "theology." According to Collingwood, the classic concern of Greek philosophy was to formulate the new convictions that had replaced the older Homeric beliefs. Thales is important because he gave expression to the new belief that the multiform spheres of nature are at bottom one, and Heraclitus because he saw that all change is according to law. These, according to Aristotle, are *divine* matters. Far from being hostile to art, ethics, and knowledge, these matters were the foundations upon which Greek achievement rested. They were also the measure of its limitations. The failure of the Greek polis and the later collapse of the Roman Empire are traced by Collingwood to metaphysical causes; that is, to inadequacies in the fundamental axioms of the Hellenic mind. People could not overcome the impression that the world falls into irreconcilable parts: necessity and contingency, eternity and time, or virtue and fortune. The sense of the contradictions in human existence that this worldview entailed left people unnerved in the face of the progressively greater challenges to which their own achievements gave rise.

When Christianity arrived, it offered a different metaphysics. According to Collingwood, Saint Athanasius and Saint Augustine are only the best known of a number of first-rank intellects who would have been drowned in a sea of trivialities if they had not been able to extract from the Gospel the basis for a new science. Their Trinitarian statements are properly understood as a highly fruitful solution to the metaphysical problem that had defeated the Greeks. In this connection, Collingwood chides English historian Edward Gibbon, claiming that he obscured an important truth in order to be clever. Gibbon said that the doctrine of the Logos was taught in the school of Alexandria in 300 B.C.E. and revealed to the Apostle John in 97 C.E. As Collingwood points out, Gibbon took this fact from Augustine, but he omitted the point that Augustine went on to make and that proved the key to Christianity's success; namely, that the Christians for the first time bridged the chasm between time and eternity, inasmuch as the Logos was made flesh. One must, Collingwood says, "regret the slipshod way in which Gibbon speaks of Plato as having 'marvelously anticipated one of the most surprising discoveries of the Christian revelation.'"

Collingwood maintains that Christian theology not only provided a rallying point for good minds during the decline and Fall of Rome but also furnished the fundamental assumptions that enabled European science to make significant advances over that of the Greeks. In part, Aristotle's presuppositions agree with those of modern humanity—that there is one god and that there are many modes of that god's activities—but they also disagree, notably on the question as to the origin of motion, which Aristotle tried to explain but which modern science takes as a presupposition. In this connection, Collingwood analyzes the statement of belief in the Trinity. That this statement contains the words "I believe" indicates from the very first that it is not a proposition but a presupposition. The doctrine of a single god, in whom, however, is contained not only the principle of being but also those of order and of motion, places all these severally and together on the plane of absolute presuppositions. According to Collingwood, this doctrine, and not the metaphysics of Pythagoras, Plato, Aristotle, or

Plotinus, provided the indispensable foundation upon which Galileo and Isaac Newton founded modern science.

Metaphysics as a Science

In Collingwood's view, it is not the job of metaphysicians to say what absolute presuppositions one should or should not hold. Their business is merely to discover the presuppositions, and they are most likely to find them not in the writings of philosophers but in those of constructive workers in the various fields of human interest such as physics or law. Essentially, metaphysicians are historians—for it makes no difference whether one investigates the "so-called past" or the "so-called present." In either case, one has to do firsthand historical work, and the things one studies—namely, absolute presuppositions—are historical facts. It is in this way that metaphysics takes its place among the sciences. Collingwood states that an absolute presupposition, taken in relation to the truths based upon it, is not a truth; however, viewed historically, it is. In order to preserve the distinction, Collingwood provides a special rubric to be applied to every metaphysical proposition: "In such and such a phase of scientific thought it is (or was) absolutely presupposed that. . . ." The statement as a whole is a proposition that may be true or false.

Taken in this way, metaphysics plays the same important role as any other kind of history: namely, to help people understand the human enterprise. According to Collingwood, when metaphysics studies the present, it has the special utility of disarming reactionary thinkers who, because of inattention to historical tensions, remain wedded to the errors of the past. Such reactionaries can be found among pseudometaphysicians, who are committed to eternal truths and deductive proofs. However, they can also be found among antimetaphysicians, many of whom, in their ignorance of the role played by absolute presuppositions, perpetuate outmoded assumptions under the guise of intuitions or inferences. Collingwood cites examples of new realists and analysts who continue to affirm the "law of causation." For instance, John Wisdom states, "I do not know *how* we know that things are as they are because they were as they were. However, *we* do know it." Wisdom's "we," says Collingwood, can only be a group or society of persons whose reverence for the past has blinded them to the developments of twentieth century science. The group does not include contemporary natural scientists or those philosophers who understand what the natural scientists are doing. He quotes Bertrand Russell: "The law of causality, I believe, like much that passes muster among philosophers, is a relic of a bygone age, surviving, like the monarchy, only because it is erroneously supposed to do no harm."

In Collingwood's opinion, the sciences (both natural and historical) are flourishing, and prospects for their growth were never more promising—if the anti-intellectual threat does not overpower them. He sees two great danger spots: a political order in which reason is replaced by emotion and an academic atmosphere in which pseudosciences are nurtured alongside the true sciences. Collingwood feels it is his duty to warn people of the danger, as he does in this work.

Jean Faurot

Additional Reading

Boucher, David. "The Significance of R. G. Collingwood's *Principles of History*." *Journal of the History of Ideas* 58, no. 2 (April, 1997): 309-330. Boucher, from the University of Wales, Swansea, provides a very interesting and informative account of the mysteries surrounding Collingwood's missing manuscript, *Principles of History*, which was discovered in 1995. His analysis of the manuscript helps elucidate Collingwood's philosophy of history while providing interpretations that are likely to ignite new controversy.

Dobbins, William, ed. *Essays in the Philosophy of History: R. G. Collingwood*. New York: McGraw-Hill Paperbacks, 1966. These eight essays focus on Collingwood's philosophy of history and include a discussion of the philosopher's criticism of Benedetto Croce's philosophy of history. The editor's introduction provides a good, brief account of Collingwood's life.

Dray, W. H. *Re-enactment and History*. New York: Oxford University Press, 1995. This work focuses on Collingwood's concept of re-enactment, a central part of his philosophy of history.

Johnson, Peter. *R. G. Collingwood: An Introduction*. Bristol, England: Thames Press, 1997. This biography incorporates some of the latest discoveries and theories regarding Collingwood's work.

Mink, Louis O. *Mind, History, and Dialectic*. Bloomington: The University of Indiana, 1969. Some critics of Collingwood have focused on his use of a priori imagination as the criterion by which historians evaluate and criticize sources. Mink sees a priori imagination as an absolute presupposition of history.

Ridley, Aaron. *R. G. Collingwood*. New York: Routledge, 1999. An excellent biographical introduction to the thoughts of the philosopher, clearly presented and requiring no special background. Bibliography.

Rubinoff, Lionel. *Collingwood and the Reform of Metaphysics*. Toronto: University of Toronto Press, 1970. This work deals with the issue of a priori imagination as a criterion for evaluating historical sources.

Wayne M. Bledsoe

Auguste Comte

Comte was the father of positivism, a philosophy that saw the evolution of new ideas as the shaping force in history and regarded the empirical method of science as the only valid basis of knowledge. Comte sought to extend the method of science to the study of humankind, coining the word "sociology."

Principal philosophical works: *Considerations sur le pouvoir spirituel*, 1826; *Cours de philosophie positive*, 1830-1842 (6 volumes; *The Positive Philosophy of Auguste Comte*, 1853); *Discours sur l'esprit positif*, 1844 (*A Discourse on the Positive Spirit*, 1903); *Système de politique positive*, 1851-1854 (4 volumes; *System of Positive Polity*, 1875-1877); *Catéchisme positiviste*, 1852 (*The Catechism of Positive Religion*, 1858); *Synthèse subjective*, 1856.

Born: January 19, 1798; Montpellier, France
Died: September 5, 1857; Paris, France

Early Life

Isidore-Auguste-Marie-François-Xavier Comte, the eldest of four children, was born in the French university town of Montpellier on January 19, 1798. His father, Louis-Auguste Comte, was a tax official, a man of strict habits and narrow interests; his mother, Félicité-Rosalie Boyer, twelve years older than her husband, was a warm, emotional person who devoted her life to her children. Both parents were devout Catholics and royalists.

Young Comte was nearsighted and small—his head and trunk seemed too large for his limbs. He had an extraordinary memory, however, and proved to be a brilliant student in the local *lycée*, winning prizes in Latin and mathematics, on occasion substituting for his teacher. At the age of fifteen, he was admitted to the prestigious École Polytechnique in Paris. There his diligence and acuteness led his awed classmates to nickname him "the philosopher." Napoleon I had given this school, like Comte's *lycée*, a military tone and discipline. Yet Comte, who at age fourteen had already rebelled against the religion of his parents by becoming an atheist, was one of the most unruly students at the school. Comte was a prominent spokesperson for the students when

they supported Napoleon during his futile attempt to regain control of France in 1815. Later, Comte was judged by authorities to be a ringleader of a student effort to oust an unpopular professor, a conflict so heated that it served as a pretext for temporarily closing the school. He was sent home and placed under police surveillance.

In 1817, Comte returned to Paris, studying independently and tutoring students in mathematics to support himself. The possibility of an offer to teach in a new American polytechnical school led Comte to immerse himself in the writings of Thomas Paine and Benjamin Franklin, but the project was not funded. Comte therefore became secretary to the exuberant social philosopher Claude-Henri Rouvroy, comte de Saint-Simon, borrowing the broad outlines of many of his own later doctrines while writing essays and articles that appeared under Saint-Simon's name. Comte served Saint-Simon for seven years but was uncomfortable with the religious bent of Saint-Simon's late writings and believed that his social theory needed a more systematic theoretical foundation. A critical preface by Saint-Simon to an essay Comte published under his own name precipitated the end of the relationship in 1824.

By then, the headstrong Comte had dropped his first name, Isidore, in favor of Auguste; had fathered, by an Italian woman, an illegitimate daughter who would die at the age of nine; and was living with Caroline Massin (herself the offspring of an unmarried provincial actress), whom he had known for three years and would marry in 1825. He praised her kindness, grace, wit, and cheerful disposition; in her mid-teens, she had been sold by her mother to a young lawyer and was by this time a registered prostitute. It was partly to help her get her name off police rolls that he agreed to the marriage. Their union was marred by his seeming indifference to their straitened economic circumstances and her occasional disappearances. A final separation came in 1842. Nevertheless, she provided needed support through the difficult period when he produced his most important work, the six-volume *The Positive Philosophy of Auguste Comte*. The most important part of this support came shortly after he had begun the series of seventy-two lectures out of which this book grew, when he had a nervous breakdown so severe that he was incapacitated for more than a year (1826-1827), was judged incurably insane by one physician, and attempted suicide.

Auguste Comte. *(Library of Congress)*

Life's Work

Comte wanted to be a philosopher-prophet, like Francis Bacon, Nicolas Condorcet, or his mentor Saint-Simon. Living in an era scarred by deep social antagonisms and warring ideologies, he dreamed of creating a persuasive philosophical synthesis that could restore both spiritual and social order to European society. Such solid intellectual underpinning was lacking, he believed, in Saint-Simon's thought. Comte reasoned that if the method of science could be extended to every aspect of life, the intellectual unity that had characterized medieval Europe could be restored on a more lasting basis, and unity of thought would bring social order.

Comte interpreted the rise of science and its extension to the study of humankind in the context of a general theory of human intellectual development he borrowed, via Saint-Simon, from the eighteenth century economist and statesman Jacques Turgot. The "law of the three stages" held that as positive knowledge of nature gradually replaces earlier tendencies to attribute much in life to unseen powers, thought moves from a theological to a metaphysical stage, replacing imagined divinities with nonobservable abstractions. Yet they too fall to skepticism, and a scientific or positive outlook triumphs.

For Comte, this concept constituted a general theory of history, accounting for institutional as well as intellectual development. Thus, he held that theological societies have military political systems; metaphysical societies have a juristic social organization; and positivist societies have an industrial polity. A positivist approach to phenomena came first in the simple sciences, such as astronomy and physics, while metaphysical or even theological modes of thought linger where phenomena are more complex. Because sciences dealing with the latter must rest on the foundation of more general, simpler ones, of necessity new positive sciences emerged in the following order: mathematics, astronomy, physics, chemistry, biology, physiology, and sociology. Although the later volumes of the book contain many prescriptive judgments about the future needs of society that now would not be termed scientific, *The Positive Philosophy of Auguste Comte* was a tour de force, a landmark in both philosophy and the historical study of science.

With its publication and the growth of his reputation, Comte secured academic posts at the Institut Laville and the École Polytechnique. His outspoken criticisms of some academicians at École Polytechnique led to the rejection of his candidacy for a chair there. He retaliated by appealing to European public opinion through a bitter attack on his opponents in the preface of the last volume of *The Positive Philosophy of Auguste Comte*, an action that brought his final break with Caroline and cost him his positions. His financial difficulties led admirers in both France and England (including John Stuart Mill, who later became a critic) to raise funds on his behalf.

Comte lived modestly in his last years. The most significant episode in this period was a passionate emotional relationship with a beautiful but unhappy and ill young woman, Clotilde de Vaux. He had known her only a year and a half when she died in the spring of 1846 from tuberculosis, yet her memory absorbed him through his remaining years. He dedicated his late work to her, including a second monumental book, the four-volume *System of Positive Polity*. He declared that it was she who had taught him the importance of feelings.

System of Positive Polity is a work that prophesies in great detail the future of Western society.

Its vision is in part a realization of the plan of Comte's youth, but it reveals a remarkable shift in emphasis from reason and scientific understanding to the emotions. He had come to regard as futile his earlier dream of achieving intellectual unity through science. In this work, he made humanity's wants (morality) the foundation for intellectual unity in positivism. The emphasis in this work had been presaged in his 1826 work, *Considerations sur le pouvoir spirituel* (considerations on spiritual power), in which he wrote that the Catholic Church, shorn of its supernaturalism, might provide an ideal structural model for positivist society. It was probably Comte's intense feelings for de Vaux that brought this hitherto inveterate rationalist to emphasize the heart above intelligence and knowledge and to prescribe a cult of womanhood as the emotional center of his secular religion.

The object of worship in this system, which T. H. Huxley dubbed Catholicism minus Christianity, was humanity itself: past, present, and future. Scientist-priests were to control both religion and education, positivist in content, which would be the foundation of the new social order. Actual political power, Comte declared, would rest with bankers and industrialists, whom economic developments were already thrusting to the fore. They would, however, operate under the spiritual guidance of the priests. The new industrial working class, its morals strengthened by religion and examples of feminine virtue, would accept the dominion of the industrialists but also give full backing to the priests. The latter, as shapers of powerful public opinion, would ensure that the workers' interests were safeguarded.

Thus, Comte, who earlier had declared the intellect his lord, now saw feelings, not reason, as the key to social unity. He contended that man has a benevolent instinct—coining the word "altruism" to describe it—but that it is weak unless nurtured by good institutions. This need provided Comte a rationale for dictating the features of his positivist utopia in obsessive detail, from career paths to private devotions, from indissoluble marriage and perpetual widowhood to the particular heroes of human progress who were to be honored on each day of the (thirteen-month) positivist calendar.

Influence

Like many in his age, including his German contemporary Georg Wilhelm Friedrich Hegel, Comte was a visionary, a self-proclaimed prophet for the ages who believed that he had unveiled profound truths with sweeping social implications. As was true of most other utopian visionaries, his concrete predictions were off the mark. Therefore, while many were dazzled by the younger Comte's brilliance as an interpreter of the evolution of science and defender of its method in all realms of thought, the impact of his later writings was quite limited. Whereas a number of intellectuals, including Hippolyte-Adolphe Taine, Ernest Renan, and the logical positivists of the twentieth century, inherited his skepticism about nonempirical thinking, his religion of humanity was essentially stillborn, even though it championed the humanism made popular by the Enlightenment. In emphasizing the limits of reason and the importance of emotions, he was at one with the Romantic movement, as were many other major writers of the nineteenth century. His sympathy for medieval institutions, if not medieval belief, was also widely shared by other intellectuals of his time, particularly in literature and art—it was the period of writer Sir Walter Scott and Gothic revival, the period when the works of Dante Alighieri (whom Comte much admired) were finally translated into English.

Comte's humorless preoccupation with order and perfection was not well suited to winning for him a broad and enthusiastic following. He antagonized onetime supporters such as Mill with his obsession with ordering—down to the level of minute details of thought and feeling, artistic creation, and religious devotion—the life of positivist society, for which he planned to be the high priest. His indifference to democracy and individual freedom separated him from the liberals of his day. His interest in old forms without old content alienated conservatives, and he had no interest in the growing nationalism that was to provide yet another basis for ideology in the decades that followed him. Yet, curiously, his thought had an affinity to a modern development for which he could have had little sympathy. In his obsession with uniformity and order, his vision of a society that sought to control every facet

of humanity's intellectual and emotional life for social ends dictated by a small elite group, he was a precursor of the totalitarian movements of the twentieth century.

R. Craig Philips

The Positive Philosophy of Auguste Comte

Type of philosophy: Epistemology, ethics, social philosophy

First published: Cours de philosophie positive, 1830-1842 (6 volumes; English translation, 1853)

Principal ideas advanced:

◊ Social dynamics is the science of history; positive philosophy provides a law of three stages to make historical facts significant.

◊ In the *theological* state of a society, people invent gods and arrange society accordingly, and priests rule; in the *metaphysical* stage, intellect deifies itself, authority is challenged, religion becomes sectarian, and individuals abandon their social responsibilities; in the *positive* stage, the positive sciences provide certainties that make order possible, inspire a moral regeneration, and make social concerns primary for all.

◊ Sociology completes the body of philosophy by tracing out the unity to be found in the various sciences.

◊ The natural sciences, like human societies and people themselves, have passed through the theological, metaphysical, and positive stages.

◊ The various sciences can be arranged according to their degree of complexity and their dependence on others; beginning with the most general (after mathematics, which is not a natural science), the order is astronomy, physics, chemistry, biology, physiology, and sociology.

Auguste Comte had two distinct aims in writing *The Positive Philosophy of Auguste Comte*. The first and "special" aim was to put the study of society on a positive foundation like those on which the natural sciences rested. The second and "general" aim was to review the natural sciences in order to show that they are not independent of one another but are "all branches from the same trunk." The two aims are inseparable.

Comte divided the study of society—sociology or "social physics," as he called it—into two parts, following a distinction that he believed runs through all the sciences: social statics and social dynamics. The former seems not to have interested him especially. He maintained that in its broader aspects, at least, it was deducible from human physiology, which demands that people live in society, that they form families, and that they obey political authorities. On these grounds, he held that woman is inferior to man and bound to subservience, and that some people and races are constitutionally suited to obey and others to command.

However, Comte dealt with these matters only in passing. His interest was not so much in the generic traits that are found in all human societies as in the laws that govern the transition of a society from one condition to another. This is what he intended by the term "social dynamics." His work was to be nothing less than a science of history. History, said Comte, had compiled many facts but had been unable to contribute anything of importance to understanding humankind's condition because, like the data of meteorology, its facts needed a law to become significant. Comte thought that he had discovered that law; he called it the "law of the three stages."

The Law of the Three Stages
According to this law, in the first, or *theological*, stage, people invent gods in order to explain the world to themselves, and in so doing, they create the conditions that make possible the specifically human kind of society. Belief in gods gives people some purpose in living beyond the satisfaction of mere bodily wants. At first, the gods are merely tribal fetishes, which do not demand much by way of social organization. As these are exchanged for astral deities, and eventually for a single god, discipline and order are imposed on the whole community. Authority characteristically comes to be vested in a priesthood. A military caste arises, with responsibility for defense, and agricultural labor becomes the foundation of the economy. From the sociological point of view, it is a happy, prosperous condition. A

common faith and goal give coherence and strength to the community.

There is, however, a serpent in the garden. The intellectual turn of mind that made people invent the gods is never content with its creation. Turning critical, it denatures divinity into a set of first principles and eternal essences. Comte called this the *metaphysical* stage. Intellect practically deifies itself, owning allegiance only to truths of reason. Not only theological beliefs but theological institutions come under criticism. The principle of authority is challenged, and notions of equality and popular sovereignty are offered in its place. As the new attitude permeates the masses, individuals abandon their social responsibilities and compete with one another to improve their private conditions. Religion becomes sectarian; peasants drift to the cities; military might declines. Sociologically, it is a negative moment, a time of dissolution and decay.

According to Comte, these two stages have appeared again and again in the history of the world, and hitherto there has been no way of saving a society that has passed into the metaphysical stage. However, modern Western civilization has the means of breaking out of the old cycle. The negative moment, represented in European history by the Reformation, the Renaissance, and the Enlightenment, has marked the end of a Catholic-dominated culture and, of itself, promises nothing but moral and political chaos. Coincident with the rise of libertarian thinking and laissez-faire economics and politics, however, the positive sciences have also made great gains. It is the assured results of these latter that, according to Comte, provide a remedy for metaphysics and make it possible for the human mind to move forward into a new *positive* stage. Like the theological stage, it will be a time when people will know what to believe. This time, however, there will be no illusion about it— and no chance that the certainties will be overthrown.

The new certainties will make possible a reorganization of society, provide a rational system of command, and inspire complete devotion in the hearts of the people. A moral regeneration will make coercive government almost a superfluity. Such regulation of life as the new society requires will rest with a managerial class arising out of industry, while ultimate authority will reside in a new spiritual class, the positive philosophers. Meanwhile, people will have cast away private ambition and personal rivalry and will have learned to consider all functions as social. They will see the "public utility in the humblest office of cooperation, no less truly than in the loftiest function of government," and will feel "as the soldier feels in the discharge of his humblest duty, the dignity of public service, and the honor of a share in the action of the general economy."

Comte devoted hundreds of pages to the analysis of Western history along the lines indicated. His work is, from one point of view, a speculative undertaking. He considered that he had put history on an indisputably scientific foundation with his theory of evolution.

It certainly appears to me that the whole course of human history affords so decisive a verification of my theory of evolution that no essential law of natural philosophy is more fully demonstrated. From the earliest beginnings of civilization to the present state of the most advanced nations, this theory has explained, consistently and dispassionately, the character of all the great phases of humanity; the participation of each in the perdurable common development, and their precise filiation; so as to introduce perfect unity and rigorous continuity into this vast spectacle that otherwise appears desultory and confused. A law that fulfils such conditions must be regarded as no philosophical pastime, but as the abstract expression of the general reality.

From another point of view, however, this Herculean labor was a blueprint for a Brave New World. A youthful disciple of utopian socialist Claude-Henri Rouvroy, comte de Saint-Simon, Comte had as his ultimate purpose in developing the positive philosophy the moral and spiritual regeneration of the West. He believed that by providing an infallible system of truth, he was doing the one thing that could bring this regeneration to pass.

Sociology and the Natural Sciences

The second aspect of Comte's philosophy was his review of the natural sciences. All the sciences,

with the exception of sociology, had already achieved the status of positive knowledge in Comte's time, but their true significance could not be discerned without sociology because, according to Comte, it was a function of the positivist philosopher (himself a sociologist) to trace out the unities and analogies of the sciences. Thus, sociology completes the body of philosophy, not merely by being the last of the sciences but by "showing that the various sciences are branches from a single trunk; and thereby giving a character of unity to the variety of special studies that are now scattered abroad in a fatal dispersion." Had people been endowed with an angelic intelligence, all the sciences would have sprung into being at the same time, and their hierarchical relation would be evident in an a priori fashion. However, because people have slowly and painfully arrived at the truth, the only intelligible account of the relationship between the sciences is the empirical one that traces their development. Thus, "all scientific speculations whatever, in as far as they are human labors, must necessarily be subordinated to the true general theory of human evolution," which, being the proper study of sociology, is the warrant for "the legitimate general intervention of true social science in all possible classes of human speculation."

Comte's science of history declared that the social evolution of humankind is a function of intellectual evolution and that, broadly speaking, the knowledge of humankind has passed through three stages—theological, metaphysical, and positive. It is not surprising, therefore, that the same cycle governs the development of particular sciences as governs the evolution of knowledge as a whole.

According to Comte, this development is clear on empirical grounds. Every science that has reached the positive stage bears the marks of having passed through the others. Astronomy, for example, became truly scientific in Hellenistic times, when observations of the heavens were first coordinated by means of geometrical principles. However, myth and astrology are reminders of times when celestial phenomena were explained in terms first of divine will and afterward of impersonal fate. In fact, the more primitive beliefs linger among less progressive parts of the population; according to Comte, they are recapitulated in the development of the mind of each civilized person, who in childhood is a theologian, in youth a metaphysician, and in adulthood a natural philosopher.

However, Comte held that the empirical account could be supported by reflection and that it is a priori evident (*post factum*) that knowledge must pass through three stages. Like philosopher Francis Bacon, he held it as a fundamental principle that mere facts are not sufficient to arrive at truth—the mind must form theories; but because intelligent theories cannot be formed without facts, one seems to be confronted with a vicious circle. At least, according to Comte, here is the reason why primitive people did not arrive at scientific truth. Caught, as it were, "between the necessity of observing facts in order to form a theory, and having a theory in order to observe facts, the human mind would have been entangled in a vicious circle but for the natural opening afforded by theological conceptions." Granted that primitive people's speculations owed more to imagination than to experience and reason—what matters is that, by hypothesizing about the gods, they were launched on the intellectual enterprise that could not have been started in any other way. Similarly, according to Comte, the metaphysical stage is necessary before the positive stage can be reached: Its abstract and impersonal conceptions prepare the mind for positive knowledge, which is too radically different from theological beliefs for people to accept it immediately.

Comte maintained that different kinds of knowledge have passed through the three stages at different paces. Astronomy became a science before terrestrial physics, physics before chemistry, chemistry before biology, biology before physiology, and physiology before sociology. According to Comte, who developed a hierarchy of the sciences, it had to be this way. Not only is physics simpler than sociology—it is more general, and hence more fundamental. The principle on which this hierarchy is based is essentially that of nominalistic logic, according to which the extension of a term is inversely proportional to its intension. Physics has greater extension than biology; that is, more objects of different kinds come under its laws, including both living and nonliving bodies. In Comte's language, physics is

more general than biology. Conversely, biology has greater intension than physics; that is, although its laws apply to objects of only one kind, they comprehend more of their aspects. In Comte's language, biology is more complex than physics.

On this principle, Comte arranged the sciences in hierarchical order. Mathematics he placed first, because it is the most general, the simplest, and the most independent of all and serves as the basis of all others. However, because of its abstract character, Comte did not regard mathematics as a "natural science." Natural sciences he divided into inorganic and organic. That the latter are more complex than the former is self-evident, inasmuch as organization is a complexity. So, within the two divisions, on the inorganic level, astronomy is less complex than physics, and physics than chemistry; likewise, on the organic level, physiology, which relates to individuals, is less complex than sociology, which relates to aggregates. It may be observed that Comte did not leave a place for psychology in the hierarchy, a notable omission in view of the fact that John Stuart Mill, in his *A System of Logic, Ratiocinative and Inductive* (1843), was to maintain that associationist psychology is as fundamental to all the human sciences as mechanics is to all the physical sciences. Comte argued, however, that because psychology proceeds by the method of introspection and assumes the actuality of the self, mental states, ideas, and the like, it is a relic of the metaphysical stage. Its counterpart in the positive system is cerebral physiology, which had newly come to the fore. In fact, Comte held that it was the discovery of the physiology of the brain that brought biology to perfection and made possible for the first time the new science of sociology.

Comte said of his classification of the sciences that, although it is artificial, it is not arbitrary. It is artificial because it marks out boundaries where none exist in the actual sciences. One of Comte's deepest concerns was to preserve the unity and integrity of intellectual pursuit, which he considered threatened to the point of sterility by increasing specialization in his day. He favored the development of a new kind of scientific worker whose task it would be to formulate the general principles of the respective sciences and to connect new discoveries with known truth. By making it possible to keep the whole structure of knowledge in view, these scientific workers would lay a new foundation for education. At the same time, they would further research by serving as consultants (for, according to Comte, investigators are often handicapped by their ignorance of what is well known by specialists in other fields).

Although Comte was eager to preserve the unity of knowledge, he maintained that the special sciences are essentially autonomous. Therefore, he insisted that the classification was not arbitrary, and he opposed the view that the sciences can eventually be reduced to one master science and all phenomena explained by a unitary law. "Our intellectual resources," he said, "are too narrow, and the universe too complex, to leave any hope that it will ever be in our power to carry scientific perfection to its last degree of simplicity." The only real unity to science, he said, is that of the positive method, which spurns the idea of asking questions about origins and ends (theological questions) or about essences and causes (metaphysical questions), and settles down to the business of analyzing the circumstances of phenomena and connecting them by the relations of succession and resemblance. It is this method that has led to the division of knowledge into several specialties, so that, in delineating the divisions, positive philosophy was following the requirements of the method itself.

Comte's book derives much of its bulk from the detailed account he gives of all the natural sciences at that time. However, he said that it was not his aim to teach the sciences as such: To do so would be endless and would demand more knowledge than one person could hope to muster. In any case, it would miss the point, which was "only to consider each fundamental science in its relation to the whole positive system, and the spirit which characterizes it." He said that his book was a course not in positive science but in positive philosophy. In his view, however, positive philosophy was "a whole, solid and entire." From the time of Bacon, it had been slowly forming until, in the nineteenth century, only one major gap remained—social physics—that was about to be filled.

Jean Faurot

Additional Reading

Gould, F. J. *Auguste Comte*. London: Watts, 1920. This biography, though brief, provides a balanced survey of Auguste Comte's life and thought. It provides information on his intellectual circle and a full treatment of his ideas. The curious positivist calendar is appended.

Harp, Gillis J. *Positivist Republic: Auguste Comte and the Reconstruction of American Liberalism, 1865-1920*. University Park: Pennsylvania State University Press, 1995. This book examines how Comte's thoughts influenced the political arena.

Lévy-Bruhl, Lucien. *The Philosophy of Auguste Comte*. Translated by Kathleen de Beaumont-Klein. New York: G. P. Putnam's Sons, 1903. A thorough and sympathetic treatment of Comte's thought by a highly regarded French scholar. Takes issue with John Stuart Mill's contention that there are serious discrepancies between Comte's early and later writings.

Manuel, Frank. *The Prophets of Paris*. Cambridge, Mass.: Harvard University Press, 1961. This survey of a number of important French social philosophers devotes an illuminating chapter to Comte and provides a good perspective from which to assess Comte in relation to his intellectual milieu. Seen in the company of other visionaries, his detailed prescriptions are somewhat less puzzling.

Mill, John Stuart. *Auguste Comte and Positivism*. Ann Arbor: University of Michigan Press, 1961. First published in 1865, this critical assessment of Comte's ideas remains one of the most important books by an English author on Comte. Highly critical of Comte's later writings, it slights the elements of continuity they share with the rest of his work.

Mill, John Stuart, and Auguste Comte. *The Correspondence of John Stuart Mill and Auguste Comte*. Translated and edited by Oscar A. Haac. New Brunswick, N.J.: Transaction, 1994. These eighty-nine letters, written between 1841 and 1847, address important issues of mid-nineteenth century philosophy, science, economics, and politics. Cumulatively, they provide a humanistic view of Western Europe and its social problems.

Pickering, Mary. *Auguste Comte: An Intellectual Biography*. Cambridge, England: Cambridge

University Press, 1993. First volume of a projected two-volume intellectual biography. Offers a reinterpretation of Comte's "first career," the period between 1798 and 1842, when he completed the scientific foundation of his philosophy, and describes the interplay between Comte's ideas and the historical context of postrevolutionary France.

Scharff, Robert C. *Comte After Positivism*. New York: Cambridge University Press, 1995. An in-depth treatment of Comte's ideas.

Sokoloff, Boris. *The "Mad" Philosopher, Auguste Comte*. New York: Vantage Press, 1961. A brief, readable biography that summarizes Comte's chief ideas while treating more fully the biographical context within which they developed. Gives more attention to his youth and his relationships with women than to his ties to other intellectuals.

Standley, Arline Reilein. *Auguste Comte*. Boston: Twayne, 1981. An effort to integrate the larger pieces of Comte's worldview. Suitable for undergraduates.

Whittaker, Thomas. *Comte and Mill*. London: Archibald Constable, 1908. Comte and Mill, though antithetical in some respects, sprang from the same movement in modern thought. This straightforward study is especially strong on Comte's early writings and the transition to later work.

R. Craig Philips, updated by Grant A. Marler

Confucius

Through Confucius's disciples and followers, Confucianism became China's official state philosophy in the second century B.C.E., and its texts became the basis of formal education. Confucianism remained the dominant philosophy of China until the early twentieth century and still has a major influence on people throughout East Asia.

Principal philosophical works: *Lunyu*, late sixth or early fifth century B.C.E. (*Analects*, 1861)

Born: 551 B.C.E.; state of Lu, China
Died: 479 B.C.E.; Qufu, state of Lu, China

Early Life

The name Confucius is the latinized version of a formal title, Kong Fuzi, meaning the Master Kong. He was born as Kong Qiu (styled Zhong Ni) somewhere in the state of Lu (in the present-day province of Shandong), into a family that was part of the official class but had fallen on hard times. His great-grandparents are thought to have emigrated from the neighboring state of Song. Confucius is believed to have lost his father when still a small child and to have been reared in poverty by his mother.

Nevertheless, Confucius learned the arts of a courtier, including archery and charioteering; at age fifteen, he began to study ancient texts. In his mid-twenties, Confucius held minor posts in Lu, first as a bookkeeper and later as a supervisor of royal herds. His approach to the problems of statecraft may have begun in his thirties, but he is best known for the period after the age of fifty when he was an established teacher or philosopher-master to young men. The actual teachings that have been handed down are contained in epigraphic and somewhat disjointed form in the *Analects*. The work is a compilation of moral teachings, usually in the form of brief dialogues between Confucius and a questioner, who might be either a high feudal lord or one of Confucius's own disciples. Tradition holds that Confucius had an ungainly personal appearance, but nothing is actually known about his looks.

He was married and had a son.

During Confucius's lifetime, China was divided into contending states under the nominal rule of the Zhou Dynasty (1122-221 B.C.E.). By the eighth century B.C.E., the Zhou rulers had lost all effective control over their subordinate lords, who became independent rulers. By Confucius's day, these rulers often were themselves figureheads, controlled by powerful individuals or families close to the throne. Murder, intrigue, and double-dealing had become the common coin of political exchange. Moreover, established authority and traditional social distinctions were violated in daily life. In this atmosphere of treachery and uncertainty, Confucius emerged as a teacher who valued constancy, trustworthiness, and the reestablishment of the rational feudal order contained in the codes of the Zhou Dynasty.

Life's Work

Confucius was already known as a teacher but desired to become an adviser or government minister when, sometime before his fiftieth year, he went to live in the powerful neighboring state of Qi. The duke of Qi honored Confucius as a moral teacher but did not give him an important position in the government; eventually, Confucius returned to Lu.

When the ruler of Qi asked Confucius the best way to govern, he replied, "Let the ruler be a ruler, the subject a subject, the father a father, and the son a son." The ideas contained in this moral maxim are central to Confucius's teaching. He taught that social order and stability could be

This statue of Confucius in an altar demonstrates the importance of his thought, which remained a significant part of Chinese education until the early twentieth century. *(Library of Congress)*

achieved at a societal and a personal level if individuals studied and followed the proper standards of behavior. Confucius taught that if one acted properly in terms of one's own social role, others would be influenced positively by the good example. That worked for a ruler in state and for an individual in his or her daily life. Thus, Confucianism, from its earliest teachings, contained an approach useful for both practical living and governing.

Virtue (*de*) displayed by living properly brought one into harmony with the correct human order, called "the Way" (*dao*, or *tao*). Confu-

cius acknowledged the existence of an overarching force in life called Heaven (*tian*) but did not accept any concept of a god or gods. He specifically opposed belief in spirits and was not interested in the immortality of the soul.

For Confucius, the human order and human character are fundamentally good, but there is a tendency to slip away from proper behavior through laxity and lack of understanding. A primary responsibility of leaders and elders is to uphold the social ideals through positive demonstration in their own lives. In Confucianism, the most complete statement of this approach is called the doctrine of the rectification of names (*zhengming*). One begins with study to establish the original meaning of the Zhou feudal order. Once that understanding is gained, individuals should alter their behavior in order to fulfill completely and sincerely the social roles they are assigned, such as minister, father, or brother. This entire process constitutes the rectification of names, which Confucius believed would restore the ideal social order.

Upon his return to Lu around the year 500 B.C.E., Confucius took up an official position under the sponsorship of Ji Huanzi, the head of the Ji clan, who were the real power holders. His post was not an important one, and Confucius resigned shortly over a question of improper conduct of ritual sacrifices. Ritual (*li*) plays a central role in Confucius's teachings. He downplayed the supernatural or religious aspects of ritual but taught that meticulous and sincere observance of rituals imparted moral improvement.

The state of Lu, where Confucius lived, derived from a collateral line of the Zhou Dynasty and was known for careful preservation of Zhou ritual practices. Confucius used this tradition as a proof of the importance of rituals. In addition to the moral training acquired by the mastery of ritual, Confucius taught ritual as a means to acquire the practical skills needed to carry out the functions of high office.

In 497 B.C.E., after his resignation over the ritual issue, Confucius set out, with a few disciples, as a wandering philosopher-teacher, looking for a ruler who would try his methods of governing. This long trek, which lasted from 497 to 484 B.C.E., led to his enhanced reputation for uprightness and wisdom, but he never obtained a significant office. In his mid-sixties, he was called back to Lu, possibly through the influence of his disciple Ran Qiu, who had become the chief steward of the Ji family. Upon his return, however, Confucius denounced Ran Qiu's tax policies as exploitative of the common people.

Confucius's approach to government stressed that the ruler should be benevolent and sincerely concerned about the well-being of his subjects. In Confucius's hierarchical conception of the social order, the ruler's concern for his subjects would be repaid by obedience and support. Confucius believed that the same hierarchical yet reciprocal principles applied to all social relationships.

Although later Confucius came to be deified as a sage of infinite powers, in the *Analects* he appears as a dignified, austere, but gentle man who suffered ordinary human disappointments. Significantly, his ideas are colored by a strong humanism. His teachings as recorded in the *Analects* emphasize benevolence (*ren*), meaning a love of one's fellows, as the key virtue of the ideal person, whom he referred to as a "gentleman" (*junzi*). Benevolence begins with straightforwardness (*zhi*) of character and then is trained or modified through practice of the rituals. Ritual and music impart the inner character needed by the ideal person. Confucius taught that the ideal person would have other virtues as well, such as loyalty (*zhong*), righteousness (*yi*), altruism (*shu*), and filial piety (*xiao*). This last virtue—the love and concern of children for their parents, which expresses itself in dutiful and sincere concern for their well-being—became particularly important in Chinese and East Asian civilization. All Confucius's teachings about social relationships demand the subordination of the individual; thus, Confucius was neither an egalitarian nor a libertarian.

During his last years, Confucius lived in Lu and was often consulted by the titular ruler, Duke Ai, and the new head of the dominant Ji clan, Ji Kangzi, but still was never an important minister. Many of his statements from this period are preserved in summary form and enhance the elliptical tone of the *Analects*.

Confucius, before his death at the age of seventy-two, completed the editing of several ancient texts. Both tradition and modern scholarship connect him with three classical texts. These are the *Shu Jing* (classic of history), which contains pronouncements by the founders of the Zhou Dynasty, the *Shi Jing* (classic of poetry), which preserves 305 songs from the time before 600 B.C.E., and the *Chun Qiu* (spring and autumn annals). The last is a terse chronicle of events in the state of Lu from 722 to 481 B.C.E. and has been closely studied through the centuries, for it was believed that Confucius edited it with the intent of transmitting moral messages about good government. Confucius also studied the *I Ching* (*Yi Jing*), eighth to third century B.C.E. (English translation, 1876; also known as *Book of Change*, 1986), but the tradition that he edited that cryptic ancient book of divination is not widely accepted today.

Confucius's concern to compile correct versions of ancient texts fits the image of him that survives in the *Analects*. There Confucius stressed his own role as simply a transmitter of the knowledge and ways from the past. Confucius's model from history was the duke of Zhou, who acted as regent for the infant King Cheng, the Completed King, who reigned from 1104 to 1067 B.C.E. Confucius taught that the duke of Zhou was the perfect minister who served his ruler and carried out his duties in complete accord with the feudal codes of the Zhou. The story of the duke of Zhou, as a good regent and loyal minister, emphasizes the exercise of power in accord with the established social codes. Much of the appeal of Confucianism to later dynasties can be found in Confucius's emphasis on loyalty to proper authority.

At the same time, Confucius's teachings have been seen as democratic, in that what he valued in others was their good character, benevolence, humanity, and learning rather than their social position, cunning, or strength of will. His teaching that anyone may become a "gentleman," or ideal person, with proper training and devotion established the important Chinese social ideal of personal cultivation through study.

Influence

Confucius died in 479 B.C.E., disappointed in his own career, upset at some disciples for their inability to follow his own high standards of conduct, and saddened by the deaths of both his own son and his favorite disciple, Yan Hui. Like the Greek sage Socrates, Confucius became known primarily as a teacher through the preservation of his teachings by his disciples. Some of those disciples went on to government service and others took up their master's calling as teachers.

By the second century B.C.E., the study of Confucian texts had become the norm for those aspiring to official posts. Young men were trained to memorize a set group of Confucian texts. That educational regime remained the heart of learning in China until the early twentieth century. The flourishing of Confucius's pedagogical approach is eloquent testimony to the philosopher's genius. His concepts of the goodness of humankind and the importance of benevolence and humanity in political and personal affairs were developed by Mencius and given a more practical and realistic interpretation by the philosopher Xunzi. By the second century B.C.E., students of Confucian teachings were highly valued for their skills in ritual, knowledge of ancient texts, and mastery of other learning that rulers needed to regulate their courts and administer their states. During the former Han Dynasty, Confucianism became the official court philosophy and then was elevated to a state cult. Confucianism continues to be a powerful philosophy in China, Japan, and other states of East Asia.

David D. Buck

Analects

Type of philosophy: Chinese philosophy, ethics, political philosophy
First transcribed: Lunyu, late sixth or early fifth century B.C.E. (English translation, 1861)

Principal ideas advanced:

◇ *Ren,* the ideal relationship among human beings, is the perfect virtue of humankind.
◇ People are basically close to *ren* by their very nature, but their actions should be controlled by *li,* the rules of propriety.
◇ The *junzi,* or ideal person, is one who practices *ren* in accordance with *li;* consequently, the individual treasures and seeks the *dao,* the right Way.

Confucius, to whom most of the sayings in the *Analects* are ascribed, was a descendant of an influential family of the state of Lu in the present-day eastern Chinese province of Shandong. His family name was Kong. His personal name was Qiu and he was also known as Zhong Ni. Later he was known as Kong Fuzi, meaning Master Kong, out of respect. At the time of his birth, his family was already in reduced circumstances, but he could boast of a long line of illustrious ancestors, dating to before the Zhou Dynasty (1122-221 B.C.E.). Because of Confucius's fame, his family history is perhaps the most complete and extensive genealogy in the world.

Orphaned at an early age, Confucius went to work while still in his teens. He held a number of minor posts in the government and in the employ of the nobility. His service record and his self-cultivation soon won for him wide recognition. Students gathered around him for instruction in ethics, literature, and the art of government service. He was particularly respected for his knowledge of ancient rituals. Among his followers were men of diverse interests and temperaments. Myth and legend grew around the historical Confucius over the centuries, and the story of the ancient sage's life has become anything but monotonous. Confucius is said to have had to put up with one student who was too stingy to let his master borrow his umbrella; consequently, Confucius was drenched in the rain at least once. Confucius, so the legend says, had constantly to restrain a second student whose hot temper involved himself and his master in frequent difficulties. Confucius is believed to have had a narrow escape from a third disciple whose reaction against his master's ceaseless moralistic admonitions amounted to a murderous intent.

Confucius divided his time among lecturing to

his students, editing reading materials for his students, and trying to persuade the men in government to adopt his ideas. If he failed in the last, he certainly succeeded remarkably well in the first two tasks, as his *Analects* and its lasting influence testify. Being a collection of remembered dialogues recorded by his disciples and their pupils, there is clearly a question about the accuracy of the statements in the *Analects*. In addition, the extremely terse style of these dialogues lends itself to a variety of interpretations. However, upon a careful perusal of these sayings, many key ideas of the Confucian system emerge with clarity.

Benevolence

Of the central idea that is discernible in Confucian thought, the idea of *ren* is perhaps the greatest in importance. *Ren* is the foundation of Confucian ethics because *ren* stands for the ideal relationship among human beings. The etymological significance of the Chinese character *ren* yields a key to this idea: The symbols that form this character mean "two human beings," hence the suggestion of "the ideal relationship between any two human beings." *Ren* suggests gentility, magnanimity, humanity, goodness of character, and benevolence. The last sense is the one most frequently used to translate this term. In short, *ren* is the perfect virtue of human beings; it is the only road to the peace and harmony of a society. One who embraces the principle of *ren* will treat people gently and humanely; and for this person, everything will go well.

In answering his disciples' questions on the existence and functions of *ren*, Confucius stressed the importance not only of internalizing the principles of *ren* to make them a part of a person's natural disposition but also of putting them into daily practice. He wanted his students to practice courtesy, magnanimity, good faith, diligence, and kindness everywhere and all the time. He came close to advocating an infinite compassion when he summed up his own exposition with a succinct command: to practice *ren* is to "love mankind" universally. Most frequently Confucius emphasized that *ren* was not a lofty metaphysical abstraction beyond the comprehension of the ordinary person. On the contrary, he insisted that *ren* lay close at hand for everyone to grasp. The

difficulty, as he saw it, was that few people could remain firm for long. Even among his distinguished disciples, he mentioned only one who succeeded in practicing *ren* with constancy.

A note of earnestness that verges on religious fervor can be detected when Confucius speaks of the importance of *ren*. With unmistakable clarity, he asserts that good people sacrifice their lives in order to maintain *ren* and that they would never alter *ren* in order to survive any crisis. In this light, the Confucian principles of *ren* become more than relative standards of desirable social behavior; they are notions of absolute right and justice. However, Confucius explains, the seeds of these notions are not to be found outside humankind's basic nature. Without giving a clear statement anywhere of his view on humankind's nature, Confucius nevertheless reveals his assumption that people are born basically the same and that direct expressions of the original nature of humankind approach much closer to *ren* than any affectation could. Confucius insists on only one condition: Any direct expression of one's own nature has to be restrained by li (the rules of propriety) in order to adhere to the principles of *ren*.

The Rules of Propriety

Strictly speaking, the rules of propriety, the *li*, taken literally could mean rites, etiquette, good form, or decorum, but clearly Confucius uses this term to mean much more than mere outward expressions of formality. As an expert and an authority on ancient rites, Confucius preferred to have his students look beyond the music and pomp, the "jade and silk," and other features usually accompanying the rituals. In the *Analects*, he stresses the essence of *li* as the distinguishing quality of humanity without which humankind and wild animals would be the same and human society would cease to exist. He also tells his own son to study *li* because if he does not know *li*, he will not know how to behave like a man.

Li, consequently, is upheld as the evidence of humankind's civilization. *Li* is essential to sophisticated, cultured, and orderly living, which is the central aim of the Confucian social teachings. With *li*, people can tame the wild animal in themselves and make themselves better members of society. In more than one statement, Confucius suggests the psychological use of *li* to bring calm and poise to people at critical moments. *Li* is the Confucian prescription to save society from chaos and disorder.

True to his status as a self-appointed standard-bearer of traditional culture, Confucius does not spare any effort to impress his students with the importance of rituals. He himself would not eat unless the meal was presented and the seat arranged in the proper manner; he would not walk on foot when he kept company with the dignitaries; he would not look, listen, speak, or move until he was sure his every action was in accordance with the rules of propriety (*li*). Indeed, his own sayings and other statements about him in the *Analects* show a man of meticulous care for proper manners. Confucius may have purposely done so to dramatize the cultural heritage of his state of Lu, which was closely linked to the Zhou Dynasty. In his philosophy, Confucius champions a revival of the Zhou institutions, which in his political vision represent a golden past. Confucius holds the spirit, the appropriateness, and the sincerity behind the rites above the formalities. He instructs his students to observe simplicity, not lavish display, as the general principle of all rites, and to ascertain the genuine sentiment behind any ritual observance rather than the mere physical presence of etiquette. The spirit of *li*, according to Confucius, obtains only when the person practicing *li* has *ren*. Here the two key Confucian ideas come together to form the basis for the concept of *junzi*.

The Ideal Person

Originally *junzi* meant no more than "the son of the lord." Its more extensive use acquired for it the broader meaning of "any person of good breeding." In the repeated appearance of this term in the Confucian statements, the element of good breeding or family origin is no longer stressed, and *junzi* becomes simply "good person" or "the best of people" in contradistinction with *xiaoren*, "small person" or "petty person." The sense of the term in the *Analects* can also be quite adequately expressed as the "superior person" in contrast to the "inferior person."

Confucius paints in *junzi* a picture of the ideal person. This perfect person has a thorough understanding of *ren* and constantly practices it. The individual always acts according to *li*, and

the rules of propriety are so much a part of the person's nature that he or she never can violate them. The individual's uprightness, or the expressions of the person's genuine nature, is perfectly blended with that proper amount of refinement, so that the ideal person is neither pedantic nor rustic. In dealing with others, the *junzi* is warm-mannered. The ideal person has a will of steel and always appears calm because *ren* keeps the individual from experiencing anxieties. The person's wisdom guards against perplexities, and courage dispels any possible fear. Although petty-minded people think of profit, the *junzi* is always mindful of what is right. The ideal person may not possess much technical knowledge about details but the individual's mind is capable of grasping what is essential and significant. Above all, the *junzi* treasures and seeks the *dao*, or the Way.

Dao and Heaven

The Confucian *dao*, or the Way, is vastly different from the Dao of mystic Daoism. Confucius speaks of the *dao* of the ancient Sage Kings, meaning the Way to an ideal government and society, and of the *dao* of a virtuous man, meaning the right Way of being a man. At times, Confucius treats the word *dao* as another name for righteousness and sagacity. As he does with *ren*, Confucius also speaks of *dao* with occasional outbursts of pious feeling. He declares, "He who hears of *dao* in the morning may die content at night." In these instances, Confucius does come close to expressing a religious dedication.

On the whole, Confucius's silence on the supernatural is eloquent. In the *Analects*, he does not defend, nor does he attempt to destroy, the prevailing ideas about the world of the spirits. Instead, he unequivocally instructs his disciples to keep their minds on the affairs of humankind and not to be bothered by questions about the spirits. He informs them that they must first learn enough about life before they inquire into life hereafter, and he himself throughout his life remained too busy studying this world to deal with the other world. When his student asks him about the relationship between the rites and the spirits, Confucius's answer is that since sincerity is the essence of the rituals, one must conduct the sacrificial rites to one's ancestors "as if they were present," and to the spirits also "as if they were present." Beyond this, so says Confucius, one should not go. It is enough "to respect the spirits and stay away from them."

Small wonder that one of his disciples declares his disappointment in trying to learn Confucius's expositions on "Heaven's ways." Confucius may be suspected of dodging the question. He may also be suspected of having no formulated ideas about the spirits, but he cannot be accused of total silence on the question of Heaven. For in many passages in the *Analects*, Confucius refers to Heaven, sometimes as an invincible moral force, at other times as a supreme being, willful and purposeful.

Heaven to Confucius is the supreme being that decides in favor of the moral and the right, and Confucius envisages himself as having been commissioned by the heavenly authority to perpetuate the Sage Kings' Way on earth. So he declares, when his life is threatened by the people of Kuang, "If Heaven is not going to let this culture decline, what can the people of K'uang [Kuang] do to me?" On another occasion of distress, Confucius comforts his friends by saying, "Heaven has created this virtue in me; what can Huan T'ui [Huan Tui] do to me?" That Confucius views Heaven's will as always in favor of the good and always beneficial is further evinced in his statement about the regularity of the seasons and the thriving of myriad creatures. This statement has been taken by many students of Confucianism as a proof of Confucius's belief in the spontaneity of a universal amoral force that is omnipotent. This view could be correct, but if one judges by the majority of Confucius's remarks concerning Heaven, the force of the foregoing statement still tends to describe Heaven as a beneficent force that works benevolently without "elaborate explanations."

Heaven's *dao* in Confucian terms is Heaven's Way or Heaven's will. This will is supreme and above human interference. If Confucius's use of the term Heaven is perfectly consistent, then Heaven's will should also be moral and in favor of the good. Here another Confucian term is introduced, the *ming*. *Ming* can mean either a command or a destiny. When it appears in connection with Heaven as "Heaven's *ming*," it usually means "Heaven's command," or "Heaven's

will." When it appears alone, *ming* can mean "fate" or "destiny." What makes Confucius's position on Heaven's will unclear is his statement that if the Way (*dao*) is to prevail, it is fate (*ming*); and if the Way is to fail, it is also fate (*ming*). If this is the same *ming* as Heaven's command, then Heaven may not always be intent on making the Great Way prevail. This idea is what is generally understood as Confucian fatalism. In other words, fate, as a shadowy necessity beyond the comprehension and control of human beings, also appears in Confucian thought.

Filial Piety

Enough is said in the *Analects* to illuminate some other Confucian ideals with regard to social and political institutions. The importance of the family as the microcosm of society is clearly implied when Confucius reminds his students to practice filial piety within the family before trying to learn how to read and write well. The significance of filial piety in the Confucian system as seen in the *Analects*, however, is not as great as has been generally believed. Confucius describes this virtue as important because people who are respectful toward their parents are not likely to violate the law and order of society and because to be thankful to one's parents is a good sentiment that should be encouraged.

However, to uphold filial piety as the supreme human virtue is not Confucius's intent in the *Analects*; rather, it is a later development in the Confucian school of thought, elaborated and reinterpreted by the Confucian commentators on these texts. Confucius himself does not preach total, blind obedience to one's parents. He sees the virtue of a son shielding his sheep-stealing father, but he also teaches the son to remonstrate, mildly but persistently, with his erring father.

Attaining Knowledge

As an educator, Confucius was equally earnest in teaching his students, regardless of their social status and family origins. He believed in the equal teachability of people, but he recognized the difference in intellect and talent among them. In the *Analects*, he accepts those "who are born with knowledge" as the best, and those who learn after industrious study as the second type of mind. Nowhere in this book does Confucius suggest that each person is born socially equal and is entitled to the right to self-rule. He urges the ruler to learn the right Way to govern; he urges his students to learn to be the best ministers possible in order to assist the ruler. Confucius's view on the function of the government is that government must rule by moral excellence—a view that anticipates the whole political philosophy of Mencius.

Confucius's remark about people "born with knowledge" is extremely provocative, but unfortunately, the *Analects* does not yield any adequate exposition on Confucius's view of knowledge. In discussing how to study, Confucius acknowledges his own intention "to observe and commit to memory what is observed," because he confesses that he "cannot do anything without knowing about it first." When these statements are examined together, Confucius does hint at the possibility that some people are born with knowledge; hence, these people can act spontaneously without the effort of learning how to act and without being aware of their knowledge. However, Confucius carefully declines the company of people of such super intellect, and he admits that the source of his knowledge is observation and intensive study. He also rules out the attainment of knowledge through meditation without the aid of books because once he "tried to think the whole day without eating and the whole night without sleeping, but nothing came of it." Furthermore, he does not separate the attainment of knowledge from action and practice.

Names and Actuality

More important than the relation between action and knowledge is the exact identification of name with actuality, according to the Confucian teachings. The times were chaotic and the social order was confused. Therefore, Confucius urged the king to behave like a king and the minister to act as one of his rank should. If the name is not correctly applied, says Confucius, then language is no longer a medium of communication. Consequently, nothing can be accomplished and people will not even know where to "put their hands or feet." From a moralistic start with a practical aim, the Confucian doctrine of rectification of names developed into a serious effort to define terms. Confucius's concern with this matter reveals his underlying assumption that the name is not just a representation of a thing but is the very essence of the thing itself. The germ of this idea can be found in pre-Confucian thought in China's high antiquity, but Confucius's effort has added significance to this idea and made it an important development in Chinese philosophy.

Survival of Confucianism

In spite of its brevity, the *Analects* remains the most authentic and rewarding source for the study of Confucius—the man and his thought. Besides setting forth the key ideas of original Confucianism, the book illuminates certain aspects of life in ancient China. The fragments of dialogues between Confucius and a few political leaders show the role the intellectuals played in a society where values were undergoing dramatic change. The dialogues also reveal how totally without restraint the states vied for supremacy in a power struggle that followed the collapse of an ancient feudal order.

The fact that certain key statements in the *Analects* have been interpreted in different ways has certainly contributed to the survival of the Confucian system. The book contains something for everyone, from the most radical to the most conservative. Indeed, much has been read back into the Confucian teachings, and what Confucius did actually teach has been, as a result, distorted. In spite of differences of interpretation, it seems important to note that Confucius valued most highly an orderly, peaceful, and harmonious society. To this goal, he channeled all his thought and teaching. His *dao* was the Way to achieve this ideal; his *de* (virtue) was his claim that he had been invested with the knowledge of the Way; his *wen* (refinement, cultural heritage) was the heritage of institutions prevailing in an imaginary golden past derived from the ancient texts. To be sure, Confucius insisted that society would not be peaceful if each individual did not behave properly, according to social station. This meant that for Confucius the individual was important, but only insofar as the person could help bring about peace and harmony in society. If Confucius speculated on the position of humanity in the universe or dealt with other metaphysical matters, he did not record it in the *Analects*.

Kai-yu Hsu

Additional Reading

Allito, Guy. *The Last Confucian*. Berkeley: University of California Press, 1979. Based on the life and work of Liang Shuming, who tried to reestablish Confucian ideas in the early twentieth century. Includes his attempt to use Confucius as a basis for reform that would revitalize rural China. His goal was to stop the growing influence of communism. Discusses the different reactions to China's problems by Liang and the communist leader, Mao Zedong.

Berthrong, John H. *Transformations of the Confucian Way*. Boulder, Colo.: Westview Press, 1998. A lucid guide through the many changes to the canon of Confucianism.

Chai, Ch'u, and Winberg Chai, eds. *The Sacred Books of Confucius and Other Confucian Classics*. New York: University Books, 1965. Introduction evaluates Confucianism both as humanism and as a religion. Includes as excellent glossary of Chinese terms used by Confucius and other writers. Covers later writings to the second century B.C.E. Contains a very readable translation of *Analects*.

Dawson, Raymond. *Confucius*. New York: Oxford University Press, 1982. A short introduction and biographical sketch of Confucius, written for a series on great individuals. Stresses Confucius's ethical and moral influence.

De Bary, William Theodore. *The Unfolding of Neo-Confucianism*. New York: Columbia University Press, 1975. Discusses the reemphasis on Confucian thought that fueled the transition from the Ming Dynasty to the Qing (Manchu) Dynasty. Explains how Confucianism stimulated a Buddhist revival in the late Ming period.

Fingarette, Herbert. *Confucius: The Secular as Sacred*. New York: Harper & Row, 1972. An interpretive essay that attempts to reconcile Confucius's attention to ritual with his humanism. In discussing *Analects*, the author believes that Confucius was ahead of his time; with ideas similar to the European Enlightenment of the eighteenth century.

Hsu, Leonard Shihlien. *The Political Philosophy of Confucianism: An Interpretation of the Social and Political Ideas of Confucius, His Forerunners, and His Early Disciples*. New York: E. P. Dutton, 1932. The authoritative discussion of the Confucian principle of *li*, an unwritten code of justice for sovereigns, their ministers, and the people themselves.

Liu, Shu-hsien. *Understanding Confucian Philosophy: Classical and Sung-Ming*. Westport, Conn.: Greenwood Press, 1998. Liu attempts to uncover the key to Confucian philosophy through its spiritual origin.

Schwartz, Benjamin. *The World of Thought in Ancient China*. Cambridge, Mass.: Harvard University Press, 1985. Contains a long chapter that compares Confucius to ancient Western philosophers. Emphasizes Confucius as a teacher who was a perpetuator of tradition as well as an innovator.

Smith, D. Howard. *Confucius*. New York: Charles Scribner's Sons, 1973. A biographical sketch that includes a discussion of Daoism, the contemporary opposition to Confucius, as well as the later opposition of Buddhism. Evaluates the impact of Confucianism on the major dynasties of Chinese history.

Sloate, Walter H., and George A. De Vos, eds. *Confucianism and the Family*. Albany: State University of New York Press, 1998. A collection of essays that examine the psychocultural aspects of the Confucian family.

David D. Buck, updated by Glenn L. Swygart

Ananda Kentish Coomaraswamy

As an advocate of the perennial philosophy, Coomaraswamy pursued the seemingly paradoxical task of advocating a cosmopolitan pursuit of the true, good, and beautiful, while simultaneously being a staunch advocate of a renewal of traditional Indian culture and art.

Principal philosophical works: *Medieval Sinhalese Art*, 1908; *The Indian Craftsman*, 1909; *Essays in National Idealism*, 1909; *Selected Examples of Indian Art*, 1910; *The Arts and Crafts of India and Ceylon*, 1913; *Buddha and the Gospel of Buddhism*, 1916; *The Dance of the Siva*, 1918; *History of Indian and Indonesian Art*, 1927; *A New Approach to the Vedas*, 1933; *The Transformation of Nature in Art*, 1934; *Elements of Buddhist Iconography*, 1935; *Hinduism and Buddhism*, 1943; *Why Exhibit Works of Art?*, 1943; *Figures of Speech or Figures of Thought*, 1946; *Time and Eternity*, 1947.

Born: August 22, 1877; Colombo, Ceylon (now Sri Lanka)
Died: September 9, 1947; Needham, Massachusetts

Early Life

Ananda Kentish Coomaraswamy's pedigree presaged the intellectual and cultural concerns that formed the nexus of his scholarship. He was born into a distinguished Ceylonese family. His father, Sir Mutu Coomaraswamy, was an accomplished barrister and legislator who in his spare time studied Eastern and Western classics. His mother, Elizabeth Clay Coomaraswamy, née Beeby, was of an old English family of Kentish origin. Seventeen years younger than her husband, she was widowed five years after their marriage, at the age of twenty-seven. She devoted the rest of her life to the rearing in England of her only child, Ananda.

Ananda Coomaraswamy was educated first at Wycliffe College, at Stonehouse in Gloucestershire, and later at the University of London, where he obtained a doctorate of science in 1906. Significantly, he was educated when the influence of art critic John Ruskin and artist William Morris pervaded English cultural life. Both Ruskin and Morris were concerned with the detrimental effects of modern industrialism on contemporary Western culture. Their concerns were reflected in those of Coomaraswamy, who later saw Western industrialization as a source of great social evil that adversely affected traditional Eastern culture. Coomaraswamy heartily concurred with and quoted Ruskin's aphorism, "Industry without art is brutality." He thought that the Enlightenment, with its concurrent industrialization, had ravaged the West and was ravaging the East.

In 1903, while pursuing his doctoral studies, Coomaraswamy was appointed director of the Mineralogical Survey of Ceylon and served in Ceylon in that capacity until 1906. Articles written during that three-year period were submitted and accepted as his dissertation for the doctorate of science. It was during that same three-year period that Coomaraswamy was first struck by the contrast between contemporary Western industrialism and traditional Eastern culture. In response, he started two societies, the Kandyan Association and the Ceylon Social Reform Society, both dedicated to the preservation and promotion of the arts of Ceylon.

At the termination of his appointment as director of the Mineralogical Survey, in 1906, Coomaraswamy left Ceylon for a three-month tour of India. This marked the beginning not only of a physical tour but also of a scholarly and spiritual tour from which he emerged with his mission in life. He became a champion of traditional Eastern culture and a critic of the modernist West. He did so by forcefully advocating the perennial philosophy.

Life's Work

Coomaraswamy's scholarly career can be divided into two periods: 1908-1932 and 1932-1947. The earlier period centers on empirical scholarship, the later on more mystic and metaphysical studies. However, the distinction between the two is never absolute in Coomaraswamy's work.

Coomaraswamy critically confronts two aspects of the modernist West: the pursuit of empirical facts and the belief in cultural relativism and subjectivism. He asserts that a mere empirical study of Eastern culture denies that culture's content and its significance. In addition, to study traditional Eastern or traditional Western culture via a modernist perspective is to deny the validity of those traditions being studied. A modernist study centers on a paradigm of facts, feelings, and style, but traditional Eastern and Western cultures consist of more than facts—they contain a belief in truth, goodness, and beauty. To give the facts concerning, for example, the worldview of Hinduism without discussing whether those facts are actually true, reduces the Hindu (or any other nonmodernist) cultural tradition to the realm of nostalgic historical fact and subjective cultural preference. It avoids and denies the possibility that Hinduism could be true. To study a nonrelativistic culture from an empirical and relativistic perspective is to deny the intrinsic validity of traditions that are not empirical and relativistic. It is in addressing this realization that the philosophical content of Coomaraswamy's thought and scholarship began to blossom.

Coomaraswamy early established his ability as an empiricist scholar by publishing a number of important works and presenting various important scholarly papers. In addition to his early published works in the area of natural science, in 1908 he published a well-illustrated monograph, *Medieval Sinhalese Art*, and presented an important paper at the International Congress of Orientalists at Copenhagen, "The Influence of Greece on Indian Art." However, his work increasingly advanced beyond the limitations of empirical scholarship with the publication of *The Indian Craftsman*, followed by *Selected Examples of Indian*

Art, The Arts and Crafts of India and Ceylon, and *Buddha and the Gospel of Buddhism*.

During this same period, Coomaraswamy published *Essays in National Idealism* and presented a series of lectures proclaiming the need for an aesthetic and spiritual awakening in the East. Not surprisingly, as a critic of modern Western civilization, he found himself increasingly at odds with the empirical methods employed by the dominant modernist scholarly and artistic community as well as with various cultural and political forces associated with modernism. The philosophical premise that increasingly informed Coomaraswamy's scholarship was expressed in the preface to *The Arts and Crafts of India and Ceylon*: "The Hindus have never believed in art for art's sake; their art, like that of mediaeval Europe, was an art for love's sake."

It was in the midst of a worsening situation that Coomaraswamy received an offer in 1917 to become a research fellow at the Museum of Fine Arts, Boston. He spent the next thirty years at that museum, and it was there that his scholarship in philosophy and metaphysics thrived. His scholarship increasingly differed from his earlier empiricist scholarship (his scientific publications) and from his earlier empirical and aesthetic efforts as an art historian. His mature scholarship focused increasingly on the metaphysical. His later scholarship centered on his dedication to the notion of the perennial philosophy.

The term "perennial philosophy" was first coined by Gottfried Wilhelm Leibniz in reference to the notion that there is a divine reality to the world of things, lives, and minds. This philosophy holds that reality and life ultimately make sense, that it is beyond the capacity of natural science to discern that ultimate meaning, and that the perennial philosophy is a cosmopolitan and enduring alternative to modernist Western culture.

Advocacy of the notions associated with the perennial philosophy that became so central to Coomaraswamy's mature scholarship is evidenced by the philosopher's early and continuing interest in the theme of Nataraja, the dancing Siva. In 1912, Coomaraswamy published an essay titled "The Dance of Siva." Later republished in various collections, this essay is considered to be a classic work not only of art history but also of theology and philosophy. It is clearly not a modernist piece of scholarship. It speaks not of what the iconography meant nor how the iconography makes one feel; instead, the essay speaks of how this work of art explains reality and life. The dancing Siva, a traditional theme in Hindu religion and art, addresses the relationship of being and becoming and of matter becoming meaningful. The traditional theme synthesizes science, religion, philosophy, and art, as does Coomaraswamy's essay. His essay of the dancing Siva and of the art objects that depict that theme, rather than being a factual and nostalgic analysis of an exotic style of art and theology, constitutes an actual attempt to explain the nature of the world and life.

As Coomaraswamy's philosophy became more metaphysical, he produced a major contribution to the study of Indian art in its historical, theological, and philosophical context, *History of Indian and Indonesian Art*. That text was soon followed by *The Transformation of Nature in Art*, in which Coomaraswamy developed his comparison of Eastern and medieval Western culture, a comparison that lies at the core of his advocacy of the perennial philosophy. Just as the perennial philosophy advocates a unity of science (in the sense of a body of knowledge), religion, philosophy, and art, in *The Transformation of Nature in Art*, Coomaraswamy concludes that "Heaven and Earth are united in the analogy of art, which is an ordering of sensation to intelligibility and tends toward an ultimate perfection in which the seer perceives all things imaged in himself."

Why Exhibit Works of Art?, a collection of essays published in 1943, provides an overview of the direction of Coomaraswamy's work and thought. In this work, he covers the philosophic and religious experience of the premodern world, East and West, concluding that premodern cultures were merely different dialects in a common, cosmopolitan language.

The essence of the perennial philosophy is vitalist and mystic rather than empirical or rationalistic (in the modernist sense). Beginning with the premise that reality is necessarily singular although it appears to be multiple, the mystic attempts to escape the illusory world of multiplicity, conflict, and death by identifying with the universal and enduring absolute. By properly un-

derstanding the illusory appearance of the world of multiplicity, conflict, and death, one comes to the mystic realization that becoming is not a contradiction of being but the epiphany of being. These concepts are fully developed in Coomaraswamy's opus magnus *Time and Eternity*. Published in the last year of his life, this work is a cross-cultural comparison of the notions of time and eternity. Coomaraswamy discusses how the key to happiness is found in imitating and in identifying with that living and enduring principle that informs reality and life. That vitalistic force, whether it is called Atman, Logos, or Dharma, passes out of eternity into time for no other purpose than to assist beings in passing out of time into eternity. It is that passage that is key to obtaining genuine happiness and bliss. Coomaraswamy applies the results of this line of reasoning to the production of art, concluding that art is eternity crystallized in time.

Influence

Since Coomaraswamy's death, interest in his work has declined in the West, and attempts to maintain or revive interest in his work have been primarily Indian. That decline has several probable sources, both intellectual and sociopolitical. The overwhelming dominance of empirical and scientific thought in the modernist West and the materialistic presuppositions of postmodernity are adverse to the thrust of the perennial philosophy. Modernity embraces both British empiricism and the Kantian notion that attempts to understand reality are personal or social constructs; this leads to the postmodern conclusion that facts are objective, but all attempts to understand reality are ultimately subjective and often the expression of mere power. From such a point of view, the perennial philosophy is, in philosopher Jeremy Bentham's words, "nonsense on stilts." Philosopher Immanuel Kant would view it as a hypothetical construct, and philosopher Friedrich Nietzsche would see it as a mask for power. This last critique has some sting to it, in that Coomaraswamy's defense of the caste system in India is difficult for many to understand; his praise for Nietzsche is equally troubling.

Alternatively, the perennial philosophy is an intellectually viable alternative to the modernist and postmodernist West; its sociological and political implications are subject to various interpretations. Indeed, the critique of the perennial philosophy pales in comparison with the telling critique of the intellectual and social defects of modernity, so convincingly argued by Ananda Coomaraswamy.

Arthur Pontynen

Time and Eternity

Type of philosophy: Indian philosophy, metaphysics
First published: 1947
Principal ideas advanced:
◇ Time is associated with death, as eternity is associated with life.
◇ To the philosopher, time is distinct from eternity; to the mystic, eternity is untouched by time; to the artist, art is a means of participating in eternity.
◇ The philosopher attempts to understand the relationship of time and eternity as well as that of death and life; the mystic attempts to live in the realm of the eternal, thus escaping time and death; the artist attempts to make things that escape time and death.
◇ Life is found in participation with the eternal; art is eternity crystallized in time.

Time and Eternity is the culminating work of Ananda Kentish Coomaraswamy's career, a career increasingly dedicated to an advocacy of the perennial philosophy. The essence of the perennial philosophy is vitalist and mystic rather than empirical or rationalistic (in the modernist sense). The mystic begins with the premise that reality is necessarily singular although it appears to be multiple and identifies with the universal and enduring absolute in order to escape the illusory world of multiplicity, conflict, and death. Once one gains a proper understanding of the illusory appearance of the world of multiplicity, conflict, and death, one comes to the mystic realization that becoming is not a contradiction of being but the epiphany of being.

This work, published in the last year of Coomaraswamy's life, is a comparison of the notions of time and eternity across several cultures. According to the philosopher, the key to happiness is in imitating and identifying with the living and enduring principle that informs reality and life. That vitalistic force, variously labeled, passes out of eternity into time in order to help beings pass out of time into eternity. This passage is crucial for obtaining genuine happiness and bliss.

The book opens with a brief introduction, followed by chapters on Hinduism, Buddhism, Grecian philosophy, Islam, and Christianity and modernity. In each chapter, Coomaraswamy examines the culture's understanding of time and eternity, making numerous cross-cultural comparisons. The introduction defines the terms that are the central focus of the book and defends the appropriateness of philosophical discourse on the topic of time and eternity.

Empirical and Philosophical Definitions of Time
Coomaraswamy distinguishes between empirical opinion and axiomatic truth, the "bastard" truth of fact and the legitimate truth of intelligible reason. Citing philosophers such as Gottfried Wilhelm Leibniz and Democritus of Abdera, Coomaraswamy argues that modernist, scientistic attempts to "explain" the nature of time are naïve, disingenuous, or both. From the viewpoint of the perennial philosophy, empirical descriptions are "explanations" only to the foolish and shallow-minded. Facts describe how phenomena act, while failing to explain why they act the way they do. Whether facts are considered singularly or grouped together into narratives, they at best establish a superficial probability. They lack both certainty and genuine understanding.

In contrast to the descriptive probabilities of empirical scientism, philosophical reflection on the nature of time and eternity results in certain clear possibilities. Coomaraswamy discusses how a review of time begins with two possibilities: It can be viewed as all or any part of the continuum of past and future, or as that present point of time that distinguishes the past from the future. Similarly, eternity can be viewed as either a duration without beginning or end, or that unextended point of time that is "now."

Coomaraswamy states that the idea that time has a beginning and an end— unlike eternity, which is everlasting in duration—is absurd. Citing Saint Augustine's famous question, Where was God before God made the universe?, Coomaraswamy observes that because time and the world presuppose each other, the word "before" in such a question has no meaning whatever. Hence, the world began not in time but originated in the first principle. God created, and is now still creating, the world. Because the metaphysical doctrine of the perennial philosophy contrasts time as a continuum with the eternity that is not in time, then the eternal cannot properly be called everlasting. The alternative to time is not an eternity of endless time; eternity is now.

If time is a continuum within creation, and both time and creation are dependent upon now, then the question of what is ultimately real arises. Relying upon a cosmopolitan variety of sources, the perennial philosophy concludes that things are false in the sense that an imitation, though it exists, is not the real thing; the philosophy distinguishes between the relative reality of the artifact and the greater reality. The particular is real but not as real as the universal ideal toward which it aspires. There are then degrees of reality, just as there are degrees of quality. A central principle of the perennial philosophy is the qualitative principle that the ideal is more real than that which temporally imitates the ideal.

Time and Eternity Across Cultures

In the first chapter, Coomaraswamy examines the Hindu understanding of time and eternity. That tradition holds that time is the source of past and present, uniting procession, recession, and stasis and, therefore, reality. According to the Katha Upanishad, Brahma is the "Lord of what hath been and shall be; He is both today and tomorrow." Brahma has both a time and timeless form. The timeless form of Brahma is the creator of time, of the moments, hours, days, and years that have separate existences. A moment is the ultimate minimum of time, and the uninterrupted flow of moments is called time. The cumulative result of all those moments of time makes up the world. By using those moments, people can be, or fail to be, all that they ought to be. The proper use of those moments of time is in seeking the timeless eternity; that timeless eternity is the ultimate reality, known as Brahma. In so doing, people can escape both time and death.

In the third chapter, Coomaraswamy examines the Buddhist understanding of time and eternity. Buddhism's essential observation on the subject is that change is constant in the world and that all change is dying. Ultimately, then, beings and the self are both unreal because they are not stable. Time is past, future, or present: In the past thought-moment one lived; in the future thought-moment one will live; and in the present thought-moment one is alive. The association of the world, time, and death is axiomatic to Buddhist philosophy, but reality is not limited to those conditions.

In the spirit of the perennial philosophy, Coomaraswamy cites philosophers Aristotle, Heraclitus of Ephesus, and even Saint Augustine to support a Buddhist point. All agree that it is only the realm of time and sense that continues subject to destruction and generation. However, there is a realm of stability and constancy that is neither empirical nor temporal. In the Buddhist view, time is a continuum and the immanent moment in time is not a part of time. It is in the realm of the immanent moment where stability is found and death and suffering can be escaped. Those who realize this experience an awakening. This timeless or instantaneous awakening occurs when the individual achieves a mystic union with the eternal that is not part of time.

The Greek tradition is introduced by reference to Parmenides, who argues that in contrast to things that are momentary and in decay, there exists a realm of that which is complete, immoveable, and endless. For Plato, the world was made by Zeus according to the same stable eternity. Time and the universe are generated together according to the paradigm of the everlasting nature. Time and the universe are therefore temporal imitations of an eternal ideal, an eternal ideal that is ultimately most real. The distinction of things being less or more real, or as they are rather than as they ought to be, is clarified in Plato's *Philēbos* (c. 360-347 B.C.E.; Philebus, 1804). In this work, Plato explains that there is one authentic self and another, which is ever pursuing something other than itself. It is the authentic self that is most real and that exists out of the realm of time. As Aristotle puts it, the most real self exists in the eternity that is not in time. The Greek view of time and eternity is concluded by reference to Plutarch and Plotinus. Plutarch reflects that what is ultimately real is eternal, unborn, and unperishing—unaffected by time. For Plutarch, this serves as a definition of God. Plotinus also identifies life as an imitation of eternity and identifies eternity with God who reconciles time with now.

A variety of understandings of time and eternity exist within Islam. One Islamic view, the Ash'arite, holds that time is made up of "nows," or present moments, each of which is continuously created by Allah. Accordingly, only Allah holds together the whole stream of the existence of the world. Therefore, the conception of causality in the universe is limited to the workings of Allah. This understanding of time is associated with an atomistic view of creation. The world is made of atoms that have no quantity, but out of which compounds can be made that possess quantity. Time and space appear to be continuous but in fact consist of a series of atomistic moments, whose source is Allah, who is the only ultimate reality.

Coomaraswamy briefly discusses possible Buddhist and Vedic origins for this Muslim atomism. Consistent with the perennial philosophy to which he is devoted, however, he notes that the important question is not one of historical origin but rather of ontology. From the viewpoint of ontology, Coomaraswamy finds fault with this particular vision of time, space, and eternity, concluding that the Sufi understanding of time as an indivisible instant is more coherent. He notes that the Sufi Islamic (and Christian) doctrines of time and eternity could have been derived from Platonic-Aristotelian sources. The Sufi hold that phenomena are perpetually changing and being created anew, while God remains as he is. Coomaraswamy summarizes the Sufi vision of time as being an imitation of eternity, much as becoming is of being and as thinking is of knowing. Now devours future and past; Time (now) is the devourer of time. Time is that whereby a person becomes independent of past and future; those who possess it are happy with God in the present. Indeed, being thus situated between the past and the future is the most precious of human things. The Sufi concept of the momentary existence of accidents does not exclude causality, butthe operation of this causality is deemed mysterious.

The Christian and modern doctrines of time and eternity share an essential idea with the previously discussed traditions. That idea is that corruptibility is inseparable from any existence in time, and that there is only one escape from that corruption: passing over from the flux of temporal existence to a present eternity in which there is neither a yesterday nor a tomorrow. The reality of the eternal present is found in the Holy Ghost, whose actions are immediate. They are immediate because the instant, in which God dwells, terminates time—and space as well. Time and space are continuous, not atomistic; indeed, Augustine notes that God "is" where "has been" and "will be" cannot be. Because God "is," then the problem of free will is resolved. Because God views as present what appears to people as the future, there can be no predestination that precludes free will. Further, Boethius compares time to the circumference of a circle of which the center is eternity; the closer one is to the center, the less one is subject to the necessity of fate, since fate is grounded in time, space, and motion. Thus, philosopher Meister Eckhart speaks of the world as a circle centered on God. The center of that circle is where time (the past and present) are transcended by Time (the eternal now). It is in the unified experience of the eternal now that the processes of creation and destruction are transcended.

Legacy of Perennial Philosophy

Time and Eternity is widely recognized as a work of erudite and cosmopolitan scholarship. The question of its importance as a philosophical work elicits radically different responses. For those who believe that reality is purposeful, *Time and Eternity* presents a cosmopolitan and penetrating ontological analysis. For those who embrace the empirical and Kantian foundations of modernity, Coomaraswamy's critique of modernity is unconvincing and even reactionary. Similarly, as he states in his last chapter, those who elect to live in a merely existential world without meaning will benefit neither from his scholarship nor from the perennial philosophy to which he is devoted. As Coomaraswamy concludes, those are the people who fail to see the world in a grain of sand and eternity in an hour.

Arthur Pontynen

Additional Reading

Bagchee, Moni. *Ananda Coomaraswamy: A Study.* Varanasi (Benares), India: Bharata Manisha, 1977. This biographical work presents a picture of Ananda Kentish Coomaraswamy not only as a scholar, philosopher, and theologian but also as a private, public, and international personality. The author discusses the paradox of writing a biography for Coomaraswamy, given that his work and his beliefs denied the importance of biography.

Coomaraswamy, Ananda Kentish. *The Wisdom of Ananda Coomaraswamy: Being Glimpses of the Mind of Ananda Coomaraswamy.* Presented by S. Durai Raja Singham. Petaling Jaya, Malaysia: S. Durai Raja Singham, 1979. This volume is a wide-ranging annotated anthology of Coomaraswamy's most telling aphorisms. Arranged topically, the aphorisms include Coomaraswamy's thoughts on art, beauty, Indian women, music, competition, religion, and political figures.

Dasgupta, Kalyan Kumar, ed. *Ananda Coomaraswamy: A Centenary Volume.* Calcutta, India: Calcutta University, 1981. This collection of essays pays tribute to Coomaraswamy's contributions to the study of Indian art, iconography, philosophy, aesthetics, religious history, and contemporary politics. The preface of this book provides an exposition of the intellectual journey of Coomaraswamy from empiricist to mystic and from art historian to metaphysician. For advanced undergraduates.

Livingston, Ray. *The Traditional Theory of Literature.* Minneapolis: University of Minnesota Press, 1962. The author presents a concise study of the works of Coomaraswamy from which he develops a perennial philosophy of literature. While using concepts presented by Coomaraswamy in an Eastern context, he explicates and applies those concepts within the historical continuum of Western literature.

Narasimhaiah, C. D. *Ananda Coomaraswamy: Centenary Essays.* Prasaranga, India: University of Mysore, 1982. This tribute to Coomaraswamy presents a collection of essays on his work and ideas. These essays center on three realms of scholarly study that Coomaraswamy finds symbiotic: metaphysics, politics, and art. For advanced undergraduates.

Quinn, William W. *The Only Tradition.* Albany: State University of New York Press, 1997. Surveying the work of Ananda Coomaraswamy and Rene Guenon, this book explores the first principals of perennial philosophy and suggests the decline of Western society is due to the decreasing importance placed on these principals.

Raja Singham, S. Durai, comp. *Ananda Kentish Coomaraswamy: A Handbook.* Malaysia: s.n., 1979. This volume provides an extensive compendium of works published by Coomaraswamy. Includes an annotated chronological bibliography, topical listings, and lists of articles and reviews.

Sastri, P. S. *Ananda K. Coomaraswamy.* India: Arnold-Heinemann, 1974. The author emphasizes that although Coomaraswamy is well known as an art historian, his major contributions to scholarship are in the realms of religion, mysticism, and metaphysics. In those realms, he is the proponent of the perennial philosophy, which, in the philosopher's view, is the basis of all significant thought in the East and West. A critical evaluation of that position is lacking.

Arthur Pontynen

Benedetto Croce

Croce, modern Italy's premier philosopher, made major contributions to European culture with his extensive writings on philosophy, history, aesthetics, and literary criticism. For his reserved but firm opposition to Benito Mussolini's regime, Croce became recognized worldwide as an anti-Fascist symbol and as the intellectual guardian of Italy's democratic political heritage.

Principal philosophical works: *Materialismo storico ed economia marxistica*, 1900 (*Historical Materialism and the Economics of Karl Marx*, 1914); *Estetica come scienza dell'espressione e linguistica generale*, 1902 (*Aesthetic as Science of Expression and General Linguistic*, 1909); *Ciò che è vivo e ciò che è morto della filosofia di Hegel*, 1907 (*What Is Living and What Is Dead of the Philosophy of Hegel*, 1915); *Logica come scienza del concetto puro*, 1909 (*Logic as the Science of the Pure Concept*, 1917); *Filosofia della pratica: Economica ed etica*, 1909 (*Philosophy of the Practical: Economic and Ethic*, 1913); *Problemi di estetica e contributi alla storia dell'estetica italiana*, 1910; *La filosofia di Giambattista Vico*, 1911 (*The Philosophy of Giambattista Vico*, 1913); *Breviario di estetica*, 1913 (*The Breviary of Aesthetic*, 1915); *Cultura e vita morale*, 1914; *Teoria e storia della storiografia*, 1917 (*Theory and History of Historiography*, 1921); *Contributo alla critica di me stesso*, 1918 (*An Autobiography*, 1927); *Frammenti di etica*, 1922 (*The Conduct of Life*, 1924); *Elementi di politica*, 1925 (*Politics and Morals*, 1945); *Etica e politica*, 1931 (includes *The Conduct of Life, Politics and Morals*, and *An Autobiography*); *La poesia: Introduzione alla critica e storia della poesia e della letteratura*, 1936 (*Poetry and Literature: An Introduction to Its Criticism and History*, 1981); *La storia come pensiero e come azione*, 1938 (*History as the Story of Liberty*, 1941); *Discorsi di varia filosofia*, 1945 (2 volumes); *Filosofia e storiografia*, 1949; *Indagini su Hegel e schiarimenti filosofici*, 1952; *Filosofia, poesia, storia*, 1951 (*Philosophy, Poetry, History: An Anthology of Essays*, 1966).

Born: February 25, 1866; Pescassèroli, Italy
Died: November 20, 1952; Naples, Italy

Early Life

Benedetto Croce was born in the southern Italian region of Abruzzi. His family's substantial property wealth afforded him a comfortable childhood in Naples. After his parents died in an earthquake in 1883, Croce moved to Rome to live with his uncle, Silvio Spaventa, a prominent intellectual and conservative politician. The Italy of Croce's youth was a country struggling with all the problems attendant to a newly formed nation-state. The heroic era of the national unification movement—the Risorgimento—had ended in 1871. In the years that followed the Risorgimento period, Italian political life settled into the more uninspiring routine of parliamentary politics, budgetary battles, and electoral campaigns.

Croce's early exposure to politics came from the lively social and political gatherings at the Spaventa household. As a young man, he demonstrated little interest in politics, and his uncle's conservative rhetoric only reinforced his apolitical disposition. Croce later recalled his time in Rome as "a bad dream . . . the darkest and most bitter years of my life." His only consolation was in attending lectures on philosophy at the University of Rome.

Life's Work

In 1886, Croce returned to Naples. His inheritance enabled him to devote his entire life to scholarship. Over several decades, he accumulated an impressive private library and made his residence in the Palazzo Filomarino, an important center of intellectual activity in Italy. Croce's early research and writing dealt with local history and culture. He discovered in Naples a rich intellectual heritage that included the eighteenth century idealist philosopher Giambattista Vico and the Risorgimento literary critic Francesco De Sanctis. Like many of the scholars of his generation, Croce became intrigued with the economic theories of Karl Marx. After several years of intense study, he wrote a critique of Marxism, *Historical Materialism and the Economics of Karl Marx*, in 1899 and published it in 1900. Croce followed his rejection of Marx's "scientific" socialism with a broader criticism of the pervasive influence of science among European intellectuals.

During the late nineteenth century, European thought was dominated by positivism—the belief that the methods of empirical science were the best means of arriving at a true understanding of all natural phenomena. Even human behavior became a valid subject of scientific inquiry through pioneering work in psychology and sociology. Croce took the lead in the intellectual "revolt against positivism." He had little regard for scientific methodology, especially when applied to the study of human activity. He sought to defend those expressions of human creativity—especially art, poetry, and literature—from "scientific" critiques. He also argued that history, like art, was subjective. He denied that history could be written or understood with the detached objectivity of a scientist. Croce's assertion that "all history is contemporary history," refers to the manner in which the historian's own time and place and personal biases are reflected in his understanding and writings about the past. Croce attempted a systematic approach to the fundamental problems of aesthestics, logic, practical philosophy, and history in his monumental four-volume *Filosofia come sciensa dello spirito* ("philosophy of spirit"), which is made up of *Aesthetic as Science of Expression and General Linguistic*, *Logic as the Science of the Pure Concept*, *Philosophy of the Practical: Economic and Ethic*, and *Theory and History of Historiography*.

In addition to the ideas of Vico and De Sanctis, Croce drew heavily on German philosophy—most notably the thought of Georg Wilhelm Friedrich Hegel. He modified Hegel's idealism by emphasizing the importance of the manifestation of the ideal in human creativity in a given time and place. Croce's synthesis of Hegelian idealism and historical relativism gave new life to idealist philosophy. Croce reiterated and further developed his ideas in his journal of Italian culture, *La Critica*, which he cofounded with Giovanni Gentile in January, 1903. For more than forty years, Croce published this highly regarded journal and reviewed current developments in the cultural life of Italy.

The Italian government acknowledged Croce's intellectual contribution in 1910 by appointing him Senator of the Realm—a position for life. As a senator, he initially opposed Italian intervention on the side of England and France in World War I. He

Benedetto Croce. *(Library of Congress)*

urged neutrality not only because of high regard for German culture but also because of a sincere belief that Italy had no valid reason for joining in the conflict. When the Italian parliament finally decided the issue, he voted for war and supported the war effort as his duty. At the same time, he tried to mitigate some of the anti-German hysteria, especially among Italian intellectuals.

Croce joined the government of Giovanni Giolitti as Minister of Public Instruction following World War I. The government lasted only a year, until 1921, and Benito Mussolini seized power the following year. At first, Croce and many other conservative intellectuals welcomed the change in government, hoping that Mussolini might resolve the postwar political crisis and bring a new vitality to the nation. He later came under criticism for his early endorsement of Fascism. During the first years of Mussolini's regime, Croce slowly moved to the opposition. He became increasingly concerned with the government's harsh suppression of political dissent and its attempts to restrict the nation's intellectual and cultural life. In 1925, Croce published his "Manifesto of Anti-Fascist Intellectuals," in which he defended the principle of intellectual and cultural freedom. Croce's manifesto was a landmark in the history of the anti-Fascist resistance movement. In a movement dominated by Socialist and Communist factions, his became the conservative voice of opposition. Many Italians who had been reluctant to join with the opposition because of the radical elements were reassured by Croce's dissent and rallied to the anti-Fascist ranks. Although Croce established himself as a leading critic of the Fascist government, his opposition often appeared subtle and reserved. The esoteric character of his criticism and his international prestige protected him from government persecution while he continued to publish *La Critica* through the Fascist period.

The Fascist era in Italy marked the most productive years for Croce as a historian. The works that signaled a new direction in his studies included *Storia d'Italia dal 1871 al 1915* (1928; *A History of Italy, 1871-1915*, 1929), *Storia d'Europa nel secolo decimonono* (1932; *History of Europe in the Nineteenth Century*, 1933), and *History as the Story of Liberty*. In these histories, Croce sought to refute the prevailing interpretation by radicals on both the right and left, who argued that Europe had entered into a period of profound social crisis at the end of the nineteenth century and that democratic governments were so laden with incompetence and corruption that only revolutionary changes could save Europe from total collapse. Croce instead highlighted the political progress and cultural achievements of late nineteenth century Europe. He admonished those who depreciated the mundane political life of post-unification Italy simply because it failed to match the excitement and heroics of the Risorgimento. He conceded that parliamentary democracy, particularly in Italy, had been severely flawed, but he emphasized that such imperfections were an unavoidable part of the natural development of liberal political institutions. Croce's writings in the 1920's and 1930's challenged the Fascist government's negative assessment of postunification Italy and held out the prospects for a restoration of democratic government and political freedom.

During Mussolini's dictatorship, Croce had come to symbolize the anti-Fascist resistance for many Italians. As a consequence, following the fall of the Fascist regime in 1943 he lent political prestige to the liberation government by serving as an adviser and helped reorganize the conservative party. Yet Croce never had a great love for politics. He was a scholar and preferred his library-study to the parliamentary chambers. He retired from political life shortly after the war and continued his studies until his death in 1952.

Influence

In modern Europe, no thinker has dominated the intellectual life of his country as did Croce. He never received an academic degree, aside from those that were honorary, nor did he hold a university position. Yet his scholarship by itself has become an intellectual tradition in Italy, and he has influenced a generation of European scholars. He left behind several books and hundreds of essays dealing with an incredible range of subjects: aesthetics, economics, ethics, literary criticism, philosophy, history, and historiography. Croce's thought represents a continuation of the humanist-idealist philosophical tradition in Western civilization—an intellectual legacy that spans two thousand years, from the Greek philosopher Plato to modern times. Croce attempted to reconcile this tradition with the growing influence of more scientific and pragmatic philosophies, especially positivism, in the modern world. At the turn of the century, he sought to counter the cynicism and pessimism among European intellectuals with a new optimism, a revitalized faith in the progress of humanity. Even after World War I, when Europe experienced severe political and economic crises and many countries—including Italy—fell under the control of authoritarian governments, Croce retained his hope for the future and reaffirmed the idea of history as the advance of human freedom.

Michael F. Hembree

Aesthetic as Science of Expression and General Linguistic

Type of philosophy: Aesthetics, epistemology, ethics
First published: Estetica come scienza dell'espressione e linguistica generale, 1902 (English translation, 1909)
Principal ideas advanced:
◇ Art is intuition, and intuition is the expression of impressions.
◇ A sense impression or image becomes an expression, or intuition, when it is clearly known as an image, and when it is unified by the feeling it represents.
◇ The externalization of works of art by the fashioning of physical objects that will serve as stimuli in the reproduction of the intuitions represented is not art.
◇ Art is not concerned with the useful, the moral, or the intellectual.
◇ The fanciful combining of images is not art.
◇ Intuitions are of individuals, not universals.
◇ The theoretical activity of the spirit has two forms: the aesthetic and the logical; the practical activity is composed of the economic and the moral.
◇ The aesthetic values are the beautiful (the expressive) and the ugly; the logical values are the true and the false; the economic values are the useful and the useless; and the moral values are the just and the unjust.

Benedetto Croce's *Aesthetic as Science of Expression and General Linguistic* is the first of four volumes in his *Filosofia come sciensa dello spirito* ("philosophy of spirit"); the other three are *Logica come scienza del concetto puro* (1909; *Logic as the Science of the Pure Concept,* 1917), *Filosofia della pratica: Economica ed etica* (1909; *Philosophy of the Practical: Economic and Ethic,* 1913), and *Teoria e storia della storiografia* (1917; *Theory and History of Historiography,* 1921). Croce is generally regarded as an inspired proponent of the idealist strain in philosophy, and *Aesthetic as Science of Expression and General Linguistic,* the introduction to his theory, continues to be the work for which he is best known, and it is by his aesthetic theory that he is judged.

The entire thesis of *Aesthetic as Science of Expression and General Linguistic* rests on the concept of intuition, and because of the ambiguity of that term, Croce's work in translation never received the critical attention that the original Italian did. No English term, used without careful qualification, has enough levels of meaning, enough systematic ambiguity, to carry the burden of Croce's central idea. If, in addition, as may very well be the case, one must bring to the reading of *Aesthetic as Science of Expression and General Linguistic* a certain tolerance of mind that the prevailing empiricist temper makes difficult, it becomes even more evident that one must resist the temptation to understand Croce all at once. The idea, however deceptively direct its initial expression, must be built with great care, according to Croce's plan.

With this warning in mind, it becomes possible to take certain phrases as initial statements of Croce's position, retaining them as expressions to be illuminated by further discussion and reflection, for otherwise they are practically meaningless. Thus, for Croce, art is intuition; intuition is expression; art is the expression of impressions; and expression is the objectification of feelings by way of representative images. Many negations follow from these affirmations; of them, the most important, for those who would understand Croce, is the denial that the work of art is a physical object.

Art as Intuition
Croce begins *Aesthetic as Science of Expression and General Linguistic* with a careful elaboration of the

distinction between intuitive and logical knowledge; it is a distinction that bears some resemblance to philosopher Henri Bergson's distinction between intuitive and scientific or conceptual knowledge, but there is a difference. Bergson argued that certain matters cannot be understood analytically or by classes; they must be *felt*, in their internal particularity—to know by *being* is intuition. For Croce, the distinction between the object as known from the outside and as realized by itself is not the critical distinction, although it is encompassed by the distinction he does stress. For Croce, intuitive knowledge is the possession of images, but of images clarified by the attention of spirit, freed of all vagueness by the act of apprehension. The idea is remarkable enough to need and deserve amplification, and fortunately there are examples that clarify Croce's idea of intuition.

Croce asks how a person can be said to have an intuition of a geometrical figure or of the contour of the island of Sicily, if he cannot draw it. The notion that the artist is skilled in the act of transferring an image from the mind to some physical surface, as if his peculiar gift were in the handling of a pencil or brush, is repudiated by Croce. Unless one possesses a sensation or impression contemplatively, realizing it as an individual image, expression has not taken place. Under the influence of sentiment, one may suppose that one intuits, but unless one knows an image as an expression, one deceives oneself.

To enforce his point, Croce points out that the term "expression" is generally limited to verbal expression, but he uses it to cover nonverbal expressions of line, color, and sound. Apparently, for Croce, expression is not merely the clear apprehension of an image; the image is expressive of the feeling that it evokes, and it is through the expression of feeling that it becomes full expression or intuition. Thus, in *Breviario di estetica* (1913; *The Breviary of Aesthetic*, 1915), Croce writes that "what gives coherence and unity to the intuition is feeling: the intuition is really such because it represents a feeling, and can only appear from and upon that." He then goes on to affirm that "Not the idea, but the feeling, is what confers on art the airy lightness of the symbol: an aspiration enclosed in the circle of a representation—that is art."

The Breviary of Aesthetic, which is in many respects a superior expression of Croce's aesthetic theory, is interesting because of the series of denials by which the positive import of Croce's idea is brought out by contrast. To claim that art is intuition, that the artist produces an image which is expressive of feeling, and that he realizes this image in its full individuality, involves the denial that art is a physical fact (for physical facts, according to Croce, "*do not possess reality*"). It also denies that art is concerned with the useful, with pleasure and pain, and that art is a moral act (for art, unlike morality, "is opposed to the practical of any sort"). Finally, it denies that art is conceptual knowledge (for intuition is unconcerned with the distinction between reality and unreality).

Croce distinguishes between "fancy," which he describes as "the peculiar artistic faculty" and "imagination"; unfortunately, the translation of this passage of *The Breviary of Aesthetic* is misleading, for by "imagination" Croce meant the fanciful combination of images, while by "fancy" he meant the production of an image exhibiting unity in variety. The distinction can be grasped by reversing the terms: The mere fanciful handling of images is not art, and the composite image thereby produced is not a work of art; but if the imagination holds on to a sense impression, realizing its presence, taking an interest in it because it serves as the embodiment of feeling, then the image is a work of art.

The esoteric character of Croce's central idea diminishes as one realizes that Croce was concerned to emphasize the artist's ability to see more clearly what others only vaguely sense. "The painter is a painter," he writes in *Aesthetic as Science of Expression and General Linguistic*, "because he sees what others only feel or catch a glimpse of, but do not see."

Having argued that art is intuition and that intuition is expressive knowledge, Croce considers the critical rejoinder that, although art is intuition, not all intuition is art. He rejects the sophisticated notion that art is the intuition of an intuition—that is, the expression of intuitions. He argues that there is no such process and that what critics have regarded as the expression of expression is, as intuition, the expression of a more complex field of impressions than is ordinarily covered by intuition. He goes on to suggest that the word "art" is often used to call attention to intuitions more extensive in their scope than ordinary intuitions. However, from the philosophical point of view—which is concerned with essence and not with quantity—all intuition is art.

If the question arises as to whether content or form is the distinctive aesthetic element in intuition, and by content is meant impressions and by form, expression, then the aesthetic fact, the distinctive aesthetic element, is form.

Because art is the elaboration of impressions, the unifying of impressions into a single, intuited image expressive of feeling, it is a means of liberation for people; the objectification of the passions frees people from their practical influence. Artists are people of passion who are nevertheless serene; that is because they use sentiment in the intuitive activity, and by that activity, they liberate and purify themselves. The paradox of artists is resolved once it is realized that sensation is passive, but intuition, as the contemplative and creative activity of realizing images as expressive symbols, is active; through activity artists dominate what would otherwise dominate them.

Art is intuitive knowledge and not conceptual knowledge because knowledge by concepts, according to Croce, is knowledge of the relations of intuitions. Thus, conceptual knowledge depends on the intuitive, and the latter cannot be reduced to the former. Furthermore, concepts are universals; an intellectual conception is concerned with what is common to a number of things, or intuitions. However, intuitions are of particulars; individuals images become expressions and serve as works of art. Croce concludes his discussion of this point with the remark that "The intuition gives the world, the phenomenon; the concept gives the noumenon, the Spirit." However, this statement is misleading unless we remember that the world presented in intuition is one in which distinctions between actual and possible, true and false, pleasant and unpleasant, and good and bad are irrelevant.

Criticism of Other Theories

Croce passes from a positive statement of his aesthetic theory to a criticism of rival theories. He considers briefly, and in turn, the theories that hold art to be an imitation of nature, the representation of universals, the presentation of symbols or allegories, or the portrayal of various forms of life. All such theories commit the fallacy of mistaking the intellectual for the artistic, confusing the concept with the intuition. Once people concentrate on the *type* of subject matter, the *mode* of treatment, the *style* exhibited, they lose the aesthetic attitude; they have passed on to the scientific or intellectual activity, the exercise of logic, which is concerned with concepts, or universals. "The science of thought (Logic) is that of the concept," he insists, "as that of fancy (Aesthetic) is the science of expression."

As the criticism continues, the outlines of Croce's philosophy of spirit become better defined. The theoretical activity of the spirit has two forms: the aesthetic and the logical; the practical activity also has two forms: the useful or economical, and the moral. "Economy is, as it were, the Aesthetic of practical life; Morality its Logic." Economy is concerned, then, with the individual and his or her values (just as aesthetic is concerned with the individual intuition and its value), while morality is concerned with the general, with the values of the universal. Nevertheless, the economic will (the practical will) is not the egoistic will; it is possible to conduct oneself practically without being limited to a concern for self. To act morally, one must act economically; but the reverse is not necessarily the case. To conduct oneself economically is to adjust means to ends, but to conduct oneself morally is to adjust means to *ideal* ends, to what the spirit would desire were it rational, aiming at the noumenon, the spirit, of the self. Just as aesthetic is concerned with phenomena, and logic with noumena, so the economic is concerned with the phenomena and morality with the noumena, the ideal.

Values

The beautiful, considered as aesthetic value, is defined by Croce as *successful expression*, but realizing that expression that is not successful is not expression, Croce concludes by writing that beauty is expression. Consequently, the ugly is unsuccessful expression, or the failure to achieve expression.

Corresponding to the polar values of beauty and ugliness in the aesthetic are the values of truth and falsity for the intellectual, the useful and the useless for the economic, and the just (or good) and unjust (or evil) for the moral. In every case, the positive value results from the successful development of spiritual activity.

Croce's central criticism of any form of aesthetic hedonism—of any theory that regards art as the production of the pleasurable—is that aesthetic hedonism fails to distinguish between the beautiful, which is the pleasurable as expression, and other sources of pleasure. He scornfully rejects any theory that finds the source of artistic activity in the sexual, in the desire to conquer. He admits that "one often meets in ordinary life poets who adorn themselves with their poetry, like cocks that raise their crests," but he argues that such a person is not a poet, but "a poor devil of a cock or turkey."

For Croce, the physical reproduction of intuitions, the making of physical objects that will stimulate those who experience them to the activity of recreating the intuitions, is an aid to memory, or a way of preserving intuitions. Physical reproduction is called "externalization," and it is defined as the activity of producing stimuli to aesthetic reproduction.

In ordinary language, the physical objects found on the walls of art museums, the statues of stones or metal that stand in gardens, and other such physical, created objects are works of art; but for Croce only intuitions are works of art; the inner image guides the production of the physical "reproduction," but the physical object is never the aesthetic fact. To confuse the techniques necessary for the externalization of art with the art activity itself is to confuse "Physic" with "Aesthetic." Externalization is a practical activity, while aesthetic is a theoretic activity. Art is thus independent not only of the intellectual, the useful, and the moral; it is independent of the activity of externalization (which is one kind of useful activity). The effort to reproduce the expression by means of the physical object involves the effort to restore the conditions under which the physical object was produced by the artist; works that are to serve as stimuli to expressions are *historically conditioned.*

Croce concludes his *Aesthetic as Science of Expression and General Linguistic* with a chapter in which he explains why he chose to include the words "and general linguistic" in the title. Aesthetic is the science of expression because, for Croce, art is expression (intuition), and aesthetic is the systematic attempt to acquire knowledge about expression. However, Croce claims that aesthetic and linguistic are a single science; philosophical linguistic is aesthetic; "Philosophy of language and philosophy of art are the same thing." Aesthetic is the science of general linguistic, then, because language is expression, and aesthetic is the science of expression. The defense of his thesis depends on Croce's decision to mean by "Linguistic" a rational science, the pure philosophy of speech, and by "speech," any mode of expression.

Ian P. McGreal

Additional Reading

Brown, Merle E. *Neo-Idealistic Aesthetics: Croce-Gentile-Collingwood.* Detroit. Mich.: Wayne State University Press, 1966. The author devotes the first five chapters of this work, more than half the entire book, to Benedetto Croce. He emphasizes the development of Croce's theory of art, which began with the view that art is representation and culminated by arguing that it is feeling objectified. The author addresses the influence of Giovanni Gentile on Croce's changing views.

Casale, Giuseppe. *Benedetto Croce Between Naples and Europe.* New York: Peter Lang, 1993. The author argues that Croce sought to offer through his concept of historicism an alternative to both traditional religion and the culture of science. He places Croce's ideas within the context of both Neapolitan and European culture.

Moss, M. E. *Benedetto Croce Reconsidered: Truth and Error in Theories of Art, Literature, and History.* Foreword by Maurice Mandelbaum. Hanover, N.H.: University Press of New England, 1987. Arguing for Croce's continuing philosophical significance, the author addresses his philosophical conceptions of truth, error, and objectivity and analyzes his theory of intuition.

Roberts, David D. *Benedetto Croce and the Uses of Historicism.* Berkeley: University of California Press, 1987. This critical reassessment is the best intellectual biography of Croce available in English. The author includes an impressive

417

bibliography, covering major themes of modern European intellectual history.

Ryn, Claes G. *Will, Imagination, and Reason: Babbitt, Croce, and the Problem of Reality*. New Brunswick: Transaction Publishers, 1997. A good assessment of Croce's thought.

Sprigge, Cecil. *Benedetto Croce: Man and Thinker*. New Haven, Conn.: Yale University Press, 1952. Sprigge's admiring, though not uncritical, account of Croce's life and thought is probably the best general biography of Croce available in English.

Ward, David. *Antifascisms: Cultural Politics in Italy, 1943-46: Benedetto Croce and the Liberals, Carlo Levi and the "Actionists."* Madison, N.J.: Fairleigh Dickinson University Press, 1996. A valuable treatment of Croce's political philosophy.

Michael F. Hembree, updated by Gary Land

Dao De Jing

Written sometime between the sixth and third centuries B.C.E. and traditionally attributed to the sage Laozi, the *Dao De Jing* is a central text of Daoism, a Chinese philosophy and popular religion that advocates the need for living in accordance with the *dao*, the animating force of the natural world.

Authorship and Context

So little is known of Laozi, to whom the *Dao De Jing* is often attributed, that some scholars think he is a purely legendary figure. His name, which means Old Master, does little to establish a credible identity. The earliest literary reference to him can be found in Sima Qian's *Shi-ji* (first century B.C.E.; *Records of the Grand Historian of China*, 1960, rev. ed. 1993), one of the earliest extant volumes of Chinese history. According to this work, Laozi was born sometime in the late sixth century B.C.E. and served as official archivist in the capital Zhou. Renowned for his knowledge of ritual, he was purportedly visited by his younger contemporary Confucius, who was much impressed by his wisdom. After retiring from his civil career, however, Laozi decided to lead a hermit's life. As he was leaving for the frontier, a gatekeeper asked him to write a book that would preserve his vast store of wisdom; he therefore composed the poetic treatise that has come to be known as the *Dao De Jing*. He divided the book into two sections: one devoted to explicating the nature of the *dao* and the other analyzing *de*, its power or effects. After completing the work—reputedly at a single sitting—he disappeared into the wilderness, where, the historian writes, Laozi lived to the advanced age of 160 or perhaps 200 years. As if plausibility has not been strained enough, Sima Qian then speculates that Laozi may even have lived into the fourth century B.C.E.—more than one hundred years after the death of Confucius—when he returned to civilization to serve as Grand Historian to the duke of Zhou. Complicating matters even further is Sima Qian's possible identifi-

cation of Laozi with an obscure figure named Lao Lai Zi, who is mentioned in the other major work of Chinese Daoism, the *Zhuangzi* (c. 300 B.C.E.; *The Divine Classic of Nan-hua*, 1881; also known as *The Complete Works of Chuang Tzu*, 1968; commonly known as *Zhuangzi*, 1991).

Although early Chinese historiography willfully mixed fact and legend, it seems unlikely that Laozi is a complete fabrication. Sima Qian's reference to Laozi's reputation as a master of traditional rites militates somewhat against the argument that the "Old Master" was a product of Daoist propaganda because Daoists were ordinarily dismissive of such practices. Moreover, while Daoist folklore is replete with legendary immortals who are able to shape-shift and perform miracles, the figure of Laozi, the humble civil servant who founded the creed, is positively mundane by comparison. (Stories of legendary encounters between Laozi and Confucius, usually at the latter's expense, do exist—most notably in the *Zhuangzi*; yet, even there Laozi remains very much a mortal figure.) Certainly Laozi's position as an official archivist would qualify him to be the author of the work attributed to him. Whether a contemporary of Confucius in the fifth century B.C.E. or an adviser to the duke of Zhou in the fourth, an archivist would be one of the few individuals in China at that time with the ability to read and write. Finally, in an era in which no distinction was made between a literary work and its author, the work's original title was simply the *Laozi*, a term that most scholars continue to use. Its subsequent title, *Dao De Jing*, literally "the classic of *dao* and *de*," was not adopted until the first century B.C.E.

Dating *Dao De Jing* is as perplexing as identifying its reputed author. Traditional scholarship, which assumed Laozi to have been the author, dated the manuscript to the Spring and Autumn period (770-476 B.C.E.), making it as old as such classics as the Confucian *Lunyu* (late sixth or early fifth century B.C.E.; *Analects*, 1861) and the *I Ching* (*Yi Jing*, eighth to third century B.C.E.; English translation, 1876; also known as *Book of Changes*, 1986). However, modern scholars who have debated the identity of Laozi and questioned his authorship of the *Dao De Jing* have generally placed its composition in the Warring States period (403-222 B.C.E.). A number of strong argu-

ments, based on internal and external evidence, seem to point to the latter period. For instance, the work's preoccupation with the individual's survival in a chaotic world seems to reflect the political instability of the Warring States period. Moreover, the work's identification of *dao* with the Creator is certainly atypical of the Spring and Autumn period, in which *tian*, or Heaven, most often serves in that capacity. Its use of rhyme and lack of dialogue also differentiate it from older wisdom books such as the *Analects* and the *Mozi* (fifth century B.C.E.; *The Ethical and Political Works of Motse*, 1929; also known as *Mo Tzu: Basic Writings*, 1963). The dearth of contemporary references to the *Dao De Jing* in works belonging to the Spring and Autumn period would also seem to weigh against the earlier date (although one can argue that if the *Analects* do not refer to the *Dao De Jing*, neither does the *Dao De Jing* refer to the *Analects*). The earliest references to the *Dao De Jing* are quotations from the work included in the *Zhuangzi*, a product of the Warring States period. However, even this supposed "fact" is at best ambiguous because the *Zhuangzi* is itself most likely a redaction of earlier works.

Whether written by Laozi or compiled by a latter-day Daoist, the *Dao De Jing* is ultimately a product of China's fervent intellectual climate of the fifth and fourth centuries B.C.E., a period often referred to as the "one hundred schools" for its philosophic diversity. This period witnessed the rise of competing schools of thought centered on charismatic expositors such as Confucius, Mozi, Mencius, and Yang Zhu. At times the *Dao De Jing* seems bewildering, if not perverse, unless this philosophic context is taken into account. Indeed, the work alternately affirms and rejects positions and even the terminology of the competing schools. For instance, its famous first line, "the *dao* that can be named is not the true *dao*," seems a deliberate re-

The *Dao De Jing* has been attributed to Laozi, an ancient Chinese sage about whom little is known for certain, although there are many stories about him. *(Corbis/Bettman)*

buke to the *fa jia*, or Legalist, school, which sought to remedy contemporary social ills through accurate naming. Similarly, chapter 3 borrows the Mohist phrase "worthy men" to make a decidedly anti-Mohist point— that *not* praising worthy men is the best way to keep from stirring the ambitions of the common people. Chapter 31's advocacy of defensive warfare finds the author in agreement with Mozi, but in opposition to Yang Zhu's more extreme pacifism. Even the emphasis on *dao* (or "Way"), a common word in the philosophic parlance of the time, seems a calculated attempt to undermine the authority of the other schools—as if to imply that the "Daoist" is the ultimate school of thought.

The reflexive nature of the *Dao De Jing* is perhaps the best argument for late authorship because the other schools' positions and terminology presumably would have to have been well established in order for the work to subvert them. If one accepts the late authorship, then the figure of Laozi becomes a necessary fiction to an emergent school of thought competing with other schools centered on a sage philosopher. On the other hand, a sixth century B.C.E. Laozi may have anticipated the philosophic debate of the "one hundred schools period"—or perhaps the positions and terminology of the period themselves belong to an earlier, largely preliterate society.

Some scholars entirely reject the premise that the *Dao De Jing* is the work of a single author, whether Laozi or a latter-day scribe writing under his name. Instead they explain the unusual work as a collection of sayings belonging to Daoist oral tradition. According to this hypothesis, the social unrest of the Warring States period produced a subclass of disaffected gentlemen, or *shi*, who withdrew from the chaos of their culture into "Laoist" communities based upon the quietist principles attributed to Laozi. The *Dao De Jing* thus becomes the work of a Laoist editor (or editors) who collected and perhaps elaborated upon the traditional Daoist proverbs attributed to Laozi. Certainly the *Dao De Jing* is full of statements with memorable images and a proverblike ring, such as "To rule a country is like cooking a small fish" (that is, it is easy to spoil) and "Heaven and Earth are not kind—to them all things are straw dogs" (insignificant items burned in ritual sacrifice). Such utterances seem

to owe less to literary metaphysics than to the practical affairs of an oral culture. This may explain the seemingly haphazard nature of some chapters, in which groups of proverbs seem artificially stitched together. For instance, the line about cooking a small fish is juxtaposed to the lines "When *dao* brings everything into harmony/Demons have no power." The *Dao De Jing* also includes a number of similar lines that seem to be based upon oral formulas. For instance, the line "*Dao* endures without name" (in Chinese, *Dao chang wu ming*) reappears in a later chapter as "*Dao* is hidden without name" (*Dao yin wu ming*).

Whether such formulas were originally used by Laozi, who would have been writing in the context of a predominantly oral culture, or by latter-day Laoists adapting traditional oral proverbs, both the individual chapters and the work as a whole have a collage effect—as if the author or Laoist editors were deliberately trying to subvert the discursive nature of the literary medium. Indeed, the power of the *Dao De Jing*, and its freshness to modern readers, seems to come from its informal ability to speak directly to them, seemingly bypassing the conventions and limitations of the manuscript or printed page. Even in translation, the work at times seems less like proverbial wisdom or literary poetry than a collection of song lyrics—a connection underscored by the rhyming structure of some chapters, which makes them reminiscent of Daoist hymns like those scattered throughout the *Zhuangzi*.

No original manuscript of the *Dao De Jing* exists. If it was a product of the fifth century B.C.E., it may have been written on bamboo stalks rather than paper—which may explain the lack of an extant copy. The earliest available complete text of the *Dao De Jing* is the edition of Wang Bi (226-249 C.E.), which includes his commentary. Although this continues to serve as the standard text, it suffers from some obvious errors. For instance, some of Wang Bi's commentaries refer to Chinese characters that are different from those in the passages glossed, while others refer to passages not included in the text. Subsequent editors, including Fu Yi, Ma Xulun, and Chen Zhu, have attempted to resolve these errors and eliminate obscurities in the text with the hope of "restoring" it to Laozi's original. Such redaction has led at times to rather extreme practices. For instance, guided by the belief that an older contemporary of Confucius authored the work, some editors have substituted older forms of Chinese characters in use in the sixth century B.C.E. for the newer variants in the Wang Bi text. Other editors with an eye on numerology have even reduced the number of characters in the Wang Bi text from 5,250 to an even 5,000.

Whether Wang Bi first divided the work into two books with a total of eighty-one chapters (thirty-seven devoted to *dao* and forty-four to *de*) remains unknown. However, most editors have agreed that the original text (or anthology) was not divided into chapters at all, allowing them to divide and rearrange the work as they have seen fit. If the *dao* that can be named is not the true *dao*, then it would seem that the *Dao De Jing* that can be definitively identified is not the true *Dao De Jing*. As if following Daoist principle, the book remains very much a living document, a work in progress as editors and scholars continue to debate not only the meaning of the text but the text itself. It remains one of the most translated works in world literature, second only to the Bible.

Luke A. Powers

Overview

Type of philosophy: Ethics, metaphysics, political philosophy

First transcribed: Dao De Jing, late third century B.C.E. (*The Speculations on Metaphysics, Polity, and Morality, of "the Old Philosopher, Lau-Tsze,"* 1868; better known as *Dao De Jing*)

Principal ideas advanced:

◇ *Dao*, the Way, is the nameless beginning of things, the universal principle underlying everything, the supreme, ultimate pattern, and the principle of growth.

◇ If one takes possession of the *dao*, the universal principle, one becomes a sage fit for ruling the world.

◇ By observing nature, one learns to follow the Way, the *dao*.

◇ One who possesses *dao* must hide power and appear soft and weak, for the people who show their power are without power, and the soft overcomes the hard.

◇ To attain *dao*, a person must return to the state of infancy, avoid action, and preserve the breath, the life-force, by breath control.

Perhaps more than any other ancient Chinese text, the *Dao De Jing* has been a center of philological dispute through the centuries. The first question is its authorship. The work is often attributed to Laozi. Sima Qian's *Shi-ji* (first century B.C.E.; *Records of the Grand Historian of China*, 1960; rev. ed. 1993), identifies Laozi as an official archivist in the capital Zhou, who lived in the late sixth century B.C.E. He was said to have composed the *Dao De Jing* all by himself shortly before he vanished beyond the mountains on the back of a blue water buffalo. In fact, the *Dao De Jing* contains many telltale features that point to its collective authorship; most probably it was not written by any single author but has grown into its present shape.

An understanding about the authorship of this work is important for a proper grasp of the central ideas behind the eighty-one short but epigrammatic and sometimes cryptic chapters in this work—for however poetically integrated these ideas may be around the central theme of a mystic quietism that dates as far back as the dawning of Chinese history, there are passages in this book alluding to the many different schools of thought that contended for intellectual dominance in the early Warring States period (403-222 B.C.E.). The voice (or voices, hereafter called the Daoist) speaking behind these epigrams is arguing against the Legalists (also called Realists), the Confucians, and the Mohists, but the voice also seems to borrow some of the arguments of its rivals. The borrowings are possibly due both to the coexistence of these arguments, as part of the common knowledge of the intellectuals at the time this book was first put together, and to the subsequent interpolations of commentaries that became hopelessly enmeshed with the original text.

The Dao

A vague notion of the *dao* existed among the proto-philosophical ideas in ancient China long before any Daoists or Mohists or Confucians expounded their respective views on this concept. It stemmed, apparently, from an early effort of the Chinese mind to search into the mystery of the universe and to discover the rationale, if any, behind things. To name the unnamable, the Chinese borrowed this term, *dao*, or the Way. The ambiguous nature of this term allows it to serve several doctrines. Hence, to Confucius, *dao* means the Sage King's way to social harmony; to Mozi, *dao* means the way to ample supply of staple foods and a populous state; and to Mencius, *dao* means the way to moral (and spiritual) perfection. However, to a Daoist, *dao* could mean all these and more.

Throughout this work (and particularly in chapter 25), *dao* is described as the nameless beginning of all things, even prior to Heaven and Earth. *Dao* is unchanging and permeates everything; hence, *dao* must be a kind of constant, universal principle that underlies all phenomena. *Dao* has always existed and has no beginning of itself; hence, it must be comparable to the first cause. Everything in the universe patterns itself after the dictates of a higher being; humans, for example, pattern their ways after those of Heaven. However, *dao*, being supreme, follows itself. Hence, it suggests the ultimate pattern. *Dao* "is so of itself," without any outside force or influence. Above all, *dao* is "always so" because it is the dynamic principle of change. It dictates the rhythm of growth and decay, but because it is itself the principle of growth, it remains constant.

This argument is a frontal attack against the Legalists. The Legalists divide phenomena into rigid categories, and they demand that the rigidity of their system be maintained at all costs because they see no other essence of anything except its name. The Daoists point out, in chapter 1, that the named are but the manifestations of essence. They are only the crust. What lies behind them is the real essence, which is the source of all mysteries of the universe. In its application, the Daoist argument thus refutes the Legalists' emphasis on rules and regulations as the essential order of things.

As the first cause and the ultimate pattern, *dao* possesses infinite power without being powerful. It does not force anything to follow its way; yet everything by virtue of being itself will of itself follow *dao*, just as water will ultimately flow downward. Any interruption of this ultimate pattern can be only temporary. Why, then, should a ruler employ force, as the Legalists insist rulers must, in order to conquer and reign over the world? Violence contrived by people is against *dao*; if only the king possesses *dao*, all the world will obey him; even Heaven and Earth will bless him and come to his aid.

The Daoists speak metaphorically of *dao*, identifying it as the secret of all secrets, but they also go on to suggest a way of comprehending *dao*. Because *dao* is the unchanging universal principle that dwells in everything, everything in its original state reflects *dao*. In humans, the original state of existence, infancy, comes closest to this idea. If one does not tamper with one's heart (mind), so that the heart remains untainted, one has the best chance of comprehending this mysterious universal principle. Unspoiled, the *dao* in a tree trunk is as great and as efficacious as the *dao* filling the universe, so long as the tree trunk remains an "uncarved block." If carved, the block of wood becomes a few ordinary articles of daily use. However, if one takes possession of the universal principle within an "uncarved block," one becomes a sage fit for ruling the world.

Nonactivity and Unspoiled Nature

Like the Confucians, the Daoists also talk about the sages. However, the Daoist sage is not one who studies the classics, disciplines himself according to the rules of propriety, and preaches constantly to the rulers to be benevolent (as is recommended in Confucius's *Lunyu* (late sixth or early fifth century B.C.E.; *Analects*, 1861). On the contrary, Daoist sages have little use for words, because the words of *dao* are "simple and flavorless." They do not occupy themselves with such useless motions as seeking audience with the rulers or teaching students, activities that kept the Confucians and the Mohists busy, because "*dao* never does, and yet through it all things are done." The life of the people becomes proportionately impoverished as Confucian rituals and decorum multiply; thieves and bandits redouble at the same rate as the laws are promulgated. The Daoist sage "does nothing," and the people of themselves behave properly. The anti-intellectual attitude of the Daoists leads them to stress nonactivity because only by refraining from useless motions can the state of the "uncarved block" be preserved.

Clearly nature in its primeval stage is the best example of the "uncarved block." Consequently, unspoiled nature is regarded by the Daoists as the best place to observe the revelation of the universal principle, or *dao*. By observing nature, one learns to follow nature's way, the Way of *dao*. This acceptance of the way of nature as inevitable, regular, and normal leads to an attitude of resignation. It is not a negative attitude undertaken with a deep sigh of regret, but a joyful acceptance of what is the perfect pattern of things and events. Daoists do not hesitate to discourage humankind's efforts to undo what nature has done. They regard such efforts as useless even should people, out of ignorance and perversion, attempt to disobey the universal principle revealed in nature. *Dao* is like an immense boat that drifts freely and irresistibly according to its own will, the Daoists say, and therefore people do well to avoid butting their heads uselessly against this huge boat and instead to ride along in it. In this idea is found the seed of the Chinese concept that the strongest is the person who makes use of his or her enemy's strength—a concept that finds its prosaic expression in the theory of Chinese boxing. Behind this concept lies the reason that Daoists respect whatever appears to be soft, weak, and yielding.

The multiple metaphors in this work comparing the nature of *dao* to the secret, the "dark," and the "mysterious" are not merely poetic embellishment but revelations of the strand of primitive quietism in Daoism. Among the proto-philosophical ideas of ancient China is the notion of *yin-yang* (negative-positive, or female-male), a pair of mutually complementary forces that are at work in and behind all phenomena. The *yin* force or element is characterized as passive, receiving, and meek (at least in appearance). Yet like the idea of the female or mother, *yin* also possesses the potential of infinite creation. Hence the *yin* principle is closer to *dao*. *Dao* is compared to "a ravine that receives all things" and, therefore, has "unlimited power." In consonance with the *yin* characteristics, one who possesses *dao* (a sage) must hide power, for one who shows that power is really without power. A Daoist sage appears to be soft and weak because it is the "soft

that overcomes the hard, and the weak, the strong," and because *dao* itself is unostentatious; *dao* "produces, clothes, and feeds" all beings without claiming mastery over them, yet everything submits itself to *dao*. For the same reason, Daoists praise the infant who is soft and weak and yet is most strong because in the child the universal essence is not dissipated and the harmony of *yin* and *yang* is still perfect.

In this concept lies the Daoist relativity of attributes. To Daoists, nothing is absolute except *dao* itself. Without "short," there cannot be "long." Thus, a Daoist dismisses the validity of the effort of members of the School of Names to distinguish the white of a white horse from the white of a white jade. In doing so, the Daoists also dismiss the Confucian effort to distinguish good from bad as useless trifling. Just as long and short have nothing to do with the essence of things, death and life are also two manifestations of what is so of itself (natural). To treasure the good, to prefer the rich, and to cherish life are equally meaningless, equally foolish to one having arrived at *dao*.

Because there is no real difference between acting and not acting, the person who does nothing accomplishes most. This concept of nonactivity, coupled with the idea that the person who "moves not" endures the longest, strengthens the Daoist belief in quietism.

Throughout the *Dao De Jing*, there are repeated hints at a process of attaining *dao*. The Daoist urges people to retain their untainted and untampered hearts and to return to a state of infancy, desirable because of its undissipated essence. The expression for "essence" here is *qi*. Generally understood as "gaseous matters," *qi* in ancient Chinese cosmology is closely tied in with "spirit" as distinguished from "physical substance." In people, *qi* is identified with breath as separate from flesh and bones. The Daoist regards people's *qi* as part of the universal *qi*, or humanity's life-force. Hence, to avoid dissipation, people must attempt to preserve their life-force, and this effort turns out to be a process of breath control. Indeed the subsequent development of magical Daoism shows many features parallel to the esoteric Indian yoga. Practitioners of Daoist magic can always cite certain passages from this work for authority. For instance, at least one line (in chapter 55) tends to support the practice of sexual hygiene as a means of achieving *dao*.

Mysticism thickens around Daoists when they claim that neither poisonous insects nor wild animals can harm the infant, or that by fixing one's gaze in meditation one can achieve longevity. Three aspects are involved in these claims. First, the Daoist actually believes in a certain kind of yoga practice to prolong this life on earth. Second, in the Daoist vocabulary, the word for longevity may mean endurance. That which endures in people is their essence, which is part of the universal essence. People may die, but as long as they do not lose their essence, they actually endure. The manifestation of a person's essence may take different forms, such as a tree or a rock, but an individual's essence remains unchanged, resulting in longevity. Third, by promoting life-nurture, the Daoist stood opposed to another school of thought prevailing at that time. Led by a philosopher named Yang Zhu, this school advocated total gratification of the physical senses as the real goal of life and the road to salvation, a doctrine clearly contrary to the Daoist emphasis on quietism.

To be with *dao* is to be free, according to the *Dao De Jing*. People who are with *dao* are free because they have the infinite power that enables them to do whatever they please while they stay within *dao*. Metaphysically this freedom should mean spiritual emancipation and salvation—a liberation of people from the bondage of their limited orbit in this earthly world. However, it can readily be seen how a person with political ambitions or a magical bent of mind could make use of this theory. This work contains mystic references to "travels in spirit" that take a person with *dao* through space and time to ethereal realms. It has been suggested that this work must have had a southern Chinese origin, as some passages in it allude to a southern setting. The area south of the Yangzi (Chang Jiang) River was rich in shamanistic tradition, and a book of southern songs, collected at about the same time as the *Dao De Jing*, contains descriptions of similar "spirit travels." These supernatural feats were probably part of the shamanistic belief common in the Warring States period along the middle reaches of the Yangzi River. The shamans induced trances with prayers and dances as well as through con-

centration and yogalike hypnotism. Later in magical Daoism there appears a True Person, a Daoist adept at having acquired the powers to perform these superhuman feats.

Nature

The *Dao De Jing*, like most Chinese classics originating during the Warring States period, was intended to serve more as a political manual than as a purely metaphysical treatise. However, the metaphysical speculations in this book are provocative enough to have inspired many developments—some occult, some seriously philosophical—in the history of Chinese thought. The concept of nature is one of them.

Nature in the *Dao De Jing* is amoral because it is one manifestation of the universal essence. Nature does not house more *dao* than an infant or a tree trunk, yet nature by its grandeur has a special appeal to the Daoist. The unchanging mountains, as contrasted with the changing affairs of humanity, symbolize for the Daoist the principle of nonactivity, and a calm lake expresses the idea of quietude. A profound appreciation of nature, at once aesthetic and mystic, stems from this Daoist attitude and forms the basis of a concept of nature that has played an important role in Chinese poetry and art. In philosophy, the concept of nature became the native stock on which Indian Mahayana Buddhism was grafted to bear the fruits of Chinese Chan (Zen) Buddhism.

Nature also has its violent moods. Its wild destructive forces must have been the inspiration behind the passage in the *Dao De Jing* that refers to Heaven and Earth as unkind because "they treat all beings like straw dogs," or expendable sacrificial objects. However, kindness has no place in *dao* which is "always so" and unchanging. The Daoist making the foregoing remark is not criticizing nature but rather is stating an actuality. This attitude has encouraged many people to embrace a political absolutism that they justify and defend using the *dao*.

The esoteric elements in Daoism encouraged the accumulation of magical formulas and alchemy, and through the years, they influenced a large area in Chinese folk religion. A city of Daoist gods has been constructed. A Daoist clerical and lay tradition and a library of Daoist scriptures have grown to impressive proportions.

The *Dao De Jing* deserves credit as an enduring expression of basic Chinese philosophy. The belief in the existence of a universal principle, having received such eloquent and poetic expression in this book, leads contemplative minds to search for the profound and the true in nature and in humanity.

Kai-yu Hsu, updated by John K. Roth

Additional Reading

Chan, Wing-tsit. *The Way of Lao Tzu*. Indianapolis, Ind.: Bobbs-Merrill, 1963. The best one-volume study of the *Dao De Jing*, with exhaustive discussion of the controversies surrounding its dating and the identity of its author. Good analytical comparisons between the philosophies of Laozi, Confucius, and Zhuangzi.

Graham, A. C. *Disputers of the Tao: Philosophical Argument in Ancient China*. La Salle, Ill.: Open Court, 1989. A thorough intellectual history of Daoism's place within the "one hundred schools."

Kohn, Livia. *Early Chinese Mysticism: Philosophy and Soteriology in the Taoist Tradition*. Princeton, N.J.: Princeton University Press, 1991. An exploration of the cross-fertilization of Daoism and Chan (or Zen) Buddhism.

Kohn, Livia, and Michael LaFargue, eds. *Lao-tzu and the "Tao-te-ching."* Albany: State University of New York, 1998. This work compares traditional Chinese and Western interpretations of the *Dao De Jing* and Eastern and Western views of Laozi. Includes index.

LaFargue, Michael. *The Tao of the Tao Te Ching: A Translation and Commentary*. Albany: State University Press of New York, 1992. The commentary includes a detailed summary of the author's oral tradition theory.

_____. *Tao and Method: A Reasoned Approach to the Tao Te Ching*. Albany: State University Press of New York, 1994. Excellent exposition of the theory that the work was derived from oral tradition by a group of "Laoist" editors.

Tao Te Ching. Translated by Stephen Addis and Stanley Lombardo. With an introduction by Burton Watson. Indianapolis, Ind.: Hackett, 1993. An English translation that includes both Chinese characters and romanized spellings in the text. Includes a glossary and pronunciation guide.

Tao Te Ching. Translated by D. C. Lau. Middlesex, England: Penguin Books, 1963. The translation is at times bland, but the introduction effectively places the work within the context of Chinese literary history.

Tao Te Ching. English Commentary on the Lao Tzu by Wang Pi. Translated by Ariane Rump in collaboration with Wing-tsit Chan. Honolulu: University Press of Hawaii, 1979. A readable translation of the Wang Bi edition and commentary.

Waley, Arthur. *The Way and Its Powers: A Study of the Tao Te Ching and Its Place in Chinese Thought*. London: George Allen & Unwin, 1934. One of the best known translations in English. The introduction is long and meandering, but the background material on the "one hundred schools" is enlightening.

Wong, Eva. *The Shambhala Guide to Taoism*. Boston: Shambhala, 1997. An informal introduction to Daoist philosophy.

Luke A. Powers

Charles Darwin

Darwin's theory of evolution through natural selection, which he set forth in *On the Origin of Species by Means of Natural Selection*, revolutionized biology by providing a scientific explanation for the origin and development of living forms.

Principal philosophical works: *Journal of Researches into the Geology and Natural History of the Various Countries Visited by H.M.S. Beagle, 1832-36*, 1839 (journal; commonly known as *The Voyage of the Beagle*); *The Structure and Distribution of Coral Reefs*, 1842; *Geological Observations on the Volcanic Islands Visited During the Voyage of H.M.S. 'Beagle,'* 1844; *Geological Observations on South America*, 1846; *On the Origin of Species by Means of Natural Selection: Or, The Preservation of Favoured Races in the Struggle for Life*, 1859; *On the Movements and Habits of Climbing Plants*, 1865; *Variation of Animals and Plants Under Domestication*, 1968; *The Descent of Man and Selection in Relation to Sex*, 1871; *The Expression of the Emotions in Man and Animals*, 1872; *The Power of Movement in Plants*, 1880; *The Formation of Vegetable Mould, Through the Action of Worms, with Observations on Their Habits*, 1881; *The Autobiography of Charles Darwin, 1809-1882, with Original Omissions Restored*, 1958.

Born: February 12, 1809; Shrewsbury, Shropshire, England
Died: April 19, 1882; Downe, Kent, England

Early Life

Charles Robert Darwin was born on February 12, 1809, in Shrewsbury, Shropshire, England, the fifth of six children. His mother, Susannah, the daughter of famed potter Josiah Wedgwood, died when he was eight, leaving him in the care of his elder sisters. His father, Robert Waring Darwin, was a robust and genial country doctor with a wide practice. In 1818, young Darwin entered Dr. Butler's Shrewsbury School, where he learned some classics but little else. At home he was a quiet, docile child, with an interest in solitary walks and collecting coins and minerals.

In 1825, Darwin was sent to Edinburgh to study medicine because his family hoped he would enter his father's profession. He proved to be a poor student, showing little interest in anatomy and disliking the crude operations performed without anesthetics. When he left Shrewsbury, his father rebuked him, saying, "You care for nothing but shooting, dogs, and rat-catching, and you will be a disgrace to yourself and all your family."

As a last resort, the young Darwin was sent to Christ's College, Cambridge, to prepare for the ministry, a profession for which he felt no more enthusiasm than he did for medicine, and he soon fell in among the sporting set. Though not a distinguished student, Darwin took an interest in natural science and was influenced by Alexander von Humboldt's *Personal Narrative of Travels to the Equinoctial Regions of the New Continent During the Years 1799-1804* (1814-1829) and Charles Lyell's *Principles of Geology* (1830-1833). He met John Stevens Henslow, a botany professor who encouraged his interest in natural history and helped to secure for him a position as naturalist aboard HMS *Beagle*, soon to depart on a five-year scientific expedition around the world. The *Beagle* sailed from Devonport on December 31, 1831. Darwin's experiences during the voyage from 1831 to 1836 were instrumental in shaping his theory of evolution.

The voyage of the *Beagle* took Darwin along the coast of South America, where the crew spent twenty-nine months charting the waters off the Pacific coast. Darwin explored the Andes and the pampas and kept detailed journals in which he carefully observed differences among the South American flora and fauna, particularly on the

Charles Darwin. *(National Archives)*

Galápagos Islands, where he found a remarkable divergence among the same species from different islands. Before he began his voyage, he had no reason to doubt the immutability of species, but from his firsthand experiences, he gradually began to doubt the creationist view of life. He would later draw upon these extensive field observations to formulate his theory of natural selection. Darwin was able to draw together from his travels vast amounts of scientific evidence to buttress his arguments against scientific and religious challenges. When he returned to England on October 2, 1836, he was an accomplished naturalist, collector, and geologist with a new view of the natural history of life.

After his return to London, Darwin settled in an apartment and began a detailed study of coral reefs. He became secretary to the Geological Society and a member of the Royal Society. He mar-

ried his first cousin, Emma Wedgwood, in January, 1839. Because his health was poor, the couple settled outside London, in Kent. There, despite his infirmities, Darwin did his most important work. A thin man, about six feet tall, Darwin walked with a stoop that made him appear shorter, especially as his illness worsened later in life.

Life's Work

At Downe House in Kent, Darwin worked for the next twenty years on his journals from the *Beagle* trip, gathering information to support his theory of evolution through natural selection. In 1837, Darwin had begun his first notebook on the "species question." A chance reading of Thomas Robert Malthus's *An Essay on the Principle of Population, As It Affects the Future Improvement of Society* (1798) in 1838 introduced him to the idea of the struggle for existence, which Darwin thought applied better to plants and animals than to humans, who can expand their food supply artificially. Darwin had returned from his voyage with many unanswered questions. Why were the finches and tortoises different on each of the Galápagos Islands, even though the habitats were not that different? Why were similar creatures, such as the ostrich and the rhea, found on separate continents? Why did some of the South American fossils of extinct mammals resemble the skeletons of some living creatures? The species question fascinated him, and gradually Darwin formulated a theory of the mutability and descent of living forms, although he was still unsure about the mechanisms of adaptation and change.

Two preliminary sketches of 1842 and 1844 presented Darwin's theory of evolution in rudimentary form, but he was determined to amass as much detail as possible to support his deductions. He turned to the work of animal breeders and horticulturalists for evidence of artificial selection among domesticated species. His preliminary work might have continued indefinitely if he had not received on June 18, 1854, an essay from Alfred Russel Wallace, a field naturalist in the Malay Archipelago, outlining a theory of evolution and natural selection similar to his own.

Darwin immediately wrote to his friends, Sir Charles Lyell and Joseph Hooker, explaining his dilemma and including an abstract of his own theory of evolution. Lyell and Hooker proposed that in order to avoid the question of precedence, the two papers should be presented simultaneously. Both were read before a meeting of the Linnean Society in Dublin on July 1, 1858, and were published together in the society's journal that year.

Darwin then began writing an abstract of his theory, which he entitled *On the Origin of Species by Means of Natural Selection*. All 1,250 copies sold out on the first day of publication in London on November 24, 1859. Darwin argued that because all species produce more offspring than can possibly survive and because species populations remain relatively constant, there must be some mechanism working in nature to eliminate the unfit. Variations are randomly introduced in nature, some of which will permit a species to adapt better to its environment. These adaptations are passed on to the offspring, giving them an advantage for survival. Darwin did not understand the genetic mechanism by which offspring inherit adaptations. It would take another seventy years before the forgotten work of the Austrian geneticist Gregor Mendel was rediscovered and Sir Ronald Fisher integrated the theories of Darwinian selection and Mendelian genetics.

A quiet and retiring man, Darwin was surrounded by a storm of controversy after the publication of *On the Origin of Species by Means of Natural Selection*. Objection came from both orthodox clergy and unconvinced scientists. At Oxford in 1860, there was a famous debate on evolution between Thomas H. Huxley and Bishop Samuel Wilberforce, in which Huxley answered the creationist arguments against evolution and silenced the religious critics. For the rest of his life, Darwin worked at home on orchid- and pigeon-breeding experiments and successive editions of *On the Origin of Species by Means of Natural Selection*, as well as further studies on plant and animal domestication, climbing plants, cross-fertilization, orchids, the expression of emotions, and his famous *The Descent of Man and Selection in Relation to Sex*. His wife, Emma, nursed him during his bouts of illness, whose origin is uncertain. She also reared their ten children, seven of whom survived to adulthood, three to become distinguished scientists and members of the Royal Society. In his later years, Darwin regretted the loss of his appreciation for poetry and music, complaining that his mind had become a "machine for grinding general laws out of large collections of facts." Still, he maintained a wide correspondence and enjoyed entertaining close friends and occasional visitors at home. He died on April 19, 1882, at Downe House in Kent, and was buried with full honors in the scientists' corner at Westminster Abbey, next to Sir Isaac Newton.

Influence

Perhaps more profoundly than any other single work, Charles Darwin's *On the Origin of Species by Means of Natural Selection* shaped the development of modern biology and, more broadly, the modern view of human nature. No longer was it possible to accept uncritically the biblical view of Creation, with the implied special place of humanity in the divine order. The human being became a creature among creatures, with a traceable evolution and descent from earlier hominoid forms. Darwin's ideas exerted a wide cultural influence, with a popular version of "the survival of the fittest" diffusing into the politics, literature, and sociology of the age, especially through Herbert Spencer's "social Darwinism." Unfortunately, Darwin's ideas were often mistakenly used to justify racism, discrimination, and repressive laissez-faire economic practices. Though Darwin drifted toward agnosticism and did not believe in a divinely sanctioned morality, neither did he condone a world of amoral violence and brute struggle for domination. He believed that human morality was the product of social and cultural evolution and that it did confer survival benefits. A gentle man who abhorred violence and cruelty, he would have been horrified at the political and social misapplications of Darwinian principles. Nevertheless, Darwin was not a Victorian liberal and accepted many of the unenlightened views of his age concerning "primitive" cultures.

During his lifetime, Darwin faced formidable challenges to his evolutionary theory, first from the scientist Fleeming Jenkin, who argued that fortuitous adaptations would be "swamped" and disappear in larger populations, and later from Sir William Thomson (Baron Kelvin), who mistakenly questioned Darwin's estimate of the geological age of the earth on the basis of the laws of thermodynamics. These challenges led Darwin to revise *On the Origin of Species by Means of Natural Selection* extensively in successive editions and to back away from some of his earlier claims about the long time span needed for slow, evolutionary changes to take place. In order to accommodate Kelvin's shortened estimate of the earth's age, Darwin moved toward a neo-Lamarckian position concerning the inheritance of acquired characteristics. Darwin had no way of knowing that Mendel's discoveries in genetics would have answered many of his doubts about the sources of variation and the mechanisms of inheritance.

Darwin has had an immeasurable influence on the development of modern biology, ecology, morphology, embryology, and paleontology. His theory of evolution established a natural history of the earth and enabled humans to see themselves for the first time as part of the natural order of life. A lively debate continues among scientists about revisionist theories of evolution, including Stephen Jay Gould's notion of "punctuated equilibria," or sudden and dramatic evolutionary changes followed by long periods of relative stability. Although they disagree about details, modern biologists agree that neoevolutionary theory remains the only viable scientific explanation for the diversity of life on earth.

Andrew J. Angyal

On the Origin of Species by Means of Natural Selection

Or, The Preservation of Favoured Races in the Struggle for Life

Type of philosophy: Epistemology, philosophy of science
First published: 1859
Principal ideas advanced:

◇ A species is a class of individuals, a population, each member of which varies in structure and instinct. A species is not a fixed cookie-cutter collection of immutable individuals.

◇ Some of the ways in which each member differs, however slight, will be favored by environmental circumstances, making more likely the survival of the organism so favored. Darwin named this mechanism "natural selection."

◇ Many of these differences of individuality are heritable and accumulate in successive generations.

◇ Species are thus transformed by small steps over great expanses of time into varieties, and eventually into new species, displacing transitional forms that then become extinct. Species are all necessarily interrelated by common descent.

◇ Natural selection is not the only mechanism of evolution, merely the most important; it organizes and makes intelligible a wide range of biological and geological facts, and it is superior to acts of special creation as an explanation for the origin of species.

◇ It implicitly follows (and was argued openly by Darwin in later works) that there is continuity of mind and emotion from lower to higher species. The mental and moral faculties of humans are of natural origin and fully a part of the natural world.

◇ What at first appeared to be a case of complex design, created by a Designer, is shown to be a product of the principles of variation, selection, and inheritance.

The prevailing view in British scientific and theological communities when Charles Darwin began his inquiries was that species were fixed, immutable types, created by God. The complex and intricate design of organisms was taken as evidence of creation by a Designer. William Paley, a natural theologian, developed the argument, which Darwin studied during his education at Cambridge.

However, the idea that species are not immutable but can be transmuted had many advocates before Darwin. They can be found as far back as the pre-Socratics, but the view was greatly advanced in early nineteenth century scientific discussions by Jean-Baptiste-Pierre-Antoine de Monet de Lamarck in his *Philosophie zoologique:*

Ou, Exposition des considérations relative à l'histoire naturelle des animaux (1809; *Zoological Philosophy: An Exposition with Regard to the Natural History of Animals*, 1914). What Lamarck and other early evolutionary theorists lacked was an adequate mechanism to explain how evolution occurred.

Charles Lyell, in his *Principles of Geology* (1830-1833), argued that geological formations had been shaped by the same physical forces that acted on them today, a doctrine known as uniformitarianism. Although Lyell was not a transmutationist until after *On the Origin of Species by Means of Natural Selection*, he did acknowledge in the volumes that Darwin read that changing environments could lead species to undergo accommodations, migrations, and extinctions.

Natural Selection and Evolution

By Darwin's own testimony, the idea of natural selection as the mechanism of evolutionary change occurred to him upon rereading in 1838 *An Essay on the Principle of Population, As It Affects the Future Improvement of Society* (1798) by Thomas Malthus, a clergyman and political economist. "The doctrine of Malthus applied with manifold force to the whole animal and vegetable kingdoms" is how Darwin described his theory of descent through modification by natural selection. Malthus asserted that because populations grow geometrically while crops grow arithmetically, there would be a struggle among creatures for survival. The fittest would prevail.

The thesis of *On the Origin of Species by Means of Natural Selection* is that species are created not by special acts of a Designer but by the process of evolution through natural selection. In each generation, more organisms are produced than can live to the point of reproducing. Those organisms that possess even a slight advantage in adapting to the demands of climate, food supply, and competition over fellow organisms (and other species of organisms) will have higher reproduction rates, will survive long enough to reproduce, and thus will pass their favored structures and instincts on to their offspring. Adaptations will accumulate over generations; internal organs, external structures, and behavior will be altered. New varieties, "incipient species" as Darwin called them, will appear and, over many genera-

tions, will come to be recognized as new species. Darwin does not explain the origin of life by his theory but rather how the diversity and complexity that is life came to be.

To speak persuasively for his theory, Darwin constructed what he described as "one long argument." The book consists of arguments and evidence. The evidence is numerous illustrations of geological and biological facts about rocks, animals, and plants. The arguments and inferences support the superiority of natural selection and other natural causes of evolution as opposed to special creation as an explanation of the facts. The facts were not just those of the vast diversity of species, but also the innumerable details of their structures, behaviors, development, and interrelationships—facts that Darwin's theory could integrate in a logical manner.

Darwin begins by discussing the variability that exists among members of a species, individual differences in structure and instinct, and the fact that some of these differences are inherited by offspring. What causes the variability is unknown to Darwin, although he speculates on changed environmental and life conditions that affect the organism both directly and through its reproduction system. These individual differences, the variability in structure and function, are used by breeders of domesticated animals to create new forms; they artificially select in a manner analogous to the way, Darwin would later argue, that nature selects. Breeders select for the qualities they desire: fancy tail feathers in pigeons, high milk yields in cows. Nature selects without regard to any particular quality, other than the ability to survive. The slight individual differences are the first small steps that lead to varieties, and varieties at the extreme cannot be distinguished from species. No rigid category lines or types exist.

Members of a species are competing among themselves as well as with other species in a struggle for life and for reproduction. The struggle for existence is created when more individuals are born than can survive under existing conditions. In this struggle, any slight advantage will increase the likelihood of living and, more important, the likelihood of leaving progeny. Thus, the ultimate struggle is not so much to live as it is to live long enough and well enough to leave offspring. Any advantage in doing so, to the degree that it is hereditary, will be preserved in subsequent generations and will accumulate to produce new forms of life, structure, and behavior. The process of preserving accumulated advantages is what Darwin called "natural selection," which he regarded as the main force behind evolution.

If it were not for two other forces that Darwin named the "principle of divergence" and the "principle of geographical isolation," natural selection would make individuals better suited to their environment but would not transform them. Because competition is most keen between those organisms that are most alike, the more individuals differ, the greater are their chances of survival, leading to greater and ever-increasing divergence in structure and instinct. Moreover, if members of a common species are separated from one another—as they naturally are by islands or mountain ranges—different features may be selected by the local conditions, leading in the course of time to different varieties and thus to new species. By these principles, Darwin said, small differences over the great expanse of geological time yield greater differences. New forms follow.

Other Causes of Evolution

Natural selection is not the only cause of evolution, merely the most important. Darwin discussed several others that may lead to transmutation but may not necessarily produce changes in the organism that are adaptive. Sexual selection resulted from competition among males for mating with females. Males that failed in the competition to secure and attract female mates had no or fewer offspring. The development of fighting or defensive organs may be explained by sexual selection. In later works, Darwin added a second kind of sexual selection, female choice or preference, which he argued explained the beauty of the male peacock tail feathers or the generally more colorful male of most bird species. Other mechanisms of evolution Darwin discussed were the alteration of parts by use and disuse (the Larmarckian idea of the inheritance of acquired characteristics), spontaneous variation (later understood as genetic mutations), direct action of the environment, and correlated variation, in which a change in one part of a structure or instinct was necessarily accompanied by a change in another part.

Beginning with the first edition of *On the Origin of Species by Means of Natural Selection*, Darwin addressed difficulties with his theory, and in later editions he expanded his remarks to objections that had been raised to the theory by critics. Among the objections that Darwin answered were the sterility of species when first crossed compared to the fertility of varieties, the seeming difficulty of natural selection to construct complex organs in small steps (the eyes, for example), and the absence of intermediate or transitional forms among the fossils. (The answer he gave to the latter was that the geological record was necessarily incomplete and imperfect.) He also addressed how organisms acquire complex abilities, such as the ability of bees to build hives. Organisms show variability in fixed behavioral patterns, instincts, as they do in structure. Natural selection acts on behavior as it acts on structures and organs, Darwin argued. His discussion of instincts, a kind of primitive mentality, set the stage in later works for Darwin to argue for the evolutionary foundations of human mentality.

Darwin explained how the geographical distribution of plants and animals developed and why the nature of the distribution is compatible with natural selection but not special creation. He demonstrated that his theory yielded a better system of classification of organisms (taxonomy), one based on a genealogical arrangement that reflected the fact of common descent of species rather than one based on the logic of their superficial features. He also argued that the structures (morphology) of related species, their development as individuals until birth (embryology), and their possession of partially formed bodily parts (rudimentary organs) were all scattered facts of nature that were rendered intelligible by a theory of natural selection but not by the belief in special creation. Darwin's theory is easily summarized with his own few key words: descent with modification through variation and natural selection.

Influence on Philosophy

On the Origin of Species by Means of Natural Selection may be the most important scientific book of the nineteenth century. It was the critical work of Darwin's life and of all his books the one that most directly influenced nearly every field of philosophy. Darwin demonstrated that what appeared to be an object of design could be produced without a Designer. Not only was the tradition of natural theology and its argument for God's existence by design threatened, but also, more important, mechanism was showed to be capable of yielding creativity. Mind could be produced by mindlessness. Darwin's views also threatened essentialism, the doctrine, prominent since Plato and Aristotle, that each member of a class or species had some shared essence that made it a member and thereby defined the class. Darwin's theory conceived of classes or categories as populations, in which class membership did not depend on an essence of whatever form but on members who would necessarily display variability in all of their identifying features. *On the Origin of Species by Means of Natural Selection* produced philosophical influences that were naturalistic, emphasizing development, function, and adaptation and that held selection as a powerful principle of change.

The influence of Darwin may be seen in the nineteenth century work of Charles Peirce, William James, and other American pragmatists who held that beliefs should be judged by their consequence; in essence, they are selected by their effects. John Dewey and his instrumentalism was also influenced by Darwinian ideas. Dewey conceived of thought as something that evolves to fit and solve a problem. Darwinism also led to a crass political philosophy, social Darwinism. The doctrine envisioned society as a struggle for survival of the fittest. The distribution of economic resources was in accord with natural selection processes, American sociologist William Graham Sumner said. Social welfare programs could only interfere. The view owed more to Herbert Spencer, a nineteenth century British social thinker, than to the work of Darwin. Karl Marx, who dedicated *Das Kapital* (1867, 1885, 1894; *Capital: A Critique of Political Economy*, 1886, 1907, 1909; better known as *Das Kapital*) to Darwin, perceived evolutionary theory as supporting his dialectical materialism. Other philosophers argued for a naturalistic, evolutionary-based ethic, one that would derive what was good from what

was functional and natural. In the twentieth century, Daniel Dennett proclaimed the principle of natural selection as the solution to many philosophical puzzles, an idea that is still greatly resisted.

Terry J. Knapp

Additional Reading

Bowler, Peter J. *Charles Darwin: The Man and His Influence*. Cambridge, England: Cambridge University Press, 1996. Combines biography with cultural history. Bowler shows how Charles Darwin's contemporaries were unable to comprehend the scientific importance of Darwin's theory in the development of modern culture. Darwin's relationships with other prominent scientists of the period are also portrayed.

Brackman, Arnold. *A Delicate Arrangement: The Strange Case of Charles Darwin and Charles Russel Wallace*. New York: Times Books, 1980. Brackman argues that Darwin and his friends conspired to deny Wallace credit for having first discovered the theory of biological evolution.

Clark, Ronald W. *The Survival of Charles Darwin: A Biography of a Man and an Idea*. New York: Random House, 1984. A study of Darwin's life and work, concentrating on the genesis of evolutionary theory and its development after Darwin's death.

Colp, Ralph, Jr. *To Be an Invalid: The Illness of Charles Darwin*. Chicago: University of Chicago Press, 1977. A detailed study of the various theories about what caused Darwin's chronic, debilitating illness after the voyage of HMS *Beagle*.

De Beer, Gavin. *Charles Darwin: A Scientific Biography*. New York: Doubleday, 1965. The standard authorized biography of Darwin by an English scientist who enjoyed full access to the Darwin Papers at Cambridge University.

Desmond, Adrian, and James Moore. *Darwin: The Life of a Tormented Evolutionist*. 1991. American ed. New York: W. W. Norton, 1994. Lively and enjoyable to read, this book has been hailed as the definitive biography of Darwin. The authors portray Darwin within the context of Victorian society and explain how he came to his momentous and controversial conclusion, which he kept secret for twenty years. Includes maps, photos, drawings, and extensive chapter notes.

Eiseley, Loren. *Darwin's Century: Evolution and the Men Who Discovered It*. New York: Doubleday, 1958. A rigorous intellectual history of the concept of evolution and its antecedents, from Darwin's precursors through the publication of *On the Origin of Species* and its reception.

Irvine, William. *Apes, Angels, and Victorians: The Story of Darwin, Huxley, and Evolution*. New York: McGraw-Hill, 1955. A detailed cultural study of Darwinism and its impact on the Victorian mind.

Stefoff, Rebecca. *Charles Darwin and the Evolution Revolution*. New York: Oxford University Press, 1996. This thoroughly researched biography emphasizes Darwin's influence on and contributions to scientific, social, and political circles. Extensive photographs of family, colleagues, and reproductions of public notices and cartoons humanize the subject. Sidebars detail terms and concepts so as not to bog down the text.

Andrew J. Angyal,
updated by Lisa A. Wroble

Donald Davidson

Davidson's work in action theory, the ontology of events, and especially the semantics of natural language was groundbreaking throughout the latter third of the twentieth century.

Principal philosophical works: *Decision Making: An Experimental Approach*, 1957 (with Patrick Suppes); "Actions, Reasons, and Causes," 1963; "Theories of Meaning and Learnable Languages," 1965; "Truth and Meaning," 1967; "Radical Interpretation," 1973; "On the Very Idea of a Conceptual Scheme," 1974; "What Metaphors Mean," 1978; *Essays on Actions and Events*, 1980; "Rational Animals," 1982; "A Coherence Theory of Truth and Knowledge," 1983; "Communication and Convention," 1983; *Inquiries into Truth and Interpretation*, 1984; "A Nice Derangement of Epitaphs," 1986; "The Myth of the Subjective," 1989; "The Second Person," 1992; "Dialectic and Dialogue," 1994; "The Folly of Trying to Define Truth," 1996.

Born: March 6, 1917; Springfield, Massachusetts

Early Life

Donald Herbert Davidson, son of Clarence and Grace Davidson, graduated from Harvard University with a B.A. in 1939. Awarded a Teschemacher fellowship in classics and philosophy, he received an M.A. in 1941. After serving in the military during World War II, he returned to Harvard and completed a dissertation on Plato's *Philēbos* (c. 360-347 B.C.E.; *Philebus*, 1804), receiving his Ph.D. in 1949. While finishing his graduate work, Davidson taught at Queen's College, leaving for a position at Stanford University, where he stayed from 1951 to 1967. He subsequently accepted positions at Princeton University, Rockefeller University, and the University of Chicago. In 1981, he returned to California to teach at the University of California, Berkeley.

Life's Work

Although Davidson was trained in the classics, his earliest writings during the 1950's were in value theory and decision making. These culminated with the publication of his first book, *Decision Making: An Experimental Approach*, which he coauthored with Patrick Suppes. However, the work that first brought Davidson to the attention of most philosophers was his 1963 essay, "Ac-

Donald Davidson. *(Princeton University Library)*

tions, Reasons, and Causes." Contrary to the prevailing behaviorist views, Davidson argued that human action needed to be understood in terms of reasons, including attitudes, beliefs, and intentions. This flew in the face of the predominant sentiment that human action, or behavior, is to be understood in terms of stimulus-response and operant conditioning. In addition, Davidson claimed that reasons function as causes of human action, not merely as one mode of explanation of human action.

Besides his important writings in action theory and philosophy of mind, Davidson produced seminal work in the philosophy of language. His first essay in this area was "Theories of Meaning and Learnable Languages," in which Davidson argued that any theory of meaning must reconcile people's finite abilities as users of the language with the infinite number of meaningful sentences of which the language is capable. His efforts resulted in a systematic program of significant and influential essays, including "Truth and Meaning." In this work, he argued for a truth-conditional analysis of meaning. That is, he argued that the meaning of a sentence could be understood by understanding the conditions under which the sentence was true (or false). Just as his writings on action theory had run counter to the prevailing behaviorist views, his truth-conditional analysis of meaning also ran counter to the predominant view of meaning as use proposed by philosopher Ludwig Wittgenstein. P. F. Strawson responded to Davidson's essay with his own, "Meaning and Truth" (1969), in which he claimed that Davidson's formal semantic analysis failed to appreciate the communicative-intentional basis of meaning (and language in general). Davidson's immediate response was that a theory of meaning is a semantic theory that should give an account of how people can understand and interpret language; a speaker's communicative and intentional concerns are important pragmatic elements of language use but not features of a semantic theory.

Over his career, Davidson returned to the concerns about communication and the pragmatics of language, though he did not abandon his truth-conditional approach. In two essays written in the 1980's, "Communication and Convention" and "A Nice Derangement of Epitaphs," he ar-

gued that people's communicative intentions and linguistic conventions, though important features of language and ones that ultimately need to be covered in theories of language, cannot serve as the basis for language or for people's understanding of language because rule-based conventions are often broken without loss of meaning or understanding.

Throughout the 1970's, Davidson produced numerous important essays in action theory and philosophy of mind, but especially in the philosophy of language. Two in particular were landmarks: "Radical Interpretation" and "On the Very Idea of a Conceptual Scheme." Both were motivated by and in response to the work of W. V. O. Quine. In various writings, Quine had argued that the basis of meaning is perceptual stimulation coupled with the association of that stimulation with language. For example, people learn the meaning of the word "red" by being presented with red objects and hearing the word "red" in association with those presentations. People learn the meaning of sentences by noting the assent and dissent of speakers when they are presented with stimuli. Therefore, having acquired the meaning of "red," upon a later presentation of a colored object, one might ask if that, too, is red; the subsequent assent or dissent helps secure the meaning of "red." Davidson balked at the underlying behaviorism of this view and insisted that interpretation is a matter of both learning and relying on others' beliefs as well as the meaning of words and sentences. That is, the assent or dissent given by the other person does not necessarily distinguish that person's beliefs about red from the meaning of "red." As Davidson said, "Only by studying the *pattern* of assents to sentences can we decide what is meant and what believed."

In the second essay, "On the Very Idea of a Conceptual Scheme," Davidson questions the claim that there are incommensurable conceptual schemes or languages (that is, that there are conceptual schemes or languages such that there is no possibility of cross-communication or understanding). A popular view, both inside and outside academia, is that languages, or conceptual schemes, determine how speakers comprehend the world and that different conceptual schemes divide up the world in such different ways that speakers cannot really comprehend each other and, indeed, in a sense, live in different worlds so that there is an ontological relativity (to use Quine's famous term). Davidson argued that this view is mistaken. Unless there is some point of contact and agreement, people could not know where they disagreed. Although particular terms might not be amenable to easy translation, the claim of complete intranslatability (incommensurable conceptual schemes) is incoherent. A theme that emerges from these essays and is carried out throughout his later writings is a rejection of wholesale relativism and subjectivism. People all bump into the world and they tend to understand one another, and people tend to get things right when they engage with the world.

As noted above, an overarching concern for Davidson was to provide a semantics for natural language. From his earliest writings on, he recognized that natural languages involve much more than declarative statements, that is, those that have truth values. For example, there are questions and commands, neither of which can be said to be true or false. In addition, there are aspects of natural languages that are not literal, such as similes and metaphors. In the context of a growing body of literature on nonliterality, Davidson created a stir with his essay, "What Metaphors Mean." Unlike most of his contemporaries, Davidson denied that there is any special metaphorical meaning separate from literal meaning. What words mean and what they do (or what people do with them) are related but distinct matters. Words function metaphorically, he claimed, only because they rely on their literal meaning. For example, the meaning of the word "man" does not change from its use in "Man is a mammal" and "Man is a wolf." The latter sentence is metaphorical only because people understand that the words "man" and "wolf" have their literal meanings and are being used in a nonliteral way. This is not to deny that metaphors expand the literal meaning of words or get people to see things in new and different ways. It is simply to say that people's ability to account for metaphors and their workings is not dependent upon special metaphorical meaning.

A basic commitment of Davidson's views, that people need to understand how they engage in the world, reveals a coherence and consistency across his work in action theory and in semantics.

People are agents, with beliefs and intentions about the world and about themselves; people are also speakers who engage in a social linguistic world. Although some of his writings focused on agency and others on language use, all were aiming at developing theories to account for people's engagement in the world.

In the 1980's and 1990's, this concern took a more explicitly epistemological turn, with Davidson writing on what it is for people to know the world and know language and know others. In his essay "Rational Animals," he employed the metaphor of triangulation, a method of locating an object by determining its placement relative to two other known objects. This notion of elucidating concepts such as belief, meaning, or truth by locating them relative to other concepts rather than by definitional reduction applied to his work in action theory, to his concerns about Quine's theory of meaning and interpretation, and to truth in his later essays, including "A Coherence Theory of Truth and Knowledge" and "The Folly of Trying to Define Truth."

For Davidson, much as the possibility of disagreement depends on the preponderance of agreement, people's subjective knowledge (knowledge of one's own thoughts and sensations) depends on knowledge of an external, objective world. Indeed, all propositional knowledge, he claimed, whether of oneself or the world, requires possession of the concept of objective truth, which in turn requires communication and knowledge of other minds. The latter, though conceptually basic, is possible only within a shared, objective world. The acquisition of knowledge, then, does not progress from the subjective to the objective but emerges holistically and intersubjectively. In "The Second Person," he reiterated this point by arguing that to even have thoughts requires a second person capable of understanding them, with that understanding itself dependent upon "the mutual and simultaneous responses of two or more creatures to common distal stimuli and to one another's responses." In his writings in the 1990's, Davidson carried out this intersubjective, holistic theme in the context of returning to his classical, Platonic academic roots. In his essay, "Dialectic and Dialogue," he suggested that most of the concepts with which philosophers wrestle in fact cannot be defined by reducing them to simpler concepts, and, therefore, it was no wonder that Plato's Socratic dialogues seemed never to succeed in producing satisfactory definitions of piety, justice, and so on. Rather, Davidson claimed, his dialectic could be construed as a method for deciding how important concepts should be used by triangulating them and seeing how they both clarify and are clarified by neighboring concepts.

Influence

Davidson's work in action theory, ontology, and semantics was profound throughout the last third of the twentieth century. In action theory and philosophy of mind, his insistence on reasons as causes weaned many philosophers away from behaviorism while at the same time avoided any commitment to a dualism of mind and body. He helped make respectable a cognitive approach to investigating the nature of mind and mentality. His work on the ontology of events and the logic of action statements was truly seminal and definitive. His writings in the semantics of natural language, though, will no doubt be his lasting legacy. Davidson's truth-conditional analysis of meaning remains paramount for many philosophers of language, as do his views on interpretation and the shared commonality of knowledge and truth. At a time when many proclaimed the fragmentation and even the end of philosophy, Davidson offered a rigorous, systematic attempt to understand people as speakers and agents, as persons.

David Boersema

Essays on Actions and Events

Type of philosophy: Epistemology, philosophy of mind
First published: 1980
Principal ideas advanced:
◇ Reasons are causes of human action and are explanatory.
◇ Events are a real ontological category, separate from objects and properties.
◇ Mental events, while identical with physical events, are not deterministic or lawlike in any

physical sense. Davidson calls this "anomalous monism."
◇ Causality is the underlying, unifying theme in describing and explaining human action.

Among the perennial ontological issues that philosophers have addressed are the relation between the mental and the physical and the fundamental categories of reality. The former issue, the relation of the mental and the physical, is often termed "the mind-body problem" and involves questions concerning the nature of the mind and how, if at all, a nonphysical entity (mind) can influence or be influenced by a physical entity (body). The latter issue, the fundamental categories of reality, can be traced back to the pre-Socratic philosophers, who questioned whether there was some single unifying reality that underlay the multiplicity of entities of everyday experience. In addressing this issue, philosophers have asked questions such as whether the physical world is "really real" and whether the world is made up basically of things, as opposed to, for example, processes. Are properties (such as being tall) real? Are relations (such as being taller than another person) real? Are events, as opposed to things, real? These are the types of issues and questions that Donald Davidson addresses in these essays.

This book consists of fifteen essays, written between 1963 and 1978, grouped into three clusters covering intention and action, event and cause, and philosophy of psychology. In the book's introduction, Davidson enunciates a common theme to the essays: the role of causal concepts in the description and explanation of human action. He also insists that there is one, ordinary notion of cause employed both in scientific accounts of human action and in commonsense experiential accounts. As Davidson puts it: "The concept of cause is what holds together our picture of the universe."

Reasons as Causes and Explanations

The first essay, "Actions, Reasons, and Causes" in the collection is probably the best known. Writing during the heyday of behaviorism, Davidson challenged the prevailing sentiment that a person's intentions, motives, or beliefs could neither cause that person's actions (because actions are physical and reasons are not) nor serve to explain that person's actions (because explanations require lawlike regularity in a physical sense). Acting for a reason, Davidson claimed, involves having both an attitude and a belief. Davidson demonstrates how an action is made reasonable (in Davidson's words, "how a reason of any kind rationalizes an action") by connecting one event (having an attitude and belief) with another event (the action). Reasons provide an interpretation of action by placing it within a broader context. For example, if one wants to know why a person raised his or her arm, one interprets that action, describing it as a case of, for example, a person signaling someone else, seeing how high he or she could reach, or trying to touch something over his or her head, and so on. These various descriptions of that event of arm raising show the person's action to be reasonable by placing it within a set of events (such as signaling). These notions of events being variously characterized and of the role of interpretation in explanatory accounts play important roles throughout Davidson's writings.

Agency, Intention, and Free Will

Given an attempt to account for human action, a number of basic concepts are necessarily invoked: agency, intention, and free will. In the remaining essays in this section of the book, Davidson spells out how these concepts relate to his understanding of actions, reasons, and causes. According to Davidson, what makes a particular event an action is the component of agency. A rock falling off a cliff is an event but not an action; a rock being thrown off a cliff is an event that is an action. The difference is the involvement of an agent in the latter event. Although this seems plausible, something more is needed because in both cases the event was preceded by another event that was sufficient to cause the event in question. In the case of the rock falling, the preceding event was, perhaps, a strong gust of wind that dislodged the rock and caused it to fall. In the case of the rock being thrown, the preceding event was, perhaps, someone's desire to see how far he or she could throw the rock. Therefore, agency cannot simply be "having a preceding cause"; otherwise, the wind would have been an agent in the falling of the rock. A

strong wind cannot be an agent because it has no intentions, and intention seems to be necessary (if not sufficient). In his essay "Intending," Davidson reconnects the concept of intention, or intendings, to the having of attitudes and beliefs. Intendings, he says, are judgments that are directed toward an agent's future actions, in light of that agent's beliefs.

Having characterized action as involving reasons, which, in turn, are causes, Davidson addresses two challenges, one facing reasons and the other facing causality. The first challenge has to do with giving an account of unreasonable or irrational human action. If human action is accounted for in terms of reasons and reasonable interpretations, then how does this explain unreasonable human action? Although Davidson does not directly answer this question, he does insist that any account of action must make sense of forms of intentional, though perhaps irrational, action, including weakness of will and self-destructive behavior. The second challenge, concerning causality, involves explaining human action as being caused (because even reasons are causes) and yet free. For Davidson, the very freedom to act is itself causally efficacious but incapable of analysis or definition except via intentionality. Action is explained in terms of reasons and causes, which are in turn explained in terms of agency and intentionality, which are then explained in terms of reasons and causes. This produces not a foundationalist analysis, with one or two elemental concepts defining the others, but rather a coherentist one, with various concepts offering an interweaving net of support and explanation.

Event Ontology and Semantics

The second set of essays in this book focuses on issues related to the ontology of events and the semantics of event statements. Because particular events, such as the raising of one's arm, can, for Davidson, be described as various sorts of actions (signaling, reaching, and so on), events should be seen as particulars, or ontological individuals, distinct from the various ways in which they are described. In answer to the question as to what individuates events, Davidson states that events are identical, and hence individuated, if and only if they have the same causes and effects.

(Davidson later came to abandon this criterion for the individuation of events when philosopher W. V. O. Quine pointed out that Davidson had already defined events in terms of causes and effects, so his criterion was circular.)

Davidson raises two issues regarding the semantics of event statements. The first concerns how formal semantic theory should characterize event statements, and the second, how formal semantic theory should correctly capture the truth values of event statements. About the first issue, Davidson says to treat events as objects that are handled semantically like other objects; in other words, they fall within the scope of formal quantifiers. For example, the statement "The battle of Waterloo ended Napoleon's reign" should be treated as "There is an x such that x is the battle of Waterloo and there is a y such that y is Napoleon's reign and x ended y." An added wrinkle is how to treat adverbial modifiers. For example, does one treat "Jones buttered the toast slowly and deliberately" as one event or two? In terms of formal semantic analysis, does one treat this statement as one sentence or two? Davidson's answer is to treat adverbs as predicates, so that the statement becomes "There is an x such that x is a buttering and x is slow and x is deliberate." Although this sounds informally awkward, it coheres well with formal semantic analysis and maintains ontological intuitions (such as only one event, not two, occurred).

A second issue related to the semantics of event statements is the correct capturing of truth values of event statements. As normally analyzed, the truth of a statement depends upon the predicate of that statement being satisfied by the subject of the statement, which in turn requires the existence of the subject. The truth of the sentence "The Queen laughed at the King's cravat" requires that there be a queen. If an event such as the buttering of the toast by Jones is an ontological individual (or if "the buttering of the toast by Jones" is a singular term), then the truth of that sentence requires the existence of that individual. Davidson's analysis is, again, to treat this as "There is an x such that x is the buttering of the toast by Jones, etc." Although such a paraphrase might seem informally awkward, it preserves the formal rigor and coherence of standard formal semantic analysis.

The Philosophy of Psychology

The third group of essays, on the philosophy of psychology, returns more directly to matters of mind and introduces Davidson's famous doctrine of "anomalous monism." Davidson's concerns with causality, lawlike accounts of action, and ontology naturally led him to investigate more fully what the mind is and how it fits in with the causal understanding of the world. In his essay "Mental Events," he argues for the ontological identity of mental and physical events while at the same time denying a physical, lawful account of mental events. Davidson claims that events are particulars and, although events are characterizable under various descriptions, they are not identical with those characterizations. The actual cause-effect relations between events, being a matter of ontology, exist regardless of the descriptive characterizations that might be given. A particular mental event, such as one's remembering a dental appointment, might cause some other event, such as one's getting in the car, but there is no nomological, or lawful, necessary connection between those two events, because such nomological connections are always given under descriptions. For Davidson, then, there is ontological monism (a single kind of ontological entity) that is nevertheless anomalous (not accountable within strict physical, causal laws).

From his stance of anomalous monism, Davidson questions the fecundity of physiological and neurological findings about the brain and cognitive functions with respect to the understanding of mentality. Understanding of mental events, he says, requires interpreting those events within broader contexts (within descriptions of types of events). Remembering a dental appointment, as an instance of remembering, causally depends upon physiological events and states but, for Davidson, is not reducible in any way that explains what remembering is. Mental events and states might well supervene on physical events and states (they might well ontologically emerge out of physical events and states) so that physical events are necessary conditions for mental events, but physical accounts of mental events can never be explanatorily sufficient because interpretation and descriptive characterizations are not physical.

Controversy and Impact

Many of the essays contained in *Essays on Actions and Events* brought renown to Davidson. His insistence on taking cognitive states and functions seriously during the time that behaviorism reigned made his views controversial and guaranteed that they could not be ignored. The growth of action theory as a philosophical concern especially during the 1960's and 1970's was in large part a result of Davidson's writings. His work on the ontology of events and the semantic analysis of event sentences is regarded as groundbreaking and definitive. Davidson's writings on actions and events, also captured in the 1984 collection *Inquiries into Truth and Interpretation*, shaped many of the latter twentieth century notions of the nature of language and interpretation and how they relate to ontological issues such as the nature of mind.

David Boersema

Additional Reading

Audi, Robert. *Action, Intention, and Reason*. Ithaca, N.Y.: Cornell University Press, 1993. This thorough treatment of contemporary issues and views in action theory includes coverage of Donald Davidson.

Evnine, Simon. *Donald Davidson*. Stanford, Calif.: Stanford University Press, 1991. This very clear survey of Davidson's thought focuses equally on issues in action theory and philosophy of mind and issues in meaning and interpretation.

LePore, Ernest, ed. *Truth and Interpretation: Perspectives on the Philosophy of Donald Davidson*. Oxford: Basil Blackwell, 1986. This anthology of papers from a conference on Davidson held at Rutgers University in 1984 includes several important papers by Davidson. The papers deal with issues relating to Davidson's work in semantics (language, truth, and meaning). Papers from the same conference relating to Davidson's work in action theory and ontology were published in a separate volume.

LePore, Ernest, and Brian P. McLaughlin, eds. *Actions and Events: Perspectives on the Philosophy of Donald Davidson*. New York: Basil Blackwell, 1985. This companion volume to *Truth and Interpretation: Perspectives on the Philosophy of Donald Davidson* contains papers, including three by Davidson, presented at a 1984 conference held at Rutgers University. This volume focuses on issues of action theory (intention and action) and ontology (events and causes).

Malpas, J. E. *Donald Davidson and the Mirror of Meaning: Holism, Truth, Interpretation*. Cambridge, England: Cambridge University Press, 1992. This sophisticated treatment of Davidson focuses on issues of holism, truth, and interpretation. Malpas relates the work and concerns of Davidson to contemporary continental thinkers such as Hans-Georg Gadamer and Martin Heidegger.

Passmore, John. *Recent Philosophers*. La Salle, Ill.: Open Court, 1985. This clear, thematic introduction to contemporary concerns about logic, language, and ontology includes a chapter on Davidson and Michael Dummett.

Preyer, Gerhard, Frank Siebelt, and Alexander Ulfig, eds. *Language, Mind, and Epistemology: On Donald Davidson's Philosophy*. Dordrecht, Netherlands: Kluwer, 1994. Collection of essays focusing on three major topics in Davidson's work: philosophy of language, epistemology, and action theory. Several papers are in German.

Ramberg, Bjorn T. *Donald Davidson's Philosophy of Language: An Introduction*. Oxford: Basil Blackwell, 1989. In this short, clear introduction to Davidson's work in philosophy of language, Ramberg focuses on issues of truth, interpretation, and the development of Davidson's views on the nature of language.

Stoecker, Ralf, ed. *Reflecting Davidson: Donald Davidson Responding to a Forum of International Philosophers*. Berlin: W. de Gruyter, 1993. This anthology is made up of papers presented at the Center for Interdisciplinary Research in Bielefeld, Germany, in 1991. The papers cover the gamut of Davidson's thought, including truth, interpretation, mental concepts, action theory, and metaphor. Each paper includes a reply by Davidson.

Vermazen, Bruce, and Merrill Hintikka, eds. *Essays on Davidson: Actions and Events*. Oxford: Clarendon Press, 1985. This anthology brings together papers analyzing and critiquing various aspects of Davidson's work. Replies by Davidson are included.

David Boersema

Gilles Deleuze

Deleuze has provided important interpretations of crucial figures in the history of philosophy, including Immanuel Kant, Friedrich Nietzsche, David Hume, Baruch Spinoza, and Gottfried Wilhelm Leibniz. He has also developed what he has called a philosophy of difference.

Principal philosophical works: *David Hume: Sa vie, son œuvre, avec exposé de sa philosophie*, 1952 (with A. Cresson); *Empirisme et subjectivité: Essai sur la nature humaine selon Hume*, 1953 (*Empiricism and Subjectivity: An Essay on Hume's Theory of Human Nature*, 1991); *Nietzsche et la philosophie*, 1962 (*Nietzsche and Philosophy*, 1983); *La Philosophie critique de Kant: Doctrines des facultés*, 1963 (*Critical Philosophy: The Doctrine of the Faculties*, 1984); *Marcel Proust et les signes*, 1964 (*Proust and Signs*, 1972); *Le Bergsonisme*, 1966 (*Bergsonism*, 1988); *Différence et répétition*, 1968 (*Difference and Repetition*, 1994); *Spinoza et le problème de l'expression*, 1968 (*Expressionism in Philosophy: Spinoza*, 1990); *Logique du sens*, 1969 (*The Logic of Sense*, 1990); *Spinoza: Philosophie pratique*, 1970 (*Spinoza: Practical Philosophy*, 1988); *Capitalisme et schizophrénie*, volume 1, *L'Anti-Œdipe*, 1972 (with Félix Guattari; *Capitalism and Schizophrenia*, volume 1, *Anti-Oedipus*, 1977); *Kafka: Pour une littérature mineure*, 1975 (*Kafka: Toward a Minor Literature*, 1986); *Capitalisme et schizophrénie*, volume 2, *Mille Plateaux*, 1980 (with Félix Guattari; *A Thousand Plateaus*, 1987); *Francis Bacon: Logique de la sensation*, 1981; *Cinéma 1: L'Image-mouvement*, 1983 (*Cinema 1: The Movement-Image*, 1986); *Cinéma 2: L'Image-temps*, 1985 (*Cinema 2: The Time Image*, 1989); *Foucault*, 1986 (*Foucault*, 1988); *Le Pli: Leibniz et le baroque*, 1988 (*The Fold: Leibniz and the Baroque*, 1993); *Qu'est-ce que la philosophie?*, 1991 (with Félix Guattari; *What Is Philosophy?*, 1994); *Critique et clinique*, 1993 (*Essays Critical and Clinical*, 1997).

Born: January 18, 1925; Paris, France
Died: November 4, 1995; Paris, France

Early Life

Gilles Deleuze was born in 1925 into a conservative, bourgeois family living in the seventeenth arrondissement of Paris. Deleuze's father, a veteran of World War I, was an engineer and inventor whose first business failed just before World War II. When the Germans invaded France from Belgium in the summer of 1940, the Deleuze family was in Deauville (in Normandy) on vacation. Because of the invasion, the family stayed in Deauville, and Deleuze attended the *lycée* there. At the *lycée*, Deleuze met a young teacher, Pierre Halwachs, who was the son of a famous sociologist. Deleuze refers to this encounter with Halwachs as an enlightening experience. Halwachs introduced Deleuze to the works of writers such as André Gide, Anatole France, and Charles Baudelaire. The two spent so much time together that suspicions were aroused about the nature of their relationship.

After a year in Deauville, Deleuze returned to Paris and attended the Lycée Carnot. Deleuze's father worked in a factory that originally made dirigibles but had been turned into a rubber raft factory by the Germans. The income from this job was minimal, and therefore Deleuze was forced to attend public rather than private schools. While at the *lycée*, where Maurice Merleau-Ponty was a professor, Deleuze was placed in a class with a philosophy professor named Vialle. Deleuze greatly admired Vialle for the enthusiasm and energy he brought to his classes. In Vialle's class, Deleuze acquired a love for learning philosophical concepts and realized that he wanted to spend the rest of his life doing philosophy. From this point, he excelled academically.

In 1944, Deleuze graduated from the Lycée Carnot and entered the Sorbonne to further his studies in philosophy. Deleuze's primary teachers at the Sorbonne were Ferdinand Aliquié (a René Descartes specialist and expert in Surrealism), Georges Canguilhem (who was Michel Foucault's supervisor), and Jean Hyppolite (a Georg Wilhelm Friedrich Hegel specialist). Deleuze's friends at the Sorbonne included Michel Butor, Michel Tournier, and François Châtelet. In 1948, Deleuze passed his *agrégation de philosophie*, a difficult postgraduate examination for teaching positions at *lycées*, and until 1957, he taught philosophy at various *lycées*. He first taught at the *lycée* in Amiens, then moved on to teach in Orleans, and finally returned to Paris to teach at the Lycée Louis-le-Grand. In 1953, Deleuze published a study on the English philosopher David Hume titled *Empiricism and Subjectivity: An Essay on Hume's Theory of Human Nature*. The book was well received and is perhaps largely responsible for Deleuze's being offered a position at the Sorbonne, a position Deleuze took. From 1957 until 1960, Deleuze taught the history of philosophy at the Sorbonne.

Life's Work

Deleuze left the Sorbonne to pursue his own research, and in 1960, he joined the Centre National de Recherche Scientifique, where he would meet Félix Guattari. Deleuze published numerous book reviews and articles during this time, many of which would later be expanded into books, but by far the most important and influential work was his book on Friedrich Nietzsche, *Nietzsche and Philosophy*. This book immediately established Deleuze as an important new voice on the French philosophical scene, and it perhaps single-handedly renewed interest in Nietzsche, for two years later, at the 1964 conference at Royaumont, Nietzsche's writings would be discussed by those who would later become the most important philosophical figures in France. Among those who participated in this conference besides De-

leuze were Michel Foucault, Jacques Derrida, Sarah Kofman, Jean Granier, and Eric Blondel. In the same year as the Royaumont conference, Deleuze published a book on Marcel Proust, *Proust and Signs*, which was also well received, though not as influential as his book on Nietzsche. In part because of the book's success, Deleuze received an academic appointment at the university level, and at the urging of Foucault, Deleuze accepted an appointment at the University of Lyon that was to begin in 1969.

Deleuze's appointment at the University of Lyon was conditional upon a successful defense of a major and minor thesis. Deleuze had been quite prolific while at the Centre National de Recherche Scientifique, so it was simply a matter of defending previously written texts. Deleuze's defense was the first to be conducted following the events surrounding the May, 1968, protests. The ongoing protests caused Deleuze to protest that the professors conducting the defense seemed to be more concerned about the potential for students barging in than the substance of his major thesis, *Difference and Repetition*. Deleuze also defended his minor thesis, *Expressionism in Philosophy: Spinoza*. After easily passing his defense, Deleuze published these two theses later that year.

Gilles Deleuze. *(AP/Wide World Photos)*

While at the University of Lyon, Deleuze began his collaborative work with Félix Guattari. Guattari was a practicing psychoanalyst who, since the 1950's, had been at La Borde, an experimental psychiatric clinic founded by Lacanian analyst Jean Oury. Deleuze met Guattari soon after the publication of his book *The Logic of Sense*. In this work, Deleuze emphasizes the nature of becoming, of breaking down oppressive sociocultural stereotypes and expectations, including the identity of being an "author." This breaking down of stereotypes was precisely what Guattari attempted to do in his psychoanalytic practice. Guattari sought to promote what he called "human relations that do not automatically fall into roles or stereotypes but open onto fundamental relations of a metaphysical kind that bring out the most radical and basic alienations of madness or neurosis." What Guattari needed, he felt, was a more sophisticated philosophical expression and formulation of his approach, and he believed that Deleuze could assist in this regard. Similarly, Deleuze hoped to get beyond philosophy into realms of practice, and by working with Guattari, he could test philosophical concepts within an actual practice. Moreover, by working together, Deleuze believed they would create a work that could not be strictly identified with either Deleuze or Guattari, but rather Deleuze would be, to use Deleuze's (and Guattari's) terminology, "becoming-Guattari," and Guattari would be "becoming-Deleuze." The collaboration worked well for both Deleuze and Guattari, and with *Anti-Oedipus*, volume 1 of *Capitalism and Schizophrenia*, they created a sensation that went well beyond the philosophical community.

Soon after the publication of *Anti-Oedipus*, Deleuze joined the faculty at the University of Paris in Vincennes. Deleuze would remain at Vincennes until his retirement from teaching in 1987. While at Vincennes, Deleuze often taught classes containing a wide mix of students, including psychiatrists, musicians, drug addicts, and people from many different countries. Deleuze thrived on this heterogeneous mix of students and found that any time he visited a more traditional university setting, he felt he had taken a step backward in time. Moreover, the diversity of students in these classes fed into Deleuze's own philosophical attempts to understand the synthesis of heterogeneous elements, an attempt Deleuze first began with his work in *Difference and Repetition*.

During the 1970's, Deleuze, a recognized philosophical voice in France, became more politically active. Deleuze joined with Foucault in an effort to initiate prison reforms, and he was involved with the gay rights movement. He wrote less, focusing primarily on his political involvements and on his teaching; however, he did publish several essays with Guattari that would later become part of *A Thousand Plateaus*, volume 2 of *Capitalism and Schizophrenia*. In addition to this work, Deleuze and Guattari wrote a book on Franz Kafka entitled *Kafka: Toward a Minor Literature*.

As the 1980's began, and with the publication of *A Thousand Plateaus*, Deleuze's international recognition began to grow. At this point in time, among French philosophers, only Foucault and Derrida were more readily recognized. Deleuze rarely traveled, however, because he did not like to travel and also because he was generally in poor health, having been diagnosed with tuberculosis in 1968. Deleuze primarily stayed in Paris, taught his seminars at Vincennes, and continued with his research. Much of this work was dedicated to film, and in 1983, he published the first of two volumes on film, *Cinema 1: The Movement-Image*, followed in 1985 with *Cinema 2: The Time-Image*. Deleuze then turned to the history of philosophy and wrote a book on Gottfried Wilhelm Leibniz, *The Fold: Leibniz and the Baroque*. By 1988, however, Deleuze's health began to deteriorate, and he was no longer able to muster the energy he felt he needed to teach his classes as he would have liked. Deleuze retired from Vincennes and dedicated nearly all his time to his research, his wife, Fanny, and their two children, and friends. Late in 1988, Deleuze agreed to give a televised interview with Claire Parnet. Deleuze rarely gave interviews; he insisted on responding to questions in writing, distrusting himself to be adequate with answers in an oral context. Deleuze granted this interview on the condition that it be shown posthumously.

The last few years of Deleuze's life continued, despite his poor health (he contracted emphysema in the early 1990's), to be productive with respect to his work. In 1990, Deleuze once again joined forces with Guattari, and in 1991, they published their last collaborative work, *What Is Philosophy?*, before Guattari's death in 1992. Deleuze's health made it increasingly difficult for him to work, and he would publish only one more book, a collection of essays he had written on literature over the preceding twenty years. The book, *Essays Critical and Clinical*, was published in 1993, and two years later, on November 5, 1995, Deleuze committed suicide by throwing himself out of his second-floor apartment window. In his interview with Parnet, Deleuze had said that suicide in a young man is tragic, but in one who has lived his life and has nothing more to accomplish, it is not tragic. Apparently Deleuze believed his declining health left him unable to work, and concluding that he had done all that he could, he took his own life.

Influence

After Deleuze's death, his reputation increased. Many of Deleuze's early books were translated into other languages. *Difference and Repetition* was first translated into English in 1994, and *The Logic of Sense* was translated into English in 1990. In the 1990's, Deleuze's books on film were beginning to be studied by film theorists. Foucault once said, largely in jest, that the twentieth century might one day be known as Deleuzian. Late in the twentieth century, Deleuze's writings began to receive the exposure that might lead others to agree with Foucault. Deleuze certainly would not want a school of thought to be formed as the sole voice of Deleuzian thought, nor would he want disciples to spread his philosophy. Rather, Deleuze sought to engender thinking, to cause changes in people's attitudes, and to have philosophy initiate becomings (changes or variations) in realms outside philosophy. The extent to which his works accomplish this might reveal the ultimate range of his influence.

Jeffrey A. Bell

Difference and Repetition

Type of philosophy: Epistemology, metaphysics
First published: Différence et répétition, 1968 (English translation, 1994)

Principal ideas advanced:

◇ Difference is understood not as a difference between identifiable terms or entities, but as the difference that allows for determination and identification *as such*.

◇ Because "representation" presupposes the identity of what is represented, Deleuze's philosophy of difference is thus a critique of representational theories of thought such as that of Immanuel Kant.

Difference and Repetition is arguably Gilles Deleuze's most important work. It was Deleuze's major thesis and his first statement of his own philosophical position and of the approach to issues he had explored in earlier works, including his books on Friedrich Nietzsche, David Hume, and Marcel Proust. Deleuze's reputation, especially in the United States, was largely established as a result of his later collaborative works with Félix Guattari, which include the first volume of *Capitalisme et schizophrénie* (*Capitalism and Schizophrenia*), titled *L'Anti-Œdipe* (1972; *Anti-Oedipus*, 1977), the second volume, titled *Mille Plateaux* (1980; *A Thousand Plateaus*, 1987), and *Qu'est-ce que la philosophie?* (1991; *What Is Philosophy?*, 1994). However, he first developed many of the themes expressed in these collaborative works in *Difference and Repetition*.

Difference and Repetition is a critical text in that it solidly and explicitly places Deleuze's philosophical project within the "philosophies of difference" tradition as found in the works of Jacques Derrida, Jean-François Lyotard, and Julia Kristeva. In fact, Deleuze is quite straightforward in stating that his work, beginning with *Difference and Repetition*, is concerned with thinking about "difference in itself." By this he meant that he was attempting to think about difference without reducing it to a difference between already identified terms and without relying on a metaphysical foundation of "identity" such as God, substance, or spirit.

Defining Difference

In his effort to develop a philosophy of difference, Deleuze admits to formulating a philosophy that does not seek to ground the identifiable differences of the world in the way that the Greek philosopher Aristotle grounded differences upon the self-identity and stability of substance. The mistake, or what Deleuze calls "illusion," of those who criticize this affirmation of "groundlessness" is that they assume that groundlessness "should lack differences, when in fact it swarms with them." The groundless ground, so to speak, is therefore not an undifferentiated abyss; however, the differences that exist within it are not differences between identifiable terms or those that can be thought of in terms of identity. So, then, what are these differences? Answering this question is the task Deleuze sets for himself in *Difference and Repetition*.

In the chapter "Difference in Itself," Deleuze notes that difference is the means for distinguishing or determining things; it is "determination *as such*." He divides differences into two categories: extrinsic and intrinsic. "The difference 'between' two things is only empirical, and the corresponding determinations are only extrinsic." In contrast to an extrinsic form of determination, Deleuze calls for a more fundamental difference, an intrinsic difference that "makes itself." An intrinsic difference is one that "makes the difference" between identifiable things, and it is this understanding of difference that is the focus of Deleuze's attention not only throughout the remaining chapters of *Difference and Repetition* but also throughout the rest of his writings. In *Difference and Repetition*, the groundlessness that "swarms" with differences is understood to swarm with these intrinsic differences; in *A Thousand Plateaus*, and again in *What Is Philosophy?*, this groundlessness is understood to be chaos, and the differences that "make the difference" are in this context defined as "abstract machines."

Deleuze argues that this chaos is not to be understood in terms of an order or identity that it negates. Chaos lacks consistency and order not because it negates these terms but because it contains elements of infinite speed that exceed consistency or because the differences that "make the difference" between identifiable terms exceed an identity. The groundless ground therefore is not a lack or negation of consistency and order or the negation of a ground; it is an excess incapable of being caught within the parameters of a consistent, ordered, and stable ground. More important, this groundlessness is the condition for the possibility of the consistent systems that emerge

by virtue of the differences that "make the difference" between identifiable terms, or for what Deleuze and Guattari later refer to as the abstract machines that allow for the slowing down of infinite speeds and hence for the possibility of consistency. Therefore, the groundlessness that is the condition for the possibility of consistency and order, for determination *as such*, is referred to as the groundless ground.

Calculus and Chaos
To explain what it means to speak of infinite speeds or of an excess that must be slowed and filtered in order for it to be transformed into finite, consistent speeds, Deleuze refers to differential calculus on a number of occasions in *Difference and Repetition*. In discussing the French mathematician Albert Lautman, for example, Deleuze notes that Lautman makes a fundamental distinction between the "distribution of individual points in a field of vectors" and "the integral curves in their neighborhood." The manner in which these points are distributed in the field is the central issue. Chaos, per Deleuze's reading, consists of infinitesimal vectors that cannot be reduced to a level of consistency, or in the language of differential equations, these points cannot be integrated. The distribution of individual points must therefore be transformed into an integrable distribution of points, or points consistent enough for the integral curves to be drawn in their neighborhood. The abstract machine, the difference that "makes the difference," performs the function of filtering the nonintegrable field of points (chaos) and transforming it into an integrable distribution. The integration of these distributed points, or the integral curve in their neighborhood, is, as Deleuze makes clear, "the thing that brings about or *actualizes* relations between forces" in that it actualizes the differences "between" identifiable terms.

Deleuze and Leibniz
In *Le Pli: Leibniz et le baroque* (1988; *The Fold: Leibniz and the Baroque*, 1993), Deleuze's book on Gottfried Wilhelm Leibniz, the philosopher refers to a sense of "anxiousness" arising from a confrontation with the nonintegrable forces or vectors of chaos. What is needed, therefore, is a taming or subduing of this chaos, or what Deleuze calls an "accord."

I produce an accord each time I can establish in a sum of infinitely tiny things differential relations that will make possible an integration of the sum—in other words a clear and distinguished perception. It is a filter, a selection.

These differential relations or series from which an integral curve can be formed are not, however, differential series or relations that could, if taken as a whole, converge upon a complete and total picture of the universe. To assume this would be to attribute a comprehensive unity or identity to the universe, an identity that the differential series would approximate. It is clear that this is the assumption Leibniz makes, for in discussing the monads (differential series) in his *La Mondologie* (written 1714, published 1840; *Monadology*, 1867), Leibniz uses the analogy of the perspectives on a city to show that although there are an infinite number of monads that are different from one another, each monad nevertheless is a different expression of one and the same universe. Deleuze, however, breaks with this faith in a pre-existent totality or identity, and it is with his notion of chaos (the groundless ground) that he argues instead for a nonidentifiable inconsistency that exceeds identity and is identified only once the chaos is filtered or an accord is produced. Consequently, for Deleuze, the relationship between differential series is not one of accord, as it was for Leibniz, but one of divergence, wherein the excess of chaos entails the possibility of undermining the consistency and unity. In *Difference and Repetition*, Deleuze is explicit on this point.

> Each series tells a story: not different points of view on the same story, like the different points of view on the town we find in Leibniz, but completely distinct stories which unfold simultaneously. The basic series are divergent: not relatively, in the sense that one could retrace one's path and find a point of convergence, but absolutely divergent in the sense that the point or horizon of convergence lies in a chaos or is constantly displaced within that chaos.

These divergent series are nonetheless put into relation with one another, for despite their divergence, lines of communication are opened. For example, Deleuze speaks of the "dark precursor" as that which "by virtue of its own power . . . puts them [the heterogenous differential series] into immediate relation to one another." Deleuze immediately addresses the logical criticism of this position: If there is a "dark precursor" that enables the heterogeneous series to communicate, must there not then be an identity to this precursor and a resemblance between the two series that enables them to communicate with each another? Deleuze's response is that indeed "there is an identity belonging to the precursor, and a resemblance between the series it causes to communicate. This 'there is', however, remains perfectly indeterminate." Deleuze then asks, "Are identity and resemblance here the preconditions of the functioning of the dark precursor, or are they, on the contrary, its effects?" Deleuze's answer is that identity and resemblance are the effects of the dark precursor, and not vice versa. In other words, the precursor is the indeterminate (he also refers to it as the "virtual") which is real although neither individuated nor determined, and it is what makes individuation and determination possible.

To clarify these issues, Deleuze examines the psychoanalytic theories surrounding the effect of repressed memories on present behavior. The past, according to Deleuze, does not have the same status or identity as the present. The past (past present) is part of an extended series of identities, or presents. Nor does the past act on the present through resemblance. (An example of the past acting on the present through resemblance would be a person repeating certain child-like behaviors because of the resemblance between a person in the present and the individual's mother, a person in the past.) Deleuze argues that this repetition of behavior "is constituted not from one present [past present] to another [present present], but between the two coexistent series [series of past and present] that these presents form in function of the virtual object [or the dark precursor]." It is not the resemblance between the mother and a present person that accounts for the repetition of childhood patterns; rather, the virtual object (or dark precursor) is the indeterminate object that is to be identified with neither the mother nor the present person, yet it is the condition that allows for the possibility of seeing the resemblance, and hence for the repetition of the behavior. The virtual object is the difference that allows for the possibility of relating two heterogeneous series (a series of pasts with a series of presents; a series of expressions with a series of content), or it is difference in itself, the difference that makes the difference between repeated behaviors.

A Definitive Statement

Difference and Repetition had an immediate influence on other philosophers in France following its publication in 1968. Although Deleuze received his greatest accolades, both in France and abroad, for his work with Guattari, *Difference and Repetition* is viewed as the most important statement of Deleuze's own philosophical position and approach, an approach further refined and modified in the books he wrote with Guattari. Since its publication in English in 1994, *Difference and Repetition* has reached a wider audience. Because this work explicitly confronts themes broached by Deleuze's more famous contemporary, Jacques Derrida, it provided scholars a fresh perspective on these themes. Deleuze's ultimate influence, therefore, largely rests on the arguments and positions developed in this book.

Jeffrey A. Bell

Additional Reading

Boundas, Constantin V., and Dorothea Olkowski, eds. *Gilles Deleuze and the Theater of Philosophy*. New York: Routledge, 1994. This is a very helpful collection of essays that present varying perspectives upon most aspects of Deleuze's work.

Deleuze, Gilles, and Claire Parnet. *Dialogues*. Translated by Hugh Tomlinson and Barbara Habberjam, 1977. New York: Columbia University Press, 1987. This work provides a glimpse into the philosopher's life and thought.

Patton, Paul, ed. *Deleuze: A Critical Reader*. Cambridge, Mass.: Blackwell, 1996. This is a helpful text for those who want a more in-depth, detailed analysis of Deleuze's work.

Pearson, Keith Ansell, ed. *Deleuze and Philosophy: The Difference Engineer*. New York: Routledge, 1997. This collection of essays is a useful resource for acquiring a quick overview of aspects of Deleuze's writings.

Schrift, Alan D. *Nietzsche's French Legacy: A Genealogy of Poststructuralism*. New York: Routledge, 1995. This is a good overview of the French philosophical tradition within which Deleuze's work appeared. It places Deleuze's work solidly within the French tradition that cites Friedrich Nietzsche as its major influence rather than Edmund Husserl. This tradition also includes philosophers Jacques Derrida, Michel Foucault, Hélène Cixous, and Sarah Kofman.

Jeffrey A. Bell

Democritus

Democritus worked out a far-reaching atomism, which he applied to science, metaphysics, and ethics. His view that the world is made up of changing combinations of unchanging atoms addressed one of the central questions of his age—How is change possible?—and provided a model of reasoning that was mechanistic, materialist, and nonsupernatural.

Principal philosophical works: Only fragments exist, c. fourth century B.C.E. (*The Golden Sentences of Democrates*, 1804).

Born: c. 460 B.C.E.; Abdera, Thrace
Died: c. 370 B.C.E.; Abdera, Thrace

Early Life

Democritus was born, probably to wealthy parents, in the city of Abdera, Thrace. Although Leucippus, the philosopher who became his teacher, can properly be regarded as the founder of Greek atomism, Leucippus himself wrote very little, and very little is known about him. Democritus, however, was a prolific writer who developed a well-reasoned atomistic view and applied it to a wide variety of fields, including science, metaphysics, and ethics.

As a young man, Democritus traveled to Egypt, Persia, and Babylonia. Some ancient sources hold that he went as far south as Ethiopia and as far east as India, but modern scholars consider this doubtful. It is reported that Democritus boasted that he had visited more foreign lands and carried out more extensive inquiries and investigations than anyone else of his time. He traveled both for the "broadening" experience that occurs for any inquisitive traveler and in order to receive instruction from those who were considered wise in many lands. When he returned to Greek soil, he earned a reputation for wisdom. He carried with him an aura of the exotic, having delved into cultures that the Greeks thought of as exotic and foreign: those of Egypt, Persia, and Babylonia.

In character, Democritus is reported to have been a man of serenity, strength, and cheerfulness. The ancient Romans referred to him as "the laughing philosopher," alluding, perhaps, to his attitude toward the typically human fault of taking oneself too seriously. As a thinker and writer, he addressed the most pressing philosophical and intellectual issues of the age in his works, which numbered at least fifty. Unfortunately, his texts have survived only in fragmentary form.

Life's Work

During the years following his travels, when Democritus began to develop his philosophical system, the Greek intellectual world was occupied with grave difficulties arising from the philosophy of Parmenides of Elea and his followers, the Eleatics. Parmenides was a practitioner of strict deductive logic. Taking premises that he thought would be generally acceptable, he argued logically to necessary conclusions. Many people admired his strong reliance on reason and thought; nevertheless, Parmenides arrived at conclusions that were deeply problematic. He concluded that there is no such thing as change and that only one thing exists. This clearly conflicts with common experience, which seems to show constant change and plurality. Still, Parmenides held fast to logic and reasoning as sources of knowledge that are more reliable than sense experience. If reason rules out change and plurality, he thought, then change and plurality do not exist.

The basis of his argument—an argument with which Democritus and Leucippus had no choice but to grapple—is the idea that reason either apprehends something or it apprehends nothing. If it apprehends nothing, then it is not reason (that

Democritus of Abdera. *(Library of Congress)*

One of the great achievements of Democritus and the atomists lies in overcoming this argument—an argument that probably seemed much more convincing to the ancient Greeks than to modern thinkers—while retaining some of its logical points and, at the same time, acknowledging the reality of change, plurality, and other common-sense ideas that Parmenides apparently denied.

It is a fundamental principle of Democritean atomism that "nothing exists but the atoms and the void." The atoms (literally, in Greek, "the indivisibles" or "the uncuttables") are the smallest units of matter, the smallest pieces of being, and cannot be further divided. The void, considered nonbeing, is thought to be just as real as the atoms. It was very important for Democritus that both exist: being and nonbeing, the atoms and the void. In a sense, the atoms are individually much like the One of Parmenides. They do not come into existence or pass out of existence, and they do not change (internally). Nevertheless, the void—a necessary feature of atomism—makes it possible for the atoms to combine and separate and recombine in changing arrangements.

As Democritus envisioned them, atoms differ from one another only in shape, size, and position. Qualities such as color and flavor were said to arise from the particular arrangements of (inherently colorless and flavorless) atoms and their interaction with the senses of the observer.

Atoms are constantly in motion, according to Democritus's theory. They do not require any force or intelligence to put them into motion. Surrounded by the void, they are not held in any one position but move quite freely. Atoms crash into one another, become entangled with one another, and sometimes establish regular motions or streams of motion. There is no limit to the void or to the number of atoms, and Democritus thought that the universe visible to human beings was only one among countless worlds, many of which must also contain stars, planets, and living things.

is, not an apprehending) after all. Thus, reason apprehends what exists, not nothing. Now, if things came into existence or passed out of existence, or if things changed their qualities over time, then reason would have to think of the things or qualities as not existing at some time (that is, before coming into existence or after passing out of existence). Reason would then, however, be apprehending nothing—and this, it was said, cannot occur. Similarly, if more than one thing existed, and there was empty space between the things, reason would again have to apprehend nothing. The conclusion is that only one thing exists, and this one thing is eternal, never coming into existence, never passing out of existence, and never changing. This one thing Parmenides called "the One."

The atomism of Democritus was a reaffirmation of the reality of change as experienced in everyday life, yet it agreed with Parmenides concerning the unchanging reality that lies behind observed phenomena. The theory attempted to do justice to both experience and reason, change and permanence. Democritus envisioned a world in which combinations and configurations of atoms change within the void, but the atoms themselves never undergo internal change. Thus, it is the void that makes change possible. Ironically, it could be said that in the theory of Greek atomism it is really the void (and not the atoms) that is innovative and enables the theory to escape from the unpalatable conclusions of Parmenides and the Eleatics.

Democritus also addressed questions raised by an entirely new movement in Greek thought. Before the time of Democritus, Greek philosophers had been almost exclusively concerned with physical and metaphysical questions—for example, questions about being and change. Around the time of Democritus, however, a revolution in philosophy was brought about by the Sophists and Socrates, who raised questions about human nature, society, and morality rather than questions that focused on the physical world.

Democritus approached all these questions through his atomism. The soul, he surmised, is made up of highly mobile spherical atoms, which disperse at death. He hypothesized that people who seem to die but who "come back to life" have actually retained their atomic integrity all the while; they did not really die and come back to life. Eventually, in a real death, the atoms in the body begin to lose their connections with one another. This process is gradual, however, so that hair and fingernails might grow for a while even after the life-breath and the necessary spherical atoms are gone. Then, as the atoms lose their connections, the entire body decays.

Democritus taught that people should have no fear or apprehension concerning supernatural matters or an afterlife. Because the totality of reality consists of the atoms and the void, when the atoms of a person disperse and the person dies, the person no longer exists. Therefore, according to Democritus, there is nothing to fear in death. The corollary conclusion is that people should not delay pleasures in anticipation of an afterlife.

It is in this life—this arrangement of atoms—that human beings can find their only fulfillment and happiness.

The best life is one that is characterized by contentedness and cheerfulness. Democritus believed that passions are powerful, disturbing factors that tend to upset the natural harmony and balance in the arrangement of atoms in human beings. Democritus used his atomism to support traditional Greek views that strong passions can cause much trouble and that moderation is best. The key to moderation and to the achievement of happiness in life is knowledge. Knowledge determines one's proper goals and activities, while passion is a threat.

It is important, however, to distinguish Democritus's knowledge-passion polarity from that of many later Platonic thinkers. Platonic thinkers (and some Christian Neoplatonists) are dualists. They distinguish between one's spiritual or intellectual part—the seat of reason, which is divine and immortal—and one's physical or irrational part—the seat of passion, which is animal and mortal. The first is the spiritual soul and lives forever; the second is the body, which suffers death and decay. In contrast, Democritus was a thoroughgoing naturalist and materialist; he believed that all the atoms disperse at death and nothing survives. Knowledge was seen as important and passion was seen as a threat, not for religious or supernatural reasons but because of their import for human contentedness and cheerfulness.

Ancient sources agree that Democritus lived to a remarkably advanced age. Few details of his later life, however, are known. The legend that he blinded himself (in order to root out lustful desires, according to Tertullian) is denied by Plutarch. Democritus is thought to have died in Thrace around the year 370 B.C.E.

Influence

The theory of atomism was not favored by Plato and Aristotle, the two major Greek philosophers who followed Democritus, but it was adopted by the Greek Epicurus and the Roman Lucretius. Epicurus was attracted to the moral teaching of Democritus and held that human well-being is best achieved by eliminating pain and the painful desire for things that people cannot (or cannot easily) obtain. Consequently, he aimed to live a life of utmost simplicity. Both Epicurus and Lucretius followed Democritus in denying supernatural influences on human life and rejecting the idea of an afterlife. Moreover, all these thinkers believed that their position on these points was not only true but also useful in freeing people from superstitions that lead to pain and suffering.

Atomism, as an essentially physical and mechanical account of the world that leaves no place for "higher purposes" or "meanings," was particularly unacceptable to religious and theological writers of the Christian tradition, which dominated Western philosophy from about the fourth to the fourteenth century. In the wake of the Renaissance and the scientific revolution (since about the fifteenth and sixteenth centuries), however, the influence of Democritus has again become apparent in philosophy and science. Modern science, like ancient Democritean atomism, deals with the world purely in terms of observable or theorized physical objects operating according to natural laws; the question of higher purposes or meanings is considered to lie beyond the scope of science. In some points of detail, there is significant agreement between ancient atomism and the modern scientific view. In both accounts, for example, qualities such as the color of a book or the taste of a cup of coffee are thought to be attached not to individual atoms—there are no red atoms or coffee-flavored atoms—but to combinations of atoms in interaction with a perceiver. One obvious difference between the two forms of atomism, however, is that in the Democritean view atoms cannot be split, while the modern scientific view upholds the existence of many kinds of subatomic particles and has even led to the development of atom-splitting technology that can unleash great power.

It must be remembered, however, that the atomism of Democritus is not a scientific theory and does not pretend to be based on experiment, experience, and observation. It is basically a philosophical theory, based on argument, which was designed to refute the theory and the arguments of Parmenides and the Eleatics. Thus, interesting as it is to compare ancient and modern atomism, it is not really fair to think of the two views as competing in the same arena. Democri-

tus and the Greek atomists succeeded in developing an attitude toward the world that enabled them to look on it as thoroughly physical and mechanical, and it is this attitude, or significant aspects of it, that many modern scientists have shared. According to this view, observable phenomena are explainable in terms of unseen movements that occur according to natural (not supernatural) law.

Stephen Satris

Democritus: Fragments

Type of philosophy: Metaphysics
First transcribed: c. fourth century B.C.E. (*The Golden Sentences of Democrates*, 1804)
Principal ideas advanced:
◇ Nothing can come from nothing, change really occurs, and motion requires a void; therefore, reality must consist of atoms moving in a void.
◇ The only inherent properties of atoms are size, shape, and solidity; color, sweetness, bitterness, and other such qualities are attributed to objects because of the sensations occurring within experiencing organisms, but such qualities have no existence in objects.
◇ The sensations that come from experiencing various kinds of atoms vary according to the shapes of the atoms.
◇ The best form of government is the democratic.
◇ The wise person is one who limits ambition according to ability.

In all probability, credit for the fundamental ideas of the atomic theory—Greek speculation's greatest achievement—should go to Leucippus of Miletus rather than to his pupil, Democritus. However, almost nothing is known of Leucippus.

Rational speculation about the nature of the world began not earlier than the sixth century B.C.E. Four or five generations later it had progressed, in Democritus, to an essentially correct account of the nature of matter. This amazing fact has led to both exaggeration and underestimation of the Greek achievement. Some people conclude that science stood still until the revival of the atomic theory in the seventeenth century. However, scientists point out that modern atomic physics rests on evidence derived from careful quantitative experimentation of which the Greeks knew nothing; therefore, it is said, the ancient theory was merely a lucky guess—and the Greeks made all possible guesses. A brief review of the development of early Greek physics will show that while Democritus did not have English chemist and physicist John Dalton's reasons for asserting that the world consists of atoms moving in the void, he nevertheless had some very good ones.

Early Assumptions

The men of Miletus, especially Anaximander, who made the break with mythological world accounts in the early sixth century B.C.E., took over from previous creation myths two important assumptions. First, Milesians accepted the belief that there *was* a creation, or rather a development: The world was not always as it is now but had in the beginning been something simple and homogeneous, like the "chaos" of the myths. Differentiation, complexity, and organization have a history. Second, the Milesians accepted the theory that there exists an impersonal force making for order and "justice" in the universe at large. The Milesians were the first philosophers; they dispensed altogether with the "will of the gods" as an explanatory principle because they assumed that the natural forces that made the universe what it is were still operative. The problem, as they conceived it, was to identify the original simple world stuff out of which all things had come and to describe the process that had differentiated and organized it into the present world. Not "divine" inspiration but ordinary human reason, they thought, was capable of solving the problem. Because conclusions based on reasons invite criticism and modification, unlike revelations, which can be only accepted or rejected, the history of rational speculation was progressive.

In addition to the ideas of ultimate oneness, development, and "justice" inherited from religion, the earliest philosophers assumed with "common sense" that nothing can come out of nothing or be absolutely destroyed and that our senses reveal directly the constituents of the world, at least as it is now. We feel heat and cold; we taste sweetness and bitterness; we see red and green. Heat, cold, sweetness, bitterness, red, and green are therefore *parts* of the objective world; together they make it up. These are now regarded as *qualities* of matter, but early Greek thought does not make this distinction; "the hot," "the cold," "the wet," "the dry," and so on, in various combinations, *are* the stuff of things. One must simply find out the unity underlying this diversity. For example, Anaximenes, the third of the Milesian "physicists," held that the fundamental stuff is mist. Everything is really mist; the things that do not appear to be mist are mist that has been thickened or thinned. Very thin mist is fire; mist somewhat thickened is water; thickened still more, mist is stone.

Parmenides' Objections

There is an inconsistency here that Parmenides (in effect) pointed out. No doubt the theory of Anaximenes squares with observation, for fire, when cooled and "thickened," becomes smoke and smoke is easy to regard, at this stage of thought, as a kind of fog or mist. Condensed mist is water, and water thickened still more becomes ice, a solid, a kind of stone. However, is the theory compatible with logic? Fire is (identical with) "the hot and dry"; water is (identical with) "the cold and wet." How, then, can the one be transformed into the other without violating the fundamental principle that nothing can come from nothing? Where did the *cold* come from? Where has the *hot* gone? If cold and hot are thought of as substances, it seems that there can be no satisfactory answer to this question. Something has come out of "nothing"; something has disappeared into "nothing." Worse still, as Parmenides saw, if there is ultimately just one stuff, that stuff must be just the kind of stuff it is, so that it cannot logically be both hot and cold, both wet and dry. Therefore *change is impossible*. If things seem to change (as they do), this must be mere illusion, for logic pronounces it contradictory.

It is important to see that Parmenides was right, given his assumptions of monism, nothing from nothing, and identity of things and qualities. Parmenides had another argument (a fallacious one) to show that the kind of change called motion cannot really occur. Parmenides said that

453

if a thing moves, there must be room for it to move into—that is, there must be empty space. However, there cannot be any empty space, for empty space would be just "nothing," "that which is not," and the assertion that there is empty space amounts to saying "That which is not, is," a statement of contradiction.

Empedocles and Anaxagoras Respond

The philosophers Empedocles and Anaxagoras tried to develop systems that would meet the logical objections of Parmenides without flying in the face of common sense. They argued that motion could occur without empty space if the moving thing *displaced* what was in front of it, as a fish swims in water. For the rest, they abandoned monism. Empedocles said that there are six basic stuffs, while Anaxagoras held that the number of stuff is infinite—that there are as many stuffs as there are sensible discriminations—and all things are made by the mixture and separation of these stuffs.

The philosophy of Anaxagoras successfully met Parmenides' criticism, but at too high a price. Although it is hard to say precisely just what it is that we are asking for when we demand an explanation of something, at any rate it is clear that an explanation is not satisfactory unless in *some* sense the ideas used in the explanation are simpler, or more unified, than the thing to be explained. However, if one's explanatory principles are as diverse as the things to be explained, the requirement cannot be met. "Flour is a mixture in which flour-stuff predominates, and water is a mixture in which water-stuff predominates, and the two make bread because when they are mixed and baked the bread-stuff in both of them comes to the fore." This may be true, but it is too easy and it does not *explain* anything.

Leucippus and Democritus Respond

Leucippus and Democritus discovered a better way of answering Parmenides. As to motion, Leucippus flatly declared that "nothing" *does* exist; Democritus more appropriately dismissed Parmenides' quibble with another: "'Hing' exists no more than 'not-hing,'" the point of the joke being that if "'Nothing' does not exist" is a truth of *logic*, elimination of the double negative must also produce a logical truth: "'Hing' does exist."

However, "hing," so far from existing, is not even a word. (Greek for "nothing" is *mēden*, of which *mē* means "not," while *den* has no meaning in isolation.)

There is, then, a *void*, and things that move in it. These things are *atoms*—"uncuttables." Each separate atom is like the "reality" of Parmenides, uncreated, indestructible, unchanging. The matter in an atom is homogeneous, and nothing can happen to one internally; that is, each atom is infinitely hard. Atoms differ from one another in size and shape—that is all. They do not differ in color, for instance, but not because they are all the *same* color. They do so because they have no color at all (not even black or gray). Similarly for heat, moisture, taste, and odor. Atoms have always been (and always will be) in motion—"like the motes in a sunbeam." They jostle one another, and in their jostlings, two kinds of processes occur that result in the "coming-into-being" of the large-scale aggregates with which we are familiar. One is vortex motion, the effect of which is to separate random aggregates according to likenesses, the heavier—that is, the bigger—atoms going to the center, the lighter ones to the periphery. The other process is the hooking on to each other by atoms of like configurations.

One atom can affect another only by colliding with it; and the outcome of a collision (hooking, or change of direction or speed) is *determined* by the sizes, shapes, and velocities of the atoms involved in the collision. However, the sizes and shapes are eternal, and the velocities in their turn are outcomes of previous collisions. Therefore, there is no such thing as "chance" in nature; "Nothing happens at random," Leucippus pronounced in the one sentence of his that has survived, "but everything from a rationale and by necessity." Ideally, explanation should consist in finding out the laws of motion and impact and using these to show how one atomic configuration came about from a previous one. Such a complex act is of course impossible; however, Democritus sought to apply the fundamental idea of *mechanical causation* to observable phenomena.

An ancient story illustrates Democritus's method and highlights its difference from traditional concepts. Considerable interest had been aroused by the extraordinary death of a prominent man. When he was strolling along a beach, an eagle had dropped a turtle on his head. Why? It was recalled that an oracle had said that he would die of "a bolt from Zeus." This had been thought to be a prediction of death by a stroke of lightning. However, someone pointed out that the eagle was a bird sacred to Zeus; thus, the oracle was fulfilled. This explanation satisfied most Greeks but not Democritus. He went to the beach and observed the habits of eagles. He found that they were fond of turtle meat. In order to get at it, an eagle would seize a turtle in his talons, fly into the air with it, and drop it on a rock to crack the shell. This observation, together with the fact that the deceased had been bald, provided an explanation that satisfied Democritus. The curious event was shown to be one item in a natural regularity or pattern. It was unnecessary to postulate the purposes of unseen beings to account for the fact. Aristotle complained, quite unjustifiably, that Democritus "reduced the explanation of nature to the statement, 'Thus it happened formerly also.'" Actually, Democritus understood the character of scientific explanation far better than did Aristotle.

In sum, Democritus's reason for asserting that reality consists of atoms moving in the void is that this statement can be *deduced* from the premises: Nothing can come from nothing, change really occurs, and motion requires a void. That this explanation must be mechanistic also follows from these assumptions if it is further allowed that all interaction is impact. Democritus's mechanism was also the culmination of the rejection of animistic and supernatural will or forces by all his philosophical predecessors.

Democritus's atomism, and still more his mechanism, agree in principle with the fundamental tenets of modern physical science. What modern physicists have that Democritus lacked is a conception of controlled, quantitative experimentation, together with a technique of mathematical manipulation of the data. For this reason, Democritus, though he declared that he would "rather discover one causal explanation than gain the kingdom of the Persians," failed utterly to add to detailed knowledge of nature. In fact, he was much behind his own times, still believing, for instance, that the earth is a flat disc, though the Pythagoreans had long understood its sphericity. In detailed explanations, Democritus

could do no better than this: "Thunder is produced by an unstable mixture forcing the cloud enclosing it to move downward. Lightning is a clashing together of clouds by which the fire-producing atoms rubbing against each other are assembled through the porous mass into one place and pass out. And the thunderbolt occurs when the motion is forced by the very pure, very fine, very uniform and 'closely-packed' fire-producing atoms, as he himself calls them." (The foregoing is an ancient paraphrase, not a quotation from Democritus.) It must be admitted that this account of lightning is no worse than any other prior to that given by American Benjamin Franklin, and a considerable improvement over "Zeus is angry."

Qualities and Sensations

"By convention color, by convention sweet, by convention bitter; but in reality atoms and void." Thus Democritus states his theory. The atoms alone are real, and their only inherent qualities (Democritus distinguished clearly between thing and quality) are size, shape, and solidity. Then what about color, sweet, bitter, and the rest? They are "by convention." What does this mean? Democritus held that a person's soul consists of particularly fine and spherical, hence mobile, atoms. When certain "images" from the external world—the images being, of course, themselves assemblages of atoms—impinge on the soul atoms, a sensation is produced. The sensation occurs only within the ensouled body; hence, it is not "out there" because the external world is colorless and odorless. This is a part of the meaning of "by convention," a phrase that might be rendered as "subjective." The sensations are also subjective in the sense that they lead us to suppose, falsely, that the world is colored and odorous.

There are two forms of knowledge, one genuine, one obscure. Of the obscure sort are all these: sight, hearing, smell, taste, touch. The genuine is distinguished from this. . . . Whenever the obscure cannot sense any farther into the minute by seeing or hearing or smelling or tasting or touching, but [it is necessary to pursue the investigation] more finely, [then the genuine, which has a finer organ of knowing,] comes up.

The organ of "genuine knowledge" would seem to be the "Pure Reason" that led Democritus to deduce the atomic nature of matter. However, Democritus was worried, as well he might have been, about the "obscure." He portrayed the senses speaking thus to the mind: "'Wretched mind, getting from us your confidences you cast us down? That is your own downfall.'" For the information on which even the atomic theory is based is, after all, derived ultimately from observation through the senses.

If reality consists of matter with only its "primary qualities," what kind of reality do sensation, thought, and consciousness in general have? This problem besets all forms of materialism and is often alleged to be fatal to it as a worldview. Democritus spent much effort in trying to account for sensations on atomic principles. Thus, he claimed that sour fluids consist of angular and twisted atoms, while honey is made of rounded, rather large ones. This was, of course, inconsistent with his claim that tastes are subjective effects. He could have patched up the account to some extent by considering not only the atomic constitution of the food but also that of the tongue that interacts with it; but there is no evidence that he did so. Perhaps it was despair at this problem that led him to exclaim, "In reality we know nothing. For truth is in a depth."

Materialists *should* say that sensations are not *things* at all; but Democritus held that they are illusory things. This, at any rate, is the impression we get from ancient discussions of his theory of knowledge. It may be mistaken, for the accounts all come from hostile critics who may well have misunderstood or misrepresented Democritus.

Unlike most Greek philosophers, Democritus was a partisan of democracy. He said: "Poverty in a democracy is as much preferable to so-called prosperity in an autocracy as freedom is to slavery." By "democracy" he meant a constitutional government, directed by public-spirited, intelligent people in the interest of all citizens.

Democritus was one of the most prolific authors of antiquity, having written, we are told, more than sixty works. The fragments that remain fill about ten pages of ordinary print, of which eight are concerned with ethics, politics, education, and child rearing. (Democritus thought it a risky and thankless business to have children.) Many of the ethical reflections are platitudinous: "In good fortune it is easy to find a friend, in misfortune hardest of all." Others are shrewd and worldly-wise: "If you cannot understand the compliments, conclude that you are being flattered." The general tenor of the maxims is advocacy of "cheerfulness," that is, of prudence, contentment with what one has, not worrying too much.

> He who would be cheerful must not busy himself with many things, either by himself or in company; and whatever he busies himself with, he should not choose what is beyond his own power and nature. However, he should be so on his guard that when a stroke of fortune tempts him to excess, he puts it aside, and does not grasp at what is beyond his powers. For being well-filled is better than being stuffed.

There are some fragments, however, that embody teachings often credited to others and used unfairly to belabor crude "materialism": "Refrain from wrongdoing not from fear but from duty"; "The doer of injustice is unhappier than the sufferer"; "Goodness is not merely in refraining from being unjust, but in not even wishing to be"; and "The cause of error is ignorance of the better."

Wallace I. Matson, updated by John K. Roth

Additional Reading

Brumbaugh, Robert S. *The Philosophers of Greece.* Albany: State University of New York Press, 1981. An important interpreter of Greek philosophy discusses the place of Democritus, atomism, and materialism within Greek philosophical theory.

Burnet, John. *Greek Philosophy: Thales to Plato.* London: Macmillan, 1953. Burnet's overview contains a brief but helpful account of Democritus's philosophy.

Cartledge, Paul. *Democritus.* New York: Routledge, 1999. An excellent biographical introduction to the thoughts of the philosopher, clearly presented and requiring no special background. Bibliography.

Cleve, Felix M. *The Giants of Pre-Sophistic Greek Philosophy: An Attempt to Reconstruct Their Thoughts.* The Hague: Martinus Nijhoff, 1969.

Cleve concentrates especially on Democritus's physical theories and his views about sense perception.

Copleston, Frederick. *A History of Philosophy: Greece and Rome*. Garden City, N.Y.: Doubleday, 1962. Copleston's brief treatment of Democritus is clear, and it places this pre-Socratic atomist in his historical context.

Curd, Patricia, ed. *A Presocratics Reader: Selected Fragments and Testimonia*. Translations by Richard D. McKirahan, Jr. Indianapolis, Ind.: Hackett, 1996. This volume includes text fragments from Democritus. Contains insightful editorial commentary.

Guthrie, W. K. C. *A History of Greek Philosophy*. Cambridge, England: Cambridge University Press, 1965. Democritus has been called an encyclopedic thinker, and Guthrie shows the truth of this remark by exploring many of Democritus's philosophical concerns.

Hussey, Edward. *The Presocratics*. Indianapolis, Ind.: Hackett, 1995. This accessible and comprehensive overview of the history of ancient Greek philosophy includes discussion of Democritus.

Kirk, G. S., and J. E. Raven. *The Presocratic Philosophers*. Cambridge, England: Cambridge University Press, 1960. Democritus's physical and ethical theories are discussed in this book, which includes the actual Greek texts of the philosophers accompanied by English translations.

McKirahan, Richard D., Jr. *Philosophy Before Socrates: An Introduction with Texts and Commentary*. Indianapolis, Ind.: Hackett, 1994. An excellent source that contains helpful discussion of Greek atomism and the thought of Democritus in particular.

Taylor, C. C. W., ed. *From the Beginning to Plato*. New York: Routledge, 1997. Taylor provides a good starting point for understanding Democritus's contributions to the origins of Western philosophy.

Stephen Satris, updated by John K. Roth

Daniel C. Dennett

Dennett brought cognitive science and philosophy closer together by discussing the physical structures of the brain and artificial intelligence in his philosophy. Arguing convincingly against Cartesian dualism, Dennett became known as a staunch defender of a materialist philosophy of mind.

Principal philosophical works: *Content and Consciousness*, 1969; *Brainstorms: Philosophical Essays on Mind and Psychology*, 1978; *Elbow Room: The Varieties of Free Will Worth Wanting*, 1984; *The Intentional Stance*, 1987; *Consciousness Explained*, 1991; *Darwin's Dangerous Idea: Evolution and the Meanings of Life*, 1995; *Kinds of Minds: Towards an Understanding of Consciousness*, 1996; *Brainchildren: Essays on Designing Minds*, 1998.

Born: March 28, 1942; Boston, Massachusetts

Early Life

Daniel Clement Dennett was born to an academic family. His father, Daniel Clement Dennett, Sr., was a historian and diplomat. His mother, Ruth Marjorie Leck Dennett, was a teacher and editor. An outstanding student, the young Dennett entered Harvard and graduated cum laude in 1963. While at Harvard, he married Susan Elizabeth Bell on June 8, 1962. Dennett has reported that he developed a fascination with the mind-body problem during his first year in college, when he read the work of the seventeenth century French philosopher René Descartes. Following his graduation, Dennett went to England to study philosophy at Oxford University, where he received a doctorate in philosophy in 1965. His chief mentor at Oxford was the philosopher Gilbert Ryle. Ryle and Dennett's Harvard mentor, W. V. O. Quine, influenced Dennett's style of writing as well as his materialist approach. Both of these older thinkers, Dennett later explained, always attempted to avoid jargon-laden writing and tried to write as though their readers would be nonphilosophers.

After he returned to the United States, Dennett took a position as assistant professor at the University of California, Irvine, in 1965 and remained there until 1971, having been promoted to the level of associate professor in 1970. He wrote his first book, *Content and Consciousness*, based on his doctoral dissertation, while in California. He moved to Tufts University in Medford, Massachusetts, in 1971. Although he would travel widely and serve as visiting professor at numerous universities, he continued to be on the faculty of Tufts throughout his career.

Life's Work

Content and Consciousness established many of the themes that would appear in Dennett's writings. It was in this book that he developed the idea of intentional systems, physical systems that could best be understood by seeing them as rational decision makers. The idea of intentionality was derived from the work of nineteenth century psychologist and philosopher Franz Brentano, who drew a distinction between mental phenomena and physical phenomena. Brentano maintained that mental phenomena could not be reduced to physical and mechanical events because mental phenomena show intentionality; they are directed upon objects in intentions, goals, wishes, desires, and interests. Dennett believed that Brentano's distinction was a useful one. Dennett, however, argued that it was possible to see intentionality as a consequence of relations among material parts and not as a characteristic of spirit or soul. His argument drew heavily on Darwinian evolution, another theme that would continually reappear in his work. Dennett paid a great deal of attention to brain mechanisms, a focus that caused some philosophers to question whether his work should really be classified as philosophy.

In 1975, Tufts University promoted Dennett from associate professor to full professor in recognition of his many contributions to philosophy journals and of his growing professional reputation. The following year, he became head of the philosophy department at Tufts.

While serving in this position, he published a book of essays, *Brainstorms: Philosophical Essays on Mind and Psychology*. These essays extended and revised the theory of the mind Dennett had put forth in his first book. They discussed the nature of intentional systems, implications of Dennett's philosophy for psychology, the nature of mental phenomena, and questions of morality and personhood.

Philosopher Douglas R. Hofstadter collaborated with Dennett in editing the volume *The Mind's I: Fantasies and Reflections on Self and Soul* (1981). This was an unusual book for professional philosophers. It was a wide-ranging anthology of stories, fantasies, and speculative essays about the nature of the self and of consciousness, designed to stimulate imaginations and provoke questions, rather than to answer philosophical questions.

Dennett's interest in exploring the relationship between the freedom of decision making and scientific concepts of causality led to his fourth book, *Elbow Room: The Varieties of Free Will Worth Wanting*. In this book, he reexamined the old philosophical question of whether human beings have free will. Most materialist thinkers would argue that thinking, as a product of physical determinants, cannot be free. Dennett, however, maintained that the deliberations of people are critical points in the process of producing actions. Therefore, people can be seen as having free will, even though the universe operates in a deterministic manner. A member of the American Civil Liberties Union, Dennett saw the question of free will as a political one and not simply as a disinterested philosophical issue.

In 1985, Dennett received the title of Distinguished Arts and Sciences Professor, and he became director of the Center for Cognitive Studies. This center consisted primarily of Dennett and an administrative assistant, and its function was to provide the philosopher with time to research, think, and write. Through the late 1980's and 1990's, Dennett produced a succession of books that were best-sellers by the standards of academic philosophy. In *The Intentional Stance*, he explored further his idea of the intentional system. The best way to predict the behavior of an animal or an information-processing machine is to suppose that these have beliefs and desires. He

Daniel C. Dennett. *(Susan Dennett)*

argued that beliefs and other types of intentional phenomena in people and other animals are virtual properties of brains that are similar to software in computers.

The application of the intentional stance to humans led Dennett to his theory of consciousness, expressed in his best-known and most controversial book, *Consciousness Explained*. In this work, Dennett argued against seeing consciousness as a "Cartesian theater," as a *homunculus* (Latin for "little person") inside the head viewing mental events from a command center. Such an explanation would make it necessary to in turn explain the thinking of the *homunculus* in terms of another little person inside of it and could lead to an infinite regression. Drawing on evidence from research in neurology, Dennett proposed a "multiple drafts" theory of mental activity. Versions of events are created through electrochemical processes throughout the brain. Consciousness, Dennett maintained, is an illusion of short-term memory. Consciousness developed through the course of evolution to enable humans to communicate with themselves, giving them the power to make decisions by providing them with the appearance of a single, unified flow of events. One of Dennett's most provocative claims was that qualia, the intrinsic qualities of things in our experience, are also just illusions.

Dennett's use of thought experiments and imaginative examples to build his argument made *Consciousness Explained* an intriguing book. It offered a convincing case for seeing human thinking as different from the processes of computers only in complexity and perhaps design but not in type of activity. Dennett offered one of the best challenges to the Chinese room thought experiment of philosopher John Searle. Searle had claimed that one could put a person who had no knowledge of the Chinese language in a room with detailed rules on how to construct sentences from Chinese characters. The sentences would seem meaningful to those outside of the room, even though the individual creating them did not really understand them. Nonconscious computing systems differ from humans, Searle maintained, because humans actually do understand the content of their own communication. Dennett's response was that conscious beings seem to themselves to be doing something mysterious

and ineffable called "understanding," but that this understanding is really only a way of assembling and regulating information.

Some of Dennett's critics have complained that *Consciousness Explained* was really "consciousness explained away." They have asserted that detailing how consciousness might come into existence is different from saying what it is. Saying that it is an "illusion" is simply giving it a label. This label may also be misleading because there are mental representations that do approximate events in the world and other mental representations that do not, and only the latter are illusions in the normal use of the world. Finally, some critics have accused Dennett of simply replacing one set of metaphors, such as the "Cartesian theater," with another set of metaphors, such as "multiple drafts."

Darwinian evolution occupied a key place in Dennett's explanation of consciousness. His next book, *Darwin's Dangerous Idea: Evolution and the Meanings of Life*, was a detailed philosophical examination of Darwinian ideas. He claimed that Darwinism is a "dangerous idea" because it affects every area of life. It is a "universal acid" that eats away all of our traditional assumptions and leaves only a radical materialism. Natural selection can explain all phenomena and there is nothing to be explained by conscious design.

Kinds of Minds: Toward an Understanding of Consciousness was based on a series of Dennett's public lectures. In it, he looked at old questions about different types of minds: Can fish think? Do lizards feel pain? Do developing fetuses have mental lives? He argued that these questions are unanswerable because they are badly posed. They are asked without knowing how fish or lizards or fetuses function in an intentional manner and without being clear about just what kinds of intentional behavior should be defined as conscious, given the lack of a clear demarcation between consciousness and "unconscious" intentional action. *Brainchildren: Essays on Designing Minds* followed similar themes. The last book was a collection of Dennett's essays, book reviews, and other short writings from the previous two decades. These were divided into three sections, on philosophy of mind, artificial intelligence, and animal minds.

Influence

Over the course of his career, Dennett came to be recognized as one of the foremost and widely read authors in the philosophy of mind. His ability to make his arguments with witty anecdotes and vivid analogies and his avoidance of jargon gave his books an appeal beyond the narrow academic readership of most philosophy books. Within five years of its publication, *Consciousness Explained* had sold one hundred thousand copies, a huge sales figure for a serious work of philosophy. *Darwin's Dangerous Idea* also reached a large number of readers and offered a convincing defense of strict Darwinian ideas in rebuttal of Darwinian revisionists and pseudo-scientific creationist theory.

Dennett's works provided a way of seeing the mind that was materialistic without being behavioristic. In his early writings, the concept of intentional systems challenged the stimulus and response views of B. F. Skinner and other behaviorists who found no place for the mind in scientific theories. According to Duke University philosopher Owen Flanagan, Dennett's idea of the intentional stance was a tremendous contribution to philosophy. At the same time, Dennett was deeply critical of those who wanted to rely on what he called "skyhooks," ideas that seemed to hang from immaterial nothingness. He made special efforts to refute scientists who seemed to be looking for higher-order explanations that would give meaning to human life. Dennett's materialistic insistence that consciousness was only an illusion made much of his work controversial. In particular, he engaged in a long and bitter debate with University of California philosopher John Searle, who maintained that there was a fundamental difference between human consciousness and the processes of computers.

Dennett played a central part in the development of the scientific study of consciousness and in the development of cognitive science. His willingness to draw on the work of psychologists, computer scientists, evolutionary biologists, and physicists helped to convince philosophers that these disciplines could contribute to philosophy. In turn, he demonstrated that when scientists attempted to understand their own work, they could be seen as doing philosophy.

Carl L. Bankston III

Brainstorms

Philosophical Essays on Mind and Psychology

Type of philosophy: Epistemology, metaphysics, philosophy of mind
First published: 1978
Principal ideas advanced:
◇ Philosophy of mind, cognitive psychology, and artificial intelligence are different ways of approaching the same problem.
◇ The mind is a product of the physical brain.
◇ Although the mind is a product of the brain, the mind is an intentional system, to be understood in terms of thoughts, beliefs, desires, and intentions rather than in terms of physical occurrences, such as chemical reactions or electrical impulses.

The nature of the mind and the relation of the mind to the body and to the physical world have been vexing problems for modern philosophy. French mathematician, philosopher, and physiologist René Descartes formulated the most influential version of dualism, the view that the mind and the body are two different types of entities. As a physiologist, Descartes understood that the human body could be understood as a mechanism. He believed that the mind, being rational, could not be reduced to mechanistic physics. Therefore, he concluded that human beings consist of two distinct parts, a mind that is pure thought and a body that is extended in physical space. This raised questions of how pure thought could cause bodily action and how sensations in the flesh could be communicated to the spiritual half.

Many materialists have argued that the mind-body problem created by Descartes's dualism is a result of a mistaken adherence to the concept of a nonphysical soul. Scientists have been able to identify areas of the brain responsible for speech, memory, and even personality traits. If the mind is seen as nothing but the electrochemical operations of the brain, though, this can create further problems. Thoughts, images, and emotions are not just influences on human behavior; they are also experiences in awareness, and it is difficult to find awareness in discharges of neurotransmitters.

In the preface to one of his later books, *Consciousness Explained* (1991), Daniel C. Dennett remarked that he had been hooked on the mind-body problem ever since his first year in college, when he read Descartes. Dennett's first book, *Content and Consciousness* (1969), was an attempt to develop a unified, comprehensive theory of the mind as a product of mechanistic, physical forces. The seventeen essays in *Brainstorms* were efforts to revise and extend this theory by addressing different aspects of the nature of the mind.

A Theory of the Mind

In the introduction to *Brainstorms*, Dennett asserts that the essays collected in the book express a theory of the mind. He distinguishes his theory from two other physical theories. The first, and simplest, is what he calls "type identity theory." This approach asserts that mental events are identical with physical events in the brain. Further, when two creatures have the same mental event, their brains must have something physical in common. Although Dennett accepts the identity of mental events and brain events, he denies that mental phenomena require common physical states. He points out that a clock and a sundial can both express the idea of "ten o'clock" while having no features in common except their purpose or function.

He calls the second theory of mind "Turing machine functionalism." From this point of view, two computing, thinking, or feeling beings have the same mental event when they are in the same logical state, as when two different computers have the same program and are at the same place in this program. However, Dennett argues that two people may share the same idea, even though individuals vary in their backgrounds and physical-chemical brain structures, making it difficult to maintain that they have identical "programs." Moreover, to say that mental events are logical states adds no real information to the description of mental states.

Dennett refers to his own theory as a version of "intentionalism." Minds are intentional systems and mental events are intentional in character. An intentional system does consist of physical operations, but it cannot be reduced to these operations. Instead, it must be understood as possessing information and pursuing goals.

From Dennett's perspective, we do not understand beliefs or opinions by reducing them to neural activities but by examining carefully and critically the language that we ordinarily use to talk about beliefs or opinions in order to see how these are oriented toward goals.

Intentionalism

The essays are divided into four parts. The three chapters of part 1 introduce the concept of an intentional system and examine arguments for Dennett's version of intentionalism. An intentional system is one whose behavior can be understood and best predicted as a matter of beliefs, desires, and other such orientations. These systems can be entirely mechanical. A chess-playing computer, for example, is an intentional system because its activities can best be understood by thinking about it as following strategies to achieve goals.

Part 2 looks at the philosophical foundations of psychology. Dennett argues against the behaviorism of psychologist B. F. Skinner, who denied the scientific value of approaching psychology in terms of mental events. Skinner maintained that people and other animals should be understood in external, physical terms, as matters of behavioral responses to stimuli. Talking about behavior in terms of internal, mental occurrences such as desires, from Skinner's perspective, involves a return to the mind-body dualism of Descartes. Further, if we say that action results from decisions or wishes, this is like saying they are consequences of an "inner man" making decisions or wishes. This would be no explanation at all because we would then have to explain how those desires or wishes were produced in the "inner man." Dennett is sympathetic to Skinner's physicalism, but maintains that Skinner fails to make the distinction between explaining and explaining away. Using the computer metaphor again, Dennett argues that we cannot understand why a computer playing chess makes a particular move just by looking at its design or programming; we need to look at what the machine "wants" to achieve. When human beings face new situations, we can grasp their behavior not by looking at what kind of stimuli have programmed them to set responses, but by examining the intentions people have in these situations.

In the chapter "Why the Law of Effect Will Not Go Away," Dennett offers suggestions on how intentional behavior occurs in people. He cites the French poet Paul Valéry, who claimed that every act of intention involves two parts within a person: one part that makes up combinations and the other part that selects among the combinations. Dennett calls this psychological model "generate and test." An organism designed to generate possibilities and choose among them, Dennett maintains, would have an evolutionary advantage over organisms that simply behave according to their conditioning in a behaviorist manner.

The four chapters of part 3 look at some of the traditional concerns of philosophers of mind. These chapters deal with the nature of sensations, dreams, mental images, and pains. Dennett maintains that philosophical problems regarding these concepts are often a matter of the language in which the concepts are expressed, which tends to present processes as things. For example, in the chapter "Why You Can't Make a Computer That Feels Pain," he demonstrates that when we use the word "pain," we may be referring to the physical stimulus of pain, to the conscious interpretation of the stimulus, or to the remembered experience of suffering. Thus, we cannot make a computer that feels pain because we do not adequately define what pain is, not because there is an unbridgeable gap between human awareness and artificial intelligence.

The Intentional Stance

Part 4 is the least technical section of the book, but it deals with some of the most profound implications of Dennett's materialist perspective. Can human beings be seen as free moral agents from this perspective? The behaviorists answer that this is not possible because all human behavior is the result of operant conditioning. The Cartesian dualists would hold that the independence of the mind from physical and material influence is a precondition of freedom and moral responsibility. In the chapter "Mechanism and Responsibility," Dennett lays out the different ways in which we can see the actions of organisms and other systems. We can, he says, take a "design stance," in which we explain actions in terms of the way a system is designed. If we

explain a computer's activity by referring to its programming or human behavior by referring to the design of the nervous system, we are taking a design stance. We can also take a "physical stance," in which the description of a system is based on knowledge of the system's physical state. We generally take this stance when talking about why a machine will not work or when interpreting human behavior as a matter of physical or mental illness. Intentional systems, though, are just too complex to be explained in terms of design and the physical stance is usually only useful when the system is malfunctioning. Therefore, we take the "intentional stance," in which we understand actions as choices among alternatives. Systems that make choices should be seen as responsible for those choices. For this reason, Dennett maintains that attributing responsibility is a matter of taking an intentional stance. Moral responsibility is entirely consistent with a mechanistic explanation of human nature.

What becomes of the individual person in Dennett's scheme of things? In the final chapter, "Where Am I?," he implies that the person, like a pain or a sensation, may be a process that ordinary language describes as a thing, with sometimes confusing results. In this humorous ending to the book, he tells how government scientists separated his brain from his body, connecting the two by radio signals. Did this mean that he was where his brain was or where his body was? When his body suffered an accident, losing contact with the brain, did he automatically transfer from the body to the brain? When his brain functions are loaded into a computer, is he in the computer? Dennett's fiction, originally written as an afterdinner talk, is entertaining, but it raises serious questions about the relationship between brain and body and about the nature of the human person.

Beyond Behaviorism

Because the essays in *Brainstorms* were meant to be delivered as talks, they are generally somewhat more approachable than Dennett's first book. These essays therefore helped to bring the author's ideas about intentionalism to a wider readership. The book received positive reviews in both specialized philosophical journals, such as the *Philosophical Review*, and in mainstream periodicals, such as *Psychology Today* and *The New York Review of Books*. The philosopher Douglas Hofstadter, in one review, praised *Brainstorms* as one of the most important pieces of thinking about thinking yet written.

Dennett's chief achievement in this work was to demonstrate how one could take a materialistic approach to mental activity without reducing mental functions to the simple stimulus-and-response mechanisms of behaviorism. Many of the ideas in *Brainstorms*, such as the concept of the intentional system, the role of Darwinian evolution in shaping mental activity, and the "generate and test" model of thinking became key elements of Dennett's later work.

The greatest impact of the book may have been its bringing engineering, artificial intelligence, and neurology into philosophical considerations of the mind-body problem and of the nature of human intelligence. Cognitive science, considered the domain of psychologists and computer scientists before Dennett began his work, became a central concern of philosophy because of the influence of *Brainstorms* and similar writings during the 1970's. Dennett also helped to demonstrate the unity of cognitive science, showing how philosophers, engineers, and researchers in artificial intelligence could be seen as working on different aspects of the same problems.

Carl L. Bankston III

Additional Reading

Churchland, Patricia S. *Neurophilosophy: Toward a Unified Science of the Mind/Brain*. Cambridge, Mass.: MIT Press, 1986. An influential introduction to philosophy of mind based on research into brain structures, this is written by one of Daniel C. Dennett's philosophical critics.

Dahlbom, Bo, ed. *Dennett and His Critics: Demystifying Mind*. Oxford: Blackwell, 1993. This is a collection of eleven essays that criticize and defend Dennett's ideas. It includes an essay by Dennett himself, "Back from the Drawing Board." The editor's introduction is a good summary of the controversies surrounding the philosopher's concepts. Some of the pieces strongly oppose Dennett's theories. Readers should see especially "Fillin in: Why Dennett is Wrong," by Patricia S. Churchland and V. S. Ramachandran.

Dawkins, Richard. *The Extended Phenotype: The Long Reach of the Gene*. Rev. ed. Oxford: Oxford University Press, 1999. A readable introduction to Darwinian biology by a thinker who influenced Dennett. Dennett wrote the afterword for this book.

Dennett, Daniel C. "A Conversation with Daniel C. Dennett." Interview by Tom Flynn and Tim Madigan. *Free Inquiry* 15, no. 4 (Fall, 1995): 19-21. In this interview, Dennett discusses his view that consciousness is an illusion that arises from short-term memory. He also argues that ideas about ethics do not necessarily depend on religion or on the existence of an immortal soul.

_____. "Daniel C. Dennett." Interview by Robert K. J. Killheffer. *Omni* 17, no. 8 (Fall, 1995): 119-120. An interview with Dennett about *Consciousness Explained*, artificial intelligence, Darwinian theory, and other topics. The interview takes place at Dennett's farmhouse and it gives a good sense of the man behind the theories.

_____. Interview by editors of the *Journal of Cognitive Neuroscience*. *Journal of Cognitive Neuroscience* 7, no. 3 (Summer, 1995): 408-414. The interview focuses on Dennett's views on the connections between cognitive science and philosophy.

Searle, John. *Intentionality: An Essay in the Philosophy of Mind*. Cambridge, England: Cambridge University Press, 1983. A view of the intentional nature of the mind that offers an alternative to Dennett's view, written by one of Dennett's chief philosophical opponents.

Shafto, Michael G., ed. *How We Know*. New York: Harper & Row, 1985. A collection of essays about the nature of thinking, including an essay by Dennett and several that are relevant to Dennett's thinking.

Carl L. Bankston III

Jacques Derrida

Derrida is the author and principal exponent of grammatology, a writing-centered theory of language, and of the associated critical practice known as deconstruction. As one of the leading figures in poststructuralism and postmodernism, he has argued forcefully against philosophical, scientific, and religious efforts to institutionalize some preferred system of meanings as "truth."

Principal philosophical works: *L'Origine de la géometrie*, 1962 (*The Origin of Geometry*, 1974); *La Voix et le phénomène: Introduction au problème du signe dans la phénoménologie de Husserl*, 1967 ("*Speech and Phenomena*," and *Other Essays on Husserl's Theory of Signs*, 1973); *L'Écriture et la différence*, 1967 (*Writing and Difference*, 1978); *De la grammatologie*, 1967 (*Of Grammatology*, 1976); *La Dissémination*, 1972 (*Dissemination*, 1981); *Marges de la philosophie*, 1972 (*Margins of Philosophy*, 1982); *Positions: Entretiens avec Henri Ronse, Julia Kristeva, Jean-Louis Houdebine, Guy Scarpetta*, 1972 (*Positions*, 1981); *L'Archéologie du frivole*, 1973 (*The Archeology of the Frivolous*, 1980); *Glas*, 1974 (English translation, 1986); *Éperons: Les Styles de Nietzsche*, 1976 (*Spurs: Nietzsche's Styles*, 1979); *Fors*, 1976 (English translation, 1988); "Signature Event Context," 1977; "Limited Inc.," 1977; *Titus-Carmel*, 1978; *La Vérité en peinture*, 1978 (*The Truth in Painting*, 1987); "Living On: Border Lines," 1979; *La Carte postale: De Socrate à Freud et au-delà*, 1980 (*The Post Card: From Socrates to Freud and Beyond*, 1987); *Scribble*, 1980; *D'un ton apocalyptique adopté naguère en philosophie*, 1983; *Oreille de l'autre*, 1984 (*The Ear of the Other: Otobiography, Transference, Translation*, 1985); *Otobiographies: L'Enseignement de Nietzsche et la politique du nom propre*, 1984; *Signéponge*, 1984 (*Signéponge-Signsponge*, 1984); *Taking Chances: Derrida, Psychoanalysis, and Literature*, 1984; *Feu la cendre*, 1984 (*Cinders*, 1991); *La Faculté de juger*, 1985; *Mémoires for Paul de Man*, 1986; *De l'esprit*, 1987 (*Of Spirit: Heidegger and the Question*, 1989); *Du droit à la philosophie*, 1990; *Le Problème de la genese dans la philosophie de Husserl*, 1990; *L'Autre Cap: Suivi de La Démocratie ajournée*, 1991 (*The Other Heading: Reflections on Today's Europe*, 1992); *Donner le temps*, 1991 (2 volumes; *Given Time*, 1992); *Mémoires d'aveugle*, 1991 (*Memoirs of the Blind: The Self-Portrait and Other Ruins*, 1993); *Acts of Literature*, 1992; *Donner la mort*, 1992 (*The Gift of Death*, 1995); *Points de suspension: Entretiens*, 1992; *Aporias: Dying—Awaiting*, 1993; *Khora*, 1993; *Passions*, 1993; *Sauf le nom*, 1993; *Spectres de Marx: L'État de la dette, le travail de deuil et nouvelle Internationale*, 1993 (*Specters of Marx: The State of the Debt, the Work of Mourning, and the New International*, 1994); *Force de loi*, 1994; *Politiques de l'amitié: Suivi de L'Oreille de Heidegger*, 1994; *Points . . . Interviews, 1974-1994*, 1995; *On the Name*, 1995 (English selections of writings); *Mal d'archive: Une Impression freudienne*, 1995.

Born: July 15, 1930; El Biar, Algeria

Early Life

Jacques Derrida was born in El Biar, Algeria, on July 15, 1930, of "assimilated" Sephardic Jewish parents. One of his earliest and most frightening memories was of the persecution directed against Jews in the period preceding the French-Algerian War. His anxiety in the face of mounting racial tension was heightened after the Allied victory in World War II, when "racial laws" were enacted in Algeria. In 1945, he was enrolled at the Jewish *lycée* but refused to attend classes for a year because of the growing racial and ethnic unrest. Despite the obstacles, he managed to complete his *baccalauréat* in 1948.

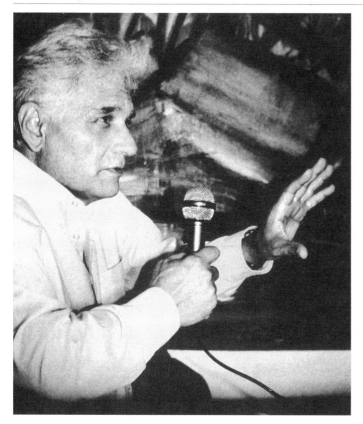

Jacques Derrida. *(Archive Photos/Erwin Schenkelback)*

Near the completion of his studies at the *lycée*, Derrida became interested in French existential philosophy, particularly in the political engagement of Albert Camus and Jean-Paul Sartre. After going to France for his military service, he stayed on in 1950 to do philosophical research on Georg Wilhelm Friedrich Hegel, Edmund Husserl, and Martin Heidegger, among others, at the École Normale Supérieure. His philosophical studies were distinguished enough to earn for him a one-year visiting scholarship at Harvard University in 1956, which marked the beginning of his fruitful association with the American intellectual community. At that time, he was already becoming disillusioned with structuralism and phenomenology, the two dominant contemporary philosophical alternatives in the continental tradition. While teaching at the Sorbonne between 1960 and 1964, he developed a critical vocabulary from his meditations on literary theory that he would later deploy against both of these theoretical positions.

Life's Work

Beginning in the mid-1960's, the main purpose of Derrida's work was to dethrone the deeply entrenched philosophical tradition of logocentrism. Common to the epistemic paradigms of ancient, medieval, and modern philosophy, according to Derrida, is the belief that the rational subject is capable of discovering timeless, universal truths. With appropriate precautions against the influence of prejudice and presuppositions, the logocentric inquirer is purportedly in a position to discover the essential nature or meaning (the logos) of things.

The strategy that Derrida developed to combat logocentrism is known as deconstruction. To deconstruct a text is to undermine its foundation by revealing the suppressed weaknesses and uncertainties that, despite the suppression, are present in the "margins," the meaningful interstices one finds "between the lines." According to Derrida, the margins of a text are an integral part of the text itself, rich in unintended and unmanaged meaning. The margins of both structuralist and phenomenological writings, for example, reveal the hidden weaknesses of the respective theories.

In 1966, Derrida burst upon the American scene with his lecture "Structure, Sign and Play in the Discourse of the Human Sciences" at The Johns Hopkins University. Previewed as a sympathetic introduction to Claude Lévi-Strauss's structuralist anthropology, the lecture instead announced the defeat of structuralism. On the question of Lévi-Strauss's theory, which fixes meaning by positing a stable structural framework, Derrida "decenters" the alleged fixity by revealing that the play of signifiers has led to the positing of the structure, thus inverting the hierarchical arrangement between structure and the play of signifiers. The published version of this lecture remains the clearest illustration of Derrida's decentering strategy and one of the most incisive critiques of structuralism available. Along with Derrida's *Of Grammatology*, which appeared the following year, the essay provided the impetus for the poststructuralist movement.

One key to understanding Derrida's writings is to appreciate the subtlety of his objections to structuralism. His argument should not be seen as antistructuralist but rather as hyper-or super-structuralist. Derrida outdoes structuralism and undoes it at the same time by exposing implications that were "always already" present in its earliest theoretical formulations. Most significantly, he exploits the central tenet of Ferdinand de Saussure's structural linguistics, according to which meaning is a function of the opposition or difference within a system of signifiers rather than a function of reference to something outside the system (to a "transcendental signified"). Whereas Saussure balked at admitting the ultimate implications of his thinking, Derrida recognized that Saussure's semantic theory allows one to dispense with reference to extralinguistic entities.

The year 1967 was pivotal in Derrida's career. In that year, he published three important philosophical works: *"Speech and Phenomena," and Other Essays on Husserl's Theory of Signs*, *Of Grammatology*, and *Writing and Difference*. The first is a sustained attack on the "phonocentrism" at the heart of Husserl's phenomenology. A phonocentric theory privileges speech, contending that the spoken word is unproblematically connected to mental representations or meanings. Deriving from Aristotle and finding support in Jean-Jacques Rousseau's writings on language, this theory holds that there is a natural unity of sound and sense because the meaning of speech is intimately bound to the consciousness of the speaker. Phonocentrism, according to Derrida, serves logocentrism by tying meaning to that which is present in the consciousness of the speaker. According to phonocentrism, writing is a mere shadow of speech, at one remove from meaning. Derrida's critique of Husserl calls for a reappraisal of any semantic theory that seeks meaning in extralinguistic entities and for an alternative theory that eschews the "metaphysics of presence." In his confrontation with phenomenology, Derrida's aim is to reveal the absence of presence, that is, the absence of meanings immediately accessible to consciousness.

As Saussure had demonstrated, there is an alternative semantic theory that does not depend on reference to transcendental signifieds. The second and third of Derrida's books published in 1967 make this alternative explicit. Though he is reluctant to admit it, grammatology is the theory that informs the practice of deconstruction. (His reluctance comes from the recognition that deconstruction has itself become a doctrine, much to his chagrin. According to Derrida, his theory should be constantly "under erasure," present only as a critical tool and not as a new "truth.") In *Of Grammatology*, sometimes ironically called the "bible of deconstruction," Derrida goes so far as to claim that writing is prior to speech, that the latter is a mere shadow of the former. The thesis that writing, as the most perspicuous example of a signifying system in which meaning arises from the difference among signifiers, can play an explanatory role in understanding all signification, Derrida calls "arche-writing." Accordingly, signifying systems as diverse as choreography, music, sculpture, painting, and politics can be viewed as "texts."

Of Grammatology and *Writing and Difference* develop two other central concepts of Derrida's theory. First, *différance*, spelled with an *a* instead of an *e*, is a French neologism combining the verbs "to differ" and "to defer." *Différance*, which can only be recognized in writing as its pronunciation is identical in French to that of *différence*, indicates both the unbridgeable gap between the signifier and the signified and the indefinite postponement of the moment when meaning can finally be established. Both aspects of *différance* are related to the notion of the trace. For Derrida, a trace is a sign of something having gone before, giving the impression that it is standing in for something more substantial or real, that is, for a signified. When one tries to track a sign to a signified, however, all that one finds is the trace of another signifier located where the signified was presumed to be.

Derrida's deconstructive strategies are evident in his treatments of such bipolar oppositions as philosophy/literature, speaking/writing, and structure/free play. Regarding the interpretations of texts, one of the most important oppositions is between "origin" and "supplement." In his criticism of Rousseau's theory of language, Derrida argues that a sign always has greater meaning than the author intended. He rejects the thesis that the text possesses essential or original properties in contrast to the supplemental constructions offered by interpreters. He maintains that the allegedly supplemental meaning was "always already" in the original text, thus obliterating a distinction that would tend to reintroduce questions about the truth or correctness of interpretations.

The range of targets for Derrida's deconstruction has not been limited to structuralism and phenomenology. In general, any position that aspires to global theoretical closure (as epitomized by metaphysics, science, and religion), thereby obstructing the generation of alternative meanings, invites deconstruction. Complementing the poststructuralist strand of Derrida's thinking, his attempt to subvert the repressive, totalizing tendencies of "ontotheology" plays a major role in the postmodernist struggle against theoretical hegemony.

His critical vocabulary essentially intact in 1967, Derrida's later works are by and large further elaborations of these ideas (for example, _Dissemination_ and _Margins of Philosophy_) or applications to particular fields (such as _Truth in Painting_). Having argued that the pursuit of truth, which distinguishes philosophy and science from such disciplines as literature, is a mere pretension of logocentrism, Derrida cannot consistently maintain a firm distinction between philosophy and literature. His writings after 1967 therefore became increasingly literary. In particular, _Glas_ and _The Post Card: From Socrates to Freud and Beyond_ are on the borderline between philosophy and literature. For readers accustomed to rigid boundaries, his later works are frustrating, leading some critics to doubt his seriousness. When viewed in the overall context of his writings, however, Derrida's crossing of boundaries is not surprising, nor is his attention to margins, even (particularly) the margins of his own work.

In 1972, Derrida began dividing his teaching between the École Normale Supérieure in France and such American institutions as The Johns Hopkins University, Yale University, and the University of California at Irvine. In France, he actively campaigned for a _lycée_ curriculum that includes the study of philosophy and against what he regards as repressive measures in education. Through his teaching in the United States, his influence spread, primarily in the field of literary criticism and also in fields such as political theory, art theory, and history. Despite the hostile

initial reception that Derrida received, the importance of Derrida's writings was eventually recognized by the philosophical community.

Influence

Beginning with his argument against Husserl's phenomenology and his rereading of Saussure's structuralism, Derrida became a forceful critic of the logocentric tendency to repress systematically all meanings that fall outside institutionally preferred doctrine. In the skeptical tradition of René Descartes, Michel Eyquem de Montaigne, and Friedrich Nietzsche, Derrida's thought not only challenges particular doctrinal readings that make exclusive claims to truth but also casts suspicion on the notion of truth itself. Such notions as God, Being, presence, and structure, he persuasively argues, tend to foreclose interpretations in the name of "truth."

Deconstruction, the strategy Derrida developed to combat attempts to establish hegemonic theoretical closure, was inspired by a theory of language. Using writing as the model for all signification, deconstruction subverts closure by showing that meaning, which is a function of intra- and intertextual opposition and difference, is in a state of constant expansion or "dissemination." Repression is thus necessarily implicated in the quest for closure.

Derrida's claim that the episteme shared by philosophy and science owes its dominance to the systematic repression of alternative viewpoints has not endeared him to the scholarly community. The hostility with which his work was received is also a result of the fact that it is exasperatingly difficult to read. In expressing his ideas, Derrida faced three formidable challenges. First, in order to subvert logocentrism, he had to use the analytical and rhetorical tools available within the logocentric tradition. Second, constrained to work within the logocentric tradition, his critique also had to be a reflexive critique of the ideas informing the critique in progress. Third, he had to be sufficiently persuasive to support his positions while somehow preventing them from becoming part of the philosophical canon with their own preemptive claim to truth.

Successful in meeting the first two challenges, Derrida largely failed to meet the third. Responses to his ideas are sharply divided between outright rejection and outright acceptance. Although his many critics lament his impact, he nevertheless has had a substantial influence on literary criticism and on such disciplines as theology, art, history, feminist studies, and legal studies.

Jeffery L. Geller

Of Grammatology

Type of philosophy: Epistemology
First published: De la grammatologie, 1967 (English translation, 1976)
Principal ideas advanced:

◇ The notion of stable, identifiable truth underlies all assumptions of Western philosophy.
◇ The basic premise relies upon definition in the form of binary opposites, in which the first is always superior to the second, as right/ wrong, life/death.
◇ The most extensive and basic of all binaries is that of speech/writing.
◇ The application of the binary structure inevitably represses, subjugates, and persecutes the inferior term.
◇ The effect of such structures extends beyond philosophy and linguistics to form the basis for all Western cultural operations.
◇ The structuralist recognition of meaning by difference retains a flawed dependence upon a stable signified.
◇ Identifying the play of difference at the level of the signified reveals the constant deferral of meaning through play of difference, or *différance.*
◇ The ongoing play of difference that produces meaning and maintains a continual potential is a nonmaterial "arche-writing" that affects all meaning in culture.
◇ Perceiving meaning as constantly deferred and produced by the play of difference allows a movement from a restrictive linguistics to grammatology, the study of arche-writing.

A fundamental poststructuralist document, *Of Grammatology* introduced deconstruction to the field of critical theory and defined the rupture with traditional Western philosophy that oc-

curred during the late 1960's in Western Europe. In it, Jacques Derrida drew upon and modified ideas from key Western philosophers such as Martin Heidegger and Friedrich Wilhelm Nietzsche, producing a new understanding of Western philosophy. In *Of Grammatology*, Derrida moved beyond Heidegger's *destruktion*, which disclosed the mechanisms of a system, to introduce deconstruction and analyze systems on their own terms, seeking their internal contradictions. Though Derrida began by analyzing the work of philosophers such as Edmund Husserl and investigating specific aspects of culture, in *Of Grammatology* he merges various analytic strands and demonstrates their application to all areas of Western culture. Issuing from a literal burst of writing that produced two other significant texts, *La Voix et le phénomène: Introduction au problème du signe dans la phénoménologie de Husserl* (1967; *"Speech and Phenomena," and Other Essays on Husserl's Theory of Signs*, 1973) and *L'Écriture et la différence* (1967; *Writing and Difference*, 1978), *Of Grammatology* clarifies Derrida's attempt to reinvigorate philosophy and infuse it with a sense of creativity and innovation.

In the preface to *Of Grammatology*, Derrida suggests the work's general separation into theory and application. He avoids the implication of a bounded structure, alerting the reader that the work proceeds in relation to an axis, rather than in strictly linear order. The metaphor introduces the broader notion of writing or philosophical elaboration that breaks with the tradition of unified, predetermined direction. In that sense, the introduction begins Derrida's strategy of merging commentary and process that permeates *Of Grammatology*, permitting him to analyze or deconstruct both his own text and the concepts under scrutiny.

Speech/Writing
Part 1, "Writing Before the Letter," proceeds along several interwoven courses, all of which converge on what he terms "logocentrism," the fundamental dependence of Western philosophy on a notion of original and essential truth as a fixed point, a definitive source from which all thought and meaning evolves. Derrida identifies that center point as a "transcendental signified," a stable source of all meaning, the basis for all

subsequent assumptions of natural order, leading to the development of hierarchies in Western culture. Hierarchies, in his analysis, draw their priorities through a system of binary oppositions such as good/evil, day/night, in which the first member of the pair is valued over the second and considered its polar opposite, its antithesis. He bases his analysis on the fundamental philosophical bias for speech above writing, citing the Western tradition of assigning values to sign systems as primary evidence.

The analysis precisely defines deconstruction in that Derrida applies Western philosophy's specific logic to reveal its inner contradictions. Rather than imposing a new set of oppositions for the old, he applies the system's own syllogisms to argue that the basic paired terms are not polar opposites, but in fact overlap, each unit or term being and containing part of the other. He neither argues for writing as superior to speech, thus merely constructing a new binary system, nor proposes to destroy or supplant the old structure or its basic units. He simply demonstrates the internally flawed logic of binary pairs and their assumed opposition, demonstrating instead a free play of difference.

Starting with the Greek philosopher Plato, Derrida analyzes speech's privileged status as a reaffirmation of the notion of an identifiable origin or source of meaning. The requirement for an identifiable origin, a speaker, in order for speech to occur forms the central idea of Western philosophy, which Derrida identifies as a "metaphysics of presence." A system that requires a fixed origin or truth source and depends upon binary opposition favors presence; speech requires presence as a condition of origin, thus shares status with truth, thought, or logos. Writing and absence acquire negative value as opposites to speech and presence. Their parallel status acquires even greater negative value by association with origin's binary opposite, death. Derrida depicts the "metaphysics of presence" as both corollary and basis for Western religious metaphysics, forming a mutual corroboration at the core of Western culture.

Structuralism Deconstructed

Continuing his deconstructive process, Derrida expands Ferdinand de Saussure's structuralist analysis of linguistic systems, developing an internal critique of both structuralism and the "transcendental signified." Derrida employs Saussure's own analysis to reveal the fundamental flaw in this phrase and to clarify structuralism's metaphysical dependence. In Saussure's sign structure, an essential concept or meaning, a signified, is represented by a signifier, the utterance or sound that refers to it. Derrida argues that Saussure's structure repeats the metaphysical operation. The signified occupies an inner or intellectual position, a center, and the signifier occurs outside, separate from the intellectual process, yet connected by reference. Writing, for Saussure, is a degraded representation, referring not to the signified, the central meaning, but by duplication, to the signifier, speech. Thus, Saussure considers writing to be a threat to meaning because it disguises the role of speech, seeming to replace it but representing only the sound, not the meaning.

Derrida's basic critical maneuver is to accept Saussure's sign-based analysis but then call attention to the fact that Saussure must rely on writing to communicate his analysis. This maneuver introduces the suggestion that speech may not be sufficient even for Saussure. More crucially, Derrida also acknowledges Saussure's claim that signs of meaning, signifiers or spoken words, acquire meaning by their difference from other signs or groups of sound, instead of through any inherent meaning in the sound. Thus, "cat" refers to a concept of the specific animal because its sound is different from "bat" or any other word in the language. Its meaning is not exclusive, however, since *gato* refers to the same concept within a different language.

Derrida accepts the notion of language as reliant on meaning through difference as Saussure develops it, but then insists that if such is the case, there can be no direct or "natural" connection between speech, the signifier defined by difference, and a stable, fixed concept. Following Saussure's logic, the signified gains meaning by its difference from other signifieds; it, too, is defined by difference. Its meaning is not fixed but constantly reliant on other meanings. Derrida coins the term *différance* to suggest this continual deferral of essential meaning produced by *différence*, or constant difference. However, Derrida points out that the graphic signs, or writing, that Saussure must use to explain his linguistic structure also derive meaning by their difference from other signs. The written signs are, then, not opposites, but merely different aspects of the constant interaction of difference that produces language. Derrida identifies this ongoing contingency, the reliance between signs, as "arche-writing," an intangible negotiation of difference that makes meaning possible but constantly latent and deferred.

By the end of part 1, Derrida has worked through two deconstructive maneuvers: He has identified the central concept that forces meaning into oppositions or binaries, and he has subverted the binary order, suggesting writing is vital to the expansion of meaning. His suggestion of "arche-writing" and Saussure's self-contradiction implies a further step, anticipating the extension of his analysis in the second part of the work.

Nature and Culture

In part 2, "Nature, Culture, Writing," Derrida clarifies logocentrism's ultimate implications and completes his deconstruction by reference to philosophers Jean-Jacques Rousseau and Claude Lévi-Strauss. Derrida establishes Rousseau's dependence on a nature/culture opposition and carefully demonstrates the binary's precise conformity to the "metaphysics of presence." The connections to religious, moral, and aesthetic codes in Rousseau's parallel of speech/writing with his nature/culture opposition corroborate Derrida's depiction of fundamental hierarchy as institutionalized throughout Western culture.

In a conclusive deconstructive maneuver, Derrida then applies Rousseau's own analysis to reveal meaning's inherent instability. Accepting writing's depiction as "supplemental" to speech, Derrida notes that Rousseau acknowledges speech's deficiency by identifying a supplement that, by definition, completes.

Rousseau's opposition thus overturns itself, allowing Derrida to observe that speech and writing, in fact, contain aspects of each other, requiring each other for existence. Accordingly, they no longer can be considered opposites but must be recognized as an example of the constant play of meaning and difference expressed in "arche-writing." In that sense, both speech and writing may be placed under "erasure," signify-

ing their individual inadequacy and mutual necessity. It is not so much that their relationship cannot be articulated, but rather that there is no specific relationship; it constantly redefines itself.

As Derrida elaborates Rousseau's nature/culture opposition, he draws the parallel with that of Claude Lévi-Strauss, disclosing logocentrism's historical persistence and emphasizing its precepts' universal application through Western culture. Introducing anthropology allows Derrida to elaborate the impact of logocentric systems as inevitably producing a "violent hierarchy," predisposed to exclude and marginalize devalued opposites. He typifies that violence by the ethnocentrism and implicit colonialism that grants status to phonetically based language as a "natural" link to speech, to the detriment of any other system, such as Asian pictographic writing.

Thus, though Derrida does not proceed through *Of Grammatology* in strictly linear fashion, his various analytical strands describe logocentrism's pervasive function not only as a standard for linguistic discourse but also as a determining structure for all aspects of Western culture. Simultaneously, he demonstrates in practice rather than definition the deconstruction process by first locating the metaphysical biases central to Western cultural discourse from Plato through Lévi-Strauss. Further, he avoids origin-based linearity both in method and discourse, blending analyses of various positions, for example, moving backward from Lévi-Strauss to Rousseau, rather than arguing an evolutionary influence.

Upon identifying the basis for a structure, Derrida then applies the system's own logic, as in the case of Rousseau and Saussure, to overturn basic oppositional premises, suggesting the primacy of the degraded terms. Finally, he demonstrates the absence of opposition, arguing that each term in a binary, as speech and writing, is both inadequate and present in the other. By extension, he proposes a movement from the linearity of linguistics into grammatology, an exploration of difference and referentiality in arche-writing, the crucial switch to the free play of *différance*, the difference and deferral of final meaning.

Derrida's Impact

This most widely known study from Derrida's large body of work remains, for many, a vital point of access to his discourse. *Of Grammatology*'s publication in 1967 generally coincided with Derrida's 1966 appearance before the International Colloquium on Critical Languages and the Sciences of Man at The Johns Hopkins University, where he analyzed structuralism's internal flaws, generating immediate controversy. *Of Grammatology* vastly expanded that presentation and coalesced many of the deconstructive ideas he had developed in his previous writing. Derrida stated subsequent to the English-language publication of *Of Grammatology* that the work represented a significant event in his own development, in that it brought coherence to his perception of the interrelation of Western culture and writing. The work also retains a key position in the introduction and development of poststructuralism.

Because it appears to follow a "traditional" book structure, many experts view *Of Grammatology* as Derrida's most accessible work. That view runs counter to the central purpose not only of the work but also of Derrida's deconstructive perspective. It also risks overlooking the fact that the work does not stand separate from Derrida's writing as the one "traditional" work. Rather, the work tends to use its position within a recognizable textual tradition and its implicit susceptibility to customary analytical reading as a deconstructive device; the text illustrates the discourse. *Of Grammatology* enacts many of the ideas and theories detailed in Derrida's previous writing, but, perhaps inescapably, eludes thorough development without a reading of Derrida's other works. In that sense, Derrida succeeded in producing a work with the apparent structure of a traditional book that resists a sense of containment, confinement, closure, and definitive meaning. In that sense, the work's significance may also lie in its position as a deconstruction of the book both as a tradition and as a self-contained product.

Ron West

Additional Reading

Johnson, Christopher. *Derrida*. New York: Routledge, 1999. An excellent biographical introduction to the thoughts of the philosopher, clearly presented and requiring no special background. Bibliography.

Lamont, Michele. "How to Become a Dominant French Philosopher: The Case of Jacques Derrida." *American Journal of Sociology* 93, no. 3 (1987). Serves as a brief synopsis of the life of Jacques Derrida and his importance to French and North American philosophy. Contains an appendix that includes a list of secondary sources.

Morag, Patrick. *Derrida, Responsibility and Politics*. Brookfield, Vt.: Ashgate, 1997. Morag's examination is directed toward the foundations of legal, moral, and political authority and at the questioning of form itself as it relates to the ethico-political significance of deconstruction.

Norris, Christopher. *Derrida*. Cambridge, Mass.: Harvard University Press, 1988. This text introduces Derrida in a post-Kantian light without delving too far into technical detail. Norris covers a broad spectrum of ideas while focusing on the subtle logic that surrounds Derrida's reasoning. Its emphasis on the philosophical importance of ontology presents the reader with a solid foundation for further inquiry.

Powell, Jim. *Derrida for Beginners*. New York: Writers & Readers, 1996. Powell offers a superb introduction to the thought and life of Derrida. Recommended for readers who are approaching Derrida's ideas for the first time.

Sallis, John. *Deconstruction and Philosophy: The Texts of Jacques Derrida*. Chicago: University of Chicago Press, 1988. This text represents the first attempt to compare Derrida's deconstruction to Western philosophy up to and including Heidegger. Includes a work by Derrida previously unavailable in English.

Salusinszky, Imre. "Jacques Derrida." In *Criticism in Society*. New York: Methuen Press, 1987. Focuses on the application of Derrida's deconstruction to education. Includes an introduction to the main ideas of grammatology and deconstruction.

Whitford, Margaret. "Jacques Derrida." In *Makers of Modern Culture*, edited by Justin Wintle. New York: Facts on File, 1981. Summarizes the life, work, and philosophical significance of Derrida.

Howard Z. Fitzgerald

René Descartes

Descartes's cardinal contribution is the extension of the mathematical method to all fields of knowledge. He is the father of analytic geometry and the author of the most universally appropriate version of mind-body dualism in the history of philosophy.

Principal philosophical works: *Le Monde*, 1633 (*The World*, 1998); *Discours de la méthode*, 1637 (*Discourse on Method*, 1649); *Meditationes de prima philosophia*, 1641 (*Meditations on First Philosophy*, 1680); *Principia philosophiae*, 1644 (*Principles of Philosophy*, 1983); *Les Passions de l'âme*, 1649 (*The Passions of the Soul*, 1950); *Regulae ad directionem ingeni*, 1701 (*Rules for the Direction of the Mind*, 1911); *The Philosophical Writings of Descartes*, 1984-1991.

Born: March 31, 1596; La Haye, Touraine, France
Died: February 11, 1650; Stockholm, Sweden

Early Life

René Descartes was born to one of the most respected families among the French-speaking nobility in Touraine. His father, Joachim, held the post of counselor to the Parlement de Bordeaux. Descartes's mother died of tuberculosis only a few days after giving birth to her son, leaving a frail child of chronically poor health to the sole care of his father. René's physical condition remained delicate until he was in his twenties.

Joachim Descartes was a devoted and admiring father, determined to obtain the best education for "his philosopher." When Descartes was ten, he was sent to the Collège de La Flèche, newly established by the Jesuits under the auspices of Henry IV.

Descartes was an exemplary student of the humanities and of mathematics. When, at the age of sixteen, he began his study of natural philosophy, he came to the insight that would later give rise to his revolutionary contributions to modern thought. Uncertainty and obscurity, he discovered, were hallmarks of physics and metaphysics. These disciplines seemed to attract a contradictory morass of opinions that yielded nothing uniform or definite. By contrast, Descartes's studies in mathematics showed him something firm, solid, and lasting.

René Descartes. *(Library of Congress)*

473

He was astonished to find that while mathematical solutions had been applied to scientific problems, the method of mathematics had never been extended to important practical matters. At La Flèche, Descartes concluded that he would have to break with the traditions of the schools if he were to find knowledge of any worth.

Descartes left his college without regret, and his father subsequently sent him to Paris. Social life there failed to amuse him, and he formed his most intimate friendships with some of France's leading scholars and teachers. When he was twenty-one, he joined the army but spent little time campaigning. In his spare time, he wrote a compendium of music and displayed his mathematical genius by instantaneously solving puzzles devised for him by soldiers in his company.

Descartes was housed with a German regiment in winter quarters at Ulm, waiting for active campaign, when the whole core of his subsequent thought suddenly took shape. On the night of November 10, 1619, after a day of intense and agitated reflection, Descartes went to bed and had three dreams. He interpreted these dreams as a divine sign that he was destined to found a unified science based on a new method for the correct management of human reason. Descartes's sudden illumination and resolve on that night to take himself as the judge of all values and the source of all certainty in knowledge was momentous for the world of ideas.

Life's Work
Descartes spent the next ten years formulating his method while continuing scientific researches, and he occupied himself with travel in order to study what he called "the great book of the world." He had come to the view that systems of human thought, especially those of the sciences and philosophy, were better framed by one thinker than by many, so that systematizing a body of thought from the books of others was not the best method. Descartes wanted to be disabused of all the prejudices he had acquired from the books of others; thus, he sought to begin anew with his own clear and firm foundation. This view was codified in his first substantial work, *Rules for the Direction of the Mind*. In this work, Descartes set forth the method of rational inquiry he thought requisite for scientific ad-

vance, but he advocated its use for the attainment of any sort of knowledge whatever.

Descartes completed a scientific work entitled *The World* in 1633, the same year that Galileo was condemned by the Inquisition. Upon hearing this news, Descartes immediately had his own book suppressed from publication, for it taught the same Copernican cosmology as did Galileo, and made the claim that indicted Galileo's orthodoxy: that human beings could have knowledge as perfect as that of God. A few years later, Descartes published a compendium of treatises on mathematics and physical sciences that were written for the educated but nonacademic French community; this work obliquely recommended his unorthodox views to the common people of "good sense" from whom Descartes hoped to receive a fair hearing. This work was prefaced by his *Discourse on Method* and contained the *Geometry*, the *Dioptric*, and the *Meteors*.

Discourse on Method provided the finest articulation of what has come to be known as Descartes's method of doubt. This consisted of four logical rules:
1. to admit as true only what was so perfectly clear and distinct that it was indubitable.
2. to divide all difficulties into analyzable elements.
3. to pass synthetically from what is easy to understand to what is difficult.
4. to make such accurate enumerations of the steps of reasoning so as to be certain of having omitted nothing.

The method is fundamentally of mathematical inspiration, and it is deductive and analytical rather than experimental. It is a heuristic device for solving complex problems that yields explicit innovation and discovery. Descartes employed his method to this end in the tract on geometry when he discovered a way to resolve the geometric curves into Cartesian coordinates. Such an invention could hardly have come from the traditional Euclidean synthetic-deductive method, which starts from assumed axioms and common notions in order to generate and prove logically entailed propositions.

Descartes's new method was akin to those found in the writings of Francis Bacon and Galileo, and it was the architectonics of the "new science." "Old" science, leftover from ancient and medieval researches, merely observed and classified, and explained its findings in terms of postulated natural purposes of things. The new science inaugurated in the seventeenth century sought, in Descartes's words, to make people the "masters and possessors of nature." This goal involved invention and discovery, the generation of new and nonspeculative knowledge, to be put in the service of practical ends. For Descartes and the other seventeenth century new scientists, human wonder and understanding were without intrinsic value; what was without practical use or application for humankind, Descartes remarked in *Discourse on Method*, was absolutely worthless. The new science aimed to create effects, not merely to understand causes.

Descartes intended his method not for mathematics and science only. He envisioned the unity of all knowledge. He employed his method in a purely metaphysical inquiry in *Meditations on First Philosophy* to "establish something firm and lasting in the sciences." He fashioned in this a primary certainty by rejecting at the outset everything about which it was possible to have the least doubt.

He set aside as false everything learned from or through the senses and the truths of arithmetic and geometry. Only the proposition *Cogito, ergo sum*, or "I think, therefore I am," remained an indubitable truth. One cannot doubt one's existence, Descartes reasoned, without existing while one doubts. Thus, *Cogito, ergo sum* became his first and most certain principle. Further days of meditation on this principle revealed the certitudes that he was a substance whose whole essence it was to think, entirely independent of his body and of all other material things. His primary truth also enabled him to prove the existence of God.

In this one epochal week of meditations, Descartes made privacy the hallmark of mental activity, moved the locus of certitude to inner mental states, and rejected faith and revelation in favor of clarity and distinctness. Reason itself had previously governed the coherence of what had to be taken as truth; now inner representation, and its correspondence with the external, material world, governed the kingdom of relevant truth. Most philosophers after Descartes have followed his conception of inner representations as the foundation of knowledge of all outer realities. Only in the twentieth century was this position, and its attendant problems, systematically examined and contested.

The years that followed the publication of *Meditations on First Philosophy* were marked by controversies resulting from attacks by theologians. Descartes's orthodoxy was impugned and his arguments were assailed. In 1647, formal objections to the Cartesian metaphysics, along with the author's replies, were published as a companion volume to a second edition of the *Meditations on First Philosophy* in French translation.

Descartes's next project was to be his last. *The Passions of the Soul* was a treatise of psychology that explained all mental and physiological phenomena by mechanical processes. This work has striking moral overtones as well. Descartes's implicit prescription for the best human life is reminiscent of that of the ancient Stoics: People should strive to conquer their passions in order to attain peace of mind. Descartes maintained in *The Passions of the Soul* that while people who feel deep passions are capable of the most pleasant life, these passions must be controlled with the intervention of rational guidance. In the end, he claimed that teaching one to be the master of one's passions was the chief use of wisdom.

In 1649, Descartes responded to the request of Queen Christina of Sweden to join a distinguished circle of scholars she was assembling in Stockholm to instruct her in philosophy. As a result of the Swedish climate and the rigorous schedule demanded by the queen, Descartes caught pneumonia and died the following year.

Influence

The thinking of Descartes epitomizes the transition from the medieval epoch of the Western world to the modern period. Modern humanity came to deify personal freedom. This tendency originated with the privatization of consciousness and the drive to overcome the rigors of nature. For Descartes, only absolutely certain knowledge counted as wisdom. Descartes envisaged wisdom as having practical benefits for the many, as opposed to being a mere cerebral exaltation for the educated few. Descartes saw the improvement of the mental and physical health of humankind as the best of these benefits of wisdom. This prospect was ratified by the enterprises of centuries to come.

Descartes was no less important as one of the pioneers of modern mathematics, which cannot be extricated from his philosophy. He conceived the possibility of treating problems of geometry by reducing them to algebraic operations and devised the necessary means for making geometric operations correspond to those of arithmetic. He also introduced the notion of deducing solutions from the assumption of the problem's being solved. This has become such a fundamental technique in algebra and higher mathematics that one can scarcely imagine its having had a genesis.

Finally, Descartes's radical distinction between mind and body and his revolutionary method of metaphysical inquiry had a profound effect on the history of philosophy as well as modern strands of philosophical inquiry.

Patricia Cook

Discourse on Method

Type of philosophy: Epistemology, metaphysics
First published: Discours de la méthode, 1637 (English translation, 1649)
Principal ideas advanced:

◇ The proper method for philosophy is as follows: Never accept any idea as true that is not clearly and distinctly beyond doubt; divide each complex question into simple, basic questions; proceed from the simple to the complex; review all steps in reasoning.

◇ If this method is put into practice, there seems to be no proposition that cannot be doubted except the following: I think, therefore I am (*Cogito, ergo sum*).

◇ As thinking substance, I have the idea of God; and because the idea of a perfect being could not have been derived from my own experience or being, God must exist as the source of my idea.

◇ Furthermore, imperfect and dependent beings could not exist unless there were a perfect being, God, who made their existence possible; in addition, God by his very nature exists, for

if God did not exist of necessity, he would not be perfect.

◇ God provides the ground for people's knowledge about the external world if people are careful to accept as true only those ideas that are clearly and distinctly beyond doubt once the reliability of the senses and of the reason can be seen to be derived from God.

In 1633, the year that Italian scientist Galileo was forced to recant by the Inquisition, René Descartes was just finishing his first major scientific treatise, *Le Monde* (*The World*, 1998). In the work, Descartes had used the Copernican theory for which, in part, Galileo had been condemned, so prudence dictated that the work be withheld from publication. However, a strong sense of the importance of his discoveries caused him to issue three token essays and to compose a kind of prospectus of his work to date for publication under the same cover. The latter is the *Discourse on Method*. Besides explaining the author's method and reviewing his labors, it summarizes his metaphysical reasoning and sketches the plan of the larger, unpublished volume. Strangely, perhaps, for one whose declared intention was to set all human knowledge on impersonal foundations, the *Discourse on Method* is a highly personal communication. It begins with a biographical reminiscence.

The Young Descartes

Familiar with books from childhood, the young Descartes entered the new Jesuit Collège de La Flèche with high expectation, but he early fell victim to the skepticism that attended the passing of the Renaissance. The study of ancient tongues, classic treatises on morals and philosophy, and jurisprudence and medicine were excellent for ornamenting the person and preparing one for a life of riches and honor, but Descartes decided that they yielded nothing that could be called knowledge. The only good to come from the revival of learning, so far as truth is concerned, was the rediscovery of mathematics, which, however, he was inclined to take without the Pythagorean mystifications that so delighted German astronomer Johannes Kepler. The thing that pleased Descartes in mathematics was the certitude and evidence that accompanied its demonstrations, and he was surprised to find that no higher science had been erected on such solid foundations. By contrast, philosophy, on which so much had been based, could exhibit no single claim that was not in dispute.

The young graduate had no further incentive toward books or toward the past. On the hunch that practical people might be wiser than scholars, in that they cannot entertain follies with impunity, Descartes resolved to see the world and talk with people of every rank and occupation. He soon found, however, that practical people disagree as much as do philosophers, and as for the experience of traveling in foreign lands, nothing so quickly undermines one's confidence in the judgment of one's fellow humans.

A Turning Point

Then came the turning point in Descartes's life. While he was still in his early twenties, he made the discovery—for which he is celebrated in the history of mathematics—that it is possible to bring geometry and algebra together into a single science by plotting equations along rectangular axes. This startling discovery encouraged him to look into his own mind for still more fundamental truths:

> I resolved at length to make myself an object of study, and to employ all the powers of my mind in choosing the paths I ought to follow.

It was the winter of 1619-1620, and Descartes was in Germany, serving in the army, twenty-three years old. For another nine years, he was content to travel, assuming the role of spectator rather than actor in the affairs of the world. However, he was not wasting his time. Part of his program consisted in systematic doubt; by painstaking reflection upon every matter that could be a source of error, he deliberately attempted to destroy beliefs that were not certainly true.

At the end of this period, he moved to Holland, ready to undertake the recovery of truth. His first step was to replace the old metaphysics with one founded on his newly formed principles, which he did in *Meditationes de prima philosophia* (1641; *Meditations on First Philosophy*, written in 1628-1629 although not published for more than ten years). This accomplished, he was free to set about his main enterprise, which was to lay bare the secret laws that govern the world of matter. In the next eight years, his progress was astonishing. However, the innumerable experiments that kept suggesting themselves required many hands. His motive in presenting the summary of his ideas in the *Discourse on Method* was to recruit workers.

Out of Skepticism

There is evidence independent of the *Discourse on Method* that the first powerful conviction that lifted Descartes out of skepticism was the discovery of certain rules for the direction of the mind. In the *Discourse on Method*, he associates this phase of his development with the winter in Germany when he was twenty-three. It antedates his enterprise of systematic doubt and, indeed, is presupposed by it, the doubt being but the first step toward carrying through the rules.

The brilliant young mathematician was led to conclude that just as the most difficult demonstrations in geometry can be arrived at easily by a long chain of simple steps, so

> all things, to the knowledge of which man is competent, are mutually connected in the same way, and . . . there is nothing so far removed from us as to be beyond our reach, or so hidden that we cannot discover it, provided only we abstain from accepting the false for the true, and always preserve in our thoughts the order necessary for the deduction of one truth from another.

What Descartes had discovered, he believed, was a key that would open for humankind all the doors to knowledge. No new power of insight or of reasoning was needed—every person, essentially, has as much insight and reason as any other. The failure of previous inquirers stemmed from no natural deficiency but from clumsiness and inexperience. Chiefly, people had been seduced by the powerful claims of their senses and imagination so that the sober witness of reason had been obscured. What people needed was a set of rules that would help them to keep faithfully to truths that, once the debris had been removed, would shine upon the mind with a natural light.

The Method

Descartes was, therefore, a bold exponent of what is known as the deductive or a priori method. Still, his approach must not be confused with the Scholasticism that, in philosopher Francis Bacon's words, "flies from the senses and particulars to the most general axioms, and from these principles, the truth of which it takes for settled and immoveable, proceeds to judgment and to the discovery of middle axioms." The fault of the Aristotelian syllogism, Descartes said, was that, although it helps people reason persuasively about things they already think they know, it is of no help in investigating the unknown. Thus, Descartes's method was more radically a priori than Aristotle's, which drew its premises from induction.

Turning his back on traditional logic and taking his cue from geometry, Descartes envisaged a chain of linear inferences that would progress from an initial truth so simple and obvious as to be self-evident to a second that would be seen at once to be included in the first, and thence to a third, and so forth. In practice, the problem would always be to find the simple truth to which the chain could be anchored; afterward, all that would be necessary would be to preserve the true order. Each particular truth along the way would be entirely obvious to anyone who understood what was being affirmed—just as in arithmetic, a child who understands a sum fathoms everything that is within reach of the greatest genius who contemplates the same set of figures.

For convenience, Descartes summed up his principles in four rules:

1. Never accept any idea as true that is not so clearly and distinctly true as to be beyond all possibility of being doubted.
2. Divide each complex question into simple ones.
3. Order thoughts from the simplest to the most complex.
4. Review the series of inferences to make sure there are no breaks or false links in the chain.

If these rules were rigorously followed, an obscure matter, such as the function of the lungs in the body, would be rendered perfectly intelligible. Such, at least, was the promise that inspired the youthful Descartes and launched him on his great career.

The Metaphysical

The biographical narrative and the exposition of method make up the first half of the *Discourse on Method*. Part 4 is an abridged version of the *Meditations on First Philosophy*. Descartes's preeminently scientific interests seem somewhat incompatible with his foray into the metaphysical. However, as he explained, to have ventured at once into the difficulties of the sciences would have been contrary to right order because he regarded all such particular truths as dependent on principles borrowed from philosophy.

The investigation of the principles set forth in part 4 was "so metaphysical and uncommon" that Descartes questioned whether his readers would find it acceptable. It is, in fact, the only part of the *Discourse on Method* that makes serious demands upon the intelligence. Yet, because the *Meditations on First Philosophy* had not been published in 1637, he felt obliged to include a précis of that work. This review of the work places it in its proper perspective—as the first serious attempt to make use of the method of doubt and as the foundation for physics and physiology rather than an end in itself. Lacking this perspective, one might suppose that Descartes's preoccupation with God and the soul stemmed from a religious interest. His Scholastic-styled proofs suggest to the modern reader that he is laboring to shore up traditional beliefs. However, when Descartes speaks of soul, he means "thinking" (and ideally "reasoning," for all the rest of the conscious life is illusion), and when he speaks of God, he means the "ordered necessity" against which all apparent "contingency" is rendered intelligible. Therefore, far from seeking to preserve the Christian view of the world, he is substituting for it an uncompromising formulation of the presuppositions of seventeenth and eighteenth century science. Just how far his philosophical work strengthened the cause of science and speeded its development is impossible to say, but it seems likely that his metaphysics was more useful than his method.

Thought and the Existence of God

The method required that Descartes discover a truth so simple and self-evident that it could not be further reduced and yet would verify itself. Yet every belief he considered seemed to him to be a possible error. He supposed that even his strongest convictions might have been planted in him by a malevolent and deceiving god. However, finally it struck him that even though his beliefs were mistaken and he could not go beyond the activity of doubting, the doubting itself existed; thinking existed; and if thinking, then he, as thinking substance, also existed. He expressed his conclusion in the triumphant words *Cogito, ergo sum*, or "I think, therefore I am."

When he sought to discover the ground of his certainty, he found nothing that guaranteed the truth of the proposition "I think, therefore I am" other than his seeing "very clearly that in order to think it is necessary to exist." He thus took as a general rule for further philosophical investigations the principle "that all the things which we very clearly and distinctly conceive are true." At the same time, he admitted the difficulty of deciding which of the objects of thought were being conceived "clearly and distinctly."

Descartes then realized that he, as one who doubted, was not perfect, and yet he had the idea of perfection and of a perfect being. He found nothing in his own experience to account for his having arrived at the idea of perfection, and he finally concluded that the idea must have been placed in him by a being possessing all the perfections he conceived, namely, by God himself. Descartes was thus led to a renewed conviction in God's existence.

Other arguments in support of the belief in God's existence were quickly generated. All imperfect bodies and intelligences show by their imperfection their dependency on the perfect, on God; hence, God exists. Furthermore, the idea of a perfect being entails the idea of the existence of such a being; for if a being otherwise perfect did not exist, he would lack an essential perfection. (This ontological argument, reminiscent of Saint Anselm's more famous version, was regarded by Descartes as having the same rigorous character as a geometric proof.) Finally, Descartes decided that no belief whatsoever could be accepted as a "metaphysical certitude" except by presupposing the existence of God. Even the principle of clarity—that clear and distinct ideas are true—depended for its certainty upon God's perfection and existence.

It has seemed to many critics of Descartes that to prove the certainty of a principle by reference to a God whose existence is proved by the use of that very same principle is certainly a circular procedure. However, Descartes probably would have argued that clear and distinct ideas are certainly true regardless of whether one knows the ground of one's certainty. He presumed that by his arguments, he revealed the ground of all certainty: God, the perfect being, the independent support of all dependent beings and of all truths endorsed by reason.

Having reassured himself and his readers of the reliability of reason and of the method he had outlined, Descartes then proceeded to summarize the conclusions of his unpublished treatise, *The World*. According to his account, the treatise was a comprehensive work containing "all that . . . I thought I knew of the nature of material objects." Beginning with light, it touched upon the sun and the stars, on the heavens, the planets, the comets, and the earth, upon terrestrial bodies, and finally, upon humans considered as organized matter. Out of caution, Descartes adopted the device of speaking about an imaginary world rather than about one created as described in the Bible. Suppose that there is matter "without form and void" in some imaginary space; if it is governed by the laws which God's perfection has established and fixed in our minds, it must work itself out of its initial chaos and arrange itself in a manner like our heavens and our earth. Tides, air currents, mountains and seas, summer and winter, minerals and vegetables are all accounted for in terms of fixed laws of nature. One has to turn to the original work to find the laws stated. Perhaps the most significant point Descartes communicates in his summary is the important principle that the nature of anything is more easily conceived when understood in terms of its origin than when viewed simply in its completed state.

Human Physiology

The greater part of the summary is given to human physiology. Continuing his hypothetical mode of argument, Descartes asks one to think of God as forming the body of a person exactly like one's own but without a rational soul. This being granted, Descartes undertook to show how, according to the same laws as obtain everywhere else in nature, all the internal and external motions of the body must take place exactly as they are observed to take place, with the exception of intelligent speech and certain inventive actions. The circulation of the blood is taken as an example. Its motion through the body, as Descartes explains it, is the result of the presence in the heart of one of those fires-without-light (the kind present in processes of fermentation). The heat purifies the blood, and the resulting expansion and contraction drives it through the cavities of the heart. Hot blood warms the stomach, enabling digestion to take place. The lungs serve as condensers that cool the blood before returning it to the left ventricle. This cooling releases the animal spirits that are the "most agitated" part of the blood. These go to the brain because the arteries leading in that direction are nearly straight, and "according to the rules of Mechanics, which are the same with those of Nature . . . the weaker and less agitated parts must necessarily be driven aside by the stronger which alone in this way reach" their destination.

This example is sufficient to make clear the character of Descartes's scientific work. However, the datedness of these theories should not obscure the original quality of Descartes's purely mechanistic account of vital phenomena. Although he continued to hold that the mind is perfectly adjusted to the body (one's feelings and appetites are evidence of this), he was careful to stress their complete mutual independence. As for animals other than humans, they are simply very cunningly contrived machines without any kind of mind or soul.

Descartes learned circulation of the blood not from his method but from the physician William Harvey. Like everyone else, Descartes had to combine experiences and inference from observation and experimentation in order to obtain knowledge of the existing world. However, Descartes thought that it is a mistake to begin with experiment. He believed that ordinary observation provides adequate material to arrive at the laws of nature, provided only that one reflects on it, for the germs of the most general truths exist naturally in the mind. Thus, he found no special observation necessary to account for the gross aspects of the universe—the motions of the heavenly bodies, the properties of the elements that make up the earth. However, when he came to particular problems, the situation altered. There

are so many ways God might have worked that it is impossible for one to infer which is the case. In general, the laws by which a clock measures time are known; however, one must look behind the face of a particular clock to see what combinations of wheels and weights or springs the mechanic has employed. Similarly, in the case of the motion of the blood, once one has observed the arrangement of the heart with one's eyes and felt the temperature of the blood with one's fingers, one can understand the method that God has employed and can demonstrate by the laws of physics why the motion must take place as it does.

Experimentation became increasingly important to Descartes the further he progressed in scientific studies. However, he did not lay aside his youthful preference for demonstrative knowledge. His program for future studies, as he hinted at the close of the *Discourse on Method*, was to devote himself exclusively "to acquire some knowledge of Nature which shall be of such a kind as to enable us therefrom to deduce rules of Medicine of greater certainty than those at present in use."

Jean Faurot, updated by John K. Roth

Meditations on First Philosophy

Type of philosophy: Epistemology, metaphysics
First published: Meditationes de prima philosophia, 1641 (English translation, 1680)
Principal ideas advanced:
◇ Perhaps everything one believes is false.
◇ There seems to be no way of avoiding the skeptical consequences of systematic doubt.
◇ If one is doubting, one exists; and this is the starting point for a philosophy based on certainty.
◇ If one exists, one is a thinker, a mind; and because one conceives of a God whose conception is beyond one's powers, there must be such a being.
◇ If God exists, then one can count on one's sense experience and one's reason, provided one is careful to believe only what is clearly and distinctly true.

In *Meditations on the First Philosophy*, René Descartes delves into epistemology, or the theory of knowledge. He asks questions such as whether there is such a thing as knowledge, and if so, what distinguishes it from opinion. However, in order to answer these questions and to validate knowledge, it was necessary to raise the fundamental questions of being.

Descartes chooses to present his thoughts as meditations; he represents himself as seated before a fire in a cozy Dutch dwelling, wrapped in his dressing gown, freed from worldly care, and ready to devote himself to a task to which he had for some time looked forward, a kind of mental housecleaning. On six successive days, he pursues his meditation, step by step, clearing his mind of all error.

In *Discours de la méthode* (1637; *Discourse on Method*, 1649), Descartes reveals that the work was actually composed in very similar circumstances. In 1628, Descartes was in his thirties and living in Holland; he had withdrawn from a more active life for the special purpose of carrying on his philosophical and scientific investigations. *Meditations on First Philosophy* was circulated in manuscript, and when it was published in 1641, it included a lengthy appendix composed of objections by leading philosophers—including Thomas Hobbes and Pierre Gassendi—together with Descartes's replies.

The First Meditation

The First Meditation is, in a way, distinct from the rest. It describes Descartes's effort, which in fact engaged him for many years, to accustom himself not to think of the world in the imagery of the senses or according to the notions of common sense and the traditions of various schools of thought.

Can it be, Descartes wonders, that all beliefs that he had formerly held are false? Perhaps not, but if he is to achieve his goal of building up a body of incontrovertible truth, he must exercise the same rigor toward beliefs that are merely uncertain as toward those that are demonstrably untrue. That is to say, he must make *doubt* his tool. Instead of allowing it to hang over him, forever threatening, he must grasp it firmly and lay about until he has expunged from his mind every pretended certainty.

The first to go are those beliefs that depend on the senses—notably one's belief in the existence of one's own body and of everything that appears to the sight and touch. One's habitual judgment protests. What can be more certain, Descartes asks himself, than that I am seated by the fire holding this paper in my hand? However, he writes, when one reflects that one's dreams are sometimes attended with equal confidence, one is forced to conclude that there is no infallible mark by which one can know true perceptions from false.

Of course, what one doubts is, in this case, only that one's ideas *represent* something beyond themselves. Descartes is one of the first philosophers to use the word "idea" in the modern sense. He means by it "whatever the mind directly perceives." However, he distinguishes between the idea taken only as a mode of thought and the idea as a representation of reality. Even in dreams, one cannot deny the former. What one challenges is the "truth" of the ideas—Descartes calls it "objective reality"—and of judgments based on them. His question is whether there is anything in sense-images that testifies unmistakably to the truth of what they represent. Obviously not in those that one initiates in dreams and fantasies, and no more, he argues, in those that come from without, through the senses, or else how could one make mistakes as to sounds and sights?

There is, he says, another class of ideas that one seems neither to originate nor to receive from without but to be born with—those, for example, that make up the science of mathematics. Two plus three equals five, even in dreams, for this sum does not require material counters to make it true. Yet, the ideas of numbers profess to be something besides modes of thought. They do have "objective reality." However, people have been mistaken about mathematical matters, so they are no more self-authenticating than sense-images. People's habitual trust in them resembles that which they place in their senses and has the same foundation, namely, that people are creatures of a benevolent deity who would not deceive them. Suppose that this is not the case, and that mathematics is merely a fancy of one's mind. Or, worse, suppose it is an illusion deliberately imposed upon people by a malicious demon who has access to the workings of their minds. This is not unthinkable.

Instead of supposing that the providence of God sustains his thinking, Descartes resolves to hold fast to the hypothesis that he is constantly being deceived by an evil spirit, so that all his ordinary beliefs are false. In this manner, while he seems to make no progress in the knowledge of truth, he at least habituates himself to suspend judgment concerning things that he does not certainly know. However, this is not easy. Descartes pleads with his readers (in the replies to his objectors) not merely to give the exercise such time as is required for reading the meditation through but to take "months, or at least weeks" before going on further. He suggests how reluctant one is to break old habits of thinking by describing a slave who, when sleeping, dreads the day and conspires to weave the sounds of gathering dawn into his dreams rather than to embrace the light and labors that it brings.

The Second Meditation

Descartes's aim in the Second Meditation is to discover, if possible, some foundation of certainty that doubt is powerless to assault. He has doubted the reality of the world presented to him through his senses. Shall he affirm that some god (or devil) must exist to put these ideas into his mind? That hardly seems necessary, for perhaps he has produced them himself. One thing, however, seems now to loom up in Descartes's mind: "I myself, am I not something?" Suppose all his ideas are hallucinations, whether self-induced or planted in him by some god or devil. In this, at least, he cannot be deceived: "I am, I exist, is necessarily true each time that I pronounce it, or that I mentally conceive it."

Here, then, for the first time, Descartes presents a self-validating judgment. It is the unique instance in which people immediately encounter the existence that is represented to them by an idea: One has an idea of "oneself." Like other ideas, this one claims to have objective reality. However, unlike other ideas, this one's claim is open to inspection—by the self. Both the idea and the existence that it represents are present each time one thinks them. In a simple act of "mental vision" (to use Descartes's expression), one

knows that one exists. As the philosopher John Locke would say, one knows one's own existence intuitively.

With this certitude to serve as a cornerstone, Descartes proceeds to raise his palace of Truth. If one explores the structure of one's inner consciousness, one will find the clue to universal Being. For instance, one can ask the question "What am I?" The answer lies at hand: "I am a thing that thinks." For was it not in the act of thinking (taken broadly to include all conscious activities) that one found the reality of the idea of oneself? Contrast this with the traditional view that a person is a body that contains a subtle essence, a very fine grade of matter, known as spirit: There is nothing certain, or even intelligible, about this idea. If one presses ahead with methodical doubt, one discovers that most of the ideas habitually associated with matter are illusory. Take a piece of wax fresh from the honeycomb: One thinks of it in terms of color, taste, odor, and texture. However, none of these is essential to the wax. Place it near the fire, and all the qualities that engross the imagination are altered. All that remains unchanged and can be called essential to the wax is "something extended, flexible, movable," properties that are knowable to the intellect and not to the senses. In any case, whether one has a body, it is not as body that one knows the self when one beholds the self as existing. The realm of being that one discovers there has nothing about it of extension, plasticity, or mobility. One is a thinking being, Descartes concludes, a mind, a soul, an understanding, a reason.

The forward progress during the second day's meditation was all made along the path of doubt. It was the act of doubting that gave Descartes the certainty both that he existed and that his nature was mind. However, the implications of his consciousness of doubt have not been exhausted. Does not doubt carry with it, and actually presuppose, the idea of certainty, just as error carries with it the idea of truth? Descartes finds in his mind the idea of a perfect being by comparison with which he is aware of his imperfections, a self-sufficient being by which he knows that he is dependent. Following this lead, he proceeds in his Third Meditation to demonstrate the existence of God.

The Third Meditation

Descartes's argument takes two forms. First, he asks directly concerning the *idea* of a perfect being, whence it could have come into his mind: From some other creature? From himself? Or must there exist a perfect being to originate the idea? His answer is obscured for the modern reader by the late-medieval philosophical framework in which it is expressed. The idea of God contains more "objective reality" than any other idea (including one's idea of self). However, a more perfect idea cannot be generated by a less perfect being. Therefore, the idea of God in his mind must have been placed there by God himself.

The second form of the argument proceeds from the contingent quality of his own existence, made up as it is of fleeting instants, not one of which is able either to conserve itself or to engender its successor. Much in the argument is reminiscent of the traditional Aristotelian proof; but there is this difference, which makes it clear that the new argument is only another version of the first: What needs explanation is not merely the existence of a contingent being or of a thinking being but of "a being which thinks and which has some idea of God." Thus, the principle that there must be at least as much reality in the cause as in the effect precludes the possibility that any being less perfect than God could have created Descartes—or any person.

This argument is of scarcely more than historical interest. The same is true of the argument from the Fifth Meditation that, since existence is a perfection, the idea of a Perfect Being entails the existence of that Being. However, it must be pointed out that behind the framework of traditional theistic proof lies a claim that rationalistic philosophers have found valid even in modern times:

> I see that in some way I have in me the notion of the infinite earlier than the finite—to wit, the notion of God before that of myself. For how would it be possible that I should know that I doubt and desire, that is to say, that something is lacking to me, and that I am not quite perfect, unless I had within me some idea of a Being more perfect than myself, in comparison with which I should recognize the deficiencies of my nature?

Here, in effect, is a new kind of reasoning. The Scholastics were committed to demonstrate the existence of God by syllogisms, and whether through expediency or inadvertency, Descartes makes a show of doing the same. However, in Descartes a new, quasi-mathematical way of reasoning was pushing the syllogism to one side. His true ground for affirming the existence of God was not that it *follows from* but that it is *implicit in* his consciousness of himself.

Blaise Pascal's famous memorial that insists that the God of the philosophers is not the God of faith is a useful reminder to the general reader. There is no need, however, to suppose that Descartes needed it. The certainty of God's existence is a great triumph—but for scientific, rather than for religious, reasons. It is the *sine qua non* of all further knowledge, since "the certainty of all other things depends on it so absolutely that without this knowledge it is impossible ever to know anything perfectly." Such obvious mathematical truths as two plus three equals five are not self-validating because they bear no evidence of the competency of one's thought. In replying to his objectors, Descartes says atheists cannot be sure, hence their knowledge cannot be called science. Doubt may never rise to trouble him; but if it does, he has no way of removing it. However, the doubt is removed when a person recognizes that his mind owes its constitution and working to the creativity of God, and that God is no deceiver.

Knowledge of the World

Much of the rest of *Meditations on First Philosophy* is devoted to determining just how far people can trust the faculties that the beneficent Deity has implanted in them. First, one must distinguish between impulses that incline one to belief (such as "the heat that I feel is produced by the fire") and insights into necessary truths (such as "a cause must be as great or greater than its effect"). Both are natural, and owing to the good offices of the Creator. However, the former can be doubted, even after one has discovered the truth about God; the latter, which Descartes speaks of as "the light of nature," cannot be doubted at all. They are the principles of reason in our minds by which we arrive at knowledge. One has no other means of distinguishing between true and false.

Second, one must consider the causes of error. It is axiomatic that God can never deceive people and that if they make proper use of the abilities received from the Deity, they can never go wrong. Yet obviously, God has chosen to make people fallible. This situation arises from the fact that the intellect is finite, together with the fact that the will is infinite. One can see why both these things must be and how, as a consequence, people do not easily stay within the narrow realm of truth. The crux of the matter is that, for Descartes, judgment involves the will (in the form of "assent" or "dissent"). It is within people's power to withhold judgment when convincing evidence is wanting and to give it only when the light of reason demands. Indeed, Descartes held that people have a duty to bring judgment under this rule. Failure to do so involves not merely error but sin.

Third, one's knowledge of the external world creates a number of problems. Descartes examined a piece of wax to find what constitutes the essence of matter. He observed that the sensible qualities that people most readily believe to be in matter are not part of the nature of wax, as are such attributes as extension, figure, and mobility, which are not properly sensible but intelligible. Comparing the two ways of thinking about things in nature, Descartes concludes (following the lead of Galileo) that the senses provide people only the most confused notions of matter—they arise from the influence upon the mind of the body to which it is united rather than from the mind's apprehension by its own light of the necessary attributes of being. It is by the latter that people obtain true knowledge of nature, which henceforth is seen to possess only those qualities that can be described in mathematical terms. In other words, the physical world has to be envisaged as a vast, complicated machine—but not the way the senses view machines, rather the way they are viewed on the drawing board and in the mind of the engineer.

So far reason leads people, Descartes says. If there is a material world, its nature must be as classic mechanics conceives it. However, it does not follow that a material world actually exists. It is conceivable that each time one receives and recognizes the idea of a body, God himself impresses it on one's mind. Nothing in the idea of matter is inconsistent with its nonexistence. All that one can discover that inclines one to assent to its existence is an instinctive impulse such as attaches to all one's sense perceptions; this, of course, is no reason.

Descartes's only recourse is to appeal to the good faith of God. Thus, he writes that if God were the cause of our ideas of matter, he would undoubtedly have given us the means of knowing that this is the case, for he is no deceiver. In granting us free will, he has, indeed, opened the door to falsity and error, but he has not permitted any error without placing within one's reach the means of avoiding it, or, at least, correcting it once it has been made. The claims of one's sense-images, which reason disproves, is an example. However, no analysis disproves the natural inclination that one has to believe that corporeal objects do exist. Hence, one is justified in affirming, along with the existence of finite mind (one's own) and infinite Being, the actuality of the material world. (Apparently, for Descartes, the existence of other minds is never more than an inference.)

The upshot of *Meditations on First Philosophy* is, then, to replace the commonsense picture of nature with one that is amenable to rational investigation. The new cosmology that was being shaped by scientists and thinkers such as Johannes Kepler, Galileo, William Gilbert, and others rested upon fundamental assumptions that were not clear to the investigators themselves. It was the task of Descartes to give these principles their classic formulation.

Jean Faurot

Additional Reading

Chappell, Vere, ed. *Descartes's Meditations: Critical Essays*. Lanham, Md.: Rowman & Littlefield, 1997. A significant collection of essays by scholars who carefully assess the perspectives and problems in one of Western philosophy's most important texts.

Copleston, Frederick. *A History of Philosophy: Modern Philosophy*. Garden City, N.Y.: Doubleday, 1964. Copleston situates René Descartes in the history of philosophy with an accessible discussion of Descartes's major theories.

Cottingham, John, ed. *The Cambridge Companion to Descartes*. New York: Cambridge University

Press, 1992. A helpful collection of essays focusing on a variety of topics in Descartes's thought.

_____. *Descartes*. New York: Basil Blackwell, 1986. Taking a broad view of Descartes's philosophy, Cottingham focuses on Descartes's views about human nature as well as on his theory of knowledge.

_____. *Descartes*. New York: Routledge, 1999. An excellent biographical introduction to the thoughts of the philosopher, clearly presented and requiring no special background. Bibliography.

Foley, Richard. *Working Without a Net: A Study of Egocentric Epistemology*. New York: Oxford University Press, 1993. A careful exposition of Descartes's analysis of skepticism and the prospects human beings have for obtaining knowledge.

Gaukroger, Stephen. *Descartes: An Intellectual Biography*. New York: Oxford University Press, 1995. A veteran interpreter of Descartes offers an important account of Descartes's intellectual development and the times and places in which it took place.

Jones, W. T. *A History of Western Philosophy: Hobbes to Hume*. New York: Harcourt, Brace & World, 1969. Offers a clear and accessible introduction to Descartes's philosophy.

Keeling, S. V. *Descartes*. New York: Oxford University Press, 1968. This analysis of the merits and defects of Descartes's philosophy provides a good overview of his thought and influence.

Kenny, Anthony. *Descartes: A Study of His Philosophy*. New York: Random House, 1968. A standard commentary for beginning students of Descartes's philosophy, which gives particular emphasis to his theory of knowledge.

Rorty, Amélie Oksenberg, ed. *Essays on Descartes' "Meditations."* Berkeley: University of California Press, 1986. Prominent philosophers, representing different perspectives, offer well-crafted studies of Descartes's best-known work.

Sepper, Dennis. *Descartes's Imagination: Proportion, Images, and the Activity of Thinking*. Berkeley: University of California Press, 1996. Explores Descartes's views about the nature of human experience and its prospects for obtaining knowledge about reality.

Strathern, Paul. *Descartes in Ninety Minutes*. Chicago: Ivan Dee, 1996. A quick but helpful introductory overview to key points in Descartes's thought.

Vinci, Thomas C. *Cartesian Truth*. New York: Oxford University Press, 1998. An evaluation of the strengths, weaknesses, and implications of Cartesian approaches to questions about knowledge and truth.

Williams, Bernard. *Descartes: The Project of Pure Enquiry*. Harmondsworth, England: Penguin Books, 1978. A detailed, analytic dissection of the careful structure of Descartes's most important philosophical arguments.

Yolton, John W. *Perception and Reality: A History from Descartes to Kant*. Ithaca, N.Y.: Cornell University Press, 1996. Yolton appraises the significance of Descartes's attempts to show how it is possible for human beings to obtain knowledge in spite of skepticism.

Patricia Cook, updated by John K. Roth

John Dewey

Dewey's instrumentalism, his version of William James's pragmatism, applied directly to the industrial problems of the United States and made pragmatism an operative concept in American politics. His contributions to the concept of functionalism earned for him a permanent place in the development of American psychology.

Principal philosophical works: *Psychology*, 1887; *The School and Society*, 1899; *Studies in Logical Theory*, 1903; *The Influence of Darwin on Philosophy*, 1910; *How We Think*, 1910; *Democracy and Education*, 1916; *Essays in Experimental Logic*, 1916; *Creative Intelligence*, 1917; *Reconstruction in Philosophy*, 1920; *Human Nature and Conduct*, 1922; *Experience and Nature*, 1925; *The Public and Its Problems*, 1927; *Individualism, Old and New*, 1929; *Experience and Nature*, 1929; *The Quest for Certainty*, 1929; *Philosophy and Civilization*, 1931; *Ethics*, 1932; *Art as Experience*, 1934; *A Common Faith*, 1934; *Liberalism and Social Action*, 1935; *Experience and Education*, 1938; *Logic: The Theory of Inquiry*, 1938; *Intelligence in the Modern World*, 1939; *Education Today*, 1940; *The Problems of Men*, 1946; *Knowing and the Known*, 1949 (with A. P. Bentley).

Born: October 20, 1859; Burlington, Vermont
Died: June 1, 1952; New York, New York

Early Life

John Dewey was born October 20, 1859, in Burlington, Vermont. His mother, née Lucina Artemisia Rich, was twenty years younger than his father, Archibald Dewey, who owned a grocery business in the community. John was the third child in a family of four. Although the Civil War separated the family for six years when Archibald enlisted in the army, by 1866, they had returned to Burlington, where Archibald entered the cigar and tobacco business.

In the years that followed, John Dewey grew up in a middle-class world where native-born Americans, along with the Irish and French Canadians, shaped his early social experiences. Dewey's parents encouraged his wide-ranging reading and his outdoor activities. His mother's evangelical piety, however, influenced Dewey's values well into adulthood. On the whole, his childhood was a pleasant one, and his parents were warm and supportive, although his mother's pietistic worrying about Dewey's behavior upset him.

After a good high school education in the classics, Dewey entered the University of Vermont. In addition to the classical curriculum, he took biology courses and read widely in the literature of the emerging Darwinian controversies over evolution and its social implications. His interests were moving him toward the study of philosophy. What he read and what he had experienced in his young life contributed to the philosophical dualisms such as body-soul, flesh-spirit, and nature-mind, but Dewey wanted a unity of knowledge that overcame such divisions. Dewey was graduated from the University of Vermont in 1879. For the next two years, he taught high school in Oil City, Pennsylvania, a community much in flux from the rapid growth of the oil business.

In Oil City, two events greatly shaped Dewey's life. First, Dewey's religious doubts (or fears) came to seem foolish to him. He felt a oneness with the universe, and although he continued attending church for the next dozen years, he left the religious faith and practice of his parents. Over the course of his long and productive life, after his abandonment of evangelical Christianity, Dewey embraced the absolute Idealism of

Georg Wilhelm Friedrich Hegel, with its emphasis on the unity of existence. Later, Dewey accepted humanistic naturalism, with its continuity of nature and humanity drawn from the thought of Charles Sanders Peirce and William James.

In 1882, Dewey entered The Johns Hopkins University for graduate study in philosophy. A serious but sly student, Dewey was quietly exploring the relationship between religion and morals in late nineteenth century American life. At Johns Hopkins, Dewey accepted neo-Hegelianism. Dewey and his whole intellectual generation were seeking something new, something to explain life, a transformation of values. Dewey's fully developed naturalism was, however, in the future. He had begun the transformation of his religious beliefs by ruling out the supernatural but placing its values into the natural. In time, as a philosopher, Dewey placed in the natural world a faith that had previously been assigned to a coming kingdom of God.

In 1884, he joined the department of philosophy at the University of Michigan. During the next four years, he broadened his interests in social affairs and educational matters, and he wrote and published. In 1886, he married Harriet Alice Chipman, a bright and capable woman who encouraged Dewey to pursue his ideas. Wife, mother, and critic, she was a source of encouragement until her death in 1927. *Psychology*, Dewey's first book, was published in 1887; it combined empirical psychology with German metaphysical Idealism. After a year at the University of Minnesota, Dewey returned to Michigan as chairman of the department of philosophy. Until 1894, when he went to the University of Chicago, Dewey built up the department's faculty and cut his final ties to organized religion. His interests became increasingly secular. He accepted an appointment at the University of Chicago as chairman of the department of philosophy, psychology, and pedagogy.

Within two years, he had established the Laboratory School, which provided the institutional expression of progressive education. He expressed his ideas in *The School and Society*. Dewey did not neglect his other interests; he wrote *Studies in Logical Theory*. At

Chicago, Dewey was active in academic, civic, and reform matters. A brilliant group of scholars was on the faculty at that time. Unfortunately, both Dewey and his wife, who held an appointment in the school of education, resigned because of a misunderstanding over the terms of her position.

Life's Work

Dewey joined the department of philosophy at Columbia University in 1904 and taught there until 1930. His greatest achievements and contributions were before him. By 1910, Dewey had sketched out his mature philosophy. Although scholars disagree about the relative influences of Hegel and Charles Darwin, the judgment is that Dewey never completely divorced himself from their influences. His philosophy was a fusion of Hegelian Idealism and Darwinian naturalism, expressed in a context of reform for the industrial United States. Ideas had significant consequences

John Dewey. *(Library of Congress)*

for human life; they were instruments to shape the world and place values, albeit human ones, into human affairs. As part of the natural world, all human activity, including the use of intelligence, was a process that existed in nature and not in an independent (or dualistic) mode of being. As a biological function, reflective intelligence meant that, by naturalistic metaphysics, people adapt to environmental situations. His 1896 essay "The Reflex Arc Concept in Psychology" is indicative of his functionalism in psychology and instrumentalism in philosophy. From physical to mental, continuity was the key concept. Language, in conjunction with other cultural elements (and here the anthropologist Franz Boas influenced Dewey's thinking), contributed to the cultural transformation from the biological to the logical.

Science, or the scientific method, was the basis of Dewey's message. Within ten years, he published four major books: *Reconstruction in Philosophy*, *Human Nature and Conduct*, *Experience and Nature*, and *The Quest for Certainty*. In these books, Dewey argued that scientific truth was an instrument to control and direct human experience or culture. Means and ends were one in nature and in society, particularly a democracy. A reconstructed philosophy, "active and operative," was relevant to the twentieth century by reorganizing the environment. Scientifically removing specific trouble areas would increase human happiness and productivity. He wanted a rational and critical mediation between the self and other human beings as expressed in *Individualism, Old and New*.

During his years at Columbia, Dewey was active in reform movements and public lectures in the United States and abroad. As the years passed, the honors increased; he became the United States' national philosopher. As one historian remarked, he was the "guide, the mentor, the conscience of the American people . . . for a generation no major issue was clarified until Dewey had spoken." Dewey continued to write and lecture after his retirement in 1930. He was a real intellectual presence during the New Deal, during World War II, and afterward. His political activities often drew criticism, and traditionalists saw dire social consequences in his progressive educational ideas. After his first wife died in

1927, he married Roberta L. Grant in 1946. Suffering from complications of a broken hip, Dewey died on June 1, 1952. His ashes are now buried on the campus of the University of Vermont. Over the course of his long life, Dewey had written forty books and seven hundred articles on a wide range of subjects.

Influence

Dewey is a major presence in U.S. history as well as philosophy. Many formal expressions such as lectureships, institutes, and university buildings bear his name. A society and foundation were established to help spread Dewey's ideas on democracy and educational reform. His portrait was included in the U.S. Post Office's Prominent Americans series.

As a philosopher, Dewey was the creator of instrumentalism, his version of William James's pragmatism, applied more directly and completely to the industrial problems of the United States. His work made pragmatism an operative concept in American politics. His efforts, particularly late in the nineteenth century, in contributing to the concept of functionalism earned for him a permanent place in the development of American psychology. Although he was often criticized for the excesses of progressive education, his educational writings contributed to the reform of American public schools. Finally, his writing and teaching, particularly in the first half of the twentieth century, made him a leading American liberal. Concerned always about individual self-realization and reconstruction of American society for a just life for all, Dewey practiced in his own life what he advocated for others.

Donald K. Pickens

Human Nature and Conduct

Type of philosophy: Ethics, pragmatism
First published: 1922
Principal ideas advanced:

◇ Moralities of the past were deficient in that they were based on arbitrary rules rather than on a scientific understanding of human nature as formed within a social environment.

◇ Human nature is continuous with the rest of nature; ethics is thus allied with physics and biology and with sociology, law, and economics.

◇ Vices and virtues are habits developed during the interaction of the human organism and the social environment.

◇ Morals are ways of action invented to meet specific situations; reactions to them become habits and acquire prescriptive character.

◇ Education must enable the organism to modify its behavior in the face of novelty.

◇ Reflection upon conduct has as its objective the satisfying resolution of a problem arising from the incompatibility of various impulses.

John Dewey believed that to understand oneself and others, one must study human nature and the social institutions in which it functions because both forces work to shape the individual. Morality is the interaction between the two. In the preface to *Human Nature and Conduct*, Dewey says that his book "sets forth a belief that an understanding of habit and of different types of habit is the key to social psychology while the operation of impulse and intelligence gives the key to individualized mental activity. However, they are secondary to habit so that the mind can be understood in the concrete only as a system of beliefs, desires and purposes which are formed in the interaction of biological aptitudes with a social environment."

Dewey criticizes the morality of the past as based largely on arbitrary rules rather than on a scientific understanding of human beings. The few have given and administered rules that the many have obeyed with reluctance, if at all. Such morality is largely restrictive, concerned with what should *not* be done. Many people conform, but others circumvent the morality in their practice, while giving lip service to it or by having a theory that avoids it. The Romantic device of the glorification of impulse as opposed to knowledge is such a theory. Those who attempt to live by a morality divorced from an adequate theory of human nature inhabit a world in which the ideal and the real are sharply separated. They must renounce one world or live uneasily in a world split in two.

It is Dewey's contention that knowledge can solve moral problems and that scientific method holds the best promise of providing knowledge. The moral life operates in an environmental setting that is both natural and social. Human nature is continuous with the rest of nature, and as a result, ethics is allied with physics and biology. Because the activities of one person are continuous with those of others, ethics is allied with such social sciences as sociology, law, and economics. Even the past is not irrelevant. One can study history to understand the present as derived from the past and to help determine the structure of the future.

Habits and Morality

The moral acts of a person are closely related to habits. Habits are compared by Dewey to psychological functions. Both require the cooperation of the organism and its environment. Vices and virtues are not private possessions of a person; they are the result of the interaction of human nature and environment. "All virtues and vices are habits which incorporate objective forces." They can be studied and understood and, as such, can serve as the basis of moral discussion.

Everyone is familiar with bad habits. They are tendencies to action that somehow command people but that people usually have acquired without conscious intent. Because they command, they are will in a clear sense of this word. Because they are demanding and determine what one regards as significant and as trivial, they are the self. Dewey uses this view to replace the belief that will is a separate faculty that, if exercised, can achieve whatever the individual wishes to achieve. A person with a bad habit is not simply failing to do the right thing; the individual has formed a habit of doing the wrong thing. Habits cannot be dismissed by a simple effort of will any more than rain can be brought on by a simple act of dancing. As one must understand the conditions that cause drought and bring rain, so one must understand the objective conditions that cause and continue habit. Neither reason nor will can be separated from habit. What one reasons about, what one decides upon, how one acts on decisions is determined by the relation of the human organism to an environment.

Many people have thought that social institutions are the result of individual habits. The contrary is true for Dewey. He believes social institutions are the source of information about habits, in the sense that the individual must acquire habits that conform with those of the social group. This explains the meaning of such terms as group mind, collective mind, and crowd mind. They can mean nothing more than "a custom brought at some point to explicit, emphatic consciousness, emotional or intellectual." Dewey adds, "In short, the primary facts of social psychology center about collective habit, custom."

One might expect that democracy would encourage individuality, but democracy as it is lived seems, on the contrary, to encourage conformity. Conformity is due to the unfavorable influence of past custom as it affects beliefs, emotions, and purposes. An education tied to the past "becomes the art of taking advantage of the helplessness of the young; the forming of habits becomes a guarantee of the hedges of custom." However, habit is not necessarily conservative. It is any ability formed through past experience. One can acquire the habit to seek new solutions to new problems as easily as the habit to attempt to solve all problems in old ways. Dewey does not describe habit as simply a way of acting; it is also a way of thinking, because thinking requires energy and energy is organized by habit.

Dewey's view of habit places him in opposition to a central contention of the great majority of moralists. They have held that ethical decisions can or must be made by the intellect, unencumbered by nonrational dispositions such as habits or customs. Morality involves relating a set of ideal laws to particular situations and deciding on a course of action that resolves the situation and is in accord with these laws. What classical moralists do not account for, Dewey contends, is the source of ideal laws. Such laws do not suddenly appear, fully formulated, carrying with them their own demand for obedience. On the contrary, they grow like language from incoherent mutterings to complex systems of communication, requiring adherence to rules that are a product of after-the-fact reflection and that acquire a prescriptive character. Morals are ways of acting invented to meet specific situations. When these situations are repeated, the reaction

to them becomes a habit and acquires a prescriptive character. Morality refers to social institutions to which one must defer if one is to live. However, deference is not implicit obedience. Indeed, implicit obedience to any rule of action is impossible. The rule is derived from the environment, and conditions change. In a completely static world, rules might forever remain the same; but the world is not static, and new rules arise from inevitable change.

Impulses and Social Training

One must distinguish between impulses and habits. All human beings love, hate, desire, and avoid; and these impulses have been embodied in social institutions. However, these institutions are highly varied. Dewey points out that different societies use the same impulses in many ways: the communism of the South Sea islanders, the pacifism of the Chinese, the militarism of the ancient Persians, the variety of class morality in almost every society.

The infant is largely potentiality. It is born in an adult environment that provides channels for its impulses; indeed, without these channels the impulses have no meaning, because although an activity stems from the impulse, the nature of the activity comes from the social environment. This environment may be intensely tight, narrow, and restrictive, or it may be loose, wide, and tolerant. Dewey advocates the latter sort:

> With the dawn of the idea of progressive betterment and an interest in new uses of impulses, there has grown up some consciousness of the extent to which a future new society of changed purposes and desires may be created by a deliberate human treatment of the impulses of youth. This is the meaning of education; for a truly humane education consists in an intelligent direction of native activities in the light of the possibilities and necessities of the social situation.

Dewey describes insistence on conformity as training, not education. Education, properly speaking, must enable the organism to modify its behavior in the face of novelty, rather than to withdraw timidly. Dewey says again and again that no old set of habits will ever be adequate to meet new situations. One fact about the future one can be sure of is that it will contain novelty. Old rules sometimes meet new situations but only because the old rules are vague.

By defining human nature as this combination of impulses and social conditioning, Dewey is able to claim that human nature can be changed. As social conditions change, new ways must be devised to meet the change; old impulses are directed into new channels and a new human nature is formed. Indeed, the very words used to describe human nature—selfishness, greed, altruism, generosity—are social terms and have no meaning apart from one's interaction with the environment. People act with regard to the consequences of their acts, and a part of these consequences is what others will think of these acts.

Instincts provide the motive for action but do not determine the character of the action. To attribute all business activity to the acquisitive instinct is an oversimplification, tending to obscure the study of business enterprise. Another case in point is pleasure. The moral literature of the world is full of tirades branding pleasure as evil. Certainly some excesses of pleasure do harm, but pleasure is as necessary to the human organism as work, which is often taken as its opposite. It is through art and play that new and fresh meanings are added to the usual activities of life. Both have a moral function. Both bring into use the imagination, which often finds no part to play in our mundane activities. Both heighten and broaden the meaning of our ordinary concerns. Art and play release energy in a constructive way.

Intelligence and Action
The constructive release of energy is in the direction of meeting new situations by modifying old ways of action. The alternatives are frozen custom or unbridled revolution. What Dewey wants is conscious, reflective reconstruction of society. One must act, but one must act constructively, guided by intelligence.

What, then, is the place of intelligence in conduct? Dewey has already discussed habits. They are related to intelligence in two ways. The first is restrictive. Habits confine intelligence to the problem at hand; however, if this were its only function, the goal of intelligence would be mindless action. Intelligence offers the solution; habit takes over and repeats the solution again and

again. However, habit is not only restrictive. In its second function, it presents alternatives. The more numerous people's habits, the greater are the possibilities of action. In explaining this second function of habit, Dewey says that people "know how by means of our habits." This means that through habits of inquiry, people recognize the novelty in a situation and marshal their previous experience by means of the channels of habit to meet it. This focus of habits on a problem and the solution that results is an essential function of intelligence. Unless one has habits of inquiry, there is no approach to the problem. One must learn until it becomes habit that problems can be recognized and that to solve them one must recollect, observe, and plan.

Some psychologists believe that intelligence and moral conscience are separate faculties that are unconditioned by experience but that operate on the subject matter of experience when it falls within their realm. Dewey does not share this view. For him, both develop in the human organism as the organism develops. The organism grows in height, learns to swim, evinces a desire for knowledge, accepts, and rejects. Every habit is an impulse. Children learn something, like what they learn, and then want to learn more. That children may want to learn more is no more mysterious than that they may want to swim better or that they may want to act morally.

To act morally is to act in the best or wisest way. Such a course of action requires deliberation. To deliberate is to examine with the mind the possible courses of action and their consequences. The possible courses of action that are considered are the result of habit. The choice of one course rather than others simply means that "some habit or some combination of elements of habits and impulse finds a way fully open. Then energy is released. The mind is made up, composed, unified." Deliberation is always the search for a way to act, not an end in itself.

Dewey disagrees with the utilitarians. Their theory, he believes, is that the intellect calculates the consequences of various courses of action and then chooses the one that will result in the most pleasure. His first objection to this theory is that it depends on the misapprehension that reason leads directly to action. On the contrary, habit furnishes the force of action, not reason nor even the anticipation of feelings. Second, there is the difficulty of predicting future pleasures. Future pleasures depend on one's bodily state at some future moment and on the environment of that state. Both of these are independent of present action. "Things sweet in anticipation are bitter in actual taste, things we now turn from in aversion are welcome at another moment in our career." What makes utilitarianism seem plausible to its advocates is their assumption that the organism and its surroundings will remain constant through time. They project the present into the future.

Dewey's Ethics

There is seen to be but one issue involved in all reflection upon conduct: The rectifying of present troubles, the harmonizing of present incompatibilities by projecting a course of action which gathers into itself the meaning of them all.

In this sentence, Dewey summarizes his ethical theory as he formulated it in *Human Nature and Conduct*. Good means the unity that the organism experiences in an action that harmonizes incompatibilities. A moral act is the solution to a problem. Moral aims are not expressed in precepts that exist outside action; they are consequences or natural effects of action. People like some consequences and attempt to achieve them again. In this attempt at realization, consequences function as ends. An end is like a dream in which present conflict is ended, the environment is corrected, and the future is seen in terms of a concrete course of action. The dream of fixed ends at which all action should aim is another expression of humanity's hope for certainty in action. That this hope is vain is the subject of another of Dewey's books, *The Quest for Certainty* (1929).

The function of intelligence is to foresee the future insofar as this can be done by means of principles and criteria of judgment. These principles are like habits. When they become fixed and are regarded as changeless, they can restrict action. However, it must be remembered, Dewey warns, that these principles were derived originally from concrete situations and that they deserve the deference due to any generalization that results from experience. They are hypotheses

with which to experiment and whose use is to forecast the consequences of action.

What part does desire play in moral judgment? Most theories evaluate desire in terms of its object. However, reflection shows that a desire can have a variety of objects. Psychologically, desire drives the organism forward. It gives activity to life. The projected object of the desire and the attained object never agree, however close they may approach one another. Desire acting without will misses its object because action is not controlled. Desire acting with intelligence, Dewey concludes, is led toward its object.

No person who acts can control the future; one's control is limited to the present. One may die before one's goal is reached or one may no longer desire it as a goal. Neither can one provide for all contingencies. If one attempts to do so, one will never act at all. One must act in the present. A new house may be a future goal, but it has to be built in some present if it is to be lived in. Future goals are attained by learning through action in the present. Dewey applies these ideas to education. "If education were conducted as a process of the fullest utilization of present resources, liberating and guiding capacities that are now urgent, it goes without saying that the lives of the young would be much richer in meaning than they are now." This principle can also be applied to modern industrial production. Workers confronted with article after article that they will never use soon lose the interest that might motivate them to make their work efficient. Their work seems senseless.

Moral Conduct

For Dewey, the scope of morals extends to all cases in which there are alternative possibilities of action. The word "conduct" covers every act that is judged better or worse. Morality is not to be severed from other life activities. Every type of conduct incorporates value and gives for good or ill a meaning of life.

Any doctrine of moral conduct that replaces adherence to precepts with a naturalistic theory must explain the fact of freedom. Whatever happens in accord with a law of nature is not free; and if morality is not somehow separated as different in kind from natural facts, moral actions will not be free and people will become automatons. Dewey must meet this problem. To do so, he defines a freely acting person as having three characteristics: the ability to plan and act in accord with the plan, the capacity to vary plans to meet new conditions, and the conviction that desire and choice are a significant factor in action. The capacity to plan presupposes intelligence, and so intelligence is a precondition to freedom. There are two sorts of freedom, freedom-to and freedom-from. Freedom-from is necessary but restrictive. It must leave room for freedom to act, which requires desire, deliberation, and choice.

According to Dewey, people live in a social world. People are conditioned by education, tradition, and environment. The materials on which intelligence operates come from the community life of which people are a part. Morals are social, and both the school and other social institutions have a responsibility toward them. The knowledge of how to fulfill moral responsibility must come from the social sciences. Just as a castaway on an uninhabited island has no moral problems, so morality is a natural outgrowth of social living. The question, "Why be moral?" has no meaning in a social context. The moral situation is a part of the social environment in which everyone lives, changing and dynamic, but always present, always presenting its obligations. Morals are actualities. In moral acts, people express their awareness of the ties that bind each person to every other.

John Collinson, updated by John K. Roth

The Quest for Certainty

Type of philosophy: Epistemology, pragmatism
First published: 1929
Principal ideas advanced:
◇ In the past, the quest for certainty, to be achieved by the discovery of eternal truths and ultimate reality, led to the misleading distinction between theory and practice.
◇ Science and philosophy, by becoming experimental and operational, have shown that idea and practice work together as instruments: Ideas relate experiences and make predictions possible, and by experience, ideas are tested.

◇ Statements about present enjoyments are factual, and value judgments indicate attitudes to be assumed; such judgments are instrumental and corrigible.

The Quest for Certainty, considered against the background of traditional philosophies, is a revolutionary work. John Dewey does not claim that all the ideas in his book are original, but he justifiably asserts that if the ideas outlined in his book were implemented, a revolution comparable to the Copernican would be effected not only in philosophy but also in the moral, social, and economic dimensions of daily life. That this claim is a valid one is partially verified by the pervasive influence of Dewey's teachings on many phases of American culture, especially on education. That Dewey's works should have such an influence is especially appropriate in view of his constantly recurring emphasis on the importance of an intimate, reciprocal relationship between theory and practice. Regardless of whether one finds all of Dewey's methods and conclusions acceptable, it is undeniable that the author's searching criticism of older theories combined with constructive suggestions of remedial and progressive measures have profound practical import.

The Separation of Theory and Practice
The quest about which Dewey writes is an ancient one, originating as a need for security from the perils of primitive life. This security was sought first, perhaps, by prayers and rites performed in an attitude proper to the holy or by magical manipulations of fortunate or lucky tangible objects. Mystery and glamour attended the former, while the latter were regarded as more amenable to practical control. Gradually this distinction was generalized and abstracted into that between the spiritual and intellectual and the material and practical; the distinction was also between superior and inferior respectively and resulted in an isolation of theory and knowledge from practice that has hampered human progress ever since.

Action is notoriously subject to failure or at least unforeseen results; material objects are only partially amenable to human control. Consequently, people were led to seek certainty in an eternal, immaterial realm of thought not subject to the risks of action. This was conceived as the realm of true Being or ultimate reality, unchanging, thoroughly rational, and governed by the laws of logic, and hence the only object of genuine science. The mundane world, on the contrary, was regarded as infected with nonbeing, unreality, and change; it was irrational and the object only of belief or opinion, not genuine knowledge. Moreover, the good was identified with the real so that value was attainable only by knowledge, and both were dissociated from action.

The developments of these distinctions have had ramifications in almost every traditional philosophical theory, Dewey argues. The ideals of certainty in knowledge, various metaphysical views, theories about mind and how it knows—even when formulated by strongly opposing schools—have stemmed from the jealously guarded barrier between theory and practice erected in the quest for certainty. Because modern philosophy has accepted the conclusions of natural science while retaining doctrines about mind, knowledge, and values formulated in prescientific ages, it has found itself increasingly isolated from the actual problems and values of contemporary life. Consequently, the basic problem for philosophy is the integration of beliefs about existence and those about values, especially since this gap has been widened by misinterpretations of certain developments of modern science.

Science and Philosophy

Greek science, says Dewey, was basically aesthetic in character; its explanatory and descriptive categories, such as harmony, symmetry, and proportion, were used to organize logically the qualitative characteristics of experienced objects into kinds of species. Thus nature, considered only an inferior kind of reality patterned after the eternal forms, was known—insofar as it was an object of knowledge at all rather than of opinion or belief—by reason rather than by experience. Greek natural philosophy was also teleological, holding that things and events tended toward their own proper ends or goods and thus toward the highest and best. This outlook, lasting through the Middle Ages, fostered an attitude of acceptance rather than an art of control such as that made possible by modern science.

Galileo and other founders of the new science effected a revolution by eliminating the qualitative and purposive and substituting the quantitative interpretation of scientific objects. Rather than classifying things into species defined by and tending toward eternal forms, the new science saw them as reducible to a few basic categories of space, time, mass, and motion. Phenomena such as heat, light, mechanical motion, and electricity could be converted or translated into one another; homogeneity replaced the heterogeneity basic to the Greek view, and "All that counted for science became mechanical properties formulated in mathematical terms." The revolution was not completed at once, however. Though Sir Isaac Newton ostensibly subscribed to the empirical approach, remnants of the old metaphysics were obvious in the scientist's belief that change occurred only in the external relations between particles of permanently fixed natures. This postulate of permanence was really evidence of the long-standing quest for certainty rather than a hypothesis experimentally verified. Even the most avowedly empiricist school showed this same bias; for them, knowledge was founded on sensory impressions given by an antecedent reality unaffected by knowing. Later, objective idealists held that reflective thought merely reproduces the rational structure of a universe constituted by an absolute reason. Realism continues to hold that valid inquiry apprehends prior existence—it does not modify it. All these views presuppose that inference and judgment are not originative.

As the new science became truly experimental, however, this premise was abandoned; science began to "substitute data for objects." This meant that science, instead of taking qualitative objects such as stars and trees as finalities waiting only for logical classification, takes them as problematic, inviting further interpretation and investigation. This investigation is undertaken in response to problems and unresolved difficulties that are never wholly theoretical but are always ultimately rooted in the need for practical security; these problematic situations determine the lines of inquiry and the criteria of successful solution. Experimental knowledge, inference, or judgment then becomes originative in a very real sense; its "procedure is one that installs doing as the heart of knowing." Change, once regarded as evidence of the inferiority of the experienced world to the ideal and eternal, now becomes useful: "The method of physical inquiry is to introduce some change in order to see what other change ensues; the correlation between these changes, when measured by a series of operations, constitutes the definite and desired object of knowledge." The objects of scientific knowledge are not qualitative entities, but *events*, mathematically formulated relations between changes undergone by experienced objects, and most important, *consequences*.

Experimental Empiricism

Dewey takes physical science as a model for experimental philosophy because, on the whole, the former yields the best authenticated and reliable knowledge, while at the same time, its conclusions are corrigible and its hypotheses subject to revision in the light of future evidence and problems. Besides, in its technological applications, physical science is the dominant feature of modern life. Philosophy can learn from it, Dewey believes, how to approach the basic modern problem of reintegrating beliefs about existence with those about values as well as how to avoid some of the more technical philosophical problems to which traditional theories inevitably led.

Dewey cites with approval American physicist Percy Williams Bridgman's statement in *The Logic of Modern Physics* (1927): "We mean by any concept nothing more than a set of operations; the concept is synonymous with the corresponding set of operations." The philosophical implications of such an experimental empiricism (as distinguished from traditional sensational empiricism), understood at the time by only a few thinkers such as William James and Charles Sanders Peirce, are very far reaching. The statement shows that neither sensational empiricism nor a priori rationalism was wholly right or wholly wrong: Ideas are empirical in origin, but sensory qualities, to be significant, must be related by ideas; the new method's concepts of scientific objects are neither a priori nor reducible to sensation. The object of knowledge is "eventual; that is, it is an outcome of directed experimental operations, instead of something in sufficient existence before the act of knowing." Thus the sensory and rational elements of knowledge do not compete but cooperate; the latter are used to organize and direct, the former to test and verify or correct. Conclusions, not the previously given, are *truly known*; but conclusions of former investigations become in turn instrumental to the achievement of new solutions.

Operational Method

The operational method makes mind a participant rather than a mere spectator in the knowing situation. As is illustrated by the Heisenberg principle of indeterminacy, the act of observation is itself an essential ingredient in what is known. From this point of view, then, nature is neither rational nor irrational as it has been described traditionally, but is, rather, intelligible; it is *to be* known through intelligence. This approach also yields new definitions of intelligence, thought, and mind. Merely mechanical and animal responses to uncertain and perilous situations are reactions or direct actions, but "response to the doubtful as such" is definitive of mind and thinking, and when responses "have a directed tendency to change the precarious and problematic into the secure and resolved, they are *intellectual* as well as mental." Misinterpretations of Newtonian science, by emphasizing the difference between ordinary perceptual experience and the scientific formulation of nature, had reinforced the metaphysical distinction between mind and body, but in Dewey's view, "There is no separate 'mind' gifted in and of itself with a faculty of thought; such a conception of thought ends in postulating the mystery of a power outside nature and yet able to intervene within it." As defined above, thinking is observable behavior, whereas traditional theories on the contrary tried to explain the more by the less obvious. Now with greater understanding of the relation between sensory organs and perception, it is possible to conceive of the same relation as holding between the brain and thought.

One stronghold of the rationalistic and mentalistic schools, however, and one not adequately accounted for by traditional empiricism, was the structure of mathematics. Because mathematics seemed to rest on self-evident axioms known intuitively and appeared to have universality, immutability, ideality, and logical necessity, mathematics was thought to demonstrate the subsistence of a realm of eternal essences and a nonphysical reality. The applicability of mathematics to the physical world, moreover, seemed to show a rational element. Does the operational theory of ideas, together with its implications concerning the nature of mind and thought, break down here? Dewey thinks not. One must distinguish between overt and symbolical operations, operations to be enacted and those merely possible but without actual consequences. Just as the concepts of space, time, and motion were finally seen to be ways of correlating observations rather than as reflecting properties of Being, and their worth was found in the former function, so logical and mathematical principles and relationships may be interpreted. They may have arisen from practical needs for manipulation and organization of physical things and later been developed more fully and independently of immediately instrumental purposes. People then become interested in such operations as operations which, when symbolized, can be performed without any direct reference to existence. That this is the case seems most clearly illustrated by the history of geometry, which originated in the need for measurement of utilitarian objects. The formal order and internal relations such systems show are analogous to the self-consistent structure of a machine designed for a certain purpose. The means-consequence relation as exemplified in the operation of a machine may be *thought* abstractly as an operation to which the imperfections of actual machines are irrelevant; so conceived, the function has the ideality, immutability, internal necessity, and universality that characterizes the realm of essence supposedly encountered in logic and mathematics.

Values

The worth of a machine is judged by the efficacy with which it performs the function for which it was designed, and the more abstractly this function is conceived—the more it is idealized—the more clearly it can be understood. However, in the conception of function, ideas for improvement are germinated. Thus, the operational or experimental method is capable of projecting new goals and values and of instituting its own standards. It is imperative that this lesson learned from science be applied in the moral, social, and political life, where it is not yet fully operative. The apparent value-sterility of quantitative and operational science can now be regarded as illusory, the illusion being rooted in the notion that science discloses reality. The experimental method is an effective way of thinking of things, but because it is not the only way to think of them, it is not actually inimical to qualitative experience, and it can make positive contributions to the qualitative aspects of human life by affording means of making values more available and secure. According to Dewey, the main problem for modern philosophy is to reintegrate beliefs about existence and values. It is obvious that his purpose in tracing the development of operationalism and instrumentalism is to show their significance for what he calls, typically, the "construction" of good, suggesting thereby that values, like objects of knowledge, are not so much given as achieved.

By "value" Dewey means "whatever is taken to have rightful authority in the direction of conduct." However, there are still rival theories about the status of values comparable to the traditional epistemological opposites, empiricism and rationalism. Some writers would equate goods with actual enjoyments, while others see them as eternal, universal, absolute. Dewey favors the empirical and subjective theories to the extent that they relate "the theory of values with concrete experiences of desire and satisfaction," but the operational approach again makes a significant emendation: Values are not antecedently given but are enjoyments attained as *consequences*. Previous goods and present enjoyments are problematic, as are immediately experienced qualitative objects in relation to knowledge. The crucial differences here are indicated in the very suffixes of terms such as "the enjoyed and the enjoyable, the desired and the desirable, the satis*fying* and the satis*factory*." This is in no sense to derogate immediate enjoyments and likings, but mere feelings have no claim over people as ideals and future goods, any more than objects as immediately experienced are adequate as scientific objects. Whereas propositions about present enjoyments are factual and may be of instrumental worth, value judgments and appraisals indicate attitudes *to be* assumed and hence do make claims on people. Dewey summarizes this view in what he describes as his main proposition: "Judgments about values are judgments about the conditions and the results of experienced objects; judgments about that which should regulate the formation of our desires, affections and enjoyments."

Value judgments, then, like their counterparts in science, are relational in nature. They, too, are instrumental and never final, and are thus corrigible. There are criteria of goods—for example, genuine goods are not later regretted; in achieving goods, concern is centered on the valuable object rather than on the mere feeling of satisfaction—but such criteria are never absolute and fixed. It is thus impossible to set up a detailed catalog of values in hierarchical order. Dewey's approach "would place *method and means* upon the level of importance that has, in the past, been imputed exclusively to ends," for as long as ends alone are considered ideal and of true worth, while means are scorned as merely practical, ends fail to be realized. Although failure to achieve the good has been attributed to perversity of will, the real obstacle has been lack of adequate knowledge of means. Hence, the traditional elevation of spirit over matter is similarly mistaken, for the material serves as means.

The Role of Philosophy

The traditional separation of ends and means, another reflection of that of theory and practice, has left action without the guidance afforded only by knowledge. Consequently, some means, such as material wealth, have been overvalued as ends in the absence of any adequate philosophy of values appropriate to contemporary problems. The technological applications of science have been used selfishly and irresponsibly. Nowhere is the failure properly to relate ends and means more evident than in industrial life, and the resulting tragedy is that enjoyment of the highest social and cultural values, the truly human goods, is dependent on economic conditions ignored by many ethical philosophers. The economy tends, therefore, to evade moral guidance as irrelevant and to be frankly materialistic, but the remedy is not to treat economics as beneath the notice of ethics; it is rather to apply here the instrumentalist approach.

Whereas mechanistic philosophy rejected the concept of purpose as explanatory of natural events, the developments of modern science have made clear the role of the observer in knowledge, and Dewey holds that in a significant sense purpose has been restored to nature, since "distinctively human conduct can be interpreted and understood only in terms of purpose." By removing the artificial barriers between knowledge and practice, science and values, and the consequent false problems such as those of the relationships between mind and body, spirit and matter, nature can be regarded as the ultimate source of all ideals and goods. To remove such obstacles, to free people's minds and hearts from slavery to the past, to turn them from the quest for an illusory certainty to discoverable paths to enjoyable goods, is the task of contemporary philosophy. No longer in competition with science through claims to sole superior knowledge of reality, philosophy takes up the task of exploring the richly various ways of putting science to truly human use.

Marvin Easterling

Art as Experience

Type of philosophy: Aesthetics, ethics
First published: 1934
Principal ideas advanced:

◇ When experience is satisfactory, when it combines memory of the past with anticipation of the future, when it is an achievement of the organism in the environment in which it functions, the experience is an experience.

◇ Any experience that is, in this unified and consummatory way, an experience is an aesthetic experience.

◇ Art is to be understood as an experience made possible by the organizing and unifying process in which the artist engages; the spectator meets the interest of the artist with an interest of his own in the reciprocal process of going through a similar operation.

◇ Art supplies mediums of communication, making community of experience possible.

◇ All arts share a common form: they are organized toward a unified experience; they all operate through sensory mediums such as stone, watercolors, oil paints, and words; and they are all concerned with space and time.

Art as Experience is the most extensive and, many say, the best book on aesthetics from the pragmatic point of view. Dewey believed that aesthetic theory should attempt to explain how works of art come to be and how they are enjoyed in experience. How is it that something produced to fill a need becomes in addition a source of aesthetic enjoyment? How is it that ordinary activities can yield a particular kind of satisfaction that is aesthetic? These and similar questions must be answered by an adequate aesthetic theory.

The Aesthetic Experience
Dewey's interest in biology influenced his description of the aesthetic experience. An organism lives in an environment through which it fulfills certain needs. The process of fulfilling these needs is called "experience" and may be more or less satisfactory to the organism. When experience seems to be completely satisfactory, when it is a happy experience that combines memories of the past and anticipations of the future, when it is an achievement of the organism in the world of things, Dewey calls it "an experience." *An* experience, realized by a human being, is aesthetic. Thus, there is no sharp line between animal and human experience. Animals could have an aesthetic experience, but no one would be likely to call it that.

Aesthetic experiences are not found in museums or in libraries alone. As a matter of fact, such settings often make enjoyment impossible by putting works of art beyond ordinary human activities and concerns. For Dewey, an intelligent worker performing a job, interested in it, and finding satisfaction in doing it well is having an experience. The worker is artistically engaged and is finding aesthetic enjoyment. Consequently, everyday activities are the ones most meaningful to the average person. To the average person, the most vital arts are popular music, comic strips, newspaper accounts of crime and love, and articles on the intimate doings of popular entertainers. These things are a significant

part of the concerns of an organized community, just as in the past rug, mat, and cloth making; dancing; music; and storytelling were an integral part of day-to-day living.

Modern museums and institutions segregate art and remove it from the concerns of most people. Dewey criticizes the modern artist for reflecting the view that art is isolated and for not attempting to reach anyone except those whom the artist regards as having a superior cultural status. The object that the artist produces may be thought of as a work of art, but the actual work of art is to be understood as what affects human experience. The problem of the artist should be to show that artistic activity can be connected with the actual processes of living.

Dewey points to other properties of the aesthetic experience. In their practical concerns with the real world, people think in terms of effect and cause. They convert these for their own use into ends they wishes to achieve and devices for achieving them; that is, into consequences and means, organizing the world in terms of needs and environment. Art, too, involves organization and may be related to any activity of the living organism. The great work of art is a complete organization, and in this completeness lies the source of aesthetic pleasure.

No experience is a unity, Dewey says, unless it has aesthetic quality. The integrated, the well-rounded, the emotionally satisfying make up the artistic structure of the experience that is immediately felt. Because of its relation to experience, art is always a part of the process of doing or making something. Like all experience, it involves emotion and is guided by purpose. Artists organize, clarify, and simplify material according to their interest. Spectators must go though these same operations according to their own interests to have an aesthetic experience from their relation to the art object. They must be creative when confronted by an art object, just as the artist was creative when producing it. What the spectator creates is an experience that is enjoyed and is satisfying for its own sake.

The Characteristics of Experience
What are the characteristics of experience for Dewey? Experience begins with an impulsion of the whole organism, outward and forward. The

organism moves to satisfy a need, but the nature of this motion is determined by the environment and the past experiences of the organism. Emotion always accompanies an experience. Without emotion there is no action.

A work of art does not simply evoke an emotion. The material in it becomes the content and matter of emotion when it is a part of the environment that satisfies a need in relation to the past experiences of an organism. Art objects may be inadequate or excessive in relation to the emotional needs of the spectator. Art is not nature; it is nature organized, simplified, and transformed in such a way that it places the individual and the community in a context of greater order and unity.

Therefore, for Dewey, a work of art represents nature as experienced by the artist. It organizes the public world by taking the scattered and weakened material of experience, then clarifying and concentrating it. However, a work of art does not lead to another experience of the world; it is *an* experience. Only secondarily, as it becomes a part of the past experiences of a person, does it transform everyday existence. Painters, for example, perceive the world just as everyone else does. However, certain lines and colors become more important to them, and they subordinate other aspects of what they are perceiving to relations among them. What they view as important is influenced by their past experiences, by their theories of art, by their attitudes toward the world, and by the scene itself.

A Medium of Communication

One reason for the importance of art, claims Dewey, is that it supplies "the only media of complete and unhindered communication between man and man that can occur in a world full of gulfs and walls that limit community of experience." Since art communicates, it requires, like language, a triadic relation of speaker (the artist), the thing said (the art product), and the hearer (the spectator). All language involves what is said and how it is said—substance and form. In art, substance is the content of the work itself; form is the organization of this content.

Each art has its own medium, fitted for a particular kind of communication. When there is a complete set of relations within a chosen me-

dium, there is aesthetic form. Form is relation, and relations are modes of interaction: pushes, pulls, lightness, heaviness. In a successful work of art, the stresses are so adapted to one another that a unity results. The work of art satisfies many ends, none of which is laid down in advance. Artists experiment. They communicate an individual experience through materials that belong to the public world. They mean the work of art, and the work of art means whatever anyone can honestly get out of it.

Art as Experience differentiates between the art product and the work of art. The art product—the statue, the painting, the printed poem—is physical. The work of art is active and experienced. When the art product enters into experience, it takes part in a complex interaction. It is the work of art with its fixed order of elements that is perceived. However, the work of art is like an organism: It manifests movement, it has a past and present, a career, a history. Energy is organized toward some result. The spectator interacts with the work of art so that energies are given rhythmic organization, are intensified, clarified, concentrated.

The fact that art organizes energy explains its power to move and to stir, to calm and to tranquilize. Paintings that seem dead in whole or in part are those that arrest movement rather than carry it forward toward a dynamic whole. Thus aesthetic perception differs from ordinary perception. The latter results in classification: Those are rain clouds, so I must carry an umbrella. Aesthetic perception is full, complete, and rhythmical.

"What properties do all of the arts share?" Dewey asks. In the past, it had been argued that they have a common subject matter. However, the tendency in the arts is to go beyond limits. New artists have new interests and express them through innovative uses of material. Yet, the arts do share a common form to the extent that they are all organized toward a unity of experience. Further, all arts operate through sensory mediums. A material such as stone, watercolor, oil paints, or words becomes a medium when it is used to express a meaning other than that of its commonplace physical existence. Different mediums give different qualities to works of art; pastel differs from oil. "Sensitivity to a medium as a medium is the very heart of all artistic creation and esthetic perception." The medium is a *mediator*; it relates the artist and the perceiver. Another property that all arts share is that they are concerned with space and time. The arts are dynamic, and all action must occur in space and time. Spatiality is mass and volume; temporality is endurance.

The aesthetic experience, Dewey contends, is located in the interaction between the spectator and the art product. Thus, art products cannot be classified into aesthetic categories. There can be as great a variety of works of art as there can be a variety of unified experiences. The work of art comes into existence when a human being cooperates with the art product. This cooperation results in an experience that is enjoyed because of its liberating and ordered properties. Thus, for Dewey, no art is inherently superior to any other. Every medium has its own power, its own efficacy and value. The important thing is that it communicates by making common, related, and available what had been isolated and singular.

Every work of art contains something of the particular personality of the artist. In practical action, one must divide reality into subject and impersonal object. No such division characterizes aesthetic experience for Dewey. Art is a unity of subject and object. Like rite and ceremony, it has the power to unite people through shared celebration to all the concerns and anticipations of life.

Aesthetic experience, indeed all experience, is imaginative. Imagination helps to adjust the old to the new, connecting the new with its physical past and the past of the person involved. Aesthetic experience is the paradigm of experience, experience freed from the factors that would impede and thwart its development.

Thus, if Dewey is right, it is to aesthetic experience that philosophers must turn if they are to understand the nature of experience itself. In the past, philosophers have explained aesthetic experience as but one type of experience. Instead, they should have taken experience in its most complete form, the fusion of the self with the objective order and law of the material that it incorporates, and used this—aesthetic experience—as the model for understanding experience in general.

Some Problems of Aesthetics

Dewey uses the principles delineated in *Art as Experience* to solve what he takes to be some of the major problems of aesthetics. Does art express the universal or the unique and particular? In Dewey's opinion, it does neither exclusively. It forms a new synthesis that is both. The expression is neither objective nor subjective, neither solely personal nor completely general.

Does art convey knowledge? It is true that it makes life more intelligible, says Dewey, but not through concepts in the way that knowing does. Art clarifies by intensifying experience. Both philosophy and art depend on the imaginative power of the mind. Art is a manifestation of experience *as* experience, of experience unalloyed. Because of this manifestation, it can provide a control for the imaginative ventures of philosophy.

The Critic

Dewey has much advice for the critic. Criticism is a judgment about art. If one is to understand the nature of criticism in the arts, one must first understand the nature of judgment. The material that judgment uses is supplied by perception. This material in a mature judgment must be controlled and selected. In viewing a work of art, the spectator conducts a controlled inquiry, which requires an extensive background and developed taste. The spectator must discriminate and unify, but unlike the jurist he has no socially approved rules to apply. The law is conservative, but criticism must be sensitive to new forms of expression that stem from spiritual and physical changes in the environment.

At the opposite extreme from Dewey is the impressionistic critic. Mere impression can never organize experience; unification and discrimination always involve reference to some theory. If works of art are not to be judged by impressions, they are also not to be judged by fixed standards. In the primary sense, a standard is a physical object that measures quantitatively. The critic measures qualitatively.

How, then, can critics make objective judgments? The qualities that they are judging are those of an object, and their judgment requires a hypothesis. It is this hypothesis that provides a criterion for judging the critics themselves. Their theories of criticism must be adequate to enable them to point to properties of the art object that will evoke an aesthetic experience. They must discuss form in relation to matter, the function of the medium, the nature of the expressive object. They must lead rather than dictate. They must discover a unifying pattern that pervades the work of art, perhaps not the only one, but one that can be shown to be maintained throughout the parts of the art object.

Art as Experience identifies two fallacies of aesthetic criticism. The first of these is reduction. The reduction fallacy occurs when some aspect of the work of art is taken as the whole. The work of art is a self-contained unity; it combines many things, none of which has aesthetic priority. The second fallacy results from a confusion of categories. Works of art provide data for students of art, for example, for the art historian. However, to identify the historian's account of the work of art with aesthetic criticism is to be guilty of a confusion of categories.

Another type of category confusion concerns values. The most obvious example is found in moralistic criticism. A work of art may well make moral judgments, but these are not the sole criterion of its aesthetic value. Art is a medium of communication in its own right, not a substitute for religion, science, philosophy, or moral exhortation. The function of the critic is to delineate the aesthetic experience, which has its own inherent value, to reeducate so that others may learn from the criticism to see and to hear.

The artist, the critic, and the aesthetician must face one problem, the relation between permanence and change. Human beings and their environments are continually subjected to change operating within a structure of laws. This structure is in turn subject to gradual change. Art must reflect such changes. Artists and critics have only begun to realize that the rise of industrialism is a source of new patterns and of new materials. Art can show that there is permanence in the changing and change in the permanent.

Art and Civilization

In a broad sense, aesthetic experience reveals the life and development of civilization. Art is a magnificent force that brings together conflicting elements found in every period of history. The customs and rituals of a people, all of their communal activities, unite the practical, social, and educative into an aesthetic unity.

The art of the past must have something to say to the present to be worthy of present consideration. An art can die just as can any other human institution. However, great art, for Dewey, is a revelation of self and always has something to say to succeeding peoples under different environments; it tells of the ordered movement of the matter of some experience to a genuine fulfillment.

Ancient civilizations are often thought of in terms of their art products. The art of the past reveals elements of civilization; in the modern world, art is affected by two new elements: natural science in its application to industry and commerce through machinery. These new factors have yet to be absorbed into the attitudes of most people. Science has given people a new conception of the environment and of their relation to it. Science tends to portray people as a part of nature and gives rational support to people's desire to control themselves and the environment. It enables them to understand themselves in relation to their past, present, and future.

Industry creates an environment in which more and more people leave the rural world of nature for the manmade world of the machine. This new setting can have aesthetic quality. Objects with their own internal functional adaptations can be combined with humanity in a way that yields aesthetic results. The artist can create a physical and moral environment that will shape desires and purposes, that will determine the direction of the interest and attention of human beings. Artistic experience, says Dewey, can and must shape the future.

John Collinson

Additional Reading

Alexander, Thomas M. *John Dewey's Theory of Art, Experience, and Nature: The Horizons of Feeling.* Albany: State University of New York Press, 1987. A thoughtful consideration of John Dewey's understanding of experience and the role of aesthetics and the arts within it.

Bernstein, Richard J. *John Dewey.* New York: Washington Square Press, 1966. A brief, clear, and reliable overview of Dewey's philosophy.

Boisvert, Raymond D. *John Dewey: Rethinking Our Time*. Albany: State University of New York Press, 1998. Tracking the implications of Dewey's thought, this study shows Dewey's significance for contemporary social and philosophical issues.

Conkin, Paul K. *Puritans and Pragmatists: Eight Eminent American Thinkers*. Bloomington: Indiana University Press, 1976. In discussing several eminent American thinkers, this book provides a solid, although technical, account of Dewey's place in American thought.

Festenstein, Matthew. *Pragmatism and Political Theory: From Dewey to Rorty*. Chicago: University of Chicago Press, 1997. A careful and critical analysis that shows how pragmatism, Dewey's included, has affected political theory and practice.

Hickman, Larry A., ed. *Reading Dewey: Interpretation for a Postmodern Generation*. Bloomington: Indiana University Press, 1998. Important interpreters of Dewey's thought explore his continuing significance for inquiry concerning knowledge and ethics.

Kuklick, Bruce. *Churchmen and Philosophers: From Jonathan Edwards to John Dewey*. New Haven, Conn.: Yale University Press, 1985. An important study that deals with Dewey's thought in the context of the interconnections between religion and American philosophical thought.

Moore, Edward Carter. *American Pragmatism: Peirce, James, and Dewey*. New York: Columbia University Press, 1966. An older but still reliable comparative study of the three classical figures in American pragmatism.

Popp, Jerome A. *Naturalizing Philosophy of Education: John Dewey in the Postanalytic Period*. Carbondale: Southern Illinois University Press, 1998. A worthwhile appraisal of Dewey's philosophy of education and its significance in ongoing debates within educational theory.

Rockefeller, Steven C. *John Dewey: Religious Faith and Democratic America*. New York: Columbia University Press, 1991. A detailed and important study of Dewey's life and thought, focusing on his views about religion and democracy.

Smith, John E. *The Spirit of American Philosophy*. Rev. ed. Notre Dame, Ind.: University of Notre Dame Press, 1983. Attempting to locate a common American spirit among five varied thinkers, this classic study interprets the philosophies of Charles Sanders Peirce, William James, Josiah Royce, and Alfred North Whitehead as well as the thought of John Dewey.

Stroh, Guy W. *American Philosophy from Edwards to Dewey: An Introduction*. Princeton, N.J.: D. Van Nostrand, 1968. An introductory account that places Dewey in relation to his most important predecessors in American philosophy.

Welchman, Jennifer. *Dewey's Ethical Thought*. Ithaca, N.Y.: Cornell University Press, 1995. A sympathetic but critical analysis of Dewey's moral philosophy and its implications.

Westbrook, Robert B. *John Dewey and American Democracy*. Ithaca, N.Y.: Cornell University Press, 1991. A readable and carefully done study of Dewey's influence on American culture and politics.

Donald K. Pickens, updated by John K. Roth

Denis Diderot

As editor of and contributor to the *Encyclopedia*, Diderot codified and promulgated the views of the French Enlightenment. He developed a philosophy of nature and promoted biology and chemistry with physiological investigations.

Principal philosophical works: *Pensées philosophiques*, 1746 (English translation, 1819; also as *Philosophical Thoughts*, 1916); *Lettre sur les aveugles*, 1749 (*An Essay on Blindness*, 1750; also as *Letter on the Blind*, 1916); *Notes et commentaires*, 1749; *Encyclopédie: Ou, Dictionnaire raisonné des sciences, des arts, et des métiers*, 1751-1772 (coedited with Jean Le Rond d'Alembert, 17 volumes of text, 11 volumes of plates; partial translation, *Selected Essays from the Encyclopedy*, 1772; complete translation, *Encyclopedia*, 1965); *Lettre sur les sourds et muets*, 1751 (*Letter on the Deaf and Dumb*, 1916); *Pensées sur l'interprétation de la nature*, 1754 (partial translation, *Thoughts on the Interpretation of Nature*, 1927); *Entretiens sur "Le Fils naturel,"* 1757; *Discours sur la poésie dramatique*, 1758 (English translation of chapters 1-5 in *Dramatic Essays of the Neo-Classical Age*, 1950); *Les Salons*, 1759-1781 (serial), 1845, 1857 (book); *De la suffisance de la religion naturelle*, 1770 (wr. 1747); *Entretien d'un père avec ses enfants*, 1773 (*Conversations Between Father and Children*, 1964); *Essai sur Sénèque*, 1778 (revised and expanded as *Essai sur les règnes de Claude et Néron*, 1782); *Essais sur la peinture*, 1796 (wr. c. 1765); *Pensées détachées sur la peinture*, 1798; *Plan d'une université pour le gouvernement de Russie*, 1813-1814 (wr. c. 1775-1776); *Paradoxe sur le comédien*, 1830 (wr. 1773; *The Paradox of Acting*, 1883); *La Promenade du sceptique*, 1830 (wr. 1747); *Le Rêve de d'Alembert*, 1830 (wr. 1769; *D'Alembert's Dream*, 1927); *Diderot's Early Philosophical Works*, 1916 (includes *Letter on the Blind*, *Letter on the Deaf and Dumb*, *Philosophical Thoughts*); *Concerning the Education of a Prince*, 1941 (wr. 1758); *Correspondance*, 1955-1970 (16 volumes); *Œuvres philosophiques*, 1956; *Œuvres esthétiques*, 1959; *Œuvres politiques*, 1962.

Born: October 5, 1713; Langres, France
Died: July 31, 1784; Paris, France

Early Life

The son of Didier and Angélique Vigneron Diderot, Denis Diderot was born on October 5, 1713, in Langres, France. Although the family was involved in trade—Didier Diderot was a master cutler and his wife the daughter of a tanner—a number of relatives had entered the Catholic Church, among them the canon of the cathedral at Langres. Diderot's brother, Didier-Pierre, and his sister, Angélique, would follow this ecclesiastical path, the former becoming a priest and the latter a nun. Diderot, despite his later atheism, also showed an early inclination in this direction. Tonsured at the age of twelve, he

made the 150-mile journey north to Paris three years later to study at the Jesuit Collège Louis-le-Grand or the Jansenist Collège d'Harcourt; he may have taken courses at both. When he received his degree in 1732, though, it was from the University of Paris, and his interest had shifted to philosophy and rhetoric.

Because Diderot had abandoned a career in the Church, his father apprenticed him to the Parisian lawyer Clément de Ris. This field suited him no better than religion, and after enduring two years of legal studies, Diderot turned to a life of letters. His father refused to approve of so uncertain a course, so for the next decade Diderot survived on the meager earnings he garnered as tutor and hack writer, supplemented by occasional small sums from his mother. On Novem-

Denis Diderot. *(Library of Congress)*

ber 6, 1743, he married Anne-Toinette Champion, the daughter of a poor linen-shop owner; this step further alienated his father, who so opposed the match that he had Diderot locked up in a monastery to prevent the wedding. Diderot escaped; he realized, however, that he could not rely on his parents to support his family and recognized that he needed a secure source of income.

Life's Work

Diderot therefore turned to the booksellers, offering his fluency in English and his literary talent. In 1743, he translated Temple Stanyan's *Grecian History* (1707) for the publisher Briasson, who was sufficiently pleased with the result to ask Diderot for a French version of Robert James's

A Medical Dictionary (1743-1745). At the same time that he was translating James's treatise, he was adapting *An Inquiry Concerning Virtue in Two Discourses* (1699), by Anthony Ashley Cooper, the third earl of Shaftesbury. Much in Shaftesbury's work appealed to Diderot and deeply influenced his views. He admired the Englishman's tolerance and emphasis on reason, and he adopted the notion that religion and morality should be judged according to their social effects. Diderot also agreed with Shaftesbury that emotions play an important role in fostering socially proper conduct. He was less prepared to accept Shaftesbury's optimism, his notion of an innate aesthetic appreciation, and his criticism of organized religion.

Diderot's first original philosophical work, *Pensées philosophiques*, written over Easter weekend, 1746, to earn fifty gold pieces for Madame de Puissieux, his mistress, built on this adaptation. Diderot was still not prepared to reject the Church—the fifty-first *pensée* reaffirms his belief in Catholicism—but he does urge that faith be tested by reason and that the passions, deemed by the orthodox to be dangerous, be seen as necessary to morality and creativity. Published anonymously, it was sufficiently impressive to be attributed to such well-known intellectuals as Voltaire or Étienne Bonnot de Condillac. It was also regarded as sufficiently radical to be condemned by the Parliament of Paris in July, 1746.

La Promenade du sceptique (1830; the promenade of a skeptic) revealed Diderot's increasing doubts about religion; the manuscript was seized before publication, and the police began to watch Diderot closely. His bawdy satire on Louis XV and Madame de Pompadour, *Les Bijoux indiscrets* (1748; *The Indiscreet Toys*, 1749), further antagonized the authorities, and his *An Essay on Blind-*

ness, which questioned the deistic argument that cosmic order proves God's existence, led to his arrest and solitary confinement for three months in the fortress of Vincennes.

This experience shook him deeply. Previously he had published his controversial works anonymously; henceforth, he would rarely publish them at all. His reputation in the eighteenth century, therefore, was lower than it would become after his death. Much of his contemporary acclaim derived from the project that would occupy him for the next fifteen years, the *Encyclopedia*. His translations and other writings not only had exposed Diderot to new knowledge but also had made him a logical choice for coeditor, with Jean Le Rond d'Alembert, of the ambitious project to translate and supplement Ephraim Chambers's five-volume *Cyclopaedia: Or, Universal Dictionary of the Arts and Sciences* (1728).

As realized by conservative opponents, who twice succeeded in having the *Encyclopedia* condemned, the work was not an innocent compilation of existing knowledge. In its pages nature replaced providence and determinism superseded God's will as the guiding forces of the world. Instead of relying on authority and tradition, Diderot and his fellow philosophers urged readers to judge by experience and experimentation. In a world of monarchies, the article "Political Authority" proclaimed that "no man has received from nature the right to command other men. Freedom is a present from heaven, and every individual of the same species has the right to enjoy it as soon as he enjoys reason." By 1758, d'Alembert was sufficiently frightened by official reaction to resign as coeditor, leaving Diderot with the responsibility of writing and soliciting contributions to complete the seventeen volumes of text and twelve of plates.

In the midst of these labors, Diderot found time to produce a number of other works. The theater had long interested him. Late in life, he would state that he had debated between studying at the Sorbonne and becoming an actor, and in *Letter on the Deaf and Dumb*, he claimed to know much of French drama by heart. In the latter half of the 1750's, he indulged this interest by writing two plays, *Le Fils naturel* (1757; *Dorval: Or, The Test of Virtue*, 1767) and *Le Père de famille* (1758; *The Father of the Family*, 1770). As the subtitle of *Dorval* reveals, Diderot regarded these works, as he saw all of his writings, as having a moral purpose. In an article in *Encyclopedia*, he had spoken of actors' ability to engender in audiences the love of virtue, and an essay on Geneva, also in the *Encyclopedia*, by d'Alembert urged the city to permit dramatic productions because they promote morality.

In addition to reforming society, Diderot hoped that his plays would alter theatrical techniques and practices, which he regarded as unrealistic. To the published version of each play he added comments on stagecraft, urging actors to pretend that no audience faced them. He wanted the people on stage to interact naturally with one another, not perform for observers. Diderot also argues, in *The Paradox of Acting*, that the actor must be ruled by the intellect rather than by his emotions if he wishes to convey passion consistently. This view incidentally suggests that Diderot was beginning to question his earlier agreement with Shaftesbury on the primacy of sentiment in guiding action.

Questioning does not, however, mean rejecting. As he matured, Diderot would become increasingly skeptical—of his own views as well as others'—stating that "scepticism is the first step towards the truth." In *Le Neveu de Rameau* (1821, 1891; *Rameau's Nephew*, 1897), he seems to prefer Apollonian reason to Dionysian passion, but he also acknowledges the necessity of emotion for creativity. This same ambivalence shows itself in the aesthetic criticism that he wrote for Friedrich Melchior Grimm's *Correspondance littéraire* (1845-1857), a newsletter that circulated in manuscript, from 1759 to 1781. In an essay from 1766 on painting, he instructed the artist, "Move me, astonish me, rend me; make me shudder, weep, tremble; fill me with indignation." At the same time, he recognized that reason must balance enthusiasm.

Though uncertain about the means by which art should achieve its effects, Diderot had no doubt that its end must be the promotion of virtue. Hence, he preferred the sentimental paintings of Jean-Baptiste Greuze to the more sensuous works of François Boucher. Greuze appealed to the heart, Boucher only to the eye. Similarly, though he was an atheist, he admired religious art because it inspired virtuous feelings.

By the time his work on the *Encyclopedia* ended in 1765, Diderot had gained the reputation of being an important French intellectual. A flattering sign of Diderot's growing reputation came from Jean-Honoré Fragonard and Catherine the Great of Russia. In his series of paintings honoring the various arts, Fragonard chose Diderot to represent literature. His hair short, his forehead high, his mouth turned up in an enigmatic smile of reason, the philosopher holds a volume of the *Encyclopedia* and appears to be a Roman citizen wearing an eighteenth century dressing gown. Catherine the Great relieved Diderot of financial concerns in 1765 by buying his library for fifteen thousand livres and appointing him curator for life at a salary of another one thousand livres a year. She agreed not to take formal possession until after Diderot's death.

In 1773, Diderot went to Russia to thank the empress for her patronage. The trip inspired a number of works reflecting on politics and education, and during this time, Diderot probably completed his best-known novel, *Jacques le fataliste et son maître* (1796; *Jacques the Fatalist and His Master*, 1797). A clever picaresque, it once more reveals Diderot's skepticism. Although he had, like his character Jacques, believed in determinism earlier in his life, in this work, he questioned this view. Despite Jacques's claim that no one has free will, Jacques behaves as if he can choose whatever course of action he wishes to pursue, and the authorial intrusions indicate that chance rules the world. Readers may draw their own conclusions—or conclude nothing.

Similar doubts characterize other writings of this period. "Beware of those who impose order," he warned in the *Supplément au voyage de Bougainville* (1796; *Supplement to Bougainville's "Voyage,"* 1956). The dialogue form, which Diderot used repeatedly, allows for the presentation of various positions without requiring the author to endorse any. This method, drawn from Plato, appealed to Diderot because it was safe should authorities secure a copy of the manuscript, and it also permitted Diderot to explore various viewpoints. *Est'il bon? Est'il méchant?* (1781; Is it good? Is it evil?), his last and best play, questions, without deciding, whether one can be virtuous if one performs good deeds in a manner that embarrasses the beneficiaries. Skeptical to the end, Diderot's

last words to his daughter were, "the first step towards philosophy is disbelief."

Influence

Since his death on July 31, 1784, Diderot's reputation has grown. With the benefit of the perspective brought by time, one can recognize the truth of German scholar Carl Becker's observation that Diderot epitomized his age, both in the profundity of his thought and in the occasional shallowness of his observations. One can appreciate more fully his courage in speaking out, guiding the *Encyclopedia* to completion despite an official ban, telling Catherine the Great that she should abandon autocracy for democracy, and the like. One of his essays was sufficiently bold in its criticism of the *ancien régime* to earn for him a severe reprimand from the police commissioner of Paris. With the publication of many of his best works, one can at last see his greatness as a writer as well as a thinker.

Even more important to the increasing appreciation of Diderot is the fact that his empiricism and skepticism match the modern mood. In his own day, Voltaire referred to him as Socrates, a title that fits well. Like Socrates, Diderot questioned the accepted wisdom of his day, risked much for his beliefs, and contributed to the intellectual progress of his age. Writing of eccentrics, Diderot remarked, "If one of them appears in company, he is like a piece of yeast which ferments and restores to everyone a portion of his natural liberty. He shakes and stirs things up; he calls forth praise and blame; he brings out the truth." In these lines from *Rameau's Nephew*, Diderot wrote his own epitaph.

Joseph Rosenblum

Thoughts on the Interpretation of Nature

Type of philosophy: Epistemology, philosophy of science,
First published: Pensées sur l'interprétation de la nature, 1754 (partial translation, 1927)
Principal ideas advanced:
◇ The rationalistic approach to nature is useless;

to study nature, one must proceed from facts by the use of methods of inference.

◇ Inferences should be checked by experiments; reflection and observation should supplement each other in empirical inquiry.

◇ By acts of interpretation, one succeeds in becoming more than a mere observer of nature; by drawing general conclusions from the order of things, one arrives at an understanding of the world's order.

◇ There is one causal principle operative in the world, but there are numerous elements, divisible into molecules that are themselves indivisible.

◇ Experimental physics is the basis of all true knowledge.

A small book consisting of fifty-eight numbered paragraphs, Diderot's *Thoughts on the Interpretation of Nature* was composed with a view to arousing young people's interest in scientific experimentation. It did not propose to instruct them but to excite them. "A more capable one than I will acquaint you with the forces of nature: it is sufficient if I have made you employ your own," he wrote in his dedicatory epistle, "To Young Men Who Are Disposed to Study Natural Philosophy."

That an essay of this sort was called for in France as late as the middle of the eighteenth century was not entirely because of religious censorship. Quite as much as Scholastic metaphysics, the rationalistic temper of Cartesian science had prejudiced French thinkers against the experimental methods that had been in vogue for a century in England. Voltaire's *Letters Concerning the English Nation* (1733), written after two years spent in exile in that country, had endeavored to acquaint the French people with such thinkers as John Locke and Isaac Newton. Diderot's *Thoughts on the Interpretation of Nature*, although not expressly mentioning the British authors, had a similar intention.

At a time when ability to read English was rare among the French, Diderot mastered the language and employed himself in translating English works for publication. The present work is clearly an echo of the work of philosopher Francis Bacon, whose *Novum Organum* (1620; English translation, 1802) also dealt with the interpretation of nature.

A New Approach to Nature

Diderot was convinced that the rationalistic approach to nature, which supposed that there is an exact correspondence between the processes of logic and the laws of the universe, held little promise. The followers of French philosopher René Descartes were accustomed to regarding geometry as the only true science because of the certitude of its results. They left to experimenters only the task of deciding that mathematical expressions happened in fact to fit the order of nature. In Diderot's opinion, this plan reversed the true procedure. Insofar as it merely elaborates the connection between ideas, mathematics is, he said, merely a branch of metaphysics. It is a kind of game that does nothing to increase understanding of the world. He acknowledged that mathematics had been put to good use by astronomers, but he believed that there was little more to be hoped for in that direction. He predicted that mathematics had reached its zenith and that a hundred years hence there would not be three great geometers in the whole of Europe.

On the other hand, Diderot found no promise in the methods employed by "naturalists" such as Carolus Linnaeus, whose system of classification he ridiculed because it placed humans in the class of quadrupeds and (admittedly) lacked means of distinguishing them from apes. He called such investigators "methodists," on the ground that they revised the world to fit their method, instead of revising their method to fit the world.

The proper method for studying nature, according to Diderot, was to proceed from facts by way of inference to further facts. Thoughts, he said, are significant only insofar as they are connected with external existence, either by an unbroken chain of experiments, or by an unbroken chain of inferences that starts from observation, or by a series of inferences interspersed with experiments "like weights along a thread hung by its two ends." He favored the latter. "Without these weights, the thread will be the plaything of the least breath of air."

Diderot distinguished three stages of experimental reasoning. First is the observation of nature, by which one becomes acquainted with the facts; second is reflection, by which the facts are combined in the mind; third is experiment, by which the combination is tested with reference to further facts. In a simile reminiscent of Bacon, he said that the scientist is like a bee: he must constantly pass back and forth from reflection to the senses. The bee would wear out its wings to no purpose if it failed to return to the hive with its burden, but it would accumulate only useless piles of wax if it were not instructed how to fashion its harvest into honeycomb.

In contrast to the facile optimism with which many enthusiasts for science have written about method, Diderot recognized that the path of the experimenter is straight and narrow and that there are few who find it. The mysterious combination of gifts that makes up "creative genius" intrigued him. People who combine the insight necessary for fruitful observation with powers of reflection and with the skill and patience required for fruitful experiment are exceedingly rare, he said; and he saw nothing that could be done about it. Like a maladroit politician who finds it impossible to take hold of a situation, the average person can spend an entire life observing, say, insects, whereas another takes a passing glance and discovers a whole new order of life.

It was the hope of Diderot that experimenters could learn a lesson from skilled craftspeople, who, without any formal teaching but purely as a result of long experience in handling materials, are able to "smell out" the course of nature and adapt their methods to its ways. As the son of a master cutler, Diderot retained throughout his life a high regard for technical skills, as numerous articles and engravings in the famous *Encyclopédie* (1751-1772; partial translation, *Selected Essays from the Encyclopedy*, 1772; complete translation, *Encyclopedia*, 1965), which he edited, attest. The workers themselves, he said, believe that they divine the ways of nature through a kind of "familiar spirit." However, he explained their gift as no more than the faculty of perceiving analogies between the qualities of objects that have certain things in common and a massive knowledge of the ways things affect one another when brought into combination. With this insight into the workings of the craftsperson's mind, the experimenter should be able not merely to equal but to surpass the person in ability.

Diderot would have some sympathy with the person who said that genius is 99 percent perspiration and only 1 percent inspiration, and he recognized that discoveries are often happy accidents, in which error and folly have a share. To make his point, he adapted the story of the man who on his deathbed told his lazy sons that there was treasure buried in the orchard. They spent the summer digging it over. Though they failed to find the object of their greed, they did receive an unusually good crop of fruit. So, said Diderot, experimentation commonly fails to unlock the secrets of the universe in the way people expect, although it yields a reward in pragmatic truth.

Diderot continued the parable. The next year one of the boys told his brothers that in the course of digging over the orchard he had noticed a peculiar depression in one corner. With his mind still on treasure, he convinced them that because the prize did not lie near the surface, it must have been hidden in the bowels of the earth. In this way, he persuaded them to join him in the strenuous task of sinking a deep shaft. After many days, they were at the point of abandoning the project when they came upon not the treasure that they had hoped for but an ancient mine, which they began to work with profit. "Such," concluded Diderot, "is sometimes the outcome of experiments suggested by a combination of observation with rationalist theories. In this way chemists and geometers, while trying to solve problems which are probably unsolvable, arrive at discoveries more important than the solutions which they sought."

Interpreting Nature

The strength and originality of Diderot's book has sometimes been said to lie in the philosopher's peculiar ability to "smell out" directions that were far beyond the intellectual horizon of the typical eighteenth century philosopher. This gift appears not only in his insights into experimental method but also in his own "interpretation of nature," for Diderot was not a positivist and had no intention of limiting human knowledge to the results of observation and experimentation.

One of the main differences between the observer of nature and the interpreter of nature is that the latter takes as his point of departure the place where the former leaves off. He conjectures from that which is known that which is yet to be known. He draws from the order of things conclusions abstract and general which have for him all the evidence of sensible and particular truths. And he arrives at the very essence of the world's order.

Thoughts on the Interpretation of Nature includes several paragraphs devoted to Diderot's own "conjectures" as to the direction that science should take—suggestions such as "that magnetism and electricity depend upon the same causes." It also includes an ironical analysis of the philosophy of Pierre-Louis Moreau de Maupertuis, whose *Système de la nature* (1751; system of nature) had recently appeared. Diderot agreed, on the whole, with Maupertuis's position, and he assumed a critical air in order to develop further implications of the theory while professing to be scandalized at the outcome. Diderot had already spent three months in prison for advanced thinking and had learned to envelop his speculations in studied ambiguity.

Perhaps the "thought" that governs all the rest of Diderot's "interpretations of nature" is that when people discover that every event must have a cause, they have reached the frontier of metaphysical knowledge. There is no point in speculating about any higher cause, nor in asking "why" things are constituted the way they are. At an earlier stage of his development, Diderot had embraced the deistic account of origins that he found in the third earl of Shaftesbury's *Characteristicks of Men, Manners, Opinions, Times* (1711). In the present work, he took his stand on the side of what today would be called naturalism, which at that time was called Spinozism.

Elements and Evolution

It seemed to Diderot that the possibility of experimental science rested on the assumption that there is only one causal principle operative in the world. However, he was so much impressed by the variety that nature exhibits at every level that he shied away from the view that the world is made of a uniform substance. Instead, he favored the materialistic version of Gottfried Wilhelm Leibniz's philosophy suggested in Maupertuis's book. In this view, every "element" that goes to make up nature is essentially different from every other. Each element is divisible into molecules, themselves incapable of further division. Moreover, the molecules must be thought of as "organic," endowed with the rudiments of desire and aversion, of feeling and thought. Only thus could one account for the whole range of nature.

In his oblique fashion, Diderot gave thanks for the biblical account of Creation. If people had been left to their own speculations, he said, the best they could do would be to infer that the elements of living beings had been mingled with other elements from all eternity in the total mass, and that they have joined together to form beasts and people "merely because it was possible for it to happen!" He allowed himself to speculate that a species of animals might come into being, reach maturity, and perish—just as happens in the case of individual members of a species. Giving full rein to his imagination, he suggested that living beings must have passed through infinite stages of development, acquiring in turn "movement, sensation, imagination, thought, reflection, consciousness, sentiments, passions, signs, gestures, sounds, articulate sounds, speech, laws, sciences, and arts," with millions of years between each of these acquisitions—that perhaps still other developments are yet to come, of which we are ignorant; that the process may come to a standstill; and that eventually the product of these transformations may disappear from nature forever. "Religion," he said, "spares us all these wanderings and the mental labor which it would require to follow them out."

Diderot's interest in biological evolution was not merely of this speculative sort. Familiar with comparative anatomy, he observed that every one of the quadrupeds is patterned on the same "prototype," that nature merely lengthens, shortens, modifies, or multiplies the same organs. "Imagine the fingers of a hand bound together and the material of the nails increased to envelop the whole: in place of a man's hand you would have a horse's hoof." Such considerations led him to conclude that there is no real division between the animal kingdoms. Nature, he said, is like a woman who loves to vary her costume. She does not require many different outfits because she knows how, by varying a sleeve or a collar, adding a pleat or letting down a hem, to achieve an infinite number of effects while using the same pattern.

Humanity and Nature

Diderot's greatest boldness, however, lay in the view that he took of humanity's role in nature and of the role of science in human affairs. The Copernican revolution had convinced enlightened thinkers that the earth is not the center of the universe, but the majority of them continued to think of humans as occupying a favored position. In rejecting deism and turning back to the more expansive tradition of philosophers Giordano Bruno and Baruch Spinoza, Diderot sharply challenged the optimism of his day, particularly as it pertained to the advancement of learning.

In principle, Diderot admitted that, just as mathematicians, in examining the properties of a curve, find the same properties present under different aspects, so experimental physicists may eventually find a single hypothesis that covers such different properties as weight, elasticity, electricity, and magnetism. However, how many intermediary hypotheses, he exclaimed, had to be found before the gaps could be filled in. Nor could there be any shortcut, such as exists in mathematics, where intermediary propositions can be arrived at by deduction. On the contrary, he saw a deplorable tendency for various branches of science to build mutually exclusive systems of explanation. Classic mechanics was such a system. Diderot said it was a labyrinth in which people must wander without hopes of ever reaching understanding with other sciences.

Diderot expressed most vividly the disparity between our fragmentary knowledge and the vastness and variety of nature. "When one begins to compare the infinite multitude of the phenomena of nature with the limits of our understanding and the weakness of our faculties, can one be surprised that our work lags and frequently drags to a halt, and that all which we possess is a few broken and isolated links of the great chain of being?" Suppose that experimental philosophy should continue for several centuries. Where is the mind that could take it all in? How many volumes would be required to record it? How far would any one person be able to read? Are people not, he asked, "as foolish as the men of Babel? We know the infinite distance that separates earth from heaven, yet we do not cease to build the tower." A confusion of tongues is bound to result that will lead to an abandoning of the effort.

This pessimism was directed against barren intellectualism, the attempt to understand the world in abstract terms, and finds its counterpart in Voltaire's *Candide: Ou, L'Optimisme* (1759; *Candide: Or, All for the Best*, 1759), where wisdom is said to consist in cultivating one's garden instead of speculating about matters too high for one. Diderot complained that people are content to live in hovels while raising uninhabitable palaces that reach to the clouds. It was his hope that experimental science would alter that condition and would bring into being vast stores of knowledge that would alleviate the human condition. However, he predicted that when this change had come about, people would lose interest in science just as they had (in his opinion) already lost interest in geometry:

> Utility circumscribes everything. It is utility that, in a few centuries, will set the limits to experimental physics as it is on the point of doing to geometry. I accord several centuries to this study because the sphere of its utility is infinitely more extensive than that of any abstract science, and because it is undeniably the basis of all true knowledge.

Jean Faurot

Additional Reading

Blum, Carol. *Diderot: The Virtue of a Philosopher*. New York: Viking Press, 1974. Focuses on Denis Diderot's concern for the moral life and his intellectual quest to define what such an existence involves. A well-written study that draws on biography, letters, and published writings.

Bremner, Geoffrey. *Order and Chance: The Pattern of Diderot's Thought*. Cambridge, England: Cambridge University Press, 1983. Bremner seeks a pattern in Diderot's thought and concludes that, in his best works, order and chance are complementary concepts. Interesting insights, suitable for advanced undergraduates.

Brewer, Daniel. *The Discourse of Enlightenment in Eighteenth-Century France: Diderot and the Art of Philosophizing*. Cambridge Studies in French, No. 42. Cambridge, England: Cambridge University Press, 1993. This somewhat difficult study examines the interplay between critical knowledge and its representation. Examining Diderot's work in philosophy, science, the fine arts, and literature, Brewer points to its remarkable similarity to aspects of modern critical theory.

Crocker, Lester G. *Diderot's Chaotic Order: Approach to Synthesis*. Princeton, N.J.: Princeton University Press, 1974. Sets forth the view that Diderot dealt with order and disorder as categories of experience and modes of thought. Argues that, for Diderot, the tension between these two opposites constitutes a universal process. For advanced undergraduates.

Fellows, Otis. *Diderot*. Boston: Twayne, 1977. This chronological overview touches briefly on almost all of Diderot's works. It stresses Diderot's modernity, traces the evolution of his thought, and imparts some of the excitement of his writing. Contains a helpful annotated bibliography.

France, Peter. *Diderot*. New York: Oxford University Press, 1983. A good, short introduction concentrating on Diderot's ideas. Arranged topically, it covers Diderot's political, social, and aesthetic views, and includes a useful annotated bibliography.

Rex, Walter E. *Diderot's Counterpoints: The Dynamics of Contrariety in His Major Works*. Oxford: Voltaire Foundation, 1998. This books offers some history and criticism of Diderot's work.

Simon, Julia. *Mass Enlightenment: Critical Studies in Rousseau and Diderot*. Albany: State University of New York Press, 1995. An examination of the social and political thought in the work of Rousseau and Diderot.

Umdank, Jack, and Herbert Joseph, eds. *Diderot: Digression and Dispersion, a Bicentennial Tribute*. Lexington, Ky.: French Forum, 1984. Presents nineteen essays that cover Diderot's many activities and interests. In their diversity, the contributions mirror the editors' view that Diderot did not seek unity but rather regarded diversity as the rule of nature.

Wilson, Arthur M. *Diderot*. New York: Oxford University Press, 1972. The definitive biography. Places Diderot within the context of the Enlightenment and considers the development of his ideas on such matters as religion, emotion and reason, order and diversity, determinism and chance.

Joseph Rosenblum, updated by Grant A. Marler

Wilhelm Dilthey

Combining major aspects of German idealism and British empiricism, Dilthey formulated humanistic methods for understanding and interpreting human behavior. He is known for his work to establish a distinction between the methodology of the humanities from that of the natural sciences.

Principal philosophical works: *Grundriss der Logik und des Systems der philosophischen Wissenschaften; Für Vorlesungen*, 1865; *Das Lebel Schleiermachers*, 1867-1870; *Einleitung in die Geisteswissenschaften*, 1883 (*Introduction to the Human Sciences*, 1988); "Ideen über eine beschreibende und zergliedende Psychologie," 1894 ("Ideas Concerning a Descriptive and Analytic Psychology," 1977); *Das Erlebnis und die Dichtung*, 1905 (partial translation in *Poetry and Experience*, 1985); *Der Aufbau der geschichtlichen Welt in den Geisteswissenschaften*, 1910 (and related writings, 1905-1910; partial translation, *Meaning in History: W. Dilthey's Thoughts on History and Society*, 1961); *Gesammelte Schriften*, 1914-1990; *Briefwechsel zwischen Wilhelm Dilthey und dem Grafen Paul Yorck von Wartenbrug, 1877-1897*, 1923; *Von deutscher Dichtung und Musik: Aus den Studien zur Geschichte des deutschen Geistes*, 1933; *Die grosse Phantasiedichtung und andere Studien zur vergleichenden Literaturgeschichte*, 1954 (partial translation, *Selected Writings*, 1976); *Selected Works*, 1985-1996.

Born: November 19, 1833; Biebrich am Rhein, near Wiesbaden, Duchy of Nassau (now in Germany)

Died: September 30, 1911; Seis am Schlern, near Bozen, Austrian Tirol, Austro-Hungarian Empire

Early Life

Wilhelm Dilthey's father was a liberal Reformed clergyman with a strong interest in history, philosophy, and politics. His mother was the daughter of a conductor and was talented in music. Both parents had a profound influence on his development. In addition to his work in philosophy and history, he wrote many essays on music and always enjoyed playing the piano. After completing his secondary education in Wiesbaden, he intended to study theology and to become a clergyman. In 1852, he enrolled at the University of Heidelberg, and the following year he moved to Berlin. As a student, he regularly worked from twelve to fourteen hours a day, and he was recognized as a competent scholar in Greek and Hebrew, as well as the classic works of literature, theology, and philosophy. Although especially interested in German idealists such as Immanuel Kant and Georg Wilhelm Friedrich Hegel, he was also attracted to the history of science and British empiricists such as John Stuart Mill.

Dilthey gradually determined that he lacked the religious faith that would be necessary for a career as a clergyman, and he decided to become a university professor. He was supported by his parents during his long period of study, and his letters of the time, later published by his daughter, demonstrate an extremely close relationship with his family. In 1860, Dilthey was invited to complete an edition of philosopher Friedrich Schleiermacher's correspondence, and he was awarded two prizes for an essay on Schleiermacher's hermeneutics. In 1864, he was awarded a doctorate for his dissertation on Schleiermacher's ethics, and his "habilitation writing" on ethical theory was also approved, which meant that he was qualified to lecture in a university.

Life's Work

After he completed his doctorate, Dilthey spent the rest of his life as a respected and dedicated university teacher and scholar. He continued to work grueling hours, and although he published only a few books in his lifetime, his published articles and unpublished drafts totaled seventeen volumes. In 1866, Dilthey was appointed to a chair of philosophy at Basel, and for the first time he was free of financial worries. At Basel, he was influenced by the Renaissance historian Jacob Burckhardt and began a serious study of psychology and physiology. He was called to the University of Kiel in 1868, and he remained there for three years. During this period, Dilthey spent much of his time doing research for a two-volume biography about Schleiermacher.

In 1867-1870, Dilthey finally published the first volume of the biography, which was quite detailed and massive. In writing the biography, Dilthey developed a thesis about the reciprocal interaction between a strong-willed individual and his or her environment. Although largely shaped by cultural and social forces, a strong-willed individual could nevertheless exert a powerful influence on the environment. In order to illustrate the relationship of the parts to the whole, the biography examined matters such as religious groups, philosophical works, friendships, and even cities that were relevant to Schleiermacher's life. Because Dilthey believed in the interdependence of empirical and philosophic activities, moreover, he did not believe that his work in intellectual history and biography was separate from his work in philosophy. These themes, expressed in a variety of ways, would constantly reappear in Dilthey's theoretical writings. Although Dilthey continued to do research and write drafts for the promised second volume, his interests kept going in other directions, and he never completed the ambitious project. However, the first volume firmly established his academic reputation, and in 1871, he was called to a more prestigious position at Breslau.

Because Dilthey cherished his privacy, only limited information is available about his personal life. In 1870, he was engaged for less than a year, but the engagement ended abruptly after he discovered that his fiancée was the mother of an illegitimate child. At the age of forty-one, in 1874, he married Katharine Püttzmann, and the couple eventually had three children, including Clara, who became his helper and confidante. Although the couple generally seemed happy, they had their disagreements. Dilthey wanted to work all the time, but his wife was more interested in entertainment and travel. Fortunately for his work, Dilthey did not have to worry about any financial distractions, and he was able to hire enough servants to take care of daily tasks such as cleaning and cooking.

While at Breslau, Dilthey's study of Mill and the positivists led him to make a sharp dichotomy between the sciences of nature (*Naturwissenschaften*) and the various studies dealing with human reality (*Geisteswissenschaften*). At the same time, he recognized a fundamental similarity among all the human studies, including fields as

Wilhelm Dilthey. *(Library of Congress)*

513

diverse as history, sociology, economics, psychology, philosophy, and poetry. In 1875, he published his first essay devoted to this issue. In 1882, Dilthey was called to Berlin to occupy the prestigious chair of philosophy that Georg Wilhelm Friedrich Hegel had earlier held.

Shortly after moving to Berlin, Dilthey published the first volume of his influential *Introduction to the Human Sciences*. After devoting two-thirds of the book to the historical emancipation of the human intellect from religion and metaphysics, Dilthey sketched a general approach to the epistemology of the human sciences. Influenced by both idealists and empirical thinkers, he argued that knowledge is acquired by "lived experience" (*Erlebnis*), although this experience is mediated through self-reflections. He then attempted to show that knowledge in all the human sciences was based on the same mental processes. Although willing to examine reality from different perspectives, he was seeking a consistency in approach that would provide for objective knowledge in all aspects of human affairs, and at this point in his career, he had a great deal of confidence that psychologists such as Wilhelm Wundt could provide such a foundation. Dilthey had no difficulty in demonstrating the interconnectedness of the various human sciences, but he was unable to establish much methodological consistency among them. He hoped that in his second volume, he would be able to incorporate all his disparate ideas into a systematic and dependable method for arriving at objective knowledge, including a "critique of historical understanding." Despite several drafts and many sleepless nights, Dilthey would never resolve numerous contradictions, and his anticipated second volume was never completed.

During the period from 1883 to about 1896, Dilthey wrote a number of historical and philosophical essays devoted to the topics of educational psychology, ethics, and aesthetics. In an 1888 essay about "the possibility of a universally valid pedagogical science," he emphasized the importance of volition and purposiveness to human development. In 1894, he wrote a controversial essay that outlined his ideas concerning "descriptive and analytic psychology," expressing a strong skepticism about the ability of psychology to provide valid explanations. Rather, he proposed that psychology should have the more modest goal of providing descriptions about the structure and development of the human psyche. This essay appeared to anticipate Dilthey's later methodological writings about "understanding" and hermeneutics.

Philosopher Wilhelm Windelband's seminal lecture of 1894, "History and the Natural Sciences," initiated an important epistemological controversy between Dilthey and the neo-Kantians. Windelband argued that Dilthey's distinction between the natural sciences and the human sciences was inadequate, especially when applied to psychology. Rather than Dilthey's subject-matter distinction, the crucial distinction was between the "nomothetic" sciences and the "idiographic" sciences, with the former establishing lawful uniformities and the latter describing unique historical patterns. Responding to Windelband in his 1895 essay "On Comparative Psychology," Dilthey insisted that psychology was indeed one of the human sciences, and he advocated a psychology based on reflections of "inner experience." More significant, he rejected any rigid nomothetic-idiographic separation, and he argued that historical material could become meaningful only when considered in connection with general regularities. The dispute with Windelband apparently had an impact on Dilthey's thinking. In his later works, he showed less interest in psychology and acknowledged a distinction between descriptive historical studies and the "systematic human studies," such as economics, which established causal regularities.

Although the concept of "understanding" (*Verstehen*) had appeared in some of Dilthey's early writings, it was following the Windelband dispute that Dilthey increasingly emphasized this concept in place of psychology. By the term "understanding," Dilthey basically referred to the process by which one person attempts to understand the motives and activities of another person. He assumed that all "life assertions" were products of cognition within the human mind and that all human minds were similar in their fundamental structures, despite great differences in beliefs, capacities, and knowledge. By carefully examining the words and actions of another person, therefore, it was possible that the observer would be able to infer the "inner" experience of another person, whether dead or alive. People share many of the same perceptions and subjective experiences (*Erlebnis*), and this allows one person to empathetically feel (*Einfuhlung*) someone else's experiences. Thus, it was even possible to relive (*nacherleben*) such experiences.

From 1896 to 1905, Dilthey devoted the bulk of his efforts to writing works of intellectual history and biography, with an emphasis on German thinkers of the eighteenth and nineteenth centuries. Topics included Gottfried Wilhelm Leibniz and his age, Frederick the Great, leaders of the Enlightenment, scientific historians, and the intellectual development of the young Hegel. His popular book *Das Erlebnis und die Dichtung* (1905; partial translation in *Poetry and Experience*, 1985) consisted of literary biographies of four romantic writers. Dilthey's historical studies provide concrete illustrations of what he meant by *Verstehen*/understanding and interpretation, and he often referred to these studies as "historical research with a philosophical aim."

In the middle of his historical period, Dilthey published his essay "Entstehung der Hermeneutik" (1900; "The Rise of Hermeneutics," 1996), in which he sketched the methodological approach that he would advocate during the last decade of his life. Influenced by Schleiermacher's hermeneutic theories, the basis idea of the essay was that understanding others should begin with an interpretation of outward expressions, especially oral and written communications. Dilthey also emphasized the concept of a "hermeneutic circle," meaning that the parts make sense only in terms of the whole. Every human expression, therefore, should be interpreted from the perspective of its historical context. Apparently Dilthey meant for his hermeneutics to provide objective balance to the subjectivity inherent in "understanding," and he conceived of the two methods as complementary to one another.

After his retirement in 1905, Dilthey returned to the task of attempting a "critique of historical understanding." He conceived of his 1910 essay, *Der Aufbau der geschichtlichen Welt in den Geisteswissenschaften* (1910; and related writings, 1905-1910; partial translation in *Meaning in History: W. Dilthey's Thoughts on History and Society*, 1961), as a continuation of his 1883 book, *Introduction to the Human Sciences*. In contrast to the earlier book,

however, the essay did not emphasize the importance of psychology, and it reflected his later theories about understanding and interpretation. In addition, Dilthey appeared less certain about the possibility of neutral descriptions, and he gave more explicit recognition of the role of the observer's presuppositions in constructing interpretations. He continued, nevertheless, to insist that objectively valid interpretations of human motives were somehow possible.

Dilthey continued to work on some of his unfinished projects, but at the age of seventy-seven he died unexpectedly from an infection while vacationing in the Tirol.

Influence
In view of Dilthey's emphasis on interpretation, it is interesting to observe the extent to which his own writings are open to numerous interpretations. It is not difficult to find tensions and even contradictions in his works, and he sometimes tended to write in a rather loose and tentative style. For this reason, scholarly studies of Dilthey disagree about basic issues, such as whether there was continuity in his thought during his long career. At the same time, readers with a variety of viewpoints find that Dilthey's works are full of provocative and challenging ideas, and almost everyone is able both to agree and to disagree with various aspects of his works. As a result, few people have considered themselves to be disciples of Dilthey, but different aspects of his writings have clearly influenced numerous writers and intellectual movements of the twentieth century.

Any listing of Dilthey's influences would have to include Edmund Husserl's methods of phenomenology, Max Weber's combination of empiricism and ideal types in sociology, Martin Heidegger's version of existentialism, Hans-Georg Gadamer's philosophical approach to hermeneutics, R. G. Collingwood's approach to "reenactment" in historical analysis, and Karl Popper's method of "situation logic." It should be emphasized, however, that most of these writers have sharply disagreed with many of Dilthey's ideas. Although his project for a life philosophy has enjoyed some appeal, he is primarily remembered for his methodological theories about "understanding" and hermeneutics.

Although humanistically oriented historians have often found that these methods are useful to their craft, philosophers and social scientists have tended to exploit Dilthey's ideas as a springboard for moving in other directions.

Thomas T. Lewis

Meaning in History

W. Dilthey's Thoughts on History and Society

Type of philosophy: Epistemology, philosophy of history

First published: Der Aufbau der geschichtlichen Welt in den Geisteswissenschaften (1910) and related writings, 1905-1910 (partial translation, 1961)

Principal ideas advanced:

◇ The sciences that investigate nature are fundamentally different from the human studies such as history, philosophy, economics, poetry, music, and psychology.

◇ Humans are able to understand one another because of shared experiences in life and because of the human capacity to feel empathetically the subjective experiences of others.

◇ The natural scientists attempt to "explain" lawlike phenomena of nature, whereas students of the human studies seek to "understand" the activity of the human mind.

◇ Interpretations of human behavior must take into account the total cultural and historical environment, with an appreciation for the relationships between the parts and the whole.

◇ Critical hermeneutic methods based on understanding a person within a historical context can result in objectively true interpretations.

◇ Humans are historical beings, and all knowledge is acquired through experience rather than introspection.

After publishing the first volume of *Einleitung in die Geisteswissenschaften* (1883; *Introduction to the Human Sciences*, 1988), Wilhelm Dilthey intended to write a second volume that was to include an analysis of the nature of historical understanding. (*Verstehen*) Because of other projects, however, he was never able to complete the sec-

ond volume. After 1896, Dilthey began to emphasize the method of using empathy in human understanding, and about 1900, he combined this approach with hermeneutics, or the systematic interpretation of human expressions. From about 1905 until his death, Dilthey used these two methods to attempt to produce an analysis of the nature of historical understanding. As part of this effort, he presented his essay, "De Aufbau der geschichtlichen Welt in den Geisteswissenschaften" (the construction of the historical world in the human sciences) to the Prussian Academy in January, 1910, and the essay was published in the academy's proceedings later that year. After his death, Dilthey's collaborators included this essay in a volume of his collected works, which contained other writing on historical methods. In 1961, Hans Peter Richman produced an English translation of the most significant parts of this volume, *Meaning in History*, a relatively concise introduction to the key ideas in Dilthey's mature thought.

An Understanding of History

Dilthey's goal in *Meaning in History* is to formulate a valid "critique of historical reason." By the term "historical reason," he referred to the process of understanding the phenomena of human history, and he did not mean to suggest that history had any ultimate purpose or intelligence of its own. He hoped that his work would be a continuation of Immanuel Kant's critiques of pure and practical reason. As a strong partisan of the historical school, Dilthey assumed that an objective understanding of history was entirely possible, and therefore much of his effort is directed at answering the epistemological question: How is it possible to acquire understanding in human history? His answer was that the human mind is able to understand what other human minds have done and created. He wrote: "The fact that the investigator of history is the same as the one who makes it, is the first condition which makes scientific history possible."

In arguing that historians were able to produce "scientific" knowledge, Dilthey meant that they could write statements about historical reality that were objectively true, even in regard to the motives of other people. His epistemology was tacitly based upon a correspondence theory of truth. In contrast to the natural sciences, the study of history dealt with unique and nonrepeating phenomena, with motivated choices as the effective causes for most human actions. Thus, historians were limited in their capacity to explain events according to established laws or theories. At the same time, however, historians could formulate and utilize general knowledge based upon certain regularities of human nature. Dilthey did not appear to appreciate sufficiently the inherent limits of all interpretations of motives, especially when using a subjective approach such as empathetic understanding. Despite his strong aversion to historical relativism, Dilthey did allow for some pluralism of perspectives by different observers, but he might have further strengthened his case by recognizing a distinction between absolute truth and verisimilitude, or the approximation of truth.

Dilthey looked upon history as encompassing the entire sphere of human life, including both the present and the past. While accepting the principles of Darwinian evolution, Dilthey was not especially interested in the biological nature of humans, and his conception of history was limited to the activities of *Homo sapiens*. Because his specialties were philosophy and the history of ideas, Dilthey tended to approach history from something of an elitist perspective, and he had only limited concern about the historical experiences of the inarticulate masses.

Meaning and Hermeneutics

Reflecting his optimistic temperament, Dilthey believed that all life is meaningful in the sense that individuals find meaning by acting in pursuit of their goals. A confirmed skeptic in matters of religion and metaphysics, he did not see any evidence that a meaning resides in history apart from human consciousness. One of the goals of the historian was to understand and interpret meaning within the minds of the historical actors. Although one human could not directly penetrate into the mind of another, the outward expressions of an individual "originated as the expression of a mental content and thus helps towards the understanding of that content." As examples of such outward expressions, Dilthey pointed to the poetry of Johann Wolfgang von Goethe, the scientific writings of Sir Isaac New-

ton, and the politics of Otto von Bismarck. Dilthey did not deny that people sometimes were deceitful or unaware of their own motives, but he apparently believed that a careful study of the total context of an outward expression would allow a thoughtful observer to detect instances of conscious or unconscious deception.

Recognizing that each normal person finds meaning in a complex pattern that is unique to that individual, Dilthey analyzed meaning, dividing it into various categories. In contrast to Kant's categories of "pure reason," Dilthey considered that all categories of meaning were derived from life experiences. Such categories, which were perhaps unlimited in number, include general concepts such as value, purpose, development, and power. The content of history includes both individual and social memories, and both individuals and societies remember those experiences that are relevant to "a conception of the meaning of life." In human life, moreover, the parts are significant only if they are relevant to the whole, and "the whole is only there for us when it becomes comprehensible through its parts."

This recognition of the interaction between the parts and the whole was one of the major components of Dilthey's hermeneutics. The process of interpreting a human activity was like interpreting the meaning of a sentence. Often words have different meanings; therefore, sometimes a word's meaning is inferred from the context of the entire sentence, while the understanding of any sentence depends on knowing the meaning of the individual words. He called this interaction, which operates as a kind of shuttlecock movement, a "hermeneutic circle." Dilthey also believed in a similar interaction between the subject and object, which presumably facilitated historical interpretations that were objectively true.

The Importance of Biography

Because of his concentration on individual meaning, Dilthey's view of history naturally included an emphasis on the values of biography and autobiography. Believing that a person acquires self-knowledge from the study of other lives, he wrote that "the possibility of scientific biography lies in the fact that the individual does not face a limitless play of forces in the historical world." In other words, one person can understand another because all people share common life experiences and similar emotions, although in vastly different combinations. Even a militant atheist, for example, might identify with the appeal of Saint Augustine's religious experiences. Although recognizing Thomas Carlyle's contribution to modern historiography, Dilthey never suggested that history is only the story of individual persons. Rather, he insisted that one cannot understand an individual apart from the totality of the historical context. One cannot begin to understand Bismarck, for instance, without a broad knowledge of Prussian politics and social institutions.

Because one of Dilthey's long-standing goals was to formulate a "philosophy of life," his main objective in history was to know and understand individual people, and he was concerned about factual data only when they had meaning for human lives. Thus, he looked upon autobiography as one of the major building blocks of history. Although he recognized that autobiographies rarely expressed scientific truth, they nevertheless presented windows into the cognitive experiences of others. Because he had earlier tried to organize worldviews into a logical typology, it is not surprising that Dilthey classifies autobiographies into three ideal types: Saint Augustine's autobiography as an example of religious meditation, Rousseau's as an example of self-justification, and those of people like Goethe, used to defend their historical importance.

Understanding and Interpretation

Despite his radical skepticism in religion and metaphysics, Dilthey was certainly not a materialist, for he believed that all historical outcomes were the products of the human spirit (or mind). Rejecting pantheism, he saw no evidence of any transcendent intelligence, such as Hegel's notion of a world spirit. Throughout *Meaning in History*, Dilthey uses the term "objective mind," but by this term, he really meant no more than the concrete realizations of human thinking, as expressed in things such as works of art, scientific achievements, or political institutions. Influenced by Giambattista Vico, he emphasized that one human mind could understand what other minds had created, and this assumption was ba-

sic to his epistemological method. He insisted, "Understanding and interpretation is the method used throughout the human studies, and all functions unite in it. It contains all the truths of the human studies."

In writing about the processes of understanding and interpretation, Dilthey often appears to have described the common sense of a reasonably intelligent and educated person, with or without any formal training in philosophy. In fact, competent historians since Herodotus have always practiced many of Dilthey's suggested methods, whether or not they have spent much time in reflecting about the methodology and epistemology of the historical craft. Apparently Dilthey recognized that much of what he was writing was simply a description of common sense at its best, but he seemed to assume that a systematic analysis of methodology could help historians do a better job of understanding and interpreting human activity. The same principles, of course, would also be used by lawyers, sociologists, journalists, and even novelists.

Numerous critics have noted a basic contradiction in Dilthey's thought. Horrified by the notion of relativism, he insisted on historical truth rather than mere opinion. On the other hand, his methods of understanding and interpretation relied upon the subjective evaluation of the fallible observer. Reflecting the climate of opinion at that time, Dilthey underestimated the extent to which the beliefs and paradigms of an observer will help determine what the observer sees, and he did not really consider the role of unconscious motivations in making interpretations. Although Dilthey's prescribed methods are a reasonable means for arriving at verisimilitude, it is difficult to see how such methods can achieve the degree of certainty that he demanded.

The Philosopher's Influence

Dilthey is primarily remembered for his methodological approaches to understanding (*Verstehen*) and hermeneutics, and these two aspects of his work are most clearly articulated in his later works, including *Meaning in History*. His ideas have had their greatest impact on philosophers. Although it is unlikely that many historians and social scientists have spent much time reading Dilthey, these scholars often have general notions about his views on methodology. Scholars with humanistic sympathies usually are attracted to such methods. On the other hand, social scientists who refer to themselves as behaviorists and positivists usually aspire to emulating the methods of the natural sciences, and they are more impressed with quantitative data than with the subjective understandings of motives. In describing Dilthey's methods, unfortunately, there is often a tendency to present an oversimplified summary. It is commonly overlooked, for example, that Dilthey was a flexible thinker who was open to a pluralism of different methods, including the use of statistics whenever appropriate.

In the twentieth century, Dilthey's greatest influence was on German and European thinkers, but he also had considerable influence in North America. There appears to be a consensus that he made important contributions to the intellectual movements of phenomenology, existentialism, critical theory, and postmodern hermeneutics. Often these movements have tended to discard his optimism, his positive views of the Enlightenment, and especially his concern for objective truth. Dilthey never intended to establish a distinct philosophical school, and not many thinkers have referred to themselves as his disciples. Sometimes the ideas in *Meaning in History* appear obvious and even commonsensical to contemporary readers. One possible explanation is that Dilthey's ideas have filtered down to the educated public over the years, but an alternative view is that he was simply describing approaches that are natural and efficient means for trying to understand the thoughts and actions of other people.

Thomas T. Lewis

Additional Reading

Bambach, Charles. *Heidegger, Dilthey, and the Crisis of Historicism.* Ithaca, N.Y.: Cornell University Press, 1995. Although he does not establish a "crisis of historicism," Bambach provides a coherent treatment of Wilhelm Dilthey's thought, recognizing a continuing contradiction between his historical view of "truth" and his demand for objective knowledge.

Ermarth, Michael. *Wilhelm Dilthey: The Critique of Historical Reason.* Chicago: University of Chicago Press, 1978. Ermarth emphasizes the continuity in Dilthey's thought and interprets Dilthey's project as an attempt to synthesize idealism and positivism, a perspective that Ermarch calls "ideal-realism."

Hodges, Herbert. *The Philosophy of Wilhelm Dilthey.* London: Routledge & Kegan Paul, 1952. Despite its age, this remains one of the most readable and scholarly studies of Dilthey's thought. Especially good on his relationship to other philosophers.

Hughes, H. Stuart. *Consciousness and Society: The Reconstruction of European Social Thought, 1890-1930.* New York: Random House, 1958. A standard work that places Dilthey in the context of "a revolt against positivism." Although sympathetic, Hughes concludes that Dilthey attempted "a synthesis too mighty for the human mind" and that he was unable to overcome the "relativist implications" of his methods and ideas.

Iggers, George. *The German Conception of History.* Middletown, Vt.: Wesleyan University Press, 1968. Highly recommended for readers who wish a broad historical perspective, with an excellent summary of Dilthey's thought. Iggers emphasizes the subjective character of his interpretive methods.

Makkreel, Rudolf. *Dilthey: Philosopher of the Human Studies.* Princeton, N.J.: Princeton University Press, 1975. Emphasizes Dilthey's theories of aesthetics and the imagination, and argues that his views on historical understanding are in the Kantian tradition. Includes a good account of the dispute with Windelband and Rickert. Not for beginners.

Owensby, Jacob. *Dilthey and the Narrative of History.* Ithaca, N.Y.: Cornell University Press, 1994. While accepting some poststructural criticisms, Owensby defends Dilthey's hermeneutics as undiminished. The first part of the book has an excellent account of Dilthey's career and a useful guide to secondary literature. Parts of the book are rather vague and abstract.

Plantinga, Theodore. *Historical Understanding in the Thought of Wilhelm Dilthey.* Toronto: University of Toronto Press, 1980. Divides Dilthey's development into three periods, criticizes his attempts at psychology in the 1890's, and is highly favorable toward his approach to interpreting life experiences during the post-1900 years. Not the place for beginning students of Dilthey to start.

Richman, Hans Peter. *Wilhelm Dilthey: Pioneer of the Human Studies*. Berkeley: University of California Press, 1979. Richman, a philosopher who has devoted many years to Dilthey's writings, presents a very readable introduction. Richman sometimes gives too much attention to commonplace ideas and probably exaggerates the continuity in Dilthey's thought. Recommended for the general reader.

Tuttle, Howard. *Wilhelm Dilthey's Philosophy of Historical Understanding: A Critical Analysis*. Leiden: E. J. Brill, 1969. In this small but perceptive account, Tuttle argues that Dilthey's methods of understanding and interpretation, while somewhat useful in biography, are ambiguous, incomplete, undeveloped, and unable to account for nondeliberative actions.

Thomas T. Lewis

The Doctrine of the Mean

Originally a chapter of the *Li Ji* (sixth to fifth century B.C.E.; *Book of Rites*, 1885), titled *Zhong Yong* (English translation, 1861), *The Doctrine of the Mean* was selected by the twelfth century neo-Confucian philosopher Zhu Xi as one of the Four Books that form the primary canonical texts of Confucianism. Though tradition dates its composition to the fifth century B.C.E., the work was significantly redacted over several centuries prior to the common era as Confucianism absorbed elements of rival creeds such as Daoism and Buddhism.

Authorship and Context

The authorship of *The Doctrine of the Mean* is problematic. Tradition ascribes the work to Kong Ji, more commonly known as Zi Si (or Chu Hsi, 483-402 B.C.E.), the grandson and disciple of Confucius. Zi Si is credited with founding one of eight schools of Confucianism in the wake of Confucius's death and is said to have served as mentor to Mencius, the so-called "second sage" of Confucianism.

Although he functioned as a link between the two preeminent figures of Confucianism, Zi Si remains a somewhat obscure figure, remembered primarily in anecdotes scattered through various Confucian texts. Perhaps the best-known legend regarding him portrays the child Zi Si approaching his uncharacteristically despondent grandfather and asking him if he were upset because his descendants would not be able to carry on his legacy. Confucius reportedly brightened at Zi Si's perspicacity, knowing that his teachings would flourish. After Confucius's death, Zi Si received a traditional education in the classics and rites from his grandfather's disciple Zengzi, reputed author of the *Da Xue* (c. end of first century B.C.E.; *The Great Learning*, 1861), another of the Four Books. The pupil's prowess made him the equal of his teacher on one occasion noted in the *Book of Rites*: When Zengzi boasted that he had abstained from food and drink for seven days after the death of his parents, the student upbraided his elder's display of filial piety as excessive, noting that the ancients prescribed only a three-day mourning period.

This innate sense of moderation, a key concept in *The Doctrine of the Mean*, may explain the work's traditional attribution to Zi Si. However, the adult Zi Si is remembered more as a stickler for the rules of propriety than for his even-temperedness. Several anecdotes recall the poverty-stricken adult refusing much-needed offers of food and clothing because he would be unable to reciprocate the gift. Like his grandfather, Zi Si also traveled to a number of Chinese states, offering his services as an adviser, and like his grandfather, he was fairly unsuccessful in this pursuit. During a sojourn in Song, his unflattering honesty with a court official nearly cost him his life; however, the duke of that state intervened to spare him. Citing the historical precedent of his grandfather writing the *Chun Qiu* (spring and autumn annals), a chronicle of events in the state of Lu from 722 to 481 B.C.E., after a similar rescue, Zi Si is said to have composed *The Doctrine of the Mean* to show his appreciation. Although this account places its composition in his early manhood, another, less colorful tradition has him writing the work at the end of his life, when, again like his grandfather, he had returned to his home state of Lu.

Despite the traditional attribution, both internal and external evidence points to an author other than Zi Si—for at least part of the text. If Zi Si is the sole author, it seems odd that he makes no personal references to his grandfather; indeed, the hyperbolic eulogy to Confucius in chapters 30-32 reads more like a literary exercise than the heartfelt memory of a direct descendent. Even the quotations of the sage seem to have come not from personal experience but from literary sources such as *Lunyu* (late sixth or early fifth century B.C.E.; *Analects*, 1861) and the *Mengzi* (early third century B.C.E.; *The Works of Mencius*, 1861). More important, the text vacillates between the highly organized *lun* or thematic essay genre (pioneered by Mozi's followers in the fourth century B.C.E.) and the older, relatively formless *jing* or collection of anecdotes (best illustrated by the *Analects*). If Zi Si is the sole author of *The Doctrine of the Mean*, his work would constitute one of the earliest examples of the *lun* or essay genre in China and it would remain anomalous for the Confucian school of his period. It seems more likely that the text is a considerable amplification of a traditional text (perhaps written Zi Si or one of his followers), undertaken by one or possibly several redactors during the Warring States period (475-221 B.C.E.) as Confucianism reacted to the emerging philosophies of Daoism, Legalism, Mohism, and Buddhism.

Beginning with its willfully ambiguous title that resists simple translation, *The Doctrine of the Mean* seems to reject Confucius's insistence on precise naming for Daoist antinomialism. Indeed, an opening statement seems reminiscent more of Laozi than Confucius: "Unroll [this scroll] and it fills the universe; roll it up and it retires and lies hid in mysteriousness." Yet, while the text coopts certain aspects of Daoism, a more immediate impulse for its composition may have been the refutation of the utilitarian philosophies of Mozi and the Legalists. In effect, *The Doctrine of the Mean* is an elaborate philosophic justification for the traditional rituals preserved in the *Book of Rites*— practices such as the traditional funerary customs that Mozi had attacked as extravagant and outmoded.

Scholars Fung Yu-lan and E. R. Hughes, who together performed a thorough examination of the authorship of *The Doctrine of the Mean*, agree that the work is most likely the work of at least two different writers separated by several hundred years. Both are willing to accept Zi Si, or one of his immediate circle, as the author of the *jing*, or anecdotal, sections of the text, particularly chapters 2-26. However, they assign the *lun*, or essay, sections, including the masterful opening chapter, to a much later figure who belongs to the Mencian line of Confucianism. Hughes dates this

part of the work to a period beginning with the Qin Dynasty (221-207 B.C.E.) and ending with the early Han Dynasty (207 B.C.E.-220 C.E.). He justifies the division of the work on the basis of internal evidence such as the use of the word *tian* (heaven): In the purportedly earlier sections, it still denotes the personified Creator, while in the later, it has adopted its more deistic sense.

Hughes also hazards that the original work may have been amplified by a Confucianist of the Qin or early Han imperial court with an eye to winning official approval for the sect: With its emphasis on hierarchy and social harmony, the text can be seen as a propaganda for the Qin and Han goal of a unified Chinese empire. The amplifier of *The Doctrine of the Mean* may have had several reasons for concealing his identity. While writing remained a dangerous activity, particularly during the repressive Qin period, Chinese literature has a long tradition of anonymous "transmission" of older works. In fact, works such as the Daoist *Zhuangzi*, correctly attributed to its eponymous author, remain the exception rather than the rule in ancient China. With its focus on tradition, its reverence for the ancients, and, especially after Mencius, its increasingly corporate structure, Confucianism naturally encouraged such creative editing of relatively "ancient" works. Indeed, Confucius himself, purported editor of the Five Classics, claimed to be a merely a transmitter rather than an original writer.

Though its origins lie in pre-Han China, *The Doctrine of the Mean* came to prominence relatively late in the history of Confucianism. During the "Neo-Confucian" revival of the Song Dynasty (960-1279), the scholar Zhu Xi (1130-1200) elevated the obscure chapter in the *Book of Rites* to its position as one of the Four Books of Confucianism—placing it in the rarefied company of the *Analects*, *Mengzi*, and *The Great Learning*, another text similarly elevated from the *Book of Rites*. *The Doctrine of the Mean*'s origination in the *Book of Rites* helps to explain scholars' difficulty in establishing a definitive text: Of the Five Classics, the *Book of Rites* seems to have fallen in the most disrepair in the centuries following Confucius's death. Most likely its subject matter, the arcane rituals of the Shang (c. 1384-1122 B.C.E.) and Zhou (1122-221 B.C.E.) Dynasties, prevented it from attaining the popularity of the other classics in an increasingly rationalistic Confucian canon. Moreover, the text itself remained indeterminate because the oldest copies had been preserved on bamboo slips, many of which had been either misplaced or misarranged. Finally, the *Book of Rites* suffered more than the other classics during the burning of the books of the Qin regime in 213 B.C.E.; after the restoration of learning during the early Han Dynasty, a definitive text was never fully established, and it remained neglected for almost a millennium. Though Confucianism had been named the official state philosophy by the Han emperor Wu in the second century B.C.E. and in subsequent centuries had developed into a popular religion based on idealization of the master, the repopularization of Daoist practice beginning with the second century B.C.E. neo-Daoist movement of Huainan and the subsequent introduction of Buddhism near the beginning of the common era witnessed the final eclipse of the traditional ritual set forth in the *Book of Rites*.

Zhu Xi edited and published *The Doctrine of the Mean* as a separate work in 1189; the text includes not only his commentary but also examples of his "creative" editing as he sought to reconcile the contradictions and fill in the gaps of the older versions. Though modern scholars quibble with the editor's interpolations of the text, his *Zhong Yong* remains by default the standard edition. In a sense, Zhu Xi's edition of the work simply continues the "transmission" process that had led earlier writers to revise the work. Although the Qin or Han era revisionists had alternately assimilated and rejected aspects of competing philosophies, Zhu Xi used his edition to respond to the ideologies of his day. Indeed, the work's emphasis on *zhong*, or centrality, resembles the "middle path" of the Buddha—thereby reclaiming for traditional Chinese thought an idea supposedly "introduced" from the alien Indian philosophy.

Zhu Xi's selection of *The Doctrine of the Mean* may be best understood in terms of the *dao tong*, a phrase he coined in his introduction to the work. Adapted from Mencius, the term (literally, "the tradition of the Way") refers to the Confucian belief that every five hundred years or so a "transmitter" would emerge to articulate Chinese traditional wisdom to a new era. According to

Zhu Xi, the *dao tong* had begun with the mythical Sage Kings Yao and Shun and had continued to include historical figures such as the duke of Zhou and Confucius (who made no claims to be an innovative thinker but declared that he was simply a transmitter of the wisdom of the ancients). After Confucius, the *dao tong* has followed a distinctly Mencian branch of Confucianism, including such exemplars as Zengzi and Zi Si. Indeed, Zhu Xi may have rescued the text from obscurity as much for its numerous references to *dao tong* figures as for its purportedly "Confucian" message. As he notes in his introduction, *The Doctrine of the Mean* reads like a who's who of the *dao tong*: In addition to its supposed authorship by Zi Si, the text is liberally sprinkled with quotations from Yao, Shun, and Confucius himself. In reintroducing Confucianism to his contemporaries, Zhu Xi may have hoped to avoid the doctrinal disputes that had fragmented the movement in earlier periods. His promotion of *The Doctrine of the Mean* and *The Great Learning* in effect constitutes an identification of an "authorized" line of Confucianism: from Confucius to Zengzi to Zi Si to Mencius. Zhu Xi's success in this enterprise is underscored by the fact that Confucianism has elevated Zhengzi, Zi Si, and Mencius as to the lofty position of "Transmitters of the Sage."

Luke A. Powers

Overview

Type of philosophy: Chinese philosophy, ethics, metaphysics
First transcribed: Zhong Yong, fifth to fourth century B.C.E. (English translation, 1861)
Principal ideas advanced:
◇ The harmony of the universe can be the harmony within a person, and a unity of nature and humankind can be achieved.
◇ A sincere effort to learn will enable a person to find the Way of Heaven and to follow the *dao* of human nature.
◇ The harmony of Heaven's Way provides the path of duty; the original nature of humankind is in equilibrium, but when feelings are

aroused and are balanced, a state of harmony results.

◇ The superior person is an embodiment of the mean, of equilibrium-harmony, of the *zhong yong*.

◇ The mean can be attained in ordinary action, but there are many who are too arrogant or too foolish to find the Way.

◇ The superior person is benevolent and righteous; he attains inner sincerity, which is the Way of Heaven.

The Doctrine of the Mean, like the *Da Xue* (c. end of first century B.C.E.; *The Great Learning*, 1861), was originally part of the *Li Ji* (sixth to fifth century B.C.E.; *Book of Rites*, 1885), and with Confucius's *Lunyu* (late sixth or early fifth century B.C.E.; *Analects*, 1861) and Mencius's *Mengzi* (early third century B.C.E.; *The Works of Mencius*, 1861), as drawn together by Zhu Xi, formed the Four Books of Confucianism that became part of the central emphasis in Chinese education for more than eight hundred years. Scholars do not agree on the authorship of *The Doctrine of the Mean*, but it is often attributed to Confucius's grandson Zi Si (483-402 B.C.E.), who is also regarded by some scholars as the author of *The Great Learning*. Although scholar E. R. Hughes argues that it is probable that Zi Si wrote the major part of *The Doctrine of the Mean*, scholar Wing-tsit Chan suggests that the work may have been the product of several authors over a considerable period of time.

The Meaning of Zhong Yong

The proper translation and understanding of the title, *Zhong Yong*, is also a matter of dispute, although there tends to be agreement that the English title—not a literal translation—namely, *The Doctrine of the Mean*, is at least acceptable. The term *zhong* means, according to Chan, what is central, and the term *yong* means what is universal and harmonious. Chan argues that, taken together, the title refers to human nature (what is "central") and to harmony, thereby making the point that the harmony of the universe underlies human nature.

Scholar Tu Wei-ming calls attention to the ancient tradition according to which the human being "embodies the centrality of heaven and

earth" and is thus unified with both. Tu argues that "centrality" is an "ontological condition" rather than a state of emotional quiescence. Centrality is the ground of human existence; harmony is the path. His own work on *The Doctrine of the Mean* is entitled *Centrality and Commonality: An Essay on Chung-yung*, reflecting his interpretation of the original *Zhong Yong*.

Zhu Xi (the compiler of the Four Books) wrote, in James Legge's translation, "Being without inclination to either side is called *chung* [*zhong*]; admitting of no change is called *yung* [*yong*]. By *chung* is denoted the correct course to be pursued by all under heaven; by *yung* is denoted the fixed principle regulating all under heaven." In Chan's translation, the same passage reads, "By *chung* (central) is meant what is not one-sided, and by *yung* (ordinary) is meant what is unchangeable. *Chung* is the correct path of the world and *yung* is the definite principle of the world."

Finally, Hughes writes that although the term *zhong* ordinarily means "the centre," in the title of the book it tends to mean what philosophers call "the Mean"; and he adds, "the other, *yung*, [is] the word used for denoting a common workman or the tasks such a man performs." He concludes: "The idea, therefore, seems to be of a Mean to be found in all types of action."

The convergence of opinion seems to indicate the idea that a course of equilibrium, a balanced course (in which one is in the center, at the mean between extremes), is the right way of action for humankind and that the form of that action is the universal harmony that can be embodied in any person.

Equilibrium and Harmony

The Doctrine of the Mean is usually published with the comments of Zhu Xi, who not only gave the work prominence by abstracting it from the *Book of Rites* but also influenced the reading of the work through his commentary. The book begins with the proposition that Heaven (nature) gave people human nature and that the path of duty, the *dao* for humankind, is to follow that nature. Education or instruction provides the regulation of that path. Because the dutiful Way is, in effect, prescribed by Heaven, it ought not, even for a moment, to be departed from; consequently, the morally exemplary person is careful not to lapse in the effort to act as nature requires.

Then the text reads (in Chan's translation): "Before the feelings of pleasure, anger, sorrow, and joy are aroused it is called equilibrium (*chung*, centrality, mean). When these feelings are aroused and each and all attain due measure and degree, it is called harmony." The conclusion of the first chapter (a two-paragraph passage) is that "When equilibrium and harmony are realized to the highest degree, heaven and earth will attain their proper order and all things will flourish." (Zhu Xi remarks that the scholar Yang—identified by Chan as Yang Shi, or Yang Guishan (1053-1135)—regarded this first chapter of *The Doctrine of the Mean* as "the quintessence of the whole work.") Humankind is the meeting place of Heaven and earth; therefore, achieving superiority as a person is succeeding in attaining the state of balance or equilibrium made possible by following the universal Way of Heaven, the unchangeable harmony that is the foundation of the being of a human being.

The Superior Person

The Doctrine of the Mean quotes Confucius as declaring that the superior person (*junzi*) embodies the mean, while the inferior person (*xiaoren*) acts in a way that is contrary to the mean. The mean course is difficult to follow, however. Confucius adds: The intelligent (or those who presume themselves to be so) go beyond it; the stupid fall short. However, one can see in Shun (the legendary Sage King) one who could take hold of the extremes in what people said, find the mean, and apply it in his ruling over the people.

The superior person attains harmony within and in dealings with others, Confucius says (in chapter 10 of *The Doctrine of the Mean*); the superior person holds the middle position and is not thrown off balance by whatever happens in public or private life. The strength of the person from the south is that he or she is gentle in teaching and shows forbearance; the strength of the person from the north consists in bearing arms and meeting death without regret. The cultivation of oneself should be whatever following the Way requires. The Way to be followed applies everywhere and to everyone, whatever a person's intelligence or station. According to Confucius (to whom *The Doctrine of the Mean* repeatedly alludes and whom it purportedly quotes at length), the Way of the superior person has its simple expression in the relation between men and women, "but in its utmost reaches, it is clearly seen in heaven and on earth."

In chapter 13, Confucius is quoted as saying that anyone who pursues the Way without being involved with other persons cannot be regarded as following the Way. One must be conscientious and cultivate the universal principle of one's own nature, and one must be concerned about serving others according to the same principle. "What you do not wish others to do to you, do not do to them," Confucius teaches, but he follows the negative form of what has come to be called the Golden Rule with positive forms of the rule in speaking of one's duties in serving one's father, ruler, elder brothers, and friends: for example, "To serve my father as I would expect my son to serve me. . . . To serve my ruler as I would expect my ministers to serve me. . . ."

To be superior, one's words must suit one's actions; one's actions, one's words. What is required, then, is an "entire sincerity" (Legge); the superior person must be "earnest and genuine" (Chan). The superior person does what is proper to his or her station, and under whatever circumstances, the individual remains true to the self. This person blames neither Heaven nor people. In a striking image, the superior person is compared to an archer who, upon missing the center of the target, looks for the fault within himself. Confucius emphasizes the requirement that the superior person find harmony within the family, seeking happy union with a spouse and children and living with siblings in enduring harmony. In this way, like the traveler, the superior person starts from the nearest point and, if a height must be ascended, starts from below.

Virtuous conduct has great rewards, according to Confucius in *The Doctrine of the Mean*. The Sage King Shun is an example of this, for he gained eminent position, wealth, fame, and long life. (However, such worldly rewards of virtue were probably meant by Confucius to be symbolic of the spiritual rewards that virtue brings; the person in harmony with Heaven, with others, with his or her family, and with his or her own nature is a person of spiritual eminence; this person knows and enjoys the power of the *dao*, or Way.) By reference to various examples of filial piety, Confucius stresses the importance of respect for parents and ancestors.

Rulers

When rulers are superior people, following the course of the mean and attaining moral equilibrium through conduct prescribed by the universal Way, government flourishes, Confucius teaches. Good government requires rulers whose characters are formed by cultivation of the Way, and cultivation of the Way consists in realizing one's humanity (*ren*) through benevolent action. Righteousness (*yi*) consists in doing what is right, especially in honoring the worthy according to principles of propriety. One's duties to rulers, family, friends, and associates can be met only if one develops the three universal virtues: wisdom, humanity, and courage (understanding, benevolence, and conscientiousness).

According to Confucius, as reported in *The Doctrine of the Mean*, the wise person, by cultivating personal life and character, learns how to govern others—how to govern the empire, its states, and its families. There are nine principles of governing to follow: to develop one's own character, to honor the worthy, to be affectionate toward relatives, to be respectful toward great ministers, to secure the well-being of the officers, to treat the common people as one's own children, to bring in and encourage artisans, to be considerate toward visitors from other lands, and to have a kind and constructive influence on the feudal lords.

The Path of the Mean

Sincerity (*cheng*) is the way of Heaven, Confucius teaches in chapter 20 of *The Doctrine of the Mean*. The sincere person is in harmony with the Way; the individual chooses the good and maintains it. To be sincere, Confucius explains, is to develop one's nature, to complete the self. Chapter 25 states the Confucian view that by completing the self all things are completed: Humanity and wisdom are achieved; the internal and the external are united.

The superior person honors his or her moral nature and persists in inquiry and study. By following the path of the Mean, the individual

achieves spiritual greatness and is thereby able to "order and adjust the great relations of mankind, establish the great foundations of humanity, and know the transforming and nourishing operations of heaven and earth."

Although *The Doctrine of the Mean* fosters the metaphysical proposition that the Way of Heaven determines the nature of humanity and consequently the direction of people's spiritual or moral development, the emphasis is on the moral course that the superior person must take and on the genesis of spiritual greatness through development of the self and the realization of one's humanity in the right and proper relations with one's family, friends, and associates. Sincerity in the sense of being true to one's fundamental nature is the key virtue of the human being, according to the Confucian ethics of *The Doctrine of the Mean*.

Ian P. McGreal

Additional Reading

Berthrong, John H. *Concerning Creativity: A Comparison of Chu Hsi, Whitehead, and Neville.* Albany: State University of New York, 1998. This work examines creativity and various religious concepts in the thought of Alfred North Whitehead, Robert Cummings Neville, and Zhu Xi.

_____. "The New *Tao-t'ung.*" In *Chu Hsi: New Studies.* Honolulu: University of Hawaii Press, 1989. This essay analyzes Zhu Xi's influential edition of *The Doctrine of the Mean* in the light of his concept of the *dao tong*, or "tradition of the Way."

Chan, Wing-tsit. *A Source Book in Chinese Philosophy.* Princeton, N.J.: Princeton University Press, 1963. This anthology includes Chan's translation of *The Doctrine of the Mean* (which follows the Zhu Xi edition). His introduction to the text concentrates on the work's appeal to Daoists and, later, Buddhists.

Fang, T. H. *The Chinese View of Life: The Philosophy of Comprehensive Harmony.* Taipei: Linking, 1981. This work posits a historical trend in Chinese philosophy toward achieving consensus rather than accentuating differences between the Confucian and other schools of thought.

Fingarette, H. *Confucius: The Secular as Sacred.* New York: Harper & Row, 1972. This standard critical biography of Confucius explores the nuances of his philosophy by analyzing his relationships with various disciples such as Zengzi and Zi Si.

Fung Yu-lan. *A History of Chinese Philosophy*. Vol. 1. Translated by Derek Bodde. Princeton, N.J.: Princeton University Press, 1952. This standard history of Chinese philosophy (originally published in Chinese in 1913) posits the "two-author" theory of *The Doctrine of the Mean* and interprets the work within the context of the *Book of Rites*.

Hughes, E. R. *The Great Learning and the Mean-in-Action*. New York: E. P. Dutton, 1943. An urbane and highly readable English translation with a detailed introductory essay on the authorship and date of *The Doctrine of the Mean*.

Legge, James. *The Confucian Analects, The Great Learning, and The Doctrine of the Mean*. Hong Kong: J. Legge, 1861. Reprint. Vol. 1. Oxford: Clarendon Press, 1893. Despite the cultural biases of its late nineteenth century Christian missionary author, this studious translation (widely disseminated on the Internet) remains the de facto standard edition of *The Doctrine of the Mean*.

Schwartz, Benjamin I. *The World of Thought in Ancient China*. Cambridge, Mass.: Harvard University Press, 1985. This broad intellectual history of pre-Han China discusses *The Doctrine of the Mean* within the context of Mencian Confucianism.

Stein, William Bysshe, ed. *The Four Books*. Translated by Rev. David Collie. A facsimile edition. Gainesville, Fla.: Scholars' Facsimiles and Reprints, 1970. A highly readable early nineteenth century English translation of the Four Books (which include *The Doctrine of the Mean*); Stein's introduction discusses the influence of Collie's translation on the American transcendentalist movement.

Tu Wei-ming. *Centrality and Commonality: An Essay on Chung-yung*. Honolulu: The University Press of Hawaii, 1976. While conceding the possibility of multiple authors, this study of *The Doctrine of the Mean* locates an underlying thematic unity in its concept of *junzi* or "profound person."

Luke A. Powers

W. E. B. Du Bois

One of the principal founders of the National Association for the Advancement of Colored People and editor of several influential journals, Du Bois was for many years the leading black intellectual in the United States. Through his teaching, writings, and speeches, he advocated economic, political, and cultural advancement of African Americans not only in the United States but also abroad.

Principal philosophical works: *The Suppression of the African Slave-Trade to the United States of America, 1638-1870*, 1896; *The Conservation of Races*, 1897; *The Philadelphia Negro*, 1899; *The Souls of Black Folk: Essays and Sketches*, 1903; *John Brown*, 1909; *Darkwater: Voices from Within the Veil*, 1920; *The Gift of Black Folk: The Negroes in the Making of America*, 1924; *Black Reconstruction: An Essay Toward a History of the Part Which Black Folk Played in the Attempt to Reconstruct Democracy in America, 1860-1880*, 1935; *Black Folk Then and Now: An Essay in the History and Sociology of the Negro Race*, 1939; *Dusk of Dawn: An Essay Toward an Autobiography of a Race Concept*, 1940; *Color and Democracy: Colonies and Peace*, 1945; *The World and Africa: An Inquiry into the Part Which Africa Has Played in World History*, 1947; *In Battle for Peace: The Story of My Eighty-Third Birthday*, 1952 (with Shirley Graham); *The Autobiography of W. E. B. Du Bois*, 1968.

Born: February 23, 1868; Great Barrington, Massachusetts

Died: August 27, 1963; Accra, Ghana

Early Life

William Edward Burghardt Du Bois (pronounced DU-boyce) was born of mixed African, French Huguenot, and Dutch descent in Great Barrington, Massachusetts, on February 23, 1868. His father, Alfred Du Bois, was the son of Alexander Du Bois, a light-skinned man born of a union between a mulatto slave girl in Santo Domingo and a wealthy American of French Huguenot descent. He lost his father early and was reared by his mother, Mary Burghardt, whose family traced its roots to a freed slave in the days of the American Revolution. The Burghardts were proud of their long, stable residence in Massachusetts as free farmers, but because they were black, they remained outside the social elite.

Du Bois grew up as part of a small black community of about fifty people among some five thousand whites in Great Barrington. Though his childhood was basically happy, he learned early that African Americans were not fully accepted as equal, even in New England. Determined to be a leader of his people, Du Bois studied hard and dreamed of getting a degree from Harvard. Books and writing interested young Du Bois more than athletics, although he did enjoy games and socializing with his friends. When he was graduated from high school in 1884 at the age of sixteen, he was the only African American in his class of twelve and was already urging African Americans to take advantage of their opportunities to advance through education and other forms of self-help.

The death of his mother shortly after his graduation, lack of funds, and his young age forced deferment of his plans to attend Harvard. After working several months and receiving scholarship aid from some interested churches, however, he was able to enter Fisk University in Nashville, Tennessee, in the fall of 1885. Because of his superior academic background, he was admitted at the sophomore level. Fisk was a radically different world from that of Great Barrington, and, significantly, it provided him with the long-sought opportunity to relate to African Americans his own age. Now living among the two hundred African Americans at Fisk, he felt a stronger sense of identification with other African Americans and continued his instinctive efforts to make his fellow blacks more conscious of what they could accomplish. He also learned more about the deep-rooted racial discrimination of the South after Reconstruction. Summers were spent teaching in small western Tennessee schools, adding to the profound influence of his Fisk years.

Du Bois was graduated from Fisk in 1888 and at last was able to attend Harvard. With financial aid, he matriculated that fall at the junior level. In 1890, he earned a second baccalaureate degree, and the next year a master's degree. From 1892 to 1894, he interrupted his Harvard doctoral program to take advantage of a fellowship to study at the University of Berlin. There he came into contact with some of Europe's most prominent scholars, such as sociologist Max Weber, Heinrich von Treitschke, and Rudolf von Gneist. Like George Santayana and the famous psychologist-philosopher William James at Harvard, these seminal thinkers left a deep mark on his formative mind. Again, he used his summers to good advantage by traveling on the Continent. This European experience did not lessen his commitment to uplifting African Americans, but it did, he recalled, help him emerge "from the extremes of my racial provincialism . . . and to become more human."

Du Bois returned to Harvard in 1894 and completed his dissertation, *The Suppression of the African Slave-Trade to the United States of America, 1638-1870*. Its acceptance for publication by Harvard marked the beginning of a career in writing and scholarship. When he was graduated in 1895—the first African American to earn a Ph.D. at Harvard—he was ready to enter the academic world and become part of what he called the Talented Tenth— the intellectual elite that he believed was the key to the advancement of African Americans. He was chosen to speak at the commencement ceremonies and was recognized for his oratorical abilities.

Life's Work

Du Bois's first appointment was at Wilberforce College in Ohio as an instructor in classics, a field in which he had excelled both at Fisk and at Harvard. He was not happy there, however, and in 1896 took a position at the University of Pennsylvania in Philadelphia, where his primary responsibility was to undertake a study of African American society in the city's Seventh Ward slums. His experience in Philadelphia was another disappointment. His apartment in the slum area brought him close to the worst effects of poverty, and he felt slighted by the university leadership. On the positive side, his year there produced his second major work and the first serious sociological study of American black social life, *The Philadelphia Negro*, which was published in 1899 after he moved to Atlanta.

W. E. B. Du Bois. *(Library of Congress)*

From 1897 to 1910, Du Bois headed the economics and history program at Atlanta University and for the first time settled into a rewarding job. During that crucial period when African Americans were going through many important changes, Du Bois developed his ideas in *Atlanta University Studies* and wrote for prominent journals such as the *Atlantic Monthly*. In 1903, he compiled his thoughts in his best-known work, *The Souls of Black Folk*. By then, he was openly challenging the ideas of fellow African American leader Booker T. Washington, head of the Tuskegee Institute in Alabama. Washington had rapidly risen to prominence after his Atlanta Exposition address of 1895, in which he urged African Americans to acquire industrial education, property, and good personal habits rather than push immediately for political rights or social equality.

The Washingtonian approach has been called accommodationism, while Du Bois's strategy emphasized immediate acquisition of rights such as voting, education, and access to public facilities. Known as a "radical" at that time, in contrast to the more conservative Tuskegee mentality, Du Bois became an intense rival of Washington, who nevertheless remained the most influential black spokesperson until his death in 1915. In 1905, Du Bois led a group of like-minded people in the formation of an organization to counter the Tuskegee approach. Meeting on the Canadian side of Niagara Falls in July, they established the Niagara Movement, a short-lived group that never attracted much popular support. Its program was in some ways the opposite of Washington's. It emphasized integration of education, voting rights for black men, and more rapid development of black people's economic resources. Washington had urged African Americans: "Cast down your bucket where you are." Du Bois and the Niagara Movement insisted that they must actively protest against inequality and seize every opportunity to move into the mainstream of American life.

The Niagara Movement failed by 1909, but that same year, Du Bois worked with Mary White Ovington and other interested whites in formally establishing the National Association for the Advancement of Colored People (NAACP). It grew out of an interracial meeting triggered by the violent racial disturbances in Springfield, Illinois, in

1908. Du Bois left Atlanta University in 1910 to become director of publicity and research for the NAACP. He also established a new journal, *The Crisis*, which became a semiofficial organ of the NAACP and afforded Du Bois larger opportunities than *The Horizon*, the Niagara Movement's journal, to promulgate his ideas on the Talented Tenth, racial solidarity of African Americans and many other issues. *The Crisis* became essentially self-supporting, and Du Bois often argued with other NAACP leaders about its content. Regarding it essentially as his, he felt that *The Crisis* was actually the spearhead of the movement rather than of the parent NAACP organization.

Du Bois's career after 1910 went through many changes that reflected the varying conditions of race relations in the United States. He retained his editorial position until his break with the NAACP in 1934, but he frequently departed from official NAACP positions. Increasingly, he advocated black separatism in the economic sphere, a modified version of Marxist socialism, and pan-Africanism. Du Bois organized the first important pan-African congress in Paris in 1919 and became a major rival of Marcus Garvey, the famous Jamaican who led the "back-to-Africa" movement between the world wars. Until the end of his life, Du Bois advocated various versions of pan-Africanism and became known in Africa for both this and his many involvements in peace organizations. A distinguished looking man with a mustache and goatee, he contrasted physically with most Africans but, nevertheless, identified with them. By the time his book *Black Reconstruction* was published, he was openly supporting socialism and racial separatism.

A third stage of his career began in 1934 as he returned to teaching at Atlanta University. From then until 1944, he resumed his academic work and added to his growing list of publications: *Black Folk Then and Now*; his autobiographical *Dusk of Dawn*; after returning to an NAACP job in 1944, *Color and Democracy*; and *The World and Africa*.

After World War II, Du Bois continued to change as the history of African Americans in the United States and the world evolved. The persistence of colonial rule after the war disturbed him, and he frankly criticized the great powers for not totally freeing their dependencies. While he continued to see the Soviet Union as a model in some respects, he did not refrain from criticizing that country's domination of Eastern Europe and other areas. His displeasure with U.S. foreign policy further alienated him from his own country, and in 1951, he was charged with failing to register as an agent for a foreign power because of his pivotal position in the Peace Information Center. Although he was acquitted, he never felt at home in the United States after that. He was invited by Kwame Nkrumah to the 1957 ceremonies marking the end of British colonial rule in Ghana but was not allowed to go—although Vice President Richard Nixon and black leader Martin Luther King, Jr., were present. Eventually, in 1961, he joined the Communist Party and left his native land for Ghana. Du Bois became a citizen of Ghana and died there, at age ninety-five, in 1963.

Influence

The life of W. E. B. Du Bois was a mirror of the growing independence of African American thought. On the surface, he embodied many contradictions: capitalism and socialism, separatism and integration, militancy and accommodationism. Yet the common thread of his evolving thought was his awareness of the racial question and the necessity to resolve it. "The problem of the Twentieth Century," he wrote in *The Souls of Black Folk*, "is the problem of the color-line." To him, it would yield only to determination and information. His commitment to scientific sociological research was so profound that some have said that he relied too much upon it.

Du Bois, however, was not merely a social scientist. He took pride in his blackness even as he recognized its complexity. He sensed in himself and all black Americans a dual identity:

One ever feels his two-ness,—an American, a Negro; two souls, two thoughts, two unreconciled strivings; two warring ideals in one dark body, whose dogged strength alone keeps it from being torn asunder.

The history of the American Negro is the history of this strife,—this longing to attain self-conscious manhood, to merge his double self into a better and truer self.

Thus, science and poetry flowed together in Du Bois's mind as he wrestled with the universal problem of racism and ways to deal with it.

Du Bois anticipated several salient themes of modern black history, including the emphasis upon development of capital resources by African Americans and cultural identification with Africa. Although he left the United States, he was widely respected among mainstream black reformers for his literary and personal contributions to black liberation. Ironically, his death occurred on August 27, 1963, as more than 200,000 people were assembling to march on Washington. They paused to honor Du Bois, and on the next day NAACP head Roy Wilkins paid tribute to him at the Lincoln Memorial, where Martin Luther King, Jr., delivered his historic "I Have a Dream" speech.

Thomas R. Peake

The Souls of Black Folk

Essays and Sketches

Type of philosophy: Ethics, social philosophy
First published: 1903
Principal ideas advanced:

◇ The biggest problem of the twentieth century is the problem of the color line.

◇ "Soul" functions as a philosophical category, signaling a shared humanity that transcends racial boundaries.

◇ African American "double-consciousness" is a result of black people's historical experience in the United States, which gives African Americans a dual African and American heritage that places their identities in dynamic tension.

◇ The political, economic, and spiritual well-being of the post-Reconstruction United States depends on the nation's ability to incorporate, value, and advance the knowledge generated through African American experience.

◇ African Americans must develop effective, community-originated, and self-defined leadership (the "Talented Tenth").

◇ Political power (via voting rights), civil rights (via full civic/legal equality), and education of youth according to ability (via access by black students to all levels of education) are nonnegotiable and immediately necessary conditions for African American freedom.

Written at the opening of the twentieth century, after the relative failure of federal Reconstruction efforts and during accelerating national tensions regarding race relations, *The Souls of Black Folk* is a complex work of philosophy, history, sociology, political theology, and literary creativity. Structurally linked by a few recurrent metaphors (soul, veil, double-consciousness), the book consists of fourteen distinct essays that together present W. E. B. Du Bois's analysis of conditions in the United States. Du Bois pays special attention to the challenges facing black and white citizens in their interrelations but also poses a sharp critique of the spiritual and economic directions of the United States as a whole. Race figures as a central concern in the work, with particular attention to the perspectives and knowledge emerging from African American experience. *The Souls of Black Folk* is rhetorically directed on one level to white readers but is also positioned in the dialogue toward "self-definition" among black intellectuals at the opening of the twentieth century. It is also a central twentieth century text of American political philosophy and social criticism. *The Souls of Black Folk* has been included by philosophers in the tradition of American pragmatism, especially given Du Bois's focus on ideas and meaning within historical or social contexts, as well as his advocacy of political action based on reason and social analysis.

Each essay in *The Souls of Black Folk* is introduced by a quotation from European literary tradition, with the author named, followed by an unlabeled musical notation, which readers later learn is a few bars from a song of the African American spiritual tradition. Most critics have assumed that this visual epigraphic pattern was meant by Du Bois to emphasize the close relationships between white and black culture. However, other commentators have suggested that the visual pairing suggests just the opposite: the separation between the two cultural traditions and the relative unknown status of African American cultural expression. This contrast in interpretations points to a strong internal philosophical tension in *The Souls of Black Folk* between Du Bois's "rational optimism" about the possibility of human progress and his more pessimistic analysis of American culture and race relations.

Color Line, Veil, and Double-Consciousness

In "The Forethought," Du Bois offers his now famous diagnosis: "The problem of the Twentieth Century is the problem of the color-line." In the opening essay, entitled "Of Our Spiritual Strivings," he challenges white perceptions that black experience itself is the "problem," and he asserts that the path to transcending that perception (for whites and blacks) is through a fuller exploration of the spiritual depth of black experience and "the souls of black folk." This spiritual metaphor functions as an explicit political theology: Du Bois asserts cross-racial spiritual identity and shared humanity during a period in which racial categories emphasized separation, and many white Americans were committed to an explicit ideology of white supremacy.

Du Bois introduces the two other central metaphors of the book in this opening chapter: he reveals "the veil" and describes African American "double-consciousness." The veil, a visual and symbolic wall of separation, returns again and again in *The Souls of Black Folk* to emphasize racial boundaries (social and psychological) and black "invisibility" in U.S. history. Double-consciousness is a psychological, political, and philosophical category of black experience for Du Bois, and the following quotation illustrates the ontological and epistemological implications of this key concept:

> The Negro is a sort of a seventh son, born with a veil, and gifted with second-sight in this American world,—a world which yields him no true self-consciousness, but only lets him see himself through the revelation of the other world. It is a peculiar sensation, this double-consciousness. . . . One ever feels his twoness,—an American, a Negro; two souls, two thoughts, two unreconciled strivings; two warring ideals in one dark body, whose dogged strength alone keeps it from being torn asunder.

The history of the American Negro is the history of this strife—this longing to attain self-conscious manhood, to merge his double self into a better and truer self. In this merging he wishes neither of the older selves to be lost. He would not Africanize America, for America has too much to teach the world and Africa. He would not bleach his Negro soul in a flood of white Americanism, for he knows that Negro blood has a message for the world. He simply wishes to make it possible for a man to be both a Negro and an American, without being cursed and spit upon by his fellows, without having the doors of Opportunity closed roughly in his face.

The philosophical stakes here are clear, in terms of a quality of "being" (ontology) and "knowing" (epistemology) unique to, and grounded in, African American experience. This contextual philosophy provides an undercurrent to the detailed account of African American history that follows. By exploring the sociological and political complexities of black history, Du Bois builds his argument that the "souls of black folk" are ultimately the souls of the nation, and the progress of the United States as a whole is inherently linked to the progress of African Americans. Du Bois, in essays such as "Of the Dawn of Freedom," "Of the Meaning of Progress," "Of the Black Belt," and "Of the Quest of the Golden Fleece," details federal efforts, largely failed, at national Reconstruction after the Civil War. He analyzes the Freedmen's Bureau, educational reform in Southern black communities, and the dangers and seductiveness of purely "material" gains made at the expense of intellectual and spiritual progress. He argues simultaneously for the importance of university liberal arts education for qualified African American students and for the dignity inherent in manual labor. Even when his focus is to provide historical detail, his writings contain an ever-present challenge to all readers to confront racism, violence, and inhumanity wherever they are revealed in American life.

A Rejection of Accommodationism

In "Of Mr. Booker T. Washington and Others," Du Bois directly confronts what he considers "accommodationist" (to whites) politics in the black community and argues vehemently against the gradualist strategies advanced by African Ameri-

can Booker T. Washington, head of the Tuskegee Institute in Alabama. In this essay, Du Bois is revealed as a social critic fully engaged with democratic political philosophy, working within the crosscurrents of political dialogue among African Americans as well as in relation to broader American debates over civil rights, race relations, suffrage, and public education. The essay examines the tension among the emerging black leadership of the post-Reconstruction period and deals with questions as to how African Americans should deal with the tensions between immediate and gradual change and how to achieve the goals of economic progress and civil rights. Du Bois examined how to effectively conduct black-defined political initiatives given the counterforces of white-defined social and political agendas. Du Bois was clearly at odds with Washington on all these issues, but the essay calls for open debate among African American intellectuals and advocates that action be based on careful analysis of specific social and historical conditions. In this essay, Du Bois's philosophical confidence in the power of reason is apparent, as is an underlying optimism about the progressive potential of Enlightenment and U.S. political tradition. He closes the essay by invoking the Declaration of Independence, positioning *The Souls of Black Folk* within familiar frameworks of Western philosophy, as does Du Bois's frequent use of classical quotations and reference to Roman and Greek antiquity. Chapter 4, "Of the Wings of Atlanta," is especially revealing of this complex fusion of Western classical tradition and African American history, with Du Bois arguing against the "deification of Bread" by invoking the power of the university as a source of reasoned "truth."

A More Somber Tone

Toward the end of the book, the essays in *The Souls of Black Folk* shift in form and focus. In two of the later essays, Du Bois tempers his earlier philosophical optimism: In "Of the Passing of the First Born," an account of the tragic death of his young son, Du Bois, the grieving father, asks if it is not, on some profoundly troubling level, better that his son died early rather than bear the racial injustice of the country into which he had been born. In "Of the Coming of John," Du Bois clearly questions the reformative power of education and seems to imply, through complex themes dealing with religion, sexuality, and political power, that psychological and historical patterns of American racism will lead the country to spiritual death and physical destruction.

The tragic and pessimistic tone of these two chapters is eased, but only partially, by the final chapter, "The Sorrow Songs." Here, Du Bois somberly celebrates the strength of slave song and African American spirituals. He calls this tradition "the sole American music" and "the singular spiritual heritage of the nation and the greatest gift of the Negro people." Although much of the music he draws upon here originates in the tradition of the black church, Du Bois's focus is more broadly metaphoric, pointing again toward spirituality as a philosophical category of shared humanity rather than a specifically Christian concept. The political theology and philosophy of *The Souls of Black Folk* is especially striking in the humanistic emphasis of Du Bois's "prophetic" call in "The Afterthought." His closing political challenge is addressed to the nation as he reasserts the power of reason as the starting point for social action: "Thus in Thy good time may infinite reason turn the tangle straight, and these crooked marks on a fragile leaf be not indeed." The God to whom these lines is directed is, tellingly, "the Reader": Du Bois to the end keeps his eyes on history and the thought and actions of human beings.

Initial Moves Toward Civil Rights

Du Bois published *The Souls of Black Folk* soon before initiating the Niagara Movement (1905), a gathering in which African American intellectuals challenged accommodationist politics in the African American community and argued for their receiving immediate and full civil rights. Du Bois believed, and stated in *The Souls of Black Folk*, that the Talented Tenth, the best-educated African Americans, should lead the black community in pursuit of a better life. In 1909, Du Bois helped start the National Association for the Advancement of Colored People (NAACP), a multiracial civil rights organization. In these projects, Du Bois tested the ideas of *The Souls of Black Folk* within the realities of U.S. racial and economic politics. The book established him as a philosopher and social critic, just as his earlier books had established him as a scholar. *The Souls of Black Folk* provoked animated debate among African Americans and challenged white readers to abandon the mental and political habits of white supremacy.

Subsequent influence of *The Souls of Black Folk* has been profound, both as a cornerstone text of black studies and African American literature, and as an exemplary work of early twentieth century American pragmatism. Du Bois can be read along with William James and John Dewey, important figures of American pragmatism. A wide range of writers continue to apply Du Bois's "problem of the color-line" as an analytical framework, albeit a historically shifting one, as they grapple with American race relations. Psychological and philosophical categories from *The Souls of Black Folk*, such as the "veil" and "double-consciousness," have proved of continued interest to literary artists, social critics, and philosophers. The book set a precedent for philosophical focus on the "subjectivity" of the African American experience and for contextual analysis of African American history.

Du Bois's philosophical shift from "blackness as problem" to "blackness as source of knowledge" is a shift in epistemology that was politically provocative in the United States of 1903 and has continued to challenge American and pan-African thinkers ever since.

Sharon Carson

Additional Reading

Broderick, Francis L. *W. E. B. Du Bois: Negro Leader in a Time of Crisis*. Stanford, Calif.: Stanford University Press, 1959. An older work still valuable for understanding the evolving views of W. E. B. Du Bois. It contains much biographical information and is especially incisive in capturing the troubled spirit of Du Bois through his many difficult transitions. The seemingly surprising changes such as his break with the NAACP in 1934 are seen as flowing naturally from certain racist tendencies he had from his youth. The book credits Du Bois with two major accomplishments: emphasis upon equal rights for African Americans and his service to black Americans' morale.

Byerman, Keith E. *Seizing the Word: History, Art, and Self in the Work of W. E. B. Du Bois*. Athens:

University of Georgia Press, 1994. Examines Du Bois in terms of contemporary literary and cultural theory. Discusses the work of Du Bois and its influence on nineteenth and twentieth century America.

Lewis, David Levering. *W. E. B. Du Bois: Biography of a Race, 1868-1919*. New York: H. Holt, 1993. This 1994 Pulitzer Prize-winning book chronicles the major impact Du Bois's controversial thinking had on the United States. It focuses on a crucial fifty-year period in Du Bois's life and in the nation's civil rights struggle.

Rampersad, Arnold. *The Art and Imagination of W. E. B. Du Bois*. Cambridge, Mass.: Harvard University Press, 1976. One of the few good treatments of Du Bois's creative genius. Essentially a biography, this work traces Du Bois's life from his New England beginnings to his last years in Ghana. Not so much concerned with controversies and rivalries as with his literary accomplishments, especially his fiction. Du Bois comes through as a concerned man, not a self-styled propagandist.

Rudwick, Elliott M. *W. E. B. Du Bois: Voice of the Black Protest Movement*. Champaign: University of Illinois Press, 1982. A well-documented study; covers the full sweep of Du Bois's career from his youth to his later involvements in pan-Africanism and peace promotion. Presents Du Bois as both a realist and an idealist, a skilled propagandist, and a devoted believer in equality. Rudwick suggests that although Du Bois erred in predicting socialism as the answer to the needs of African Americans, he accurately forecast the strong African orientation of contemporary black culture.

Thomas R. Peake, updated by Lisa A. Wroble

Michael Dummett

By investigating metaphysical issues concerning the objectivity of reality in terms of meaning-theoretic concepts such as truth and understanding, Dummett makes the case that realism is an incoherent conception of thought and the world.

Principal philosophical works: *Frege: Philosophy of Language*, 1973; *Elements of Intuitionism*, 1977; *Truth and Other Enigmas*, 1978; *The Interpretation of Frege's Philosophy*, 1981; *Frege and Other Philosophers*, 1991; *Frege: Philosophy of Mathematics*, 1991; *The Logical Basis of Metaphysics*, 1991; *The Origins of Analytical Philosophy*, 1993; *The Seas of Language*, 1993.

Born: June 27, 1925; London, England

Early Life

Michael Anthony Eardley Dummett, the son of a prosperous London businessman, George Herbert Dummett, and his wife, Iris Dummett, was educated at Sandroyd School and Winchester College. Although he was from a Congregationalist background, he became a devout Roman Catholic when he was eighteen. He joined the British army in 1943 and served in the Intelligence Corps while stationed in India and Malaya. By the time of his discharge in 1947, he had made the rank of sergeant. After his army service, he attended Oxford University and received his B.A. (with first class honors) in 1950 and his M.A. in 1954. Dummett was made a fellow of All Souls College in 1950.

Philosophy at Oxford during the 1950's was dominated by the ordinary language philosophy of J. L. Austin, a philosophical orientation that eschews generality and replaces systematic theorizing with piecemeal descriptions of the everyday usage of language. During this period, Dummett regarded himself as a follower of Ludwig Wittgenstein, and he has said that this inoculated him against the influence of Austin. In the mid-1950's, while at the University of California, Berkeley, on a Harkness fellowship, he witnessed the early struggles against segregation in the United States and met Dr. Martin Luther King, Jr. He and his wife, Ann, whom he married in 1951,

became active in the fight for racial justice and equality in Britain.

Life's Work

In the late 1950's and the 1960's, Dummett began exploring in a series of papers, many of which were later published in *Truth and Other Enigmas*, the debate between realism and a view he calls "antirealism." Realism, in general, is the view that reality exists independently of our knowledge of it. One of Dummett's insights was that while this is not a single issue, the various instances of the debate are structurally similar enough to make a unified treatment of them profitable. The debate between realism and antirealism arises for a variety of aspects of the world. Perhaps the best known concerns the physical world of medium-sized objects: Commonsense realism says that they are mind-independent objects apprehended in sense experience, while antirealism (typically some version of idealism or phenomenalism) holds that sense experiences are constitutive of the physical world. Another area is mathematics, where realism (called in this context Platonism) maintains that mathematicians *discover* the constitution of a preexisting mathematical reality, while antirealism holds that their activity *creates* mathematical reality. Dualism is a form of realism about the mental according to which observable behavior is merely evidence of someone's inner states; in contrast, the behaviorist version of antirealism holds that pain is nothing over and above pain-behavior. As even a short list such as this suggests, a realism/antirealism dispute can arise for any area of thought, knowledge, or experience.

What do these various issues over realism have in common? Rejecting the traditional answer that they concern whether entities of a certain sort exist, Dummett suggests what they have in common is that the realist employs a notion of truth subject to the principle of bivalence: the principle that reality renders statements either true or false independently of our capacity to discover their truth value. The central contention of antirealism is that no intelligible conception of truth is so radically divorced from people's capacity to discover it. One argument used by the antirealists focuses on people's acquisition of the concept of truth. When people learn what it is for a sentence to be true, they are presented with evidence that is accessible to them. How, then, are people to get from this training a conception of truth that transcends their capacity to discover it? It appears the realist's conception of truth is not one that people could acquire. This leads the antirealist to abandon the principle of bivalence and with it the idea of reality as fully determinate in the sense of rendering each statement as either true or false. The picture of reality that emerges is a reality that becomes fully determinate only as people investigate it.

Dummett's first book was his study of Gottlob Frege, a nineteenth century German mathematician and logician. This work, titled *Frege: Philosophy of Language*, was published in 1973 and makes the case that Frege was a revolutionary thinker who altered the course of philosophy. Because Frege is the founder of mathematical logic, his stature as a logician has never been in doubt. It is Dummett's contention, however, that Frege's greatness does not lie solely, or even principally, in virtue of his great achievements in logic. Rather, Dummett argues, Frege's greatness lies in having initiated a revolution in philosophy comparable in significance to the revolution initiated by philosopher René Descartes in the seventeenth century. Descartes's revolution consisted of making questions of knowledge and justification the fundamental problems in philosophy; epistemology thus came to be regarded as the foundation of the rest of philosophy. Frege's

revolution, according to Dummett, consisted of making questions of meaning fundamental; from this perspective, it is the theory of meaning (or philosophy of thought) that is rightly viewed as the foundation of philosophy. Dummett regards this as a great achievement because for the first time in the history of philosophy, the proper object and methodology of philosophy had been identified. Frege had identified the goal of philosophy as the analysis of the structure of thought, and the proper way of performing such an analysis is the analysis of language. Philosophy, then, is not concerned with seeking out new facts or telling people what reality is; rather it seeks to understand how people think about reality. Because Dummett regards this perspective as constitutive of what is known as "analytic philosophy," he names Frege as the founder of the type of philosophy that has been dominant in Great Britain, Scandinavia, and the United States in the twentieth century.

In 1979, Dummett succeeded A. J. Ayer as the Wykeham Professor of Logic at Oxford. Both before and after taking this prestigious post, his main philosophical concern was with outlining an adequate theory of meaning. Important papers in this regard are "The Philosophical Basis of Intuitionistic Logic" (collected in *Truth and Other Enigmas*), "What Is a Theory of Meaning? (II)," and "What Do I Know When I Know a Language?" (both collected in *The Seas of Language*). This investigation was also the focus of Dummett's William James Lectures, delivered at Harvard University in 1976. These lectures were published in book form as *The Logical Basis of Metaphysics*.

According to Dummett, a theory of meaning is an attempt to describe what is known when someone knows the meaning of a sentence. The most popular answer in contemporary philosophy is given by the truth-conditional theory of meaning. This theory holds that what is known is the truth condition of the sentence—the condition that must be satisfied in order for that sentence to be true. Because this condition is held to be either satisfied or not satisfied irrespective of whether anyone can make that determination, the concept of truth employed satisfies the principle of bivalence, and hence, truth-conditional theories are committed to realism.

Building on Wittgenstein's ideas underlying the slogan "meaning is use," Dummett argues that the truth-conditional theory of meaning cannot give an acceptable account of what it is to understand a sentence. An adequate account of meaning and understanding must specify how a speaker manifests or displays an understanding of a sentence: The understanding must be correlated to a practical ability. If the meaning of a sentence is its truth condition, then the relevant practical ability would be the capacity to recognize whether that condition is satisfied in a variety of circumstances. However, this gives rise to a problem for truth-conditional theories. There are sentences whose truth conditions transcend people's capacity to recognize whether they are satisfied; for these sentences, it is therefore impossible to correlate the speaker's understanding with a practical ability. Dummett takes this to mean that the central notion in a theory of meaning cannot be a concept such as truth, which can transcend people's capacity to recognize it, but rather should be some nontranscendent notion such as verification. It does not escape Dummett's notice that verificationist theories of meaning have antirealist implications. Because there are sentences that are neither verifiably true nor verifiably false, bivalence will fail for these sentences, and this implies, once again, that reality cannot be viewed as fully determinate.

Dummett retired in 1992, becoming professor emeritus at Oxford. In addition to his professional philosophical work, Dummett avidly pursued a wide range of other interests and hobbies. He wrote a book on the theoretical underpinnings of voting procedures and a monograph on the role of the Catholic Church in social issues. An internationally recognized authority on tarot cards as artistic objects and on the games of skill that can be played with them, Dummett published a book, *The Game of Tarot*, in 1980 and several articles on the subject. In writing on tarot cards, he tried to discredit their use as instruments for divining the future. In the preface to *The Game of Tarot*, Dummett remarked that this hobby probably would not have gripped him to the degree it did if he had not needed a refuge from the emotional strain of his involvement in the late 1960's in the fight against racism in Britain. Along with his wife, Ann, Dummett played a major role in

the struggle for racial justice. The Dummetts were founding members of the Oxford Committee for Racial Integration and have written scores of articles and letters to the editors in support of the cause. They also served in the trenches of the struggle, spending many hours, for example, at Heathrow Airport helping Asians avoid being turned back by the immigration authorities and picketing Oxford businesses that refused service to black customers.

Influence
Dummett's influence on philosophy, especially in Britain, has been great. One area of influence has been the belated recognition that Frege was a philosophical genius of the first rank. Before Dummett, Frege was acknowledged as a great logician, but his achievements were seen as technical advances and tangential to the main concerns of philosophy. Dummett makes the case that Frege's achievements, far from being confined to a technical area, led to a revolutionary change in perspective that gave birth to analytic philosophy. If Frege is now seen as just as important in the development of analytic philosophy as philosophers Bertrand Russell and Wittgenstein, and a philosopher comparable in importance to the Greek philosopher Aristotle or the German philosopher Immanuel Kant, this is largely because of the efforts of Dummett. Related to his role in bringing about a reappraisal of Frege has been Dummett's vigorous defense of the view that the theory of meaning is the foundation of philosophy and that this is the only proper method for approaching philosophical problems. Dummett himself suggested that if he has made any worthwhile contribution to philosophy, it is in developing the view that the theory of meaning underlies metaphysics.

Dummett's analysis of the realism/antirealism debate probably is the aspect of his thought that has exerted the greatest influence on contemporary philosophy. (Dummett coined the expression "antirealism" in 1959, terminology that has become a part of the contemporary philosophical lexicon.) Issues over realism go back to the beginnings of philosophy. However, despite this being well-trod ground, Dummett has articulated a novel approach to the issue that many philosophers have found illuminating. He shows that when the issue of realism is approached through the theory of meaning, the problems of realism are made more visible. Although almost everyone comes to this issue with a strong predilection toward realism, Dummett shows that philosophical progress is not made by merely consulting our intuitive convictions; it is made by deeper and deeper analyses of the arguments for a position and the counterarguments against it. Even those not convinced by Dummett's case against realism have gained a deeper understanding of what they are believing when they believe in realism.

David Haugen

The Logical Basis of Metaphysics

Type of philosophy: Logic, metaphysics, philosophy of language
First published: 1991
Principal ideas advanced:

◇ The best approach to metaphysical issues is a "bottom-up" strategy in which one first attempts to get a clear view of how people think about reality before turning to questions about reality itself; the competing strategy is "top-down," in which metaphysical problems are tackled directly.

◇ The bottom-up strategy should be used in the controversy over realism, the view that the world exists independently of thought and knowledge.

◇ Underlying realism is the truth-conditional theory of meaning, which holds that understanding a statement is a matter of knowing how reality must be in order for that statement to be true.

◇ The concept of truth employed by the truth-conditional theory is subject to the principle of bivalence (the principle that every statement is determinately either true or false regardless of whether anyone can determine which), and this principle underlies classical logic.

◇ The central problem with the truth-conditional theory is that it does not account for a speaker's grasp of truth conditions because there is no way for the speaker to manifest a grasp of verification-transcendent truth conditions.

◇ If the truth-conditional theory of meaning proves to be untenable, then the most promising alternative is a verificationist theory that employs a notion of truth constrained by people's capacity to recognize it; this in turn yields a nonclassical (intuitionistic) logic and an antirealist metaphysics according to which reality is not fully determinate.

In 1976, Michael Dummett delivered the William James Lectures at Harvard University. These lectures are usually published by Harvard University Press shortly after they are given, but professional commitments kept Dummett from making the necessary revisions until the late 1980's, and the lectures were not published until 1991. The effects of the delay were not, however, entirely negative. It gave Dummett time to revise and expand the lectures so that the resulting book, *The Logical Basis of Metaphysics*, can fairly be seen as the definitive expression of his position on a number of the logical, semantic, and metaphysical issues that have been the focus of his career. Although the book may be the definitive statement of his views on these issues, Dummett does not regard it as providing a definitive solution to them. He says the book is merely his attempt to establish a base camp for future assaults on the metaphysical peaks still looming in the distance; he does not claim to take the expedition any further than the foothills of metaphysical truth.

The Logical Basis of Metaphysics begins with the observation that the nonprofessional expects philosophers to answer deep questions about the nature of the world. Such questions, concerning, for example, whether the will is free, whether the soul is immortal, or whether God exists, have traditionally been at the center of philosophical thinking. However, from the nonprofessional's perspective, this no longer seems to be true of practitioners of contemporary analytic philosophy. To the outsider, these philosophers seem to be playing a complicated but pointless game, using overly sophisticated techniques to answer trivial questions. Dummett believes that this reaction, while understandable, is not justified. However, he does agree that if philosophy fails to take on the great metaphysical issues of the past, then it is no longer a worthwhile enterprise.

The metaphysical issues that are the focus of *The Logical Basis of Metaphysics* concern the objectivity of various aspects of the world and the extent to which reality in general is independent of our thought and knowledge. These issues arise for a variety of subject matter including the commonsense world of physical objects, mathematics, minds, ethics and the objectivity of moral judgments, the theoretical entities of science, and issues regarding the reality of time. In each of these areas, debate arises between realists, who maintain that the facts and truths of that subject matter are objective, and antirealists, who deny that the facts are as objective as portrayed by the realist.

Top-Down and Bottom-Up Strategies

Realists and antirealists have traditionally tackled these issues directly and then from their metaphysical positions derived conclusions about meaning and logic—an approach Dummett calls the "top-down" strategy. The debate between Platonists (the realists) and intuitionists (the antirealists) over the existence of mathematical objects and the objectivity of mathematical truth provides a clear example of this. Platonists hold the metaphysical view that there is a mind-independent world of mathematical structures. This metaphysical view is then invoked to justify the principles of classical logic including, in particular, the law of excluded middle: For any proposition *P*, either *P* or not-*P* is true. The belief that this logical principle is universally valid for mathematical statements is, then, based on the metaphysics of Platonism: Because there is an objective and fully determinate mathematical reality, it will determine that either *P* is true or not-*P* is true independently of whether it is possible to discover which of these is in fact the case. The traditional intuitionists also employ a top-down approach. Their basic metaphysical thesis is the idealist view that mathematical objects and truths are created by the construction of mathematical proofs and hence do not have a mind-independent existence. This leads them to deny the universal validity of the law of excluded middle: Because a mathematical statement is true only if there exists a proof of it, and because no guaran-

tee exists that for every *P* someone can either prove it or its negation, it follows that the law of excluded middle is not universally valid.

Rather than the top-down strategy employed by the participants of the traditional dispute, Dummett recommends the "bottom-up" approach in which the issues concerning meaning and logic are dealt with before metaphysical concerns are addressed. His basic reason for preferring this strategy is that it is difficult to give a clear content to these metaphysical disputes except in terms of what the meaning of the statements are taken to be and which logical principles are appropriate for the subject matter under investigation. What exactly does it mean to believe that there are abstract mathematical objects or that future facts exist *now* as the Platonist and realist believe? These are really just "pictures" whose substance obstructs the view of the meaning, truth, and logic underlying them. Metaphysical disputes are, according to Dummett, really disputes about the contents of one's thoughts about reality; once one gets clear about the content of one's thoughts, there are no further metaphysical problems that need to be solved. The bottom-up strategy recommends, therefore, that before endeavoring to say how reality *is*, people first try to understand how they think about reality. Once people attain an understanding of this, they will have a clear view of the nature of reality itself.

The Truth-Conditional Theory and Verification

The most developed approach to meaning is the truth-conditional theory of meaning. According to this theory, the meaning of a sentence is its truth condition—the condition that must be satisfied in order for the sentence to be true. Therefore, understanding a sentence is a matter of grasping the condition that must be satisfied in order for it to be true. Truth, in this view, is in no way constrained by people's capacity to discover it. This view endorses the principle of bivalence, which holds that sentences are determinately true or false independently of people's capacity to discover their truth-value. The principle of bivalence supports classical logic: Because statements are true or false independently of one's power to determine truth or falsity, the principles of classical logic, including the law of excluded middle, are the right ones. The metaphysical picture that emerges from the truth-conditional theory is realistic. Because statements are true or false independently of people's access to the facts that determine their truth-value, people will find the picture of reality as mind-independent and fully determinate almost irresistible.

Although the truth-conditional theory of meaning is the most developed and widespread approach to meaning, Dummett believes that it fails to do what any adequate theory of meaning must do: provide an illuminating account of what it is for a speaker to understand the meaning of a sentence. The truth-conditional theory identifies what a speaker knows, but Dummett's charge is that the theory cannot say what possession of such knowledge means by relating that knowledge to the speaker's practical abilities. Because it is knowledge of truth conditions that is in question, the relevant practical ability would be manifested by a capacity to recognize whether these conditions are satisfied or not satisfied. One implication of the truth-conditional theory, due to its acceptance of bivalence and the idea that truth is in no way constrained by people's capacity to recognize it, is that there are sentences whose truth conditions transcend a speaker's capacity to recognize whether they are satisfied. Examples of such sentences from natural language include those about remote regions of space and sentences about the distant past or the future. The sentence, for example, "Caesar had eggs for breakfast the morning before he crossed the Rubicon" is either true or false even though no one is now in a position to make that determination. Dummett's focus is on the alleged grasp of an unrecognizable truth condition such as this because, plainly, a speaker cannot manifest a grasp of its truth condition by recognizing, when suitably positioned, whether it is satisfied or not satisfied. The truth-conditional theory, therefore, implies the absurd result that the knowledge involved in speaking a language is unconnected with the practical abilities involved in being a competent speaker. This, Dummett contends, shows that the attribution of such knowledge to a speaker (or to oneself) is idle and without substance.

If the truth-conditional theory proves to be untenable, then, in Dummett's opinion, the most promising approach to meaning would focus on verification. This type of theory of meaning employs a notion of truth that is constrained by people's powers to detect it, implying that understanding a sentence is a matter of grasping the conditions under which it would be verified. This theory then keeps the speaker's knowledge of meaning connected with the practice of speaking the language. Making verification the central notion has logical and metaphysical implications. If truth is constrained by people's capacities to recognize it, then the correct logic would be a nonclassical type such as intuitionistic logic. The mere fact, for example, that both P and not-P imply Q will not entail Q because there no longer is a guarantee that either P is true or not-P is true. A metaphysical picture will emerge as well: Because there will be statements that are neither true nor false, people will no longer be entitled to think of reality as fully determinate in the sense of making all statements either true or false. The metaphysical picture that emerges is one of reality as coming into being or becoming fully determinate as it is investigated.

Dummett and the Debate over Realism
Dummett devoted his career to articulating and exploring many of the themes of *The Logical Basis of Metaphysics*, so many of the ideas in this work exercised an influence long before the book itself was published. The aspect of Dummett's work that has had the greatest impact is undoubtedly his analysis of the realism/antirealism dispute. More than anyone else, Dummett has redirected attention to this central philosophical issue, and his approach to it, the bottom-up strategy, dominates recent philosophical thinking on this topic. Even those philosophers dealing with the realism issue who do not accept the bottom-up approach to issues over realism feel compelled to explain why they reject it.

However, to acknowledge Dummett's influence on contemporary philosophy is not, of course, to say that he has converted the philosophical world to antirealism or convinced it that the bottom-up approach is the proper way of doing metaphysical business. The position Dummett has staked out on the realism issue is controversial, so it is not surprising that he has had critics. Some have said, for example, that underlying the bottom-up strategy is nothing more than the positivist dogma that metaphysical theses are not resolvable by empirical means and so are meaningless. Others have argued that Dummett's central argument against the truth-conditional theory of meaning presupposes epistemological behaviorism, at best a highly controversial view. Why, it is asked, must a speaker's grasp of truth conditions be manifested in the observable behavior of recognizing that the condition is satisfied? Still other critics might bluntly suggest that any retreat from realism reveals not philosophical sophistication but a serious lack of a robust sense of reality. Even Dummett himself has sometimes expressed doubts about the coherence of global antirealism. However, in spite of these criticisms—and perhaps even because of them—the central ideas of *The Logical Basis of Metaphysics* have contributed enormously to the debate over realism.

David Haugen

Additional Reading

Devitt, Michael. *Realism and Truth*. Princeton, N.J.: Princeton University Press, 1991. An interpretation and assessment of most contemporary forms of antirealism from a naturalistic and physicalist standpoint. Devitt devotes a lengthy chapter to a detailed exposition and criticism of Michael Dummett's antirealism.

French, P., T. Uehling, and H. Wettstein, eds. *Realism and Antirealism*. Vol. 12 in *Midwest Studies in Philosophy*. Minneapolis: University of Minnesota Press, 1988. A collection of papers exploring many aspects of the realism/antirealism debate. Many of the papers discuss issues raised by Dummett's treatment of realism and antirealism.

Heck, Richard G., ed. *Language, Thought, and Logic: Essays in Honour of Michael Dummett*. Oxford: Oxford University Press, 1997. Many of the papers in this collection focus on Dummett's contributions to the philosophy of language, especially issues concerning the rela-

tionship between thought and language. Others concern Dummett's views on the nature of time, Gottlob Frege, and the philosophy of mathematics.

Luntley, Michael. *Language, Logic, and Experience*. La Salle, Ill.: Open Court, 1988. Building on Dummett, the author articulates and defends an antirealist account of logic, truth, and reality. For advanced undergraduates.

McGuinness, B., and G. Oliveri, eds. *The Philosophy of Michael Dummett*. Dordrecht, Netherlands: Kluwer Academic, 1994. This collection contains papers on Dummett's philosophies of language, mathematics, time, mind, and religion. Also includes Dummett's replies to his critics.

Taylor, Barry, ed. *Michael Dummett: Contributions to Philosophy*. Dordrecht, Netherlands: Martinus Nijhoff, 1987. Although most of the essays in this collection focus on Dummett's antirealism, the book also includes papers on two of his nonphilosophical passions: the history of playing cards and card games and the struggle for racial justice and equality in Britain. Also contains Dummett's responses.

Wright, Crispin. *Realism, Meaning, and Truth*. Oxford: Basil Blackwell, 1987. A collection of Wright's papers on Dummett and topics relating to antirealism. Wright's introductory essay is especially valuable for beginning students of the realism/antirealism debate.

_____. *Wittgenstein on the Foundations of Mathematics*. London: Gerald Duckworth, 1980. While the nominal subject of the book is Ludwig Wittgenstein's philosophy of mathematics, many of Dummett's central ideas are explored. A difficult book but worth the effort.

Young, James O. *Global Anti-realism*. Aldershot, England: Avebury, 1995. A brief and readable defense of antirealism. Recommended for undergraduates interested in realism and antirealism.

David Haugen

John Duns Scotus

With his closely woven synthesis of Scholastic philosophical and theological thought, Duns Scotus created the school of Scotism. His rigorous and subtle critical method and fresh theoretical formulations influenced important later thinkers, from his own time to the present.

Principal philosophical works: *Commentaria Oxoniensia ad IV libros magistri Sententiarum*, after 1300 (*Proof for the Unicity of God*, 1950; better known as *Ordinatio: Philosophical Writings*, 1962); *Quaestiones subtilessimae super libros metaphysicorum Aristotelis*, after 1300 (*Questions on the "Metaphysics" of Aristotle*, 1997); *Collationes*, after 1300; *Quaestiones scoti super universalia Porphyrii*, after 1300; *Reportatio parisiensis*, 1302-1305; *Quaestiones Quodlibetales*, 1306 (*The Quodlibetal Questions*, 1975); *De primo principio*, 1308 (English translation, 1949; best known as *A Treatise on God as First Principle*, 1966); *Philosophical Writings*, 1962; *Duns Scotus on the Will and Morality*, 1986.

Born: c. March, 1266; Duns, Scotland
Died: November 8, 1308; Cologne (now in Germany)

Early Life

Little is known for certain about the life, early or late, of John Duns Scotus, both because of the period in which he was born and because his life was not one of action but of thought; he was a thinker rather than a doer. The exact date of Duns Scotus's birth is unknown, but evidence suggests that he was born in the town of Duns in March of 1266. He evidently was the son of a well-to-do landowner known as Ninian Duns of Littledean. The Duns family was noted as a longtime benefactor of the Friars Minor, or Franciscans, the religious order founded in 1210 by Saint Francis of Assisi. Indeed, Duns Scotus's paternal uncle was a member of this order under the name Father Elias Duns. In 1278, Elias Duns was appointed vicar general of the Friars Minor of Scotland. Because the boy Duns Scotus evidently displayed a brilliant intellect as well as pious religious devotion, his uncle, who was stationed at the friary of Dumfries, arranged for the twelve-year-old grammar school student to come to the friary.

John Duns Scotus. *(Library of Congress)*

543

Because Duns Scotus was not yet fifteen, however, he had to wait until 1280 before he could be accepted as a novice friar. In 1282, he became a candidate for the bachelor's degree, which required four years of philosophical training, and entered Oxford for this purpose, although no extant documentation sustains this assumption. Before his studies were completed, he was ordained into the priesthood by Oliver Sutton, the bishop of Lincoln, Oxford being in this diocese, at St. Andrew's Church in Northampton on March 17, 1291. Duns Scotus apparently received his bachelor's degree from Oxford in the following year.

In 1293, Duns Scotus was sent to the University of Paris to obtain his master's degree. There he studied under Gonsalvus of Balboa until 1296. For some reason, however, he then returned to Oxford without having completed his master's requirements. At Oxford, from 1297 to 1301, he lectured on Peter Lombard's *Sententiarum libri IV* (1148-1151; *The Books of Opinions of Peter Lombard*, 1970, 4 volumes; commonly known as *Sentences*). In 1302, he returned to Paris and resumed his studies. In 1303, however, he was forced to leave the university and return to England because he supported Boniface VIII in the pope's controversy with the French king, Philip the Fair. Duns Scotus's presence at Oxford from 1300 to 1301 is attested by documentation: His name is listed among the twenty-two Oxford Franciscans who were presented to Bishop Dalderby on July 26, 1300, and a disputation of a master of theology, Philip of Bridington, names Duns Scotus as the bachelor respondent. Following a brief exile, Duns Scotus returned to the University of Paris, where he received his master's degree in 1305.

Duns Scotus was evidently a devout monk, a zealous teacher, and an ambitious writer, but the essence of his personality must be extrapolated from his writing style, which, in general, is impersonal in line with his intention to attain absolute objectivity. Utilizing the dialectical approach to the discussion of a topic, Duns Scotus deliberately suppresses the identities of those with whom he enters into dialogue. Yet despite his meticulous analysis and his effort to be precise, his style is difficult and often obscure. Nevertheless, despite his efforts to be impersonal, his style is not fully dehumanized, however lacking it is in emotion and a sense of humor. Never seeking to portray himself in any favorable light, he sometimes falls from grace and displays pettiness, narrow-mindedness, prejudice, and even fanaticism.

His reception of the master's degree from the University of Paris in 1305 stimulated Duns Scotus to ambitious literary activity. Having started on his *Ordinatio* at Oxford in 1300, he set about to complete this notable work by drawing not only on his original Oxford lecture notes but also on those made at Cambridge (exactly when he taught at Cambridge is not known, but possibly this occurred during his exile) and at Paris. This remarkable commentary on Lombard's *Sentences* has proven to be the most important of his works, although it remained unfinished at his death.

Life's Work

In 1305, Duns Scotus was appointed regent master in the Franciscan chair at the University of Paris, and he lectured and disputed there in this capacity until 1307. During this period, Duns Scotus conducted several disputations that are worthy of note. In one, he locked horns with the Dominican master Guillaume Pierre Godin regarding the principle of individuation, or what makes one thing different from another of the same species. Godin held that matter was the principle of individuation. Duns Scotus denied that that was so. In fact, he held, it was neither matter nor form nor quantity. Rather, he contended, the principle of individuation was a property in itself that was added to the others. Scotists later referred to this property as the *haecceitas*, that is, the "thisness" of a thing, which individualized it. At the same time, Duns Scotus recognized that individualized created natures must have some common denominator if scientific knowledge were to be gained of them.

Duns Scotus also conducted an important quodlibetal disputation. This was a disputation in which the master accepted questions of any kind on any topic (*de quodlibet*) and from any bachelor or master present (*a quodlibet*). Duns Scotus accepted twenty-one such questions to be disputed that concerned God and creatures. Later, he revised, enlarged, and organized them into a work called *The Quodlibetal Questions*. Like his *Ordinatio*, however, this work was unfinished at his death. Nevertheless, *The Quodlibetal Questions* proved scarcely less important than the *Or-*

dinatio. Indeed, the former represented his most advanced thinking. Altogether, his fame depends chiefly on these two works.

Another important disputation in which Duns Scotus engaged at this time was his defense of his theory of the Immaculate Conception. During the Middle Ages, many doctors of the Church were disturbed by the very idea of the Immaculate Conception. Was not Mary a product of human propagation? Was she therefore not a child of Adam and Eve, one who had inherited the Original Sin of her primordial parents? If so, did she not need Christ as her Redeemer? Therefore, how could Mary, virgin birth notwithstanding, have been free of original sin at her conception of Christ? Although Duns Scotus agreed with the skeptics that Mary would necessarily have needed Christ as her Redeemer, he proposed that mother and Son had been united in the Incarnation and Redemption by virtue of divine predestination and hence were joined together in their life, mission, and privileges. Therefore, he concluded, Mary had been preserved from both original and actual sin by Christ's Redemption. This theory, however, was not received well by Duns Scotus's secular and Dominican colleagues and was heatedly debated. Indeed, the idea of the Immaculate Conception continued to be controversial for five centuries before it became approved Catholic dogma.

Although Duns Scotus worked out of the Augustinian-Franciscan tradition, he was influenced by a variety of predecessors. He belonged to no particular school except the one he founded. Near the end of 1307, Duns Scotus was suddenly called away from Paris, having been unexpectedly appointed to a professorship at Cologne, Germany. According to some scholars, the reason for this abrupt departure is that his teacher and loyal friend, Master Gonsalvus of Balboa, had transferred him to Germany because he feared for his protégé's life, given the heated resistance to his defense of the Immaculate Conception. Duns Scotus's theory at this time seemed to many to conflict with the Church's doctrine of Christ's universal redemption, and he had been hotly challenged by his secular and Dominican colleagues. Indeed, at one quodlibetal disputation the secular master Jean de Pouilly had denounced the thesis as heretical and hinted

that Duns Scotus deserved severe punishment.

This threat came at a particularly unpropitious time, for King Philip IV of France, supported by Pope Clement V of Rome, had but recently instituted trial proceedings against the military religious order known as the Knights Templars. The Knights Templars, who had originated in the Crusades, were rich and powerful. Their chief rival was another military religious order, which had also originated in the Crusades, called the Knights Hospitallers. The Knights Hospitallers were favored by the pope. King Philip distrusted the power of the Knights Templars and coveted their possessions. Consequently, he lodged charges of heresy and immorality against them. Under these circumstances, Duns Scotus's life was surely in danger if a charge of heresy could have been proved against him.

In any case, Duns Scotus had not long to live. He lectured at Cologne until near the end of 1308, when he died prematurely, on November 8. His body was buried in the Franciscan church at Cologne, where it still lies. Although canonical proceedings for his beatification have been initiated twice since his death—once in the early twentieth century—he has never been canonized by the Church. In the Franciscan order, however, he is known as "Blessed" Duns Scotus, and his name is included in the Franciscan martyrology. He is also thus venerated in the German dioceses of Cologne and Nola.

The basis of Duns Scotus's metaphysics is "being" (*ens*). For him, being is the primary object of human intellect. He distinguishes, however, between spiritual and material beings. God, the Divine Spirit, is the Supreme Being: He is "pure" being, self-generated and uncreated. Although angels are in like manner immaterial, their spirit is less pure than that of the Divine Spirit; having been created, they are distanced from God. The human soul is also immaterial; breathed into the body by God to give it life, it lodges temporarily in its prison house, further distanced from "pure" being until it is released by death. For Duns Scotus, all created substances are composed of matter (*materia*) and form (*forma*). He calls the common substate of all created beings *materia prima.* Passive and receptive to corporeal forms, it is the subject of substantial and accidental change without the mediation of any substantial form. In other words, it is a *terminus creationis*. Duns Scotus insists on the unity and homogeneity of matter in all created beings. Everything that is created partakes univocally of this *materia prima*, which is indeterminate, matter without form, and only just removed from "nothing."

Duns Scotus distinguishes between "essence" (what makes a thing what it is) and "existence" (actual being). Between the two, he holds, is a *distinctio formalis a parte rei*, a formal property that is partly logical and partly real. Because an imaginary being has essence without having existence, however, substance (*substancia*) is an essence that has existence. In attempting to solve the questions of what gives existence to an essence and what constitutes the individual thing, Duns Scotus proposes that every created thing is composed of two realities: the "universal" and the "particular." The universal essence is the *natura* (what is common to all concrete realities of the same species). It is "form" that confers *natura* on matter. Form and matter constitute concrete substance in the "real" world, or what is taken to be reality. Matter in itself is indeterminate, but form is determining. It is form that communicates being to matter by determining "genus" and "species." Compounded, form and matter make a "unity."

It is *haecceitas*, however—the principle of individuation—that confers singularity and uniqueness on a thing. Thus haecceity, like matter and form, has its own unity. According to Duns Scotus, between the *natura* and the *haecceitas* is a difference that is partly conceptional but is also partly an objective ground in reality itself and independent of the mind. The unity of this composite is less than the numerical unity of the individual as such. What actually constitutes the individual as a concrete object is neither matter nor form nor *compositum* as such, for all three of these factors can be conceived of logically as universals. Hence the singular and unique thing is a composite of this matter, this form, and this *compositum*. Duns Scotus's view that the universal has an objective ground in reality is termed in philosophy "moderate realism."

Influence

Duns Scotus, inheritor of the Augustinian-Franciscan tradition, founded the Scholastic school of Scotism. Franciscan teachers tended to follow his lead. In the fourteenth century, the principle Scotists were Francis of Mayron and Antonio Andrea. During the fourteenth and the fifteenth centuries, there appeared the following Scotists: John of Basoles, John Dumbleton, Walter Burleigh, Alexander of Alessandria, Lychetus of Brescia, and Nicholas De Orbellis. Among the Scotists of the period that marks the transition from Scholasticism to modern philosophy were John the Englishman, Johannes Magistri, Antonius Trombetta, and Maurice the Irishman.

The high quality of Duns Scotus's thought is attested by his influence on modern philosophers and literary figures of the nineteenth and twentieth centuries. He exerted a direct influence on such twentieth century philosophers as the American pragmatist Charles Sanders Peirce, the German existentialist and phenomenologist Martin Heidegger, and the French paleontologist, cosmic evolutionist, and Jesuit priest Pierre Teilhard de Chardin. Two modern literary figures, the late nineteenth century English poet and Jesuit priest Gerard Manley Hopkins and the American poet, religious writer, and Trappist monk Thomas Merton, were both deeply impressed by the thought of Duns Scotus, and their ideas and poems show his influence.

Duns Scotus is not to be taken simply as another medieval Scholastic. His philosophy contains much that is original, even unique. Emphasizing criticism, his thinking displays rigor as well as subtlety and depth as well as brilliance. It is true that he composed no single work in which the whole of his philosophy is clearly set forth as a system; nevertheless, a fairly well-rounded system can be extracted from his two major works: *Ordinatio* and *The Quodlibetal Questions*. Duns Scotus had the courage of his convictions and mercilessly attacked those masters whom he considered either inconclusive or erroneous in their thinking. He cared not that their schools might be distinguished or that their names were authoritative and prestigious. His Latin style has been criticized, not unjustly, for its difficulty of comprehension; it does require sustained concentration if it is to be comprehended. Duns Scotus is by no means inferior to Saint Thomas Aquinas as a thinker.

Richard P. Benton

A Treatise on God as First Principle

Type of philosophy: Metaphysics, philosophical
  theology
First transcribed: De primo principio, 1308 (English
  translation, 1949; best known as *A Treatise on
  God as First Principle,* 1966)
Principal ideas advanced:
◊ God, the First Principle, is the most perfect
  Being, that which causes but is not itself
  caused, that which is independent and on
  which everything else is dependent.
◊ The First Principle is possible because an infinite series of causes is impossible; such an uncaused being must be necessary in itself.
◊ There is but one First Principle, for multiple
  first principles are not necessary.
◊ The First Principle is simple, infinite, wise, indefinable, intelligent, and endowed with will.
◊ God created the natural order by a free act of
  will.

John Duns Scotus wrote in conscious opposition
to Saint Thomas Aquinas, as William of Ockham
did after him. Duns Scotus and Ockham felt there
were certain deficiencies in Thomas's position,
especially as it related to Christian doctrine. Both
were somewhat more avowedly philosophical
than Thomas, and both preferred to separate
more radically philosophy and theology as disciplines. The appearance of Aristotle in translation
was new in Thomas's day, and both Duns Scotus
and Ockham seem closer to Aristotelianism than
does Thomas, perhaps because the Aristotelian
corpus had had more time to be appraised, with
erroneous impressions corrected and Platonic
glosses removed.

A Metaphysical Analysis
Even a brief glimpse of *A Treatise on God as First
Principle* reveals that it is not in any sense a devotional work, even though its subject is God. No
practical or religious goals are specifically in
view, and in place of "God," Duns Scotus uses an
abstract title, the First Principle. The work is a
technical consideration of metaphysical structure
and attributes, and it deals directly with the central speculative questions that surround the divine nature. Theory of knowledge and arguments

for God's existence are present, but they are secondary to this straightforward metaphysical
analysis of the First Principle of all things.

Although *A Treatise on God as First Principle* has
few religious overtones, Duns Scotus begins with
the traditional prayer for divine assistance in his
task. He then considers "being" as the primary
name for God, which shifts the discussion on to a
metaphysical plane from which it seldom returns. He then discusses the traditional "division
of orders," the various meanings for and divisions of "being."

Cause and the First Principle
Eminence versus dependence is the first and traditional division. Whatever is perfect and nobler
in its essence is prior, according to Duns Scotus.
That which causes but is itself uncaused is first,
and everything of a more dependent nature is
posterior. The prior is whatever is able to exist
without the posterior, whereas the posterior cannot exist without the prior. This division is accurate even if the prior produces the posterior orders necessarily. After this first and essential
division of being, the posterior orders may then
be subdivided.

Duns Scotus goes on to quote Saint Augustine
with approval: There is not anything at all that
brings itself into being. Nothing that we know
from its nature to be an effect can be its own
cause. Some aspects are ruled out as being inci-
dental. Only certain crucial relations and orders
are to be considered, not all data. The goal of
such a delimited investigation is an understanding of the first cause in causing, although in
addition to this, myriad efficient causes are
needed to account for the majority of temporal
events. An efficient cause acts for the love of
some end; a first cause produces from itself without ulterior motive. No causation, therefore, is
perfect other than that which comes from a first
cause itself uncaused; lesser causes necessarily
have some imperfections connected with them.

Duns Scotus departs from Aristotle in making
"matter" prior according to independence,
whereas Aristotle completely subordinates matter to form. However, Duns Scotus reasserts with
Aristotle the priority of form according to eminence, because it is more perfect. Turning then to
Plotinus and to the Neoplatonic tradition, he af-

firms the traditional preference for unity: Plurality is never to be posited without necessity. Order is due to simplicity. It is really the preference for simplicity that dictates that the fewest possible principles should be introduced, and this is one of the strongest arguments for positing only a single first principle.

Then Duns Scotus offers his version of the traditional "proofs" for God's existence, phrasing it as being a demonstration "that some one nature is simply first." However, Duns Scotus prefers to couch his argument in terms of "possibles," rather than to argue from the nature of the actual natural world. If his reasoning holds for all possible states, he argues, then it would hold for whatever set of states happens to be actual, whereas an argument based on actualities need not hold necessarily for possible states. With Duns Scotus, and later with Ockham, an increasing stress is placed on simply considering the order of possible entities as something prior to (and thus nearer to God than) the actual order of nature.

Duns Scotus follows the traditional view that an ascent through an infinite series of prior levels or causes is impossible. He concludes merely that it is possible that some single causal principle should be simply first, not the assumed existence of a God. As a preliminary step, and as the limit of philosophical argument, God is proved simply to be possible, and then only in the form that "an efficient causality simply first is possible." Metaphysics explores possible arguments; it does not support dogmatic conclusions.

Furthermore, Duns Scotus never attempts to prove that such a cause that is simply first is necessarily itself uncaused. He simply goes on to argue that this is possible, because it is not affected by anything else and yet it affects other things independently. A first cause in the possible order is then shown to be required to bring some set of possibles into actual existence. From this point on, such a being can be examined as to its nature, although it is merely a being whose possible existence (although perhaps it has now become probable) has been established. Duns Scotus reasons: Such an uncaused being must be necessary in itself because it depends upon no prior causes. Of itself, it is impossible for such a first cause not to be.

Singularity and Simplicity

It becomes evident that there could be only one being of such a nature, because the kind of necessity that belongs to a being that owes its existence to no outside cause cannot be shared. Because there cannot be multiple beings all of whom derive the necessity of their existence from themselves, the unique perfection of such a single and preeminent nature is ensured. Duns Scotus turns from the internal consideration of such a first principle to argue that, moreover, there is nothing about the multiple entities in the world that requires more than a single first principle for their explanation. Because multiple first principles are not necessary, it would be foolish to posit more than the single first cause that the explanation requires.

A multitude cannot be from itself; a first cause is required to explain such existence. A unitary and unique being requires no previous cause; it can explain multiple beings without itself requiring explanation. Explanation ends when simplicity is reached. In the essential orders, an ascent is made toward unity and fewness, ending in one cause. Such a first efficient cause contains every possible actuality. No possible entities can be conceived of as being outside its nature. Thus it is perfect.

Nothing shares perfectly unless it shares, not of necessity, but from the liberality of its nature. Such a consideration of what perfection means leads Duns Scotus on to consider the divine will. If such a first principle must share its being with other beings, due to its natural liberality, then "will" must have an important place in such a nature as essential to its perfection. Along with this necessary endowment of will, Duns Scotus describes his God as being simple, infinite, and wise. Such essential simplicity excludes all possible composition in the divine nature. It is not a being made up of parts as other beings are. None of its perfections are really distinct from the others, although our language and the process of analysis force us to consider each perfection as if it were in some way separate and distinct.

Contingency and Will

It seems perfectly acceptable to Duns Scotus to say that the First Efficient is intelligent and endowed with will, although such assertions require special argument to support them and special qualifications to accept them. For instance, most intelligence looks to some end outside itself, but Duns Scotus's First Efficient is made unique by being said not to love any end different from itself. Thus the traditional categories are used to describe such a First Principle, but they are qualified in a way that makes their application unique. However, it is when Duns Scotus turns to the question of contingency that he becomes the most radical and the most subject to innovations.

The First Cause causes contingently, Duns Scotus asserts; consequently, it causes freely. The classical tradition had been united in making the creation of lesser orders in nature necessary and in viewing necessity often as the very hallmark of the perfection characteristic of a First Principle. Christian theologians, in considering God's creative activity, had modified this somewhat, although necessity still seemed to be preferred. Duns Scotus for the first time raises contingency to a central place in the divine nature and designates the creation of the natural order as a free act.

Duns Scotus sees that if any freedom of action is to be preserved for humans, some freedom of action must first be found to be possible in God. For if the First Cause moves necessarily, every other cause is moved necessarily and everything is caused necessarily. The locus of the problem of freedom is not in human nature; it really revolves around an issue concerning God's initial action. If God's creative act is necessary, if he has no freedom of movement in originating the natural order, then it is hardly likely that people could move contingently or freely when even God cannot.

Now Duns Scotus turns to the question of human will. If there is to be freedom in humans' causal activity, then people must act contingently. If such contingent action is to be possible, God must first of all have been open to such possibilities in his initial creative act. However, nothing, says Duns Scotus, is a principle of contingent operation except will. This is the source of Duns Scotus's "voluntarism." Anything other than an action that is contingent on the will is a necessary action, so that the possibility of allowing for contingency depends upon upholding a doctrine that gives a primary place to the will, both in

humans and in God. Contingency means that the act is dependent on the will's direction. Any view that wishes to preserve at least some human actions as being free must begin with the divine nature and preserve will as an independent power within that nature. Will can give rise to contingent actions and opens a freedom to humanity, through the similarity discovered between the activity of human will and God's.

The First Principle wills nothing outside its nature of necessity; consequently neither does it cause any effect necessarily. There could be no contingency in any second cause in causing unless there were contingency in the First Principle in willing. The presence of evil demands that God be free either to will or not to will this less perfect order into existence. Thus God's freedom in willing allows humans a similar freedom in willing and opens the way for contingent causation. Every effect in nature is contingent, because it depends upon the efficiency of the First Principle, whose efficiency is contingent.

God's Infinity
Will becomes identical with the First Nature although no act of God's understanding can be an accident. Thus, God's understanding of all things is necessary, but the action of his will in causing is not. Necessary cognition of everything whatsoever is a part of the divine nature, which means that God understands everything continually. Thus God must understand everything he wills, and this removes the possibility of a blind action by the divine will. With humans, no such necessary understanding exists, so that ignorant action is always possible. God is unique in this respect.

The possible intelligible concepts are infinite, and God must actually understand them all eternally and simultaneously. An intellect capable of such comprehension must itself be infinite and in turn must reside in a nature also actually infinite. God's infinity is claimed as a consequence of the infinity of possible objects of understanding and of his necessary grasp of them all.

If a being is infinite, then Duns Scotus argues that its various aspects are not formally distinct. Because simplicity must be predicated on God as a primary perfection, Duns Scotus concludes that God must be infinite. Only an infinite principle seems to be free of the distinctions within its nature that cause disruptive multiplicity. A finite entity is subject to division, whereas one characterized by infinity holds all of its attributes together in an essential unity.

How can we understand the infinite? Duns Scotus answers that it is through the finite, for the infinite can be defined only through the use of the finite. The meaning of the infinite is grasped negatively, as that which exceeds any given finite limit. Because finiteness itself does not belong essentially to the meaning of being, the natural intellect can easily come to see that "being" may be classified as either finite or infinite. This means that the human intellect apprehends being in general as neither finite nor infinite and then goes on to see whether the particular being it is dealing with is or is not actually finite (subject to limits) or whether it is to be understood negatively as exceeding all finite limits. Such a doctrine allows a much more direct and natural understanding of the divine nature than is usual among theologians.

What is infinite can also be a being, although other beings are finite. The natural intellect finds nothing repugnant or difficult about understanding the concept of an infinite being. On the contrary, "infinite being" seems to be the most perfectly intelligible concept. The argument for the intelligibility of infinity comes from the will. The human will is never satisfied by any finite object. It is always restless, always seeking something greater than any finite end. After this is understood, it is possible to grasp what infinity means: a lack of any specifiable limit or end.

God has the power to actualize all possible states simultaneously, but he does not choose to do so. Some states mutually exclude one another at any given moment, and other possibilities his will does not choose to actualize. If all possible states existed simultaneously, our world would be absolutely unlimited. Duns Scotus believes the natural order to be finite, its limits representing the original self-restraint of the divine will in creating.

Thus Duns Scotus's First Principle comes to have some of the attributes (will, contingent choice, freedom) that are usually associated with human activity, although in other respects (power, unlimited knowledge, infinity) it belongs to no natural genus. Here is a view that, in certain respects, makes the First Principle very much like a human and in other respects distinguishes it radically. Yet more important than this is the overall modernity of Duns Scotus's thought. "Freedom" and "will" predominate in these considerations, and a tentative quality pervades the argument as a whole. Duns Scotus represents not so much the decline of medieval theology as the beginning of a modern metaphysical spirit.

Frederick Sontag, updated by John K. Roth

Additional Reading

Bettoni, Efrem. *Duns Scotus: The Basic Principles of His Philosophy*. Edited by Bernardine Bonansea. Washington, D.C.: Catholic University of America Press, 1961. A clear account of John Dun Scotus's metaphysics, epistemology, theology, and ethics.

Copleston, Frederick. *A History of Philosophy: Medieval Philosophy*. Garden City, N.Y.: Doubleday, 1962. An excellent historian of Western philosophy provides a helpful interpretation of Duns Scotus's thought and its significance in the medieval period.

Cross, Richard. *Duns Scotus*. New York: Oxford University Press, 1999. An accessible account of Scotus's religious thought that focuses not only on the distinctive features of his philosophy but also on his lasting insights.

Gilson, Étienne. *The Spirit of Medieval Philosophy*. London: Sheed & Ward, 1936. An older but still important account of medieval thought, including the views of Dun Scotus, by a major twentieth century interpreter.

Langston, Douglas C. *God's Willing Knowledge: The Influence of Scotus' Analysis of Omniscience*. University Park: Pennsylvania State University Press. 1986. A worthwhile appraisal of Dun Scotus's important efforts to interpret the relationship between God's knowledge, will, and freedom.

Ryan, J. K., and B. W. Bonansea, eds. *John Scotus, 1265-1965*. Washington, D.C.: Catholic University of America Press, 1965. Important interpreters discuss a wide range of philosophical and theological topics in the thought of Duns Scotus.

Weinberg, Julius R. *A Short History of Medieval Philosophy*. Princeton, N.J.: Princeton University Press, 1966. Provides a careful analysis of the key concepts and theories in the philosophical theology of Dun Scotus.

Wolter, Allan B., ed. Introduction to *A Treatise on God as First Principle*, by John Duns Scotus. Chicago: Forum Books, 1966. Wolter explains Duns Scotus's views about logic, necessity, contingency, and freedom and shows how those concepts are crucial for Scotus's understanding of God.

Wolter, Allan B., and Marilyn McCord Adams, eds. *The Philosophical Theology of John Duns Scotus*. Ithaca, N.Y.: Cornell University Press, 1990. This volume reflects a late-twentieth century revival of interest in medieval philosophy and theology and the work of Duns Scotus in particular.

Richard P. Benton, updated by John K. Roth

Émile Durkheim

Durkheim was one of the founders of modern sociology, a discipline that he demonstrated was not reducible to psychology or biology. His concept of society as a moral construct had a great impact on anthropology, history, religion, law, and political theory.

Principal philosophical works: *De la division du travail social*, 1893 (*The Division of Labor in Society*, 1933); *Les Règles de la méthode sociologique*, 1895 (*The Rules of Sociological Method*, 1938); *Le Suicide: Étude de sociologie*, 1897 (*Suicide: A Study in Sociology*, 1951); "De quelques formes primitives de classification: Contribution à l'étude des représentations collectives," 1903 ("On Several Primitive Forms of Classification: Contribution to the Study of Collective Representations in Primitive Classification," 1963); *Les Formes élémentaires de la vie réligieuse: Le Système totémique en Australie*, 1912 (*The Elementary Forms of the Religious Life*, 1915); *Éducation et sociologie*, 1922 (*Education and Sociology*, 1956); *Sociologie et philosophie*, 1924 (*Sociology and Philosophy*, 1953); *L'Éducation morale*, 1925 (*Moral Education*, 1961); *Le Socialisme*, 1928 (*Socialism and Saint-Simon*, 1958); *L'Évolution pédagogique en France*, 1938 (*The Evolution of Educational Thought*, 1977); *Leçons de sociologie*, 1950.

Born: April 15, 1858; Épinal, France
Died: November 15, 1917; Paris, France

Early Life

Émile Durkheim was born April 15, 1858, to a family of rabbinical scholars living in the Vosges region of France. Although he broke with his Judaic heritage by becoming an agnostic, the ordered and respectable nature of his home life would have a lasting effect upon his attitudes and interests. After studying at the Collège d'Épinal and the Lycée Louis-le-Grand in Paris, he entered the famous École Normale Supérieure in 1879, receiving instruction from the philosopher Émile Boutroux and the historian Fustel de Coulanges. Although his mental brilliance and serious demeanor earned for him the nickname the Metaphysician, Durkheim did not do well at the École Normale, whose academic standards he thought were marred by literary dilettantism, and he finished second to last among successful graduates in 1882. Over the next five years, he taught at *lycées* in Sens, Saint-Quentin, and Troyes, except for 1885-1886, which he spent in Germany, visiting the psychophysical laboratory of Wilhelm Wundt. In 1887, he married Louise

Dreyfus; the couple eventually had two children, Marie and André. The same year he was appointed to teach a social science course created especially for him at the University of Bordeaux; nine years later, he was promoted to the first sociology chair in France.

Among the early influences on Durkheim's thought were the philosophers Immanuel Kant and Charles Renouvier, both concerned with establishing objective grounds for morality, and the English anthropologist of religion Robertson Smith. Work and contact with Alfred Espinas led to the development of the important Durkheimian notion of collective representations, the common ideas and symbols of a community. In this, Durkheim was also influenced by Auguste Comte's notion of a social consensus, and he especially identified with his predecessor's efforts to establish an autonomous science of sociology. In his second dissertation, *Quid secundatus politicae scientiae instituendae contulerit*, written in Latin and published in 1892, he recognized Montesquieu as the first to attempt an understanding of society in terms of universal laws. With the addition of an essay on Jean-Jacques Rousseau, the work appeared in English as *Montesquieu and*

Rousseau: Forerunners of Sociology (1960). Durkheim's eloquent and forceful defense of this thesis before hostile examiners did much to advance his reputation as a spokesperson for sociology.

Life's Work

For Durkheim, the primal union that created society also created religion; the totem represented not only god but also the clan. No religion was "false" inasmuch as all served a social function. Public rituals reaffirmed the identification between the state and its religious origins, wrapping social authority in an inviolable aura of sanctity that served to make antisocial aggressions unthinkable. Although Durkheim was interested in the ethical foundation of society from the earliest stages of his career, it was only in teaching a course on religion in 1895 that the subject became a principal focus of his work, most extensively addressed in his book *The Elementary Forms of the Religious Life*.

Another well-known aspect of Durkheimian sociology, closely related to his ideas about the religious foundations of society, is the concept of the "conscience collective," a term having a dual meaning inasmuch as "conscience" can be translated as both consciousness and conscience. Durkheim recognized that the social order was ultimately dependent upon an implicit system of values shared by members of a society. These values were developed intellectually in a society's culture and were internalized emotionally in the personality of its members.

Durkheim developed these concepts against both empirical utilitarianism, the belief that social union arose in the pursuit of mutual interests, scientifically recorded, and German idealism, the philosophy that the universe could be understood through subjective consciousness, known intuitively. In the first case, he attacked a long tradition stretching from Thomas Hobbes to Herbert Spencer, which under the banner of "science" insisted that humans were self-interested animals motivated solely by their wants. In the second case, he criticized the lack of empiricism in the idealists' notion of a

transindividual consciousness. Collective representations were "social facts" that could be studied empirically in cultural, religious, and legal practices, and thus the social system was as much a reality determining collective human experience and as subject to scientific observation as the physical environment. The utilitarian notion that social systems were simply arrangements of power and law that allowed the plurality of individuals to pursue their own interests Durkheim found reductive. Instead, he developed a philosophy that understood social causation in terms other than individual interest or individual action. Human motivations were also rooted in collective spiritual experiences that in cultural and legal institutions existed outside, and in fact acted on, individual consciousness.

Durkheim showed an interest in the problem of establishing a moral order in modern indus-

Émile Durkheim. *(Library of Congress)*

trial society from his earliest work. In *The Division of Labor in Society*, his doctoral dissertation published in 1893, Durkheim addressed the question of how to achieve stability in a society in which citizens were motivated by what has become known as possessive individualism. Utilitarians, who saw society as simply a system of contractual relations satisfying private wants, held that the increasing division of labor in modern society promoted greater happiness because it led to economic prosperity. In fact, Durkheim noted, newly industrialized societies were characterized by increasing rates of suicide. Social life began before both the division of labor and the exchange of goods, and a more primary form of social cohesion prevented differentiation and competition from degenerating into a Hobbesian state of war among all. Contracts were themselves dependent upon preexisting noncontractual elements; cooperation had its own intrinsic morality.

Social solidarity came in two forms, depending on its stage of development. Mechanical solidarity, by which individuals were attached directly to the group and mutually dependent, was characteristic of the primitive horde. Here the force of collective sentiments, like-minded and undifferentiated, was powerful and required no formal legal codification. Organic solidarity, by which more advanced societies integrated subgroups into the collectivity, used functional divisions of labor to create interdependence and regulated conflicts of interest by constraints and punishments. Nevertheless, collective identification with common underlying principles, such as the value of individuality, was still necessary under these more complex social arrangements.

Increasing differentiation in industrial society had, however, disintegrated the mechanical unity of the collective conscience, as was evident in the increase in deviant and anomic behavior. These were problems explored in Durkheim's famous work on suicide, published in 1897. In its subtle correlation of data concerning nationality, religion, age, sex, marital status, family size, geographic location, and economic conditions, *Suicide: A Study in Sociology* became a model for later sociological studies that used statistical evidence to support theory. Breaking with conventional categorizations, Durkheim explained suicide in terms of an individual's relationship to normative structures. The taking of one's own life was to be understood basically in terms of three attitudes: *egoism*, arising from the isolation of an individual from others; *anomie*, arising from the collapse of individual faith in an ordered worldview; and *altruism*, arising from individual sacrifice to a great cause. An anomic social environment, where there was no longer collective agreement about regulatory norms, occurred when failed expectations about reality destroyed the meaning of an individual's orientation toward society.

In 1902, Durkheim was invited to the Sorbonne as a lecturer in education, but because of continued academic resistance against sociology, he did not become a professor of the discipline by name until 1913. As an educator, Durkheim wanted to apply sociological ideas about the moral health of society to the Third Republic. After rejecting what he regarded as the glitteringly superficial intellectual life of the École Normale Supérieure, he had argued that a science of society must have practical application. Yet his remedy for social ills prescribed neither conservativism nor revolution. The distinction between "normal" and "pathological" forms of social behavior was actually relative to a particular stage in the development of a society; deviant beliefs simply led to the formation of new normative codes. As he argued in *The Division of Labor in Society*, individualism was not symptomatic of a pathological condition in modern society but, on the contrary, was a normal characteristic of the transformations engendering more advanced forms of social solidarity. Such a line of reasoning, developed by subsequent sociologists into functionalism, was open to criticism from radical thinkers inasmuch as it appeared to legitimate the status quo. For Durkheim, the sociologist, like a doctor, should try to maintain the normal state.

Nevertheless, social and ethical reform was a concern running throughout his lectures, most published posthumously. His political ideas were rooted in a Rousseauean notion of democratic individualism, by which the personal will defined itself in the general will and individual freedom was understood as moral action in the community. He was profoundly shaken by the

Dreyfus affair at the turn of the century and in 1898 published an article defending the ideal of moral individualism, under whose principles intellectuals had the right to denounce social injustices. With the outbreak of World War I, which took the lives of more than half of his former students at the École Normale Supérieure as well as that of his only son, Durkheim wrote several nationalistic pamphlets that are markedly in contrast to his scholarly work. The strain of the war undoubtedly weakened his health, and he died of a heart attack in Paris on November 15, 1917.

Influence

Durkheim recruited around his journal, *Année sociologique*, begun in 1898, a distinguished group of disciples, such as Henri Berr, Célestin Bouglé, Georges Davy, Marcel Granet, Maurice Halbwachs, Marcel Mauss, Robert Hertz, and François Simiand, who were to define the "French school" of sociology for years to come. Because their focus upon the moral order coincided so neatly with pedagogical reforms of the Third Republic, the school had considerable influence upon university appointments in France, exaggeratedly referred to as State Durkheimianism. A large number of twentieth century sociologists and anthropologists came to work within the tradition of Durkheimian sociology. Jean Piaget and Claude Lévi-Strauss recognized Durkheim's importance in the development of structuralism. Alfred Radcliffe-Brown brought Durkheimian ideas into British anthropology. The development of functionalism in the United States, in the work of Talcott Parsons, for example, is particularly indebted to Durkheim. Contemporary scholarly work on contractual systems, suicide rates, primitive religions, and symbolic representations of authority is still very much influenced by his work.

Bland Addison, Jr.

Sociology and Philosophy

Type of philosophy: Ethics, social philosophy
First published: Sociologie et philosophie, 1924 (English translation, 1953)

Principal ideas advanced:

◇ Individual "representations" (sensations, images, or ideas) are not mere epiphenomena, or by-products of the brain's neural process.
◇ Collective representations are not mere epiphenomena of individual lives.
◇ Individual representational life is characterized by its "spirituality," social life by its "hyperspirituality," terms that Durkheim ambiguously asserts designate "nothing more than a body of natural facts which are explained by natural causes."
◇ Morality derives from society, not from the individual.
◇ Value judgments express the relationship of things to ideals.

Émile Durkheim's *Sociology and Philosophy* contains the essays "Représentations individuelles et représentations collectives" ("Individual and Collective Representations"), "La Détermination du fait moral" ("The Determination of Moral Facts"), and "Jugements de valeur et jugements de réalité" ("Value Judgments and Judgments of Reality"). The immediate motive for writing "Individual and Collective Representations" in 1898 was to head off an attack Durkheim knew was coming from Gabriel Tarde, a criminologist, statistician, and sociologist who headed the French Ministry of Justice. Tarde was a fierce opponent of the exponents of biologism in sociology—thinkers such as Herbert Spencer and Albert Espinas—and he founded his own school of interpsychology, a theory that reduced all social behavior to statistically measurable imitations of beliefs and desires. The 1906 essay "The Determination of Moral Facts" represents Durkheim's effort to provide a structure for a sociology of morality according to rules he had formulated earlier. The essay deploys a favorite rhetorical strategy of Durkheim, setting up dualisms, in this instance between the moral and the sacred. In the 1911 essay "Value Judgments and Judgments of Reality," Durkheim struggles to link sociology with a concern for ideals.

Individual and Collective Representations
Durkheim begins "Individual and Collective Representations" by attacking proponents of the psychophysiological school, such as Thomas

Huxley, who maintained that mental processes were simple epiphenomena of the brain—in other words, that the mind has no nonphysical properties and names only the poorly understood workings of the brain. Durkheim turns the epiphenomenalists' own metaphor against them. To claim, as they do, that the mind is a "light which accompanies, but does not constitute, those [cerebral] processes" is mistaken, Durkheim says, because this light is itself "a reality which testifies to its presence by its peculiar effects." The act of understanding one's own behavior contributes in itself to one's freedom from a mere "system of reflexes."

Much of Durkheim's argument against epiphenomenalism is directed against psychologist William James's account of memory as "a purely physical phenomenon" that follows familiar pathways in the brain. If James is right, Durkheim asserts, and memory is "solely a property of the tissues," then it is hard to understand how a representation—a "sensation, image, or idea"— could be revived because "ideas cannot be linked unless the corresponding points in the cerebral mass are materially linked." Thus, for Durkheim, memory is a "specifically mental phenomenon." Moreover, splitting mental life into "myriads of organic elements" makes incomprehensible the unity and continuity the mind reveals. Durkheim's explanation of the ontological status of representations is blurry, for it is not necessary, he says, to think of them as having a separate existence, but only to understand them as phenomena "endowed with reality."

The last section of "Individual and Collective Representations" pleads first for agreement that collective representations are "produced" by the interactions of individual minds but do not "derive" from them. They even "surpass" them. The relationship between individual and collective representations is completely analogous to that between the brain's neural processes and the individual's mental life. This argument is simple to grasp if not necessarily easy to agree to, but it is only anterior to the main point Durkheim has been driving at all along:

While one might perhaps contest the statement that all social facts without exception impose themselves from without upon the individual, the doubt does not seem possible as regards religious beliefs and practices, the rules of morality and the innumerable precepts of law—that is to say, all the most characteristic manifestations of collective life. All are expressly obligatory, and this obligation is the proof that these ways of acting and thinking are not the work of the individual but come from a moral power above him, that which the mystic calls God or which can be more scientifically conceived. The same law is found at work in the two fields.

Later, speaking of the mysterious actions that produce both individual and collective representations, Durkheim concedes that "It is for metaphysics to find the concepts which will render this heterogeneity in an acceptable form." Durkheim names this indefinable property of individual representations "spirituality," and the larger property of collective representations "hyperspirituality." In his last word on the subject of spirituality, Durkheim concludes unhelpfully, "Despite its metaphysical appearance, this word designates nothing more than a body of natural facts which are explained by natural causes."

Moral Facts

"The Determination of Moral Facts" identifies obligation and desirability as the two essential characteristics of moral acts, which history reveals are never identified with individuals acting in their own interest but instead are always devoted to the good of society, *with the condition that society be always considered as being qualitatively different from the individual beings that compose it.* Moral rules differ from others in that they are synthetic, not analytic. That is, getting sick from violating commonsense rules of hygiene is understood by analyzing the behavior involved: The punishment is inherent in the violation. However, no consequence is necessarily entailed by violation of a moral rule; the blame—the "sanction," as Durkheim calls it—is synthetic in that it accrues from violating a preestablished rule. Sanctions can also proceed from conformity to moral rules, in which case the consequences are favorable. In all instances, the sanctions derive not from the act itself but from the violation or the observance of the preestablished rules, none of which are absolute in all places for all times but are constructed by each society in keeping with its own needs.

These rules are related to sacredness, which also implies obligations, or duty, and a desire to seek the good for its own sake. Neither duty nor desirability has priority over the other, and neither can be derived from the other. The obligatory nature of moral rules derives from their moral authority, and Durkheim stresses the parallels between the moral and the sacred with the apparent intention of rooting the moral in the religious. Morality and religion have always been closely associated. Thus, "there must, then, be morality in religion and elements of the religious in morality."

Just as collective representations are more than the sum of individual representations, collective morality is more than the sum of the morals of individuals: "We arrive then at the conclusion that if a morality, or system of obligations and duties, exists, society is a moral being qualitatively different from the individuals it comprises and from the aggregation from which it derives." Durkheim notes how similar this argument is to Kant's argument for the existence of God. Kant said that morality was unintelligible without God; Durkheim fixes morality in society because "otherwise morality has no object and society no roots." Durkheim professes to be indifferent to the question of which is the source of morality, God or society: "I see in the Divinity only society transfigured and symbolically expressed."

However, the individual's role in moral activity must not be overlooked, for although society "transcends" the individual, it is also "immanent" in each person. Society's moral force produces civilization, "the assembly of all the things to which we attach the highest price," and everyone is human only to the extent that we share the "ideas, beliefs, and precepts" of our civilization. This "*sui generis* force" that we all "shelter under" is "an intelligent and moral force capable, consequently, of neutralizing the blind and amoral forces of nature." However, there is no universal moral force governing all societies, for each society has its own appropriate morality, and any other would be "fatal." Moreover, each society has its ideal type of individual whom all

members "realize is the keystone of the whole social system and gives it its unity."

"The Determination of Moral Facts" was originally presented as a seminar, and appended to it are several of Durkheim's most cogent answers to questions raised by his listeners. For example, he judges it impossible that morality and religion will ever be separated but explains his own position. He will not accept the utilitarians' view of morality as merely a useful set of guidelines but neither will he go along with the theologians in hypostatizing a "transcendent Being." Instead, he will frame the source of morality in rational language that remains faithful to its nature. To another questioner, he insists on the moral authority of the collective, and he compares people's awe in the face of the collective's moral authority to the awe felt by believers on their knees before their God. One must respect society even with its "pettiness," he says, concluding with a remark that gives a new slant to most theodicies: "If we were only able to love and respect that which is *ideally perfect*, supposing the word to have any definite meaning, God Himself could not be the object of such a feeling, since the world derives from Him and the world is full of imperfection and ugliness." Sort of a corollary to this observation is the point that each person is immoral to a degree because nobody can perfectly embody the "communal moral conscience."

Judgments

Durkheim makes a simple distinction in "Value Judgments and Judgments of Reality." Judgments are simple statements of preference that describe the state of the subject (for example, "I like hunting"), whereas judgments of value attribute worth to something and correspond to some objective reality. These objective values derive not from "a *mean type* found in the majority of individuals" in a given society because the average person is mediocre, but from the effect an object has on the collective subject, society. The moral authority of society constrains individuals in their judgments and even "ridicules those whose aesthetic inspiration is different," making society both a legislator and a "creator and guardian" of civilization's goods.

Value resides not in the thing, Durkheim says, but in the relationship between things and ideals.

These ideals, though, are not transcendent and universal but specific to different societies, arising from each culture's respect for human dignity. Durkheim emphasizes that whereas there are different types of value, they are all, including the economic, "species of the same genus." Finally, Durkheim arrives at the relationship between value judgments and judgments of reality, asserting that because ideals are themselves real, though of a "different order," the two kinds of judgments do not differ "in nature." This reasoning brings Durkheim to the point he was working toward all along: The "injustice" of the accusation that sociology has "a fetish for fact and a systematic indifference to the ideal."

Legacy and Criticisms

Durkheim is always named with Max Weber as one of the founders of sociology, and the concerns of these three essays are central to his whole project. In studying sociology, one studies the whole universe, the many aspects of which "converge in society" to create new and richer syntheses. "In a word, society is nature arrived at a higher point in its development, concentrating all its energies to surpass, as it were, itself." Sociology, then, has the noblest goals, and these three essays—even when making the most arbitrary proclamations—often impress with their perception and manner of formulation. However, their core of sociological science remains evasive, always blurred by Durkheim's postulation of some entity that he maintains is not metaphysical even though he "see[s] in the Divinity only society transfigured and symbolically expressed."

Scholars have viewed the attack on epiphenomenalism in "Individual and Collective Representations" as weak and uninformed, lacking a convincing account of the mind-body relationship. Exactly a hundred years after Durkheim's dismissal in 1898 of William James's remarks on memory, neuroscientists at Harvard and Stanford used magnetic resonance imaging to focus on the prefrontal lobes and the parahippocampal cortex as crucial to good memory, basically negating Durkheim's thought. In "The Determination of Moral Facts," Durkheim admits to being criticized for a theory of morality that subjugated the individual to a collective social morality, a charge that he answers by posing a slippery distinction

between appearance and ideal. Finally, in "Value Judgments and Judgments of Reality," his aim of putting value judgments on a firm scientific foundation by merging them with personal preferences via the claim that "all judgment brings ideals into play" is a sleight-of-hand trick that does not work in the view of most scholars. To say that value judgments represent the relations of things to ideals is unexceptionable, but it is hard to get from that claim to the position that statements such as "I prefer beer to wine" are concerned with ideals.

Frank Day

Additional Reading

Allen, N. J., W. S. F. Pickering, and W. Watts Miller, eds. *On Durkheim's Elementary Forms of Religious Life*. New York: Routledge, 1998. An examination of Durkheim's social and political thought.

Bierstedt, Robert. *Émile Durkheim*. New York: Dell, 1966. A clear introduction to the major themes surrounding Émile Durkheim's work.

Fenton, Steve, et al. *Durkheim and Modern Sociology*. Cambridge, England: Cambridge University Press, 1984. This text examines Durkheim's influence on modern sociology in various areas, including the division of labor, social conflict and deviance, state authority, education, and religion.

Giddens, Anthony. *Émile Durkheim*. New York: Viking Press, 1979. A concise and informative introduction to the life and writings of Durkheim.

Lukes, Steven. *Émile Durkheim: His Life and Work*. New York: Harper & Row, 1973. One of the leading authorities of Durkheim's thought presents the reader with an account of his life and influence.

Nielsen, Donald A. *Three Faces of God: Society, Religion, and the Categories of Totality in the Philosophy of Émile Durkheim*. Albany: State University of New York Press, 1999. A very readable presentation of the influences in Durkheim's thought.

Pearce, Frank. *The Radical Durkheim*. London: Unwin Hyman, 1989. A radical stance on Durkheim, this text is exemplary of the various ways in which he can be interpreted.

Schmaus, Warren. *Durkheim's Philosophy of Science and the Sociology of Knowledge: Creating an Intel-

lectual Niche. Chicago: University of Chicago Press, 1994. In this magnificent account of the links between philosophy of science and scientific practice, Schmaus explains the relationship between Durkheim's philosophy and his sociology. Through a revolutionary interpretation of Durkheim's major works, Schmaus argues that Durkheim, in his empirical observations, demonstrated how a philosophy of science can bring about a new science.

Walford, Geoffrey, and W. S. F. Pickering, eds. *Durkheim and the Modern Education*. New York: Routledge, 1998. A selection of revised papers highlighting Durkheim's views on education.

Wolff, Kurt H., ed. *Essays on Sociology and Philosophy, with Appraisals of Durkheim's Life and Thought*. New York: Harper, 1964. A collection of essays that explores the intellectual contexts of Durkheim's thought.

Howard Z. Fitzgerald

Ronald Dworkin

Dworkin has eloquently articulated a liberal philosophy of law that emphasizes the individual's affirmative rights to equal concern and fundamental liberties.

Principal philosophical works: "Is the Law a System of Rules?," 1967; *Taking Rights Seriously*, 1977; "What Is Equality? Equality of Welfare," 1981; "What Is Equality? Equality of Resources," 1981; *A Matter of Principle*, 1985; *Law's Empire*, 1986; "Foundations of Liberal Equality," 1991; *Life's Dominion*, 1993; *Freedom's Law*, 1996.

Born: December 11, 1931; Worcester, Massachusetts

Early Life
Ronald Myles Dworkin majored in philosophy at Harvard University, where he graduated with a B.A. in 1953. Two years later, he earned an M.A. in jurisprudence from Oxford University. Discovering that his major interests were in law, he returned to Harvard to complete an LL.B. in 1957, and he then served as a law clerk for the legendary American judge Learned Hand, who trusted only his clerks with the tasks of reading and criticizing his written opinions. Although Dworkin greatly admired Hand, he was never influenced by Hand's strong distrust of judicial power. In 1958, Dworkin married Betsy Ross, and he frequently expressed appreciation for her help and encouragement. The Dworkins raised one son and one daughter.

After his admission to the New York bar in 1959, Dworkin worked for more than two years as an associate for the famous law firm Sullivan & Cromwell. Many years later, he stated that he enjoyed practicing law, but it appeared unlikely that he would ever have become a courtroom lawyer. Although he had not really thought about an academic career, in 1962 Yale University unexpectedly offered him a position as assistant professor of law. Dworkin decided that the work of teaching and writing would allow him to combine his two interests of law and ethical philoso-phy and would also give him the freedom to work on those problems that he found the most interesting.

Life's Work
Dworkin advanced extremely rapidly in his academic career. In 1963, he published his first important article, a critique of utilitarianism, which appeared in the *Journal of Philosophy*, and he was promoted to the rank of professor two years later. His critique of legal positivism in the 1967 article "Is the Law a System of Rules?" established his reputation as a significant philosopher of law. In 1969, he was named to succeed Herbert Hart as the professor of jurisprudence at Oxford University, an unusual honor for an American citizen. In 1975, he was given a joint appointment as professor of law at New York University, where he typically taught courses and seminars during the fall semesters. In addition, numerous universities—including Harvard, Stanford, and Cornell—would either appoint him as a visiting professor or invite him to give special lectures.

In contrast to many academic scholars, Dworkin believed it was important to apply philosophical analysis to current legal and political issues. He became especially fascinated by the controversial cases decided by the United States Supreme Court. A committed liberal, he endorsed the Court's liberal decisions while Earl Warren and Warren Burger were chief justices, and he was angered by Republican politicians who attacked the Court. Dworkin especially supported those constitutional rulings that upheld a woman's right to obtain a legal abortion, that approved the use of court-ordered busing for desegregating schools, and that allowed the use of affirmative action to benefit minorities. In an attempt to influence public opinion, he began to publish articles for a broad reading public in *The New York Review of Books*. An extremely articulate writer, Dworkin soon became recognized as an important voice for the left wing of the Democratic Party. He served as chairman of Democrats Abroad in 1972-1974, and he was chosen a delegate to the Democratic National Convention in 1972 and 1976.

Dworkin's first book, *Taking Rights Seriously*, is mostly a collection of his early articles analyzing both philosophical problems and current legal issues. The articles are loosely unified by their defense of a "liberal theory of law" based on individual rights, especially the equal right to concern and respect. In rejecting legal positivism and utilitarianism, Dworkin argued that the law was composed of general principles as well as specific rules, and that individual rights should be recognized as "trumps" whenever they compete with public policies designed to promote the general welfare. The law contains both broad concepts and specific conceptions, and whenever judges encounter abstract concepts such as "due process of law," they should not hesitate to use philosophical analysis to make the law as good as it can become. To achieve this, Dworkin postulated an ideal judge, named Hercules, who would be able to discover the one correct decision in "hard cases." Hercules is a judge who operates within the Anglo-American legal system, and his decisions make use of philosophical principles embedded in constitutional texts, statutes, and judicial precedents.

In his later writings, Dworkin reacted to criticisms by expanding and refining various aspects of the theories found in *Taking Rights Seriously*, and he also responded to the constantly changing issues of the law, especially the constitutional decisions of the U.S. Supreme Court. In 1985, he collected nineteen articles into a second book, *A Matter of Principle*. By this time, the issue of affirmative action had grown in importance, and Dworkin was an outspoken advocate of the pol-

icy. In one of the most revealing articles, he defended Justice William Brennan's interpretative approach in *United Steelworkers of America v. Weber* (1979), which had been based on the spirit and purpose of the relevant statute rather than on its literal wording. In another revealing article, he moderated his position on "one-right-answer" in hard cases. He wrote that more than one right answer might exist in "extremely rare" cases, and he also acknowledged that there are no objective standards for evaluating which opinion is correct.

Dworkin's book *Law's Empire* is a treatise that integrates his earlier ideas into a systematic theory of legal hermeneutics (methods of interpretation of laws), and it is usually considered to be his most sophisticated achievement in jurisprudence. *Law's Empire* criticizes two hermeneutical approaches: conventionalism and pragmatism. Conventionalist doctrine resembles legal positivism insofar as it accepts established authority as the only source of the law. Dworkin refutes the version of pragmatism that considers societal results rather than principles of the right. Dworkin calls his alternative approach "law as integrity," which formulates constructive interpretations made from precedents that uphold principles of justice, fairness, and democratic ideals. Comparing law to literature, he writes that a judge should think of himself as "an author in the chain of common law." Such a judge would look upon judicial precedents as part of a long story that he must interpret and apply in new conditions, and he would seek "to make the developing story as good as it can be." The judge's decision would be based on an interpretation that "both fits and justifies" the principles of earlier decisions.

In the rather poetic conclusion of *Law's Empire*, Dworkin personifies law so that it has consciousness and reflects on the nature of "law beyond the law" in an ideal utopia. "The courts," he declares, "are the capitals of law's empire, and judges are its princes." In addition, philosophers are the "seers and prophets" of this empire, and their task is "to work out law's ambitions for itself, the purer form of law within and beyond the law we have."

By the time that *Law's Empire* appeared, Dworkin was one of the few philosophers recognizable to readers outside the academic community. In 1987, he was interviewed for American public television in the series *Bill Moyers: In Search of the Constitution*. That same year, he bitterly opposed the confirmation of Robert Bork to the U.S. Supreme Court. Bork not only was committed to conservative policies, but he also argued that judges should make narrow constructions of the Constitution based on the intent of the framers. About this time, also, Dworkin entered into a controversy with Catherine MacKinnon and other feminists who wanted to proscribe pornography in the name of gender equality.

Although Dworkin's writings usually emphasized legal issues in the United States, he was also interested in British affairs. His short volume *A Bill of Rights for Britain* (1990) advocated that the European Convention on Human Rights should be incorporated into Britain's domestic law, which would give British judges the power of judicial review. Explaining why such a change would be consistent with democracy, he argues that "true democracy" is not just a "statistical democracy" in which anything a majority wants is legitimate, but it is a "communal democracy" in which the majority decides within a system that guarantees equality and basic rights.

Dworkin's book *Life's Dominion* provides a thoughtful analysis of the controversial issues of abortion, euthanasia, and the sanctity of human life. While recognizing the "intrinsic value" of human life, Dworkin argues that the interests of a nonviable fetus are much less compelling than a woman's right to control her body. Dworkin is willing to follow *Roe v. Wade* (1973) in allowing government to proscribe abortions after the fetus reaches the development required to live on its own, and he asserts that there is a universal consensus "that abortion becomes steadily more problematic morally as a fetus develops toward infanthood." On the issue of euthanasia, Dworkin defends the right of a competent person to refuse medical procedures even if death results, but he arrives at no clear position on the difficult question of doctor-assisted suicides.

In contrast to his early works, Dworkin was no longer rejecting a generic right to liberty, but he had decided that the right to fundamental liberties was inseparable from the right of equal respect and concern. "It is generally agreed," he writes, "that adult citizens of normal competence

have a right to autonomy, that is, a right to make important decisions defining their own lives for themselves." He continued to believe, of course, that government should limit economic liberties in the interest of greater equality.

Dworkin further refines his interpretative theory in *Freedom's Law*, a collection of seventeen of his articles, mostly taken from *The New York Review of Books*. By a "moral reading," he basically means that judges and others should broadly interpret abstract constitutional concepts in ways that enhance human dignity and equality, a position already expressed in his law-as-integrity model. In three essays, he denounces Robert Bork's methods of reading the Constitution, especially Bork's "originalism" and his "crude positivism." According to Dworkin's political morality, the First Amendment's concept of free expression means that government cannot prohibit either pornography or hate speech. In keeping with his emphasis on principles, he does not defend free expression on the basis of utilitarian or pragmatic considerations; rather, he argues that censorship is morally wrong because it disrespects the individual's inherent right to express and to examine all points of view, even dangerous ideologies such as Nazism.

Influence

Following the publication of *Taking Rights Seriously* in 1977, Dworkin became one of the most influential philosophers of law in the English-speaking world. Although the bulk of his work is specifically concerned with Anglo-American jurisprudence, many continental philosophers such as Jürgen Habermas have taken a keen interest in his ideas. Time and again, Dworkin wrote about topics at the right moment. For instance, he began to criticize the schools of legal positivism and utilitarianism during the Vietnam War, when many people in the West were thirsting for philosophical alternatives that included moral content. Dworkin's emphasis on fundamental rights appears to offer the emotional satisfaction provided by natural law theory but without its metaphysical baggage. His insistence that law is composed of both general principles and specific rules seems especially appropriate for a normative approach to jurisprudence, and he has demonstrated that it is possible to combine abstract philosophical ideas with the analysis of concrete issues and legal cases. Even critics of Dworkin's ideas can appreciate the clarity, conviction, and precision in his writings.

Among philosophers and jurists, Dworkin's greatest influence was in the area of hermeneutics and constitutional interpretation. Writing at a time when conservative jurists were defending methods of strict textual analysis and original intent, he presented a coherent alternative that provided justification for judiciary activism. Although he did not originate the distinction between broad concepts and more specific conceptions, he did much to popularize the notion that judges should look upon abstract legal terms as concepts of political morality. In law schools, Dworkin's ideas were in step with those held by the majority of teachers and students, even though most jurists probably agree with Lawrence Tribe's reservations about his subjective methods that rely so greatly on the judge's moral values. Although certain of his normative theories are considered extreme, he has always been a man of practical realism, reflected in the fact that his methods and conclusions often coincided with those of Justice William Brennan and other liberals on the Supreme Court. Public opinion is important in a system of representative democracy, and Dworkin's popular articles in *The New York Review of Books* attracted an extremely large audience. Unfortunately, his articles dealing with particular cases will inevitably become less relevant with the passing years.

Thomas T. Lewis

Taking Rights Seriously

Type of philosophy: Ethics, political philosophy, philosophy of law
First published: 1977
Principal ideas advanced:
◇ Legal systems contain both rules and principles, the latter of which are especially important in "hard cases."
◇ Legal systems should recognize human rights as "trumps" in relation to other considerations.

◇ The most fundamental of rights is the right of equality, which means "the right to equal concern and respect."
◇ Legal positivism and utilitarianism are flawed insofar as they do not give priority to individual rights.
◇ Individuals have no valid claim to a generic right to negative liberty but only rights to specific positive liberties.
◇ There can and should be no absolute separation between law and ethical philosophy.
◇ Legal rights have no metaphysical foundations, but they are constructed on the reasoned analysis of existing laws and judicial precedents.
◇ In any legal dispute, there is only one right decision.

Taking Rights Seriously is a collection of thirteen essays written by Ronald Dworkin, two that were new and eleven originally published between 1966 and 1976. At the time the essays were written, legal positivism and utilitarianism were considered to be the two dominant schools of Anglo-American jurisprudence, but Dworkin attracted a great deal of attention by proposing a liberal alternative based on natural law and individual rights. In most ways, his ideas agreed with those found in John Rawls's famous book *A Theory of Justice* (1971). This was a period of great political and legal controversy, with many of the controversial issues involving general principles of equality and liberty. The U.S. Supreme Court, for instance, was ruling on important matters such as the legality of abortions, affirmative action for disadvantaged groups, and the use of busing for school desegregation. The Court's majority was usually upholding liberal positions, but it was also stimulating a strong conservative reaction. As both a lawyer and a philosopher, Dworkin was passionately committed to a liberal, left-of-center point of view. His goal was to develop systematic theories of jurisprudence and ethics relevant to the analysis of specific issues, and his intended audience included philosophers, lawyers, and the general reading public.

Because *Taking Rights Seriously* is a collection of essays, each chapter can be approached as an independent unit and the chapters need not be read in the order in which they appear. Some of the essays were written primarily for academic philosophers, and others were written for a broader public in *The New York Review of Books*. Several of the essays deal with abstract principles of jurisprudence, and others apply these principles in analyzing particular issues of policy, such as the moral justification of giving preferences to racial minorities and women.

Refuted Legal Positivism and Utilitarianism

In the introduction, Dworkin explains that his major purpose is to define and defend "a liberal theory of law" that is based on individual rights, and he rejects two alternative models, legal positivism and utilitarianism. According to his analysis, legal positivism holds that law is a "duty-based" system of rules, and it recognizes only those personal rights established by authoritative political institutions. He considers Herbert Hart's Concept of Law as the best example of this perspective. Dworkin understands utilitarianism as primarily a "goal-based" system in which individual rights are considered subordinate to maximizing the aggregate happiness of the majority.

In his refutation of legal positivism, Dworkin argues that a legal system consists of both specific rules and general principles. This distinction between rules and principles is especially relevant to the Anglo-American tradition of common law, in which judges interpret laws according to judicial precedents. In illustrating the distinction, Dworkin endorses the reasoning used in the New York case of *Riggs v. Palmer* (1889), where the named heir in a will had murdered his grandfather in order to obtain his inheritance. Although the applicable statute (a rule) had provided that a valid testament would determine the terms of the inheritance, the court decided to overrule the statute with the common law principle that a person should not be permitted to profit from his own crime. Dworkin argues that such general principles of equity are grounded in the state's interest in seeking justice and protecting individual rights. Such principles, moreover, should serve as "trumps" whenever they conflict with other legal considerations.

In complex legal systems, such as those in the United States and Great Britain, Dworkin insists that "no ultimate distinction can be made between legal and moral standards." Lawyers and judges should not only look to the black-letter rules that appear in statutes but also have some discretion to take into account moral principles. He does not suggest that judges should create new principles without preexisting materials, but he does believe that they can discover relevant principles within existing laws and prior cases. Although judges should not act as Platonic philosopher-kings with unlimited discretion to invent new laws, they should be encouraged to interpret and reorganize legal precedents in order to make the laws more just.

The Right to Equal Concern and Respect

Because established rights sometimes come in conflict with one another, certain rights must have priority over others. "Our intuitions about justice," Dworkin writes, "presuppose not only that people have rights but that one among these is fundamental and even axiomatic. This most fundamental of rights is a distinct conception of the right to equality, which I shall call the right to equal concern and respect." As an unambiguous example of invidious discrimination, Dworkin points to Jim Crow segregation, which stigmatized African Americans as unworthy of equal rights. The principle of equality, however, does not always require equal treatment for each person. He argues, for instance, that the goal of providing "equal concern and respect" is not inconsistent with affirmative action policies that give preferences to members of racial minorities who suffer the harmful effects of past discrimination. Although such policies might mean that nonminorities will enjoy fewer opportunities in education or employment, Dworkin argues that the policies are not invidious because they do not insult nonminorities or imply that they are inferior.

In order to promote his expansive view of equality, he is willing to place considerable restraints on the individual's liberty to do as he wishes, especially in the economic realm. "Laws," he writes, "are needed to protect equality, and laws are inevitably compromises of liberty." Although he asserts in chapter 12 that it is "absurd" to suppose that people possess any "general right to liberty," he strongly defends those specific liberties that are consistent with the more fundamental right of equality. Examples of such protected liberties include the right to practice one's religion, the right to purchase pornography, and the right of women to obtain safe abortions. Critics observe that Dworkin's choice of protected freedoms is based on his own hierarchy of values.

Although Dworkin asserts that his philosophy is within the natural rights tradition, he explicitly rejects any reliance on metaphysical or religious foundations, and he does not explicitly defend his rights theory by reference to a universal human nature. His epistemology emphasizes coherence rather than correspondence with reality. Although he endorses John Rawls's concept of "justice as fairness," he clearly recognizes that the hypothetical experiment of an "original observer" cannot logically obligate actual people to agree with the choices of such an observer. In determining which rights are to be protected, he is primarily interested in those rights that have developed within the Anglo-American tradition, whether located in constitutions, legislative statutes, or judicial opinions. Also, he sometimes justifies particular rights by referring to intuition or to a societal consensus.

Judge Hercules

Dworkin does recognize that legislatures and ordinary citizens have a legitimate part in the making of law, but his emphasis is always on how judges should make their decisions. He posits an ideal judge, named Hercules, in order to illustrate his proposed method of adjudication. Hercules, like any judge, would decide when a legal dispute is clearly covered by established law. If faced with a "hard case," however, Hercules would consider all relevant constitutional provisions, statutes, and judicial precedents, and his judicial opinion would emphasize those sources that are consistent with the most satisfactory concepts of moral philosophy. Hercules, in other words, would discover principles from the legal heritage in which he worked, and he would strive to make the best possible analysis of the material at his disposal. Because he respects the work of democratic legislatures, Hercules would accept the authority of a statute that he regrets as mistaken, but he would try to limit its "gravitational force" whenever possible.

Judge Hercules would especially have the op-portunity to employ his constructive hermeneutics whenever called upon to render decisions in hard cases of constitutional law. He would, of course, begin with the normal meaning of the text, but he would not speculate about the specific intent of the people who wrote and ratified the document. Closely related to the priority of general principles over specific rules, Hercules would also recognize a distinction between narrow "conceptions" and broad "concepts." Such a distinction would have great implications in constitutional texts that use abstract terms such as "due process of law" or "establishment of religion," because Hercules would interpret these terms according to the abstract political concepts that they currently evoke. For instance, the Eighth Amendment of the U.S. Constitution, which prohibits "cruel and unusual punishments," is a concept that is open to moral interpretation, and Hercules would decide its contemporary meaning rather than look at the narrow conceptions of "cruel and unusual" when the amendment was written in the eighteenth century. He would not inquire, therefore, about whether or not the framers of the Constitution endorsed capital punishment, but he would inquire about whether capital punishment is consistent with current principles of justice.

Dworkin takes his constructive hermeneutics to its logical conclusion, and he assumes that judicial discretion generally promotes the expansion of rights. For example, he strongly defends the Supreme Court's interpretation of the due process clauses of the Fifth and Fourteenth Amendment so that they protect broad substantive rights such as the "right to privacy." Going farther, the two clauses would logically protect one's freedom of speech even if there were no First Amendment. In effect, Dworkin does not recognize any real distinction between interpreting and amending the Constitution and certainly not a distinction between enumerated and unenumerated rights. Some critics warn that such a degree of discretion can produce judicial abuses such as the decisions in the *Scott v. Sandford* (1857) and *Lochner v. New York* (1905) cases.

Dworkin postulates that a competent judge such as Hercules can determine the one correct decision in value-laden "hard cases." Such a decision makes use of the most satisfactory moral arguments and is based on a "good fit" between the case and established legal materials. Although often criticized for this position, Dworkin appears to consider that the correct decision is only a theoretical possibility, for he never formulates any objective standards for knowing whether the correct decision has been rendered. In the litigation of legal disputes in the real world, he expects that competent judges should and will disagree with one another, and that deductions from either liberal or conservative values will be legitimate components of a judge's decisions.

A Provoking Theory

Legal philosophers were already familiar with most of Dworkin's ideas when *Taking Rights Seriously* was published, but the appearance of the book created something of a sensation. Reviewers praised the book for its rigor, its clarity, and its stimulating ideas. In contrast to many serious philosophical works, it was written in a style that was accessible to nonphilosophers within the educated public, and it dealt with issues of public policy that were being debated at the time. The book established Dworkin's reputation as one of the major jurisprudential thinkers of the time. Legal and philosophical journals were soon full of articles debating all aspects of the book, and Dworkin enjoyed responding to his many critics. Whether or not one agrees with his point of view, it is impossible to deny that *Taking Rights Seriously* provoked a great deal of fascinating and good writing in the field of legal philosophy and in the analysis of current legal issues.

Although most readers probably did not accept all the theories defended in *Taking Rights Seriously*, Dworkin did make a persuasive case for a reconsideration of the assumptions within legal positivism and utilitarianism. Even many of his critics were willing to acknowledge the validity of his arguments for using general principles and abstract concepts when analyzing the law. Although the book had only a marginal impact on the legal culture, it did help to determine the framework of discourse among philosophers of law, and it also provided considerable ammunition for those already committed to broad constructionism, judicial activism, and liberal policies on issues such as affirmative action.

In his later works, Dworkin continued to defend and to refine most of the ideas found in *Taking Rights Seriously*. He made two major revisions: He moderated his claims about the likelihood of there existing only one right decision in hard cases, and he explicitly recognized that a generic right to liberty is not incompatible with the principle of equality. His later works, moreover, have attempted to formulate a much more systematic theory of legal interpretation.

Thomas T. Lewis

Additional Reading

Burke, John A. *The Political Foundation of Law and the Need for Theory with Practical Value: The Theories of Ronald Dworkin and Roberto Unger*. San Francisco: Austin & Winfiel, 1993. Argues that Dworkin's theory does not have much practical value and that his antipositivism makes it difficult to identify the law. Interesting, but it overlooks Dworkin's flexibility and agreement with numerous judicial decisions.

Cohen, Marshall, ed. *Ronald Dworkin and Contemporary Jurisprudence*. Totowa, N.J.: Rowman & Allanheld, 1983. This collection includes especially good essays on utilitarianism by Rolf Sartorius and Herbert Hart, followed by Dworkin's reply to his critics. Many of the essays are abstract and for advanced students.

Covell, Charles. *The Defense of Natural Law*. New York: St. Martin's Press, 1992. The fourth chapter gives an excellent analysis of Dworkin's ideas, emphasizing that he rejected the classical tradition of natural law, which assumed the existence of universally valid truths based on human nature.

DeRosa, Marshall. *The Ninth Amendment and the Politics of Creative Jurisprudence*. New Brunswick, N.J.: Transaction, 1996. A stimulating but polemical work that argues that Dworkin's natural rights perspective, combined with his judicial activism, results in a nondemocratic ideology.

Gaffney, Paul. *Ronald Dworkin on Law as Integrity: Rights as Principles of Adjudication*. Lewiston, N.Y.: Mellen University Press, 1996. An excellent critique that argues that Dworkin does not have an adequate foundationist theory to support his claims in behalf of natural rights. Gaffney finds that Dworkin's defense of affirmative action contradicts his theory concerning the priority of individual rights.

Guest, Stephen. *Ronald Dworkin*. Stanford, Calif.: Stanford University Press, 1991. Although dated, this is the best general introduction to Dworkin's political philosophy and his theories of legal interpretation. The work is sympathetic but considers valid criticisms by other philosophers.

Honeyball, Simon, and James Walter. *Integrity, Community, and Interpretation: A Critical Analysis of Ronald Dworkin's Theory of Law*. Brookfield, Vt.: Ashgate/Dartmouth, 1998. The authors describe Dworkin as "the leading legal philosopher of our time." They argue that Dworkin's later works moved from an analytic to an interpretative theory of law. They provide excellent comparisons among Dworkin and other contemporary philosophers, with a useful bibliography.

Hunt, Alan, ed. *Reading Dworkin Critically*. New York: Berg, 1992. Left-wing critiques written primarily for British and Canadian readers. Hunt's interesting introduction argues that there is no real linkage between Dworkin's theory of adjudication and his political philosophy. Some of the essays take rather extreme positions.

Murphy, Cornelius. *Descent into Subjectivity: Studies of Rawls, Dworkin, and Unger in the Context of Modern Thought*. Wakefield, N.H.: Longwood Academic, 1990. Argues that the extreme subjectivity in Dworkin's theory of interpretation allows judges a dangerous degree of discretion. Murphy suggests that Dworkin, by encouraging judges to seek desired results, virtually accepts pragmatism as a philosophical outlook.

Thomas T. Lewis

Meister Eckhart

The medieval mystic Scholasticism of Eckhart served as a bridge between the classic Scholasticism of thirteenth century figures such as Albertus Magnus and Saint Thomas Aquinas and northern Renaissance scholars such as Desiderius Erasmus.

Principal philosophical works: *Reden der Untensweisung*, c. 1300 (*The Talks of Instruction*, 1941); *Quaestiones Parisienses*, c. 1302-1303, volumes 1-3, c. 1311-1313, volumes 4-5 (*Parisian Questions and Prologues*, 1974); *Das Buch der göttlichen Tröstung*, c. 1307-1320 (*The Book of Divine Consolation*, 1941); *Von dem edlen Menschen*, c. 1307-1320 (*The Nobleman*, 1941; also known as *The Aristocrat*); *Liber Benedictus*, c. 1308-1318 (*Book of Benedictus*, 1931); *Opus Tripartitum*, c. 1311-1326 (part 1, *Opus propositionum*; part 2, *Opus quaestionum*; part 3, *Opus expositionum*, includes *Expositio libri Genesis*, *Liber parabolorum Genesis*, *Expositio libri Exodi*, *Sermones et lectiones super Ecclesiastici Cap. XXIV*, *Expositio libri sapientiae*, *Expositio Sancti evangelii secumdum Iohannem*, *Sermones*); *Von Abgeschiedenheit*, c. 1315 (*On Detachment*, 1941; also known as *About Disinterest*); *Meister Eckhart's Sermons*, 1909; *Meister Eckhart: The Essential Sermons, Commentaries, Treatises, and Defense*, 1981; *Meister Eckhart, from Whom God Hid Nothing: Sermons, Writings, and Sayings*, 1996.

Born: c. 1260; Hochheim, Franconia (now a province of Thuringia, Germany)
Died: 1327 or 1328; Avignon, France?

Early Life

In medieval times, dates and places for births and deaths, except for royalty and others of significance, were rarely recorded. The best secondary sources indicate that Johannes Heinrich Eckhart von Hochheim was born about 1260 in the village of Hochheim, probably the village near Erfurt, in the province of Thuringia in Germany. His early years were spent in a knight's castle, of which his father was the steward, in the Thuringian forest. Accounts indicating that Eckhart himself was of noble birth are inaccurate, but his contact with nobility may have influenced his later view of God. His life in a castle, perhaps one on high ground, may have led to his comparison of a castle to a human soul, exalted so high by pride that even God could not penetrate it. His plan to "detach" himself from this pride and all things material may be why he spoke and wrote very little about himself, the result being that knowledge about his early life is very limited.

Probably at age fifteen, Eckhart became a novice in the Dominican order of preachers at Erfurt. The Dominicans were one of the most scholarly monastic orders of the Roman Catholic Church. After a one-year novitiate, Eckhart was accepted as a monk into the order and began his eight to ten years of study for the priesthood. The usual course of study began with Latin grammar and the liberal arts. Before March of 1277, Eckhart was sent to the University of Paris to study arts and philosophy. This was a rare honor for a novice and reveals an early recognition of his academic ability.

From Paris, he was sent for higher studies at the Dominican institute in their monastery at Cologne, where he may have sat under Albertus Magnus (Albert the Great), the leading Scholastic teacher of the time. Later, as in his Easter sermon of 1294, he quoted Albertus as if he had heard him in person. Because Albertus died in 1280, Eckhart's contact with him would have been brief. At Cologne, Eckhart also was influenced by the ideas of Saint Thomas Aquinas, another student of Albertus, although Thomas died a few years before Eckhart arrived. Eckhart himself embraced Scholasticism at Cologne, and there he received a bachelor of theology degree. In 1293-1294, as a requirement for a master's degree, Eckhart lectured on Peter Lombard's *Sententiarum libri IV* (1148-1151; *The Books of Opinions of Peter Lombard*, 1970, 4 volumes; commonly known as *Sentences*) at the Dominican College of Saint-Jacques in Paris. He earned a master of theology degree at the University of Paris in 1302. It was also then, in recognition of his ability, that Pope Boniface VIII conferred on him the official title of Meister, which means authority. From that time on, he was known as Meister Eckhart.

Life's Work

About 1290 Eckhart was elected prior of the Dominican convent at Erfurt, and shortly thereafter he became the vicar for the district of Thuringia. He probably wrote *The Talks of Instruction* about 1300. This is the earliest of his writings still in existence, and it provides the first glimpse into his inner life. Although he had not yet gone beyond Roman Catholic orthodoxy, he separated the essentials from the nonessentials in human life. For example, Eckhart declared that it was better to help a sick person in need than to fast with a heavenly countenance.

In Paris about 1300, while studying for his master's degree, Eckhart defended the Dominican position in theological debates with the Franciscans, another leading monastic order. These debates are probably the cause of later Franciscan attacks on the orthodoxy of Eckhart. About 1303, soon after receiving his degree in Paris, Eckhart returned to serve his order in Germany. He was first chosen as provincial prior for the Dominican order for Saxony, an area stretching from Thuringia to the North Sea and including fifty-one monasteries and nine nunneries. In 1307, he became vicar general for Bohemia but soon returned to his old position in Saxony. In 1311, Eckhart briefly returned to Paris, but in 1312, he began his distinguished tenure as head of the Dominican order in Strassburg, which was then one of the major religious centers of Europe. Eckhart served as prior, professor of theology, spiritual director, and preacher for the order. He was also in charge of the ring of Dominican convents surrounding the city.

In Strassburg, Eckhart reached his full potential as a teacher and a preacher. He used his excellent knowledge of Latin to convey his ideas in the convents, and he used vernacular German dialects to preach to the laity. However, while Eckhart was in this position, his orthodoxy was questioned, primarily because his thoughts were so deep that most religious leaders could not grasp them. He was supported by the Dominican order, but perhaps because of the opposition, in 1320, he left Strassburg to become prior at Frankfurt. Eckhart was called back to Cologne in 1323 and became regent master of the Studium Generale, the position once held by Albertus. Eckhart was still held in high esteem by most in the Roman Catholic Church, and his writings were affecting much of Europe.

During the most productive years of his life, Eckhart was strongly influenced by like-minded individuals who were seeking change in the medieval Roman Catholic Church. Among these were the Beguines (the word *beguines* may simply have meant "religious"). The Beguines were mostly women, although a few men, called Beghards, belonged. They took vows of celibacy and followed an ascetic lifestyle but did not live in monasteries. Eckhart was especially influenced by three Beguine women: Hadewijch of Brabant, a Dutch mystic who lived about 1240; Mechthild von Magdeburg, who wrote *Das Fliessende Licht de Gottheit* (*The Flowing Light of the Godhead*, 1953), a book that evidently helped shape Eckhart's view of God and the Godhead; and Marguerite Porete, who wrote *Miroir des simples âmes* (c. 1300; *The Mirror of Simple Souls*, 1968) and was burned at the stake as a heretic by the Paris Inquisition on June 1, 1310.

Although his teaching and preaching were extremely popular and edifying to those who heard him, the most enduring part of Eckhart's work was his writing. He wrote in Latin and German, and although the exact dates of publication are unknown, most of his works were probably written during the last twenty years of his life. He wrote four major treatises in German: *The Talks of Instruction*; *The Book of Divine Consolation*, which was dedicated to the queen of Hungary; *The Nobleman*; and *On Detachment*. These four works define four stages of human relationship to God: dissimilarity, similarity, identity, and breakthrough. The driving force behind this process is what Eckhart called detachment. Eckhart's Latin works, *Opus tripartium*, are more scholarly than the German works and won him the respect of the academic community, as evidenced by his being called back to Cologne in 1323.

For most of his life, Eckhart faced very little opposition. However, this changed during his last few years. The trouble began with his return to Cologne, where the archbishop was Heinrich von Virneburg (or Henry of Virneburg), a Franciscan who had no love for the Dominicans, especially none for Eckhart. To stem the tide of opposition that had arisen in Strassburg and to pacify the archbishop, Nicholas of Strassburg, who was a Dominican papal representative, conducted an investigation of Eckhart's ideas. Although Nicholas pronounced Eckhart free of heresy, Heinrich initiated an inquisitorial process in 1325. An inquisitorial commission was established to again investigate Eckhart's orthodoxy. He was also accused of leading others astray in faith and morals.

Eckhart gave his first defense to the commission on September 26, 1326. In a spirited opening statement, he questioned the jurisdiction of such a commission over a member in good standing of an exempt order, especially an individual who was held in high esteem by much of Europe. He also cast doubt on the scholarship of the commission members, who had found only twelve objectionable articles in his *Expositio libri Genesis* (commentary on the book of Genesis), which he said contained many more serious deviations from orthodoxy that they had not grasped. Eckhart then told the commission that he might have erred in doctrine, and he agreed to correct the errors if they could be revealed to him. However, he declared that he could never be a heretic because heresy was a matter of the will and not of the mind. Above all else, Eckhart desired to die as a member in good standing of the Roman Catholic Church.

Eckhart eventually responded to several lists of objectionable articles from his writings and sermons, but there was no final decision by the committee. He feared that the delay would lead to public scandal that would damage not just his own work but the entire Dominican order and the laity as well. Therefore, on January 24, 1327, he appealed his case to the papal court at Avignon, France, the headquarters of the Roman Catholic Church. On February 13, he delivered

his Declaration of Orthodoxy in the Dominican Church at Cologne. This is the last date on which Eckhart was known to be alive; however, it seems likely that, after making his declaration, he traveled to Avignon to defend himself. He was accompanied by several of his Dominican superiors, demonstrating that he still had the support of his order. In Avignon, he would have joined others, such as William of Ockham, a Franciscan philosopher from England, who were awaiting trial on similar charges.

The charges against Eckhart were gradually reduced to a more manageable list of twenty-eight. It is likely that Eckhart appeared before the papal commission as indicated by William of Ockham in one of his writings but died before the commission issued its verdict. On April 30, 1328, Pope John XXII replied to an inquiry from Heinrich von Virneburg concerning the proceedings against Eckhart. In this reply, the pope referred to Eckhart as being dead, and he assured the archbishop of a quick disposition of the case. That disposition was accomplished by the papal bull *In agro dominico* (March 27, 1329), in which Eckhart was either partially or wholly condemned on all twenty-eight charges. However, Eckhart himself was never officially declared a heretic.

Influence

Pope John XXII ordered that the bull against Eckhart's ideas be published in all areas under Heinrich von Virneburg but not in other parts of Europe. This indicates that he wanted to satisfy Heinrich but still limit the scope of his decree. Several of Eckhart's disciples, who were with him during his final difficult years, perpetuated and circulated his beliefs. The best known were John Tauler (who probably best understood his former teacher), Henry Suso, and Jan von Ruusbroec, all members of the Friends of God, a mystic group based primarily on Eckhart's ideas.

Eckhart's philosophical contributions were unique. To his own mystic Scholasticism, he added Greek, Arabic, and classic Scholastic ideas. The universality of his philosophy is attested by its partial incorporation in the philosophy of Friedrich Nietzsche, Marxism, Zen Buddhism, and various New Age movements.

In 1980, a process was initiated by the Dominican order to clear Eckhart's name. Pope John Paul II expressed approval of this process in September, 1985. Although *In agro dominico* is not likely to be reversed, the action by John Paul II was interpreted as a practical rehabilitation of the reputation of Eckhart and of his philosophical contributions to the modern world.

Glenn L. Swygart

On Detachment

Type of philosophy: Ethics, metaphysics, philosophical theology

First transcribed: Von Abgeschiedenheit, c. 1315 (English translation, 1941; also known as *About Disinterest*)

Principal ideas advanced:

◇ To be empty of all creatures is to be filled with God.

◇ A heart detached from the world must rest in nothingness.

◇ Once a person is detached, God must pour himself, in his entirety, into that person.

◇ As far as a person detaches the self from all things, that far, no less and no more, does God pour himself into that person.

◇ A detached person in not broken by adversity or carried away by prosperity.

◇ The immensity of the sweetness of God in a person extinguishes all other delights.

◇ A person who truly loves God receives all things as having been willed by God.

This treatise by Meister Eckhart marks the climax of his German writing. It is the last of four treatises describing four stages of the union between the human soul and God. The first of these stages is dissimilarity, and it is discussed in *Reden der Untensweisung* (c. 1300, *The Talks of Instruction*, 1941) in which Eckhart declared that all creatures are pure nothingness until they receive their being from God. They can receive that being only though the Son of God. To receive it, a person must be aware of the nothingness. The second stage, similarity, is described in *Das Buch der göttlichen Tröstung* (c. 1307-1320; *The Book of Divine Consolation*, 1941). Once people recognize that

their being is from God, they also recognize themselves as images of God. The third stage is identity. *Von dem edlen Menschen* (c. 1307-1320; *The Nobleman*, 1941; also known as *The Aristocrat*) describes this stage as identity with God in operation, not identity in substance. The human soul is uncreated and beyond time and space, and it operates as a part of God. The final stage is breakthrough, in which a person goes beyond God the Creator into the Godhead, the origin of all things. *On Detachment* describes how this can be done. Detachment is the driving force behind the entire process of union with God, and it is accomplished through the Cross of Jesus Christ. The three previous treatises also discuss detachment.

Detachment Defined

Although he was a Dominican monk, Eckhart's idea of detachment transcends monastic vows and traditional asceticism. By detachment, he meant complete metaphysical detachment rather than self-denial or physical separation. According to Eckhart, a person detached in this way is actually in God. Eckhart, who emphasized service to others, said a person could be surrounded by other people, be serving other people, and still be detached.

Understanding *On Detachment* requires an examination of Eckhart's use of the German word *Abgescheidenheit*, which is an abstract noun from a verb meaning "to depart from." Because Eckhart was speaking about giving up self-interest, some translators have used the word "disinterest" rather than detachment. To strengthen his meaning, Eckhart used various forms of the word and related words with meanings such as "to put off" and "become a stranger to."

Detachment is the way to achieve breakthrough, the fourth step in union with God, and it also has four steps. First, all perishable things are taken away. Second, those things are destroyed. Third, the things are forgotten as if they had never existed. Four, detachment is achieved. The human soul is in God, which produces happiness far beyond any temporal or carnal pleasure. Only detachment has no negative effect, and only detachment leads to a joy that is no more moved by earthly circumstances than a mountain is moved by a gentle breeze.

Detachment as a Virtue

Eckhart's earlier treatise, *The Book of Divine Consolation*, initiated a divine journey for the human soul. Eckhart began *On Detachment* with the description of his own journey. He began by reading the writings of pagan and Christian philosophers and both the Old Testament and the New Testament of the Bible. He quotes from and refers to much from these sources in his treatise. Eckhart was seeking advice on how one could draw closer to God, or how one could become by grace what God is by nature. His conclusion was the admonition of Jesus Christ to Martha (Luke 10:42) that the one thing she needed to become like her sister Mary was "choosing that good part," or as Eckhart translated it, "detachment." He then explained the details of that conclusion by taking virtues praised by other philosophers and showing how detachment was better than each of them.

He first explained why detachment is better than love. The authority he uses is the Apostle Paul in First Corinthians 13:1-2. Eckhart explained that even though love made him love God, it was better for God to love him, because his blessing in eternity depends on being identified with God. He realized that the identification begins with God and that he gives himself only to those who are detached. Eckhart refers here to Boethius in *De consolatione philosophiae* (523; *The Consolation of Philosophy*, late ninth century). Then, he said that love enabled him to suffer for God, but that detachment ranks above love because it made him sensitive only to God. Love is an experience, and an experience must be of something. Detachment creates nothingness so that God can fill the detached heart with himself.

Other philosophers praise humility, but Eckhart declared that although humility is a great virtue, detachment is far better. Humility can exist with detachment but detachment cannot exist with humility. Humility requires self-denial, but in detachment, there is nothing to deny. In humility, people prostrate themselves before other creatures and therefore must pay attention to those creatures. However, detachment stays within itself; thus, as Eckhart quotes David in Psalm 45:13, "the king's daughter is all glorious within." A perfectly detached person has no regard for anything higher or lower than his or her own position. Eckhart again refers to Boethius,

then points out that even though the Virgin Mary gloried in her humility (Luke 1:48), this was not a contradiction to detachment. Mary spoke what God told her to speak. Therefore, her declarations were a result of her detachment and were addressed to God. Eckhart said that both humility and detachment are virtues attributed to God. The Son of God, Jesus Christ, exhibited ultimate humility by becoming human and dying for the sins of humanity, but he also was the ultimate of detachment.

The third virtue described by Eckhart is mercy. Eckhart states that mercy is a great virtue because it causes a person to go out and meet the needs of others, and as with love and humility, mercy is the result of detachment. Eckhart concludes his comparison of detachment to other virtues by saying that after surveying them, he could find none as flawless or as conductive to God as detachment.

A Detached Mind

Eckhart next turns to the condition of a detached mind. He quotes Avicenna, a Muslim physician and philosopher, who stated that whatever a detached mind sees is true and that whatever it desires or commands will be carried out. Eckhart added that such a mind is a free mind and that God is compelled to enter it. God's attributes then begin to affect the mind so that it is caught up in eternity. The transitory things of this world no longer matter and the person is dead to this world. Eckhart quotes the apostle Paul, "I live; yet not I, but Christ liveth in me" (Galatians 2:20). The truly detached mind is unmoved by affection, sorrow, honor, slander, or vice.

The constant example given by Eckhart for detachment is God himself. God the Creator is so unmovably detached that even his creation of Heaven and Earth affects him as little as if he had not created them. God is not affected by the prayers and good works of his human creations. God in his sovereignty and omnipotence has already heard the prayers and knows of the good works in eternity, and in eternity, he has already answered and rewarded them. The ultimate of God's detachment is that he was not even moved by his Son becoming human, suffering on Earth, and then dying a horrible death on the cross. Eckhart quotes Philippus, a Roman emperor who reportedly became a Christian, as saying that God ordains the course of all things and holds all things to their course. He also refers to Isidore of Seville, a Spanish bishop who emphasized the immutability of God, that there was never a departure in God and that all things existed in the mind of God before creation. Eckhart declareA that God, in his detachment, works differently with different parts of his creation. He compareS this to an oven whose heat has a different effect on different kinds of dough.

Some questioned Eckhart about the statement of Christ in the Garden of Gethsemane, "My soul is exceeding sorrowful unto death" (Mark 14:34). Eckhart answered by saying that a person is in reality two persons: an outward or sensual person and a spiritual person. He declares the it was the outward person in Christ that cried out to God in Gethsemane, and that his spiritual person remained as unmovable as a hinge on a door when the door is opened. Eckhart's own lamentation at this point is that some people squander the strength of their souls on the outward person, thus robbing the spiritual person of the possibility of detachment.

Eckhart switches back to a human mind by saying that it will dwell in nothingness until it receives a message form God. If ideas are already there, the message from God cannot be fully received. A detached mind, because it wants nothing, will offer no prayer to God. Eckhart quotes one of his favorite writers, Pseudo-Dionysius, the Areopagite, who wrote *Peri t/e-macrons ouranias hierarchias* (c. 500; *The Celestial Hierarchy*, 1894), as saying that in the apostle Paul's comment (First Corinthians 9:24) concerning running a race, Paul meant a race to union with God.

Eckhart discusses the excellence of total detachment. The fastest way to attain that goal is through suffering, which seems to indicate the influence of Buddhism on Eckhart. Eckhart gives five admonitions to those who want total detachment in this life:
1. Be aloof among men
2. Do not engage in any idea you get
3. Free yourself from things that accumulate and cumber you
4. Set your mind to virtue
5. Dedicate it all to one end, the goal of perfection

Eckhart never claims to have reached the goal of perfection, and he realizes that a person living in this world cannot achieve this goal. However, he believes that all people should still pursue it, because it is always better to draw closer to God.

Most philosophies are based on the ability of the human intellect to answer the basic questions of life. However, for Eckhart, that intellect must first be detached and be therefore controlled by God. Detachment was the launching pad for Eckhart's theory of divine knowledge. All knowledge is a gift from God, and to possess divine knowledge, the mind must be undisturbed by the process of how it is given. Knowledge can then be activated by the faith that moves mountains.

Eckhart's Legacy

Late medieval reformers were greatly influenced by *On Detachment*. John Tauler and other disciples of Eckhart took the idea of detachment and made it more practical and more devotional by condemning more directly than Eckhart the external ceremonies and dead works that characterized medieval worship. Gerhard Groote founded a semimonastic group called the Brethern of the Common Life. The educational work of this group influenced later mystic leaders. Thomas à Kempis wrote *Imitatio Christi* (c. 1427; *The Imitation of Christ*, c. 1460-1530), which helped connect Eckhart's idea of detachment to the Reformation period of the sixteenth century.

In addition to having a significant impact on the philosophical thought of medieval Europe, *On Detachment* remains useful to those who want to live a life dedicated more to the service of God than to the service of self.

Glenn L. Swygart

Additional Reading

Colledge, Edmund, and Bernard McGinn. *Meister Eckhart*. Classics of Western Spirituality series. New York: Paulist Press, 1981. Excellent introduction and detailed historical data and theological summary. Contains good notes on Meister Eckhart's writing and an extensive bibliography. Includes the full text of the papal bull condemning the ideas of Eckhart.

Hollywood, Amy. *The Soul as Virgin Wife: Mechthild of Magdeburg, Marguerite Porete, and Meister Eckhart*. Notre Dame, Ind.: University of

Notre Dame Press, 1995. Puts the teaching of Eckhart in the context of the Beguine mystics and reveals the impact of those women on Eckhart. Attempts to give a clear picture of Eckhart's idea of detachment.

Jones, Rufus. *Studies in Mystical Religion*. London: Macmillan, 1919. Discusses the mystic groups and individuals of the medieval period. Includes a chapter on the life and influence of Eckhart and examines several quotes from his writings. Also has a chapter on the Friends of God, led primarily by disciples of Eckhart.

Kelley, Carl Franklin. *Meister Eckhart on Divine Knowledge*. New Haven, Conn.: Yale University Press, 1977. A detailed explanation of Eckhart's theory of divine knowledge and the difficulty in understanding exactly what he meant. Examines the influence of Saint Thomas Aquinas and the differences between the classic Scholasticism of Thomas and the mystic Scholasticism of Eckhart. Has thirty pages of excellent notes.

McGinn, Bernard, ed. *Meister Eckhart and the Beguine Mystics*. New York: Continuum, 1994. Put together by one of the leading Eckhart scholars, this is an excellent collection of essays by a variety of authors on the mutual influence between Eckhart and the Beguine mystic women, including Hadewijch of Brabant. Reveals both the complexity and the simplicity of medieval mysticism.

Perry, Ray C., ed. *Late Medieval Mysticism*. Philadelphia: Westminster Press, 1957. Puts Eckhart in the context of others with similar beliefs. Gives background and introductory material as well as a good synopsis of Eckhart's writings. Has both a general index and an index of biblical references for Eckhart's work.

Schmidt, K. O. *Meister Eckhart's Way to Cosmic Consciousness: A Breviary of Practical Mysticism*. Lakemont, Ga.: Center for Spiritual Awareness Press, 1976. Schmidt draws from the writings of Eckhart many concepts that he believes help define the idea of cosmic consciousness. He lists ten levels to achieve that elusive goal.

Schurmann, Reiner. *Meister Eckhart: Mystic and Philosopher*. Bloomington: Indiana University Press, 1978. Translations of Eckhart by the author, with commentary and analysis. Gives insight into terms used by Eckhart. Appendix discusses the use of Eckhart by Zen Buddhism.

Smith, Cyprian. *The Way of Paradox: Spiritual Life as Taught by Meister Eckhart*. London: Darton, Longman & Todd, 1987. Designed for modern spiritual seekers, as well as for a general audience. Attempts to summarize the major elements in the teachings of Eckhart.

Tobin, Frank. *Meister Eckhart: Thought and Language*. Philadelphia: University of Pennsylvania Press, 1986. Good coverage of life of Eckhart, including his trial and the condemnation of his ideas. Discusses major concepts in Eckhart's *On Detachment*. Includes the influence on Eckhart on Bernard of Clairvaux.

Glenn L. Swygart

Jonathan Edwards

The greatest Puritan theologian in America, Edwards tried to establish an intellectual foundation for Puritanism, to find a rational interpretation of predestination, and to justify the ways of God to humanity.

Principal philosophical works: *God Glorified in the Work of Redemption*, 1731; *A Faithful Narrative of the Surprising Work of God*, 1737; *Some Thoughts Concerning the Present Revival of Religion in New England*, 1742; *A Treatise Concerning Religious Affections*, 1746; *True Grace*, 1753; *A Careful and Strict Enquiry into the Modern Prevailing Notions of That Freedom of Will*, 1754 (commonly known as *Freedom of the Will*, 1957); *The Great Christian Doctrine of Original Sin Defended*, 1758; "Personal Narrative," 1765 (in *The Life and Character of the Late Reverend Mr. Jonathan Edwards*); *A Jonathan Edwards Reader*, 1995.

Born: October 5, 1703; East Windsor, Connecticut
Died: March 22, 1758; Princeton, New Jersey

Early Life

Jonathan Edwards was born in East Windsor, Connecticut, on October 5, 1703. East Windsor was still frontier, where worshipers carried muskets to church. Edwards was the only boy in his family, with ten sisters, but there were seven male cousins living next door and a number of boys attending school under Edwards's father, the Reverend Timothy Edwards. Educated by his father, Edwards was a precocious child who was ready for college at the age of thirteen. When he was eleven, he wrote a paper on flying spiders that is remarkable for both its scientific observation and its literary skill. As a teenager, Edwards was already dedicated to religion as his unquestioned calling. Sober and meditative by temperament, he had a private place of prayer deep in the woods.

In 1716, he entered Yale College, founded only fifteen years earlier, with a freshman class of ten. At this time, Edwards experienced an intense religious struggle, which he later described in his "Personal Narrative"; in particular, he had been "full of objections against the doctrine of God's sovereignty, in choosing whom he would to eternal life, and rejecting whom he pleased; leaving them eternally to perish, and be everlastingly tor-

mented in hell." This doctrine appeared horrible to him, but somehow he managed to accept it and to delight in God's absolute sovereignty. After graduating from Yale at seventeen, in 1720, Edwards studied theology for two years in New Haven, after which he served for a year and a half as pastor to a Presbyterian church in New York City. For the next two years, Edwards was a tutor at Yale. On February 22, 1726, he was ordained at Northampton, Massachusetts, as assistant minister to his eighty-four-year-old grandfather, Solomon Stoddard. About twenty-five miles north of East Windsor, on the Connecticut River, Northampton was then an isolated frontier village, cut off by forests from the wider world. In July of 1727, Edwards married Sarah Pierrepont, the daughter of a founder of Yale. Edwards was then twenty-three, his bride seventeen. She was apparently the ideal wife for him: a capable manager, a devoted mother to their surviving three sons and seven daughters, and a deeply religious person able to share her husband's spiritual life. When the famous evangelist George Whitefield visited the Edwards family in 1740, he was so impressed with Mrs. Edwards that he wished he could marry someone like her. When Solomon Stoddard died in 1729, Edwards, at twenty-six, became the minister of the chief parish of western Massachusetts.

Life's Work

Coming of age when the Puritan oligarchy had crumbled and when Puritan theology was being challenged by Deism and by more liberal Christian denominations, Edwards tried to create a philosophical justification for Calvinist dogma. Calvinism can be summed up in the acronym TULIP: total depravity, unconditional election, limited atonement, irresistible grace, and perseverance of the saints. First proclaimed in John Calvin's *Institutes of the Christian Religion* (1536), these doctrines had been the backbone of Puritanism. The thorniest of them were the ideas that humanity is not merely in a state of Original Sin (which is not total and is balanced by human goodness) but is totally depraved; everyone deserves damnation, and most will receive it; and only a limited few will be saved by God's inscrutable mercy. Along with this doctrine is the idea

of predestination: There is no free will, and every detail of each individual's life is predetermined by God, including salvation and damnation, which are ordained before birth, so that no amount of good works can merit salvation for one who is not among the elect.

Calvin offered no proof of these grim doctrines; he merely maintained that God's majesty is so great that humanity is nothing beside it. By Edwards's time, the Puritans had lost their monopoly on the northern colonies; other denominations preached a more merciful creed, according to which salvation was available (though not guaranteed) for everyone, while Deism threw out Christianity altogether, denying miracles, Original Sin, the Incarnation and Resurrection, and proclaiming that "whatever is, is right."

Edwards has been maligned as the quintessential "hellfire and brimstone" preacher, chiefly because of a sermon entitled "Sinners in the Hands of an Angry God," which he gave at Enfield, Connecticut, on July 8, 1741. In it he dramatized the concept of total depravity, arguing that everyone deserves to be cast into Hell, so that divine justice never stands in the way, for sinners are already under a sentence of condemnation and only God's restraints keep them out of Hell. Yet people cannot count on those restraints, for "the God that holds you over the pit of hell, much as one holds a spider, or some loathsome insect over the fire, abhors you, and is dreadfully provoked." The flaming mouth of Hell gapes wide, "the bow of God's wrath is bent," the wrath of God is like great waters dammed but ready to be released. Edwards piles up more metaphors for God's wrath but then urges his congregation to repent so that they may receive divine mercy.

Indeed, it is that mercy that Edwards stressed in most of his work. In his entire career, he gave only two sermons on hellfire, the other being "The Justice of God in the Damnation of Sinners" (1734). Edwards was no ranter; he was slender and shy, with a thin, weak voice; he spoke his sermons with

Jonathan Edwards. *(Library of Congress)*

quiet intensity. What made them eloquent was his immense preparation, his ability to paint pictures that made the abstract visible in terms of familiar experience, and the sense of authority that made him seem merely the mouthpiece for God. He was not a fiery preacher, nor was he an ecclesiastical scold giving lurid exposés of community sins and laying down blue laws.

The problem with which Edwards tried to cope was that of reconciling a loving and merciful God with a God who predestined most of humankind to Hell before they were even born. If salvation or election is already determined, why should individuals strive for salvation, when they have no free will? Why should ministers call sinners to repentance?

Nevertheless, Edwards tried, stressing "the excellency of Christ," and in 1734 he preached so eloquently that a revival broke out in Northampton (though he had not calculated to start one) and quickly spread to other towns. Seemingly wholesome at first, it turned to frenzied hysteria, with numerous suicides and attempted suicides. Edwards tried to tone down such bizarre behavior and "bodily manifestations," writing in *A Faithful Narrative of the Surprising Work of God* that "multitudes" felt suicide "urged upon them as if somebody had spoke to them, 'Cut your own throat. Now is a good opportunity.'"

The Northampton revival foreshadowed a much broader one, ushered in in 1740 by the visiting evangelist George Whitefield, who, unlike Edwards, was an itinerant preacher using the devices of theatrical showmanship. Lord Chesterfield said Whitefield could make people weep simply by the way he said "Mesopotamia." Following Whitefield, a revival frenzy broke out all over New England, called the Great Awakening. After its initial inspiration passed, novelty took over, with ecclesiastical juvenile delinquents trying to take over services and with zeal considered more important than knowledge; there was a danger that fanaticism would triumph.

In response, Edwards wrote one of his major works, *A Treatise Concerning Religious Affections*, preached in 1742-1743 and published in 1746, in which he tried to distinguish between genuine and false religious experiences. Edwards said that the church should be concerned with souls, not bodily symptoms. He did not study the bi-

zarre details but tried to examine the laws of human nature behind such behavior. Turning to John Locke's *An Essay Concerning Human Understanding* (1690), Edwards denied innate ideas and said that all knowledge comes through sensation, whereby one apprehends those ideas that God has willed to communicate. Accordingly, the imagination conjures up things that are not present objects of sense, and here is "the devil's grand lurking place." Edwards divided the mind into the Understanding and the Will; Reason belongs to the former, and though it is important, it is not, as the Deists maintained, sufficient, for Edwards believed that true religion comes from "holy love," which is not in the Understanding but in the Will. Thus, echoing Saint Paul, Edwards wrote that "he that has doctrinal knowledge and speculation only, without affection, never is engaged in the business of religion." Those who have received a divine light do not merely notionally believe that God is glorious but have a sense of the gloriousness of God in their hearts. Rational understanding alone is insufficient. There is, then, an essential emotional element in religion.

Edwards attempted to distinguish between the false emotionalism of revivalism, generated by mass hysteria, and a true religion whereby regenerate individuals receive a supernatural light from divine grace and are touched by the Holy Ghost, which acts within them as an indwelling vital principle. Therefore, enthusiastic delusions and bodily manifestations are merely from the imagination, not of love from and for God.

For modern readers, *A Treatise Concerning Religious Affections* is likely to be the most meaningful of Edwards's works. In his day, *Freedom of the Will* was thought to be his masterpiece. In it, he tries to reconcile human choice with the doctrine of predestination. Briefly, his reasoning is that each act of the will depends on a preceding act of the will, back to the original act of creation in the mind of God. Accordingly, he concluded that one is free to do what one will but not to will what one will.

In 1747, when David Brainerd, missionary to the Indians, died, Edwards edited his life and diary, producing a popular book that spurred missionary activities. Then in June of 1750, Edwards's congregation dismissed him after twenty-three years as minister. He had been too aristocratic for Northampton tastes, but the actual break came over the question of whether the unconverted should be admitted to Communion. When Edwards refused to admit those who would not acknowledge faith, he was defeated by a rigged election. Afterward, he moved to Stockbridge, Massachusetts, as missionary to the Indians. He did not consider the Indians depraved; he respected their customs, was an able administrator and earned the friendship and trust of the Stockbridge Indians, who protected him when the French and Indian War broke out in 1754. At Stockbridge, Edwards wrote *Freedom of the Will* and "The Nature of True Virtue" (1765), in which he argues that true virtue must be disinterested benevolence. Unlike his contemporary, Benjamin Franklin, a Deist who tried to make himself morally perfect by a thirteen-point program of good works, Edwards argued that true virtue comes not from repeated good choices but only from the grace of God.

In 1757, Edwards was offered the presidency of the College of New Jersey (which later became Princeton University). A week after his induction on February 16, 1758, he allowed himself to be inoculated against smallpox; a month later, he died of smallpox at age fifty-four. A week later, his daughter Esther Burr also died of smallpox, and the following autumn, his wife died in Philadelphia. One of Edwards's grandsons, Timothy Dwight, became a poet and president of Yale; another, Aaron Burr, became vice president of the United States.

Influence
Though Perry Miller, a leading scholar on American Puritanism, traced a line of influence from the Puritan Edwards to the Transcendentalist Ralph Waldo Emerson, most leading nineteenth century thinkers reacted against Edwards. Herman Melville, Oliver Wendell Holmes, Leslie Stephens, and Harriet Beecher Stowe were all hostile to his Puritan doctrines, chiefly predestination, total depravity, and limited atonement. Among other things, Moby Dick (of Melville's novel of the same title, 1851) symbolizes the Puritan God of wrath and vengeance; to Captain Ahab, this God is a tyrant whose "right worship

is defiance." Nathaniel Hawthorne never wrote directly about Edwards, but Edwards's somber theology and psychology may have influenced such Hawthorne tales as "The Minister's Black Veil." The twentieth century, with its horrors, in some measure rediscovered Original Sin, and Edwards was reappraised, though few scholars accept Calvinism uncritically. In the late twentieth century, marked by militant fundamentalism and biblical literalism as well as cults and gurus, Edwards's *A Treatise Concerning Religious Affections* takes on a new relevance, and though his reasoning in *Freedom of the Will* may seem logic-chopping, many modern doctrines—behaviorism, Freudianism, and communist dialectical materialism, to name a few—deny free will on secular but similar grounds. Edwards is now recognized not only as a writer of poetic prose but also as the major philosophical and psychological thinker and writer of the colonial era in America.

Robert E. Morsberger

Freedom of the Will

Type of philosophy: Metaphysics, philosophical theology
First published: A Careful and Strict Enquiry into the Modern Prevailing Notions of That Freedom of Will, 1754 (commonly known as Freedom of the Will, 1957)
Principal ideas advanced:
◊ The will is the ability people have of choosing one course of action rather than another.
◊ The will is determined when, as a result of certain actions or influences, a decision is made.
◊ The will is always determined by the greatest apparent good.
◊ To be free is to be able to do as one wills.
◊ Freedom is compatible with determination of the will; if the will were not determined, there would be no possibility of moral motivation and no sense in praise or blame.
◊ The Arminians claim that the will is self-determining and that it wills indifferently and without cause; but this idea is inaccurate and self-contradictory; furthermore, it makes vir-

tuous action impossible and moral injunctions senseless.

The problem of the freedom of the will, like many of the traditional issues, remains a problem for many philosophers because of the manner of its formulation. Even determining the appropriate question is difficult. Is it *whether* the will is free? Or is it *how* the will is free? Or is it a question as to *what* the will is? Or freedom? Does it even make sense to talk about the will as free? A person can be free, but what is the sense of saying that the *will*—whatever that is—can be free? Or is the question whether the will is free or determined?

Jonathan Edwards, the great Puritan philosopher of the eighteenth century, taking his cue from John Locke, whose *An Essay Concerning Human Understanding* (1690) he admired, recognized the difficulties involved in the formulation of the problem. Consequently, his careful study of the problem begins with explanations of the terms involved in discourse concerning freedom of the will; he begins with "will" and proceeds to "determination," "necessity," "liberty," and other terms whose ambiguity and vagueness have made the problem a particularly troublesome one for philosophers. Also unlike many philosophers, Edwards did not use the occasion of definition as an opportunity for framing the problem to suit his own purposes. With analytic acumen, he hit on the meanings relative to common use, and he clarified those meanings without neglecting consideration of the function of terms in conventional discourse. Thus, in considering "liberty," he noted that, "in the ordinary use of language," the words "freedom" and "liberty" mean the "power, opportunity, or advantage, that anyone has, to do as he pleases."

In recognizing that to be free is to be able to do as one pleases, Edwards prepared the way for his next point, that it is nonsense to talk about the will as free. It is nonsense because the will is not an agent, not a person who is somehow able to do as he or she pleases. Thus, Edwards wrote, "It will follow, that in propriety of speech, neither liberty, nor its contrary can properly be ascribed to any being or thing, but that which has such a faculty, power or property, as is called 'will.'" It makes sense to talk about a free *person*, for a

person can be in a condition of being able to do as he or she pleases, but it violates "propriety of speech" to talk about a free *will*, as if a will could do as it pleased, could act as *it* wills.

If, then, to have free will is to be able to do as one wills, and if the will, the power of choice, is determined by the apparent values of the alternatives brought to the attention of the person, it follows that free will is determined: An individual, who is able to choose, is *free* if, when his or her choice is *determined* by various considerations, he or she *can do as he or she pleases*. If this is the resolution of the problem—and, except for introducing the careful definitions, the arguments, and the qualifications, this is the essential resolution as Edwards presents it—then it is apparent that the formulation of the problem is misleading. It is misleading to consider the "freedom of the will," as if the will were an agent, capable of doing as it willed, and it is misleading to take the problem as the one put by the question, "Is the will free *or* is it determined?"—as if the alternatives were incompatible. Edwards deserves credit not only for resolving the problem in a manner that continues to win the admiration of professional philosophers but also for making his method clear: the method of destroying a problem by clarifying its formulation.

A Strict Calvinist
Edwards was a vigorous defender of Calvinism, a minister who was an effective combination of intellectual and emotional power. As minister at Northampton, Massachusetts, he argued for predestination, the depravity of man, and the doctrine of irresistible grace. He held with Puritan fervor to the conviction that God is unlimited in his use of grace; he can save whomever he chooses. In support of these hard doctrines, he employed a remarkable talent for developing, defending, and propounding ideas. However, he did not expect to win anything by the use of intellect alone; although he disdained religious emotionalism, he declared the necessity of conversion and faith. His extraordinary personality brought about an enthusiastic movement in support of the faith he defended; the church at Northampton became the origin and center of religious revival that came to be known as the Great Awakening.

His strict Calvinism eventually had its effect; as a result of an argument concerning the qualifications for communion, probably only the focal point of a number of doctrinal quarrels, he was dismissed in 1750 from the ministry of Northampton. He moved to the Indian mission at Stockbridge and continued work on the problem of the freedom of the will, an enterprise undertaken sometime in 1747. Written in support of the Calvinistic doctrine of predestination and of the necessity which it entails, the resultant work is nevertheless philosophically relevant to the general problem of the freedom of the will.

The *Freedom of the Will* was Edwards's answer to Arminianism, a doctrine based on the ideas of Jacobus Arminius, a sixteenth century Dutch Reformed theologian. To Edwards, the most objectionable feature of Arminianism, which was a view calling for a moderation of Calvinist doctrine, was the claim that divine grace is resistible. Arminianism, in advocating a less strict conception of election and redemption, prepared the way for an increasing emphasis on the moral and the human, with decreasing emphasis on the divine and on the absolute dependence of humanity on God. The "modern prevailing notions" referred to in the title of the work are the Arminian notions, in particular the Arminian idea of the liberty of the will. According to Edwards, the Arminians regarded the will as acting contingently, not necessarily, and without cause—a conception often referred to as indeterminism of the will.

The *Freedom of the Will* has four major parts and a concluding section. The first part defines the terms of the inquiry and explains the problem. Part 2 considers the Arminian conception of the freedom of will, inquiring whether there is any possibility that the will is indifferent, that is, free from any influence by causal or determining factors. Part 3 deals with the question whether liberty of the will in the Arminian sense is necessary to moral agency. Part 4 continues the criticism of the Arminian conception of the freedom of will by examining the reasons offered in support of that conception. The conclusion reaffirms the basic Calvinistic doctrines: universal providence, the total depravity and corruption of humanity, efficacious grace, God's universal and absolute decree, and absolute, eternal, personal election.

The Will Defined

Edwards begins his treatise with an analysis of the meaning of the term "will." He quite sensibly reminds the reader that definition would probably not be necessary had not philosophers confused the issue. The will, then, is "that by which the mind chooses anything"; it is the power to choose. There is no suggestion that the will is a substantial entity of some sort, an internal mechanism that hands out decisions. The will is what common discourse makes it to be: simply the faculty that a person has of choosing to do one thing rather than another. Where there is no inclination one way of the other, there is no act of will, no volition.

Next, he considers what is meant in talking about the "determination" of the will. The answer is that the will is "said to be determined, when, in consequence of some action, or influence, its choice is directed to, and fixed upon a particular object." To say that the will is determined, then, means simply that choices are caused.

The "good" is defined as the agreeable, whatever wins acceptance or "tends to draw the inclination." Thus, Edwards points out, "the will always is as the greatest apparent good is." In other words, if the will is the power to choose, and if choices are inclinations toward some alternatives at the expense of others, and if the greatest apparent good is what most of all provokes the interest, the inclination, of the person, then what is chosen, in every case, is whatever is the greatest apparent good. The factors affecting choice are several: They include the apparent characteristics of the object considered (allowing for the possibility that the object is not precisely what it appears to be), the apparent degree of difficulty involved in attaining the object, and the apparent time it would be before the object was attained. The apparent good, according to Edwards, is a function not only of the apparent character of the object considered but also of the manner in which the object is viewed or considered, and the circumstances of the mind that views. There is no objection to saying that the greatest apparent good *determines* the will—indeed, that is a proper way of speaking—but to say that the will "is" as the greatest apparent good "is" serves to emphasize the point that an object's appearing most agreeable and its being chosen are not two distinct acts.

The term "necessity" is critical in the problem of freedom of the will. Edwards states his intention of showing that necessity is not inconsistent with liberty. He rejects several customary definitions of necessity, showing that either they say very little or else they ignore the relativity of necessity: Anything that is necessary is so *to us* "with relation to any supposable opposition or endeavor *of ours*." The necessity relevant to a consideration of free will is philosophical necessity, defined as "the full and fixed connection between the things signified by the subject and predicate of a proposition which affirms something to be true."

A distinction is then drawn between natural necessity and moral necessity. Natural necessity is the result of natural causes other than such moral matters as habits, dispositions, motives, or inducements. Thus, by a natural necessity, falling bodies move downward. We are naturally unable whenever we cannot do something, even if we will it; we are morally unable when we are not sufficiently motivated to do a particular act. "Freedom" or "liberty" signifies the power to act as one wills.

The Arminian Concept of Free Will

Having completed the definition of crucial terms, Edwards turns to an explication and criticism of the Arminian conception of the free will. According to the Arminians, the will is self-determining. Edwards points out the impropriety of saying that the *will* determines its own choices; after all, the will is not an agent. However, even if it be contended that not the will, but the soul, determines the will, and does so without causal influence of its action, the further difficulty remains that every act of choice would be determined by a preceding act of choice. If a first act of choice, in a series of acts, is self-determined, it must be the consequence of a previous choice and, thus, be not first: a contradiction. If, on the other hand, it is not self-determined, then it is not free in the Arminian sense. In either case, the Arminian notion is self-defeating.

The next important consideration is whether it would be possible for an event to occur (say, an act of volition) without a cause of its occurrence.

Defining a cause as any antecedent on which the existence or nature of something depends, Edwards claims that no event could occur without cause. He affirms the principle of universal causation as one on which all reasoning about matters of fact depends, and he adds that no proof of the being of God would be possible without that principle. If no event could occur without a cause, then no act of volition could occur without a cause.

The argument that the will has the freedom of indifference—that is, that the will can choose any course indifferently, on its own, without being influenced, or that the soul's power of choice is in that way indifferent—is rejected by Edwards because of the contradiction involved in the implicit claim that the soul, while indifferent (in a state of *not* being inclined one way rather than another), chooses (is in a state of being inclined one way rather than another).

Referring to the Arminian contention that the will is contingent in the sense that acts of will are free from all necessity, Edwards argues that there could not be any act free from both cause and consequence. He adds that, even if an act could in this way be free from necessity, it could not be an act of volition, for acts of volition are *necessarily* connected with motives. To will is to be moved to action by the greatest apparent good; volition, then, necessarily involves being moved, or motivation; consequently, an act entirely unnecessary could not be an act of will.

In order to strengthen further his point that volitions are not contingent, in the sense of being without necessity, Edwards maintains that God's foreknowledge of events is possible only because of the necessity of those events, a necessity he recognizes.

Virtue and Necessity

In part 3, Edwards argues that the Arminian notion of an indifferent will, a will free from all causal necessity, is not only not necessary to moral virtue but also inconsistent with it. To establish his point, he advances a number of considerations to show that necessity is not incompatible with virtue or vice. God's moral excellence, the holiness of Jesus' acts, the sin of humanity—these are all necessary, but surely God's nature is virtuous and praiseworthy, as are

Jesus' acts; and the acts of the sinner, although morally necessary, are nevertheless instances of vice and blameworthy.

Having argued that necessity is not incompatible with virtue, Edwards then maintains that the freedom of indifference is not compatible with virtue, for virtue cannot reside in a soul that is indifferent; what common judgment requires is that one commit the self, that one be inclined toward commendable action.

The conclusion is that virtue depends on necessity; if a person could not be moved by exhortations, considerations, and inducements, neither virtue nor vice would be possible, and neither praise nor blame would be sensible. Even the commands of God would have to be acknowledged as senseless if a virtuous soul could not be moved by those commands without losing its moral freedom.

Answers to Objections
In part 4, Edwards considers, among other objections to the doctrine he proposes, the claims that if choices are determined, people are machines; that if choices are necessary, fate rules people; that the doctrine makes God the author of sin and (ironically) encourages atheism; and, finally, that the doctrine is metaphysical and abstruse.

Answering the charges, Edwards argues that people are entirely different from machines in that people are able to reason, to will, to do as they will, to be capable of moral acts, and to be worthy of praise, love, and reward. According to the Arminian conception, however, people would be worse than machines, the victims of "absolute blind contingence." If fate, as conceived by the Stoics, involves any limitations of human liberty, as Edwards has described it, then he rejects that notion of fate. It is misleading, Edwards continues, to argue that God is the author of sin, for even if God permits sin and so orders events that sin occurs, he does so for holy purposes and must be distinguished from the human agents who are the actual sinners. If atheists have embraced the doctrine of the determined will and have used it to defend their ways, Edwards argues, that in no way implies that the view is to blame. To the charge that his philosophy is metaphysical and abstruse, Edwards replies that it seems to be the other way about: The Arminian philosophy de-

pends on vague and undefined ideas and self-contradictory suppositions.

Edwards concludes by claiming that the chief objections to Calvinism have been met by his discourse. The principal objections against the notions of God's universal and absolute decree and the doctrine of personal election are that they imply a necessity of human volitions and of the acts of humanity; but the argument has shown that unless choices and acts are necessary, in the causal sense described, no volition is possible, and no judgment of moral action is justifiable.

Ian P. McGreal, updated by John K. Roth

Additional Reading

Chai, Leon. *Jonathan Edwards and the Limits of Enlightenment Philosophy*. New York: Oxford University Press, 1998. Situates Jonathan Edwards in the context of the Enlightenment and shows his similarities and differences with that tradition.

Cherry, Conrad C. *The Theology of Jonathan Edwards: A Reappraisal*. Garden City, N.Y.: Doubleday Anchor Books, 1966. Treating Edwards as a major figure in American literary and intellectual history, Cherry analyzes how Edwards's philosophy and theology affect each other.

Elwood, Douglas J. *The Philosophical Theology of Jonathan Edwards*. New York: Columbia University Press, 1960. Emphasizing Edwards's concern to integrate scientific, philosophical, and theological understanding, this work also explores Edwards's views about evil and God's grace.

Fiering, Norman. *Jonathan Edwards's Moral Thought and Its British Context*. Chapel Hill: University of North Carolina Press, 1981. A study of seventeenth century moral philosophy and its influence on Edwards.

Jenson, Robert W. *America's Theologian: A Recommendation of Jonathan Edwards*. New York: Oxford University Press, 1988. Clarifies Edwards's views on personal freedom, sin, the meaning of history, and the nature of God.

McClymond, Michael J. *Encounters with God: An Approach to the Theology of Jonathan Edwards*. New York: Oxford University Press, 1998. Focuses on Edwards's important philosophical understanding of religious experience.

Miller, Perry. *Jonathan Edwards*. New York: Meridian Books, 1959. A leading scholar on Edwards and American Puritanism focuses on Edwards's views about human freedom and moral responsibility.

Smith, John Edwin. *Jonathan Edwards: Puritan, Preacher, Philosopher*. Notre Dame, Ind.: University of Notre Dame Press, 1992. One of the most important Edwards scholars presents a reliable overview of Edwards's multifaceted career and philosophical perspectives.

Steele, Richard B. *"Gracious Affection" and "True Virtue" According to Jonathan Edwards and John Wesley*. Metuchen, N.J.: Scarecrow Press, 1994. An instructive comparative study that explores the life and work of two men who were among the most influential theologians and religious leaders of their day.

Stroh, Guy W. *American Philosophy from Edwards to Dewey: An Introduction*. Princeton, N.J.: D. Van Nostrand, 1968. An introductory account that identifies Edwards as one of the key sources for an American philosophical tradition.

Yarborough, Stephen R. *Delightful Conviction: Jonathan Edwards and the Rhetoric of Conversion*. Westport, Conn.: Greenwood Press, 1993. This study shows how Edwards shaped his preaching, theology, and philosophy so that they would have a persuasive, converting effect on his listeners and readers.

Robert E. Morsberger, updated by John K. Roth

Ralph Waldo Emerson

Emerson's invocation to humanity to live in harmony with nature became the impetus for the American Transcendentalist movement, which held that human beings could transcend sensory experience and rejected the Lockean notion that all knowledge comes from and is rooted in the senses.

Principal philosophical works: *Nature*, 1836; *An Oration Delivered Before the Phi Beta Kappa Society, Cambridge*, 1837 (better known as *The American Scholar*); *An Address Delivered Before the Senior Class in Divinity College, Cambridge . . .* , 1838 (better known as *Divinity School Address*); *Essays: First Series*, 1841; *Opinions, Lectures, and Addresses*, 1844; *Essays: Second Series*, 1844; *Addresses and Lectures*, 1849; *Representative Men: Seven Lectures*, 1850; *English Traits*, 1856; *The Conduct of Life*, 1860; *Representative of Life*, 1860; *Society and Solitude*, 1870; *Works and Days*, 1870; *Letters and Social Aims*, 1875; *Lectures and Biographical Sketches*, 1884; *Miscellanies*, 1884; *Natural History of Intellect*, 1893; *The Journals of Ralph Waldo Emerson*, 1909-1914 (10 volumes); *The Letters of Ralph Waldo Emerson*, 1939 (6 volumes); *The Journals and Miscellaneous Notebooks*, 1960-1982 (16 volumes).

Born: May 25, 1803; Boston, Massachusetts
Died: April 27, 1882; Concord, Massachusetts

Early Life

The fourth child of Unitarian minister William Emerson and Ruth Haskins Emerson, Ralph Waldo Emerson was born in Boston, Massachusetts, on May 25, 1803. His father's death in 1811 left the family poor, and his mother had to maintain a boardinghouse to support the family of six young children.

Despite this poverty, Emerson's education was not neglected. He attended the prestigious Boston Latin School (1812-1817) and in 1821 was graduated from Harvard. Even when he was an undergraduate, his interest in philosophy and writing was evident. In 1820, he won second prize in the Bowdoin competition for his essay "The Character of Socrates," and the following year he won the prize again with "The Present State of Ethical Philosophy." In these pieces, he demonstrated his preference for the present over the past, praising the modern Scottish Common Sense philosophers more highly than Aristotle and Socrates.

This preference derived largely from his belief that the modern philosophers offered more guidance in how to live. Despite the mysticism that informs much of Emerson's writing, he remained concerned with daily life. Thus, his purpose in *Representative Men* was to draw from the lives of great men some lessons for everyday behavior, and in the 1850's, he gave a series of lectures collected under the title *The Conduct of Life*.

After graduation from Harvard, Emerson taught school for his brother William before entering Harvard Divinity School in 1825. In 1826, he delivered his first sermon in Waltham, Massachusetts; typically, it dealt with the conduct of life. Emerson warned that because prayers are always answered, people must be careful to pray for the right things. One sees here another strain that runs through Emerson's writings, the optimistic view that one gets what one seeks.

Three years later, in 1829, Emerson was ordained as minister of Boston's Second Church, once the Puritan bastion of Increase and Cotton Mather. In the course of his maiden sermon there, he spoke of the spiritual value of the commonplace. He reminded his audience that parables explain divine truths through homey allusions and noted that if Jesus were to address a nineteenth century congregation, he "would appeal to those arts and objects by which we are surrounded; to the printing-press and the loom, to the phenomena of steam and of gas." Again one finds this love of the commonplace as a persistent theme throughout his work. As he states in *Nature*, "The meal in the firkin; the milk in the pan; the ballad in the street; the news of the boat" all embody universal truths.

In the same year that Emerson became minister of the Second Church, he married Ellen Louisa Tucker. Her death from tuberculosis in 1831 triggered an emotional and psychological crisis in Emerson, already troubled by elements of Unitarianism. In October, 1832, he resigned his ministry, claiming that he could not accept the church's view of communion, and in December embarked for a year in Europe. There he met a number of his literary heroes, including Samuel Taylor Coleridge, William Wordsworth, and Thomas Carlyle. He was less impressed with these men (Carlyle excepted) than he was with the Jardin des Plantes in Paris. At the French botanical garden, he felt "moved by strange sympathies. I say I will listen to this invitation. I will be a naturalist."

Returning to Boston in 1833, Emerson soon began the first of numerous lecture series that would take him across the country many times during his life. From the lectern, he would peer at his audience with his intense blue eyes. Tall and thin, habitually wearing an enigmatic smile, he possessed an angelic quality that contributed to his popularity as a speaker. The subject of his first lectures was science, a topic to which he often returned. His literary debut came, however, not from a scientific but from a philosophical examination of the physical world.

In 1835, Emerson married Lydia Jackson (rechristened Lidian by Emerson), and the couple moved to Concord, where Emerson lived the rest of his life. The next year Waldo, the first of their four children, was born.

Life's Work
In 1836, Emerson published a small pamphlet called *Nature*. Condemning the age for looking to the past instead of the pre-

sent, he reminded his readers that "the sun shines to-day also." To create a contemporary poetry and philosophy, all that was necessary was to place oneself in harmony with nature. Then

> swine, spiders, snakes, pests, madhouses, prisons, enemies" would yield to "beautiful faces, warm hearts, wise discourse, and heroic acts . . . until evil is no more seen. . . . Build therefore your own world.

The volume was not popular: It sold only fifteen hundred copies in the United States in the eight years following its publication, and a second edition was not published until 1849. It served, though, as the rallying cry for the Transcendentalist movement. In literature, this group looked to Carlyle and Johann Wolfgang von Goethe; indeed, Emerson arranged for the publication of Carlyle's book, *Sartor Resartus* (1836), in

Ralph Waldo Emerson. *(Library of Congress)*

the United States some years before it found a publisher in England. In philosophy, the Transcendentalists followed Immanuel Kant in believing that humanity can transcend sensory experience (hence the movement's name); they thus rejected the view of John Locke, who maintained that all knowledge comes from and is rooted in the senses. In religion, this group rejected miracles and emphasized instead the Bible's ethical teachings.

Addressing the Phi Beta Kappa Society at Harvard on August 31, 1837, Emerson returned to his theme in "The American Scholar." He warned against the tyranny of received opinion, particularly as it appeared in books: "Meek young men grow up in libraries, believing it their duty to accept the views, which Cicero, which Locke, which Bacon have given," but "Cicero, Locke, and Bacon were only young men in libraries, when they wrote these books." The American scholar should, therefore, read the book of nature and should do so confidently, believing that "the law of all nature, . . . the whole of Reason" resides in the self.

Thus guided by his own insight and revelation rather than by outdated cultures, the scholar would lead others to a union with the spiritual source of life. This enlightened individual was to be American as well as scholarly, for the nature he (today we would add "or she") was to take as his mentor was that of the New World rather than the Old.

In 1838, Emerson presented the controversial "Divinity School Address." To his audience of intellectual, rational Unitarians he preached the doctrine of constant revelation and called each of his listeners "a newborn bard of the Holy Ghost." Once more, he was urging the rejection of the past—in this case, historical Christianity—in favor of the present and trust in personal feelings rather than doctrine and dogma. His criticism of what he saw as the cold lifelessness of Unitarianism so shocked his listeners that he was barred from Harvard for almost three decades.

Such a reaction, though, was what Emerson was seeking; he wanted to shock what he saw as a complacent nation into regeneration through an appreciation of the present. "What is man for but to be a Reformer," he wrote. First a person was to reform, that is remake, himself; hence, Emerson

took little interest in political parties or the many Utopian experiments—some started by members of the Transcendental Club—of the 1840's. When enough individuals reformed themselves, society would necessarily be improved.

Among those who shared Emerson's vision were a number of neighbors: Bronson Alcott, Ellery Channing, Margaret Fuller, Elizabeth Peabody, Jones Very, and Henry David Thoreau. From 1840 to 1844, this group published *The Dial*, a quarterly magazine rich in literature that expressed the Emersonian vision. Emerson frequently contributed to the journal, and for the magazine's last two years, he was its editor also. Emerson's new philosophy spread well beyond Concord. In his journal in 1839, Emerson recorded that "a number of young and adult persons are at this moment the subject of a revolution [and] have silently given in their several adherence to a new hope."

In 1841, Emerson published the first series of his *Essays*, which includes what is probably Emerson's most famous piece, "Self-Reliance." The themes of the essays were by now familiar, but the expression was forcefully aphoristic. Attacking contemporary religion, education, politics, art, and literature for their adherence to tradition, he declared, "Whoso would be a man must be a nonconformist." In 1844 appeared *Essays: Second Series*, with its call for an American poet who would sing of "our logrolling, our stumps, . . . our fisheries, our Negroes, and Indians, . . . the northern trade, the southern planting, the western clearing, Oregon, and Texas." The American poet would not care for "meters, but metermaking argument."

Emerson attempted to fill this role himself. His aunt Mary Moody had encouraged his youthful efforts in this area, and at the age of ten, he had begun a poetic romance, "The History of Fortus." His early efforts had earned for him the role of class poet when he was graduated from Harvard in 1821. *Poems* (1847) suggests, however, that he lacked the ability or inclination to follow his own advice. The poems often remain tied to meter and rhyme rather than the rhythms of natural speech. In "Days," one of his more successful pieces, he described himself as sitting in his "pleached garden" and forgetting his "morning wishes." In "The Poet" he lamented, "I miss the grand design." Shortly before his second marriage, he had written to Lidian that though he saw himself as a poet, he knew he was one "of a low class, whose singing . . . is very husky." Some poems, though, such as "The Snow Storm," reveal the power and beauty of nature through language that is fresh and immediate. Others, such as "Brahma" and "The Sphinx" (Emerson's favorite), use symbols well to convey spiritual messages and suggest the correspondence among man, nature, and the spiritual world that is one of the tenets of Transcendentalism.

In the next decade, Emerson published three important works based on his lectures: *Representative Men*, *English Traits*, and *The Conduct of Life*. His lectures were not always well attended, even though he was in great demand. One course of lectures in Chicago brought only thirty-seven dollars; another audience in Illinois quickly left when it found a lecture lacking in humor. The books that emerged from these lectures are more sober than his earlier writings. His youthful idealism is tempered by a darker sense of reality. In "Fate," the first chapter of *The Conduct of Life*, he recognizes the tyrannies of life and notes that man is subject to limitations. In the concluding essay of the book, he reaffirms liberty and urges again, "Speak as you think, be what you are," but he concedes, too, the power of illusion to deceive and mislead.

After the Civil War ended in 1865, Emerson published two more collections of his essays, *Society and Solitude* and *Letters and Social Aims*, the second with the help of James Elliot Cabot. Much of the content of these books is drawn from lectures and journal entries written decades earlier. Although he was reusing old ideas, his popularity continued to grow. In 1867, he was invited to deliver the Phi Beta Kappa address again at Harvard; the previous year, the school had indicated its forgiveness for the "Divinity School Address" by awarding Emerson an honorary doctorate. When he returned from a trip to Europe and the Middle East in 1873, the church bells of Concord rang to welcome him back, and the townspeople turned out in force to greet him.

Emerson recognized, however, that his powers were declining. In "Terminus" he wrote, "It is time to be old/ To take in sail/ . . . Fancy departs." The great naturalist and conservationist

John Muir saw him in California in 1871 and was amazed at the physical transformation, one mirrored by his fading mental abilities as his aphasia worsened. After John Burroughs attended a lecture by Emerson in 1872, he described the address as "pitiful." When Emerson attended the funeral of his neighbor Henry Wadsworth Longfellow in March, 1882, he could not remember the famous poet's name. A few weeks later, on April 27, 1882, Emerson died of pneumonia and was buried near his leading disciple, Thoreau.

Influence
Emerson said that Goethe was the cow from which the rest drew their milk. The same may be said of Emerson himself. Walt Whitman derived his poetic inspiration from "The Poet," as Whitman acknowledged by sending a copy of the first edition of *Leaves of Grass* (1855) to Concord. Emerson was among the few contemporary readers of the book to recognize its genius. Thoreau, though an independent thinker, also took much from Emerson. In "Self-Reliance," Emerson had written, "In the pleasing contrite wood-life which God allows me, let me record day by day my honest thoughts without prospect or retrospect. . . . My book should smell of pines and resound with the hum of insects." That is a summary of *Walden: Or, Life in the Woods* (1854). Emerson's emphasis on the miraculous within the quotidian may even have influenced William Dean Howells and other American realists later in the century.

As an advocate of literary nationalism, of a truly American culture, he urged his countrymen to look about them and celebrate their own surroundings. His was not the only voice calling for an intellectual and cultural independence to mirror the country's political autonomy, but his was an important and influential one. Oliver Wendell Holmes, Sr., referred to "The American Scholar" as "our intellectual Declaration of Independence." In calling for a Renaissance rooted in the present of the New World rather than the past of the Old, Emerson was paradoxically joining the mainstream of the American spirit. Like John Winthrop in his sermon aboard the *Arbella* in 1630, he was advocating a new spirit for a new land.

Like his Puritan forerunners, too, Emerson stressed spiritual rather than material salvation.

Having grown up poor, he harbored no illusions about poverty. He knew that "to be rich is to have a ticket of admission to the masterworks and chief men of every race." Because of such statements, journalist H. L. Mencken said that Emerson would have made a fine Rotarian. This misreading of Emerson ignores the view that he expressed near the end of his life: "Our real estate is that amount of thought which we have." For Benjamin Franklin, the American Dream meant the opportunity to earn money. For Emerson, as for the Puritans, it meant the opportunity to live in harmony with oneself, to save not one's pennies but one's soul. Emerson's lectures and essays forcefully articulate a vision of the United States that has continued to inform American thought and writing.

Joseph Rosenblum

Essays

First Series

Type of philosophy: Ethics, metaphysics
First published: 1841
Principal ideas advanced:
◇ History is subjective and relative, not objective and absolute.
◇ Individual conscience should have ultimate authority.
◇ Moral laws work themselves out in people's lives and are not imposed externally.
◇ In love, whether erotic or platonic, people do not surrender their freedom to the beloved but paradoxically discover a greater freedom in self-giving.
◇ Our individual selves are extensions of a "cosmic consciousness," or "over-soul," which Emerson does not specifically associate with God.

Ralph Waldo Emerson's first series of essays grew out of the public lectures he gave after resigning as pastor of the Second Church of Boston. Though a great number of parallels exist between the essays—"Love" and "Friendship" are clearly companion pieces, and the thesis of "Self-Reli-

ance" is a corollary of the thesis of "History"—there is no intended coherence in the volume as a whole. The ideas expressed in *Essays* show the influence of German and British Romanticism; the German writers reached Emerson mostly through the Englishmen Thomas Carlyle and Samuel Taylor Coleridge. These tendencies of Romantic thought include the privileging of idealism over realism, imagination over reason, and the inner or psychological over the outer or objective. What was original in Emerson's thought, however, arose from his own struggles with ecclesial authority and with his personal experience of the young American nation that was still inventing itself. Emerson's peculiarly American form of Romanticism became known as "Transcendentalism," the term he himself preferred.

Essays is an ecclectic gathering of a dozen essays in the following order: "History," "Self-Reliance," "Compensation," "Spiritual Laws," "Love," "Friendship," "Prudence," "Heroism," "The Over-Soul," "Circles," "Intellect," and "Art." Although there may be no significance to the order of all the essays, scholars since the mid-twentieth century have generally agreed that beginning the collection with "History" and "Self-Reliance" is significant. The notion that what is called "history" is not one immutable, objective reality, but something incarnated in the human individual, is the premise that leads not only to Emerson's concept of over-soul but also to that of self-reliance. The over-soul connection is obvious when Emerson begins "History"—and, therefore, the whole collection of essays—with "There is one mind common to all individual men." Less obvious is the connection with "Self-Reliance," but the logic proceeds as follows: If everyone has equal access to this "common mind," then no one has particular authority. The individual conscience is the highest moral authority. The ideas in *Essays*, therefore, overlap.

"History"
"History" condenses an entire series of lectures on the philosophy of history that Emerson had delivered after giving up his Unitarian pulpit in 1839. The philosophy is essentially mystical: History is the record of the universal mind, and people are "inlets" to that universal mind (which in the ninth lecture Emerson will call the over-soul)

in that they have unmediated access to the wisdom of the ages. The essay might be summarized in an aphorism found in the eighth paragraph: "There is properly no history; only biography." Individual experience shows us universal experience.

"Self-Reliance"

"Self-Reliance" is, quite appropriately, Emerson's most anthologized essay. Not only does it capture Emerson's liberal mysticism, but it also captures the "spirit of the age" of nineteenth century Western thought and the essence of American individualism, which was just beginning to define itself. Emerson turns the Delphic oracle's "know thyself" into "trust thyself," which becomes a mantra echoing through the essay. Emerson posits a Philistine "Society" against which the individual must struggle. In a rare Socratic moment, this notion leads Emerson to a definition of the "self," which, as the previous essay asserted, is part of the divine. It also leads to the criticism of organized religion, which, to the absolute individualist, is following somebody else's creed.

"Compensation"

The influence of Eastern religion on Emerson's thought can be seen most clearly in the next essay, "Compensation," which is Emerson's term for the law of Karma, or metaphysical checks and balances. The idea that all evils are punished metaphysically, regardless of whether the punishment comes materially or even in this world, is of course not exclusive to Eastern thought. It is seen throughout classical myths, and in Judeo-Christian thought ("as ye sow, so shall ye reap," Galatians 6:7). However, Emerson goes beyond this concept of reciprocity to a very un-Western notion, the central moral tenet of the Bhagavad Gita, that from a divine vantage point, what appears evil to people may not be so. Emerson's poem "Brahma" echoes the philosophy of "Compensation."

"Spiritual Laws"

The fourth essay, "Spiritual Laws," springs organically from several points in the previous two essays. From the latter end of "Self-Reliance" Emerson resumes the criticism of organized religion or, more generally, systematic morality, by

once again asserting the individual soul as the seat of morality. From "Compensation," Emerson picks up the image of time smoothing the harshness of calamity. In fact, the closing paragraph of "Compensation" virtually blends into the first paragraph of "Spiritual Laws," wherein Emerson demonstrates the propensity of memory for improving things. However, because the modern soul has been surrendered to system, even people's virtues do not bring them happiness, as they ought. Unless people allow the spiritual laws of their own souls to dictate their morality, and not a cold and external system, they can neither do good nor be happy.

"Love" and "Friendship"

The next two essays, "Love" and "Friendship," are complementary essays that are most fruitfully read together. The first raises erotic love to a noble eminence as the foundation of all "domestic and civic relations" that "gives permanence to human society." The second essay raises platonic friendship to the level of romantic love. Both essays follow directly from the premise laid down in "Self-Reliance," but by a curious detour. "Self-Reliance" insists on the autonomy of the self, yet the very nature of love is a surrendering of self. Emerson gets around this difficulty by demonstrating that the paradox of love is that in giving one's self to the beloved or the friend, one is not diminished but expanded. People do not lose their liberty in love but rather gain a higher liberty in releasing themselves. Here Emerson uses the image of the widening circle as an analogy, which he will explore in more detail in "Circles."

"Prudence"

The individualism of "Self-Reliance" is continued in the next two essays. "Prudence" restates the critique of conventional morality as stifling, not just to the will but to the spirit as well. The essay stands as a marker for the change of the concept of prudence as a Christian virtue to that of *prudery*, which is almost a vice. The pejorative word "prude" had already been around for a century by Emerson's time, but this essay stamped even the older and more positive word of "prudence" with a negative character. "Prudence" for Emerson becomes the watch-cry of the potentially self-reliant individual surrendering to the moral rule of the crowd rather than following "spiritual laws."

"Heroism"

The irony that British essayist Thomas Carlyle's *Sartor Resartus* (1838) inspired Emerson's essay "Heroism" is compounded by the fact that virtually simultaneously with this essay, Carlyle published *On Heroes, Hero-Worship, and the Heroic in History* (1841), expanding on the very ideas Emerson distilled. Indeed, Carlyle's wife once complained that Emerson did not have a single idea that did not originate in Carlyle. Yet what is distinctly Emersonian in this essay is the equation of the heroic with the self-reliant. Those who surrender their dreams to the demands of society or convention never become heroes, though all have the capacity for heroism. The hero is one who maintains self-reliance despite opposition.

"The Over-Soul"

The next essay, "The Over-Soul," is almost as well-known as "Self-Reliance," though notoriously more difficult. It is essentially Emerson's digestion (or, some critics suggest, partial digestion) of German Transcendental philosophy of the early nineteenth century, though the idea in the West goes back to Plotinus. Emerson had already developed the image of a universal self from which the individual self, in Plotinus's term, "emanates." Here Emerson gives that universal self, if not a local habitation, at least a name: the over-soul.

"Circles"

"Circles" develops one of the most crucial images of Transcendental thought, already established in "Love," of the emanating self as the ever-widening circle. The opening sentence summarizes the image, and the essay: "The eye is the first circle; the horizon which it forms is the second; and throughout nature this primary figure is repeated without end." This image, embodying the pun of "eye-I," expresses the central tenets of Transcendental philosophy: the dissolution of the mundane self into the higher self of the over-soul. It is this process of transcendence that gives the name to Emerson's philosophy. Five years earlier, in *Nature*, Emerson had described the transcendental experience not only with the image of the circle but also with the image of the eye. As "all mean egotism vanishes," he wrote, "I become a transparent Eyeball." While the image leads easily to ridicule, recent scholarship has demonstrated that the widening spiral is both an apt description of Transcendental thought and an emblem for Emerson's prose style, which abandons the linearity of classical style.

"Intellect"

In the penultimate essay of his 1841 volume, "Intellect," Emerson not only echoes the preceding essay in describing the intellect as the outward-flowing circle of the self but also returns to the opening image of "History" as the record of the universal mind. People are "prisoners of our ideas," he writes, a more negative expression of the hopeful statement in "History" that the ideas of the past can be claimed as people's own. That inescapable doctrine of self-reliance returns at the end of the essay, where Emerson argues that the proper training of the intellect is toward resisting the potential "prison" of received ideas. The intellect must be as self-reliant as the soul.

"Art"

In the realm of art, the final essay in the volume, self-reliance takes the form of the relatively new Romantic aesthetic of "originality." True to the image of the ever-widening circle, however, Emerson is not content simply to condemn imitation in art and lionize originality. Instead, the artist builds on the art of the past, enlarging and building upon the insights of previous artists. "Because the soul is progressive," the essay begins, "it never quite repeats itself." This statement has implications for Emerson's circular style of expressing an idea by circling around it, repeating the central idea in slightly different forms. The artist, Emerson says, will use the language of his day to convey age-old truths, so that they are ever new. Yet Emerson also cautions the artist not to remove himself too much from the world in the idealism of creation; he minimizes the distinction between the "fine" and the "useful" arts.

Impact on American Thought

Emerson's *Essays* gave American Transcendentalism a philosophical and poetic language for expressing the peculiarly American form of individualism, especially as expressed in the political concept of civil disobedience (a phrase coined by Emerson's friend and disciple, Henry David Thoreau). It can be argued, in fact, that the rest of the nineteenth century, especially the horror of the American Civil War (1861-1865), played out the conclusions of Emersonian self-reliance. It should be no surprise that the ideas of a New England liberal with abolitionist tendencies would find expression in a war fought in part for the self-determination of the nation's black slaves. However, on the other hand, the very right of the Confederate states to their own self-determination also invokes the principle of self-reliance in the act of secession.

In metaphysics, Emerson's claim of moral autonomy for the individual anticipates that of existentialism. In fact, his response to the anticipated objection of the traditoinal moralist, that such a philosophy is moral sloth, is almost verbatim that of Jean-Paul Sartre. "If any one imagines that this law is lax," challenges Emerson, "let him keep its commandment one day." The ideas of Emerson's *Essays* continue to be felt, and his language of "Over-Soul," "Self-Reliance," and "Transcendentalism" can scarcely be avoided in modern discourse.

John R. Holmes

Additional Reading

Allen, Gay Wilson. *Waldo Emerson: A Biography.* New York: Viking Press, 1981. An excellent biography, at once scholarly and readable. Deals with the personal as well as public side of Emerson and shows the evolution of his ideas by citing the stages of their development in journal entries, letters, essays, and poems.

Bode, Carl, ed. *Ralph Waldo Emerson: A Profile.* New York: Hill & Wang, 1969. Biographical sketches by Emerson's friends and scholars that relate how his contemporaries viewed him and as well as how perspectives on him have changed since his death.

Goodman, Russell B. *American Philosophy and the Romantic Tradition.* New York: Cambridge University Press, 1990. Includes a chapter on Emerson's philosophical perspective on the romantic idea of the "marriage of the self and the world."

Jacobson, David. *Emerson's Pragmatic Vision: The Dance of the Eye.* University Park: Pennsylvania State University, 1993. A discussion of Emerson's insistence that a practical application of learning and philosophy leads to empowerment. Includes an index.

Leary, Lewis Gaston. *Ralph Waldo Emerson: An Interpretive Essay.* Boston: Twayne, 1980. An intellectual biography with a thematic arrangement. Focuses on Emerson's ideas and their relationship to his life.

Lopez, Michael. *Emerson and Power: Creative Antagonism in the Nineteenth Century.* DeKalb: Northern Illinois University Press, 1996. Focuses on Emerson's emphasis on power and force in the development of his American philosophy. Includes an index.

McAleer, John J. *Ralph Waldo Emerson: Days of Encounter.* Boston: Little, Brown, 1984. Contains eighty short chapters that treat stages of Emerson's growth as a person, thinker, or writer. Much of the book deals with actual encounters between Emerson and his contemporaries to illustrate their mutual influence.

Robinson, David M. *Emerson and the Conduct of Life: Pragmatism and Ethical Purpose in the Later Work.* New York: Cambridge University Press, 1993. Focuses on Emerson's writings as they relate to pragmatic rather than merely transcendental purposes. Includes an introduction that reviews various perspectives on Emerson. Contains an index.

Richardson, Robert D. *Emerson: The Mind on Fire.* Berkeley: University of California Press, 1995. A first-rate biography on Emerson that includes a life chronology, genealogy, and index.

Whicher, Stephen E. *Freedom and Fate: An Inner Life of Ralph Waldo Emerson.* New York: A. S. Barnes, 1953. Still a solid introduction to Emerson's life and thought. Includes a life chronology, bibliography, and index.

Yannella, Donald. *Ralph Waldo Emerson.* Boston: Twayne, 1982. A good introduction to Emerson's life and thought. Includes a life chronology, select bibliography, and index.

Joseph Rosenblum, updated by Richard M. Leeson

Empedocles

Empedocles was one of the earliest of the Greek philosophers to provide a unified theory of the nature of the world and the cosmos.

Principal philosophical works: *Peri physeos*, fifth century B.C.E (*On Nature*, 1908); *Katharmoi*, fifth century B.C.E. (*Purifications*, 1908); only fragments of these texts remain and no consensus exists as to which fragments belong to which texts.

Born: c. 490 B.C.E.; Acragas, Sicily
Died: c. 430 B.C.E.; in the Peloponnese, Greece

Early Life

Born c. 490 B.C.E. in Acragas, Sicily, Empedocles was a member of the aristocracy. Much of his life has become shrouded in legend; however, it is known that he spent some time with Greek philosophers Zeno and Parmenides in the city of Elea. Some time after that, he studied with the school of Pythagoras. Later, he left the Pythagoreans for reasons that are not completely clear and returned to Acragas, where he became a political figure. He eventually participated in a movement to depose a tyrant, despite his aristocratic background. Empedocles made enemies, however, and during one of his absences from Acragas, these enemies used their influence to banish him from his home. He would spend much of his life in exile.

Life's Work

Empedocles' two main works, *On Nature* and *Purifications*, exist only in fragments. *On Nature*, an essay on the ability of humans to experience the world, reveals Empedocles to be a cosmic philosopher and one of the earliest natural scientists. Parmenides believed that the world can be apprehended through the use of reason; Empedocles, however, believed that neither reason nor the senses can provide a clear picture of reality. In his view, reason is a better instrument for dealing with abstraction, and the physical senses are best suited for the phenomenological world.

Empedocles assumed that the universe is in motion and that it is composed of a multitude of separate parts, but unlike Parmenides, he believed that the nature of the parts is such that the senses can perceive neither the motion nor the great plurality of living and spiritual forms that inhabit the natural world. In his conception, the basic building blocks of true reality lie in the four archaic "roots": earth, air, fire, and water. In the abstract, these four elements are also represented by spiritual beings: Aidoneus is associated with earth, Hera with air, Zeus with fire, and Nestis with water. The elements can neither be added to the natural world nor deleted from it because the universe is a closed system. The elements can be mixed with one another, however, and the mixture of these elements in various proportions constitutes the stuff of the perceived world. Every physical entity is a composite of the four elements, in varying forms and degrees of mixture. Empedocles likened the blending of the elements to the creation of a painting: A few basic colors on the palette could be blended to produce all the colors of the rainbow.

Empedocles saw living things as only a matter of appearance. While alive, they have control over their corporeal forms and assume that the forms of life are as they perceive them. At the time of their death, when the bonds that hold together the elements of which they are composed are loosened, they die.

Empedocles believed that two opposing principles, Love and Strife (also variously called love and hate, harmony and disharmony, attraction and repulsion), are engaged in a constant struggle in the universe, a process that gives rise to a continual mixing and shifting of the basic particles of earth, air, fire, and water. The two principles alternate in their dominance in a great cosmic cycle that involves the whole universe. When Love dominates, the particles of matter are brought into a homogeneous mass. When Strife is in the ascendant, the effect is to separate the mixed elements into four separate and discrete masses. These alternating states form the poles of existence. The periods when neither Love nor Strife dominated were times of flux during which the power of one principle gradually increased as the power of the other waned. The human world is one where Strife is in the process of slowly overcoming Love—a place of relative disintegration.

In the beginning of the cycle, the elements are separated, under the control of Strife. As the powers of Love manifest themselves, the integrative process creates from the earth random or unattached portions of animals. These combine in various haphazard ways, creating monsters. A similar integrative process creates unattached human parts: disembodied heads, shoulderless arms, unattached eyes. Through chance wanderings, the parts begin to join, creating human monsters, such as many-handed creatures with double faces, cattle with human faces, and people with the faces of oxen. Nevertheless, some join in a manner that allows them to survive. As time and chance do their work, more and more improvements allow certain forms to prosper; eventually, human form, because of its relatively high survival value, becomes established and flourishes. The same process brings about the various orders of beasts.

After a relatively short period, the flux begins again. Strife becomes gradually more powerful, and the cycle is eventually completed. Empedocles may have meant his theory of Love and Strife to apply to human experience as well: These two forces, acting in the human world, are the causes of the harmony of friendship and the disharmony of hatred.

Empedocles thought that every entity in the universe was endowed with par-

ticular consciousness. In addition to being conscious of each other, Love and Strife are aware of their effect on the elements. The elements in turn are conscious of the workings of Love and Strife. Finally, the four elements—fire, air, earth, and water—are aware of one another, both pure and in their various mixtures, and therefore, humans have consciousness, if only on a lower level, as well. Everything in the world constantly releases emanations consisting of the particles of which it is made into the atmosphere. As these particles pass through the air, humans absorb them through their pores, transmitting them throughout the body by the blood.

In addition, the four elements and their combinations are aware of themselves. For example, the water in the air is conscious of the water in a human body. A particle that enters the human body is eventually transported to the heart,

Empedocles of Acragas. *(Library of Congress)*

which is a particularly sensitive organ: It is closely associated with the creation and perception of human thought. The blood is the prime medium for this transfer because it contains equal proportions of the four elements. The operation of the senses also is based on the awareness of the elements. The particles in the air are perceived differentially by the particles in the sense organs.

After Empedocles completed *On Nature*, he apparently changed many of his beliefs—probably after he had studied among the Pythagoreans. Especially attractive was the Pythagorean doctrine concerning the transmigration of the soul. Earlier, Empedocles seems to have thought that because humans were formed from the four elements, when they died, both body and soul ceased to exist. In *Purifications*, however, Empedocles seems to have adopted the Pythagorean idea that an individual's soul survives physically, going through a series of incarnations. Each soul has to pass through a cycle somewhat like the cosmic cycle of Love and Strife.

Sinfulness, as conceived in Christian thought, was not a factor in the Greek world. Nevertheless, *Purifications* reflects a concept of sin and atonement. The most likely source for such an abstraction would be the Buddhist Middle East, and Empedocles was probably aware of certain Buddhist doctrines.

Empedocles linked his cycle of incarnations with the concept of sin. The soul is initially in a state of sinlessness when it enters the world. In this stage, it is pure mind—a beatific state. As it resides in the world, the soul becomes tainted, especially by the sin of shedding the blood of humans or animals. The sinful soul is condemned to undergo a series of physical incarnations for thirty thousand seasons (an indeterminate time; Empedocles never defined the length of a season). The soul is incarnated in bodily forms that are in turn derived from air, water, earth, and fire. Empedocles recounted some of his own incarnations: He was a boy, a girl, a bird, a bush, and a fish at various times. Each successive incarnation allows the sincere soul an opportunity to better itself. Declaring that he had progressed to the company of such people as doctors, prophets, and princes, Empedocles hoped to be reborn among the gods.

One interesting facet of Empedocles' greatness is his pioneering work in the field of biology. Implicit in his observations on anatomy is the assumption that he conducted experiments on the bodies of animals and humans. He conjectured that blood circulates throughout the body in a system powered by the heart, that respiration occurs through the pores of the skin, and that some of the organs of the human body are similar in function to the organs of animals. He also observed that the embryo is clearly human in form in the seventh week of pregnancy.

Most interesting of Empedocles' theories is his concept of evolution. In *On Nature*, he assumed that the first creatures were crudely formed monstrosities and that some of these were, by chance, better adapted to survive than others. As the millennia passed, certain mutations (Empedocles did not use this word) made some forms more efficient in basic matters, such as eating and digesting and adapting their anatomy to catch and kill prey. With the passage of time, the successful body forms became nearly perfectly adapted to living in a particular environment.

Despite the great differences in the forms of various animals, Empedocles still saw unity in the whole of life. All organisms adapted safeguards against predation; all reproduced, breathed air, and drank water; and all had a particular consciousness—they rejoiced in the act of living and grieved at physical death.

Empedocles seems to have been many-faceted. According to contemporary accounts, his wardrobe was idiosyncratic, and some of his actions were bizarre. In his own works, and according to other testimony, he claimed to be a god. This claim seems to have gained credence: He boasted that crowds of people followed him, entreating him to use his magical healing powers. He claimed to be able to resurrect the dead as well as to have some control over the weather.

Several versions of Empedocles' death exist. He is said to have hanged himself, to have died after falling and breaking his thigh, and to have fallen from a ship and drowned. From the second century B.C.E., one version superseded all others: He disappeared in a brilliant light when a voice called his name. The best-known version, however, is that made famous by English poet and critic Matthew Arnold in his poem "Empedocles on Etna," in which Empedocles jumped into the crater of the erupting Mount Etna, apparently to prove that he was immortal.

Influence

In many ways, Empedocles influenced medieval and Renaissance conceptions of science and anticipated modern theories. For example, despite some criticism, Greek philosphers Plato and Aristotle adopted his biological theories. His conception of the four elements, probably derived from the work of Hippocrates, thus had influence until the scientific revolution in the seventeenth century. Finally, his ideas on human and animal evolution foreshadow modern theories, and his concept of a universe in which elements maintained a constant though ever-changing presence presages the law of the conservation of energy.

His accomplishments were honored by his contemporaries, and his memory was revered. Greek philosopher Aristotle called him the father of rhetoric, and Greek physician Galen considered him the founder of the medical arts. According to the Roman poet Lucretius, Empedocles was a master poet, and the extant fragments of his works support this claim. His main contribution was philosophical, however, and his two works were an important influence on early Greek philosophy.

Richard Badessa

Empedocles: Fragments

Type of philosophy: Metaphysics
First transcribed: Peri physeos, fifth century B.C.E (*On Nature*, 1908); *Katharmoi*, fifth century B.C.E. (*Purifications*, 1908); only fragments of these texts remain and no consensus exists as to which fragments belong to which texts.
Principal ideas advanced:
◇ Earth, air, fire, and water—stirred by Love and Strife—compose the world.
◇ The universe is eternal, but it is not always arranged in the same pattern.
◇ Particular things exist in the two intermediate stages of the cycle created by the alternating domination of Love and Strife.

Besides being a philosopher, Empedocles was a democratic statesman, the founder of an important school of medicine, and a religious leader and reformer. He also claimed to be a god.

Empedocles was the first thinker to try seriously to reply to the Greek philosopher Parmenides. Parmenides, a great genius and the founder of logic, claimed that all that really exists is a solid sphere within which there is no differentiation, no change, and no motion. He showed that three assumptions, taken as self-evident by all investigators up to and including himself, logically entailed his worldview. The first of these assumptions was that nothing can come from nothing or disappear into nothing. Nothing just pops up or vanishes without a trace. The second was that there is fundamentally just one reality, one stuff of which particular things are modifications. The third was that whatever really exists is identical with whatever properties it really has. This last assumption was so taken for granted that no one had ever stated it explicitly, and it is doubtful whether anyone at the time could have done so, as no alternative had yet been conceived. Modern thinkers distinguish between water itself and its properties of being wet and cold, but to the early Greeks, water was simply "the cold and wet."

Once the nature of this last assumption is grasped, it becomes obvious that Parmenides was right, for if there is only one kind of stuff, then that stuff, being identical with its properties (whatever they are), cannot possibly change. Suppose the stuff is hot—that is, it *is*, or equals, "the hot." Then the stuff cannot get cold, for if it did, "the hot" would have to disappear into nothing and "the cold" would have to come out of nothing. Previous thinkers had supposed, naturally enough, that one particular thing might get cold without violating the rule of nothing from nothing as long as something else got hot to compensate for it. However, Parmenides pointed out, this was shoddy reasoning. If there is just *one* reality, and it *is*, or equals, hot, then it is contradictory to say that it *is* also cold.

Probably because of a propensity for religious mysticism, Parmenides' conclusions were quite agreeable to him. The fact that they were utterly opposed to experience did not bother him. If logic tells people one thing and the senses tell them something else, so much the worse for the senses. "Keep your thinking clear of this way of inquiry," he warned, "nor let much-experienced habit force you down this road, where the unseeing eye and the noisy ear and the tongue rule. However, decide by logic the much-disputed proof that I utter." Empedocles, however, was not prepared to abandon his senses. In an "empiricist" vein he wrote: "Come now, consider with all your powers in what way each thing is clear. Hold not your sight in greater credit as compared with your hearing, nor value your resounding ear above the clear instructions of your tongue; and do not withhold confidence in any of the other parts of your body in which there is an opening for understanding, but consider everything in the way it is clear."

On Nature: The Four "Roots"

Empedocles also did not abandon logic. He realized that Parmenides' conclusion was validly drawn; therefore, if it was to be rejected, at least one of the premises leading to it would have to be discarded. Empedocles could not throw out the third for the simple reason that he did not realize that it was a premise of the argument. (This fact in due time dawned on atomists Leucippus and Democritus; the distinction that they drew between thing and quality eventually made modern physics possible.) The first premise also could not be discarded. Parmenides had said: "Nor will forceful credibility ever allow that anything besides itself can arise from nonbeing. . . . Thus is generation extinguished and destruction not to be heard of." Empedocles repeated this thought: "Fools!—for they have no far-reaching thoughts—who deem that what before did not exist comes into being, or that aught can perish and be utterly destroyed. For it cannot be that aught can arise from what in no way exists, and it is impossible and unheard of that Being should perish." Both Parmenides and Empedocles were fighting straw men, for no Greek ever questioned the maxim of nothing from nothing.

By elimination, only the second assumption, monism, could be questioned. Empedocles declared that stuff was not singular but made of four parts: the great world-masses of earth, air, fire, and water. Greek philosopher Aristotle later called these "the elements" but Empedocles

called them "roots": "Hear first the four roots of all things: shining Zeus [air], life-bringing Hera [earth], Aidoneus [fire], and Nestis [water] whose teardrops are a wellspring to mortals." These roots, like Parmenides' Being, are ungenerated, indestructible, and unchanging. Particular perishing things are temporary combinations of them: "There is no nature [phusis, essential being] of any of all the things that perish nor any cessation for them of baneful death. They are only a mingling and interchange of what has been mingled. 'Nature' is but a name given to these things by men."

The Possibility of Motion

However, before he could successfully assert a theory of change as a mixing of the unchanging, Empedocles had another Parmenidean hurdle to get over: the denial of the possibility of motion. Parmenides had argued (independently of his main doctrine) that if anything moves, there must be empty space for it to move into. However, empty space, or void, would be mere "nothing," or "that which is not," and because it would be logically contradictory to say that "that which is not" exists, there can be no void, hence no motion. Empedocles agreed that there is no void: "In the All there is naught empty and naught too full." He had an empirical reason for this view. He was probably the first person to realize that where there seems to be only empty space, there is really matter—namely, air. Empedocles' discovery of air, as distinguished from wind and mist, was his principal contribution to science. He illustrated the existence of air by means of the klepsydra, a Greek kitchen gadget. The tool, a metal tube with a perforated bottom and an open top small enough to be stopped by holding a finger on it, was used to remove small quantities of liquid from narrow-mouthed jars too heavy to be poured conveniently. Empedocles explained its working.

When a girl, playing with a klepsydra of shining brass, puts the orifice of the pipe upon her comely hand, and dips the klepsydra into the yielding mass of silvery water—the stream does not then flow into the vessel, but the bulk of the air inside, pressing upon the close-packed perforations, keeps it out till she uncovers the compressed stream; but then air escapes and an equal volume of water runs in. In the same way, when water occupies the depths of the brazen vessel and the opening and passage is stopped up by the human hand, the air outside, striving to get in, holds the water back at the gates of the gurgling neck, pressing upon its surface, till she lets go with her hand. Then, on the contrary, just in the opposite way to what happened before, the wind rushes in and an equal volume of water runs out to make room.

Motion could nevertheless occur without a void and without flouting logic, Empedocles maintained, as long as the obstacle in front of the moving object could be *displaced*, as the water could not move into the *klepsydra* unless an exit was provided for the air. In general, one thing could mix with another, he held, if there were tiny *pores*, like the tube of the *klepsydra*, for the substance to penetrate. He thought that when people inhale, air rushes into their bodies through the pores of the skin, the blood retiring to the center of the body; when they exhale, the blood comes back to the surface, forcing the air out.

Love and Strife, and Evolution

Besides "Fire and Water and Earth and the boundless height of Air," there exist "dread Strife, too, apart from these, of equal weight to each, and Love in their midst, equal in length and breadth. . . . It is she that is believed to be implanted in the frame of mortals. It is she that makes them have thoughts of love and work the works of peace. They call her by the names of Joy and Aphrodite." Love and Strife are the forces that cause motion, though Empedocles at the same time seems to regard them as kinds of matter. However, they are not conscious beings: "Aphrodite" is just whatever it is inside people that impels them to form unions. Cosmically, it causes unlike to mix with unlike. Strife, the opposite force of repulsion, causes separation and, as a result, union of like with like. The four roots, plus Love and Strife, are all that exists.

Behold the sun, everywhere bright and warm, and all the immortal things that are bathed in heat and bright radiance. Behold the rain, everywhere dark and cold; and from the earth

issue forth things close-pressed and solid. When they are in strife, all these are different in form and separated; but they come together in love and are desired by one another. For out of these have sprung all things that were and are and shall be—trees and men and women, beasts and birds and the fishes that dwell in the waters, yea, and the gods that live long lives and are exalted in honor. For there are these alone; but running through one another, they take different shapes—so much does mixture change them.

Empedocles believed that the universe is eternal, but it is not always arranged in the same pattern. Love and Strife alternate in dominance. There is a time when Love unites all the roots; in this condition, the universe is a sphere, a homogeneous mixture of the roots and Love, with Strife separate and outside the universe. Then Strife enters the sphere and begins its work of separation, which, when complete, leaves each of the four roots gathered together in unmixed purity. Then Love begins a process of mingling, eventuating in the sphere, and the cycle repeats.

Particular things exist in the two intermediate stages of the cycle when neither Love nor Strife has attained supremacy. There are two kinds of "evolution" of living things corresponding to these two periods. When Love is coming in and displacing Strife, "on the earth many heads spring up without necks and arms wander bare and bereft of shoulders. Eyes stray up and down in want of brows." These various unattached parts are united by Love, for the most part into monsters: "Many creatures with faces and breasts looking in different directions arise; some, offspring of oxen with faces of men, while others, again, arise as offspring of men with the heads of oxen, and creatures in whom the nature of women and men is mingled, furnished with sterile organs." Only the few that happen to be capable of nourishing themselves and reproducing their kind survive. This concept contains the germ of the idea of evolution by adaptation and survival of the fittest. However, it is inferior both in form and in underlying reasoning to the older theory of Greek astronomer Anaximander.

In the period when Strife is gaining ascendancy over Love (which, according to Empedocles, was the present stage of the world), "Fire as it was separated caused the night-born shoots of men and tearful women to arise. . . . Whole-natured forms first arose from the earth. . . . These showed as yet neither the charming form of the limbs, nor yet the voice and organ that are proper to men." That is, they were bisexual creatures, later separated further by Strife into men and women.

Purifications

The poem *Purifications* begins with a curiously charming proem in which Empedocles describes his own divinity.

> Friends, that inhabit the great town looking down on the yellow rock of Acragas, up by the citadel, busy in goodly works, harbors of honor for the stranger, men unskilled in meanness, hail. I go about among you an immortal god, no mortal now, honored among all as is meet, crowned with fillets and flowery garlands. Whenever I come to men and women, in the flourishing towns, straightway is reverence done me; they go after me in thousands asking of me what is the way to gain; some desiring oracles, while some, who for many a weary day have been pierced by the grievous pangs of all manner of sickness, beg to hear from me the word of healing. . . . But why do I harp on these things, as if it were any great matter that I should surpass mortal, perishable men?

Empedocles literally believed himself to be a god, though a fallen one:

> There is an oracle of Necessity, an ancient ordinance of the gods, eternal and sealed fast by broad oaths, that whenever one of the divinities . . . has sinfully polluted his hands with blood, or followed strife and forsworn himself, he must wander thrice ten thousand seasons [an indeterminate time; Empedocles never defined the length of a season] from the abodes of the blessed, being born throughout the time in all manners of mortal forms, changing one toilsome path of life for another. For the mighty Air drives him into the Sea, and the Sea spews him forth on the dry Earth; Earth tosses him into the beams of the blazing

Sun, and he flings him back to the eddies of Air. One takes him from the other, and all reject him. One of these I now am, an exile and a wanderer from the gods, for that I put my trust in raving Strife.

During this time, he says, he has been incarnated as a boy, girl, bush, bird, and fish. His original sin, it appears, was meat eating, for all living creatures are akin. However, deliverance is in sight:

> At the last, they appear among earth-dwelling men as prophets, song-writers, physicians, and princes; and thence they rise up as gods exalted in honor, sharing the hearth of the other gods and the same table, free from human woes, safe from destiny, and incapable of being hurt.

The principal problem posed by *Purifications* is its evident inconsistency, in teaching transmigration of souls, with *On Nature*, according to which there is "no cessation of baneful death" for particular things. The only possibility of reconciling the works seems to lie in supposing that the soul that transmigrates is a piece of Love. The soul cannot be a mixture, for all mixtures are perishable, and it is not plausible to identify it with any of the roots. Nor could it be Strife, for its sin consisted in "putting trust in raving Strife." It might be thought that if the soul is Love, then Love is conscious, contrary to the express statement of Empedocles that "the blood round the heart is the thought of men." However, according to a very ancient tradition of the Greeks, a person has two "souls," a blood-soul that is the seat of consciousness and a breath-soul that is the vivifying principle. It seems possible that Empedocles identified the latter with the Love that admittedly is in the human body; and a particular piece of Love might somehow retain its identity even through thirty thousand seasons. However, this is speculation, for which there is no explicit warrant either in the fragments of Empedocles' poems or in the ancient commentaries.

Wallace I. Matson

Additional Reading

Guthrie, W. K. C. *A History of Greek Philosophy*. Cambridge, England: Cambridge University Press, 1962-1981. Volume 2 of this set contains a 143-page chapter on Empedocles. Guthrie's writing is clear and his scholarship is superb, making this the best place for a nonspecialist to begin studying Empedocles.

Inwood, Brad. *The Poem of Empedocles*. Toronto: University of Toronto Press, 1992. This excellent work proceeds on the unorthodox thesis that the extant fragments come from a single poem rather than from two very different poems. It contains a long introduction in which the author presents his interpretation of Empedocles' philosophy as well as the fragments in Greek with Inwood's translations and textual notes. It is clear and accessible to students.

Kingsley, Peter. *Ancient Philosophy, Mystery, and Magic: Empedocles and Pythagorean Tradition*. New York: Oxford University Press, 1995. This book examines important aspects of ancient Greek philosophy.

Kirk, Geoffrey S., John E. Raven, and M. Schofield. *The Presocratic Philosophers*. 2d ed. Cambridge, England: Cambridge University Press, 1983. Much of the material on pre-Socratic philosophers is subject to interpretation; this book presents both sides of dozens of equivocal topics. It has a useful chapter on Empedocles.

Lambridis, Helle. *Empedocles: A Philosophic Investigation*. Tuscaloosa: University of Alabama Press, 1976. This book begins with a preface by Marshall McLuhan entitled "Empedocles and T. S. Eliot." The book is both a good and comprehensive survey and the best analysis of the poetry of Empedocles. Both modern and ancient Greek criteria are brought to bear on the poetry.

Millerd, Clara E. *On the Interpretation of Empedocles*. Chicago: University of Chicago Press, 1908. Reprint. New York: Garland Publishing, 1980. This important study discusses a number of topics concerning the intellectual background and development of Empedocles' ideas. The discussions are well written and knowledgeable. Though by no means obsolete, the book is somewhat dated.

Mourelatos, Alexander P. D., ed. *The Pre-Socratics: A Collection of Critical Essays*. Princeton, N.J.: Princeton University Press, 1993. This collection contains two papers on specific aspects of Empedocles' philosophy and one on the concept of mind (*nous*) in pre-Socratic philosophy in general, including a substantial section on Empedocles. Written by eminent ancient scholars, these papers represent serious detailed scholarship.

O'Brien, D. *Empedocles' Cosmic Cycle*. Cambridge, England: University of Cambridge Press, 1969. The most comprehensive and scholarly discussion of Empedocles' *On Nature*. Contains a useful section of notes, following the text, in which relatively minor but interesting topics are discussed. Contains an exhaustive annotated bibliography.

Sedley, D. N. *Lucretius and the Transformation of Greek Wisdom*. New York: Cambridge University Press, 1998. This book shows how Lucretius used the literary example of Empedocles to write his great poem, *De Rerum Natura*.

Wright, M. R. *Empedocles: The Extant Fragments*. New Haven, Conn.: Yale University Press, 1981. This modern critical work includes the Greek text of Empedocles' works, a translation, and a closely written and copious set of notes. Wright's detailed commentary on the fragments is valuable, though students will be put off by frequent lapses into untranslated Greek.

Richard Badessa, updated by Priscilla K. Sakezles

Epictetus

Epictetus revived early Greek Stoicism, emphasizing tolerance of pain and the freedom of the soul. His teachings were admired by early Christians, who found them consonant with their own reactions to persecution.

Principal philosophical works: *Diatribai*, second century C.E. (*Discourses*, 1670); *Encheridion*, c. 138 C.E. (English translation, 1567).

Born: c. 55; Hierapolis, Phrygia
Died: c. 135; Nicopolis, Epirus (now Greece)

Early Life

Epictetus was born a slave around the year 55 in the commercially significant city of Hierapolis between the rivers Maeander and Lycus in the country of Phrygia (modern-day Turkey), which was the eastern stretch of the Roman Empire. His master, Epaphroditus, was a freed slave who worked under Emperor Nero as an administrative secretary. The name Epictetus is Latin from the Greek word for "acquired," and Epictetus's master may have given him this name as a joke about his slave status, or it may have been a nickname Epictetus either chose or accepted.

Epictetus was a frail, bashful, feeble man who had a pronounced limp. Some observers claimed he was only weakened late in life with rheumatism or that he had always walked with a limp. A legend persists, however, that Epaphroditus once twisted Epictetus's leg in anger. The fledgling Stoic warned his master that he would break the leg by using so much force. The leg then broke, and Epictetus merely noted that he had been correct.

Slaves were prevalent in the late Roman Empire, and masters often educated or trained their slaves to be tutors or craftspeople in order to rise in prestige among their peers. Epaphroditus took Epictetus to Rome while he was still a minor so that he could attend lectures by the most prominent Stoic teacher of the time, Musonius Rufus, who was imprisoned for the crime of being wise, according to the writer Philostratus. According to Epictetus, Rufus was an overbearing, intense lecturer who held the class's attention by making each student feel chastised for having great ignorance.

Epictetus continued to serve under Epaphroditus, who allegedly accompanied Nero when he was forced to flee Rome in the year 68. Epaphroditus then assisted Nero in his suicide, and for this crime, the new emperor Domitian had him killed some time before the year 89. At his master's death, Epictetus was presumably freed, although no record of a manumission exists. He remained in Rome until around the year 94, when Domitian exiled all philosophers and teachers from Italy. The reason for this action is usually seen as Domitian's fear of their influence on Romans' minds and his belief that intellectuals favored republicanism over a dictatorship. Epictetus subsequently left Rome and settled in Nicopolis in Epirus on the northwest coast of present-day Greece, where he founded a Stoic school for elite young men that soon became large and famous.

Life's Work

Epictetus spent the rest of his career as a teacher in Nicopolis, making short visits to Athens and Olympia. A contemporary of Plutarch and Tacitus, he wrote nothing, perhaps in acknowledgment of his hero Socrates, whom he emulated by questioning people in the streets before founding his school. Many of his lectures and conversations, however, were recorded by one of his students, Arrian of Nicomedia, who prepared an eight-book transcription of lectures entitled *Discourses* (only four books of which are extant) and a shorter list of aphorisms from the *Discourses* entitled *Encheridion* (manual). Arrian wrote down the lectures when he was a student around the age of twenty during the years around 110 and published his work after Epictetus's death after he noticed unauthorized copies in circulation. The delay was occasioned by the supposed subversive nature of Epictetus's lectures. Arrian also wrote a biography of Epictetus, which has since been lost.

Epictetus read from the writings of Stoics, and he would assign papers on technical Stoic subjects, which would be read and criticized in class. Epictetus's classes, however, were usually characterized by informal discussions in which he would try to shock the students and encourage them to argue with him. Students observed that he had a strong personality and was an enthusiastic lecturer. Epictetus would relate homilies as he taught ethics, and he constantly brought up current events or well-known recent historical events to show examples of human behavior. Sometimes he would relate anecdotes about himself, his master, or other people he knew to prove a point. When presented with a recalcitrant class, Epictetus would forgo arguing with his students and create dialogues in which he would argue with himself. Because some of the dialogues concern visitors from Rome speaking with Epictetus, some scholars have suggested that Epictetus would not have private conversations with these visitors, but that he would argue with them in front of the class for Arrian to record. Others claim that Arrian fictionalized these dialogues, though he wrote using the Greek dialect in which Epictetus spoke, a dialect different from that in which Arrian usually wrote, indicating their probable authenticity.

Because of the nature of Epictetus's lectures, many readers find it hard to determine when Epictetus is being truthful to his own beliefs and when he is inventing a ridiculous argument that he intends to refute. For example, Epictetus is generally believed not to condone suicide except in extreme cases, yet at one point, he advocates suicide rather than having one's beard cut off. After careful study, however, some consistent beliefs do emerge. Epictetus taught as if education were defined as a painful alteration of attitudes. He taught his students to be independent. He wanted to guide their natural sense of the good into a mature acknowledgment of virtue, with ethical actions determined through the use of their reason. Much of what he taught was practical ethics. Epictetus emphasized adherence to duty, self-control, and modes of living that would tend toward personal achievement, not just a sense of doing good. As a Stoic, Epictetus stressed personal freedom that came from an indifference to events outside one's control. He also regarded the inner life of the soul as under one's control and hence changeable. In other words, he taught that such outer occurrences as torture must be tolerated as beyond one's control, but the serenity achieved through maintaining one's own beliefs is what his students should strive toward.

Epictetus lived alone, never married, and never had children. He wore a beard and a rough cloak. His house was small with no furniture except a straw mattress. Epictetus did not lock his doors, so at one point his iron lamp was stolen.

Epictetus. (*Giraudon/Art Resource*)

Presumably to deter thieves, Epictetus replaced the iron lamp with a clay one. After his death, this cheap lamp was sold for quite a bit of money. The buyer insisted that with this lamp one could become as enlightened as Epictetus was.

Once Epictetus advised an acquaintance to procreate, but the friend pointed out that Epictetus did not practice what he preached. At another time, Epictetus advised an important visitor to care for his daughter when she was ill. Epictetus obviously believed that compassion was appropriate, even logical, and in his old age, he did change his hermit status to assist another. When he learned that an unwanted child was to be exposed to the elements to die, he took the child in and hired a nursemaid to care for it. His interaction with children during his lifetime caused him to mention that the true Stoic saw life as a children's game. Life was not to be taken seriously, and the sad fact of life that one must accept is that there are not enough winners.

Epictetus died around the year 135 in Nicopolis. People who knew of his teachings eulogized him. An anonymous epigram of the time called him a "friend of the immortals."

Influence

In an era historians see as in intellectual decline with a lack of originality, Epictetus stood out. At the time, Stoicism was in fashion and Christianity had not yet begun to be popular. Epictetus at one point mentions Christians, whom he saw as rather insignificant bearers of a new religion, calling them "Galileans," but he was not familiar with the New Testament. Admirers of Epictetus include the Roman medical writer Galen, the Roman emperor Hadrian, and the Roman emperor Marcus Aurelius, who actively persecuted Christians during his reign. Despite the Stoics' tendency to ignore or demean Christianity, many of Stoicism's tenets were adaptable to the new religion, so much so that famous Christian theologians and priests such as Gregory of Nazianzus and Saint Augustine claimed to be admirers of Epictetus's teachings.

Epictetus's philosophy related to Christianity in numerous ways in addition to the Stoic advice to accept martyrdom while standing by one's beliefs and the Stoic disparaging of status and ambition. For example, Epictetus advocated ethical actions, for in doing good, a person acts for the good of others. Epictetus eschewed possessions, focusing instead on a person's mental gifts as the only true human possession. The Stoic philosophy turned away from the world and refuted egotism, emphasizing the need for hard work and chastity. Epictetus, while not a believer in Christian theology, sought the divine, which he claimed to be a part of humanity, existing within a person as a soul as well as outside a person as a sort of guardian. All these beliefs coincided with early Christian tenets.

Besides its influence on Christianity, Stoicism continued to play a part in philosophical study in modern times. Neo-Stoicism arose obliquely in the works of seventeenth and eighteenth century philosophers such as René Descartes, Blaise Pascal, Baruch Spinoza, and Immanuel Kant. Descartes's major thesis was the rejection of the outside world in favor of the inner, knowable soul, and Pascal discussed theology in a manner that supported the Stoic belief that there are two sides to every question. Spinoza and Kant, like Epictetus, discussed ethics and morality as if they were strongly supported by reason and logic.

Stoicism emphasized rationality and denied the uncertainty of probability, yet its teachings in many ways also anticipated the philosophical thought of the nineteenth and twentieth centuries. For instance, Epictetus explained that humans are observers and interpreters of what they receive through their senses. This point was taken up further by Georg Wilhelm Friedrich Hegel and later philosophers. Despite a reliance on logic, Epictetus mentions that what is rational for one person is not necessarily rational for another. Pluralistic reason hence has a precedent in Stoicism. Other ideas that originated with the Stoics are humanism, individualism, anarchism, a universal stance that rejects nationalism, tolerance that eschews dogmatism, and equality between the sexes and among races and classes.

Stoicism in some aspects was a precursor of modern psychoanalysis in that it stressed management of the self and the control of raging desires. Self-analysis was practiced by Stoics, much as psychoanalysis patients seek out the causes of their mental disorders. Psychiatry emphasizes coping with pain, not the pursuit of happiness, much as the Stoic Epictetus sought to deal with misery caused by the outer world.

Stoicism had negative features that fore-shadow currents in twentieth century society. Epictetus's works were frequently published between the years 1905 and 1925, a time of anomie and reconsideration of society's basic values. Epictetus believed that freedom must come from within, that citizens can believe in anything they wish but in practice they must obey the state. His cynicism is reflected in the modern tendency to view intellectual and political freedom ironically. Many modern thinkers and novelists reflect the Stoic attitude of nonchalance toward punishment so far as to advocate motiveless crime, as does writer Albert Camus in *L'Étranger* (1942; *The Stranger*, 1946). On a more positive note, the acceptance of a certain amount of control over one's life coupled with a tolerance for an inevitable lack of control has been the topic of many self-help books published in recent times.

Rose Secrest

Discourses *and* Encheridion

Type of philosophy: Ethics
First transcribed: Diatribai, second century C.E. (*Discourses*, 1670); *Encheridion*, c. 138 C.E. (*Encheridion*, 1567)
Principal ideas advanced:

◇ The good life is a life of inner tranquillity that comes from conforming to nature—to reason and to truth.

◇ To achieve the good life, one must master one's desires, perform one's duties, and think correctly concerning oneself and the world.

◇ To master desire, one has only to bring desire to the level of facts; one should be concerned only with what is within one's power.

◇ Every individual has a duty to others because each person is a citizen of the world, one of its principal parts.

◇ To discover one's duty, one should be skilled in elementary logic, in the art of disputation, and in the right use of names.

As far as is known, Epictetus left no philosophical writings. The *Discourses* is a transcription of some of his lectures made by a pupil, Arrian. Originally there were eight books, of which only four are known to modern scholars. The *Encheridion*, a condensed selection from the *Discourses*, was also composed by Arrian. The *Encheridion* is a good summary of Epictetus's main doctrines, but the *Discourses* is rewarding for the vivid picture it calls up of Epictetus as a teacher. It catches the vigor and warmth of a wise and witty man in the act of informally expounding his philosophy. He wore his technical equipment lightly as he answered questions concerning practical difficulties, pointed out dangers in contemporary customs, and delivered short homilies suggested by current events.

For Epictetus, the goal of philosophy was not so much to understand the world as to achieve the good life, which, for him, consisted of inner tranquillity. The Stoics, of whom he was a representative, had a well-developed philosophy of nature, based on the Heraclitean doctrine that Logos, or Reason, governs all change. They were also competent logicians. However, their chief interest lay in personal ethics, to which they applied a knowledge of physics and logic. Inner serenity, they held, consists of conforming to nature (following reason) or discovering and living by the truth. Epictetus alluded to logic from time to time but rarely mentioned philosophy of nature. When he spoke of philosophy, he meant "philosophy of life." In his view, the philosopher is the wise person.

Epictetus noted three stages in the achievement of the good life. The first concerns mastering one's desires; the second, performing one's duties; and the third, thinking correctly concerning one's self and the world. He complained that students are prone to neglect the first two, which are the most important, and to overvalue the third because they are less concerned with achieving moral excellence than with gaining a reputation as disputants. As a result, the world is flooded with vain, passionate, fault-finding people who have so little self-mastery that a mouse can frighten them to death; yet they boast the name of philosopher.

Mastery of Desires
Epictetus put the mastery of desires first because he regarded the main business of philosophy to

be the achievement of a tranquil mind. In his view, all perturbations are the result of a disproportion between people's wills and the external world. The natural person supposes that happiness is possible only when the external world comes up to the individual's expectations. Philosophers know that this condition rarely exists and that if people build on any such hope, they are doomed to endless sorrow, which in turn leads to envy and strife. Instead of trying to bring the world up to their desires, people should bring their desires to the level of actuality. Happily, this is quite within the realm of possibility because people's wants are in their power, although external things are not.

In effect, philosophers tell themselves that things that are not in their power are matters of indifference, and all that matters is the use they can make of these things. Philosophers may be exiled—that they cannot prevent—but does any person hinder them from going with a smile? They must die—but must they die lamenting? Their legs may be fettered—but not even Zeus can overpower their will.

Epictetus recognized the difference between saying these things and doing them, and he sought various means of inculcating the habits of self-mastery. One should daily write and meditate on extreme situations, such as how to comport oneself if subjected to a tyrant's torture. When enjoying anything, one should form the habit of calling up contrary appearances; for example, when embracing one's child, one should whisper, "Tomorrow you will die." To overcome passions such as anger, each person should write down every offense in a daybook. These are the concerns that should occupy philosophers' thoughts. "Study not to die only, but also to endure torture, and exile, and scourging, and, in a word, to give up all which is not your own." Without such practice, people will not be prepared when unexpected trials descend upon them.

Epictetus liked to speak of the "handles" that things present to people. "Everything has two handles, the one by which it may be borne, the other by which it may not." He cited the example of a man whose brother uses him unjustly: If the man thinks of the injustice, he will not bear it; if he thinks of him as a brother, he will.

Duties

The second of Epictetus's main concerns was duty. It was an important part of his teaching that a human being is not a detached entity but part of a whole. In a passage that is quite similar to one in the writings of Saint Paul (1 Cor. 12), Epictetus compares man to one of the organs of the human body: "Do you know that as a foot is no longer a foot if it is detached from the body, so you are no longer a man if you are separated from other men? For what is a man? A part of a state, of that which first consists of gods and men; then of that which is called next to it, which is a small image of the universal state." The whole duty of humankind is inscribed here. A human being is, as Epictetus liked to say, "a citizen of the world" and, unlike the lower animals, is not one of the subservient parts but "one of the principal parts, for you are capable of comprehending the divine administration and of considering the connection of things." The lower creatures fulfill their functions without knowing what they do. It is the prerogative of humankind to understand the "connection of things," and in these connections lie an individual's duties.

"Duties," Epictetus said, "are universally measured by relations." Among the most important for the ordinary person he listed "engaging in public business, marrying, begetting children, venerating God, taking care of parents, and generally, having desires, aversions, pursuits of things and avoidances, in the way in which we ought to do these things, and according to our nature." The Cynics, who were in some respects the predecessors of the Stoics, used to place nature and society in opposition and to make a great issue of obeying the former and flouting the latter. That the Stoics of Epictetus's day should see their way to including society as part of nature is noteworthy.

However, Epictetus was not ready simply to follow conventional conceptions as to what people's duties are. The view that an individual was a citizen of the cosmos before that person was a citizen of Rome has important implications. One of these is that all people, in virtue of possessing reason, are "sons of Zeus." Another is that all men are brothers. To the slave owner, Epictetus said, "Will you not bear with your own brother, who has Zeus for his progenitor, and is like a son from the same seeds and of the same descent from above? . . . Will you not remember who you are, and whom you rule, that they are kinsmen, that they are brethren by nature, that they are the offspring of Zeus?" Conversely, the fact that a man happened to wear the emperor's crown was, in itself, no reason for obeying him. One must examine the stamp on the coin, whether it be that of a Roman emperor such as Trajan—gentle, sociable, tolerant, affectionate—or that of an emperor such as Nero—passionate, resentful, violent.

Just as people have duties toward their fellows, said Epictetus, they have duties toward the gods: "to have right opinions about them, to think that they exist, and that they administer the All well and justly; and you must fix yourself in this principle, to obey them, and yield to them in everything which happens, and voluntarily to follow it as being accomplished by the wisest intelligence." Epictetus spoke of the place appointed to an individual as being like the role assigned an actor. The actor should not complain about the role, whether it is the part of a lame man or of a magistrate. "For this is your duty, to act well the part that is given to you; but to select the part belongs to another." In another figure, he spoke of God as resembling a trainer of wrestlers who matches athletes with suitable partners in order to bring out the best in them. Difficulties, in other words, are designed to test our souls. "For what purpose? you may say. Why, that you may become an Olympic conqueror; but it is not accomplished without sweat." Again he varied the figure: "Every man's life is a kind of warfare, and it is long and diversified. You must observe the duty of a soldier and do everything at the nod of the general."

Some of these thoughts seem far removed from the ideal of inner tranquility that Epictetus had as his ultimate goal. "Give me a man who cares how he shall do anything, not for the obtaining of a thing." Such a passage seems close to the view that urges duty for duty's sake. However, Epictetus also said that faithfulness is accompanied by the consciousness of obeying God and performing the acts of a wise and good man. What higher peace is there, he asked, than to be able to say, "Bring now, O Zeus, any difficulty that thou pleasest, for I have means given to me by thee and powers for honoring myself through the things which happen"?

Right Thinking

The third stage in the education of a philosopher, in Epictetus's program, concerns the discipline of logic and disputation. Because right thinking is a prerequisite both to the rational control of appetite and to discovering one's duty to God and humankind, it is imperative that every individual should study to avoid "deception and rashness of judgment." However, how far formal logic is necessary for this purpose was, for Epictetus, an open question. Mostly, logic was useful in debating with Sophists and rhetoricians—and with Epicureans. A knowledge of elementary fallacies seemed to him sufficient for most purposes.

Of the problems that arise in connection with moral judgments, three were particularly noticed by Epictetus. The first had to do with right names. If man's duty is prescribed by relations, it is important to see things as they are. "Does a man bathe quickly? Do not say that he bathes badly, but that he bathes quickly." The right name puts the thing in the right light. Like Confucius in his *Lunyu* (late sixth or early fifth century B.C.E.; *Analects*, 1861), Epictetus urged his disciples to consider what is meant by "father," "son," "man," and "citizen." Right names disclose true relations.

Similarly, inferences should be studied, so that people do not conclude from a proposition more than it really says. Epictetus used as an example the inference "I am richer than you are, therefore I am better than you." This is invalid. Nothing follows necessarily from the premise except judgments on the order of "I have more possessions than you." Epictetus explained the function of inference as establishing assent and that of critical thinking as teaching us to withhold assent from what is uncertain.

Finally, a philosopher needed to learn the art of testing whether particular things are good. According to Epictetus, all people are by nature endowed with common moral conceptions, such as of what is good and what is just, but nature does not teach people to apply these in detail. Individuals begin to be philosophers when they observe that people disagree about what is good or when they cast about for some rule by which they may judge between them. There is no simple rule, but there is what Epictetus called "the art of discussion," which draws out the consequences of one's conception so that one may see whether it agrees or conflicts with what one really wants. If it is maintained that pleasure is the good, one should ask such questions as these: "Is the good something that one can have confidence in?" Yes. "Can one have confidence in what is insecure?" No. "Is pleasure insecure?" Yes. Here is the answer: Pleasure is not the good. Epictetus supposed that his art of discussion was the same as Socrates' dialectic, and he advised his pupils to read Xenophon's *Symposion* (late fifth or early fourth century B.C.E.; *Symposium*, 1750, also known as *The Banquet of Xenophon*) in order to see Socrates in action and "how many quarrels he put an end to."

Socrates was one of those held to be "saints" by the later Stoics. Another was Diogenes the Cynic. These men were, in Epictetus's view, "messengers from Zeus to men about good and bad things, to show them that they have wandered and are seeking the substance of good and evil where it is not."

Jean Faurot

Additional Reading

Arnold, Edward Vernon. *Roman Stoicism*. 1911. Reprint. New York: Arno, 1971. This book focuses on the Stoics of Epictetus's era. Chapter 4 discusses Epictetus's life and influence, and later chapters emphasize his views on religion, morality, duty, and death. Includes bibliography.

Barnes, Jonathan. *Logic and the Imperial Stoa*. New York: Brill, 1997. A detailed examination of particular texts from *Discourses*.

Bonhèoffer, Adolf F. *The Ethics of the Stoic Epictetus: An English Translation*. Translated by William O. Stephens. New York: Peter Lang, 1996. A look at Epicurean thought. Contains a bibliography and index.

Hicks, R. D. *Stoic and Epicurean*. 1911. Reprint. New York: Russell & Russell, 1962. An excellent discussion of some of the tenets within Stoic, Epicurean, and Skeptical thought. Chap-

ter 4, "The Teaching of the Later Stoics," is a thorough discussion of Epictetus's beliefs and three-stage method of instruction. Contains time line and bibliography.

Inwood, Brad. *Ethics and Human Action in Early Stoicism*. New York: Oxford University Press, 1985. Traces the development of ethics in Stoics, including Epictetus. The emphasis is on textual analysis and interpretation of key terminology. Includes bibliography.

Lebell, Sharon. *A Manual for Living: Epictetus*. New York: HarperCollins, 1994. An excellent introduction to the wisdom of Epictetus. This new translation relates his sayings to modern life.

Rist, J. M. *Stoic Philosophy*. London: Cambridge University Press, 1969. A chronological narrative of all Stoic philosophy. Rist discusses Epictetus's speculation on phenomenology, suicide, and metaphysics.

Sandbach, F. H. *The Stoics*. New York: W. W. Norton, 1975. An introductory summary of the history of Stoic philosophy that pinpoints areas such as ethics, fate, and logic. Epictetus is granted a section that clearly describes his most significant insights. Includes annotated bibliography, glossary of Greek and Latin terms, and time line.

Stadter, Philip A. *Arrian of Nicomedia*. Chapel Hill: University of North Carolina Press, 1980. A look at the man known for the transcription of Epictetus's lectures, the only extant examples of Epictetus's thoughts. Chapter 2 details Arrian's time as a student of Epictetus. Includes a map that shows Epictetus's homeland Phrygia, present-day Turkey.

Xenakis, Iason. *Epictetus: Philosopher-Therapist*. The Hague, Netherlands: Martinus Nijhoff, 1969. The first book-length commentary published in English devoted solely to Epictetus. Includes a brief biography. Chapters discuss Epictetus's view on practical living, logic, religion, values, ethics, and the study of human personality and behavior, thus connecting his observations with modern psychology. Includes bibliography.

Rose Secrest

Epicurus

Epicurus founded the Garden School of Greek philosophy, a hedonistic school known for its pursuit of pleasure and tranquillity of mind and body, which was to be achieved through avoiding pain and living a simple, aesthetic life.

Principal philosophical works: *Peri physeōs*, third century B.C.E. (only fragments exist; "Fragments," 1926); *Kyriai doxai*, third century B.C.E. (*Principal Doctrines*, 1926); *Epikourous Hērodotoi Khairein*, c. 305 B.C.E. (*Letter to Herodotus*, 1926); *Epikourous Pythoklei Khairein*, c. 305 B.C.E. (*Letter to Pythocles*, 1926); *Epikourous Menoikei Khairein*, third century B.C.E. (*Letter to Menoeceus*, 1926); *Epicurus: The Extant Remains*, 1926.

Born: 341 B.C.E.; Greek island of Samos
Died: 270 B.C.E.; Athens, Greece

Early Life

Epicurus was born on the Greek island of Samos, about two miles off the coast of Turkey. His father, Neocles, was an immigrant from an old Athenian family who had moved to the distant island for economic reasons and who made his living as an elementary school teacher. Epicurus was forever disadvantaged in the eyes of the people of Athens because of his rustic birth and the low social status of his father's occupation. To make matters worse, his mother was reputedly a fortune-teller. His experiences as her apprentice might well account for Epicurus's later criticism of all kinds of superstitions and even for his controversial renunciation of the ancient Greek myths and stories.

Epicurus shared a happy family life with his parents and three brothers, Neocles, Chaeredemus, and Aristobulus, who would eventually become his disciples. It is recorded by Diogenes Laërtius that Epicurus began to study philosophy at the age of fourteen because he was not satisfied with his schoolmasters' explanations of the meaning of "chaos" in Hesiod. Others contend that he was drawn to philosophy by the works of Democritus, echoes of which can be seen in Epicurus's later writings.

At eighteen, Epicurus served his two years of compulsory military duty in Athens, at an exciting time when both Xenocrates and Aristotle were lecturing. He clearly familiarized himself with the works of Aristippus, Socrates, and Pyrrhon of Elis. He served in the garrison with the future playwright Menander, with whom he established a close friendship; many critics believe that they see the impress of Epicurus's ideas on Menander's later plays.

After his military service, Epicurus rejoined his family, who, with other Athenian colonists, had been expelled from Samos by a dictator and had subsequently moved to Colophon. Not much is known of the ten years that Epicurus spent at Colophon, but it might be surmised that he spent much of his time in study and contemplation, perhaps even visiting the intellectual center of Rhodes. At around the age of thirty, he moved to Mytilene, on the island of Lesbos, to become a teacher. As he developed his own philosophy, he came into conflict with the numerous followers of Plato and Aristotle on that island, and after only a short stay, he left. He took with him, however, Hermarchus, a man who would become a lifetime friend and perhaps more important, after Epicurus's death, the head of his Athenian school.

Hermarchus and Epicurus moved to Lampsacus on the Hellespont for the fertile years between 310 and 306 B.C.E. At Lampsacus, Epicurus gathered around him the devoted disciples and the influential patrons who would make it possible for him, at the age of thirty-five, to move to Athens and begin the major stage of his career.

607

Epicurus. *(Library of Congress)*

They presented to him the house and the garden in the outskirts of Athens that would be both his school and his home for the rest of his life.

Life's Work

Once established in Athens, Epicurus founded his Garden School, whose name came from the practice of the resident members, who in almost monastic fashion provided for their own food by gardening. The many statues, statuettes, and engraved gems that bear the image of Epicurus's long, narrow, intelligent face, with its furrowed brows and full beard, attest the devotion of his followers and the unusually enduring influence of his ideas.

Epicurus organized his Garden School in a strict hierarchical system, at the apex of which stood only himself: the Master. One of the common slogans of the school was "Do all things as if Epicurus were looking at you." Although this motto may sound dictatorial, it represented a be-

nevolent tyranny to which all the disciples and students of Epicurus happily adhered, and it no doubt accounts for the consistently accurate promotion of his philosophical ideas, even after his death. Three men—Metrodorus, Hermarchus, and Plyaenus—reached the rank of associate leaders in the Garden School and were understood to follow in their master's footsteps so closely that they might teach the Epicurean doctrine in its purest form. Beneath them were the many assistant leaders, unfortunately unknown to modern scholars by name, and the numerous students. It is important to mention that among Epicurus's students were women (for example, the distinguished Leontion) and slaves (Epicurus's own slave Mys was one of his favorite students). The accessibility of the Epicurean philosophy, which eschewed most classical learning, ensured a remarkably heterogeneous following.

Despite many later slanders against him, by writers who misconstrued his emphasis on pleasure as a license for sensory excess, the overwhelming evidence supports the idea that Epicurus lived in his Garden School simply and privately, following his own dictate to "live unobtrusively." His health, which was delicate and complicated by bladder or kidney stones, would certainly not have survived the riotous living ascribed to him by his detractors.

Fortunately, both Epicurus and his closest disciples were prolific writers, and in some ways the home of Epicurus was a kind of publishing house for their works. Still, only a small portion of that original writing is extant, and an even smaller part is translated into English. Of Epicurus's three hundred or more books (it is best to think of them as scrolls), all that remains are some fragments of his central work *Peri physeōs* (on nature), three important letters recorded by Diogenes Laërtius in the early third century B.C.E., and some miscellaneous correspondence, which shows Epicurus's affectionate relationship with his friends. Yet, as Plato had his Socrates, Epicurus had the Roman poet Lucretius, from whose book *De rerum natura* (c. 60 B.C.E.; *On the Nature of Things*, 1862) much of our understanding of Epicurus's ideas comes.

Through the works of Lucretius, one is introduced to Epicurus's theories on matter and space, the movements and the shapes of atoms, life and the mind, sensation and sex, cosmology and sociology, and meteorology and geology. In addition to Epicurus's atomic theory, which in some interesting respects presages modern physics, the parts of Epicurus's philosophy that still have the power to move people are the simple axioms of behavior around which he organized life at the Garden School.

Rejecting much of traditional education because it did not foster happiness through tranquillity (which was the ultimate goal of life), Epicurus had a more profound respect for common sense than for classical learning. Prudence was an important virtue, and the senses were the ultimate sources of all knowledge. The highest good in life was attaining a secure and lasting pleasure. To Epicurus, pleasure was not unbridled sensuality but freedom from pain and peace of mind. These two goods could easily be obtained by simple living, curbing one's unnecessary desires, and avoiding the stresses and compromises of a public life. It might even be profitable to avoid love, marriage, and parenting because they usually bring more pain than pleasure. Friendship, on the other hand, was regarded as one of the highest and most secure forms of pleasure.

Epicurus thought that the great aim of philosophy was to free people of their fears. Epicurus was not an atheist, but he considered the gods to be very remote—living in Epicurean serenity—and not likely to be tampering viciously with people's lives. For Epicureans, the soul dies with the body and, therefore, not even death is to be feared.

Perhaps the most salient criticisms of Epicurus's ethics of self-reliance and free will are that they are very negative (viewing wisdom as an escape from an active, hazardous, but possibly full life) and very selfish (placing the good of the individual above the needs of society or the state). Although these criticisms may be valid, the life of Epicurus showed that there was much everyday merit in his philosophy. He was blessed with many lifelong friendships that became legendary throughout Greece. His enthusiastic followers kept his ideas alive long into the fourth century. Even on his deathbed, he exhibited that almost Eastern detachment and calm that was the major goal of his philosophy. In a letter that he wrote to friends at his last hour, he commented that the extreme pain of his abdomen was considerably relieved by the happy thoughts he had of his talks with them.

Influence

Epicurus's thought outlived most other important Greek philosophical systems, but it too was finally overwhelmed in the fourth century by Christianity, which considered it just another pagan creed. Some critics believe, however, that the writer of Ecclesiastes in the Old Testament was likely a member of the Garden School and that the Epistles of Saint Paul in the New Testament were strongly influenced by Epicurean thought.

Ironically, it was a French priest, Pierre Gassendi, who revived interest in Epicurus in the seventeenth century with his short treatise *De vita et moribus Epicuri libri octo* (1647; eight books on the life and manners of Epicurus). This interest was manifested in English by Walter Charleton and further fueled by Sir William Temple, a renowned seventeenth century English essayist. In the early nineteenth century, the United States had an avowed Epicurean as its president: Thomas Jefferson.

Discoveries of inscriptions and manuscripts in Asia Minor and Herculaneum have kept scholars debating the issues raised in the works of Epicurus up to the present day. Richard W. Hibler, for example, focused on what Epicurus has to teach about pedagogy. There is no question that as long as humans worry about ethics, strive after the good life, or try to make sense of the universe, the voice of Epicurus will continue to be heard.

Cynthia Lee Katona

Principal Doctrines *and* Letter to Menoeceus

Type of philosophy: Ethics
First transcribed: Kyriai doxai, third century B.C.E. (*Principal Doctrines*, 1926); *Epikourous Menoikei Khairein*, third century B.C.E. (*Letter to Menoeceus*, 1926)
Principal ideas advanced:
◇ Pleasure is the standard by which every good and every right action is to be judged.

⬦ No pleasure is in itself bad, and all pleasures are alike in quality.

⬦ Certain natural desires are necessary, and the gratification of such desires is preferable to the gratification of unnecessary natural desires or desires attaching to artificially cultivated tastes.

⬦ The three human needs are equanimity, bodily health and comfort, and the exigencies of life.

⬦ To achieve the good life, a life of moderate and enduring pleasure, a person must cultivate the virtues, particularly prudence, and study philosophy.

⬦ Death is nothing to fear, for while we live death is not with us; when death comes, we no longer exist.

The *Principal Doctrines* is a collection of forty of the most important articles of Epicurus's teaching, presumably extracted by a disciple from the master's voluminous works. It was widely known in ancient times and was preserved by Diogenes Laërtius (probably third century B.C.E.) in his *Peri biōn dogmatōn kai apophthegmatōn tōn en philosophia eudokimēsantōn* (third century C.E.; *The Lives, Opinions, and Remarkable Sayings of the Most Famous Ancient Philosophers*, 1688). Together with the *Letter to Menoeceus*, also found in Diogenes' works, it constitutes our only firsthand source for the ethical teachings of Epicurus. The most important supplementary source is Lucretius's poem, *De rerum natura* (c. 60 B.C.E.; *On the Nature of Things*, 1862).

Pleasure as a Standard

Epicurus's central teaching was that pleasure is the standard by which every good is to be judged. He distinguished between feelings of pleasure and judgments concerning good and right, and in the *Letter to Menoeceus*, he maintained that the latter, insofar as they have meaning, must refer to the former. "For we recognize pleasure as the first good innate in us, and from pleasure we begin every act of choice and avoidance, and to pleasure we return again, using the feeling as the standard by which we judge every good."

No pleasure, said Epicurus, is in itself bad. He maintained that pleasures are all the same kind. Some pleasures are more intense than others,

some last longer, and some satisfy a greater portion of the body; but if these differences could be set aside, one pleasure could not be distinguished from another. Unfortunately, however, the limitations of human existence compel us to distinguish between pleasures. In actuality, no pleasure can be chosen in isolation, and the conditions that are necessary to our enjoying some pleasures are also annexed to pains. In the *Letter to Menoeceus*, he stated, "For this reason, we do not choose every pleasure, but sometimes pass over many pleasures, when greater discomfort accrues to us as the result of them."

Desires

Therefore, Epicurus turned his attention to the consideration of desires. Some desires, he said, are natural and others are illusory. By the latter, he meant physical desires of the sort that neither arise from any deprivation nor admit of definite satisfaction—desires that attach to artificially cultivated tastes. Already in his day, the public supposed that he and his followers pursued the pleasures of profligacy and vice. Such was far from the case. The reason was that such artificial desires inevitably come into conflict with natural desires that are far more important. Indeed, Epicurus held that not all natural desires are to be satisfied. He distinguished between natural desires that are necessary and those that are merely natural. The necessary ones are so exacting that we are counseled to concentrate on them alone.

The strength of Epicurus's philosophy, compared with the Cyrenaic and other philosophies of pleasure, derives from its deeper understanding of the psychology of human needs. People have three kinds of needs that will not be denied: equanimity or peace of mind, bodily health and comfort, and the exigencies of life itself. Fortunately, according to Epicurus, few things are necessary in order to sustain life and keep the body in health, and they are comparatively easy to obtain. Illness is unavoidable, but as he pointed out, acute pain rarely lasts long, and chronic illnesses permit a predominance of pleasure over pain in the flesh. On the whole, Epicurus seems to have expended but little thought on the necessities of life and bodily health. His main concern was with peace of mind, how to avoid unpleasantness, how to escape the pangs of conscience, how to avoid worry about the future, including the life beyond the grave. Such considerations gave Epicurus's philosophy a predominantly somber tone, so much so that he rarely spoke of pleasure except in a negative way, as "freedom from pain in the body and from trouble in the mind." Speaking of the three necessary desires in the *Letter to Menoeceus*, he said, "The right understanding of these facts enables us to refer all choice and avoidance to the health of the body and the soul's freedom from disturbance, since this is the aim of the life of blessedness."

Thus, although the good in life is always simple and immediate, namely, feelings of pleasure, the art of achieving a life abundant in goodness requires great skill and constant application. To this end, Epicurus recommended two sorts of means: first, the cultivation of virtue; second, the study of philosophy.

Prudence

Of these two, virtue is the more important. "The man who does not possess the virtuous life cannot possibly live pleasantly," he declared. Among virtues, he held prudence to be chief because all other virtues were, in his view, merely special kinds of prudence.

By prudence, he meant what author Fyodor Dostoevski once called "solving the problem of existence." Prudence consists of knowing both the worth and the cost of various satisfactions. Sometimes we have to choose pain in order to secure greater pleasure; for example, having a wisdom tooth extracted. Sometimes we have to forgo pleasure because of resultant pain; for example, we might stop drinking wine to avoid becoming ill afterward. Epicurus spoke of a scale of comparison that the prudent person uses to judge prospective courses of action in terms of their advantages and disadvantages.

One of the best counsels of prudence, he thought, was to make oneself independent of desire and, to this end, to accustom oneself to simple food and plain surroundings. His motive was not an ascetic one—he saw no good in deprivation for its own sake. However, he contended that anyone who has learned to be satisfied with the necessities of life is freed from most of the cares of the future because changes of fortune are un-

likely to reduce one to starvation, whereas the slightest turn may deprive one of luxuries. Moreover, he maintained that there is an actual surplus of pleasure in the abstemious life. Bread and water produce as great pleasure to one who needs them as the luxuries of a wealthy table do to the reveler. Moreover, plain fare is better for health of body and alertness of mind. Furthermore, one whose taste is not spoiled by habitual indulgence is better able to appreciate fine food and drink when, at long intervals, these become available.

Another counsel of prudence was to retire from the world of human affairs. Epicurus, somewhat like English philosopher Thomas Hobbes, regarded humanity as its own greatest enemy. To secure protection from others is a natural want. However, how shall one go about it? Epicurus doubted the wisdom of those who undertake to find security by competing for public honor and position. In his opinion, this is not "safe." Instead, he recommended "the immunity which results from a quiet life and the retirement from the world."

Justice

It is in connection with the harm that we may expect from others that Epicurus introduced the virtue of justice. In opposition to the teaching of Greek philosophers Plato and Aristotle but in agreement with that of Greek philosopher Democritus, he denied that justice has its foundation in nature. All justice, he said, originates in "a pledge of mutual advantage to restrain men from harming one another and save them from being harmed." It does not exist among primitive tribes, and what is considered just in one country may be quite different from what is considered just in another. In fact, within the same land, as circumstances change, what was once considered just may be so no longer. For the justice of a law ultimately depends on its being to the mutual advantage of both parties.

Epicurus raised the question that Glaucon raised in Plato's *Politeia* (middle period, 388-368 B.C.E.; *Republic*, 1701), book 2, whether it is not to one's advantage secretly to act unjustly if one can do so without detection. The answer is that one can never be confident that one will escape detection, and that anxiety would spoil the fruits of the crime. "The just man is most free from trouble, the unjust most full of trouble."

Philosophy

After virtue, Epicurus considered philosophy the second most important means for securing the life of bliss. "Let no one when young," he wrote to Menoeceus, "delay to study philosophy, nor when he is old grow weary of his study." Epicurus was not recommending philosophy as a solace against the sorrows of existence nor as a diversion that yields a satisfaction of its own. By philosophy, Epicurus meant a kind of mental hygiene, based on a naturalistic worldview that, if its implications were understood, would free people's minds from superstitious fear and moral anxiety.

The view of nature that recommended itself to him was that of Democritus, who denied that the world was created by the gods or that there is any ultimate purpose in life, all things having been formed by the accidental collision of atoms falling through empty space. One who is convinced that this is the case has, according to Epicurus, two great advantages over those who hold to traditional beliefs: First, one is freed from religious scruples; second, one is freed from the fear of death.

Epicurus did not deny the existence of the gods, which he identified with the heavenly bodies. He held that they are composed of the same fine, smooth atoms that make up human souls and are the basis of reason and feelings. However, because the gods are eternal and blessed in their regular motions, Epicurus found no reason to suppose that they are exacting and vengeful, or indeed that they pay any attention to humans. He explained the traditional view, that the gods are the source of human misfortune and of blessedness, as arising from the tendency people have to view other beings as acting like themselves. He denied that such a belief is founded on sensation or has any foundation in reason. Eclipses, solstices, and other celestial phenomena that the ancients were accustomed to regard with superstitious awe, he said, are capable of explanation according to natural principles.

The fear of death seemed to him as groundless as fear of the gods. At death, the soul-atoms leave the body and are dispersed through space; there-fore, one's consciousness is dissipated, the separate atoms no longer possessing the same power and sentience that they had when together in the bodily sheath. However, good and evil consist of sensations and nothing else. Therefore, according to Epicurus, there is nothing terrible in death. If we persuade ourselves of this, the anticipation of death ceases to be painful. In the *Letter to Menoeceus*, he stated, "So death, the most terrifying of ills, is nothing to us, since so long as we exist death is not with us; but when death comes, then we do not exist. It does not then concern either the living or the dead, since for the former it is not, and the latter are no more." Nor does the wise person seek length of days. "Just as with food he does not seek simply the larger share and nothing else, but rather the most pleasant, so he seeks to enjoy not the longest period of time but the most pleasant." Such is the sweetness introduced into life by the knowledge that death is nothing, that we no longer have any thirst for immortality.

Epicurus was moved to modify the philosophy of Democritus in one respect. The latter held to a strictly deterministic theory of causation, but Epicurus said that, though some events happen by necessity and chance, others are within our control. It was, he said, more foolish to become "a slave to the destiny of the natural philosophers" than to follow the myths about the gods. The myths leave us some hope—the determinists only despair. The part of wisdom in these matters seemed to him, very much as it did to the Stoic Epictetus, to consist of understanding the limits of the human condition and in not expecting more than is reasonable. One who knows these things laughs at destiny. All that one asks is companionship, and then one "shall live like a god among men."

Jean Faurot, updated by John K. Roth

Additional Reading

Durant, Will. *The Life of Greece*. New York: Simon & Schuster, 1939. Contains an excellent chapter, "The Epicurean Escape," which places Epicurus in the context of his times and also evaluates the tenets of his philosophy.

Edwards, Paul. *The Encyclopedia of Philosophy*. 4 vols. New York: Macmillan, 1967. Contains a lucid, short explanation of Epicurus's complex theory and a scholarly bibliography (now somewhat outdated).

Englert, Walter G. *Epicurus on the Swerve and Voluntary Action*. Atlanta, Ga.: Scholars Press, 1987. A fascinating study of an infamously peculiar facet of Epicurean physics: the atomic swerve. This book focuses on Epicurean physics and the ramifications for psychology. Also contains an extended comparison of Aristotelian and Epicurean theories of voluntary action.

Frischer, Bernard. *The Sculpted Word: Epicureanism and Philosophical Recruitment in Ancient Greece*. Berkeley: University of California Press, 1982. A somewhat eccentric work whose premise is that the sculptures and other images of Epicurus, which were so common in the ancient world, were used by the Epicureans as charismatic recruitment devices. The book contains an important set of plates showing many of the images of Epicurus in statues and in print.

Hibler, Richard W. *Happiness Through Tranquillity: The School of Epicurus*. New York: University Press of America, 1984. Hibler's interest in Epicurus is primarily as a great teacher; consequently, he follows his discussion of the philosopher's life and works with a summary of twenty points that are especially relevant to readers who wish to know more about Epicurus's educational methodology.

Hicks, R. D. *Stoic and Epicurean*. New York: Russell & Russell, 1961. Hicks compares the Stoics with the Epicureans. He gives an excellent, extended account of Epicurus's theory. This book contains a useful chronological table and is well indexed.

Long, A. A., and D. N. Sedley. *The Hellenistic Philosophers*. 2 vols. Cambridge, England: Cambridge University Press, 1987. Volume one contains translations of the principal sources and excellent philosophical commentary; volume two contains the Greek and Latin texts with extensive notes and bibliography. Approximately 125 pages of each volume is devoted to Epicureanism.

Lucretius. *On the Nature of the Universe*. Translated by Ronald Latham. Baltimore, Md.: Penguin Books, 1964. This philosophical poem forms the basis of the modern reading of Epicurus. Lucretius, in true Epicurean fashion, avoided the usual occupations of his times—war and politics—to devote himself to extensive exposition of Epicurus's teachings.

Rist, J. M. *Epicurus: An Introduction*. New York: Cambridge University Press, 1972. Rist describes his book as an unambitious and elementary account of the philosophy of Epicurus. It is, in fact, a fine introduction to the thought of Epicurus and takes full advantage of the most important developments in Epicurean scholarship.

Sharples, R. W. *Stoics, Epicureans, and Sceptics: An Introduction to Hellenistic Philosophy*. London: Routledge, 1996. Very interesting and readable. This book contains chapters on various aspects of Hellenistic philosophy, comparing and contrasting Stoic, Epicurean, and Skeptic theories within each chapter. Provides an excellent view of the relationship between Epicurean philosophy and its contemporary rivals.

Cynthia Lee Katona, updated by Priscilla K. Sakezles

Desiderius Erasmus

Erasmus transmitted and adapted the Renaissance spirit to northern Europe. Taken together, his writings reflect a rare combination of practical Christian piety, biblical and patristic scholarship, and broad humanistic learning.

Principal philosophical works: *Adagia*, 1500 (*Proverbs or Adages*, 1622); *Enchiridion Militis Christiani*, 1503 (*The Manual of the Christian Knight*, 1533); *Moriæ Encomium*, 1511 (*The Praise of Folly*, 1549); *De Duplici Copia Verborum ac Rerum*, 1512 (*On the Twofold Abundance of Words and Things*, 1978; better known as *De Copia*); *De Rationae Studii*, 1512 (*A Method of Study*, 1978); *Institutio Principis Christiani*, 1516 (*The Education of a Christian Prince*, 1936); *Querela Pacis*, 1517 (*The Complaint of Peace*, 1559); *Colloquia Familiaria*, 1518 (*The Colloquies of Erasmus*, 1671); *Antibarbarum*, 1520 (*The Book Against the Barbarians*, 1930); *De Libero Arbitrio*, 1524 (*On the Freedom of the Will*, 1961); *Dialogus, Cui Titulus Ciceronianus Sive, de Optimo Dicendi Genere*, 1528 (*The Ciceronian*, 1900); *Opus Epistolarum*, 1529 (partial translation, *The Epistles*, 1901, 3 volumes)

Born: October 28, 1466?; Rotterdam, Holland
  (now the Netherlands)
Died: July 12, 1536; Basel, Switzerland

Early Life

Erasmus was born in Rotterdam, or possibly in the Dutch village of Gouda, on October 28 in the late 1460's (the exact year is disputed) to Margaret, a physician's daughter, and a priest probably named Gerard, for whom she served as housekeeper. As one of two illegitimate sons born to this couple, the sensitive Erasmus (he took the additional name Desiderius later in life) would endure shame and legal problems, but his parents lived together for many years and appear to have been devoted parents. Erasmus's childhood coincided with the ongoing war between the Duchy of Burgundy, which controlled Holland, and France. He grew to despise the Burgundian knights, whose cruelty belied the chivalric ideal expressed by Charles the Bold. He also developed an aversion to the provinciality and social rigidity of his homeland.

Around 1478, Erasmus's mother enrolled the two boys at a school in Deventer, about seventy-five miles inland, conducted by the Brethren of the Common Life, a lay society dedicated to the

imitation of primitive Christianity. Although Erasmus later expressed contempt for the Brethren's teaching methods, both their piety and a humanistic strain that entered the school at this time helped shape the young student. His schooling at Deventer ended in 1483 or 1484, when the plague claimed the lives of both his parents. Three guardians appointed by his father sent Erasmus to another more conservative and even less congenial of the Brethren's schools for three additional years.

He entered the Augustinian priory at Steyn about 1487. There, the critical young man learned to dislike the ascetic routine and prevailing mysticism, but he enlarged his grasp of classical literature and wrote the first two of his many books, a conventional treatise on monastic life and a book of Latin verse. His years at Steyn climaxed with his ordination as priest on April 25, 1492.

Life's Work

About a year after his ordination, Erasmus accepted a post as Latin secretary to the ambitious Henri, Bishop of Cambray. While in his service, Erasmus wrote, in the form of a Platonic dialogue, an attack on Scholasticism, the dominant philosophy of the Catholic Church, although the book remained unpublished for nearly thirty years. In 1495, Bishop Henri assisted Erasmus in gaining entrance to the University of Paris, a hotbed of Scholasticism, presumably to study for his doctorate in theology. At the College of Montaigu in Paris, he made humanist friends, including an elderly man named Robert Gaguin, who had been a pupil of the noted Florentine Platonist Marsilio Ficino, and who now encouraged Erasmus to study the Neoplatonists. Constantly seeking the independence that would enable him to spend his life studying in reasonable comfort, he accepted in 1499 the patronage of the Englishman William Blount, Lord Mountjoy, and thus visited England for the first time. There he established friendships with leading scholars such as William Grocyn, Thomas Linacre, John Colet, and—preeminently—Sir Thomas More.

Already the wandering pattern of the man who later called himself a citizen of the world was being established. He returned to France the next year and began a routine of scholarly activity that included the study of Greek, the compilation of a book of proverbial wisdom, *Proverbs or Adages*, and a manual of Christianity written for the laity from the point of view of a monk who, at this point, was living in the manner of a principled Christian layman. *The Manual of the Christian Knight* became the best-known of his works in this genre. His study of Lorenzo Valla's exegesis of the New Testament, a work that he edited and published in 1506, quickened his determination to master the original Greek. After another sojourn in England with his humanist friends, he accepted a tutoring appointment that took him to Italy.

His work took him on a tour that included Turin, at whose university he received a doctorate in divinity in 1506, and Florence, Bologna, and Venice, where he met the distinguished printer Aldus Manutius, with whom he worked to produce a handsome revision

of *Proverbs or Adages*. In Rome, he witnessed the growing corruption of the papal court, after which Mountjoy persuaded him to return to England. It has been argued that had the now influential Erasmus remained in Rome during the next crucial decade, he might have furthered the cause of reform, prevented the excommunication of Martin Luther, with whom he corresponded, and thus changed the course of religious history.

After reaching London, while awaiting the arrival of his books, he lived in Thomas More's house where he wrote a book, *The Praise of Folly*, which he certainly did not consider among his most important but which, more than any other, has immortalized him. By a species of pun congenial to him and to his host, the title also signifies "the praise of More," though without any suggestion that More was foolish. Although the book is, like Sebastian Brant's *Narrenschiff* (1494; *Ship of Fools*, 1509), a satire on human folly, Erasmus's characterization of Folly is a rich and origi-

Desiderius Erasmus. *(Library of Congress)*

nal conception depicting not only gradations of conventional foolishness but also ultimately figuring the Christian fool, whose folly is in reality wisdom.

Later, he became the first man to teach Greek at Cambridge. During his two and a half years on the faculty of the English university, he wrote *De Copia*, which would hold its place as a standard textbook on literary style for two centuries. Nevertheless, Erasmus was not happy at Cambridge, blaming the cold, damp climate for undermining his always frail health and finding Cambridge intellectually mediocre and provincial. His more enlightened humanist English friends resided, for the most part, in London.

He was even less pleased with the prospect of returning to monastic life at Steyn, to which he was recalled in 1514, more than two decades after gaining permission to leave: Erasmus relayed his firm intention to return; it required, however, dispensation from Pope Leo X, which took him three years to acquire, to free himself from all possibility of further obligation to his order. While this appeal was pending, he completed his own Latin version of the New Testament, based on Greek manuscripts and more accurate in many (though not all) details than the standard Latin Vulgate. His translation reflected his conviction that Christ's teachings are easily understandable and not meant to be encrusted by the commentary of theologians. Strategically, he dedicated his work to Leo and also recommended that the Bible be translated into the vernacular tongues so that it might be accessible to the less educated.

Among his other works in this busy period were a nine-volume edition of the works of Saint Jerome and a manual, *The Education of a Christian Prince*. Sharply contrasting with Niccolò Machiavelli's *Il principe* (1532; *The Prince*, 1640), Erasmus's advice to the prince included pleas for restraint in taxation and in the waging of war. Unlike Machiavelli, Erasmus regarded politics as a branch of ethics in the classical manner. Unenthusiastic about the tyranny of princes, Erasmus could see no other acceptable alternative to anarchy. In this work and in two other treatises of this period, Erasmus's thought tended toward pacifism, a shocking philosophy in an age that looked on the willingness to wage war as a certification of one's conviction.

During a stay at Antwerp in 1516-1517, Erasmus was painted by Quentin Massys, the first of three famous artists for whom he sat. In this portrait, Erasmus, then middle-aged, is at his writing desk, intently serious. Portraits by Albrecht Dürer and Hans Holbein the Younger a few years later interpret the Dutch scholar quite differently, but all three artists agree that Erasmus had a very long, somewhat aquiline nose, a wide mouth with thin lips, and a strong chin. Both Dürer and Holbein (in a late portrait of about 1532) endow the writer with a faint, enigmatic smile, which many viewers have seen as mocking human weakness, as does his character Folly. All of these portraits show Erasmus wearing a flat cap.

From 1517 to 1521, Erasmus lived at Louvain. He published one of his most enduring works, *The Colloquies of Erasmus*, and also continued his task of editing the early fathers of the Church, spending all day and much of the night at his writing desk and turning out a stupendous volume of work for publication and hundreds—probably thousands—of gracefully written letters to correspondents all over Europe. Having made a number of severe criticisms of the Church, Erasmus received overtures from his fellow Augustinian Martin Luther, but while refusing for years to denounce Luther—many of whose famous ninety-five theses he anticipated—he did not support him either. In the interests of Christian unity, more important to Erasmus than most of the theological points on which Luther challenged the Church, he attempted to mediate the quarrel, but observing the intransigence of both Church and reformers, he refused an invitation to the Diet of Worms, where, in 1521, Luther's doctrines were condemned. Solicited by both sides but widely viewed as cowardly for his unwillingness to back either unequivocally, Erasmus made many enemies. Although he had little reason to fear the Protestant majority in Basel, where he lived during most of the 1520's, he refused to endorse even tacitly the city's denial of religious liberty to Catholic citizens and left for Freiburg in 1529.

He unsuccessfully urged the warring Christians to compromise and focus on the Turkish threat in the Balkans and continued to prepare editions of early Christian thinkers. In 1535, his own health failing, he learned of King Henry

VIII's execution of his good friends More and Bishop John Fisher. In the final months of his life, he returned to Basel, dying there on July 12, 1536. In 1540, a wooden statue of Erasmus was erected in Rotterdam, the city he claimed as his birthplace, and Johann Froben published an edition of his collected works in Basel. The statue did not survive the Spanish occupation of the Netherlands and many of his books were burned, but the centuries that followed have proved Erasmus ineradicable.

Influence

Before the heyday of the Protestant Reformers, Erasmus articulated his dismay at the excesses of an increasingly worldly and corrupt Church and urged a return to Christian essentials. His numerous editions of early Christian theologians and his Latin version of the New Testament signaled his contempt for the decadent but still-prevailing Scholasticism, and his manuals of practical piety reflected his conviction that what he called "the philosophy of Christ" was a simple and achievable attainment.

Erasmus's tolerance and pacifism, which owed something to his physical timidity but more to his capacity for rational analysis and insight into the futility of religious confrontation, turned both the Catholics and Protestants against him. In an ecumenically minded world, however, what appeared to his contemporaries as cowardice or indecisiveness looks more like wisdom.

As the greatest of the northern humanists, he communicated not only the learning of the ancients but also their spirit of inquiry and independence to educated people of his time. He saw harmony in the best of classical and Christian thought. He also understood the potentialities of mass-produced books—a new development in his lifetime—and thus devoted his life to incessant writing. A bibliographical analysis by an Erasmian scholar in 1927 produced an estimate that two million copies of his books had been printed, one million of them textbooks. Erasmus never understood, however, why more people did not submit to the logic of his arguments. Paradoxically, his books enjoyed more popularity in the later sixteenth and seventeenth centuries, when his personal reputation was ebbing; today a torrent of scholarly works interpret his charac-

ter much more favorably, but he is much less read. Only *The Praise of Folly* is still widely admired for its wit, subtlety, and the universality of its analysis of human folly. Readers who find their way to *The Colloquies of Erasmus*, however, discover that no writer since Plato has used dialogue so well to express his thought in a persuasive and readable form.

Taken as a whole, Erasmus's writings cast more light on the great European movements of his time—the Renaissance and the Reformation—than do the work of any other eyewitness. This wandering Augustinian monk was an intellectual seismograph who registered the brightest hopes and most profound disappointments of Western civilization in the stormy period of his life.

Robert P. Ellis

On the Freedom of the Will

Type of philosophy: Ethics, philosophical theology
First published: De Libero Arbitrio, 1524 (English translation, 1961)
Principal ideas advanced:

◇ Contrary to Martin Luther's thesis, faith alone without good works is not enough to lead to people's salvation.

◇ Theological grace, which all receive from God, complements and does not limit free will.

◇ According to the writings of Church fathers and the New and Old Testaments, only those who freely choose to do good and avoid evil are leading morally exemplary lives.

◇ Because of one's limited understanding of God's intentions, it is haughty to affirm, as German monk Martin Luther had, that God has granted humans no free will.

◇ People are not predestined for hell or heaven.

With the publication in 1516 of his critical edition of the New Testament in Greek and his accompanying Latin translation, Desiderius Erasmus established his expertise in the field of biblical exegesis. His annotation of the New Testament also demonstrated that he had effectively used the writings of numerous Church fathers in order to support traditional Catholic interpretations of both the New and Old Testaments.

Free Will and Predestination

German monk Martin Luther presented his belief in predestination both in the ninety-five theses that he placed in 1517 on the main door of the Cathedral of Wittenberg and his assertions published in 1521. In these works, Luther stated that it was meaningless to talk about free will because everything takes place in conformity with God's intentions. Luther's break with the Roman Catholic Church created a schism in Christianity.

In 1521, the newly elected Pope Adrian VI, who like Erasmus was from Holland, asked Erasmus to attempt to reestablish Christian unity by writing a well-organized treatise in which the contentious issue of free will would be carefully and calmly analyzed. After some hesitation, Erasmus agreed to compose such a treatise, which was published in 1524 as *On the Freedom of the Will*. Just one year later, Martin Luther published his treatise *De Servo Arbitrio* (1525; *On the Bondage of the Will*, 1823) in which he systematically criticized Erasmus's arguments in favor of the reality of free will. The publication of these two treatises served to define very clearly incompatible positions between Catholics and Lutherans on the contentious issues of free will and grace.

In the preface to his treatise on free will, Erasmus reminds readers that he has an open mind and is skeptical about people who claim that they alone possess absolute truth. As a Christian, he firmly believed that the Bible contained God's revealed truths and he asks his readers how a single person, such as Luther, could be so haughty as to believe that he alone definitely knew how God wanted people to interpret the Bible. Erasmus then argues that even if Luther were correct in asserting that people possess no free will and that all happens as a result of absolute necessity, such theories should not be shared with the general public because it might encourage amoral people to yield to temptation and violate God's commandments. Discussions about predestination might be harmless in a theology class, but they might have an unintended negative effect on those who are looking for any excuse to yield to their base instincts. Erasmus is very careful to suggest that Luther would cer-

tainly not want his theological views to harm society.

Erasmus then discussed rather inflexible positions by Luther, who claimed that Christians should ignore fifteen centuries of Christian writings and rely solely on their own judgment in interpreting the Bible. Erasmus suggests that such an approach is unwise because it prevents people from appreciating insights into the meanings of the Bible by such respected and learned theologians as Saints John Chrysostom, Augustine, Jerome, and Thomas Aquinas. Erasmus wonders why it is sensible to conclude that every Christian theologian had misinterpreted the Bible whereas Luther's readings are the only ones with which one should agree. Despite his great respect for the fathers of the Church, Erasmus agrees to play by Luther's rules and base his analysis of free will solely on the canonical works of the Old and New Testaments.

Grace

In two parallel chapters, Erasmus explains very clearly that numerous texts from the Old and New Testaments demonstrate that God had granted men and women the freedom to choose between good and evil. Erasmus wonders if it would have been fair for God to have expelled Adam and Eve from the Garden of Eden if they had not been responsible at all for their sins. No Christian would presume that God was cruel and punished people for no justifiable reason. Luther had claimed that virtuous people received grace, which enabled them to do good deeds whereas sinners were denied this necessary grace.

Erasmus argues that grace is a complex concept that people can never fully understand. He indicates that there are, in fact, four types of grace. The first type of grace is common sense, which discourages people from doing that which is harmful to themselves or their neighbors. The second type of grace encourages sinners to repent and reform their lives. The third type of grace, which Erasmus calls efficient or cooperative grace, leads men and women toward the love of God, and the final grace makes possible eternal salvation. An orthodox Christian belief is that Christ so loved all people that he willingly accepted a painful death on the cross so that everyone could be saved. Erasmus suggests that God loves people and gives them many forms of help and assistance so that they can be saved, but God does not force people to choose good over evil. People are free to lead a virtuous or a rakish life. Erasmus asks his readers if sin can mean anything if people are not at all free to resist temptation. Erasmus then explains that those biblical passages that seem to deny the efficacy of free will can nevertheless be interpreted so that they are compatible with freedom of choice.

Exodus 9:12 states that God "made the Pharaoh obstinate." The Egyptian Pharaoh who enslaved the Jews could, however, have resisted his evil tendencies and treated the Jews with human dignity. It would be preposterous to claim that God had forced the Pharaoh to commit evil actions. Erasmus argues that it is important to distinguish between God's foreknowledge of future events and Luther's belief in predestination. God may well know that certain evil men and women will sin egregiously, but God does not force them to do that which displeases him. This was an important distinction for Erasmus, but in his treatise *On the Bondage of the Will*, Luther affirmed that such a distinction was meaningless.

Despite the very real differences between Catholic theologians and Luther, Erasmus very much wanted to put an end to the schism. In his chapter on Luther's proofs against free will, he complements Luther several times. Erasmus argues that Luther's analysis of the basic weakness of human nature is insightful and agrees with Luther's interpretation of Saint Paul's comment "If I do not have love, I am nothing" in 1 Corinthians 13:2, but Erasmus adds that love (*agapē* in Greek) is the greatest of all gifts or graces from God because it enables people to make the right moral choices and leads them to eternal life in heaven. Erasmus firmly believed that it was possible to reconcile Luther's comments on God's omnipotence with the reality of free will. Erasmus argues that Luther had not properly defined the complex relationship between divine power and human freedom when he claimed that because God is omnipotent, men and women have no real free will as concerns their eternal lives. Erasmus suggested the need for a moderate position that would reconcile Catholicism and Lutheranism and thus reestablish order and unity in Christianity. Catholics believed in free will whereas Luther and his followers believed with equal fervor in the efficacy of grace. A simple or moderate solution would be to state that grace enriches and does not destroy free will. Erasmus expressed his effort to reconcile Catholic and Lutheran positions in these terms: "Man is able to accomplish all things, if God's grace helps him."

Pope Adrian VI hoped that Erasmus would somehow succeed in persuading Luther and numerous Catholic theologians to put an end to their bickering and to consider the general welfare of all Christians. Despite his best efforts to develop a moderate position that would please both Lutherans and Catholics, Erasmus only succeeded in angering both groups. Just one year after the publication of Erasmus's treatise on free will, Luther published his *On the Bondage of the Will*, which was four times longer than Erasmus's essay. Luther accused Erasmus of having distorted the meaning of numerous biblical passages and he rejected Erasmus's efforts to reconcile grace with free will. Numerous Catholic theologians criticized Erasmus for not having affirmed that Luther was completely wrong on the question of free will. Both Catholic and Lutheran positions hardened. Although Erasmus later argued that Catholics and Lutherans should "tolerate" each other, few of his contemporaries felt that this schism could be ended. Erasmus was tolerant of those with whom he disagreed, but his tolerance was not shared by most of the Catholic and Lutheran theologians of his day.

Edmund J. Campion

Additional Reading

Augustijn, Cornelis. *Erasmus: His Life, Works, and Influence*. Translated by J. C. Grayson. Toronto: University of Toronto Press, 1991. Augustijn puts Desiderius Erasmus's life in the context of the political, economic, and intellectual climate of the time, sketches his education and early career; and examines the nature, significance, and impact of his major works—all in the light of recent scholarship.

DeMolen, Richard L., ed. *Essays on the Works of Erasmus*. New Haven, Conn.: Yale University Press, 1978. DeMolen assembles a collection of fourteen essays by leading scholars on the individual works of Erasmus in order to provide an interpretation of a central theme in each work.

Dickens, A. G. *Erasmus the Reformer*. London: Mandarin, 1995. An examination of Erasmus's life, work, and legacy.

Faludy, George. *Erasmus of Rotterdam*. London: Eyre & Spottiswoode, 1970. This excellent general reader's biography explains the historical and intellectual contexts of Erasmus's work clearly. Although it uses few notes, it displays a thorough grasp of scholarship.

Friesen, Abraham. *Erasmus, the Anabaptists, and the Great Commission*. Grand Rapids, Mich.: William B. Eerdmans, 1998. A look at Erasmus's influence in religious thought.

Halkin, Léon E. *Erasmus: A Critical Biography*. Translated by John Tonkin. Oxford: Blackwell, 1993. First issued in 1987, Halkin's study aims to understand Erasmus through Erasmus; hence, he quotes extensively from his works, including his letters, so readers can trace Erasmus's intellectual and spiritual journey and learn of his successes, struggles, ambitions, and setbacks.

Huizinga, Johan. *Erasmus and the Age of Reformation*. Translated by F. Hopman. New York: Harper, 1957. Originally published as *Erasmus of Rotterdam* in 1924, this biography has worn well. Not only was Huizinga a recognized expert on Erasmus's era, but he also understood his subject's psychology as few others have.

McConica, James K. *Erasmus*. New York: Oxford University Press, 1991. McConica's life of Erasmus concentrates on his spiritual and intellectual development by examining his contributions to education, to biblical scholarship, and to the study of the Church fathers.

Mangan, John Joseph. *Life, Character, and Influence of Desiderius Erasmus of Rotterdam*. 2 vols. New York: Macmillan, 1927. Although some of its interpretations are dated, this biography prints translations of many of Erasmus's writings, especially the letters. Its last chapter investigates Erasmus's later influence as indicated by editions and translations of his works.

Phillips, Margaret Mann. *Erasmus and the Northern Renaissance*. London: English Universities Press, 1949. Rev. ed. Woodbridge, England: Boydell Press, 1981. This somewhat elementary introduction to Erasmus and his age are useful for beginning students of the Renaissance.

Smith, Preserved. *Erasmus: A Study of His Life, Ideals, and Place in History*. New York: Frederick Ungar, 1962. This reprint of a scholarly life with its bibliography of nineteenth and earlier twentieth century studies chiefly by European scholars was issued in 1923. Although less useful on Erasmus as humanist, it views him as champion of "undogmatic Christianity" and emphasizes his ideas' relationship with those of Protestant reformers.

Tracy, James D. *Erasmus of the Low Countries*. Berkeley: University of California Press, 1996. A readable, clear account of Erasmus's life and thoughts.

Robert P. Ellis, updated by Albert J. Geritz

Johannes Scotus Erigena

Erigena provided the first Latin translations of and commentaries on the works of the great Greek fathers of the early Christian church. His sometimes controversial Neoplatonic works were a synthesis of medieval theology and philosophy.

Principal philosophical works: *De divina praedestinatione*, 851 (*Treatise on Divine Predestination*, 1998); *De divisione naturae*, c. 862-866 (also known as *Periphysion*; best known in partial translation as *On the Division of Nature: Book 1*, 1940; complete translation, *Johannis Scotti Eriugenae Periphyseon [De divisione naturae]*, 1968-1981); *Homilia in prologum Sancti Evangelli secundum Joannem*, c. 870 (*The Voice of the Eagle: Homily on the Prologue to the Gospel of St. John*, 1990).

Born: c. 810; Ireland
Died: c. 877; France or England

Early Life

Johannes Scotus Erigena was born in Ireland—hence the designation "Scotus," or "Scot," which in the ninth century meant "Irishman," and the possible construing of "Erigena" as "Ireland-born." His place of birth and his education in an Irish monastery account for a great deal of his importance for Western philosophy because in Erigena's day, the Irish monasteries were one of the last remaining places in Western Europe where Greek was taught.

Little is known about Erigena's early life, except for where he received his schooling, and that is merely inferred. Like most great writers of the Middle Ages, however, he is at the center of many legends. The story that he traveled in Greece, Italy, and Gaul in his early years is probably based on a confusion of Erigena with a Spaniard with a similar name. Stories that he was invited to France by Charlemagne and that he helped found the University of Paris cannot be substantiated.

However, although the connection with Charlemagne cannot be proved, it is known that Erigena served in the court of emperor Charles the Bald. Prudentius, Bishop of Troyes, left that court in 847 and later recalled spending time there with Erigena, placing Erigena's service somewhere between 843 (the accession of Char-

les) and 847. Erigena's position was headmaster of the court school. He must have enjoyed some degree of eminence in the court, if an anecdote told by William of Malmsbury is true. According to William, Erigena was seated at dinner opposite Charles when the king riddled, "What is the distance between a Scot and a sot?" Erigena replied, "That of a table." Delivering such a quip to an emperor implies a great deal of security and familiarity.

Life's Work

The continuity of Western thought, both across time (from the Neoplatonists to the modern idealists, as scholar Henry Bett put it) and across European space (from Greece to the British Isles) owes much to Erigena's synthesis of the minds of the ancient Greeks and the essentially Germanic mind of Carolingian Europe. Erigena's leanings were Neoplatonic, particularly influenced by Pseudo-Dionysius. Although his first published work, a treatise on the Eucharist, no longer exists, commentaries suggest that in this work Erigena argued that the Eucharist was only symbolically the body of Christ (though it must be kept in mind that to a Neoplatonist "symbolic" reality was higher, more real, than the merely material). Though this teaching was declared heretical a few years later, ecclesial authorities do not seem to have associated it with Erigena, for the Bishop of Riems requested him to respond to a treatise on predestination by the Saxon monk Gottschalk.

Erigena's heterodoxy, apparently not readily evident in his lost work on the Eucharist, was unmistakable in his *Treatise on Divine Predestination*. Gottschalk's fatalistic predestinarianism was ably refuted by Erigena but in a scurrilous, name-calling fashion and by asserting that philosophy and religion were identical. Erigena's treatise was condemned by the Synod of Valence in 855, which, in language as strong as Erigena's, called it *pultes Scotorum*, or "Scot's gruel."

Erigena's next work, a translation of Pseudo-Dionysius, was commissioned by the emperor Charles. It must have been completed by the late 850's, for Pope Nicholas I (installed in 858) wrote to Charles the Bald in 860, rebuking Charles and Erigena for publishing the translation without his papal approval. Nicholas also mentioned previous works, which he cited in the letter, apparently questioning their orthodoxy. He demanded that Erigena come to Rome or that he be banished from the court of Charles the Bald. Neither appears to have occurred.

Erigena's translation of the *Ambigua* (seventh century; ambiguities) of Maximus the Confessor probably belongs to the same period as his translations of the works of Pseudo-Dionysius and is related in content. Maximus's work is a set of commentaries on the most obscure passages in Pseudo-Dionysius and Gregory Nazianzen. Maximus greatly influenced the thought of Erigena, particularly in the area that corresponds to modern-day psychology. Maximus refuted the heresy known as *monothelitism*, the notion that Christ had two natures, divine and human, but only one will. Though the controversy was no longer an issue in Erigena's day, it had implications for the medieval view of the nature of personality. By demonstrating that the monothelites confused personality with the single will, Erigena paved the way for later discussion of individual consciousness.

Erigena's greatest work, both in bulk and in significance, is *On the Division of Nature*. The work, which presupposes and builds on his translations and his work on predestination, is most likely a work of the late 860's. Written in five books and a quarter of a million words, *On the Division of Nature* takes the form of a dialogue between master and disciple. Erigena's scheme of dividing nature is fourfold: God as source of all

(book 1), primal causes that mediate God and nature (book 2), creation itself (book 3), and the return of all to God (books 4 and 5). This is the essence of Erigena's philosophy.

In *On the Division of Nature*, Erigena anticipates a controversy that would lead, two hundred years later, to the "great schism" between Eastern and Western Christianity. The pupil in the dialogue discusses the *filioque* clause in the Nicene Creed, an early expression of Christian doctrine. The Latin word *filioque* means "and the son" and represents a statement about the Trinity, that the Holy Spirit proceeds from the Father and the Son. Though that formulation exists in the writings of the early Greek fathers, some Eastern writers began to object to the phrase "and the son." In Erigena's dialogue, it is the disciple who raises the question: Does the Holy Spirit proceed from the son after the son is begotten, and is it from the essence or the substance? The master resolves this question by resorting to Erigena's translations of works by Pseudo-Dionysius, Maximus, and Nazianzen, demonstrating the extent to which Erigena's great work is a synthesis of his earlier writings. The question of the relationship among the members of the Trinity points to the central theme of the work, represented by the word "divisions" in the title. "Divisions" in nature refer to the Neoplatonic doctrine of Plotinus that the "Many," the multiplex created things in the universe, are fallen forms and need to return to the "One," which is God. That pattern of individuation and return is clear in the five books of *On the Division of Nature*.

The dialogue form, though common in philosophy since the Greek philosopher Plato, allows for a great deal of creativity on Erigena's part in *On the Division of Nature*. Erigena's style contributes a great deal to the effectiveness of his writings, and it is clear from the Latin verse that survives that writing was for him more than a mechanism for transmitting ideas. The character of the student in Erigena's great dialogue is fully developed, rather than the mindless foil for the master one usually finds in such colloquies. Also unlike the character of Socrates in Plato's dialogues, the master in Erigena's work does not so much correct the errors of the pupil as restate more clearly the insights the pupil has discovered.

Concerning the later life of Erigena, confusion reigns, with legend merging into fact. A dedicatory poem he wrote for a church founded in Compiègne in 877 has been used as evidence that Erigena was still in France at that time. However, later that year, his patron Charles the Bald died, and Alfred the Great defeated the Danes the following year, both circumstances lending credence to the report by William of Malmsbury that Erigena came to England at Alfred's invitation at this time. William writes that Erigena taught at the abbey of Malmsbury, which would account for William's familiarity with Erigena, and scholar Bett noted that the abbey of Malmsbury was founded by an Irish monk and maintained an Irish tradition, circumstances that would have made Erigena welcome. What makes this very plausible tradition suspect is the end of the story, in which William asserts that Erigena's students stabbed him to death with their pens. However, this bizarre element is the only implausible item in the story.

Influence

Erigena's most marked influence on later writers was among mystics, particularly the Victorine school, although he also strongly influenced the heretical sects of the thirteenth century, particularly the Albigensians and Cathari. The Scholastic philosophers of the later Middle Ages never quote Erigena, but that is to be expected, as his works were under a papal ban. However, nineteenth century scholars demonstrated a direct line from Erigena to the late medieval Schoolmen. For example, when they quote the doctrinally "safe" Avicebron (Ibn-Gebirol), who was virtually a commentator on Erigena, they are in reality quoting Erigena. Saint Thomas Aquinas's refutations of the heretics Amalric of Bena and David of Dinant (both early thirteenth century) appear to be treatments of Erigenism.

There is also some reason to believe that Erigena's thought was influential in the nominalist controversy of the tenth century. The question among philosophers was whether or not abstract qualities such as "whiteness" had any real existence. In a tenth century chronicle, several minor philosophers are listed as partaking in the controversy and identified as followers of "John the Sophist." Because sophism, or arguing a case for

the purpose of winning rather than arriving at the truth, was one of the charges against John the Scot in his papal condemnation, it has been conjectured that this otherwise unknown "John the Sophist" was in fact Erigena. For this reason and because some of his arguments anticipate the nominalist position in the controversy (that "whiteness" is only a word and not a real quality), Erigena has been called "the first nominalist."

Paradoxically, however, he has also been called "the first realist," which is the opposite position. This seeming contradiction can be reconciled when we realize that Erigena, like most of his contemporaries, was first and foremost a Neoplatonist. That is, the highest reality for him is the ideal, a world beyond the merely physical one known through the senses, wherein abstract concepts and transcendental beings (such as God and the angels) have their being. In this context, to say that "whiteness" is "real" does not necessarily mean that its reality is accessible to our senses in the same way that an individual white thing is. Erigena's statements on the subject would have been found in both camps of the controversy, the realist and the nominalist.

In the early Renaissance, two distinct and influential intellectual movements were demonstrably influenced by Erigena, in both cases through a single writer. The Christian humanism of northern Europe felt Erigena's doctrine through Nicholas of Cusa, who refers to him as "Scotigena," and German mysticism felt it through the writings of Meister Eckhart. There is no doubt that Erigena's thought continues to influence philosophy in that most subtle and least detectable way—by becoming basic presuppositions of which one is often no longer conscious.

John R. Holmes

On the Division of Nature

Type of philosophy: Metaphysics, philosophical theology

First transcribed: De divisione naturae, c. 862-866 (also known as *Periphyseon*; best known in partial translation as *On the Division of Nature:*

Book 1, 1940; complete translation, *Johannis Scotti Eriugenae Periphyseon [De divisione naturae]*, 1968-1981)

Principal ideas advanced:

◇ God created humanity in such a manner that humans share the nature of other animals as well as the celestial nature.

◇ Our minds are ignorant and unwise, but in God the mind finds its discipline; humanity is an intellectual idea formed eternally in the divine mind, and for humans to know they must come to full consciousness and recall the eternal ideas.

◇ The idea by which people know themselves is their substance; consequently, people may be known through intellectual causes or by effects.

◇ Humanity exists in the divine mind, for humanity is by its essence divine idea.

◇ People are by nature omniscient, but they lost the knowledge of themselves and of their creator when they sinned; insofar as people can know, it is by the grace of God, who allows people to become aware of essences by acts of understanding in which the idea in people's minds and in God's mind are one.

Johannes Scotus Erigena is often regarded as the first of the real medievals. Boethius and Saint Augustine, from several centuries earlier, are his only substantial predecessors. Erigena was familiar with Boethius, about whose life he wrote, and he introduced classical Neoplatonism into the formative years of the medieval period through his translations from Pseudo-Dionysius. He was also familiar with the fathers of both the Latin Church and the Greek Church. Yet, more than the fact that he is the first major writer to appear in several centuries, his importance to the Middle Ages lies in his production of one of the first complete metaphysical schemes, his *On the Division of Nature*. The Middle Ages became noted for its systematic, speculative, and constructive effort, and the tone for such effort is set here in Erigena's major work.

His Platonistic tendencies are immediately evident in the use he makes in his writing of the dialogue form. Master and disciple question and answer each other, although the form is more that of alternating brief essays than that of Plato's

more dramatic rapid reply. Of course, Plato also tends to adopt a more sustained form of speech in his later dialogues, and it is perhaps primarily from the Neoplatonists that Erigena learned his writing style. Another similarity to Neoplatonism (in contrast to Plato) can be seen in the cosmic perspective that Erigena adopts. Plato's metaphysics is more fragmentary; the Neoplatonists tend naturally to deal with problems in the total setting of a cosmic scheme. Erigena outlines such a scheme in book of *On the Division of Nature*.

Human Nature

Erigena's disciple asks why God created humans as one of the family of animals instead of in the form of some higher celestial creature? Humans need their terrestrial bodies and can perceive only with the aid of perceptions received from without. With angels it is not so; no such limitations bind them, and yet humans are supposed to have been made in God's image. Humanity's sin and fall from grace cannot account for this animal nature because even if humans had not sinned they would still be animals. It is not by sin but by nature that humans are animals. The human position is even stranger considering that in a future life, a human may be transmuted into a celestial form of being.

To answer his disciple's question, the master resorts to the divine will, saying that why God willed this is beyond inquiry because the causes of the divine will cannot be known. Why God willed it is beyond all understanding.

However, one can say that the whole of created nature, both visible and invisible, is present in humans, and this is a valuable position. What is naturally present in the celestial essences subsists essentially in humans. We can say rationally, therefore, that God wished to place humans in the genus of animals because he wished to create every creature in humans, and for this to be possible, humans had to share in all nature, not only in celestial nature. No irrationality is implied, for everything from God can be understood and anything not from God cannot be understood because it simply is not. Things exist outside the knower, and they are what produces knowledge of them in humans. The ideas of things and the things themselves are of different natures. In addition, things must be granted to be of a more excellent nature than the ideas of them.

That which understands is better than that which is understood, and taking it one step further, the idea of intelligible things is older than the intelligible things themselves. The human mind derives its knowledge from things, but the things themselves were originally formed from intelligible ideas (existing in God's mind). Although the human mind is born inexpert and unwise, nevertheless it is able to find in itself its God, its expertness, and its discipline. As in God, so in humanity, there is a kind of trinity: mind, learning, and art. However, only the divine mind possesses the true idea of the human mind because the human mind cannot of itself comprehend itself. To define humanity truly we must say: Humanity is an intellectual idea formed eternally in the divine mind.

What results is a Platonic doctrine of recollection, now transferred to the divine mind. What humans essentially are, all the knowledge they can possess, is eternally contained as idea in the divine mind. To know, then, is to come to full consciousness, to recall this set of ideas eternally formed. Self-consciousness means increased knowledge of the divine nature. A true knowledge of all things is implanted in human nature, although its presence is concealed until by divine light, the soul is turned to God. What else is there, then, except ideas? Accordingly, the very idea by which humans know themselves may be considered their substance. Yet, how could it be that humans are not always and naturally seen as this divine idea? Because (as philosopher Baruch Spinoza was to say later) all things in nature may be viewed through two perspectives: Either as creatures in the word of God in which all things have been made or as individuals considered in themselves without reference to their divine origin.

God's Nature

Humans have one substance understood both through its creation in intellectual causes and by its generation in effects. Accordingly, one and the same thing is spoken of as double because it is twice observed. What difficulties does this theory present? In order to know the human essence properly, God's nature must first be understood,

for here is the true focus of knowledge. Yet Erigena holds to the traditional assertion: It is in no way granted to the human mind to know what the essence of God is, although humans may know "that it is." The result is that, although humans were first rendered intelligible by understanding their essence as an idea in the divine mind, because of this, the knowledge of humanity is subjected to all of the traditional difficulties surrounding the knowledge of God.

God is entirely uncircumscribed and is to be understood through no thing because God is infinite. What about humans? Erigena denies that the human mind is *anything* and affirms only that it *is*. If the human mind were circumscribable, it could not express the image of its creator wholly, which means that because the human mind is so much like the divine, it also cannot be grasped directly. The same problems that surround the divine nature now surround the human mind's understanding of its own essence because this cannot be grasped except as part of the divine mind. Amazingly enough, even infinity is transferred to the human mind: Just as the divine essence is infinite, human determination is also not limited by any certain end. It is understood only to be, but what it *is* is never understood. Infinity, once God's unique possession, humans now come to share, and they immediately become subject to its rational difficulties.

An Idea in the Divine Mind

Aristotle rejected infinity as an attribute of divine perfection because of its inaccessibility to rational comprehension. Transcendentalists applied unlimitedness to God in spite of the difficulties for knowledge. Erigena, by defining the essence of humanity as a divine idea, subjects the understanding of human nature to the same insurmountable difficulties because God's mind must be understood before humanity's essence can be found. In God, however, there is no ignorance, except the divine darkness that exceeds all understanding. Because humans subsist more truly an in idea than in themselves, they must be understood in and through an idea, and this is located in God, who is himself not fully knowable. Yet this cannot be avoided, for when a thing is known better, it must be judged to exist more truly. Humans, then, exist more truly as an idea in the divine mind than they do in themselves, which means that God's understanding (and darkness) is involved in the knowledge of the true existence of all things, humans included.

For example, geometrical figures do not exist in themselves, but only in the theoretical structure of the discipline in which they are the figures. Humans do not exist in themselves truly but exist in the divine plan of which they are a part. If, therefore, geometrical bodies subsist only in their rational ideas, what is there so astonishing about the fact that natural bodies should subsist in that nature (God) in which there is the idea of them? Reality is never ultimately located in the natural world; it is in the divine mind. Intelligible things are actually prior to sensible things in the mind that understands them. The thing understood, furthermore, is preceded by the understanding soul that perceives it. Finally, the divine nature is prior to the human soul because it provides the locus for both the soul's self-understanding and its ultimate existence.

Why should it be so difficult for humans to learn these facts about their nature and their understanding? If humans had not sinned, the reply comes, they certainly would not have fallen into so profound an ignorance. In the fall, human nature perished entirely in all people, except in the Redeemer of the world, in whom alone it remained incorruptible. He alone was joined in a unity of substance to the word of God, in whom all the elect by grace are made sons of God and participants of the divine substance. Before sin, each creature had implanted in it a full knowledge of both itself and its creator, so that if human nature had not sinned, it would assuredly be omniscient. Sin alone separates humanity from God and human from divine nature. First, Erigena made humans infinite by linking their self-understanding with God's understanding. Then he showed that humans are omniscient by nature, losing this quality only through the bondage of sin.

Knowledge

According to Erigena, human nature retained this perfect knowledge, of itself, of its creator, and of all things (present before sin), but this perfect knowledge is held in possibility alone. In

the highest humans, this knowledge becomes actual again. All things are known in and are created by the word of God; thus, the created wisdom of humanity knew all things before they were made. In fact, everything in the human understanding proceeds from and through the idea of the creative wisdom. All things subsist in the divine understanding causally and in the human understanding effectually. In knowledge and in dignity, but not in time and place, the creation of humanity precedes those things that were created with it and by it. Yet, in the end, no created intellect can know what a thing is because the essence of everything is involved in the problem of divine ignorance.

Humans' rational processes are so great, in fact, that their understanding would naturally be equal with that of the angels—if they had not sinned. Humans and angels are by nature so alike that they reciprocally understand each other. In fact, any two human understandings can essentially become one because they can both apprehend ideas, and human essence and understanding are not two things but one. Humans are essentially their understanding. This is incorporeal and, ultimately, is to be seen as an idea in the divine mind. Humans' one true and supreme essence is the understanding made specific in the contemplation of truth. This is an antecedent to French philosopher René Descartes's definition of humanity as a "thinking substance." This final identification makes humans in their real nature so much like God and thus involves the understanding of humanity in the difficulties of comprehending God. Humans are their knowledge; humans are their ideas, whose locus is in the divine mind.

God created by separating light from darkness; were there no dark element, all would be angelic nature and understanding. As it is, darkness precipitated humans into ignorance as a penalty for their pride, and people could neither foresee their fall nor their misery. Were it not for the unshapeliness of darkness, all creatures would cling immutably to their creator, and humans would not need to struggle for understanding. As it is, humans must first see God, the presence of the idea of humanity in the divine mind, in order to understand their own nature. However, this requires overcoming the ignorance of sin and grasping the divine nature—surely a job for an angel, unless humans are first restored by divine grace.

A speculative system of such scope and daring as Erigena presented is quite difficult for the modern mind to grasp for many reasons. Such pure speculation is no longer prevalent, and speculation of such vigor is quite unexpected as the first philosophy of consequence since Saint Augustine, who wrote nearly four centuries earlier. Here Erigena easily ranges between God and humanity, comprehending in his theory the whole of creation with the greatest of ease. Modern caution has restrained us from such far-ranging flights of philosophical reasoning. Erigena's thoughts were considered unorthodox by his own church, but they exerted a powerful influence (particularly in Platonic circles) in the following centuries and stand as a monument to independent and original speculative construction.

Frederick Sontag

Additional Reading

Bett, Henry. *Johannes Scotus Erigena: a Study in Mediaeval Philosophy*. Cambridge, England: Cambridge University Press, 1925. Reprint. New York: Russell & Russell, 1964. Although dated, this work, the first complete study of Johannes Scotus Erigena in English, is still a valuable introduction to this complex thinker. Bett tirelessly traces Erigena's sources in earlier writers and his influence on later ones. The author marshals considerable evidence to debunk some legends about John the Scot as well as to corroborate others.

Gibson, Margaret T., and Nelson, Janet L., eds. *Charles the Bald: Court and Kingdom*. Rev. ed. Aldershot, England: Variorum Editions, 1990. This collection of essays provides valuable background on the court in which Erigena served as schoolmaster. All of the essays have some bearing on Erigena, but the most direct is John Marenbon's "John Scottus and Carolingian Theology."

Jeauneau, Edouard, and Paul Edward Dutton. *The Autograph of Eriugena*. Turnholti: Typographi Brepols Editores Pontificii, 1996. A good source of textual criticism.

McGinn, Bernard, and Otten, Willemien, eds. *Eriugena East and West*. Notre Dame, Ind.: University of Notre Dame Press, 1994. This collection of essays is the proceedings of a scholarly conference on Erigena sponsored by Notre Dame University in 1991. McGinn's introduction to the volume is a helpful starting place for the beginning student of Erigena and a good tool for determining which of the other articles in the book will be most helpful.

O'Meara, J. J. *Eriugena*. Oxford: Oxford University Press, 1988. A comprehensive study of Erigena's philosophy, this volume is for the advanced student. O'Meara places Erigena's thought in the context of the Neoplatonic philosophy of his era, but this book presupposes some basic knowledge of medieval philosophy.

O'Meara, J. J., and Bieler, L. *The Mind of Eriugena*. Dublin: Irish University Press, 1973. This collection of essays is the proceedings of a colloquium on Erigena in Dublin in 1970. Although not all of the articles are in English (nine are in French, and one in German), this book contains some important essays in English, including A. H. Armstrong's study of Erigena's Greek sources and R. Russell's essay on Augustinian sources.

Otten, Willemien. *The Anthropology of Johannes Scottus Eriugena*. Leiden: E. J. Brill, 1991. Though narrower in scope than other studies mentioned here, this book presents the implications about human nature in Erigena's philosophy, especially in his discussions on monothelitism and the Trinity.

John R. Holmes

Emil L. Fackenheim

Fackenheim used Jewish resources to interpret non-Jewish philosophy and Western techniques on Jewish texts and history. He defined an authentic Jewish philosopher—and an authentic Jew—as one who has opened the self to the historical uniqueness of the Holocaust and one who actively supports the building of the State of Israel as past, present, and future home for the Jews.

Principal philosophical works: *Metaphysics and Historicity*, 1961; *The Religious Dimension in Hegel's Thought*, 1967; *Quest for Past and Future: Essays in Jewish Theology*, 1968; *God's Presence in History: Jewish Affirmations and Philosphical Reflections*, 1970; *Encounters Between Judaism and Modern Philosophy*, 1973; *The Jewish Return into History: Reflections in the Age of Auschwitz and a New Jerusalem*, 1978; *To Mend the World: Foundations of Future Jewish Thought*, 1982; *The God Within: Kant, Schelling and Historicity, Essays by E. L. Fackenheim*, 1996.

Born: June 22, 1916; Halle, Germany

Early Life

Emil Ludwig Fackenheim was raised by a piously Jewish mother and a father who not only was a successful lawyer but who also daily recited traditional Jewish prayers in Hebrew. After completing *Gymnasium* (college-prep high school) studies in the rigorous German school system, with an emphasis on Greek and classical philology, Fackenheim traveled to Berlin in 1935 in order to study Judaism at the Hochschule für die Wissenschaft des Judentums with the intent of becoming a rabbi. However, following the November, 1938, Nazi pogrom of the Jews known as Kristallnacht (night of the broken glass), his six-year rabbinical program was permanently interrupted when he was arrested by the Gestapo and sent to the Sachsenhausen labor camp for three months. Released on February 8, 1939, Fackenheim finished an abbreviated rabbinical training in two months and was ordained as a rabbi.

Significantly, Fackenheim insists that what most markedly characterized him and a small group of friends from the rabbinical school was that they never questioned their faith in God. In contrast, they rejected self-pity and focused on husbanding their strength for survival. They were some of the few who survived.

Life's Work

On May 12, 1939, Fackenheim fled Germany one step ahead of another Gestapo roundup and spent a year studying in Aberdeen, Scotland. Afterward, he was interned in Britain, then sent for a year and a half further internment in Canada. Upon release, he entered the Graduate School of Philosophy at the University of Toronto while also serving as a rabbi in Hamilton, Canada, from 1943 to 1945. Under the influence of scholars such as Leo Strauss and Jacques Maritain, Fackenheim formed a philosophy of history and wrote *Metaphysics and Historicity*, in which he attempted his first refutation of Martin Heidegger's philosophy. In this work, Fackenheim was already drawing on traditional philosophic and Jewish sources for his critical analysis in attacking Heidegger, and both his refutation of Heidegger's choice to support Hitler and Nazism and his own appropriation of significant elements of Heidegger's existentialism would, in one way or another, dictate his philosophical endeavors for the rest of his career.

Although strongly influenced by the existentialist elements in Heidegger's philosophy, Fackenheim drew much more regularly and extensively on Georg Wilhelm Friedrich Hegel's philosophy, especially his logic of the dialectic. When Fackenheim first joined the faculty at the University of Toronto in 1948, no courses were being taught in German idealism and so Fackenheim began what he called a decades-long encounter beginning with Hegel's *Phénoménologie des Geistes* (1807; *The Phenomenology of Mind*, 1910). In 1960, Fackenheim was made a professor on the faculty, which enabled him to continue his work in German idealism including how it related to his Jewish heritage. His research resulted in the publication of one of the most significant analyses of Hegel's philosophy of religion in the twentieth century, *The Religious Dimension in Hegel's Thought*, in 1967. This work is his most important contribution to the branch of philosophy concerned with German idealism and formed the cornerstone of his ongoing critique of the limits of philosophy to adequately deal with history.

Although primarily Hegelian, Fackenheim's philosophical interests range broadly, as he includes critical commentaries within his texts on many other modern non-Jewish philosophers, especially Immanuel Kant, Johann Gottlieb Fichte, Friedrich Wilhelm Joseph Schelling, Søren Kierkegaard, A. J. Ayer, Heidegger, and Jean-Paul Sartre. Baruch Spinoza, Karl Marx, and Ernst Bloch merit special attention by Fackenheim because of their disavowal of their Jewish origins. Additionally, many Jewish philosophers, including Maimonides, Franz Rosenzweig, Leo Strauss, and especially Martin Buber, have also deeply influenced his work.

Although Fackenheim was profoundly marked by these and many other philosophers, he consistently returns to Hegel's philosophical reflections to construct his own formulations, such as his original version of dialectical encounter. The thesis of encounter is one that Fackenheim plays out in each of his succeeding works and is based on the notion that although Jewish thinkers need to take non-Jewish philosophy seriously and have done so (as Fackenheim's own work demonstrates), philosophers also need to take Jewish thought and existence seriously, which has not been the case. Consequently, Fackenheim ends *The Religious Dimension in Hegel's Thought* by noting that Hegel accepts the frag-

mentation of the modern world as a modern necessity, "yet believes in the power of the Spirit to re-create as a new unity beyond fragmentation." Despite his judgment that "philosophers are an isolated order of priests" who have to leave the world, he counsels that "philosophic thought must move beyond the extremes of partisan commitments, and grope for what may be called a fragmented middle." Rooted in his reading of Hegel's commitment to existential-historical conditions, it seems that with his *The Religious Dimension in Hegel's Thought*, Fackenheim could still hope for metaphysical comprehensiveness.

However, although Fackenheim attends to this "fragmented middle" throughout the remainder of his career, coincidentally with his publication of the Hegel text, he became convinced that it is impossible to attain any kind of philosophical comprehensiveness on what he calls Planet Auschwitz. A world that has not authentically taken into account the radical, unique evil of Adolf Hitler, Nazism, and Auschwitz and that allows for the possibility of absolute destruction is a world that is marked not only by wonder that originally spurs on philosophical reflection but also the horror of inexplicable evil. Hence, to Fackenheim, the year 1967 represents not only the year of publication of his text on Hegel but also the year of the Six-Day War in Israel that precipitated his decision that he could no longer remain an isolated philosopher-priest. Fackenheim, based on his Holocaust-oriented historical analysis, saw the attack on Israel by the Arab states as a logical extension of the attempt to annihilate Jewish existence by the Nazis. The response of the Jews to this military attack on their very existence as a people was an extension of another Holocaust-related experience, namely, the Warsaw ghetto response of fierce, autonomous resistance thirty-five years earlier. Although the Jews demonstrated their commitment and will to fight for survival in both situations, the decisive difference, according to Fackenheim, was that in Israel in 1967, the Jews had the military training and arms—the power—to execute success. During this war, the Israelis also took full control of the city of Jerusalem.

Fackenheim's *Quest for Past and Future* is a collections of essays concerning his response to those historical events, in particular, how to make sense philosophically of the events of the Holocaust from 1933 to 1945 and the formation of the modern state of Israel in 1948. In this work, he coined the phrase that brought his work popular exposure: his declaration of the "614th Commandment" as a Holocaust-inspired addition to the 613 commandments referred to in the traditional Halakah of the Jews. That commandment presupposes that God is still present in history, and out of the inexplicable horror of the Holocaust emerges God's command not to give Hitler a posthumous victory by giving up Jewish faith in the ongoing historical effectiveness of God. Rather, Jews should act in concrete, historical ways by forsaking martyrdom, fighting for their very survival and raising their children as traditional Jews in order to continue to bear witness to God and to their hope for a better world.

He clarifies and develops these themes during the next decade in several collections of essays: *God's Presence in History: Jewish Affirmations and Philosophical Reflections*, *Encounters Between Judaism and Modern Philosophy*, and *The Jewish Return into History: Reflections in the Age of Auschwitz and a New Jerusalem*. These volumes each serve to prepare Fackenheim to produce what he called his magnum opus, *To Mend the World: Foundations of Future Jewish Thought*, published in 1982, his first systematic work since *The Religious Dimension in Hegel's Thought*. One year after finishing that work, Fackenheim acted on his own beliefs and moved permanently to Israel.

In 1970, Fackenheim and his wife had made their second trip to Jerusalem, stopping along the way with a group of Holocaust survivors making a pilgrimage to Bergen Belsen. That trip began what was to become a gradual commitment to traveling more and more often to Jerusalem with his family and spending more and more time there, eventually securing a position as a fellow at the Institute of Contemporary Jewry at the Hebrew University of Jerusalem.

Over the course of his life and work, a clear pattern emerged that showed the growing force of Fackenheim's commitment to live out in practical and political ways his understanding of his Jewish heritage. What characterizes Fackenheim's work is a verification that people are still left with the historical fragments of a broken Hegelian middle and that dealing with the remaining religious content is the most important task, especially for Jews. Philosophically, Fackenheim came to the conclusion that all systematic philosophical thinking, including even that of key systematic Jewish philosophers such as Maimonides and Rosenzweig, is anachronistic post-Holocaust. Rather, what remains is the "systematic labor of thought" and the existential verification of a commitment to authentic Jewish life. In fact, his move to Jerusalem in 1983 after finishing his last major work, *To Mend the World*, exemplifies his own acting out of Rosenzweig's prescription at the end of *Der Stern der Erlösung* (1921; *The Star of Redemption*, 1970) that one's faith must be verified in life and that study is but a prelude that establishes the gates through which one must humbly walk into life with others and with one's God.

Influence

Although Fackenheim's interpretation of Hegel continues to attract scholars of continental philosophy, especially because of his erudite analysis of religion in Hegel's work, his influence in Jewish philosophy is much more pronounced. However, that influence is clearly mixed. On the one hand, he significantly contributed to increasing awareness of the importance for Jews of confronting the Holocaust and for promoting its importance as a world historical event and therefore as a significant event for all peoples. Additionally, he redefined Jewish Zionism and the establishment of the modern state of Israel in functional terms of protecting current and future Jewish existence. However, not all Jews accept such a linkage and, in fact, Fackenheim's insistence that his redefined Zionism is the only mark of authentic Jewish existence is problematic not only for any Jew committed to living outside Israel or in Diaspora but also for a traditional understanding of Judaism. Traditionally, Judaism has always taught that survival is a religious duty, and according to secular and religious Jews not committed to living in Israel as a response to the Holocaust, categorically proclaiming the 614th Commandment as revelatory and beyond question does not allow for any further exploration of how non-Israeli Jews may or may not continue to act in the world.

Julius J. Simon

God's Presence in History

Jewish Affirmations and Philosophical Reflections

Type of philosophy: Ethics, Jewish philosophy, philosophy of religion

First published: 1970

Principal ideas advanced:

◇ A standard of biblical faith is used to confront the atheism and secularism of modern Jews as well as the modern Enlightenment values of rational explanation and progressive socialism.

◇ The Holocaust of the Jews by the Nazis is an epoch-making event equivalent in moral authority for the Jews, and therefore the rest of humanity, to God's liberating actions in choosing the Jewish people out of Egyptian slavery and in God's revelation as commanding power revealed at Mount Sinai.

◇ Other epoch-making events are the destruction of the two temples, the political emancipation from European ghettos, and the establishment of the modern state of Israel.

◇ Each of these events challenges the formative Jewish "root experiences" of the Exodus and the revelation at Mount Sinai, but the Holocaust provides a unique challenge.

The text of *God's Presence in History* is a written revision of three lectures delivered by Emil L. Fackenheim as the Charles F. Deems Lectures at New York University in 1968 about how world historical Jewish events such as the Holocaust and the establishment of the modern state of Israel categorically entail concrete responses by Jews to ensure Jewish survival. The event that directly precipitated this work was the 1967 surprise attack by the Arab states surrounding Israel (the Six-Day War) and the total lack of support by any other nation in the world. An additional impetus was Fackenheim's assertion that responses to the Holocaust such as the death of God movement of the 1960's or the rise of secular and nonobservant Jews was threatening the future existence of the Jewish people as a whole. However, it could easily be argued that Fackenheim was working toward just such an apologetic response his entire life.

Jews as Witnesses

Fackenheim begins his text by dedicating it to Holocaust survivor and activist Elie Wiesel, to whom he credits his use of a midrashic method in exploring the faith-commitment of Jews post-Holocaust and their support of the modern state of Israel. His opening, a midrashic interpretation of a scriptural passage, provides the cornerstone of his argument that post-Holocaust Jews have the right and duty to judge others because they survived the attack on their ongoing existence as a people. Hence, Fackenheim begins with his telling of an "ancient Midrash [which] affirms God's presence in history" and demonstrates how that presence becomes historically effective through Jewish witness. However, modernity challenges such testimony in two ways: First, the modern scientist has to expel God from nature because of a lack of verifiable proof, and the modern historian expels God from history because of the incompatibility of the supernatural with natural history. Second, and consequently, modern Jewish and Christian theologians can only affirm a provident God who uses nature and humans but is absent from history. Adding to the modern rejections, Fackenheim challenges a commitment of faith by asking: After Auschwitz and Hiroshima, who can still believe in a God who manifests himself as a superintending providence, or in an ideal kind of progress based on the promises of modern, enlightened technological advances?

In wake of the Holocaust, the Jewish people must still believe because they have a unique status based on the phenomenon of collective survival, a claim that serves as the key term for understanding Fackenheim's entire thought. Fackenheim argues that this collective survival has significance for both Jewish people and the rest of humanity because the God of Israel is not a mere tribal God but is someone who is Creator of the world and is concerned for universal humanity. However, Fackenheim's conception of God is nonetheless of one who does not have a presence-in-general but is, rather, present to particular people in particular situations. For Fackenheim, these "implications, however, are manifest only in the particular; and they make of the men to whom they are manifest, not universalistic philosophers who rise above their situations, but rather witnesses, in, through, and because of

631

their particularity to the nations." He then asks, How is the modern Jew today, after Auschwitz, able to be a witness to the world?

His answer is that Jews can continue to draw upon their foundational root experiences, that is, the historical events of Exodus and Sinai that ensure continuity in how they are relived in rituals. Accordingly, Fackenheim contends that the past is able to be relived in the present; the root experience is a public event in which there is a transformation of the earth and which decisively affects all future Jewish generations. Later generations have access to the founding event and can and do reenact them as present reality.

The Religious Experience and History

Fackenheim links philosophy to his religious heritage via the congruence of starting points that he establishes between the religious experience and the philosophical experience of the world, principally the historical concept of wonder. For Fackenheim, the religious experience is an astonishing experience of an event that enters the system of cause and effect and becomes transparent, thus allowing a glimpse of the sole power at work that is not limited by any other. Moreover, he draws on Martin Buber to support his claim that, like the philosophical experience of wonder, the religious experience is an "event which can be fully included in the objective, scientific nexus of nature and history" with the proviso that it includes a "vital meaning [which] for the person to whom it occurs, destroys the security of the whole nexus of knowledge for him, and explodes the fixity of the fields of experience named 'Nature' and 'History.'"

Based on such historical effectiveness, for example, the believer in and practitioner of ritual relates to the Red Sea event during the Jewish ritual of Passover. By reenacting the event, practitioners reenact the abiding astonishment and make, thereby, the historical event their own, which results in a continuation of the sole power that is God. Hence, memory enacted becomes living faith and hope, and the root experience is able to legislate from the past to the present and future.

Questions arise, however, about the nature of God as one that is on the one hand transcendent and on the other involved. In short, the question

of human control of the earth leads to judgments of the nature and relationship of an historically effective God to such an earth. If God were present at that particular moment of the Exodus and exercised power on behalf of the Jewish people, as sole power, God necessarily should be able to fight oppressive evil once again, demonstrating God's status as Creator and as absolute sovereign of the world. Fackenheim accepts this paradox and responds with a recourse to traditional Jewish thought that God does act and is involved in history and is not merely the consummation or transfiguration of history, that is, God does not stand over the entirety of the historical continuum.

Such a present God is the object of Messianic faith where the believing Jew responds to historical instances of evil and threats to existence by pointing to the future where evil will ultimately be vanquished and human freedom and divine freedom are reconciled. Furthermore, such a future is anticipated in a reenacted past, that is, the reenactment of the root experiences through ritual. Such reenactment is what Fackenheim understands as the midrashic experience, which he argues is "consciously fragmentary" and "yet destined to an ultimate resolution."

Philosophical Challenges

As Fackenheim relates at the end of the first part of the work, two of the strongest criticisms of God's presence in history have to do with the Holocaust. Given the actuality of God's presence as it is affirmed in Judaism and Christianity, to still believe in God post-Holocaust entails that Auschwitz is punishment for Jewish sins, which slanders a million innocent children in an abortive defense of God, and that any God connected with Auschwitz must have decreed Auschwitz, and such a God must be dead.

Fackenheim takes these criticisms seriously and spends the next two parts of his text in elaborating his rejection. In his analysis, the metaphysical foundations for such a rejection are based on how the Jewish people are rooted in the actuality of history. Because of their dialectical balance and playing out of the oppositions of the particular and the universal facets of their own lives, they are concretely situated within the overarching temporal framework of past, present, and future relations with other nations and their God.

Specifically, Fackenheim confronts a series of philosophical challenges, the greatest coming from modern positivists such as Auguste Comte, who reject God as a hypothesis that is empirically unverifiable. Fackenheim rejects the reduction of religious experience to scientific explanation and the positivist's assertion that a resort to absolutes is a mere logical mistake by contending that such a reduction eliminates wonder and ongoing historical effectiveness of abiding astonishment. The alternative is to replace that wonder with mere scientific or historical curiosity. What Fackenheim argues is that faith and modern secularism are irreconcilable because they are mutually irrefutable and that in order for historians, secular and Jewish, to exercise genuine impartiality, they should be required to suspend judgment between faith and secularism, resulting in a more nuanced philosophical stance of "criticism of criticism."

Fackenheim criticizes those who spoke out against the Jews, including German philosopher Friedrich Nietzsche, because of his predilection for Hellenic aristocracy and aestheticism and the Marxists who, based on a kind of Jewish Messianic expectation, nonetheless preached that Jews had a universal duty to assimilate into general humanity. Philosopher Ludwig Feuerbach taught that Jews are nothing more than egoists projecting an idea of God to themselves as an instance of self-worship. Karl Marx, for the sake of ideological consistency, claimed that Jews are merely self-interested hucksters who worship money and are dialectically false because they are so bound up with capitalism.

Fackenheim reserves his final critique for Ernst Bloch's philosophy of hope. He tempers his critique with a generally sympathetic reading of Bloch because of his affirmative acceptance of the survival of the Jewish people. The problem, however, is that Bloch relocates his version of Messianism to Moscow, not Palestine, thus committing a very old Jewish act, namely, premature Messianism.

Finally, the shortfall of all modern philosophers is their iterations of various versions of the death of God theme. Consequently, Fackenheim ends part 2 of the work by referring approvingly

of philosopher Martin Buber's conceptualization of an eclipse of God rather than the death of God, viewing it as an authentic Messianic response to the unique challenge of Auschwitz and the abiding human experience of horror.

After Auschwitz

The culmination of Fackenheim's own dialectic is fueled by his Jewish faith, as quintessential good, that is confronted by Adolf Hitler, as quintessential evil. Thus, Fackenheim asks, post-Auschwitz: Although Hitler failed to kill all the Jews, did he ultimately succeed postmortem by destroying Jewish faith? Fackenheim responds: "Yet we protest against a negative answer, for we protest against allowing Hitler to dictate the terms of our religious life. If not martyrdom, there can be a faithfulness resembling it, when a man has no choice between life and death but only between faith and despair."

After Auschwitz, Jews are left with existential fragments related to the problems of being uniquely targeted for destruction and yet, as part of their destiny with God, are demanded to survive. Moreover, such survival must be existentially grounded and faith-committed. After Auschwitz, he argues, the defiant success of the Jew to survive despite many challenges, especially the ultimate challenge of extermination, testifies to their endurance. However, mere survival is not enough, and in order to avoid madness, Jews desire to endure precisely because of the testimony to the voices of the prophets of their heritage with the living presence of God in history. Hence, Jews must continue to pray, after Auschwitz, as proof against madness in defiant particularity and as witnesses.

Fackenheim's analysis of modern philosophical and psychological perspectives and certain forms of social theory continues to provide powerful arguments that other philosophers of religion have continued to debate. Fackenheim continued to publish refined versions of his argument, eventually resulting in his most philosophically systematic work, *To Mend the World: Foundations of Future Jewish Thought*. However, even this text carries on the basic insights about the Holocaust, the state of Israel, and the failure of philosophy that Fackenheim initially presented in *God's Presence in History*. According to

Fackenheim, the reason for the surprising success of the Israeli defense forces against the attack by the surrounding Arab states in 1967 was that the Israelis responded with "a new song of defiance in the midst of hopelessness—the song of the Warsaw Ghetto Jewish Underground." For many Jews, both inside and outside Israel, Fackenheim provides a voice for their general concerns regarding the inexplicable horror of the Holocaust. Indeed, his call for a renewed defense of Israel was in tune with a general move not only by Jews the world over to resist further attacks on Israel but also especially by the initiation of the support of the U.S. government, which emerged in the second half of the twentieth century as a strong and faithful ally of Israel.

Julius J. Simon

Additional Reading

Cohn-Sherbok, Dan. *Holocaust Theology*. London: Lamp Press, 1989. Emil L. Fackenheim's views on the Holocaust are succinctly and critically set out in this comparative study, which includes several other key Jewish writers who take definitive positions with respect to the Holocaust. Other figures include Elie Wiesel, Richard Rubenstein, and Marc Ellis.

Fackenheim, Emil L. *Jewish Philosophers and Jewish Philosophy*. Edited by Michael L. Morgan. Bloomington: Indiana University Press, 1996. Morgan's introduction to this overview provides helpful orientation through Fackenheim's assessment of several Jewish philosophers who have influenced his own philosophy. Many of the selections were previously unpublished and include commentaries on Hermann Cohen, Franz Rosenzweig, Martin Buber, and Leo Strauss.

Greenspan, Louis, and Graeme Nicholson, eds. *German Philosophy and Jewish Thought*. Toronto: Toronto Studies in Philosophy, 1992. This book includes ten essays by several international philosophers and former students of Fackenheim who present critical views of several of Fackenheim's central ideas. The book concludes with an original essay by Fackenheim responding to the arguments of the ten authors.

Raaven, Heidi M. "Observations on Jewish Philosophy and Feminist Thought." *Judaism: A Quarterly Journal of Jewish Life and Thought* 46, no. 4 (Fall, 1997): 422-439. This article presents a creative critique of both Fackenheim's position and certain feminist philosophical projects because of their similar insistence on the fragmentation of the liberal, modern tradition of Enlightenment-inspired philosophy. Raaven's argument hinges on her rejection of Fackenheim's narrowing of the philosophical enterprise to particularist national and ethnic isolations.

Samuelson, Norbert. *An Introduction to Modern Jewish Philosophy*. Albany: State University of New York Press, 1989. Although the section on Fackenheim is only ten pages long, it provides a clear and balanced summary of Fackenheim's central philosophical positions. Also, the commentary is situated as the capstone of the text because of Samuelson's assessment of Fackenheim's importance for late twentieth century Jewish philosophy.

Seeskin, Kenneth. *Jewish Philosophy in a Secular Age*. Albany: State University of New York Press, 1990. Seeskin deals with a philosophical problem he terms "Universality and Particularity." In the final chapter of his work, he concludes a dialogue between contemporary secular philosophers and Jewish philosophers. Fackenheim represents the chief protagonist in the form of Jewish existentialism. Aligning himself with another modern Jewish rationalist philosopher, Steven Schwarzschild, Seeskin opposes Fackenheim's ideas of Jewish historical particularity and rupture.

Julius J. Simon

Frantz Fanon

Fanon argued that race was the most important factor in colonial relationships and articulated a theory of global revolution for colonized people that emphasized the need for each member of society to participate in the decolonization process.

Principal philosophical works: *Peau noire, masques blancs*, 1952 (*Black Skin, White Masks*, 1967); *L'An V de la révolution algérienne*, 1959 (*Studies in a Dying Colonialism*, 1965); *Les Damnés de la terre*, 1961 (*The Damned*, 1963; better known as *The Wretched of the Earth*, 1965).

Born: July 20, 1925; Fort-de-France, Martinique
Died: December 6, 1961; Bethesda, Maryland

Early Life

Frantz Omar Fanon was born on July 20, 1925, on the Caribbean island of Martinique, then a French colony. His father was a customs inspector and his mother was a shopkeeper. Fanon was the fifth of eight children. He had three older brothers, one older sister, and three younger sisters. The Fanons were a black middle-class family whose social status fell between that of the wealthy white ruling minority and that of the poor black majority. At the time, France's policy was to "improve" the lives of people in the nation's colonies by injecting more French culture into the local culture. The Fanons taught their children to identify with French customs and with the culture of metropolitan France. This included encouraging them to speak French instead of the more popular Creole spoken among blacks living in Martinique. Many blacks living in Martinique hoped that identifying with French culture would provide more opportunities and higher social status.

A detailed account of Fanon's childhood does not exist. Fanon's mother, who died in 1981, was interviewed at least once by Peter Geismar, a biographer of Fanon; however, he was only moderately interested in the details of Fanon's childhood and focused more on Fanon's life as a revolutionary. Fanon's brothers and sisters recall

him as very rigid and committed to making his words match his actions—a trait he would be known for later in life—and as a practical joker, who once, with the help of his friends, pinned the skirts of a number of women together in church.

The Fanons were able to afford the tuition to send Frantz to the Lycée Schoechler, the only secondary school in the French Caribbean. Only about 4 percent of blacks living on Martinique could afford to pay tuition to this prestigious school. Fanon attended the *lycée* and became a student of the poet and political activist Aimé Césaire, who taught language and literature. Césaire and his philosophy of negritude had a great impact on Fanon. Negritude, cofounded by Césaire and the Senegalese poet Léopold Senghor, was devoted to promoting African culture and encouraged blacks to reject the culture imposed upon them by French colonialism. Césaire's attacks on Western civilization and French culture helped Fanon begin to stop identifying with French culture.

However, Fanon's transformation was far from complete, and in 1943, he joined the fight to liberate France from the Germans, who had defeated the French in 1940 during World War II. Against his family's wishes, Frantz went to Dominica and received six months of training before returning to Martinique and officially joining the Free French Army with his two best friends during a recruitment drive. Despite his idealism and willingness to risk his life for the freedom of

France, Fanon suffered racism, beginning in the transport ships. Fanon became especially upset with the members of the Martinique women's corps who slept with French officers on these ships.

Fanon's first assignment was in the Fifth Battalion in Morocco, where he experienced additional racism. Black soldiers, whether from the Caribbean or Africa, were treated with contempt by the white soldiers in the French army. While in North Africa, Fanon began to see the larger picture regarding French colonialism. He began to connect the ill treatment of black Africans with the treatment of blacks from the Caribbean by white French people. In France, the populace, whom Fanon and other black soldiers had come to defend, treated them with contempt, and blacks were shunned at victory celebrations and dances, a blatant insult to those who had risked their lives in battle against the Nazis. Additionally, Fanon mentioned in letters home that French peasants would not fight, an action that made Fanon seriously reconsider his involvement in the war. Fanon was wounded in combat and awarded the Croix de Guerre. When he returned to Martinique in 1945, Fanon was reevaluating his colonial identity as a Frenchman. He worked on the election campaign of Césaire, who was elected mayor of Fort-de-France as a Communist Party candidate in 1945.

In 1947, Fanon completed his examinations at the *lycée* and went back to France to attend a university with the help of a veteran's scholarship. Before Frantz left, his father died, which forced Frantz to go abroad with more limited resources than he had expected. Fanon wanted to chose a career that would be practical for the people of Martinique, and his first choice was medicine. However, he was unwilling to spend the years it would take to complete medical training and instead opted for a career in dentistry. Fanon left the school of dentistry and Paris because of boredom (caused by both the course of study and the city) and enrolled in medical school at the University of Lyons, specializing in psychiatry. During this time, Fanon became nominally involved in the negritude movement as a form of escape from racism; he wrote three plays and edited a newsletter for black students. However, he separated himself from negritude

and from Césaire for good in 1958 when Césaire advocated a policy of total integration with France. By this time, Fanon was considering solutions to the colonial problem that involved separation, not integration.

Life's Work

While at the medical school in Lyons, Fanon became interested in the work of philosophers Maurice Merleau-Ponty and Jean-Paul Sartre. Also while in school, Fanon met Marie-Josephe Dublé, a white French woman, whom he married in 1953. In 1952, while he was still in medical school, Fanon published his first book, *Black Skin, White Masks*. Its original title was *Essay for the Dis-alienation of the Black*, which accurately describes Fanon's French experience. He expected to be treated as an equal while in France, which is what French colonial rhetoric taught. However, he was confronted with strong racism that revealed itself not only in people's actions but also in the way they looked at Fanon.

In *Black Skin, White Masks*, Fanon presented a clinical study of group racial identity. The work shows the influence of Césaire, Sartre, and psychiatric pioneers Sigmund Freud and Alfred Alder. Fanon argues that through colonialism, black people have been taught to desire to be white. This causes an identity crisis among many blacks, who are never accepted by the culture to which colonial schools and society have taught them they belong. Fanon also argues that colonialism will not die of natural causes and that it is up to the colonized peoples to take action, an idea he would later fully develop in *The Wretched of the Earth*.

Fanon defended his medical thesis in 1951 and briefly returned to Martinique, but he went back to France in 1952 for residency training under the renowned psychiatrist Francois Tosquelles at the Saint Alban-de-Lozere Hospital. In 1953, Fanon passed all his examinations and became the clinical director of a French psychiatric hospital near Normandy. However, this position lasted only a few months; Fanon wanted to be transferred to a country that was under French colonial domination because he had come to believe that he could do the most good by helping colonized people deal with the psychiatric impact of colonial relationships. In 1953, Fanon was appointed medical chief of Blida-Joinville, the largest psychiatric hospital in Algeria. He transformed his ward by pursuing a policy of "normalization." He released his patients from their straitjackets and restrictive devices. He focused on turning his ward into a community complete with a café and redecorated the ward in a more Algerian and less French motif. Although not major breakthroughs in psychiatry, these were revolutionary treatments in Algeria at the time.

While in Algeria, Fanon became sympathetic to the freedom struggle of the Front de Libération Nationale (FLN), and he secretly supplied the FLN with medical supplies and provided medical training for FLN nurses from 1954 to 1956. His sympathy came from a combination of his previous colonial experience, his experience with racism, and his psychiatric diagnoses of his patients. He believed a large number of his patients' psychiatric problems were caused by living in colonial society. He held this to be true for both the colonized (Algerians) and colonizers (white French living in Algeria).

In 1956, Fanon resigned his position at the psychiatric hospital in solidarity with a general strike on the part of the Muslim employees. He went to work full time for the FLN. In January, 1957, Fanon received a letter of expulsion stating that he had forty-eight hours to leave Algeria. He went to Tunis, FLN headquarters, and served as spokesperson for the Algerian freedom struggle, editor of the official FLN paper *El Moudjahid*, and medical doctor. He also lectured at the University of Tunis. Many of the articles and essay's Fanon wrote for *El Moudjahid* are collected in the work *Pour la révolution africaine* (1964; *Toward the African Revolution*, 1967). This work provides a glimpse of the month-to-month changes in Fanon's thought as he became more involved in the Algerian revolution.

Fanon took a three-week break from his activities with the FLN and wrote *Studies in a Dying Colonialism*, which was banned in France six months after publication. *Studies in a Dying Colonialism* is a report on the Algerian revolution, specifically how an Algerian national identity was formed in order to combat French colonialism. He used such everyday cultural items as the veil, the radio, and medicine to demonstrate how identity was reshaped during the revolution. He

also ventured to predict how this Algerian identity would affect the society of the future. Algeria was presented not only as a singular case study but also as one component of a much larger process, a global decolonization process.

In 1959, Fanon was severely injured when his jeep hit a land mine while establishing new supply lines for the FLN in the Sahara desert. Fanon was flown into Rome for medical treatment. While in Rome, his hospital room number was published in the newspaper, and that night, his bed was sprayed with machine-gun fire. However, Fanon avoided injury because after seeing the article in the paper, he had moved to a different hospital room. While Fanon was on his way to the airport after being discharged from the hospital, the car he was supposed to be in was destroyed by a bomb. Fanon's FLN activities had become too much for the organization's enemies to tolerate. Fanon had become the spokesperson for the FLN and was on his way to becoming the spokesperson for the Third World.

In December, 1960, while looking for new supply routes for Algerian freedom fighters, Fanon fell ill. He was diagnosed with leukemia and taken to a Moscow hospital for treatment. Doctors there suggested he go to the United States where leukemia treatment was more advanced. While he was in Tunis debating whether to make the trip, he wrote *The Wretched of the Earth*. It took him only ten weeks.

In *The Wretched of the Earth*, Fanon call for the decolonization of all colonized people. He describes decolonization as a naturally violent phenomenon. After all, there would be no need for decolonization had there not first been colonization, which, Fanon argues, is intrinsically violent and has absolutely no positive effect on the colonized. For Fanon, violent tactics cleanse the decolonization movement because they force the participants to be conscious of their activity and place personal responsibility on each individual. He directly links decolonization with colonization, claiming that the amount of violence in any particular decolonization movement will be in direct proportion to the amount of violence used by the colonizers in the area.

In this work, Fanon also argues that mass repression causes the formation of a national consciousness. As their consciousness rises, colonized people become sick of their status as "slaves" and begin extorting concessions from the colonizers, thus initiating decolonization. However, Fanon states, the type of national consciousness that develops in response to colonization also acts as a separating force. Colonialism only exploits part of a country, which allows some local people to become wealthy and therefore causes them to support the colonial system. Fanon says these people are typically the ones who acquire political power upon independence. He argues that these political groups are not a direct expression of the masses but rather spokespeople for a small greedy collection of local exploiters who came to a friendly agreement with the colonizers.

The FLN and Central Intelligence Agency (CIA) arranged for a secret transfer of Fanon to Washington, D.C., for medical treatment. He was suspicious of the arrangements but felt his health forced him to go through with it. Fanon was left in a hotel room in Baltimore, Maryland, for ten days before receiving medical attention. Many have speculated that the CIA wanted an opportunity to get information from Fanon concerning FLN and other African operations of which Fanon was aware. Once he was finally placed in the custody of the National Institutes of Health in Bethesda, Maryland, Fanon contracted double pneumonia after a massive blood transfusion. He died December 6, 1961. His body was smuggled out of the country and buried in an FLN cemetery in Algeria.

Influence

Fanon and his work have been of critical interest to many of the leading intellectuals in underdeveloped countries because underneath all of Fanon's work is a deep concern with how the process of decolonization is to occur. Fanon did not think decolonization could occur on a nation-by-nation basis; instead, he believed that the people of different nations would have to help one another through this process. This made Fanon a leading theorist in the development of global solutions for the colonial problem. Fanon also became extremely influential in some of the more radical elements of the U.S. Civil Rights movement.

Eric L. Martin

The Wretched of the Earth

Type of philosophy: Ethics, social philosophy
First published: Les Damnés de la terre, 1961 (*The Damned*, 1963; better known as *The Wretched of the Earth*, 1965)
Principal ideas advanced:

◇ Decolonization is a global process and must be approached from within this dynamic; the success of any decolonization movement that isolates itself from other decolonization movements is questionable.

◇ Colonialism is inherently a violent phenomenon because it involves an oppressive relationship; therefore, decolonization is also a violent phenomenon.

◇ The extent of the violence during decolonization depends on the amount of violence practiced by the colonizer in the colonial setting.

◇ Mass repression under colonialism forces the oppressed to create national identities; decolonization unifies colonized people.

◇ Political control of the former colonies passes from the hands of an elite foreign repressing class to an elite local repressing class.

Frantz Fanon's principal work, *The Wretched of the Earth* has sold millions of copies and has been translated into twenty-five languages. Essentially, *The Wretched of the Earth* is an analysis of the process of decolonization that was occurring at a rapid pace while Fanon was writing this book. The sense of urgency that pervades the book is partly a result of Fanon's condition. He was dying of leukemia and knew he had only a limited amount of time left to contribute to the destruction of colonial relationships everywhere, but especially in Africa.

Fanon was from the French colony of Martinique, now a department of France, and was trained as a psychiatrist in France. Eventually Fanon was assigned to a psychiatric hospital in Algeria, where he treated both Algerians, who he felt were victims of colonialism, and white French people, who he felt were oppressors in Algeria. Fanon believed that many of the psychiatric problems he was treating in Algeria, in both Algerians and white French people, were due to the unequal colonial relationship that permeated every aspect of Algerian society. This unequal relationship affected Fanon so much that during the Algerian war, Fanon became sympathetic to the Algerians' cause and joined the FLN. Through the FLN, Fanon became the spokesperson not only for the Algerian revolution but also for anticolonial resistance all over the world, especially in Africa. In *The Wretched of the Earth*, Fanon drew on many of the ideas he had developed in his earlier writings, notably *Peau noire, masques blancs* (1952; *Black Skin, White Masks*, 1967); *L'An V de la révolution algérienne* (1959; *Studies in a Dying Colonialism*, 1965); and a number of essays collected in *Pour la révolution africaine* (1964; *Toward the African Revolution*, 1967).

In *The Wretched of the Earth*, Fanon called for the decolonization of all colonized people. *The Wretched of the Earth* is not a retrospection of events that have long since passed; in fact, a large part of this book is written in the present tense. Fanon sees the process of decolonization and potential decolonization percolating throughout the underdeveloped world, and through this book, he attempts to influence the process. In the preface, philosopher Jean-Paul Sartre wrote that *The Wretched of the Earth* was not intended for a white Euro-American audience, but that it was precisely this audience who should "have the courage to read this book." Sartre, however, assumes that the only people who are concerned with the unequal colonial relationship are the colonized. In fact, Fanon wrote this book with a much larger audience in mind, optimistically hoping that there were "anticolonialists" throughout the world who wanted to understand the decolonization process. However, Sartre is correct on the general level; this is a book intended for those involved in anticolonial struggles.

A Violent Process

In the chapter "Concerning Violence," Fanon painted a slightly bipolar vision of decolonization. At one point, he described decolonization as the "veritable creation of new men." This suggests that decolonization is a creative process in which humanity invents something new. However, in another portion of the same chapter, he describes decolonization as "quite simply the replacing of a certain 'species' of man by another 'species' of man." These contrasting views on de-

colonization most likely reflect the difference between Fanon's ideal and what would become reality.

Fanon describes decolonization as a naturally violent phenomenon. He argues that decolonization would not be necessary if there had not first been colonization, which is intrinsically violent and has no positive effect whatsoever on the colonized. Violence is a key element to Fanon's decolonization, for it is the way in which colonized people find their freedom. He believed that violent tactics cleanse the decolonization movement because they force movement participants to be conscious of their activity and they require that each individual accept personal responsibility for his actions and beliefs. Fanon is often criticized for writing this chapter. Many people believe that he is promoting violence; however, Fanon was attempting to explain human behavior. These critics disregard the fact that colonialism is a physically, economically, and psychologically violent phenomena. Furthermore, Fanon is not calling for massive bloodshed in the streets of every colony and former colony. He claims that the processes of decolonization and colonization are linked; the amount of violence in any particular decolonization movement will be in direct proportion to the amount of violence used by the colonizers.

The Role of the Native

In the chapter "The Pitfalls of National Consciousness," Fanon tackles the question of why decolonization takes place. Fanon argues that mass repression results in the formation of a national consciousness. Decolonization unifies people because the key to colonialism is the separation of people. Decolonization takes place because colonized people become sick of their status as repressed people and begin demanding concessions from the colonizers. Fanon wrote, "The native must realize that colonialism never gives anything away for nothing. Whatever the native may gain through political or armed struggle is not the result of the kindness or goodwill of the settler; it simply shows that he cannot put off granting concessions any longer."

Fanon further argues that the type of national consciousness that develops in response to colonization can also act as a separating force. Colonialism only exploits part of a country; this allows some native people to become wealthy, which causes them to be generally supportive of the colonial system. Fanon states that typically it is these people who acquire political power when a country gains independence. He argues that the political groups formed by these wealthy natives do not represent the masses but rather function as spokespeople for a small greedy collection of local exploiters who have reached a friendly agreement with the colonizers. After independence, this local elite seeks to follow in the footsteps of the colonizers and, using a slightly modified version of the colonial system, to generate profit for themselves. Therefore, Fanon says, political parties in underdeveloped areas rarely represent the masses. In addition, these political parties use divisive tactics in order to maintain their members' economic advantage. Fanon states that social separation is most widespread between urban dwellers, who hold most of the formal political power, and rural people, who make up the large majority of the population.

The major problem in fostering permanent nationalism in underdeveloped countries, according to Fanon, is the development of a bourgeoisie that does not care about the common people and is unable to deal effectively with the West. Fanon believed this class was in political control of the underdeveloped world. Some critics of Fanon have argued that the philosopher was unable to see a political unit other than the modern nation state. This is a common criticism of philosophers Karl Marx and Georg Wilhelm Friedrich Hegel as well. Perhaps this represents the ultimate colonization of Fanon's thinking, that he was unable to escape the political terms established by "the West," or perhaps he was being a realist in acknowledging the power of the modern nation state and realizing that any region's political future depended on establishing a strong national consciousness. Either way, Fanon remained trapped in this dynamic.

The Colonized and the Colonizer

In the chapter "On National Culture," Fanon argues that universal standards of civility and barbarism, based on Euro-American criteria, do not actually exist. In fact, Fanon argues that the educational system is one of the major tools used by colonialists. Native schoolchildren are taught the cultural tradition of the colonizer, France in Fanon's case. Furthermore, these children are taught that their heritage is one of barbarism. In addition, Fanon tackled the problem of the difference between a political party that claims to speak for a nation and the people who make up that nation. Fanon argued that political parties in the former colonies (or anywhere else) do not represent the masses and that the concept of a "nation" as a singular entity is a dangerous fiction.

In the chapter "Colonial War and Mental Disorders," Fanon provides the case notes for a number of the patients, both colonized people and colonizers, he treated while in Algeria. Through these notes, Fanon provide a firsthand account of what colonialism does to people's minds. In his brief conclusion, Fanon reminds the reader that in order for the colonized to be successful, they must look for models other than the one provided by Europeans and that these models can be found within themselves.

Political and Cultural Legacy

The impact of *The Wretched of the Earth* has been tremendous because this book, like much of Fanon's work, expresses a deep concern with how the process of decolonization is to occur. Since his death, interest in Fanon's thought has been steady among those who are concerned with colonialism and neocolonialism. He and his work became well known throughout the colonial world, affecting such African leaders as Kwame Nkrumah, Sekou Touré, and Juilius Nyerere. Additionally, *The Wretched of the Earth* was influential in some of the more radical elements of the U.S. Civil Rights movement. Black Panther Party members Bobby Seale, Huey P. Newton, and Eldridge Cleaver read Fanon and credited him for providing a framework for their work in the United States.

Fanon thought that decolonization could not occur on a nation-by-nation basis; instead, the people of different nations would have to help one another through this process. This made Fanon a leading theorist in the development of global solutions for the colonial problem. Many scholars criticize the formation of worldwide solutions, arguing that mass generalizations are usually wrong. However, because Fanon was attempting to describe what he saw as a global problem, some generalization would seem necessary and appropriate. In addition, he was entirely aware of the dangers of such mass generalizations and warned readers to beware of this pitfall.

The Wretched of the Earth has also been used as a launching point in cultural studies. Fanon's interest in examining the way people's minds and thought were affected by the colonial relationship, especially in regard to racism, made him a pioneer in the field, although Fanon was not writing for an academic audience.

Eric L. Martin

Additional Reading

Bulhan, Hussein Abdilahi. *Frantz Fanon and the Psychology of Oppression*. New York: Plenum Press, 1985. A biography of Frantz Fanon from a psychiatric perspective. Fanon is treated essentially as a contributor to the field of psychiatry, and his revolutionary activity is placed primarily in the context of his interest in the psychology of oppression.

Geismar, Peter. *Fanon*. New York: Dial Press, 1971. The most authoritative biography on Fanon, based on Geismar's interviews with members of Fanon's family and his friends. Geismar claims to have been influenced very little by the secondary literature on the topic of Fanon, asserting that as of his publication date, little informative secondary literature on Fanon existed. This book is a good introduction to Fanon and provides a sympathetic and easy-to-read account of Fanon's life.

Gendzier, Irene. *Frantz Fanon: A Critical Study*. New York: Pantheon, 1973. One of the few sbiographies on Fanon. This book should be standard reading for any serious inquiry into Fanon's life.

Gordon, Lewis R., T. Denean Sharpley-Whiting, and Renée T. White, eds. *Fanon: A Critical Reader*. Cambridge, Mass.: Blackwell, 1996. This compilation contains twenty-one essays by different authors produced for a Fanon conference in 1995. These essays are grouped into six main sections and cover the following themes: oppression, questions regarding the human sciences, identity and the dialectics of recognition, the emancipation of women of color, the postcolonial dream, neocolonial realities, resistance, and revolutionary violence.

Sharpley-Whiting, T. Denean. *Frantz Fanon: Conflicts and Feminism*. New York: Rowman & Littlefield, 1998. This book reevaluates Fanon's commitment (or noncommitment) to feminism through an examination of his commitment to antiracism. It also revisits many of the previous interpretations of Fanon and feminism. Sharpley-Whiting finds Fanon to be profeminist, which is counter to the majority of feminist critique of Fanon and his work.

Wyrick, Deborah. *Fanon for Beginners*. New York: Writers and Readers, 1998. Combines a detailed account of Fanon's life with a critical view of his major works. Accompanied by cartoon illustrations to help make the author's points clearer. Contains a glossary, and many terms are defined in the text. A good source to be read in conjunction with one of Fanon's works because it helps place any individual Fanon work in the larger context of his life.

Eric L. Martin

Ludwig Feuerbach

Through a sustained critique of theology and speculative Idealism, Feuerbach developed an anthropological account of religious needs and a materialist, sensationalist epistemology for the philosophy of the future.

Principal philosophical works: *Gedanken über Tod und Unsterblichkeit*, 1830 (*Thoughts on Death and Immortality*, 1980); *Darstellung der Geschichte der neueren Philosophie*, 1833-1837; *Abelard und Heloise*, 1834; *Pierre Bayle*, 1838; *Das Wesen des Christentums*, 1841 (*The Essence of Christianity*, 1854, rev. ed. 1957); *Vorläufige Thesen zur Reformation der Philosophie*, 1842; *Grundsätze der Philosophie der Zukunft*, 1843 (*Principles of the Philosophy of the Future*, 1966); *Das Wesen des Glaubens im Sinne Luthers, ein Beitrag zum Wesen des Christentums*, 1844 (*The Essence of Faith According to Luther*, 1967); *Das Wesen der Religion*, 1845; *Ludwig Feuerbach's Sämtliche Werke*, 1846-1866; *Vorlesungen über das Wesen der Religion, nebst Zusätzen und Anmerkungen*, 1851 (*Lectures on the Essence of Religion*, 1967); *Die Unsterblichkeitsfrage von Standpunkt der Anthropologie*, 1846; *Theogonie*, 1857; *Ludwig Feuerbach Sämtliche Werke*, 1903-1911 (10 volumes, reprint 1959-1964; 3 supplemental volumes, 1962-1964); *Historical-critical edition: Ludwig Feuerbach Gesammelte Werke*, 1964-   , multiple volumes); *The Fiery Brook: Selected Writings of Ludwig Feuerbach*, 1972.

Born: July 28, 1804; Landshut, Bavaria (now Germany)

Died: September 13, 1872; Rechenberg, Bavaria

Early Life

Ludwig Andreas Feuerbach was the fourth son of a jurist noted for studies in criminal law. In 1823, Feuerbach began studying theology at Heidelberg before turning to the study of philosophy under Georg Wilhelm Friedrich Hegel in Berlin. When political events caused Feuerbach to lose a government stipend in 1826, he moved to the University of Erlangen. He received his doctoral degree in 1828 with a dissertation on the Hegelian analysis of reason, and he worked as a docent from 1829 to 1835, lecturing on modern philosophy. In 1830, he published an analysis of religious ideas, *Thoughts on Death and Immortality*, which was seen as an attack on religion. He was never able to secure a university appointment. Drawing from his studies for his lectures as docent, Feuerbach published a three-volume work on the history of modern philosophy, *Darstellung der Geschichte der neueren Philosophie* (1833-1837;

presentations of the history of modern philosophy). He married Berta Low and moved to Bruckberg, living in solitude with income from his wife's dowry, which contained shared ownership in a porcelain factory. In Bruckberg, he studied geology but soon turned back to religion and philosophy.

Life's Work

Although Feuerbach learned from Hegel how to attack religious problems, his first publication, *Thoughts on Death and Immortality*, reflected little of this learning. His next effort, *Darstellung der Geschichte der neueren Philosophie*, a three-volume set on the history of modern philosophy, plunged directly and deeply into Hegelian Idealism as the culmination of modern philosophy. Hegel's dialectical method gave the three-volume history its structure, although the work contained an empiricist conclusion that became the foundation for Feuerbach's subsequent thinking.

In the first volume, *Geschichte der neueren Philosophie von Bacon von Verulam bis Benedict Spinoza* (1833; the history of modern philosophy from Bacon to Spinoza), Feuerbach examined the epistemologies of Francis Bacon, Thomas Hobbes, and Pierre Gassendi as well as those of René Descartes, Cartesians Arnold Geulincx and Nicolas de Malebranche, and Baruch Spinoza. According to Feuerbach, modern philosophy began with materialist theories regarding bodies in motion that freed philosophy from theistic constraints. However, materialism proved unable to resolve problems of knowledge that dealt with relationships of matter and consciousness. In this volume, Feuerbach praised Descartes's method of doubt, describing his positive achievement of certainty in the activity of a thinking, reasoning self. Feuerbach also found clues toward the resolution of the basic Cartesian split of mind and body in the pantheism of Spinoza.

In the second volume of the history, *Darstellung, Entwicklung und Kritik der Leibniz'schen Philosophie* (1836; exposition, development, and critique of Leibnizian philosophy), Feuerbach critiqued the German philospher Gottfried Wilhelm Leibniz. This volume marked Feuerbach's commitment to a course of thinking that led to naturalistic concrete individualism. Leibniz's monadology, which deals with monads as the elements of all things, did not answer Feuerbach's questions about the relationship of the universal (in reason) with the particular (in sensation). He also felt that Leibniz's concept of the will was too irrational to resolve the Cartesian mind-body split. Leibniz did, however, provide pathways through belief toward anthropological materialism.

In *Pierre Bayle*, Feuerbach addressed differences between belief and knowledge and between faith and reason. Modern philosophy had turned God into Reason without confirming the reality of matter and nature. Feuerbach believed the key to reconciliation was the relationship of reason and belief. He considered skepticism and dogma to be the underlying causes for the Cartesian dualism with which Leibniz contended. Descartes was also a victim of this underlying conflict, because he professed a religious faith despite his philosophical method of skepticism.

In his 1839 essay, "Zur Kritik der Hegelschen Philosophie" (translated as "Toward a Critique of Hegelian Philosophy" and published in *The Fiery Brook*), Feuerbach focused on the basic contradiction in Hegel's philosophy of the absolute, which sees disunity between consciousness (thought, ideal spirit) and sensation. In *Phänomenologie des Geistes* (1807; *The Phenomenology of Spirit*, 1872, also known as *The Phenomenology of Mind*, 1910) and *Wissenschaft der Logik* (1812-1816; *Science of Logic*, 1929), Hegel had shown that the fulfillment of the Idea is in having pure thought as its own object. Feuerbach, using a reductionist technique, rejected this as nonsense, as "no-thinking." To fill this emptiness, this abstract reason of Idealism, without rejecting the form of Reason was the object of Feuerbach's project to put *humanity* into the emptiness of Idea. Modern philosophy had not understood the importance of sense perception in knowledge, and that led to an alienation and fragmentation of Being, which was improperly retained as a displaced deity by speculative philosophy in the name of Reason. Hegel had turned theology inside out (making God into Thought, or Absolute Spirit); Feuerbach's new philosophy would make Thought into Humanity by showing that Absolute Spirit is nothing but the hypostatization of self-consciousness. Feuerbach rejected Hegelian Idealism but used it as the ground for truth, or species-knowledge, in his new conception of the human community.

Resisting efforts by friends to move to Heidelberg, where he might have worked in a vigorous intellectual community, Feuerbach pursued his own agenda, publishing *The Essence of Christianity*, the next stage for unveiling the true meaning of existence. It was increasingly difficult to pursue that truth in a place and time that discouraged intellectual freedom. *The Essence of Christianity* was banned in Austria, and police raided Feuerbach's home, searching for evidence against a politically active acquaintance. This affected Feuerbach's style, making him direct and deliberately unsystematic.

In *The Essence of Christianity*, one of Feuerbach's best known works, he showed how the divine has origins in human consciousness. All religious ideas and images—the Incarnation, the Trinity, prayer, and immortality—were human projections. The origins of traditional religious ideas are unveiled by reversing their subjects and predicates: For example, "God is love" becomes "Love is God." The attributes of God were simply features or characteristics of individual human beings made into universals. Feuerbach showed theology to be anthropology and the Christian religion to be atheism. He followed Hegel's interpretation of history as a dialectical unveiling of the absolute in images and concepts of Christianity. Feuerbach took this to the next stage of understanding, stating that Hegel's Absolute Spirit is the human species.

Feuerbach unveiled truth by using the Hegelian dialectic against itself. The self, "I," finds itself objectified in another, "Thou," and becomes conscious of itself as a part of a community, one of a species with a social nature. Thus does the Spirit become an object that is alienated as the Trinity in Christian doctrine until it develops into the next, synthesizing stage of history, which is nothing less than self-recognition. Imagination, an instrument of feeling, misrepresented the alienated object in symbols and mythology. Philosophy's task is to strip away the disguises and uncover the source of happiness in human desire. Once found, it would dissolve the forces of alienation that were sustained by religion, theology, and the speculative philosophy of Idealism. Feuerbach became a philosophical anthropologist.

It was the purpose of his next work, *Principles of the Philosophy of the Future*, to provide the world with a new philosophy to replace religion. A year later, Feuerbach published *The Essence of Faith According to Luther* to meet the popular demand created as a result of *The Essence of Christianity*. With these publications, he caught the attention of a public pleased with his critique of religion and the old speculative philosophy of Idealism. He redirected philosophy into an empiricist route, promoting materialist humanism when positivism and natural science were gaining strength. He gave philosophical respectability to the science of biblical scholarship, and he inspired political philosopher Karl Marx and socialist Friedrich Engels in the domains of economics and politics.

By 1846, he had sufficient confidence in his philosophical accomplishment that he began publishing a ten-volume collection of his essays, *Ludwig Feuerbach's Sämtliche Werke* (collected works of Ludwig Feuerbach). He had become the intellectual leader of the new Hegelians, includ-

ing Marx, who spoke of himself as one of many Feuerbachians. During the revolutionary activities of 1848, Feuerbach solidified the ideological structures for the principles of the revolution. In this atmosphere, he lectured in Heidelberg, from December, 1848, to March, 1849, on the topic of religion; these lectures were published as *Lectures on the Essence of Religion*. He contemplated living in the United States, where he had admirers; however, he decided to remain in Bavaria. He continued publishing elaborations and extensions of his new principles in several works, including *Die Unsterblichkeitsfrage von Standpunkt der Anthropologie* (the question of immortality from the standpoint of anthropology) and *Theogonie* (theogony). These built upon Feuerbach's *The Essence of Christianity* and *Principles of the Philosophy of the Future*, emphasizing anthropology, materialism, and humanism. All continued the open and simple style appropriate to a new philosophy of humanism. His was a philosophy of common sense.

In 1860, the porcelain factory in Bruckberg suffered serious economic losses. To cope with his reduced income, Feuerbach moved to Rechenberg, where he lived until his death in 1872. There he wrote and published *Die Geheimniss des Opfers oder der Mensch ist was er isst* (1862; the mystery of sacrifice, or man is what he eats). He read the first volume of Marx's *Das Kapital* (1867, 1885, 1894; *Capital: A Critique of Political Economy*, 1886, 1907, 1909; better known as *Das Kapital*) and thought it a profound analysis of political economy. He joined the Social Democratic Party, a Marxist party, in 1870, making a public commitment to the socialist principles that he had promoted with his anthropological philosophy. He died two years later and was buried in Nuremberg.

Influence

As a critic of Hegelian Idealism, Feuerbach translated Idealist abstractions into concrete and popular humanist forms. He shifted philosophical concerns toward scientific positivist and materialist ideas of nineteenth century naturalism. From David Friedrich Strauss's *Das Leben Jesu, kritsch bearbeitet* (1835; *The Life of Jesus, Critically Examined*, 1846) to the writings of Karl Barth in the twentieth century, Feuerbach has had a profound influence on religious and theological ideas. By examining psychological sources for religious beliefs, he secured legitimacy for the biblical scholars of the new criticism, one product of philosophical efforts by the "young Hegelians," who included, besides Feuerbach and Strauss, Bruno Bauer, Arnold Ruge, Ferdinand Lassalle, and Karl Marx. Through her translations of *The Life of Jesus* and *The Essence of Christianity*, author George Eliot (Mary Anne Evans) extended Feuerbach's influence to English readers.

Important for modern history was the philospher's direct influence on Marx and Engels, who wrote critiques of Feuerbach. Marx used Feuerbach's notion of species-being, an intersubjectivity of consciousness shared through the senses, as a principle of labor alienated by capital. Marx and Engels used Feuerbach's method of inversion, whereby subjects and predicates are reversed. Although Engels charged that Feuerbach's philosophy was too abstract, he championed Feuerbach for bringing German Idealistic philosophy to an end. Through Marx and Engels, Feuerbach radicalized thought in the modern world. Feuerbach gave philosophical direction to Martin Heidegger with the concept of *Dasein* (human being), theological direction to Martin Buber with ideas of I-Thou relationships, and psychological/psychoanalytical directions to Sigmund Freud and R. D. Laing with notions of human anxiety and existential self-alienation.

Richard D. McGhee

Principles of the Philosophy of the Future

Types of philosophy: Metaphysics, philosophy of religion

First published: Grundsätze der Philosophie der Zunkunft, 1843 (English translation, 1966)

Principal ideas advanced:

◇ The history of modern philosophy, from René Descartes to Georg Wilhelm Friedrich Hegel, is a systematic displacement of theology and religion.

◇ Hegel's Idealist philosophy is the fulfillment of modern philosophical development.

◇ Hegelian philosophy is nothing but rationalized theology.

◇ Idealist concepts are negative abstractions of concrete human consciousness and experience.

◇ The new philosophy is a positive, concrete structure of anthropology, sensationism, and materialism.

◇ The ontologically true and primary concept is finite being.

◇ The primacy of finite being lies in individual consciousness universalized as sensation through species-being.

◇ The new philosophy must unveil these truths by negating the false perceptions of previous thought.

The success of Ludwig Feuerbach's book *Das Wesen des Christentums* (1841; *The Essence of Christianity*, 1854) raised expectations for more from the philosopher. He was seen as the heir to his teacher, Georg Wilhelm Friedrich Hegel, whose work he had analyzed, using the Hegelian dialectical method, in the light of a universal need for religious belief. He was looked to for a new philosophy to replace that of his great predecessor, and he wrote *Principles of the Philosophy of the Future* to satisfy those expectations.

Feuerbach believed that philosophy needed to escape the abstractions of transcendental Idealism that philosophers such as Immanuel Kant, Johann Gottlieb Fichte, Friedrich Wilhelm Joseph von Schelling, and Hegel had constructed. In addition, philosophy needed to incorporate the skepticism of modern atheist philosophers from David Hume to Arthur Schopenhauer. Finally, the new philosophy should take into account the successes of empiricism, sensationism, and materialism in the natural sciences of physics, geology, chemistry, biology, and human physiology. At the same time that Feuerbach was critiquing Idealist speculative philosophy, empiricism was leading to the positivism of John Stuart Mill in England, Auguste Comte in France, and, through biology, to the philosophy of Herbert Spencer in England and Eduard von Hartmann in Germany. These later movements intensified intellectual focus on the psychology of individual human experience and on the sociology of human experience in groups. A stirring of cries for political freedom, which would erupt in the rebellions of 1848, excited minds anxious for philosophical justifications and ideological commitments to principles of political and economic liberty. Feuerbach's new philosophy engaged the challenges of these tendencies of thought.

Methodology

Feuerbach begins with a review of the history of modern speculative philosophy. In the course of his review, he applies his method of inversion, whereby he turns predicates into subjects and vice versa. He had employed this tactic in *The Essence of Christianity*, where he demonstrated that the subject "God" is really a predicate by reversing "God is love" to "Love is God." This revealed that God is nothing less than an idealized abstraction of very human features. In his review of modern philosophical history, Feuerbach reverses the subject "Being" with predicates such as "necessity" and "infinity" to show that philosophy's Being is human consciousness hypostatized as an object. The method of inversion serves a process of reduction. The Absolute Being of the Idea is reduced to the consciousness of an individual human, dependent for existence on a community of human beings in material nature. These were positions Feuerbach had been developing from his earliest publications. Hegel taught him how to undo Hegel's own philosophy and, at the same time, to advance the dialectic to a new level of synthesis.

The structure and organization of *Principles of the Philosophy of the Future* have the Hegelian characteristic of thesis-antithesis-synthesis. There are sixty-five, often aphoristic statements, or paragraphs, which easily divide into three parts: The first eighteen are a historical review of modern philosophy as the humanization of God; the middle twelve (nineteen through thirty) constitute a focused critique of Hegel's culminating philosophy; and the last thirty-five propose a new philosophy. The second part is the antithesis, or negation, of the first: modern philosophy is the negation of theology, which is negated by Hegel as a displaced theology with a new contradiction. The third part is the negation of the negation, or synthesis, producing a new affirmation: The new philosophy is the realization of Hegelian philosophy without contradictions.

Modern Speculative Philosophy

In the first section, modern speculative philosophy is found to originate in the thought that replaces God with Reason. To the theistic philosopher, God is an object of Reason; to the speculative philosopher, Reason, or Thought, is its own object. Hegel and other speculative Idealist philosophers had rescued God from the obscurities of mystery, but at the same time they produced a basic contradiction of absolute thought with nothing to think about—not even itself.

This process of speculative philosophy began with René Descartes, who first abstracted mind from sensation and matter. Gottfried Wilhelm Leibniz showed that the only limitation of mind was matter, beyond which mind must advance. After Leibniz, mind became absolute and idealized as the ground of ideas whose objectivity was purged of sensuousness. Things ceased to exist except as thoughts: Matter is mind. Kant's limited idealism, empirically based and subordinating the appearances of matter to the shaping powers of mind, yielded place to the ideas of Fichte, who resolved the contradictions into activity of the Ego.

Baruch Spinoza's pantheism unified appearance and truth, affirming nature as divine and mind as matter. Feuerbach sees pantheism as consistent with theism and compares Spinoza to the biblical Moses. The next step in this developing philosophy is to reveal that materialists are rationalists because, in pantheism, matter is elevated to reason, and reason is idealism. The object, matter, is the same as the subject, reason. Therefore, idealism reveals itself as the truth of pantheism. The priority of Being lies in the subject itself after all, and Fichte, for whom God is the Ego itself, advanced philosophy from Spinoza and Kant by showing that outside Ego, there is no God. Feuerbach calls Fichte the messiah of modern speculative philosophy because Fichte rescued Ego from theism, but he did so without preserving the attributes of extension and materiality. Hegel would reclothe the Ego with these attributes, but he would do so at the cost of creating a new contradiction. Thus, Feuerbach completed his move from a critique of religion, through a critique of philosophy, to a confrontation with Hegelian Idealism itself.

Questioning Hegelian Idealism

The fundamental principle of Hegelian philosophy is that Being is ideal. Even matter is mind at its boundary, merely a limit to be overcome by the dialectical process of Becoming. The only activity of a thinking Being is to think, and this thinking is a process of liberation from the boundaries that confine its fullest expression. The paradox is that these boundaries are self-generated even as Being overcomes them in the process of Becoming. Feuerbach identified the contradiction as a logical one in which Being posits itself as nonbeing and the self as other, in what Hegel called self-alienation of spirit. Matter is nothing less than "not-mind," which is posited by mind itself out of itself. Mind negates itself in the process of becoming itself. To become something, everything must first be nothing.

Feuerbach sees through this contradiction to find that essence is nothing less than existence set free from the limits of nature. Hegel had, in effect, made Thought into a divine and absolute Being. Hegelian philosophy was little more than rationalized theology. The next logical step, to Feuerbach, was to place Thought where it began, in the consciousness and experience of the individual human being. Feuerbach would strip Hegel of the old theological mistakes that had set God off as distinct and separate from humanity, because Hegel had done the same thing in his system of abstracting Ideal Thought. Once relocated where it belongs, Thought (as well as mind) has objective and real being, confirmed by the presence and pressure of others in a community of being, what Feuerbach would call species-being, an intersubjectivity of consciousness shared through the senses. Individual consciousness, like individual being, cannot be separated from the objective reality that makes itself known through feelings, wants, and needs. Just as an individual human being needs air to breathe, so does mind need objective reality to exist. Feuerbach thus found in Hegel a basic contradiction between Thought and Being when Hegel separated the general from the particular, negating the differences by positing everything in Thought itself. Feuerbach asserts a new philosophy to break through the prison of Thought created by his teacher Hegel. As if to dramatize his differences, Feuerbach eschews systematic argument in favor of aphorisms and assertions. Using this style, he demonstrates the existential, as opposed to the logical and rational, origin of truth. Thought does not follow a straight line; it interrupts itself in sensuous perception. Truth is not linear; it is fractal.

Hegel found objectivity to be the limit of the Subjective Ideal, which realizes itself in an act of alienation. For Feuerbach, this discovery led to a prison of consciousness. Hegel had done no more than clarify the facts of the prison. He felt there had to be more truth than Hegel revealed. Thought thinks only about itself, swallowing up all matter in the abstractions of itself. Spinoza's pantheism had provided clues for finding the key that would break through the prison of Hegelian Absolute Thought. What lay all about the prison of consciousness was nothing less than material reality.

The New Philosophy

The power for this philosophical liberation is in the experience of sensation as a feeling of need. Idea is sensation, and sensation is truth. Sensuous beings affect one another as "I" to "Thou." Abstract philosophy had dissolved this dependence, denied the ground for self-awareness from the presence and pressure of others. Being for the new philosophy is a being of the senses, perception, feeling, and love. Materialism is the real existence of human beings, who are made conscious of material reality by their own dependence on matter, of objects and others, through the senses. Human needs, including thought itself, make themselves felt through the senses. Matter is a mode of consciousness that has independent reality established by the needs and desires of consciousness itself. Hegelian and speculative philosophy had proposed the Infinite as the ontological source of the finite; the new philosophy would reverse this, to assert that the Finite is the source of the infinite. In the human is infinity.

That infinity has been disguised by imagination in a cultural process of mystification. Even though material reality presents itself with immediacy, it cannot immediately be recognized by the uneducated person. This is the result of an ideological conditioning by religious and political institutions that are the historical products of theistic and idealistic philosophies. The new philosophy has, therefore, to negate those ideological forces, purge the mysteries, and restore the immediacy of sensuous reality. It must reveal that sensation is the source of knowledge about a real and material world, that thought is a product of sensation, and that active sensation is a specifically human experience. In their awareness of themselves as suffering, sensuous beings, human beings assert the universality of sensation. Universal sensation is mind. Because the specifically human experience of sensation is necessary for the existence of being and consciousness, its truth and reality can be discovered and appreciated only by a philosophy that concentrates on the human as a whole and complex community. New philosophy makes humankind the object of philosophy. Anthropology is the universal science. Wherever humanity has its being, there is the subject of the new philosophy.

The direct impact of *Principles of the Philosophy of the Future* was mitigated by the more dramatic influence of *The Essence of Christianity* two years earlier. Nevertheless, *Principles of the Philosophy of the Future* worked to extend and develop further the exciting ideas of the earlier book. Together these works energized a new generation of artists, politicians, and philosophers. They set the terms for the ensuing debates of the later nineteenth century in Europe and the United States because they brought forward the strengths of Hegel's dialectical method and the discoveries of natural science, and they gave philosophical justification for the new sciences of sociology, economics, psychology, and, of course, anthropology. Feuerbach's work was a contribution to the most radical of intellectual achievements in modern European history, from Karl Marx's dialectical materialism to, arguably, Sigmund Freud's methods of psychoanalysis.

Richard D. McGhee

Additional Reading

Barth, Karl. "Feuerbach," in *Protestant Thought: From Rousseau to Ritschl: Being the Translation of Eleven Chapters of 'Die Protestantische Theologie im 19 Jahrhundert.'* Translated by Brian Cozens. New York: Harper, 1959. Barth sees through Feuerbach's philosophical skepticism and atheism to recognize and appreciate the philosopher's love of theology.

Brudney, Daniel. *Marx's Attempt to Leave Philosophy*. Cambridge, Mass.: Harvard University Press, 1998. This book shows the influence Feuerbach had on Karl Marx's work.

Harvey, Van A. *Feuerbach and the Interpretation of Religion*. Cambridge, London: Cambridge University Press, 1995. An extended essay in appreciation of Feuerbach's contributions to the modern philosophy of "suspicion," that is, religious skepticism. Although the book is limited by its theme, it provides valuable insights into Feuerbach as a philosopher whose impetus was determined by religious concerns and theological training. The book also illuminates the value of Feuerbach as a contributor to existentialism, with some similarities to Søren Kierkegaard, and as an influence on the development of psychology, psychiatry, and psychoanalysis.

Hoffding, Harold. *A History of Modern Philosophy: A Sketch of the History of Philosophy from the Close of the Renaissance to Our Own Day*. Vol. 2. Translated by B. E. Meyer. New York: Dover, 1955. There is a valuable chapter on Feuerbach's psychology of religion and ethics in which Feuerbach is presented as a transitional figure who brought philosophical discourse back to first presuppositions.

Hook, Sidney. *From Hegel to Marx: Studies in the Intellectual Development of Karl Marx*. New York: Humanities Press, 1950. Still a good book for appreciating the importance of Feuerbach in the development of Marxism as a major force in the making of the modern mind.

Kamenka, Eugene. *The Philosophy of Ludwig Feuerbach*. London: Routledge & Kegan Paul, 1970. Contributes to an understanding of the context for Feuerbach's philosophy.

Wartofsky, Marx. *Feuerbach*. Cambridge, London: Cambridge University Press, 1977. This is a full and comprehensive study of Feuerbach's philosophical development as a Hegelian dialectical process whereby Feuerbach discovered himself as he analyzed the philosophy of his teacher Georg Wilhelm Friedrich Hegel. After establishing the Hegelian foundation that Feuerbach laid with his doctoral dissertation, Wartofsky proceeds to extract the essential philosophical achievements at each step of Feuerbach's career. There is a particularly valuable concluding chapter on Feuerbach's later works on materialism and anthropologism. This is the best study in English of Feuerbach.

Wilson, Charles A. *Feuerbach and the Search for Otherness*. American University Studies, Series V, Philosophy 76. New York: Peter Lang, 1989. This is useful for understanding and appreciating Feuerbach's importance for contemporary thought.

Richard D. McGhee

Johann Gottlieb Fichte

Fichte's philosophy of ethical idealism served as the pivotal theory in the development of idealism within the German philosophical community. His emendations of Immanuel Kant's conception of the human mind paved the way for the development of Absolute Idealism by Georg Wilhelm Friedrich Hegel.

Principal philosophical works: *Versuch einer Kritik aller Offenbarung*, 1792 (*Attempt at a Critique of All Revelation*, 1978); *Über den Begriff der Wissenschaftslehre*, 1794 (*Concerning the Concept of the "Wissenschaftslehre,"* 1988); *Grundlage der gesamten Wissenschaftslehre*, 1794 (*The Science of Knowledge*, 1868); *Einige Vorlesungen über die Bestimmung des Gelehrten*, 1794 (*The Vocation of the Scholar*, 1847); *Grundriss des Eigenthümlichen der Wissenschaftslehre in Rüksicht auf das theoretische Vermögen als Handschrift für seine Zuhörer*, 1795 (*Outline of the Distinctive Character of the "Wissenschaftslehre," with Respect to the Theoretical Faculty*, 1988); *Grundlage des Naturrechts nach Principien der Wissenschaftslehre*, 1796 (*The Science of Rights*, 1869); *Das System der Sittenlehre nach den Principien der Wissenschaftslehre*, 1798 (*The Science of Ethics as Based on the Science of Knowledge*, 1897); *Die Bestimmung des Menschen*, 1800 (*The Vocation of Man*, 1848); *Sonnenklarer Bericht an das grössere Publikum über das eigentliche Wesen der neuesten Philosophie*, 1801 (*A Crystal Clear Report to the General Public Concerning the Actual Essence of the Newest Philosophy*, 1987); *Über das Wesen des Gelehrten, und seine Erscheinungen im Gebiete der Freiheit*, 1806 (*On the Nature of the Scholar and Its Manifestations*, 1845); *Die Grundzüge des gegenwärtigen Zeitalters*, 1806 (*The Characteristics of the Present Age*, 1847); *Reden an die deutsche Nation*, 1808 (*Addresses to the German Nation*, 1922); *Die Anweisung zum seligen Leben: Oder, Auch die Religionslehre*, 1806 (*The Way Towards the Blessed Life*, 1844); *The Popular Works of Johann Gottlieb Fichte*, 1848-1849 (2 volumes); *Fichte: Early Philosophical Writings*, 1988; *Introduction to the Wissenschaftslehre and Other Writings, 1797-1800*, 1994.

Born: May 19, 1762; Rammenau, Saxony (now in Germany)
Died: January 27, 1814; Berlin, Prussia (now in Germany)

Early Life

Johann Gottlieb Fichte was born into poverty. His father, Christian Fichte, managed only a meager living by making and selling ribbons. At an early age, the young Fichte displayed severe conscientiousness, stubbornness, and tremendous intellectual talents. As legend has it, a local nobleman, Baron von Miltitz, missed the Sunday sermon and was informed that Johann could recite it verbatim. The baron was so impressed with this feat that he undertook to have the poor boy formally educated. Fichte was sent to the school at Pforta (1774-1780). This was followed by studies in theology at the Universities of Jena, Wittenberg, and Leipzig. No longer supported by Miltitz, Fichte was forced to terminate his education in 1784 and support himself by tutoring. His proud temperament and radical ideas forced him to change locations frequently. In 1788, he traveled to Zurich as a tutor for a wealthy hotel owner. There he befriended Johann Kasper Lavater, the most important pastor of Zurich, with whom he came to share theological interests. Lavater in turn introduced him to Inspector Hartman Rahn (a brother-in-law of the poet Friedrich Klopstock). Fichte fell in love with the inspector's daughter Johanna. Because of his financial situation, however, they remained unmarried for several years.

Life's Work

During his engagement, Fichte studied the work of Immanuel Kant, the dominant philosopher in Germany during this period and the figure responsible for Fichte's intellectual development. Initially, Fichte endorsed the doctrine of determinism. He became convinced, however, that a philosophical reconciliation between determinism and human freedom was possible within a Kantian framework. In fact, Fichte was so enthusiastic about Kant's philosophy that he traveled to Königsberg to meet the aging savant but received a rather cold reception.

In spite of this rebuff, Fichte immediately went to work on his first major philosophical treatise, *Attempt at a Critique of All Revelation*, in which he interpreted revealed religion in terms of Kant's moral theory. He argued that the experience of duty (the analysis of which he deduced from Kant) is the real supernatural element in human life; in short, one's experience of the moral law is one's experience of the divine. Thus, revealed religion amounts to an acknowledgment of being bound by a principle (of morality) that cannot be deduced from the world of sensation.

When the work was published, the author's name was omitted and the reading public assumed that Kant was the author. Eventually, Kant denied authorship, praised the work, and cited the rightful author. This error on the part of the publisher made Fichte's career. The year after publication, he married Johanna.

After their marriage, Fichte and his wife continued to live in Switzerland. During this time, Fichte published two pamphlets anonymously, *Zurückforderung der Denkfreiheit von der Fürsten Europens* (1793; reclamation of the freedom of thought from the princes of Europe) and *Beitrag zur Berichtigung der Urteile des Publikums über die französische Revolution* (1793; contributions designed to correct the judgment of the public on the French Revolution). In these works, he was influenced by Gotthold Ephraim Lessing's concerns with freedom of thought and toleration and defended the ideal of free speech as an inalienable right. Unfortunately, these political views earned for him the label of a radical.

In 1794, at the age of thirty-two, he was appointed to a professorship at the University of Jena on the recommendation of Johann Wolfgang von Goethe. Fichte had been working on foundational problems in epistemology and metaphysics for some time and now com-

bined these domains of philosophical investigation into a science of knowledge, the *Wissenschaftslehre*. His first major texts on the subject, *Concerning the Concept of the "Wissenschaftslehre"* and *The Science of Knowledge* were published the year of his appointment.

Kant lies at the basis of all Fichte's writings, but even though Fichte embraced Kant's moral philosophy, he completely rejected Kant's metaphysical notion of the thing-in-itself (*Ding-an-ich*). This concept refers to that which lies "behind" and causes experience. Yet there can be no answer to the question of whether the world is identical to the way it is experienced (because an answer would entail taking a viewpoint that stands above experience and measuring its correspondence). Because one cannot know in principle if there is perfect correspondence between one's experience and the thing that causes that experience, one is forced to conclude that the thing-in-itself is absolutely unknowable. Because Fichte rejected the notion of such a cause of experience, only the phenomenal realm was left. This

Johann Gottlieb Fichte. *(Library of Congress)*

is the starting point of all idealistic philosophies, the world as it appears in one's experience.

The great problem for Fichte was to account for the fact that experiences are of two sorts, namely subjective and objective, or what appears to be coming from one's own mind and what does not. The philosopher conceptually isolates the two fundamental facts of experience, the subject and the object, and attempts to explain all experience in terms of one or the other. The attempt that begins with the object (of experience) must ultimately make recourse to the thing-in-itself and is labeled dogmatism by Fichte. The other approach, idealism, begins with the subject (of experience) and explains experience ultimately through recourse to the thought that lies behind the conscious subject. Only this approach allows for freedom of action. Most important, Fichte argued that the choice between these two is ultimately based on the character of the philosopher. Because freedom belongs to the realm of the subject, a philosopher aware of and concerned with the fact of freedom will choose idealism.

Within this general idealistic approach, Fichte argued that there are three fundamental principles that characterize the metaphysical structure of the universe. All the particular sciences are derived from these principles, which do not admit of further justification or grounding. The first, and logically ultimate principle, is "the ego posits itself," or, in effect, reality is conceived of as activity. Fichte has already ruled out the thing-in-itself, so reality is not ultimately material, it is ideal, or thought or spirit. Yet even as ideal, the fundamental nature of reality is not substance, it is thought activity. This activity is the absolute ego, by which Fichte does not mean the individual self, soul, "I," or whatever might be meant by the term "ego" in contemporary psychology. He means the primordial, total, infinite activity of existence. The second principle is that this prime activity creates for itself a "field." The transcendental ego posits the nonego and in so doing limits and defines itself by creating the domain within which it realizes itself. The third principle is that the absolute spirit posits a limited ego in opposition to a limited nonego. One now has the particular subjects and objects of empirical knowledge, that is, knowers and what is known.

In Kant's philosophy, the concept of the tran-

scendental ego had served the function of making the experience and moral action of the individual possible. Fichte argued that a transexperiential, unindividuated ego was the ground or source of all being, including finite, experiencing selves.

In the following years, Fichte developed the ethical aspect of his philosophy. In 1796, he published *The Science of Rights* and in 1798 he published *The Science of Ethics as Based on the Science of Knowledge*. In Fichte's moral philosophy, the choices of the individual are expressions of the striving of the absolute ego, if the individual acts in accord with the moral law. The free activity of the absolute spirit has as its end increased self-determination or definition (as free, self-defining activity). Because the absolute ego expresses its free, determining activity through individual selves, each individual self strives to determine itself to strive after complete freedom. Thus, freedom itself becomes the end of moral activity. With these developments of his moral philosophy, Fichte had become the preeminent philosopher in Germany.

While at Jena, Fichte coedited a monthly philosophical journal, the *Philosophisches Journal einer Gesellschaft teutscher Gelehrten*. In 1798, he published an article in this journal entitled "Concerning the Foundation of Our Belief in Divine Government of the World," in which he argued that if the world is considered from a standpoint outside itself, then it is seen to be only a "reflection of our own activity." Accordingly, God is not needed to explain the existence of the sensed world. Fichte iterated an identification of God with the moral order of the universe (equating God with the absolute ego). On the basis of these claims, he was charged, in a series of anonymous pamphlets, with atheism and unfitness for teaching. The Saxon government ordered the Universities of Leipzig and Wittenberg to impound all copies of the journal in which the articles appeared and requested the governments of the neighboring German states to follow suit. Fichte responded by publishing two essays insisting that his views were not atheistic though they differed from the Judeo-Christian conception of a personal God. The Grand Duke of Weimar was finally approached concerning the issue and, because he was dedicated to free research, would have been content with a censure of Fichte. Anticipating this, Fichte declared in writing to the authorities that he would not submit to censure, which, when acknowledged by the government, was tantamount to dismissal. Fichte left the university in 1799 and settled in Berlin. Surprisingly, though Goethe had supported Fichte's acceptance at Jena, he now became an ardent supporter of his dismissal. In addition, Kant published a statement in which he emphatically separated his own philosophy from that of Fichte.

In the year after his dismissal, Fichte published a popularization of his moral views, *The Vocation of Man*. In 1805, Fichte accepted a professorship at Erlangen. Yet within two years, he returned to Berlin and shortly thereafter published *Addresses to the German Nation*. In this work, he advocated national educational policies that emphasized the development of the individual's conscience and capacity for moral action. When these traits were fully realized in adulthood, according to Fichte, the German people would be worthy of being spiritual leaders of the world. Fichte believed that the German people were best fitted for such leadership because Napoleon I had betrayed the ideals as expressed in the French Revolution.

Fichte's metaphysics took on deeply religious overtones toward the end of his life. He came to equate the absolute ego with the god of traditional religion. In 1806, he published *The Way Towards the Blessed Life*. In this work, Fichte claimed that the whole purpose of life is to attain knowledge of and love of God.

The final university appointment came for Fichte in 1811, when he was made rector of the newly formed University of Berlin. Because his temperament made it difficult to work with him, he did not remain at this post for long. He did continue to lecture throughout 1812-1813. During these years, Johanna worked at a hospital nursing the sick and those wounded in the Napoleonic Wars. In the course of her work, she contracted a fever and while Fichte was nursing her back to health, he also became ill. The malady proved fatal in his case, and he died on January 27, 1814.

Influence

Fichte exercised a tremendous influence on philosophy in Germany. He personally knew the leading figures of the Romantic movement.

While he was Fichte's student in 1796, Friedrich Schlegel closely followed the intellectual footsteps of his master. Schlegel later turned to Baruch Spinoza and Gottfried Wilhelm Leibniz and eventually became the most prominent leader of the German Romantic movement. Friedrich Wilhelm Joseph Schelling, a professor at Jena, argued that the absolute ego could be apprehended in a direct intuition (and not merely posited by pure practical reason, as in Fichte's system). One of Schelling's early journal articles was a comparison of the philosophies of Fichte and Spinoza. Fichte met Friedrich Schleiermacher during his Berlin years. He was, however, very critical of the free morals and glorification of sentimentality of the Romantics and quickly dissociated himself from the movement.

Most important, Fichte influenced Hegel, who had succeeded Fichte in 1800 as professor of philosophy at Jena. Hegel's first book was a comparison of the philosophies of Fichte and Schelling. Fichte's change of the Kantian transcendental ego into an unindividuated absolute activity paved the way for Hegel's development of Absolute Idealism. Fichte's philosophy also influenced Thomas Carlyle.

In his own day, Fichte was respected as much for his moral character as for his philosophy. He was regarded as extremely conscientious, self-demanding, and disciplined. The epigraph on his tomb reads "Thy teachers shall shine as the brightness of the firmament, and they that turn many to righteousness as the stars that shine for ever and ever."

Mark Pestana

The Vocation of Man

Type of philosophy: Epistemology, ethics, metaphysics
First published: Die Bestimmung des Menschen, 1800 (English translation, 1848)
Principal ideas advanced:
◇ Each self appears to be a self-conscious, intelligent, willing element in a rigidly determined system that results from a fundamental forming power in nature.

◇ However, the world of experience (together with the causal laws that appear to govern it) is a construction by the self.
◇ The self, therefore, is free and morally responsible.
◇ By faith the self is assured of the existence of other selves; and by action humans fulfill their moral obligation, to act, to do—this is humanity's vocation.

Johann Gottlieb Fichte is a transitional figure in the history of German philosophy. His philosophical impetus came from Immanuel Kant, and his work began the modifications of Kant that ultimately resulted in the Absolute Idealism of Georg Wilhelm Friedrich Hegel. He had some trying experiences as a young man, finding himself in financial want during the latter days of his formal education and during the five years that passed between his engagement to his future wife and their marriage. He was forced to scrape along as a tutor during his early career, work that was not always satisfying and rewarding. However, during these early years as a private tutor, he came across the writings of Kant, and these provided him with background and inspiration for his career as a philosopher. In fact, his emergence from obscurity to national recognition almost overnight resulted from his being mistaken for Kant. A book of Fichte's on philosophy of religion was published without his name appearing as author. The literary world assumed the book had been written by Kant himself. Kant then made it known that the book was from Fichte's pen, not his own, and he also praised the work, thereby immediately making Fichte a national figure.

Fichte and Kant

Fichte was attracted most strongly to the ethical views of Kant. He saw himself in his youth as a Spinozist, but he was not happy with philosopher Baruch Spinoza's rigid determinism. He had considerable passion and enthusiasm, and he apparently also had a need to feel that his acts were subject to ethical appraisal in that he himself was a free and responsible ethical agent. In the Spinozistic world, of course, all acts followed from their causal antecedents in a necessary way. This view comforted Spinoza, but it was too somber for Fichte. Kant's conviction, expressed in the *Kritik der praktischen Vernunft* (1788; *The Critique of Practical Reason*, 1873), that men are free ethical agents, opened a new philosophical possibility for Fichte.

However, even Kant was not strong enough for Fichte, because Kant did not begin his philosophy with a free ethical agent but with an account of the world of experience that the scientist investigates. Kant's metaphysics and epistemology only made it *possible* that there are free, ethically responsible selves; proof that such is indeed the case was not given. Because Fichte wanted a firmer base than this for his own philosophy, he introduced modifications that, although they seemed innocent enough at first, ultimately resulted in a noticeably different kind of idealism from that of Kant. Kant was moved by both the heavens above and the moral law within; Fichte was too much involved with the moral law within to pay much attention to the heavens.

On the epistemological side, Fichte dropped out the Kantian *Ding-an-sich* (thing-in-itself). For Kant, the world of experience is a world constructed out of the sensuous material given in the manifold of intuition as ordered by the forms of space and time, a construction that is ordered by the categories. However, the manifold of sense is caused by the unknown and unknowable *Ding-an-sich*. We can know only the world of our experience; we cannot know anything of the things-in-themselves. (Except, perhaps, that they cause the sensuous manifold out of which we produce the world of our experience.) Things-in-themselves, then, initiate a process that ultimately yields the world of our experience, but the world of experience, as we are able to know it, includes no things-in-themselves, and it is, furthermore, something that we ourselves unconsciously construct. We do not experience things-in-themselves; we cannot know them. It is a short step from this idea of things-in-themselves to saying that we do not need them and that they are therefore not real. This is the step Fichte made. The world of experience was for Fichte, as it was for Kant, a construction made unconsciously by the self. However, while Kant saw this construction as a kind of response to the stimulus of an unknown and unknowable thing-in-itself, Fichte did away with the thing-in-itself and merely said that the world of experience is an unconscious construction by the self.

Fichte, however, did offer a causal account to explain how the world of experience comes to be constructed, an account that results from his fundamentally ethical orientation. At the base of Fichte's system is the self as an ethical agent. The self, in becoming aware of itself, sees itself as a free ethical agent, and therefore posits the ego. The self, or ego, posits its own existence. It is as if Fichte were offering a variation of French philosopher René Descartes's *Cogito, ergo sum* ("I think, therefore I am") argument; we might paraphrase Fichte's starting point as "I am obligated, therefore I am." It is not the knowledge problem with which Fichte begins, but the ethical problem. However, after the ego posits itself, it finds that there is need for an additional posit. One cannot be ethical in a vacuum; there must be an arena of action—one must be obligated to other persons. It is this circumstance that produces the world of experience. The ego, having posited itself as ethical agent, also posits the nonego as a world of experience (which includes other selves) in order that the ego may have an arena in which to perform its tasks and discharge its obligations. The world of experience is not fundamental in its own right in Fichte's philosophy as it is in Kant's. Rather, the world of experience exists in order that a person can be ethical.

It is against this background that *The Vocation of Man* must be viewed. It is less technical than most of Fichte's writings, and it is addressed to the ordinary reader rather than to the professional philosopher. Fichte says in the preface that the book "ought to be intelligible to all readers who are able to understand a book at all." He therefore avoids the words "ego" and "nonego," as well as other technical terms that appear elsewhere in his writings. Nevertheless, the position is the same. This avoidance of technicality is one of the considerable merits of this book, as contrasted with Fichte's *Grundlage der gesamten Wissenschaftslehre* (1794; *The Science of Knowledge*, 1868). The latter is liberally sprinkled with technical terminology and arguments that Fichte himself thought important and sound but that recent philosophers have judged to be almost the opposite. *The Vocation of Man* is thus the most

understandable and the most popular statement of Fichte's position.

The book has three divisions: "Doubt," "Knowledge," and "Faith." Roughly, they may be said to represent the Spinozistic, the Kantian, and the Fichtean positions, at least as Fichte understood them.

The Spinozistic Position

Book 1, "Doubt," has the tone of Descartes's *Discours de la méthode* (1637; *Discourse on Method*, 1649) or his *Meditationes de prima philosophia* (1641; *Meditations on First Philosophy*, 1680). Fichte writes in the first person and addresses himself to the problem of discovering what he can know about himself and the world in which he lives. He considers the information he gets from sense-experience and draws conclusions about what the world is like. He accepts the view that there are independently real objects, each occupying a place in a system that is connected throughout by necessary causal relations. Each object or each event in nature is what it is and is what it must be. Nothing could possibly be other than it is. Removing even a single grain of sand, Fichte says, would change the entire structure of nature; all past and future history would be different.

Each man, including Fichte himself, is, of course, "a link in this chain of the rigid necessity of Nature." There is a "forming power" in nature, or perhaps better, behind or lying under observed nature, which gives rise to all the objects and events that make up the system of nature. Fichte himself was produced by the forming power. As he becomes aware of this power, he says, he feels himself sometimes free, sometimes restrained, and sometimes compelled. Yet this is merely Fichte's awareness of how the underlying power operates in his own existence and consciousness. It explains his own consciousness, his awareness of himself as a discrete item in the system of nature. However, this self-consciousness of the forming power as manifested in himself provides the ground from which he infers that the forming power also manifests itself in other objects in nature. There are varieties of individual selves, each resembling Fichte. Finally, the summation of the self-consciousnesses of these selves makes up the "complete consciousness of the universe." Fichte, as a self, then, is one element—a self-conscious, intelligent, willing element—in a rigidly determined system that is the result of a fundamental forming power in nature.

Yet this Spinozistic system of nature fails to satisfy Fichte. There is no freedom in it. If Fichte, together with all his acts, is merely a set of necessary consequences in a rigidly determined system, then he is not an ethical agent. Whatever he does, he necessarily has to do, and his conduct is therefore not subject to ethical evaluation or to praise and blame. This is the outcome of his reflection. However, what he desires, on the other hand, is to know that he is free and ethically responsible. He wants to be, in some sense, himself the cause of his behavior, instead of feeling that his behavior is merely the effect of external causes.

The conclusion reached in book 1 of *The Vocation of Man*, then, is this: Fichte has stated two possibilities: Either he is merely one element in a rigidly determined system, or else he is a free moral agent. One view, he says, satisfies his heart, while the other destroys his own sense of worth. Which view should he adopt? This is the issue he must resolve, but he is left, at the end of book 1, in doubt.

The Kantian Position

Book 2, "Knowledge," is a dialogue, not unlike George Berkeley's *Three Dialogues Between Hylas and Philonous* (1713). Fichte writes that he is tormented by the doubt that issued from the first attack on the problem, and he awakens in the night, his sleep interrupted by the unresolved problem. A Spirit then comes to him to lead him out of doubt and into knowledge. The knowledge offered is subjective idealism, and book 2 is as fine a statement of the position as is generally available.

The Spirit begins by questioning Fichte about how he knows objects in the external world, to which Fichte replies that he knows them by sensation. However, the sensations are merely modifications of Fichte himself, the Spirit points out, and so Fichte has knowledge only of his own condition—not knowledge of the independently real, external world. "In all perception," the Spirit points out, "thou perceivest only thine own condition."

Fichte is not yet convinced, however. The argument moves on to consider the ordinary belief that sensations are caused by independently real, external objects. However, such independent objects cannot be known by sense, for if Fichte has sensations, they are merely modifications of Fichte himself, not characteristics of independent objects. If there are external, independent objects, they cannot be known by sense, at any rate. They can only be known in virtue of applications of the principle of causality. However, how can the principle of causality itself be justified? Certainly not by appealing to the fact that sense objects are causally connected, for that would be to argue in a circle. The argument would then go: I know there are independent objects because of the principle of causality, and I know the principle of causality because independent objects are examples of it. Such an argument fails to do the required job. The principle of causality must, therefore, be justified in another way.

The alternative taken is that the causal principle is a statement of how humans really do interpret experience; that is to say, the principle is contributed by the knower, not by the objects known. The principle is thus another modification of Fichte himself, not a feature of the world he believes is external to himself. If this is the case, however, the justification previously given for believing that there are independent objects that cause sensations collapses, and Fichte's world of experience loses all of its independent status. Kant's things-in-themselves are removed from the philosophical terrain because they are erroneously inferred from an inadequately formulated version of the causal principle. The world of experience is not a response to a set of stimuli from independently real things in themselves; instead, it is from beginning to end a projection of, or a construction out of, the self's own modifications. The "object" of knowledge is only a modification of the knower, and, as such, is (in Fichte's terminology) a "subject-objectivity." Subject and object merge into the subjectivity of the knower.

Such is the subjective idealism developed in the second book of *The Vocation of Man*. His subjective idealism was developed by Fichte in order to settle the doubt that marked the outcome of book 1. Fichte wanted to reject rigid determinism but needed a ground that would justify the rejection. He saw subjective idealism as providing such a ground. If the world of experience is constructed freely by the self, then the self need no longer labor under the onus of rigid determinism. The Spirit tells Fichte that he need "no longer tremble at a necessity which exists only in thine own thought; no longer fear to be crushed by things which are the product of thine own mind."

The Fichtean Position

However, other selves, the necessary additional elements that make the ethical situation plausible, do not have fundamental reality in the subjective idealism that is presented in book 2. The doubt of book 1 is replaced by knowledge, yet this knowledge does not assure a fundamental reality for other selves. To get full reality for other selves Fichte must go still further; he must go beyond knowledge. If knowledge must be transcended, it is inadequate. The opinion is what lies behind the strikingly strange statement Fichte makes near the end of book 2, that "knowledge is not reality, just because it is knowledge." Knowledge does not disclose reality, according to Fichte. Its function differs from this commonly held view. Really, knowledge is less powerful. Fichte writes that "it destroys and annihilates error," but it "cannot give us truth, for in itself it is absolutely empty." Knowledge is not the avenue to reality. It must make way for a higher power; it must make way for faith, the subject of book 3. Faith assures the self that there are really other selves.

Book 3 opens with Fichte's dissatisfaction at the outcome of book 2. If all there is to the world is the construction Fichte himself unconsciously makes out of the modifications of his own self, then the world is empty. Yet this is all one can get from knowledge. However, knowing does not exhaust human life; there is more to it than just that. "Not merely TO KNOW, but according to thy knowledge TO DO, is thy vocation," Fichte declares. The "doing" here is clearly an *ethical* doing; it is striving, achieving, fulfilling obligations. Fichte regards himself as under an immediate and underived sense of obligation to *act*; this is his, it is all humanity's, vocation. Yet if one is to act, there must be an arena in which to act; there

must be an externally real world to act in and to act on. To justify such a world on the basis of knowledge is not possible. One must transcend knowledge and place his reliance in faith. Early in book 3, Fichte resolves to do just this. He turns from knowledge to faith, from intellect to will, and thus he arrives at a real, external world that is populated with other selves related to Fichte and to one another by mutual ties of ethical obligation.

This discussion brings to a conclusion the strictly philosophical segment of *The Vocation of Man*. Fichte goes on for quite a time, however, into what is really more religion than philosophy. Once he has established his own existence and the existence of a world in which he can strive, he sermonizes about fulfilling his obligations. If book 1 is similar to Descartes and book 2 is similar to Berkeley, it can be said with equal justice that book 3 resembles a sermon enjoining strenuous ethical striving. Fichte tries to sound a clear call to plain living and high thinking, and his fervor, if not the details of his message, cannot fail to strike the reader.

Essentially the position he took is a mystical one. Somehow or other, according to his account, Fichte's own ethical will merged with the Universal Will, a kind of metaphysical ultimate that functioned as Fichte's God. He seemed to feel affinities with Saint John's Gospel, but he insisted on de-anthropomorphizing God, and he thus lost what has always been at the center of the devotional life of the saints. Fichte had much of the emotion of the Christian mystic, but little sympathy for the object of Christian devotion. He replaced Saint John's incarnate Word (Jesus Christ) with a pantheistic extension of his own ethical sensitivity. The result is quite a frightening projection of Fichte's own passions set up as God. The control exercised over the saint by his worship of a truly transcendent God is missing in Fichte; he remained an egocentric German Romantic.

The Vocation of Man is a kind of guided tour beginning with Spinoza, leading through Kant, and ending in a subjective ethical idealism with deep Romantic footings. It is an excellent introduction to the philosophy of nineteenth century Germany, and it shares with that general movement its characteristic strengths and weaknesses.

The logic is often unsound, feeling often over-rules reason, selfish concerns are sometimes read out as the Will of God. Yet the Romantics generally, and Fichte among them, certainly were ethically concerned; they were trying to spell out the moral ideal and to set people moving toward a better world.

A Transitional Figure

However, while *The Vocation of Man* is a fine example of Romantic idealism, it is at the same time, paradoxically, a work that foreshadows significant developments in philosophy of a sort opposed in spirit and method to much of what Fichte endorsed. In rejecting the *Ding-an-sich* of Kant, in emphasizing the role of the self in the effort to know reality, in basing his philosophy on the self's declaration of its own existence, and particularly in urging the definitive importance of action, Fichte suggested the basic ideas of later pragmatic and existentialistic philosophies. Of course, Fichte remains a subjective idealist, and he never developed the pragmatic and existentialistic features of his thought; philosophically speaking, he remains a nineteenth century German idealist. However, the resolution of the paradox of moral action—the paradox in which humans as free moral agents find themselves involved because of their presence in a causally determined universe—is similar to the resolution achieved by the existentialists, Christian and atheistic alike. To begin with the striving self, to regard humans as what they can become as a result of their moral efforts, to take their moral "vocation" as prior to their essence—all of this is strikingly similar to the ideas later to be defended by such radically different philosophic personalities as Søren Kierkegaard and Jean-Paul Sartre.

It is the emphasis on will which makes a philosopher such as Fichte a transitional figure, borrowing from the old idealistic philosophy and suggesting the lines of development of the new pragmatic-existentialistic philosophy. A thinker who extends the principle of the will to the entire universe, deifying will and rejection all else on its behalf, exhibits a metaphysical radicalism that is today's philosophical conservatism. However, one who regards will, the striving of the stubbornly independent self, as definitive of self, of

humans, but not of all reality—such a one may very well oppose oneself to the idealist, at the same time refusing to commit oneself to realism; this thinker remains pragmatic, testing not only one's own nature, but the nature of everything else, in terms of action and consequences.

In arguing that the moral will involves the assumption of a moral law that admits no exceptions, and in regarding the Infinite Will as that law—"a Will that in itself is law"—Fichte shows that he is in the great tradition of idealistic philosophy. However, in arguing that it is "the vocation of our species to unite itself into one single body" through the moral striving of the free self, and in suggesting that "All my thoughts must have a bearing on my action," Fichte passes from the metaphysical to the moral, and from the moral to the pragmatic and existential. In his philosophy, then, the old and the new combine, neither one in a pure state but each aspect enlivened by the presence of the other.

Robert E. Larsen

Additional Reading

Adamson, Robert. *Fichte*. Edinburgh: William Blackwood and Sons, 1881. Contains a long biography. Devoted to tracing the evolution of *The Science of Knowledge* from early phase to later phase. Argues that this philosophy never rids itself of subjective idealism and that only in its earlier formulations was the doctrine influential.

Breazeale, Daniel, and Tom Rockmore, eds. *Fichte: Historical Contexts/Contemporary Controversies*. Atlantic Highlands, N.J.: Humanities Press, 1994. A collection of thirteen essays, selected from a 1992 conference, exemplifying a wide range of approaches to Fichte's work. Includes comprehensive bibliographies of English translations of writings by Fichte and of work in English about Fichte.

Everett, Charles Carroll. *Fichte's "Science of Knowledge": A Critical Exposition*. Chicago: S. C. Griggs, 1884. Compares Georg Wilhelm Friedrich Hegel's and Arthur Schopenhauer's philosophies to Fichte's. Argues that Fichte fails to reconcile the concept of finitude with the doctrine of the absolute. More than half of the work is devoted to exposition of Fichte's three fundamental principles.

Gopalakrishnaiah, V. A. *Comparative Study of the Educational Philosophies of J. G. Fichte and J. H. Newman.* Waltair: Andhra University Press, 1973. Stresses the importance of the university to the community, the social function of education, and the provision of scientific research by the university in Fichte's educational theories and contrasts these themes with their contraries in John Henry Newman.

Hohler, T. P. *Imagination and Reflection: Intersubjectivity Fichte's "Grundlage" of 1794.* The Hague: Martinus Nijhoff, 1982. Devoted to the problem of finitude and the philosophy of the "I" in Fichte's early writings only. Argues that the transcendental "I" is essentially and inherently intersubjective; that is, intersubjectivity is argued to be a transcendental constituent of "I-ness."

Neuhouser, Frederick. *Fichte's Theory of Subjectivity.* New York: Cambridge University Press, 1990. Outlines the development of Fichte's early writings that attempt to construct a unified and coherent theory of subjectivity.

Rockmore, Tom. *Fichte, Marx, and the German Philosophical Tradition.* Carbondale: Southern Illinois University Press, 1980. Compares the philosophical positions of Fichte and Karl Marx, often taken to be intellectual opposites, with a view toward establishing their common ground within the context of nineteenth century German thought.

Rockmore, Tom, and Daniel Breazeale, eds. *New Perspectives on Fichte.* Atlantic Highlands, N.J.: Humanities Press, 1996. A collection of thirteen essays on Fichte's philosophy, selected from a 1993 conference.

Talbot, E. B. *The Fundamental Principle of Fichte's Philosophy.* New York: Macmillan, 1906. Concentrates on the changes that Fichte made in his fundamental principle between the early and later periods of his development. Argues that differences noted by critics are overstated and that the fundamental characterization as activity remains constant throughout.

Mark Pestana, updated by William Nelles

Jerry A. Fodor

Attempting to vindicate people's commonsense psychological views, Fodor provided a staunch defense of a representational theory of mind and the language of thought that such a theory presupposes.

Principal philosophical works: *Psychological Explanation*, 1968; *The Language of Thought*, 1975; *RePresentations: Philosophical Essays on the Foundations of Cognitive Science*, 1981; *The Modularity of Mind*, 1983; "Semantics, Wisconsin Style," 1984; *Psychosemantics: The Problem of Meaning in the Philosophy of Mind*, 1987; "Connectionism and Cognitive Architecture," 1988 (with Z. Pylyshyn); *A Theory of Content, and Other Essays*, 1990; *Holism: A Shopper's Guide*, 1992 (with Ernest LePore); *The Elm and the Expert: Mentalese and Its Semantics*, 1994; *Concepts: Where Cognitive Science Went Wrong*, 1998.

Born: April 22, 1935; New York, New York

Early Life

After an undergraduate education at Columbia University in New York City, Jerry A. Fodor received his Ph.D. from Princeton University in 1960. He began his academic career at the Massachusetts Institute of Technology (MIT) in 1959, first as an instructor and then, in 1961, as an assistant professor. Around that time, he also published his first article, "What Do You Mean?" (1960), in *Journal of Philosophy*.

Early in his career, Fodor spent a year visiting at the University of Illinois, where he worked closely with Charles Osgood, one of the pioneers of psycholinguistics. He also married Janet Dean, a linguist with a Ph.D. from MIT, with whom he often collaborated in his early work. Added to the fact that the philosophy department at MIT was closely connected with the linguistics department, it is not surprising that Fodor's work would draw significantly from the discipline of linguistics.

Life's Work

Many of Fodor's early articles were collaborative, interdisciplinary efforts, as he worked together with psychologists and linguists such as Zenon Pylyshyn, Jerrold Katz, Merrill Garrett, and Thomas Bever. In the early 1970's, Fodor once again joined forces with Bever and Garrett, this time to produce a book that surveyed the literature in psycholinguistics, a field that begun to blossom only in the previous decade. Much of the material in the text they wrote, *The Psychology of Language: An Introduction to Psycholinguistics and Generative Grammar* (1974), was then revisited by Fodor in his subsequent book *The Language of Thought*. This book clearly reveals Fodor's debt to Noam Chomsky, distinguished member of the faculty at MIT and a towering figure in linguistics.

Though Fodor's work had been generating discussion for a number of years, in many ways *The Language of Thought* is the book that put him on the philosophical map. An argument for realism about the mental, this book presents Fodor's first comprehensive argument for the representational theory of mind (RTM), a theory that he has vigorously continued to defend throughout his career. The fundamental claim of RTM is that to have a propositional attitude (for example, a belief or a desire) is to be in a certain relation to an internal representation. As such, RTM postulates an infinite set of internal representations and this, as the title of the book suggests, is the language of thought, an innate system of representation. This claim of innateness is one respect in which Chomsky's influence can be clearly seen, and much of the argument for the existence of a language of thought in the book's second chapter calls upon Chomskian linguistic theory. It is important to note, however, that the innateness claim does not commit Fodor to the view that children are born with every concept that there is, including even complex concepts such as "airplane" or "telephone." Rather, all that must be innate are the basic elements out of which those more complex concepts can be constructed.

A useful description of RTM and its relation to the language of thought, which Fodor often employs, invokes the metaphorical notion of propositional attitude boxes. For example, when one has the belief that one's car's gas tank is full, this puts the appropriate language of thought symbols corresponding to "the gas tank is full" in one's belief box. Were one instead to desire that the gas tank be full, the symbols would be put in one's desire box. The presence or absence of certain symbols in someone's belief and desire boxes will then issue an action. For example, the conjunction of "the gas tank is empty" in someone's belief box and "the gas tank is full" in that same person's desire box will, other things being equal, lead to subsequent behavior such as a trip to the gas station. It is by showing how it is scientifically possible for behavior to be connected to the representational content of mental states that RTM vindicates folk psychology.

It is important that, although the language of thought is not supposed to be a natural language such as English or French, it is supposed to be a language—that is, it is supposed to have a syntax. That such a language be syntactical is important because Fodor wants to maintain that the relations between propositional attitudes and the language of thought symbols that are their objects are computational, and computational relations must be able to be formally (or syntactically) specified.

Having postulated a language of thought, Fodor next had to explain how symbols in such a language could refer to items in the world. The problem of finding a suitable property or relation to explain such reference has become known as the problem of psychosemantics, a term coined by Fodor in his long manuscript, "Psychosemantics: Or, Where Do Truth Conditions Come From?" Though this manuscript was widely circulated among his philosophical circle in the 1980's, he decided not publish it, having changed his mind about the adequacy of the the theory offered therein. Ultimately, he revisited the problem of psychosemantics in his book *Psychosemantics: The Problem of Meaning in the Philosophy of Mind*. In the original manuscript, which he eventually consented to having published in the much-respected anthology *Mind and Cognition* (1990), Fodor had offered a teleological answer to the problem of psychosemantics. In the later book, he explicitly rejects the teleological approach, dismissing it as unsatisfactory. The theory that replaces it is a causal one, where symbols in the language of thought refer to objects and properties in the world in virtue of being caused by instantiations of such objects and properties.

Like much of Fodor's work, *Psychosemantics* continually invokes the figures of both Granny and Aunty, largely fictionalized versions of his actual aunt and grandmother. Both are characterized as no-nonsense women, full of folksy wis-

Jerry A. Fodor. *(Courtesy of Jerry Fodor)*

dom and aphorisms, who speak with the voice of the establishment. Granny and Aunty thus serve as dialectical foils, forcing Fodor to defend controversial claims, but they also serve as humorous means for Fodor to put himself in his place. Granny, for example, is portrayed as wont to grin from her rocking chair and say "I told you so" in response to some of Fodor's theories, and Aunty's chiding advice to her nephew closes *Psychosemantics*: "Children should play nicely together and respect each other's points of view."

After spending twenty-seven years as a faculty member at MIT, in 1986 Fodor departed for the City University of New York (CUNY) Graduate Center. Then, only two years later, he moved from CUNY to Rutgers University, where he was appointed State of New Jersey Professor of Philosophy. While at Rutgers, Fodor worked closely with his colleague Ernest LePore, associate director for the Rutgers Center for Cognitive Science. In addition to collaborating on several articles, Fodor and LePore wrote *Holism: A Shopper's Guide* (1992).

Fodor has a reputation for being not only an engaging writer but an engaging speaker as well, which accounts for frequent invitations to participate in distinguished lecture series. In 1993, for example, he was asked to give the inaugural Jean Nicod Lectures in Paris, France. Jean Nicod was a French philosopher and logician, and the lecture series in his name was inaugurated on the occasion of the hundredth anniversary of his birth. The Centre National de la Recherche Scientifique, which sponsors the annual lectures, seeks to foster the development of the discipline of cognitive science in France by hosting the lectures of a leading philosopher of mind or philosophically minded cognitive scientist. Fodor's lectures have been published as *The Elm and the Expert: Mentalese and Its Semantics*. The title refers to a much-discussed example put forth in "The Meaning of 'Meaning'" (1975), by Hilary Putnam, one of Fodor's main philosophical influences.

Fodor also delivered the highly prestigious John Locke Lectures at Oxford University in 1996. An extended version of those lectures has been published as *Concepts: Where Cognitive Science Went Wrong*. Once again, Fodor invoked Aunty, and characterized the book as what Aunty would call "constructive criticism" of the enter-

prise of cognitive science. *Concepts* was also meant to be an internal critique, since Fodor himself is deeply committed to the traditional program of cognitive science. His criticism centers on the anti-atomist approach that traditional cognitive science has taken with respect to concepts, and Fodor offers an atomistic theory of concepts in an effort to solve many of the problems with which cognitive scientists have struggled.

Influence
Fodor has often been characterized as irreverent, and insofar as he has been prepared to depart from the philosophical mainstream, the characterization seems apt. Other adjectives that are offered to describe Fodor are "infuriating" and "irritating," and though these may understandably have negative connotations, in Fodor's case such descriptions are actually not meant to be unflattering. As evidence for this interpretation, consider the fact that the book jacket for *Concepts* proclaims, "This is surely Fodor's most irritating book in years." Fodor is irritating in the sense that he has, time and again, provided the philosophical community with stimuli for argument. In this respect, being an irritant is a philosophical virtue.

Perhaps the most important respect in which Fodor has been a philosophical irritant is that, throughout his career, he has defended RTM in part by challenging his opponents to produce an adequate competitor. According to Fodor, the representational theory is the only serious proposal on the playing field that accounts for the production of bodily behavior by the mind—it is, so to speak, the only game in town. RTM prevails by default. This argumentative strategy has often infuriated his opponents. As a result, many cognitive scientists working on, for example, connectionist theories of the mind see their endeavor, at least in part, as an explicit effort to meet Fodor's challenge and prove him wrong. Thus, whether cognitive science ultimately turns out to be the way that Fodor envisions it or the way that his opponents envision it, he will have played a large part in its development.

There is no doubt that as future philosophers look back on late twentieth century philosophy, they will regard Fodor as the period's preeminent defender of the commonsense conception of mind. Though his representational theory of mind is, after all, a philosophical theory, it is nonetheless true that at bottom it aims to vindicate the commonsense presuppositions of folk psychology. Throughout his career, Fodor has revisited, reworked, and revised this theory, but he has never abandoned it. In fact, as he notes in *Concepts*, in his characteristically humorous style, "I seem to have grown old writing books defending RTMs; it occurs to me that if I were to stop writing books defending RTMs, perhaps I would stop growing old." Alas, not even Fodor—as irreverent and infuriating and irritating as he is—can stop the march of time, but the arguments that he will leave behind in his voluminous corpus of published work ensure his place in history.

Amy Kind

RePresentations

Philosophical Essays on the Foundations of Cognitive Science

Type of philosophy: Epistemology, philosophy of mind, philosophy of science
First published: 1981
Principal ideas advanced:

◇ Fodor puts forth a version of "functionalism": Propositional attitude states (such as beliefs and desires) are relational; the correct theory of such states will analyze them in terms of the functional or causal role they play in the life of the organism.

◇ Cognitive science should adopt a strategy of methodological solipsism, focusing solely on the narrow content of mental states.

◇ Any adequate theory of mental content demands an ontological commitment to mental representations; that is, we must adopt Realism about mental representations. The resulting theory that Fodor develops is referred to as the representational theory of mind (RTM).

◇ Mental representations, like sentences in a natural language, are symbolic structures that have both syntactic and semantic properties. This hypothesis is often referred to as the language of thought hypothesis.

The ten articles in *RePresentations* were all written in the 1960's and 1970's, fairly early in Fodor's career. With the exception of the final essay, entitled, "The Present Status of the Innateness Controversy," all of the essays were previously published in anthologies or philosophical journals such as *Journal of Philosophy* and *The Philosophical Review*. The fact of their previous publication gives rise to the pun of the title: Not only are the essays about the subject of mental representation but they are also, in this volume, re-presented.

Methodological Solipsism and Thought Experiments

RePresentations contains a number of highly influential papers. One such paper is "Methodological Solipsism Considered as a Research Strategy in Cognitive Psychology," originally published in 1980 in the interdisciplinary journal *Behavioral and Brain Sciences*. The term "methodological solipsism" comes from "The Meaning of 'Meaning'" (1975), in which Hilary Putnam defined it as the assumption that the existence of any particular psychological state does not require anything other than the existence of the mind whose psychological state it is. In the remainder of the paper, Putnam presented a series of thought experiments to show that this assumption is misguided.

The most famous of these thought experiments is the case of Twin Earth, a planet remarkably like Earth and populated with people who speak a language remarkably like English. However, Twin Earth differs from Earth in one important respect: the clear liquid there called "water," which flows in the rivers and streams and is used for drinking and bathing, has the molecular composition not of water (H_2O) but rather the composition XYZ (a fictional chemical composition that is different from H_2O). Consider now your Twin Earth counterpart, a being who is, molecule for molecule, identical with you. When you are in the mental state "water is wet," you are thinking about H_2O, but when your counterpart thinks "water is wet," she is thinking about XYZ. It thus seems that you and your counterpart must be in different types of mental states. However, since you and she are, by hypothesis, microphysical duplicates of one another, the fact that your mental state is the state that it is depends on something external to you. In this case, for example, the fact that your mental state is the state that it is, rather than the one that your counterpart is in, depends on the fact that your environment contains H_2O and not XYZ.

Notice, however, that although your mental state is about H_2O and your twin's mental state is about XYZ, it nonetheless seems that there is some sense in which you and your twin are in the same mental state. This intuition leads to the distinction between two kinds of mental state content: wide content (with respect to which you and your twin's mental states are different) and narrow content (with respect to which you and your twin's mental states are the same). Methodological solipsism commits one to doing psychology without wide content, and throughout his essay, Fodor argues forcefully that such a strategy is preferable. One reason he offers is that to focus on wide content is, in essence, to give up on the possibility of psychology altogether. If one had to do psychology in terms of wide content, one would have to wait for the outcome of all science; for example, your thoughts about water could be explained only after the completion of chemistry. As Fodor says, "No doubt it's all right to have a research strategy that says 'wait awhile.' However, who wants to wait *forever*?"

It bears noting that Fodor's embrace of the assumption of methodological solipsism is strongly reminiscent of the views of René Descartes, and Fodor himself acknowledges that in many respects the theory of mind he puts forth is a Cartesian one. It is important, however, that he does not endorse the ontological commitments of the Cartesian theory of mind; unlike a Cartesian dualist, Fodor is not committed to the existence of a nonphysical mind distinct from the physical body. Fodor's own position on the relationship between mind and body is a functionalist one.

Functionalism

The development of functionalism in the 1960's and 1970's brought about a significant transformation in the philosophy of mind. The functionalist theory, underlying the discussion of several of the essays in *RePresentations*, emerged from the ashes of behaviorism and the identity theory. Behaviorism, espoused in the first half of the twentieth century by theorists such as Carl Hempel and Gilbert Ryle, attempted to define mental states solely in terms of behavior and dispositions to behave. Unfortunately for the behaviorists, however, significant problems with their theory soon became evident and were extensively detailed in numerous publications, such as Putnam's "Brains and Behavior" (1965). Most problematic, perhaps, is the fact that the behaviorist is forced to deny a mental life to any creature that does not exhibit the standard behavioral patterns.

The other precursor to functionalism, the identity theory, was developed in the middle of the century by theorists such as J. J. C. Smart and U. T. Place as a materialist alternative to behaviorism. Instead of identifying a mental state with a particular pattern of behavior, the identity theorists identified mental states with particular physical states, usually neurophysiological states of the brain. Unlike the behaviorist, the identity theorist was thus able to account for the existence of mental states when there is not the appropriate behavior; moreover, by identifying mental states with brain states, the identity theorist was able to provide a highly satisfactory account of the causal powers mental states have with respect to behavior. However, the identity theory itself soon ran into trouble, due to its unfortunate exclusivity: According to this theory, the only creatures that can have mental states are creatures with brains that are exactly like human brains.

Functionalism retains the best elements of these two preceding theories, combining the behaviorists' insight that mental states are relational with the insight of the identity theorists that people need to take seriously the causal relation between mental states and behavior. Roughly put, functionalism defines mental states in terms of their relations to sensory input, behavior, and other mental states. It is no accident that the development of functionalism coincided with the rise of computer science. Functionalism is grounded in a computational metaphor—viewing cognition as the "program" of the brain—and the early functionalists relied on the idea of a Turing machine, borrowed from computer science, to lay out their theories.

Fodor's version of functionalism is outlined in "What Psychological States Are Not," an essay cowritten with Ned Block. More generally, however, his functionalist leanings shape the discussions of mental representation in several other essays in *RePresentations*. For example, one corollary to Fodor's functionalism is his rejection of psychological reduction, the view that psychological kinds (like propositional attitudes such as belief and desire) are reducible to neurological kinds. This theme is addressed most directly in "Special Sciences." As Fodor argues, to provide a theory of the mind, people should focus not on the neurological composition of the brain but rather on the functional organization of cognition. His reasons are not simply epistemological; that is, he is not simply arguing that people should not focus on the brain because their experimental access to it is limited in various respects. Rather, people need to focus on the functional organization because neurological theories cannot adequately account for the propositional attitudes.

Criticism of Dennet's "Intentional Stance"

As this suggests, Fodor is a realist about the propositional attitudes and a staunch champion of the folk psychological theory that posits them. Several of the articles in *RePresentations*, including both "Propositional Attitudes" and "Three Cheers for Propositional Attitudes," defend against antirealist views that seek to eliminate the propositional attitudes. "Three Cheers for Propositional Attitudes" is largely a criticism of some work by Daniel Dennett, particularly the consequences he draws from his "intentional stance." According to Dennett, in their interactions with other beings and objects, people can choose to adopt one of three different stances: the physical stance, the design stance, and the intentional stance.

When people adopt the physical stance toward something, they predict its behavior on the basis of its physical constitution; when they adopt the design stance, they predict its behavior on the basis of its purpose or design. In contrast, when they adopt the intentional stance toward something, they predict its behavior on the basis of what it would be rational for that thing to do. Which stance people adopt, according to Dennett, is a wholly pragmatic matter. This, however, implies that there are no intentional facts that correspond to the ascriptions people make when they adopt the intentional stance. Against this, Fodor argues that the reason that the intentional

stance is useful in making behavioral predictions about other beings, and in developing psychological theories, is that it is true. People are inclined to adopt the intentional stance toward their friends and neighbors not simply because it is pragmatically beneficial for them to do so but also because there is no other reasonable framework for them to use in making psychological generalizations.

Representational Theory of Mind

Fodor's criticism of Dennett is only one way in which he champions realism in *RePresentations*. Another linchpin in this defense is his representational theory of mind (RTM). This theory claims that the propositional attitudes should be understood in terms of relations to mental representations. (The theory is extensively defended in *The Language of Thought*, a book that was written at about the same time as the essays in *RePresentations*.) Because the mental representations have semantic content, the RTM provides an explanation of what it is for propositional attitudes to have representational content. It is important that, although such an explanation is not provided directly by functionalism, it is fully consistent with it. Moreover, the conjunction of RTM and functionalism is what constitutes Fodor's computationalist approach to the mind: Cognition can be understood as transformations on mental representations, and such transformations proceed based entirely on the syntactic properties of the symbols involved in such representations. Such symbols do, of course, have semantical properties, and Fodor thinks that there are important parallels between symbols' syntax and their semantics.

Several of the essays in *RePresentations* are rightly recognized as contemporary philosophical classics. Perhaps the most influential is "Methodological Solipsism Considered as a Research Strategy in Cognitive Psychology." This paper, along with Tyler Burge's "Individualism and the Mental" (1979), spawned a vast literature on the distinction between narrow and wide content and its ramifications. "What Psychological States Are Not" and Fodor's other writings on functionalism also generated a great deal of secondary literature. Though not every paper in the collection has made a similarly indelible mark on temporary philosophical discourse, each none-theless makes an important contribution to the development of contemporary philosophy of mind and cognitive science in general, and to the development of Fodor's own research program in particular.

Amy Kind

Additional Reading

Block, Ned, et al. "Commentary on 'Methodo-logical Solipsism Considered as a Research Strategy in Cognitive Psychology.'" *Behavioral and Brain Sciences* 3, no. 1 (March, 1980): 73-109. As is the practice of this journal, Fodor's article was followed by an open peer commen-tary. Altogether, there are twenty-five short es-says, contributed by philosophers and other cognitive scientists.

Dennett, Daniel. "The Logical Geography of Computational Approaches: A View from the East Pole," in *The Representation of Knowledge and Belief*, edited by Myles Brand and Robert M. Harnish. Tucson: University of Arizona Press, 1986. In this humorous and easy-to-read discussion of computational approaches to the mind, Dennett contrasts two extremes: High Church Computationalism and Zen Holism. He casts Fodor as the "archbishop" of the for-mer view.

Fodor, Jerry A. "The Folly of Simulation." In *Speaking Minds: Interviews with Twenty Eminent Cognitive Scientists*, edited by Peter Baumgart-ner and Sabine Payr. Princeton, N.J.: Princeton University Press, 1995. This interview with Fo-dor presents many of his views about the dis-cipline of cognitive science. The book in which the interview appears contains an extensive glossary of terms common to discussions of cognitive science.

Heil, John. "Functionalism and the Representa-tional Theory of Mind." In *Philosophy of Mind:*

A Contemporary Introduction. New York: Rout-ledge, 1998. This summary of the representa-tional theory of mind and the language of thought is especially well suited to the under-graduate philosophy student. In addition to providing an exposition of Fodor's views, it discusses some simple problems with such views. The chapter ends with suggestions for further reading.

Loewer, Barry, and Georges Rey, eds. *Meaning in Mind: Fodor and His Critics*. Oxford, England: Blackwell, 1986. The fourteen essays in this book constitute extensive critical commentary on many different aspects of Fodor's work. Following the essays, Fodor contributes a lengthy reply. The editors' introduction is a useful overview of Fodor's views, and the book contains a comprehensive bibliography of Fodor's works. Anyone who has come across Fodor's invocations of Granny in his work will be interested in the photograph of her that opens the book.

Sterelny, Kim. *The Representational Theory of Mind: An Introduction*. Oxford, England: Blackwell, 1990. In this work, designed to bridge the gap between introductory texts in philosophy of mind and scholarly literature, Sterelny de-fends both the representational theory of mind and the existence of a language of thought. In doing so, he makes frequent contact with Fo-dor's views on these subjects. Written in a style that should be accessible to undergraduates. Glossary.

Stich, Stephen. *From Folk Psychology to Cognitive Science: The Case Against Belief*. Cambridge, Mass.: MIT Press, 1983. In presenting a com-prehensive argument against folk psychology, Stich takes a critical look at much of Fodor's work. Chapters 3, 7, and 8 are especially rele-vant to Fodor.

Amy Kind

Michel Foucault

Foucault was a controversial thinker and theorist who examined structures of societal and political power in Western thought and how they related to discourse and language as well as to human sexuality.

Principal philosophical works: *Maladie mentale et personnalité*, 1954 (revised and expanded as *Maladie mentale et psychologie*, 1962; *Mental Illness and Psychology*, 1976); *Folie et déraison: Histoire de la folie à l'âge classique*, 1961 (*Madness and Civilization: A History of Insanity in the Age of Reason*, 1965); *Naissance de la clinique: Une Archéologie du regard médical*, 1963 (*The Birth of the Clinic: An Archaeology of Medical Perception*, 1973); *Raymond Roussel*, 1963 (English translation, 1978); *Les Mots et les choses: Une Archéologie des sciences humaines*, 1966 (*The Order of Things: An Archaeology of the Human Sciences*, 1970); *L'Archéologie du savoir*, 1969 (*The Archaeology of Knowledge*, 1972); *L'Ordre du discours*, 1971 (*The Discourse on Language*, 1971); *Surveiller et punir: Naissance de la prison*, 1975 (*Discipline and Punish: The Birth of the Prison*, 1977); *Histoire de la sexualité*, 1976-1984 (3 volumes; *The History of Sexuality*, 1978-1987, includes *La Volonté de savoir* [*An Introduction*], *L'Usage des plaisirs* [*The Use of Pleasure*], and *Souci de soi* [*The Care of the Self*]); *Language, Counter-Memory, Practice: Selected Essays and Interviews*, 1977; *Power/Knowledge: Selected Interviews and Other Writings, 1972-1977*, 1980.

Born: October 15, 1926; Poitiers, France
Died: June 25, 1984; Paris, France

Early Life

Michel Foucault was born on October 15, 1926, in Poitiers, France, into the middle-class family of Dr. Paul Foucault and his wife, the former Anne Malapert. After attending the local Catholic school, in 1944 the promising young scholar was sent to the Lycée Henri IV in Paris, where he prepared for the entrance examinations to the prestigious École Normale Supérieure. There and at the Sorbonne, he studied under Jean Hippolyte, a philosopher specializing in Georg Wilhelm Friedrich Hegel; Georges Canguilhem, a historian of science; and Louis Althusser, a Marxist theoretician interested in structuralist thought. Foucault received his undergraduate degrees in philosophy, in 1948, and in psychology, in 1950.

Perhaps as a result of Althusser's influence, Foucault became a member of the Communist Party, but he soon found its ideological rigidity too confining and resigned in 1951. He received his diploma in psychopathology from the Uni-

versity of Paris in 1952, and then—in an unusual step for a French intellectual of his time—embarked upon a period of teaching at foreign institutions. From 1953 to 1957, he was a member of the French department at the University of Uppsala in Sweden, then spent a year as director of the Warsaw Institut Français, and from 1959 to 1960, he occupied the same position at the Institut Français in Hamburg.

Life's Work

Foucault returned to France in 1960, taking up a professorship at the University of Clermont-Ferrand in Auvergne. He remained there until 1968, when he accepted a post at the University of Paris at Vincennes.

In the 1950's and early 1960's, Foucault's investigations into the history of how those classified as social or psychological deviants were perceived by their peers led to an interest in the nature of language. In books such as *Madness and Civilization* and *The Birth of the Clinic*, he conceptualized this understanding primarily in terms of power relationships similar to those hypothe-

Michel Foucault. *(Corbis/Bettmann-UPI)*

sized in Louis Althusser's epistemological Marxism and stressed the use of such institutions as agents of control and repression that exclude their inmates from meaningful participation in society.

The obvious political implications of such views made Foucault one of the heroes of France's would-be revolutionaries of 1968; they are also evident in his prominence as a defender of the rights of women, homosexuals, and other oppressed groups. After his 1970 appointment to the chair in the history of systems of thought at Collège de France in Paris, Foucault became something of a public figure, forming the Groupe d'Information sur les Prisons (group for information on prisons) as a spur to penal reform and campaigning vigorously for the rights of women and homosexuals.

Foucault's development took him well beyond the orthodoxies of the kind of Marxist social science so popular in Western culture during the 1950's and 1960's. Instead of simply accepting the idea that language is nothing more than a function of one class's dominance over another, Foucault considered how the strategies with which language is employed—those specific modes of discourse that appropriate words into highly technical vocabularies—are in fact the means of exercising power upon its subjects. In the 1977 work *Discipline and Punish*, he came to the conclusion that power is a set of techniques for organizing human knowledge; while not inconsistent with Marxist ideology, this idea was such an essentially intellectual construct that Foucault ceased to be considered a reliable friend of the Left. He criticized the repressive nature of the Eastern European bloc countries and became associated with the general wave of disillusionment with Communism so characteristic of French intellectual life in the 1970's and 1980's.

The key word in this reorientation of Foucault's thinking is "discourse," which he uses in the sense of language as rhetorical persuasion, as the determinant of the boundaries within which it speaks, and as the hidden workings of operations obscured by the superficial objectivity of its constituent words and sentences. It is when one tries to think about the concept of discourse—to discourse upon discourse, as it were—that one starts to break through to levels of meaning denied to those who take language at its face value. As Foucault puts it in *The Archaeology of Knowledge*:

> The question posed by language analysis of some discursive fact or other is always: according to what rules has a particular statement been made, and consequently according to what rules would other similar statements be made? The description of the events of discourse poses a quite different question: how is it that one particular statement appeared rather than another?

In undertaking such examinations, Foucault usually begins with paradoxes aimed at breaking down the conventional formulations of thinking on particular subjects. In *The Archaeology of Knowledge*, it is the supposed unity of the concepts of the book, the body of the author's work, and the author's character that he demolishes before proceeding onward; in volume 1 of *The History of Sexuality*, it is the detestation of sex attributed to the Victorians that attracts his subversive attentions. What he wants to do for any given branch of knowledge is "to account for the fact that it is spoken about, to discover who does the speaking, the positions and viewpoints from which they speak, the institutions which prompt people to speak about it and which store and distribute the things that are said. . . . The essential aim will not be to determine whether these discursive productions and these effects of power lead one to formulate the truth . . . but rather to bring out the 'will to knowledge' that serves as both their support and their instrument."

Foucault sees such assaults upon traditional modes of thought as a necessary prelude to those investigations of "positivity," of the material realities of history, which constitute the middle sections of his books. These typically range over an extraordinarily wide panorama of empirical evidence, display an erudition that reflects his extensive studies in philosophy and the social sciences, and make illuminating connections among phenomena that at first sight seem completely disparate. Because Foucault considers inherited notions about the need for logical coherence and linear organization as obstacles, and not aids, to knowledge, he presents his researches in an allusive, unrestrained manner that seems simply to break off rather than come to manifest conclusions. Although this method can be maddening for the reader expecting to be told what to think, it can also spark the kind of creative reordering of experience that results in genuinely fresh insights.

The problematic aspects of such a methodology are obvious and are squarely faced by Foucault himself. The possibility of an infinite regress of discourses—of discourses that merely recede into ever-murkier depths of disguised assumptions—certainly threatens his work, and he does his best to avoid it by striving for a discourse that

> is trying to operate a decentering that leaves no privilege to any centre . . . it does not set out to be a recollection of the original or a memory of the truth. On the contrary, its task is to make differences . . . it is continually making *differentiations*, it is a *diagnosis*.

Foucault's selection of specific pieces of evidence, which he wishes to be random and unrestrained, is also open to question: His belief that he is working outside conventional discourse may in fact simply mean that he is operating within an unconventional, but nevertheless constraining, discourse of his own, and he tends to assume that materials from the same historical period must exhibit the same fundamental characteristics. The openness of Foucault's approach ensures that he is always cognizant of these problems, although much of the debate about his work centers on the extent to which he has actually managed to transcend them.

In fact, Foucault's explorations of the history of madness, of prisons, and of sexuality—his probes into the subject matter of particular intellectual disciplines—have had relatively little influence on the disciplines themselves: It is not the world's psychiatrists, criminologists, and sexologists who have made Foucault's writings a basic unit of modern intellectual currency. It is in the humanities, and especially in philosophy and literary studies, that his ideas have been adopted as important sources of insight.

Foucault's interest in history and his use of historical materials as a means of examining an era's normative characteristics have strongly appealed to those postmodernists who resist philosopher Jacques Derrida's call for the complete deconstruction of texts. It is in his public disagreements with Derrida that Foucault has probably exercised his greatest degree of influence. These conflicts between Derrida's efforts to deconstruct history in order to set free its hidden possibilities and Foucault's attempts to experience history as a means of making explicit its latent structures have generated numerous scholarly commentaries, many of which seek either to reconcile or selectively choose from the work of these two French thinkers.

The difficulty of Foucault's style and the sheer complexity of his thought have tended to limit his direct influence to the realm of the university, and even there his work has often been dismissed as chaotic or useless by more traditional scholars.

Foucault's work centers on the nature of language rather than the nature of literature. He does not differentiate between literature and non-literature in ways that exalt the status of the former, and indeed, his writings tend to subvert traditional notions of literature's distinctive qualities. In addition, his researches almost always reflect a spirit of open-ended inquiry rather than a search for absolute truths. He accepts paradox as a source of potentially valuable insights and is never ashamed to admit that he has changed his mind.

When he died on June 25, 1984, from a rare neurological disorder that he had kept a secret from all but his closest friends, he was engaged in making major revisions to the first volume of *The History of Sexuality*, a fact that underlines his commitment to projects that would in a sense always remain unfinished.

Influence

Foucault had a profound effect on philosophy and literary theory. His probing into the historical archaeology of human culture places great emphasis on the forces operating behind the concepts of "discourse" and "the word." Foucault's well-publicized disagreements with Derrida have served as the starting point for many a book and article, and literary critics such as Frank Lentricchia, Timothy Reiss, Michel Serres, and Edward Said have acknowledged Foucault as a source of fruitful ideas and suggestions.

Paul Stuewe

Power/Knowledge

Selected Interviews and Other Writings, 1972-1977

Type of philosophy: Ethics, social philosophy
First published: 1980
Principal ideas advanced:

◇ In the modern era, power manifests itself not as a visible force emanating from a central authority, or sovereign, but as an invisible web of material and ideological relations.
◇ Power is not merely a mode of repression but a productive, creative force.
◇ The individual, or the self, is a product of power; power lacks a subject.

◇ Since the eighteenth century, new forms of knowledge—particularly the human sciences—have served as the vehicle for the development of new and more insidious methods of control, which function not through command and obedience but through normalization.
◇ Truth is a function of power; power is fashioned by and circulated through the discourses of truth.
◇ The modern idea of sexuality is a part of the new technology of control through normalization.

Power/Knowledge is a loosely related collection of writings and interviews that cover a crucial transitional period in Michel Foucault's development as a thinker and theorist of power—his enduring theme. Three distinct periods can be discerned in his work. The first, which begins in the late 1950's and continues roughly until the late 1960's, may be called the "archaeological" period—a term that Foucault himself used to characterize his early methodology. The principal book of this phase is his *Les Mots et les choses: Une Archéologie des sciences humaines* (1966; *The Order of Things: An Archaeology of the Human Sciences*, 1970). In this work, Foucault is concerned primarily with the investigation of communities of discourse and the way in which particular languages or disciplinary codes define those communities. This early phase in his work is heavily influenced by structuralism, especially by the structuralist emphasis upon *synchronic* rather than *diachronic* modes of analysis. This privileging of space over time, paradigm over progress continues in the second phase of Foucault's work; however, after 1968 he gradually abandoned his earlier claims for the primacy of discourse.

In the second, or "genealogical" phase, Foucault's emphasis shifted to an examination of power. The principal book of this second period is *Surveiller et punir: Naissance de la prison* (1975; *Discipline and Punish: The Birth of the Prison*, 1977). In that work, "genealogy," as adapted from philosopher Friedrich Nietzsche, refers to an investigative method that assumes that "truth," wherever it appears, is always relative to an order of power. Now discourse is but one among an array of social practices that may all be understood as matrices of power.

Finally, in the last years of his life, Foucault did not so much abandon the genealogical method as adapt it for political and moral purposes. This period, which may be termed Foucault's "ethical" phase, is concerned above all with the modern notion of sexuality and its origins in Christian ideas of the self. The principal work of this final period is *Histoire de la sexualité* (1976-1984, 3 volumes; *The History of Sexuality*, 1978-1987). Although most of the interviews and essays in *Power/Knowledge* focus on the second and third phases of Foucault's career, the reader will also find useful clarifications of the early research.

A Theory of Power

Chapter 5 of *Power/Knowledge*, two lectures delivered in France in 1976, serves as an overview of Foucault's genealogical research. In this chapter, Foucault, in a retrospective mood, attempts to explain the evolution of his theory of power. In the first of these lectures, he outlines the breakup after World War II of all the totalizing political and ideological systems dating from the Enlightenment. The status of the term "knowledge" has been profoundly altered. The privilege once bestowed upon universal, hierarchical, and essentialist knowledge claims is now disrupted by what Foucault calls an irruption of "subjugated knowledges." Subjugated knowledge is knowledge under the signs of the repressed, the marginal, the fragmented, and above all, the local. Subjugated knowledges are those voices or traditions that were silenced by the discourses of modernity. Foucault implies that such repressed or degraded knowledge has already begun to sprout through the cracks in the once-shining façade of the Age of Reason; however, he also argues the need for critical, erudite researchers such as himself, molelike students of hidden knowledge who will burrow deep beneath the foundations of progressivist historiography to uncover the irrational, the discontinuous, and the uncanny. Such an antifoundationalist history, or genealogy, Foucault believes, will serve an emancipatory purpose; it will liberate local knowledge and local histories from the oblivion to which the dominant theoretical paradigms have consigned them.

In these lectures, Foucault rejects the Marxist tendency to reduce all relations of power to economic terms as well as the more traditional analyses that focus on questions of sovereignty and contract, examining, for example, in whom authority is vested and what the rights of the sovereign, state, and individual are. Foucault instead puts a Nietzschean spin on Prussian army officer Karl von Clausewitz's well-known dictum that war is politics continued by other means. In fact, he reverses the dictum: Power, claims Foucault, is war continued by other means. The radical move here is essentially to refuse any reduction of the essence of power, that is, to refuse to explain it as the secondary effect of some other more fundamental principle or mechanism. Power resides not so much in the vested rights of sovereigns or individuals but instead "circulates" in society in a much less tangible but all the more pervasive manner. Genealogists should concern themselves not with the way in which one individual dominates another, with how "rights" can be adjudicated, but with how power is embodied in institutions not obviously political, in material practices and techniques such as the methods of, for example, psychiatry. Most provocatively, Foucault argues that the traditional approach is most deeply flawed when it assumes that power is the prerogative of the individual will, that power is a manifestation of a unified subject or stable identity. The reality, he suggests, is that subjects (individuals, selves) are *constituted* by power; that is, stable identities, unified selves, are in fact the necessary fictions of power as it shapes people through a matrix of social and bodily relations.

Prisons

The manner in which power in the modern age manifests itself through institutions of normalization is discussed extensively in chapters 2 and 3 of *Power/Knowledge*, both of which consist of interviews conducted in 1975, the year of the French publication of *Discipline and Punish*—Foucault's study of the modern penal system and the manner in which it evolved from a system of punishment to one of disciplinary surveillance. In these interviews, Foucault responds to his critics and attempts to clarify and elaborate upon the arguments found in that work. Central to his thesis is the notion that the appearance of the idea of prison reform in the early nineteenth century corresponds to (and is covertly linked to) the decline of sovereign authority in the person of the monarch. Traditional criminal punishment was, he notes in chapter 2 ("Prison Talk"), an exercise of power from above; every form of criminality was, in essence, a threat to the sovereign. Thus punishment was conceived as exemplary vengeance. With the rise of democratic states and the decentralization of political authority, punishment ceases to be conceived of as vengeance and is, instead, promoted as reform. Although it is often thought that the movement for prison reform arose only after certain abuses had become apparent, Foucault argues that the discourse of reform was apparent from the very inception of the modern prison. Further, reform functioned principally through methods of surveillance, a term that signifies for Foucault the paradigm for the new methods of power and control that were emerging alongside the prisons—in medical and psychiatric practices, in hospitals, in schools, in the military, and elsewhere.

In chapter 8, "The Eye of Power," an interview first published as the preface to a 1977 French edition of Jeremy Bentham's *Panopticon* (1791), Foucault elaborates upon the importance of prison surveillance as a testing ground or model (one of several) for the methods of observation and control that would later become the norm in advanced technological societies. The title of Bentham's work refers to an ingenious architectural plan for the observation of prisoners that Bentham hoped to see implemented in England. The plan consisted of a central observation tower and a circular, walled enclosure honeycombed with individual cells. Each cell contained two windows: one facing the inner tower, another facing outward. From the central tower, the overseers were able to monitor every movement of the prisoners, each isolated in his virtually transparent cell. Although the panopticon as he envisioned it was never constructed, Bentham's plan was widely studied in the nineteenth century and inspired many similar plans for the construction, not only of prisons but also of schools, hospitals, and military housing. For Foucault, the importance of Bentham's plan was its effectiveness as a metaphor for the Enlightenment's preoccupation with visibility or transparency. In France, philosopher Jean-Jacques Rousseau and the ideological founders of the Revolution dreamed of a society in which all vestiges of medieval darkness had been removed, not only the darkness of unreason and superstition but also the hidden and secret places of the aristocratic regime—places in which repressive power might reside undetected by the masses. Bentham's dream, according to Foucault, is also one of total visibility in society (for which the panopticon is a microcosm), but visibility organized explicitly to serve the ends of a centralized power or overseer. Surveillance, then, became one of the chief means of effecting political control. Just as the prisoner under the constant gaze of the overseers would, it was thought, learn to habituate himself to the disciplinary norms of prison life, so also common soldiers, students, or psychiatric patients under a similar scrutiny would habituate themselves to the new behavioral norms of modern society.

Sexuality and the Self

The final chapters of *Power/Knowledge*, particularly chapter 10, "The History of Sexuality," indicate the new direction that Foucault's research had begun to take in the final years of his life. Certainly there is a shift away from genealogy understood as the study of how subjects (selves) are fashioned and constrained by institutions; but the genealogical method is not so much abandoned as adapted to the study of how subjects are fashioned vis-à-vis self-imposed ethical codes or systems. More particularly, the shift involves a movement away from the study of power toward the study of the origins of modern sexuality which, at least since psychoanalyst Sigmund Freud, has been the primary source for the individual's self-understanding. In other words, Foucault is arguing that modern notions of the self cannot be properly understood outside a genealogy of *sexual ethics*. What is most radical in Foucault's inquiry into the history of sexuality is his claim that sexuality as such is in fact not some state of nature but a social *invention* of recent vintage. His thesis reverses the romantic claim that subjects somehow possess an inherent, biologically given sexual role that is closely related to the truth of one's innermost nature. Foucault seeks to destroy this fundamental idea of a unique inner nature that can be explored, with the help of experts, and liberated from repressive external forces, that is, societal conventions, religious taboos. On the contrary, he argues, human sexuality (or any other expression of this supposed inner nature) is the *effect* of those same conventions. Moreover, when twentieth century subjects turn to the enormous variety of therapies and techniques that promise liberation from the repressive taboos of the past, they are deluded. For such techniques provide not liberation, not some release of an authentic self, but subtler control of the self.

The idea of an inviolable interiority requiring expert assistance (as in psychoanalysis) to be uncovered in its pristine state, Foucault traces ultimately back to late antiquity (the Stoics) but especially to Christianity. For it is out of Christianity that the idea of a uniquely created soul destined for eternal life emerges with greatest clarity. Furthermore, it is the Christian church of the Middle Ages that, in the confessional, first developed that mode of interrogation of the self that may be understood as a precursor of Freudian psychoanalysis. What both have in common, Foucault suggests, is the assumption of a certain interiority, a "depth" within the confines of the self that must be questioned and stripped of the trappings of culture and convention. In both cases, however, the assumption of such an inner sanctum deludes people and encourages them in the belief that the self is somehow autonomous (an a priori essence) when in fact it is merely the product, always and everywhere, of power.

Foucault's Impact

Although *Power/Knowledge* cannot be regarded as one of Foucault's seminal works, it has nonetheless exerted a significant influence across a number of disciplines. One reason for this influence is the timing of the work, appearing as it does at a crucial moment of transition between the middle and late phases of his career. Another reason is that *Power/Knowledge* is far more accessible than most of Foucault's texts, probably because of the exigencies of the interview format. In this regard, it is also worth noting that the interview is a highly regarded genre in French intellectual circles and is often used by scholars to introduce major clarifications and/or qualifications of earlier work, as well as to outline plans for works in progress. In the English-speaking world, *Power/Knowledge* is among Foucault's most often cited texts.

Because Foucault's work, including *Power/ Knowledge*, is transdisciplinary, its impact has been impressively broad. Disciplines as diverse as historiography, philosophy, political theory, geography, art history, literary criticism, sociology, and linguistics all have practitioners whose research and teaching reflect the influence of Foucault's powerful adaptation of Nietzsche's genealogical mode of analysis. The influence of *Power/Knowledge* has been especially evident among British and American literary critics. It is no exaggeration to say that the so-called New Historicism, the most prominent school of American literary theory in the 1990's, would not have been possible without Foucault's notion that literary works are not themselves autonomous aesthetic objects but rather the products of discursive networks of power.

Jack Trotter

Additional Reading

Arac, Jonathan, ed. *After Foucault: Humanistic Knowledge, Postmodern Challenges*. New Brunswick, N.J.: Rutgers University Press, 1988. This book contains essays on Michel Foucault presented in 1985, the year after Foucault's death, at a conference sponsored by the Institute for the Humanities of the University of Illinois at Chicago. Includes bibliography and index.

Barker, Phillip. *Michel Foucault: An Introduction*. Edinburgh: Edinburgh University Press, 1998. This book provides an introduction to Foucault and his thought. Includes bibliographies and an index.

Bernauer, James William. *Michel Foucault's Force of Flight: Toward an Ethics for Thought*. Contemporary Studies in Philosophy and the Human Sciences series. Atlantic Highlands, N.J.: Humanities Press International, 1990. This work, part of a series on modern philosophers, examines Foucault's views on ethics in the twentieth century. Includes bibliography.

Boyne, Roy. *Foucault and Derrida: The Other Side of Reason*. London: Unwin Hyman, 1990. This volume looks at the ongoing debate between Foucault and deconstructionist Jacques Derrida. Includes bibliographical references and index.

Davidson, Arnold I. *Foucault and His Interlocutors.* Chicago: University of Chicago Press, 1997. This book includes essays by several French thinkers who were influenced by Foucault. These authors take up the breadth of Foucault's life's work and provide a firm foundation by which to understand his writing.

Foucault, Michel, ed. *I, Pierre Riviere, Having Slaughtered My Mother, My Sister, and My Brother . . . : A Case of Parricide in the Nineteenth Century.* Lincoln: University of Nebraska Press, 1990. A literal account of the murder of a family by a "madman" that simultaneously analyzes the "murder" of free will and responsibility.

Nehamas, Alexander. *Art of Living: Socratic Reflections from Plato to Foucault.* Berkeley: University of California Press, 1998. Nehamas focuses on the importance of Socrates to Foucault and produces an accessible evaluation of the idea of personhood as described by each.

Howard Z. Fitzgerald

Viktor Emil Frankl

Frankl turned his experiences as a prisoner in Nazi concentration camps into an enduring work of survival literature and originated logotherapy, a existential system of psychological treatment emphasizing that the search for meaning in life is the key to psychological health.

Principal philosophical works: *Trotzdem Ja zum Lebel sagen*, 2d ed., 1947; *Zeit und Verantwortung*, 1947; *Ärztliche Seelsorge*, 4th ed., 1947 (*The Doctor and the Soul: An Introduction to Logotherapy*, 1955; also published as *The Doctor and the Soul: From Psychotherapy to Logotherapy*, 1965); *Ein Psycholog erlebt das Konzentrationslager*, 1946 (*From Death-Camp to Existentialism: A Psychiatrist's Path to a New Therapy*, 1959; revised and enlarged as *Man's Search for Meaning: An Introduction to Logotherapy*, 1962); *Logos and Existenz*, 1951; *Theorie and Therapie der neurosen: Einführung in Logotherapie and Existenz-analyse*, 1956; *Das Menschenbild der Seelenheilkunde*, 1959; *Die Psychotherapie in der Praxis*, 1961; *Der umbewusste Gott*, 1966 (*The Unconscious God: Psychotherapy and Theology*, 1975); *Psychotherapy and Existentialism: Selected Papers on Logotherapy*, 1967 (with James C. Crumbaugh, Hans O. Gerz, and Leonard T. Maholick); *The Will to Meaning: Foundations and Applications to Logotherapy*, 1969; *Psychotherapie für Jedermann*, 1971; *Der Wille zum Sinn: Ausgewaehlte Vortraeger über Logotherapie*, 1972; *The Unheard Cry for Meaning: Psychotherapy and Humanism*, 1979.

Born: March 26, 1905; Vienna, Austria
Died: September 2, 1997; Vienna, Austria

Early Life

Born and raised in Vienna, Austria, Viktor Emil Frankl was the middle child of Gabriel Frankl, a high-ranking civil servant, and Elsa Lion, a descendant of Jewish religious leaders. Frankl described his family, religiously observant middle-class Jews, as close and warm. In an autobiography, he described his early life as safe and secure, even amid the upheaval caused by World War I, which broke out when he was nine years old.

As early as age three, Frankl decided to become a physician. As a teenager, he did brilliantly in his studies, including a course in Freudian theory that prompted him to write to Sigmund Freud. A correspondence ensued, and in one letter, he included a two-page letter on mimicry that Freud forwarded to the *International Journal of Psychoanalysis*, which published it three years later. At age nineteen, Frankl was walking through a Viennese park when he saw a man with an old hat, a torn coat, a silver-handled walking stick, and a face he recognized from photographs. It was none other than Freud himself. Frankl began to introduce himself but was interrupted when the man stated Frankl's exact address. The founder of psychoanalysis had remembered the young man's name and address from their earlier correspondence.

Frankl studied medicine at the University of Vienna, where he broke from his initial attraction to Freudian theory and began studying psychoanalysis under Alfred Adler. However, he came to disagree with Adler's position that people do not have the freedom of choice and willpower to overcome their problems. In 1927, a schism in the Society for Individual Psychology, an association of Adlerians, led to the breakdown of Frankl's relationship with Adler and to his expulsion from the group.

Life's Work

Frankl began working as a psychotherapist even before he graduated in 1930 and continued to work at the University of Vienna for two years before going on staff at the Am Steinhof Psychiatric Hospital in Vienna, where he worked with suicidal female patients. While there, he developed his theory that behavior is driven by a subconscious and conscious need to find meaning and purpose. In 1937, he went into private practice and began writing articles on this theory.

At this time, anti-Semitism was on the rise in Europe. After the invasion of Austria in 1938, Frankl, like other Jewish professionals, tried desperately to obtain a visa that would enable him to work in the United States. Finally, in 1941, he was offered the visa, but with the provision that only he would be allowed to leave. His elderly parents would have to stay behind. Frankl knew that his parents would be sent to a concentration camp if he left, so he risked his life by letting his visa lapse.

Viktor Frankl. *(Archive Photos/Reuters/Herwig Prammer)*

In 1940, Frankl began working at the Rothschild Hospital in Vienna, at that time Austria's only hospital still employing Jewish staff. While there, he managed to save numerous psychiatric patients from euthanasia by falsifying diagnoses (for example, labeling schizophrenia as aphasia or depression as fever-induced delirium) and thus certifying the patients as eligible for nursing home care.

For a time, Frankl's work at Rothschild kept him from being sent to a concentration camp and permitted him to keep his parents with him. In December, 1941, Frankl married Mathilde Frosser, a nurse. They were among the last couples allowed to wed at the National Office for Jewish Marriage, a bureau set up by the Nazis. One month later, in 1942, Frankl was arrested and deported to Theresienstadt, a Nazi concentration camp. Around this time, his entire family, except one sister who had already left the country, was deported to concentration camps. Expecting the roundup, his wife had sewn the book that he had written on his theory into the lining of his coat. The Nazis destroyed it along with all his other possessions. They also separated him from his family and killed his pregnant wife, his brother, and both parents. Frankl spent a total of three years at Auschwitz, Dachau, and other camps.

While imprisoned, Frankl noticed that some prisoners seemed to will themselves to die, while others suffering equally from brutality, disease, and starvation struggled to survive. He helped save many prisoners from dangerous despair, doing his best to reassure them that human life is meaningful under any circumstances. He urged that they "not lose hope but should keep their courage in the certainty that the hopelessness of our struggle did not detract from its dignity and meaning." He also attempted to restore their inner strength by showing them some future goal. His idea was that "it did not really matter what we expected from life, but rather what life expected from us."

In the concentration camp, Frankl recreated his book, writing notes on pilfered paper with a pencil stub given by a fellow prisoner as a present for his fortieth birthday. Released in 1945, Frankl wrote about his death-camp experiences and his logotherapeutic system from those notes. The resulting book, *Man's Search for Meaning*, was published in 1946. At the urging of friends, Frankl reluctantly agreed at the last minute to include his name on the title page, having originally planned to publish it anonymously. At the time of his death, it had been reprinted seventy-three times, translated into twenty-four languages, and used as a text in high schools and universities, and it had sold more than 10 million copies. In a 1991 survey by the Library of Congress and the Book-of-the-Month Club, people who regarded themselves as lifetime general-interest readers rated it as one of the ten most influential books they had ever read.

In 1947, after the Red Cross verified that his first wife had indeed been killed in the camp, Frankl married Eleanor Schwindt, with whom he would have a daughter. In 1949, he earned a Ph.D. in psychiatry, having returned to the University of Vienna as head of the Department of Neurology, a position he held for twenty-five years. In 1970, he started working at U.S. International University, a position he held until his retirement, although he took several visiting professorships throughout these years.

Despite the broad popularity of his book, the application of his theories into a distinct school of psychotherapy was slow in coming. Perhaps one reason was the wartime interruption and the lingering effects of anti-Semitism in Vienna at a critical point in his career. Perhaps another reason was that Frankl concentrated more on writing and lecturing than in developing followers among his therapist contemporaries. Interest in his approach to therapy increased after fellow concentration camp prisoner Joseph B. Fabry, who moved to the United States and became a successful lawyer, founded the Viktor Frankl Institute of Logotherapy in Berkeley, California, in 1977. Logotherapy societies have been established in twenty-two countries in Europe, Asia, North and South America, and Africa.

In the postwar years, Frankl wrote thirty-three other books on his theories of theoretical and clinical psychology. He also wrote on a variety of religious and spiritual issues as well as on other topics related to people, including love, sex, de-

pression, and hunger in the Third World. Toward the end of his life, he voiced an opposition to physician-assisted suicide. He believed that the physician should act as an agent of the sick person's will to live and as supporter of the patient's right to live. This duty, Frankl believed, remains binding, even when the physician confronts a patient who has attempted suicide and whose life now hangs by a thread.

Frankl was a visiting professor at Harvard University, Stanford University, Southern Methodist University, and Duquesne University. He lectured at more than one hundred colleges and universities in the United States, Australia, and Africa. He was recognized by many organizations in many countries for his life's work. He received more than twenty-five honorary doctorates, and other honors including the Oskar Pfister Award from the American Association of Psychiatrists, the John F. Kennedy Star, the Albert Schweitzer Medal, and the City of Vienna Prize for Science.

Frankl's logotherapy is often referred to as the Third Viennese School of Psychotherapy, Freud's psychoanalysis being the first and Adler's individual psychology being the second. Logotherapy represents a major change from the strictures of Freud and Adler, who attributed neuroses to, respectively, sexual repression and unconscious conflicts and unfilled desires for power and feelings of inferiority. To Frankl, behavior is driven by a need for meaning. Also in contrast to many other schools of psychotherapy, which focus on patients' inner lives or drives, logotherapy requires the patient to make connections with the outside world in order to find fulfillment. In addition, logotherapy differs from many other systems of psychotherapy in its belief that individuals have the power to control their own actions and reactions and are not at the mercy of unconscious forces or environmental contingencies.

Lillian M. Range

Man's Search for Meaning

Type of philosophy: Ethics, existentialism, philosophical psychology

First published: Ein Psycholog erlebt das Konzentra-tionslager, 1946 (*From Death-Camp to Existential-ism: A Psychiatrist's Path to a New Therapy*, 1959; revised and enlarged as *Man's Search for Mean-ing: An Introduction to Logotherapy*, 1962)

Principal ideas advanced:

◇ People possess an innate "will to meaning."

◇ The search for significance in one's life is the key to psychological well-being.

◇ The primary cause of neurotic behavior is an inability to find meaning.

◇ Even tragic suffering can be turned into a hu-man achievement by if one adopts the right attitude.

◇ Life involves each individual's taking the re-sponsibility to find the right answer to life's problems and to fulfill the tasks that life con-stantly sets.

◇ People are capable of controlling their actions and reactions; they are not at the mercy of their unconscious or external contingencies.

A version of this largely autobiographical book was originally written while Viktor Emil Frankl was director of the Department of Neurology at the University of Vienna. The book was lost when he was forced into a concentration camp, and he re-created the book by writing notes on pilfered strips of paper while he was imprisoned for three years in four different Nazi concentration camps, including Auschwitz and Dachau. The book con-sists of two parts: a description of life in the con-centration camps and people's reactions to that life and an explanation of logotherapy.

Life in a Concentration Camp

In the first part of *Man's Search for Meaning*, Frankl describes the daily humiliation and vio-lence that stripped many people of their dignity and their very humanity in the concentration camps and of his own struggle to maintain a sense of meaning in the face of such brutality. He did so primarily by focusing on his wife, with whom he held imaginary conversations; on the work he hoped to resume after leaving the camp; and on the rare acts by some of those in charge that demonstrated, if not kindness, at least a rela-tive absence of malice. Along with these personal recollections, Frankl presents the inmates' reac-tion to camp life during its three phases: the pe-

riod following incarceration, the period of be-coming entrenched in camp routine, and the pe-riod following release and liberation.

Following incarceration, most inmates suf-fered from shock. In some cases, shock preceded the formal incarceration, and it was often accom-panied by delusions of reprieve. As all illusions were destroyed, most inmates were overcome by a grim sense of humor. Another common sensa-tion was curiosity; the inmates' minds somehow detached from their surroundings, which came to be regarded with a kind of objectivity. Most peo-ple entertained the thought of suicide, at least briefly.

During the second phase, when inmates be-came entrenched in camp routine, they often de-scended from a denial of their situation into a stage of apathy and the beginning of a kind of emotional death. As their illusions dropped away and their hopes died, they watched others perish without experiencing any emotion. At first, the lack of feeling served as a protective shield. Then, however, many prisoners plunged with surpris-ing suddenness into depressions so deep that the sufferers could not move, wash themselves, or leave the barracks to join a forced march. No entreaties, no blows, no threats had any effect. No one could extricate them. There was a link, Frankl found, between their loss of faith in the future and this dangerous giving up. Some inma-tes, however, were able to discover meaning in their lives, if only in helping one another through the day. These discoveries gave them the will and strength to endure.

For Frankl, the only meaning in his camp life was to help his fellow inmates restore their psy-chological health. He believed that he had to learn himself and teach the despairing men that it did not matter what he expected from life but rather what life expected from him. He described a day when he became disgusted with the fact that his mind was totally preoccupied with the trivialities of camp life. To overcome this preoc-cupation, he forced himself to think of another subject: He imagined giving a lecture on the psy-chology of camp life. "Both I and my troubles became the object of an interesting psychoscienti-fic study undertaken by myself." One way that Frankl helped others was to attempt to prevent suicides. Nazi jailers forbade prisoners from interfering with a suicide attempt. For example, no one could cut down a man attempting to hang himself. Therefore, Frankl's goal was to prevent the act before the attempt. Healthy prisoners such as Frankl would remind the despondent person that life expected something from them. For example, perhaps a child waited for the individual outside prison, or work remained to be completed. Thus, healthy prisoners taught others not to talk about food when starvation was a daily threat and to hide a crust of bread in a pocket to stretch out the nourishment. They urged others to joke, sing, take mental photographs of sunsets, and replay valued thoughts and memories.

Frankl maintained that it was essential to keep practicing the art of living, even in a concentration camp. "We needed to stop asking about the meaning of life but instead to think of ourselves as those who were being questioned by life, daily and hourly. Our answer must consist not in talk and medication, but in right action and in right conduct. Life ultimately means taking the responsibility to find the right answer to its problems and to fulfill the tasks which it constantly sets for each individual."

The third stage began at liberation. Initially, although most inmates experienced total relaxation when they learned they would be released, they were not particularly pleased or joyful. They had lost the ability to experience these emotions and had to relearn them slowly. One continuing danger was to their moral and spiritual health. Finally free, some inmates thought that they should use their freedom licentiously and ruthlessly. Two other dangers to their moral and spiritual health were bitterness and disillusionment upon returning to former lives.

Logotherapy
In the second part of the book, Frankl sketches his view of psychotherapy, which he termed "logotherapy" from the Greek word "logos," or "meaning." Logotherapy focuses on the meaning of human existence and on people's search for such meaning. It teaches that even the tragic and negative aspects of life, such as unavoidable suffering, can be turned into a human achievement by the attitude that people adopt toward their predicament.

Logotherapy attempts to offer solutions to human concerns as they exist in the moment rather than trying to locate their roots in the past as in Freudian psychiatry. A central tenet is that to live is to suffer and to survive is to find meaning in the suffering. Further, each person must find a purpose; no one can tell another what this purpose is. Each person's meaning is unique and specific in that it must and can be fulfilled by that person alone; only then does it achieve a significance that will satisfy the individual. If one succeeds at this task, one will continue to grow in spite of all indignities.

A person's "will to meaning," or will to find meaning, can be frustrated so that the person experiences what Frankl termed "existential frustration." Existential frustration in itself is neither pathological nor pathogenic. For example, an American diplomat came to see Frankl after five years of treatment with an analyst in New York. The analyst attributed the patient's continuing problems with U.S. policy to the fact that the patient viewed the U.S. government and his superiors as father images. Consequently, the analyst believed the patient's job dissatisfaction was due to his unconscious hatred toward his father. After seeing Frankl for a few sessions, the patient changed jobs. Frankl viewed this treatment as neither psychotherapy nor logotherapy. This patient actually longed to be in some other kind of work; he remained contented in his new occupation more than five years later, when Frankl made his final follow-up. Frankl's view was that not every conflict is neurotic. Similarly, suffering is not always pathological, especially if the suffering flows out of existential frustration.

Because the goal of logotherapy is to help individuals find the hidden meaning in their life, it is an analytical process. The search may arouse inner tension rather than inner equilibrium. This tension is inherent in the human being and is an indispensable prerequisite of mental health. What people need is not a tensionless state but rather the striving and struggling for a worthwhile goal, a freely chosen task. For example, Frankl believed that the goal of recreating his manuscript should he ever be liberated was a force that helped him live through the rigors of concentration camp life.

Conversely, Frankl believed that existential vacuum was a widespread phenomenon of the twentieth century. One reason for this vacuum is the loss of basic animal instincts, which provide security. Because these instincts are lost, people have to make choices. Further, people have suffered the loss of traditions to buttress their behavior. No instinct tells people what to do; no traditions tell people what they ought to do. Evidence of this vacuum is boredom. Boredom causes more psychological troubles than distress. For example, "Sunday neurosis" is a kind of depression that afflicts people who become aware of the lack of content in their lives when the rush of the busy week is over and the void within themselves becomes apparent.

In the search for meaning, abstract answers are irrelevant. Everyone has a specific vocation, or mission in life, to carry out a concrete assignment that demands fulfillment. Logotherapy sees the very essence of human existence in responsibility and tries to make patients fully aware of their responsibility. Therefore, the logotherapist imposes no value judgments on patients and refuses to let the patient pass the responsibility of judging to the logotherapist. Patients must decide whether to interpret life's task as being responsible to society or to their own conscience. The logotherapist's role is to widen and broaden the visual field of the patient so that the whole spectrum of potential meaning becomes conscious and visible.

According to logotherapy, people can discover the meaning in life in three ways: first, by creating a work or doing a deed; second, by experiencing something or encountering someone; and third, by adopting an appropriate attitude toward unavoidable suffering. The first way is self-explanatory. The second way may involve experiencing a quality such as goodness, truth, or beauty or something concrete such as nature and culture. Additionally, it may involve experiencing the uniqueness of another human being and loving that person. Love is the only way to grasp another human being in the innermost core of personality. No one can become fully aware of the very essence of another human being without loving that person. Love enables people to see the essential traits and features of the beloved person as well as that person's potential. Love

fosters actualization and enables potentialities to become realities. The third way involves bearing witness to the uniquely human potential at its best by transforming a personal tragedy into a triumph and turning one's predicament into a human achievement.

One procedure that Frankl advocated to accomplish his goals in logotherapy was to make use of the specifically human capacity for self-detachment. This basic capacity to detach, called paradoxical intention, enables patients to put themselves at a distance from their neuroses. The use of this technique is demonstrated in Frankl's treatment of a bookkeeper. This man had previously been treated extensively but unsuccessfully for writer's cramp, which had become so severe that he was in danger of losing his job. The logotherapist recommended that instead of trying to write neatly and legibly, he should write with the worst possible scrawl. Paradoxically, he was unable to do so, because as soon as he tried to write in this way, his writer's cramp disappeared.

Unlike many European existentialists, Frankl was neither pessimistic nor antireligious. On the contrary, he took a surprisingly hopeful view of people's capacity to transcend their predicament and discover an adequate guiding truth. His widely critically acclaimed book, *Man's Search for Meaning*, helped broaden postwar thinking and exploration in psychology. It introduced logotherapy as a new existential approach to psychotherapy and focused on the spiritual dimension of the human psyche, previously ignored by most psychotherapists. It challenged people to face their problems and find meaning in their individual lives. Discovering meaning is what gave concentration camp inmates the will and strength to endure and is what Frankl recommends for all people.

Lillian M. Range

Additional Reading

Belkin, Gary S. *Contemporary Psychotherapies*. 2d ed. Monterey, Calif.: Brooks/Cole, 1987. This text presents the current major systems of psychotherapy and offers, through clinical case studies, realistic examples of each. Landmark cases are presented by well-known therapists, including Viktor Frankl. This book is directed to the introductory student or clinical trainee who is interested in understanding the nomenclature, major theoretical constructs, and day-to-day workings in contemporary psychotherapy.

Drapela, Victor J. *A Review of Personality Theories*. Springfield, Ill.: Charles C Thomas, 1987. This text explores the major theories of personality, including Frankl's. Each chapter contains a study guide to review the salient points of the personality theory discussed and suggestions to apply these concepts to professional counseling practice. Explanatory drawings used throughout the text lend a degree of concreteness to the abstract ideas.

Fabry, Joseph B. *The Pursuit of Meaning: Viktor Frankl, Logotherapy, and Life*. New York: Pocket Books, 1968. Rev. ed. Foreword by Viktor E. Frankl. New York: Harper & Row, 1980. Fabry, a fellow concentration camp survivor and founder of the Viktor Frankl Institute of Logotherapy in Berkeley, California, writes cogently about Frankl's life and work.

Gould, William Blair. *Viktor E. Frankl: Life with Meaning*. Pacific Grove, Calif.: Brooks/Cole, 1993. An important treatment of Frankl's contributions to philosophy.

Hoeller, Keith, ed. *Readings in Existential Psychology and Psychiatry*. Atlantic Highlands, N.J.: Humanities Press International, 1992. The volume begins with basic theoretical considera-tions and proceeds immediately to the practice of psychotherapy. The chapters deal with major issues raised by existential psychology and are arranged in alphabetical order from "Anxiety" to "Will." It is meant to serve both as an introduction to the field and as a refresher for the expert.

Lantz, James E. *Existential Family Therapy: Using the Concepts of Viktor Frankl*. Northvale, N.J.: Jason Aronson, 1993. This volume consists of twelve revised classic papers on existential family therapy, Franklian family therapy, and family logotherapy that were published in the fifteen years before the book's publication. The book is intended for mental health practitioners who wish to help families discover the meaning of life as a primary part of the treatment process.

Meier, Levi, ed. *Jewish Values in Bioethics*. New York: Human Sciences Press, 1986. In this insightful volume, the dilemmas posed by medical ethics are thoroughly explored by leading physicians, clinicians, ethicists, and clergy. Edited by a noted rabbi-psychotherapist, these essays integrate the advances of modern medicine with the wisdom of traditional Jewish ethics and scholarship. This book is directed toward physicians, bioethicists, attorneys, rabbis, and mental health professionals as well as laypersons.

Lillian M. Range

Gottlob Frege

Frege is the founder of modern symbolic logic and the creator of the first system of notations and quantifiers of modern logic.

Principal philosophical works: *Begriffsschrift: Eine der arithmetischen nachgebildete Formelsprache des reinen Denkens*, 1879 ("*Begriffsschrift*: A Formula Language, Modeled upon That of Arithmetic, for Pure Thought," 1967; better known as *Conceptual Notation*, 1972); *Die Grundlagen der Arithmetik: Eine logische mathematische Untersuchung über den Begriff der Zahl*, 1884 (*The Foundations of Arithmetic: A Logico-Mathematical Enquiry into the Concept of the Number*, 1950); *Funktion und Begriff*, 1891 ("Function and Concept," 1952); "Über Begriff und Gegenstand," 1892 ("On Concept and Object," 1952); "Über Sinn und Bedeutung," 1892 ("On Sense and Nominatum," 1949; better known as "On Sense and Reference," 1952); *Grundgesetze der Arithmetik*, 1893-1903 (2 volumes; partial translation, *The Basic Laws of Arithmetic*, 1964); "Der Gedanke: Eine logische Untersuchung," 1918 ("The Thought: A Logical Inquiry," 1956).

Born: November 8, 1848; Wismar, Mecklenburg-
  Schwerin (now in Germany)
Died: July 26, 1925; Bad Kleinen, Germany

Early Life

Friedrich Ludwig Gottlob Frege was the son of the principal of a private girls' high school. While Frege was in high school in Wismar, his father died. Frege was devoted to his mother, who was a teacher and later principal of the girls' school. He may have had a brother, Arnold Frege, who was born in Wismar in 1852. Nothing further is known about Frege until he entered the university at the age of twenty-one. From 1869 to 1871, he attended the University of Jena and proceeded to the University of Göttingen, where he took courses in mathematics, physics, chemistry, and philosophy. By 1873, Frege had completed his thesis and had received his doctorate from the university. Frege returned to the University of Jena and applied for an unsalaried position. His mother wrote to the university that she would support him until he acquired regular employment. In 1874, as a result of publication of his dissertation on mathematical functions, he was placed on the staff of the university. He spent the rest of his life at Jena, where he investigated the foundations of mathematics and produced semi-

nal works in logic.

Frege's early years at Jena were probably the happiest period in his life. He was highly regarded by the faculty and attracted some of the best students in mathematics. During these years, he taught an extra load as he assumed the courses of a professor who had become ill. He also worked on a volume on logic and mathematics. Frege's lectures were thoughtful and clearly organized, and were greatly appreciated by his students. Much of Frege's personal life, however, was beset by tragedies. Not only did his father die while he was a young man but also his children died young, as did his wife. He dedicated twenty-five years to developing a formal system, in which all of mathematics could be derived from logic, only to learn that a fatal paradox destroyed the system. During his life, he received little formal recognition of his monumental work and, in 1925, died virtually unnoticed by the academic world.

Life's Work

Frege's first major work in logic was published in 1879. Although this was a short book of only eighty-eight pages, it has remained one of the most important single works ever written in the field. In *Conceptual Notation*, Frege created a formal system of modern logic that could be used more readily than ordinary language. Frege was by no means the first person to use symbols as representations of words; Aristotle had used this device and was followed by others throughout the history of deductive logic.

Earlier logicians, however, had thought that in order to make a judgment on the validity of sentences, a distinction was necessary between subject and predicate. For the purposes of rhetoric, there is a difference between the statements "The North defeated the South in the Civil War" and "The South was defeated by the North in the Civil War." For Frege, however, the content of both sentences conveyed the same concept and hence must be given the same judgment. In this work, Frege achieved the ideal of nineteenth century mathematics: If proofs were completely formal and no intuition was required to judge the correctness of the proofs, there could be complete certainty that these proofs were the result of explicitly stated assumptions. During this period, Frege began to use universal quantifiers in his logic, which cover statements that contain "some" or "every." Consequently, it was now possible to cover a range of objects rather than a single object in a statement.

In 1884, Frege published *The Foundations of Arithmetic*, his attempt to apply similar principles to arithmetic as he had to logic. He first reviewed the works of his predecessors and then raised a number of fundamental questions on the nature of numbers and arithmetic truth. Throughout the work, which was more philosophical than mathematical, Frege enunciated three basic positions concerning the world of philosophical logic: First, mental images of a word as perceived by the speaker are irrelevant to the meaning of a word in a sentence in terms of its truth or falsity. The word "grass" in the sentence "the grass is green" does not depend on the mental image of "grass" but on the way in which the word is used in the sentence. Thus the meaning of a word was found in its usage. Second, words only have meaning in the context of a sentence. Rather than depending on the precise definition of a word, the sentence determined the truth-value of the word. If "all grubs are green," then it is possible to understand this sentence without necessarily knowing anything about "grubs." Also, it is pos-

sible to make a judgment about a sentence that contains "blue grubs" as false, since "all grubs are green." Third, a distinction exists between concepts and objects. This distinction raises serious questions concerning the nature of proper names, identity, universals, and predicates, all of which were historically troublesome philosophical and linguistic problems.

After the publication of *The Foundations of Arithmetic*, Frege became known not only as a logician and a mathematician but also as a linguistic philosopher. Although the notion of proper name is important for his system of logic, it also extends far beyond those concerns. An extended debate existed as to whether numbers such as "1, 2, 3, . . . " or directions such as "north" were proper names. Frege argued that it was not appropriate to determine what can be known about these words and then see if they can be classified as objects. Rather, like his theory of meaning, in which the meaning of a word is determined by its use in a sentence, if numbers are used as objects, they are proper names.

His insistence on the usage of words extended to the problem of universals. According to tradition, something that can be named is a particular, while a universal is predicated of a particular. For example, "red rose" is composed of a universal "red" and a particular "rose." Question arose as to whether universals existed in the sense that the "red" of the "red rose" existed independently of the "rose." Frege suggested that universals are used as proper names in such sentences as "The rose is red."

Between 1893 and 1903, Frege published two volumes of his unfinished work *The Basic Laws of Arithmetic*. These volumes contained both his greatest contribution to philosophy and logic and the greatest weaknesses of his logical system. Frege made a distinction between sense and reference, in that words frequently had the same reference but may imply a different sense. Words such as "lad," "boy," and "youth" all have the same reference or meaning but not in the same sense. As a result, two statements may be logically identical, yet have a different sense. Hence, 2 + 2 = 4 involves two proper names of a number, namely "2 + 2" and "4," but are used in different senses. Extending this idea to a logical system, the meaning or reference of the proper names and the truth-value of the sentence depend only on the reference of the object and not its sense. Thus, a sentence such as "The boy wore a hat" is identical to the sentence "The lad wore a hat." Because the logical truth-value of a sentence depends on the meaning of the sentence, the inclusion of a sentence without any meaning within a complex statement means that the entire statement lacks any truth-value. This proved to be a problem that Frege could not resolve and became a roadblock to his later work.

A further problem that existed in *The Basic Laws of Arithmetic*, which was written as a formal system of logic including the use of terms, symbols, and derived proofs, was the theory of classes. Frege wanted to use logic to derive the entire structure of mathematics to include all real numbers. To achieve this, Frege included, as part of his axioms, a primitive theory of sets or classes. While the second volume of *The Basic Laws of Arithmetic* was being prepared for publication, he received a letter from Bertrand Russell describing a contradiction that became known as the Russell Paradox. This paradox, sometimes known as the Stranger Loop, asks, Is "the class of all classes that are not members of itself" a member of itself or not? For example, the "class of all dogs" is not a dog; the "class of all animals" is not an animal. If the class of all classes is a member of itself, then it is one of those classes that are not members of themselves. Yet if it is not a member of itself, then it must be a member of all classes that are members of themselves, and the loop goes on forever. Frege replaced the class axiom with a modified and weaker axiom, but his formal system was weakened, and he never completed the third volume of the work.

Between 1904 and 1917, Frege made few contributions to his earlier works. During these years, he attempted to work through those contradictions that arose in his attempt to derive all of mathematics from logic. By 1918, he had begun to write a new book on logic, but he completed only three chapters. In 1923, he seemed to have broken through his intellectual dilemma and no longer believed that it was possible to create a foundation of mathematics based on logic. He began work in a new direction, beginning with geometry but completed little of this work before his death.

Influence

In *Conceptual Notation*, Frege created the first comprehensive system of formal logic since the ancient Greeks. He provided some of the foundations of modern logic with the formulation of the principles of noncontradiction and excluded middle. Equally important, Frege introduced the use of quantifiers to bind variables, which distinguished modern symbolic logic from earlier systems.

Frege's works were never widely read or appreciated. His system of symbols and functions was forbidding even to the best minds in mathematics. Russell, however, made a careful study of Frege and was clearly influenced by his system of logic. Also, philosopher Ludwig Wittgenstein incorporated a number of Frege's linguistic ideas, such as the use of ordinary language. Frege's distinction between sense and reference later generated a renewed interest in his work, and a number of important philosophical and linguistic studies are based on his original research.

Victor W. Chen

The Foundations of Arithmetic

A Logico-Mathematical Enquiry into the Concept of the Number

Type of philosophy: Epistemology, logic, philosophy of mathematics
First published: Die Grundlagen der Arithmetik: Eine logische mathematische Untersuchung über den Begriff der Zahl, 1884 (English translation, 1950)
Principal ideas advanced:
◊ Arithmetic can be reduced to logic: All arithmetical notions are definable in terms of purely logical ones and the truths of arithmetic can be deduced from axioms that are purely logical in character.
◊ Numbers exist independently of our apprehension of them, and the truths of arithmetic are true independently of our knowledge of them.
◊ Empiricism is false: Not all knowledge is empirical knowledge; our knowledge of mathematics, for example, is independent of experience and does not depend on any sort of empirical investigation.

◇ Psychologism is false: The subjective process of thinking should be sharply distinguished from the object of thought; and logic, properly understood, is not merely a description of how humans as a matter of fact think and reason.

◇ A fruitful strategy for dealing with metaphysical and epistemological problems is to recast them as problems concerning the meaning of problematic terms or expressions.

In 1879, Gottlob Frege, a German mathematician and logician, published a slim volume entitled *Begriffsschrift: Eine der arithmetischen nachgebildete Formelsprache des reinen Denkens* ("*Begriffsschrift*, a Formula Language, Modeled upon That of Arithmetic, for Pure Thought," 1967; better known as *Conceptual Notation*, 1972), in which, for the first time in the history of logic, the fundamental ideas and principles of mathematical logic were set out. In this remarkable book, Frege achieved a much deeper analysis of deductive inference than had previous logicians; for example, the problem of deductive inferences involving multiply embedded expressions of generality (for example, "everyone loves someone") was finally solved. Frege realized that the formal system of logic he had devised was precisely the instrument needed for realizing philosopher Gottfried Wilhelm Leibniz's dream of reducing arithmetic to logic. Frege believed that before attempting this daunting task, an informal overview and defense of the project should be given; *The Foundations of Arithmetic* was written for that purpose. Frege later attempted the rigorous reduction of the concepts and truths of arithmetic to those of logic in *Grundgesetze der Arithmetik*, 1893-1903 (two volumes; partial translation, *The Basic Laws of Arithmetic*, 1964).

Others' Notions Refuted

Frege's concern in *The Foundations of Arithmetic* is with basic philosophical issues concerning the nature of numbers and the truths of arithmetic: What are numbers? How do we apprehend them? Why are the truths of arithmetic *true*? How do we know these truths? Adequate answers to these simple and basic questions would seem necessary for understanding this elementary branch of mathematics, but Frege came to believe

that the answers given by previous writers were shallow and confused. Frege accordingly devotes the first half of *The Foundations of Arithmetic* to an examination and criticism of the views of his predecessors and contemporaries on the nature of numbers and arithmetical truth.

One prominent approach to foundational issues in mathematics is the empiricism of John Stuart Mill. Empiricism in general is the philosophical theory that all substantive knowledge is acquired by experience. Numbers, in Mill's view, are properties of physical objects or collections of physical objects and therefore are conveyed to people through sense perception. The truths of arithmetic, according to Mill's empiricism, are high-level inductive generalizations: Because, for example, when two objects are added to three objects the result is almost always a collection of five objects, we can conclude that 2 + 3 = 5. Frege points out, first of all, that numbers are not simply collections of physical objects or properties of physical objects. The same physical situation can be described as one deck, four suits, or fifty-two cards depending on the concept employed. Frege concludes that it is concepts, not physical things themselves, to which numbers are primarily ascribed. As far as the truths of arithmetic being inductive generalizations, Frege points out that induction presupposes probability theory, which in turn presupposes arithmetic. Furthermore, it is simply quite implausible to think that the process of adding a quart of water to a quart of popcorn should shake our confidence that 1 + 1 = 2.

Another approach to the foundations of mathematics is psychologism. This view holds that numbers are subjective mental entities and that the laws of arithmetic are descriptions of how humans as a matter of fact calculate. Psychologism views arithmetic as ultimately resting on naturalistic facts about human beings—facts about their ideas and mental processes. Frege believes that psychologism completely misconceives the nature of mathematics and logic. Because subjective ideas are private and can be apprehended only by their owners, psychologism implies, for example, that all humans think about a different object when they think about the number six. However, if each of us has our own number six, there would be nothing to prevent someone from legitimately asserting that six is a prime number—for how could this claim be rebutted? If psychologism is true, only that person has access to the number being discussed. It is obvious that arithmetic as a body of objective truths cannot rest on a view such as this. The claim that the laws of arithmetic are merely descriptions of how humans think implies that in the situation in which, because of some sort of mass hallucination, most people came to believe that 2 + 2 = 5, it would be true that 2 + 2 = 5. However, are the truths of arithmetic so dependent on what people happen to believe? This view ignores the normative character of mathematics and logic. These subjects are not concerned, as psychology and anthropology are, with how people reason and calculate; they are concerned with how we *should* reason and calculate.

Realism and Logicism

Frege's criticisms of empiricism and psychologism prepare the way for his own view about the nature and status of numbers and the truths of arithmetic. Frege is a realist (or Platonist) about numbers; he maintains that they exist independently of our knowledge of them and that they have properties that are independent of our knowledge. The truths of arithmetic are, therefore, independent of our recognition of these truths. Numbers are not physical entities, but it does not follow from this that they are subjective mental entities. They are, rather, abstract logical objects. Numbers are nonactual in the sense that they cannot causally act on our sense organs. However, while not actual, they are objective: The way they are is independent of the way we might happen to think they are; and they are public entities in that all rational beings can apprehend the same numbers and arithmetical truths. Although it may seem that nothing could be both nonactual and objective, Frege points out that we think of things such as the equator in this way. It is not a physical or perceivable line, but for any point on Earth, it is an objective fact whether or not it is on the equator.

In addition to realism, the other main strand of Frege's philosophy of arithmetic is the thesis that arithmetic can be reduced to logic, a view that has come to be known as *logicism*. Frege expresses his view using German philosopher Immanuel Kant's distinction between analytic and synthetic propositions. According to Frege, a proposition is analytic if it is either a truth of logic or follows deductively from truths of logic; it is synthetic otherwise. Frege's logicism is, then, the thesis that the truths of arithmetic are analytic. While expressing his view using Kantian terminology, Frege disagrees with Kant, who held that the propositions of arithmetic are synthetic. Kant's reason for denying that the truths of arithmetic are analytic is that they are informative and constitute substantive knowledge, but the stock examples of analytic truths (for example, "all bachelors are unmarried") hardly seem to have this status. Frege argues that Kant's view is mistaken because it depends on a simplistic conception of analyticity and fails to recognize that knowledge is extended when we come to see analytic connections we did not see before. Frege suggests that the analytic consequences of a concept are not contained in it like the beams in a house, apparent to us through casual observation, but as plants are contained in their seeds. By becoming aware of these consequences through deductive reasoning, we acquire knowledge we did not have by merely knowing the meanings of the terms.

Frege's logicism can be thought of as having two main stages: Numbers and arithmetical operations are first defined in terms of logical concepts, then the truths of arithmetic are deduced from axioms of a purely logical character. The first step in defining numbers in purely logical terms is the observation that an ascription of number is an assertion about a concept. For Frege, the expression "the number belonging to the concept *F*" refers to the number of objects falling under *F*. For example, the number belonging to the concept "natural satellite of Mars" is two because Mars has two moons. He next notes that a fundamental type of assertion involving numbers is when two concepts are said to have the same number belonging to them: "The number belonging to the concept *F* is the same as the number belonging to the concept *G*." What Frege wants to do is explain how the content of this proposition can be expressed without mentioning numbers. His basic insight is that two concepts have the same number belonging to them if the objects falling under the concepts can be placed in a one-to-one correspondence. For example, the number of Gospels is the same as the number of suits in bridge because each Gospel can be paired with one of the suits: Matthew with hearts, Mark with spades, and so on. Thus, the content of a proposition asserting that two concepts have the same number can be expressed without mentioning numbers: "The objects falling under *F* can be put into a one-to-one correspondence with the objects falling under *G*." The notion of a one-to-one correspondence is not a mathematical concept; it is a logical concept. A waiter does not have to know how to count in order to make sure the table has the same number of plates and knives; all he has to do is make sure there is a knife beside each plate. Thus, Frege has devised a way of capturing the content of a proposition asserting that the number of *F*'s is the same as the number of *G*'s in purely logical terms. This definition provided Frege with the basis for the rest of his definitions of arithmetical concepts and the ultimate deduction of the truths of arithmetic.

A Paradox

In 1902, shortly before the second volume of *The Basic Laws of Arithmetic* was to be published, philosopher Bertrand Russell wrote Frege informing him of a contradiction, or paradox, in his system of logic. Frege's system assumes that every concept determines a set; the concept "natural satellite of Earth," for example, determines a set with the Moon as its only member. Two types of sets can be distinguished: sets that are members of themselves (the set of abstract objects is a member of itself because it itself is an abstract object) and sets that are not members of themselves (the set of mammals is not a mammal and so is not a member of itself). The contradiction can be generated by asking whether the set of all sets that are not members of themselves is itself a member of itself: If it is, then it is not; if it is not, then it is. Frege attempted to amend his system so that the contradiction would be blocked, but he soon came to the conclusion that his version of logicism could not be repaired.

Once Frege realized that it was impossible to construct a version of logicism employing only self-evident logical principles that would therefore provide a foundation for the knowledge of arithmetic, he simply lost interest in logicism. The

program of logicism continued through the work of Russell and others, though because of the apparatus needed to block the contradiction, it could no longer be held to reduce arithmetic to self-evident axioms that are purely logical in character.

The Foundations of Arithmetic reached beyond the confines of logic and the philosophy of mathematics to general philosophy by influencing the approach philosophers take in dealing with problems. A striking example of this new approach occurs in section 62, in which the issue is how we can apprehend numbers given that they are not physical entities (and so are not perceivable) and given that they are not subjective mental entities available to us through introspection. Frege deals with this epistemological problem by recasting it as the problem of what propositions containing number terms *mean*. Also once we have an adequate answer to this question, perhaps the central question of *The Foundations of Arithmetic*, it is possible to maintain that we apprehend numbers by grasping the sense of propositions in which number terms occur. This strategy of translating metaphysical and epistemological issues into questions about language, meaning, and understanding is constitutive of what is known as the *analytic* tradition in philosophy. *The Foundations of Arithmetic* can be regarded, therefore, as the fountainhead of analytic philosophy.

David Haugen

Selected Essays

Type of philosophy: Epistemology, logic, philosophy of language

First published: "Funktion und Begriff," 1891 ("Function and Concept," 1952); "Über Begriff und Gegenstand," 1892 ("On Concept and Object," 1952); "Über Sinn und Bedeutung," 1892 ("On Sense and Nominatum," 1949; better known as "On Sense and Reference," 1952); "Der Gedanke: Eine logische Untersuchung," 1918 ("The Thought: A Logical Inquiry," 1956)

Principal ideas advanced:

◇ The True and the False are indefinable, primitive objects.

◇ Reality is three-tiered: At the level of *signs* is language; at the level of *sense* is thought; at the level of *reference* are objects.

◇ The significant expressions of a language have both a sense and a reference.

◇ Thoughts are unchanging and eternal; unlike ideas, they are common property and have no owners.

Four essays express the essence of Gottlob Frege's mature philosophy of language: "Function and Concept," "Concept and Object," the classic "On Sense and Reference," and the later "The Thought." (All are collected in *The Frege Reader*, 1997.) Although Frege conceived these papers as ancillary to the logicist project, they became the foundation of modern semantic theory. They contain significant revisions of Frege's earlier views, yet they basically adhere to the three principles of *Die Grundlagen der Arithmetik: Eine logische mathematische Untersuchung über den Begriff der Zahl* (1884; *The Foundations of Arithmetic: A Logico-Mathematical Enquiry into the Concept of the Number*, 1950): "There must be a sharp separation of the psychological from the logical, the subjective from the objective"; "the meaning of a word must be asked for in the context of a proposition, not in isolation"; and "the distinction of concept and object must be kept in mind."

Functions and Concepts

"Function and Concept" was the first essay to clarify and systematize the semantic theses of Frege's earlier works. The notion of function is taken from mathematics. In the expression "$2x^2 + 2$," if x is replaced with 1, the result is 4. Frege says that "people call x the argument," which is a useful way to think of it. However, for Frege an argument is defined as that which is not part of a function but combines with it to form a complete expression. The number signified by the whole expression is its *value*. For any argument there is only one value, and for mathematical functions it is always a number. The *value-range* of a function is thus a series of pairs of arguments and values. The value-ranges of two functions are identical if the functions always have the same value for the same argument. Thus, "$x^2 - 2x$" and "$x(x-2)$" have the same value-ranges. When a function lacks an argument, Frege refers to it as incomplete, or

"unsaturated." When an argument is present, the function is complete, or "saturated." A function has a value only for an argument.

Frege extended his definition of function from mathematical to universal use by considering functions such as $x^2 = 4$. He posited that the *value* of this function is a truth-value, either the True or the False. There are only two arguments, –2 and 2, for which the function's value is the True; for all other arguments, it is the False. Therefore the expression "$2^2 = 4$" signifies the True just as "2^2" signifies 4. He defines a function whose value is always a truth-value as a *concept*. Any predicate formed by omitting a proper name from a sentence will express a concept. However, a functional expression such as "the father of . . . " will not, because for any appropriate argument (Mary), the value of the function is not a truth-value but a person (John).

The *extension* of a concept is a series of pairs, with one member being an object and the other a truth-value. This is an advance over the traditional conception, in which the extension of a concept consists of the objects that fall under it. According to that view, *unicorn* cannot signify a concept because no objects fall under it. This undesirable result is avoided by Frege's theory, because for any argument there will be a truth-value—albeit for *unicorn* this is always the False.

As is perhaps now evident, Frege's definitions of function and concept apply to statements of all kinds. For example, in the sentence "Caesar conquered Gaul," the expression "conquered Gaul" contains an empty place; it is an incomplete expression. Only when this place is filled with a proper name (Caesar) or definite description does the sentence make sense. When used as such, however, arguments are not names but *objects*, and may, where appropriate, be persons, places, truth-values, value-ranges, extensions of concepts, or any other entity that is not a function. Moreover, a concept must be bounded: "It must be determinable, for any object, whether or not it falls under the concept."

Objects and Concepts

The principal contention of "Concept and Object" is that concepts and objects are exclusive categories: Objects may fall under concepts but not the reverse. Frege anticipated a number of possible objections. One is that concepts can have properties, and to have a property must be to fall *under* a concept. Frege replied that a first-level concept can be subordinate to another first-level concept; for example, the concept *mammal* is subordinate to the concept *animal*. A concept may also fall *within* a second-level concept. We may say, "The concept *unicorn* is not instantiated (has no objects)," where instantiation is a property. Another possible objection stems from Frege's criterion that any expression preceded by a definite article designates an object rather than a concept. How, then, does one construe sentences such as "The concept *horse* is a concept?" Because "the concept *horse*" begins with a definite article, it must refer to an object; yet because of its content, it must refer to a concept. Frege argued that "the concept *horse*" designates an object, even though it forced him to the awkward and controversial conclusion that "The concept *horse* is a concept" is false.

Sense and Reference

Frege's seminal distinction between sense and reference was introduced in "Function and Concept" and developed in "On Sense and Reference," one of the most influential works in analytic philosophy. In it Frege grappled with two language puzzles. The first concerns statements of identity such as "$3 + 2 = 5$," "The morning star is identical to the evening star," and "Regina is Davis's mother." These statements all take the form "$a = b$," where "a" and "b" are either names or descriptions that designate individuals. The truth of "$a = b$" requires that the expressions flanking the identity sign refer to the same object. For example, "$3 + 2 = 5$" is true only when "$3 + 2$" and "5" refer to the same number. Similarly, "The number of planets is nine" is true only when "The number of planets" is the same number as "nine." This assumes that identity expresses a relation between signs, as indeed it did in Frege's *Begriffsschrift: Eine der arithmetischen nachgebildete Formelsprache des reinen Denkens* (1879; "*Begriffsschrift*, a Formula Language, Modeled upon That of Arithmetic, for Pure Thought," 1967; better known as *Conceptual Notation*, 1972).

The puzzle arises from the fact that the truth conditions for "$a = b$" are no different from those of "$a = a$." Compare these two sentences: (1) The evening star is the evening star, and (2) The morning star is the evening star.

If, as astronomers have shown, the morning star and the evening star are just different aspects of the planet Venus, then (2) should be obtainable from (1) by substituting "the morning star" for "the evening star." There is no difference between (1) and (2) at the level of reference because they refer to the same object. However, whereas (1) is almost trivially true (2) conveys genuine knowledge. Frege's insight was that, because "the morning star" and "the evening star" express different *thoughts*, it follows that (1) and (2), though they share the same reference, also differ in the thoughts they express. Names are arbitrary signs; we can name an object anything we choose. Frege concluded that if "$a = b$" signifies a relation between signs, it expresses no knowledge about the extra-linguistic world.

The sense-reference distinction attempts to overcome this difficulty. Here, identity is a relation not between signs but between objects, or *references*; the informativeness of identity statements is explained by differences in the senses of the expressions flanking the identity sign. The sense of a linguistic item is what we grasp when we understand it; it is a common property—objective, immutable, and timeless. Senses are neither ideas nor objects. As Frege puts it, an idea is a subjective "mode of the individual mind" and may vary with person and place: It has an *owner*. In an ideal language, Frege asserts, every sign would have a unique sense. However, in natural languages, different signs may express the same sense. Moreover, not every sense has a reference; for example, "the least rapidly convergent series" has a sense but refers to no object. Fictional names also have a sense but no referent. If a supposedly fictional name is found to have a reference, then the thought remains the same but is "transposed from the realm of fiction to that of truth," which further shows that sense is independent of reference. Ordinarily, though, the use of names presupposes that they have a reference.

Not only do proper names and definite descriptions have senses and references, but so do entire sentences. The sense of a sentence is the thought it expresses, and its reference is its truth-value, the object known as the True or the False. Every seriously propounded indicative sentence is the *name* of one or the other of these objects. It is by making a *judgment* that we take a sentence from the level of thought to the level of reference. Frege explicitly ignores sentences that do not make assertions because his aim is to describe, and where necessary to construct, a language that serves the needs of science. The reference of expressions within sentences is explained in terms of the contribution they make to the reference of the sentences in which they occur. For example, the reference of a predicate is a concept, and the reference of a quantifier, such as "all" or "some," is a second-order concept, a function from concepts to truth-values.

Frege held that the references of complex expressions are determined by the references of their parts. This gives rise to the second linguistic puzzle, one concerning intensional contexts, in which expressions ascribe a "propositional attitude" such as "X knows that p," "X believes that p," and so on. Compare the following propositions: (3) Venus is the morning star, (4) Gottlob believes that the morning star is the morning star, and (5) Gottlob believes that Venus is the morning star.

In accordance with (3), the substitution of "Venus" for "the Morning Star" in (4) will yield (5). However, (4) is almost trivially true, whereas (5) is not, for it may be either true or false that Gottlob holds this belief. Frege interpreted this apparent failure of reference in intensional contexts as further evidence that a purely referential theory—one lacking senses—cannot account for the logical behavior of certain expressions. His reaction was not to deprive the expressions of referential status but to change the reference. In the resulting theory of *indirect reference*, belief is a relation between a believer and a thought. The reference is a not a truth-value but the sense of what is believed (or disbelieved).

Thought

The later essay "The Thought: A Logical Inquiry" explicates its subject and much more, for in it Frege develops his mature theories of truth and judgment. Here the True and the False are presented as indefinable, primitive objects. Frege's three-tiered system is clearer than ever: At the level of *signs* is language, at the level of *sense* is thought, and at the level of *reference* are objects, which include truth-values as the references of

thoughts. This translates into three realms of existent things: physical entities, mental entities, and a "third realm" of entities that are neither physical nor mental. Frege's theory of judgment is marked by three levels: the grasping of a thought, the judgment that the thought is true (or false), and the assertion (or denial) of the thought. The first two are mental acts, whereas the third is an external manifestation of the judgment. The sense-reference distinction gives the notion of thought more clear-cut form because, for the most part, linguistic structures mirror the senses that they express. Although two or more expressions may share a reference yet differ in sense, no expression has more than one sense (in a given context). The greatest virtue of Fregean semantics is the clarity with which it can distinguish linguistic from other kinds of knowledge.

Relegating thoughts to a third realm results from Frege's desire to preserve the objectivity of knowledge. The cost, however, was a weighty metaphysics that entails, for example, a causal relation between nonphysical entities and human cognition. Some argue that thoughts need not have this special status to fulfill their purpose. The question of whether all expressions have both a sense and a reference and what these are for each class of expressions has spawned much research. In some interpretations, the realm of sense is not independent of thinkers; rather, it contains humanity's store of "accumulated knowledge." Despite these disagreements, all philosophers of language owe a debt to Frege for providing the framework for such investigations.

Grant A. Marler

Additional Reading

Beaney, Michael. *Frege: Making Sense*. London: Duckworth, 1996. An analysis of Frege's logic and resulting philosophy.

Currie, Gregory. *Frege: An Introduction to His Philosophy*. Brighton, England: Harvester Press; Totowa, N.J.: Barnes & Noble, 1982. Offers an introduction to the central points of Gottlob Frege's philosophical program and traces the historical development of his views. It provides a very clear explanation of Frege's formal system, philosophy of mathematics, and philosophical logic. Recommended for advanced undergraduates.

Dummett, Michael. *Frege: Philosophy of Language*. 2d ed. Cambridge, Mass.: Harvard University Press, 1981. Although Dummett's interpretations are hotly contested, this magisterial study is the definitive work on Frege. A very long work, it presupposes knowledge of the main currents of analytic philosophy and of symbolic logic in places, but the summaries impart key arguments very clearly. For advanced undergraduates.

_____. *The Interpretation of Frege's Philosophy*. Cambridge, Mass.: Harvard University Press, 1987. This book is a reply to criticisms of Dummett's *Frege: Philosophy of Language*. It is also shorter, less technical, and places Frege in a broader historical setting, thus making it suitable as an introduction.

Grossman, Reinhardt. *Reflections on Frege's Philosophy*. Evanston, Ill.: Northwestern University Press, 1969. The author sees "On Sense and Reference" as the solution—though not a faultless one—to a number of problems emerging from Frege's earlier work. This is a superb introductory text for the advanced undergraduate.

Kenny, Anthony. *Frege*. New York: Penguin Books, 1995. This marvelous survey briefly explains and assesses the full range of Frege's work. Accurate but nontechnical, this is perhaps the most accessible introduction to Frege for the student or general reader.

Kneale, William, and Martha Kneale. *The Development of Logic*. Oxford: Clarendon Press, 1962. Though lacking the benefit of recent scholarship, this classic and authoritative text contains a profound yet accessible analysis of Frege's career, his relation to his predecessors, and his theory of number. It devotes a chapter to his general logic, including expositions of his *Conceptual Notation*, the theory of sense and reference, and *The Basic Laws of Arithmetic*.

Schirn, Matthias, ed. *Frege: Importance and Legacy*. New York: Walter de Gruyter, 1996. This book examines Frege's analytical philosophy and its lasting legacy.

Sluga, Hans D. *Gottlob Frege*. Boston: Routledge & Kegan Paul, 1980. A readable account of Frege's theories set against the philosophical concerns of late nineteenth century Germany. Traces the influences of Gottfried Wilhelm Leibniz, Immanuel Kant, and later philosophers on Frege and his contemporaries.

Walker, Jeremy D. B. *A Study of Frege*. Ithaca, N.Y.: Cornell University Press, 1965. A thoughtful exposition, especially strong on the philosophy of language of Frege's middle and late periods. Suitable for advanced undergraduates.

Weiner, Joan. *Frege in Perspective*. Ithaca, N.Y.: Cornell University Press, 1990. Though not expansive enough to serve as an introduction, this study is not addressed solely to specialists. It discusses Frege's writings on number theory and the laws of thought and seeks to discover Frege's motivation for attempting to prove the truths of arithmetic.

Victor W. Chen, updated by Grant A. Marler

Paulo Freire

Although Freire's major contribution was to help impoverished and illiterate residents of South America, his educational pedagogy has become the worldwide model for institutions and instructors wishing to liberalize their curriculums.

Principal philosophical works: *Educação como prática da liberdade*, 1967 ("Education and the Practice of Freedom," 1973); *Extensíon o comunicación?*, 1969 ("Extension or Communication," 1973); *The Cultural Action Process: An Introduction to Its Understanding*, 1969; *Cultural Action for Freedom*, 1970; *Pedagogía del oprimido*, 1970 (*Pedagogy of the Oppressed*, 1970); *Education for Critical Consciousness*, 1973 (also published as *Education, the Practice of Freedom*, 1976); *Education for Liberation: Addresses*, 1975 (bound with *Critical Reflections on Indian Education* by J. P. Naik); *Cartas à Guiné-Bissau: Registros de uma experiência em processo*, 1977 (*Pedagogy in Process: The Letters to Guinea-Bissau*, 1978); *Christian Ideology and Adult Education in Latin America*, 1982; *Por uma pedagogia da pergunta*, 1985 (with Antonio Faundez; *Learning to Question: A Pedagogy of Liberation*, 1989); *Literacy: Reading the Word and the World*, 1987 (with Donaldo Macedo); *A Pedagogy for Liberation: Dialogues on Transforming Education*, 1987 (with Ira Shor).

Born: September 19, 1921; Recife, Brazil
Died: May 2, 1997; São Paolo, Brazil

Early Life

Paulo Freire, the son of Joaquim Themisodes Freire and Edeltrus Neves Freire, was born in Recife, a seaport and center of great poverty in northeast Brazil. Unlike the majority of the city's population, Freire spent his early life in middle-class comfort; however, in 1929, when the repercussions from the Great Depression in the United States trickled southward, the Freire family lost its financial stability and joined the masses gripped by destitution. In 1931, in an effort to improve his economic situation, Joaquim Freire relocated to Jabatoa but died soon after, leaving his wife and child in even more penurious circumstances.

With every thought ruled by extreme hunger and deprivation, Paulo Freire fell two years behind in school. His performance was so below par that many of his teachers diagnosed him as mentally retarded. These unfortunate circumstances caused the young Freire to vow to dedicate his life to the "struggle against hunger." As the effects of the Depression faded and financial conditions improved, Freire compensated for his educational deficiencies, completed his schooling, and entered the University at Recife to study law, including classes in philosophy and the psychology of language. He married Eliza Maia Costa Oliveria, a grade-school teacher, in 1944; the union produced three daughters and two sons. Following the birth of his first child, his interest in education and educational theories grew, and soon Freire was reading more in education, philosophy, and sociology than he was in law.

Life's Work

After graduating from the university, Freire passed the bar examination but abandoned the profession of law to work for the welfare department and later to become the director of the Department of Education and Culture for the social service in the state of Pernambuco. In this capacity, he came into direct contact with the urban poor and began to formulate his pedagogical theories. He returned to school and was awarded a doctoral degree in adult education from the University of Recife in 1959.

In the early 1960's, Brazil was in a state of political and social unrest, produced in part by the government's policies. Although a type of democratic electoral policy was in place, using elections to alter the power structure was difficult primarily because peasants who were legally unable to vote because of their illiteracy made up the majority of the population. In an effort to erase this inequity, the University of Recife developed the Cultural Extension Service, which was to undertake the literacy training of thousands of the disenfranchised. Freire, as the first director of this service, realized the difficulties inherent in learning what one does not understand and insisted that the program be both social and political. He attempted to change the ingrained mindset of the peasants by teaching not only adult literacy but also democratic skills. He refused to use the traditional literacy texts because he felt the sentences, advocating middle-and upper-class values, had no meaning for the peasants. He altered the face of literacy education by concentrating on teaching critical thinking rather than employing the conventional curriculum of memorization and recitation. In this manner, he transformed the established pedagogy from paternalism, which kept the peasants captives of the historical cycle, to humanism, through which they could gain liberation from that cycle. Freire did not give credence to theories of determinism, Social Darwinism, or behaviorism because he held that behavior can be modified by willing it to be changed.

Although Freire's views were utopian, the methods that he employed to achieve his ends were overwhelmingly successful. The literacy movement officially began in 1963, and three hundred people learned to read and write in only forty-five days. In June, Paulo de Tarso, a friend of Freire, became minister of education, and the program was expanded to serve the peasant population of the entire nation. Freire was appointed director of the national literacy campaign. Thousands enrolled, and college students volunteered as coordinators. After only one year of operation, plans were underway to establish twenty thousand centers across Brazil that would serve 20 million illiterates.

As word of Freire's success reached officials of the government, newly established by a military coup, they began to fear that his work would give thousands of peasants a political voice and countered by labeling the educator a politicizing radical. The politicians, encouraged by the editorial support of the right-wing newspaper *Globo*, had Freire arrested for "subversive" activities, and in April, 1964, he was jailed along with 150 other political prisoners. While incarcerated, Freire began working on "Education and the Practice of Freedom," his first written account of his attempts in humanistic education and his analysis of why those attempts failed to produce change. After seventy days in confinement, the educator was released, stripped of his citizenship, and exiled to Chile.

A man of passionate optimism in spite of poverty, imprisonment, and exile, Freire continued his mission in Santiago, Chile, by accepting a position with the Agrarian Reform Training and Research Institute and by serving as a consultant to the United Nations Educational, Scientific, and Cultural Organization (UNESCO). Freire worked for five years in Chile as an adult educator connected to the agrarian reform movement, a philosophical undertaking designed not to increase production for the overseers but to humanize the industry for the workers. Freire believed the peasants were conditioned and dehumanized by history and society and that they had been forced through traditional education to adapt to the values of the majority. As an alternative, he designed classroom activities to enrich rather than replace the peasant culture. His pedagogical methods investigated the background and customs that shaped the lives of his students, and his training focused on terms and concepts of importance to their daily activities. The reading vocabulary for these students therefore concentrated on familiar words such as "shanty," "well," "work," "plow," and "slum," which led to known themes such as housing, dirt, clothing, and health. By slowly piecing together these words and themes, Freire was successful in guiding the peasants toward identifying concepts in written form. His national literacy campaign won Chile a UNESCO award for successfully eliminating illiteracy among the adult population.

In the late 1960's, Freire accepted an invitation to be a visiting professor at the Harvard Center for Studies in Education and Development. It was a chaotic period in U.S. history, and the Brazilian was enlightened by the discovery that political and economic injustice was not limited to the Third World. As he observed the active political protests of the period, engendered by the economic and social inequities experienced by African Americans, women, and youth, he became aware of the universality of inequality and acquired an increased interest in violence as a means of altering the status quo.

Between 1969 and 1970, Freire wrote two articles for the *Harvard Educational Review* that were reprinted in a booklet, *Cultural Action for Freedom*. The work reemphasized his thesis that education could not be neutral. In 1970, his masterwork, *Pedagogy of the Oppressed*, was translated and published in the United States. It offered many American educators their first taste of Freire's philosophy. Many of those initially examining the theories were appalled by the sprinkling of quoted material from world leaders whom some educators considered unsavory, including Communist leaders Vladimir Lenin, Karl Marx, and Mao Zedong. *Pedagogy of the Oppressed* was critiqued for its socialism and justification of revolutionary violence, as well as its vagueness, redundancy, and complex sentence structure. Some considered the work a handbook for revolutionary education, advocating revolt as the only method for social and political change.

In 1972, Freire relocated to Geneva, Switzerland, to work as the special education consultant to the World Council of Churches. In this capacity, he traveled to assist the educational programs of newly independent countries in Asia and Africa. He was also chairman of the executive committee of the Institut d'Action Culturelle, a nonprofit organization created to train educators in the Freirean method. This training process does not offer a method or a final solution but instead promotes the theory that respect for people and open dialogue can lead to social justice.

In 1979, Freire returned to his homeland under political amnesty and accepted a faculty position at the University of São Paulo. While at the university, he found money to offer teachers an equitable salary, empowered teachers and parents, challenged students to think critically, had damaged buildings repaired, and continued to help the poor and disenfranchised through efforts to change the curriculum. He died on May 2, 1997, of a heart attack.

Influence

Freire's influence extended beyond the classroom; he had an impact on national development through the enfranchisement of thousands of people in South America who acquired literacy through his teachings. Freire offers something to educators, Christians, Marxists, and minorities, and he has been viewed variously as a neo-Marxist, an idealist, a communist, a "theologian in disguise," a phenomenologist, and an existentialist.

The Freirean method of education, though considered radical and subversive at the time, is really quite simple. Freire's main tenet was that it is easier to educate if one can communicate. He believed that students must be addressed in their idiom, study that with which they identify, and learn more than what is offered through the traditional curriculum and textbooks. He felt that if schools negate the students' day-to-day experience and their culture and language, students will ultimately resist learning by refusing to hear the language of the teacher. Consequently, he believed that the conventional form of education—the "banking system," in which the teacher makes a deposit of knowledge and the student listens, memorizes, and regurgitates—would not halt the process of dehumanization he encountered among the population. It was his belief that students and teachers should realize that knowledge is an ongoing process and that both groups learn from and teach each other. To ensure that this exchange took place, he employed dialogue and introduced critical thinking to obviate what he called the "culture of silence" that ruled the lives of many of those with whom he interacted.

Through the use of generative words, those with which the student was familiar, Freire enabled thousands of illiterate people not only to read and write but also to become more fully human and to be in their world, not merely of it. Generative words carry emotion and meaning; they express the anxiety, fears, and dreams of the group. This emotional push moves the student toward literacy as well as enlightenment. Freire compared this mental liberation to childbirth in that the student leaves the process as a new person.

Although Freire was obviously influenced by world leaders, writers, and educators who came before him, he developed a perspective uniquely his own in relation to the milieu and reality of his world. Because the majority of his work was carried out in South America, his impact is most evident there, where he gave thousands of the illiterate population skills, liberation, and hope. This, however, is not the limit of his reach. Through his work with the World Council of Churches, he extended his method throughout most of the Third World and served as a model for educators worldwide, particularly in higher education, who have detected something inherently missing in standardized curriculums and who seek a better way.

Joyce Duncan

Pedagogy of the Oppressed

Type of philosophy: Ethics, philosophy of education, social philosophy

First published: Pedagogía del oprimido, 1970 (English translation, 1970)

Principal ideas advanced:

◇ The dehumanization of individuals, particularly of the impoverished and illiterate, is tied to an existing patriarchal order and traditional educational curricula.

◇ Students should be instructed through generative words, words that are within the idiom of the students and that generate new ideas, leading to themes of import (a thematic universe).

◇ The "banking concept" of education, wherein the teacher deposits knowledge and the student listens, memorizes, and recites, should be discarded.

◇ Conscientization, which allows students to become critical thinkers and to take part in their world, is integral to the educational process.

◇ Dialogical teaching uses problem posing and lets students and their teachers communicate while realizing that each is simultaneously teacher and student.

Having survived a childhood of extreme poverty, Paulo Freire was intimately aware of the dehumanization that deprivation creates. At a young age, he vowed to dedicate his life to the "struggle against hunger," and as an adult, he kept that vow by undertaking the education of thousands of illiterate Brazilian and Chilean peasants who were the victims of paternalism, indigence, and disenfranchisement. His views on education and the struggle for liberty are captured in *Pedagogy of the Oppressed*, the first of his writings to be translated and published in the United States and, therefore, the work that introduced his research and methodology to the American academic world and general public. Some critics found the work vague, redundant, and needlessly complex, however, the greatest objections were caused by its content. Some felt the work advocated revolution and others criticized the work for its liberal use of quotes and concepts from socialist and communist leaders Vladimir Lenin, Karl Marx, Mao Zedong, and others. It was obvious, however, that Freire had developed a unique educational method that worked within the parameters of his environment.

Literacy and Liberty

During the twentieth century, South America was a region marked by political unrest and turmoil. Although a democratic election policy was in place in Brazil, the population consisted largely of peasants whose illiteracy made them legally unqualified to vote. In an effort to remedy this problem, the University of Recife in Brazil created the Cultural Extension Service, which undertook the literacy training of thousands. Freire was named the first director of this organization.

When he began the education process, Freire was appalled at the curriculum and texts that were then in use. The curriculum was structured in accordance with what he labeled the "banking system of education," wherein the teacher speaks and the students listen, memorize, and recite. The textbooks were compiled using a sophisticated vocabulary and imbued in middle- and upper-class values. Freire felt this information would be of little use to a primarily agrarian, impoverished population. Therefore, he devised a workable system based on the milieu of the people, employing their day-to-day language and concepts and encouraging dialogue and critical thinking. He felt that true education could not be accomplished until the teacher and student realized that each simultaneously plays both roles. Additionally, he believed peasants should be empowered through the educational process, so he undertook their political, sociological, and historical training.

He was intimately aware of the "culture of silence" surrounding the peasant population of his native South America and felt that the economic, social, and political isolation of these people, as well as the paternalism of social institutions including the educational system, kept them enslaved to the status quo. Further, it was his thesis that the world is not a reality to be accepted or adjusted to but a problem to be worked out and solved. This ultimate solution was to be found through literacy training; as people discovered the written word, they would unleash their creativity.

Humanization and Freedom

Freire posited that this process could be achieved through humanization. He held that humankind's "vocation" was the struggle to recover its lost humanity. Humanization can be achieved only when people realize they have been subjected to dehumanization through injustice, exploitation, oppression, and violence. Furthermore, the oppressed must recover from the fear of freedom by refusing to conform to the ideas of others and thereby breaking the cycle of repression and violence. He observed that when a person is elevated from slave to overseer, the theories of the oppressor persist, and violence worsens to appease the owner. When the prevalent order has not been altered, the oppressed take on the values of the oppressor, and the cycle of violence continues.

Freedom requires autonomy and responsibility, and Freire compares liberation to childbirth in that the oppressed individual emerges as a new person. The educational model, or pedagogy, for this liberation is created in two stages: First, the oppressed sees the world as it is and commits himself or herself to its transformation; second, that vision of the world becomes shared by everyone as the old myths are expulsed and permanent liberation begins. This utopian view frees the oppressed from being objects or things with no purpose other than that prescribed for them by their oppressors. Furthermore, it eliminates

public assistance systems, which were considered the pathology of an otherwise healthy society.

In *Pedagogy of the Oppressed*, Freire calls himself a humanist who engages in the struggle rather than merely supplies gifts to ease the struggle. He asserted that one cannot support a cause while considering those involved in that cause to be totally ignorant. When people are told repeatedly that they are ignorant, they begin to accept it as true. This self-deprecation causes them to develop an emotional dependence on their oppressor or, if students, to defer to the instructor's point of view because he or she is the one with knowledge. Freire affirmed that the avenue leading away from this route was conscientization, the introduction of critical thinking and acknowledgment of the students' intelligence through dialogue in which the teacher and students simultaneously learn from and educate one another.

Conscientization

In *Pedagogy of the Oppressed*, Freire critiques what he labels the "banking system of education," wherein the teacher narrates and the students listen, memorize words and concepts of little relevance to their lives, and regurgitate the information in order to excel on an examination. In this process, the student is viewed as a container, an object, to be filled by the all-knowing instructor, and Freire states emphatically that education is suffering from "narration sickness." Bankers, he feels, are against any form of critical thinking because it jeopardizes the status quo; by considering student ignorance as absolute, teachers can justify their own existence. On the other hand, conscientization teaches transformation of the social order to allow the oppressed to become "beings for themselves" rather than to merely adapt to the prevailing order. This view was considered radical, subversive, and dangerous by many who observed Freire or read his work.

Freire believed this transformation could be achieved through dialogical education, "problem posing" carried out via conversations that constantly unveiled reality. Dialogue must include both action and reflection and requires faith, humility, hope, and critical inquiry from all involved. It creates communication, and communication creates true education. Communication could be fostered only through a common language; rather than attempting to raise the students' language to the level of the instructors, educators must communicate in the language of the people. Freire accomplished this and the burgeoning of literacy by allowing students to learn written language through generative words, or words familiar to them and part of their everyday lives, including shanty, well, work, plow, and slum. Subsequently, these words led to themes such as housing, clothing, and health. Moving from the particular to the general allowed the peasants to create a thematic universe with interacting historical themes, to decode their world, and to communicate in ways previously unavailable to them.

Old Myths

Pedagogy of the Oppressed concludes with a discussion of cultural revolutions, and an in-depth discussion of the oppressor. Freire deduces that society is impeded by old myths, such as humanity is free, jobs are available if one seeks them, entrepreneurism is always possible, all people are equal, and the elite are inherently good because of their charitable contributions. Further, he insists that these myths must be replaced by a new order before humanity can be fully liberated.

Oppressors, according to Freire, have their own set of myths that encode as behaviors. The most prevalent myth is messianism, wherein they see themselves as saviors of the people, which logically leads to paternalism. Others include the belief that it is best to force others to adapt to the status quo, which engenders cultural invasion, and the practice of dividing and ruling, which translates into manipulation.

Education and the Route to Freedom

Many of Freire's ideas, as expressed in *Pedagogy of the Oppressed*, were utopian although some were socialistic. Whatever his political viewpoint, Freire serves as a universal model for the ability to use education to forward liberty, and he must be credited for fearlessly taking on the system to offer freedom to the oppressed of the Third World. In 1964, Freire's beliefs were considered a threat to the political regime in Brazil, and he was imprisoned, stripped of his citizenship, and exiled. A man of passionate optimism in spite of adverse circumstances, he successfully continued his work in Chile and later imported his methods to the United States, Europe, Asia, and Africa.

Freire believed that although education is the true route to freedom, antiquated systems often reinforce the old order and become a major source of oppression. He believed that the memorization and recitation mode of learning was passé and needed to be replaced. Subsequent educational research supported Freire's idea that students learn more completely through discussion, projects, and hands-on activity than through memorization. In this respect, Freire resembles educators such as John Dewey, Ivan Illich, and Socrates, who were considered radical in their time, and his efforts with literary training and consciousness-raising can be compared to movements for equality for African Americans, women, and the poor in the United States.

Freire's theory of eduation must be given high marks for its student-centered emphasis. Students cannot learn what they do not understand, and they cannot communicate in a language that is unfamiliar to them. Arguments similar to Freire's surfaced in the battle over ebonics and multilingual education that erupted in the 1980's and 1990's. An educator who consistently speaks "over the heads" of students may discover that he or she is not communicating because the students tend to stop listening to what they cannot comprehend. Freire's implicit assumption that the prevailing order must ultimately be changed to create lasting freedom is generally considered valid. Freire did not believe in integrating minority cultures or groups into the majority but in creating a society in which all cultures, value systems, and people were held in equal regard. In this lies the crux of his humanism and also, perhaps, his lasting value as a philosopher.

Joyce Duncan

Additional Reading

Collins, Denis. *Paulo Freire: His Life, Works, and Thought*. New York: Paulist Press, 1997. This book, written by a Jesuit educator, provides biographical information and an overview of Freire's educational and sociological theories.

Elias, John L. *Conscientization and Deschooling*. Philadelphia: Westminster Press, 1976. The work compares and contrasts the educational and theological theories of Paulo Freire and Ivan Illich. It contains some biographical information and illustrates the effect religion had on Freire's educational philosophy and content. An extensive bibliography for both Freire and Illich is included.

_____. *Paulo Freire: Pedagogue of Liberation*. Malabar, Fla.: Kreiger Press, 1994. The text analyzes the historical background of Freire's work and the concepts included in his theories of education. It also examines the influences on his work, from existentialism to Catholic theology to Marxism, and explores the impact of Vladimir Lenin, Karl Marx, Mao Zedong, and others on his beliefs.

Horton, Myles, and Paulo Freire. *We Make the Road by Walking: Conversations on Education and Social Change*. Philadelphia: Temple University Press, 1990. One of two works that Freire created in collaboration, the book is written in interview format and features a dialogue that compares Freire's teaching methods to liberal educational programs in the United States and elsewhere.

MacLaren, Peter, and Peter Leonard. *Paulo Freire: A Critical Encounter*. London: Routledge Press, 1993. A collection of essays by imminent scholars and educators reflecting their assessments of Freire's life, theories, and methods.

Shor, Ira. *Freire for the Classroom: A Sourcebook for Liberatory Teaching*. Portsmouth, N.H.: Boynton/Cook, 1987. Designed for use by educators, the book demonstrates various ways in which Freire's pedagogical approaches can be adapted to a variety of classrooms. Noneducators will find the work understandable.

Shor, Ira, and Paulo Freire. *A Pedagogy for Liberation: Dialogues on Transforming Education*. South Hadley, Mass.: Bergin & Garvey, 1987. This work, written in interview format, contains a definition of the dialogical method employed by Freire, discussion of the fears and risks associated with transformation, and a design for overcoming language difficulties with students. The focus of the work is on classroom activities and makes this work of particular interest to educators.

Joyce Duncan